About the author

Respected wine critic and vigneron James Halliday AM has a career that spans forty-five years, but he is most widely known for his witty and informative writing about wine. As one of the founders of Brokenwood in the Hunter Valley and thereafter of Coldstream Hills in the Yarra Valley, James is an unmatched authority on every aspect of the wine industry, from the planting and pruning of vines through to the creation and marketing of the finished product. His winemaking has led him to sojourns in Bordeaux and Burgundy, and he has had a long career as a wine judge in Australia and overseas. In 1995 he received the wine industry's ultimate accolade, the Maurice O'Shea Award. In 2010 James was made a Member of the Order of Australia for his services to the wine industry.

James has written or contributed to more than 70 books on wine since he began writing in 1979. His books have been translated into Japanese, French, German, Danish, Icelandic and Polish, and have been published in the United Kingdom and the United States, as well as in Australia. He is the author of *Varietal Wines, James Halliday's Wine Atlas of Australia, The Australian Wine Encyclopedia* and *A Life in Wine*.

ONE YEAR
WEBSITE & MAGAZINE MEMBERSHIP
ONLY $49

Visit: winecompanion.com.au/
become-a-member

Enter unique code word *wcb2017* at checkout before
30th November 2016 to redeem this offer

Halliday

WINE COMPANION

ESTABLISHED 1986 · WINECOMPANION.COM.AU

The bestselling and
definitive guide
to Australian wine

2017

hardie grant books

Wine zones and regions of Australia

NEW SOUTH WALES

WINE ZONE		WINE REGION	
Big Rivers	(A)	Murray Darling	1
		Perricoota	2
		Riverina	3
		Swan Hill	4
Central Ranges	(B)	Cowra	5
		Mudgee	6
		Orange	7
Hunter Valley	(C)	Hunter	8
		Upper Hunter	9
Northern Rivers	(D)	Hastings River	10
Northern Slopes	(E)	New England	11
South Coast	(F)	Shoalhaven Coast	12
		Southern Highlands	13
Southern New South Wales	(G)	Canberra District	14
		Gundagai	15
		Hilltops	16
		Tumbarumba	17
Western Plains	(H)		

SOUTH AUSTRALIA

WINE ZONE		WINE REGION	
Adelaide Super Zone includes Mount Lofty Ranges, Fleurieu and Barossa wine regions			
Barossa		Barossa Valley	18
		Eden Valley	19
Fleurieu	(J)	Currency Creek	20
		Kangaroo Island	21
		Langhorne Creek	22
		McLaren Vale	23
		Southern Fleurieu	24
Mount Lofty Ranges		Adelaide Hills	25
		Adelaide Plains	26
		Clare Valley	27
Far North	(K)	Southern Flinders Ranges	28
Limestone Coast	(L)	Coonawarra	29
		Mount Benson	30
		Mount Gambier	31
		Padthaway	32
		Robe	33
		Wrattonbully	34
Lower Murray	(M)	Riverland	35
The Peninsulas	(N)	Southern Eyre Peninsula*	36

VICTORIA

WINE ZONE		WINE REGION	
Central Victoria	(P)	Bendigo	37
		Goulburn Valley	38
		Heathcote	39
		Strathbogie Ranges	40
Gippsland	(Q)	Upper Goulburn	41
		Alpine Valleys	42
North East Victoria	(R)	Beechworth	43
		Glenrowan	44
		King Valley	45
		Rutherglen	46
North West Victoria	(S)	Murray Darling	47
		Swan Hill	48
Port Phillip	(T)	Geelong	49
		Macedon Ranges	50
		Mornington Peninsula	51
		Sunbury	52
		Yarra Valley	53
Western Victoria	(U)	Ballarat*	54
		Grampians	55
		Henty	56
		Pyrenees	57

* For more information see page 50.

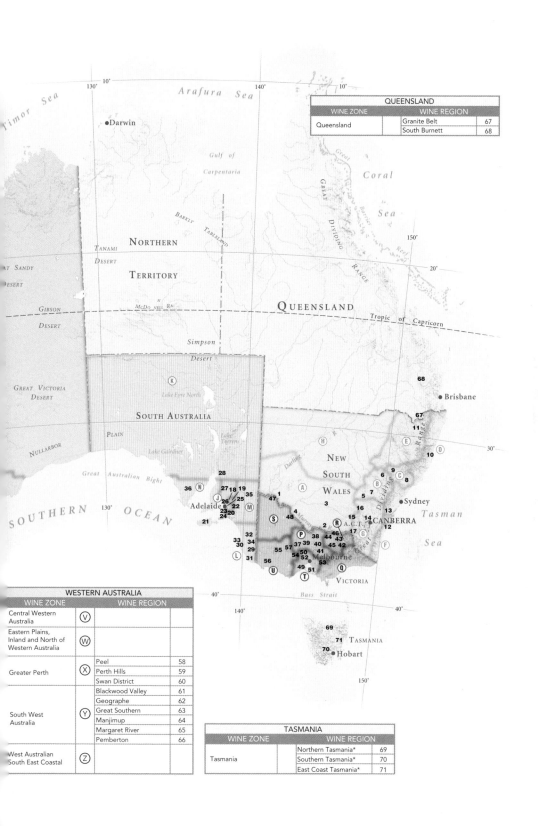

Published in 2016 by Hardie Grant Books, an imprint of Hardie Grant Publishing

Hardie Grant Books (Melbourne)
Ground Floor, Building 1
658 Church Street
Richmond, Victoria 3121
www.hardiegrant.com.au

Hardie Grant Books (London)
5th and 6th Floors
52–54 Southwark Street
London SE1 1UN
www.hardiegrant.co.uk

ISBN 978 1 74379 172 1

Typeset by Megan Ellis
Cover design by Philip Campbell Design
Author photograph by Julian Kingma
Printed and bound in Australia by McPherson's Printing Group

Contents

Introduction

Why should you, the readers of this *Wine Companion*, be concerned about the economic health of Australia's winemakers? Well, in the broad sense it is self-evident: profitable operation will allow winemakers who care about the quality of their wine to reinvest some or all of their profit in their vineyards and/or their wineries.

The chilling reality is that less than 20% of Australia's 2800-plus wineries make a profit. How much less, and the method of calculation, are the devils in the detail. It seems topical to say that most of the 1700 wineries crushing less than 100 tonnes per year are negatively geared.

Those that may be profitable are mostly in regions with a high level of wine, food and lifestyle tourism activity. It is these wineries that were attracted to invest by the (maximum) $500 000 per annum rebate of the 29% wine equalisation tax (WET), which they would otherwise pay on the proceeds of sales direct to the public at their cellar door or online.

When GST was created, the rationale was that there would be a single rate of 10% for all goods except food, medicine and education et al. Only three products retained a higher tax rate: luxury motor vehicles, perfume and wine. The WET was exacted on top of the 10% GST. It left the wine industry with the dubious distinction of having the highest tax on domestic wine of all significant wine producing countries.

The idea that the WET exemption isn't justified comes with the implicit, and bizarre, assertion that 'only' 100 producers would be impacted by a reduction of the WET ceiling. The most successful wineries provide the greatest economic benefits to the rural regions in which they operate.

Moving on, total domestic sales have been declining for the past five years, down by 2.5% for the 2015–16 financial year. Imports (led by New Zealand sauvignon blanc) have increased by 40% (on value) since 2011. Exports decisively increased in the 12 months to March 2016, growing by 13% to $2.1 billion. Growth was heavily weighted by exports over $10 per litre; indeed the $15–$20 band increased by 56%, and the $50–$100 band grew by 46%.

China continues to be the roaring dragon. Exports to this destination were $397 million, an increase of 64%, taking it past the United Kingdom. If the exports of $129 million (up 17%) to Hong Kong are aggregated with those of China, it becomes Australia's largest market. Given that the United States (in first place) recorded a 4% gain, and China a 64% gain, in another 12 months China may well be in first place all on its own – unless its economy implodes.

Will there be enough wine to sustain these exports (and those to Japan and South Korea, sharing free trade agreements with China)? When the WET tax was introduced, the then Liberal minister's response was to let the wineries eat cake – in other words, export their wines, which attract no tax on sales (just on overall profit). I discuss the supply side on pages 42–45. A silver lining perhaps.

How to use this book

Wineries

Mount Pleasant ★★★★★

401 Marrowbone Road, Pokolbin, NSW 2320 **Region** Hunter Valley
T (02) 4998 7505 **www.**mountpleasantwines.com.au **Open** 7 days 10–4
Winemaker Jim Chatto, Adrian Sparks **Est.** 1921 **Dozens** NFP **Vyds** 88.2ha
McWilliam's Elizabeth and the glorious Lovedale Semillon were generally
commercially available with four to five years of bottle age; they were treasures
with a consistently superb show record. The individual vineyard wines, together
with the Maurice O'Shea memorial wines, add to the lustre of this proud name.
However, the appointment of Jim Chatto as group chief winemaker in 2013,
and the '14 vintage, the best since 1965, has lifted the range and quality of the
red wines back to the glory days of Maurice O'Shea in the 1930s and '40s.
Henceforth it will be known as Mount Pleasant, severing the (name) connection
with McWilliam's. With seven shirazs scoring between 97 and 99 points, supported
by three semillons scoring more than 95 points, it was the only possible choice as
Winery of the Year in this *Wine Companion*.

Winery name   Mount Pleasant

The name appearing on the front label as the producer is used throughout the book.

Winery rating ★★★★★

I look at the ratings for this and the previous two years; if the wines tasted this year
justified a higher rating than last year, that higher rating has been given. If, on the
other hand, the wines are of lesser quality, I take into account the track record over
the past two years (or longer where the winery is well known) and make a judgement
call on whether it should retain its ranking, or be given a lesser one. In what I call
the mercy rating, in most instances a demotion is no more than half a star. Where
no wines were submitted by a well-rated winery with a track record of providing
samples, I may use my discretion to roll over last year's rating.

While there are (only) 1302 wineries profiled in this edition, there are more than
2800 wineries to be found on www.winecompanion.com.au.

The percentage at the end of each rating on page 10 is that of the total number
of wineries in the respective category in the *Wine Companion* database at the time
of going to print. Two caveats: first, I retain a discretionary right to depart from the
normal criteria. Second, the basis of the rating will best be understood on the website,
where all wine ratings appear.

Some may think my ratings are too generous, but less than half (45.4%) of the
wineries in our database that are believed, or known to be, active are given ratings in
this book, spread across the eight categories. Moreover, if I were to reduce the number
of wineries in each category by (say) 50% the relative ranking would not change, other
than a massive increase in the NR category, providing no useful guidance for the reader.

★★★★★ Outstanding winery regularly producing wines of exemplary quality and typicity. Will have at least two wines rated at 95 points or above, and had a five-star rating for the previous two years. 282 wineries, 10%

Where the winery name itself is printed in red, it is a winery generally acknowledged to have a long track record of excellence in the context of its region – truly the best of the best. 102 wineries, 3.6%

★★★★★ Outstanding winery capable of producing wines of very high quality, and did so this year. Will also usually have at least two wines rated at 95 points or above. 181 wineries, 6.3%

★★★★☆ Excellent winery able to produce wines of high to very high quality, knocking on the door of a five-star rating. Will normally have one wine rated at 95 points or above, and two (or more) at 90 and above, others 87–89. 245 wineries, 8.4%

★★★★ Very good producer of wines with class and character. Will have two (or more) wines rated at 90 points and above (or possibly one at 95 and above). 357 wineries, 12.6%

★★★☆ A solid, usually reliable, maker of good, sometimes very good wines. Will have one wine at 90 points and above, others 86–89. 107 wineries, 3.7%

★★★ A typically good winery, but often has a few lesser wines. Will have wines at 86–89 points. 28 wineries, 1%

NR The NR rating mainly appears on www.winecompanion.com.au. The rating is given in a range of circumstances: where there have been no tastings in the 12-month period; where there have been tastings, but with no wines scoring more than 88 points; or where the tastings have, for one reason or another, proved not to fairly reflect the reputation of a winery with a track record of success. NR wineries in the book are generally new wineries with no wine entries. 0 wineries.

Contact Details 401 Marrowbone Road, Pokolbin, NSW 2320 **T** (02) 4998 7505

The details are usually those of the winery and cellar door, but in a few instances may simply be a postal address; this occurs when the wine is made at another winery or wineries, and is sold only through the website and/or retail outlets.

Region Hunter Valley

A full list of Zones, Regions and Subregions appears on pages 50–53. Occasionally you will see 'Various' as the region. This means the wine is made from purchased grapes, from a number of regions – often a winery without a vineyard of its own.

www.mountpleasantwines.com.au

An important reference point, normally containing material not found (for space reasons) in this book.

Open 7 days 10–4

Although a winery might be listed as not open or only open on weekends, some may in fact be prepared to open by appointment. Many will, some won't; a telephone call will establish whether it is possible or not. For space reasons, we have simplified the open hours listings, taking out 'or by appt' as superfluous; also, convoluted opening hours dictated by winter, summer, or whatever, do not appear. The assumption is the details can be found via their website.

Winemaker Jim Chatto, Adrian Sparks

In all but the smallest producers, the winemaker is simply the head of a team; there may be many executive winemakers actually responsible for specific wines in the medium to large companies (80 000 dozens and upwards). Once again, space constraints mean usually only two winemakers are named, even if they are part of a larger team.

Est. 1921

Keep in mind that some makers consider the year in which they purchased the land to be the year of establishment, others the year in which they first planted grapes, others the year they first made wine, and so on. There may also be minor complications where there has been a change of ownership or break in production.

Vyds 88.2ha

Shows the hectares of vineyard(s) owned by the winery.

Dozens NFP

This figure (representing the number of 9-litre/12-bottle cases produced each year) is merely an indication of the size of the operation. Some winery entries do not feature a production figure: this is because the winery (principally, but not exclusively, the large companies) regards this information as confidential.

Summary McWilliam's Elizabeth and the glorious Lovedale Semillon were generally commercially available with four to five years of bottle age; they were treasures with a consistently superb show record. The individual vineyard wines, together with the Maurice O'Shea memorial wines, add to the lustre of this proud name.

Surely self-explanatory, except that I have tried to vary the subjects I discuss in this part of the winery entry.

New wineries

 The vine leaf symbol indicates the 68 wineries that are new entries in this year's *Wine Companion*.

Tasting notes

There has been a progressive adoption of the 100-point system in wine shows and in reviews by other commentators. The majority follow the system outlined below, which I used in precisely this form in the 2016 *Wine Companion*. Space means that only 3963 notes are printed in full in this book, with points, drink-to dates and prices for a further 3645 wines. Tasting notes for all wines receiving 84 points or above appear on www.winecompanion.com.au. See also page 26.

Ratings

Points	Medal	Glasses	Description
97–99	GOLD	🍷🍷🍷🍷🍷	**Exceptional.** Wines that have won a major trophy or trophies in important wine shows, or are of that standard.
95–96		🍷🍷🍷🍷🍷	**Outstanding.** Wines of gold medal standard, usually with a great pedigree.
94	SILVER	🍷🍷🍷🍷🍷	Wines on the cusp of gold medal status, virtually indistinguishable from those wines receiving 95 points.
90–93		🍷🍷🍷🍷	**Highly Recommended.** Wines of silver medal standard; wines of great quality, style and character, and worthy of a place in any cellar.
89	BRONZE	🍷🍷🍷🍷	**Recommended.** Wines on the cusp of silver medal standard, the difference purely a judgement call.
86–88		🍷🍷🍷🍷	Wines of bronze medal standard; well-produced, flavoursome wines, usually not requiring cellaring.
		✪	**Special Value.** Wines considered to offer special value for money within the context of their glass symbol status.
84–85		🍷🍷🍷	**Acceptable.** Wines of good commercial quality, free from significant fault.
80–83		🍷🍷🍷	**Over to You.** Everyday wines, without much character, and/or somewhat faulty.

🍷🍷🍷🍷🍷 **Maurice O'Shea Shiraz 2014** 'Arguably, one of the greatest red vintages in living memory,' says Mount Pleasant. The flagship wine. Has the gently throbbing power of a Rolls Royce; superb, deep crimson-purple hue, itself rare in the Hunter Valley. Countless layers of black fruits have absorbed the oak and put the undoubted tannins into limbo land. O'Shea would have died a happy man had this been his last wine. Dissecting it now is an academic exercise at best, so great is its future. This is as close to a 100-year potential as you are ever likely to find. Screwcap. 14% alc. **Rating** 99 **To** 2064 $250

The tasting note opens with the vintage of the wine tasted. This tasting note will have been made within the 12 months prior to publication. Even that is a long time, and during the life of this book the wine will almost certainly change. More than this, remember the tasting is a highly subjective and imperfect art. The price of the wine is listed where information is available. Tasting notes for wines 95 points and above are printed in red.

The initials CM or TS appearing at the end of a tasting note signifies that Campbell Mattinson or Tyson Stelzer tasted the wine and provided the tasting note and rating.

To 2064

Rather than give a span of drinking years, I have simply provided a (conservative) 'drink-to' date. Modern winemaking is such that, even if a wine has 10 or 20 years' future during which it will gain greater complexity, it can be enjoyed at any time over the intervening months and years.

Screwcap

This is the closure used for this particular wine. The closures in use for the wines tasted are (in descending order): screwcap 88.4% (last year 90.7%), one-piece natural cork 5.8% (last year 5.5%), Diam 4.5% (last year 3.1%). The remaining 0.7% (in approximate order of importance) are ProCork, Twin Top, Crown Seal, Zork and Vino-Lok. I believe the percentage of screwcap-closed wines will continue to rise for red wines; 98.4% (last year 98.4%) of white wines tasted are screwcapped, leaving little room for any further increase.

14% alc.

As with closures, I have endeavoured to always include this piece of information, which is in one sense self-explanatory. What is less obvious is the increasing concern of many Australian winemakers about rising alcohol levels, and much research and practical experimentation (picking earlier, higher fermentation temperatures in open fermenters, etc) is occurring. Reverse osmosis and yeast selection are two of the options available to decrease higher than desirable alcohol levels. Recent changes to domestic and export labelling mean the stated alcohol must be within a maximum of 0.5% difference to that obtained by analysis.

$250

I use the price provided by the winery. It should be regarded as a guide, particularly if wine is purchased retail.

Winery of the year

Mount Pleasant

Mount Pleasant was so named by Maurice O'Shea, its sole owner from 1922–32, its co-owner (with McWilliam's) until 1941 and then simply its winemaker and manager until his death in 1956. And before I continue the story, I cannot help but say how utterly remarkable McWilliam's role was. Based in the Riverina, they were makers of fortified wines. While it was (and remains) a mighty clan, I have not read or heard of a senior clansman who had an understanding of light to medium-bodied shirazs in the 1920s or 1930s.

Indeed, there were all too few customers who had such knowledge. The reality was that the wines were difficult to sell at prices that barely covered the cost of production.

Fast forward to 2013 and the appointment of Jim Chatto, and tectonic plates move again. Chatto walked through every metre of vines (as O'Shea would have done) with retiring winemaker Phil Ryan, tasted every wine still in barrel or tank, and tasted all bottled wine stock yet to be sold. One of Maurice O'Shea's great strengths was his ability to taste wines near or at the end of fermentation, and know where they would fit under the Mount Pleasant label.

Chatto has adopted an O'Shea approach to the vineyards of Mount Pleasant, notably the 3.1ha Old Hill (planted 1880) and the 0.74ha Old Paddock (planted 1921 with cuttings from the Old Hill). A forensic palate, and a vine-by-vine observation are his tools.

Just below the Old Hill is Steel City, a 0.4ha block planted in 1988 ('very promising'); above on the next rise is The Contours, a 0.67ha block planted in 1963, which now makes Mountain D Full Bodied Dry Red. Adjacent to the Old Paddock is 8 Acre (2.79ha planted in 1986 which, says Chatto, 'Makes some of the best shiraz from the estate').

Rosehill, across the road from Lake's Folly, is a 27ha mosaic of shiraz blocks planted in 1946, 1965, 1968 and1990, and replanting in 2015 and 2016. Instead of a single wine, we now have the 1946 Plantings (ex 5.44ha in three blocks) and the 1965 Plantings (6.56ha in three blocks, the first fronting Broke Road). Like the plantings around the winery, the soil is deep red.

The 31ha Lovedale semillon block on sandy flats fronting Allandale Road has also been under the dissection microscope, with identified block releases maturing in bottle. Equally important is the decision that as from 2014, Elizabeth Semillon is 100% ex Lovedale Vineyard.

This year's tastings produced one shiraz (2014 Maurice O'Shea) with 99 points; two with 98 points; four with 97 points; and five with 96 points. Three semillons received 98, 97 and 95 points. An awe-inspiring array.

Previous Winery of the Year winners are Paringa Estate (2007), Balnaves of Coonawarra (2008), Brookland Valley (2009), Tyrrell's (2010), Larry Cherubino Wines (2011), Port Phillip Estate/Kooyong (2012), Kilikanoon (2013), Penfolds (2014), Hentley Farm Wines (2015) and Tahbilk (2016).

Winemaker of the year

Sarah Crowe

I'm prepared to believe Sarah Crowe has ESP or some method of seeing the future. How else would someone whose professional career has been in the Hunter Valley have two Flying Winemaker stints in Oregon with Adelsheim Vineyard and Ponzi Vineyards respectively? Her third Flight was to Paul Jaboulet Aîné in 2008, the connection with syrah/shiraz obvious. But there was nothing to suggest she would be heading to the Yarra Valley in the foreseeable future.

Her career started with Brokenwood as vineyard hand in 2001. She then absented herself for the 2002 vintage as cellarhand at First Creek Winemaking. She returned to Brokenwood, becoming assistant winemaker. By sheer chance, I was in the audience at the Hunter Valley Legends and Wine Industry Awards in 2009 when she was named Rising Star of the Year. The emotion in the room was palpable, as was the pleasure with which her award was received.

She moved to Swish Wine as chief winemaker in 2010, then was senior winemaker at Bimbadgen until she was offered the top winemaking position at Yarra Yering in late September of 2013. I don't think I am gilding the lily by saying Iain Riggs greatly regretted her departure from Brokenwood, but accepted it was inevitable.

Her winemaking career was enhanced by her roles as a Len Evans Tutorial Scholar (2010); in the Future Leaders Program (2010); as Chair of the Hunter Valley Winemaking Sub-Committee (2011–12); in the Hunter Valley Wine Industry Association Executive Committee (2010–12); as Session Chair of the Australian Wine Industry Technical Conference (July 2013); and as Chair of the Yarra Valley Wine Show Committee (2014).

Threaded through all of this is the deep regard and loyalty she engenders, whichever hat she wears. I had nothing to do with her appointment as Yarra Yering's winemaker, but would have immediately given my support if anyone had asked my opinion.

Would I have guessed she would make wines of the calibre of the 2014 wines? No, I would not. It would be hard to find two regions so different in their make up: climate, terroir and varieties are but a starting point. And 2014 was not of the same class as 2010, 2012, 2013 and 2015 in the Yarra Valley.

The foretaste of the 2015 Pinot Shiraz would be compelling even if there was no other evidence, but all the Yarra Valley makers regard 2015 as a very, very good vintage. There are still many wines from the best producers awaiting release as this book goes to print. My mouth dribbles at the thought of the Yarra Yerings.

I'm sure that Sarah's experience will grow exponentially over the coming years as she accumulates knowledge about the strengths and weaknesses of the blocks within the vineyard. If there are hard decisions to make, she won't shirk the challenge. Her bubbly personality and pocket-rocket size shouldn't fool anyone. Staring down those with a long connection to the vineyard and its wines, who were horrified at the thought of a new red wine and the *lèse–majesté* of resorting to screwcaps were dealt with firmly but politely, histrionics nipped in the bud before things got out of hand.

Wine of the year

Best's Thomson Family Great Western Shiraz 2014

There were two ways of seeking fame and fortune in the Victorian gold rush decades of the second half of the 19th century. One was to buy a miner's licence, a high risk with an occasional high return. The other was to feed hungry miners and slake their thirst with wine and/or beer.

Brothers Joseph and Henry Best were in the latter camp, opening a butcher's shop in Ararat. Realising it was only a question of time before the gold ran out, Joseph planted his first vines in 1862. As they grew and came into bearing, and the gold became scarcer, he employed out-of-work gold miners to excavate the massive underground drives (or cellars) of today's Seppelt. Henry Best followed suit in 1866 by planting vines on a 30ha property he acquired at nearby Concongella Creek.

One 1.02ha experimental block had 32 varieties, including what is now the oldest pinot noir and pinot meunier in the world, but there was also a small block of 15 rows of shiraz planted in 1867.

It is commonplace for wineries to release an icon wine for the first time saying it will only be released in the best vintages, but then releasing it virtually every year. Since 1992 (the first release), this wine has been made in 14 vintages, and not made in nine. Indeed, since 1999 it has only been made every second year.

It's obvious that the self-set standards have been stricter with a succession of highly qualified winemakers, none more so than present incumbent Justin Purser (and before him, Adam Wadewitz). The fruit selection is rigorous; some of the fruit from the 15 rows was discarded, replaced by fruit from mature vines grown by cuttings taken from the old block.

That the wine is not 'stretched' with younger material is self-evident given the number of years it is not made at all, and that 2200 bottles were made in 2014, compared with (for example) 4200 in 2010.

It is open-fermented in small tubs, and matured for 18–24 months in French oak; there is no recipe for the percentage, nor for the percentage of new oak (usually around 50%, but can be higher).

It is handled with kid gloves in the winery, as the tasting note on page 110 shows. It is a truly glorious wine.

Best value winery

Larry Cherubino Wines

I have an unpublished and non-binding principle that no person or winery can win the same award twice in an indefinite period. But as our Prime Minister would say, it is an exciting time for Australian wine, and opportunities are unlimited. New varieties, new wineries and new regions are popping up all over the place.

Natural wines are basking in a small square of sun. If they are (when young) yellow, brown or simply muddy to look at, or sparkling when they aren't meant to be, I don't want to taste them. I get irritated, if not downright angry, when it is implied that a wine that has not been filtered and/or fined is somehow superior to a wine that has been so treated, when in the vast majority of cases, the opposite is true.

But when I taste a pale straw-green white wine that has been fermented on its skins and that has an electric freshness to its mouthfeel and flavours, or a red wine fermented and matured on its skins, pips and lees in an amphora that is supple and full of fruit, I applaud.

Truth is a moving target. I had been making red wine for 17 years before I became seriously interested in wild/indigenous/natural (the three names are interchangeable) yeast fermentation of red wines, and it was almost 30 years before I thought that some white wines might benefit from primary fermentation at warm temperatures well outside my comfort zone.

What, I hear you say, has all this got to do with Larry Cherubino? First up, in 2011 his eponymous winery was honoured as Winery of the Year. Second, in 15 years he has traversed all the challenges and practices of the issues I discuss above.

And he has done it in style. In this year's *Wine Companion*, 15 of the 17 wines scoring 95 points or above had the red value star, these days determined by a mathematical formula applying to all wines in the *Wine Companion*. All up, 35 of Larry Cherubino's wines appear, 28 (80%) of which have the value rosette: those 28 include fiano, pinot gris, riesling, sauvignon blanc, semillon sauvignon blanc, chardonnay, a field blend of four white varieties, syrah grenache, grenache, shiraz, cabernet sauvignon, cabernet merlot and cabernet malbec.

His Laissez Faire wines have no additions or adjustments of any kind other than SO_2, itself normally added not long before the wine is bottled. A six-week fermentation/maceration for Margaret River cabernet sauvignon isn't unprecedented, but it's at the outer limit of a normal envelope.

And he's got a sense of humour. Franklin Tate has a virtual winery, which he established in 2007, called Miles from Nowhere (all the grapes come from Margaret River), met, as it were, by Cherubino's Ad Hoc Middle of Everywhere Shiraz.

Best new winery

Bondar Wines

This is the business of Andre Bondar and wife Selina Kelly, he the 'Winemaker, Grapevine Hacker, the Boss', she 'Marketing, Taste-Tester, the (Real) Chief'. An interesting start. But it gets another dimension when you come across this: 'Selina began her working life as a lawyer but soon realised that the long, boring hours behind a desk were far from what suited her. Selina has a passion for luxury: fashion, diamonds, champagne. And it was this love of the finer things in life that directed her career change towards marketing and the world of wine.'

It's written in the third person, but you know who the author is. It's a pity not to continue the story in her own words.

'Bondar wines began its life in March 2012, when Andre, Selina and a small group of their family and friends hand-picked a couple of tonnes of shiraz grapes for their first ever wine. It was a beautiful, calm, warm summer's evening, and when the sun went down, the McLaren Vale sky lit up with one of the most spectacularly beautiful sunsets any of us had ever seen. The Violet Hour Shiraz is named in its honour.'

Paradoxically, that first vintage from the great 2012 vintage caused them to abandon their initial plan (hatched in 2009) of buying an existing winery close to McLaren Vale's beaches, restaurant and *la dolce vita*. It was proving hard to find, and they decided to seek a vineyard that had a track record of producing great shiraz and grenache.

You make your own luck, and they were in the right place at the right time to be able to buy one of McLaren Vale's best vineyards, Rayner. The sale went through in 2013, but after that year's vintage.

There are some dots that need to be connected. Selina's first marketing position was with Hentley Farm, Winery of the Year in the 2015 *Wine Companion*. She is now marketing manager for Yangarra Estate and Hickinbotham Clarendon Vineyard (both very distinguished and both owned by Jackson Family Wines of California).

Andre Bondar began his winemaking career in 2001, making vintages around the world and in Australia before becoming winemaker at Nepenthe, a position he held for seven years. This has given him contacts throughout the Adelaide Hills, hence the Bondar chardonnay, and the syrah they have in their sights.

But their ultimate success (or unthinkable failure) will turn on the Rayner vineyard. A ridge bisects the property, with the Blewitt Springs sand on the eastern side, and the Seaview heavier clay loam soils over limestone on the western side. It is an exceptional site for a cellar door, with views over the hills and out to the sea. They hope to have it open for business in 2018.

There is also scope for further plantings; 1ha of bush vine trained grenache was planted on the bony, sandy top of the Blewitt Springs side in the spring of 2015. Then there are experimental 0.1ha plantings of counoise, cinsaut and carignan (which sounds like advice from Yangarra's winemaker, Peter Fraser).

It looks to me that Andre Bondar has great fruit available, and that he needs to make the best possible wine from it to keep Selina's wardrobe in current vintage order, diamonds as her best friend, and the refrigerator permanently stocked with champagne.

Ten of the best new wineries

Each one of these wineries making its debut in the *Wine Companion* has earned a five-star rating. They are thus the leaders of the 68 new wineries in this edition, although a number of other first-up wineries also achieved five stars. The ultimate selection criteria included the number of wines earning 95 points or above, and also value for money.

BEST NEW WINERY
Bondar Wines McLaren Vale / PAGE 122
The story of Bondar appears on page 18; further details appear in its winery entry on page 122.

Charlotte Dalton Wines Adelaide Hills / PAGE 171
Charlotte Hardy explains that when she and her three brothers were tucked into bed at night, their mother always said 'Love me, love you.' And Dalton is her middle name, and was her Hardy grandfather's Christian name. Love and her family to one side, she made wine in a string of great New Zealand, Californian and Bordeaux wineries for 15 years before coming home to roost.

Fikkers Wine Yarra Valley / PAGE 260
If you say Fikkers Two Bricks quickly enough, the laidback Australian humour needs no further explanation. Anthony Fikkers started his winemaking life in the Hunter Valley, before moving to the Yarra Valley. Here he worked with Mac Forbes, using the same philosophy and modus operandi. He seeks out small parcels of grapes for his two ranges. At the top are the single vineyard wines led by chardonnay and pinot noir, and quasi-alternative varieties for the Two Bricks range, with a two-tiered price structure of $35 and $26 respectively. Simplicity itself.

Hentyfarm Wines Henty / PAGE 329
Initially just a bit of fun for Jonathan (Jono) Mogg (Best's marketing honcho) and partner Belinda Low, Best's winemaker Adam Wadewitz and partner Nikki. They purchased chardonnay from a renowned Henty grape grower, and made it for personal consumption. It was a hit, so more was made the next year, and sold to a few key restaurants and retailers. Over the next five years pinot noir, pinot gris and pinot meunier have been added to the portfolio, Adam and Nikki are no longer involved, after having moved to Shaw + Smith.

Muster Wines Barossa Valley / PAGE 472
David Muster was the inaugural winner of the Negociants Working With Wine Fellowship in 1998. Over the years he's worked for a select group of wineries including Seppeltsfield, Samuel Smith & Sons, Petaluma, Argyle (in Oregon) and Kilikanoon. Its two brands are radically different, the labels of the newly introduced Mars Needs are not easy to describe – arresting perhaps. Riesling is Muster's strong suit, but with solid backup from Barossa Shiraz.

R. Paulazzo Wines Riverina / **PAGE 538**

Rob Paulazzo has seen and done it all. Raised on the family vineyard in the Riverina, it was inevitable he would work for McWilliam's, but the rest of his career has been anything but inevitable. He has worked in Marlborough and for Giesen in New Zealand; he has also worked four vintages in Burgundy, plus vintages in Tuscany, the Napa Valley, and in Canada. Now operating out of his family's property, he is sourcing high quality grapes from Hilltops, Tumbarumba, Orange, Canberra District and homebase for Botrytis Semillon.

Rouleur Yarra Valley / **PAGE 566**

Wine was in Matt East's blood, for he was only young when his father planted a vineyard in Coldstream. He moved off the land and into sales and marketing, with a 16-year career stretching from 1999–2015. Retiring as national sales manager for Wirra Wirra, he formed Mr East Wine Industry Consulting in Melbourne. Thus Rouleur's reach into McLaren Vale and the Yarra Valley was preordained. His Grenache is made at Dennis Winery, the Yarra Valley wines are made by Rob Hall.

Ruckus Estate Wrattonbully / **PAGE 568**

Merlot may yet recover from the indifferent reputation it has in Australia by the upper class of winemakers, wine judges, retailers and so forth. The public at large has been indifferent to the views of the experts, flocking to the soft, sweet, plum-accented flavours of most examples. Ruckus Estate has five clones of merlot, most recently selected in Bordeaux and imported here. Ruckus is one to watch.

Twinwoods Estate Margaret River / **PAGE 684**

Twinwoods Estate has multicultural roots. It involves Hans Michael Jebsen, of distinguished Hong Kong wine importer and distributor, Jebsen Fine Wines; Gavin Jones, managing director of Jebsen; and Aldo Bratovic, of Italian parentage, a town planner turned winemaker. Finally, there is the 25ha property, and its 8.5ha of cabernet and shiraz, some dating back to the early 1990s, with first class wines made at Deep Woods Estate.

Zerella Wines McLaren Vale / **PAGE 752**

Jim Zerella's grandfather left Campania, in Italy, in 1950, seeking (and establishing) a better life for his family. Son Vic founded Tatachilla, where Jim rose from cellarhand to controller of the thousands of tonnes of grape purchases each year. He also purchased land in McLaren Vale and planted it, the first of three estate vineyards. Zerella has the pick of the crop, selling most of its annual production.

Ten of the best value wineries

The selection of the 10 wineries is largely mathematical – that is, the percentage/strike rate of wines receiving the red value rosette compared with the total number of wines tasted for this edition. Penfolds and Henschke would always be in the 10, but I feel (rightly or wrongly) that they are above this award category.

BEST VALUE WINERY
Larry Cherubino Wines Western Australia / **PAGE 391**
See the entry for Best Value Winery on page 17.

Alkoomi Frankland River / **PAGE 68**
Alkoomi is not on any of the main tourist trails in the southwest of Western Australia; you have to set out with a specific mission, but when you arrive, you'll be happy. With 22 wines tasted for this edition, 17 received the value rosette, all of the major varieties covered.

Bleasdale Vineyards Langhorne Creek / **PAGE 118**
Always one of the pacesetters, with 87% (13 out of 15) of its wines being awarded. Most, of course, are shiraz, cabernet sauvignon and malbec from Langhorne Creek, but it also produces juicily priced varietals from the Adelaide Hills. Winemaker Paul Hotker is a star.

Brown Brothers King Valley / **PAGE 135**
Brown Brothers has the greatest suite of vineyards covering northeast Victoria, all the way through central Victoria and on to Tasmania, with Rutherglen muscat through to pinot noir on its estate books – a unique spread of 570ha. Small wonder its 24 entries garnered 15 value rosettes.

d'Arenberg McLaren Vale / **PAGE 208**
Given d'Arenberg's sheer weight of numbers, it might normally have been selected as the Best Value Winery, not one of. It was just the unstoppable force of Cherubino that prevailed. As it is, 30 of d'Arenberg's 44 tasted wines received the rosette, with virtually every variety grown in McLaren Vale.

De Bortoli (Victoria) Yarra Valley / **PAGE 216**
I have long held De Bortoli in the highest esteem; it is not only the largest maker in the Yarra Valley, but also has the broadest portfolio, covering virtually all price points, with two-thirds having value rosettes. The acquisition of Lusatia Park Vineyard may well be the jewel in the crown.

Stella Bella Wines Margaret River / **PAGE 624**

2016 marked the 20th vintage for Stella Bella Wines, an extremely successful owner-operated but relatively low-profile winery in the Margaret River. Its 50 000-case production is of the highest quality, all but two of its 15 value wines rating 94 points or above. The prices are truly mouthwatering.

Tahbilk Nagambie Lakes / **PAGE 637**

Tahbilk is one of my favourite places on the Australian wine scene. It exudes history from every pore, with many of the buildings having National Trust classification. It leads the field this year with its strike rate of 88% (15 out of 17 wines with the value rosette), so there's every reason to visit.

Woods Crampton Barossa Valley / **PAGE 733**

This is the joint venture of marketing wunderkind Nicholas Crampton and winemaker friend Aaron Woods. They use the Sons of Eden winery to secure some of the best grapes South Australia has to offer (Tumbarumba being an outpost). Seventeen out of 22 wines received the value rosette.

Xanadu Wines Margaret River / **PAGE 737**

Xanadu is in danger of becoming a serial offender, so frequently do its wines receive high points; and here, 20 out of 22 wines received the value rosette. It blitzes chardonnay and cabernet sauvignon, but is a worthy warrior with SBS and shiraz.

Ten dark horses

To qualify for this award, each winery has to have received a five-star rating for the first time, and have a history of lesser ratings. Arlewood Estate is Dark Horse of the Year, and accordingly heads the list; the remaining wineries are in alphabetical order.

DARK HORSE OF THE YEAR
Arlewood Estate Margaret River / **PAGE 82**
Arlewood Estate dates back to 1988 and is located in the south of Margaret River, not the centre. It went through several ownership changes and is now owned and run by Garry Gossatti, who spent 2008–12 living on what was a very run-down vineyard. It was a hands-on, near full-time (one day per week in Perth) job. Now the vineyard is as he wanted it to be; he lives in Perth but spends every weekend on the vineyard.

Anderson Rutherglen / **PAGE 75**
Father and daughter team Howard and Christobelle Anderson bring a wide range of skills and experience to their eponymous winery. Howard's first and only occupation after leaving school was as a (trainee) winemaker, after which he spent 14 years as a senior winemaker at Seppelt Great Western, with particular involvement in making sparkling wines. Christobelle brings a first-class honours degree (2005) from the University of Adelaide, and Flying Winemaker stints in Alsace, Champagne and Meursault.

Atze's Corner Wines Barossa Valley / **PAGE 85**
Andy Kalleske is the sixth-generation descendant of one of several branches of two Kalleske families who arrived in South Australia in the 1830s and 1840s. His parents, John and Barb, purchased the Atze Vineyard in 1975, with its precious small blocks of shiraz planted in 1912 and 1951 respectively. Andy is first and foremost a viticulturist content to oversee the making of the wines, but very much the leader of the move to plant new varieties, and responsible for the sale of the production surplus to requirements.

Claymore Wines Clare Valley / **PAGE 182**
Claymore has been knocking on the door for the past 11 years, with 4½ stars its dominant rating. It has two major resources, the first its impressive vineyards. There are five at Penwortham, producing the grapes for the red wines in the portfolio; the Joshua Tree Vineyard at Watervale provides the riesling. The second resource has been its winemakers' experience. Donna Stephens made the wines that took Claymore Wines to five stars, but incoming winemaker Marnie Roberts (who took over from 2016) has had a long and successful career.

Ernest Hill Wines Hunter Valley / **PAGE 252**
The Wilson family's vineyard is by far the closest to the town of Cessnock, and was chosen by district veteran viticulturist Harry Tulloch for Seppelt Wines in the

early 1970s. I passed by it virtually every weekend, and daily during vintage in the formative years of Brokenwood. Seppelt lost interest in it, and in 1999 the Wilson family purchased the upper (superior) half of 9ha. They have methodically built the portfolio, and the appointment of Mark Woods as winemaker has lifted the quality of the 2014 shirazs to unprecedented levels.

Lightfoot & Sons Gippsland / PAGE 404

Brian and Helen Lightfoot have established 29ha of pinot noir, shiraz, chardonnay, cabernet sauvignon and merlot, the lion's share to pinot noir and shiraz planted on soil very similar to that of Coonawarra, with terra rossa over limestone. With the arrival of Alastair Butt (formerly of Brokenwood and Seville Estate), supported by son Tom, production has increased. After four years with a 4.5 star rating, Lightfoot finally broke through to five stars this year with two beautiful wines, a Chardonnay and a Pinot Noir.

Piano Piano Beechworth / PAGE 519

The development of Marc Scalzo and wife Lisa's business may have been slow, but it was carefully considered. Marc had already obtained his degree in oenology from CSU, along with practical experience in Australia and New Zealand when, in 1997, they purchased and planted their Brangie Vineyard in the King Valley, followed by their Beechworth vineyard in 2006. Marc's main job is winemaker for Rutherglen Estates.

Sew & Sew Wines Adelaide Hills / PAGE 597

The name Sew & Sew comes from Jodie Armstrong's annual visits to Jakarta to meet expat friends. She heard about a group of women who lived and worked on a Jakarta garbage dump, sorting through the refuse for recycling. A local Samaritan had taught them how to sew scraps of cloth together to eke out a living. Jody hit on the idea of having them sew wine gift bags; 100% of the proceeds go to the women who are empowered to leave the dump and find work in Jakarta's clothing trade.

Shaw Vineyard Estate Canberra District / PAGE 599

This family-owned and run business has languished with a 4.5 star rating for each of the past five years, not a record that one would necessarily look for. The glass half full then points out it is the reason that it has qualified as a Dark Horse this year. It is the largest vineyard in the region, and has turned part of the working shearing shed into a gallery space for the first weekend in September, October and November, and over Easter. And, of course, there is the cellar door.

Two Rivers Hunter Valley / PAGE 687

A significant part of the viticultural scene in the Upper Hunter Valley, with 67.5ha of vineyards. Part of the fruit is sold under long-term contracts, and part is made for the winemaking and marketing operations of Two Rivers. The emphasis is on chardonnay and semillon, its 2011, 2013 and 2015 Semillons all rated 95 or 96 points. A contemporary cellar door adds significantly to the appeal of the Upper Hunter Valley as a wine-tourist destination. The appointment of highly talented winemaker Liz Silkman was a coup.

Best of the best by variety

There is a major change in the way these lists are presented in this year's *Wine Companion*. The categories are the same as in prior years, as is the link of each wine with its region. But the number of wines within each category is far less than in previous years so that only the very best are listed. That said, the cut-off point does reflect the strength of the particular category.

Riesling

The game of musical chairs continues with riesling: the Clare and Eden Valleys tied with the Great Southern subregions, but only because there were two vintages from two Great Southern wineries. Canberra District, Henty and Tasmania rounded off a glorious celebration of this great variety.

RATING	WINE	REGION
98	2015 Seppelt Drumborg Vineyard	Henty
97	2015 Willoughby Park Ironrock Kalgan River	Albany
97	2015 Helm Premium	Canberra District
97	2015 Nick O'Leary	Canberra District
97	2015 Shaw Vineyard Estate	Canberra District
97	2015 Gaelic Cemetery Premium	Clare Valley
97	2015 Grosset Polish Hill	Clare Valley
97	2015 Grosset Springvale	Clare Valley
97	2015 Mount Horrocks Watervale	Clare Valley
97	2015 Naked Run The First Clare Valley	Clare Valley
97	2015 Steve Wiblin's Erin Eyes Pride of Erin Single Vineyard Reserve	Clare Valley
97	2015 Henschke Julius Eden Valley	Eden Valley
97	2015 Frankland Estate Isolation Ridge Vineyard	Frankland River
97	2015 Frankland Estate Poison Hill Vineyard	Frankland River
97	2015 Crawford River	Henty
97	2008 d'Arenberg The Dry Dam	McLaren Vale
97	2015 Forest Hill Vineyard Block 1	Mount Barker
97	2014 Forest Hill Vineyard Block 1	Mount Barker
97	2010 Abbey Creek Vineyard Museum Release	Porongurup
97	2015 Duke's Vineyard Magpie Hill Reserve	Porongurup
97	2014 Duke's Vineyard Magpie Hill Reserve	Porongurup
97	2015 Ghost Rock Vineyard	Tasmania
97	2015 Riversdale Estate Roaring 40s	Tasmania

Chardonnay

The usual battle royal between Margaret River (10) and Yarra Valley (9) wines continued, Leeuwin Estate's two 98-point wines the *coup de grâce*. It was an equally close contest for third place on the podium, albeit with wines of different styles, the supple/fleshy Mornington Peninsula wines (5) edging out the steely intensity of Tasmania (4).

RATING	WINE	REGION
98	2014 Golden Ball là-bas	Beechworth
98	2014 Castelli Estate Il Liris	Denmark
98	2012 Leeuwin Estate Art Series	Margaret River
98	2013 Leeuwin Estate Art Series	Margaret River
98	2013 Xanadu Stevens Road	Margaret River
98	2015 Serrat	Yarra Valley
97	2014 Penfolds Reserve Bin A	Adelaide Hills
97	2014 Rockcliffe Single Site	Denmark
97	2014 Singlefile Family Reserve	Denmark
97	2013 Staniford Co Great Reserve	Great Southern
97	2014 Burch Family Howard Park	Great Southern/ Margaret River
97	2015 Burch Family Howard Park	Great Southern/ Margaret River
97	2013 Flowstone Queen of the Earth	Margaret River
97	2013 Peccavi	Margaret River
97	2013 Streicker Ironstone Block Old Vine	Margaret River
97	2014 Vasse Felix Heytesbury	Margaret River
97	2014 Windows Estate	Margaret River
97	2014 Xanadu Reserve	Margaret River
97	2014 Xanadu Stevens Road	Margaret River
97	2014 Dexter	Mornington Peninsula
97	2015 Garagiste Le Stagiaire	Mornington Peninsula
97	2014 Garagiste Le Stagiaire	Mornington Peninsula
97	2014 Garagiste Merricks	Mornington Peninsula
97	2012 Scorpo	Mornington Peninsula
97	2015 Yabby Lake Vineyard Single Block Release Block 6	Mornington Peninsula
97	2014 Pepper Tree Single Vineyard Venus Block	Orange
97	2014 Derwent Estate Calcaire	Tasmania
97	2014 Pipers Brook Vineyard	Tasmania
97	2013 Tolpuddle Vineyard	Tasmania
97	2014 Tolpuddle Vineyard	Tasmania
97	2014 Hardys Eileen Hardy	Tasmania/Yarra Valley
97	2015 Coldstream Hills Reserve	Yarra Valley
97	2015 Giant Steps Giant Steps Lusatia Park Vineyard	Yarra Valley
97	2014 Giant Steps Giant Steps Tarraford Vineyard	Yarra Valley
97	2015 Little Yarra	Yarra Valley
97	2014 Mount Mary	Yarra Valley
97	2014 Oakridge Local Vineyard Series Willowlake Vineyard	Yarra Valley
97	2015 Rochford Terre	Yarra Valley
97	2012 Toolangi Vineyards Block F Reserve	Yarra Valley
97	2010 Toolangi Vineyards Reserve	Yarra Valley

Semillon

There's a single, although very potent, message here. Semillon bursts into siren song with five-plus years bottle age.

RATING	WINE	REGION
98	2009 Mount Pleasant Lovedale	Hunter Valley
97	2011 David Hook Aged Release Old Vines Pothana Vineyard Belford	Hunter Valley
97	2009 Keith Tulloch Museum Release	Hunter Valley
97	2010 Mount Pleasant Lovedale Single Vineyard	Hunter Valley
97	2011 Tyrrell's Museum Release Vat 1	Hunter Valley

Sauvignon Blanc

Cherubino, true to form, has found a patch of great sauvignon blanc vineyard, and simply protected that. The other four wines are heavily influenced by the philosophy and techniques of their makers.

RATING	WINE	REGION
97	2014 Geoff Weaver Ferus Lenswood	Adelaide Hills
97	2014 Flowstone	Margaret River
96	2015 Larry Cherubino Wines Cherubino	Pemberton
96	2015 Freycinet Wineglass Bay	Tasmania
96	2014 Out of Step Lusatia Park Vineyard	Yarra Valley

Semillon Sauvignon Blends

Why does anyone outside of Margaret River bother? Not only does it monopolise the field on points, the wines typically have mouthwatering prices.

RATING	WINE	REGION
96	2013 Cape Mentelle Wallcliffe	Margaret River
96	2015 Clairault Sauvignon Blanc Semillon	Margaret River
96	2014 Fraser Gallop Estate Parterre Semillon Sauvignon Blanc	Margaret River
96	2015 Hay Shed Hill Block 1 Semillon Sauvignon Blanc	Margaret River
96	2015 Moss Wood Ribbon Vale Vineyard Sauvignon Blanc Semillon	Margaret River
95	2015 The Lake House Denmark Premium Reserve Single Vineyard Semillon Sauvignon Blanc	Denmark
95	2010 Arlewood Estate Reserve Semillon Sauvignon Blanc	Margaret River
95	2014 Cowaramup Reserve Limited Edition Semillon Sauvignon Blanc	Margaret River
95	2015 Cullen Mangan Vineyard Semillon Sauvignon Blanc	Margaret River
95	2015 Evans & Tate Metricup Road Semillon RiverSauvignon Blanc	Margaret
95	2015 Fraser Gallop Estate Semillon Sauvignon Blanc	Margaret River
95	2014 Happs Three Hills Eva Marie	Margaret River
95	2015 Larry Cherubino Pedestal Semillon Sauvignon Blanc	Margaret River
95	2015 Laurance of Margaret River Semillon Sauvignon Blanc	Margaret River

95	2015 McHenry Hohnen Rocky River Semillon Sauvignon Blanc	Margaret River
95	2015 Pierro L.T.C.	Margaret River
95	2015 Stella Bella Semillon Sauvignon Blanc	Margaret River
95	2015 Windows Estate Grown Semillon Sauvignon Blanc	Margaret River
95	2015 Clemens Hill Fume Blanc	Tasmania

Other White Wines and Blends

Only seven wines, but with the usual spread of regions.

RATING	WINE	REGION
97	2015 Scott La Prova Pinot Grigio	Adelaide Hills
97	2007 Tahbilk 1927 Vines Marsanne	Nagambie Lakes
97	2008 Tahbilk 1927 Vines Marsanne	Nagambie Lakes
97	2015 Ben Haines B Minor Marsanne Roussanne	Upper Goulburn
96	2014 Yalumba The Virgilius Viognier	Eden Valley
96	2015 Ros Ritchie Dead Man's Hill Vineyard Gewurztraminer	Upper Goulburn
96	2015 St Huberts Roussanne	Yarra Valley

Sparkling

All of these wines have been available at some point (and tasted by Tyson Stelzer or myself) over the past 12 months. I am aware that some practitioners, and some critics, are less convinced than I am about the quality of the Arras wines, but I am unrepentant.

White and rose

RATING	WINE	REGION
97	2005 House of Arras Blanc de Blancs	Tasmania
97	2009 Jansz Tasmania Single Vineyard Vintage Chardonnay	Tasmania
96	1998 House of Arras 20th Anniversary Late Disgorged	Tasmania
96	2003 House of Arras Anniversary EJ Carr Late Disgorged	Tasmania
96	2006 House of Arras Blanc de Blancs	Tasmania
96	2006 House of Arras House of Arras Grand Vintage	Tasmania
96	2005 House of Arras Rose	Tasmania

Sparkling Red

A tiny group of wines unique to Australia, eagerly sought by those who understand the peculiarities of the style and who, better still, are prepared to cellar them, the longer the better.

RATING	WINE	REGION
96	NV Primo Estate Joseph Sparkling Red	Adelaide
96	2008 Ashton Hills Sparkling Shiraz	Adelaide Hills
96	2010 Peter Lehmann Black Queen Sparkling Shiraz	Barossa Valley
95	2008 Charles Melton Sparkling Red	Barossa Valley
95	NV Rockford Black Shiraz	Barossa Valley

Sweet

Suffice it to say *caveat emptor*, and read the tasting notes of the rieslings (off dry to luscious and intense) that monopolise the category this year.

RATING	WINE	REGION
97	2015 Derwent Estate Late Harvest Riesling	Tasmania
96	2015 Frankland Estate Smith Cullam Riesling	Frankland River
96	2015 Bellarmine Riesling Half Dry	Pemberton
96	2015 Bellarmine Riesling Select	Pemberton
96	2014 Gala Estate Late Harvest Riesling	Tasmania

Rose

Roses are the ultimate all-purpose wines, to be enjoyed when people meet for a drink, or with any Asian cuisine, with seafood, with entrees of almost every kind, and yet more. These wines are of world class, all full of vibrant fruits (mainly red), but dry.

RATING	WINE	REGION
96	2015 Deep Woods Estate Rose	Margaret River
95	2015 Hahndorf Hill Rose	Adelaide Hills
95	2015 Charles Melton Rose of Virginia	Barossa Valley
95	2015 Head Grenache Rose	Barossa Valley
95	2015 Turkey Flat Rose	Barossa Valley
95	2015 Wines by KT Rosa Garnacha Tempranillo Rosada	Clare Valley
95	2015 Farr Rising Geelong Saignee	Geelong
95	2015 Harcourt Valley Vineyards Rose	Heathcote
95	2015 Merindoc Vintners Willoughby Bridge Rose	Heathcote
95	2013 Vinea Marson Rose	Heathcote
95	2015 Laurance of Rose	Margaret River
95	2015 Victory Point Rose	Margaret River
95	2015 Domaines & Vineyards Pemberley Rose	Pemberton
95	2015 Levantine Hill Estate Rose	Yarra Valley
95	2015 Rochford Rose	Yarra Valley

Pinot Noir

Put these wines alongside Burgundies of similar age, and they won't yield any ground. The same can be said of Central Otago; as each year goes by, the number of first-class pinots increases. Yet there is still a long way to go on this journey, with new clones slotting in alongside MV6, an old clone unique to Australia. The average age of vines is also rising – the oldest are now more than 40 years old.

RATING	WINE	REGION
98	2014 Farrside by Farr	Geelong
98	2014 Bass Phillip Premium	Gippsland
98	2014 Bass Phillip Reserve	Gippsland
98	2015 Rochford Premier	Yarra Valley
97	2014 Ashton Hills Reserve	Adelaide Hills
97	2012 Henschke The Alan	Adelaide Hills
97	2015 Rockcliffe Single Site	Denmark
97	2015 Clyde Park Vineyard Single Block D Bannockburn	Geelong

97	2014 Sangreal by Farr	Geelong
97	2013 Tout Pres by Farr	Geelong
97	2014 Bindi Block 5	Macedon Ranges
97	2014 Garagiste Terre de Feu	Mornington Peninsula
97	2014 Montalto Single Vineyard Main Ridge Block	Mornington Peninsula
97	2013 Moorooduc Estate The Moorooduc McIntyre	Mornington Peninsula
97	2014 Moorooduc Estate The Moorooduc McIntyre	Mornington Peninsula
97	2015 Yabby Lake Vineyard Single Block Release Block 6	Mornington Peninsula
97	2015 Chatto Isle Huon Valley	Tasmania
97	2014 Dawson & James	Tasmania
97	2013 Gala Estate Constable Amos	Tasmania
97	2014 Home Hill Kelly's Reserve	Tasmania
97	2013 Stoney Rise Holyman Project X	Tasmania
97	2014 Tolpuddle Vineyard	Tasmania
97	2015 Coldstream Hills Deer Farm Vineyard	Yarra Valley
97	2015 Giant Steps Giant Steps Applejack Vineyard	Yarra Valley
97	2015 Giant Steps Giant Steps Lusatia Park Vineyard	Yarra Valley
97	2015 Giant Steps Giant Steps Sexton Vineyard	Yarra Valley
97	2014 Oakridge 864 Single Block Release B-Block Lusatia Park Vineyard	Yarra Valley
97	2014 Punch Lance's Vineyard Close Planted	Yarra Valley
97	2013 Toolangi Vineyards Block E	Yarra Valley
97	2014 Yarra Yering	Yarra Valley
97	2013 YarraLoch Stephanie's Dream Whole Bunch	Yarra Valley

Shiraz

These wines are truly the crème de la crème of Australian shiraz, coming from all points of the compass. It may be decades before the Hunter Valley has the most wines in future lists, but 2014 is the best vintage since 1965, itself a celebrated exception.

RATING	WINE	REGION
99	2010 Henschke Hill Of Grace	Eden Valley
99	2014 Best's Thomson Family Great Western	Grampians
99	2014 Mount Pleasant Maurice O'Shea	Hunter Valley
99	2010 Tahbilk 1860 Vines	Nagambie Lakes
99	2014 Yarra Yering Carrodus	Yarra Valley
98	2014 Elderton Neil Ashmead Grand Tourer	Barossa Valley
98	2013 Hare's Chase Lepus	Barossa Valley
98	2013 Giaconda Estate Vineyard	Beechworth
98	2006 Henschke Hill Of Grace	Eden Valley
98	2012 Hutton Vale Farm	Eden Valley
98	2014 Mount Langi Ghiran Vineyards Langi	Grampians
98	2014 Margaret Hill Vineyard Kudo	Heathcote
98	2014 Brokenwood Graveyard Vineyard	Hunter Valley
98	2011 Mount Pleasant Mountain A Medium Bodied Dry Red	Hunter Valley
98	2014 Mount Pleasant Old Paddock & Old Hill	Hunter Valley
98	2013 Pepper Tree Single Vineyard Reserve Tallawanta	Hunter Valley

98	2014 Tyrrell's Winemaker's Selection 4 Acres	Hunter Valley
98	2013 Hardys Eileen Hardy	McLaren Vale
98	2014 Yarra Yering Underhill	Yarra Valley

Shiraz Viognier

Cool regions provide the best shiraz viogniers, in which fragrance, spice and red fruits are the flavour cornerstones.

RATING	WINE	REGION
98	2015 Clonakilla	Canberra District
98	2015 Serrat	Yarra Valley
98	2013 Yering Station Reserve	Yarra Valley
97	2014 Yering Station Reserve	Yarra Valley

Cabernet Sauvignon

The affinity of cabernet sauvignon with a maritime climate is put beyond doubt by its home in Bordeaux's Medoc region. So it comes as no surprise to find that most (but not all) of Australia's top quality cabernets come from regions with climates similar to Bordeaux's. The dominance of Margaret River is likely to continue; not only is the climate ideally suited, but is far more consistent than that of any other Australian region.

RATING	WINE	REGION
99	2012 Cullen Vanya	Margaret River
99	2014 Yarra Yering Carrodus	Yarra Valley
98	2014 Purple Hands Planta Circa Ancient Vine	Barossa Valley
98	2013 Singlefile The Philip Adrian	Frankland River
98	2013 Deep Woods Estate Grand Selection Wilyabrup	Margaret River
98	2013 Domaine Naturaliste Morus	Margaret River
98	2012 Moss Wood Wilyabrup Cabernet Sauvignon	Margaret River
98	2013 Xanadu Reserve Cabernet Sauvignon	Margaret River

Cabernet and Family

A thoroughly diverse range of Bordeaux blends and varieties on the one hand, and the classic Australian blend of cabernet and shiraz on the other.

RATING	WINE	REGION
98	2012 Penfolds The Max Schubert Coonawarra Cabernet Shiraz	Barossa Valley/ Coonawarra
98	2014 Cullen Diana Madeline	Margaret River
98	2013 Hickinbotham Clarendon Vineyard The Peake Cabernet Shiraz	McLaren Vale
98	2014 Yarra Yering Dry Red No. 1	Yarra Valley
97	2012 Henschke Cyril Henschke	Eden Valley
97	2013 Moss Wood Ribbon Vale Vineyard Wilyabrup Merlot	Margaret River
97	2012 Vasse Felix Heytesbury	Margaret River
97	2014 3 Drops Great Southern Cabernets	Mount Barker
97	2012 Ross Hill The Griffin	Orange
97	2014 Major by Mitchell Harris	Pyrenees
97	2014 Mount Mary Quintet	Yarra Valley

Shiraz and Family

A South Australian stronghold, indeed stranglehold, mostly with some or all of shiraz, grenache and mourvedre.

RATING	WINE	REGION
98	2014 Yarra Yering Dry Red No. 2	Yarra Valley
98	2015 Yarra Yering Light Dry Red Pinot Shiraz	Yarra Valley
97	2012 Hemera Estate Tier 1 Shiraz Cabernet Sauvignon	Barossa
97	2013 Charles Melton Nine Popes	Barossa Valley
97	2012 Grant Burge Abednego Mourvedre Grenache Shiraz	Barossa Valley
97	2014 Hentley Farm H Block Shiraz Cabernet	Barossa Valley
97	2014 Hentley Farm The Quintessential Shiraz Cabernet	Barossa Valley
97	2014 Singlefile Wines Clement V	Frankland River
97	2012 d'Arenberg The Ironstone Pressings Grenache Shiraz Mourvedre	McLaren Vale
97	2013 Yangarra Estate Vineyard High Sands Grenache	McLaren Vale
96	2010 Chateau Tanunda The Everest Old Bush Vine Grenache	Barossa Valley
96	2012 Hewitson Old Garden Mourvedre	Barossa Valley

The Italians and Friends

With each year the quality (and quantity) of sangiovese and nebbiolo increases, with greater vine age and winemaking experience the drivers. Paradoxically, plantings of these two are becalmed.

RATING	WINE	REGION
97	2014 Ravensworth Sangiovese	Canberra District
97	2013 Greenstone Vineyards Sangiovese	Heathcote
96	2014 Mr Riggs Montepulciano d'Adelaide Hills	Adelaide Hills
96	2013 SC Pannell Nebbiolo	Adelaide Hills
96	2014 Boireann La Cima Superiore Barbera	Granite Belt
96	2014 Ravensworth Nebbiolo	Hilltops
96	2012 A.T. Richardson Hard Hill Road Nebbiolo	Pyrenees

Fortified Wines

The points speak for themselves. These wines are unique to Australia in terms of their age, their complexity, their intensity, and their varietal make up. They arguably represent the best value of all Australian wines given the cost of production, notably in the amount of working capital tied up for decades.

RATING	WINE	REGION
100	1916 Seppeltsfield 100 Year Old Para Liqueur	Barossa Valley
99	NV All Saints Estate Museum Muscadelle	Rutherglen
99	NV Chambers Rosewood Rare Muscadelle	Rutherglen
99	NV Chambers Rosewood Rare Muscat	Rutherglen

Best wineries of the regions

The nomination of the best wineries of the regions has evolved into a three-level classification (further explained on page 9. At the very top are the wineries with their names and stars printed in red; these have been generally recognised for having a long track record of excellence – truly the best of the best. Next are wineries with their stars (but not their names) printed in red, which have had a consistent record of excellence for at least the last three years. Those wineries with black stars have achieved excellence this year (and sometimes longer).

ADELAIDE HILLS

Ashton Hills ★★★★★
Bird in Hand ★★★★★
BK Wines ★★★★★
Catlin Wines ★★★★★
Chain of Ponds ★★★★★
Charlotte Dalton Wines ★★★★★
CRFT Wines ★★★★★
Deviation Road ★★★★★
Geoff Weaver ★★★★★
Guthrie Wines ★★★★★
Hahndorf Hill Winery ★★★★★
Mike Press Wines ★★★★★
Mt Lofty Ranges Vineyard ★★★★★
Murdoch Hill ★★★★★
Ngeringa ★★★★★
Ochota Barrels ★★★★★
Petaluma ★★★★★
Pike & Joyce ★★★★★
Riposte ★★★★★
Romney Park Wines ★★★★★
Scott ★★★★★
Sew & Sew Wines ★★★★★
Shaw + Smith ★★★★★
Sidewood Estate ★★★★★
Tapanappa ★★★★★
The Lane Vineyard ★★★★★
Tomich Wines ★★★★★
Wicks Estate Wines ★★★★★

ADELAIDE ZONE

Heirloom Vineyards ★★★★★
Hewitson ★★★★★
Patritti Wines ★★★★★
Penfolds Magill Estate ★★★★★

BALLARAT

Eastern Peake ★★★★★
Tomboy Hill ★★★★★

BAROSSA ZONE

Bethany Wines ★★★★★
Sons of Eden ★★★★★
St Hallett ★★★★★

BAROSSA VALLEY

Atze's Corner Wines ★★★★★
Burge Family Winemakers ★★★★★
Caillard Wine ★★★★★
Charles Melton ★★★★★
Chateau Tanunda ★★★★★
David Franz ★★★★★
Dell'uva Wines ★★★★★
Dorrien Estate ★★★★★
Dutschke Wines ★★★★★
Elderton ★★★★★
Eperosa ★★★★★
First Drop Wines ★★★★★
Gibson ★★★★★
Glaetzer Wines ★★★★★
Glen Eldon Wines ★★★★★
Grant Burge ★★★★★
Hare's Chase ★★★★★
Head Wines ★★★★★
Hemera Estate ★★★★★
Hentley Farm Wines ★★★★★
John Duval Wines ★★★★★
Kaesler Wines ★★★★★
Kalleske ★★★★★
Kellermeister ★★★★★
Landhaus Estate ★★★★★
Langmeil Winery ★★★★★
Laughing Jack ★★★★★

Massena Vineyards ★★★★★
Maverick Wines ★★★★★
Muster Wines ★★★★★
Penfolds ★★★★★
Peter Lehmann ★★★★★
Purple Hands Wines ★★★★★
Rockford ★★★★★
Rolf Binder ★★★★★
Saltram ★★★★★
Schubert Estate ★★★★★
Schwarz Wine Company ★★★★★
Seppeltsfield ★★★★★
Smallfry Wines ★★★★★
Spinifex ★★★★★
St John's Road ★★★★★
Teusner ★★★★★
Thorn-Clarke Wines ★★★★★
Tim Smith Wines ★★★★★
Torbreck Vintners ★★★★★
Turkey Flat ★★★★★
Two Hands Wines ★★★★★
Westlake Vineyards ★★★★★
Wolf Blass ★★★★★
Woods Crampton ★★★★★
Yelland & Papps ★★★★★

BEECHWORTH
A. Rodda Wines ★★★★★
Fighting Gully Road ★★★★★
Giaconda ★★★★★
Golden Ball ★★★★★
Indigo Vineyard ★★★★★
Piano Piano ★★★★★

BENDIGO
Bress ★★★★★
Harcourt Valley Vineyards ★★★★★

CANBERRA DISTRICT
Capital Wines ★★★★★
Clonakilla ★★★★★
Collector Wines ★★★★★
Eden Road Wines ★★★★★
Four Winds Vineyard ★★★★★
Helm ★★★★★
Lark Hill ★★★★★
Lerida Estate ★★★★★
Mount Majura Vineyard ★★★★★
Nick O'Leary Wines ★★★★★

Ravensworth ★★★★★
Shaw Vineyard Estate ★★★★★

CENTRAL VICTORIA ZONE
Mount Terrible ★★★★★

CLARE VALLEY
Adelina Wines ★★★★★
Atlas Wines ★★★★★
Claymore Wines ★★★★★
Crabtree Watervale Wines ★★★★★
Gaelic Cemetery Wines ★★★★★
Grosset ★★★★★
Jeanneret Wines ★★★★★
Jim Barry Wines ★★★★★
Kilikanoon ★★★★★
Knappstein ★★★★★
Leasingham ★★★★★
Mitchell ★★★★★
Mount Horrocks ★★★★★
Naked Run Wines ★★★★★
O'Leary Walker Wines ★★★★★
Paulett ★★★★★
Pikes ★★★★★
Rieslingfreak ★★★★★
Steve Wiblin's Erin Eyes ★★★★★
Taylors ★★★★★
Wendouree ★★★★★
Wilson Vineyard ★★★★★
Wines by KT ★★★★★

COONAWARRA
Balnaves of Coonawarra ★★★★★
Bellwether ★★★★★
Brand's Laira Coonawarra ★★★★★
Katnook Coonawarra ★★★★★
Koonara ★★★★★
Lindeman's (Coonawarra) ★★★★★
Majella ★★★★★
Parker Coonawarra Estate ★★★★★
Patrick of Coonawarra ★★★★★
Penley Estate ★★★★★
Rymill Coonawarra ★★★★★
Wynns Coonawarra Estate ★★★★★
Zema Estate ★★★★★

DENMARK
Apricus Hill ★★★★★
Harewood Estate ★★★★★
Moombaki Wines ★★★★★

Rockcliffe ★★★★★
The Lake House Denmark ★★★★★

EDEN VALLEY
Brockenchack ★★★★★
Flaxman Wines ★★★★★
Gatt Wines ★★★★★
Henschke ★★★★★
Hill-Smith Estate ★★★★★
Hutton Vale Farm ★★★★★
Leo Buring ★★★★★
Pewsey Vale ★★★★★
Poonawatta ★★★★★
Radford Wines ★★★★★
Robert Johnson Vineyards ★★★★★
Stage Door Wine Co ★★★★★
Yalumba ★★★★★

FRANKLAND RIVER
Alkoomi ★★★★★
Frankland Estate ★★★★★

GEELONG
Austins & Co. ★★★★★
Bannockburn Vineyards ★★★★★
Barrgowan Vineyard ★★★★★
Brown Magpie Wines ★★★★★
Clyde Park Vineyard ★★★★★
Curlewis Winery ★★★★★
Farr | Farr Rising ★★★★★
Lethbridge Wines ★★★★★
Leura Park Estate ★★★★★
McGlashan's Wallington Estate
    ★★★★★
Oakdene ★★★★★
Paradise IV ★★★★★
Provenance Wines ★★★★★
Scotchmans Hill ★★★★★
Shadowfax ★★★★★

GEOGRAPHE
Capel Vale ★★★★★
Willow Bridge Estate ★★★★★

GIPPSLAND
Bass Phillip ★★★★★
Dirty Three ★★★★★
Lightfoot & Sons ★★★★★
Narkoojee ★★★★★

GLENROWAN
Baileys of Glenrowan ★★★★★
A.T. Richardson Wines ★★★★★

GRAMPIANS
Best's Wines ★★★★★
Grampians Estate ★★★★★
Halls Gap Estate ★★★★★
Montara ★★★★★
Mount Langi Ghiran Vineyards
    ★★★★★
Seppelt ★★★★★
The Story Wines ★★★★★

GRANITE BELT
Boireann ★★★★★
Golden Grove Estate ★★★★★

GREAT SOUTHERN
Byron & Harold ★★★★★
Castelli Estate ★★★★★
Forest Hill Vineyard ★★★★★
Marchand & Burch ★★★★★
Singlefile Wines ★★★★★
Staniford Wine Co ★★★★★
Trevelen Farm ★★★★★
Willoughby Park ★★★★★

HEATHCOTE
Flynns Wines ★★★★★
Graillot ★★★★★
Heathcote Estate ★★★★★
Jasper Hill ★★★★★
Margaret Hill Vineyard ★★★★★
Paul Osicka ★★★★★
Sanguine Estate ★★★★★
Tellurian ★★★★★
Vinea Marson ★★★★★

HENTY
Crawford River Wines ★★★★★
Henty Estate ★★★★★
Hentyfarm Wines ★★★★★

HILLTOPS
Chalkers Crossing ★★★★★
Freeman Vineyards ★★★★★
Moppity Vineyards ★★★★★

HUNTER VALLEY
Audrey Wilkinson ★★★★★
Bimbadgen ★★★★★
Briar Ridge Vineyard ★★★★★
Brokenwood ★★★★★
Chateau Francois ★★★★★
David Hook Wines ★★★★★
De Iuliis ★★★★★
Eagles Rest Wines ★★★★★
Ernest Hill Wines ★★★★★
First Creek Wines ★★★★★
Glenguin Estate ★★★★★
Gundog Estate ★★★★★
Hart & Hunter ★★★★★
Hungerford Hill ★★★★★
Keith Tulloch Wine ★★★★★
Lake's Folly ★★★★★
Leogate Estate Wines ★★★★★
Margan Family ★★★★★
McGuigan Wines ★★★★★
Meerea Park ★★★★★
Mistletoe Wines ★★★★★
Mount Pleasant ★★★★★
Mount View Estate ★★★★★
Pepper Tree Wines ★★★★★
Pokolbin Estate ★★★★★
Saddler's Creek ★★★★★
Silkman Wines ★★★★★
Tallavera Grove | Carillion ★★★★★
Thomas Wines ★★★★★
Tinklers Vineyard ★★★★★
Tintilla Wines ★★★★★
Tower Estate ★★★★★
Tulloch ★★★★★
Two Rivers ★★★★★
Tyrrell's ★★★★★

KANGAROO ISLAND
The Islander Estate Vineyards ★★★★★

KING VALLEY
Brown Brothers ★★★★★
Eminence Wines ★★★★★
Wood Park ★★★★★

LANGHORNE CREEK
Bleasdale Vineyards ★★★★★
Bremerton Wines ★★★★★

John's Blend ★★★★★
Lake Breeze Wines ★★★★★

MACEDON RANGES
Bindi Wine Growers ★★★★★
Cope-Williams ★★★★★
Curly Flat ★★★★★
Granite Hills ★★★★★
Hanging Rock Winery ★★★★★
Lane's End Vineyard ★★★★★
Paramoor Wines ★★★★★

MARGARET RIVER
Amelia Park Wines ★★★★★
Arlewood Estate ★★★★★
Ashbrook Estate ★★★★★
Brookland Valley ★★★★★
Burch Family Wines ★★★★★
Cape Grace Wines ★★★★★
Cape Mentelle ★★★★★
Chalice Bridge Estate ★★★★★
Chapman Grove Wines ★★★★★
Clairault | Streicker Wines ★★★★★
Credaro Family Estate ★★★★★
Cullen Wines ★★★★★
Deep Woods Estate ★★★★★
Devil's Lair ★★★★★
Domaine Naturaliste ★★★★★
Driftwood Estate ★★★★★
Evans & Tate ★★★★★
Evoi Wines ★★★★★
Fermoy Estate ★★★★★
Flametree ★★★★★
Flowstone Wines ★★★★★
Flying Fish Cove ★★★★★
Forester Estate ★★★★★
Fraser Gallop Estate ★★★★★
Grace Farm ★★★★★
Happs ★★★★★
Hay Shed Hill Wines ★★★★★
Heydon Estate ★★★★★
Higher Plane ★★★★★
House of Cards ★★★★★
Juniper Estate ★★★★★
Knee Deep Wines ★★★★★
Laurance of Margaret River ★★★★★
Leeuwin Estate ★★★★★
Lenton Brae Wines ★★★★★
Marq Wines ★★★★★

McHenry Hohnen Vintners ★★★★★
Moss Wood ★★★★★
Night Harvest ★★★★★
Palmer Wines ★★★★★
Peccavi Wines ★★★★★
Pierro ★★★★★
Redgate ★★★★★
Rosabrook Margaret River Wine
    ★★★★★
Sandalford ★★★★★
Stella Bella Wines ★★★★★
Swings & Roundabouts ★★★★★
Thompson Estate ★★★★★
Twinwoods Estate ★★★★★
Umamu Estate ★★★★★
Vasse Felix ★★★★★
Victory Point Wines ★★★★★
Voyager Estate ★★★★★
Warner Glen Estate ★★★★★
Watershed Premium Wines ★★★★★
Wills Domain ★★★★★
Windows Estate ★★★★★
Wise Wine ★★★★★
Woodlands ★★★★★
Woody Nook ★★★★★
Xanadu Wines ★★★★★

MCLAREN VALE
Bekkers ★★★★★
Beresford Estates ★★★★★
Bondar Wines ★★★★★
Brash Higgins ★★★★★
Chalk Hill ★★★★★
Chapel Hill ★★★★★
Clarendon Hills ★★★★★
Coates Wines ★★★★★
Coriole ★★★★★
d'Arenberg ★★★★★
Dandelion Vineyards ★★★★★
Ekhidna ★★★★★
Five Geese ★★★★★
Fox Creek Wines ★★★★★
Gemtree Wines ★★★★★
Geoff Merrill Wines ★★★★★
Hardys ★★★★★
Haselgrove Wines ★★★★★
Hickinbotham Clarendon Vineyard
    ★★★★★
Hugh Hamilton Wines ★★★★★

Kangarilla Road Vineyard ★★★★★
Kay Brothers Amery Vineyards
    ★★★★★
Maxwell Wines ★★★★★
Mitolo Wines ★★★★★
Mr Riggs Wine Company ★★★★★
Olivers Taranga Vineyards ★★★★★
Paxton ★★★★★
Penny's Hill ★★★★★
Pirramimma ★★★★★
Primo Estate ★★★★★
Reynella ★★★★★
Rosemount Estate ★★★★★
Rudderless ★★★★★
Samuel's Gorge ★★★★★
SC Pannell ★★★★★
Serafino Wines ★★★★★
Shingleback ★★★★★
Shottesbrooke ★★★★★
Ulithorne ★★★★★
Way Wood Wines ★★★★★
Willunga 100 Wines ★★★★★
Wirra Wirra ★★★★★
Woodstock ★★★★★
Yangarra Estate Vineyard ★★★★★
Zerella Wines ★★★★★

MORNINGTON PENINSULA
Allies Wines ★★★★★
Circe Wines ★★★★★
Crittenden Estate ★★★★★
Dexter Wines ★★★★★
Eldridge Estate of Red Hill ★★★★★
Elgee Park ★★★★★
Foxeys Hangout ★★★★★
Garagiste ★★★★★
Hurley Vineyard ★★★★★
Jones Road ★★★★★
Kooyong ★★★★★
Lindenderry at Red Hill ★★★★★
Main Ridge Estate ★★★★★
Montalto ★★★★★
Moorooduc Estate ★★★★★
Onannon ★★★★★
Paradigm Hill ★★★★★
Paringa Estate ★★★★★
Port Phillip Estate ★★★★★
Red Hill Estate ★★★★★
Scorpo Wines ★★★★★

Stonier Wines ★★★★★
Ten Minutes by Tractor ★★★★★
Tuck's Ridge ★★★★★
Willow Creek Vineyard ★★★★★
Yabby Lake Vineyard ★★★★★

MOUNT BARKER
3 Drops ★★★★★
Plantagenet ★★★★★
Poacher's Ridge Vineyard ★★★★★
West Cape Howe Wines ★★★★★

MOUNT GAMBIER
Coola Road ★★★★★

MOUNT LOFTY RANGES ZONE
Michael Hall Wines ★★★★★

MUDGEE
Huntington Estate ★★★★★
Logan Wines ★★★★★
Robert Oatley Vineyards ★★★★★
Robert Stein Vineyard ★★★★★

NAGAMBIE LAKES
Tahbilk ★★★★★

NORTH EAST VICTORIA ZONE
Eldorado Road ★★★★★

ORANGE
Bloodwood ★★★★★
Patina ★★★★★
Philip Shaw Wines ★★★★★
Printhie Wines ★★★★★
Ross Hill Wines ★★★★★

PEMBERTON
Bellarmine Wines ★★★★★

PERTH HILLS
Millbrook Winery ★★★★★

PORONGURUP
Abbey Creek Vineyard ★★★★★
Castle Rock Estate ★★★★★
Duke's Vineyard ★★★★★

PYRENEES
Blue Pyrenees Estate ★★★★★
Dalwhinnie ★★★★★

DogRock Winery ★★★★★
Mitchell Harris Wines ★★★★★
Mount Avoca ★★★★★
Summerfield ★★★★★
Taltarni ★★★★★

QUEENSLAND ZONE
Witches Falls Winery ★★★★★

RIVERINA
De Bortoli ★★★★★
Lillypilly Estate ★★★★★
McWilliam's ★★★★★
R. Paulazzo Wines ★★★★★

RUTHERGLEN
All Saints Estate ★★★★★
Anderson ★★★★★
Campbells ★★★★★
Chambers Rosewood ★★★★★
Morris ★★★★★
Pfeiffer Wines ★★★★★
Stanton & Killeen Wines ★★★★★

SHOALHAVEN COAST
Coolangatta Estate ★★★★★

SOUTH AUSTRALIA
Angove Family Winemakers ★★★★★
Wines by Geoff Hardy ★★★★★

SOUTH WEST AUSTRALIA ZONE
Kerrigan + Berry ★★★★★
Snake + Herring ★★★★★

SOUTHERN FLEURIEU
Salomon Estate ★★★★★

SOUTHERN HIGHLANDS
Centennial Vineyards ★★★★★
Tertini Wines ★★★★★

STRATHBOGIE RANGES
Fowles Wine ★★★★★
Maygars Hill Winery ★★★★★

SUNBURY
Craiglee ★★★★★
Galli Estate ★★★★★

SWAN DISTRICT
Mandoon Estate ★★★★★

SWAN VALLEY
Houghton ★★★★★
John Kosovich Wines ★★★★★
Sittella Wines ★★★★★

TASMANIA
Bay of Fires ★★★★★
Chatto ★★★★★
Craigow ★★★★★
Dalrymple ★★★★★
Dawson & James ★★★★★
Delamere Vineyard ★★★★★
Derwent Estate ★★★★★
Devil's Corner ★★★★★
Domaine A ★★★★★
Freycinet ★★★★★
Frogmore Creek ★★★★★
Gala Estate ★★★★★
Glaetzer-Dixon Family Winemakers ★★★★★
Heemskerk ★★★★★
Holm Oak ★★★★★
Home Hill ★★★★★
House of Arras ★★★★★
Jansz Tasmania ★★★★★
Josef Chromy Wines ★★★★★
Milton Vineyard ★★★★★
Moorilla Estate ★★★★★
Pipers Brook Vineyard ★★★★★
Pooley Wines ★★★★★
Pressing Matters ★★★★★
Stargazer Wine ★★★★★
Stefano Lubiana ★★★★★
Stoney Rise ★★★★★
Tamar Ridge | Pirie ★★★★★
Tolpuddle Vineyard ★★★★★

TUMBARUMBA
Coppabella of Tumbarumba ★★★★★

UPPER GOULBURN
Delatite ★★★★★

VARIOUS
Ben Haines Wine ★★★★★
Echelon ★★★★★
Handpicked Wines ★★★★★

Ministry of Clouds ★★★★★
Stonefish ★★★★★
Smidge Wines ★★★★★

WESTERN AUSTRALIA
Domaines & Vineyards ★★★★★
Larry Cherubino Wines ★★★★★

WRATTONBULLY
Ruckus Estate ★★★★★
Terre e Terre ★★★★★

YARRA VALLEY
Bicknell fc ★★★★★
Carlei Estate | Carlei Green Vineyards ★★★★★
Chandon Australia ★★★★★
Coldstream Hills ★★★★★
De Bortoli (Victoria) ★★★★★
Denton Viewhill Vineyard ★★★★★
Dominique Portet ★★★★★
Elmswood Estate ★★★★★
Fikkers Wine ★★★★★
Gembrook Hill ★★★★★
Giant Steps ★★★★★
Greenstone Vineyards ★★★★★
Helen's Hill Estate ★★★★★
Hillcrest Vineyard ★★★★★
Hoddles Creek Estate ★★★★★
In Dreams ★★★★★
Innocent Bystander ★★★★★
Journey Wines ★★★★★
Levantine Hill Estate ★★★★★
Little Yarra Wines ★★★★★
Mac Forbes ★★★★★
Mandala ★★★★★
Mayer ★★★★★
Medhurst ★★★★★
Mount Mary ★★★★★
Oakridge Wines ★★★★★
Out of Step ★★★★★
PHI ★★★★★
Pimpernel Vineyards ★★★★★
Punch ★★★★★
Punt Road ★★★★★
Rob Dolan Wines ★★★★★
Rob Hall Wines ★★★★★
Rochford Wines ★★★★★
Rouleur ★★★★★

St Huberts ★★★★★
Santolin Wines ★★★★★
Serrat ★★★★★
Seville Estate ★★★★★
Six Acres ★★★★★
Soumah ★★★★★
Stefani Estate ★★★★★
Sticks Yarra Valley ★★★★★
Sutherland Estate ★★★★★
Tarrahill. ★★★★★
TarraWarra Estate ★★★★★
Thick as Thieves Wines ★★★★★
Tokar Estate ★★★★★
Toolangi Vineyards ★★★★★
Wantirna Estate ★★★★★
Yarra Yering ★★★★★
Yering Station ★★★★★
Yeringberg ★★★★★

Plantings and production

To remove or not to remove, that is the question. There has been continuing support for the proposition that plantings need to be reduced further if an overall balance between supply and demand is to be achieved. The elephant in the room has been the absence of any data from 2013 and 2014, due to funding cutbacks for the Australian Bureau of Statistics (ABS). The wine industry agreed that the absence could blindfold it in the middle of a prolonged downsizing commencing with the 2008 vintage, and the 2015 (and ongoing) collation of figures has been funded by the industry, even though the data now comes, once again, through the ABS.

I have been concerned for some time that there is a real chance the industry could suddenly find itself with a major deficit. The area planted with vines in production is now virtually equal to that of 2001, 132 000ha now compared with 131 000ha then.

Jim Moularadellis of Austwine, the country's largest bulk wine dealer, contrasts the situation then (300 million litres surplus, vineyard area growing and overall outlook deteriorating) with 2015 − 3 million litres shortfall, vineyard area shrinking and overall outlook improving. Both scenarios are full of internal conflicts, but each component is correctly framed.

The inconsistencies continue. Vineyards are continuing to be removed (cost of irrigation water too high, alternative crops offer better returns, etc.), but there was a price increase for Riverland grapes − small, but better than a fall − and, for the first time in more than a decade, 1,235ha of mainstream varieties were planted. Not statistically important, but there nonetheless.

The question of the size of the 2016 crop has no clear answer. The Murray Darling and Riverina regions seem likely to be slightly down in volume and quality, the premium regions of South East Australia up in terms of quality and volume.

In looking at the overall figures, one has to understand there are two quite different markets. The first is commercial wine in casks or in lightweight bottles. This type of wine is sold at a discounted price below $10 a bottle, with every input cost reduced to a bare minimum from the vineyard through to the packaged, branded producer on the chain retailer's shelves. Casks are the cheapest form of alcohol available, casks of fortified wine doubly so, both providing the anti-alcohol lobby with material it uses for all it is worth. The other is the fine wine market, with prices starting at $15 or so, and going up to $200-plus, Grange and Hill of Grace $600-plus.

The other picture provided by the table opposite is the fall in the percentage of white grapes, mirrored by the increase in the percentage of red grapes. An altogether different path, but one pointing in the same direction, is that red wines accounted for 60% (5347) of the wines tasted for this *Wine Companion* and white wines for 34.5% (3099); the remainder were fortified and sparkling wines (5.5%; 530). The fall in plantings since 2007, let alone since 2001, has been buffered by the increase in the yield per hectare. Small wonder that Jim Moularadellis is uncertain when (and in which direction) there will be a major shift in plantings.

	2007	2008	2012	2015	07 vs '15 %
CHARDONNAY					
hectares	32,151	31,564	25,491	21,442	-33.3
tonnes	366,936	428,082	348,283	340,773	-7.1
t/ha	11.4	13.6	13.7	15.9	39.3
RIESLING					
hectares	4,432	4,400	3,893	3,157	-28.8
tonnes	31,002	39,305	32,317	28,797	-7.1
t/ha	7.0	8.9	8.3	9.1	30.4
SAUVIGNON BLANC					
hectares	5,545	6,404	6,927	6,097	10.0
tonnes	36,515	62,420	81,442	83,505	128.7
t/ha	6.6	9.7	11.8	13.7	108.0
SEMILLON					
hectares	6,752	6,716	5,632	4,569	-32.3
tonnes	75,170	100,031	77,890	65,411	-13.0
t/ha	11.1	14.9	13.8	14.3	28.6
PINOT GRIS					
hectares	2,469	2,835	3,767	3,732	51.2
tonnes	12,340	26,156	50,426	61,387	397.5
t/ha	5.0	9.2	13.4	16.4	229.1
CABERNET SAUVIGNON					
hectares	27,909	27,553	25,879	24,682	-11.6
tonnes	183,052	258,066	207,558	202,672	10.7
t/ha	6.6	9.4	8.0	8.2	25.2
MERLOT					
hectares	10,790	10,764	9,286	8,477	-21.4
tonnes	90,461	125,285	117,383	111,533	23.3
t/ha	8.4	11.6	12.6	13.2	56.9
PINOT NOIR					
hectares	4,393	4,490	4,978	4,948	12.6
tonnes	26,251	43,923	34,574	43,223	64.7
t/ha	6.0	9.8	6.9	8.7	46.2
SHIRAZ					
hectares	43,417	43,977	42,012	39,893	-8.1
tonnes	283,741	441,950	362,217	395,154	39.3
t/ha	6.5	10.0	8.6	9.9	51.6
TOTAL GRAPES					
hectares	173,776	172,675	148,509	135,178	-22.2
tonnes	1,370,691	1,837,034	1,582,049	1,608,218	17.3
t/ha	7.9	10.6	10.7	11.9	50.8
PERCENTAGE (TONNES)					
White	51.19%	46.43%	49.07%	47.50%	-7.2
Red	48.81%	53.57%	50.93%	52.50%	7.6

Without wishing to belabour the point, the alternative-variety treasure hunt may well extend long into the future, but it will never be a get-rich-quick occupation. Indeed, the skimpy record we have in a country that has been growing and making wine for over 180 years points to more failures than successes.

You might say it's too early to draw conclusions about arneis and savagnin, but arneis had virtually disappeared from Italy in the early 1970s, with only two producers bottling it, and the last census in Italy showed only 745ha under vine.

Savagnin blanc, to give it its full name, was planted in Australia in the late 1990s in the belief it was alvarinho (having been misidentified by the CSIRO as such). It is one of three ancestor grapes that head the family trees of all European varieties, and is highly regarded in the Jura. Notwithstanding this, the ABS figures suggest it is being removed at a rapid rate. Genetically, it is one and the same as traminer, but there is a de facto separation of the names (and related crops) in this country.

When the two great Italian varieties, sangiovese and nebbiolo, are doing little better than treading water, the questions grow louder. As I say on page 33, the quality of the wines made from these two varieties has never been higher. Nebbiolo is the great aristocrat of Italian wine, the best wines from Barolo fashioned from it, justly bringing high prices. There are very few Australian wine drinkers – even highly wine educated – who are prepared to pay for Barolo, and even fewer who understand/ enjoy it. This means the target market is miniscule, which splashes back against the prospects for growth. Forget immediately any idea about planting it in the Murray Darling in the hope of increasing the yield and reducing the formidable tannins.

Sangiovese was first grown in Australia in the Kalimna Vineyard in the Barossa Valley by the late Italian-born and trained Carlo Corino at Montrose (itself Italian-owned) in the late 1970s, Coriole taking the bushel in the early 1980s.

The planting and production figures opposite suggest it's having a hard time holding its own, strange given the excellent quality of the leading wines of today (Ravensworth in the Canberra District the torch bearer).

The quirky zinfandel, with its extreme variation in the ripeness of berries in a given bunch (from green pea to raisin) and its dislike of being grown on a trellis (its preference single-stake bush vines), is a lost cause. Montepulciano vines are still in their infancy, which leaves tempranillo as the last man standing.

The next few years will tell the tale for tempranillo, an early ripening variety in the same group as pinot noir, and which I sought to plant on a small rocky slope at Coldstream Hills in the 1980s. I was let down by the nursery for two years in a row, losing patience and planting viognier instead, which a local wallaby believed was an entrée to its evening meal.

Jancis Robinson describes 1368 varieties in her masterwork *Wine Grapes* (Jancis Robinson, Julia Harding and Jose Vouillamoz, Ecco/Harper Collins, 2012), and estimates the total population may be as high as 10 000, so there's plenty of choice available. Chalmers is still bringing in new varieties it thinks may be suited to one part or another of Australia.

Finally, the number of wineries that grow, buy or sell wine made from the varieties opposite are those published in the 2016 *Wine Industry Directory*.

	2007	2008	2012	2015
ARNEIS (52 users 2016)				
hectares	-	-	81	38
tonnes	-	-	652	315
FIANO (63 users 2016)				
hectares	-	-	107	111
tonnes	-	-	340	685
SAVAGNIN (60 users 2016)				
hectares	-	-	140	60
tonnes	-	-	1058	509
VERMENTINO (92 users 2016)				
hectares	-	-	93	121
tonnes	-	-	839	1,842
MONTEPULCIANO (46 users 2016)				
hectares	-	-	49	74
tonnes	-	-	178	449
NEBBIOLO (135 users 2016)				
hectares	90	105	122	115
tonnes	319	420	548	410
NERO D'AVOLA (36 users 2016)				
hectares	-	-	33	77
tonnes	-	-	70	602
SANGIOVESE (309 users 2016)				
hectares	479	517	575	438
tonnes	3,552	5,630	5073	5,210
TEMPRANILLO (370 users 2016)				
hectares	354	386	712	736
tonnes	1,863	3,680	3,422	5,570
ZINFANDEL (85 users 2016)				
hectares	136	140	104	87
tonnes	780	833	492	332

Varietal wine styles and regions

For better or worse, there simply has to be concerted action to highlight the link between regions, varieties and wine styles. It's not a question of creating the links: they are already there, and have been in existence for periods as short as 20 years or as long as 150 years. So here you will find abbreviated summaries of those regional styles (in turn reflected in the Best of the Best lists commencing on page 26).

Riesling

Riesling's link with the **Eden Valley** dates back at least to when Joseph Gilbert planted his Pewsey Vale vineyard, and the grape quickly made its way to the nearby **Clare Valley**. These two regions stood above all others for well over 100 years, producing wines that shared many flavour and texture characteristics: lime (a little more obvious in the Eden Valley), apple, talc and mineral, lightly browned toasty notes emerging with five to 10 years bottle age. Within the last 20 or so years, the subregions of the **Great Southern** of Western Australia have established a deserved reputation for finely structured, elegant rieslings with wonderful length, sometimes shy when young, bursting into song after five years. The subregions are (in alphabetical order) **Albany**, **Denmark**, **Frankland River**, **Mount Barker** and **Porongurup**. **Canberra** is up with the best and **Tasmania**, too, produces high-class rieslings, notable for their purity and intensity courtesy of their high natural acidity. Finally, there is the small and very cool region of **Henty** (once referred to as Drumborg), its exceptional rieslings sharing many things in common with those of Tasmania.

Semillon

There is a Siamese-twin relationship between semillon and the **Hunter Valley**, which has been producing a wine style like no other in the world for well over 100 years. The humid and very warm climate (best coupled with sandy soils not common in the region) results in wines that have a median alcohol level of 10.5% and no residual sugar, are cold-fermented in stainless steel and bottled within three months of vintage. They are devoid of colour and have only the barest hints of grass, herb and mineral wrapped around a core of acidity. Over the next five to 10 years they develop a glowing green-gold colour, a suite of grass and citrus fruit surrounded by buttered toast and honey notes. As with rieslings, screwcaps have added decades to their cellaring life. The **Adelaide Hills** and **Margaret River** produce entirely different semillon, more structured and weighty, its alcohol 13% to 14%, and as often as not blended with sauvignon blanc, barrel fermentation of part or all common. Finally, there is a cuckoo in the nest: Peter Lehmann in the **Barossa/Eden Valley** has adapted Hunter Valley practices, picking early, fermenting in steel, bottling early, and holding the top wine for five years before release – and succeeding brilliantly.

Chardonnay

This infinitely flexible grape is grown and vinified in all 63 regions, and accounts for half of Australia's white wine grapes and wine. Incredibly, before 1970 it was all but unknown, hiding its promise here and there (**Mudgee** was one such place) under a cloak of anonymity. It was there and in the **Hunter Valley** that the first wines labelled chardonnay were made in 1971 (by Craigmoor and Tyrrell's). Its bold yellow colour, peaches and cream flavour and vanilla oak was unlike anything that had gone before and was accepted by domestic and export markets with equal enthusiasm. When exports took off into the stratosphere between 1985 and 1995, one half of Brand Australia was cheerful and cheap oak-chipped chardonnay grown in the **Riverina** and **Riverland**. By coincidence, over the same period chardonnay from the emerging cool climate regions was starting to appear in limited quantities, its flavour and structure radically different to the warm-grown, high-cropped wine. Another 10 years on, and by 2005–2006 the wine surplus was starting to build rapidly, with demand for chardonnay much less than its production. As attention swung from chardonnay to sauvignon blanc, the situation became dire. Lost in the heat of battle were supremely elegant wines from most cool regions, **Margaret River** and **Yarra Valley** the leaders of the large band. Constant refinement of the style, and the adoption of the screwcap, puts these wines at the forefront of the gradually succeeding battle to re-engage consumers here and abroad with what are world-class wines.

Sauvignon Blanc

Two regions, the **Adelaide Hills** and **Margaret River**, stood in front of all others until recently joined by **Orange**; these three produce Australia's best sauvignon blanc, wines with real structure and authority. It is a matter of record that Marlborough sauvignon blanc accounts for one-third of Australia's white wine sales; all one can say (accurately) is that the basic Marlborough style is very different, and look back at what happened with Australian chardonnay. Margaret River also offers complex blends of sauvignon blanc and semillon in widely varying proportions, and with varying degrees of oak fermentation.

Shiraz

Shiraz, like chardonnay, is by far the most important red variety and, again like chardonnay, is tremendously flexible in its ability to adapt to virtually any combination of climate and soil/terroir. Unlike chardonnay, a recent arrival, shiraz was the most important red variety throughout the 19th and 20th centuries. Its ancestral homes were the **Barossa Valley**, the **Clare Valley**, **McLaren Vale** and the **Hunter Valley**, and it still leads in those regions. With the exception of the Hunter Valley, it was as important in making fortified wine as table wine over the period 1850 to 1950, aided and abetted by grenache and mourvedre (mataro). In New South Wales the **Hilltops** and **Canberra District** are producing elegant, cool grown wines that usually conceal their power (especially when co-fermented with viognier) but not their silky length. Further north, but at a higher altitude, **Orange** is also producing fine, fragrant and spicy wines. All the other New South

Wales regions are capable of producing good shiraz of seriously good character and quality; shiraz ripens comfortably, but quite late in the season. Polished, sophisticated wines are the result. Victoria has a cornucopia of regions at the cooler end of the spectrum; the coolest (though not too cool for comfort) are the **Yarra Valley**, **Mornington Peninsula**, **Sunbury** and **Geelong**, all producing fragrant, spicy medium-bodied wines. **Bendigo**, **Heathcote**, **Grampians** and **Pyrenees**, more or less running east–west across the centre of Victoria, are producing some of the most exciting medium-bodied shirazs in Australia, each with its own terroir stamp, but all combining generosity and elegance. In Western Australia, **Great Southern** and three of its five subregions, **Frankland River**, **Mount Barker** and **Porongurup**, are making magical shirazs, fragrant and spicy, fleshy yet strongly structured. **Margaret River** has been a relatively late mover, but it, too, is producing wines with exemplary varietal definition and finesse.

Cabernet Sauvignon

The tough-skinned cabernet sauvignon can be, and is, grown in all regions, but it struggles in the coolest (notably **Tasmania**) and loses desirable varietal definition in the warmer regions, especially in warmer vintages. Shiraz can cope with alcohol levels in excess of 14.5%, cabernet can't. In South Australia, **Coonawarra** stands supreme, its climate (though not its soil) strikingly similar to that of Bordeaux, the main difference lower rainfall. Perfectly detailed cabernets are the result, with no need of shiraz or merlot to fill in the mid-palate, although some excellent blends are made. **Langhorne Creek** (a little warmer) and **McLaren Vale** (warmer still) have similar maritime climates, doubtless the reason why McLaren Vale manages to deal with the warmth of its summer/autumn weather. The **Eden Valley** is the most reliable of the inner regions, the other principal regions dependent on a cool summer. From South Australia to Western Australia, where **Margaret River**, with its extreme maritime climate shaped by the warm Indian Ocean, stands tall. It is also Australia's foremost producer of cabernet merlot et al in the Bordeaux mix. The texture and structure of both the straight varietal and the blend is regal, often to the point of austerity when the wines are young, but the sheer power of this underlying fruit provides the balance and guarantees the future development of the wines over a conservative 20 years, especially if screwcapped. The **Great Southern** subregions of **Frankland River** and **Mount Barker** share a continental climate that is somewhat cooler than Margaret River's, and has a greater diurnal temperature range. Here cabernet has an incisive, dark-berry character and firm but usually fine tannins – not demanding merlot, though a touch of it and/or malbec can be beneficial. It is grown successfully through the centre and south of Victoria, but is often overshadowed by shiraz. In the last 20 years it has ceased to be a problem child and become a favourite son of the **Yarra Valley**; the forward move of vintage dates has been the key to the change.

Pinot Noir

The promiscuity of shiraz (particularly) and cabernet sauvignon is in sharp contrast to the puritanical rectitude of pinot noir. One sin of omission or commission, and the door slams shut, leaving the bewildered winemaker on the outside. **Tasmania** is the El Dorado for the variety, and the best is still to come with better clones, older vines and greater exploration of the multitude of mesoclimates that Tasmania has to offer. While it is north of Central Otago (New Zealand), its vineyards are all air conditioned by the Southern Ocean and Tasman Sea, and it stands toe-to-toe with Central Otago in its ability to make deeply-coloured, profound pinot with all the length one could ask for. Once on the mainland, Victoria's Port Phillip Zone, encompassing the **Geelong**, **Macedon Ranges**, **Sunbury**, **Mornington Peninsula** and **Yarra Valley** is the epicentre of Australian pinot noir, **Henty** a small outpost. The sheer number of high quality, elegant wines produced by dozens of makers in those regions put the **Adelaide Hills** and **Porongurup** (also capable of producing quality pinot) into the shade.

Other Red Varieties

There are many other red varieties in the *Wine Companion* database, and there is little rhyme or reason for the distribution of the plantings.

Sparkling Wines

The patter is eerily similar to that of pinot noir, **Tasmania** now and in the future the keeper of the Holy Grail, the **Port Phillip Zone** the centre of activity on the mainland.

Fortified Wines

Rutherglen and **Glenrowan** are the two (and only) regions that produce immensely complex, long-barrel-aged muscat and muscadelle, the latter called tokay for over a century, now renamed topaque. These wines have no equal in the world, Spain's Malaga nearest in terms of lusciousness, but nowhere near as complex. The other producer of a wine without parallel is Seppeltsfield in the **Barossa Valley**, which each year releases an explosively rich and intense tawny liqueur style that is 100% 100 years old.

Australia's geographical indications

The process of formally mapping Australia's wine regions is all but complete, though it will never come to an outright halt – for one thing, climate change is lurking in the wings.

The division into States, Zones, Regions and Subregions follows; those Regions or Subregions marked with an asterisk are not yet registered, and may never be, but are in common usage. The bizarre Hunter Valley GI map now has Hunter Valley as a Zone, Hunter as the Region and the sprawling Upper Hunter as a Subregion along with Pokolbin (small and disputed by some locals). Another recent official change has been the registration of Mount Gambier as a Region in the Limestone Coast Zone. I am still in front of the game with Tasmania, dividing it into Northern, Southern and East Coast. In a similar vein, I have included Ballarat (with 15 wineries) and the Southern Eyre Peninsula (three wineries).

State/Zone	Region	Subregion
AUSTRALIA		
Australia Australian South Eastern Australia★	★ The South Eastern Australia Zone incorporates the whole of the states of NSW, Vic and Tas, and only part of Qld and SA.	
NEW SOUTH WALES		
Big Rivers	Murray Darling Perricoota Riverina Swan Hill	
Central Ranges	Cowra Mudgee Orange	
Hunter Valley	Hunter	Broke Fordwich Pokolbin Upper Hunter Valley

State/Zone	Region	Subregion
Northern Rivers	Hastings River	
Northern Slopes	New England Australia	
South Coast	Shoalhaven Coast Southern Highlands	
Southern New South Wales	Canberra District Gundagai Hilltops Tumbarumba	
Western Plains		

SOUTH AUSTRALIA

State/Zone	Region	Subregion
Adelaide (Super Zone, includes Mount Lofty Ranges, Fleurieu and Barossa)		
Barossa	Barossa Valley Eden Valley	 High Eden
Far North	Southern Flinders Ranges	
Fleurieu	Currency Creek Kangaroo Island Langhorne Creek McLaren Vale Southern Fleurieu	
Limestone Coast	Coonawarra Mount Benson Mount Gambier Padthaway Robe Wrattonbully	
Lower Murray	Riverland	
Mount Lofty Ranges	Adelaide Hills Adelaide Plains Clare Valley	Lenswood Piccadilly Valley Polish Hill River★ Watervale★
The Peninsulas	Southern Eyre Peninsula★	

State/Zone	Region	Subregion
VICTORIA		
Central Victoria	Bendigo Goulburn Valley Heathcote Strathbogie Ranges Upper Goulburn	Nagambie Lakes
Gippsland		
North East Victoria	Alpine Valleys Beechworth Glenrowan King Valley Rutherglen	
North West Victoria	Murray Darling Swan Hill	
Port Phillip	Geelong Macedon Ranges Mornington Peninsula Sunbury Yarra Valley	
Western Victoria	Ballarat★ Grampians Henty Pyrenees	Great Western
WESTERN AUSTRALIA		
Central Western Australia		
Eastern Plains, Inland and North of Western Australia		
Greater Perth	Peel Perth Hills Swan District	Swan Valley

State/Zone	Region	Subregion
South West Australia	Blackwood Valley	
	Geographe	
	Great Southern	Albany
		Denmark
		Frankland River
		Mount Barker
		Porongurup
	Manjimup	
	Margaret River	
	Pemberton	
West Australian South East Coastal		

QUEENSLAND

Queensland	Granite Belt	
	South Burnett	

TASMANIA

Tasmania	Northern Tasmania★	
	Southern Tasmania★	
	East Coast Tasmania★	

AUSTRALIAN CAPITAL TERRITORY

NORTHERN TERRITORY

Wine and food or food and wine?

It all depends on your starting point: there are conventional matches for overseas classics such as caviar (Champagne), fresh foie gras (Sauternes, riesling or rose), and new season Italian white truffles (any medium-bodied red). Here the food flavour is all important, the wine merely incidental.

At the other extreme come 50-year-old classic red wines: Grange, or Grand Cru Burgundy, or First Growth Bordeaux, or a Maurice O'Shea Mount Pleasant Shiraz. Here the food is, or should be, merely a low-key foil, but at the same time must be of high quality.

In the Australian context I believe not enough attention is paid to the time of year, which – particularly in the southern states – is or should be a major determinant in the choice of both food and wine. And so I shall present my suggestions in this way, always bearing in mind how many ways there are to skin a cat (but not serve it).

Spring

Sparkling
Oysters, cold crustacea, tapas, any cold hors d'oeuvres

Young riesling
Cold salads, sashimi

Gewurztraminer
Asian

Young semillon
Antipasto, vegetable terrine

Pinot gris
Crab cakes, whitebait

Verdelho, chenin blanc
Cold smoked chicken, gravlax

Mature chardonnay
Grilled chicken, chicken pasta, turkey, pheasant

Rose
Caesar salad, trout mousse

Young pinot noir
Seared kangaroo fillet, grilled quail

Merlot
Pastrami, warm smoked chicken

Cool climate medium-bodied cabernet sauvignon
Rack of baby lamb

Light to medium-bodied cool-climate shiraz
Rare eye fillet of beef

Young botrytised wines
Fresh fruits, cake

Summer

Chilled fino
Cold consommé

2–3-year-old semillon
Gazpacho

2–3-year-old riesling
Seared tuna

Young barrel-fermented semillon sauvignon blanc
Seafood or vegetable tempura

Young off-dry riesling
Prosciutto & melon/pear

Cool-climate chardonnay
Abalone, lobster, Chinese-style prawns

10–year-old semillon or riesling
Braised pork neck

Mature chardonnay (5+ years)
Braised rabbit

Off-dry rose
Chilled fresh fruit

Young light-bodied pinot noir
Grilled salmon

Aged pinot noir (5+ years)
Coq au vin, wild duck

Young grenache/sangiovese
Osso bucco

Hunter Valley shiraz (5–10 years)
Beef spare ribs

Sangiovese
Saltimbocca, roast poussin

Medium-bodied cabernet sauvignon (5 years)
Barbecued butterfly leg of lamb

Mature chardonnay
Smoked eel, smoked roe

All wines
Parmagiana

Autumn

Amontillado
Warm consommé

Barrel-fermented mature whites
Smoked roe, bouillabaisse

Complex mature chardonnay
Sweetbreads, brains

Aged (10-year-old) marsanne or semillon
Seafood risotto, Lebanese

Grenache
Grilled calf's liver, roast kid, lamb or pig's kidneys

Mature Margaret River cabernet merlot
Lamb fillet, roast leg of lamb with garlic and herbs

Cool climate merlot
Lamb loin chops

Fully aged riesling
Chargrilled eggplant, stuffed capsicum

Mature grenache/rhône blends
Moroccan lamb

Rich, full-bodied Heathcote shiraz
Beef casserole

Southern Victorian pinot noir
Peking duck

Young muscat
Plum pudding

Winter

Dry oloroso sherry
Full-flavoured hors d'oeuvres

Sparkling Burgundy
Borscht, wild mushroom risotto

Viognier
Pea and ham soup

Aged (10+ years) semillon
Vichysoisse (hot)

Sauvignon blanc
Coquilles St Jacques (pan-fried scallops)

Chardonnay (10+ years)
Cassoulet

2–4-year-old semillon sauvignon blanc
Seafood pasta

Tasmanian pinot noir
Squab, duck breast

Mature pinot noir
Mushroom ragout, ravioli

Mature cool-grown shiraz viognier
Pot au feu

10-year-old Grampians shiraz
Chargrilled rump steak

15–20-year-old full-bodied Barossa shiraz
Venison, kangaroo fillet

Coonawarra cabernet sauvignon
Braised lamb shanks/shoulder

Muscat (rare)
Chocolate-based desserts

Topaque (rare)
Creme brûlée

Vintage fortified shiraz
Dried fruits, salty cheese

Australian vintage charts

Each number represents a mark out of 10 for the quality of vintages in each region.

red wine   white wine   fortified

NSW

	2012	2013	2014	2015
Hunter Valley				
	2	8	10	5
	7	8	7	6
Mudgee				
	5	7	7	9
	7	8	9	8
Orange				
	7	9	5	9
	8	9	7	9
Canberra District				
	7	9	7	10
	8	9	8	10
Hilltops				
	7	9	9	8
	7	9	9	8
Southern Highlands				
	4	7	7	6
	7	8	7	8
Tumbarumba				
	-	8	9	7
	7	9	8	0
Riverina/Griffith				
	8	7	7	8
	9	8	8	8
Shoalhaven				
	6	8	9	7
	8	8	9	8

VIC

	2012	2013	2014	2015
Yarra Valley				
	10	9	7	10
	9	8	8	9
Mornington Peninsula				
	9	9	9	10
	9	8	9	9
Geelong				
	10	9	8	10
	8	8	7	9
Macedon Ranges				
	8	9	8	9
	7	9	8	8
Sunbury				
	8	9	9	8
	8	9	8	7
Gippsland				
	9	8	5	9
	9	8	9	9
Bendigo				
	9	8	9	8
	8	7	7	8
Heathcote				
	9	9	8	8
	8	6	7	7
Grampians				
	9	9	9	8
	8	8	9	8
Pyrenees				
	9	8	8	7
	7	7	8	8

	2012	2013	2014	2015
Henty				
	9	10	9	10
	9	8	10	9
Beechworth				
	8	8	8	8
	9	9	8	9
Nagambie Lakes				
	7	9	8	8
	8	7	8	9
Upper Goulburn				
	8	9	9	9
	7	9	9	7
Strathbogie Ranges				
	7	9	6	8
	7	7	7	8
King Valley				
	7	8	7	9
	8	8	9	8
Alpine Valleys				
	7	9	7	10
	9	7	8	9
Glenrowan				
	7	9	9	8
	6	7	7	7
Rutherglen				
	9	10	7	9
	-	-	-	9
Murray Darling				
	9	8	8	9
	9	87	8	7

SA

	2012	2013	2014	2015
Barossa Valley				
	10	8	7	9
	8	7	7	8
Eden Valley				
	10	8	8	9
	9	8	8	10
Clare Valley				
	9	7	8	9
	10	8	8	9
Adelaide Hills				
	10	9	8	9
	9	8	8	10
McLaren Vale				
	10	9	7	8
	9	8	8	8
Southern Fleurieu				
	9	6	8	7
	8	5	8	6
Langhorne Creek				
	10	9	9	9
	8	8	8	7
Kangaroo Island				
	10	8	8	8
	10	8	9	8
Adelaide Plains				
	8	7	7	x
	6	6	7	x
Coonawarra				
	8	9	8	9
	8	8	8	8

	2012	2013	2014	2015
Wrattonbully				
	9	9	9	9
	8	8	8	9
Padthaway				
	8	8	8	9
	8	8	9	9
Mount Benson & Robe				
	9	7	9	10
	9	8	9	9
Riverland				
	9	8	8	9
	7	8	8	8

WA

	2012	2013	2014	2015
Margaret River				
	10	9	8	8
	8	9	9	9
Great Southern				
	8	7	8	8
	8	8	8	8
Manjimup				
	7	8	9	8
	7	9	8	7
Pemberton				
	8	8	9	6
	8	9	9	8
Geographe				
	9	6	9	7
	7	7	8	7
Peel				
	8	9	8	x
	8	9	8	x

	2012	2013	2014	2015
Perth Hills				
	8	8	8	9
	7	10	10	9
Swan Valley				
	9	9	8	7
	7	10	10	9

QLD

	2012	2013	2014	2015
Granite Belt				
	10	8	9	8
	7	8	8	8
South Burnett				
	8	8	8	8
	7	9	7	8

TAS

	2012	2013	2014	2015
Northern Tasmania				
	8	7	8	8
	9	8	9	8
Southern Tasmania				
	9	8	9	9
	8	7	9	9

Australian vintage 2016: a snapshot

A vintage with an ever-repeating conundrum: below average rainfall (especially in winter), above average temperatures, above average yields, record early vintages, and good to excellent quality. I'll come back to this shortly but, as with any sweeping generalisation, there are exceptions. At the quality end of the spectrum, Western Australia had rainfall (erratic in most regions) punctuating a cool vintage, and a stiff upper lip when it came to quality. Then there are the mighty engines of the regions fuelled by the Murrumbidgee and Murray Rivers. It is these that will determine the national crush.

Coming back to the 63 regions outside the river regions spread from Queensland to Tasmania, the pattern was of vintages with very early budburst (dry soils warm more quickly than wet), and dry conditions during flowering providing perfect fruit-set. One of the less easily explained features of many regions was abundant canopies with a high number of leaves per bunch. From this point on, supplementary irrigation played a major role, but often ran out.

Once harvest was approaching (at record early dates) all varieties seemed to ripen simultaneously, and crops usually exceeded estimates. Winemakers tried in vain to find extra barrels and tanks, and some high quality grapes had to remain on the vine for days after their optimum picking dates.

The best explanation I can find for the conundrum is elevated levels of vine nutrition: CO_2.

SOUTH AUSTRALIA

The **Barossa Valley** vintage was shaped by low rainfall, 72% of the long-term average. Despite the dry conditions and hot December and February, yields were average to above average (after four vintages with below average production). The generally ideal conditions for ripening, coupled with generous yields, resulted in one winery saying vintage was like 'an intense chess game, juggling tank space to capture everything at optimal ripeness.' Shiraz and grenache were nominated as outstanding, and most of the reporting wineries are hopeful that 2016 will become part of the Barossa's fabled vintages. In the **Eden Valley**, the focus was on riesling, shiraz and cabernet sauvignon, with quality very good to excellent. The heat was alleviated by widespread rain at the end of January. The **Clare Valley** had a similar story, with ideal fruit-set promising above average yields; then a hot December reduced yield expectations, before nature threw its last dart, the rain in late January and early February, completely altering the yield forecasts with a 20% surge. Riesling, shiraz and cabernet sauvignon were the standouts. In the **Adelaide Hills** the low winter and spring rainfall required early irrigation, rare for the region. Rain in late January was worth its weight in gold, the outcome above average yields, the chardonnay and sauvignon blanc the best white wines, shiraz and pinot noir the best reds. One reporter in the **Adelaide Plains** summarised things thus: 'The best all-round vintage I have seen in 10 years of working in this area'. When you read vintage summaries such as, '2016 may well go down as one of the great **McLaren Vale** vintages in recent memory. Vines were well-balanced, crop levels were good, colour and flavour fantastic. Shiraz the pick', you cannot help but wonder whether there is an edge of embellishment. However, all the reports were in agreement, throwing in grenache and cabernet sauvignon for particular praise. The strongly maritime climate of **Langhorne Creek**, **Southern Fleurieu** and **Kangaroo Island** stood out in high relief. The warm, dry spring led to good fruit-set in all varieties, and summer was generally quite cool, with rainfall episodes in January and February very welcome. There were very few days over 35°C. Bleasdale buys grapes from the Adelaide Hills and finished that harvest before Langhorne Creek. Cabernet sauvignon is the star, one of the best in many years. Kangaroo Island rates its overall quality as very, very good, with the earliest start of vintage (March 1) and the latest finish (April 8) on record. The **Coonawarra** growing season and harvest reflected the extreme El Niño event across the Pacific, the Bureau of Meteorology likening 2016 to 1998. Budburst was two weeks early, and at no stage did that two-week start diminish, and the final stages of ripening took place in cool conditions. The colour is excellent, as is the fruit intensity and ripeness. The only question with the red wines is tannin ripeness, but it's too early to make a final call on that. **Mount Benson, Robe, Wrattonbully** and **Padthaway** were in agreement about potential yields significantly better than those in 2014 and 2015, but thereafter opinions were split: some were sanguine, some (slightly) pessimistic. Spicy shiraz was nominated by the majority of reporters, cabernet sauvignon pleasing some with its elegant medium body. The **Riverland** experienced ideal ripening conditions, leading to a compressed vintage, with yields slightly down on 2014 and 2015. However, the quality is said to be high, the white wines bright and balanced, the red wines with freshness, good fruit concentration and silky tannins.

VICTORIA

In the **Yarra Valley** a dry winter and spring, with record warmth in October, saw the vines leap out of the starting blocks and race to another very early harvest. Yields were all higher than in recent years, but even though a hot (though not windy) January was to follow, the vine canopies remained in perfect health with no leaf senescence; there was an exceptionally compressed harvest. There are high hopes for pinot noir (once again, and despite the heat), shiraz and the other red varieties; the prime white variety, chardonnay, will be good, but not a repeat of great vintages such as 2011 and 2014. The **Mornington Peninsula** threw a curve ball at global warming, with the coldest winter in 26 years. Just as in the Yarra Valley, very low rainfall created issues, October having the lowest rainfall since 1900. January rain filled out the bunches, and yields were moderate to high, particularly on the whites. The best variety was pinot noir, the overall quality average to above average. **Geelong** followed the pattern with early budburst and rapid growth through to Christmas, but January was not as hot as in some nearby regions, and some vineyards had very high yields of pinot noir: a puzzle explained only by the large size of the seeds in what were generally quite plump berries. A site-specific pattern was evident, with some nominating chardonnay as the standout variety; quality is expected to be good to very good. The **Macedon Ranges** created all sorts of records – the lowest recorded rainfall since 2006, the warmest October on record, the warmest December since 2004, a February without rain, the earliest vintage ever. The picks were pinot noir and chardonnay, the overall quality excellent. Bone-dry soils at budburst in **Sunbury** caused issues for those without water. Low to moderate yields resulted in shiraz, chardonnay and viognier with moderate alcohol and (shiraz) deep colour. **Bendigo**'s weather through to harvest was dry but of moderate heat, providing good ripening conditions. Yields were moderate, the best variety cabernet sauvignon 'hands down.' **Heathcote** had one of the coldest winters in recent memory, and the driest lead into a warm and dry spring and early summer; harvest was the earliest on record. All agreed that shiraz is of exceptional quality. The varied topography and landscape of the **Grampians** led to differences in the physical conditions of the growing season, deciding which varieties fared best. Chemical analysis was unusual, with sugar accumulation three to four weeks ahead of phenolic maturity. Very much a wait-and-see proposition. **Henty**'s temperature gauge was all over the place this year with an unusually hot November, moderate to high December temperatures, a cooler January than usual, but no rainfall in January or the first half of February. The upside was no disease pressure; the outstanding variety was riesling. In one of those unexpected outcomes, one **Pyrenees** vigneron was of the view that the growing season weather for 2015 and 2016 were very similar. One reporter nominated chardonnay and cabernet as standout varieties, the overall quality being good to high. **Beechworth** had an early start to vintage with generous yields providing the best of both worlds, chardonnay the best of the early varieties; cabernet sauvignon, sangiovese and tempranillo the best reds. Overall a vintage to remember. **Nagambie Lakes** experienced the quickest vintage on record (just over four weeks compared to the usual eight to nine weeks). Notwithstanding a thunderstorm on January 3 with 85-100mm of rain falling in two hours, dry and windy conditions after the rain prevented disease outbreaks. The simultaneous ripening of white and red varieties, and scrambling for non-existent fermentation space, was the only issue. Overall, a very good vintage in terms of quality and quantity. The **Strathbogie Ranges** shared very dry soil conditions and the earliest use of irrigation on record, but with cabernet still being picked on April 7. Vine stress undoubtedly played a role. Chardonnay and pinot noir were the standouts. **Upper Goulburn** vignerons were happy, with good quality across the board despite the very early and condensed season. The **Alpine Valleys** had the earliest harvest on record (nothing new there), after some yoyo weather changes; differing parts of the Valleys had very different outcomes. Some were happy with their reds, but not so much the whites, others had a diametrically opposed view. The **King Valley** had a basically dry, warm vintage, the yields moderate, prosecco and pinot grigio the standout varieties for some, but perhaps without the acidity of 2015. **Glenrowan** and **Rutherglen** had a warm, dry start, followed by heavy rain in early February, then a return of dry conditions ending fears about mildew and botrytis. A very good year for shiraz and durif, and even better for muscadelle (producing topaque) and muscat. The **Murray Darling** had to cope with the usual very hot conditions, which it did with ease. Viognier and chardonnay were the best whites, cabernet sauvignon, tempranillo and shiraz the pick of the reds.

NEW SOUTH WALES

The **Hunter Valley** had the narrowest of escapes with above average rainfall in December and January, the latter ending up with 338mm for the month. Then nature did a U-turn, with negligible rain throughout February and up to the conclusion of vintage. Those who ran a stringent sorting system for semillon got out of jail, although the net impact on some vineyards was a loss of 50%, others a total loss. Shiraz was picked over the course of February, with sugar levels 13.5 to 14.5 baume, and excellent colour. **Mudgee** reports that it had one of the best vintages in recent memory, rain in January providing moisture in otherwise bone-dry soils. In the harvest period of February through to April, only 16mm of rain was recorded, making it one of the driest harvests on record. The standouts were riesling, pinot grigio, chardonnay, and the usual suspects of shiraz and cabernet sauvignon. **Orange** had almost perfect weather conditions, commencing with winter and spring rainfall, which fell with regularity. All varieties ripened rapidly, the downside for vintage insufficient tank and barrel space in a very compressed vintage. Overall quality was good to very good, with cabernet sauvignon, shiraz and riesling leading the way. The **Canberra District** felt the El Niño effect with a dry spring and early summer (90mm of rain in the last week of January a blessing). Disease-free fruit with generous yields and perfect levels of ripeness were the result, winery logistics a nightmare. Shiraz and riesling were the standouts. Indeed, one winery rated its cabernet sauvignon and shiraz higher than 2015: a big call. **Hilltops** had a wild ride, but taking the drama out of the rainfall and temperature records, it was in fact an ideal growing season, with two of the major players in the region agreeing that it was exceptional, comparable with 2014. The standout variety was shiraz. The weather for **Tumbarumba** was very similar to that of Hilltops, but generalisations for Tumbarumba are hazardous because of the large variations in elevation and aspect. Chardonnay is the pick of the vintage, sauvignon blanc strong, and pinot noir riper and denser in the black fruit spectrum plus full-bodied tannins. Overall, a good but not great vintage. The **Southern Highlands** had normal winter rain and a warm, dry spring, creating growth a week or two ahead of average. A wet January slowed the ripening, but from this point on the season was favourable, sugar accumulation retarded vis-à-vis phenological flavours. In the outcome, the baume levels were low, flavour levels high. Riesling and pinot gris fared best, but all varieties performed well. The **Shoalhaven Coast** experienced high winter and early spring rainfall, the summer warm and dry, the yields very good. All the whites fared well. Tannat was the pick of the red wines. Good winter and spring rainfall in the **Riverina**, followed by multiple heatwaves from December through to February, led to a fast and furious harvest, slowed only by rain around Australia Day necessitating selective harvesting. Chardonnay, pinot grigio and arneis stood out, as did shiraz and durif in the reds, all harvested by St Patrick's Day (March 17), the earliest finish in living memory.

WESTERN AUSTRALIA

Good winter rains in **Margaret River** were followed by dry weather until 90mm fell in January, with rainfall continuing at above average levels through February and March. Rigorous control of disease (mildew, botrytis) in the vineyard was essential, and not all producers were up to the challenge. For those that were, chardonnay and cabernet sauvignon were the highlights, some rating them as superb, others very good. Albany, Denmark, Frankland River, Mount Barker and Porongurup in the **Great Southern** all experienced constant changes in rainfall patterns. This was coupled with a generally cool, cloudy and humid growing season, exacerbated by sudden, intense influxes of silvereyes. Yields were moderate, with some losses due to fruit sorting. Riesling fared well (as ever), as did shiraz; overall, complex and austere red wines will be slow to develop and show their true potential. **Manjimup** and **Pemberton**'s winter and spring rainfall was below average, then 196mm fell in two hours, 120mm of that within one hour, on January 19. The temperatures, too, fluctuated wildly: Pemberton's 2016 maximums varied from 18°C to 37°C. Overnight temperatures were cold, which helped acid retention. Riesling and shiraz were best, the overall quality good for whites, moderate for reds. **Geographe** pointed to El Niño for its hot spring and high average temperatures, which continued until January 18, when the region received 74mm of rain, with temperatures remaining cool thereafter. Yields varied, as did the success stories, shiraz and tempranillo from one producer, verdelho and malbec from another. Winter and spring in the **Swan Valley** were warmer than average, the rainfall below average. This led to an early harvest, commencing on January 2. There were three significant heatwaves, and only those who picked before the February heatwave fared well. Yields were as much as 50% below average, shiraz the best performing variety. **Perth Hills** had little winter rainfall, but spring brought some relief; thereafter the weather remained hot and dry, the yields moderate. Viognier, shiraz and merlot were the best varieties, the vignerons very pleased with the outcome.

TASMANIA

A dry winter and spring in **Southern Tasmania** along with record warmth in October saw the vines race to another very early harvest. Yields were all up on recent years, but such was vine health that almost all blocks looked balanced. Quality seems to have been shielded by a notable absence of extreme heat during the ripening phase for red varieties in particular. The **East Coast** had the coldest winter since 1966 and was drier than the long-term average. Spring went in the opposite direction, being the second warmest since 1914 and very dry. Flowering and fruit-set was uninterrupted, leading to better than average yields statewide. The summer was the warmest on record, thanks to consistently mild temperatures (and relatively few hot days). Chardonnay and pinot noir were the benchmarks for a vintage that was described by one of the most clear-eyed vignerons as 'solid, good, but not a classic, great year.' And, of course, there will always be the exceptions. **Northern Tasmania** conformed to the patterns described for the South and East, leaving little more to be said. If there is to be a standout variety, it will be pinot noir.

QUEENSLAND

The **Granite Belt** had absolutely perfect weather up to vintage except for a short week of rainfall in late January (a small frost and hail event in October 2015 did lead to a loss of 10% for some producers). Yields were moderate to high across the board; the standouts vermentino, sauvignon blanc and semillon in the whites, tempranillo, malbec, durif and shiraz in the reds. Quality is very high, on a par with 2014.

Acknowledgements

One of the inescapable outcomes of age is that for most of us, myself very definitely included, things take longer to do. It's far distant from those years when you didn't even realise you were hard wired to instantly recall memories of all kinds. It didn't seem remarkable, it was just what one did, said or wrote. The insidious change is not groping for a name or a word (you can learn tricks to prompt recall), but the cumulative loss of time. Thus I'm not doing any more than I used to, but I have to work longer hours to achieve the same result.

It's lucky I have got two helpers in the office (downstairs in my house) and another upstairs. They are my faithful servants Paula Grey, with a quarter of a century on the job, and Beth Anthony, with 16 years. They put up with my skill in constantly losing emails, printouts – anything physical – in the Bermuda Triangle of my desk, and print another copy, and another …

My wife, Suzanne, is most certainly not my servant, but that doesn't stop her looking after all I could possibly need. Among many other attributes is her ever-inventive cuisine, some of it very time-consuming, but always wine-friendly.

Then there are the tribes at Hardie Grant who look after both the pre- and postnatal welfare of the *Wine Companion* in all its forms. All are important, some more important than others. From my selfish point of view, Sandy Grant is the *sine qua non* – he had the faith to form a joint venture, which I treasure dearly in all its forms.

Julie Pinkham, Simon McKeown and Fran Berry are all in the frontline of decision-making, and I have never had a cross word – not even a niggle of annoyance – with or from any of them.

Then there is the one and only Annie Clemenger, who had the preposterous idea of having a book launch for the 2014 *Wine Companion*. I told her to forget it entirely, saying I regarded such events as a complete waste of time. I am still bewildered at the runaway success of the Wine Companion Awards event, and sincerely thank the winemakers and wineries that so willingly support it.

The newcomer to the tasting team next year will be Ned Goodwin MW, who was dux of the Len Evans Tutorial in 2012. He will join Campbell Mattinson, whose support and contribution over the past three years has been invaluable. Tyson Stelzer's knowledge of Champagne and Australian sparkling wine is profound, and I thank him for his continuing support. Stephen Creber, a near-Yarra Valley resident (a former winemaker, and thereafter professional wine taster) has also agreed to come on board in moments of need.

Loran McDougall became editor of this edition at short notice, and has had a baptism by fire. Loran, I promise you it won't be so trying next time. The magic wand of Megan Ellis in typesetting the *Wine Companion* in the blink of an eye continues to amaze me.

Finally, my thanks to the unnofficial couriers who spring to my aid in the worst times of the year (four solid months) and likewise to Tracy and Alan at the Coldstream Post Office.

Australian wineries and wines

A note on alphabetical order
Wineries beginning with 'The' are listed under 'T'; for example,
'The Bridge Vineyard'. Winery names that include a numeral are
treated as if the numeral is spelt out; for example, '2 Mates'
is listed under 'T'.

A. Rodda Wines

PO Box 589, Beechworth, Vic 3747 **Region** Beechworth
T 0400 350 135 **www**.aroddawines.com.au **Open** Not
Winemaker Adrian Rodda **Est.** 2010 **Dozens** 800 **Vyds** 2ha

Adrian Rodda has been winemaking since 1998, almost entirely working with David Bicknell
at Oakridge. He was involved in the development of the superb Oakridge 864 Chardonnay,
his final contribution to 864 coming in 2009. At the start of 2010 he and wife Christie, a
doctor, decided to move to Beechworth, and it was no coincidence that he was a long-term
friend of viticulturist Mark Walpole. Coincidences came with the Smith Vineyard and winery
being available for lease; he now shares it with Mark, who makes his Beechworth wines there.
Even more propitious was the availability of Smith Vineyard chardonnay, planted in 1974. The
quality of the portfolio has been consistently excellent.

99999 **Willow Lake Vineyard Yarra Valley Chardonnay 2015** White peach,
melon and grapefruit are backed by complex wild yeast and barrel fermentation
providing the background of funk. Intense and superbly balanced, it drives on and
on with grapefruit pith and the finest of acid lines. Of the single vineyard releases
this vintage, Willow Lake is the clear favourite. Screwcap. 13% alc. **Rating** 96
To 2025 $42 ○

Smiths Vineyard Beechworth Chardonnay 2014 From the celebrated
47yo vineyard. Bright green-gold, it has that extra dimension the best Beechworth
(Giaconda) exhibits most vintages. White peach, nectarine and rockmelon are
folded into the gentle hand of oak, the requisite length present and correct,
likewise a Burgundian hint of funk. Screwcap. 13% alc. **Rating** 95 To 2022 $42

Willow Lake Vineyard Yarra Valley Chardonnay 2014 Willow Lake Vineyard
is high in the Yarra Valley, planted in '79, well before any others in the Upper
Yarra. Here the impact is derived from the length and balance of the fruit profile,
grapefruit joining the white peach, fresh acidity evident from the outset. A breath
of fresh air. Screwcap. 13% alc. **Rating** 95 To 2024 $38

Smiths Vineyard Beechworth Chardonnay 2015 A complex and intriguing
effort. Lemon rind, mealy and smoky, spicy oak; the palate is finely poised and
wound tightly around a backbone of fine acid. Screwcap. 13% alc. **Rating** 94
To 2020 $42

Beechworth Cuvee de Chez 2014 66% cabernet sauvignon, 24% merlot,
6% petit verdot, 4% malbec. The red fruit-accented bouquet is backed by mulberry
and tobacco, the palate medium-bodied and finely extracted, long and well
balanced. Screwcap. 13.5% alc. **Rating** 94 To 2024 $36

A.T. Richardson Wines

103 Hard Hill Road, Armstrong, Vic 3377 **Region** Grampians
T (02) 9460 3177 **www**.atrichardsonwines.com **Open** Not
Winemaker Adam Richardson **Est.** 2005 **Dozens** 2000 **Vyds** 7ha

Perth-born Adam Richardson began his winemaking career in 1995, along the way working
for Normans, d'Arenberg and Oakridge Estate. Since that time he has held senior winemaking
roles, ultimately with TWE Americas before moving back to Australia with wife Eva and
children in late 2015. But in 2005 he put down small roots in the Grampians region, acquiring
a vineyard with shiraz from old clones from the 19th century, and riesling. The wines are
exceptionally good, and given his experience and the quality of the vineyard, that should not
come as a surprise. As well as having hands-on experience in winemaking for the smallest to
the largest producers, he has firsthand knowledge of the US market, and contacts in many
parts of the world. He has set up a wine consultancy business, drawing on experience that is
matched by few consultants based in Australia. Exports to the UK and the US.

99999 **Hard Hill Road Pyrenees Nebbiolo 2012** Nebbiolo made to look easy. It
has unusually good colour, and all the perfumed rose petal, violet and dark cherry
aromas you are meant to see on the bouquet, but which are so often missing in
action; the palate follows suit and, best of all, the tannins are supple. Yes, it was

a good vintage, but this is an utterly exceptional result. Tasted 18 months later (Sept '15), it has barely changed. Screwcap. 14% alc. **Rating** 96 **To** 2032 $60 **◐**

ŸŸŸŸ° Chockstone Grampians Chardonnay 2015 **Rating** 92 **To** 2023 $22 **◐**

Abbey Creek Vineyard

2388 Porongurup Road, Porongurup, WA 6324 **Region** Porongurup
T (08) 9853 1044 **Open** By appt
Winemaker Castle Rock Estate (Robert Diletti) **Est.** 1990 **Dozens** 800 **Vyds** 1.6ha
This is the family business of Mike and Mary Dilworth, the name coming from a winter creek that runs alongside the vineyard and a view of The Abbey in the Stirling Range. The vineyard is split between pinot noir, riesling and sauvignon blanc. The Rieslings have had significant show success for a number of years.

ŸŸŸŸŸ Museum Release Porongurup Riesling 2010 So fresh, so intense, so perfectly articulated you could easily believe it's only 1 or 2 years old. This is vibrantly alive, lime and mineral flavours clinging together so tightly you can't separate them. I am totally confident this will continue on an upwards course for another decade, then plateau for who knows how long. Screwcap. 12.5% alc. **Rating** 97 **To** 2040 $30 **◐**

ŸŸŸŸŸ Porongurup Riesling 2013 The easiest of the museum releases to understand and enjoy, the Abbey Creek fruit profile appearing immediately, and content to let it loose for all to taste and revel in its slightly softer expression. Not, mind you, much different from how it expressed itself when last tasted 2 years ago in the wake of its two trophies from the National Cool Climate Wine Show '13. Screwcap. 12.5% alc. **Rating** 96 **To** 2033 $25 **◐**
Museum Release Porongurup Riesling 2011 All three Abbey Creek Rieslings from '10 to '15 have the same pale quartz-green colour – amazing. This takes its time in waking up as you taste it to tease out its secrets, then as quick as a flash it takes hold on the finish and aftertaste, unsweetened lime and mineral exploding. Screwcap. 12.5% alc. **Rating** 96 **To** 2036 $25 **◐**
Porongurup Riesling 2015 Light straw-green; ultra-classic Porongurup, so crisp it's almost brittle (it's not); the delicacy of the wine is sustained in the face of purity and intensity – or the other way around. The extreme length of the wine is its secret, the key to unlock and fully understand the wine; the '13, '11 and '10 vintages are now available as museum releases, all at $25, bar the magnificent '10 at $30. Screwcap. 12.5% alc. **Rating** 95 **To** 2040 $25 **◐**
Porongurup Pinot Noir 2012 Has retained a youthful hue; clear-cut varietal expression, red berry fruits interlaced with sweet spices. I'll stick to the original drink-to date and points. Screwcap. 13.5% alc. **Rating** 94 **To** 2019 $30 **◐**
Porongurup Pinot Noir 2010 Exceptional retention of bright hue; it has now realised its potential since first tasted 3 years ago, my tasting note then 'Bright, clear crimson-purple; helps to advance the argument that this region has to be taken seriously as a pinot producer. It has a mix of red and black cherry and spicy/savoury/stemmy notes that pull in different directions on the mid-palate before joining together in a juicy stream on the finish and aftertaste.' The only changes are adding 4 years to the drink-to date, and upgrading the points from 92. Screwcap. 13% alc. **Rating** 94 **To** 2020 $30 **◐**

ŸŸŸŸ Museum Release Porongurup Pinot Noir 2006 **Rating** 89 **To** 2016 $30

Adelina Wines

PO Box 75, Sevenhill, SA 5453 **Region** Clare Valley
T (08) 8842 1549 **www.**adelina.com.au **Open** Not
Winemaker Colin McBryde, Jennie Gardner **Est.** 2002 **Dozens** 400
Established by Jennie Gardner and Col McBryde, both having prior experience in Australia (and elsewhere). The winery and vineyard (owned by the Gardner family) are set in the Springfarm Valley, just south of the Clare township. The old vineyard, part dating back to

1910, is divided into three small blocks, with 1ha each of shiraz and grenache, and just under 0.5ha of cabernet sauvignon. The winery is a simple shed with the basic requisites to process the grapes and make wine. Most is estate-grown, along with grapes from a few sites in the Adelaide Hills.

ΨΨΨΨΨ **Clare Valley Shiraz 2012** Clear, bright colour; made using biodynamic principles, and whatever influence that may have had is moot, because this is a lovely wine, supple, smooth and long, fruit, oak and silky tannins all in astral alignment. As ever, a great label. Screwcap. 13.9% alc. **Rating** 95 **To** 2027 $60
Clare Valley Shiraz Mataro 2014 We have a live one here. The price is almost double-take territory; before it was revealed I was expecting it to be far higher. It's one of those 'complex but seductive' wines. It's all black cherry and plum, but it's meaty and smoky too, with inlays of earth and roasted nuts. It's not overly intense but it feels vital; a 7-iron of a wine. Jump at this wine if you get the chance. Screwcap. 14% alc. **Rating** 95 **To** 2030 $29 CM ✪
Adelaide Hills Nebbiolo Rose 2014 From a single Woodside vineyard. Light russet-red; has maximum impact on the bone-dry, savoury palate with a blend of sour and morello cherry, plus a pinch of spice coming through on the lingering finish. High quality rose. Screwcap. 13% alc. **Rating** 94 **To** 2016 $27 ✪

ΨΨΨΨΨ **Polish Hill River Clare Valley Riesling 2015 Rating** 93 **To** 2023 $25 CM ✪
Clare Valley Shiraz 2014 Rating 93 **To** 2039 $60
Adelaide Hills Nebbiolo 2012 Rating 93 **To** 2020 $40
Watervale Clare Valley Riesling 2015 Rating 92 **To** 2022 $25 CM ✪
Clare Valley Grenache 2014 Rating 91 **To** 2024 $40
Adelaide Hills Arneis 2014 Rating 90 **To** 2017 $27

After Hours Wine   ★★★★

455 North Jindong Road, Carbunup, WA 6285 **Region** Margaret River
T 0438 737 587 **www**.afterhourswine.com.au **Open** Fri–Mon 10–4
Winemaker Phil Potter **Est.** 2006 **Dozens** 3000 **Vyds** 8.6ha
In 2005 Warwick and Cherylyn Mathews acquired the long-established Hopelands Vineyard, planted to cabernet sauvignon (2.6ha), shiraz (1.6ha), merlot, semillon, sauvignon blanc and chardonnay (1.1ha each). The first wine was made in '06, after which they decided to completely rework the vineyard, which required many hours of physical labour. The vines were retrained, with a consequent reduction in yield and rise in wine quality and value.

ΨΨΨΨΨ **Margaret River Sauvignon Blanc Semillon 2015** Tropical fruit ex sauvignon blanc has emerged the driver of the wine. The full range is on display, from passionfruit through to kiwi fruit and lychee, balanced by cleansing lemony acidity ex the semillon. Gold medal Australian Cool Climate Wine Show '15. Screwcap. 12.5% alc. **Rating** 94 **To** 2017 $19 ✪
Margaret River Chardonnay 2014 Barrel-fermented with cultured yeast in new (35%) and 2yo (65%) French oak, matured for 10 months, then the best barrels selected. Has it all exactly where it should be for a secure future, allowing the white peach and grapefruit to expand on the already long palate. Screwcap. 13% alc. **Rating** 94 **To** 2024 $26 ✪

ΨΨΨΨΨ **9 to 5 Semillon Sauvignon Blanc 2015 Rating** 92 **To** 2018 $15 ✪
Margaret River Cabernet Merlot 2013 Rating 90 **To** 2019 $19 ✪
Margaret River Cabernet Sauvignon 2014 Rating 90 **To** 2024 $25

Alkoomi   ★★★★★

Wingebellup Road, Frankland River, WA 6396 **Region** Frankland River
T (08) 9855 2229 **www**.alkoomiwines.com.au **Open** 7 days 10–5
Winemaker Andrew Cherry **Est.** 1971 **Dozens** 70 000 **Vyds** 104.5ha
Established in 1971 by Merv and Judy Lange, Alkoomi has grown from a single hectare to be one of Western Australia's largest family-owned and -operated wineries, with a vineyard

of 104.5ha. Now owned by Merv and Judy's daughter, Sandy Hallett, and her husband Rod, Alkoomi is continuing the tradition of producing high quality varietally expressive wines which showcase the Frankland River region. Presently Alkoomi is actively reducing its environmental footprint; future plans will see the introduction of new varietals. Alkoomi operates cellar doors in Albany and the winery (which also has a function centre). Exports to all major markets.

ΨΨΨΨΨ **Black Label Frankland River Shiraz Viognier 2013** Five per cent viognier co-fermented, matured in French oak (20% new) for 18 months. There's a lot of wine here for the money, the complex bouquet arresting and complex, with red and black fruits and multi-spices leading into a medium to full-bodied palate that is a three-dimensional replay of the bouquet, tannins and oak providing gravitas. Exceptional value. Screwcap. 14.4% alc. **Rating** 96 **To** 2038 $24 ✪

Wandoo Frankland River Semillon 2013 Free-run juice is fermented in two parcels: half in French oak, half in stainless steel, 5 months on lees. Long experience with this approach shows its capacity to progressively build even more complexity. While the Meyer lemon core will always be the centrepiece of the wine, honey is not far around the corner. Screwcap. 11.3% alc. **Rating** 95 **To** 2028 $35 ✪

Black Label Frankland River Chardonnay 2014 From the oldest estate blocks, fermented in new and used French oak and matured for 8 months on lees. Totally delicious and harmonious, the fruit with all the right flavours of fresh-cut white peach and a squeeze of grapefruit; immaculate length and balance, the oak entirely soaked up by the fruit. Screwcap. 13.1% alc. **Rating** 95 **To** 2024 $24 ✪

Jarrah Frankland River Shiraz 2011 Open-fermented, hand-plunged, extended skin contact, fermentation completed in French oak (33% new), matured for 20 months. From the oldest estate vines, and has deceptive elegance, masking the underlying power of the wine. Black cherry, plum and blackberry join in unison with the help of fine, ripe tannins and cedary French oak. Screwcap. 13.8% alc. **Rating** 95 **To** 2036 $45

Blackbutt 2010 80% cabernet sauvignon, 14% malbec, 5% cabernet franc and 1% merlot, fermented in small open vats, hand-plunged, matured in French oak for 20 months. The colour is still fresh, and sets the agenda for the bouquet and palate with cassis and cedary oak, soft and ripe tannins initially ignored because of that ripeness. All up, a 6yo wine looking like a 3yo, but also ready for work. Screwcap. 13.6% alc. **Rating** 95 **To** 2025 $62

Black Label Frankland River Malbec 2014 Two blocks planted '71 and '89, fermented in small open vats, hand-plunged, matured in French hogsheads for 16 months. The '71 planting gave rise to one of Alkoomi's earliest successes, and to this day its deeply coloured Malbec has a unique savoury/spicy combination on the palate that blurs the normal distinction between texture and flavour. Screwcap. 14.5% alc. **Rating** 94 **To** 2034 $24 ✪

Hail Riesling 2015 90% of the vineyard was destroyed by hail early in the growing season, immediate repruning of the vines aiding their recovery, free-run juice, cool-fermented. 19.8g/l residual sugar. The considerable residual sugar is balanced by mouthwatering acidity. A totally delicious wine made in the most unexpected circumstances. Screwcap. 10.2% alc. **Rating** 94 **To** 2025 $24 ✪

ΨΨΨΨΨ **Black Label Sauvignon Blanc 2015** Rating 93 To 2017 $24 ✪
Black Label Cabernet Sauvignon 2014 Rating 93 To 2034 $24 ✪
White Label Riesling 2015 Rating 92 To 2030 $15 ✪
Wandoo Semillon 2007 Rating 92 To 2020 $35
White Label Semillon Sauvignon Blanc 2015 Rating 92 To 2018 $15 ✪
Black Label Chardonnay 2015 Rating 92 To 2025 $24 ✪
Black Label Cabernet Sauvignon 2013 Rating 91 To 2028 $24

All Saints Estate ★★★★★

All Saints Road, Wahgunyah, Vic 3687 **Region** Rutherglen
T 1800 021 621 **www**.allsaintswine.com.au **Open** Mon–Sat 9–5.30, Sun 10–5.30
Winemaker Nick Brown, Chloe Earl **Est.** 1864 **Dozens** 25 000 **Vyds** 33.46ha
The winery rating reflects the fortified wines and table wines alike. The one-hat Terrace restaurant makes this a must-see stop for any visitor to North East Victoria. The towering castle façade is classified by the Historic Buildings Council. All Saints and St Leonards are owned and managed by fourth-generation Brown family members Eliza, Angela and Nicholas (Nick). Eliza is an energetic and highly intelligent leader, wise beyond her years, and highly regarded by the wine industry. The Brown family celebrated the winery's 150th anniversary in 2014. Exports to the UK, the US, Canada, Singapore and China.

♟♟♟♟♟ **Museum Rutherglen Muscadelle NV** This has Formula One acceleration from zero to 100km/hr in the blink of the eye. The concentration and texture are such that you want to (and do) physically bite on the wine in the mouth. Amid the fireworks and white light display there is a certain calm for the so-fine spirit, the flavours equally amazing. It is based on 80yo components (compared to 20+ years for the Rare) and sits outside the normal Rutherglen classification. It is only bottled on order. 375ml. Vino-Lok. 18% alc. **Rating** 99 **To** 2018 $1000
Rare Rutherglen Muscadelle NV Olive on the rim; a heady perfume of tea leaf, toffee and spice introduce the intensity and drive of the palate, where malt and shortbread join the choir of the bouquet; the finish is never-ending, but miraculously dries while its flavours are still with you, as much on your brain as in your mouth. 375ml. Vino-Lok. 18% alc. **Rating** 98 **To** 2018 $120 ✪
Rutherglen Museum Muscat NV The ultimate in complexity and concentration; from a solera started in 1920, and only 250 litres are released in 500 bottles of 500ml each year, the presentation doing it full justice. It is a deep olive-brown, and pours reluctantly from the bottle so viscous is it. This is at once more concentrated, complex and labyrinthine, yet is amazingly light on its feet, with no spirit burn whatsoever. Its ultimate quality and rarity is the extraordinary length that sets it apart. Vino-Lok. 18% alc. **Rating** 98 **To** 2017 $1000
Rare Rutherglen Muscat NV Darker colour than the Muscadelle; liqueured raisins lead the Christmas pudding and heady spice aromas of the perfumed bouquet, morphing seamlessly into treacle, raisin and Christmas pudding with hard sauce. 375ml. Vino-Lok. 18% alc. **Rating** 97 **To** 2018 $120 ✪

♟♟♟♟♟ **Grand Rutherglen Muscadelle NV** The faint hint of red colour at the heart of the Classic has gone, dark walnut grading to lighter olive-brown on the rim. Less luscious, but more intense and penetrating, tea leaf and burnt toffee to the fore; overall, a little more complex than the Grand Muscat. 375ml. Vino-Lok. 18% alc. **Rating** 96 **To** 2018 $72 ✪
Grand Rutherglen Muscat NV Is a neat match with the Grand Muscadelle; here it is richly fruity, with raisins, caramelised ginger and grilled nuts on the mid-palate, changing to an elegant back-palate with a pantry full of spices of Arabia; the overall balance is exceptional, especially for muscat. 375ml. Vino-Lok. 18% alc. **Rating** 96 **To** 2018 $72 ✪
Family Cellar Durif 2012 A textbook example of a variety known for its generosity, but less for its medium-bodied elegance. This nails both, its flavours rolling along the tongue, tannins and oak simply marking the boundaries of the game. Screwcap. 14% alc. **Rating** 95 **To** 2027 $62
Classic Rutherglen Muscadelle NV Golden brown, the clear rim showing age; exceptional complexity and depth for this level, the bouquet showing the range of flavours to come; terrific viscosity, rolling with Christmas cake and Callard & Bowser toffee wreathed in rancio drying the finish. A massive step up from the entry point wine. 375ml. Vino-Lok. 18% alc. **Rating** 95 **To** 2018 $35 ✪
Barrel Reserve Shiraz 2011 55 months in oak for an '11 shiraz? Well, much of the grapes came from 125yo vines planted in the aftermath of phylloxera, and it celebrated All Saints' 150th birthday. If all this were not enough, it was pressed

in the rehabilitated 1880s French basket press. The wine is genuinely good, the flavours sweet, not green. Screwcap. 13.8% alc. **Rating** 94 **To** 2021 $40

Rutherglen Muscadelle NV Pale golden brown; the scented bouquet of butterscotch and honey leads into a beautifully balanced and silky palate building on the flavours of the bouquet, before a gloriously fresh finish. While some may have been aged in oak for up to 5 years, this is all about freshness and nascent, youthful, varietal character. 375ml. Vino-Lok. 17% alc. **Rating** 94 **To** 2018 $25 **◐**

Classic Rutherglen Muscat NV The voluminous bouquet of essence of raisins leaps out of the glass; this has a wonderful mix of exuberant juicy muscat fruit on the one hand, and an elegantly cleansing finish demanding the next taste. 375ml. Vino-Lok. 18% alc. **Rating** 94 **To** 2018 $35

The Vintage 2005 Made to celebrate All Saints' 150th anniversary. It spent 9 years in large barrel, bottled in '14. Extremely potent and powerful, it still has some red in the dark colour, but is largely deep brown; luscious on the way through the palate, it freshens up on the finish and long aftertaste of spices, raisins and dark chocolate. If not consumed for weeks after opening, should be kept refrigerated. Screwcap. 20.5% alc. **Rating** 94 **To** 2026 $35

Marsanne 2015 Rating 93 To 2025 $25 **◐**
Rutherglen Muscat NV Rating 92 To 2018 $25 **◐**
Pierre 2014 Rating 91 To 2025 $36
Chardonnay 2015 Rating 90 To 2019 $24
Rosa 2015 Rating 90 To 2017 $28
Durif 2014 Rating 90 To 2029 $30

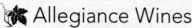

Allegiance Wines ★★★★

Scenic Court, Alstonville, NSW 2477 **Region** Various
T 0434 561 718 **www**.allegiancewines.com.au **Open** Not
Winemaker Contract **Est.** 2009 **Dozens** 15 000
When Tim Cox established Allegiance Wines in 2009 he had the decided advantage of having worked in the Australian wine industry across many facets for almost 30 years. He worked on both the sales and marketing side, and also on the supplier side with Southcorp. He started Cox Wine Merchants to act as distributor for Moppity Vineyards, and successfully partnered with Moppity for over 5 years. It is a virtual wine business, owning neither vineyards nor winery, either having wines made for the business or purchased as cleanskins or as bulk wine.

The Fighter McLaren Vale Tempranillo 2014 On skins for 8 days with plunging and pump-overs, matured for 10 months in used puncheons. Excellent crimson-purple hue to an interesting wine: varietal characters (red, black and sour cherries) battle with regional character (chocolate) for supremacy, neither winning, but both lengthening the palate. Screwcap. 14% alc. **Rating** 91 **To** 2024 $25

The Artisan Coonawarra Cabernet Sauvignon 2013 Cultured yeast, fermented on skins for 9 days, with a combination of pump-over and submerged cap using header boards late in the fermentation, matured in French and American oak (15% new) for 15 months. A well-painted and detailed portrait of medium-bodied Coonawarra Cabernet, with cassis to the fore on the medium-bodied palate, savoury tannins to close. Screwcap. 13.5% alc. **Rating** 90 **To** 2023 $30

The Artisan Coonawarra Shiraz 2014 Rating 88 To 2022 $30

Allies Wines ★★★★★

15 Hume Road, Somers, Vic 3927 (postal) **Region** Mornington Peninsula
T 0412 111 587 **www**.allies.com.au **Open** Not
Winemaker David Chapman **Est.** 2003 **Dozens** 900 **Vyds** 2.6ha
A former chef and sommelier, David Chapman began Allies in 2003 while working at Moorooduc Estate. He aims to make Pinot Noir, emphasising the diversity of the Mornington Peninsula by making a number of wines sourced from different districts. David spends much of his time in the vineyard, working to ensure well-exposed and positioned bunches to

achieve ripe, pure flavours and supple tannins. His winemaking focuses on simple techniques that retain concentration and character. No added yeasts, and no fining or filtration, are standard practices. Production of Allies wines is tiny and will probably remain that way, given that any expansion will limit the number of vines David can personally tend.

ŸŸŸŸŸ Assemblage Mornington Peninsula Pinot Noir 2015 The firm hand of quality; takes you on a meticulously planned ride. Redcurrant, black cherry, infusions of wood smoke, foresty herbs. It has an easy air of confidence; as a drinker you find yourself hanging on its every move. It's light but it's also so magnificently assured. Screwcap. 13.4% alc. **Rating** 96 **To** 2023 $40 CM ✪

ŸŸŸŸŸ Merricks Pinot Noir 2015 Rating 93 **To** 2021 $40 CM

Alta Vineyards   ★★★☆

102 Main Street, Hahndorf, SA 5245 **Region** Adelaide Hills
T (08) 8388 7155 **www**.altavineyards.com.au **Open** 7 days 11–5
Winemaker Sarah Fletcher **Est.** 2003 **Dozens** 4000 **Vyds** 23ha
Sarah Fletcher came to Alta after seven years working for Orlando Wyndham. There she came face to face with grapes from all over Australia, and developed a particular regard for those coming from the Adelaide Hills. So she joined Alta, which had already established a reputation for its Sauvignon Blanc. The portfolio has been progressively extended with varieties suited to the cool climate of the Adelaide Hills.

ŸŸŸŸŸ Adelaide Hills Sauvignon Blanc 2015 A persuasive outcome of attention to detail and lateral thinking. Taken together, they make this an interesting (and enjoyable) wine that surges on the finish and aftertaste with a mix of gently tropical and citrus flavours. Screwcap. 12.5% alc. **Rating** 94 **To** 2017 $20 ✪

ŸŸŸŸ Adelaide Hills Shiraz 2014 Rating 89 **To** 2029 $20

Amadio Wines   ★★★★

461 Payneham Road, Felixstow, SA 5070 **Region** Adelaide Hills
T (08) 8337 5144 **www**.amadiowines.com **Open** Wed–Sun 10–5.30
Winemaker Danniel Amadio **Est.** 2004 **Dozens** 75 000 **Vyds** 250ha
Danniel Amadio says he has followed in the footsteps of his Italian grandfather, selling wine from his cellar (cantina) direct to the consumer. He also draws upon the business of his parents, built not in Italy, but in Australia. Amadio Wines has substantial vineyards, primarily in the Adelaide Hills and Barossa Valley, and also contract-grown grapes from Clare Valley, McLaren Vale and Langhorne Creek, with a strong suite of Italian varieties. Exports to the UK, the US, Canada, Denmark, Russia, India, Indonesia, South Korea, Singapore, Hong Kong and China.

ŸŸŸŸŸ Block 2a Adelaide Hills Shiraz 2012 It takes time to be coaxed forward and therefore, especially if drinking it young, can use a decant. It's a substantial wine but a well-balanced one, with black cherry, plum and undergrowth flavours given a thorough infusion by toasty, (dark) chocolatey oak. Tannin is ultrafine and length doesn't disappoint. It almost feels old school, but in a well-polished way. Screwcap. 14.5% alc. **Rating** 94 **To** 2028 $60 CM

Vintage Sparkling 2009 A pristine pale straw hue does nothing to betray four years on yeast lees (and a further 2 years in bottle since), though such a creamy bead, seamless integration and subtle texture could come from nowhere else. Upholding the elegant precision of lemon and red apple fruit, set against a backdrop of brioche and completed with a subtle dosage of 5g/l on a long finish defined by pristine Tasmanian acidity. Diam. 12.5% alc. **Rating** 94 **To** 2019 $39 TS

ŸŸŸŸŸ Adelaide Hills Pinot Grigio 2015 Rating 92 **To** 2017 $22 CM ✪
Adelaide Hills Cabernet Sauvignon 2013 Rating 92 **To** 2025 $25 CM ✪
Vino di Famiglia Adelaide Hills Arneis 2015 Rating 91 **To** 2017 $13 CM ✪

Amato Vino

PO Box 475, Margaret River, WA 6285 **Region** Margaret River
T 0409 572 957 **www.**amatovino.com.au **Open** Not
Winemaker Brad Wehr, Contract **Est.** 2003 **Dozens** 5000
Brad Wehr has long walked on the wild side with his wines and his labels. The three brands within his portfolio are wine by brad, Mantra and Amato Vino (the last based on SA's Riverland). It's not altogether surprising that he has become the Australian importer for California's Bonny Doon Vineyard; some of the quirky humour of Bonny Doon is exemplified by the wine by brad label. Exports to Ireland, Canada, South Korea and Singapore.

ΨΨΨΨΨ **Bela 2015** Made with slancamenca bela grapes, a Balkan grape variety. Basket-pressed and wild-fermented in stainless steel. It's a thrilling wine, highly aromatic and textural, with rich salty/floral characters adding excitement to the palate. Screwcap. 13.6% alc. **Rating** 94 To 2017 $25 CM ✪

ΨΨΨΨΨ **Amato Nebbiolo 2014** Rating 93 To 2024 $40 CM
Amato Tempranillo 2014 Rating 93 To 2023 $28 CM
Amato Montepulciano 2015 Rating 93 To 2024 $25 CM ✪
Amato Fiano 2015 Rating 92 To 2017 $25 CM ✪
Amato Teroldego 2014 Rating 92 To 2021 $40 CM
Mantra Sauvignon Blanc 2015 Rating 91 To 2017 $22 CM ✪
wine by brad Sauvignon Blanc Semillon 2015 Rating 91 To 2017 $19 CM ✪
Mantra Barrel-Aged Sauvignon Blanc 2015 Rating 90 To 2019 $35 CM
wine by Brad Cabernet Merlot 2013 Rating 90 To 2022 $19 CM ✪

Amberley

10460 Vasse Highway, Nannup, WA 6275 **Region** Margaret River
T 1800 088 711 **www.**amberleyestate.com.au **Open** Not
Winemaker Lance Parkin **Est.** 1985 **Dozens** NFP
Initial growth was based on its ultra-commercial, fairly sweet Chenin Blanc. Became part of Accolade, but is now simply a brand, without vineyards or winery. Exports to the UK, Canada and the Pacific Islands.

ΨΨΨΨ **Secret Lane Margaret River Sauvignon Blanc 2015** A good example of what the region delivers for $20 or less. Citrus, passionfruit and gooseberry control the scene, green grass/vegetable notes barely perceptible. Screwcap. 13% alc.
Rating 89 To 2017 $20
Secret Lane Margaret River Semillon Sauvignon Blanc 2015 Quartz-white; juicy citrus, gooseberry, guava and lychee make a wine for any and all occasions; an added bonus is its capacity to develop a touch. Screwcap. 12.5% alc.
Rating 89 To 2017 $20
Shiraz 2014 Good colour; a particularly well composed medium to full-bodied shiraz, its blackberry, black cherry and plum fruit with a wash of warm vanilla bean oak and pliable tannins. Screwcap. 14% alc. **Rating** 89 To 2022 $17 ✪

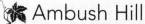 Ambush Hill

PO Box 239, McLaren Vale, SA 5171 **Region** McLaren Vale
T 0434 566 047 **www.**ambushhill.com.au **Open** Not
Winemaker Phil Christiansen **Est.** 2007 **Dozens** 200 **Vyds** 5.5ha
John, Mark and Shaun are the third generation of the Ledson family, which has owned the vineyard since it was planted by grandfather Syd Ledson in the 1950s. From that time until the present, the quality of the grapes has meant there has always been a ready market for them. They decided some years ago to put their toe into the water – or, rather, wine – by having a small part of the crush contract-made. The Ambush Hill name comes from the 19 century, when Ambush Hill was a landmark on the hills to the north of McLaren Vale, with tales of derring-do by smugglers of illegal alcohol and tobacco.

🍷🍷🍷🍷🍷 **McLaren Vale Shiraz 2012** Open-fermented, 8 days on skins, hand-plunged, basket-pressed, 18 months maturation (the back label says 21) in new and used American oak. Deep colour; exceedingly powerful, with some warmth on the finish, albeit with some savoury aspects to the black fruits. 190 dozen made. Screwcap. 14.9% alc. **Rating** 91 **To** 2027 $24

Amelia Park Wines   ★★★★★

3857 Caves Road, Wilyabrup, WA 6280 **Region** Margaret River
T (08) 9756 7007 **www**.ameliaparkwines.com.au **Open** 7 days 10–5
Winemaker Jeremy Gordon **Est.** 2009 **Dozens** 20 000 **Vyds** 9.6ha
Jeremy Gordon had a winemaking career starting with Evans & Tate and thereafter Houghton, before moving to the eastern states to broaden his experience. He returned to Margaret River, and after several years he and wife Daniela founded Amelia Park wines with business partner Peter Walsh. Amelia Park initially relied on contract-grown grapes, but in 2013 purchased the Moss Brothers site in Wilyabrup, allowing the construction of a new winery and cellar door. Exports to the UK, the US, Russia and China.

🍷🍷🍷🍷🍷 **Reserve Margaret River Cabernet Sauvignon 2013** The fragrant bouquet and the finely detailed cassis/blackcurrant fruit, with touches of black olive and bay leaf, all effortlessly communicate with the medium-bodied palate, relying on the innate quality of the grapes. Screwcap. 14% alc. **Rating** 96 **To** 2033 $50 ✪
Frankland River Shiraz 2014 Matured for 12 months in French oak, it has a scented allspice and Cherry Ripe bouquet, moving smartly to blackcurrant, blackberry and licorice on the medium to full-bodied palate; it's fruit-driven, but there's still room for a wave from the oak, and a salute from the tannins. Screwcap. 14.5% alc. **Rating** 95 **To** 2029 $29 ✪
Reserve Frankland River Shiraz 2013 Black fruits and spice leap from the glass, filling the bouquet; the palate is intense and powerful, yet remains light on its feet; black cherry, plum and licorice fill the mouth with persistent flavour; its lightness is due to silky tannins. Screwcap. 14.5% alc. **Rating** 95 **To** 2038 $50
Margaret River Cabernet Merlot 2014 Matured in French oak for 12 months. The varieties are locked in combat (part due to oak) and you have to wait for the blackcurrant and redcurrant promised by the bouquet to resonate, mulberry adding its weight. Screwcap. 14.5% alc. **Rating** 94 **To** 2029 $29 ✪
🍷🍷🍷🍷🍷 **Margaret River Semillon Sauvignon Blanc 2015 Rating** 92 **To** 2020 $22 ✪

Amherst Winery   ★★★★☆

285 Talbot-Avoca Road, Amherst, Vic 3371 **Region** Pyrenees
T 0400 380 382 **www**.amherstwinery.com **Open** W'ends & public hols 11–5
Winemaker Luke Jones, Andrew Koerner (Consultant) **Est.** 1989 **Dozens** 1500 **Vyds** 5ha
In 1989 Norman and Elizabeth Jones planted vines on a property with an extraordinarily rich history, commemorated by the name Dunn's Paddock. Samuel Knowles was a convict who arrived in Van Diemen's Land in 1838. He endured continuous punishment before fleeing to SA in 1846. He changed his name to Dunn and in 1851 married 18-year-old Mary Taaffe. They walked to Amherst, pushing a wheelbarrow carrying their belongings, the original lease title in his name. Amherst Winery is sited on land once owned by Samuel Dunn. In Jan '13 son Luke and wife Rachel Jones acquired the Amherst Winery business. Luke has a wine marketing diploma and a diploma in Wine Technology. Exports to China.

🍷🍷🍷🍷🍷 **Walter Collings Pyrenees Shiraz 2013** Seriously good. This slams the pedals of flavour hard without resorting to excessive alcohol. It tastes of licorice, prune, dark chocolate and fresh redcurrant, and comes bolted with firm, sturdy tannin. Floral nuances make a subtle but important guest appearance. A cracking red. Screwcap. 14% alc. **Rating** 96 **To** 2033 $50 CM ✪
Bonindra Vineyard Pyrenees Shiraz 2014 Terrifically inviting. It's one of those 'I could smell this all night' wines. It's floral, berried, ripe and yet savoury all at once, though the emphasis is clearly on pretty, buoyant, eager-to-please fruit. Beautifully turned out. Screwcap. 14% alc. **Rating** 94 **To** 2027 $28 CM ✪

ΨΨΨΨႳ Daisy Creek Shiraz 2014 Rating 93 To 2024 $20 CM ◯
Daisy Creek Sauvignon Blanc 2015 Rating 90 To 2017 $18 CM ◯

Anderson ★★★★★

1619 Chiltern Road, Rutherglen, Vic 3685 **Region** Rutherglen
T (02) 6032 8111 **www.**andersonwinery.com.au **Open** 7 days 10–5
Winemaker Howard and Christobelle Anderson **Est.** 1992 **Dozens** 2000 **Vyds** 8.8ha
Having notched up a winemaking career spanning 28 years, including a stint at Seppelt (Great Western), Howard Anderson and family started their own winery, initially with a particular focus on sparkling wine but now extending across all table wine styles. Daughter Christobelle graduated from Adelaide University in 2003 with first-class honours, and has worked in Alsace, Champagne and Burgundy either side of joining her father full-time in 2005. The original estate plantings of shiraz, durif and petit verdot (6ha) have been expanded with tempranillo, saperavi, brown muscat, chenin blanc and viognier.

ΨΨΨΨΨ Cellar Block Shiraz 2008 Released Aug '15, all Cellar Block wines held for a minimum of 5 years, and only made in the best years from the best parcels of the dry grown estate vines. Exceptional depth and vibrancy of colour for a 7yo wine, and the palate lives up to the promise, with a rich, velvety array of luscious dark fruits, and a twist of licorice and chocolate on the farewell. Screwcap. 14.9% alc. **Rating** 95 **To** 2048 $35 ◯
Cellar Block Petit Verdot 2008 Anderson's top-of-the-range Petit Verdot. The deep colour and inky/graphite bouquet accurately signal a full-bodied palate, but the tannins are (relatively) fine, and against the odds, the wine aspires to some elegance. It is clearly varietal, and served with a large, thick charcoal-grilled T-bone, would be a major winner. Screwcap. 14.9% alc. **Rating** 95 **To** 2038 $35 ◯
Verrier Basket Press Durif Shiraz 2008 60/40%, designed with durif to be dominant, shiraz to add roundness to the mid-palate. Gold medals Rutherglen Wine Show '11 and '12. It is unapologetically full-bodied and fleshy, the shiraz certainly achieving its task, the flavours all in a black fruit/licorice/earth spectrum. In its particular idiom, impressive. Screwcap. 14.5% alc. **Rating** 94 **To** 2038 $32

ΨΨΨΨႳ Basket Press Reserve Petit Verdot 2008 Rating 90 To 2028 $26
Cellar Block Durif 2008 Rating 90 To 2018 $40

Anderson Hill ★★★★

407 Croft Road, Lenswood, SA 5240 **Region** Adelaide Hills
T 0412 499 149 **www.**andersonhill.com.au **Open** W'ends & public hols 11–6
Winemaker Ben Anderson, Brendon Keys **Est.** 1994 **Dozens** 500 **Vyds** 8ha
Ben and Clare Anderson planted their vineyard in 1994. A substantial part of the grape production is sold (Hardys and Penfolds have been top-end purchasers of the chardonnay) but enough is retained to produce their three wines. The cellar door has panoramic views, making the venue popular for functions ranging from weddings and birthdays to other special occasions and group get-togethers.

ΨΨΨΨΨ Quacking Mad Lenswood Sauvignon Blanc 2014 While conventionally cool-fermented in stainless steel, it has well above average intensity and drive, lemon and grapefruit to the fore, diverse hints of passionfruit and cut grass in the background; exemplary length. Screwcap. 12.5% alc. **Rating** 94 **To** 2016 $22 ◯

ΨΨΨΨႳ Lila Agars Lenswood Chardonnay 2013 Rating 90 To 2018 $28
The Black Cat Lenswood Shiraz 2013 Rating 90 To 2023 $30

Andevine Wines

247 Wilderness Road, Rothbury, NSW 2320 **Region** Hunter Valley
T 0427 948 880 **www.**andevinewines.com.au **Open** Fri–Mon 10–5
Winemaker Andrew Leembruggen **Est.** 2012 **Dozens** NFP

Andrew Leembruggen has been a Hunter Valley boy since his cadetship at Mount Pleasant in 1998; he led winemaking operations for Drayton's Family Wines before his departure in '12 to create Andevine Wines. Andrew has made wine in the Rhône Valley, Bordeaux, Napa Valley and Coonawarra. There are three ranges of wines: Vineyard Reserve for 100% Hunter Valley (available exclusively from the cellar door); Hunter Valley varietals (available exclusively through Naked Wines); and Regional Collection wines, sourced from regions across NSW.

🍷🍷🍷🍷🍷 **Reserve Hunter Valley Shiraz 2014** Rich and luscious and sporting a heavy dose of creamy, coffeed oak. The fruit is up to the task, but it's a close-run thing. Ultrafine-grained tannin ripples through a mainstay of cherry, plum and earth notes. Lengthy finish. It arguably would have been better again had there been a lighter hand on the oak tiller but the grandness of the fruit, and vintage, ultimately shines through. Screwcap. 14% alc. **Rating** 95 **To** 2034 $30 CM ☉
Hunter Valley Pinot Shiraz 2014 Both powerful and understated at once. The fruit beavers away beneath a glide of creamy oak, tannin then gathering all components and propelling them out through the finish. In short, it works in the most impressive of ways. Red berry notes add lift; dry spice/earth/game notes add a sense of complexity. Screwcap. 13% alc. **Rating** 94 **To** 2026 $30 CM ☉

🍷🍷🍷🍷🍷 **Hunter Valley Semillon 2015 Rating** 90 **To** 2021 $17 CM ☉

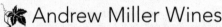

🍇 Andrew Miller Wines ★★★

17 Main South Road, Auburn, SA 5451 **Region** Clare Valley
T 0412 569 445 **www**.andrewmillerwines.com.au **Open** 7 days 10–5
Winemaker Contract **Est.** 2010 **Dozens** 2500 **Vyds** 90.55ha
This is a long-distance business, owner Dr Andrew Miller living in Casuarina in the Northern Territory. In 1998 he acquired the St Clare Vineyard, originally planted over 80 years ago, substantially reworked and replanted in the 1980s. Andrew has further improved the vineyard, which is now 90ha, planted to shiraz (44ha), cabernet sauvignon (32ha), riesling (9ha) and grenache (5ha). It was not until 2010 that he decided to retain some of the grapes (right from the outset most of the production has been sold) and chose the Velvet & Willow brand, named after twins delivered by Andrew. Exports to Thailand.

🍷🍷🍷🍷 **Velvet & Willow Clare Valley Riesling 2014** An honest, dyed-in-the-wool example of the synergy between place and variety. Lime/lemon/mandarin share the same umbilical cord, and gain strength from each other, especially on the all-important back-palate and finish. Drink whenever the mood takes you. Screwcap. 12.5% alc. **Rating** 89 **To** 2021 $19 ☉
Velvet & Willow Clare Valley Shiraz 2013 Open-fermented, matured in new and used oak. Deeply coloured, its back label claim to be full-bodied is 100% correct unless you wanted to write 'very' before 'full-bodied'. Alcohol, tannins and oak circumnavigate the black fruits without pausing for a breath. Screwcap. 15% alc. **Rating** 88 **To** 2020 $24

Andrew Peace Wines ★★★☆

Murray Valley Highway, Piangil, Vic 3597 **Region** Swan Hill
T (03) 5030 5291 **www**.apwines.com **Open** Mon–Fri 8–5, Sat 12–4
Winemaker Andrew Peace, David King **Est.** 1995 **Dozens** 180 000 **Vyds** 270ha
The Peace family has been a major Swan Hill grapegrower since 1980, moving into winemaking with the opening of a $3 million winery in '96. Varieties planted include chardonnay, colombard, grenache, malbec, mataro, merlot, pinot gris, riesling, sangiovese, sauvignon blanc, semillon, tempranillo and viognier. The planting of sagrantino is the largest of only a few such plantings in Australia. Exports to all major markets.

🍷🍷🍷🍷 **Estate Chardonnay 2013** Easy to enjoy; special lots kept for small batch treatment, with some French barriques getting involved in the fermenting and/or maturation. Screwcap. 13% alc. **Rating** 89 **To** 2017 $18 ☉

Estate Chardonnay 2012 When this wine might have been blitzed by the very distinguished chardonnays around it on the tasting table, it just put up its hand and shouted 'hey, don't forget about me'. Screwcap. 13% alc. **Rating** 89 **To** 2016 $18 ✪

Angas Plains Estate ★★★★

317 Angas Plains Road, Langhorne Creek, SA 5255 **Region** Langhorne Creek
T (08) 8537 3159 www.angasplainswines.com.au **Open** 7 days 11–5
Winemaker Peter Douglas **Est.** 1994 **Dozens** 3000 **Vyds** 15.2ha
In 1994 Phillip and Judy Cross began the Angas Plains Estate plantings, firstly with cabernet sauvignon, secondly shiraz and thirdly a small block of chardonnay predominantly used for a sparkling base. The location, on ancient Angas River flood plains, together with cooling evening breezes from the local Lake Alexandrina, proved to be ideally suited to the red varieties. Skilled contract winemaking has resulted in some excellent wines from the estate-grown shiraz and cabernet sauvignon. Exports to Singapore, Hong Kong and China.

🍷🍷🍷🍷🍷 **Emily Cross Langhorne Creek Shiraz 2013** Machine-harvested at night, open-fermented with 8 days on skins, fermentation finished in barrel, every barrel tasted and the best chosen, the majority new French with 15% new American. A very impressive full-bodied shiraz, full of fruit, oak, tannins and alcohol (the last despite only 13.9%). The question is whether a slightly lighter touch would have made a more elegant wine. Diam. **Rating** 93 **To** 2028 $40
Special Reserve Langhorne Creek Cabernet Sauvignon 2013 Machine-harvested at night, open-fermented with 8 days on skins, fermentation finished in barrel, the majority new French. Langhorne Creek provides cabernet with the unusual combination of clear-cut cassis fruit and soft tannins, an ability that Wolf Blass recognised, and made his fortune from. This is a classic example. Diam. 13.3% alc. **Rating** 93 **To** 2028 $40
Special Reserve Langhorne Creek Shiraz 2012 Machine-harvested at night, open-fermented with 8 days on skins, fermentation finished in barrel, the majority new French with 15% new American. Full-bodied and lush; the components are still manoeuvring for their place, and some egg white fining might have reduced the tussle, softening the blows. Diam. 14% alc. **Rating** 92 **To** 2027 $40

Angelicus ★★★★

Lot 9 Catalano Road, Burekup, WA 6227 **Region** Geographe
T 0429 481 425 www.angelicus.com.au **Open** W'ends & public hols 11–4
Winemaker John Ward, Sue Ward **Est.** 1997 **Dozens** 500 **Vyds** 1.65ha
Dr John and Sue Ward moved from Sydney to WA with the aim of establishing a vineyard and winery. They moved to the Geographe region, where they purchased a 51ha block of granite-strewn rocky hillside facing north and west, looking towards the Indian Ocean. In 2009 they began the planting of their vines, the lion's share to grenache (bush vines, managed biodynamically), five clones of tempranillo, and verdejo. They purchase grenache, mourvedre and shiraz from local growers.

🍷🍷🍷🍷🍷 **Rosa 2015** Made from estate-grown bush vine grenache, cold-soaked for 2 days and then fermented. Clear, light crimson; a perfumed bouquet of spice, nougat and liqueur cherries moves decisively into an unexpectedly dry, crisp palate. In doing so, it has the best of both worlds. Unusual, ultra-delicious and compelling value. Screwcap. 12.5% alc. **Rating** 94 **To** 2016 $18 ✪

🍷🍷🍷🍷 **Garnacha 2014 Rating** 91 **To** 2016 $25

Angove Family Winemakers ★★★★★

Bookmark Avenue, Renmark, SA 5341 **Region** South Australia
T (08) 8580 3100 www.angove.com.au **Open** Mon–Fri 9–5, Sat 10–4, Sun 10–3
Winemaker Tony Ingle, Paul Kernich, Ben Horley **Est.** 1886 **Dozens** 1 million **Vyds** 480ha

Exemplifies the economies of scale achievable in the Riverland without compromising quality. Very good technology provides wines that are never poor and sometimes exceed their theoretical station in life. The vast Nanya Vineyard is currently being redeveloped with changes in the varietal mix, row orientation and a partial move to organic growing. Angove's expansion into Padthaway (chardonnay), Watervale (riesling) and Coonawarra (cabernet sauvignon) via long-term contracts, and the purchase of the Warboys Vineyard in McLaren Vale in 2008, have resulted in outstanding premium wines. A large cellar door and café on the Warboys Vineyard at the corner of Chalk Hill Rd/Olivers Rd, McLaren Vale, is open 10–5 daily. Exports to all major markets.

ΨΨΨΨΨ **The Medhyk Old Vine McLaren Vale Shiraz 2014** Hand-picked, destemmed to open fermenters, plunged/trodden, basket-pressed to French oak, tasted at 9 months, the best matured for a further 6 months. Deeply coloured, it has the power of a Rolls Royce, but shares the smooth as silk delivery of that power; blackberries, poached plum, star anise and licorice are perfectly framed and presented by quality French oak, now perfectly integrated. Screwcap. 14.5% alc. **Rating** 97 **To** 2039 $70 ✪
The Medhyk Old Vine McLaren Vale Shiraz 2013 From four sites with vines 40-60yo, half-tonne open fermenters, basket-pressed, matured for 18 months in French puncheons, each assessed for inclusion. Pushes the envelope with its far-ranging suite of flavour and texture, but does so with sure-footed confidence. Blackberry, satsuma plum, cedary oak and ripe tannins all contribute to an outstanding McLaren Vale shiraz. Screwcap. 14.5% alc. **Rating** 97 **To** 2043 $65 ✪

ΨΨΨΨΨ **Warboys Vineyard McLaren Vale Shiraz 2014** Hand-picked, 25% whole bunches in the bottom of the fermenter with destemmed and crushed fruit on top, 3 days cold soak, wild yeast, matured for 11 months in French hogsheads. The fragrant bouquet of red and black fruits leads into a multifaceted palate of licorice, wild blackberries eaten straight from the vine, spices and a savoury salute. Screwcap. 14.5% alc. **Rating** 95 **To** 2034 $42
Single Vineyard Limited Release Blewitt Springs McLaren Vale Shiraz 2014 Hand-picked, destemmed, plunged/foot-stomped, wild yeast, basket-pressed, 9 months in used French oak. Bright, clear, full crimson-purple; the bouquet and medium-bodied palate sing in perfect harmony. Blewitt Springs' cooler climate gives the elegance and length to this wine, its perfumed aromas and juicy red and black fruits utterly compelling. Screwcap. 14% alc. **Rating** 95 **To** 2034 $38
Warboys Vineyard McLaren Vale Shiraz Grenache 2014 57/43%, the shiraz chilled for 7 days, then placed at the bottom of small fermenters with just-picked grenache crushed on top, other fermenters had whole bunch grenache layered with whole berries; matured in used French oak. A textbook exercise in the blend, with a perfumed bouquet and supple medium-bodied palate of satsuma plum and red berry fruits held in a fine web of tannins and ghostly oak. Screwcap. 14% alc. **Rating** 95 **To** 2030 $42
Single Vineyard Limited Release Sellicks Foothills McLaren Vale Shiraz 2014 From the coolest Angove site, destemmed, cultured yeast, open concrete fermenters, matured in used French oak for 9 months. A powerful, intense shiraz with an Aladdin's cave of spice, bitter chocolate and black fruits finishing with a savoury flourish. At the very dawn of its life. Screwcap. 14.5% alc. **Rating** 94 **To** 2034 $38
Warboys Vineyard McLaren Vale Grenache 2014 Hand-picked and sorted, 50% of the bunches placed in the bottom of half-tonne fermenters, destemmed and crushed fruit on top, matured in used French oak for 11 months. Light colour, although bright (like pinot, never judge a grenache for light colour as long as the hue is good) spiced plum, raspberry and cherry fruit flavours coalesce in juicy union. Screwcap. 14.5% alc. **Rating** 94 **To** 2024 $42
Average Age 15 Years Rare Tawny Port NV 11 gold medals in capital city shows. It is pungently aromatic, the bouquet and palate with great rancio and a myriad of burnt toffee/butterscotch, fruitcake (especially with a teaspoon of this

wine poured over it), roasted almonds, even a little singed bitter chocolate. It shares excellent richness with the 10 Year Old Grand Tawny. 500ml, bottled Jul '15. Screwcap. 19.8% alc. **Rating** 94 **To** 2018 $45

πππππ **Single Vineyard Limited Release Willunga McLaren Vale Shiraz 2014** **Rating** 93 **To** 2039 $38
Alternatus McLaren Vale Carignan 2015 Rating 93 **To** 2021 $25 ✪
Alternatus McLaren Vale Tempranillo 2015 Rating 92 **To** 2020 $25 ✪
Family Crest McLaren Vale Shiraz 2014 Rating 91 **To** 2024 $22 ✪
Family Crest Cabernet Sauvignon 2014 Rating 91 **To** 2029 $22 ✪
Alternatus McLaren Vale Fiano 2015 Rating 90 **To** 2017 $22
Grand Tawny Average Age 10 Years NV Rating 90 **To** 2018 $25

Angullong Wines ★★★★

Victoria Street, Millthorpe, NSW 2798 **Region** Orange
T (02) 6366 4300 **www.**angullong.com.au **Open** Fri–Mon & public hols 11–5
Winemaker Jon Reynolds **Est.** 1998 **Dozens** 18 000 **Vyds** 216.7ha
The Crossing family (Bill and Hatty, and third generation James and Ben) has owned a 2000ha sheep and cattle station for over half a century. Located 40km south of Orange, overlooking the Belubula Valley, more than 200ha of vines have been planted. In all, there are 15 varieties, with shiraz, cabernet sauvignon and merlot leading the way. Most of the production is sold. Exports to China.

πππππ **Fossil Hill Orange Sangiovese 2014** Bright mid-red; spice, oak, a touch of tobacco and the hallmark cherry. The medium-bodied palate has nice shape and feel, finishing with a savoury kick. Screwcap. 14% alc. **Rating** 93 **To** 2024 $24 ✪
Orange Sauvignon Blanc 2015 Purity of fruit. Swish texture. Pineapple dripping with passionfruit, then edging into apple and citrus. Bang on. Screwcap. 13% alc. **Rating** 92 **To** 2016 $19 CM ✪
Crossing Reserve Shiraz 2014 Good depth to the purple-crimson hue; medium-bodied, with a fragrant, spicy bouquet with both purple fruits and oak on parade, then a spicy/peppery/savoury dark-fruited palate with tannins ex fruit and oak. All up plenty to chew on. Screwcap. 14.5% alc. **Rating** 92 **To** 2029 $48
Orange Chardonnay 2014 To be measured not by its depth or complexity, but by its vigour and drive, riding on the back of white peach and pink grapefruit; some French oak is also there to provide a hand in support. I'd drink it now, but it won't fall over anytime soon. Screwcap. 13% alc. **Rating** 90 **To** 2021 $19 ✪

ππππ **Orange Pinot Grigio 2015 Rating** 89 **To** 2016 $19 CM ✪
Orange Shiraz 2014 Rating 89 **To** 2021 $19 ✪

Annie's Lane ★★★★☆

Quelltaler Road, Watervale, SA 5452 **Region** Clare Valley
T (08) 8843 2320 **www.**annieslane.com.au **Open** Mon–Fri 10–4.30, w'ends 10–4
Winemaker Alex MacKenzie **Est.** 1851 **Dozens** NFP
The Clare Valley brand of TWE, the name coming from Annie Wayman, a turn-of-the-century local identity. The brand consistently offers wines that over-deliver against their price points. Copper Trail is the flagship release, and there are some very worthy cellar door and on-premise wines. Exports to the UK, the US and Europe.

πππππ **Quelltaler Watervale Riesling 2015** From the Carlsfield Vineyard, planted in '35 (Geisenheim clone). A powerful, classic riesling; lime and lemon blossom aromas allow some apple blossom to assist, but when it comes to the palate, apple is discarded, flinty acidity taking its place. A distinguished riesling with a proud history. Screwcap. 13% alc. **Rating** 95 **To** 2030 $27 ✪

πππππ **Copper Trail Clare Valley Shiraz 2013 Rating** 91 **To** 2028 $80

Anvers

633 Razorback Road, Kangarilla, SA 5157 **Region** Adelaide Hills
T (08) 8374 1787 **www**.anvers.com.au **Open** Not
Winemaker Kym Milne MW **Est.** 1998 **Dozens** 10000 **Vyds** 24.5ha
Myriam and Wayne Keoghan's principal vineyard is in the Adelaide Hills at Kangarilla (16ha
of cabernet sauvignon, shiraz, chardonnay, sauvignon blanc and viognier), the second (96-year-
old) vineyard at McLaren Vale (shiraz, grenache and cabernet sauvignon). Winemaker Kym
Milne has experience gained across many of the wine-producing countries in both northern
and southern hemispheres. Exports to the UK and other major markets.

🍷🍷🍷🍷🍷 **Kingsway Adelaide Hills Shiraz 2014** A heavy glove of oak wraps around a
powerful hand of fruit. Anise, black cherry, cloves and violet, with resiny/toasty oak
adding the velvet. A foresty/spearmint-like edge adds something extra. Just needs
time to settle into itself. Screwcap. 14.5% alc. **Rating** 94 **To** 2030 $30 CM ❂

🍷🍷🍷🍷🍷 **Adelaide Hills Chardonnay 2014** Rating 93 To 2019 $28 CM
Razorback Road Sauvignon Blanc 2015 Rating 92 To 2017 $20 CM ❂
Kingsway Adelaide Hills Chardonnay 2015 Rating 92 To 2020 $30 CM
Brabo Riesling 2014 Rating 90 To 2019 $15 CM ❂
Razorback Road Adelaide Hills Shiraz 2014 Rating 90 To 2021 $20 CM ❂
Brabo Cabernet Sauvignon 2014 Rating 90 To 2020 $15 CM ❂

Appellation Ballarat

67 Pickfords Road, Coghills Creek, Vic 3364 **Region** Ballarat
T 0408 059 454 **www**.appellationballarat.com **Open** By appt
Winemaker Owen Latta **Est.** 2007 **Dozens** 280 **Vyds** 3.8ha
The striking name and label design are the work of Owen Latta, whose family planted Eastern
Peake in 1983. Owen was born during the first growing season of that vineyard and has always
been involved in Eastern Peake. Indeed, aged 15, and while still at school, he took control of
the winemaking when his father suffered concussion after a fall in the winery. Since then he
has travelled widely, making wine in Burgundy, the Yarra Valley, Geelong and the Pyrenees. His
aim is to have a Pinot Noir that is affordable, yet distinctive.

🍷🍷🍷🍷 **Pinot Noir 2014** Light and savoury, but with enough fruit to see it swinging
more-or-less confidently through the finish. Juicy/tangy acidity keeps the energy
levels high. Screwcap. 13% alc. **Rating** 89 **To** 2020 $32 CM

Apricus Hill

550 McLeod Road, Denmark, WA 6333 **Region** Denmark
T 0427 409 078 **www**.apricushill.com.au **Open** Fri–Mon 11–5, 7 days school hols
Winemaker James Kellie **Est.** 1995 **Dozens** 750 **Vyds** 8ha
When the then owners of Somerset Hill Vineyard, Graham and Lee Upson, placed the
vineyard on the market, James and Careena Kellie (owners of Harewood Estate) purchased
the vineyard with two purposes: first, to secure a critical fruit source for Harewood, and
second, to make and market a small range of single vineyard, single-varietal wines for sale
exclusively through the spectacular cellar door, with its sweeping vista. Thus Somerset Hill is
now Apricus Hill.

🍷🍷🍷🍷🍷 **Single Vineyard Denmark Sauvignon Blanc 2015** 30% was barrel-fermented
in new French oak, with 9 months maturation, 70% tank-fermented. The new
French oak adds substantially to the flavour and texture with juicy citrus and
tropical fruits; good length, and a bright finish. Screwcap. 12.5% alc. **Rating** 95
To 2019 $28 ❂
Single Vineyard Denmark Chardonnay 2015 Machine-harvested, crushed/
destemmed, fermented in French oak (35% new) for 10 months. Very tight and
vibrant, with grapefruit to the fore, backed by juicy white peach and stone fruit.
A mouthwatering style, with oak reduced to a means, not an end. Screwcap.
13% alc. **Rating** 95 **To** 2025 $28 ❂

🍷🍷🍷🍷♀ Single Vineyard Denmark Semillon 2015 Rating 93 To 2028 $28
Single Vineyard Denmark Pinot Noir 2015 Rating 90 To 2025 $28

Arakoon   ★★★★

7/229 Main Road, McLaren Vale, SA 5171 **Region** McLaren Vale
T (08) 8323 7339 **www**.arakoonwines.com.au **Open** By appt
Winemaker Raymond Jones **Est.** 1999 **Dozens** 3500 **Vyds** 3.5ha
Ray and Patrik Jones' first venture into wine came to nothing: a 1990 proposal for a film about the Australian wine industry with myself as anchorman. Five years too early, say the Joneses. In 1999 they took the plunge into making their own wine, and exporting it along with the wines of others. As the quality of the wines has improved, so has the originally zany labelling been replaced with simple, but elegant, labels. Exports to Sweden, Denmark, Germany, Singapore, Malaysia and China.

🍷🍷🍷🍷♀ **Sellicks Beach McLaren Vale Shiraz 2014** Crushed and destemmed into open fermenters, 2 days cold soak, 5 days fermentation with cultured yeast, the last stage of fermentation and mlf in oak (85% American, 15% French), 19 months in barrel. Deep crimson-purple; a rich bouquet of blackberries and spice is followed by a medium to full-bodied palate that, despite its weight and concentration, is nimble on its feet, with those same spices at work, joined by fine, ripe tannins and integrated oak. Great value. Screwcap. 14.5% alc. **Rating** 92 To 2034 $20 ●
Lighthouse Fleurieu Shiraz Cabernet 2014 60/40%, the shiraz machine-picked, the cabernet hand-picked, crushed and destemmed into open fermenters for 2 days cold soak, 5 days fermentation with cultured yeast, the last stage of fermentation and mlf in oak (85% American, 15% French), 19 months in barrel. The alcohol needle on the palate dial barely twitches, and both the bouquet and palate benefit from the gently cedary oak, the tannins also light and lithe. Its value is a wonder to behold – and savoury. Best of all, it's ready to go right now. Screwcap. 15% alc. **Rating** 90 To 2020 $16 ●

🍷🍷🍷🍷 **Vale Cru Grenache Shiraz Mataro 2014** Rating 88 To 2017 $18

Aravina Estate   ★★★★

61 Thornton Road, Yallingup, WA 6282 **Region** Margaret River
T (08) 9750 1111 **www**.aravinaestate.com **Open** 7 days 10.30–4
Winemaker Jodie Opie **Est.** 2010 **Dozens** 10 000 **Vyds** 28ha
In 2010 seventh-generation Steve Tobin and family acquired the winery and vineyard of Amberley Estate from Accolade, which retained the Amberley brand. Steve has turned the property into a multifaceted resource with a host of attractions: a restaurant, sports car collection, wedding venue and so forth. Exports to Indonesia, Malaysia, Hong Kong and China.

🍷🍷🍷🍷♀ **Margaret River Shiraz 2013** You get a core of blackberried flavour and a glide of creamy, chocolatey oak. Solid and smooth. Gum leaf and earth-like nuances, and perhaps some chewed tobacco, take care of the complexity angle. It's not the chirpiest of wines but what it does say carries weight. Screwcap. 14.5% alc. **Rating** 92 To 2024 $28 CM

Arcadia Wines   ★★★★☆

2875 Red Gum Pass Road, Kendenup, WA 6323 **Region** Mount Barker
T (08) 9851 4020 **www**.arcadiawines.com.au **Open** Fri–Sun 10–4
Winemaker James Kellie **Est.** 1998 **Dozens** 850 **Vyds** 4ha
John and Gaye Robinson came to Kendenup from Perth one weekend while looking for a getaway property. The last thing on their mind was buying a vineyard, but before they knew it, the bank had lent them the money, and what they imagined would be a part-time occupation had taken control of their lives. Given the quality of their wines, it's hard to imagine they are having second thoughts.

🍷🍷🍷🍷🍷 **Mount Barker Cabernet Sauvignon 2012** Mid-deep red; a brooding and deeply scented bouquet, with blackberry, cassis, earth and a positive leafy background. The palate is equally serious, with superfine tannins impeccably balanced against black fruits and a seamless, long finish. An extremely polished effort. Screwcap. 14% alc. **Rating** 96 **To** 2030 $22 ✪

🍷🍷🍷🍷🍷 **Mount Barker Riesling 2015 Rating** 92 **To** 2024 $18 ✪

Argyle Forest Estate ★★★

101 Ormond Esplanade, Elwood, Vic 3184 (postal) **Region** Heathcote
T (03) 9531 5370 **www**.argyleforestestate.com.au **Open** Not
Winemaker Mark Matthews **Est.** 1995 **Dozens** 400 **Vyds** 4ha
In 2009 Jenny, Tony and Alice Aitkenhead acquired an 8ha property situated in the middle of the lightly wooded Argyle Forest. It had (and has) 4ha of clone PT23 shiraz, which had been planted in the mid-1990s. Both Jenny and Tony have a diploma in viticulture and winemaking, while Alice undertook a number of wine units during her biomedicine degree at the University of Melbourne. They are content that the low-yielding vines should produce less than 2.5 tonnes per hectare (1 tonne per acre) and hand-prune the vines accordingly.

🍷🍷🍷🍷 **Betelgeuse Heathcote Shiraz 2013** 20yo vines, hand-picked and sorted, crushed/destemmed, wild yeast open fermentation, 20 days on skins, matured in used French oak for 20 months. A very powerful wine in a curate's egg style: the colour, oak and tannins all good, but there is the same edgy finish and aftertaste noted in the '12. I wonder whether some of the barrels have volatile acidity from previous usage. Screwcap. 14.6% alc. **Rating** 89 **To** 2024 $49

Arlewood Estate ★★★★★

Cnr Bussell Highway/Calgardup Road, Forest Grove, WA 6286 **Region** Margaret River
T (08) 9757 6676 **www**.arlewood.com.au **Open** Sat 11–5 or by appt
Winemaker Stuart Pym **Est.** 1988 **Dozens** 3000 **Vyds** 8ha
Over the years, the antecedents of today's Arlewood shifted several times; they might interest a PhD researcher, but – with one exception – have no relevance to today's business. That exception was the 1999 planting of the vineyard by the (then) Xanadu winemaker Jurg Muggli. Garry Gossatti purchased the run-down, close-planted vineyard in 2008, and lived in the onsite house from 2008–12, driving to Perth one day per week for his extensive hospitality/hotel business (which paid Arlewood's bills). His involvement in the resurrection of the vineyard was hands-on, but the cool site in the south of Margaret River was, and remains, his obsession. He now drives down every weekend from Perth to talk to viticulturist Russell Oates and contract winemaker Stuart Pym, clearly believing that the owner's footsteps make the best fertiliser.

🍷🍷🍷🍷🍷 **Reserve Margaret River Semillon Sauvignon Blanc 2010** 67/33% When tasted 4 years ago, a drink-to date of '16 was given, a bold prediction; this gleaming straw-green wine still has time to run as it builds on its citrus/honey/toast palate. It's totally delicious, ready now. Screwcap. 12% alc. **Rating** 95 **To** 2018 $25 ✪
Margaret River Chardonnay 2014 Fermented and matured in French oak (30% new) for 10 months. The bouquet is elegant, the fruit on the palate in precisely the midpoint between citrus and stone fruit, grapefruit and white peach, cashew and acidity. Lovely stuff. Screwcap. 13% alc. **Rating** 95 **To** 2024 $30 ✪
Margaret River Cabernet Sauvignon 2013 Matured for 2 years in French barriques (50% new), so don't be surprised by the oak: this is a wine designed to stay, not sprint. Red and blue fruits have freshness, and sufficient tannins to provide enduring structure. Screwcap. 14% alc. **Rating** 95 **To** 2033 $40
Margaret River Sauvignon Blanc Semillon 2015 70/30%, the sauvignon blanc tank-fermented, the semillon matured in used French oak for 2 months. It all comes together well, with a seamless fusion of green pea/grass, lemongrass and vibrant tropical notes coming from harvesting the sauvignon blanc in two parcels, one early, the other later. Screwcap. 13% alc. **Rating** 94 **To** 2018 $20 ✪

Artwine ★★★★

72 Bird in Hand Road, Woodside, SA 5244 **Region** Adelaide Hills/Clare Valley
T (08) 8389 9399 **www**.artwine.com.au **Open** 7 days 11–5
Winemaker Joanne Irvine **Est.** 1997 **Dozens** 5000 **Vyds** 27ha
Artwine is the venture of Judy and Glen Kelly. It has three vineyards, two in Clare Valley:
one on Springfarm Rd, Clare, the other on Sawmill Rd, Sevenhill, which also has two
B&B cottages. The third vineyard is in the Adelaide Hills in Woodside, which houses their
cellar door. Artwine currently has 15 varieties planted. The Clare Valley vineyards comprise
tempranillo, shiraz, riesling, pinot gris, cabernet sauvignon, fiano, graciano, grenache,
montepulciano, viognier and cabernet franc. The Adelaide Hills vineyard has prosecco, pinot
noir, merlot and albarino. Exports to Singapore.

ΨΨΨΨΨ **Wicked Stepmother Clare Valley Fiano 2015** Streaks of smoke and hay lend
this fruity white a certain something extra. It's most appealing. Grapefruit, sea spray
and citrus notes work themselves towards a dry, sophisticated finish. Screwcap.
12.5% alc. **Rating** 92 **To** 2016 $22 CM ✪
The Kelly Surrender Clare Valley Shiraz 2014 Firm but fruit-filled. Archetypal
'drink now or later' wine. Leather and plum notes with highlights of woody spice
and choc-mint. Well balanced. Feels mellow but also as though it has some positive
development ahead. Screwcap. 14.5% alc. **Rating** 92 **To** 2022 $30 CM
Grumpy Old Man Clare Valley Grenache 2014 Toffeed vanillan oak strides
into town, leaving earthen/raspberried fruit largely obscured. It makes for a love
or loathe style, in many ways, though the overall impact of flavour is impressive.
Braids of tannin aid the cause. Screwcap. 14.5% alc. **Rating** 91 **To** 2020 $30 CM
Vivacious Clare Valley Viognier 2014 Fresh face of the variety. Tropical fruit
and spice, perhaps some crisp pear. Has some grip, some texture, but for the most
part it races through to the finish. Screwcap. 12% alc. **Rating** 90 **To** 2016 $22 CM
Hola Clare Valley TCG 2014 Tempranillo, cabernet franc, cabernet sauvignon
and graciano. Unlikely blend but it works. Juicy raspberry and blackberry meet
assorted dry herb and ferrous-like notes. Firmish finish. Made for drinking sooner
rather than later. Screwcap. 14% alc. **Rating** 90 **To** 2020 $28 CM
Graciano 2014 Works a treat. Jubey red-berried flavours gather good easygoing
momentum as they move through the mouth. Simple but effective in the lighter
toss-it-down style. Screwcap. 14.5% alc. **Rating** 90 **To** 2018 $28 CM

ΨΨΨΨ **Prego Clare Valley Pinot Grigio 2015** Rating 88 **To** 2016 $22 CM
The Doghouse Adelaide Hills Merlot 2013 Rating 88 **To** 2020 $30 CM

Arundel Farm Estate ★★★★

321 Arundel Road, Keilor, Vic 3036 **Region** Sunbury
T (03) 9338 9987 **www**.arundelfarmestate.com.au **Open** W'ends 10–5
Winemaker Mark Matthews, Claude Ceccomancini **Est.** 1984 **Dozens** 2000 **Vyds** 7.4ha
The first stage of the vineyard in 1984 was 0.8ha of shiraz and cabernet sauvignon. Rick
Kinzbrunner of Giaconda made the first vintage in 1988 and for some years thereafter, but the
enterprise lapsed until it was revived with new plantings in '96 and 2000. Today it is planted
solely to shiraz and viognier. In October '11 Claude and Sandra Ceccomancini acquired the
business and appointed Mark Matthews as winemaker.

ΨΨΨΨΨ **Sunbury Viognier 2014** Light and shade. Powerful fruit flavours but it feels
light on its feet; it's riddled with stone fruit, ginger and spice notes but it's not
overbearing; indeed it's remarkably more-ish. Screwcap. 14.5% alc. **Rating** 93
To 2017 $23 CM ✪

Ashbrook Estate ★★★★★

379 Tom Cullity Drive, Wilyabrup, WA 6280 **Region** Margaret River
T (08) 9755 6262 **www**.ashbrookwines.com.au **Open** 7 days 10–5
Winemaker Catherine Edwards, Brian Devitt **Est.** 1975 **Dozens** 12500 **Vyds** 17.4ha

This fastidious producer of consistently excellent estate-grown table wines shuns publicity and is less well known than is deserved, selling much of its wine through the cellar door and to an understandably very loyal mailing list clientele. It is very much a family affair: while founder Tony Devitt retired in Nov 2013, his brother Brian is at the helm, winemaking is by his daughter Catherine, and viticulture by son Richard (also a qualified winemaker). Exports to the US, Canada, Germany, Indonesia, Japan, Singapore, Hong Kong and China.

ŸŸŸŸŸ **Reserve Margaret River Chardonnay 2013** Planted between '76 and the early '80s on five blocks, hand-picked over 3 days, crushed and pressed to tank with cultured yeast, and transferred to new barriques once the fermentation was fully established, matured on undisturbed lees for 8 months, no mlf.. There has been some development of colour and varietal fruit richness, taking the wine onto another level and justifying 28 months of cellar maturation. A joy to drink with its panoply of white peach and grapefruit, oak and acidity handmaidens in support. Screwcap. 13.6% alc. **Rating** 96 **To** 2023 $65 ✪

Margaret River Sauvignon Blanc 2015 From two estate blocks planted '76 and '90, the old block converted to a lyre trellis in the early '90s, this and a thick composted mulch have enhanced the primary fruit intensity. Classic Margaret River style, complex and intense, yet not OTT. The flavours run from herbaceous through citrus, thence tropical, yet the line and length are perfect, the intensity a plus. Screwcap. 13.6% alc. **Rating** 95 **To** 2017 $24 ✪

Margaret River Chardonnay 2014 Made in similar fashion to the '13 Reserve Chardonnay, the difference fruit selection. Tasted side by side, you can see exactly how this wine will develop over both the short and long term; the fruit line is tensed like the string of a bow, oak and acidity ready to act in support as the wine ages; the flavours are quintessentially varietal, with melon, apple, grapefruit and white peach all straining at the leash. Screwcap. 13.5% alc. **Rating** 95 **To** 2024 $32 ✪

Margaret River Shiraz 2012 15yo estate vines; matured for 2 years in French oak (25% new). The colour is bright and clear, the bouquet and palate fragrant and elegant, red cherry and redcurrant fruit shot through with spice and pepper, the finish long and refreshing; the oak is a distinct plus, present, but largely a means to the end. Screwcap. 14.7% alc. **Rating** 95 **To** 2032 $29 ✪

Margaret River Cabernet Sauvignon Merlot 2012 77% cabernet sauvignon, 10% merlot, 7% petit verdot and 6% cabernet franc, hand-picked over 2 weeks, destemmed, not crushed, and small batch open-fermented, matured in French oak (15% new) for 2 years, bottle-matured for a further 18 months. Very good hue and depth are part of a distinguished blend of cassis, bay leaf and perfectly pitched tannins. Screwcap. 14.5% alc. **Rating** 95 **To** 2042 $29 ✪

Reserve Margaret River Cabernet Sauvignon 2011 Includes 7% cabernet franc, 4% merlot 3% and petit verdot, estate-grown (the cabernet planted '76), hand-picked, open-fermented, the wine was matured in French barriques (40% new) for 2 years, then bottle-aged for 18 months. Has great length to its full-bodied palate, varietal expression loud and clear, blackcurrant and black olive to the fore, firm tannins and oak to the rear. Screwcap. 14.7% alc. **Rating** 95 **To** 2042 $65

Reserve Margaret River Cabernet Sauvignon 2012 Estate-grown vines planted '76, hand-picked, immediately destemmed, transferred to temperature-controlled open red fermenters, both pre-fermentation cold soak and post-ferment maceration before pressed to French barriques (40% new) for 24 months maturation. A cedary, slightly earthy wine with notes of dried herb to the fore. Slightly disappointing in the context of such a distinguished producer and such old vines. Screwcap. 14% alc. **Rating** 94 **To** 2027 $65

ŸŸŸŸŸ **Margaret River Semillon 2015** **Rating** 92 **To** 2025 $24 ✪
Margaret River Verdelho 2015 **Rating** 90 **To** 2023 $24

Ashton Hills

Tregarthen Road, Ashton, SA 5137 **Region** Adelaide Hills
T (08) 8390 1243 **www**.ashtonhills.com.au **Open** W'ends & most public hols 11–5.30
Winemaker Stephen George **Est.** 1982 **Dozens** 1500 **Vyds** 3ha
Stephen George made Ashton Hills one of the great producers of Pinot Noir in Australia, and by some distance the best in the Adelaide Hills. With no family succession in place, he sold the business to Wirra Wirra in April 2015. It had been rumoured for some time that he was considering such a move, so when it was announced, there was a sigh of relief that it should pass to a business such as Wirra Wirra, with undoubted commitment to retaining the extraordinary quality of the wines made by Stephen. He will continue to live in the house on the property, and provide ongoing consulting advice.

ŶŶŶŶŶ **Reserve Pinot Noir 2014** Below average yield of high quality from clones 777, D5V12 and MV6, 33% matured in new French oak. Has the extra depth and complexity typical of this label, the low yield obvious in its layered power. It has at least 10 years in front of it, yet the perfect line, length and balance make it a hedonistic pleasure to drink right now, revelling in its sumptuous plum and black cherry fruit. Screwcap. 14% alc. **Rating** 97 **To** 2029 $91 **✪**

ŶŶŶŶŶ **Riesling 2015** It's easy to see why Stephen George was reluctant to remove the tiny patch of riesling on the estate. This is all about purity and elegance, floral and fine. You don't want to analyse it, simply drink it for the sheer pleasure it provides. A riesling lover's riesling. Screwcap. 12.5% alc. **Rating** 96 **To** 2030 $40 **✪**
Sparkling Shiraz 2008 The price of this wine has increased by $20 since Wirra Wirra acquired Ashton Hills earlier this year, but it is still underpriced. It has supreme elegance, so difficult to achieve with this style; red fruits and licorice serenade each other through the long, balanced finish. Cork. 13% alc. **Rating** 96 **To** 2038 $64 **✪**
Estate Pinot Noir 2014 The yield was well below average, made from four of the best five clones, 25% matured in new French oak. Has the generosity that is the Adelaide Hills thumbprint, yet remains light on its feet as it moves gracefully through the palate, plum and cherry equally important, neatly supported by subtle oak. Screwcap. 14% alc. **Rating** 95 **To** 2024 $60

ŶŶŶŶŶ **Piccadilly Valley Blanc de Noirs 2011** **Rating** 91 **To** 2016 $40 TS

Atlas Wines

PO Box 458, Clare, SA 5453 **Region** Clare Valley
T 0419 847 491 **www**.atlaswines.com.au **Open** Not
Winemaker Adam Barton **Est.** 2008 **Dozens** 3000 **Vyds** 8ha
Owner and winemaker Adam Barton had an extensive winemaking career before establishing Atlas Wines: in McLaren Vale, the Barossa Valley, Coonawarra, the iconic Bonny Doon Vineyard in California, and most recently at Reillys Wines in the Clare Valley. He has 6ha of shiraz and 2ha of cabernet sauvignon grown on a stony ridge on the eastern slopes of the region, and also sources small batches from other distinguished sites in the Clare and Barossa valleys. The quality of the wines is extraordinarily good and extraordinarily consistent. No new wines were received for this edition, the rating has been maintained. Exports to Canada, Singapore, Hong Kong and China. Wines were received too late for the book, but tasting notes can be found on www.winecompanion.com.au.

Atze's Corner Wines

Box 81, Nuriootpa, SA 5355 **Region** Barossa Valley
T 0407 621 989 **www**.atzescornerwines.com.au **Open** By appt
Winemaker Contract, Andrew Kalleske **Est.** 2005 **Dozens** 2000 **Vyds** 30ha
The seemingly numerous members of the Kalleske family have widespread involvement in grapegrowing and winemaking in the Barossa Valley. This venture is that of Andrew Kalleske, son of John and Barb Kalleske. In 1975 they purchased the Atze Vineyard, which included a

small block of shiraz planted in 1912, but with additional plantings along the way, including more shiraz in '51. Andrew purchases some grapes from the family vineyard. It has 20ha of shiraz, with small amounts of mataro, petit verdot, grenache, cabernet, tempranillo, viognier, petite sirah, graciano, montepulciano, vermentino and aglianico. The wines are all estate-grown and made in the onsite winery. Exports to the US.

♥♥♥♥♥ Zen Master 1912 Centurion Vineyard Barossa Valley Shiraz 2013 This is the second release, open-fermented and basket-pressed, matured in a new French hogshead for 20 months, 50 dozen made. This cannot be judged by normal standards – quite apart from anything else, the difference between 103yo, 64yo and plantings between is not of itself preordained: a 20yo vineyard may produce better grapes. Here the alcohol heat does really spear through, but as the song goes, some like it hot. Cork. 15.5% alc. **Rating** 95 **To** 2033 $140

Forgotten Hero 1951 Survivor Vineyard Barossa Valley Shiraz 2013 From a vineyard planted by the Atze family in '51, acquired and nursed back to health by Andrew Kalleske's parents in '83; destemmed, open-fermented, matured in two new French barriques for 24 months, 50 dozen made. This has slightly more elegance than its siblings, but that is simply in the context of the three wines – it's still massive. Incidentally, the vineyard should be 70yo (or more) to be called Survivor. Cork. 15% alc. **Rating** 95 **To** 2033 $100

Eddies Old Vine Barossa Valley Shiraz 2013 Part from a vineyard planted in 1912, part from two estate blocks planted much later, matured in new and used French and American hogsheads, 120 dozen made. Massively built, one of a trio of '13 Old/Survivor/Centurion Shirazs that share more things in common than those that might differentiate them. My personal opinion is that by one means or another (all legal, of course) these three wines would have been better with a maximum of 14% alcohol, still unashamedly full-bodied, but less challenging. Cork. 15% alc. **Rating** 95 **To** 2033 $55

♥♥♥♥♡ The Giant Barossa Valley Durif 2014 Rating 92 **To** 2024 $28 CM
White Knight Vermentino 2015 Rating 90 **To** 2016 $20 CM ○

Audrey Wilkinson   ★★★★★

750 De Beyers Road, Pokolbin, NSW 2320 **Region** Hunter Valley
T (02) 4998 1866 **www**.audreywilkinson.com.au **Open** 7 days 10–5
Winemaker Jeff Byrne, Xanthe Hatcher **Est.** 1866 **Dozens** 30 000 **Vyds** 35.33ha
One of the most historic properties in the Hunter Valley, set in a particularly beautiful location and with a very attractive cellar door, has been owned by Brian Agnew and family since 2004. The wines are made from estate-grown grapes, the lion's share to shiraz, the remainder (in descending order) to semillon, malbec, verdelho, tempranillo, merlot, cabernet sauvignon, muscat and traminer; the vines were planted from the 1970s to the '90s. Also has a 3.45ha McLaren Vale vineyard of merlot and shiraz. Exports to the UK, Canada and China.

♥♥♥♥♥ The Lake Shiraz 2014 Excellent colour; a wine of maximum power and concentration in Hunter Valley terms; intense red and black cherry fruit is cradled by French oak and ripe, but fine, tannins; its near-unique feature is the fresh acidity that appears on the finish, obliterating any suggestion of heat or dehydrated fruit. Screwcap. 14.5% alc. **Rating** 97 **To** 2044 $80 ○

♥♥♥♥♥ The Ridge Semillon 2015 Hand-picked 40yo estate vines, whole bunch-pressed, cold-settled, cool-fermented in stainless steel with cultured yeast, early bottled. 1yo semillon shouldn't have as much character and multiple flavours as this; curiously, but happily, it was picked later than the Winemakers Selection, but has much better acidity. Screwcap. 11.5% alc. **Rating** 95 **To** 2030 $45

Winemakers Selection Hunter Valley Shiraz 2014 French oak. 25% whole bunches. The old vines of the historic Hunter property. It's resulted in a medium-bodied wine with fine, firm, spicy tannin reaching far back through the palate. This tannin doesn't necessarily dominate, but it sets a cellar-worthy tone, and creates an environment of dryness. Cherries, earth and mineral notes lay a cloth of

flavour over it all. It's well built. And it tastes good. Years/decades await. Screwcap.
14.5% alc. **Rating** 95 **To** 2035 $36 CM
The Oakdale Chardonnay 2013 This is the renamed 'Reserve' range. It's
grown on 40yo vines and sees 50% new oak, but no mlf. Both those decisions are
fairly obvious. It's racy with acidity but softened by a cushion of cedary/spicy oak.
Peach, flint and citrus flavours keep the wine's rhythm going. Most impressively,
it sets sails of dry, chalky flavour on what becomes a very long finish. Screwcap.
13% alc. **Rating** 94 **To** 2020 $38 CM

 Winemakers Selection Semillon 2015 Rating 93 To 2025 $28
The Oakdale Chardonnay 2015 Rating 93 To 2022 $38
Hunter Valley Shiraz 2014 Rating 93 To 2029 $22 **○**
Hunter Valley Semillon 2015 Rating 92 To 2024 $22 CM **○**
Hunter Valley Semillon Sauvignon Blanc 2015 Rating 92 To 2017 $22
CM **○**
Winemakers Selection Orange Arneis 2015 Rating 92 To 2017 $28
Hunter Valley Rose 2015 Rating 90 To 2016 $22 CM
Orange Merlot 2013 Rating 90 To 2020 $22

Austins & Co.   ★★★★★

870 Steiglitz Road, Sutherlands Creek, Vic 3331 **Region** Geelong
T (03) 5281 1799 **www**.austinsandco.com.au **Open** By appt
Winemaker Scott Ireland **Est.** 1982 **Dozens** 20 000 **Vyds** 61.5ha
Pamela and Richard Austin have quietly built their business from a tiny base, and it has
flourished. The vineyard has been progressively extended to over 60ha. Son Scott (with a
varied but highly successful career outside the wine industry) took over management and
ownership in 2008. Scott Ireland is full-time resident winemaker in the capacious onsite
winery, and the quality of the wines is admirable. Exports to the UK, Canada, Hong Kong,
Japan and China.

Custom Collection Ellyse Chardonnay 2014 A superb example of Geelong
chardonnay, citrus, melon and stone fruits leading to a remarkably fine and tightly
wound palate. Mineral, chalky and pithy, it lingers gracefully with great precision
and purity. Screwcap. 13% alc. **Rating** 96 **To** 2028 $60 **○**
Custom Collection Spencer Shiraz 2014 Hand-picked fruit was further
passed along a sorting table in the winery, wild-fermented and after 7 days post-
ferment maceration pressed to thick-staved 600l puncheons and a 600l concrete
egg. A full-bodied wine deriving part of its power from structural elements and
part from the tightly focused black fruits. Like its less expensive sibling, is tightly
furled up, pleading for time, but has so much of its future obvious I'll recognise its
quality now. Screwcap. 14% alc. **Rating** 95 **To** 2039 $60

Geelong Chardonnay 2014 Rating 93 To 2025 $35
Custom Collection Delilah Pinot Noir 2013 Rating 93 To 2020 $60
Geelong Shiraz 2014 Rating 93 To 2035 $35
Geelong Rose 2015 Rating 91 To 2016 $25
6Ft6 King Valley Prosecco 2014 Rating 91 To 2016 $20 **○**
Geelong Riesling 2015 Rating 90 To 2023 $25

Australian Domaine Wines   ★★★★

PO Box 13, Walkerville, SA 5081 **Region** South Australia
T (08) 8234 5161 **www**.ausdomwines.com.au **Open** By appt
Winemaker Pikes (Neil Pike), Charles Wish **Est.** 1998 **Dozens** 5000
Australian Domaine Wines is a business owned by Ben and Mario Barletta, who started
their own brand business for leading Adelaide retailer Walkerville Cellars, which they then
owned. The wines are made at Pikes using tanks and barrels owned by the Barlettas. Grapes
are sourced from the Clare Valley, McLaren Vale and the Barossa Valley. Exports to the US,
Germany, Switzerland, France, Japan and Sweden.

ΨΨΨΨ **The Hattrick 2012** Shiraz, grenache and cabernet sauvignon. It's just starting
to mellow, and drink well, but raspberry and boysenberry-like flavour maintain a
keen sense of freshness. Woodspice and leather flavours are the steak knives in an
elegant flavour equation. Screwcap. 14.5% alc. **Rating** 92 **To** 2022 $45 CM
Deaf Galah McLaren Vale Red 2012 Licorice, leather and raspberry flavours
combine to create an attractive, medium-bodied red. Spice and herb notes
are modest but part of the show. Entering peak drinking zone now. Screwcap.
14.5% alc. **Rating** 91 **To** 2020 $23 CM **○**

ΨΨΨΨ **Alliance McLaren Vale Shiraz 2014 Rating** 88 **To** 2020 $18 CM

Auswan Creek   ★★★★☆

218 Murray Street, Tanunda, SA 5352 **Region** Barossa Valley
T (02) 8203 2239 **www**.auswancreek.com.au **Open** Wed–Sun 10–5
Winemaker Ben Riggs **Est.** 2008 **Dozens** 30000 **Vyds** 12ha
The Swan Wine Group was formed through the merger of Inspire Vintage and Australia
Swan Vintage. The jewel in the business is a 10ha vineyard in Angaston, with 1.7ha of shiraz
planted in 1908, 0.86ha planted in the '60s, 5.43ha of younger shiraz, topped up with 1.76ha
of cabernet sauvignon and 1.26ha of grenache. The 2ha cellar door and winery vineyard
in Tanunda provide the home base. The major part of the production comes from grapes
purchased from growers across SA, and Ben Riggs' experience as a winemaker needs no
comment. The focus of the group is exports to Singapore, Thailand and China.

ΨΨΨΨΨ **1908 Vineyard Centenarian Barossa Valley Shiraz 2013** Vines planted
in 1908, hand-picked, matured in new French oak. A full-bodied shiraz with
black fruits, licorice, tar and earth that has made light work of the French oak.
The tannin structure is robust, and the wine will live for decades. Cork. 15% alc.
Rating 95 **To** 2038 $150

ΨΨΨΨ **Master Selection Langhorne Creek Shiraz 2014 Rating** 91 **To** 2029 $35

Avani   ★★★★☆

98 Stanleys Road, Red Hill South, Vic 3937 **Region** Mornington Peninsula
T (03) 5989 2646 **www**.avanisyrah.com.au **Open** By appt
Winemaker Shashi Singh **Est.** 1987 **Dozens** 500 **Vyds** 4ha
Avani is the venture of Shashi and Devendra Singh, who have owned and operated restaurants
on the Mornington Peninsula for over 25 years. This inevitably led to an interest in wine, but
there was nothing inevitable about taking the plunge in 1998 and purchasing an established
vineyard, Wildcroft Estate. Shashi enrolled in viticulture at CSU, but moved across to the wine
science degree course. Phillip Jones began making the Avani wines in 2000, and in '04 Shashi
began working at Bass Phillip, her role in the winery steadily increasing. Changes to the
vineyard increased the planting density to 4000 vines per hectare, and reduced the cropping
level to a little over 1 tonne per acre. There was a move to organic in '05, and thereafter to
key biodynamic practices in the vineyard. Even more radical was the decision to convert the
existing plantings of five varieties to 100% shiraz. Shashi took total control of making the
Avani wines at Phillip's Leongatha winery in '09, and in '12 they established their small onsite
winery, of which they can be truly proud.

ΨΨΨΨ **Mornington Peninsula Syrah 2014** Given 8 days pre-maceration before being
wild fermented over 2 weeks. Matured in 100% new French oak for 12 months;
hand-bottled unfined and unfiltered. Low alcohol but it's not unripe; whether
or not it lacks power is another thing. It's a wine that demands something of the
drinker; it requires you to slow down and see things from its perspective. Light
cherries, hints of meat and game, wood smoke. The texture is satiny, the finish dry.
Cork. 11.6% alc. **Rating** 90 **To** 2025 $65 CM

Axiom Wines

15 George Street, Parkside, SA 5063 (postal) **Region** South Australia
T 0409 579 708 **www**.axiomwines.com.au **Open** Not
Winemaker Stephen Clarke **Est.** 2004 **Dozens** 2200

TWM Wine Consultancy was established by the husband and wife team of Catherine and Stephen Clarke over 20 years ago, while they were living in the UK. The business continues to help wineries produce wines of consistent quality and style suited to the current market. The long story began when Stephen emigrated to Australia in 1970 with his parents. After graduating from high school, he worked temporarily in the chemistry department of Roseworthy, moving to Stanley Leasingham in the Clare Valley in '78. Thereafter, he enrolled at Roseworthy, completing the degree in oenology in '83, and through the rest of that decade worked in the Barossa. In '89 he returned to the UK with his family, undertaking what he describes as 'an apprenticeship in the international wine trade'. He worked for a wine writer, a wine importer/distributor, and also made wines in the Cape District of South Africa, Alsace, Burgundy, the Ukraine, Bulgaria and (for six years) Macedonia. Returning to Australia in 2000, he took up the post of senior winemaker and lecturer at the University of Adelaide, and continues some consultancy work with wineries across the globe, but is now focusing ever more on Axiom wines. Exports to the UK and China.

ỹỹỹỹỹ **Mathieu GSM 2013** 50/45/5% grenache, shiraz and mourvedre from Blewitt Springs and Willunga, the shiraz matured in 2yo French and American barriques, the remainder in older French and American puncheons, all for 2½ years. Has a wealth of red and black cherry fruit, and bunches of dark chocolate and licorice, all within a firm structure. A fine display of McLaren Vale GSM. Screwcap. 14.5% alc. **Rating** 93 **To** 2023 $25 ❂

Heddwyn Shiraz 2013 A powerful, full-bodied wine; good colour and a black fruits bouquet with the impact of 30 months in 2yo French and American oak obvious, but not OTT; the line of the palate needs to mend the interruption between the fruit on entry to the mouth and the tannins (part fruit, part oak) on the finish. Its source from 80yo vines suggests time will be on its side. Screwcap. 14.5% alc. **Rating** 91 **To** 2033 $40

Adelaide Hills Pinot Gris 2014 Full blush salmon-pink (eye of the partridge) from 12 hours' skin contact; full of flavour, with some spicy nuances first up, then a pot pourri of dried and fresh tropical fruits – even glacé – balanced by crisp acidity on the finish. Has plenty to say. Screwcap. 13% alc. **Rating** 90 **To** 2016 $20 ❂

McLaren Vale Grenache 2013 From the cool Blewitt Springs district, open-fermented and matured in used French and American barriques for 10 months. Bright, clear colour announces a light to medium-bodied wine with an enticing array of red fruits and just enough tannin support – as it should be. A delicious wine for immediate consumption. Screwcap. 14.5% alc. **Rating** 90 **To** 2017 $20 ❂

ỹỹỹỹ **Moonshadow Shiraz 2012 Rating** 89 **To** 2027 $40

Baarmutha Wines

1184 Diffey Road, Beechworth, Vic 3747 **Region** Beechworth
T (03) 5728 2704 **www**.baarmuthawines.com.au **Open** By appt
Winemaker Vincent Webb **Est.** 2006 **Dozens** 170 **Vyds** 2ha

Vincent Webb is a modern-day Renaissance man. He is a graduate of oenology and viticulture at CSU, but his full-time occupation is scheduler with Ausnet Services. He manages the vineyard and winery with 'plenty of help' from wife Sharon, and their young sons. Family and friends hand-select the fruit at harvest, and small quantities of wine are made using precisely what you would expect: a basket press, open vat fermenters, wild yeast fermentation, and maturation in new and used French oak. This is yet another start-up winery in the Beechworth region, which has many attractions for both winemakers and wine consumers.

ŢŢŢŢŢ **Beechworth Shiraz 2014** Wild-fermented, matured in new and used French oak, not filtered. Deep colour; luxuriant black fruits with notes of licorice, chocolate and pepper ease their languid way from the start to the finish of the palate. A delicious hedonistic style, doesn't really need age, but will stay the distance. Screwcap. 13.5% alc. **Rating** 94 **To** 2034 $42

BackVintage Wines

2/177 Sailors Bay Road, Northbridge, NSW 2063 **Region** Various
T (02) 9967 9880 **www**.backvintage.com.au **Open** Mon–Fri 9–5
Winemaker Julian Todd, Nick Bulleid MW, Mike Farmilo (Contract) **Est.** 2003
Dozens 10 000
BackVintage Wines is a virtual winery in the fullest sense; not only does it not own vineyards, nor a winery, but also it sells only through its website or by phone. The winemaking team sources parcels of bulk or bottled wines it considers represent excellent quality and value for money, and is then responsible for the final steps before the wine goes to bottle. The value for money offered by these wines is self-evident, and quite remarkable.

ŢŢŢŢŢ **Watervale Riesling 2015** From the dry-grown Neil Grace Vineyard, hand-picked at night, destemmed, crushed, pressed, cool-fermented with cultured yeast in stainless steel. You discover the quality of this wine on the back-palate and finish, with its surge of lemon zest and juice, sustained by good acidity. Particularly easy to drink right now, but give a few bottles a chance to show their real worth. Screwcap. 12.4% alc. **Rating** 94 **To** 2028 $13 ✪

ŢŢŢŢŢ **Hunter Valley Semillon 2014** Rating 93 **To** 2029 $13 ✪
Reserve Barossa Valley Shiraz 2013 Rating 93 **To** 2023 $20 CM ✪

Baddaginnie Run

PO Box 579, North Melbourne, Vic 3051 **Region** Strathbogie Ranges
T (03) 9348 9310 **www**.baddaginnierun.net.au **Open** Not
Winemaker Sam Plunkett **Est.** 1996 **Dozens** 2500 **Vyds** 24ha
Winsome McCaughey and Professor Snow Barlow (Professor of Horticulture and Viticulture at the University of Melbourne) spend part of their week in the Strathbogie Ranges, and part in Melbourne. The business name, Seven Sisters Vineyard, reflects the seven generations of the McCaughey family associated with the land since 1870; Baddaginnie is the nearby township. Exports to the US and China.

ŢŢŢŢŢ **Reserve Strathbogie Ranges Shiraz 2013** Estate-grown, matured in French oak for 24 months, part hand-picked 7 Mar, open-fermented, part machine-harvested 5 days later, destemmed and crushed, the majority matured in oak for 22 months (33% new). A rich and complex wine that carries its alcohol well enough, but might have been better had it been picked at 13° baume and spent less time in oak. Screwcap. 14.5% alc. **Rating** 90 **To** 2025 $40

Badger's Brook

874 Maroondah Highway, Coldstream, Vic 3770 **Region** Yarra Valley
T (03) 5962 4130 **www**.badgersbrook.com.au **Open** Wed–Sun 11–5
Winemaker Michael Warren, Gary Baldwin (Consultant) **Est.** 1993 **Dozens** 2500
Vyds 4.8ha
Situated next door to the well-known Rochford, the vineyard is planted to chardonnay, sauvignon blanc, pinot noir, shiraz (1ha each), cabernet sauvignon (0.35ha), merlot, viognier (0.2ha each), with a few rows each of roussanne, marsanne and tempranillo. The Badger's Brook wines, made onsite since 2012, are 100% estate-grown; the second Storm Ridge label uses only Yarra Valley grapes. Also houses the smart brasserie restaurant/bakery/cooking school Bella Vedere. Exports to Asia.

♥♥♥♥♀ **Yarra Valley Chardonnay 2014** Straw-green. It's a tense wine with grapefruit, green apple and melon characters buzzing through the palate. Oatmeal and sweet oak make positive contributions too. Shows well. Screwcap. 13% alc. **Rating** 91 To 2020 $25 CM

Yarra Valley Tempranillo 2014 Jumpy, almost nervy flavours of plum and boysenberry are smoothed, settled and softened by creamy vanillan oak. It has a freshness and a liveliness and, while it's not overly cohesive, time will help and it has a charm already anyway. Screwcap. 13% alc. **Rating** 91 To 2020 $25 CM

Yarra Valley Cabernet Sauvignon 2013 Fluid flavours of cassis, mint and milk chocolate glide through the mouth with noted ease; not the kind of description necessarily associated with cabernet. A handy performer, well put together. Screwcap. 13.5% alc. **Rating** 90 To 2021 $25 CM

♥♥♥♥ **Viognier Roussanne Marsanne 2014** Rating 89 To 2021 $22 CM
Yarra Valley Pinot Noir 2013 Rating 89 To 2020 $28 CM
Yarra Valley Shiraz 2013 Rating 89 To 2020 $25 CM
Storm Ridge Yarra Valley Pinot Gris 2015 Rating 88 To 2017 $18 CM
Yarra Valley Pinot Noir 2014 Rating 88 To 2020 $28 CM

Baie Wines ★★★★

120 McDermott Road, Curlewis, Vic 3222 **Region** Geelong
T 0400 220 436 **www.**baiewines.com.au **Open** By appt
Winemaker Robin Brockett **Est.** 2000 **Dozens** 2000 **Vyds** 6ha
Takes its name from the farming property Baie Park, owned by the Kuc family (headed by Anne and Peter) for over 30 years. In 2000 they established 2ha each of sauvignon blanc, pinot gris and shiraz, the first vintage following in '06. The vineyard is planted on north-facing slopes running down to the shore of Port Phillip Bay; the maritime influence is profound. Patriarch Peter Kuc is a GP, used to working long hours and with attention to detail, and he and agriculturist son Simon are responsible for the viticulture. Anne greets visitors at the waterfront estate, and Simon's wife Nadine is the marketing and sales force behind the business.

♥♥♥♥♀ **Barrique Bellarine Peninsula Pinot Gris 2015** Has exceptionally deep varietal flavours, led by pear, but with strong support from peach and fresh ginger. Served chilled, would gain (grudging) acceptance at most lunch gatherings. Screwcap. 13% alc. **Rating** 90 To 2017 $25

Bellarine Peninsula Shiraz 2014 A powerfully built shiraz, with blackberry and black cherry doing the talking, background music of spicy/savoury tannins and oak adding complexity. Needs a year or two to get its act together. Screwcap. 14% alc. **Rating** 90 To 2030 $30

♥♥♥♥ **Bellarine Peninsula Sauvignon Blanc 2015** Rating 89 To 2017 $22
Bellarine Peninsula Rose 2015 Rating 88 To 2017 $22

Baileys of Glenrowan ★★★★★

779 Taminick Gap Road, Glenrowan, Vic 3675 **Region** Glenrowan
T (03) 5766 1600 **www.**baileysofglenrowan.com.au **Open** 7 days 10–5
Winemaker Paul Dahlenburg **Est.** 1870 **Dozens** 15 000 **Vyds** 143ha
Just when it seemed that Baileys would remain one of the forgotten outposts of the TWE group, the reverse has occurred. Since 1998 the utterly committed Paul Dahlenburg has been in charge of Baileys and has overseen an expansion in the vineyard and the construction of a 2000-tonne capacity winery. The cellar door has a heritage museum, winery viewing deck, contemporary art gallery and landscaped grounds, preserving much of the heritage value. Baileys has also picked up the pace with its Muscat and Tokay, reintroducing the Winemaker's Selection at the top of the tree, while continuing the larger-volume Founder series.

♥♥♥♥♥ **Varley Shiraz 2014** Matured in a single 2800l French cask. It's simultaneously flavoursome and a picture of restraint. It's an insight into why this estate has survived for so long: it grows sensational grapes. Plum, cherry, boysenberry and anise, with smoky/spicy oak adding careful whispers of flavour throughout. More-ish quality. ProCork. 14% alc. **Rating** 96 To 2034 $75 CM ⊙

1920s Block Shiraz 2014 Svelte plum and boysenberry flavours swoosh through the palate in seamless fashion. It has depth and texture ticked off from the outset; flavour-filled length follows as a natural progression. Screwcap. 14.5% alc. **Rating** 95 To 2030 $40 CM

VP140 2013 Seek it out and buy it in number. It's a tremendously rich, sweet, exuberant fortified shiraz with both brightness and length to die for. Luscious fruit goes without saying. Screwcap. 19.5% alc. **Rating** 95 To 2038 $30 CM ⊙

Petite Sirah 2014 Thoroughly tannic but simultaneously bright and juicy. It's modern history 101. Boysenberry, red cherry, tar and saturated plum, perhaps even some leaf matter. There's a real sense of urgency to the palate, despite the spreading wealth of tannin. Screwcap. 15% alc. **Rating** 94 To 2028 $28 CM ⊙

Durif 2014 Beefy and powerful, but it maintains excellent vigour. Tar, sweet plums, toasty/malty oak and sawdust characters, underpinned by a surge of forceful tannin. Screwcap. 14.5% alc. **Rating** 94 To 2032 $28 CM ⊙

🍷🍷🍷🍷 **Shiraz 2014** Rating 93 To 2025 $28 CM
Organic Shiraz 2014 Rating 90 To 2020 $28 CM
ND Naturally Dried Nero d'Avola Cabernet Sauvignon Merlot 2014 Rating 90 To 2030 $40 CM

Baillieu Vineyard ★★★★

32 Tubbarubba Road, Merricks North, Vic 3926 **Region** Mornington Peninsula
T (03) 5989 7622 www.baillieuvineyard.com.au **Open** At Merricks General Wine Store
Winemaker Geraldine McFaul **Est.** 1999 **Dozens** 2500 **Vyds** 9.2ha
Charlie and Samantha Baillieu have re-established the former Foxwood Vineyard, growing chardonnay, viognier, pinot gris, pinot noir and shiraz. The north-facing vineyard is part of the 64ha Bulldog Run property owned by the Baillieus, and is immaculately maintained.

🍷🍷🍷🍷🍷 **Mornington Peninsula Pinot Noir 2013** Sheer velvet. Fruit and oak team to create a seductive impression. Sweet-sour cherries, strawberries and orange blossom notes meet tips of spice. Minty/cedary oak keeps the conversation moving in the right direction. Not especially long, perhaps, but most attractive flavour and mouthfeel. Screwcap. 12.5% alc. **Rating** 92 To 2021 $35 CM

Mornington Peninsula Pinot Gris 2015 Saline characters run through crisp pear and apple. The alcohol reading is relatively high but you'd not know it from tasting the wine. Crushed oyster-shell aspects to the finish. Characterful. Screwcap. 14% alc. **Rating** 91 To 2016 $30 CM

Mornington Peninsula Viognier 2015 Bright and juicy with a firmness to the finish. Doesn't play the varietal card too hard; is mostly just a fruit-filled white wine with a bit of structure. Screwcap. 13.5% alc. **Rating** 90 To 2016 $25 CM

Mornington Peninsula Rose 2015 Squeaky clean strawberry and citrus flavours. Pale colour. High refreshment factor. Screwcap. 14% alc. **Rating** 90 To 2016 $25 CM

Balgownie Estate ★★★★☆

Hermitage Road, Maiden Gully, Vic 3551 **Region** Bendigo
T (03) 5449 6222 www.balgownieestate.com.au **Open** 7 days 10–5
Winemaker Tony Winspear **Est.** 1969 **Dozens** 10 000 **Vyds** 35.28ha
Balgownie Estate is the senior citizen of Bendigo, having celebrated its 40th vintage in 2012. A $3 million winery upgrade coincided with a doubling of the size of the vineyard. Balgownie Estate also has a cellar door in the Yarra Valley (Yarra Glen). The Yarra Valley operation of Balgownie Estate neatly fits in with the Bendigo wines. Balgownie has the largest vineyard-based resort in the Yarra Valley, with over 65 rooms and a limited number of spa suites. In April 2016 Chinese Interactive China Cultural Technology Investments purchased the Balgownie Bendigo and Yarra Valley operations for $29 million. Exports to the UK, the US, Canada, Fiji, Hong Kong, Singapore, China and NZ.

🍷🍷🍷🍷🍷 Old Vine Bendigo Shiraz 2013 250 dozen. The back label suggests that hand harvesting is 'complimented' by traditional winemaking techniques. It's picked from the best 12 rows of the original '69 plantings. The wine takes volume of flavour and gives it a nudge, and does so with a masterful sense of control, even poise. It's firm, rich, warm; it's both an essay on style and a vote for substance. Screwcap. 14.9% alc. **Rating** 96 **To** 2035 $95 CM

Bendigo Shiraz 2013 With warmth comes richness and with richness comes seamlessness. It's flush with dark/sweet plum, mint and smoky/chocolatey oak, the volume of flavour making ultrafine-grained tannin feel barely discernible. Drinks well now, but will age well. Screwcap. 14.8% alc. **Rating** 94 **To** 2033 $45 CM

🍷🍷🍷🍷🍷 **White Label Yarra Valley Chardonnay 2014** Rating 93 To 2020 $45 CM
White Label Yarra Valley Pinot Noir 2014 Rating 93 To 2021 $45 CM
Black Label Sparkling Shiraz 2014 Rating 93 To 2023 $29 CM
Black Label Sauvignon Blanc 2015 Rating 92 To 2017 $25 CM ✪
Centre Block Cabernet Sauvignon 2014 Rating 92 To 2026 $45 CM
Bendigo Cabernet Sauvignon 2013 Rating 92 To 2030 $45 CM
Black Label Yarra Valley Chardonnay 2014 Rating 91 To 2018 $25 CM
Black Label Bendigo Sangiovese 2014 Rating 91 To 2020 $29 CM
Black Label Heathcote Bendigo Shiraz 2013 Rating 90 To 2021 $25 CM

Ballabourneen ★★★★

515 McDonalds Road, Pokolbin, NSW 2320 **Region** Hunter Valley
T (02) 4998 6505 **www.**ballabourneen.com.au **Open** 7 days 10–5
Winemaker Daniel Binet **Est.** 1993 **Dozens** 5000 **Vyds** 1ha
Ballabourneen had been making wines since the early 1990s and, in 2008, Hunter Valley winemaker Daniel Binet formed a joint venture with owner Alexander Stuart OAM to extend the Ballabourneen range of wines, buying grapes from well-known Hunter Valley sources, and making their wine at Tatler's Lovedale Road facility. In January '16, Ballabourneen acquired its new home at Pokolbin Hill on McDonalds Road, and is constructing a cellar door overlooking the foothills of the Brokenback Ranges. They have also planted 1ha of tannat and touriga nacional. Exports to the US and China.

🍷🍷🍷🍷🍷 **Alexander the Great Shiraz 2014** It's not big or beefy, but it gets the job done in style. We're talking the 'epitome of elegance' for the most part, but the mid-palate has real power purring neatly away, and it all rolls nicely through the finish too. Cherry, plum, earth, coffee grounds; standard fare flavours, but executed precisely. Screwcap. 14.5% alc. **Rating** 94 **To** 2034 $50 CM

🍷🍷🍷🍷🍷 **Baile Shiraz 2014** Rating 93 To 2030 $50 CM
EDS Hunter Valley Semillon 2015 Rating 91 To 2024 $35 CM
The Three Amigos Cabernet Merlot Petit Verdot 2013 Rating 91 To 2021 $35 CM

Ballandean Estate Wines ★★★★

Sundown Road, Ballandean, Qld 4382 **Region** Granite Belt
T (07) 4684 1226 **www.**ballandeanestate.com **Open** 7 days 9–5
Winemaker Dylan Rhymer, Angelo Puglisi **Est.** 1970 **Dozens** 12 000 **Vyds** 34.2ha
A rock of ages in the Granite Belt, owned by the ever-cheerful and charming Angelo Puglisi and wife Mary. Mary has introduced a gourmet food gallery at the cellar door, featuring foods produced by local food artisans as well as Greedy Me gourmet products made by Mary herself. 2012 was a stellar vintage for an energised Ballandean Estate, with smart new labels on a portfolio of excellent wines. Exports to Singapore, Taiwan and China.

🍷🍷🍷🍷🍷 **Generation 3 2012** Cabernet sauvignon and shiraz. The '12 vintage was one of the best ever in the Granite Belt, the grapes for this wine from the oldest estate vines, planted '71. Excellent colour with blackcurrant and blackberry the primary drivers of this supple, accessible medium-bodied blend. ProCork. 14.8% alc. **Rating** 94 **To** 2027 $65

🍷🍷🍷🍷🍷 Messing About Granite Belt Shiraz Viognier 2014 Rating 91 To 2022 $24
Opera Block Granite Belt Chardonnay 2014 Rating 90 To 2020 $30
Opera Block Granite Belt Shiraz 2013 Rating 90 To 2028 $30
Opera Block Cabernet Sauvignon 2014 Rating 90 To 2021 $30
Messing About Granite Belt Durif 2014 Rating 90 To 2024 $35

Ballycroft Vineyard & Cellars ★★★

1 Adelaide Road, Greenock, SA 5360 **Region** Barossa Valley
T 0488 638 488 **www.**ballycroft.com **Open** 7 days 11–5
Winemaker Joseph Evans **Est.** 2005 **Dozens** 250 **Vyds** 3.5ha
This micro-business is owned by Joe and Sue Evans. Joe's life on the land started in 1984
with a diploma of horticulture in nursery management, followed three years later by a
viticulture degree from Roseworthy/Adelaide University. Between '92 and '99 he had various
responsibilities at Rockford Wines, '92–'95 in the cellar door, '96 vintage cellar hand, and
'97–'99 vineyard manager. Since that time he has been at Greenock Creek Wines.

Balnaves of Coonawarra ★★★★★

15517 Riddoch Highway, Coonawarra, SA 5263 **Region** Coonawarra
T (08) 8737 2946 **www.**balnaves.com.au **Open** Mon–Fri 9–5, w'ends 12–5
Winemaker Pete Bissell **Est.** 1975 **Dozens** 9000 **Vyds** 74.33ha
Grapegrower, viticultural consultant and vigneron, Doug Balnaves has almost 70ha of high
quality estate vineyards. The wines are invariably excellent, often outstanding, notable for their
supple mouthfeel, varietal integrity, balance and length; the tannins are always fine and ripe,
the oak subtle and perfectly integrated. Coonawarra at its best. Exports to the UK, the US,
Canada, Japan, Hong Kong and China.

🍷🍷🍷🍷🍷 The Tally Reserve Cabernet Sauvignon 2014 Includes 5.5% petit verdot,
matured for 18 months in French oak (60% new). Counterintuitively, the wine
is every bit as approachable now as its lower-priced siblings. The colour is superb,
deep but brilliant, the bouquet laden with ripe cassis fruit, the palate threaded with
streams of black fruits, firm tannins and high quality oak. Already a great wine, and
it has only just begun its journey. ProCork. 14.5% alc. **Rating** 96 **To** 2054 $105
The Tally Reserve Cabernet Sauvignon 2012 Hand-picked grapes from the
Dead Morris Vineyard were given extended maceration post-ferment, then taken
to the best French barrels money can buy (50% new) for 20 months maturation.
The complexity of the bouquet is striking, with black fruits, spice, earth and cedar;
a complete wine in the mouth, at once supple yet firm thanks to exemplary
texture and structure. The savoury finish and aftertaste are pure cabernet. ProCork.
14.5% alc. **Rating** 96 **To** 2052 $95
Chardonnay 2014 Hand-picked, whole bunch-pressed, wild and cultured
yeast, fermented on solids in French barriques (31%), matured for 11 months.
Everything has been done to make this standout chardonnay in Coonawarra, and
indeed it's a very smart wine by any standards. The balance of fruit flavours (stone
fruit/citrus), and the integration of oak (the mouthfeel) are impeccable, but its
X-factor comes with its length. Screwcap. 13% alc. **Rating** 95 **To** 2024 $34 ✪
Chardonnay 2013 Hand-picked, whole bunch-pressed direct to Louis Latour
barriques (30% new), part wild, part bayanus cultured yeast. White peach and fresh
grapefruit flavours glide across the tongue, the finish fresh, the oak controlled. Has
flourished over the past year, elegance the key word. Screwcap. 13% alc. **Rating** 95
To 2020 $30 ✪
Shiraz 2013 Estate-grown, and matured for 19 months in the top-class Louis
Latour barriques (68% new). Deeply coloured, vibrant black cherry fruit on the
bouquet and a silky, opulent palate, tempered and balanced on the finish by fine,
ripe tannins ex the fruit and oak. Screwcap. 14.5% alc. **Rating** 95 **To** 2038 $28 ✪
Shiraz 2014 From the 40yo Paulownia Vineyard, matured for 18 months in
French oak (35% new). In the carefully considered and crafted Balnaves style, the
aim to take full advantage of the quality of the fruit, allow it free expression, but

not over-extract it. This is a full-bodied shiraz with black fruits in control, but allowing the tannins and oak to both exert some influence. Screwcap. 14.5% alc. **Rating** 94 **To** 2044 $30 ❂

The Blend 2014 56% cabernet sauvignon, 38% merlot, 6% cabernet franc, matured in fine-grained French oak for 14 months. One of the classics at this price point, over-delivering the goods year in, year out. It makes you wonder why there aren't more blends such as this in Coonawarra, as the blend has genuine integrity. Screwcap. 14% alc. **Rating** 94 **To** 2029 $22 ❂

🍷🍷🍷🍷🍷 **Cabernet Sauvignon 2014 Rating** 92 **To** 2039 $38
Sparkling Cabernet NV Rating 92 **To** 2029 $35 TS
Cabernet Merlot 2014 Rating 91 **To** 2034 $30

Banks Road

600 Banks Road, Marcus Hill, Vic 3222 **Region** Geelong
T (03) 5258 3777 **www.**banksroad.com.au **Open** Fri–Sun 11–5
Winemaker William Derham **Est.** 2001 **Dozens** 2000 **Vyds** 6ha
Banks Road is a small family-owned and -operated winery on the Bellarine Peninsula. The estate vineyard is adopting biodynamic principles, eliminating the use of insecticides and moving to eliminate the use of all chemicals on the land. The new winery not only processes the Banks Road grapes, but also makes wine for other small producers in the area.

🍷🍷🍷🍷🍷 **Geelong Chardonnay 2014** This floats to a nice place. It has an airy lightness and yet it doesn't lack flavour, or power. It's all citrus and white peach, spice and nutty oak. It scoots through the palate as if it doesn't have a care in the world; little wonder then that it's such a pleasure to have in your glass. Screwcap. 12.5% alc. **Rating** 94 **To** 2020 $30 CM ❂

Will's Selection Bellarine Peninsula Pinot Noir 2013 The mid-palate is good but it's the finish where this wine sets sail into the distance. The fabled peacock's tail is apt here. Undergrowth, cranberry and plum cherry flavours run on rails of silk. Oak adds texture more than flavour. The finish is both tangy and impressive. Screwcap. 13.2% alc. **Rating** 94 **To** 2022 $45 CM

Growers Range Rice Vineyard Grampians Shiraz 2014 Fluid and supple but ripped with tannin and spice. You wouldn't call this wine intense, necessarily, but you would call it imposing; it certainly impresses from the outset. It's finely boned, well-enough fruited, wears meaty characters easily and finishes long. The colour is light and it's mid-weight at most, but this is a victory for power over might. Screwcap. 13.4% alc. **Rating** 94 **To** 2027 $30 CM ❂

🍷🍷🍷🍷🍷 **Will's Selection Chardonnay 2012 Rating** 93 **To** 2020 $45 CM
Rob Durbridge Cabernet Sauvignon 2014 Rating 93 **To** 2030 $30 CM
Yarram Creek Pinot Noir 2014 Rating 92 **To** 2020 $24 CM ❂
Geelong Chardonnay 2013 Rating 91 **To** 2018 $30 CM
Soho Road Barrel Select Chardonnay 2013 Rating 91 **To** 2019 $55 CM
Soho Road Barrel Select Pinot Noir 2013 Rating 90 **To** 2020 $55 CM

Bannockburn Vineyards

Midland Highway, Bannockburn, Vic 3331 (postal) **Region** Geelong
T (03) 5281 1363 **www.**bannockburnvineyards.com **Open** By appt
Winemaker Matthew Holmes **Est.** 1974 **Dozens** 7000 **Vyds** 24ha
The late Stuart Hooper had a deep love for the wines of Burgundy, and was able to buy and drink the best. When he established Bannockburn, it was inevitable that pinot noir and chardonnay would form the major part of the plantings, with lesser amounts of riesling, sauvignon blanc, cabernet sauvignon, shiraz and merlot. Bannockburn is still owned by members of the Hooper family, who continue to respect Stuart's strong belief in making wines that genuinely reflect the flavours of the vineyard. Exports to Canada, China, Singapore and Hong Kong.

🍷🍷🍷🍷🍷 **Geelong Sauvignon Blanc 2015** One-third fermented on skins for 7 days, two-thirds wild-fermented on fine lees in French oak (10% new), matured for 6 months. The Bannockburn credo is to find every bit of flavour and texture in the grapes – a Mike Tyson approach. It works very well, the power of the punch of the fruit well able to withstand the extreme vinification methods. Sauvignon blanc seldom looks like this. Screwcap. 13% alc. **Rating** 95 **To** 2018 $32 ✪
Serre 2013 MV6 close-planted in '84, hand-picked, open-fermented, 100% whole bunches, 15 days on skins, pressed to French hogsheads (one-third new), after 12 months racked to older barriques for a further 7 months. Exceptional colour; whole bunch fermentation is the most frequently discussed aspect of pinot noir making, but Serre always comes through as a top pinot. Yes, there are savoury characters, but supple red and black cherry and blueberry provide the superstructure. Will be long-lived. Screwcap. 13% alc. **Rating** 95 **To** 2028 $95
Geelong Chardonnay 2013 Hand-picked, wild-fermented in French puncheons (20% new), mlf, matured in oak for 23 months. The long period in oak is very obvious on the bouquet, but the wine bounces back on the palate with white peach, creamy cashew, fig and citrussy acidity all in the frame. Screwcap. 13% alc. **Rating** 94 **To** 2018 $57
Geelong Pinot Noir 2014 Primarily MV6, but also clones 114, 115 and 777, 80% whole bunches, 20% destemmed, open-fermented, wild yeast, 25–27 days on skins, pressed to French hogsheads (one-third new), after 12 months racked to older barriques for a further 7 months. Deeply coloured; a very complex, full-bodied pinot with dark berry fruits, spice and oak on the bouquet and an opulently textured palate; firmish tannins ex whole bunches and acidity keep the wine corralled. Screwcap. 13% alc. **Rating** 94 **To** 2024 $57

🍷🍷🍷🍷🍷 **Stuart Geelong Pinot 2014 Rating** 93 **To** 2024 $75
S.R.H. 2012 Rating 92 **To** 2017 $75
Geelong Shiraz 2012 Rating 92 **To** 2032 $42

Bantry Grove   ★★★☆

25 Victoria Street, Millthorpe, NSW 2798 **Region** Orange
T (02) 6368 1036 **www.**bantrygrove.com.au **Open** Fri–Sun & Mon public hols 10–5
Winemaker Will Rikard-Bell **Est.** 1990 **Dozens** 1625 **Vyds** 12.3ha
Terrey and Barbie Johnson (and family) raise beef cattle on a property at the southern end of Orange. Seeking to diversify, the Johnsons have planted a vineyard at an elevation of 960m, making it one of the coolest in the region. The plantings began in 1990 with chardonnay and cabernet sauvignon, the latter now grafted or removed because the climate is simply too cool. Most of the 80–85-tonne production (chardonnay, merlot, sauvignon blanc, pinot noir and pinot gris) is sold to various producers making Orange-designated wines. A steadily increasing portion of the grapes is retained for the Bantry Grove label. The wines are sold through membership of Bantry Grove's Inner Circle Wine Club and local outlets.

🍷🍷🍷🍷 **Slow Wine Co Orange Sauvignon Blanc 2014** Hand-picked, half wild-fermented, then with cultured yeast in tank, transferred to French barriques (10% new), lees stirred and part wild mlf in spring, the remainder with no mlf, then blended in tank and held for 5 months before bottling. Given the counterintuitive winemaking, the wine still has ample tropical fruits in play, supported by fresh acidity. Screwcap. 12.5% alc. **Rating** 89 **To** 2016 $24
Slow Wine Co Orange Riesling 2015 Hand-picked, whole bunch-pressed, warm (26°C) ferment with solids. A first-crop wine, and the decision to vinify as shown is a curious one. That said, while the bouquet has been stifled, the wine comes to life on the finish and aftertaste thanks to citrussy acidity. Screwcap. 12.5% alc. **Rating** 88 **To** 2020 $24
Slow Wine Co Orange Pinot Noir 2013 Hand-picked, sorted, destemmed to open fermenters, cold-soaked until wild fermentation started, 2–3 weeks post-ferment maceration before pressing to French barriques (one-third new), matured

for 14 months in oak, then in stainless steel until late spring '14. All good stuff, except there wasn't enough fruit concentration to carry the vinification – it's just too light-bodied. At its best now. Screwcap. 14% alc. **Rating** 88 **To** 2017 $32

Barley Stacks Wines

159 Lizard Park Drive, Maitland, SA 5573 **Region** The Peninsulas Zone
T (08) 8834 1258 **www.**barleystackswines.com **Open** 7 days 10–5
Winemaker Colin Sheppard **Est.** 1997 **Dozens** 500 **Vyds** 10ha
Lyall and Cynthia Schulz have an organically managed vineyard near Maitland, on the western side of the Yorke Peninsula, planted to chardonnay, viognier, shiraz and cabernet sauvignon. This was, and remains, the first commercial vineyard and winery established on the traditional barley belt of the Yorke Peninsula. In 2015 Colin Sheppard, owner/winemaker at Flaxman Wines in the Eden Valley, came onboard as winemaker. He is not only a winemaker with a 5 red star rating in this Companion, but also made it to the top 10 of Masterchef '14. The wines are made onsite; there are also facilities to cater for concerts or festivals, and tours by arrangement.

🍷🍷🍷 **The Peninsulas Viognier 2014** Comes from the big end of flavour town, with apricot and ginger, all of which makes finesse a non sequitur. Still an interesting wine from somewhere outside the middle of nowhere. Screwcap. 12.5% alc. **Rating** 89 **To** 2017 $19 ❂

Barossa Valley Estate

Seppeltsfield Road, Marananga, SA 5352 **Region** Barossa Valley
T (08) 8568 6900 **www.**bve.com.au **Open** 7 days 10–4.30
Winemaker Ryan Waples **Est.** 1985 **Dozens** 141 500 **Vyds** 150.67ha
When Barossa Valley Estate was placed in receivership in 2013, a number of Australian wine businesses looked at the opportunity of acquisition, but most observers were surprised when the successful bidder was revealed as NZ-based Delegat's, and even more surprised at the price of $AUD24.7 million. Delegat's' economic engine is the Oyster Bay brand, its Sauvignon Blanc centre stage. While Barossa Valley Estate only owns 40ha of shiraz, cabernet merlot, grenache, chardonnay and marsanne, it has extensive contracts with the grapegrowers who were its shareholders when the receiver was appointed. Managing Director Jim Delegat revealed that the acquisition was funded through existing bank facilities even though Delegat's had acquired the Hawke's Bay Matariki Group for $NZ8.5 million in Jan '14, this in turn following vineyard acquisitions in '12. The arrival of Delegat's has had a dramatic effect; production has increased from 50 000 dozen to 141 500, and the estate vineyards are now almost touching 300ha, many times greater than the 40ha previously owned. Exports to the UK, Ireland, Canada, Singapore and NZ.

🍷🍷🍷🍷 **Shiraz 2014** This has a V8 turbo engine, but it also knows how to quietly mooch along for a Sunday drive. There's a lot of oak, a lot of black and purple fruits, and a lot of tannins (in that order), but there's a surprising lightness of foot, so pick your time and your speed. Screwcap. 14% alc. **Rating** 90 **To** 2029 $27
Grenache Shiraz Mourvedre 2014 Exceptional colour for this blend ex the Barossa Valley; the fruit aromas and flavours are likewise above average, lush and sweet, but not confection. Screwcap. 14% alc. **Rating** 90 **To** 2024 $27

🍷🍷🍷🍷 **Cabernet Sauvignon 2014** **Rating** 89 **To** 2029 $27

Barratt

Uley Vineyard, Cornish Road, Summertown, SA 5141 **Region** Adelaide Hills
T (08) 8390 1788 **www.**barrattwines.com.au **Open** W'ends & most public hols 11.30–5
Winemaker Lindsay Barratt **Est.** 1993 **Dozens** 2000 **Vyds** 8.7ha
This is the venture of former physician Lindsay Barratt. Lindsay has always been responsible for viticulture and, following his retirement in 2001, has taken full, hands-on responsibility

for winemaking (receiving a graduate diploma in oenology from the University of Adelaide in '02). The quality of the wines is excellent. Limited quantities are exported to the UK, Malaysia and Singapore.

♀♀♀♀♀ Uley Vineyard Piccadilly Valley Chardonnay 2014 Hand-picked, whole bunch-pressed, wild-fermented in French oak (50% new), matured for 11 months. Very well made; has great length, and a savoury element running throughout. Screwcap. 13.5% alc. **Rating** 95 **To** 2023 $32 **✪**

Piccadilly Valley Sauvignon Blanc 2015 Hand-picked, crushed and pressed, racked for cool fermentation in stainless steel. Bright straw-green, it has a flowery bouquet, then a racy, punchy palate picking up the tropical fruits promised by the bouquet, throwing in gooseberry and the odd snow pea/herbal notes for good measure. Screwcap. 13% alc. **Rating** 94 **To** 2018 $23 **✪**

♀♀♀♀♀ Uley Vineyard Piccadilly Valley Pinot Noir 2013 Rating 92 **To** 2023 $41

Barrgowan Vineyard ★★★★★
30 Pax Parade, Curlewis, Vic 3222 **Region** Geelong
T (03) 5250 3861 **www**.barrgowanvineyard.com.au **Open** By appt
Winemaker Dick Simonsen **Est.** 1998 **Dozens** 150 **Vyds** 0.5ha
Dick and Dib (Elizabeth) Simonsen began planting their shiraz (with five clones) in 1994, intending to make wine for their own consumption. With all five clones in full production, the Simonsens have a maximum production of 200 dozen, and accordingly release small quantities of Shiraz, which sell out quickly. The vines are hand-pruned, the grapes hand-picked, the must basket-pressed, and all wine movements are by gravity. The quality is exemplary.

♀♀♀♀♀ Simonsens Bellarine Peninsula Shiraz 2014 The perfume comes at you in waves. The peppers, the cloves, the violets, smoked meats, the spearmint. It's all backed by ripe cherry plum flavour; this is savoury and floral and fruity all at once, total conviction applied to each element. It's beautifully put together and beautiful to drink. Diam. 13.4% alc. **Rating** 95 **To** 2030 $25 CM **✪**

Barringwood ★★★★☆
60 Gillams Road, Lower Barrington, Tas 7306 **Region** Northern Tasmania
T (03) 6492 3140 **www**.barringwood.com.au **Open** Wed–Sun & public hols 10–5
Winemaker Josef Chromy Wines (Jeremy Dineen) **Est.** 1993 **Dozens** 1700 **Vyds** 5ha
Judy and Ian Robinson operated a sawmill at Lower Barrington, 15 minutes south of Devonport on the main tourist trail to Cradle Mountain, and when they planted 500 vines in 1993 the aim was to do a bit of home winemaking. In a thoroughly familiar story, the urge to expand the vineyard and make wine on a commercial scale soon occurred, and they embarked on a six-year plan, planting 1ha per year in the first four years and building the cellar and tasting rooms during the following two years. The recent sale of Barringwood to Neville and Vanessa Bagot hasn't seen any significant changes to the business.

♀♀♀♀♀ Mill Block Pinot Noir 2013 Grown on the estate's oldest vines. Complexity is the name of the game here. It's all undergrowth and macerated cherry, spice and forest floor. It strikes upfront then pulls you swiftly through to a second burst of flavour on the finish. Positively impressive. Screwcap. 13.2% alc. **Rating** 95 **To** 2025 $45 CM

Pinot Gris 2015 Crystal-clear varietal character with nashi pear, musk, ginger and peach all sparring with each other. Tasmania was first out of the blocks 20+ years ago with pinot gris; I have grown with it and we each treat the other with more respect these days. Screwcap. 14.2% alc. **Rating** 94 **To** 2020 $32

♀♀♀♀♀ Pinot Noir 2013 Rating 91 **To** 2023 $35 CM
Blanc de Blanc 2012 Rating 90 **To** 2027 $60 TS

Barristers Block

141 Onkaparinga Valley Road, Woodside, SA 5244 **Region** Adelaide Hills
T (08) 8389 7706 **www.**barristersblock.com.au **Open** 7 days 10.30–5
Winemaker Anthony Pearce, Peter Leske **Est.** 2004 **Dozens** 7000 **Vyds** 18.5ha
Owner Jan Siemelink-Allen has over 20 years in the industry, first as a grapegrower of 10ha
of cabernet sauvignon and shiraz in Wrattonbully, then as a wine producer from that region.
In 2006 she and her family purchased an 8ha vineyard planted to sauvignon blanc and pinot
noir near Woodside in the Adelaide Hills. Exports to the UK, Germany, Vietnam, Malaysia,
South Korea, Hong Kong, Singapore and China.

The Bully Limited Release Wrattonbully Shiraz 2013 Matured for
17 months in French hogsheads. A very attractive, supple medium-bodied shiraz
with purple and black fruits to the fore, fine tannins and integrated French oak
in support. It also has a second wind, with notes of licorice and dark chocolate
fluttering on the finish and aftertaste. Screwcap. 14.5% alc. **Rating** 93 **To** 2028 $45
Limited Release Wrattonbully Cabernet Sauvignon 2013 'Hand-selected
single vineyard fruit placed in fine-grained French hogsheads' says the back label.
A wine that waits until the last possible moment for its cassis fruit and oak to
expand dramatically on the finish and aftertaste. Screwcap. 14.5% alc. **Rating** 90
To 2023 $35

Limited Release Sauvignon Blanc 2015 Rating 89 **To** 2016 $25
The Bully Limited Release Wrattonbully Shiraz 2014 Rating 89 **To** 2029 $35
Limited Release Oaked Chardonnay 2013 Rating 88 **To** 2017 $25

Barton Estate

2307 Barton Highway, Murrumbateman, NSW 2582 **Region** Canberra District
T (02) 6230 9553 **www.**bartonestate.com.au **Open** W'ends & public hols 10–5
Winemaker Capital Wines, Gallagher Wines **Est.** 1997 **Dozens** 500 **Vyds** 7.7ha
Bob Furbank and wife Julie Chitty are both CSIRO plant biologists: he is a biochemist
(physiologist) and she is a specialist in plant tissue culture. In 1997 they acquired the 120ha
property forming part of historic Jeir Station, and have since planted 15 grape varieties. The
most significant plantings are to cabernet sauvignon, shiraz, merlot, riesling and chardonnay,
the Joseph's coat completed with micro quantities of other varieties.

Riley's Canberra Riesling 2015 A flowery, blossom-filled bouquet heralds
a totally delicious palate awash with lime juice and crisp acidity; the juicy lime
rises again on the aftertaste of the long, impeccably balanced palate. Screwcap.
11.5% alc. **Rating** 95 **To** 2028 $30 ✪

Canberra Blue Rose 2015 Rating 91 **To** 2017 $20 ✪

Barton Jones Wines

39 Upper Capel Road, Donnybrook, WA 6239 **Region** Geographe
T (08) 9731 2233 **www.**bartonjoneswines.com.au **Open** Thurs–Mon 10.30–4.30
Winemaker Contract **Est.** 1978 **Dozens** 2000 **Vyds** 3ha
The 22ha property on which Blackboy Ridge Estate is established was partly cleared and
planted to 2.5ha of semillon, chenin blanc, shiraz and cabernet sauvignon in 1978. When
current owners Adrian Jones and Jackie Barton purchased the property in 2000 the vines were
already some of the oldest in the region. The vineyard and cellar door are on gentle north-
facing slopes, with extensive views over the Donnybrook area.

Sauvignon Blanc Semillon 2015 Everything that is present is attractive. Tropical
fruit is balanced by citrus, and while the initial reaction is that it is a little light on,
retasting says there's plenty. Screwcap. 13% alc. **Rating** 89 **To** 2017 $18 ✪

Barwang

Barwang Road, Young, NSW 2594 (postal) **Region** Hilltops
T (02) 9722 1200 **www**.mcwilliams.com.au **Open** Not
Winemaker Bryan Currie, Russell Cody, Andrew Higgins **Est.** 1969 **Vyds** 100ha
Peter Robertson pioneered viticulture in the Young area when he planted his first vines in 1969 as part of a diversification program for his 400ha grazing property. When McWilliam's acquired Barwang in '89, the vineyard amounted to 13ha; today the plantings are 100ha. The Barwang label also takes in 100% Tumbarumba wines, as well as Hilltops/Tumbarumba blends. Exports to Asia.

ΨΨΨΨΨ **Tumbarumba Chardonnay 2014** Whole bunch-pressed and barrel-fermented. Citrus infused with melon and stone fruits, the palate fine and subtle with balanced acidity. Screwcap. 13.5% alc. **Rating** 91 **To** 2018 $23 ✿
Tumbarumba Pinot Gris 2015 Pear, florals and a hint of spice, the palate generous, rounded and nicely textured. Screwcap. 13.5% alc. **Rating** 90 **To** 2017 $23

Barwon Ridge Wines

50 McMullans Road, Barrabool, Vic 3221 **Region** Geelong
T 0418 324 632 **www**.barwonridge.com.au **Open** 1st w'end of month
Winemaker Leura Park (Nyall Condon) **Est.** 1999 **Dozens** 400 **Vyds** 3.6ha
In 1999 Geoff Anson, Joan Anson and Ken King (of Kings of Kangaroo Ground) planted Barwon Ridge. The vineyard nestles in the Barrabool Hills just to the west of Geelong. Geoff and Joan now operate the vineyard and they are focusing on producing premium fruit, with the wines now made at Leura Park. The vineyard is part of the re-emergence of winemaking in the Barrabool Hills, after the area's first boom through the 1840s to the 1880s. Barwon Ridge is planted to pinot noir, shiraz, cabernet sauvignon, marsanne and chardonnay. All wines are vegan compliant.

ΨΨΨΨΨ **Chardonnay 2012** A fair degree of colour development sounds a warning that turns out to be false. This has a better future than its '13 sibling, with a tighter and brighter fruit profile, crisp acidity helping to underwrite the package. Screwcap. 13% alc. **Rating** 94 **To** 2017 $24 ✿
Pinot Noir 2014 10% whole bunches, matured for 10 months in French oak (50% new), X-flow filtered. Bright personality starts with a red berry fragrance, plum joining in on the silky palate; seductive mouthfeel and length are major assets for pinot. Screwcap. 12.5% alc. **Rating** 94 **To** 2022 $36
Pinot Noir 2013 Grown in the right place and made in the right way, Geelong pinot can do battle with Central Otago, and this is such a wine. It has exceptional depth and power, overflowing with black cherry and plum fruit that stays resolutely in a true pinot flavour spectrum. Will richly repay cellaring, but by all means open a bottle now. Screwcap. 14% alc. **Rating** 94 **To** 2025 $33
Cabernet Sauvignon 2013 Although the alcohol is a touch generous, this has all the indicia of cool grown cabernet; there is a mix of cassis (dominant) and bay leaf/black olive (subservient) that ticks the boxes, the measured support of tannins doing the same thing. Screwcap. 14.3% alc. **Rating** 94 **To** 2030 $33

ΨΨΨΨΨ **Shiraz 2013** **Rating** 93 **To** 2033 $33
Cabernet Sauvignon 2014 **Rating** 92 **To** 2034 $36
Marsanne 2013 **Rating** 91 **To** 2020 $24

🌿 Basalt Wines

1131 Princes Highway, Killarney, Vic 3283 **Region** Henty
T 0429 682 251 **www**.basaltwines.com **Open** 7 days 10–5
Winemaker Scott Ireland **Est.** 2002 **Dozens** 800 **Vyds** 2.8ha
Shane and Ali Clancey are part of the Great Ocean Road's community of Irish descendants spread around Port Fairy, and have turned a former potato paddock into a small, but very

successful, wine business. During the late 1990s, Scott spent two years on the floor of Walter's Wine Bar at Southbank, It was a fast learning process and Shane then headed home to Port Fairy with brother Andrew to establish the two chef hat restaurant Portofino on Bank. During this time he began planting a multi-clone pinot noir vineyard, plus a small planting of tempranillo. Basalt Wines' grape intake is supplemented by a Drumborg vineyard, including 0.4ha of 26yo MV6 pinot noir and, even more importantly, riesling of the highest quality. Shane is viticulturist, assistant winemaker, wholesaler, and runs the cellar door, with Ali involved in various parts of the business including the small flock of babydoll sheep which graze next to the winery. Since 2012 Scott Ireland has been the contract winemaker, sharply lifting the quality of the wines.

🍷🍷🍷🍷🍷 **Great Ocean Road Riesling 2015** Light straw-green; remarkably intense lime juice fruit and minerally acidity drawing out the length. Trophy Western Victoria Wine Challenge '15 well deserved. A long life ahead. Screwcap. 11.8% alc. **Rating** 94 **To** 2025 $29 ✪
Great Ocean Road Pinot Noir 2014 Biodynamically grown. An elegant, well-made wine with perfectly ripened fruit maximising varietal expression; red cherry, wild strawberry and subtle forest floor aromas and flavours sing in unison. Screwcap. 12.9% alc. **Rating** 94 **To** 2024 $29 ✪

Basedow's | B3 Wines

2948 Barossa Valley Way, Tanunda, SA 5352 **Region** Barossa Valley
T 0418 847 400 **www**.basedow.com.au **Open** 7 days 10–5
Winemaker Richard Basedow, Rob Gibson **Est.** 1896 **Dozens** 5000 **Vyds** 214ha
Peter, Michael and Richard Basedow are the three Brothers Basedow (as they call themselves), fifth-generation Barossans with distinguished forefathers. Grandfather Oscar Basedow established the Basedow winery in 1896, while Martin Basedow established Roseworthy Agricultural College. Their father, John Oscar Basedow, died in the 1970s, having won the 1970 Jimmy Watson Trophy for his '69 Cabernet Sauvignon. As well as retaining consultant winemaker Rob Gibson, the brothers constructed a winery in the old Vine Vale Primary School property in 2008, using the schoolrooms as a cellar door. In '14 B3 Wines purchased the Basedow brand from James Estate, restoring continuity of ownership. In January '15 the (new) Basedow's cellar door was opened, just up the road from the old Basedow's winery. Exports to the UK, the US, Canada, Denmark, South Korea, Thailand, Singapore and China.

🍷🍷🍷🍷🍷 **Eden Valley Riesling 2015** Lively, fresh lime blossom aromas are a great start, and set the course for the crisp, intense palate, acidity lending its weight to a very attractive riesling at a bargain price. Screwcap. 11% alc. **Rating** 94 **To** 2025 $18 ✪
🍷🍷🍷🍷 **B3 Barossa Botrytis Semillon 2011 Rating** 89 **To** 2017 $20

Bass Phillip

Tosch's Road, Leongatha South, Vic 3953 **Region** Gippsland
T (03) 5664 3341 **www**.bassphillip.com **Open** By appt
Winemaker Phillip Jones **Est.** 1979 **Dozens** 1500
Phillip Jones handcrafts tiny quantities of superlative Pinot Noir which, at its best, has no equal in Australia. Painstaking site selection, ultra-close vine spacing and the very, very cool climate of South Gippsland are the keys to the magic of Bass Phillip and its eerily Burgundian Pinots. One of Australia's greatest small producers.

🍷🍷🍷🍷🍷 **Premium Pinot Noir 2014** Pinot noir with flavour and attitude and a scaffold of tannin is one thing, and this wine has all those things. But pinot noir with a ricochet of flavour through the finish, a sense of spread and run, an impression that the burst/explosion turned out to be greater than the package of the palate had predicted; this is far rarer territory, and it is the domain of this wine. ProCork. 13.6% alc. **Rating** 98 **To** 2028 $185 CM ✪
Reserve Pinot Noir 2014 Stunning intensity and yet completely varietal; not that such parameters have any meaning in the context of a wine of this ilk.

It creates its own exclusive domain. It's luscious, tangy, earthen and fruit-filled; it creates contradictions and makes them seem logical. On the way to creating a positive impression, it creates its own rules; Bass Phillip Pinot Noir, in its pomp, on this the grandest of days. ProCork. 13.6% alc. **Rating** 98 **To** 2035 $550 CM

ΨΨΨΨΨ **Estate Chardonnay 2014** Less polarising than the Premium and arguably higher quality. It shines bright in the glass, offers intense stone fruit and mineral flavours, and sears long through the finish. Toast, oatmeal and flint all play roles in getting that finish to sing; sweetness of fruit is also a factor. Should develop beautifully over the medium term. Cork. 13.3% alc. **Rating** 95 **To** 2022 $65 CM

Crown Prince Pinot Noir 2014 You could call it earthen, or sweet-sour, or redolent of beetroot, or gamey, and perhaps even foresty. Truth is, it's all of those things and none of them; it is simply itself. This drips with character, and performs well above its station. As strange as it may seem, it is its own kind of 'steal', in value terms. Cork. 13.9% alc. **Rating** 95 **To** 2026 $65 CM

Gamay 2014 It's hard not to marvel. It's smoky, almost into campfire; it's reductive, almost into burnt rubber; it's awash with roasted nuts and leafy spice notes; and only then is it cherried and juicy, with earthen beetroot flavours carried throughout. All these things should make it challenging at best, off-putting at worst. And yet it's a captivating wine, perhaps even brilliant. Cork. 13.9% alc. **Rating** 95 **To** 2020 $55 CM

Issan Vineyard Pinot Noir 2014 Brooding pinot with depth of both fruit and earth notes. As absurd as it sounds, there's a keen sense that this was grown from the ground up. Beetroot and twig notes do nothing to sway this impression. Its best days are ahead of it, but this is compelling even in its youth. ProCork. 13.2% alc. **Rating** 95 **To** 2027 $80 CM

Premium Chardonnay 2014 Less than 100 dozen made. It's both intense and idiosyncratic. Honey, ginger, white peach, brine, cashews; it's rich and sweet-accented and entirely luscious, and yet it frolics with tangy acidity. It's old school, new school and home-schooled. The quality is high, but it will part the crowd. Cork. 13.5% alc. **Rating** 94 **To** 2021 $85 CM

Estate Pinot Noir 2014 Forget the price and, indeed, the position this holds in the Bass Phillip hierarchy. It's all drive and dare, power and glory, the combination of satiny texture and minerally, smoky savouriness an exercise in pure seduction. ProCork. 13.7% alc. **Rating** 94 **To** 2027 $80 CM

ΨΨΨΨ **Gewurztraminer 2014 Rating** 88 **To** 2017 $33 CM

Bass River Winery   ★★★★

1835 Dalyston-Glen Forbes Road, Glen Forbes, Vic 3990 **Region** Gippsland
T (03) 5678 8252 **www**.bassriverwinery.com **Open** Thurs–Tues 9–5
Winemaker Pasquale and Frank Butera **Est.** 1999 **Dozens** 1500 **Vyds** 4ha
The Butera family has established 1ha each of pinot noir and chardonnay and 2ha split equally between riesling, sauvignon blanc, pinot gris and merlot, with both the winemaking and viticulture handled by the father and son team of Pasquale and Frank. The small production is principally sold through the cellar door plus to some retailers and restaurants in the South Gippsland area. Exports to Singapore.

ΨΨΨΨΨ **1835 Gippsland Chardonnay 2014** Plenty of vim and vigour. Oak and fruit are still coming together but there are good signs aplenty here. Flavours of cream, peppermint, lemon and barley meet pure, sweet white peach. Finishes lengthily. Screwcap. 13% alc. **Rating** 94 **To** 2021 $35 CM

Single Vineyard Gippsland Pinot Gris 2015 Hand-picked, whole bunch-pressed, part fermented in tank, part in barrel, gold medal and trophy Gippsland Wine Show '15. An à la mode style of gris, surging with flavour and attitude, pear, stone fruit and ginger supported by smart acidity. Screwcap. 12% alc. **Rating** 94 **To** 2019 $25 ✪

♀♀♀♀♀ **Single Vineyard Gippsland Riesling 2015** Rating 92 To 2025 $22 ✪
1835 Iced Riesling 2014 Rating 90 To 2017 $30 CM

Battle of Bosworth   ★★★★

92 Gaffney Road, Willunga, SA 5172 **Region** McLaren Vale
T (08) 8556 2441 **www**.battleofbosworth.com.au **Open** 7 days 11–5
Winemaker Joch Bosworth **Est.** 1996 **Dozens** 15 000 **Vyds** 80ha
Battle of Bosworth is owned and run by Joch Bosworth (viticulture and winemaking) and
partner Louise Hemsley-Smith (sales and marketing). The winery takes its name from the
battle which ended the War of the Roses, fought on Bosworth Field in 1485. The vineyards
were established in the early 1970s in the foothills of the Mt Lofty Ranges. The vines are fully
certified A-grade organic by ACO. The label depicts the yellow soursob (*Oxalis pes-caprae*),
whose growth habits make it an ideal weapon for battling weeds in organic viticulture. Shiraz,
cabernet sauvignon and chardonnay account for 75% of the plantings. The Spring Seeds
wines are made from estate vineyards. Exports to the UK, the US, Canada, Sweden, Norway,
Belgium, Hong Kong and Japan.

♀♀♀♀♀ **McLaren Vale Shiraz 2013** 'Organically grown, traditionally vinified', says the
back label helpfully. Well, it needs no explanation, because it's ultra-typical of
McLaren Vale: medium to full-bodied, laden with plush plum and blackberry fruits
and the usual coat of dark chocolate and ample, but soft, tannins. Good vintage,
good wine, that is ultra-reliable. Screwcap. 14.5% alc. **Rating** 94 To 2028 $25 ✪

♀♀♀♀♀ **Ding's McLaren Vale Shiraz 2013** Rating 93 To 2026 $45 CM
Spring Seed Wine Co Morning Bride Rose 2015 Rating 92 To 2017 $18
CM ✪
Chanticleer McLaren Vale Shiraz 2013 Rating 92 To 2028 $45 CM
McLaren Vale Chardonnay 2015 Rating 91 To 2018 $25 CM
McLaren Vale Cabernet Sauvignon 2014 Rating 91 To 2024 $25 CM
Puritan McLaren Vale Shiraz 2015 Rating 90 To 2017 $20 CM ✪
McLaren Vale Graciano 2015 Rating 90 To 2018 $25 CM
McLaren Vale Touriga Nacional 2015 Rating 90 To 2019 $25 CM

Bay of Fires   ★★★★★

40 Baxters Road, Pipers River, Tas 7252 **Region** Northern Tasmania
T (03) 6382 7622 **www**.bayoffireswines.com.au **Open** 7 days 11–5 (11–4 Jun–Aug)
Winemaker Penny Jones **Est.** 2001 **Dozens** NFP
Hardys purchased its first grapes from Tasmania in 1994, with the aim of further developing
and refining its sparkling wines, a process that quickly gave birth to House of Arras (see
separate entry). The next stage was the inclusion of various parcels of chardonnay from
Tasmania in the 1998 Eileen Hardy, then the development in 2001 of the Bay of Fires brand.
Bay of Fires has had outstanding success with its table wines, Pinot Noir was obvious, the
other wines typically of gold medal standard. Exports to the US, Asia and NZ.

♀♀♀♀♀ **Eddystone Point Riesling 2014** Quite simply totally delicious, crammed with
ripe lime juice (plus other citrus fruits) and electrifying acidity, the fruit, acid and
pH in perfect balance. Hard to resist drinking it now, which is fine, but try to keep
a few bottles for the future. Screwcap. 12.5% alc. **Rating** 96 To 2029 $25 ✪
Chardonnay 2014 Intensity, elegance and restraint are the tripods of this wine,
Tasmanian acidity playing a cleverly tempered role in extending the finish and
aftertaste to a seldom matched degree. Pink grapefruit is in the front of the
bus, white peach and a faint touch of cashew on the exit. Screwcap. 13.5% alc.
Rating 96 To 2025 $43 ✪
Pinot Noir 2014 From the Derwent River and Coal River districts. The wine
has the impact that is the hallmark of the brand, managing to harness the power of
the dark berry fruits into a long, gliding stream seemingly without end. It has an
assured future. Screwcap. 13.5% alc. **Rating** 96 To 2025 $43 ✪

Eddystone Point Pinot Gris 2015 This is so stacked with flavour – nashi pear, stone fruit and citrus, for starters – it seems it must have had at least some barrel fermentation, but it didn't. It thus stands in all its natural glory at the peak of the tank-fermented style of pinot gris. Screwcap. 13.5% alc. **Rating** 95 **To** 2020 $25 ○

Tasmanian Cuvee Pinot Noir Chardonnay Brut NV Based on the '06 vintage, this spent an astonishing 9 years on lees. The bouquet and palate sing with all the joy of bready, nutty complexity and waves of mouthfilling texture. For all this jubilation, it upholds its pinot-led substance and its acid line and lemon and apple fruit. Cork. 12.5% alc. **Rating** 95 **To** 2017 $30 TS ○

Riesling 2015 Picture of elegance, but not at the expense of fruit intensity. It has the line, the length, the flavour. Sends you out through the finish with plenty to remember. Screwcap. 12.5% alc. **Rating** 94 **To** 2027 $35 CM

Sauvignon Blanc 2015 From Coal River and the Derwent Valley. There's a rainbow of passionfruit/lychee, a sprig of fresh herbs, and cleansing acidity. It's all about the fruit, and that's entirely appropriate. Screwcap. 12.5% alc. **Rating** 94 **To** 2017 $35

Eddystone Point Pinot Noir 2014 From the Derwent River and Tamar Valley districts. Bright, clear crimson, it has a pure bouquet of cherry and cherry blossom, laying the flavour path for the palate until the pleasurably foresty notes of the finish. Screwcap. 13.5% alc. **Rating** 94 **To** 2024 $30 ○

Tasmanian Cuvee Pinot Noir Chardonnay Rose NV One-fifth matured in oak and a decade on lees in bottle ('05 base vintage) make for a pinot-led blend of captivating mouthfeel and nutty, honeyed complexity. Its cool climate sophistication finishes long and lively. Cork. 12.5% alc. **Rating** 94 **To** 2017 $30 TS ○

🏆🏆🏆🏆🏆 Pinot Gris 2015 Rating 93 To 2017 $35

Beckingham Wines ★★★

6–7/477 Warrigal Road, Moorabbin, Vic 3189 **Region** Various Victoria
T 0400 192 264 **www**.beckinghamwines.com.au **Open** W'ends 10–5
Winemaker Peter Beckingham **Est.** 1998 **Dozens** 1000
Peter Beckingham is a chemical engineer who has turned a hobby into a business, moving operations from the driveway of his house to a warehouse in Moorabbin. The situation of the winery may not be romantic, but it is eminently practical, and more than a few winemakers in California have adopted the same solution. His friends grow the grapes, and he makes the wine, both for himself and as a contract maker for others. Exports to China.

Beechworth Wine Estates ★★★★

PO Box 514, Beechworth, Vic 3477 **Region** Beechworth
T (03) 5728 3340 **www**.beechworthwe.com.au **Open** Not
Winemaker Jo Marsh **Est.** 2003 **Dozens** 1260 **Vyds** 8ha
John and Joanne Iwanuch say Beechworth Wine Estates is a family-run and owned business, with Jo and John's four children participating in all aspects of vineyard life. Situated on the Rail Trail, 4km from Beechworth, they have planted sauvignon blanc, pinot gris, chardonnay, shiraz, cabernet sauvignon, merlot, tempranillo and sangiovese. Exports to Germany.

🏆🏆🏆🏆🏆 **Chardonnay 2015** Attractive fresh white peach, nectarine and fig fruit balanced and lengthened by citrus acidity and subtle oak. Beechworth and chardonnay are blood brothers. **Rating** 93 **To** 2022 $28

Cabernet Merlot 2014 Light, clear crimson-purple; while only light to medium-bodied, the flavours and texture are attractive, with cassis and redcurrant fruits supported by fine-grained tannins and subtle oak. Screwcap. 13.5% alc. **Rating** 92 **To** 2029 $23 ○

Shiraz 2014 The bouquet is fragrant and spicy, the juicy palate picking up the spicy character and running with it; there's a touch of eucalypt mint that I have no problems with, and the finish of the light to medium-bodied palate is unencumbered by tannins. Screwcap. 13.5% alc. **Rating** 90 **To** 2025 $26

🏆🏆🏆🏆 Pinot Gris 2015 Rating 89 To 2017 $19 ○

Beelgara

Farm 576 Rossetto Road, Beelbangera, NSW 2680 **Region** Riverina
T (02) 6966 0200 **www**.beelgara.com.au **Open** Mon–Fri 10–3
Winemaker Rod Hooper, Danny Toaldo **Est.** 1930 **Dozens** 600 000

Beelgara Estate was formed in 2001 after the purchase of the 60-year-old Rossetto family winery by a group of shareholders, mostly the Toohey family. The emphasis has changed significantly, with a concerted effort to go to the right region for each variety, while still maintaining very good value for money. In 2015 Beelgara (which also owns the Moss Bros, Riddoch Run and The Habitat brands) merged with Cumulus. Exports to most major markets.

ΨΨΨΨΨ **Black Label Clare Valley Grenache Rose 2015** It doesn't pander; it just lets both the variety and the style do their thing, and to winning effect. Raspberry and spice notes, but mostly it's about perfumed refreshment before a dry finish. Screwcap. 13.5% alc. **Rating** 91 **To** 2016 $18 CM ✪
Black Label Adelaide Hills Sauvignon Blanc 2015 There's no question you get your money's worth with this wine. It opens with a burst of tropical fruits, then settles into cruise mode with the aid of citrussy acid. No more needs to be said. Screwcap. 12.5% alc. **Rating** 90 **To** 2017 $18 ✪

Bekkers

212 Seaview Road, McLaren Vale, SA 5171 **Region** McLaren Vale
T 0408 807 568 **www**.bekkerswine.com **Open** Fri–Mon 10–4
Winemaker Emmanuelle and Toby Bekkers **Est.** 2010 **Dozens** 500 **Vyds** 5.5ha

This brings together two high-performance, highly experienced and highly credentialled business and life partners. Husband Toby Bekkers graduated with an honours degree in applied science in agriculture from the University of Adelaide, and over the ensuing years has had broad-ranging responsibilities as general manager of Paxton Wines in McLaren Vale, and as a leading exponent of organic and biodynamic viticulture. Wife Emmanuelle was born in Bandol in the south of France, and gained two university degrees, in biochemistry and oenology, before working for the Hardys in the south of France, which led her to Australia and a wide-ranging career, including Chalk Hill. Exports to the UK, Canada, France and China.

ΨΨΨΨΨ **McLaren Vale Syrah 2014** From two vineyards, destemmed and machine-sorted, 15% whole bunches, 5 days cold soak, gentle pump-overs, basket-pressed to French puncheons (40% new), bottled Nov '15. Dense, deep crimson-purple; grace with power, varietal expression at once fine yet intense. The balance and mouthfeel are exceptional, and it will cruise serenely through decades to come. Class stamped on every bottle. Screwcap. 14.5% alc. **Rating** 96 **To** 2039 $110
Grenache 2014 The silk, the robes of tannin, the flesh of ripe fruit. Aristocratic grenache wearing seductive garb. Raspberry and smooth-skinned plum, smoked cedar wood and a gentle infusion of herbs. Firm tannin doesn't intrude on the impression of delicacy. Screwcap. 15% alc. **Rating** 96 **To** 2026 $80 CM
McLaren Vale Syrah Grenache 2014 The quality is certain, but so too is the creep of warming alcohol. Silken raspberry, plum, blackberry and saltbush flavours team deliciously well, the slip of integrated tannin judged just so. It feels fine and soft throughout; the warmth you need to be in the mood for. Fruit quality here, though, is superb. Screwcap. 14.5% alc. **Rating** 95 **To** 2028 $80 CM

Belford Block Eight

65 Squire Close, Belford, NSW 2335 **Region** Hunter Valley
T 0410 346 300 **www**.blockeight.com.au **Open** Not
Winemaker Daniel Binet **Est.** 2012 **Dozens** 1000 **Vyds** 6ha

The existing 2ha each of semillon, shiraz and chardonnay were planted in 2000. Despite the fact that Block Eight semillon has been purchased by Brokenwood in the past, and was the single vineyard source for the 2006 Brokenwood Belford Semillon, the vineyard had been left to its own devices for two years before Jeff Ross and Todd Alexander purchased it in 2012.

With the help of local consultant Jenny Bright, the vineyard was nursed back to health just in time for the celebrated '14 vintage. With a bit more TLC, and Daniel Binet continuing to make the wines, the future should be bright. Vines, olives, ducks, chickens, perch, yabbies and vegetables are all grown and harvested from the 40ha property.

🍷🍷🍷🍷🍷 **Hunter Valley Shiraz 2014** Destemmed, warm-fermented, 20% finishing fermentation in new oak, the remainder in tank. A very great full-bodied Hunter Valley shiraz in the making, with some of the marks of the '65 vintage, noted for both intensity and depth; rewards will increase for each decade it is stored in a good cellar. Screwcap. 14% alc. **Rating** 96 **To** 2054 $40 ○

🍷🍷🍷🍷🍷 **Estate Hunter Valley Semillon 2015 Rating** 90 **To** 2025 $29

Bellarmine Wines

1 Balyan Retreat, Pemberton, WA 6260 **Region** Pemberton
T (08) 9842 8413 **www**.bellarmine.com.au **Open** By appt
Winemaker Dr Diane Miller **Est.** 2000 **Dozens** 5000 **Vyds** 20.2ha
This vineyard is owned by German residents Dr Willi and Gudrun Schumacher. Long-term wine lovers, the Schumachers decided to establish a vineyard and winery of their own, using Australia partly because of its stable political climate. The vineyard is planted to merlot, pinot noir, chardonnay, shiraz, riesling, sauvignon blanc and petit verdot. Exports to the UK, the US, Germany and China.

🍷🍷🍷🍷🍷 **Pemberton Riesling Half Dry 2015** The back label suggests around 40g/l of residual sugar, but the silky finesse and airy delicacy of the palate shows little of that; this is a beautifully crafted wine with all the indicia of a long life as the balance slowly shifts forward to fruit. Screwcap. 10% alc. **Rating** 96 **To** 2030 $25 ○
Pemberton Riesling Select 2015 Has 75g/l of residual sugar, which it carries with the same ease as the Half Dry, a truly remarkable result. All Bellarmine Rieslings come from the same grapes, simply stopping the ferment earlier or later as required. Screwcap. 7% alc. **Rating** 96 **To** 2034 $25 ○
Pemberton Riesling Dry 2015 Pale straw-green; the bouquet is fragrant and flowery, the palate already expressive with gently ripe citrus flavours that continue until the last moment when acidity strides to the rescue, lengthening the dry finish and cleansing the aftertaste. Screwcap. 12% alc. **Rating** 95 **To** 2030 $25 ○

🍷🍷🍷🍷🍷 **Pemberton Chardonnay 2015 Rating** 92 **To** 2023 $26
Pemberton Shiraz 2014 Rating 91 **To** 2034 $28
Pemberton Sauvignon Blanc 2015 Rating 90 **To** 2017 $20 ○

Bellbrae Estate

520 Great Ocean Road, Bellbrae, Vic 3228 **Region** Geelong
T (03) 5264 8480 **www**.bellbraeestate.com.au **Open** W'ends 11–5, 7 days (Jan)
Winemaker Peter Flewellyn, David Crawford **Est.** 1999 **Dozens** 2000 **Vyds** 4.1ha
The Bellbrae Estate of 2014 is a very different business from that established in 1999. Co-founder Richard Macdougall is now the sole owner, having purchased the small, former sheep-grazing property on which the estate vineyard was planted. In '12 the mothballed Tarcoola Estate winery was reopened and refurbished for Bellbrae under the direction of winemaker David Crawford, and very successful vintages have been made under the Bellbrae Estate and Longboard labels.

🍷🍷🍷🍷🍷 **Boobs Geelong Chardonnay 2015** Hand-picked Mendoza clone, whole bunch-pressed, wild yeast for first half of fermentation, then cultured yeast, fermentation finished in new and 1yo French barriques, matured for 7 months with fortnightly stirring. Very good wine; has complexity and attitude to burn; racy grapefruit/white peach duo, oak a contributor but not OTT; a long, balanced finish. Screwcap. 12.5% alc. **Rating** 95 **To** 2025 $35 ○

🍷🍷🍷🍷♀ Longboard Geelong Pinot Gris 2015 Rating 93 To 2018 $24 ✪
Longboard Geelong Pinot Noir 2014 Rating 93 To 2021 $22 CM ✪
Longboard Geelong Sauvignon Blanc 2015 Rating 92 To 2016 $22 CM ✪

Bellvale Wine   ★★★★

95 Forresters Lane, Berrys Creek, Vic 3953 **Region** Gippsland
T 0412 541 098 **www.bellvalewine.com.au Open** By appt
Winemaker John Ellis **Est.** 1998 **Dozens** 3500 **Vyds** 22ha
John Ellis is the third under this name to be actively involved in the wine industry. His
background as a 747 pilot, and the knowledge he gained of Burgundy over many visits, sets
him apart from the others. He has established pinot noir (14ha), chardonnay (6ha) and pinot
gris (2ha) on the red soils of a north-facing slope. He chose a density of 7150 vines per
hectare, following as far as possible the precepts of Burgundy, but limited by tractor size, which
precludes narrower row spacing and even higher plant density. Exports to the UK, the US,
Denmark, Germany, Singapore and Japan.

🍷🍷🍷🍷🍷 Quercus Vineyard Pinot Noir 2014 Strung with herbs and wood smoke;
velvety texture; light colour but real presence; tannic but flush with foresty fruit.
Impeccable. Screwcap. 12.5% alc. **Rating** 94 **To** 2024 $35 CM

🍷🍷🍷🍷♀ Athena's Vineyard Chardonnay 2014 Rating 93 To 2021 $35 CM

Bellwether   ★★★★★

14183 Riddoch Highway, Coonawarra, SA 5263 **Region** Coonawarra
T 0417 080 945 **www.bellwetherwines.com.au Open** Thurs–Mon 11–5
Winemaker Sue Bell, Steve Brown **Est.** 2009 **Dozens** 2000
When Constellation decided to sell (or mothball) its large Padthaway winery, built by Hardys
little more than 10 years previously at a cost of $20 million, chief winemaker Sue Bell was
summarily retrenched. In quick succession she received a $46,000 wine industry scholarship
from the Grape & Wine Research Development Council to study the wine industry in
relation to other rural industries in Australia and overseas, and its interaction with community
and society. She also became Dux of the Len Evans Tutorial, her prize an extended trip
through Bordeaux and Burgundy. She decided to stay and live in Coonawarra, and the next
stroke of good fortune was that a beautiful old shearing shed at Glenroy in Coonawarra came
on the market – which is her winery and cellar door. Exports to the UK, Canada and France.

🍷🍷🍷🍷🍷 Coonawarra Cabernet Sauvignon 2009 The colour is still strong and
vibrant, and my tasting note from 4 years ago still stands, as do the points:
A remarkably fresh and generous cabernet, flooded with cassis, dried herbs and
an echo of regional mint; the tannins are ripe and integrated, the quality of the
oak also seamlessly woven through the palate. Screwcap. 13% alc. **Rating** 96
To 2030 $50 ✪

🍷🍷🍷🍷♀ Tamar Valley Chardonnay 2013 Rating 93 To 2023 $50
Nero d'Avola Rose 2015 Rating 93 To 2018 $25 ✪
Wrattonbully Shiraz Malbec 2014 Rating 92 To 2029 $28
Heathcote Vermentino 2015 Rating 91 To 2020 $28

Ben Haines Wine   ★★★★★

13 Berry Street, Clifton Hill, Vic 3068 (postal) **Region** Various
T 0417 083 645 **www.benhaineswine.com Open** Not
Winemaker Ben Haines **Est.** 2010 **Dozens** 1800
Ben Haines graduated from the University of Adelaide in 1999 with a degree in viticulture,
waiting a couple of years (immersing himself in music) before focusing on his career. An
early interest in terroir led to a deliberate choice of diverse regions, including the Yarra Valley,
McLaren Vale, Adelaide Hills, Langhorne Creek, Tasmania and Central Victoria, as well as time
in the US and France. His services as a contract winemaker are in high demand, and his name
bobs up all over the place. Exports to the US.

ŢŢŢŢŢ **B Minor Upper Goulburn Marsanne Roussanne 2015** A 60/40% blend
from the estate Dabyminga Vineyard planted in the mid '90s, whole bunch-
pressed, wild-fermented in French oak (15% new), matured for 10 months on lees.
Brilliant straw-green; this is a seriously good wine, full of energy, with great line
and length to its apple/citrus flavours, the balance also impeccable. It will develop
superbly. Screwcap. 12.8% alc. **Rating** 97 **To** 2028 $26 **☉**

ŢŢŢŢŢ **Warramunda Reprise Yarra Valley Marsanne 2014** Hand-picked, whole
bunch-pressed, a cool fermentation with wild yeast in French oak (10% new),
matured for 13 months on lees. As long as you have faith (as I do) in the ability
of well-made marsanne to thrive in bottle, this should be a winner. It's very well
balanced, the oak handling perfect, the honeysuckle varietal fruit equally good.
Screwcap. 12.8% alc. **Rating** 95 **To** 2029 $32 **☉**
B Minor Yarra Valley Shiraz Marsanne 2014 Hand-picked shiraz open-
fermented on marsanne skins, wild yeast, matured for 16 months in French oak
(30% new), a portion with marsanne lees, the final blend analysis 92% shiraz, 8%
marsanne. Brilliant colour; this is a thoroughly successful blend, promoting the red
fruit components of the shiraz without shifting the tannins or texture. I'd buy it.
Screwcap. 13.8% alc. **Rating** 95 **To** 2027 $26 **☉**

ŢŢŢŢŢ **Maroondah Yarra Valley Syrah 2014** Rating 93 **To** 2029 $45

Bendbrook Wines   ★★★☆

Section 19, Pound Road, Macclesfield, SA 5153 **Region** Adelaide Hills
T (08) 8388 9773 **www.**bendbrookwines.com.au **Open** By appt
Winemaker Contract **Est.** 1998 **Dozens** 2000 **Vyds** 5.5ha
John and Margaret Struik have established their vineyard on either side of a significant bend
in the Angas River that runs through the property, with cabernet sauvignon on one side
and shiraz on the other. The name comes from the bend in question, which is indirectly
responsible for the flood that occurs every 4–5 years. The Struiks have restored what was
known as the Postmaster's Residence to be their home. Exports to Hong Kong.

ŢŢŢŢŢ **Savvy Sauvignon Blanc 2014** Pale quartz hue, still with no development;
the bouquet has an unusual lychee/floral mix, the palate crisp, with lemony
acidity driving through to the finish. Gold medal Adelaide Hills Wine Show '14.
Screwcap. 12.5% alc. **Rating** 94 **To** 2016 $18 **☉**

Bent Creek   ★★★★☆

13 Blewitt Springs Road, McLaren Flat, SA 5171 **Region** McLaren Vale
T (08) 8383 0414 **www.**bentcreekvineyards.com.au **Open** W'ends 12–4
Winemaker Tim Geddes, Sam Rugari, David Garrick **Est.** 1999 **Dozens** 5000
Established in 1999, today Bent Creek is a joint partnership between Sam Rugari and
David Garrick, collectively with over 40 years' experience in the wine industry. They source
premium fruit from vineyards in McLaren Vale (with 70–100-year-old vines) to Piccadilly
Valley in the Adelaide Hills, working closely with the growers. There is an overall focus on
small parcels of high quality fruit that reflect the variety, vintage and unique terroir each has
to offer. Exports to Indonesia, Hong Kong and China.

ŢŢŢŢŢ **Black Dog McLaren Vale Shiraz 2014** Estate-grown, matured in 75%
American oak (10% new) and 25% French oak for 14 months. Deep colour;
archetypal McLaren Vale regional character on the bouquet, redoubled (in Bridge
terms) on the viscous/velvet black fruits and dark chocolate of the full-bodied
palate. Has steered clear of the rocks of dead fruit and butch tannins, but delicate
it ain't. Screwcap. 14.5% alc. **Rating** 91 **To** 2034 $25

ŢŢŢŢ **Piccadilly Valley Sauvignon Blanc 2015** Rating 89 **To** 2017 $20
Misty Lane McLaren Vale Shiraz 2014 Rating 89 **To** 2020 $15 **☉**

Beresford Estates

252 Blewitt Springs Road, McLaren Flat, SA 5171 **Region** McLaren Vale
T (08) 8383 0362 **www.beresfordwines.com.au Open** Wed–Sun 10–5
Winemaker Chris Dix **Est.** 1985 **Dozens** 30000 **Vyds** 28ha
This is a sister company to Step Rd Wines in Langhorne Creek, owned and run by VOK
Beverages. The estate plantings are of cabernet sauvignon and shiraz (10ha each), chardonnay
(5.5ha) and grenache (2.5ha), but they account for only a part of the substantial production.
Some of the wines offer excellent value. Exports to the UK, the US, Germany, Denmark,
Poland, Singapore, Hong Kong and China.

♟♟♟♟♟ **Limited Release Shiraz 2014** It doesn't roll, it creeps. It's like a lava flow of
blackberried flavour. Its bones are fortified with tannin, its inky depths layered
with sweet, cedary oak. It needs time to all come together, but it will mature (well)
over decades. Cork. 14.1% alc. **Rating** 96 **To** 2038 $80 CM
McLaren Vale Shiraz 2014 Firm and brooding with black-berried fruit stuffed
into every corner. If you're looking for a substantial red, this would be a top
choice. It tastes of blackberry, cloves, redcurrant and musk, the latter character
evident in the floral note to the bouquet too. Terrific value. Screwcap. 14.5% alc.
Rating 95 **To** 2034 $28 CM ✪
Estate Blewitt Springs McLaren Vale Cabernet Sauvignon 2014 Thick-
flavoured, but lively. Smoked cedar wood, concentrated plum, blackcurrant, bay
leaves, fresh boysenberry. An array of flavours to admire. The texture too is silken;
the tannin exquisitely well integrated. Serious intensity swings effortlessly through
a beautifully formed palate. Screwcap. 13.5% alc. **Rating** 95 **To** 2032 $50 CM
Estate Blewitt Springs Shiraz 2014 It pours on the flavour but contingencies
of tannin keep everything firmly in place. Red and black berries, a sweet
redcurrant-like note, not a lot of spice or savoury input, but clovey oak fills the
void. Quality is undeniable. Screwcap. 14% alc. **Rating** 94 **To** 2030 $50 CM
Blewitt Springs Grenache 2014 Deep and rugged. Unusual in a varietal
context. Blackberries, dry licorice, ironstone, undergrowth and malt. Its weighty
flavours creep slowly and deliberately through the palate. Along the way, more than
a little gravitas is established. Screwcap. 14.5% alc. **Rating** 94 **To** 2024 $50 CM

♟♟♟♟♟ **Barrel Select McLaren Vale G.S.M 2014** Rating 93 **To** 2025 $28 CM
McLaren Vale Cabernet Sauvignon 2014 Rating 91 **To** 2023 $28 CM

Berton Vineyard

55 Mirrool Avenue, Yenda, NSW 2681 **Region** Riverina
T (02) 6968 1600 **www.bertonvineyards.com.au Open** Mon–Fri 10–4, Sat 11–4
Winemaker James Ceccato, Bill Gumbleton **Est.** 2001 **Dozens** 1 million **Vyds** 12.14ha
The Berton Vineyard partners – Bob and Cherie Berton, James Ceccato and Jamie Bennett –
have almost 100 years' combined experience in winemaking, viticulture, finance, production
and marketing. 1996 saw the acquisition of a 30ha property in the Eden Valley and the
planting of the first vines. Wines are released under the Berton Vineyard, Oddsocks and Head
Over Heels labels. Exports to the UK, the US, Sweden and China.

♟♟♟♟♟ **High Eden The Bonsai 2012** A blend of the best barrels of shiraz and cabernet,
separately matured for 20 months in French oak and blended shortly prior to
bottling. It is fleshy and mouthfilling, with a rainbow of flavours encompassing
black cherry, plum, licorice and spice, the cedary oak providing an elegant
latticework finish. Screwcap. 14.5% alc. **Rating** 94 **To** 2037 $40

♟♟♟♟♟ **High Eden Cabernet Sauvignon 2012** Rating 92 **To** 2032 $30

Best's Wines

111 Best's Road, Great Western, Vic 3377 **Region** Grampians
T (03) 5356 2250 **www.bestswines.com Open** Mon–Sat 10–5, Sun 11–4
Winemaker Justin Purser **Est.** 1866 **Dozens** 20000 **Vyds** 34ha

Best's winery and vineyards are among Australia's best-kept secrets. Indeed the vineyards, with vines dating back to 1866, have secrets that may never be revealed: for example, one of the vines planted in the Nursery Block has defied identification and is thought to exist nowhere else in the world. Part of the cellars, too, go back to the same era, constructed by butcher-turned-winemaker Henry Best and his family. The Thomson family has owned the property since 1920, with Ben, the fifth generation, having taken over management from father Viv. Best's consistently produces elegant, supple wines; the Bin No. 0 is a classic, the Thomson Family Shiraz (largely from vines planted in 1867) magnificent. In the 2017 Wine Companion it has been awarded the mantle of Wine of the Year from a field of almost 9000 wines. Very occasionally a Pinot Meunier (with 15% Pinot Noir) is made solely from 1866 plantings of those two varieties; there is no other Pinot Meunier of this vine age made anywhere else in the world. Justin Purser brings with him a remarkable CV, with extensive experience in Australia, NZ and (most recently) Burgundy (at Domaine de Montille). Exports to the UK, the US, Canada, Sweden, Switzerland, Singapore, Hong Kong and China.

🍷🍷🍷🍷🍷 **Thomson Family Great Western Shiraz 2014** Bottle no. 39 of 2200 tells part of the story, but the front label also has, in demure typeface, 'original 1867 plantings'. This is a ravishing wine with a velvet and satin mouthfeel, and a rainbow of black, purple and blue fruits. Supple tannins are somewhere in the mix, likewise French oak, but don't bother dissecting what is an exquisite wine. As a point of principle, I'm not going to give 100 points for a table wine, but if I were, this would get the nod. Screwcap. 13.5% alc. **Rating** 99 **To** 2054 $200 ✪

🍷🍷🍷🍷🍷 **Foudre Ferment Concongella Vineyards Great Western Riesling 2015** 'Made from juice with extended skin contact and wild-fermented in a large oak foudre.' It pushes the envelope far beyond its technical limits, and succeeds brilliantly. It is supple and generous, lime and honey in abundance, yet not phenolic. Screwcap. 12% alc. **Rating** 96 **To** 2028 $35 ✪

White Gravels Hill Great Western Shiraz 2014 From an elevated block in the Concongella Vineyard with white gravels and reef quartz on a granite bedrock. Excellent colour; glorious black and red fruits are joined by a high-tension wire with its own claim on the palate, neither with the slightest chance of conceding defeat, this giving the wine exceptional length. Great value. Screwcap. 13.5% alc. **Rating** 96 **To** 2044 $35 ✪

Bin No. 0 Great Western Shiraz 2014 Full crimson-purple; a complex medium to full-bodied shiraz with blackberry, black cherry, spice, licorice, tannins and oak all contributing to the intense palate; natural acidity and freshness enhanced by the modest alcohol; it builds and builds, lengthens and lengthens each time it is retasted. Screwcap. 13.5% alc. **Rating** 96 **To** 2044 $85

Great Western Chardonnay 2015 Yet another strike. Is there anything Justin Purser can't do? This is a beautifully sculpted chardonnay, the fruit flavours spanning white peach to grapefruit, the oak evident on the bouquet, less so on the palate, acidity just so. Screwcap. 12.5% alc. **Rating** 95 **To** 2023 $25 ✪

Great Western Pinot Noir 2015 Clear but deep crimson colour; very attractive cherry (red and black) and damson plum fruit; the palate has particularly good mouthfeel, with superfine tannins threaded through the fruit. Ticks every box with quiet authority. Great value. Screwcap. 12% alc. **Rating** 95 **To** 2027 $25 ✪

Bin No. 1 Great Western Shiraz 2014 Medium to full-bodied with licorice, dark cherry and plum building the main tent of flavour; clove and eucalypt as the guy ropes; tannin stake it all firm. Outside of flavour descriptors the best way to describe this wine is to say: it will mature beautifully over 15–20 years but it's going to prove extremely difficult to keep your hands off it, even now in its youth. Screwcap. 14% alc. **Rating** 95 **To** 2035 $25 CM ✪

Great Western Cabernet Sauvignon 2014 Still a pup, but all the signs are excellent. Arms of minted blackcurrant; chubby legs of tannin; vanillan oak covering the belly. It's still growing into itself but the fruit feels so pure you'd almost label it sincere; it hasn't learned its tricks yet, but when it does, it will fascinate. Screwcap. 14% alc. **Rating** 95 **To** 2035 $25 CM ✪

🍷🍷🍷🍷🍷 **Great Western Riesling 2015 Rating** 93 **To** 2028 $25 CM ✪

Bethany Wines ★★★★★

378 Bethany Road, Tanunda, SA 5352 **Region** Barossa
T (08) 8563 2086 **www**.bethany.com.au **Open** Mon–Sat 10–5, Sun 1–5
Winemaker Geoff and Robert Schrapel **Est.** 1981 **Dozens** 25 000 **Vyds** 38ha
The Schrapel family has been growing grapes in the Barossa Valley for 140 years, and has had the winery since 1981. Nestled high on a hillside on the site of an old bluestone quarry, Geoff and Rob Schrapel produce a range of consistently well-made and attractively packaged wines. Bethany has vineyards in the Barossa and Eden valleys. Exports to the UK, Europe and Asia.

ΨΨΨΨ Reserve Eden Valley Riesling 2015 The cut and thrust of high quality riesling. This is searingly dry, but terrifically intense, its quality clear from start to finish and then some. Screwcap. 12% alc. **Rating** 95 **To** 2030 $32 CM ✪
LE Barossa Shiraz 2014 Refreshing style. It places an emphasis on brightness; on succulence. It's complex and structural, but it's bursting to please; it wants you to love it, and for a long time. All about redcurranty fruits, spice, mandarin and smoky oak. Pure but refined pleasure. Behold the alcohol. Screwcap. 13.4% alc. **Rating** 95 **To** 2032 $48 CM
GR Reserve Barossa Shiraz 2013 Complex with game, earth and spice, though it's red- and black-berried flavours, naturally enough, that beat most strongly through its heart. Tannin is fine, but (very) firm and oak is sympathetic. It's not the deepest or blackest but it's immaculate, and it will last. Cork. 13.8% alc. **Rating** 95 **To** 2035 $95 CM

ΨΨΨΨ East Grounds Project Barossa Shiraz 2014 **Rating** 93 **To** 2028 $45 CM
Eden Valley Riesling 2015 **Rating** 91 **To** 2021 $20 CM ✪
Barossa Cabernet Sauvignon 2013 **Rating** 90 **To** 2025 $35 CM

Between the Vines ★★★★

452 Longwood Road, Longwood, SA 5153 **Region** Adelaide Hills
T 0403 933 767 **www**.betweenthevines.com.au **Open** W'ends & public hols 12–5
Winemaker Matt Jackman **Est.** 2013 **Dozens** 400 **Vyds** 2.1ha
The estate vineyard (2.1ha of chardonnay) was planted in 1995, and purchased by Stewart and Laura Moodie in 2006. Between then and '12 the grapes were sold to d'Arenberg for its Lucky Lizard Chardonnay. The vineyard is fully managed by Stewart and Laura, who do all the spraying/netting/wire lifting, pruning, fruit and shoot thinning, Laura having undertaken a year-long viticulture course. They employ backpackers for labour where needed, and only bring in professional teams for the harvest. In '13, the Moodies created the Between the Vines brand, grafting 0.2ha of tempranillo (on chardonnay rootstock). Output has increased, and small quantities of Pinot Noir and Tempranillo are bottled under their label. The annual crush (between 4 and 10 tonnes) is taken to McLaren Vintners, where Matt Jackman makes the wine in consultation with the Moodies.

ΨΨΨΨ Single Vineyard Adelaide Hills Chardonnay 2014 Restrained winemaker inputs; subtle oak usage. A slightly funky/smoky bouquet is followed by an incisive and bright palate, white-fleshed stone fruits guarding the gate against any suggestion the wine is a wannabe sauvignon blanc; has good length and persistence. Screwcap. 13% alc. **Rating** 90 **To** 2019 $18 ✪
Single Vineyard Adelaide Hills Tempranillo 2013 This is a sock it to 'em tempranillo laden with red and black cherry fruit, firm acidity and controlled tannins. Retasting helps pull it back from the initially threatening pose, and cellaring will aid the cause further. Screwcap. 14.5% alc. **Rating** 90 **To** 2023 $22

ΨΨΨΨ Single Vineyard Adelaide Hills Pinot Noir 2013 **Rating** 89 **To** 2019 $22

Bicknell fc ★★★★★

41 St Margarets Road, Healesville, Vic 3777 **Region** Yarra Valley
T 0488 678 427 **www**.bicknellfc.com **Open** Not
Winemaker David Bicknell **Est.** 2011 **Dozens** 300 **Vyds** 2.5ha

This is the busman's holiday for Oakridge chief winemaker David Bicknell and (former) viticulturist (present) partner Nicky Harris. It is focused purely on chardonnay and pinot noir, with no present intention of broadening the range, nor, indeed, the volume of production. The vintages between 2011 and '13 came, with one exception, from the Upper Yarra Valley, the exception the '13 Gippsland Pinot Noir. As from '14 all of the wines will come from Val Stewart's close-planted vineyard at the top of Prices Road, Gladysdale, planted in 1988. The partners have leased this vineyard, which will become the total focus of their business. The quality of the wines so far released has been extremely high, and there is no reason to think there will be any change in the future.

🍷🍷🍷🍷🍷 **Yarra Valley Pinot Noir 2014** On the one hand it's so bright and sweet it feels happy-go-lucky, on the other it's savoury, dry and stern. It could easily seem schizophrenic, but the warring parties meet on the common ground of quality. In other words, it makes it work, the end result both complex and thrilling, yet accessible. Screwcap. 13.5% alc. **Rating** 96 **To** 2024 $39 CM ◐

Bike & Barrel

PO Box 167, Myrtleford, Vic 3736 **Region** Alpine Valleys
T 0409 971 235 **Open** Not
Winemaker Jo Marsh, Daniel Balzer **Est.** 2013 **Dozens** 280 **Vyds** 1.5ha
Brian and Linda Lewis have split their vineyard and wine interests in two. One half is a commercial vineyard of 10ha, established on undulating free-draining slopes above the valley floor, mainly supplying local wineries with chardonnay, prosecco, pinot noir and tempranillo. For Bike & Barrel they have 1.5ha of pinotage, fiano, schioppettino and refosco dal peduncolo rosso.

🍷🍷🍷🍷🍷 **Slaughteryard Creek Pinot Noir 2015** Light, bright hue; the wine is light-bodied, and there has been no attempt to bodybuild and lose the ethereal pinot bouquet and the more (naturally) punchy palate. The net result is a genuinely attractive red-berried pinot. Screwcap. 13.5% alc. **Rating** 90 **To** 2021 $30

Bill Byron Wines

PO Box 770, Narrabri, NSW 2390 **Region** Mudgee
T 0408 657 483 **www**.billbyronwines.com **Open** Not
Winemaker James Manners **Est.** 2013 **Dozens** 20 000 **Vyds** 60ha
The Findley family are farmers in the Central Ranges GI, NSW. In 1998 William (Bill) Bryon Findley began planting the now 60ha vineyard as a diversification from the core business. The intention was to simply sell the grapes, but changes in the marketplace led to changes both in viticulture (moving to organic viticulture, certification following in 2013) and the making of the first vintage in that year. Son Robin and daughter-in-law Yvonne now own the vineyard, planted to 26ha of shiraz and 17ha each of cabernet sauvignon and merlot. They have recruited James Manners, a man about Mudgee for decades as winemaker, and have developed a striking label design with various hidden meanings. Last, but not least, they have appointed Oatley Fine Wine Merchants as their distributor, the winemaking and bottling carried out at Robert Oatley Vineyards' Mudgee winery.

🍷🍷🍷🍷🍷 **Organic Shiraz Cabernet Merlot 2013** Well polished and appealing with red and black berries and sweet jubey fruit flavour running fluidly through the palate. Chocolatey/vanillan oak plays a modest but positive role. Screwcap. 13.2% alc. **Rating** 90 **To** 2020 $23 CM

Billanook Estate

280 Edward Road, Chirnside Park, Vic 3116 **Region** Yarra Valley
T (03) 9735 4484 **www**.billanookestate.com.au **Open** W'ends 10–6
Winemaker Domenic Bucci, John D'Aloisio **Est.** 1994 **Dozens** 1200 **Vyds** 14.06ha
The D'Aloisio family has been involved in the agricultural heritage of the Yarra Valley since the late 1960s, and in '94 planted the first vines on their 36ha property. The vineyard is planted

to shiraz, sauvignon blanc, cabernet sauvignon, pinot noir, merlot, nebbiolo, tempranillo, nebbiolo and barbera. Most of the grapes are sold to various wineries in the Valley, leaving a small percentage for the Billanook Estate label.

🍷🍷🍷🍷🍷 **Yarra Valley Barbera 2013** Light, although bright, hue. Hmmm, has more flavour and style than expected, berries and cherries of all kinds running around the mouth, the latter ranging from red to morello to maraschino. For chefs to take up the challenge of food matching. Cork. 13.4% alc. **Rating** 90 **To** 2028 $25

🍷🍷🍷🍷 **Yarra Valley Sauvignon Blanc 2015 Rating** 89 **To** 2017 $22
Yarra Valley Rose 2015 Rating 89 **To** 2017 $20

Billy Button Wines ★★★★☆

2d Anderson Street, Bright, Vic 3741 **Region** Alpine Valleys
T 0418 559 344 **www**.billybuttonwines.com.au **Open** W'ends & public hols 12–5.30
Winemaker Jo Marsh **Est.** 2014 **Dozens** 2500
Jo Marsh speaks quietly, if not diffidently, making light of the numerous awards she won during her studies for her Degree in Agricultural Science (Oenology) at the University of Adelaide. She continued that habit when she won a contested position in Southcorp's (now Treasury Wine Estates) Graduate Recruitment Program; she was appointed assistant winemaker at Seppelt Great Western in 2003. By '08 she had been promoted to acting senior winemaker, responsible for all wines made onsite. In '09 she won the Graham Thorp Memorial Scholarship at the Sydney Wine Show with '05 Seppelt Salinger, the first sparkling wine she had made. The following year she won the Member's Choice and Sommelier's Choice at the Wine Society Young Winemaker of the Year Award. She also was one of the 12 wine professionals selected to participate in the Len Evans Tutorial Scholarship, from a field of over 100. After resigning from Seppelt, she became winemaker at Feathertop, and after two happy years decided to step out on her own in '14 to create Billy Button Wines. She has set up a grower network – with one exception all from the Alpine Valleys (King Valley the exception) – and made a string of excellent wines in '14, the following year making 11 varietal wines.

🍷🍷🍷🍷🍷 **The Torment King Valley Riesling 2015** Grown at 800m in the upper heights of the King Valley. It's a severe, take-no-prisoners style in general but it has just enough prettiness to keep you on its side. In flavour terms: the full gamut of lime (juice, rind and blossom) set with grapefruit and slate. It darts. It lingers. Screwcap. 12% alc. **Rating** 95 **To** 2026 $25 CM ✪

🍷🍷🍷🍷🍷 **The Happy Gewurztraminer 2015 Rating** 93 **To** 2017 $25 CM ✪
The Little Rascal Arneis 2015 Rating 93 **To** 2017 $25 CM ✪
The Versatile Vermentino 2015 Rating 93 **To** 2016 $25 CM ✪
The Demure Pinot Blanc 2015 Rating 93 **To** 2017 $25 CM ✪
The Beloved Alpine Valleys Shiraz 2014 Rating 93 **To** 2025 $30 CM
The Alluring Alpine Valleys Tempranillo 2014 Rating 92 **To** 2022 $30 CM
The Fantastic Alpine Valleys Fiano 2015 Rating 90 **To** 2020 $25
The Feisty Alpine Valleys Friulano 2015 Rating 90 **To** 2020 $25
The Mysterious Alpine Valleys Malvasia 2015 Rating 90 **To** 2020 $25
The Delinquent Alpine Valleys Verduzzo 2015 Rating 90 **To** 2020 $25

Billy Pye Vineyard ★★★

PO Box 229, Ashton, SA 5137 **Region** Adelaide Hills
T (08) 8390 1332 **Open** Not
Winemaker Contract **Est.** 1997 **Dozens** 90 **Vyds** 2.1ha
The history of Billy Pye Vineyard dates back to 1868 and colourful local character WH (Billy) Pye. His property contained the largest hill in the area, known locally as Billy Pye Hill. In 1997 Sandra Schubert, a fifth-generation Grasby, began to plant a vineyard on the northern slopes of Billy Pye Hill in partnership with John Bowley, leaving the top of the hill with the native vegetation Billy had loved. The wines are made from grapes grown on a small site on the eastern slopes of the vineyard. The Glengyle Red is named after a variety of apple developed by the Grasby family.

♟♟♟♟ **Glengyle Red 2013** 55/40/5% shiraz, merlot, cabernet. It offers rounds of berried fruit with licks of dust and spice. Grippy tannin to the finish isn't entirely integrated but full marks for freshness and flavour. Screwcap. 14% alc. **Rating** 89 To 2021 $28 CM

Bimbadgen   ★★★★★

790 McDonalds Road, Pokolbin, NSW 2320 **Region** Hunter Valley
T (02) 4998 4600 **www**.bimbadgen.com.au **Open** Fri–Sat 10–7, Sun–Thurs 10–5
Winemaker Rauri Donkin, Mike De Garis (Consultant) **Est.** 1968 **Dozens** 25 000
Vyds 27ha
Bimbadgen's Palmers Lane vineyard was planted in 1968 and the McDonalds Road vineyard shortly thereafter, both sites providing a source of old vine semillon, shiraz and chardonnay. Since assuming ownership in '97, the Lee family has applied the same level of care and attention to cultivating Bimbadgen as they have with other properties in their portfolio. The small but impressive production is consumed largely by the owner's luxury hotel assets, with limited quantities available in the Sydney market. Exports to the UK, Switzerland, Germany, The Netherlands, Japan, Taiwan and China.

♟♟♟♟♟ **Signature Hunter Valley Shiraz 2014** Crushed, and given a 2-day cold soak, then a 10-day ferment and a further week on skins, matured in new and used French oak, gold medal Hunter Valley Wine Show '15. Lives up to the reputation of the vintage, effortlessly imposing its array of blackberry and plum fruit flavours on the front line, silky tannins and integrated oak supplying all the structural support needed. Screwcap. 13.2% alc. **Rating** 95 To 2044 $50

Signature McDonalds Road Hunter Valley Shiraz 2014 All French oak but only 20% new. It's the Hunter Valley on fluid display, trademark earth and spice notes stitched into plush, almost flashy fruit, and yet there are no signs of either overripeness or over-oaking. Now or many years hence, we have a medium-bodied delight. Screwcap. 13.6% alc. **Rating** 95 To 2032 $75 CM

Art Series Riesling 2015 From the Angullong Vineyard in Orange, the free-run juice cool-fermented in stainless steel, the pressings wild-fermented in used oak. The two components were blended before the wine spent 5 months on yeast lees. The bouquet and palate are laden with lime juice, at once fruity, yet minerally. This is hard to assess professionally, the urge to swallow difficult to suppress. Screwcap. 12% alc. **Rating** 94 To 2025 $22 ❂

Signature Palmers Lane Hunter Valley Semillon 2015 Wonderfully expressive and vibrant. Open for business too. Lychee, fennel and sweet lemon with spice and slate notes shooting out through the finish. Floral aspects. Texture too. Pleasure writ large. Screwcap. 11.2% alc. **Rating** 94 To 2025 $50 CM

Signature Palmers Lane Hunter Valley Shiraz 2014 Mid-weight and shy, at least on the palate, with subtle floral fragrances leading to a palate of redcurrant and black cherry, oak almost entirely tucked away. Spicy, almost coal-like notes come forward given time to breathe; it's not obvious or brash, but its underlying quality is clear. Screwcap. 13.7% alc. **Rating** 94 To 2032 $75 CM

Members Hunter Valley Shiraz 2014 An early release; has vivid varietal fruit expression, with red and black cherries both involved; there is also a polish of well-integrated new oak, the tannins firm but balanced. Attractive now, great 5-15 years down the track. Screwcap. 13.5% alc. **Rating** 94 To 2034 $35

♟♟♟♟♡ **Fortified Verdelho NV** Rating 92 To 2020 $28
Estate Hunter Valley Semillon 2015 Rating 91 To 2029 $25

Bindi Wine Growers   ★★★★★

343 Melton Road, Gisborne, Vic 3437 (postal) **Region** Macedon Ranges
T (03) 5428 2564 **www**.bindiwines.com.au **Open** Not
Winemaker Michael Dhillon, Stuart Anderson **Est.** 1988 **Dozens** 2000 **Vyds** 6ha

One of the icons of Macedon. The Chardonnay is top-shelf, the Pinot Noir as remarkable (albeit in a very different idiom) as Bass Phillip, Giaconda or any of the other tiny-production, icon wines. The addition of Heathcote-sourced shiraz under the Pyrette label confirms Bindi as one of the greatest small producers in Australia. Exports to the UK, the US and other major markets.

ΥΥΥΥΥ **Block 5 Pinot Noir 2014** Block 5 was planted in '92 on quartz-riddled soil over sandstone, mudstone and clay, open-fermented, wild yeast, 5% whole bunches, 95% whole berries, 15 days on skins, matured for 11 months in French oak (35% new). The wine combines power with elegance, the black cherry and plum flavours never challenged, the length and texture of the fruit remarkable. Bindi had a great vintage. Diam. 13.5% alc. **Rating** 97 **To** 2034 $110 **✪**

ΥΥΥΥΥ **Original Vineyard Pinot Noir 2014** Obviously enough, from the oldest vines on the estate, open-fermented, wild yeast, 5% whole bunches, 95% whole berries, 15 days on skins, matured for 11 months in French oak (30% new). The fragrant bouquet tells of the poised and focused palate that follows; here savoury, earthy nuances are the stage for the purity and elegance of the dark fruits of the palate. Diam. 13.5% alc. **Rating** 96 **To** 2030 $85

Quartz Chardonnay 2014 Wild-fermented in French oak (35% new) with 100% solids, matured for 15 months. Some colour development, not an issue; this is a complete wine, with fruit to the fore, oak and acidity of lesser importance; the mouthfeel is admirable, as is the expression of place and variety, white peach, green apple and citrus expertly hand-stitched together. Screwcap. 13.5% alc. **Rating** 95 **To** 2024 $85

Dixon Pinot Noir 2014 Estate-grown. the components from various parts of the vineyard across all soil types, wild yeast open-fermented, 5% whole bunches, 95% whole berries, 15 days on skins, matured for 11 months in French oak (20% new). The bouquet is built around a core of dark plum fruit, the palate rich and concentrated. Diam. 13.5% alc. **Rating** 94 **To** 2029 $60

ΥΥΥΥΥ **Kostas Rind Chardonnay 2014** **Rating** 93 **To** 2030 $55
Pyrette Heathcote Shiraz 2014 **Rating** 91 **To** 2029 $40

Bird in Hand ★★★★★

Bird in Hand Road, Woodside, SA 5244 **Region** Adelaide Hills
T (08) 8389 9488 **www.**birdinhand.com.au **Open** Mon–Fri 10–5, w'ends 11–5
Winemaker Kym Milne (MW), Peter Ruchs, Dylan Lee **Est.** 1997 **Dozens** 75 000
Vyds 29ha
This very successful business took its name from a 19th-century goldmine. It is the venture of the Nugent family, headed by Dr Michael Nugent; son Andrew is a Roseworthy graduate. The family also has a vineyard in the Clare Valley, the latter providing both riesling and shiraz. The estate plantings (merlot, pinot noir, cabernet sauvignon, sauvignon blanc, riesling, shiraz) provide only part of the annual crush, the remainder coming from contract growers. In 2010, a replica Bird in Hand cellar door was opened in Dalian, in China's northeastern Liaoning province, a second following in Yingkou. Exports to all major markets.

ΥΥΥΥΥ **Mt Lofty Ranges Shiraz 2014** Some whole berries, cultured yeast, fermentation temperatures allowed to peak at 30°C, 8–10 days on skins. Inoculated mlf and racked to French oak (50% new) for 16 months. Good hue; medium to full-bodied, it hangs it all out there for everyone to see – and taste; black and morello cherries lead, with slashes of licorice, bitter chocolate and toasty French oak all holding their hands up, the tannins made to measure. Screwcap. 14.5% alc. **Rating** 95 **To** 2040 $42

ΥΥΥΥΥ **Adelaide Hills Montepulciano 2014** **Rating** 92 **To** 2024 $42
Adelaide Hills Pinot Gris 2015 **Rating** 91 **To** 2017 $28
Two in the Bush Mt Lofty Ranges Shiraz 2014 **Rating** 91 **To** 2024 $23 **✪**
Honeysuckle Clare Valley Riesling 2015 **Rating** 91 **To** 2025 $25
Clare Valley Riesling 2015 **Rating** 90 **To** 2025 $25

Bird on a Wire Wines

51 Symons Street, Healesville, Vic 3777 (postal) **Region** Yarra Valley
T 0439 045 000 **www**.birdonawirewines.com.au **Open** By appt
Winemaker Caroline Mooney **Est.** 2008 **Dozens** 500

This is now the full-time business of winemaker Caroline Mooney, who grew up in the Yarra Valley and who has had (other full-time) winemaking jobs in the valley for over 10 years. The focus is on small, single vineyard sites owned by growers committed to producing outstanding grapes. Having worked at the legendary Domaine Jean-Louis Chave in the 2006 vintage, she has a special interest in shiraz and marsanne, both grown from distinct sites on a single vineyard in the Yarra Glen area. There is also a Chardonnay from the Upper Yarra Valley, now generally accepted as a perfect environment for the finest of Chardonnay styles. Exports to the UK.

🍷🍷🍷🍷🍷 **Syrah 2013** Some wines just seem ready to shine. This is one such. The aromas and flavours stride out in confident, ordered, appealing lines, like patterns, like chords. Roasted nuts, black cherries, plums, meats, wood smoke. It's ripe but fresh, fun but lengthy. Ultimately it is, simply, impressive. Screwcap. 14.1% alc. **Rating** 96 To 2028 $40 CM ✪

🍷🍷🍷🍷🍷 **Chardonnay 2013 Rating** 93 To 2021 $40 CM

BK Wines

Burdetts Road, Basket Range, SA 5138 **Region** Adelaide Hills
T 0410 124 674 **www**.bkwines.com.au **Open** By appt
Winemaker Brendon Keys **Est.** 2007 **Dozens** 3500

BK Wines is owned by NZ-born Brendon Keys and wife Kirsty. Brendon has packed a great deal of high and low living into the past decade, driving tractors in the UK, then managing a chalet in Val d'Isere (in the French Alps) for eight months. Bouncing between Australia and NZ before working a vintage in California with the well-known Paul Hobbs, he then helped Paul set up a winery in Argentina. Brendon's tag-line is 'wines made with love, not money', and he has not hesitated to confound the normal rules of engagement in winemaking. If he isn't remembered for this, the labels for his wines should do the trick. Exports to the UK, the US, Canada, Singapore, Hong Kong and Japan.

🍷🍷🍷🍷🍷 **Swaby Single Vineyard Piccadilly Valley Chardonnay 2014** Miserable yield, only three barrels made; picked for acid, not sugar; whole bunch-pressed, matured for 10 months in French oak (30% new), stirred for 9 months. Bright green-straw; it has a very complex, deliberately funky bouquet, and draws saliva from the mouth long after it has been swallowed, lively citrussy acidity the final phase of a very high quality chardonnay. Screwcap. 12.5% alc. **Rating** 96 To 2024 $55 ✪
One Ball Single Vineyard Kenton Valley Adelaide Hills Chardonnay 2014 Brendon Keys provides his chardonnay with a level of flavour, texture and structure he chooses not to achieve with his red wines. Mind you, the barrel fermentation here has been controlled from start to finish, likewise the amount of new oak; the white peach and grapefruit core has wisps of cashew verging on creamy, acidity a given. Screwcap. 12.5% alc. **Rating** 95 To 2024 $32 ✪
Saignee of Pinot Noir Lenswood Adelaide Hills Rose 2015 Wild-fermented, 4 months in used oak on lees. Pale salmon-pink; fresh, lively and juicy; strawberries and (a little) cream, dusted with spice. Balanced acidity is a feature, as is length. Screwcap. 12.5% alc. **Rating** 94 To 2017 $25 ✪
Gower Single Vineyard Lenswood Pinot Noir 2014 Tiny yield, 60% less than usual; 30% whole bunches (but few berries per bunch, so effectively 70% whole bunches), 1 month on skins, wild-fermented in French oak (30% new), matured for 10 months. Has excellent colour, clear and bright; the palate is full-bodied in pinot terms, but is not the least extractive; the balance is unquestioned, but the wine pleads for another 2–3 years in bottle to allow the perfume and spice components to grow. Screwcap. 12.5% alc. **Rating** 94 To 2026 $55

ŶŶŶŶŶ Archer Beau Single Barrel Piccadilly Valley Adelaide Hills Chardonnay
2014 Rating 92 To 2024 $85
Ovum Single Vineyard Lenswood Pinot Gris 2014 Rating 92 To 2016 $32
Sparks Blewitt Springs Grenache 2014 Rating 92 To 2020 $55
Inox Lenswood Adelaide Hills Pinot Grigio 2015 Rating 91 To 2017 $25
Skin n' Bones Lenswood Pinot Noir 2014 Rating 91 To 2020 $32
Lobethal Adelaide Hills Syrah Nouveau 2015 Rating 91 To 2020 $25

Black Bishop Wines ★★★★

1 Valdemar Court, Magill, SA 5072 (postal) **Region** Adelaide Hills
T 0422 791 775 **www.**blackbishopwines.com.au **Open** Not
Winemaker Damon Koerner **Est.** 2012 **Dozens** 2000
Black Bishop was established by three mates from school, Jack Horsnell, Damon Koerner and
Chris Bishop, each 27 years old. Chris has an ongoing love for Barossa Shiraz, and thought that
it made sense to make his own wine rather than purchasing it from others; Damon grew up
in the Watervale district of the Clare Valley, and studied oenology and viticulture at Adelaide
University, working vintages across Australia and abroad since graduation; and Jack grew up
living and working in Adelaide Hills hotels, often drinking ('way') too much local wine. A
successful small vintage from 2012 led to a significantly broader portfolio in '13, which must
have brought a smile to their faces.

ŶŶŶŶŶ Single Vineyard Barossa Valley Shiraz 2014 Barossa shiraz at 13% alcohol
is rare. Plums, cherry and a nice spicy edge to the bouquet. Soft, accessible and
particularly drinkable. Screwcap. 13% alc. **Rating** 93 To 2030 $25
Bish's Barrel Shiraz 2014 A 40yo single vineyard selection from Vine Vale,
spending 24 months in French oak. Spice and black fruits lead to a rounded and
finely grained palate. Screwcap. 13% alc. **Rating** 92 To 2024 $40
Single Vineyard Watervale Riesling 2015 Pale straw; this wine has classic lime
and citrus blossom with nice purity, leading to a relatively tighter weight palate.
A touch grippy to close. Screwcap. 12.7% alc. **Rating** 90 To 2026 $25

BlackJack Vineyards ★★★★☆

Cnr Blackjack Road/Calder Highway, Harcourt, Vic 3453 **Region** Bendigo
T (03) 5474 2355 **www.**blackjackwines.com.au **Open** W'ends & most public hols 11–5
Winemaker Ian McKenzie, Ken Pollock **Est.** 1987 **Dozens** 4000 **Vyds** 6ha
Established by the McKenzie and Pollock families on the site of an old apple and pear orchard
in the Harcourt Valley, Blackjack is best known for some very good Shirazs. Despite some
tough vintage conditions, BlackJack has managed to continue to produce supremely honest,
full-flavoured and powerful wines, all with a redeeming edge of elegance. Exports to Canada
and China.

ŶŶŶŶŶ Bendigo Shiraz 2013 In a word: beautiful. Rich but silken, awash with pure,
dark-berried flavour but admirably aided by savoury inputs and a sheer coating of
creamy oak. That its (gently peppery) tannin moves in perfect formation through
the back half of the wine is no small bonus. Screwcap. 13.5% alc. **Rating** 95
To 2030 $38 CM
Block 6 Bendigo Shiraz 2013 With each release this wine seems to find a new
level of elegance, yet it remains ripe and flavoursome. There's no tar or blackberry
here, it's cherried and plummy, and while there are gum leaf notes, there are also
elements of cracked pepper, wood smoke and fennel root, with tangy acidity
ringing through the finish. It's inherently complex but upfront fruitiness is still
there to be enjoyed. Screwcap. 13.5% alc. **Rating** 94 To 2028 $38 CM

ŶŶŶŶŶ Bendigo Cabernet Merlot 2013 Rating 91 To 2024 $28 CM

Blaxland Vineyards

2948 Barossa Valley Way, Tanunda, SA 5352 **Region** Barossa Valley
T (08) 8304 8879 **www.**blaxwine.com.au **Open** 7 days 10–5
Winemaker Chris Polymiadis **Est.** 1995 **Dozens** 150 000 **Vyds** 675ha

Founder and owner Ron Collins has prospered mightily given the headwinds that have buffeted the Australian wine industry over the past decade. Blaxland Vineyards is the 12th-largest vineyard proprietor in Australia; it owns the 320ha Tanunda Hill Vineyard in the Barossa Valley, the 266ha Old Mundulla Vineyard in the Limestone Coast, and the 89ha St Magnus Vineyard in the Adelaide Hills. It has side-stepped the cost of establishing a winery by forming ongoing arrangements with leading wineries to make its wines meeting its cost criteria, overseen by Chris Polymiadis. The wines have enjoyed considerable success in overseas wine shows, notably in China, California and Germany. The value for money is self-evident. Exports to UK, US, China and Japan.

ŶŶŶŶŶ Barossa Valley Shiraz 2014 Extended post-ferment maceration was followed by maturation in 1yo French oak for 6 months. Dense and deep, but vivid, crimson-purple hue; an impressive wine at the price, with real aspirations to elegance, French oak playing a role on both the bouquet and the light to medium-bodied palate; both black (predominant) and red fruits are associated with a pinch of spice, supported by fine tannins. Screwcap. 14.5% alc. **Rating** 92 **To** 2029 $24 **۞**

Bleasdale Vineyards

1640 Langhorne Creek Road, Langhorne Creek, SA 5255 **Region** Langhorne Creek
T (08) 8537 4000 **www.**bleasdale.com.au **Open** Mon–Sun 10–5
Winemaker Paul Hotker, Matt Laube **Est.** 1850 **Dozens** 100 000 **Vyds** 49ha

This is one of the most historic wineries in Australia, in 2015 celebrating 165 years of continuous winemaking by the direct descendants of the Potts founding family. Not so long prior to the start of the 21st century, its vineyards were flooded every winter by diversion of the Bremer River, which provided moisture throughout the dry, cool, growing season. In the new millennium, every drop of water was counted. The vineyards have been significantly upgraded and refocused, with shiraz accounting for 45% of plantings, supported by seven other proven varieties. Bleasdale has completely revamped its labels and packaging, and has headed to the Adelaide Hills for sauvignon blanc, pinot gris and chardonnay under the direction of gifted winemaker (and viticulturist) Paul Hotker. Exports to all major markets.

ŶŶŶŶŶ The Iron Duke Langhorne Creek Cabernet Sauvignon 2012 Deep crimson-purple; an immaculately crafted cabernet, ticking every box; while the blackcurrant fruit is first and foremost on the fragrant bouquet and perfectly balanced and constructed full-bodied palate, it's far from a one-trick pony. Since first tasted in Jan '15 it has grown another leg, with a quite different outcome in its style – but not its points. Screwcap. 14.5% alc. **Rating** 97 **To** 2037 $65 **۞**

ŶŶŶŶŶ Bremerview Langhorne Creek Shiraz 2014 15% whole berries, short cold soak, 9–12 days on skins, pressed to new (15%) and used French oak. Top gold National Wine Show '15, gold Adelaide Wine Show and Melbourne Wine Awards. This is right in the heart of medium-bodied shiraz, black cherry, plum and blackberry fruits encased in a silken web of tannins, and a fleeting glimpse of French oak. Yes, it's $20. Screwcap. 14% alc. **Rating** 96 **To** 2030 $20 **۞**
Generations Langhorne Creek Shiraz 2014 Matured for 12 months in new (24%) and used French oak, gold medal Queensland Wine Show '15. The aromas and flavours offer a layered canvas of spice, licorice, black cherry and plum, the frame easily provided by ripe, soft tannins and French oak. Its balance will probably mean most is consumed before it reaches its full potential. Screwcap. 14% alc. **Rating** 96 **To** 2034 $35 **۞**
Frank Potts 2014 61% cabernet sauvignon, 18% malbec, 9% merlot, 8% petit verdot, 4% cabernet franc, gold medal National Wine Show '15. Almost nonchalantly floods the mouth with blackcurrant and plum, the texture mesmeric,

focusing on the fruit, yet providing the edge of tannin that is an integral part of the quality of the wine. Screwcap. 14% alc. **Rating** 96 **To** 2034 $35 **✪**

The Powder Monkey Single Vineyard Langhorne Creek Shiraz 2014
Open-fermented, 15% whole berries, short cold soak, 9–12 days on skins, matured for 12 months in French oak (27% new), two gold medals. Deep crimson-purple; resplendent in its generosity with plum and blackberry leading the juicy fruits, licorice, spice and soft tannins all singing the same song. Screwcap. 14% alc. **Rating** 95 **To** 2034 $65

Generations Langhorne Creek Malbec 2014 Open-fermented, 20% whole berries, 3 days' cold soak, 12 days on skins, matured for 12 months in new (12%) and used French oak, gold medal Six Nations Wine Challenge (beating Argentina's best). The bouquet is spicy and almost flowery (violets); plum is the leader of the fruit band; oak adds to the proceedings, and the tannins complete the story. Screwcap. 14.5% alc. **Rating** 95 **To** 2034 $35 **✪**

Adelaide Hills Chardonnay 2015 Clones 76, 95 and Mendoza, wild yeast solids fermentation in French puncheons (25% new), partial mlf and 9 months' maturation. Skilled winemaking has left the wine bright and crisp, not in sauvignon blanc territory; it is light-bodied, but white peach and grapefruit varietal flavours hold the floor, not oak or vanilla pod mlf. Will flower over the next 2–3 years. Screwcap. 13% alc. **Rating** 94 **To** 2023 $25 **✪**

Adelaide Hills Pinot Gris 2015 Hand-picked, whole bunch-pressed, part fermented in tank, part in used French puncheons. In the same class as its best predecessors, with a textural complexity seldom achieved outside Alsace, and a convincing display of nashi pear and crunchy green apples fresh from the tree. Screwcap. 13% alc. **Rating** 94 **To** 2019 $19 **✪**

The Petrel Langhorne Creek Shiraz Cabernet Malbec 2014 59/32/9%, open-fermented, 11–15 days on skins, matured for 12 months in French oak (25% new). The bones of its structure and attitude are more obvious than most plush Langhorne Creek red wines, but if you wonder, as I did, what the result would be, the long, focused finish and aftertaste swept my reservations out the back door. Screwcap. 14% alc. **Rating** 94 **To** 2034 $30 **✪**

The Iron Duke Langhorne Creek Cabernet Sauvignon 2013 Open-fermented, 8–12 days on skins, matured for 12 months in French oak (25% new), one trophy, three gold medals. Deep crimson-purple; the Iron Duke indeed; a full-bodied cabernet taking no prisoners. Don't fight, you won't win. Just find a cool, dark place, leave it there for a minimum of 20 years and then start the discussion. Screwcap. 14% alc. **Rating** 94 **To** 2036 $65

Second Innings Langhorne Creek Malbec 2014 Open-fermented, 15% whole berries for 3 days' cold soak, 12 days on skins, matured for 12 months in new (10%) and used French oak. The structure is tighter than that of its Generations sibling, and I'm not too sure I don't prefer this wine, its freshness, balance and fine, savoury tannins all in harmonious balance. Screwcap. 14% alc. **Rating** 94 **To** 2024 $20 **✪**

♀♀♀♀♀ Mulberry Tree Cabernet Sauvignon 2014 Rating 92 To 2024 $20 **✪**
Langhorne Creek Sparkling Shiraz NV Rating 92 To 2018 $23 TS **✪**
Adelaide Hills Sauvignon Blanc 2015 Rating 91 To 2016 $19 **✪**

Bloodwood ★★★★★

231 Griffin Road, Orange, NSW 2800 **Region** Orange
T (02) 6362 5631 **www.**bloodwood.biz **Open** By appt
Winemaker Stephen Doyle **Est.** 1983 **Dozens** 4000 **Vyds** 8.43ha
Rhonda and Stephen Doyle are two of the pioneers of the Orange district, 2013 marking Bloodwood's 30th anniversary. The estate vineyards (chardonnay, riesling, merlot, cabernet sauvignon, shiraz, cabernet franc and malbec) are planted at an elevation of 810–860m, which provides a reliably cool climate. The wines are sold mainly through the cellar door and by an energetic, humorous and informatively run mailing list (see, for example, the tasting note for Big Men in Tights). Has an impressive track record across the full gamut of varietal (and

other) wine styles, especially Riesling; all of the wines have a particular elegance and grace. Very much part of the high quality reputation of Orange.

♈♈♈♈♈ Shiraz 2013 Hand-picked, one-third wild yeast open-fermented and hand-plunged, the remainder with cultured yeast in tank, matured in French oak for 18 months. The black fruits of the bouquet are liberally enriched with black pepper and licorice, then strengthened and given texture by gently savoury, fine tannins on the long, medium-bodied palate. Screwcap. 14% alc. **Rating** 95 To 2033 $28 **○**

Riesling 2015 Hand-picked, whole bunch-pressed, cool-fermented to dryness with cultured yeast, matured on fine lees in tank for 6 months. Good wine, with all the requisites of lime/citrus fruit aroma and flavour backed by citrussy acidity. Screwcap. 12.5% alc. **Rating** 94 To 2025 $25 **○**

Chardonnay 2015 Whole bunch-pressed, 25% cool-fermented in barrel and taken through mlf. In Orange territory, grapefruit and white peach are joined at the hip, barrel-ferment oak also relevant to the shaping of the wine; the balance and length are on the money. Screwcap. 12.5% alc. **Rating** 94 To 2023 $28 **○**

Cabernet Franc 2014 Planted as merlot before its true identity was discovered, but the variety and place have grown used to each other. Hand-picked and destemmed, not crushed, giving some maceration carbonique nuances; matured for 12 months in French hogsheads (30% new). It has a distinctive blend of blackcurrant and raspberry along with some flowery aromas, the finish supported by fine, yet firm, tannins. Screwcap. 13.5% alc. **Rating** 94 To 2024 $30 **○**

♈♈♈♈♉ Big Men in Tights 2015 Rating 93 To 2019 $18 **○**
Merlot Noir 2014 Rating 92 To 2024 $30
Cabernet Sauvignon 2013 Rating 90 To 2023 $28

Blue Pyrenees Estate ★★★★★

Vinoca Road, Avoca, Vic 3467 **Region** Pyrenees
T (03) 5465 1111 **www**.bluepyrenees.com.au **Open** Mon–Fri 10–4.30, w'ends 10–5
Winemaker Andrew Koerner, Chris Smales **Est.** 1963 **Dozens** 60 000 **Vyds** 149ha
Forty years after Remy Cointreau established Blue Pyrenees Estate (then known as Chateau Remy), the business was sold to a small group of Sydney businessmen. Former Rosemount senior winemaker Andrew Koerner heads the winery team. The core of the business is the very large estate plantings, most decades old, but with newer arrivals, including viognier. Blue Pyrenees has a number of programs designed to protect the environment and reduce its carbon footprint. Exports to Asia, primarily China.

♈♈♈♈♈ Section One Shiraz 2013 Formerly labelled 'Reserve', from the oldest (40yo) section of the vineyard, includes 2% viognier and 1% cabernet sauvignon co-fermented in open and closed fermenters, 2 weeks on skins, matured in new and used French and American oak (40% new) for 24 months. Four trophies plus two gold medals, all from the Riverina or Western Victoria Wine Shows. This is an attractive single block selection, medium-bodied shiraz with good oak and tannin management, and perfectly ripe fruit. Screwcap. 14.5% alc. **Rating** 95 To 2033 $36

Richardson Cabernet Sauvignon 2013 Honours the larger (by some distance) than life, much loved, figure of the late Colin Richardson. The colour is deep, but bright, and the medium to full-bodied wine ticks each and every box: great varietal expression, immaculately balanced cabernet tannins, quality French oak, and great length; seamless blackcurrant and bay leaf flavours are the order of the day. Screwcap. 14% alc. **Rating** 95 To 2043 $50

Richardson Shiraz 2013 It has good depth to its colour, and has clearly been matured in high quality oak; thanks to its full body, the blackberry, plum and spice/pepper flavours have absorbed the oak, assisted by the ripe tannins that do not detract from the overall juicy mouthfeel. Colin Richardson would have enjoyed this wine. Screwcap. 14.5% alc. **Rating** 94 To 2043 $50

Cabernet Sauvignon 2013 Includes 6% merlot and 3% cabernet franc, matured for 18 months in French and American barriques (12% new). The tannins are significantly softer than they were when first tasted in Mar '15, giving free rein to the blackcurrant fruit that leads the way. A very attractive wine is the result. Screwcap. 14% alc. **Rating** 94 **To** 2033 $20 ✪

🍷🍷🍷🍷🍷 **Pinot Noir Dry Rose 2015 Rating** 92 **To** 2018 $18 ✪
Shiraz 2013 Rating 92 **To** 2033 $20 ✪
Champ Blend Blanc 2014 Rating 90 **To** 2021 $32

Boat O'Craigo   ★★★★

458 Maroondah Highway, Healesville, Vic 3777 **Region** Yarra Valley
T (03) 5962 6899 **www.boatocraigo.com.au Open** Fri–Sun 10.30–5.30
Winemaker Rob Dolan (Contract) **Est.** 1998 **Dozens** 3000 **Vyds** 21.63ha
Steve Graham purchased the property, which is now known as Boat O'Craigo (a tiny place in a Scottish valley where his ancestors lived), in 2003. It has two quite separate vineyards: a hillside planting on one of the highest sites in the Yarra Valley, and one at Kangaroo Ground on the opposite side of the Valley. The winery has now passed on to Steve's eldest son, Travers, who is anxious to reinvigorate the brand, explore new grape varieties and wine styles, while simultaneously upgrading the cellar door. Exports to Hong Kong and China.

🍷🍷🍷🍷🍷 **Black Spur Healesville Yarra Valley Chardonnay 2015** It doesn't put a foot wrong. Sweet fruit with savoury nuances. Spicy oak, but fully integrated. A wash of juicy acidity. And clear, clean lines from start to finish. It's part of the new breed of sunny sophistication. Screwcap. 13.5% alc. **Rating** 94 **To** 2021 $28 CM ✪

🍷🍷🍷🍷🍷 **Black Cameron Shiraz 2013 Rating** 93 **To** 2024 $30 CM
Black Spur Gewurztraminer 2015 Rating 91 **To** 2017 $25 CM
Braveheart Cabernet Sauvignon 2013 Rating 91 **To** 2023 $30 CM
Black Spur Pinot Noir 2015 Rating 90 **To** 2021 $30 CM

Boireann   ★★★★★

26 Donnellys Castle Road, The Summit, Qld 4377 **Region** Granite Belt
T (07) 4683 2194 **www.boireannwinery.com.au Open** Fri–Sun 10–4
Winemaker Peter Stark **Est.** 1998 **Dozens** 1200 **Vyds** 1.6ha
Peter and Therese Stark have a 10ha property set among the great granite boulders and trees that are so much a part of the Granite Belt. They have planted no fewer than 11 varieties, including four that go to make the Lurnea, a Bordeaux blend; shiraz and viognier; grenache and mourvedre providing a Rhône blend; and a straight merlot. Tannat, pinot noir (French) and sangiovese, barbera and nebbiolo (Italian) make up the viticultural League of Nations. Peter is a winemaker of exceptional talent, producing cameo amounts of quite beautifully made red wines that are of a quality equal to Australia's best. Peter says he has decided to think about retiring, and has listed the property for sale.

🍷🍷🍷🍷🍷 **Granite Belt Shiraz Viognier 2014** Estate-grown, the viognier co-fermented with shiraz for 6 days before going to French oak (50% new). Vigneron Peter Stark has always proved his skills as a self-taught winemaker, but this takes Boireann onto another level, with the depth and power of the fusion of red and black fruits, firm tannins and French oak. Its balance is faultless, its future assured. Screwcap. 13.5% alc. **Rating** 96 **To** 2039 $65 ✪
The Lurnea 2014 Classic Bordeaux blend of 40% merlot, 36% cabernet sauvignon, 14% petit verdot and 10% cabernet franc, hand-picked, destemmed and crushed, open-fermented with cultured yeast, 1 week on skins, fermentation finished in barrel, matured in French oak (25% new) for 12 months. The colour is faultless, the bouquet fragrant, the complex palate with cassis, dried herb and black olive flavours, the oak handling impeccable, the length and balance remarkable. Screwcap. 14% alc. **Rating** 96 **To** 2034 $30 ✪

La Cima Superiore Granite Belt Barbera 2014 Destemmed and crushed, open-fermented with cultured yeast, 1 week on skins, fermentation finished in barrel. This takes its sibling onto another level, 98 octane fuel compared with standard unleaded: everything from the depth of colour, depth of fruit flavours, tannins, texture and structure to length. This is no smoothie: it's a Latin lover hot on the trail of a mate. Screwcap. 14% alc. **Rating** 96 **To** 2030 $45 **○**

Granite Belt Shiraz 2014 Hand-picked, destemmed and crushed, open-fermented with cultured yeast, 1 week on skins, fermentation finished in barrel. The only thing wrong with this wine is the price – it's far too low. The crimson-purple colour, the scented spice and cherry bouquet and the vibrant medium-bodied palate all follow each other in perfect unison; the texture and drive of the finish is exemplary. Screwcap. 13.5% alc. **Rating** 95 **To** 2034 $28 **○**

La Cima Granite Belt Nebbiolo 2014 Destemmed and crushed, open-fermented with cultured yeast, 2 weeks' post-ferment maceration, matured in used French oak for 12 months. Bright hue, clear and inviting, is not a trap for the unwary; while the varietal character of crunchy red berries is here in abundance, the tannins are as rare as, and akin to, well-behaved small children. They are part of the nebbiolo storyline, and do the job to perfection. Screwcap. 14% alc. **Rating** 95 **To** 2024 $45

La Cima Granite Belt Barbera 2014 Destemmed and crushed, open-fermented with cultured yeast, 1 week on skins, fermentation finished in barrel. Good depth and hue; you know you are enjoying the flavour of this wine before you have attempted to analyse and describe it: it's a plum and red cherry smoothie with a fresh cleansing finish. Screwcap. 14% alc. **Rating** 94 **To** 2020 $28 **○**

Granite Belt Mourvedre 2014 Hand-picked, destemmed and crushed, open-fermented with cultured yeast, 1 week on skins, fermentation finished in barrel. Has the usual, indeed invariable, impeccable crimson hue of Boireann's wines; it is fully ripe, with dusty tannins lined up in support of its black fruits. Managing this ever-increasing tribe of wines under the Boireann banner must place Peter Stark in the same position as a contract winemaker dealing with a miniature army of vignerons all demanding attention at the same time. Screwcap. 14% alc. **Rating** 94 **To** 2029 $40

♟♟♟♟♟ **Granite Belt Cabernet Sauvignon 2014** Rating 93 To 2024 $28
La Cima Rosso 2014 Rating 92 To 2029 $28
Granite Belt Tannat 2014 Rating 92 To 2030 $45
La Cima Granite Belt Sangiovese 2014 Rating 90 To 2025 $40

🍇 Bondar Wines   ★★★★★

Rayner Vineyard, 24 Twentyeight Road, McLaren Vale, SA 5171 **Region** McLaren Vale
T 0419 888 303 **www**.bondarwines.com.au **Open** By appt
Winemaker Andre Bondar **Est.** 2013 **Dozens** 500 **Vyds** 11ha
Husband and wife Selina Kelly and Andre Bondar began a deliberately unhurried journey in 2009, which culminated in the purchase of the celebrated Rayner Vineyard post-vintage '13. Andre had been a winemaker at Nepenthe wines for 7 years, and Selina had recently completed a law degree, but was already somewhat disillusioned about the legal landscape. They changed focus, and began to look for a vineyard capable of producing great shiraz. The Rayner Vineyard had all the answers, a ridge bisecting the land, Blewitt Springs sand on the eastern side, and the Seaview, heavier clay loam soils over limestone on the western side. They are continuing to close-plant counoise, and mataro, carignan and cinsaut will follow. An Adelaide Hills Syrah is in their sights. Exports to the UK.

♟♟♟♟♟ **Adelaide Hills Chardonnay 2015** Dijon clone, hand-picked, pressed straight to French oak (25% new) for wild fermentation, matured on lees with stirring for 9 months. The extreme drive and intensity of the wine is terrific, the fruit flavours of white peach and pink grapefruit dominant. A first-class example of the new style of chardonnay. Screwcap. 13% alc. **Rating** 95 **To** 2025 $32 **○**

Violet Hour McLaren Vale Shiraz 2013 From a sandy Blewitt Springs vineyard similar to Bondar's Rayner Vineyard, hand-picked, with a small proportion retained as whole bunches in a wild yeast, gently extracted, fermentation, matured for 14 months in French hogsheads (20% new) on lees, not fined or filtered. There are complex aromas and flavours spread on a complex canvas of red, purple, blue and black fruits on the medium to full-bodied palate. Given its price, the Trophy for Best Shiraz $25–$50 at the McLaren Vale Wine Show '15 is doubly impressive. Screwcap. 14% alc. **Rating** 95 **To** 2030 $28
Rayner Vineyard Grenache 2015 From a 0.7ha block planted on sand, Bondar selected the lowest-yielding vines, hand-picking two batches; one (75%) spent 35 days on skins, the other 9 days, cool-fermented to add aromatics, matured for 6 months in used hogsheads. The bouquet is indeed strikingly fruity, but no confection, the palate is firm, with as much dark as red fruit, the overall balance and extract strikingly good. A grenache that will live and live. Screwcap. 14.5% alc. **Rating** 95 **To** 2035 $38

♟♟♟♟♟ Junto McLaren Vale GSM 2014 **Rating** 93 **To** 2024 $25
Adelaide Hills Chardonnay 2014 **Rating** 90 **To** 2018 $32

Bonking Frog ★★★
7 Dardanup West Road, North Boyanup, WA 6237 **Region** Geographe
T 0408 930 332 **www.**bonkingfrog.com.au **Open** Fri–Sun 12–5
Winemaker Naturaliste Vintners (Bruce Dukes) **Est.** 1996 **Dozens** 1200 **Vyds** 3ha
Julie and Phil Hutton put their money where their hearts are, electing to plant a merlot-only vineyard in 1996. Presumably knowing the unpredictable habits of merlot when planted on its own roots, they began by planting 3500 Swartzman rootstock vines, and then 12 months later field-grafting the merlot scion material. Small wonder their backs are still aching. I don't doubt for a millisecond the sincerity of their enthusiasm for the variety when they say, 'Fruity, plummy, smooth and velvety. Hints of chocolate too. If you're new to wine and all things merlot, this is a wonderful variety to explore.' And the frogs? Well they bonk – loudly.

♟♟♟♟ Summer Geographe Merlot Rose 2015 Bright coloured and flavoured, with raspberry, strawberry and twiggy cherries doing the heavy lifting. It's fruity and ripe but finishes dry. Screwcap. 13% alc. **Rating** 89 **To** 2016 $22 CM
Foreigner Margaret River Semillon Sauvignon Blanc 2015 Sweaty and a bit disjointed but it packs plenty of tropical fruit flavour into the package. So, many will enjoy it. Screwcap. 12.5% alc. **Rating** 88 **To** 2017 $22 CM

🍃 Born & Raised ★★★★
33 Bangaroo Street, North Balgowlah, NSW 2093 (postal) **Region** Various Vic
T 0413 860 369 **www.**bornandraisedwines.com.au **Open** Not
Winemaker David Messum **Est.** 2012 **Dozens** 1000
David and Helen Messum have covered a fair bit of ground in relatively quick time since starting specalised wine and hospitality marketing agency Just a Drop in 2009. Interaction with David's clients led him to the conclusion that he should be making wine as well as finding ways for others to market their wines. Part of the realisation came from working with hipster winery Pyramid Valley and major quality-oriented producer Craggy Range, known around the world. David likes to dabble in wild ferments, odd varietal couplings, sometimes staying in the realm of conventionally made wine (wild yeast is no big deal these days) and at times going way out as he did with his 2014 Sauvignon Blanc, which spent 104 days on skins. David makes the wines in rented space at Galli Estate in Sunbury.

♟♟♟♟♟ Heathcote Grenache 2014 From the Willoughby Bridge Vineyard, hand-picked, destemmed and crushed, wild open ferment followed by 30 days on skins, basket-pressed, 13 months in French barriques (15% new), unfiltered, 6 barriques made. Very youthful, clear and bright hue; intense, juicy red berry/cherry fruit with a spicy background, and a crisp acid finish. Very attractive summer red. Screwcap. 14.3% alc. **Rating** 94 **To** 2020 $35

♟♟♟♟♟ The Super T 2013 Rating 93 To 2028 $35
Sauvignon Blanc 2015 Rating 90 To 2016 $27
The Chance Field Blend 2015 Rating 90 To 2018 $24

Bowen Estate   ★★★★☆

15459 Riddoch Highway, Coonawarra, SA 5263 **Region** Coonawarra
T (08) 8737 2229 **www**.bowenestate.com.au **Open** 7 days 10–5
Winemaker Emma Bowen **Est.** 1972 **Dozens** 12000 **Vyds** 33ha
Bluff-faced regional veteran Doug Bowen presides over one of Coonawarra's landmarks
but he has handed over full winemaking responsibility to daughter Emma, 'retiring' to the
position of viticulturist. In May 2015 Bowen Estate celebrated its 40th vintage with a tasting
of 24 wines (Shiraz and Cabernet Sauvignon) from 1975 to 2014. Exports to the Maldives,
Singapore, China, Japan and NZ.

♟♟♟♟♟ **Coonawarra Cabernet Sauvignon 2014** There's pure blackcurrant fruit
opening the batting on both the bouquet and medium-bodied palate, with
mulberry, Coonawarra earth, cedar, a wisp of mint and a flash of red berry joining
the dots. Doesn't demand time it's so well balanced, but will certainly enjoy its
10th birthday. Screwcap. 14.5% alc. **Rating** 96 To 2040 $33 **✪**

♟♟♟♟♟ **Coonawarra Shiraz 2014** Rating 91 To 2040 $33

Bowman's Run   ★★★☆

1305 Beechworth-Wodonga Road, Wooragee, Vic 3747 **Region** Beechworth
T (03) 5728 7318 **Open** By appt
Winemaker Daniel Balzer **Est.** 1989 **Dozens** 150 **Vyds** 1ha
Struan and Fran Robertson have cabernet sauvignon, riesling and small plots of shiraz and
traminer dating back to 1989. The tiny winery is part of a larger general agricultural holding.

♟♟♟♟♟ **Creek Flat Beechworth Shiraz 2013** Light to medium-weight but with ample
personality. Beef stock, black cherry, earth and deli meat characters give you plenty
to contemplate. Spearmint notes rise as the wine breathes. Plays its own game in
attractive fashion. Screwcap. 13.5% alc. **Rating** 91 To 2024 $35 CM

♟♟♟♟ **Granite Rise Cabernet Sauvignon 2012** Rating 89 To 2022 $30 CM
Seven Springs Beechworth Riesling 2015 Rating 88 To 2020 $30 CM
Jessie's Rock Beechworth Rose 2015 Rating 88 To 2017 $25 CM

Box Grove Vineyard   ★★★★☆

955 Avenel-Nagambie Road, Tablik, Vic 3607 **Region** Nagambie Lakes
T 0409 210 015 **www**.boxgrovevineyard.com.au **Open** By appt
Winemaker Sarah Gough **Est.** 1995 **Dozens** 2500 **Vyds** 31ha
This is the venture of the Gough family, with industry veteran (and daughter) Sarah Gough
managing the vineyard, winemaking and marketing. Having started with 10ha each of shiraz
and cabernet sauvignon under contract to Brown Brothers, Sarah decided to switch the focus
of the business to what could loosely be called 'Mediterranean varieties'. These days prosecco,
vermentino, primitivo and roussanne (roussanne as both a table wine and a sparkling) are the
main varieties, plus shiraz and cabernet sauvignon from the original plantings. Exports to
Singapore and China.

♟♟♟♟♟ **Roussanne 2013** Wild yeast barrel fermentation and long ageing on lees have
produced a beautifully pure and expressive roussanne. Pear, florals and a hint of
fennel lead to a tightly wound mineral palate that has layers of flavour and texture,
and admirable length. Screwcap. 13% alc. **Rating** 95 To 2022 $28 **✪**
Late Harvest Viognier 2015 This is mission impossible, yet Sarah Gough has
brought it as close to success as anyone else. It has varietal character (apricot and

peach) and citrussy acidity; the finish is not, repeat not, soapy or flat. I'd still be inclined to drink it soon. 500ml. Screwcap. 10.8% alc. **Rating** 94 **To** 2018 $22 **O**

ŸŸŸŸŸ **Primitivo Saignee 2015 Rating** 90 **To** 2017 $22

Brand's Laira Coonawarra ★★★★★

14860 Riddoch Highway, Coonawarra, SA 5263 **Region** Coonawarra
T (08) 8736 3260 **www.**brandslaira.com.au **Open** Mon–Fri 9–4.30, w'ends 11–4
Winemaker Peter Weinberg, Amy Blackburn **Est.** 1966 **Dozens** NFP **Vyds** 278ha
Three days before Christmas 2015, Casella Family Brands received an early present when it purchased Brand's Laira from McWilliams. Over the years McWilliam's had moved from 50% to 100% ownership of Brand's and thereafter purchased an additional 100ha of vineyards (taking Brand's to its present 278ha) and had expanded both the size of and the quality of the winery. Exports to select markets.

ŸŸŸŸŸ **Stentiford's Shiraz 2013** Bright crimson-purple; 110yo vines don't necessarily result in powerful fruit (and wine), but they certainly do here; it is brimful of blackberry, licorice, warm spices and French oak, the conclusion of primary fermentation taking place in that oak (new and used) and gaining the integration and mouthfeel only this technique provides. A final barrel selection produced an exceptional wine. Screwcap. 13.5% alc. **Rating** 97 **To** 2048 $75 **O**
One Seven One Cabernet Sauvignon 2013 Great colour; already so juicy, awash with cassis, it can be enjoyed now, although this has been made with the future in mind. The tannins have been polished, and already sit elegantly in the armchair of fruit and oak; it is the finish that puts this into a class of its own. Screwcap. 13.5% alc. **Rating** 97 **To** 2048 $76 **O**

ŸŸŸŸŸ **Foundation Chardonnay 2014 Rating** 93 **To** 2022 $23 **O**
Old Station Riesling 2015 Rating 91 **To** 2025 $20 **O**
August Tide Dry Red 2013 Rating 90 **To** 2023 $28

Brangayne of Orange ★★★★☆

837 Pinnacle Road, Orange, NSW 2800 **Region** Orange
T (02) 6365 3229 **www.**brangayne.com **Open** Mon–Fri 11–4, Sat 11–5, Sun 11–4
Winemaker Simon Gilbert **Est.** 1994 **Dozens** 3000 **Vyds** 25.7ha
The Hoskins family (formerly orchardists) moved into grapegrowing in 1994 and have progressively established high quality vineyards. Brangayne produces excellent wines across all mainstream varieties, ranging, remarkably, from Pinot Noir to Cabernet Sauvignon. It sells a substantial part of its crop to other winemakers. Exports to China.

ŸŸŸŸŸ **Isolde Reserve Chardonnay 2014** Seamless. Elegant. Confident. There are any number of apt words to describe it and they all point to its quality. It's not in your face or overt but it presents stone fruit, melon, honeysuckle and lactose flavours with such effortless conviction that you can't but help admire it. Screwcap. 13% alc. **Rating** 94 **To** 2021 $30 CM **O**

ŸŸŸŸŸ **Pinot Grigio 2015 Rating** 93 **To** 2017 $20 CM **O**
Cabernet Sauvignon 2013 Rating 93 **To** 2032 $35 CM
Sauvignon Blanc 2015 Rating 92 **To** 2017 $22 CM **O**
Shiraz 2013 Rating 92 **To** 2025 $32 CM
Late Harvest Riesling 2015 Rating 91 **To** 2022 $24 CM
Pinot Noir 2014 Rating 90 **To** 2021 $35 CM

Brash Higgins ★★★★★

California Road, McLaren Vale, SA 5171 **Region** McLaren Vale
T (08) 8556 4237 **www.**brashhiggins.com **Open** By appt
Winemaker Brad Hickey **Est.** 2010 **Dozens** 1000 **Vyds** 7ha

Move over TWE's 'vintrepreneurs', for Brad Hickey has come up with 'creator' and 'vinitor' to cover his role (together with that of partner Nicole Thorpe) in establishing Brash Higgins. His varied background, including 10 years as head sommelier at some of the best New York restaurants, then a further 10 years of baking, brewing and travelling to the best-known wine regions of the world, may provide some clue. More tangibly, he planted 4ha of shiraz, 2ha of cabernet sauvignon, and recently grafted 1ha of shiraz to nero d'Avola on his Omensetter Vineyard looking over the Willunga Escarpment. Export to the US and Canada.

TTTTT SHZ Site Specific McLaren Vale Shiraz 2014 Glorious shiraz to drink and admire. Tannin, fruit, length and personality. It rolls into town and promptly takes over. Blackberry and roasted plums, florals and cedary oak. Bright fruit belies its deep, dark heart. If you're going to push ripeness, this is how to do it. Diam. 14.9% alc. **Rating** 95 **To** 2035 $37 CM
GR/M Co-Ferment McLaren Vale Grenache Mataro 2014 Such a good wine. Flesh, spice, structure and length. Pretty aromas and fruits, fun and inviting, turn seriously savoury and sinewy as the flavour drives through the palate. Elegant and majestic at once. Screwcap. 14.5% alc. **Rating** 95 **To** 2026 $37 CM
Omensetter 2010 85% shiraz, 15% cabernet sauvignon. The wine tastes of blackberried fruit drenched in grainy block coffee. Oak here is as essential to the wine as fruit; always a strange result when the quality of the grapes is meant to be the reason for and purpose of the wine. That said, all the components are undeniably impressive in themselves. Cork permitting, it will mature and develop (positively) for decades. 15% alc. **Rating** 94 **To** 2040 $95 CM
CBSV Site Specific McLaren Vale Cabernet Sauvignon 2014 Basket-pressed before spending 15 months in French oak. Pitch perfect. Full of fruit but fresh; touched by chocolatey oak but only that; curranty but floral; firm but with no halt to the momentum of fruit flavour. Exemplary from start to finish. Screwcap. 14.5% alc. **Rating** 94 **To** 2030 $37 CM

TTTTT NDV Amphora Nero d'Avola 2014 **Rating** 93 **To** 2026 $42 CM
MRLO Lennon Vineyard Merlot 2015 **Rating** 92 **To** 2021 $37 CM
MRLO Lennon Vineyard Merlot 2014 **Rating** 92 **To** 2020 $37 CM
FRNC Sommerville Vineyard McLaren Vale Cabernet Franc 2015 **Rating** 91 **To** 2020 $37 CM

Brash Vineyard   ★★★★☆

PO Box 455, Yallingup, WA 6282 **Region** Margaret River
T 0427 042 767 **www**.brashvineyard.com.au **Open** Not
Winemaker Bruce Dukes (Contract) **Est.** 2000 **Dozens** 1000 **Vyds** 18.35ha
Brash Vineyard was established in 1998 as Woodside Valley Estate. While most of the grapes were sold to other Margaret River producers, Cabernet Sauvignon, Shiraz, Chardonnay and Merlot were made, and in '09 the Cabernet Sauvignon and the Shiraz earned the winery a 5-star rating. It is now owned by Chris and Anne Carter (managing partners, who live and work there), Brian and Anne McGuinness, and Rik and Jenny Nitert. The vineyard is now mature, and is producing high quality fruit.

TTTTT Single Vineyard Margaret River Sauvignon Blanc 2015 Machine-picked at night, 75% crushed and pressed to stainless steel, 25% to new French oak for cultured yeast fermentation and maturation. This has successfully built in texture and structure, focusing on mineral, snow pea and herbal flavours. A sauvignon blanc that will repay time in bottle. Gold medal Melbourne Wine Awards '15. Screwcap. 12.7% alc. **Rating** 95 **To** 2018 $23 ✪
Single Vineyard Margaret River Shiraz 2014 A wine that creeps up on you, initially fresh, cheerful and only just medium-bodied, but offering more food for thought each time you retaste it and try to pin down the myriad of shadowy, spicy notes threaded through the summer-weight doona of the palate. Ready soonish. Screwcap. 13.9% alc. **Rating** 94 **To** 2020 $35

TTTTT Single Vineyard Cabernet Sauvignon 2014 **Rating** 92 **To** 2034 $40

Brave Goose Vineyard

PO Box 852, Seymour, Vic 3660 **Region** Central Victoria Zone
T 0417 553 225 **www.**bravegoosevineyard.com.au **Open** By appt
Winemaker Nina Stocker **Est.** 1988 **Dozens** 200 **Vyds** 6.5ha
The Brave Goose Vineyard was planted in 1988 by former chairman of the Grape & Wine
Research and Development Corporation, Dr John Stocker, and wife Joanne. In 1987 they
found a property on the inside of the Great Dividing Range, near Tallarook, with north-
facing slopes and shallow, weathered ironstone soils. They established 2.5ha each of shiraz and
cabernet sauvignon, and 0.5ha each of merlot, viognier and gamay, selling the majority of the
grapes, but making small amounts of Shiraz, Cabernet Merlot, Merlot, Viognier and Gamay
under the Brave Goose label. The brave goose in question was the sole survivor of a flock put
into the vineyard to repel cockatoos and foxes. Two decades on, Jo and John handed the reins
of the operation to their winemaker daughter Nina and son-in-law John Day.

Shiraz 2014 It has both power and elegance on its side. Spearmint and cherry-
plum flavours build excellent momentum before a finely turned finish. At no point
is succulence sacrificed. Screwcap. 13.5% alc. **Rating** 93 **To** 2026 $25 CM ⦿
Cabernet Merlot 2014 95/5%. 15 days on skins post ferment. Basket-pressed
into 100% used French oak. 50 dozen made. A juicy start leads to a stern finish.
As a young wine it begs to be decanted. Spearmint, redcurrant, twists of briary
herbs, boysenberry. It doesn't feel thick, it feels lively. Or it does right up until the
finish, where slightly coarse tannin takes over. Extra time in bottle won't hurt it.
Screwcap. 13% alc. **Rating** 91 **To** 2028 $25 CM

Braydun Hill Vineyard

38–40 Hepenstal Road, Hackham. SA 5163 **Region** McLaren Vale
T (08) 8382 3023 **www.**braydunhill.com.au **Open** Thurs–Sun & public hols 11–4
Winemaker Rebecca Kennedy **Est.** 2001 **Dozens** 2000 **Vyds** 4.5ha
It is hard to imagine there would be such an interesting (and inspiring) story behind a vineyard
planted between 1998 and '99 by the husband and wife team of Tony Dunn and Carol
Bradley, wishing to get out of growing angora goats and into grapegrowing. The extension
of the business into winemaking was totally unplanned, forced on them by the liquidation of
Normans in late 2001. With humour, courage and perseverance, they have met obstacles and
setbacks which would have caused many to give up. Exports to Canada, Singapore and China.

Single Vineyard Premium McLaren Vale Shiraz 2013 Has an array of medals
from various quarters, some more convincing than others; however, there are no
questions about the regional expression of the wine, which has a thick coating of
dark chocolate wrapped tightly around the full-bodied, but pliant, black fruit core.
Screwcap. 14.9% alc. **Rating** 94 **To** 2029 $35

Bream Creek

Marion Bay Road, Bream Creek, Tas 7175 **Region** Southern Tasmania
T (03) 6231 4646 **www.**breamcreekvineyard.com.au **Open** At Dunalley Waterfront Cafe
Winemaker Greer Carland, Glenn James **Est.** 1974 **Dozens** 6000 **Vyds** 7.6ha
Until 1990 the Bream Creek fruit was sold to Moorilla Estate, but since then the winery
has been independently owned and managed by Fred Peacock, legendary for the care he
bestows on the vines under his direction. Fred's skills have seen an increase in production and
outstanding wine quality across the range, headed by the Pinot Noir. The list of trophies and
gold, silver and bronze medals won is extensive. Fred's expertise as a consultant is in constant
demand. Exports to China.

Chardonnay 2012 Hand-picked, 100% whole bunches, wild and cultured yeast,
9 months in French oak (18% new). When Campbell Mattinson tasted this last
year he prophesied that it would sort itself out. He was right, and it moved from
silver to gold (Australian Small Winemakers Show '15 and Tasmanian Wine Show
'16). Everything about the wine is now in perfect balance and harmony, and it is

exceptionally youthful. I'd love to have a dozen or so bottles in my cellar to see me through to my dotage. Screwcap. 12.7% alc. **Rating** 96 **To** 2025 $32 **O**
Pinot Noir 2013 Hand-picked and sorted, 90% whole berries, 10% whole bunches, 7-day wild fermentation, cultured yeast added, 20 days on skins, 10 months in French oak (20% new). Powerful, complex and long in the mouth, red and black cherries and wild raspberries; exemplary tannin and oak management. An astonishing 3432 dozen made. Screwcap. 13.8% alc. **Rating** 94 **To** 2028 $36

ŢŢŢŢŢ **Pinot Rose 2015 Rating** 93 **To** 2017 $26 **O**
Riesling 2015 Rating 91 **To** 2022 $26

Bremerton Wines   ★★★★★
Strathalbyn Road, Langhorne Creek, SA 5255 **Region** Langhorne Creek
T (08) 8537 3093 **www**.bremerton.com.au **Open** 7 days 10–5
Winemaker Rebecca Willson **Est.** 1988 **Dozens** 38 000 **Vyds** 120ha
Bremerton has been producing wines since 1988. Rebecca Willson (Chief Winemaker) and Lucy Willson (Marketing Manager) became the first sisters in Australia to manage and run a winery. With 120ha of premium vineyards (80% of which goes into their own labels), under the guiding hand of viticulturist Ron Keelan (Rebecca's husband), they grow cabernet sauvignon, shiraz, verdelho, chardonnay, sauvignon blanc, malbec, merlot and petit verdot. Exports to most major markets.

ŢŢŢŢŢ **Batonnage Langhorne Creek Chardonnay 2014** Estate-grown, fermented and matured in French oak for 12 months. The acidity comes at a full gallop on the first taste, but on the second time it slows down a bit. The question remains whether this has more sauvignon blanc than chardonnay in its DNA. It does have great length. Screwcap. 12.5% alc. **Rating** 94 **To** 2022 $32
Special Release Langhorne Creek Tempranillo Graciano 2014 Perfumed red berry/cherry aromas, then an intense palate that sets all the receptors tingling; a mix of predominantly red fruits, plus a savoury twist, on the farewell. Screwcap. 14% alc. **Rating** 94 **To** 2024 $24 **O**
Special Release Langhorne Creek Malbec 2014 Matured for 14 months in Hungarian oak, wild yeast, lees-stirred periodically. Deep crimson-purple; a pervasive and immediate bouquet of violets, then a plummy palate criss-crossed with bramble. Screwcap. 14.5% alc. **Rating** 94 **To** 2029 $24 **O**

ŢŢŢŢŢ **Betty & Lu Sauvignon Blanc 2015 Rating** 90 **To** 2016 $17 **O**

Bress   ★★★★★
3894 Harmony Way, Harcourt, Vic 3453 **Region** Bendigo
T (03) 5474 2262 **www**.bress.com.au **Open** W'ends & public hols 11–5 or by chance
Winemaker Adam Marks, Xavier Goodridge **Est.** 2001 **Dozens** 5000 **Vyds** 17ha
Adam Marks has made wine in all parts of the world since 1991, and made the brave decision (during his honeymoon in 2000) to start his own business. Having initially scoured various regions of Australia for the varieties best suited to those regions, the focus has switched to three Central Victorian vineyards: Bendigo, Macedon Ranges and Heathcote. The Harcourt vineyard in Bendigo is planted to riesling (2ha), shiraz (1ha) and 3ha of cabernet sauvignon and cabernet franc; the Macedon vineyard to chardonnay (6ha) and pinot noir (3ha); and the Heathcote vineyard to shiraz (2ha). Exports to the Philippines, Singapore and Hong Kong.

ŢŢŢŢŢ **Gold Chook Heathcote Shiraz 2014** 15yo vines, clones PT23 (75%) and 2626 fermented separately, hand-picked and sorted, destemmed, 50% whole bunches, wild open ferment, 15 days on skins, matured in French hogsheads (30% new) for 14 months. Good colour; oh boy, does this give you a speed-of-light ride as it throws black fruits of every description, multi-spice, black pepper, licorice, earth and tar at you in a seeming split second. Shades of Côte Rôtie. Screwcap. 13.5% alc. **Rating** 97 **To** 2039 $45 **O**

♟♟♟♟♟ **Gold Chook Macedon Pinot Noir 2014** Hand-picked, 65% whole bunches, 35% destemmed on top, 6 days' cold soak, wild open ferment, matured in French hogsheads (30% new). A very complex pinot, faithfully reflecting its vinification, with savoury/spicy/stemmy notes threaded through red and black cherry fruit. Can't be faulted once you accept the style, which I do. Screwcap. 13% alc. **Rating** 95 **To** 2026 $45

Gold Chook Macedon Fume Blanc 2015 Clever winemaking, with a 9-day barrel fermentation in new French hogsheads (François Frères), than taken to tank. This sauvignon blanc has the power of first-rate chardonnay, its natural acidity doubtless the engine that drives the citrus/gooseberry fruit with such conviction. Screwcap. 12.5% alc. **Rating** 94 **To** 2018 $35

Silver Chook Heathcote Vermentino 2015 The wine was fermented on skins, either having been destemmed or as whole bunches, for at least 5 days before being pressed. And no, it's neither yellow or orange, just tangy and dry, with flavours of lemon and apple, and a distinctly savoury finish. Food wise, the world should be its oyster. Screwcap. 11% alc. **Rating** 94 **To** 2020 $25 ✪

♟♟♟♟♀ **Silver Chook Macedon Chardonnay 2015** **Rating** 90 **To** 2021 $25

Brian Fletcher Signature Wines ★★★★

PO Box 8385 Angel Street, South Perth, WA 6951 **Region** Margaret River
T (08) 9368 4555 **www.**brianfletcherwines.com.au **Open** Not
Winemaker Brian Fletcher **Est.** 2012 **Dozens** 12000
Brian Fletcher began his winemaking career in 1978, graduating in oenology at CSU. He had an illustrious career in eastern Australia before moving to Margaret River to become chief winemaker for Evans &Tate. He has not left the region since that time, forming a partnership with the Calneggia family, major vineyard developers and owners in the region. The wines are made under the Naked Wines umbrella, whereby Naked Wines provides the capital required to make the wines and takes them at a guaranteed price.

♟♟♟♟♟ **Reserve Margaret River Chardonnay 2015** Barrel-ferment inputs are relatively subtle, but leave you in no doubt about the crafting of the wine; the fruit flavours are very similar to those of its varietal sibling, but have significantly greater depth and length, and aren't intimidated by the oak. Screwcap. 13.5% alc. **Rating** 94 **To** 2025 $27 ✪

♟♟♟♟♀ **Margaret River Cabernet Merlot 2014** **Rating** 91 **To** 2025 $19 ✪

Briar Ridge Vineyard ★★★★★

Mount View Road, Mount View, NSW 2325 **Region** Hunter Valley
T (02) 4990 3670 **www.**briarridge.com.au **Open** 7 days 10–5
Winemaker Gwyneth Olsen **Est.** 1972 **Dozens** 10000 **Vyds** 39ha
Semillon and shiraz have been the most consistent performers, underlying the suitability of these varieties to the Hunter Valley. Briar Ridge has been a model of stability, and has the comfort of substantial estate vineyards from which it is able to select the best grapes. It also has not hesitated to venture into other regions, notably Orange. In 2013 Gwyneth (Gwyn) Olsen was appointed winemaker after an impressive career in Australia and NZ. In '12 she added the distinction of graduating as Dux of the AWRI Advanced Wine Assessment course to her CV. Exports to the UK, Europe and Canada.

♟♟♟♟♟ **Dairy Hill Single Vineyard Hunter Valley Semillon 2015** Very well made and articulated; an intense, classic array of lemon citrus, lemongrass and zesty acidity on the long, precise palate, the aftertaste fresh and thirsting for more. Screwcap. 11% alc. **Rating** 96 **To** 2030 $35 ✪

Dairy Hill Single Vineyard Hunter Valley Shiraz 2014 Matured in French hogsheads. No doubt I will repeat myself, but this is a very good example of the power and depth of the '14 Hunter Valley shiraz vintage, and its similarities to '65. Its black cherry and blackberry fruits have background nuances of earth, leather and licorice, and the tannins are exactly balanced for the long haul. A great full-bodied shiraz. Screwcap. 14% alc. **Rating** 96 **To** 2044 $60 ✪

Signature Release Karl Stockhausen Hunter Valley Shiraz 2014 Red fruits and spices alongside the black fruits of the bouquet and medium-bodied palate. It pulsates with freshness, and it's no sin to hop into a bottle tonight, however great the rewards of a decade of abstinence will be. The balance and mouthfeel are simply perfect. Screwcap. 13.5% alc. **Rating** 96 **To** 2034 $35 ✪

Stockhausen Hunter Valley Semillon 2015 Typical of modern Hunter Valley semillon, ever closer to young riesling, a fact that makes no sense, but a fact nonetheless. Yeast may be involved, but the blossom-filled bouquet and Meyer lemon palate allied with electric acidity could easily make you think of riesling if tasted blind. Skilled winemaking in a difficult vintage. Screwcap. 11% alc. **Rating** 95 **To** 2030 $28 ✪

H.R.B. Single Vineyard Hunter Valley Shiraz Pinot Noir 2014 H.R.B. is a nostalgic look back to Hunter River Burgundy, its apogee the '65 Lindemans Burgundy Bin 3100. It certainly has a fragrant red berry bouquet and a silky palate, no more than light to medium-bodied, redeemed (if that be the right word) by its line, length and balance. A success. Screwcap. 13% alc. **Rating** 95 **To** 2034 $60

🍷🍷🍷🍷🍷 **Fume Semillon Sauvignon Blanc 2015** Rating 92 **To** 2018 $23 ✪
Old Vines Shiraz 2014 Rating 92 **To** 2029 $23 ✪

Brick Kiln   ★★★★☆

21 Greer St, Hyde Park, SA 5061 **Region** McLaren Vale
T (08) 8357 2561 **www.**brickiln.com.au **Open** At Red Poles Restaurant
Winemaker Linda Domas, Phil Christiansen **Est.** 2001 **Dozens** 1500 **Vyds** 8ha
This is the venture of Malcolm and Alison Mackinnon, Garry and Nancy Watson, and Ian and Pene Davey. They purchased the Nine Gums Vineyard in 2001; it had been planted to shiraz in 1995–96. The majority of the grapes are sold, with a lesser portion contract-made for the partners under the Brick Kiln label, which takes its name from the Brick Kiln Bridge adjacent to the vineyard. Exports to the UK, Canada, China, Hong Kong and Singapore.

🍷🍷🍷🍷🍷 **The Grove McLaren Vale Shiraz 2014** Open-fermented before being basket-pressed to all French oak, 50% new. The end result feels complete. It's rich in flavour but well controlled, with coffee-cream and sweet blackberry characters doing everything in their powers to seduce. Ultrafine tannin enhances the impression of quality. Screwcap. 14.9% alc. **Rating** 95 **To** 2034 $45 CM

🍷🍷🍷🍷🍷 **Single Vineyard McLaren Vale Shiraz 2014** Rating 92 **To** 2026 $25 CM ✪

Brindabella Hills   ★★★★

156 Woodgrove Close, Wallaroo, ACT 2618 **Region** Canberra District
T (02) 6230 2583 **www.**brindabellahills.com.au **Open** W'ends, public hols 10–5
Winemaker Dr Roger Harris, Brian Sinclair **Est.** 1986 **Dozens** 1500 **Vyds** 5ha
Distinguished research scientist Dr Roger Harris presides over Brindabella Hills, which increasingly relies on estate-produced grapes, with small plantings of riesling, shiraz, chardonnay, sauvignon blanc, merlot, sangiovese, cabernet sauvignon, cabernet franc and viognier. Wine quality has been consistently good.

🍷🍷🍷🍷🍷 **Canberra District Riesling 2015** The region grows in stature with its rieslings as each vintage passes, the strongly continental climate a natural host. This has a superabundance of citrus fruit, with lime juice in a silver cup of acidity providing the long, cleansing finish. Screwcap. 12.5% alc. **Rating** 94 **To** 2025 $25 ✪

🍷🍷🍷🍷🍷 **Canberra District Sauvignon Blanc 2015** Rating 92 **To** 2018 $20 ✪
Canberra District Cabernet Shiraz 2013 Rating 92 **To** 2020 $20 ✪

Brini Estate Wines

698 Blewitt Springs Road, McLaren Vale, SA 5171 (postal) **Region** McLaren Vale
T (08) 8383 0080 **www.**briniwines.com.au **Open** Not
Winemaker Adam Hooper (Contract) **Est.** 2000 **Dozens** 4000 **Vyds** 16.4ha
The Brini family has been growing grapes in the Blewitt Springs area of McLaren Vale since 1953. In 2000 John and Marcello Brini established Brini Estate Wines to vinify a portion of the grape production; up to that time it had been sold to companies such as Penfolds, Rosemount Estate and d'Arenberg. The flagship Limited Release Shiraz is produced from dry-grown vines planted in 1947, the other wines from dry-grown vines planted in '64. Exports to Canada, Vietnam, Hong Kong and China.

John Brini Reserve Shiraz 2013 Grown on vines planted in '47. Matured in all-new American and French oak hogsheads. Heavyweight McLaren Vale shiraz with oak leeching from its plum and blackberry-drenched pores. It's one with the lot, but the meat and the sauce and indeed all ingredients work positively towards a rich, firm finish. Alcohol? It's swamped here by the tide of flavour. Cork. 15% alc. **Rating** 95 **To** 2035 $125 CM
Limited Release Single Vineyard Sebastian Shiraz 2012 Matured in French and American oak for 18 months. Slippery smooth, almost resiny, with blueberry and blackberry and a seductive ooze of chocolate. Dense flavour, played well. Screwcap. 14.5% alc. **Rating** 94 **To** 2027 $50 CM

Sebastian McLaren Vale Shiraz 2010 Rating 93 **To** 2028 $30 CM
Blewitt Springs Shiraz 2013 Rating 92 **To** 2025 $22 CM ○
McLaren Vale Grenache 2013 Rating 92 **To** 2021 $20 CM ○

Brockenchack

13/102 Burnett Street, Buderim, Qld 4556 **Region** Eden Valley
T (07) 5458 7700 **www.**brockenchack.com.au **Open** By appt
Winemaker Shawn Kalleske **Est.** 2007 **Dozens** 3000 **Vyds** 16ha
Trevor (and wife Marilyn) Harch have long been involved in liquor distribution in Qld, owning one of Australia's leading independent liquor wholesalers. Over the years, he became a regular visitor to the Barossa/Eden Valley, and in 1999 purchased the Tanunda Cellars Wine Store. In 2007, Trevor and Marilyn purchased a vineyard in the Eden Valley and retained Shawn Kalleske as winemaker. The vineyard has 8ha of shiraz, 2ha each of riesling and cabernet sauvignon, and 1.3ha each of pinot noir, pinot gris and chardonnay. The name of the business is appropriately Delphic. The vast majority of wines released are labelled in honour of one or other of the Harch's family. Brockenchack comes from the first names of the four grandchildren: Bronte, Mackenzie, Charli and Jack. Exports to Japan and NZ.

William Frederick Single Vineyard Eden Valley Shiraz 2012 Named in honour of Trevor Harch's father. Estate-grown, destemmed and crushed, open-fermented, macerated 21 days, matured for 24 months in new French oak. This is a seriously good – very good – wine saturated with black fruits, spice, pepper and licorice, yet nimble on its feet. You feel the fact that the berries were still tight, not at all on the point of collapse, and that the tannin and acid balance and structure were not manipulated. Screwcap. 14.5% alc. **Rating** 97 **To** 2042 $150 ○

Mackenzie William 1896 Single Vineyard Eden Valley Riesling 2015 Rating 93 **To** 2030 $20 ○
Charli Jaye Eden Valley Chardonnay 2015 Rating 91 **To** 2018 $35

Broken Gate Wines

57 Rokeby Street, Collingwood, Vic 3066 **Region** South Eastern Australia
T (03) 9417 5757 **www.**brokengate.com.au **Open** Mon–Fri 8–5
Winemaker Josef Orbach **Est.** 2001 **Dozens** 50 000

Broken Gate is a Melbourne-based multi-regional producer, specialising in cool climate reds and whites. Founder Josef Orbach lived and worked in the Clare Valley from 1994 to '98 at Leasingham, and completed a winemaking degree at the University of Melbourne in 2010. His is a classic negociant business, buying grapes and/or wines from various regions; the wines may be either purchased in bulk, then blended and bottled by Orbach, or purchased as cleanskins. Exports to Canada, Thailand, Singapore and China.

ɳɳɳɳ **Side Gate Organic Clare Valley Riesling 2015** Generous serve of citrussy flavour. Ready to tear into now. Screwcap. 12.5% alc. **Rating** 89 **To** 2020 $15 CM ✪

Reserve Clare Valley Shiraz 2012 Blackberry smeared with peppermint cream and ground coffee. Medium weight but dark in its flavour profile. Value. Screwcap. 13% alc. **Rating** 89 **To** 2020 $17 CM ✪

Side Gate Adelaide Hills Sauvignon Blanc 2015 Tropical fruit flavour, all served upfront, with a steely grassiness to close. Both refreshing and uncomplicated. Screwcap. 12.5% alc. **Rating** 88 **To** 2017 $15 CM ✪

Brokenwood ★★★★★

401–427 McDonalds Road, Pokolbin, NSW 2321 **Region** Hunter Valley
T (02) 4998 7559 **www**.brokenwood.com.au **Open** Mon–Sat 9.30–5, Sun 10–5
Winemaker Iain Riggs, Stuart Hordern **Est.** 1970 **Dozens** 100 000 **Vyds** 64ha
This deservedly fashionable winery, producing consistently excellent wines, has kept Graveyard Shiraz as its ultimate flagship wine, while extending its reach through many of the best regions for its broad selection of varietal wine styles. Its big-selling Hunter Semillon provides the volume to balance the limited quantities of the flagships ILR Semillon and Graveyard Shiraz. Next there is a range of wines coming from regions including Beechworth (a major resource from the associated Indigo Vineyard), Orange, Central Ranges, McLaren Vale, Cowra and elsewhere. In 2015 Iain Riggs celebrated his 60th birthday, and his 33rd vintage at the helm of Brokenwood, offering a unique mix of winemaking skills, management of a diverse business, and an unerring ability to keep Brokenwood's high profile fresh and newsworthy. He has also contributed a great deal to various wine industry organisations. Exports to all major markets.

ɳɳɳɳɳ **Graveyard Vineyard Hunter Valley Shiraz 2014** It hardly needs to be said that this is a great Graveyard, shortlisted for Wine of the Year. It is full-bodied, with intense intersections and trails of black fruits, earth, leather, spice, oak and ripe tannins running in all directions. Its magic is that it remains coherent, with its line (or focus) never compromised. Screwcap. 14% alc. **Rating** 98 **To** 2054 $250

Verona Vineyard Hunter Valley Shiraz 2014 It's not a blockbuster, and it's only marginally more intense than you might normally expect. But it feels both tightly strung and effortless at once, and the formation of the tannin – like a net flung out across a sea of earth-and-fruit flavour - is quite brutal in its beauty. It's a masterpiece of fine art. Screwcap. 14% alc. **Rating** 97 **To** 2040 $90 CM ✪

Mistress Block Vineyard Hunter Valley Shiraz 2014 The very idea of having a mistress has become a mortal social sin, after thousands of years of a simple fact of life for men with the requisite wealth. But if I could have a wine mistress I could do no better (DRC excepted) than this luscious, supple and smooth blend of red and black fruits, the usual regional extras all there in support, but allowing you to concentrate on the sexy parts. It's a very great Hunter Valley shiraz. Screwcap. 14% alc. **Rating** 97 **To** 2050 $110 ✪

ɳɳɳɳɳ **Kats Block Hunter Valley Shiraz 2014** A block on the Graveyard Vineyard, replanted in '02 with cuttings from the original vines, this the inaugural vintage. A mix of crushed/destemmed, with some whole-berry and some whole-bunch fermentation, matured in new and used French oak. If you doubt that earth can smell sweet, have a whiff of this; the full-bodied palate is crammed with black fruits, ripe tannins and some smart French oak, its drink-by date over the horizon. Screwcap. 14% alc. **Rating** 96 **To** 2054 $75 ✪

Rayner Vineyard McLaren Vale Shiraz 2014 Iain Riggs is a faithful chap, and has never forgotten that McLaren Vale was where his full-time wine life started. It's fascinating how the Hunter Valley can impose its stamp on red wines from any part of Australia if they are taken there prior to bottling. But it hasn't obliterated the wine's origin, with it luscious full-bodied black fruits and dark chocolate, tannins woven into the fabric of the palate, oak of passing relevance. Screwcap. 14% alc. **Rating** 96 **To** 2044 $100

Four Winds Vineyard Canberra District Riesling 2015 This is positively charged with Bickford's lime juice flavours from start to finish, and is so full of flavour few will even think about its development potential. A knockout if offered at the cellar door. Screwcap. 11.5% alc. **Rating** 95 **To** 2030 $35 ❂

Trevena Vineyard Hunter Valley Semillon 2012 Interesting time for release. It's a very, very good semillon, so the timing isn't as important for wines destined for release when 5–6yo, or of modest dimension when young. This makes a determined effort to mix it with riesling of a similar age with the amount of lemon citrus available. Screwcap. 10.5% alc. **Rating** 95 **To** 2035 $55

Hunter Valley Shiraz 2014 Not, as one might imagine, a regional blend from many sources, but from young vines on the Graveyard Vineyard and declassified wines from the original plantings. Vivid crimson, it is a seriously good shiraz, with dark red fruits enriched with a sauce of French oak and peppered with the firm tannins that will protect its longevity: a bare minimum of 30 years. Screwcap. 13.5% alc. **Rating** 95 **To** 2044 $50

Indigo Vineyard Beechworth Shiraz 2014 A perfect season in Beechworth; the wine was matured in French puncheons for 16 months. A chameleon: one moment an elegant, cool grown style, the next richer, edging towards full-bodied, but then retreating. Supple and spicy, its vibrant palate has red and blue fruit flavours and a magic carpet ride on fine-grained tannins and French oak. Screwcap. 13.5% alc. **Rating** 95 **To** 2039 $65

Hunter Valley Semillon 2015 Has an abundance of flavours, venturing from citrus into a shadow of stone fruit, making it a drop-dead drink tonight (or whenever) proposition. Top gold medal in its class at the Adelaide Wine Show '15. Screwcap. 10.5% alc. **Rating** 94 **To** 2020 $25 ❂

Wade Block 2 Vineyard McLaren Vale Shiraz 2011 Small wonder that Brokenwood didn't hesitate to release this wine despite the very wet and cool '11 vintage. Chilled must was sent by tanker to the Hunter Valley for fermentation, then maturation in 80% French (new and used) and 20% American oak. The brightness of colour and flavour made you wonder whether some Hunter shiraz may have been added (perfectly legally up to 15%); black cherry encased in chocolate, in turn in oak. Screwcap. 14% alc. **Rating** 94 **To** 2036 $65

♟♟♟♟♟ **Beechworth Sangiovese 2014** Rating 91 To 2021 $35 CM
Forest Edge Vineyard Sauvignon Blanc 2015 Rating 90 To 2017 $30
Beechworth Pinot Noir 2014 Rating 90 To 2018 $35

Bromley Wines ★★★★

PO Box 571, Drysdale, Vic 3222 **Region** Geelong
T 0487 505 367 **www**.bromleywines.com.au **Open** Not
Winemaker Darren Burke **Est.** 2010 **Dozens** 300
In his previous life, Darren Burke worked as an intensive care nurse in Australia and the UK, but at the age of 30 he fell to the allure of wine and enrolled in the Bachelor of Applied Science (Oenology) at Adelaide University. Thereafter he successively became graduate winemaker at Orlando, then at Alkoomi Wines, fitting in a vintage in Chianti. With two successful vintages in 2005 and '06 completed, and the impending birth of wife Tammy's first child, the couple decided to move back to the east coast. There Darren worked at several wineries on the Bellarine Peninsula before taking up his winemaking post at Leura Park Estate. Says Darren, 'The essence of Bromley is family. All our wines carry names drawn from our family history. Family is about flesh and blood, sweat and tears, love and laughter.' Exports to Singapore.

🍷🍷🍷🍷🍷 **Alchemy 2015** 95% semillon, 5% sauvignon blanc, 65% wild-fermented on skins, pressed to oak and stainless steel for maturation, the remainder whole bunch-pressed, fermented on solids in stainless steel, then to a new French hogshead, bottled Jun, 192 dozen made. A lot of work, this is an excitement machine, vibrantly edgy with lemon juice and pith, minerally acidity, and layers of funky flavours. Screwcap. 12.5% alc. **Rating** 94 To 2018 $19 **○**

🍷🍷🍷🍷🍷 **Geelong Pinot Noir 2014 Rating** 92 To 2023 $30

Brook Eden Vineyard   ★★★★☆

167 Adams Road, Lebrina, Tas 7254 **Region** Northern Tasmania
T (03) 6395 6244 **www**.brookeden.com.au **Open** 7 days 11–5 Sept–May
Winemaker Winemaking Tasmania **Est.** 1988 **Dozens** 1000 **Vyds** 2.1ha
At 41° south and an altitude of 160m, Brook Eden is one of the coolest sites in Tasmania, and represents 'viticulture on the edge'. While the plantings remain small (1ha pinot noir, 0.8ha chardonnay and 0.3ha pinot gris), yield has been significantly reduced, resulting in earlier picking and better-quality grapes.

🍷🍷🍷🍷🍷 **Nero 2013** 100% estate-grown pinot noir. It presents immaculately. It's silken and fresh, has more than enough fruit and is riddled with savoury, undergrowthy inputs. Both tannin and length do nothing to distort the quality impression. It's a high-class pinot. Screwcap. 13.6% alc. **Rating** 95 To 2023 $38 CM

🍷🍷🍷🍷🍷 **Riesling 2012 Rating** 92 To 2024 $32 CM
Pinot Noir 2010 Rating 91 To 2021 $47 CM

Brookland Valley   ★★★★★

Caves Road, Wilyabrup, WA 6280 **Region** Margaret River
T (08) 9755 6042 **www**.brooklandvalley.com.au **Open** 7 days 10–5
Winemaker Courtney Treacher **Est.** 1984 **Dozens** NFP
Brookland Valley has an idyllic setting, plus its café and Gallery of Wine Arts, which houses an eclectic collection of wine, food-related art and wine accessories. After acquiring a 50% share of Brookland Valley in 1997, Hardys moved to full ownership in 2004; it is now part of Accolade Wines. The quality, value for money and consistency, of the wines is exemplary.

🍷🍷🍷🍷🍷 **Estate Margaret River Chardonnay 2014** Hand-picked, whole bunch-pressed and matured in French oak for 9 months. Speaks loud and clear of its region, with perfectly ripened, layered fruits led by nectarine, white peach and melon, balanced by citrus-tinged acidity, oak somewhere in the mix, but far from obvious. Screwcap. 13.5% alc. **Rating** 96 To 2024 $48 **○**
Estate Margaret River Cabernet Merlot 2013 Hand-picked, open-fermented, matured in French oak for 14 months. The high quality of the grapes is immediately obvious, the bouquet fragrantly inviting, the palate surging with blackcurrant, redcurrant, blackberry and cedary oak. A scaffold of ripe tannins is precisely proportioned for a wine destined to live for decades. Screwcap. 13.5% alc. **Rating** 96 To 2045 $55 **○**

🍷🍷🍷🍷🍷 **Verse 1 Margaret River Chardonnay 2015 Rating** 90 To 2018 $15 **○**
Verse 1 Margaret River Shiraz 2014 Rating 90 To 2022 $15 **○**
Verse 1 Margaret River Cabernet Merlot 2014 Rating 90 To 2024 $15 **○**

Brothers in Arms   ★★★★☆

Lake Plains Road, Langhorne Creek, SA 5255 **Region** Langhorne Creek
T (08) 8537 3182 **www**.brothersinarms.com.au **Open** By appt
Winemaker Jim Urlwin **Est.** 1998 **Dozens** 25 000 **Vyds** 85ha
The Adams family has been growing grapes at Langhorne Creek since 1891, when the vines at the famed Metala vineyards were planted. Guy Adams is the fifth generation to own and work the vineyard, and over the past 20 years has both improved the viticulture and expanded

the plantings. It was not until 1998 that they decided to hold back a small proportion of the production for vinification under the Brothers in Arms label, and now they dedicate 85ha to Brothers in Arms (40ha each of shiraz and cabernet sauvignon and 2.5ha each of malbec and petit verdot). Exports to the UK, the US, Canada, Germany, Sweden, Denmark, Singapore, Hong Kong and China.

ΨΨΨΨΨ **Langhorne Creek Shiraz 2013** Estate-grown, matured for 20 months in French barriques (67% new). Full colour is an early signal of a full-bodied shiraz, with an eager display of black fruits of every description, notes of licorice and tar, savoury tannins and cedary oak all competing for space. Simply needs more time. Screwcap. 14.5% alc. **Rating** 94 **To** 2035 $45

ΨΨΨΨΨ **Langhorne Creek Cabernet Sauvignon 2013** **Rating** 93 **To** 2028 $50
No. 6 Langhorne Creek Shiraz Cabernet 2013 **Rating** 92 **To** 2033 $22 ✪
Side by Side Langhorne Creek Malbec 2013 **Rating** 92 **To** 2028 $27

Brown Brothers ★★★★★

Milawa-Bobinawarrah Road, Milawa, Vic 3678 **Region** King Valley
T (03) 5720 5500 **www.**brownbrothers.com.au **Open** 7 days 9–5
Winemaker Wendy Cameron, Joel Tilbrook, Cate Looney, Geoff Alexander, Chloe Earl
Est. 1885 **Dozens** Over 1 million **Vyds** 570ha
Draws upon a considerable number of vineyards spread throughout a range of site climates, ranging from very warm to very cool. An expansion into Heathcote added significantly to its armoury. In 2010 Brown Brothers took a momentous step, acquiring Tasmania's Tamar Ridge for $32.5 million. In May '16 it acquired the Innocent Bystander and stock from Giant Steps, and with it a physical presence in the Yarra Valley. The premium quality varietal wines to one side, Brown Brothers has gained two substantial labels, Innocent Bystander Moscato and Innocent Bystander Prosecco. It is known for the diversity of varieties with which it works, and the wines represent good value for money. Deservedly one of the most successful family wineries – its cellar door receives the greatest number of visitors in Australia. A founding member of Australia's First Families of Wine. Exports to all major markets.

ΨΨΨΨΨ **Patricia Chardonnay 2010** First tasted 30 months ago, the note finishing 'Improvement certain. 93 points'. The prophecy wasn't hard, and was correct. This is still wonderfully fresh, but also full of white peach/grapefruit/oak/crunchy acidity, its colour still vibrantly quartz-green. 4 gold medals, 2 at the National Wine Show '12 and '14. Screwcap. 13% alc. **Rating** 96 **To** 2020 $42 ✪
Patricia Shiraz 2012 The fruit was harvested from five vineyards spread across Vic in parcels from late Feb. to mid-Apr. at baumés between 13° and 14.5°. A portion of the wine finished fermenting in barrels, then all parcels spent 18 months in 44% new French (30%) and American (14%) oak with the balance in older oak barriques and puncheons. Its power and intensity hit like a bullet, packed with pepper, spice, savoury jet black fruits and customised tannins. This could see out 50 years thanks to the length and balance of the powerhouse of fruit. Screwcap. 14% alc. **Rating** 96 **To** 2052 $65 ✪
Limited Release Single Vineyard Heathcote Durif 2013 Ribald purple. Announces itself as alive, well, and ready to party from the first splash into the glass. It's fragrant, lively, bursting with dark fruit flavour and unafraid of both flashy oak and a hum of tannin. It's hard to know whether it's marriage material or a one-night stand; it has its paws poised over all bases. In the overall scheme, the asking price offers enormous value. Screwcap. 14% alc. **Rating** 95 **To** 2025 $21 CM ✪
Patricia Chardonnay 2012 Proclaims its Yarra Valley origin from the first sip. Bright straw-green, it has a complex fruit-driven bouquet rather than simply barrel ferment (it has, of course, been barrel-fermented), the palate with white peach, nectarine and fig flavours before a long finish of citrussy acidity. Screwcap. 12.9% alc. **Rating** 95 **To** 2022 $45
Single Vineyard Heathcote Durif 2013 Cellar Door Release. Seriously good durif, marrying a fireworks display of black fruits, spice and positive oak.

Despite this abundance, its impeccable balance gives it lightness of foot. A great advertisement for the variety. Screwcap. 14% alc. **Rating** 95 **To** 2025 $21 ✪

Patricia Pinot Noir Chardonnay Brut 2010 Five years on yeast lees, the elegantly pristine lemon and apple flavours declare a vintage of precision and stamina. Wonderful texture and understated almond meal and nougat nuances of maturity underline the gently sustaining presence of its acidity. Cork. 12.5% alc. **Rating** 95 **To** 2018 $47 TS

Patricia Noble Riesling 2013 Estate-grown, hand-picked from early Apr to early May with significant botrytis. Shows the balance needed between residual sugar (117g) and titratable acidity (7.2g/l); very complex, cumquat/orange/ mandarin, plus honey. 375ml. Screwcap. 9% alc. **Rating** 95 **To** 2018 $35 ✪

Methode Traditionelle King Valley Pinot Noir Chardonnay Pinot Meunier NV A serial collector of gold medals at capital city wine shows. Chardonnay, pinot noir and pinot meunier are whole bunch-pressed, each kept separate, each taken through mlf before the final blend was made and bottled for the secondary fermentation. It has an expressive, fragrant bouquet, and a long, crisply focused palate, citrus and stone fruit to the fore, with background bready/ yeasty characters. Cork. 12% alc. **Rating** 94 **To** 2017 $27 ✪

♥♥♥♥♀ 18 Eighty Nine Tasmania Sauvignon Blanc 2015 **Rating** 93 **To** 2017 $19 ✪
125 Years Heathcote Montepulciano 2014 **Rating** 92 **To** 2020 $21 ✪
Single Vineyard King Valley Prosecco NV **Rating** 92 **To** 2017 $21 TS ✪
Patricia Cabernet Sauvignon 2010 **Rating** 91 **To** 2025 $65
Victoria Tempranillo & Graciano 2014 **Rating** 91 **To** 2020 $21 ✪
18 Eighty Nine King Valley Pinot Grigio 2015 **Rating** 90 **To** 2017 $19 ✪
125 Years Heathcote Malbec 2014 **Rating** 90 **To** 2017 $21 ✪
King Valley Vintage Prosecco 2015 **Rating** 90 **To** 2016 $20 CM ✪
Cuvee Premium Sparkling Brut NV **Rating** 90 **To** 2016 $19 TS ✪

Brown Hill Estate

Cnr Rosa Brook Road/Barrett Road, Rosa Brook, WA 6285 **Region** Margaret River
T (08) 9757 4003 **www.**brownhillestate.com.au **Open** 7 days 10–5
Winemaker Nathan Bailey, Haydn Millard **Est.** 1995 **Dozens** 3000 **Vyds** 22ha
The Bailey family is involved in all stages of wine production, with minimum outside help. Their stated aim is to produce top quality wines at affordable prices, via uncompromising viticultural practices emphasising low yields. They have shiraz and cabernet sauvignon (8ha each), semillon, sauvignon blanc and merlot (2ha each). The quality of the best wines in the portfolio is very good, and the value for money of the wines selling for less than $20 is mouthwatering.

♥♥♥♥♥ Fimiston Reserve Margaret River Shiraz 2014 It throws savoury spice at the slab of blackberried fruit, but it's like water off a duck's back: the fruit here will neither be tamed nor deflected. This is a substantial shiraz by any measure, but particularly in regional terms. It has the tannin and overall balance to make a successful fist of the style too. Screwcap. 14% alc. **Rating** 94 **To** 2032 $35 CM
Croesus Reserve Margaret River Merlot 2014 Only light to medium-bodied, but it's firmly a cellaring style. Earnest tannin ensures it is so. Mulberry and red cherry flavours come thoroughly infused with both dry and fresh garden herbs. It's hard to mount an argument for it as a drink-now proposition but it should develop beautifully. Screwcap. 14% alc. **Rating** 94 **To** 2026 $35 CM
Oroya Margaret River Malbec 2014 Grunt of this dimension rarely seems so effortless. This throws a healthy serve of earth, leather and blackberried flavour the drinker's way, dried spice and floral notes fanning the display. Impressive. Screwcap. 14% alc. **Rating** 94 **To** 2025 $35 CM

♥♥♥♥♀ Golden Horseshoe Chardonnay 2015 **Rating** 93 **To** 2021 $35 CM
Bill Bailey Shiraz Cabernet 2013 **Rating** 93 **To** 2032 $60 CM
Perseverance Cabernet Merlot 2013 **Rating** 93 **To** 2026 $50 CM

Ivanhoe Reserve Cabernet Sauvignon 2014 Rating 93 To 2030 $35 CM
Morning Star Dry Light Red 2015 Rating 91 To 2016 $19 CM ✪
Hannans Cabernet Sauvignon 2014 Rating 91 To 2025 $20 CM ✪
Lakeview Sauvignon Blanc Semillon 2015 Rating 90 To 2017 $19 CM ✪
Trafalgar Cabernet Merlot 2014 Rating 90 To 2022 $20 CM ✪

Brown Magpie Wines ★★★★★

125 Larcombes Road, Modewarre, Vic 3240 **Region** Geelong
T (03) 5266 2147 **www.**brownmagpiewines.com **Open** 7 days 11–4 Jan, w'ends
11–4 Nov–Apr
Winemaker Loretta and Shane Breheny **Est.** 2000 **Dozens** 5000 **Vyds** 9ha
Shane and Loretta Breheny's 20ha property is situated predominantly on a gentle, north-facing
slope, with cypress trees on the western and southern borders providing protection against the
wind. Vines were planted over 2001–02, with pinot noir (4ha) taking the lion's share, followed
by pinot gris and shiraz (2.4ha each) and 0.1ha each of chardonnay and sauvignon blanc.
Viticulture is Loretta's love; winemaking (and wine) is Shane's.

♟♟♟♟♟ **Single Vineyard Geelong Pinot Gris 2015** Hand-picked, whole bunch-
pressed, fermentation initiated in stainless steel, 56% taken to used French oak
for fermentation, the remainder fermented in tank and given yeast lees contact;
the barrel-ferment portion spent 6 months in oak. Picked ripe, and clearly looks
to Alsace for inspiration (the riesling bottle another pointer). If you really want
gris to be a subject of conversation, this is it. Is there some residual sugar, or is it
just the glacé ginger thrown into the conversation by Brown Magpie? Screwcap.
14% alc. **Rating** 95 **To** 2017 $27 ✪

Single Vineyard Geelong Shiraz 2014 Hand-picked and destemmed
over 2 weeks, a small proportion of each day's pick crushed, the remainder
destemmed for whole-berry fermentation, 7% pressed before dryness to complete
fermentation in barrel, the remainder pressed dry; 12 months in oak. Good
colour; as elegant as it is intense and complex; a haunting bouquet of spice, truffle
and violets leads into a palate that adds wild blackberry and superfine – but all
important – tannins. Cool climate shiraz in fine fettle. Screwcap. 13.4% alc. **Rating**
95 **To** 2029 $30 ✪

Paraparap Single Vineyard Reserve Geelong Pinot Noir 2014 The
Paraparap Reserve, given longer maturation in French oak than its standard sibling,
has absorbed that oak into the fabric of the imperious dark fruits of its bouquet
and mid-palate. It's a really tough call, but it dips a little on the finish; more time
may change the picture. Screwcap. 12.3% alc. **Rating** 94 **To** 2024 $60

♟♟♟♟♀ **Single Vineyard Geelong Pinot Grigio 2015** Rating 93 To 2020 $27 ✪

Brygon Reserve ★★★★

529 Osmington Road, Margaret River, WA 6280 **Region** Margaret River
T 1800 754 517 **www.**brygonreservewines.com.au **Open** W'ends 10–5
Winemaker David Longden **Est.** 2009 **Dozens** NFP
Since its establishment in 2009 by Robert and Laurie Fraser-Scott, this business has grown
very rapidly, although details of its production are not available. Having originally relied on
contract winemaking, it opened a winery and cellar door in February '15. The winery has its
own bottling plant and bulk wine storage facilities, with at least some of the wine produced
under contract elsewhere in Margaret River. The plethora of wines are under six major brands:
Hummingbird, The Bruce, Brygon Reserve, Flying High, Third Wheel and Mirror Image.
Unless otherwise stated, all come form the Margaret River. There are some ancillary brands
used in export or special markets, thus not sold through retail outlets in Australia. Exports to
the US, Vietnam, Macau, Taiwan, Thailand, Hong Kong, Singapore and China.

♟♟♟♟♀ **Brygon Reserve Small Batch Oak Aged Shiraz 2011** Brygon Estate may
well be the world's most over-engineered wine range. It's a bewildering line-up.
That said, some of the wines are very good, and this is one of them. It's sturdy,

it's well fruited, it carries itself through the finish well, and it generally satisfies. Screwcap. 13.5% alc. **Rating** 93 **To** 2024 $60 CM

Third Wheel Reserve Cabernet Sauvignon 2014 Powerful, supple and most importantly, persistent. Blackcurrant and gum leaf with smoky, chocolatey oak keeping it smooth. Tannin has been well managed. Can't argue with the quality or value. Screwcap. 13.5% alc. **Rating** 93 **To** 2024 $25 CM ✪

Brygon Reserve Small Batch Oak Aged Cabernet Sauvignon 2011 Subtle notes of leather and malt help give this a soft, mellow disposition. Of course there are also strong forces of blackcurrant and bay leaf at play, with gravelly fruit-rich tannin then crashing through the finish. Now or any time over the next 10 years; it will provide enjoyment. Screwcap. 13.5% alc. **Rating** 93 **To** 2027 $60 CM

Brygon Reserve Gold Label Vintage Reserve Cabernet Sauvignon 2010 Well composed and lengthy. Chocolatey blackcurrant with reductive notes adding positive complexity. Framework of tannin is there without getting in the way. Just entering its prime. Screwcap. 13.5% alc. **Rating** 93 **To** 2025 $40 CM

Brygon Reserve Small Batch Oak Aged Chardonnay 2011 The packaging is overt and obvious (the less kind might call it 'dumbed down'), an interesting approach for a $60 white. The wine itself continues the theme, more or less, with malty oak sitting atop sunny, peach-driven fruit. There's no lack of power and it certainly fills the mouth with flavour. Screwcap. 14% alc. **Rating** 92 **To** 2018 $60 CM

Brygon Reserve Gold Label Vintage Reserve Shiraz 2010 Developing steadily but well. Blackberry, beef stock and mulberry flavours come steeped in leather and dried herbs. It's brambly, almost, but it feels harmonious and in terms of volume no one is likely to have quibbles. Web of tannin through the back-palate helps elevate the impression of quality. Screwcap. 13.5% alc. **Rating** 92 **To** 2023 $40 CM

Gold Label Museum Release Chardonnay 2011 Warm flavours of brown bread, stone fruit and cooked apple lead into toasty, cedary oak. It's drinking at its peak now. Screwcap. 14% alc. **Rating** 91 **To** 2018 $40 CM

Brygon Reserve Museum Release Chardonnay 2010 Bold flavours of honeycomb, sweet peach, condensed milk and malty oak. It's well developed, but it keeps flinging the flavours at you all the way through the finish. Indeed citrussy acidity is a godsend here. Screwcap. 14% alc. **Rating** 91 **To** 2018 $50 CM

Brygon Reserve The Bruce Shiraz 2014 Works it way through a pack of flavours to record a strong finish. You wouldn't call it a pretty show, but it manages good heft and, in the end, balance. Screwcap. 14% alc. **Rating** 91 **To** 2021 $20 CM ✪

Brygon Reserve Bin 882 Shiraz 2014 In a good place. The fruit has been ripened just so, oak barely shows, and all the flavours and facets flow evenly through the finish. Value. Screwcap. 14% alc. **Rating** 91 **To** 2021 $20 CM ✪

War Horse Barossa Syrah 2012 Not a blockbuster. It has a tangy lightness of touch, its sweet-sour personality carried by boysenberry, citrus, black cherry and (at a pinch) blackberried fruit flavour. Oak is modest, so too tannin. It's a pleasant wine to drink, but a curious one given the price of admission. Screwcap. 14.5% alc. **Rating** 91 **To** 2025 $100 CM

Third Wheel Reserve Cabernet Shiraz Merlot 2014 Comforting red with all the elements working as a team. Blackcurrant, chocolate, bay leaves and tobacco-like notes push a mid-weighted palate through to a logical, satisfying conclusion. Screwcap. 14.5% alc. **Rating** 91 **To** 2023 $25 CM

Brygon Reserve Private Bin Block 9 Shiraz 2011 Sweet coconutty oak and a sweet fruit profile. It's a lush wine, abundantly soft and immediately attractive, the flavour profile (in the bottle tasted, under screwcap) showing minor signs of oxidation. Appreciating its appeal remained easy, scoring it the opposite. Screwcap. 13.5% alc. **Rating** 90 **To** 2018 $50 CM

Brygon Reserve Private Bin Block 8 Cabernet Sauvignon 2010 This is gruff with tannin and as a 6yo, the fruit is struggling to keep up. It's a close-run thing though; the fruit seems warmer and sweeter than its stated alcohol would suggest, with suede and blackcurrant jelly flavours turning dusty and dry to close. Indeed it's one of those 'almost excellent' wines. Screwcap. 13.5% alc. **Rating** 90 **To** 2022 $50 CM

Buckshot Vineyard   ★★★★☆

PO Box 119, Coldstream, Vic 3770 **Region** Heathcote
T 0417 349 785 **www**.buckshotvineyard.com.au **Open** Not
Winemaker Rob Peebles **Est.** 1999 **Dozens** 700 **Vyds** 2ha
This is the venture of Meegan and Rob Peebles, and comes on the back of Rob's 20+ year involvement in the wine industry, including six vintages in Rutherglen, starting in 1993, followed by 10 years at Domaine Chandon, and squeezing in weekend work at Coldstream Hills' cellar door in '93. It is the soils of Heathcote, and a long-time friendship with John and Jenny Davies, that sees the flagship Shiraz, and a smaller amount of zinfandel (with some shiraz) coming from a small block, part of a 40ha vineyard owned by the Davies southwest of Colbinabbin. Rob makes the wines at Domaine Chandon. Exports to the US.

ΨΨΨΨΨ **Heathcote Shiraz 2013** The driest growing season on record, with an early
           harvest. Crushed and destemmed, open-fermented with 5% whole bunches,
           3 days' cold soak, matured for 14 months in new and used French hogsheads.
           Dark crimson-purple; an intense and highly focused wine with black fruits,
           licorice and spice on its bouquet and palate alike, French oak and tannins coming
           through on the finish of the long palate. It is still very youthful, with a long life
           ahead. Screwcap. 14.3% alc. **Rating** 95 **To** 2038 $31

Bull Lane Wine Company   ★★★★☆

PO Box 77, Heathcote, Vic 3523 **Region** Heathcote
T 0427 970 041 **www**.bulllane.com.au **Open** Not
Winemaker Simon Osicka **Est.** 2013 **Dozens** 400
After a successful career as a winemaker with what is now TWE, Simon Osicka, together with viticulturist partner Alison Phillips, returned to the eponymous family winery just within the eastern boundary of the Heathcote region in 2010. Spurred on by a decade of drought impacting on the 60-year-old dry-grown vineyard, and a desire to create another style of shiraz, Simon and Alison spent considerable time visiting Heathcote vineyards with access to water in the lead-up to the '10 vintage. They ultimately decided to buy grapes from a cool slope on a vineyard owned by John Davies. It was intended that the first vintage should be in '11, but (ironically) the wet growing season precluded any idea of launching a new label with insufficient fruit flavour, so '12 (a wonderful vintage) produced the first wine. Exports to Denmark.

ΨΨΨΨΨ **Heathcote Shiraz 2014** Astute vineyard selection, great fruit from a low-
           yielding vintage and skilled winemaking have all been rewarded. The bouquet is
           highly expressive, with black fruits dominant, but not suppressing some red berry
           notes, the rich brocade of velvety mid-palate welcoming ripe, grainy tannins on
           the finish. A gold-plated certainty to develop further in bottle. Screwcap. 14.2% alc.
           Rating 95 **To** 2034 $28

ΨΨΨΨΨ **Heathcote Shiraz 2014 Rating** 92 **To** 2024 $28 CM

Buller Wines   ★★★★☆

2804 Federation Way, Rutherglen, Vic 3685 **Region** Rutherglen
T (02) 6032 9660 **www**.bullerwines.com.au **Open** Mon–Sat 9–5, Sun 10–5
Winemaker Dave Whyte **Est.** 1921 **Dozens** 10 000 **Vyds** 32ha
In 2013, after 92 years of ownership and management by the Buller family, the business was purchased by Gerald and Mary Judd, a well-known local couple and family with extensive roots in the northeast. They are hands-on in the business, and have overseen investment in the cellar, storage, operations and, importantly, the vineyards. Exports to all major markets.

ŸŸŸŸŸ **Calliope Rare Frontignac NV** Deep, dark, toffeed brown. Immensely sweet and intense. The palate really needs to be tasted to be believed: it's earthen and sweet at once, fresh but pricked by rancio. Balance is spot on. It comes at you at a million miles a minute and yet it's fascinating, even cerebral, at the same time. Screwcap. 18% alc. **Rating** 96 **To** 2018 $120 CM
Calliope Rare Tokay NV The spirit is high but the flesh is something else. This is all tea leaves and chocolate, peat and burnt, toasty sugar. It's luscious, intense, speckled with rancio on the finish, and fundamentally imposing. Whether or not the balance has been absolutely nailed is a question worth asking, though it's a moot point. 375ml. Screwcap. 18% alc. **Rating** 94 **To** 2017 $120 CM

ŸŸŸŸŸ **Fine Old Tokay NV Rating** 92 **To** 2018 $25 CM ✪
Fine Old Muscat NV Rating 91 **To** 2018 $25 CM

Bundaleer Wines   ★★★★☆

PO Box 41, Hove, SA 5048 **Region** Southern Flinders Ranges
T (08) 8294 7011 **www.**bundaleerwines.com.au **Open** Little Red Grape, Sevenhill
Winemaker Angela Meaney **Est.** 1998 **Dozens** 3500 **Vyds** 7ha
Bundaleer is a joint venture between the Meaney and Spurling families, situated in an area known as Bundaleer Gardens, on the edge of the Bundaleer Forest, 200km north of Adelaide. The red wines are produced from estate plantings (equal quantities of shiraz and cabernet sauvignon are planted), the white wines from purchased grapes from the Clare Valley. Exports to Canada, Taiwan, Hong Kong and China.

ŸŸŸŸŸ **St Gregory 2012** 52% shiraz, 48% cabernet sauvignon, matured for 3 years in new French and American oak (70/30%). Deep crimson-purple; the oak influence is, of course, profound, but the quality of the blackberry and blackcurrant fruit sustains the balance of a very good wine. Mercifully (in the biblical sense) the temptation to let the grapes ripen further was resisted. Screwcap. 14.5% alc. **Rating** 96 **To** 2047 $40 ✪

ŸŸŸŸŸ **Stony Place Clare Valley Riesling 2015 Rating** 90 **To** 2022 $20 ✪
Golden Spike Clare Valley Pinot Gris 2015 Rating 90 **To** 2017 $18 ✪
North Star Clare Valley Rose 2015 Rating 90 **To** 2017 $18 ✪

Bundaleera Vineyard   ★★★☆

449 Glenwood Road, Relbia, Tas 7258 (postal) **Region** Northern Tasmania
T (03) 6343 1231 **Open** W'ends 10–5
Winemaker Pirie Consulting (Andrew Pirie) **Est.** 1996 **Dozens** 1000
David (a consultant metallurgist in the mining industry) and Jan Jenkinson have established 2.5ha of vines on a sunny, sheltered north to northeast slope in the North Esk Valley. The 12ha property on which their house and vineyard are established gives them some protection from the urban sprawl of Launceston. Jan is the full-time viticulturist and gardener for the immaculately tended property.

Bundalong Coonawarra   ★★★★☆

109 Paul Road, Comaum, SA 5277 (postal) **Region** Coonawarra
T 0419 815 925 **www.**bundalongcoonawarra.com.au **Open** Not
Winemaker Andrew Hardy, Peter Bissell **Est.** 1990 **Dozens** 900 **Vyds** 65ha
James Porter has owned the Bundalong property for many years. In the second half of the 1980s, encouraged by an old shallow limestone quarry on the property, he sought opinions about the suitability of the soil for grapegrowing. The answer was yes, and so in '89 the first plantings of cabernet sauvignon were made, followed by shiraz. The primary purpose of the 65ha vineyard was to supply grapes to major companies, and Southcorp and its successors (now TWE) have been long-term purchasers. Trial vintages were made in '94 and '96, followed by the first serious vintage in 2008. The strategy has been only to make wine in the very best vintages in Coonawarra, with the '08, '12 and '14 the only vintages so far accredited.

ΨΨΨΨΨ **Single Vineyard Cabernet Sauvignon 2014** Perfectly balanced. Neither deeply coloured nor intensely flavoured, but it gets its message across cleanly, clearly and well. Mulberry, blackcurrant and peppermint flavours do the talking. Oak isn't a major player. But tannin is: this is firm and sure of itself. It'll age like a charm. Screwcap. 14% alc. **Rating** 94 **To** 2032 $28 CM ✪

ΨΨΨΨΨ **Single Vineyard Shiraz 2014 Rating** 92 **To** 2026 $28 CM

Bunkers Margaret River Wines ★★★★

1142 Kaloorup Road, Kaloorup, WA 6280 **Region** Margaret River
T (08) 9368 4555 **www**.bunkerswines.com.au **Open** Not
Winemaker Brian Fletcher **Est.** 2010 **Dozens** 5500 **Vyds** 34ha
Over the past 20+ years, Mike Calneggia has had his fingers in innumerable Margaret River viticultural pies. He has watched some ventures succeed, and others fail, and while Bunkers Wines (owned by Mike and Sally Calneggia) is only a small part of his viticultural undertakings, it has been carefully targeted from the word go. It has the six mainstream varieties (cabernet, semillon, merlot, chardonnay, sauvignon blanc and shiraz) joined by rising star, tempranillo, in the warm and relatively fertile northern part of the Margaret River. Brian Fletcher is winemaker and Murray Edmonds the viticulturist (both ex Evans & Tate). Mike and daughter Amy are responsible for sales and marketing. They say, 'The world of wine is full of serious people making serious wines for an ever-decreasing serious market … Bunkers wines have been created to put the "F" word back into wine: "FUN", that is.' Exports to China.

ΨΨΨΨΨ **The Box Tempranillo 2013** Hand-picked, open-fermented, 25% matured in new American oak for 1 year before blending with the stainless steel component. Vivid purple-crimson; the wine enters the mouth with a blast of red cherry fruit and vanillan oak, finishing with powdery tannins. Screwcap. 14.5% alc. **Rating** 92 **To** 2018 $20 ✪
Honeycombs Chardonnay 2014 Machine harvesting and cold-pressed clear juice fermented in French oak results in a fresh, fruit-driven style with white peach and melon flavours to the fore. Screwcap. 13.5% alc. **Rating** 90 **To** 2017 $20 ✪

ΨΨΨΨ **Guillotines Shiraz 2014 Rating** 88 **To** 2024 $20

Bunnamagoo Estate ★★★★

603 Henry Lawson Drive, Mudgee, NSW 2850 **Region** Mudgee
T 1300 304 707 **www**.bunnamagoowines.com.au **Open** 7 days 10–4
Winemaker Robert Black **Est.** 1995 **Dozens** 70 000 **Vyds** 108ha
Bunnamagoo Estate (on one of the first land grants in the region) is situated near the historic town of Rockley. Here a 6ha vineyard planted to chardonnay, merlot and cabernet sauvignon has been established by Paspaley Pearls, a famous name in the WA pearl industry. The winery and cellar door are located at the much larger (and warmer) Eurunderee Vineyard (102ha) at Mudgee. Exports to the UK, Singapore, Fiji, Papua New Guinea, Indonesia, Hong Kong and China.

ΨΨΨΨΨ **Semillon 2015** It runs on silken rails. The flavours are both fresh and intriguing. It's really quite delicious, in a sophisticated way. It can be cellared, but this is one where there's no need to. Screwcap. 11.5% alc. **Rating** 94 **To** 2024 $22 CM ✪

ΨΨΨΨΨ **Cabernet Merlot 2014 Rating** 92 **To** 2022 $24 CM ✪
1827 Handpicked Chardonnay 2014 Rating 91 **To** 2020 $40 CM
Cabernet Sauvignon 2014 Rating 91 **To** 2025 $24 CM
Riesling 2015 Rating 90 **To** 2021 $22 CM

Burch Family Wines   ★★★★★

Miamup Road, Cowaramup, WA 6284 **Region** Margaret River/Denmark
T (08) 9756 5200 **www**.burchfamilywines.com.au **Open** 7 days 10–5
Winemaker Janice McDonald, Mark Bailey, Andries Mostert **Est.** 1986 **Dozens** NFP
Vyds 189.2ha

This is the renamed Howard Park, which has two vineyards: Leston in Margaret River, and
Mt Barrow in Mount Barker; it also manages three vineyards. It practises mainly organic
viticulture in its owned and managed vineyards, Mt Barrow with a pinot noir block established
and operated using biodynamic practices. The Margaret River winery incorporates feng shui
principles, and can welcome large groups for concerts, speaking events, film evenings and
private parties. Burch Family Wines also operates a cellar door at Scotsdale Road, Denmark
(7 days 10–4). At the top of the portfolio is Howard Park Abercrombie Cabernet Sauvignon,
then follow the Rieslings, Chardonnay and Sauvignon Blanc. Next come pairs of Shiraz and
Cabernet Sauvignon under the Leston and Scotsdale labels, and the Miamup and Flint Rock
regional range. MadFish is a second label, itself with three price tiers: MadFish Gold Turtle,
Sideways and (the original) MadFish, covering the full varietal range. A founding member of
Australia's First Families of Wine. Exports to all major markets.

♀♀♀♀♀ **Howard Park Chardonnay 2015** Wow. This comes out of the glass at a rate of
knots, its intensity almost shocking, and not yielding an inch on the way through
to the finish and aftertaste. White peach, pink grapefruit, cedary/toasty oak,
electrifying acidity are fused together as they soar through the heights. Screwcap.
13% alc. **Rating** 97 **To** 2030 $54 ✪

Howard Park Chardonnay 2014 Estate-grown, hand-picked, and chilled before
hand-sorted, whole bunch-pressed direct to barrel (30% new French) for wild
fermentation, matured on lees for 9 months, part with mlf. Iron fist in a velvet
glove, more common with red wines than chardonnay, but this has awesome power,
concentration and length to its pink grapefruit, white stone fruit and pistachio,
nougat accents from the mlf. Screwcap. 13% alc. **Rating** 97 **To** 2024 $54 ✪

Howard Park Abercrombie Cabernet Sauvignon 2013 83% Mount Barker,
17% Margaret River, wild-fermented, extended maceration, matured for 20
months in French barriques (60% new). Has class stamped all over it in big letters
from start to finish. The bouquet is full of fragrant cassis fruit and high quality
cedary oak, the medium-bodied, but intense, palate with perfectly balanced fruit,
tannins and oak. That balance makes it easy to enjoy now, even though its ultimate
destiny is way down the track. Screwcap. 14% alc. **Rating** 97 **To** 2043 $125 ✪

♀♀♀♀♀ **Howard Park Scotsdale Great Southern Shiraz 2014** The purple-crimson
colour is excellent, the wine living up to that promise; the spicy/peppery bouquet
leads into a medium to full-bodied palate, black fruits, licorice and pepper all on
display. It is the structure of the tannins that clinch the deal: they are rounded and
sewn into the fabric of the wine. This and the Leston are very different, but of
equal quality. Screwcap. 14.5% alc. **Rating** 96 **To** 2044 $46 ✪

Howard Park Leston Margaret River Shiraz 2014 The dense but vibrant
hue flags the sumptuous wine that follows, flooded with blackberry, blackcurrant
and spice; while it flirts with full-bodied status, it has a supple and long, very well
balanced, palate. The 5% Great Southern component isn't identifiable per se, but
has played a role. Lovely wine. Screwcap. 14.5% alc. **Rating** 96 **To** 2040 $46 ✪

Howard Park Leston Margaret River Cabernet Sauvignon 2013 Both
opulent and fine at once. The bullseye has been hit dead centre here. Oak,
fruit, acid and tannin all pull together. Excellent wine, builds its own landscape.
Blackcurrant-like flavour, luscious, is slipped with coffee-cream, leather, cigars.
Dusty, fruit-filled tannin winds its way through, inexorable, unhurried, a river
flowing over smooth long stones. The longer you sit with it, the lower the price
seems. Screwcap. 14% alc. **Rating** 96 **To** 2030 $46 CM ✪

Howard Park Museum Release Great Southern Riesling 2011 Free-run
juice was cold-fermented, with Mount Barker and Porongurup components
blended for the final product. One sure foot down the golden path to full maturity

2 or 3 years hence; the volume of the fruit bowl has already expanded, juicy citrus now with hints of honey. Screwcap. 12% alc. **Rating** 95 **To** 2026 $41
Howard Park Jete Methode Traditionnelle NV 83% chardonnay and 17% pinot noir, traditional method based on '12 vintage, tiraged Jul '12, disgorged after 36 months on lees. Full of joyous white peach, grapefruit and apple fruit flavours, yet fresh and crisp on the long finish. Diam. 12% alc. **Rating** 95 **To** 2020 $34 ○
Howard Park Porongurup Riesling 2015 It's dry and lengthy, but it has some flesh. The combination speaks of class. Lemon pith, grapefruit, slate, lime blossom. You'd think it was easy. Screwcap. 12% alc. **Rating** 94 **To** 2028 $34 CM
Howard Park Mount Barker Riesling 2015 A line of great rieslings have appeared over the decades under the Howard Park label; here a flowery, scented bouquet leads into a complex palate with Granny Smith, Meyer lemon and a subtext of limey acidity produce yet another classy riesling, with more to come. Screwcap. 12% alc. **Rating** 94 **To** 2025 $33
Howard Park Sauvignon Blanc 2015 Thrilling intensity. You could measure the flavour here in watts. Grass, gravel, tropical fruit and lime. It all rips out through the finish. A beauty. Screwcap. 13% alc. **Rating** 94 **To** 2016 $31 CM
Howard Park Scotsdale Great Southern Cabernet Sauvignon 2013 Vines planted in '67. 40% new French oak. It's an example of effortless quality. It tastes of blackcurrant, bay leaves, smoky/creamy oak and gravel, but the way the flavour swooshes through the mouth and then slings out through the finish determines its quality. Screwcap. 14% alc. **Rating** 94 **To** 2028 $46 CM

♥♥♥♥♡ **Howard Park Miamup Sauvignon Blanc Semillon 2015** **Rating** 93 **To** 2017 $28 CM
Howard Park Miamup Chardonnay 2015 **Rating** 93 **To** 2023 $28
MadFish Pinot Noir 2014 **Rating** 93 **To** 2024 $18 ○
MadFish Gold Turtle Cabernet Sauvignon Merlot 2014 **Rating** 93 **To** 2024 $25 ○
MadFish Gold Turtle Semillon Sauvignon Blanc 2015 **Rating** 92 **To** 2019 $25 ○
MadFish Gold Turtle Chardonnay 2015 **Rating** 92 **To** 2020 $25 ○
MadFish Shiraz Rose 2015 **Rating** 92 **To** 2017 $18 ○
Howard Park Flint Rock Great Southern Pinot Noir 2015 **Rating** 92 **To** 2025 $28
MadFish Shiraz 2014 **Rating** 92 **To** 2029 $18 ○
Howard Park Flint Rock Great Southern Shiraz 2013 **Rating** 92 **To** 2026 $28 CM
Howard Park Cellar Collection Cabernet Sauvignon Shiraz 2013 **Rating** 92 **To** 2025 $32
MadFish Riesling 2015 **Rating** 91 **To** 2025 $18 ○
Howard Park Jete Methode Traditionnelle Rose NV **Rating** 91 **To** 2016 $35 CM
MadFish Premium White 2015 **Rating** 90 **To** 2022 $19 ○
Howard Park Flint Rock Mount Barker Chardonnay 2015 **Rating** 90 **To** 2019 $29
Howard Park Cellar Collection Chardonnay 2014 **Rating** 90 **To** 2019 $32
MadFish Gold Turtle Shiraz 2014 **Rating** 90 **To** 2020 $25

Burge Family Winemakers ★★★★★

1312 Barossa Way, Lyndoch, SA 5351 **Region** Barossa Valley
T (08) 8524 4644 **www.**burgefamily.com.au **Open** Fri, Sat, Mon 10–5
Winemaker Rick Burge **Est.** 1928 **Dozens** 3500 **Vyds** 10ha
Burge Family Winemakers, with Rick Burge at the helm (not to be confused with Grant Burge, although the families are related), has established itself as an icon producer of exceptionally rich, lush and concentrated Barossa red wines. 2013 marked 85 years of continuous winemaking by three generations of the family. Exports to Canada, Germany, Belgium, The Netherlands, Hong Kong, Singapore and Japan.

♥♥♥♥♥ Olive Hill Shiraz 2012 Estate-grown, spending 12 months in new and used French (Allier) barriques. The bouquet sets the antennae waving with its promise (duly delivered) of plush blackberry fruit, quality oak entirely integrated on the medium-bodied palate, the tannins ripe and soft. The best for many years. The cork is perfect. 13.8% alc. **Rating** 95 **To** 2032 $30 ❂

Maturation Reserve Release Olive Hill Premium Barossa Semillon 2012 Brilliant glowing green-yellow; now if you want toast, butter and lime marmalade, try this. A freak wine in every way, because it also treads lightly. Screwcap. 12% alc. **Rating** 95 **To** 2022 $32 ❂

Draycott Shiraz 2013 Matured for 16 months in French barriques (45% new). A microscopic yield from the Draycott block, and was always going to be full-bodied. The multiplicity and complexity of the flavours on offer is exceptional, the anise on the finish a lipsmacking farewell. Cork. 14.8% alc. **Rating** 95 **To** 2038 $35 ❂

Eden Valley Riesling 2015 Crisp lime juice flavours come heavily laden with talc Classic regional/varietal combination. Both intensity and length are very good. Screwcap. 12% alc. **Rating** 94 **To** 2028 $26 CM ❂

♥♥♥♥♡ Olive Hill Premium Semillon 2014 Rating 93 To 2020 $26 CM ❂
Draycott Shiraz Souzao 2014 Rating 93 To 2023 $25 CM ❂
Clochemerle Grenache Shiraz Mourvedre 2014 Rating 93 To 2024 $18 ❂
Wilsford Founders Reserve Three Generations Blend Old Tawny Port NV Rating 93 To 2015 $38
Draycott Shiraz Souzao 2013 Rating 91 To 2028 $25
The Spanner Tempranillo Grenache 2014 Rating 91 To 2020 $20 CM ❂
Olive Hill Roussanne Semillon 2015 Rating 90 To 2020 $28 CM
Olive Hill Mourvedre 2012 Rating 90 To 2025 $25

Burk Salter Wines   ★★★

72 Paisley Road, Blanchetown, SA 5357 **Region** Riverland
T (08) 8540 5023 **www.**burksalterwines.com.au **Open** W'ends & public hols 11–4.30
Winemaker Peter Gajewski, Eric and Jenny Semmler **Est.** 2002 **Dozens** 3000
Vyds 20.4ha
The husband-and-wife team of Gregory Burk Salter and Jane Vivienne Salter is the third generation of the Salter family to grow grapes at their Blanchetown property. They have chardonnay, semillon, colombard, ruby cabernet, shiraz, merlot, cabernet sauvignon and muscat gordo blanco; 450 tonnes are sold each year, the remaining 50 tonnes contract-made at various small Barossa Valley wineries. The cellar door and a self-contained B&B adjoin the vineyard, which has Murray River frontage.

Burke & Wills Winery   ★★★★

3155 Burke & Wills Track, Mia Mia, Vic 3444 **Region** Heathcote
T (03) 5425 5400 **www.**wineandmusic.net **Open** By appt
Winemaker Andrew Pattison, Robert Ellis **Est.** 2003 **Dozens** 1500 **Vyds** 3.4ha
After 18 years at Lancefield Winery in the Macedon Ranges, Andrew Pattison moved his operation a few miles north in 2004 to set up Burke & Wills Winery at the southern edge of Heathcote, continuing to produce wines from both regions. With vineyards at Mia Mia and Redesdale, he now has 2ha of shiraz, 1ha of cabernet sauvignon and Bordeaux varieties and 0.4ha of gewurztraminer. He still sources a small amount of Macedon Ranges fruit from his former Malmsbury vineyard; additional grapes are contract-grown in Heathcote. Exports to Malaysia.

♥♥♥♥♥ Mia Mia Heathcote Gewurztraminer 2015 Establishes its varietal make-up from the first whiff of its spiced lavender, rose and lychee fruit, the palate simply confirming that which the bouquet promised. The fruit flavours are so exotic you might think the wine has residual sugar, but the sweetness is almost entirely that of the fruit. Screwcap. 13.5% alc. **Rating** 94 **To** 2023 $28 ❂

Vat 1 French Oak Heathcote Shiraz 2014 Hand-picked, open-fermented, basket-pressed, matured in new and used French oak for 12 months. Reflects the cool climate of the border between the Macedon Ranges and Heathcote; the bouquet has spice and red fruit aromas that invite you to press on quickly to the very elegant, light to medium-bodied palate with its encore of spicy, fresh red fruits. Screwcap. 13% alc. **Rating** 94 **To** 2030 $36

The Aristocrat Heathcote Cabernet Merlot 2013 Cabernet sauvignon, cabernet franc and merlot from Redesdale, petit verdot, malbec and merlot from the estate Mia Mia Vineyard; open-fermented, hand-plunged, matured for 12 months in French oak. It is very well named, aristocratic as it is with its unyielding tannins strung through the red and black fruits of the medium-bodied palate; in the end, cassis does get the last say – or is it laugh? Screwcap. 14% alc. **Rating** 94 **To** 2030 $36

ŸŸŸŸŸ Vat 2 American Oak Heathcote Shiraz 2012 Rating 91 **To** 2027 $28

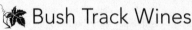 # Bush Track Wines   ★★★★

219 Sutton Lane, Whorouly South, Vic 3735 **Region** Alpine Valleys
T 0409 572 712 **www**.bushtrackwines.com.au **Open** By appt
Winemaker Jo Marsh, Eleana Anderson **Est.** 1987 **Dozens** 300 **Vyds** 9.65ha
Bob and Helen McNamara established the vineyard in 1987, the 5.53ha of shiraz with 11 different clones, the other plantings 2ha of chardonnay, 1.72ha of cabernet sauvignon and 0.4ha of sangiovese. They have made small volumes of wines since 2006, all sold locally, and given the improvement in vineyard practices, and employing the services of Jo Marsh (Billy Button Wines) and Eleana Anderson (Mayford Wines), should secure the future of Bush Track Wines.

ŸŸŸŸŸ Alpine Valley Chardonnay 2015 You can't do much more with a single vineyard Alpine Valley chardonnay than starting with the best two Dijon clones (96 and 97). White peach and nectarine open proceedings, grapefruit and apple providing the end of the palate; the oak handling has been impeccable. Screwcap. 12.5% alc. **Rating** 94 **To** 2024 $24 ✪

ŸŸŸŸŸ Alpine Valleys Shiraz 2014 Rating 93 **To** 2026 $25 CM ✪
Alpine Valleys Cabernet Sauvignon 2013 Rating 92 **To** 2028 $25 ✪

Buttermans Track   ★★★★☆

PO Box 82, St Andrews, Vic 3761 **Region** Yarra Valley
T 0425 737 839 **www**.buttermanstrack.com.au **Open** Not
Winemaker James Lance, Gary Trist **Est.** 1991 **Dozens** 600 **Vyds** 2.13ha
I became intimately acquainted with Buttermans Track in the latter part of the 1980s when Coldstream Hills, at that stage owned by my wife Suzanne and myself, purchased grapes from the Roberts family's Rising Vineyard. I had to coax a 3-tonne truck with almost no brakes and almost no engine to tackle the hills and valleys of the unsealed Buttermans Track. Louise and Gary Trist began planting a small vineyard in '91 on a small side road just off the Buttermans Track. Between then and 2003 they established 0.86ha of pinot noir, 0.74ha of shiraz and 0.53ha of sangiovese. The first tiny yield of 400kg of pinot noir was sold to a boutique winery in the Yarra Valley, and the Trist family continued to sell the grapes to Yarra Valley wineries until '08. From that year onwards a small parcel of sangiovese was retained for the Buttermans Track label, which has now extended to include the other two varieties.

ŸŸŸŸŸ Yarra Valley Sangiovese 2014 Still holding bright crimson hue; a most attractive wine with cherries of every shape and size, and exceptional, fine-grained tannins. Top class. Screwcap. 13.9% alc. **Rating** 95 **To** 2025 $32 ✪

Museum Release Yarra Valley Sangiovese 2008 Destemmed, 50% crushed, 50% whole berries, wild open ferment, 21 days on skins, matured in used French barriques for 18 months. Some colour change to be expected, but the depth of the hue is another thing again – quite exceptional; to nitpick, might be accused of some over extraction, but … Screwcap. 14% alc. **Rating** 94 **To** 2018 $75

🍷🍷🍷🍷 Yarra Valley Pinot Noir 2015 Rating 88 To 2018 $40

Buxton Ridge ★★★☆
88 Seal Rock Road, Buxton, Vic 3711 **Region** Upper Goulburn
T (03) 5774 7117 **www.**buxtonridge.com **Open** W'ends & public hols 10–5
Winemaker Michael Gelbert **Est.** 1996 **Dozens** 1300 **Vyds** 3ha
The story of Buxton Ridge is long and complicated, with sorrow and hardship, but also extraordinary tenacity. In 1996 Lorna and IT consultant husband Wolf-Ruediger Gelbert purchased a 2ha property. The first shiraz was planted in Nov '96; Wolf retired in Oct '97, and in November that year planted small quantities of sauvignon blanc, pinot noir, merlot and more shiraz. Every weekend was spent with the endless tasks of a young vineyard. Wolf died unexpectedly from a heart attack in July '98, leaving an embryonic vineyard and a building site where their dream house had only advanced to the stage of a leaky cellar. Their youngest son Michael wanted to continue, and with input from friends and experts, the business progressed, with small blocks either side of the original vineyard purchased and more vines planted. Oscar Rosa and Nick Arena from Mount Cathedral Wines took Michael under their wing, and he has made all the red wines since 2005, with Marysville an important local market. Then came the '09 bushfires, the destruction of that year's vintage by smoke, and the loss of the '11 vintage thanks to the cold and wet spring and summer.

🍷🍷🍷🍷🍷 Molly Jean Methode Traditionelle Blanc de Noir 2012 Strawberry ex pinot
noir very obvious (and attractive), but it lacks depth. Time in the bottle may help.
Diam. 12% alc. **Rating** 91 **To** 2017 $33

Byrne Vineyards
PO Box 15, Kent Town BC, SA 5071 **Region** South Australia
T (08) 8132 0022 **www.**byrnevineyards.com.au **Open** Not
Winemaker Peter Gajewski, Phil Reedman MW **Est.** 1963 **Dozens** 35 000 **Vyds** 384ha
The Byrne family has been involved in the SA wine industry for three generations, with vineyards spanning SA's prime wine-producing regions, including Clare Valley, Eden Valley, Adelaide Plains and Riverland. The vines vary from 20 to over 50 years of age. Exports to the UK, Canada, France, Germany, Denmark, Sweden, Norway, Thailand, the Philippines, Singapore, Japan and China.

🍷🍷🍷🍷🍷 Antiquarian Barossa Shiraz 2013 Matured in French barriques for 24 months,
winning silver and bronze medals in overseas shows. A supple, medium-bodied
wine that has plenty going for it, including a recurrent theme of licorice and spice
through its bouquet and palate. For once, a Barossa shiraz that seems less alcoholic
than stated, allowing plenty of room to come back several times to enjoy what it
offers. Diam. 14.5% alc. **Rating** 94 **To** 2028 $59

🍷🍷🍷🍷🍷 Limited Release Clare Valley Sangiovese 2013 Rating 90 To 2023 $59

Byron & Harold
351 Herdigan Road, Wandering, WA 6308 **Region** Great Southern
T 0402 010 352 **www.**byronandharold.com.au **Open** Not
Winemaker Luke Eckersley **Est.** 2011 **Dozens** 20 000 **Vyds** 18ha
The owners of Byron & Harold make a formidable partnership, covering every aspect of winemaking, sales and marketing, and business management and administration. Paul Byron and Ralph (Harold) Dunning together have more than 65 years of experience in the Australian wine trade, working at top levels for some of the most admired wineries and wine distribution companies. Andrew Lane worked for 20 years in the tourism industry, including in a senior role with Tourism Australia, leading to the formation of the Wine Tourism Export Council. More recently he developed the family vineyard (Wandering Lane). Luke Eckersley

has a Bachelor of Science in oenology and viticulture, and has worked in Europe and the US, then at Forest Hill and Rockcliffe. Exports to Canada, China and NZ.

TTTTT **The Partners Great Southern Pinot Noir 2015** Rich varietal aromas of sour cherry and red berry fruits are overlaid with toasty oak, hints of tobacco and savoury notes which all fit together perfectly. The palate is long and deeply flavoured, the acid and tannin in exact balance and extending the finish as far as you could wish for. Screwcap. 14.5% alc. **Rating** 96 **To** 2027 $40 ✪

The Partners Great Southern Cabernet Sauvignon 2013 Machine-picked, cold-soaked for 6–8 days in static fermenters, then fermented at 24–26°C, matured in French oak for 15 months. Excellent hue and depth; a full-bodied cabernet that imposes itself on you from the first sip through to the lingering aftertaste thanks to its pristine expression of blackcurrant, bay leaf/dried herbs and autocratic tannins. Screwcap. 14.5% alc. **Rating** 96 **To** 2043 $40 ✪

The Partners Great Southern Riesling 2015 Intense and linear, the strict citrus characters of lime and grapefruit are entwined with softer notes of blossom and talc. The acidity is the spine, running from beginning to end and imprinting itself on the finish and aftertaste. Great now, but the ageing potential is almost limitless. Screwcap. 12.5% alc. **Rating** 95 **To** 2035 $35 ✪

TTTTᵀ **The Partners Great Southern Chardonnay 2014** Rating 93 To 2024 $40
The Partners Great Southern Chardonnay 2015 Rating 92 To 2022 $40
Wheelabout St Margaret's Margaret River Chardonnay 2014 Rating 92 To 2022 $28
Wheelabout Hay View Mount Barker Shiraz 2013 Rating 92 To 2023 $28
The Partners Great Southern Shiraz 2013 Rating 92 To 2030 $40
First Mark Mount Barker Chardonnay 2014 Rating 91 To 2020 $13 ✪

Caillard Wine   ★★★★★

5 Annesley Street, Leichhardt, NSW 2040 (postal) **Region** Barossa Valley
T 0433 272 912 **www**.caillardwine.com **Open** Not
Winemaker Dr Chris Taylor, Andrew Caillard MW **Est.** 2008 **Dozens** 700
Andrew Caillard MW has had a long and varied career in wine, including vintages at Brokenwood and elsewhere, but has also taken the final step of making his own wine, with the support of wife Bobby. Andrew says the inspiration to make Mataro (and now Shiraz) came while writing the background for the Penfolds' The Rewards of Patience tastings. He learnt that both Max Schubert and John Davoren had experimented with mataro, and that the original releases of Penfolds St Henri comprised a fair percentage of the variety. For good measure, Andrew's great (times four) grandfather, John Reynell, planted one of Australia's first vineyards at Reynella, around 1838. Exports to Hong Kong and China.

TTTTT **Reynell Selection Coonawarra Cabernet Sauvignon 2013** This could double as cabernet cologne. It exhibits that gorgeous cassis and violet scent, lifted by mint and finished with aromas of dried, brown tobacco. It acts – when you finally begin to drink it – as its introduction caused you to expect, its lines of blackcurrant trained by thick, warm tannin. Classic lines. Screwcap. 14.8% alc. **Rating** 94 **To** 2030 $35 CM

Cake Wines   ★★★

162 Redfern Street, Redfern, NSW 2016 (postal) **Region** Adelaide Hills
T 0432 532 094 **www**.cakewines.com **Open** Not
Winemaker Tim Burvill, Richie Harkham, Dave Mackintosh **Est.** 2011 **Dozens** 8500
There is more to this venture than meets the eye. The simple explanation is that the business is a collective of young winemakers and young wine lovers, intent on building a wine business targeted at 'new generation' wine drinkers, people in their late 20s and early 30s. So far, so good. But the winemaking team leaders are all very experienced: Tim Burvill, consultant winemaker, once with the ultra-premium whites team at Penfolds, and thereafter winemaker and proprietor of Rockbare; Richie Harkham, based in the Hunter Valley; and

Dave Mackintosh, of the Yarra Valley, where he wears a number of hats. Much of the wine portfolio comes from Adelaide Hills: Sauvignon Blanc, Pinot Gris, Rose and Pinot Noir, plus Limestone Coast Cabernet Sauvignon and McLaren Vale Shiraz. The funding for this far-flung wine business comes from the two owners, Mike Smith and Glen Cassidy.

ŶŶŶŶ **Adelaide Hills Sauvignon Blanc 2014** Snow pea and passionfruit flavours make a decent fist of intensity and momentum. Simple, fresh, easy to enjoy. Screwcap. 12.5% alc. **Rating** 88 **To** 2016 $18 CM
Adelaide Hills Pinot Gris 2015 Clean, crisp and well made with enough fruit flavour to keep most folks happy. Screwcap. 13% alc. **Rating** 88 **To** 2016 $18 CM
McLaren Vale Cabernet Sauvignon 2014 It has depth but it also has a perfumed, minty freshness. Dusty tannin gives away its variety as much as anything. Screwcap. 14% alc. **Rating** 88 **To** 2021 $18 CM

Calabria Family Wines   ★★★★☆

1283 Brayne Road, Griffith, NSW 2680 **Region** Riverina
T (02) 6969 0800 **www**.calabriawines.com.au **Open** Mon–Fri 8.30–5, w'ends 10–4
Winemaker Bill Calabria, Emma Norbiato, Tony Steffania, Jeremy Nascimben, Sam Trimboli **Est.** 1945 **Dozens** NFP **Vyds** 55ha
Along with a number of Riverina producers, Calabria Family Wines (until 2014 known as Westend Estate) has successfully lifted both the quality and the packaging of its wines. Its 3 Bridges range, which has an impressive array of gold medals to its credit, is anchored on estate vineyards. Calabria Family Wines is moving with the times, increasing its plantings of durif, and introducing aglianico, nero d'Avola, and St Macaire (on the verge of extinction, and once grown in Bordeaux, this 2ha is the largest planting in the world). Equally importantly, it is casting its net over the Canberra District, Hilltops and King Valley premium regions, taking this one step further by acquiring a 12ha vineyard in the Barossa Valley. A producer that consistently delivers exceptional value for money across the entire range. Exports to the UK, the US and other major markets, including China.

ŶŶŶŶŶ **The Iconic Grand Reserve Barossa Valley Shiraz 2013** It's a beast that is no burden to drink. It offers a wealth of black fruit, toasty oak and swaggering tannin, and if you stand anywhere near it you're likely to get sucked into its vortex of dense, saturated flavour. It's an 'old school' style but concentration, balance and length like this never goes out of style. Screwcap. 14.5% alc. **Rating** 97 **To** 2043 $175 CM

ŶŶŶŶŶ **3 Bridges Barossa Valley Shiraz 2014** A flood of black, inky flavour meets and greets and then sweeps you through the palate. Dense blackberry, sweet coffeed oak, earthen/leathery tannin. Blockbuster style and value. Screwcap. 14.5% alc. **Rating** 94 **To** 2026 $25 CM **◐**

ŶŶŶŶŶ **3 Bridges Durif 2014** Rating 92 To 2032 $25 CM **◐**
3 Bridges Botrytis Semillon 2013 Rating 92 To 2018 $25 CM **◐**
3 Bridges Tumbarumba Chardonnay 2015 Rating 91 To 2020 $22 CM **◐**
3 Bridges Barossa Valley Cabernet Sauvignon 2014 Rating 91 To 2021 $25 CM
Cool Climate Series Eden Valley Riesling 2015 Rating 90 To 2020 $15 CM **◐**
Calabria Private Bin Aglianico 2015 Rating 90 To 2020 $15 CM **◐**

Caledonia Australis | Mount Macleod   ★★★★

PO Box 626, North Melbourne, Vic 3051 **Region** Gippsland
T (03) 9329 5372 **www**.southgippslandwinecompany.com **Open** Not
Winemaker Mark Matthews **Est.** 1995 **Dozens** 4500 **Vyds** 16.18ha
Mark and Marianna Matthews acquired Caledonia Australis in 2009. Mark is a winemaker with vintages in numerous wine regions around the world. He works as a winemaking teacher, and also runs a contract winemaking business. Marianna has experience with

major fast-moving consumer goods brands globally. The Matthews have converted the main chardonnay block to certified organic, and are rehabilitating around 8ha of wetlands with the local catchment authority. Exports to Canada and Japan.

🍷🍷🍷🍷🍷 **Caledonia Australis Gippsland Chardonnay 2013** Except for no sign of cloudiness in the appearance, I have little to add to Campbell Mattinson's original tasting note: 'Slightly cloudy appearance. Flavours of tinned pineapple, fig and peach with a creamy, spicy sauce. Remains lively throughout despite its soft, ripe profile. Good to drink now.' Screwcap. 14% alc. **Rating** 92 **To** 2018 $28
Caledonia Australis Gippsland Pinot Noir 2013 **Rating** 91 **To** 2018 $28 CM

Campbells ★★★★★

Murray Valley Highway, Rutherglen, Vic 3685 **Region** Rutherglen
T (02) 6033 6000 **www**.campbellswines.com.au **Open** Mon–Sat 9–5, Sun 10–5
Winemaker Colin Campbell, Tim Gniel, Julie Campbell **Est.** 1870 **Dozens** 36 000
Vyds 72ha
Campbells has a long and rich history, with five generations of the family making wine for over 140 years. There were difficult times: phylloxera's arrival in the Bobbie Burns Vineyard in 1898; the Depression of the 1930s; and premature deaths. But the Scottish blood of founder John Campbell has ensured that the business has not only survived, but quietly flourished. Indeed, there have been spectacular successes in unexpected quarters (white table wines, especially Riesling) and expected success with Muscat and Topaque. 99-point scores from Robert Parker and a 100-point score from Harvey Steiman (*Wine Spectator*) put Campbells in a special position. It is fair to say that the nigh-on half-century fourth-generation stewardship of Malcolm and Colin Campbell has been the most important in the history of the winery, but the five members of the fifth generation all working in the business are well equipped to move up the ladder when Colin and/or Malcolm decide to retire. A founding member of Australia's First Families of Wine. Exports to the UK, the US, China and other major markets.

🍷🍷🍷🍷🍷 **Merchant Prince Rare Muscat NV** Wines of this intensity can be a life-changing experience. If it was any thicker or denser it would be impossible to pour. It has might but it also has glory: it packs bags of tarry, toffeed, burnt fruits and honeyed flavours, but it still manages to skip through the palate at a speed more youthful wines often cannot manage. Few wines come as guaranteed to impress as this does. Screwcap. 18% alc. **Rating** 98 **To** 2016 $120 CM ✪
Isabella Rare Topaque NV A deep well of flavour, preserved and kept fresh to make the weight on our shoulders seem lighter. If you look deep into this wine's olive-mahogany hues you're likely to glimpse an insight into human existence. Such is the profound depth of flavour. Toffee apples, sweet tea, raisins and stone fruits dried and shrivelled. There's a tar-like thickness here; a burst of lime/toffee treacle. Screwcap. 18% alc. **Rating** 97 **To** 2016 $120 CM ✪

🍷🍷🍷🍷🍷 **Grand Topaque NV** Deep olive-brown, especially on the rim; gloriously intense and complex, yet satin smooth; burnt honey/toffee carries the spice and Christmas cake mid-palate, then a lovely drying, nutty, aftertaste. 375ml. Cork. 17.5% alc. **Rating** 96 **To** 2015 $65 ✪
Grand Muscat NV Intense leather, malt, black tea and burnt honey flavours with brighter notes of dried orange peel and apricot. Dense, dark Christmas cake character, in-shot with roasted nuts. They release these treasures each year; they're raved over routinely; they must never be taken for granted. Screwcap. 17.5% alc. **Rating** 96 **To** 2016 $65 CM ✪
The Sixties Block 2013 Fantastic release. A step up in class for this label. Fresh, polished, dark-berried fruits, licks of woody spice, peppercorns and slippery, smoky oak. Floral influences, succulent feel throughout, plenty of grunt but with a modern face. Screwcap. 14.5% alc. **Rating** 95 **To** 2030 $30 CM ✪
Bobbie Burns Shiraz 2013 Richness and personality. Excellent release. Blackberry, iodine, leather and toast, with musky notes adding an extra layer of

appeal. Grainy, earthen tannin gives it an authoritative stamp. Excellent value.
Screwcap. 14.5% alc. **Rating** 94 To 2028 $22 CM ✪
Limited Release Durif 2013 Fans of Rutherglen durif should seek this little
beauty out. It is laden with black fruits and subsequent concentrated and savoury
palate, coupled with firm and chewy tannins. Screwcap. 14% alc. **Rating** 94
To 2029 $28 ✪
Liquid Gold Classic Topaque NV Old sweet material brimful with life. If we
were introduced to these wines anew we would find them miraculous. Tea, dried
apricot, honey and dark, intense butterscotch. Sweet but champing at the bit to
please, and to entertain. Screwcap. 17.5% alc. **Rating** 94 To 2016 $38 CM

♀♀♀♀♀ **Classic Muscat NV Rating** 93 To 2016 $38 CM
Muscat NV Rating 92 To 2016 $18 CM ✪
Limited Release Marsanne Viognier 2015 Rating 91 To 2017 $25
Limited Release Rutherglen Roussanne 2015 Rating 90 To 2017 $25

Cannibal Creek Vineyard ★★★★

260 Tynong North Road, Tynong North, Vic 3813 **Region** Gippsland
T (03) 5942 8380 www.cannibalcreek.com.au **Open** 7 days 11–5
Winemaker Patrick Hardiker **Est.** 1997 **Dozens** 2500 **Vyds** 5ha
Patrick and Kirsten Hardiker moved to Tynong North in 1988, initially grazing beef cattle,
but aware of the viticultural potential of the sandy clay loam and bleached subsurface soils
weathered from the granite foothills of the Black Snake Ranges. Plantings began in '97, using
organically based cultivation methods; varieties include pinot noir, chardonnay, sauvignon
blanc, merlot and cabernet sauvignon. The family established the winery in an old farm barn
built in the early 1900s by the Weatherhead family, with timber from Weatherhead Hill (visible
from the vineyard); it also houses the new cellar door and restaurant.

♀♀♀♀♀ **Sauvignon Blanc 2015** Pale straw; crystal clear aromas of passionfruit and
lemongrass with real purity lead into a perfectly proportioned palate backed by
a fine spice of mineral acids; long and refreshing. Screwcap. 12.5% alc. **Rating** 93
To 2018 $32
Cabernet Merlot 2014 Incorrectly labelled Cabernet Merlot when it is 70%
merlot and 30% cabernet. Mid-red; it is a fragrant and berry-scented wine whose
vibrancy and purity flows seamlessly from aroma to palate, the finish plush and
layered. Screwcap. 13% alc. **Rating** 93 To 2024 $35
Methode Traditionnelle 2011 The elegance of this cool season is sustained in
this blanc de blancs with a pristine pale straw hue and a focused palate of lemon
and apple fruit, sustained by an excellent line of beautifully ripe acidity. Four years
on lees has brought wonderful integration and finely textured structure and just
the faintest hint of almond meal complexity. Plenty of potential yet. Diam. 11% alc.
Rating 93 To 2021 $32 TS
Chardonnay 2014 Mid-straw; citrus, melon, white peach, wrapped in well-
handled French oak; the palate is seamless, creamy, and held in check with a nice
touch of acidity. Screwcap. 13% alc. **Rating** 92 To 2020 $32
Chardonnay 2013 Darts through the mouth. High acid style. Bitter grapefruit-
like flavour, though there's plenty of pulp and flesh – and ripeness – to latch onto.
Toasty fig notes lurk. Some interest. Plenty of drive. Distinctly designed for the
dinner table. Screwcap. 13.5% alc. **Rating** 92 To 2020 $28 CM
Pinot Noir 2014 Delicate red fruits, spice and a herbal background are the main
aromas; the palate is spicy, silky and relatively soft, although the purity of fruit and
sensitive handling shine through. Screwcap. 13.5% alc. **Rating** 92 To 2022 $35
Merlot 2014 Light mid-red; leafy red fruits with some earthy notes; a light
to medium-bodied palate with savoury tannins to close. Screwcap. 13.5% alc.
Rating 90 To 2020 $35

Cape Barren Wines   ★★★★☆

PO Box 738, North Adelaide, SA 5006 **Region** McLaren Vale
T (08) 8267 3292 **www**.capebarrenwines.com **Open** By appt
Winemaker Rob Dundon **Est.** 1999 **Dozens** 11 400 **Vyds** 16.5ha

Cape Barren was founded in 1999 by Peter Matthews, who worked tirelessly to create wines of distinction from some of the oldest vineyards in McLaren Vale. Peter sold the business in late 2009 to Rob Dundon and Tom Adams, who together have amassed in excess of 50 years' experience in winemaking, viticulture and international sales. The wines are sourced from dry-grown vines between 70 and 125 years old. With changes in vineyard blocks, the '15 vintage red wines (to be released early '17) will be from 70yo shiraz and 79yo grenache. Chardonnay, sauvignon blanc and gruner veltliner are sourced from the Adelaide Hills. Exports to the US, Canada, Switzerland, Vietnam, the Philippines, Singapore, Taiwan, Hong Kong, Thailand, Japan and China.

ҮҮҮҮҮ **Native Goose McLaren Vale Shiraz 2014** From three vineyards 45–70yo, separately crushed, 8 days fermentation, pressed at 2° baume, matured in French and American oak (17% new) for 12 months. Exceptionally deep crimson-purple, holding its depth through to the rim; the palate follows on logically, dense and full-bodied, blackberry, licorice and spice oozing from every pore; there is no sign of alcohol heat, the oak is fully integrated, the tannins soft (reflecting the pressing before dryness). I would expect a $50 price tag, not a paltry $23. Screwcap. 14.7% alc. **Rating** 94 **To** 2029 $23 **❂**

ҮҮҮҮҮ **Native Goose Adelaide Hills Chardonnay 2014** **Rating** 92 **To** 2018 $23 CM **❂**

Native Goose McLaren Vale GSM 2013 **Rating** 92 **To** 2022 $23 CM **❂**
Funky Goose Adelaide Hills Gruner Veltliner 2015 **Rating** 90 **To** 2020 $21 **❂**
McLaren Vale Cabernet Sauvignon Merlot Cabernet Franc 2013
Rating 90 **To** 2023 $18 **❂**

Cape Bernier Vineyard   ★★★★

230 Bream Creek Road, Bream Creek, Tas 7175 **Region** Southern Tasmania
T (03) 6253 5443 **www**.capebernier.com.au **Open** By appt
Winemaker Winemaking Tasmania (Julian Alcorso) **Est.** 1999 **Dozens** 1800 **Vyds** 4ha

Andrew and Jenny Sinclair took over from founder Alastair Christie in 2014. The vineyard plantings consist of 2ha of pinot noir (including three Dijon clones), 1.4ha of chardonnay and 0.6ha of pinot gris on a north-facing slope with spectacular views of Marion Bay. The property is one of several in the region that are changing from dairy and beef cattle to wine production and tourism. The coastal vineyard benefits from the moderating effects of the sea in Tasmania's generally cool climate. Exports to Singapore.

ҮҮҮҮҮ **Pinot Noir 2013** Wild ferment, matured for 9 months in French puncheons. Light, bright colour; a very attractive pinot with that X-factor so many Tasmanian pinots share. Here ripe red fruits are balanced by spicy, savoury sidelights that create a sense of place, and of space. Screwcap. 13.5% alc. **Rating** 93 **To** 2025 $36

Pinot Rose 2015 Delicious strawberry fruit aromas and flavours reflect the small amount of chardonnay field-blended; citrus, rather than acidity per se, marks the long finish. Scrumptious. Screwcap. 12.7% alc. **Rating** 91 **To** 2018 $29

Chardonnay 2013 Tangy, incisive and bright, the acidity in the DNA of the flesh of this chardonnay. Unsweetened grapefruit and some preserved fruit flavours are an odd couple, especially with the hoodie of acidity. Screwcap. 13% alc. **Rating** 90 **To** 2020 $40

ҮҮҮҮ **Pinot Gris 2015** **Rating** 89 **To** 2017 $29

Cape Grace Wines

281 Fifty One Road, Cowaramup, WA 6284 **Region** Margaret River
T (08) 9755 5669 **www.**capegracewines.com.au **Open** 7 days 10–5
Winemaker Dylan Arvidson, Mark Messenger (Consultant) **Est.** 1996 **Dozens** 2000
Vyds 6.25ha

Cape Grace can trace its history back to 1875, when timber baron MC Davies settled at Karridale, building the Leeuwin lighthouse and founding the township of Margaret River; 120 years later, Robert and Karen Karri-Davies planted the vineyard to chardonnay, shiraz and cabernet sauvignon, with smaller amounts of cabernet franc, malbec and chenin blanc. Robert is a self-taught viticulturist; Karen has over 15 years of international sales and marketing experience in the hospitality industry. Winemaking is carried out on the property; consultant Mark Messenger is a veteran of the Margaret River region. Exports to Singapore and China.

🍷🍷🍷🍷🍷 **Reserve Margaret River Cabernet Sauvignon 2012** Cape Grace has fulfilled its desire to make a Reserve cabernet, a 2-barrel selection from the Estate Cabernet Sauvignon, held for an additional 4 months in barrel after the Estate had been bottled. It is a beautiful wine, graceful and elegant, the balance utterly exceptional. Screwcap. 13.5% alc. **Rating** 97 **To** 2032 $85 ❂

🍷🍷🍷🍷🍷 **Margaret River Shiraz 2013** Hand-picked and sorted, destemmed, open-fermented, 24 days on skins with hand-plunging for the first 14 days, matured in French barriques (50% new) for 12 months. Blackberry, licorice and tar flavours are framed by high quality oak and persistent, but ripe, tannins, melding power with grace. Screwcap. 13.5% alc. **Rating** 96 **To** 2038 $35 ❂

Margaret River Chardonnay 2015 Hand-picked, whole bunch-pressed cloudy juice wild-fermented, matured in French oak (33% new) for 10 months., 160 dozen made. A very classy wine, elegance its cornerstone. Will mature very slowly. Screwcap. 12.9% alc. **Rating** 95 **To** 2027 $38

Margaret River Cabernet Sauvignon 2013 Hand-picked and sorted, destemmed to an open fermenter, cultured yeast, 15 days on skins, matured for 12 months in French oak (50% new), 560 dozen made. Deep crimson-purple; it is still exceptionally youthful, cassis confronted by argumentative tannins. Attrition will ensure they both fall into step. Screwcap. 14.5% alc. **Rating** 95 **To** 2048 $55

🍷🍷🍷🍷🍷 **Margaret River Cabernet Shiraz 2014** Rating 93 **To** 2029 $25 ❂
Margaret River Cabernet Franc 2014 Rating 93 **To** 2029 $40

Cape Jaffa Wines

459 Limestone Coast Road, Mount Benson via Robe, SA 5276 **Region** Mount Benson
T (08) 8768 5053 **www.**capejaffawines.com.au **Open** 7 days 10–5
Winemaker Anna and Derek Hooper **Est.** 1993 **Dozens** 10000 **Vyds** 22.86ha

Cape Jaffa was the first of the Mount Benson wineries, its winery made from local rock (between 800 and 1000 tonnes are crushed each year). Cape Jaffa's fully certified biodynamic vineyard provides 50% of production, with additional fruit sourced from a certified biodynamic grower in Wrattonbully. Having received the Advantage SA Regional Award in '09, '10 and '11 for its sustainable initiatives in the Limestone Coast, Cape Jaffa is now a Hall of Fame inductee. Exports to the UK, Canada, Thailand, the Philippines, Hong Kong, Singapore and China.

🍷🍷🍷🍷🍷 **Limestone Coast Sauvignon Blanc 2015** No tricks to the winemaking, simply cool-fermented in stainless steel, but gold medals at the Adelaide Wine Show and Melbourne Wine Awards '15 attest to the balance and length of the tropical fruits that fill the palate. Obviously, terrific value. Screwcap. 12.5% alc. Rating 95 **To** 2016 $20 ❂

Cavaliers Limestone Coast Shiraz 2014 Reductive, but firm and rich. Smoky oak, blackberry and plum fruit, iodine and assorted woody herbs/spices. This has personality and power, and it curls on and out through the finish. It's great at the asking price. Screwcap. 14.5% alc. **Rating** 94 **To** 2028 $25 CM ❂

🍷🍷🍷🍷🍷 En Soleil Shiraz 2014 Rating 93 To 2029 $39 CM
Upwelling Cabernet Sauvignon 2014 Rating 93 To 2034 $29
Graviere Cabernet Sauvignon 2013 Rating 92 To 2026 $25 CM ✪
En Soleil Pinot Gris 2015 Rating 91 To 2017 $27 CM
Riptide Red Blend 2014 Rating 91 To 2024 $29
Anna S Limestone Coast White Blend 2015 Rating 90 To 2017 $25 CM

Cape Mentelle ★★★★★

Wallcliffe Road, Margaret River, WA 6285 **Region** Margaret River
T (08) 9757 0888 **www.**capementelle.com.au **Open** 7 days 10–4.30
Winemaker Robert Mann, Paul Callaghan, Evan Thompson **Est.** 1970 **Dozens** 105 000
Vyds 166ha
Part of the LVMH (Louis Vuitton Möet Hennessy) group. Cape Mentelle is firing on all
cylinders, with the winemaking team fully capitalising on the extensive and largely mature
vineyards, which obviate the need for contract-grown fruit. It is hard to say which of the wines
is best; the ranking, such as it is, varies from year to year. That said, Sauvignon Blanc Semillon,
Chardonnay, Shiraz and Cabernet Sauvignon lead the portfolio, and Cape Mentelle is one of
those knocking on the door the the Winery of the Year Award. Exports to all major markets.

🍷🍷🍷🍷🍷 **Wallcliffe 2013** 55/45% sauvignon blanc, semillon. Aromatics. Mouthfeel. A
power of flavour. And scorching length. This is an emphatic release. As sophisticated
as it is, simply delicious. Screwcap. 13% alc. **Rating** 96 To 2021 $45 CM ✪
Chardonnay 2014 Some wines are songs to their variety and vineyard(s) and this
is one such. It's touched by toasty, spicy oak but the wellspring is clearly the fruit,
pure and shining as it is. Gingerbread, white peach, pear and grapefruit. A match
has been struck nearby, the glow and the smoke subtly apparent. Beauty in a bottle.
Screwcap. 13% alc. **Rating** 96 To 2022 $46 CM ✪
Cabernet Sauvignon 2013 A seamless parade of varietal and regional flavour.
Gone is the brawn of yesteryear; this holds finesse and length closest to its chest.
Blackcurrant, cedar wood, dust, undergrowth and gravel/eucalypt characters
build a wealth of succulent momentum before lingering on through the finish.
Integration of tannin the final quality flourish. Screwcap. 13.5% alc. **Rating** 95
To 2030 $94 CM
Shiraz 2013 A core of black-cherried fruit champs through an array of clove and
assorted dry spice notes. This is a savoury rocket. Peppery, leafy, fruity and firm. Its
ripeness is at the upper level of comfort, but power and impact comes as a result.
Screwcap. 14% alc. **Rating** 94 To 2028 $46 CM

🍷🍷🍷🍷🍷 **Sauvignon Blanc Semillon 2015** Rating 93 To 2019 $25 CM ✪
Zinfandel 2013 Rating 93 To 2024 $50 CM

Cape Naturaliste Vineyard ★★★★☆

1 Coley Road (off Caves Road), Yallingup, WA 6282 **Region** Margaret River
T (08) 9755 2538 **www.**capenaturalistevineyard.com.au **Open** 7 days 10.30–5
Winemaker Ian Bell, Bruce Dukes, Craig Brent-White **Est.** 1997 **Dozens** 2600
Vyds 9.7ha
Cape Naturaliste Vineyard has a long and varied history going back 150 years, when it was a
coach inn for travellers journeying between Perth and Margaret River. Later it became a dairy
farm, and in 1970 a mining company purchased it, intending to extract nearby mineral sands.
The government stepped in and declared the area a national park, whereafter (in '80) Craig
Brent-White purchased the property. The vineyard is planted to cabernet sauvignon, shiraz,
merlot, semillon and sauvignon blanc, and is run on an organic/biodynamic basis.

🍷🍷🍷🍷🍷 **Reserve Single Vineyard Merlot 2012** Merlot of weight and purpose.
Integration of oak, fruit, acid and tannin is spot on here. Dark-berried fruits,
musky vanillan, gum nut and toasty/sawdusty oak. It smells accessibly sweet and
perfumed even as a young wine, but the palate has its sights set on the future.
Screwcap. 14.5% alc. **Rating** 95 To 2035 $50 CM

Torpedo Rocks Reserve Single Vineyard Cabernet Sauvignon 2012 The
hand of tannin descends on ripe, dark-berried fruit. No mucking around here.
Varietal and intense, satisfying easily on the palate before lingering through the
finish. Screwcap. 14.5% alc. **Rating** 94 **To** 2032 $60 CM

Torpedo Rocks Single Vineyard Cabernet Shiraz 2012 Dark fruit,
blackcurrant and black olive march through dry twists of bay and tobacco leaf.
With every step, tannin holds and grips. Substance is its middle name. Screwcap.
14.5% alc. **Rating** 94 **To** 2034 $50 CM

 Torpedo Rocks Single Vineyard Shiraz 2012 Rating 92 To 2024 $40 CM
Reserve Shiraz 2012 Rating 92 To 2024 $60 CM
Single Vineyard Cabernet Sauvignon 2012 Rating 92 To 2025 $40 CM
Cabernet Sauvignon 2014 Rating 91 To 2027 $25 CM
Single Vineyard Sauvignon Blanc 2015 Rating 90 To 2017 $20 CM ✪

Capel Vale ★★★★★

118 Mallokup Road, Capel, WA 6271 **Region** Geographe
T (08) 9727 1986 **www**.capelvale.com **Open** 7 days 10–4
Winemaker Daniel Hetherington **Est.** 1974 **Dozens** 50 000 **Vyds** 90ha
Established by Perth-based medical practitioner Dr Peter Pratten and wife Elizabeth in 1974.
The first vineyard adjacent to the winery was planted on the banks of the quiet waters of
Capel River. The very fertile soil gave rise to extravagant vine growth, providing 95% of
the winery's intake until the mid-1980s. The viticultural empire has since been expanded,
spreading across Geographe (15ha), Mount Barker (15ha), Pemberton (28ha) and Margaret
River (32ha). There are four tiers in the Capel Vale portfolio, Debut (varietals), Regional
Series, Black Label Margaret River Chardonnay and Cabernet Sauvignon, and at the top the
Single Vineyard Wines of Whispering Hill, Mount Barker and The Scholar Margaret River
Cabernet Sauvignon. Exports to all major markets.

ℙℙℙℙℙ Single Vineyard Series Whispering Hill Mount Barker Shiraz 2014 Shows
the synergy between Mount Barker and shiraz; go to the Rhône Valley to find a
shiraz of similar style and quality, but count yourself lucky if you only have to pay
double. Black fruits, licorice, cracked pepper – all the usual building blocks, except
that these are gold-plated. Screwcap. 14.5% alc. **Rating** 97 **To** 2039 $55 ✪

ℙℙℙℙℙ Regional Series Mount Barker Riesling 2014 This is Top Gear stuff, racing at
high speed across the palate, yet doing so with such ease and precision you arrive
at the diamond-clear finish and aftertaste in a flash, repeating the exercise as often
as you wish. Screwcap. 12.5% alc. **Rating** 95 **To** 2030 $25 ✪

Single Vineyard Series The Scholar Margaret River Cabernet Sauvignon
2014 The colour doesn't have the depth expected at this price; in all other
respects it does what is expected of it, with cassis, leaf and herb fruit, a decent
amount of French oak and disciplined tannins. Screwcap. 14.5% alc. **Rating** 94
To 2029 $80

ℙℙℙℙℙ Regional Series Margaret River Cabernet Sauvignon 2014 Rating 91
To 2024 $27

Capercaillie ★★★★☆

4 Londons Road, Lovedale, NSW 2325 **Region** Hunter Valley
T (02) 4990 2904 **www**.capercailliewine.com.au **Open** 7 days 10–4.30
Winemaker Peter Lane **Est.** 1995 **Dozens** 7000 **Vyds** 8ha
A highly successful winery in terms of the quality of its wines, as well as their reach outwards
from the Hunter Valley. The Capercaillie wines have always been well made, with generous
flavour. Following the example of Brokenwood, its fruit sources are spread across South
Eastern Australia, although the portfolio includes high quality wines that are 100% Hunter
Valley. Exports to the UK, Dubai and China.

🍷🍷🍷🍷🍷 **The Ghillie 2014** From the same red volcanic soils and 70yo vines as its less expensive shiraz sibling. Exceptional colour; it is highly fragrant, and marries elegance with its intense and complex array of red and black fruits that have soaked up the new oak. Screwcap. 14.2% alc. **Rating** 96 **To** 2044 $70 ❂

🍷🍷🍷🍷🍷 **Hunter Valley Shiraz 2014 Rating** 93 **To** 2054 $35

Capital Wines   ★★★★★

42 Cork Street, Gundaroo, NSW 2620 **Region** Canberra District
T (02) 6236 8555 **www.**capitalwines.com.au **Open** Thurs–Sun 10–5
Winemaker Andrew McEwin **Est.** 1986 **Dozens** 5000 **Vyds** 5ha
This is the venture of Mark and Jennie Mooney (of the Royal Hotel at Gundaroo) and Andrew and Marion McEwin (of Kyeema Wines). They joined forces to found Capital Wines, which purchased Kyeema Wines and its related contract winemaking in 2008. The venture saw the creation of The Ministry Series wines, with clever graphic design and generally invigorated marketing efforts. The estate vineyard is still an important source, supplemented by grape purchases. The cellar door operates in conjunction with the Grazing Restaurant in Gundaroo, in the 1830s stone stables. Exports to Thailand.

🍷🍷🍷🍷🍷 **Gundaroo Vineyard Riesling 2015** Geisenheim clone, hand-picked, whole bunch-pressed, cultured yeast, cool-fermented, four trophies, including Champion Wine of Show, Canberra Regional Wine Show. Immaculately balanced and structured, calmly going about its business, secure in the knowledge of its destiny 5–10 years hence when all its aromas will come into full flower. Screwcap. 11% alc. **Rating** 95 **To** 2035 $28 ❂
Kyeema Vineyard Reserve Merlot 2014 This is a very snappy merlot, plum shown the door, red fruits taking its place in this medium-bodied wine. The tannins are fine and soft, but sufficient to give the wine the texture it needs. Screwcap. 14% alc. **Rating** 95 **To** 2034 $48
The Whip Canberra District Riesling 2015 Geisenheim clone, hand-picked, whole bunch-pressed, cultured yeast, cool-fermented. Close on the heels of the Gundaroo Vineyard release; this is as pure as fresh driven snow, with delicate lime/lemon citrus fruit gently clasped by crisp acidity. Great value. Screwcap. 11% alc. **Rating** 94 **To** 2030 $21 ❂
The Senator Canberra District Chardonnay 2015 Hand-picked, cultured yeast, fermented and matured in French oak for 6 months. Attractive wine from the grapefruit side of the bed sheets. Has good drive and length, the oak perfectly pitched. Screwcap. 12.8% alc. **Rating** 94 **To** 2024 $25 ❂
The Frontbencher Shiraz 2014 35+yo Penfolds clone, hand-picked and sorted, some whole bunches, open-fermented, cultured yeast, matured in French oak. Has plenty of energy, but not trying to land a knockout punch first up. Juicy black cherry and blackberry flavours do have a measure of savoury tannins, but they're compressed, electoral victory in sight. Screwcap. 13.7% alc. **Rating** 94 **To** 2029 $27 ❂
Kyeema Vineyard Reserve Shiraz Viognier 2014 Hand-picked and sorted, some whole bunches, co-fermented, cultured yeast, matured in French oak. Bright and lively red fruits lifted by the viognier, the finish long and fresh, the tannins superfine, the oak subtle. Delicious now, but will hold on for years. Screwcap. 13.5% alc. **Rating** 94 **To** 2034 $52
The Ambassador Tempranillo 2014 Hand-picked and sorted, some whole bunches, open-fermented, cultured yeast, matured in French oak. Decadently, juicily rich, with plum joining the more usual cherry on both the palate and bouquet. This is deadly stuff, likely to wreak havoc on safe drinking standards. Screwcap. 13.9% alc. **Rating** 94 **To** 2029 $27 ❂

🍷🍷🍷🍷🍷 **The Backbencher Merlot 2014 Rating** 93 **To** 2029 $27 ❂
Kyeema Vineyard Reserve Shiraz 2014 Rating 92 **To** 2034 $52
Kyeema Vineyard Tempranillo Shiraz 2014 Rating 92 **To** 2025 $36

Cargo Road Wines

Cargo Road, Orange, NSW 2800 **Region** Orange
T (02) 6365 6100 **www**.cargoroadwines.com.au **Open** W'ends & public hols 11–5
Winemaker James Sweetapple **Est.** 1983 **Dozens** 3000 **Vyds** 14.65ha
Originally called The Midas Tree, the vineyard was planted in 1983 by Roseworthy graduate
John Swanson, who established a 2.5ha vineyard that included zinfandel – 15 years ahead
of his time. The property was acquired in '97 by Charles Lane, James Sweetapple and Brian
Walters. They have rejuvenated the original vineyard and planted more zinfandel, sauvignon
blanc, cabernet and riesling. Exports to the UK and Singapore.

🍷🍷🍷🍷🍷 **Orange Riesling 2015** Unambiguously good riesling, with layers of lime, lemon
and apple separated from each other by elastic acidity drawing out the very long
and persistent finish. Screwcap. 11.5% alc. **Rating** 94 **To** 2025 $28 ✪

🍷🍷🍷🍷🍷 **Orange Sauvignon Blanc 2014 Rating** 93 **To** 2017 $25 ✪
Orange Gewurztraminer 2015 Rating 91 **To** 2023 $25
Orange Cabernet Sauvignon 2013 Rating 90 **To** 2023 $35

Carlei Estate | Carlei Green Vineyards ★★★★★

1 Alber Road, Upper Beaconsfield, Vic 3808 **Region** Yarra Valley/Heathcote
T (03) 5944 4599 **www**.carlei.com.au **Open** W'ends 11–6
Winemaker Sergio Carlei **Est.** 1994 **Dozens** 10 000 **Vyds** 2.25ha
Sergio Carlei has come a long way, graduating from home winemaking in a suburban garage
to his own (commercial) winery in Upper Beaconsfield. Carlei Estate falls just within the
boundaries of the Yarra Valley. Along the way Carlei acquired a Bachelor of Wine Science from
CSU, and established a vineyard with organic and biodynamic accreditation adjacent to the
Upper Beaconsfield winery, plus 7ha in Heathcote. Contract winemaking services are now a
major part of the business. Exports to the US, Singapore and China.

🍷🍷🍷🍷🍷 **Estate Directors' Cut Central Victoria Shiraz 2007** A barrel selection that
spent 24 months in oak. Deep crimson-purple; looks as if it might have the secret
to eternal youth, so plush and rich is its panoply of velvety black fruits, licorice,
spice and pepper; the tannins and oak both contribute to the total package. Diam.
14.9% alc. **Rating** 96 **To** 2032 $90
Estate Nord Heathcote Shiraz 2012 Red Cambrian soil; a 5-day cold soak,
destemmed berries then wild-fermented plus post-fermentation maceration for
25 days, matured for 10 months in French oak (40% new). Deep crimson-purple,
a full-bodied, layered palate brings pepper, licorice and bitter chocolate into play,
backed by ripe tannins. Diam. 14.9% alc. **Rating** 95 **To** 2037 $149
Estate Sud Heathcote Shiraz 2012 Decomposed granite soils; identical
making to the Estate Nord other than slightly longer on skins. A fragrant berry
bouquet, and a lighter and softer medium to full-bodied palate will be ready well
before Nord, although it still has an attractive web of red and black fruits, licorice
and spice. Diam. 14.7% alc. **Rating** 95 **To** 2032 $69

🍷🍷🍷🍷🍷 **Estate Pinot Noir 2012 Rating** 92 **To** 2020 $49
Green Vineyards Heathcote Shiraz 2012 Rating 92 **To** 2025 $30
Green Vineyards Cardinia Ranges Pinot Noir 2012 Rating 90 **To** 2019 $27

Casa Freschi

159 Ridge Road, Ashton, SA 5137 **Region** Langhorne Creek
T 0409 364 569 **www**.casafreschi.com.au **Open** By appt
Winemaker David Freschi **Est.** 1998 **Dozens** 2000 **Vyds** 7.55ha
David Freschi graduated with a degree in oenology from Roseworthy College in 1991 and
spent most of the decade working in California, Italy and NZ. In '98 he and his wife decided
to trade in the corporate world for a small family-owned winemaking business, with a core of
2.4ha of vines established by his parents in '72; an additional 1.85ha of nebbiolo is now planted

adjacent to the original vineyard. Says David, 'The names of the wines were chosen to best express the personality of the wines grown in our vineyard, as well as to express our heritage.' A second 3.2ha vineyard has been established in the Adelaide Hills, planted to chardonnay, pinot gris, riesling and gewurztraminer. Exports to the UK, Singapore and the Philippines.

TTTTT **Adelaide Hills Chardonnay 2014** Yields were down 66%. What there is of the wine is smashingly good; put it in your mouth and it's like bugles on Anzac Day, the fruit singing proud and clear, the oak sure of its role, the trail of flavour out through the finish an enduring reminder. It's stunning in a way that will never go out of fashion. Screwcap. 12.5% alc. **Rating** 96 **To** 2021 $45 CM ◐

Profondo Old Vines 2013 55/24/21% cabernet sauvignon, shiraz and malbec, wild yeast open-fermented, pressed direct to barrel and matured for 21 months in French barriques (5% new). Has the soft, plushy fruit typical of Langhorne Creek, and is very complex, the apparent impact of oak inexplicable unless a high percentage was 1yo old. All of that said, there's plenty to enjoy. Cork. 14% alc. **Rating** 94 **To** 2030 $55

Langhorne Creek Nebbiolo 2013 Absolutely varietal. Tight with tannin, splashed with spice, juiced with cranberry and red cherry and complexed with leather, herbs, wood smoke. It's almost autumnal but mostly fruity, and yet it's dry to the nth degree. Cork. 13.5% alc. **Rating** 94 **To** 2030 $55 CM

TTTTY **Ragazzi Adelaide Hills Chardonnay 2015 Rating** 93 **To** 2020 $28
Ragazzi Adelaide Hills Pinot Grigio 2015 Rating 93 **To** 2018 $28

Casella Family Brands   ★★★★

Wakely Road, Yenda, NSW 2681 **Region** Riverina
T (02) 6961 3000 **www**.casellafamilybrands.com **Open** Not
Winemaker Alan Kennett, Peter Mallamace **Est.** 1969 **Dozens** 12.5 million **Vyds** 2891ha
The fairytale success story for Casella, gifted the opportunity to establish yellow tail as a world brand overnight by Southcorp withdrawing the distribution of (inter alia) its best-selling Lindemans Bin 65 Chardonnay in the US, is now almost ancient history. yellow tail will remain the engine room for Casella well into the future, but it has now moved decisively to build a portfolio of premium and ultra-premium wines through its acquisition of Peter Lehman in 2014, and then Brand's Laira winery, cellar door and the use of the brand name from McWilliam's in '15. McWilliam's no doubt had its reasons for the sale, but it had invested much time and money in expanding both the vineyards and the winery; the Peter Lehmann and Brand's Laira brands will transform the future shape of Casella's business. The fact that Casella now has 2891ha of vineyards spread across Australia is a case of putting its money where its mouth is. It is second only to Treasury Wine Estates in export sales (by value), followed by Pernod-Ricard and Accolade. Exports to all major markets.

Cassegrain Wines   ★★★★

764 Fernbank Creek Road, Port Macquarie, NSW 2444 **Region** Hastings River
T (02) 6582 8377 **www**.cassegrainwines.com.au **Open** Mon–Fri 9–5, w'ends & public hols 10–5
Winemaker John Cassegrain (Chief), Alex Cassegrain (Senior) **Est.** 1980 **Dozens** 50000 **Vyds** 34.9ha
Cassegrain has continued to evolve and develop. It still draws on the original Hastings River vineyard of 4.9ha, the most important varieties being semillon, verdelho and chambourcin, with pinot noir and cabernet sauvignon making up the numbers. However, Cassegrain also part-owns and manages Richfield Vineyard in the New England region, with 30ha of chardonnay, verdelho, semillon, shiraz, merlot, cabernet sauvignon and ruby cabernet. Grapes are also purchased from Tumbarumba, Orange and the Hunter Valley. Exports to Japan, China and other major markets.

TTTTY **Semillon 2015** Crisp and fresh, but offering a reasonable body of flavour. A good release. Lemon, apple and lime with woolier, fuller aspects. Screwcap. 12% alc. **Rating** 90 **To** 2020 $25 CM

Seasons Sauvignon Blanc 2015 From Orange. Plenty of passionfruit flavour but soft and creamy too. Subtle grassy notes. Draws you in. Screwcap. 13.5% alc. Rating 90 To 2017 $22 CM

🍷🍷🍷🍷 **Edition Noir Chardonnay 2015** Rating 89 To 2017 $28 CM
Shiraz 2014 Rating 89 To 2021 $22 CM
Reserve Shiraz 2011 Rating 89 To 2024 $45 CM
Edition Noir Central Ranges Riesling 2015 Rating 88 To 2018 $25 CM
Edition Noir Gewurztraminer 2015 Rating 88 To 2017 $25 CM
Edition Noir Pinot Noir 2015 Rating 88 To 2022 $35 CM

Castagna ★★★★☆
88 Ressom Lane, Beechworth, Vic 3747 **Region** Beechworth
T (03) 5728 2888 **www**.castagna.com.au **Open** By appt
Winemaker Julian Castagna, Adam Castagna **Est.** 1997 **Dozens** 1800 **Vyds** 4ha
Julian Castagna is an erudite and totally committed disciple of biodynamic grapegrowing and winemaking. While he acknowledges that at least part of the belief in biodynamics has to be intuitive, he also seeks to understand how the principles and practices enunciated by Rudolf Steiner in 1924 actually work. He purchased two egg-shaped, food-grade concrete tanks, each holding 900 litres. They are, he says, 'the most perfect shape in physics', and in the winery reduce pressure on the lees and deposit the lees over a larger surface area, which, he believes, will eliminate the need for batonnage. He has been joined by son Adam, who is responsible for the 400 dozen or so of Adam's Rib made each year, complementing the production of Castagna. Exports to the UK, France, Spain, Denmark, South Korea, Hong Kong, China and Japan.

🍷🍷🍷🍷 **Sparkling Allegro 2009** A full crimson-copper hue heralds a savoury style of spicy tomato flavour. Disgorged Sept '12 after 3 years on lees, it has now lost its primary fruit character and finishes with a touch of bitterness, though retains good persistence. Diam. 13.5% alc. **Rating** 88 **To** 2016 $45 TS
Sparkling Genesis 2008 Still a vibrant red hue after 4 years on lees, this is a complex and savoury style with tomato, spice and a subtle tropical hint from a touch of viognier. Sour acidity and bitter dark chocolate linger long on the finish. Diam. 13.5% alc. **Rating** 88 **To** 2023 $80 TS

Castelli Estate ★★★★★
380 Mount Shadforth Road, Denmark, WA 6333 **Region** Great Southern
T (08) 9364 0400 **www**.castelliestate.com.au **Open** 7 days 10–5
Winemaker Mike Garland **Est.** 2007 **Dozens** 10 000
Castelli Estate will cause many small winery owners to go green with envy. When Sam Castelli purchased the property in late 2004, he was intending simply to use it as a family holiday destination. But because there was a partly constructed winery he decided to complete the building work and simply lock the doors. However, wine was in his blood, courtesy of his father, who owned a small vineyard in Italy's south. The temptation was too much, and in '07 the winery was commissioned, with 20 tonnes of Great Southern fruit crushed under the Castelli label, and annual increases thereafter. Fruit is sourced from some of the best vineyards in WA, situated in Frankland River, Mount Barker, Pemberton and Porongurup. Exports to Singapore and China.

🍷🍷🍷🍷🍷 **Il Liris Chardonnay 2014** This wine is not about to sit down and discuss its merits. If you don't get it the first moment, get on your bike. Chardonnay seldom has as much power and drive as this, but what is more striking is that it is luscious peach and nectarine providing the flavour, not citrus or oak. All this from 13% alcohol. Amazing. Screwcap. **Rating** 98 **To** 2030 $65

🍷🍷🍷🍷🍷 **Great Southern Shiraz 2014** The bouquet sets the scene with its black pepper and licorice background to black fruits. The palate is like a black panther: you know it's going to strike, but can't help riding the waves of the spicy black fruits, the audacious tannins ripping and tearing the fabric of the wine, its layer upon layer of black fruits. A bargain for decades of enjoyment. Screwcap. 14.5% alc. Rating 96 To 2044 $32 ❂

Great Southern Shiraz 2013 Vibrant purple-crimson; a perfectly built cool grown shiraz, making you wonder why you would look elsewhere; the bouquet is highly expressive, the counterbalance of the red and black fruits, spice, pepper, fine-grained tannins and French oak perfectly judged. Has gained power since first tasted (Mar '13). Screwcap. 14.3% alc. Rating 96 To 2033 $32 ❂

Il Liris Rouge 2013 Dense, but bright, crimson-purple; the colour reflects the wine, which is also exceptionally dense, rich and velvety with a kaleidoscope of red and black berry fruit flavours; the tannins are controlled, the wine destined for a long, contemplative life. Vino-Lok. 14.6% alc. Rating 96 To 2043 $85

Great Southern Riesling 2015 A fragrant and flowery bouquet sets the scene for a palate of purity and precision, the citrus fruits and minerally acidity interwoven throughout; it also has all the length one could wish for. Screwcap. 12.5% alc. Rating 95 To 2030 $28 ❂

Empirica Great Southern Gewurztraminer 2015 Includes 8% riesling; hand-picked, wild yeast, part fermented in French oak, part in stainless steel, 4 months on lees. I really like this wine, for its overall balance, harmony and juicy mouthfeel, flavours of lemon and lime zest woven through the gossamer touch of oak. Screwcap. 13.3% alc. Rating 95 To 2025 $32 ❂

Empirica Uvaggio 2014 Grenache, mourvedre, shiraz, hand-picked and bunch-sorted, 18 days on skins, 15 months in used French oak. This really attractive GSM owes nothing to either McLaren Vale or the Barossa Valley. There isn't a scintilla of confection; instead there is a welded fusion of red and black fruits on a spicy base plate, the tannins fine, oak used for texture. Screwcap. 14.7% alc. Rating 95 To 2034 $32 ❂

The Sum Riesling 2015 The fragrant, floral bouquet is enticing, but the impact of the palate comes as a surprise; it surges with a bow wave of citrus and passionfruit that overflows with flavour. It has the acidity to provide balance and length, and puts a large 'must buy' placard around the neck of (an attractively packaged) bottle. Screwcap. 12.5% alc. Rating 94 To 2025 $16 ❂

🍷🍷🍷🍷🍷 **Empirica Pemberton Fume Blanc 2015** Rating 93 To 2018 $32
Denmark Pinot Noir 2014 Rating 91 To 2026 $32
Pemberton Chardonnay 2015 Rating 90 To 2020 $32
Empirica Iced Viognier 2014 Rating 90 To 2017 $32

Castle Rock Estate   ★★★★★

2660 Porongurup Road, Porongurup, WA 6324 **Region** Porongurup
T (08) 9853 1035 www.castlerockestate.com.au **Open** 7 days 10–5
Winemaker Robert Diletti **Est.** 1983 **Dozens** 4500 **Vyds** 11.2ha

An exceptionally beautifully sited vineyard (riesling, pinot noir, chardonnay, sauvignon blanc, cabernet sauvignon and merlot), winery and cellar door on a 55ha property with sweeping vistas from the Porongurups, operated by the Diletti family. The standard of viticulture is very high, and the vineyard itself is ideally situated. The two-level winery, set on a natural slope, maximises gravity flow. The Rieslings have always been elegant and have handsomely repaid time in bottle; the Pinot Noir is the most consistent performer in the region; the Shiraz is a great cool climate example; and Chardonnay has joined a thoroughly impressive quartet, elegance the common link. Rob Diletti's excellent palate and sensitive winemaking mark Castle Rock as one of the superstars of WA. Exports to China.

🍷🍷🍷🍷🍷 **Porongurup Riesling 2015** You often need to have tasted Castle Rock's Rieslings as they develop over a 5–10-year period to interpret them in their youth. Having said that, this has more varietal fruit (citrus, apple and citrus zest) interwoven with minerally acidity than many of its predecessors. Its aftertaste is extraordinarily persistent. Screwcap. 12.5% alc. Rating 96 To 2035 $26 ❂

A&W Reserve Great Southern Riesling 2015 Something of a riesling masterclass. Or a thesis on purity and control. Take your pick. Pristine citrus and slate with chalky characters to the texture. Bursting with quality. Gold medal WA Wine Show '15. Screwcap. 12% alc. **Rating** 96 **To** 2028 $35 CM ✪

Great Southern Pinot Noir 2014 Very good hue and clarity; a wine that goes from strength to strength as Rob Diletti's experience and the vineyard's maturity grow each vintage. Its strengths are its balance, harmony, varietal purity and length. It's hard to ask for more – this is the best Great Southern pinot. Screwcap. 13.8% alc. **Rating** 96 **To** 2025 $35 ✪

ㅇㅇㅇㅇㅇ **Skywalk Great Southern Riesling 2015 Rating** 93 **To** 2022 $20 CM ✪
Diletti Chardonnay 2014 Rating 91 **To** 2021 $30 CM

Catherine Vale Vineyard   ★★★★

656 Milbrodale Road, Fordwich, NSW 2330 **Region** Hunter Valley
T (02) 6579 1334 **www**.catherinevale.com.au **Open** W'ends & public hols 10–5
Winemaker Hunter Wine Services (John Hordern) **Est.** 1993 **Dozens** 1200 **Vyds** 4.5ha
Wendy Lawson has taken over management of Catherine Vale Vineyard for the foreseeable future after the death of Bill in Jan 2016. Bill's teaching life at Knox Grammar School extended for 28 of his 36-year teaching career, and the Bill and Wendy team continued for 20 years in the Hunter Valley, melding into the communities around Broke. This retirement venture is now 21yo with the lion's share of the vineyard planted to chardonnay and semillon, with smaller amounts of verdelho, arneis, dolcetto and barbera. The Lawsons chose to plant the latter three varieties after visiting the Piedmont region of Italy, pioneering the move to these varieties in the Hunter. In '12 Wendy received an OAM for her work in tourism, the environment and viticulture.

ㅇㅇㅇㅇㅇ **Semillon 2014** Pale quartz; pleasant young semillon, but lacks the finesse and drive of the best examples. That said, cellaring for 5 years will bring substantial rewards. Screwcap. 11.4% alc. **Rating** 90 **To** 2020 $18 ✪
Arneis 2014 Has that irrepressible attitude of arneis, with fruit skin and zest, apple, pear and citrus all possibilities; excellent acidity. Screwcap. 11% alc. **Rating** 90 **To** 2017 $20 ✪

ㅇㅇㅇㅇ **Gabrielle Dolcetto 2014 Rating** 89 **To** 2017 $18 ✪
J and B Reserve Winifred Barbera 2014 Rating 88 **To** 2017 $25

Catlin Wines   ★★★★★

39B Sydney Road, Nairne, SA 5252 **Region** Adelaide Hills
T 0411 326 384 **www**.catlinwines.com.au **Open** Not
Winemaker Darryl Catlin **Est.** 2013 **Dozens** 2000
Darryl Catlin grew up in the Barossa Valley with vineyards as his playground, picking bushvine grenache for pocket money as a child. Various stints with Saltram, the Australian Bottling Company and Vintner Imports followed in his 20s, before he moved on to gain retail experience at Adelaide's Royal Oak Cellar, London's Oddbins and McKay's Macquarie Cellars. The next stage was studying for a winemaking degree while working at Adelaide's East End Cellars. Then followed a number of years at Shaw + Smith, rising from cellar hand to winemaker, finishing in 2012 and allowing him to establish his own business the following year. Exports to the UK.

ㅇㅇㅇㅇㅇ **Adelaide Hills Sauvignon Blanc 2014** Hand-picked, basket-pressed and wild-fermented and matured in French oak for 5 months confer the funky nuances of the bouquet and the distinctly edgy complexity of the palate. It all works well, brisk acidity providing a high-tensile backbone. Will polarise opinions, but I like it. Screwcap. 12.5% alc. **Rating** 95 **To** 2016 $30 ✪
Single Vineyard Adelaide Hills Shiraz 2014 Inherently complex, but it remains accessible. This is a face of Australian red wine it's always a pleasure to encounter. It's ripped with cherry-plum flavour but also carries hints (and louder)

of charcuterie, graphite and wood smoke. Tannin seeps slowly from its pores; undergrowth notes rise from its depths. It will develop well, but it's all there to enjoy even now. Screwcap. 14% alc. **Rating** 95 **To** 2030 $45 CM

Adelaide Hills Merlot 2014 Hand-picked grapes from a vineyard with a yield of 1 tonne/acre, open-fermented, hand-plunged, and left on skins for a month before 10 months in used French oak. All this, and the perfect alcohol, has served to produce a wine with delicious cassis fruit, a trace of black olive, and a very appealing juicy mouthfeel. Screwcap. 13.5% alc. **Rating** 95 **To** 2020 $30 **○**

Clare Valley Riesling 2014 Hand-picked, whole bunch-pressed and wild-fermented. The palate is strongly textured, the chalky flavours sitting alongside apple and lime, the finish firm and dry. Cellaring for 10+ years should define its ultimate scope for improvement. Screwcap. 12% alc. **Rating** 94 **To** 2029 $30 **○**

Adelaide Hills Chardonnay 2015 Complex. Fine. Flavoursome. In this case a scintillating combination. Chalk, white peach, dry pear and struck match. Spicy oak offers support but little more. The finish doesn't disappoint, but this is one of those 'had me at hello' wines. Screwcap. 13% alc. **Rating** 94 **To** 2020 $30 CM **○**

Adelaide Hills Gruner Veltliner 2015 Wild-fermented in French oak. Said oak hasn't imparted much flavour (a positive) but it's no doubt contributed to the wine's velvety texture. Indeed this is a lovely wine to have in your mouth; plenty of texture, just enough flavour, and more than a little interest and length. Screwcap. 12.9% alc. **Rating** 94 **To** 2017 $30 CM **○**

🍷🍷🍷🍷🍷 **Adelaide Hills Sauvignon Blanc 2015** Rating 93 **To** 2017 $30 CM
The Molly Mae Clare Valley Riesling 2015 Rating 92 **To** 2022 $16 CM **○**
Adelaide Hills Montepulciano 2014 Rating 90 **To** 2024 $30

Caught Redhanded   ★★★

1 Esplanade, Sellicks Beach, SA 5174 **Region** Adelaide Zone
T 0419 252 967 **Open** Not
Winemaker Phil Rogers, Linda Domas (Consultant) **Est.** 2009 **Dozens** 500
Phil Rogers, a casualty of the 2001 Ansett Airlines collapse, enrolled at the start of '02 in the CSU Bachelor of Wine Science program, completing his first vintage in '03 at Rosemount in McLaren Vale. His practical training involved 12 months as trainee winemaker at the CSU winery, followed by a vintage at Hardys Chateau Reynella, later in the same year making Brunello di Montalcino and Chianti Classico in Tuscany, then back to commercial production in '07 with McLaren Vale Shiraz and Adelaide Hills Syrah.

🍷🍷🍷🍷 **Reserve Grenache 2012** Plenty of oomph, particularly in a varietal context, with blackberry, black cherry and malty oak flavours sliding successfully through the palate. Alcohol is more or less taken in the wine's stride. Age is just starting to mellow things. Screwcap. 15.2% alc. **Rating** 89 **To** 2020 $30 CM
The Labyrinth Grenache Shiraz 2012 Caramel-like oak has left a (too) lasting impression on raspberry and black cherry fruit. It's not unattractive by any stretch and the fruit itself is of handy quality. Alcohol warmth is at play too but not to an excessive degree. Screwcap. 14.8% alc. **Rating** 88 **To** 2020 $25 CM

Centennial Vineyards   ★★★★★

'Woodside', 252 Centennial Road, Bowral, NSW 2576 **Region** Southern Highlands
T (02) 4861 8722 **www**.centennial.net.au **Open** 7 days 10–5
Winemaker Tony Cosgriff **Est.** 2002 **Dozens** 10 000 **Vyds** 28.65ha
Centennial Vineyards, a substantial development jointly owned by wine professional John Large and investor Mark Dowling, covers 133ha of beautiful grazing land, with the vineyard planted to pinot noir (6.21ha), chardonnay (7.14ha), sauvignon blanc (4.05ha), tempranillo (3.38ha), pinot gris (2.61ha) and smaller amounts of savagnin, riesling, arneis, gewurztraminer and pinot meunier. Production from the estate vineyards is supplemented by purchases of grapes from other regions. Tony Cosgriff has not hesitated to source grapes from Orange to meet the challenge of Southern Highlands' capricious weather – Orange provides the bulk of

the 20 wines tasted for this edition that were rated 90 points and above. Exports to the US, Denmark, Singapore, China and South Korea.

🍷🍷🍷🍷🍷 **Reserve Single Vineyard Chardonnay 2013** Hand-picked, whole bunch-pressed, fermented in French oak (22% new), 50/50% wild/cultured yeast, 80% mlf, matured for 9 months. This has great mouthfeel, balance and length; white peach and nectarine lead proceedings, pink grapefruit in the second row, oak at the very back. What will they think of next? Trophy Orange Wine Show '14, golds Cool Climate and Highland Wine Shows '15. Screwcap. 12.8% alc. **Rating** 95 **To** 2022 $33 ✪

Reserve Single Vineyard Pinot Gris 2014 Hand-picked, crushed/destemmed, settled for 4 hours, fermented in used French oak, 50/50% wild/cultured yeast, matured for 9 months. The texture and structure are dramatic: this is gris as Alsace would have it. The fruit flavours are positive, with pear, joined by strawberry, apple and citrus, the residual sugar just below threshold. It is very grippy, but in the very best sense of that term; the length is also impressive. Real wine. Screwcap. 13.6% alc. **Rating** 95 **To** 2017 $26 ✪

Reserve Single Vineyard Arneis 2014 Hand-picked, whole bunch-pressed, settled for 4 hours, fermented in French oak (2% new), 50/50% wild/cultured yeast, matured for 9 months, trophy NSW Small Winemakers Show '15. The winemaking was inspired, leaving arneis with its savoury/herbal/sugar-free fruit base, but giving it context and structure. It has an almost peppery, very attractive, finish. Screwcap. 13% alc. **Rating** 95 **To** 2023 $26 ✪

Winery Block Tempranillo 2014 Hand-picked, crushed/destemmed, open-fermented, cultured yeast, 5 days on skins, matured in used French oak for 9 months, a barrel selection. Rich, supple, fruit-sweet cherry and plum run through a long, medium-bodied palate without a single tremor, leaving the mouth a happy place. From Bowral, making it all the more impressive. Screwcap. 12.5% alc. **Rating** 95 **To** 2024 $25 ✪

Reserve Single Vineyard Shiraz Viognier 2014 A co-fermented 97/3% blend from Orange (given viognier is less than 5%, it should not appear on the label). It works a treat, giving the wine a juicy quality to its cherry-accented fruit, the palate medium-bodied and very well balanced, supple all the way through to the gentle tannins of the finish and aftertaste. Diam. 14.5% alc. **Rating** 94 **To** 2029 $33

🍷🍷🍷🍷🍷 **Reserve Single Vineyard Fume Blanc 2013** Rating 93 To 2017 $25 ✪
Old Block Pinot Grigio 2015 Rating 93 To 2018 $24 ✪
Orange Sauvignon Blanc 2015 Rating 92 To 2017 $22 ✪
Reserve Single Vineyard Pinot Noir 2014 Rating 92 To 2022 $30 CM
Orange Cabernet Sauvignon 2013 Rating 92 To 2028 $25 ✪
House Block Pinot Noir 2014 Rating 91 To 2020 $27
Reserve Single Vineyard Shiraz 2014 Rating 91 To 2030 $30
Reserve Single Vineyard Sangiovese 2014 Rating 91 To 2024 $28
Reserve Single Vineyard Riesling 2015 Rating 90 To 2025 $26
Winery Block Chardonnay 2013 Rating 90 To 2018 $24
Old Block Savagnin 2014 Rating 90 To 2020 $20 ✪
Bong Bong Quattro Bianco 2015 Rating 90 To 2017 $19 CM ✪
Bong Bong Pinot Noir 2014 Rating 90 To 2019 $20 ✪
Bong Bong Quattro Rosso 2014 Rating 90 To 2019 $19 ✪
Old Block Riesling 1012 2015 Rating 90 To 2019 $25 CM

Ceravolo Estate   ★★★★

Suite 5, 143 Glynburn Road, Firle, SA 5070 (postal) **Region** Adelaide Plains/Adelaide Hills
T (08) 8336 4522 **www.**ceravolo.com.au **Open** Not
Winemaker Joe Ceravolo, Michael Sykes **Est.** 1985 **Dozens** 15 000 **Vyds** 23.5ha
Dentist turned vigneron and winemaker Joe Ceravolo, and wife Heather, have been producing single vineyard wines from their 16ha estate on the Adelaide Plains since 1999, enjoying

wine show success with Shiraz, Petit Verdot, Merlot and Sangiovese. Their son Antony, and wife Fiona, have joined to take their family business into the next generation. The Ceravolos have also established vineyards (7.5ha) around their home in the Adelaide Hills, focusing on Italian varieties such as primitivo, picolit, pinot grigio, dolcetto, barbera and cortese. Wines are released under Ceravolo and St Andrews Estate labels. Exports to Denmark, Germany, Dubai, South Korea, Japan, Taiwan and China.

🍷🍷🍷🍷🍷 Adelaide Plains Petit Verdot 2012 For smooth, concentrated flavour at a more-than-reasonable price, this takes some beating. It loads blackcurrant, violet and vanilla flavour onto the palate and sustains the show all the way through to a satisfying finish. Don't hesitate. Cork. 15% alc. **Rating** 93 **To** 2023 $22 CM ✪

Adelaide Hills Cortese 2015 Mad not to, really. If you see this and it's in your price range and a white wine is in order, go for it. It's textural and a bit different and has more than enough flavour, without getting in the way of anything. Pear, apple, grapefruit, that kind of spectrum. But with florals and brine too. Versatile. Screwcap. 12% alc. **Rating** 91 **To** 2017 $20 CM ✪

🍷🍷🍷🍷 The Emigrant Adelaide Plains Primitivo 2013 **Rating** 89 **To** 2019 $20 CM

Adelaide Hills Pinot Grigio 2015 **Rating** 88 **To** 2016 $18 CM

Ceres Bridge Estate ★★★☆

84 Merrawarp Road, Stonehaven, Vic 3221 **Region** Geelong
T (03) 5271 1212 **www**.ceresbridge.com.au **Open** By appt
Winemaker Challon Murdock **Est.** 1996 **Dozens** 400 **Vyds** 7.4ha

Challon and Patricia Murdock began the long, slow and at times very frustrating process of establishing their vineyard at the foot of the Barrabool Hills in 1996. They planted 1.8ha of chardonnay in that year, but 50% of the vines died over the next two years in the face of drought and inadequate water supply. Instead of deciding it was all too difficult, they persevered by planting 1.1ha of pinot noir in 2000, with replanting in '01, and then in '05 signified their intention to become serious by planting shiraz, nebbiolo, sauvignon blanc, viognier, tempranillo and pinot grigio. Those vines are now mature, the nebbiolo, in particular, proving its worth.

🍷🍷🍷🍷🍷 Geelong Shiraz 2013 Hand-picked, crushed and destemmed, wild and cultured yeast, matured in used French barriques for 12 months. Interesting wine: good colour of medium depth, the bouquet in tune with the colour; the sombre black as midnight fruit flavours are, to say the least, striking. Ceres Bridge aims for intensity, and has achieved that in spades. The almost, but not quite, gritty character comes from the fruit, not the tannins (although they are there). You can go on a magic carpet ride for a few pence. Screwcap. 14% alc. **Rating** 92 **To** 2038 $20 ✪

🍷🍷🍷🍷 Geelong Pinot Noir 2014 **Rating** 89 **To** 2023 $20

Geelong Nebbiolo 2014 **Rating** 89 **To** 2024 $20

Chaffey Bros Wine Co ★★★★

26 Campbell Road, Parkside, SA 5063 (postal) **Region** Barossa Valley
T 0417 565 511 **www**.chaffeybros.com **Open** Not
Winemaker Daniel Chaffey Hartwig, Theo Engela **Est.** 2008 **Dozens** 7000

Chaffey Bros was co-founded by Daniel Chaffey Hartwig, whose great-uncle Bill Chaffey founded Seaview Wines in McLaren Vale, and who was himself a descendant of the Chaffey brothers who came to Australia to create the Riverina and Riverland regions by designing and implementing the original irrigation schemes. Daniel, born and raised in the Barossa Valley, picked grapes during school holidays, and later on worked at Penfolds' cellar door. After eight years of selling and helping other people create wine labels, he became a bulk wine merchant dealing in both Australian and overseas wines and wineries and also developing a range of branded wines. Exports to Canada, Denmark, The Netherlands, Singapore, Macau, Hong Kong and China.

🍷🍷🍷🍷🍷 **Zeitpunkt Eden Valley Riesling 2015** Hand-picked from the Ahrens Vineyard. A fine, slatey, zesty wine, high on finesse, but with a fierce whip of flavour to close. Screwcap. 11.5% alc. **Rating** 94 **To** 2024 $30 CM ✪

🍷🍷🍷🍷 **Tripelpunkt Riesling 2015** **Rating** 93 **To** 2020 $24 CM ✪
Dufte Punkt 2015 **Rating** 93 **To** 2018 $25 CM ✪
Synonymous Barossa = Shiraz 2014 **Rating** 93 **To** 2024 $25 CM ✪
The Super Barossa is Shiraz + Cabernet Sauvignon 2014 **Rating** 93 **To** 2027 $35 CM
This Is Not Your Grandma's Eden Valley Riesling 2015 **Rating** 92 **To** 2022 $22 CM ✪
Evangeline Eden Valley Syrah 2014 **Rating** 92 **To** 2024 $35 CM
This Is Not Your Grandma's Barossa Valley Rose 2015 **Rating** 91 **To** 2016 $22 CM ✪

Chain of Ponds ★★★★★

C/- 83 Pioneer Road, Angas Plains, SA 5255 (postal) **Region** Adelaide Hills
T (08) 8389 1415 **www**.chainofponds.com.au **Open** Not
Winemaker Greg Clack **Est.** 1993 **Dozens** 25 000

It is long since the Chain of Ponds brand was separated from its then 200ha of estate vineyards, which were among the largest in the Adelaide Hills. It does, however, have long-term contracts with its major growers and, prior to the 2015 vintage, Greg Clack came onboard as full-time chief winemaker. In May '16 Chain of Ponds closed its cellar door and moved to Project Wine's small-batch processing facility at Langhorne Creek, completing its withdrawal from the Adelaide Hills, other than its grape purchasing contracts. Exports to the UK, the US, Canada, Singapore, Hong Kong, the Philippines and China.

🍷🍷🍷🍷🍷 **The Ledge Adelaide Hills Shiraz 2013** Single vineyard from Kuitpo. It continues the cracking form of recent releases. Bold but elegant, with cherry-plum, spice and fennel favours, slithers of smoky/cedary oak then nestled comfortably within. A fine melt of tannin and confident length. Nails it. Screwcap. 13.9% alc. **Rating** 96 **To** 2032 $38 CM ✪

Forreston Reserve Cabernet Sauvignon 2013 The elegance, the silk, the power. Quality and deliciousness, the bases are covered. Black cherry and undergrowth, sweet-sour cranberry and smoky oak. Spice. It's its own beast; it's not a slave to its variety. In this case that's a very good thing. Screwcap. 14% alc. **Rating** 95 **To** 2035 $80 CM

Forreston Reserve Shiraz 2013 It's not the brightest or most detailed wine, the fruit so intense it feels slightly baked, but it's laced with licorice and sporty with spice, and for both substance and length it has matters well sewn up. Beautiful integration of oak and fruit too, it must be said. Screwcap. 14% alc. **Rating** 94 **To** 2032 $80 CM

🍷🍷🍷🍷 **Black Thursday Sauvignon Blanc 2015** **Rating** 92 **To** 2017 $22 CM ✪
Amadeus Cabernet Sauvignon 2013 **Rating** 92 **To** 2028 $38 CM
Grave's Gate Shiraz 2013 **Rating** 91 **To** 2021 $22 CM ✪
Corkscrew Rd Chardonnay 2014 **Rating** 90 **To** 2021 $38 CM

Chalice Bridge Estate ★★★★★

796 Rosa Glen Road, Margaret River, WA 6285 **Region** Margaret River
T (08) 9319 8200 **www**.chalicebridge.com.au **Open** By appt
Winemaker Janice McDonald (Consultant) **Est.** 1998 **Dozens** 5000 **Vyds** 122ha

Planting of the vineyard (now fully owned by the Edinger family) began in 1998; there are now 29ha of chardonnay, over 28ha each of cabernet sauvignon and shiraz, 12.5ha of semillon, 18ha of sauvignon blanc, 7.5ha of merlot and a small amount of savagnin; it is the second-largest single vineyard in Margaret River. Sensible pricing helps, cross-subsidised by the sale of the major part of the annual crop. Exports to the UK, Macau, Hong Kong and China.

ŸŸŸŸŸ **The Quest Margaret River Merlot 2013** There appears to be what may be
information written by an ant on the side of the label. Given the uncertainty about
the first step, I didn't delve for my magnifying glass. In any event, the wine tells
the full story: high quality merlot opening with cassis, spice and dried herbs; high
quality oak and fine-grained tannins. Screwcap. 14% alc. **Rating** 95 **To** 2030 $30 ✿
The Quest Margaret River Cabernet Sauvignon 2014 This wine has more
in common than not with The Quest Merlot. The answer, flawed though it may
be, is that Margaret River merlots are better than those of any other region, and
stand side by side with cabernet. Screwcap. 14% alc. **Rating** 95 **To** 2030 $30 ✿
The Quest Margaret River Shiraz 2013 Full, deep crimson-purple; has the
works, indeed the kitchen sink full of luxuriant black fruits, oak and tannins. It has
achieved this off the back of moderate acidity, which has been its saviour. The
all-up effect is not dissimilar in weight and power to the big guns of the Barossa
Valley, although with very different fruit flavours. Screwcap. 14% alc. **Rating** 94
To 2038 $30 ✿
**The Chalice Limited Release Margaret River Cabernet Sauvignon
2012** The colour is of moderate depth, although the hue is still bright; it offers a
hedonistic blend of cassis fruit on the one hand and sumptuous French oak on the
other. Just how the game will play out is uncertain, but it should be fun to watch.
377 dozen made. Screwcap. 14% alc. **Rating** 94 **To** 2027 $60

ŸŸŸŸŸ **The Estate Margaret River Chardonnay 2014** **Rating** 92 **To** 2025 $20 ✿

Chalk Hill ★★★★★

58 Field Street, McLaren Vale, SA 5171 **Region** McLaren Vale
T (08) 8323 6400 **www**.chalkhill.com.au **Open** Not
Winemaker Emmanuelle Bekkers **Est.** 1973 **Dozens** 20 000 **Vyds** 89ha
The growth of Chalk Hill has accelerated after passing from parents John and Diana Harvey to
grapegrowing sons Jock and Tom. Both are heavily involved in wine industry affairs in varying
capacities. Further acquisitions mean the vineyards now span each district of McLaren Vale,
planted to both the exotic (savagnin, barbera and sangiovese) and mainstream (shiraz, cabernet
sauvignon, grenache, chardonnay and cabernet franc) varieties. The Alpha Crucis series is
especially praiseworthy. Exports to most markets; exports to the US under the Alpha Crucis
label, to Canada under the Wits End label.

ŸŸŸŸŸ **Alpha Crucis Winemakers' Series Mike Brown Shiraz 2014** Destemmed,
crushed, open-fermented, wild yeast, 16 days on skins, matured in new and
used French barriques for 18 months. Ticks all the boxes from the word go, the
bouquet promising the balance of fruit and oak that follows on the elegant and
long palate. Delivers its message without any self-doubt. The most classic of the
Alpha Crucis series. Screwcap. 14.2% alc. **Rating** 96 **To** 2034 $60 ✿
Alpha Crucis Shiraz 2014 Inky crimson-purple; the flag bearer for Chalk Hill,
and arguably for McLaren Vale as a whole; endless coils of blackberry, satsuma
plum, dark chocolate and licorice are wound with military precision along the
deck of the palate. It's that precision that stops this full-bodied wine going over the
top. Screwcap. 14.5% alc. **Rating** 96 **To** 2039 $85
Alpha Crucis Winemakers' Series Corrina Wright Shiraz 2014 Destemmed
and crushed, 3 days cold soak, open-fermented, wild yeast, basket-pressed to
American (25% new) and French (used) hogheads for completion of fermentation
and maturation, bottled Aug '15. Medium-bodied, it has warm scents and flavours
derived in part from the fruit, and in part from American oak. Very good length
and a supple finish. Screwcap. 14.5% alc. **Rating** 95 **To** 2034 $60
Alpha Crucis Winemakers' Series Tom Harvey Shiraz 2014 Destemmed,
3 days cold soak, pressed to new French hogsheads and puncheons to complete
fermentation and maturation, bottled Aug '15. One of the most elegant of the
group, roughly allied with that of Mike Brown. Obvious new French oak plays a
major role, amplified by concluding the ferment in that oak, a technique I started
using in '73 at Brokenwood, then Coldstream Hills (since '85), so I am a biased
witness. Screwcap. 14.5% alc. **Rating** 95 **To** 2034 $60

Alpha Crucis Winemakers' Series Bec Willson Shiraz 2014 Crushed, 24 hours cold soak, fermented on skins for 11 days, pressed to used French (75%) and American barriques for completion of fermentation and maturation, bottled Aug '15. Excellent colour; a strikingly complex bouquet is matched by a very full-bodied palate, throbbing with black fruits, pulled into line with the completion of fermentation in barrel. Screwcap. 14.9% alc. **Rating** 95 **To** 2034 $60

Alpha Crucis Winemakers' Series Steve Grimley Shiraz 2014 Destemmed, open-fermented for 9 days with a further 7 days on skins, matured in French barriques (20% new). The powerful black fruits of the bouquet and palate are in the same camp as that of Bec Willson; also has a delicious interplay with licorice and a flick of dark chocolate. Screwcap. 14.9% alc. **Rating** 95 **To** 2034 $60

Alpha Crucis Winemakers' Series Peter Schell Shiraz 2014 Destemmed, 40% whole bunches, wild-fermented, 14 days on skins, matured in French barriques (25% new). Pete Schell plays on the wild side with the alcohol (but is not alone on this) and gets away with it, whole bunches and French oak providing cool breezes – magically ending up with an elegant finish. Screwcap. 15% alc. **Rating** 95 **To** 2034 $60

Grenache Tempranillo 2015 50% grenache, 36% tempranillo, 14% graciano. A labrador wine that is desperate to please, wagging its tail furiously, and succeeding handsomely. The sheer purity of the red berry assemblage rests upon the modest alcohol, oak and tannins doing a disappearing trick – they're still there, but are hard to detect. Screwcap. 14% alc. **Rating** 95 **To** 2025 $25 ✪

ＰＰＰＰＰ **Luna Shiraz 2014** Rating 92 To 2029 $19 ✪
Shiraz 2014 Rating 91 To 2029 $25
Cabernet Sauvignon 2014 Rating 90 To 2029 $25
Barbera 2014 Rating 90 To 2025 $29

Chalkers Crossing ★★★★★

285 Grenfell Road, Young, NSW 2594 **Region** Hilltops
T (02) 6382 6900 **www**.chalkerscrossing.com.au **Open** Mon–Fri 9–5
Winemaker Celine Rousseau **Est.** 2000 **Dozens** 14000 **Vyds** 27ha
Chalkers Crossing's Rockleigh Vineyard was planted in 1996–97, and is supplemented by purchased grapes from Tumbarumba. Winemaker Celine Rousseau was born in France's Loire Valley, trained in Bordeaux and has worked in Bordeaux, Champagne, Languedoc, Margaret River and the Perth Hills. This Flying Winemaker (now an Australian citizen) has exceptional skills and dedication. In 2012 a subsidiary of a substantial Hong Kong-based company (Nice Link Pty Ltd) acquired Chalkers Crossing, and has appointed Celine Rousseau as manager of the business in addition to her prior and continuing role as winemaker. Exports to the UK, Canada, Germany, Denmark, Sweden, Thailand, Singapore, China and Hong Kong.

ＰＰＰＰＰ **Riesling 2015** From the 20yo estate Rockleigh Vineyard, cool-fermented in stainless steel, matured on fine lees for 4–6 months. If you haven't recognised the quality of this wine until the finish and aftertaste, you will be rudely awakened by the power and concentration of the lime/lemon citrus fruit held within a framework of minerally acidity. Screwcap. 12.5% alc. **Rating** 94 **To** 2030 $18 ✪
Reserve Shiraz 2014 From the 20yo estate Rockleigh Vineyard, open-fermented, 50% whole berries, matured for 16 months in French hogsheads (40% new). The colour is deep crimson-purple, the complex bouquet signals the balance between sumptuous black fruits and the cedary French oak of the palate. Can be enjoyed now because the tannins on the finish are barely perceptible. The question is should there be more tannin structure? Screwcap. 14.5% alc. **Rating** 94 **To** 2034 $50

ＰＰＰＰＰ **CC2 Riesling 2015** Rating 92 To 2053 $14 ✪
Semillon 2015 Rating 92 To 2020 $18 ✪
Cabernet Sauvignon 2014 Rating 92 To 2029 $30
CC2 Hilltops Chardonnay 2015 Rating 90 To 2020 $18 ✪
Hilltops Shiraz 2014 Rating 90 To 2020 $30

Chalmers

PO Box 2263, Mildura, Vic 3502 **Region** Heathcote
T 0400 261 932 **www**.chalmerswine.com.au **Open** Not
Winemaker Sandro Mosele (Contract) **Est.** 1989 **Dozens** 7500 **Vyds** 26.5ha
Following the 2008 sale of their very large vineyard and vine nursery propagation business, the Chalmers family has refocused its wine businesses. All fruit comes from the 80ha property on Mt Camel Range in Heathcote, which provides the grapes for the individual variety, single vineyard Chalmers range (Vermentino, Fiano, Greco, Lambrusco, Rosato, Nero d'Avola, Sagrantino and Aglianico). The entry-level Montevecchio label is based around blends and more approachable styles. The Chalmers and Montevecchio wines continue to be made at Kooyong. A second vineyard at Mildura is a contract grapegrower, but also has a small nursery block housing the Chalmers' clonal selections. In '13 a program of micro-vinification of the rarer, and hitherto unutilised, varieties from the Nursery Block was introduced.

ΨΨΨΨΨ **Heathcote Greco 2015** The brine, the stone fruit, the apple, the anise. This sets a serious, seafood-friendly tone and holds fast to it. Hard not to be impressed. White wine with substance. Screwcap. 12% alc. **Rating** 94 **To** 2016 $29 CM ❂
Heathcote Rosato 2015 Made with 60% sagrantino and 40% aglianico. It's a beauty. Tangy but jubey/sweet-fruited. A handful of herbs as an afterthought. Summer written all over it. If you see it, don't hesitate. Screwcap. 13% alc. **Rating** 94 **To** 2016 $25 CM ❂

ΨΨΨΨΨ **Heathcote Vermentino 2015 Rating** 93 **To** 2017 $27 ❂
Heathcote Fiano 2014 Rating 92 **To** 2017 $33
Montevecchio Heathcote Rosato 2015 Rating 91 **To** 2016 $23 CM ❂
Montevecchio Heathcote Moscato 2015 Rating 90 **To** 2016 $23 CM

Chambers Rosewood

Barkly Street, Rutherglen, Vic 3685 **Region** Rutherglen
T (02) 6032 8641 **www**.chambersrosewood.com.au **Open** Mon–Sat 9–5, Sun 10–5
Winemaker Stephen Chambers **Est.** 1858 **Dozens** 10 000 **Vyds** 50ha
Chambers' Rare Muscat and Rare Muscadelle (or Topaque or Tokay, what's in a name?) are the greatest of all in the Rutherglen firmament, the other wines in the hierarchy also magnificent. Stephen Chambers comes into the role as winemaker, the sixth generation of the Chambers family, but father Bill, with his startling light blue eyes, is seldom far away. Exports to the UK, the US, Canada, Belgium, Denmark, South Korea, Singapore, China and NZ.

ΨΨΨΨΨ **Rare Rutherglen Muscadelle NV** Dark mahogany; the impact of the wine in the mouth is as extraordinary as that of the Rare Muscat; a micro-sip floods the senses as they go into overdrive trying to capture the myriad interlocking flavours. The everlasting finish and aftertaste are the keys to understanding this wine: it is not just the 5% or so of the oldest component (say 90 years), but the 5% of the most youthful (say 5–6 years) that, by skill worthy of Michelangelo, has given the wine the vibrant freshness drawing you back again and again, but without diminishing its complexity. 375ml. Screwcap. 18% alc. **Rating** 99 **To** 2017 $250 ❂
Rare Rutherglen Muscat NV Dense mahogany; incredibly concentrated and complex, and startling viscosity as it enters the mouth, yet has a quicksilver lightness on the back-palate; the layers of flavour are almost countless, with sour cherry/morello cherry, Turkish coffee and the finest black chocolate (Swiss or Belgian). This wine is truly something that all wine lovers must experience at least once in their lives; one sip was taken for this entire note and the flavour is still building. 375ml. Screwcap. 18% alc. **Rating** 99 **To** 2017 $250 ❂
Grand Rutherglen Muscadelle NV It's the end of a day's tasting and there's no way I'm going to spit out wines of this world–class quality. Malt, mocha, wild honey, caramel and every exotic spice you can think of – all these and more flavours blaze the mouth until you have swallowed it, when the aftertaste is wondrously fresh. 375ml. Screwcap. 18% alc. **Rating** 98 **To** 2017 $100 ❂

Grand Rutherglen Muscat NV The olive rim to the walnut-brown heart of the colour sets the scene; the heady essence of raisin bouquet pushes any discussions of the fortifying spirit to the back row; in its place there is an Arabian bazaar of spices, with a nod to Turkish baklava, then a rolling wave of Christmas pudding with a garnish of dark chocolate and caramelised rose nuts. The ultimate magic of the Chambers wines lies in the freshness of the finish. 375ml. Screwcap. 18.5% alc. Rating 97 To 2017 $55 ✪

🍷🍷🍷🍷🍷 **Old Vine Rutherglen Muscat NV** Rating 93 To 2017 $25 ✪
Rutherglen Muscadelle NV Rating 92 To 2017 $20 ✪

Chandon Australia   ★★★★★

727 Maroondah Highway, Coldstream, Vic 3770 **Region** Yarra Valley
T (03) 9738 9200 **www**.chandon.com.au **Open** 7 days 10.30–4.30
Winemaker Dan Buckle, Glenn Thompson, Adam Keath **Est.** 1986 **Dozens** 120 000
Vyds 153ha
Established by Möet & Chandon, this is one of the two most important wine facilities in the Yarra Valley; the tasting room has a national and international reputation, having won a number of major tourism awards in recent years. The sparkling wine product range has evolved, and there has been increasing emphasis placed on the table wines, now released under the Chandon label. An energetic winemaking team under the leadership of Dan Buckle has maintained the high quality standards. Exports to all major markets.

🍷🍷🍷🍷🍷 **Barrel Selection Yarra Valley Shiraz 2014** Good hue and depth; this is a great example of a wine that is medium-bodied, yet has the intensity and length of a wine with much greater extract and body. Its freshness and balance are its ace in the hole, supple dark fruits married seamlessly with quality French oak, the tannins largely hidden. Screwcap. 13.5% alc. **Rating** 95 **To** 2034 $46
Yarra Valley Shiraz 2014 Takes a split second to announce its class; black cherry leads red cherry, spice leads pepper, French oak leads tannins, all happy to contribute to this perfectly balanced, cool grown shiraz. Chandon gives it 8 years, I'm doubling that. Screwcap. 13.5% alc. **Rating** 95 **To** 2030 $32 ✪
Blanc de Blancs 2012 From vineyards in the Upper Yarra Valley and the Whitlands Plateau Vineyard purchased from Brown Brothers, the Upper Yarra grapes picked 24 Feb, the Whitlands grapes 20 Mar – astonishing. Made using the traditional method, disgorged in Jun '15 after 3 years on lees. Brilliant straw-green, it is a tour de force of investing a 100% chardonnay with multi-variety complexity. Cork. 12.5% alc. **Rating** 95 **To** 2017 $41
Pinot Gris 2015 From the 30yo high-altitude Whitlands Plateau Vineyard in the King Valley, now owned by Chandon, cool-fermented in stainless steel and early-bottled. Simply by virtue of vine age and location, the wine has much more intensity and depth than is usual for pinot gris, with nashi pear, apple and citrus zest all jostling for space. Screwcap. 13% alc. **Rating** 94 **To** 2017 $25 ✪
Pinot Noir Rose 2015 Various vineyard sources, with various periods of skin contact time in open fermenters. Pale purplish-crimson; you can sense the extra degree of flavour and depth that duly manifests itself on the spiced strawberry palate and its emphatic finish. Adroitly avoids heaviness while packing a punch from the word go. Screwcap. 12% alc. **Rating** 94 **To** 2016 $32
Barrel Selection Yarra Valley Pinot Noir 2014 Low yields were chronic in the cool regions of South Eastern Australia, but the quality was good; clear-matured for 11 months in French barriques. An elegant pinot with a strong sense of place; it also speaks of the fermentation and oak regime with its foresty/stemmy nuances woven through the fruit. Screwcap. 13% alc. **Rating** 94 **To** 2024 $46

🍷🍷🍷🍷 **Brut NV** Rating 92 To 2020 $22 ✪
Brut Rose NV Rating 92 To 2020 $22 ✪
Sparkling Pinot Noir Shiraz NV Rating 91 To 2018 $32 TS
Barrel Selection Yarra Valley Pinot Meunier 2015 Rating 90 To 2022 $46
Vintage Brut 2012 Rating 90 To 2018 $41 TS

Chapel Hill

1 Chapel Hill Road, McLaren Vale, SA 5171 **Region** McLaren Vale
T (08) 8323 8429 **www**.chapelhillwine.com.au **Open** 7 days 11–5
Winemaker Michael Fragos, Bryn Richards **Est.** 1973 **Dozens** 60 000 **Vyds** 44ha
A leading medium-sized winery in the region. Owned since 2000 by the Swiss Thomas
Schmidheiny group, which owns the respected Cuvaison winery in California and vineyards
in Switzerland and Argentina. Wine quality is unfailingly excellent. The production comes
from estate plantings of shiraz, cabernet sauvignon, chardonnay, verdelho, savagnin, sangiovese
and merlot, plus contract-grown grapes. Exports to all major markets.

House Block Shiraz 2014 Hand-picked and sorted, crushed/destemmed,
open-fermented in small pots with cultured yeast, 10 days on skins, matured
in French oak (15% new) for 20 months. Deep crimson-purple; unashamedly
full-bodied, with black fruits in a swathe of fine, ripe tannins and largely unseen
oak contributing more to texture than flavour. Screwcap. 14.5% alc. **Rating** 95
To 2044 $65

Road Block Shiraz 2014 Identical vinification to House Block except 17% new
French oak. Very deep crimson-purple. While full-bodied, is quite different from
House Block; the fruit spectrum extends to purple and red, and the mouthfeel is
supple and velvety. It's got plenty of structure and depth, simply making its mark in
different fashion. Screwcap. 14.5% alc. **Rating** 95 To 2039 $65

Gorge Block Cabernet Sauvignon 2014 A very good example of what can
be achieved with cabernet in McLaren Vale. The varietal expression is crystal clear,
fully ripe, but not overripe; blackcurrant with an embroidery of bay leaf, warm
earth, tannins and integrated oak. Screwcap. 14.5% alc. **Rating** 95 To 2039 $65

The Vicar Shiraz 2014 A full-bodied McLaren Vale shiraz. with minimalist
winemaking. The concentration and intensity of the savoury, brambly black fruits is
intimidating, with some of the autocracy of cabernet sauvignon; oak is part of the
story, as are the tannins. Simply not ready yet, but it's all there under the blankets.
Screwcap. 14.5% alc. **Rating** 94 To 2039 $75

Reserve Shiraz Cabernet 2014 70% shiraz, 30% cabernet sauvignon, machine-
harvested, open-fermented for 10–12 days, matured in French oak (24% new) for
21 months. Deep crimson-purple hue; this is a Leviathan wine in ultra-McLaren
Vale style; the price suggests seriously old vines. More relevant is the wine in the
glass: full of savoury, earthy, licorice flavours and tannins to match. A wine to watch
for years to come. Screwcap. 14% alc. **Rating** 94 To 2034 $100

Bush Vine Grenache 2014 Good colour; right in the very heart of McLaren
Vale style, deeply fruited, red cherry and raspberry to the fore, a touch of plum
tucked in behind, with not a scintilla of confection in sight. Screwcap. 14.5% alc.
Rating 94 To 2030 $30 ✪

Sangiovese Rose 2015 Rating 92 To 2016 $18 CM ✪
Sangiovese Rose 2015 Rating 92 To 2017 $18 ✪
Hill Block Shiraz 2015 Rating 92 To 2021 $25 CM ✪
GSM 2014 Rating 92 To 2021 $25 CM ✪
The Parson Shiraz 2014 Rating 91 To 2020 $18 CM ✪
The Vinedresser Shiraz 2014 Rating 91 To 2020 $26 CM
The Parson GSM 2014 Rating 91 To 2020 $16 CM ✪
The Parson Cabernet Sauvignon 2014 Rating 90 To 2021 $18 CM ✪

Chapman Grove Wines

29 Troy Street, Applecross, WA 6153 **Region** Margaret River
T (08) 9364 3885 **www**.chapmangrove.com.au **Open** Not
Winemaker Richard Rowe (Consultant) **Est.** 2005 **Dozens** 7000 **Vyds** 32ha
A very successful venture under the control of CEO Ron Fraser. The wines come from the
estate vineyards planted to chardonnay, semillon, sauvignon blanc, shiraz, cabernet sauvignon
and merlot. The wines have three price levels: at the bottom end, the Dreaming Dog red

varietals and blends; in the middle, the standard Chapman Grove range; and, at the top, ultra-premium wines under the Atticus label. Exports to Canada, Hong Kong, Singapore, the Philippines, Taiwan and China.

ΨΨΨΨΨ **Atticus Single Vineyard Chardonnay 2014** Hand-picked Gin Gin clone, fermented and matured in French oak (50% new) for 10 months. The balance of fruit, oak and acidity is so immaculate it is a pointless exercise to try to deconstruct their contributions. However, the white peach and pink grapefruit flavours are as clear as a bell on the back-palate and aftertaste, the finish fresh and clean. Masterful winemaking. Screwcap. 13.1% alc. **Rating** 95 **To** 2024 $60
Atticus Single Vineyard Syrah 2014 Hand-picked, matured for 18 months in French oak (50% new). Brilliant crimson-purple; a very complex wine on the bouquet and medium to full-bodied palate alike; the new oak certainly plays a role, but it's the spiced black fruits and fine tannins that build the perfect platform for a wine with a very, very long future. Gold medal National Wine Show '15. Screwcap. 13.7% alc. **Rating** 95 **To** 2039 $80
Atticus Single Vineyard Cabernet Sauvignon 2013 Machine-harvested, matured for 18 months in French oak (50% new). Good colour; the bouquet and palate are filled with blackcurrant, bay leaf and a wisp of herbs; tannins chime in to perfection on the palate leaving no room for argument – this is a very classy cabernet. Screwcap. 13.4% alc. **Rating** 95 **To** 2038 $70
Reserve Chardonnay 2014 Machine-harvested Gin Gin clone, fermented and matured in French oak (25% new, the balance with staves). The depth of the Gin Gin clone is obvious, enhanced by the 75% tank-fermented with the staves portion, pushing stone fruit flavours forward. Needless to say, the barrel-ferment component invests the wine with texture and complexity on the mid-palate, the finish lively and fresh. Screwcap. 13.2% alc. **Rating** 94 **To** 2022 $30 ❂
Atticus Single Syrah 2013 Hand-picked, fermented and matured in French oak (50% new) for 18 months. Still very youthful, the quality French oak riding high in the saddle. This is a wine of excellent quality, ticking every box except for oak balance. Its texture and balance are admirable, the varietal character likewise. Screwcap. 13.7% alc. **Rating** 94 **To** 2038 $70
Reserve Shiraz 2011 Machine-harvested, crushed and destemmed, pressed to French oak (25% new, the balance with staves) for 14 months. The excellent retention of primary crimson colour is a reflection of the lively, juicy red fruits on its medium-bodied palate, the French oak little more than lift music. It cries out to be drunk asap. Screwcap. 14.4% alc. **Rating** 94 **To** 2021 $30 ❂

ΨΨΨΨΨ **Reserve Shiraz 2014** Rating 92 To 2034 $30
Reserve Cabernet Sauvignon 2014 Rating 91 To 2029 $30

Charles Cimicky   ★★★★☆

Hermann Thumm Drive, Lyndoch, SA 5351 **Region** Barossa Valley
T (08) 8524 4025 **www**.charlescimickywines.com.au **Open** Tues–Fri 10.30–3.30
Winemaker Charles Cimicky **Est.** 1972 **Dozens** 20 000 **Vyds** 25ha
These wines are of very good quality, thanks to the sophisticated use of good oak in tandem with high quality grapes. Historically, Cimicky was happy to keep an ultra-low profile, but he has relented sufficiently to send some (very impressive) wines. Exports to the US, Canada, Switzerland, Germany, Malaysia and Hong Kong.

ΨΨΨΨΨ **The Autograph Barossa Valley Shiraz 2014** It hits Barossa shiraz firmly in the centre of the bat. It's a sweet-spot wine. It's blackberried and dense, coffeed and mouthfilling, but it also offers various nuances of salted licorice and earth; it's not a one-trick pony. It promises plenty of warm-hearted pleasure as a result. Screwcap. 14.5% alc. **Rating** 94 **To** 2030 $25 CM ❂

ΨΨΨΨΨ **Trumps Barossa Valley Shiraz 2014** Rating 92 To 2024 $20 CM ❂
Twist of Fate Barossa Valley Merlot 2014 Rating 92 To 2025 $25 CM ❂
Reluctant Muse Barossa Valley Shiraz 2012 Rating 91 To 2024 $35 CM

Charles Melton ★★★★★

Krondorf Road, Tanunda, SA 5352 **Region** Barossa Valley
T (08) 8563 3606 **www.**charlesmeltonwines.com.au **Open** 7 days 11–5
Winemaker Charlie Melton, Krys Smith **Est.** 1984 **Dozens** 15 000 **Vyds** 32.6ha
Charlie Melton, one of the Barossa Valley's great characters, with wife Virginia by his side, makes some of the most eagerly sought à la mode wines in Australia. There are 7ha of estate vineyards at Lyndoch, 9ha at Krondorf and 1.6ha at Light Pass, the lion's share shiraz and grenache, and a small planting of cabernet sauvignon. An additional 30ha property was purchased in High Eden, with 10ha of shiraz planted in 2009, and a 5ha field of grenache, shiraz, mataro, carignan, cinsaut, picpoul and bourboulenc was planted in '10. The expanded volume has had no adverse effect on the quality of the rich, supple and harmonious wines. Exports to all major markets.

♀♀♀♀♀ **Grains of Paradise Shiraz 2013** One of the great wines of the Barossa Valley, not just because of its quality, but also its individuality of style. It is traditionally destemmed, plunged and pumped over, the oak providing the X-factor (plus high quality fruit). American oak is sent to France for 3 years air drying, then coopered using the boiling water method to soften the staves for bending, and only once half-made does it receive any fire toasting. Dargaud & Jaegle are the masters. Just relax and let the glorious black fruits sweep you away. Screwcap. 14.5% alc. **Rating** 97 **To** 2048 $54 ✪
Voices of Angels Shiraz 2013 Here 15% whole bunches and 3% co-fermented riesling give the wine the individuality it has enjoyed unchanged for 25 years. The wine remains undisturbed for the 3 years it spends in new French oak. Grains of Paradise is all about severe black fruits, and this is all about red fruits (well, mainly red) and finesse. Balance and length are shared by both wines. Screwcap. 14.5% alc. **Rating** 97 **To** 2043 $64 ✪
Nine Popes 2013 Shiraz, grenache, mataro undergoing the most complex fermentation of all Charles Melton wines: hand-plunging, whole bunch fermentation, wild and cultured yeast, with a mix of single and co-fermentation, matured in French barriques (25% new) on lees for 28 months. A richly woven tapestry of spiced red and black fruits that stands apart from and above all but one or two Barossa Valley SGMs. It is wonderfully detailed and complex, yet achieves this with a lightness of foot and freshness of face. Screwcap. 14.5% alc. **Rating** 97 **To** 2033 $68 ✪

♀♀♀♀♀ **Barossa Valley Rose of Virginia 2015** 60% grenache, 17% pinot meunier, 14% cabernet sauvignon, 8% pinot noir, 1% shiraz. Deep (for rose) crimson; it is flush with poached plum and cherry fruit flavours, yet retains vibrancy and freshness courtesy of brisk acidity. The ultimate test is the aftertaste, which is crisp and fruity, but dry. Screwcap. 13.5% alc. **Rating** 95 **To** 2017 $25 ✪
Barossa Valley Sparkling Red 2008 80% shiraz, 20% cabernet sauvignon, although it's really hard to see the impact of the cabernet. The wine was aged for 3 years in used barriques, then tiraged and given 3 years on lees before disgorgement in Nov '14. Deep colour; still very youthful and vigorous; red and black fruits, spice, licorice and (attractive) plum cake. The critical dosage has been judged to perfection. Crown seal. 14% alc. **Rating** 95 **To** 2020 $53

♀♀♀♀ **La Belle Mere GSRM 2013 Rating** 89 **To** 2033 $23

🍇 Charlotte Dalton Wines ★★★★★

PO Box 125, Verdun, SA 5245 **Region** Adelaide Hills
T 0466 541 361 **www.**charlottedaltonwines.com **Open** Not
Winemaker Charlotte Hardy **Est.** 2015 **Dozens** 700
Charlotte Hardy has been making wines for 15 years with a star-studded career at Craggy Range (NZ), Chateau Giscours (Bordeaux) and David Abreu (California), but has called SA home since 2007. Her winery is part of her Basket Range house, which has been through many incarnations since starting life as a pig farm in 1858. Much later it housed the Basket

Range store, and at different times in the past two decades it has been the winery to Basket Range Wines, The Deanery Wines and now Charlotte Dalton Wines.

🍷🍷🍷🍷🍷 **Love You Love Me Adelaide Hills Semillon 2015** 'Harvested with a firm acid', battonage, extended time on lees, fermented in used French oak. Charlotte Hardy's international experience (as well as Australian) shines through in this wine. It already has texture and structure without compromising the fresh acidity on the finish. There is little oak flavour, but the barrel ferment certainly built complexity into the wine. A true alternative to Hunter Valley or Barossa Valley styles. Screwcap. 12.5% alc. **Rating** 95 **To** 2025 $40
Love Me Love You The Deanery Vineyard Adelaide Hills Shiraz 2015 From Balhannah, Wendouree clone, 30% whole bunches, matured in French oak (20% new). Flawless winemaking; a highly expressive bouquet of variety and place, the medium-bodied palate supple and velvety, black cherry and satsuma plum with a scatter of spice and pepper, the tannins and oak both drawn into the embrace of the fruit. Screwcap. 14.2% alc. **Rating** 95 **To** 2035 $42

Charnwood Estate

253 Burrundulla Road, Mudgee, NSW 2850 (postal) **Region** Mudgee
T (02) 6372 4577 **www**.charnwoodestate.com.au **Open** At Winning Post Motor Inn 12–5
Winemaker Jacob Stein **Est.** 2004 **Dozens** 450 **Vyds** 2ha
In 2004 Greg Dowker planted the vineyard on a historic property just 5 minutes from the centre of Mudgee, nestled at the foot of the surrounding hills of the Cudgegong Valley. He has established shiraz (1.5ha) and merlot (0.5ha), the wines contract-made by former Flying Winemaker Jacob Stein.

🍷🍷🍷🍷🍷 **Mudgee Shiraz 2014** It carries a raisiny sweetness but it's otherwise a wash of red- and black-berried fruit flavours, smoky oak lending a helping hand at most. Well shaped and fruited. Screwcap. 14% alc. **Rating** 90 **To** 2021 $26 CM

🍷🍷🍷🍷 **Mudgee Semillon Sauvignon Blanc 2015 Rating** 88 **To** 2017 $20 CM
Mudgee Merlot 2014 Rating 88 **To** 2020 $25 CM

Charteris Wines

PO Box 800, Cessnock, NSW 2320 **Region** Central Otago, NZ
T (02) 4998 7701 **www**.charteriswines.com **Open** Not
Winemaker PJ Charteris **Est.** 2007 **Dozens** 170 **Vyds** 1.7ha
Owners Peter James (PJ) Charteris and partner Christina Pattison met at Brokenwood in the Hunter Valley in 1999. PJ was the chief executive winemaker at Brokenwood, and Christina was the marketing manager. Together they have over three decades of winemaking and wine marketing experience. For NZ-born PJ, finding a top pinot noir site in Central Otago was a spiritual homecoming (they claim to have searched both Australia and NZ for the right combination of site and variety). They also have a vineyard with the gold-plated address of Felton Road, Bannockburn, planted to clones 115 777 and Abel. PJ carries on a consultancy business in Australia, with some, though not all, of his focus being the Hunter Valley. Tasting notes can be found on www.winecompanion.com.au.

Chateau Francois

Broke Road, Pokolbin, NSW 2321 **Region** Hunter Valley
T (02) 4998 7548 **Open** W'ends 9–5
Winemaker Don Francois **Est.** 1969 **Dozens** 200
I have known former NSW Director of Fisheries Dr Don Francois for almost as long as I have been involved with wine, which is a very long time indeed. I remember his early fermentations of sundry substances other than grapes (none of which, I hasten to add, was the least bit illegal) in the copper bowl of an antiquated washing machine in his suburban laundry. He established Chateau Francois one year before Brokenwood, and our winemaking and fishing paths have crossed many times since. Some years ago Don suffered a mild stroke,

and no longer speaks or writes with any fluency, but this has not stopped him from producing a range of absolutely beautiful Semillons that flourish marvellously with age. I should add that he is even prouder of the distinguished career of his daughter, Rachel Francois, at the NSW bar. The semillon vines are now 47 years old, producing exceptional wine that is sold for the proverbial song year after year. Five-star value.

TTTTT **Pokolbin Semillon 2013** Has barely moved over the past two years. Has great length and crunchy acidity to go with the lemongrass and citrus fruits; the acidity is dazzling. Screwcap. 11% alc. **Rating** 96 **To** 2028 $22 **✪**
Pokolbin Semillon 2015 This wasn't an easy vintage, but the 40yo vines and the sloping hillside vineyard give it a start over many others. This is a fine, delicious wine now, but will bloom over the next 10 years, and live long thereafter. Screwcap. 11% alc. **Rating** 95 **To** 2030 $22 **✪**
Pokolbin Semillon 2014 This vintage is celebrated for its red wines, but the semillons are very good as well, picked when the fruit was perfect rather than threading the needle of impending rain. This has a gold-plated 15-year life ahead, but the lemon juice and lemon curd flavours are already evident, acidity providing both balance and length. Screwcap. 11% alc. **Rating** 95 **To** 2029 $17 **✪**
Pokolbin Semillon 2012 Gleaming straw-green; taste this wine alongside all other stainless steel-fermented wines, riesling the most obvious contender, and its mouthwatering lemon/lemongrass/lemon curd and the barest hint of honey poking through the long, crisp palate and aftertaste. Screwcap. 11% alc. **Rating** 95 **To** 2028 $18 **✪**

TTTTT **Pokolbin Shiraz 2014 Rating** 90 **To** 2029 $17 **✪**

Chateau Tanunda   ★★★★★

9 Basedow Road, Tanunda, SA 5352 **Region** Barossa Valley
T (08) 8563 3888 **www**.chateautanunda.com **Open** 7 days 10–5
Winemaker Neville Rowe **Est.** 1890 **Dozens** 130 000 **Vyds** 100ha
This is one of the most historically significant winery buildings in the Barossa Valley, built from bluestone quarried at nearby Bethany in the late 1880s. It has been restored by John Geber and family, and a new small batch basket press has been installed. Chateau Tanunda owns almost 100ha of vineyards in Bethany, Eden Valley, Tanunda and Vine Vale, with additional fruit sourced from a group of 30 growers covering the panoply of Barossa districts. The wines are made from hand-picked grapes, basket-pressed, and are neither fined nor filtered. There is an emphasis on single vineyard and single district wines under the Terroirs of the Barossa label. The grand building houses the cellar door and the Barossa Small Winemakers Centre, offering wines from boutique winemakers. Exports to all major markets have been a major reason for the increase in production from 50 000 to 130 000 dozen, success due to the unrelenting market-oriented approach of John Geber.

TTTTT **The Everest Old Bush Vine Barossa Grenache 2010** Hand-picked from the Mattschoss family vineyard at Greenock, destemmed, open-fermented and matured in three used French barriques, 65 dozen made. It is indeed a mountainous grenache, with deep, sultry fruits – as much black as red – and tannins of equal proportions. It needs a minimum of 10 years to soften its towering, indeed menacing, fruit and tannin mix. Out on its own in terms of durability and price. Cork. 15% alc. **Rating** 96 **To** 2030 $195
The Chateau Eden Valley Riesling 2014 From the relatively young Ahrens Vineyard. Its vibrant palate, with citrus fruit nestling in a trellis of natural, minerally acidity, promises much for the future, however good it is right now. Lovely wine, with a great aftertaste. Screwcap. 10.5% alc. **Rating** 95 **To** 2029 $24 **✪**
Terroirs of the Barossa Ebenezer District Shiraz 2013 A single vineyard wine, hand-picked, the grapes destemmed but not crushed, open-fermented and hand-plunged, oak-matured for 20 months, basket-pressed. While unashamedly full-bodied, the procession of black fruits glides smoothly along the tongue, with a lift on the finish that reflects the alcohol; the bright, deep hue points to good pH and acidity. Cork. 15% alc. **Rating** 95 **To** 2038 $49

The Chateau 100 Year Old Vines Shiraz 2012 From three small vineyards in the Eden Valley, Lyndoch and Nuriootpa districts, destemmed grapes were open-fermented, basket-pressed, matured for 22 months in new and used American and French oak. Mocha oak and plum cake flavours are allied with ripe, fine-grained tannins to produce a generous, medium to full-bodied wine that will please in its youth and maturity alike. Cork. 14% alc. **Rating** 95 **To** 2032 $125

50 Year Old Vines Barossa Shiraz 2012 Made from vines planted '60–'61, the standard Chateau Tanunda vinification. Retains excellent hue, and has strong focus and power, the rich fruit braced by acidity and oak. Cork. 14.5% alc. **Rating** 95 **To** 2032 $75

The Everest Barossa Shiraz 2010 From two famous vineyards, open-fermented and hand-plunged, basket-pressed to one new French puncheon and two used barriques for 2 years maturation, 90 dozen made. An Everest indeed, but K2 might have been a better proposition, for the fruit power has been boosted by its alcohol; you can have too much of a good thing. Cork. 15% alc. **Rating** 95 **To** 2035 $195

150 Year Old Vines Barossa 1858 Field Blend 2013 From a single vineyard in the Springton district planted in 1858, destemmed, open-fermented for 7 days, basket-pressed and matured in a single French puncheon for 18 months. The colour is deceptively light, for the wine packs a fiery punch that will polarise opinions, but should be eagerly sought in the US. Not an easy wine to reduce to numbers. Cork. 15.7% alc. **Rating** 95 **To** 2033 $300

125th Anniversary Limited Eden Valley Riesling 2014 From the Ahrens Vineyard. A singularly finely detailed expression of Eden Valley riesling, purity and balance its watchwords; Meyer lemon juice flavour runs in a clear, smooth stream across the palate, precisely measured acidity bracing the finish and aftertaste. Excellent value. Screwcap. 10.5% alc. **Rating** 94 **To** 2029 $17 ❂

150 Year Old Vines Barossa Semillon 2014 From the Cirillo family's single block in the Vine Vale district, planted in the 1850s, fermented in 8 French barrels followed by 7 months maturation. It is a full-bodied semillon in a traditional style, very different from the Hunter Valley. Its layered flavours provide plenty to sink one's teeth into, but will cruise along past '20 if you are curious to see how it will develop. Screwcap. 11.5% alc. **Rating** 94 **To** 2034 $49

Terroirs of the Barossa Greenock Shiraz 2013 From the 40yo Mattschoss Vineyard, and vinified in the standard Chateau Tanunda fashion for its single vineyard wines. Black fruits, a touch of bitter chocolate and rippling, soft tannins all stake their claims immediately the wine is tasted; oak, too, has made a positive contribution. All the Chateau Tanunda wines fall in the love or leave category. Cork. 15% alc. **Rating** 94 **To** 2035 $49

Newcastle Barossa Syrah Grenache Mourvedre Cinsault 2014 38/28/27/7%, each component made and matured separately in various oaks for 19 months before blending and bottling. Clever winemaking has produced the maximum result, with a suite of predominantly red fruits on a palate notable for its freshness and drinkability. Great value. Screwcap. 14.5% alc. **Rating** 94 **To** 2025 $22 ❂

♟♟♟♟♟ **Newcastle Barossa Marsanne Viognier Roussanne 2014** Rating 93 To 2019 $24 ❂
Mattiske Road Barossa Valley Shiraz 2013 Rating 93 To 2020 $30
The Chateau Single Vineyard Shiraz 2012 Rating 93 To 2027 $29
The Chateau Shiraz Primitivo Montepulciano 2013 Rating 93 To 2023 $30
Grand Barossa Dry Riesling 2014 Rating 92 To 2024 $25 ❂
125th Anniversary Limited Barossa Shiraz 2013 Rating 92 To 2025 $20 ❂
Terroirs of the Barossa Lyndoch Shiraz 2013 Rating 92 To 2043 $50
150 Year Old Vines Barossa Semillon 2015 Rating 91 To 2030 $50
The Chateau Old Bush Vine Grenache Rose 2014 Rating 91 To 2016 $24
The Chateau 100 Year Old Vines Shiraz 2014 Rating 91 To 2039 $125
The Everest Barossa Shiraz 2013 Rating 91 To 2023 $195

Dahlitz Single Vineyard Barossa Merlot 2013 Rating 91 To 2023 $20 ✪
The Chateau Bethanian Shiraz 2013 Rating 90 To 2023 $29
Barossa Tower Shiraz 2013 Rating 90 To 2020 $19 ✪
Barossa Tower Shiraz Primitivo 2014 Rating 90 To 2020 $19 ✪
Matthews Road Single Vineyard Barossa Cabernet Sauvignon 2013
Rating 90 To 2020 $15 ✪

Chatto   ★★★★★

PO Box 54, Cessnock, NSW 2325 **Region** Southern Tasmania
T (02) 4990 8660 **www**.chattowines.com **Open** Not
Winemaker Jim Chatto **Est.** 2000 **Dozens** 300 **Vyds** 1.5ha
Jim Chatto is recognised as having one of the very best palates in Australia, and has proved to
be an outstanding winemaker. He and wife Daisy have long wanted to get a small Tasmanian
Pinot wine business up and running, but having moved to the Hunter Valley in 2000, it took
six years to find a site that satisfied all of the criteria Jim considers ideal. It is a warm, well-
drained site in one of the coolest parts of Tasmania, looking out over Glaziers Bay. So far they
have planted nine clones of pinot noir, with a 5000 vines per hectare spacing. This will be a
busman's holiday for some years to come, following his appointment as chief winemaker for
McWilliam's Wine Group.

🍷🍷🍷🍷🍷 Isle Huon Valley Pinot Noir 2015 Dijon clones 777 (75%) and 115 (25%),
hand-picked and sorted, 25% destemmed whole berries, 8 days cold soak, open-
fermented, 15 days on skins, pressed to French oak (35% new) at 1° baume for
10 months maturation. Deeper colour than the standard Pinot, the bouquet
and palate following suit with darker fruits led by plums, the texture and structure
still with the outstanding mouthfeel, balance and length. Tasted in the same month
as it was bottled, which makes it unbelievably harmonious, its line, length and
balance flawless. Screwcap. 13.5% alc. **Rating** 97 **To** 2030 $75 ✪

🍷🍷🍷🍷🍷 Huon Valley Pinot Noir 2015 Eight clones, hand-picked and sorted, 25%
destemmed whole berries, 8 days cold soak, wild open ferment, 15 days on skins,
pressed to French oak (25% new) at 1° baume for 10 months maturation. Intensely
aromatic and flavoured, small red fruits in a silken web also catching precisely
balanced spices, fine tannins and wholly integrated oak. A very high quality wine
from its bouquet through to the finish, never wavering. Screwcap. 13.5% alc.
Rating 96 **To** 2028 $50 ✪

Cherry Tree Hill   ★★★★

Hume Highway, Sutton Forest, NSW 2577 **Region** Southern Highlands
T (02) 8217 1409 **www**.cherrytreehill.com.au **Open** 7 days 9–5
Winemaker Anton Balog (Contract) **Est.** 2000 **Dozens** 4000 **Vyds** 14ha
The Lorentz family, then headed by Gabi Lorentz, began the establishment of the Cherry Tree
Hill vineyard in 2000 with the planting of 3ha each of cabernet sauvignon and riesling; 3ha
each of merlot and sauvignon blanc followed in '01, and, finally, 2ha of chardonnay in '02.
The inspiration was childhood trips on a horse and cart through his grandfather's vineyard
in Hungary, and Gabi's son (and current owner) David completes the three-generation
involvement as manager of the business.

🍷🍷🍷🍷🍷 Diana Reserve Southern Highlands Chardonnay 2013 In very good shape.
It mixes pear with sweet, sunny peach, spicy oak with fennel. It feels succulent and
appealing all the way through to a satisfying finish. Screwcap. 13% alc. **Rating** 92
To 2019 $35 CM
Riesling 2015 Flavours of crystallised lime and barley sugar lend this an
idiosyncratic edge but shoots of lemon return matters closer to home. It won't be
a long-lived wine but for early drinking it's full of charm. Screwcap. 11.5% alc.
Rating 90 **To** 2020 $30 CM
Riesling 2014 Spritzy lime and mandarin flavours. Ample body. Soft and free
flowing. Screwcap. 12.3% alc. **Rating** 90 **To** 2020 $30 CM

Sauvignon Blanc 2015 Slight spritz but an attractive hit of lemongrass, gravel and gooseberried fruit flavour. It almost seems smoky with herbs. Pretty good show, all up. Screwcap. 12.5% alc. **Rating** 90 **To** 2017 $20 CM ✪

Diana Reserve Southern Highlands Chardonnay 2014 Resiny oak gives the wine a sweet smoothness; peachy fruit continues the theme. Its charms come at you with open arms but the finish is surprisingly measured. Screwcap. 13.5% alc. **Rating** 90 **To** 2018 $35 CM

ΨΨΨΨ **Reserve The Wedding Cabernet Sauvignon 2013 Rating** 88 **To** 2022 $50 CM

Chestnut Grove ★★★★

Chestnut Grove Road, Manjimup, WA 6258 **Region** Manjimup
T (08) 9722 4255 **www.**chestnutgrove.com.au **Open** 7 days 10–4
Winemaker David Dowden **Est.** 1988 **Dozens** 15 000 **Vyds** 40ha
A substantial vineyard that commenced in 1987, with a winery constructed in '98, Chestnut Grove has come full circle from founder Vic Kordic and sons Paul and Mark, to Australian Wine Holdings in 2002, and back to the Kordics in '09 under the umbrella of Manjimup Wine Enterprises Pty Ltd. Mark is general manager of the wine business. Exports to China.

ΨΨΨΨΨ **Estate Manjimup Verdelho 2015** Virtually devoid of colour, but certainly not flavour; it has exceptional drive and intensity, the usual fruit salad sauced up with pink grapefruit and pomegranate. Truly remarkable. Screwcap. 13% alc. **Rating** 94 **To** 2020 $20 ✪

ΨΨΨΨ♀ **Reserve Manjimup Chardonnay 2014 Rating** 90 **To** 2022 $40

Chris Ringland ★★★★☆

Franklin House, 6–8 Washington Street, Angaston, SA 5353 **Region** Barossa Valley
T (08) 8564 3233 **www.**chrisringland.com **Open** By appt
Winemaker Chris Ringland **Est.** 1989 **Dozens** 500 **Vyds** 2.05ha
The wines made by Chris Ringland for his eponymous brand were at the very forefront of the surge of rich, old-vine Barossa shirazs discovered by Robert Parker. As a consequence of very limited production, and high quality (albeit polarising) wine, the wine assumed immediate icon status. The production of 500 dozen does not include a small number of magnums, double-magnums and imperials that are sold each year. The addition of 0.5ha of shiraz planted in 1999, joining the 1.5ha planted in '10, has had little practical impact on availability. Exports to the UK, France, Germany, Spain, South Korea, Japan, Hong Kong and China.

ΨΨΨΨΨ **Anniversary Edition Barossa Ranges Shiraz 2012** From a single 105yo vineyard, the grapes vinified by Chris Ringland for the last 21 years. The colour is exceptional, bright, clear crimson-purple, the flavours spanning black cherry, plum and pepper, the tannins poised and fine, the oak integrated. Alcohol? No worries. Screwcap. 14.5% alc. **Rating** 96 **To** 2037 $110

CR Barossa Shiraz 2014 Dense purple-crimson; one of those uncommon back labels that precisely describes the wine: 'flavours of sweet blackberry, dark chocolate and old-fashioned fruitcake'. It's also well balanced, and there is no reason to query the 14% alcohol – there is no heat or dead fruit notes, and the wine has sure-footed longevity. Screwcap. **Rating** 94 **To** 2030 $30 ✪

Reservation Barossa Valley Shiraz 2013 Dense, deep crimson-purple; there's no point in allowing the question of alcohol to dominate the discussion of this wine: it is what it is, and Ringland is a master of the style – if you are happy with this volume of extract and alcohol, go for it. Within its terms of reference, it is well balanced, and has the requisites to age well. My score is a self-evident compromise. Screwcap. 16% alc. **Rating** 94 **To** 2038 $65

ΨΨΨΨ♀ **CR Sealed Barossa Shiraz 2013 Rating** 90 **To** 2028 $45

Chrismont ★★★★

251 Upper King River Road, Cheshunt, Vic 3678 **Region** King Valley
T (03) 5729 8220 **www**.chrismont.com.au **Open** 7 days 10–5
Winemaker Warren Proft **Est.** 1980 **Dozens** 25 000 **Vyds** 100ha
Arnie and Jo Pizzini's substantial vineyards in the Cheshunt and Whitfield areas of the upper King Valley have been planted to riesling, sauvignon blanc, chardonnay, pinot gris, cabernet sauvignon, merlot, shiraz, barbera, sagrantino, marzemino and arneis. The La Zona range ties in the Italian heritage of the Pizzinis and is part of the intense interest in all things Italian. It also produces a Prosecco, contract-grown in the King Valley. In January '16 the Chrismont Cellar Door, Restaurant and Larder was opened. As well as a 7-day cellar door, the new development can seat up to 300 guests, and is designed to host weddings, corporate events, business conferences and group celebrations. A feature is the 'floating' deck over the vineyard, which can seat up to 150 people and has floor-to-ceiling glass looking out over the Black Ranges and King Valley landscape. Exports to the Philippines and Singapore.

🍷🍷🍷🍷🍷 **La Zona King Valley Sangiovese 2014** From 17yo vines in Whitfield, fermented on skins for 12 days, drained to new and used French barriques to complete fermentation and 15 months maturation. Bright, light crimson-purple hue; sangiovese can hurt its consumer in fine S&M style, but here it is all silky red berry/cherry, with no bite on the finish. Screwcap. 13.5% alc. **Rating** 94 **To** 2024 $26 ○

La Zona King Valley Barbera 2014 14yo vines in Whitfield, fermented on skins for 7 days, drained to new and used French oak for completion of fermentation and 12 months maturation. Bright crimson-purple hue; a most attractive fresh cherry and plum combination, the juicy fruits discreetly enhanced by the barrel ferment influence. Screwcap. 13.5% alc. **Rating** 94 **To** 2023 $26 ○

🍷🍷🍷🍷 **King Valley Riesling 2015 Rating** 90 **To** 2035 $17 ○
King Valley Chardonnay 2014 Rating 90 **To** 2019 $24
King Valley Petit Manseng 2013 Rating 90 **To** 2019 $26
La Zona King Valley Nebbiolo 2014 Rating 90 **To** 2020 $30

Churchview Estate ★★★★☆

8 Gale Road, Metricup, WA 6280 **Region** Margaret River
T (08) 9755 7200 **www**.churchview.com.au **Open** Mon–Sat 10–5
Winemaker Greg Garnish **Est.** 1998 **Dozens** 45 000 **Vyds** 65ha
The Fokkema family, headed by Spike Fokkema, immigrated from The Netherlands in the 1950s. Business success in the following decades led to the acquisition of the 100ha Churchview Estate property in '97, and to the progressive establishment of substantial vineyards (65ha planted to 16 varieties), managed organically. Exports to all major markets.

🍷🍷🍷🍷🍷 **St Johns Limited Release Cabernet Sauvignon Malbec Merlot Petit Verdot 2014** 54% cabernet sauvignon, 24% malbec, 11% each of merlot and petit verdot. A convincing Bordeaux blend, one that Margaret River seems able to produce whenever asked so to do. Blackcurrant, redcurrant, blueberry, raspberry – wherever your imagination takes you, with no rude shocks from tannins: they are polished, not dry or raspy. Screwcap. 14.5% alc. **Rating** 95 **To** 2040 $35 ○

Estate Range Sauvignon Blanc Semillon 2015 An 80/20% blend grown using organic principles, tank-fermented with four cultured yeasts in two lots, one with the varieties co-fermented. The bouquet sets the scene with grass/snow pea/ lemon on the one hand, passionfruit and white peach on the other. The wine has excellent intensity and, particularly, mouthfeel and length. Screwcap. 13% alc. **Rating** 94 **To** 2019 $20 ○

The Bartondale Cabernet Sauvignon 2014 Houghton clone, cultured (Bordeaux) yeast, pumped over twice daily for 14 days, then once daily for 14 days, fermentation completed in French oak (30% new), then transferred to used French oak for 16 months maturation, 10 barrels of 30 selected. Since 30% of the barrels make it through the selection process, and since 30% of the barrels were new, it seems likely the majority of this is ex new oak. It's a powerful wine, with lashings of blackcurrant, mulberry, black olive and oak, pulling in the same direction. Screwcap. 14.5% alc. **Rating** 94 To 2034 $55

♀♀♀♀♀ St Johns Limited Release Viognier 2015 Rating 93 To 2017 $35
St Johns Limited Release Chenin Blanc 2015 Rating 92 To 2023 $35
St Johns Limited Release Marsanne 2015 Rating 91 To 2023 $35
St Johns Limited Release Petit Verdot 2014 Rating 91 To 2034 $35
The Bartondale Shiraz 2014 Rating 90 To 2024 $55
St Johns Limited Release Zinfandel 2014 Rating 90 To 2024 $35

Ciavarella Oxley Estate ★★★★

17 Evans Lane, Oxley, Vic 3678 **Region** King Valley
T (03) 5727 3384 **www**.oxleyestate.com.au **Open** Mon–Sat 9–5, Sun 10–5
Winemaker Tony Ciavarella **Est.** 1978 **Dozens** 3000 **Vyds** 1.6ha
Cyril and Jan Ciavarella's vineyard was begun in 1978, with plantings being extended over the years. One variety, aucerot, was first produced by Maurice O'Shea of McWilliam's Mount Pleasant 60 or so years ago; the Ciavarella vines have been grown from cuttings collected from an old Glenrowan vineyard before the parent plants were removed in the mid-'80s. Tony Ciavarella left a career in agricultural research in mid-2003 to join his parents at Ciavarella. Cyril and Jan retired in '14, Tony and wife Merryn taking over management of the winery.

♀♀♀♀♀ Cabernet Merlot 2013 The fruit comes forward, the tannin ushers in behind. This is a wine of flavour and poise, and therefore value. Ripe, accessible fruit comes well turned out. Screwcap. 14.2% alc. **Rating** 90 **To** 2021 $22 CM
Tempranillo 2014 It takes a running jump at life. It's highly expressive and as close to full-bodied as tempranillo tends to get, elastic tannin stretched over the back half of the wine. We're talking bitter chocolate, black cherries, sarsaparilla, that spectrum of flavours. You wouldn't necessarily call it refined; you'd pick it to open proceedings in a 20/20 but leave it out of the Test squad. Screwcap. 14.2% alc. **Rating** 90 **To** 2021 $22 CM

♀♀♀♀ Zinfandel 2014 Rating 89 To 2019 $28 CM
Pinot Grigio 2015 Rating 88 To 2017 $18 CM

Cirami Estate ★★★★

78 Nixon Road, Monash, SA 5342 **Region** Riverland
T (08) 8583 5366 **www**.rvic.org.au **Open** Mon–Fri 9–4
Winemaker Eric Semmler **Est.** 2008 **Dozens** 1000 **Vyds** 46.4ha
Cirami Estate is owned by the Riverland Vine Improvement Committee Inc., a sizeable non-profit organisation. It is named after Richard Cirami, who was a pioneer in clonal selection and variety assessment, and was on the RVIC committee for over 20 years. Richard was made a Member of the Order of Australia in 2003 for his services to the wine industry. The vineyard includes 40 varieties at 0.3ha or greater, and another 2ha planted to over 60 varieties, the latter Cirami Estate's collection of nursery plantings.

♀♀♀♀♀ Albarino 2015 Fascinating aromas of citrus, rose petal and vanilla, the palate fresh, with ripe citrus flavours. Screwcap. 13.5% alc. **Rating** 90 To 2017 $15 ✪

♀♀♀♀ Verdejo 2015 Rating 89 To 2017 $15 ✪
Lagrein 2015 Rating 89 To 2020 $18 ✪

Circe Wines ★★★★★

PO Box 22, Red Hill, Vic 3937 **Region** Mornington Peninsula
T 0417 328 142 **www**.circewines.com.au **Open** Not
Winemaker Dan Buckle **Est.** 2010 **Dozens** 800 **Vyds** 2.9ha
Circe Wines (Circe was a seductress and minor goddess of intoxicants in Homer's *Odyssey*) is the partnership of winemaker Dan Buckle and marketer Aaron Drummond, very much

a weekend and holiday venture, inspired by their mutual love of pinot noir. They have a long-term lease of a vineyard in Hillcrest Road, not far from Paringa Estate, Tucks Ridge and Montalto. 'Indeed,' says Dan, 'it is not far from the Lieu-dit "Buckle" Vineyard my dad planted in the 1980s.' Circe has 1.2ha of vines, half chardonnay and half MV6 pinot noir. They have also planted 1.7ha of pinot noir (MV6, Abel, 777, D2V5 and Bests' Old Clone) at a vineyard in William Road, Red Hill. Dan Buckle's real job is chief winemaker at Chandon Australia. Exports to the UK.

ⓎⓎⓎⓎⓎ **Hillcrest Road Vineyard Pinot Noir 2014** Exceptionally smoky, reductive, savoury wine. It detonates in the glass, shattering scent and flavour to all parts. The colour is lightish but there ends the ambivalence. It's all about long sinews of complex flavour. It's ripe enough but savoury galore. It will be fascinating to watch it develop. Screwcap. 12.5% alc. **Rating** 96 **To** 2026 $70 CM ❂
Shiraz 2014 Lots of whole bunch influence here but the fruit does not fear the examination. Peppery notes are the bridge to plush cherry-plum fruit, clovey aspects woven through. Savoury and seductive at once. Meat and great, if you will. Tannin comes with a high thread count. The '14 Circe wines are stunning. Screwcap. 13.5% alc. **Rating** 96 **To** 2028 $40 CM ❂
Hillcrest Road Vineyard Chardonnay 2014 Hand-picked, crushed, pressed, fermented and matured in French oak (25% new) for 10 months. You have to have a bushman's ability to track the footprints of humans to identify this wine's region from the front (and only) label. It's important, for this has more focus, energy and drive than most of its Mornington Peninsula peers, zesty, mouthwatering, pink grapefruit to the fore on the long palate. Screwcap. 13% alc. **Rating** 95 **To** 2022 $60

ⓎⓎⓎⓎⓎ **Pinot Noir 2015 Rating** 93 **To** 2021 $40 CM
Gippsland Pinot Noir 2015 Rating 93 **To** 2023 $40 CM
Red Hill Chardonnay 2015 Rating 92 **To** 2022 $35 CM

Cirillo Wines   ★★★★

Lot 298 Nuraip Road, Nuriootpa, SA 5355 **Region** Barossa Valley
T 0408 803 447 **Open** By appt
Winemaker Marco Cirillo **Est.** 2003 **Dozens** 600 **Vyds** 6ha
In 1973 the Cirillo family acquired one of the oldest vineyards in Australia, situated in the Light Pass district of the Barossa Valley, where the soil is deep silt sand over limestone and clay. This combination of free-draining topsoil and water-holding subsoil has sustained the 3ha of grenache, along with 1ha semillon (previously incorrectly called madeira) and 0.5ha of shiraz planted in 1850, the latter complemented by 1ha of shiraz and 0.5ha of mourvedre planted in 1988. Most of the grapes are sold to Torbreck, leaving only a small portion for Cirillo. Exports to the US and Singapore.

ⓎⓎⓎⓎⓎ **Single Vineyard Mataro 2013** Cuts a fine figure. A neck of svelte, supple, leathery fruits with herb, spice and earth notes as a kind of multiflavoured scarf. Beautifully balanced. Not heavy. Fine, dry, velvety tannin. The force of light. Screwcap. 14% alc. **Rating** 94 **To** 2021 $30 CM ❂

ⓎⓎⓎⓎⓎ **The Vincent Grenache 2014 Rating** 92 **To** 2020 $21 CM ❂
1850s Old Vine Barossa Grenache 2010 Rating 91 **To** 2021 $50 CM

CJ Wines   ★★★

65 Pettavel Road, Waurn Ponds, Vic 3216 **Region** Geelong
T 0408 474 833 **Open** Not
Winemaker David Crawford **Est.** 2014 **Dozens** 8000
CJ Wines may be a virtual winery, owning neither vineyards or winery, but it makes up for that with its people power. There may be only two partners, but their experience and skills cover all the bases needed, while keeping costs to a bare minimum. It is in this way that they are able to sell wines to the consumer for $17 a bottle which would cost $20+ when made

by conventional operators. The 'C' stands for (David) Crawford, the winemaker half of the duo, 'J' for (Phil) Joiner, the marketer. David has 29 vintages under his belt, starting with 12 in Rutherglen, then a seachange with three at Taltarni/Clover Hill, the next eight as senior winemaker at Willow Bridge Estate in Geographe, before moving back to Vic to Bellbrae Estate in Geelong, where he is currently employed. Phil began his career in the glory days of Mildara Blass/Beringer Blass, followed by work guiding smaller wine businesses for over 20 years. The Geelong St Erth Pinot Noir and Heathcote Redcastle Shiraz are both single vineyard wines, but the emphasis is on the value for money the wines offer.

♥♥♥♥ **Redcastle Single Vineyard Heathcote Shiraz 2014** Dan Murphy's exclusive. 100% Heathcote shiraz matured in American oak. Generous to a fault. Soft and sweet with dark berry and clove/dried spice notes bounding through the palate. Falling over itself to be liked. Drink now style. Screwcap. 14.2% alc. **Rating** 89 To 2019 $17 CM ◐

Clairault | Streicker Wines   ★★★★★
3277 Caves Road, Wilyabrup, WA 6280 **Region** Margaret River
T (08) 9755 6225 **www.**clairaultwines.com.au **Open** 7 days 10–5
Winemaker Bruce Dukes **Est.** 1976 **Dozens** 10 500 **Vyds** 113ha
This multifaceted business is owned by New York resident John Streicker. It began in 2002 when he purchased the Yallingup Protea Farm and Vineyards. This was followed by the purchase of the Ironstone Vineyard in '03, and finally the Bridgeland Vineyard, which has one of the largest dams in the region: 1km long and covering 18ha. The Ironstone Vineyard is one of the oldest vineyards in Wilyabrup. In April 2012 Streicker acquired Clairault, bringing a further 40ha of estate vines, including 12ha now over 40 years old. The two brands are effectively run as one venture. A large part of the grape production is sold to winemakers in the region. Exports to the US, Canada, Dubai, Malaysia, Singapore, Hong Kong and China.

♥♥♥♥♥ **Streicker Ironstone Block Old Vine Chardonnay 2013** Still pale straw-green; this is the big banana where the Streicker story began before Clairault in '03. This chardonnay has a rare inner strength (Leeuwin Estate another) that gives it prodigious length on the palate and equally prodigious longevity, but without ever having to get out of first gear or raise a mental or physical sweat. That's why the special quality of this wine can simply not be recognised. Screwcap. 14.1% alc. **Rating** 97 To 2030 $41 ◐

♥♥♥♥♥ **Clairault Sauvignon Blanc Semillon 2015** 65/35%, part cool-fermented in stainless steel, the balance in French barriques, 1 month on lees, bottled Jul, gold medal WA Wine Show '15. Maximum return from high quality grapes, the region, and very good winemaking. The barrel ferment and semillon inputs provide the framework for the melange of poached pear and yellow peach, lemony acidity running like a golden thread throughout. One of those wines causing you to regret having to spit out in tastings. Screwcap. 12.5% alc. **Rating** 96 To 2020 $22 ◐

Clairault Estate Chardonnay 2014 Both this and its '14 sibling come from estate vineyards and are made in similar fashion, yet Clairault's own notes use totally different descriptors for each. It's not a question of volume, although I think that the significantly greater volume/intensity of this wine is the difference. Strange, but then that's the everlasting fascination of wine. Screwcap. 14% alc. **Rating** 96 To 2026 $38 ◐

Streicker Ironstone Block Old Vine Cabernet Sauvignon 2012 Open-fermented, 18 months maturation in French barriques. Uncompromisingly full-bodied, with blackcurrant and mulberry supported by a phalanx of firm tannins and French oak on the long finish. Will richly repay cellaring, the longer the better. Screwcap. 14.1% alc. **Rating** 96 To 2047 $45 ◐

Streicker Bridgeland Block Sauvignon Semillon 2014 Hand-picked, whole bunch-pressed, fermented and matured in French oak. You get the whole box and dice here: texture, structure, length and weight, very similar to dry white Bordeaux.

It's the polar opposite of the fruit bomb style, and at 2yo is only now starting to welcome all who venture near. Screwcap. 13% alc. **Rating** 95 **To** 2020 $35 ✪

Clairault Chardonnay 2014 A beautifully modulated chardonnay, all its facets in a harmonious, gravity-free space. While peach leads the stone fruit, grapefruit/ citrus players; barrel fermentation has provided sotto voce notes of spice, grilled nuts and cream. Screwcap. 13% alc. **Rating** 95 **To** 2025 $27 ✪

Streicker Bridgeland Block Syrah 2013 Hand-picked, open-fermented, 18 months in French barriques. As interesting as it is complex, with a strong savoury/licorice/pepper trio wound around the blackberry fruit of the bouquet and palate; it is medium-bodied with a particularly good tannin framework for the the fruit, assisted to a degree by the French oak. Screwcap. 14.1% alc. **Rating** 95 **To** 2038 $43

Clairault Estate Cabernet Sauvignon 2012 Fermented and macerated on skins for 10 days, matured in new and used French oak for 10 months. Classic Margaret River style made from the original Clairault vines planted in '76; it is cabernet to its bootstraps with cassis/blackcurrant fruit on a pedestal of firm tannins that are unique to cabernet; cedary oak adds a further dimension. Screwcap. 14.5% alc. **Rating** 95 **To** 2037 $43

Clairault Cellar Release Cabernet Sauvignon Cabernet Franc 2013 57% cabernet sauvignon, 29% cabernet franc, 11% merlot, 3% petit verdot, hand-picked, destemmed and crushed, different batches separately handled, average 14 days on skins, matured in French barriques (50% new) for 18 months. Interesting wine; you wander through a garden of berries of all kinds, finding them all delicately sweet, and matched by sufficient sous bois characters to provide structure and balance. Screwcap. 14% alc. **Rating** 95 **To** 2028 $65

Clairault Cabernet Sauvignon 2014 There's a nuclear arsenal of black and redcurrant, cassis, wild herb, black olive and charred, tarry tannins in each bottle of this wine, so handle with care. A big rib eye steak to start, and someone to share the bottle. Screwcap. 14% alc. **Rating** 94 **To** 2044 $27 ✪

♀♀♀♀♀ **Clairault Cabernet Sauvignon Merlot 2014 Rating** 92 **To** 2027 $22 ✪

Clarendon Hills   ★★★★★

Brookmans Road, Blewitt Springs, SA 5171 **Region** McLaren Vale
T (08) 8363 6111 **www**.clarendonhills.com.au **Open** By appt
Winemaker Roman Bratasiuk **Est.** 1990 **Dozens** 15 000 **Vyds** 63ha

Age and experience, it would seem, have mellowed Roman Bratasiuk – and the style of his wines. Once formidable and often rustic, they are now far more sculpted and smooth, at times bordering on downright elegance. Roman took another major step by purchasing a 160ha property high in the hill country of Clarendon at an altitude close to that of the Adelaide Hills. Here he has established a vineyard with single-stake trellising similar to that used on the steep slopes of Germany and Austria; it produces the Domaine Clarendon Syrah. He makes up to 20 different wines each year, all consistently very good, a tribute to the old vines. Exports to the US and other major markets.

♀♀♀♀♀ **Brookman Syrah 2013** The dark and inky appearance leads to the dark and brooding bouquet, blackberry, spice and a hint of florals drawing you in. The fruit set and hugely proportioned palate is loaded with layers of firm and savoury tannins that are structured with dark and brooding fruits. Especially long. Cork. 14.5% alc. **Rating** 96 **To** 2040 $100

Astralis 2013 This monumentally proportioned wine has all the hallmarks of a classic Astralis, the bouquet with an endless array of detail. The palate is plush and expansive with layer upon layer of inky fruit and powerful tannins. Needless to say, exceptionally long and powerful. Cork. 14.5% alc. **Rating** 96 **To** 2040 $450

Piggott Range Syrah 2013 Dark and inky, the trademark density one expects from this estate; there is less detailed fruit here than in the Astralis or Brookman, but it is typically darkly fruited. The palate bodes firmer, more rustic tannins that seem to hang to the palate for minutes. Monumental and powerful. Cork. 14.5% alc. **Rating** 95 **To** 2040 $200

Liandra Mourvedre 2013 Dark, dense red with the blackest of black fruits, inky, deep and impenetrable, lashings of texture and extract completing the picture. Despite its size, it manages to remain balanced, and finishes long and intensely. Cork. 14.5% alc. **Rating** 95 **To** 2040 $55

Blewitt Springs Grenache 2013 Dark red with purple hints; a full throttle densely packed grenache, loads of sweet raspberry coulis, licorice and some spice. The palate has chalky and sandy tannins wrapped in layers of raspberry and dark berry fruit; long and grippy. Cork. 14.5% alc. **Rating** 94 **To** 2030 $75

Sandown Cabernet Sauvignon 2013 Saturated with currants, tobacco and cassis; the palate is equally inky and substantial, with grippy and powerful tannins that have a stranglehold on the finish. Cork. 14.5% alc. **Rating** 94 **To** 2040 $75

ΨΨΨΨΨ **Kangarilla Grenache 2013** **Rating** 93 **To** 2038 $75
Hickinbotham Grenache 2013 **Rating** 93 **To** 2028 $55

Clarnette & Ludvigsen Wines ★★★★☆

Westgate Road, Armstrong, Vic 3377 **Region** Grampians
T 0409 083 833 **www**.clarnette-ludvigsen.com.au **Open** By appt
Winemaker Leigh Clarnette **Est.** 2003 **Dozens** 650 **Vyds** 15.5ha
Winemaker Leigh Clarnette and viticulturist Kym Ludvigsen's career paths crossed in late 1993 when both were working for Seppelt, Kym with a 14ha vineyard in the heart of the Grampians, all but 1ha of chardonnay, 0.5ha of viognier and 0.25ha of riesling planted to rare clones of shiraz, sourced from old plantings in the Great Western area. They met again in 2005 when both were employed by Taltarni. The premature death of Kym in '13 was widely reported, in no small measure due to his (unpaid) service on wine industry bodies. With next generations on both sides, the plans are to continue the business. Exports to China.

ΨΨΨΨΨ **Grampians Shiraz 2014** Made from the St Ethel clone, said to be grown exclusively in the Grampians, with a long history. Open-fermented in small batches, it is very intense and powerful, yet paradoxically is juicy and light on its feet. There is a stream of blackberry, blueberry and plum, spice and pepper woven through the fruit, the firm tannins in balance and will underwrite the long future of the wine. Screwcap. 14% alc. **Rating** 95 **To** 2044 $35 ✪

ΨΨΨΨΨ **Grampians Riesling 2015** **Rating** 92 **To** 2025 $23
Reserve Grampians Shiraz 2012 **Rating** 90 **To** 2032 $49

Claymore Wines ★★★★★

7145 Horrocks Way, Leasingham, SA 5452 **Region** Clare Valley
T (08) 8843 0200 **www**.claymorewines.com.au **Open** 7 days 10–5
Winemaker Marnie Roberts **Est.** 1998 **Dozens** 12 000 **Vyds** 27ha
Claymore Wines is the venture of Anura Nitchingham, a medical professional who imagined that it would lead the way to early retirement (which, of course, it did not). The starting date depends on which event you take: the first 4ha vineyard at Leasingham purchased in 1991 (with 70-year-old grenache, riesling and shiraz); '96, when a 16ha block at Penwortham was purchased and planted to shiraz, merlot and grenache; '97, when the first wines were made; or '98, when the first releases came onto the market. The labels are inspired by U2, Pink Floyd, Prince and Lou Reed. Exports to the UK, Canada, Denmark, Malaysia, Singapore, Taiwan, Hong Kong and China.

ΨΨΨΨΨ **Superstition Reserve Clare Valley Riesling 2015** Made by riesling superstar Kerri Thompson. Classic Watervale aromas, lime leaf and green apple leading to a tightly wound and focused mineral-infused palate. Young and intense, but will develop extremely well. Screwcap. 13.9% alc. **Rating** 95 **To** 2028 $28 ✪

Bittersweet Symphony Clare Valley Cabernet Sauvignon 2014 The classic Clare blend of cabernet sauvignon and malbec works extremely well, and this is a fine example. Malbec tends to soften and fill out the mid-palate and temper the firm Clare cabernet tannins. Screwcap. 14.3% alc. **Rating** 95 **To** 2030 $22 ✪

Nirvana Reserve Clare Valley Shiraz 2012 A classic Clare shiraz, dark-fruited, plummy, earthy, and backed by a spicy oak lift. The palate is seamless and plush, carrying its 15.2% alcohol with ease, with a long and gravelly finish. Screwcap. **Rating** 94 **To** 2035 $45

ŢŢŢŢ **Purple Rain Adelaide Hills Sauvignon Blanc 2014** Rating 89 To 2016 $20
London Calling Clare Valley Merlot 2013 Rating 88 To 2020 $22

Clemens Hill   ★★★★☆

686 Richmond Road, Cambridge, Tas 7170 **Region** Southern Tasmania
T (03) 6248 5587 **www.**clemenshill.com.au **Open** By appt
Winemaker Winemaking Tasmania **Est.** 1994 **Dozens** 3500 **Vyds** 8ha
Clemens Hill is now jointly owned by Aurelia D'Ettorre and Dr Rob Ware. Rob has over 20 years' experience in the Tasmanian wine industry, having been a partner with Fred Peacock at Bream Creek since 1989. Clemens Hill now has two vineyards: the estate property with pinot noir, sauvignon blanc and semillon, and the Tashinga Vineyard, also in the Coal River area, but with a different climate, bringing chardonnay and additional pinot noir.

ŢŢŢŢŢ **Fume Blanc 2015** 86% sauvignon blanc, 14% semillon, gold medal Tasmania Wine Show '15, causing the judges to write 'quite Graves (Bordeaux) like', and I agree 100%. What's more, by the time it's released in '17 it will have built even more complexity. Screwcap. 13% alc. **Rating** 95 **To** 2022 $34 ✪

ŢŢŢŢŢ **Rose 2015** Rating 92 To 2017 $26
Sauvignon Blanc 2015 Rating 90 To 2019 $26
Pinot Noir 2013 Rating 90 To 2021 $36

Clonakilla   ★★★★★

Crisps Lane, Murrumbateman, NSW 2582 **Region** Canberra District
T (02) 6227 5877 **www.**clonakilla.com.au **Open** 7 days 10–5
Winemaker Tim Kirk, Bryan Martin **Est.** 1971 **Dozens** 17 000 **Vyds** 13.5ha
The indefatigable Tim Kirk, with an inexhaustible thirst for knowledge, is the winemaker and manager of this family winery founded by his father, scientist Dr John Kirk. It is not at all surprising that the quality of the wines is exceptional, especially the Shiraz Viognier, which has paved the way for numerous others to follow, but remains the icon. Demand for the wines outstrips supply, even with the 1998 acquisition of an adjoining 20ha property by Tim and wife Lara Kirk, planted to shiraz and viognier; the first Hilltops Shiraz being made in 2000, from the best vineyards; the 2007 purchase by the Kirk family of another adjoining property, and the planting of another 1.8ha of shiraz, plus 0.4ha of grenache, mourvedre and cinsaut; and in the same year, the first vintage of O'Riada Shiraz. Exports to all major markets.

ŢŢŢŢŢ **Shiraz Viognier 2015** Tim Kirk is continuing to refine and explore the myriad of possibilities from this great site. Increasingly turning to higher proportions of whole bunches in the fermentations, he is getting greater and greater detail in his flagship wine. It is a thinker's wine: it stops you, draws you in and captivates. Incredibly detailed and floral-scented, the sumptuous and finely poised palate is a masterpiece. Screwcap. 14% alc. **Rating** 98 **To** 2030 $110 ✪
O'Riada Canberra District Shiraz 2015 A strikingly fragrant and perfumed effort from Clonakilla, this wine captures you instantaneously. It is superbly constructed, aromatically fragrant, perfumed and darkly fruited; on the palate spice, superfine tannins and then a finish that just lingers and expands. Screwcap. 14.5% alc. **Rating** 97 **To** 2040 $45 ✪

ŢŢŢŢŢ **Tumbarumba Chardonnay 2015** Not content with the icon status of the Shiraz Viognier, Tim Kirk has taken cool grown chardonnay from Tumbarumba, and succeeded magnificently. Grapefruit, citrus blossom and a lovely mealy complexity dominate. The palate is poised and precise, with exceptional drive and energy. A superb effort. Screwcap. 12.5% alc. **Rating** 96 **To** 2025 $45 ✪

Shiraz Viognier 2014 The bright hue and perfumed, spicy red berry bouquet run true to type for this modern classic, setting the bar for the co-fermented blend many years ago. It has a set of flavours that are unique, and can fool even expert tasters in blind tastings: its cross-thatched flavours need careful navigation to decide whether it's from Côte Rôtie or Canberra. Screwcap. 13.5% alc. **Rating** 96 To 2034 $110

Canberra District Riesling 2015 Long fingers of flavour. Pressing intensity. The delivery of lime sherbet, florals, wet stone and talc flavours here is, simply, a terrific display of quality and class. Screwcap. 12% alc. **Rating** 95 To 2028 $35 CM ✪

Canberra District Viognier 2015 Complex and inviting; lime, honeysuckle, ginger and spice lead to a powerful and intensely concentrated palate. Viognier is a difficult variety to balance the power and retain the delicacy of, but Tim Kirk has done so admirably. Screwcap. 14% alc. **Rating** 95 To 2018 $55

Hilltops Shiraz 2015 This is another cracking release under the Hilltops label. Superbly balanced with an impeccably silky and fine palate, it is a wine you must put in the cellar: it is lovely now, but will reward those who can resist for as long as possible. Screwcap. 14.5% alc. **Rating** 95 To 2030 $35 ✪

Canberra District Semillon Sauvignon Blanc 2015 Provides great pleasure. Slips easily through the mouth but shows excellent intensity of flavour throughout. Tropical fruit, cut grass, lemon and slate. It's fresh and fruity but fine; precise. Screwcap. 12% alc. **Rating** 94 To 2017 $25 CM ✪

ŸŸŸŸŸ **Viognier Nouveau 2015** Rating 93 To 2016 $28 CM
Ceoltoiri 2015 Rating 93 To 2023 $45

Cloudbreak Wines ★★★★

5A/1 Adelaide Lobethal Road, Lobethal, SA 5241 **Region** Adelaide Hills
T 0431 245 668 **www.**cloudbreakwines.com.au **Open** Not
Winemaker Simon Greenleaf, Randal Tomich **Est.** 1998 **Dozens** 22 000 **Vyds** 80ha
Cloudbreak Wines is a joint venture between Randal Tomich and Simon Greenleaf, who share a friendship of nearly 20 years. Cloudbreak specialises in cool climate wines, grown on the Tomich family's Woodside Vineyard. Simon has been producing wines from Tomich Vineyards since 2005 and has a strong understanding of the site and fruit quality. Randal has had more than 20 years' experience in winemaking, specialising in vineyard development, and plants vineyards for brands across Aus and California. The vineyards upon which Cloudbreak Wines is based comprise chardonnay (22ha), sauvignon blanc (18ha), pinot noir (15ha), gruner veltliner (6ha), and riesling, gewurztraminer and shiraz (5ha each). Exports to Singapore and China.

ŸŸŸŸŸ **Chardonnay 2013** As is the pattern for Cloudbreak, picked at dawn, processed cool, and fermented and matured in French barriques. Retains a bright, light green hue; the flavours are fruit, rather than oak, driven, ranging through melon, fig and citrus. Screwcap. 13.5% alc. **Rating** 91 To 2019 $25

Pinot Noir 2013 The vineyard is planted to clones 114, 115 and MV6, the hand-picked bunches cold-macerated before fermentation. Light, clear colour with very good retention of hue; there is plenty of stemmy/whole bunch here adding complexity and length, but I wonder whether there is enough fruit to go the distance. Screwcap. 13.5% alc. **Rating** 91 To 2020 $30

ŸŸŸŸ **Winemakers Reserve Sauvignon Blanc 2015** Rating 89 To 2016 $19 ✪
Chardonnay Pinot Noir NV Rating 89 To 2017 $30

Clovely Estate ★★★☆

Steinhardts Road, Moffatdale via Murgon, Qld 4605 **Region** South Burnett
T (07) 3876 3100 **www.**clovely.com.au **Open** 7 days 10–4
Winemaker Luke Fitzpatrick, Sarah Boyce **Est.** 1997 **Dozens** 25 000 **Vyds** 173.76ha
Clovely Estate has the largest vineyards in Qld, with immaculately maintained vines at two locations in the Burnett Valley. There are 140ha of red grapes (including 60ha of shiraz) and

34ha of white grapes. The attractively packaged wines are sold in various styles at various price points. The estate also has a second cellar door at 210 Musgrave Road, Red Hill (open Tues–Sat 11–7). Exports to Denmark, Papua New Guinea, Taiwan and China.

ΨΨΨΨ **Left Field South Burnett Sangiovese 2014** Developed colour and savoury palate don't surprise, but there is some cherry fruit surrounded by persistent, albeit relatively fine, tannins. Screwcap. 13.5% alc. **Rating** 89 **To** 2020 $22

Clover Hill ★★★★

60 Clover Hill Road, Lebrina, Tas 7254 **Region** Northern Tasmania
T (03) 5459 7900 **www**.cloverhillwines.com.au **Open** By appt
Winemaker Robert Heywood, Peter Warr **Est.** 1986 **Dozens** 12 000 **Vyds** 23.9ha
Clover Hill was established by Taltarni in 1986 with the sole purpose of making a premium sparkling wine. It has 23.9ha of vineyards (chardonnay, pinot noir and pinot meunier) and its sparkling wine quality is excellent, combining finesse with power and length. The American owner and founder of Clos du Val (Napa Valley), Taltarni and Clover Hill has brought these businesses and Domaine de Nizas (Languedoc) under the one management roof, the group known as Goelet Wine Estates. Exports to the UK, the US and other major markets.

ΨΨΨΨΨ **Tasmanian Cuvee Methode Traditionnelle Rose NV** A rose that effortlessly walks the tightrope between elegance and character. Nuances of pink pepper accent and pretty rose petal and red cherry backdrop; an invisible 7.5g/l dosage completes a long, vibrant and elegantly focused finish. Diam. 12.5% alc. **Rating** 94 **To** 2017 $32 TS

ΨΨΨΨΨ **Tasmanian Cuvee Methode Traditionelle NV** **Rating** 92 **To** 2017 $32 TS

Clyde Park Vineyard ★★★★★

2490 Midland Highway, Bannockburn, Vic 3331 **Region** Geelong
T (03) 5281 7274 **www**.clydepark.com.au **Open** 7 days 11–5
Winemaker James Thomas, Terry Jongebloed **Est.** 1979 **Dozens** 5000 **Vyds** 10.1ha
Clyde Park Vineyard, established by Gary Farr but sold by him many years ago, has passed through several changes of ownership. Now owned by Terry Jongebloed and Sue Jongebloed-Dixon, it has significant mature plantings of pinot noir (3.4ha), chardonnay (3.1ha), sauvignon blanc (1.5ha), shiraz (1.2ha) and pinot gris (0.9ha), and the quality of its wines is consistently exemplary. Exports to the UK and Hong Kong.

ΨΨΨΨΨ **Single Block D Bannockburn Pinot Noir 2015** Inbuilt complexity, powerful in its own way, and long with tannin and flavour. This undergrowthy, herb-flecked pinot is a wonder to behold; it begs the word 'mesmerising'. Little more need be said. 165 dozen. Screwcap. 13% alc. **Rating** 97 **To** 2025 $65 CM **۞**

ΨΨΨΨΨ **Single Block B2 Bannockburn Pinot Noir 2015** 25% whole bunch. 120 dozen. Sterner than the Block D but of comparable quality. Clyde Park has clearly had a scintillating year. This is all dried herbs and meat, bright red cherries and spearmint. It hits, runs and holds, the wine's thin folds of tannin gathered to produce a collective strength. Screwcap. 13% alc. **Rating** 96 **To** 2025 $65 CM **۞**
Single Block F Bannockburn Pinot Noir 2015 100% whole bunch, though you wouldn't pick it. There's a sinewy character to the tannin but there's plenty of fruit flesh and spice notes are neatly tucked therein. Oak is beautifully integrated. Gun smoke and clove-like complexities work a treat. The hits keep coming. Screwcap. 13.5% alc. **Rating** 96 **To** 2026 $65 CM **۞**
Geelong Shiraz 2015 In immaculate shape. Silken but seriously well fruited. Cool climate but ripe. Dried spices, plums, subtle peppers, cloves and wood smoke. Ultrafine tannin. A pearler. Will reward the patient. Screwcap. 14% alc. **Rating** 96 **To** 2032 $35 CM **۞**
Geelong Sauvignon Blanc 2015 Estate-grown, hand-picked, whole bunch-pressed, wild yeast-fermented in French oak (45% new), plus 5 months maturation on lees. As much about structure, texture and length as it is about sauvignon blanc

flavour, and succeeds brilliantly year after year. The complex flavour and texture wheel is halted by the stream of citrussy acidity on the long finish. Screwcap. 13% alc. **Rating** 95 **To** 2020 $30 ⊙

Block B3 Geelong Chardonnay 2015 A bright shining beauty. As effortless as it is insistent. Flush with pear, grapefruit, white peach and smoky, sawdusty character, oatmeal as an afterthought. It draws you in and lightens your load. The perfect host. Screwcap. 13% alc. **Rating** 95 **To** 2021 $60 CM

Geelong Rose 2015 Pinot gris and saigneed pinot noir were wild-fermented separately, with 5 months maturation on lees prior to blending. Bright, light crimson, it has a particularly fragrant bouquet of crushed strawberries, the palate with an extra layer of flavour and length, ditto the aftertaste. Screwcap. 12.5% alc. **Rating** 94 **To** 2017 $25 ⊙

ＹＹＹＹＹ **Geelong Pinot Noir 2015** Rating 93 To 2023 $35 CM
Locale Geelong Pinot Noir 2015 Rating 92 To 2020 $25 CM ⊙
Geelong Chardonnay 2015 Rating 90 To 2019 $35 CM
Geelong Pinot Gris 2015 Rating 90 To 2017 $35

Coal Valley Vineyard ★★★★

257 Richmond Road, Cambridge, Tas 7170 **Region** Southern Tasmania
T (03) 6248 5367 www.coalvalley.com.au **Open** 7 days 11–5 (closed Jul)
Winemaker Alain Rousseau, Todd Goebel **Est.** 1991 **Dozens** 1500 **Vyds** 4.5ha
Since acquiring Coal Valley Vineyard in 1999, Gill Christian and Todd Goebel have increased the original 1ha hobby vineyard to pinot noir (2.3ha), riesling, cabernet sauvignon, merlot, chardonnay and tempranillo. More remarkable were Gill and Todd's concurrent lives: one in India, the other in Tasmania (flying over six times a year), and digging 4000 holes for the new vine plantings. Todd makes the Pinot Noir and Tempranillo onsite, and dreams of making all the wines. Exports to Canada.

ＹＹＹＹＹ **Pinot Noir 2014** Estate-grown 25yo vines, open-fermented, 50% wild yeast, transferred to barrel for completion of fermentation and mlf, matured in French oak (35% new) for 15 months. A strongly savoury/foresty style likely to polarise opinions; full of interest, with touches of bacon, liqueur black cherry and tannin on the back-palate. An unruly teenager with obvious potential, the length of the palate a clincher. Screwcap. 14% alc. **Rating** 93 **To** 2022 $36

TGR Riesling 2015 The tropical characters of the dry Riesling are more at home here, although in best Tasmanian fashion, the 20g/l of residual sugar is muted by the acidity. It all adds up well enough, and I don't have the slightest doubt this will flourish with 2–3 years in bottle. Screwcap. 9% alc. **Rating** 91 **To** 2023 $28

Chardonnay 2014 Pressed to tank for initiation of fermentation, transferred to French oak (25% new) for completion of fermentation and 8 months maturation. Gleaming straw-green, it is still youthful and a bit gangly, but will settle down without losing its personality. Screwcap. 13% alc. **Rating** 90 **To** 2020 $32

ＹＹＹＹ **Riesling 2015** Rating 89 To 2018 $28
Cabernet Merlot 2014 Rating 88 To 2024 $32

Coastal Estate Vineyard ★★★☆

320 Grays Road, Paraparap, Vic 3240 **Region** Geelong
T 0437 180 664 www.coastalestate.com.au **Open** Not
Winemaker Suzanne Paton **Est.** 2007 **Dozens** 400 **Vyds** 3.5ha
Winter trips to Falls Creek have taken innumerable skiers into Brown Brothers' cellar door at Milawa. Suzanne and Colin Paton's visits began in the early 1990s as 20-year-olds, and it changed their perspective on wine forever. Colin began studies in viticulture at Dookie, and then at Charles Sturt University to complete his degree, coupled with working in the Yarra Valley for periods of time, and coming into the Sergio Carlei orbit. Counterintuitively, it is in fact Suzanne who has taken on the role of winemaker and sales. The vineyard is planted to 0.6ha each of sauvignon blanc and shiraz, and 1.1ha of pinot noir with MV6 and 115 clones.

ΨΨΨΨΨ **Heathcote Shiraz 2014** From Mt Camel Range, open-fermented and basket-pressed, 12 months in barrel. Inky purple-crimson; some very good quality grapes are the source of a towering shiraz with a fountain of black fruits, licorice and ripe tannins. Lucky they who were born this year, for this will have a long life ahead. The ultimate bargain. Screwcap. 14% alc. **Rating** 94 **To** 2049 $21 ✪

ΨΨΨΨ **Surf Coast Hinterland Sauvignon Blanc 2015 Rating** 89 **To** 2016 $21

Coates Wines   ★★★★★

PO Box 859, McLaren Vale, SA 5171 **Region** McLaren Vale
T 0417 882 557 **www**.coates-wines.com **Open** Not
Winemaker Duane Coates **Est.** 2003 **Dozens** 2500
Duane Coates has a Bachelor of Science, a Master of Business Administration and a Master of Oenology from Adelaide University; for good measure he completed the theory component of the Masters of Wine degree in 2005. Having made wine in various parts of the world, and in SA, he is more than qualified to make and market Coates wines. Nonetheless, his original intention was to simply make a single barrel of wine employing various philosophies and practices outside the mainstream; there was no plan to move to commercial production. The key is organically grown grapes. Exports to the UK and the US.

ΨΨΨΨΨ **Langhorne Creek The Cabernet Sauvignon 2013** Crushed and destemmed, with wild yeast fermentation, 14 days on skins, matured for 20 months in French barriques (50% new), neither fined nor filtered. This is a celebration of the almost velvety nature of Langhorne Creek cabernet, full to the gunnels with cassis, the tannin profile soft; oak, too, plays a positive role. Screwcap. 13.5% alc. **Rating** 95 **To** 2033 $30 ✪
Adelaide Hills The Semillon Sauvignon Blanc 2015 A beautiful, fluid wine with oak adding a bit of spark to zesty tropical fruit. Price is more than reasonable. Screwcap. 13% alc. **Rating** 94 **To** 2017 $25 CM ✪
Shin Zen Bi Syrah 2012 Wild-fermented before being matured for 33 months in all-new French oak. It's resiny, creamy, musk-laden and blackberried, with sweet/tangy acidity making its presence felt before an ooze of chocolate rolls in. The fruit doesn't sit at the biggest end of town (a positive) but the winemaking does. Cork. 14.5% alc. **Rating** 94 **To** 2028 $300 CM

ΨΨΨΨΨ **McLaren Vale The Syrah 2014 Rating** 93 **To** 2027 $25 CM ✪
McLaren Vale The Syrah 2013 Rating 93 **To** 2033 $25 ✪
The Gimp McLaren Vale Shiraz 2013 Rating 93 **To** 2030 $30 CM
The Iberian 2013 Rating 93 **To** 2030 $30
Langhorne Creek Cabernet Sauvignon 2014 Rating 92 **To** 2026 $30 CM
Adelaide Hills The Sauvignon Blanc 2015 Rating 91 **To** 2017 $25 CM

Cobaw Ridge   ★★★★☆

31 Perc Boyers Lane, Pastoria, Vic 3444 **Region** Macedon Ranges
T (03) 5423 5227 **www**.cobawridge.com.au **Open** Thurs–Mon 12–5
Winemaker Alan Cooper **Est.** 1985 **Dozens** 800 **Vyds** 5ha
When the Coopers started planting in the early 1980s there was scant knowledge of the best varieties for the region, let alone the Cobaw Ridge site. They have now settled on four varieties, chardonnay and syrah always being part of the mix. Lagrein and close-planted, multi-clonal pinot noir are more recent arrivals to thrive. Cobaw Ridge is now fully certified biodynamic, and all winery operations are carried out according to the biodynamic calendar.

ΨΨΨΨΨ **Chardonnay 2014** P58 clone, hand-picked, whole bunch-pressed, barrel-fermented, mlf, 12 months maturation. A full-bodied and notably complex chardonnay with layers of white peach, grapefruit, oak and acidity, each contributing to the end result; the mlf has been particularly effective, and the new oak influence is on the money. Diam. 12.8% alc. **Rating** 95 **To** 2022 $50

ŶŶŶŶŶ L'altra Lagrein Syrah 2012 Rating 90 To 2018 $40
Lagrein 2013 Rating 90 To 2020 $60

Cockfighter's Ghost ★★★★☆

576 De Beyers Road, Pokolbin, NSW 2320 **Region** Hunter Valley
T (02) 4993 3688 **www.cockfightersghost.com.au Open** 7 days 10–5
Winemaker Jeff Byrne, Xanthe Hatcher **Est.** 1988 **Dozens** 30 000 **Vyds** 38ha
Ever the professional, David Clarke had taken steps towards the sale of Poole's Rock prior
to his death in April 2012. Discussions with neighbour Brian Agnew, owner of Audrey
Wilkinson, led to agreement between the Clarke and Agnew families for Poole's Rock to be
acquired by the Agnew interests. Audrey Wilkinson keeps its separate identity, but the changes
have been rung for Poole's Rock. The winery is now known as Cockfighter's Ghost, Poole's
Rock and Firestick brands forming part of the Cockfighter's Ghost business. Exports to the
US, Canada, Japan and China.

ŶŶŶŶŶ **Cockfighter's Ghost Reserve Coonawarra Cabernet Sauvignon 2014** It's
a sign of the times that Cockfighter's Ghost was able to make a first-time entry
into Coonawarra to buy cabernet of this quality, even if it is reflected in the price
of the wine. It abounds with cassis, a flick of Coonawarra mint and bay leaf/
dried herbs on the finish, where cabernet tannins also make their point. Screwcap.
14% alc. **Rating** 94 **To** 2034 $38

ŶŶŶŶŶ **Poole's Rock Tasmania Pinot Noir 2014** Rating 93 To 2021 $65 CM
Poole's Rock Post Office Shiraz 2014 Rating 93 To 2028 $50 CM
Cockfighter's Reserve Hunter Semillon 2015 Rating 91 To 2025 $28 CM
Cockfighter's Ghost McLaren Vale Shiraz 2014 Rating 91 To 2021 $22
CM ❂
Cockfighter's Langhorne Creek Cabernet Sauvignon 2014 Rating 91 To
2024 $22 CM ❂
Cockfighter's Adelaide Hills Pinot Gris 2015 Rating 90 To 2017 $22 CM
Cockfighter's Hunter Valley Verdelho 2015 Rating 90 To 2017 $22 CM

Cofield Wines ★★★★

Distillery Road, Wahgunyah, Vic 3687 **Region** Rutherglen
T (02) 6033 3798 **www.cofieldwines.com.au Open** Mon–Sat 9–5, Sun 10–5
Winemaker Damien Cofield, Brendan Heath **Est.** 1990 **Dozens** 13 000 **Vyds** 15.4ha
Sons Damien (winery) and Andrew (vineyard) have taken over responsibility for the business
from parents Max and Karen Cofield. Collectively, they have developed an impressively broad-
based product range with a strong cellar door sales base. The Pickled Sisters Café is open for
lunch Wed–Mon (02) 6033 2377). A 20ha property at Rutherglen, purchased in 2007, is
planted to shiraz, durif and sangiovese. Exports to China.

ŶŶŶŶŶ **Provincial Parcel Alpine Valleys Beechworth Chardonnay 2014** A 50/50%
blend of the two regions, hand-picked, whole bunch-pressed, part fermented in
stainless steel, part fermented in French oak (25% new), matured for 9 months.
An elegant and balanced stone fruit/grapefruit wine very much in tune with the
times. Screwcap. 13% alc. **Rating** 93 **To** 2022 $36
Rutherglen Shiraz Durif 2014 An 85/15% blend, matured for 14 months in
used French and American oak. Good depth to the colour is no surprise; savoury/
earthy flavours (ex the durif) marry well with plum and blackberry fruit. A
thoroughly hedonistic wine. Screwcap. 14.2% alc. **Rating** 92 **To** 2030 $24 ❂
Rutherglen Topaque NV The colour is more developed than some of its
Rutherglen siblings; the palate, too, is a little more complex, with spice, tea leaf,
burnt butterscotch and honey. Screwcap. 17.5% alc. **Rating** 92 **To** 2018 $25 ❂
King Valley Riesling 2015 BV17 clone planted '71 in Whitfield, machine-
harvested, cultured yeast cool-fermented in stainless steel. Fragrant blossom aromas
of lime and apple, the palate following on in single file behind those aromas.

It is easy to enjoy now, but will build a bit more flesh soon. Screwcap. 12% alc. **Rating** 91 **To** 2025 $18 ✪

♥♥♥♥ Pinot Noir Chardonnay 2006 **Rating** 89 **To** 2017 $45 TS

Coldstream Hills   ★★★★★

31 Maddens Lane, Coldstream, Vic 3770 **Region** Yarra Valley
T (03) 5960 7000 **www**.coldstreamhills.com.au **Open** 7 days 10–5
Winemaker Andrew Fleming, Greg Jarratt, James Halliday (Consultant) **Est.** 1985
Dozens 25 000 **Vyds** 100ha

Founded by the author, James Halliday, Coldstream Hills is now a small part of Treasury Wine Estates, with 100ha of owned estate vineyards as its base, three in the Lower Yarra Valley and two in the Upper Yarra Valley. Chardonnay and Pinot Noir continue to be the principal focus; Merlot came on-stream in 1997, Sauvignon Blanc around the same time, Reserve Shiraz later still. Vintage conditions permitting, Chardonnay and Pinot Noir are made in Reserve, Single Vineyard and varietal forms (at three price levels). In addition, Amphitheatre Pinot Noir was made in tiny quantities in 2006 and '13. In '10 a multimillion-dollar winery was erected around the original winery buildings and facilities; it has a capacity of 1500 tonnes. There is a plaque in the fermentation area commemorating the official opening on 12 October '10 and naming the facility the 'James Halliday Cellar'. Exports to the UK, the US and Singapore. The tasting notes were not written by the author or a Coldstream Hills winemaker.

♥♥♥♥♥ Reserve Yarra Valley Chardonnay 2015 With a lineage dating back to '90, the Reserve Chardonnay has an enviable reputation for producing outstanding wines. The '15 continues that fine heritage and is one of the best in recent years. From vineyards, including the original House Block at the home vineyard, planted '85. Increasing use of puncheons is having a generously positive effect on this label. The bouquet is laden with melon, stone fruit, citrus and a background of cedar and struck match, and has impressive depth. The palate is layered, pithy, minerally and exceptionally long and precise. Screwcap. 13% alc. **Rating** 97 **To** 2028 $60 ✪
Deer Farm Vineyard Pinot Noir 2015 Another seriously impressive release from the Deer Farm Vineyard in the Upper Yarra. It balances power and elegance in a way that is totally seductive. Seriously fragrant and perfumed, the bouquet is captivating. The palate is silky, plush, expansive and minutely detailed. The finish just goes on and on, revealing more as the wine opens up in the glass. A magnificent effort that will reward extended clearing. Screwcap. 13.5% alc. **Rating** 97 **To** 2035 $50 ✪

♥♥♥♥♥ Reserve Yarra Valley Chardonnay 2014 Stunning. Elegance and power combined. The lines of a sports car. Flint, funk, pristine stone fruit, gun smoke and mineral. It hits and drives and keeps on going. In the end the price looks more than reasonable; says it all. Screwcap. 13% alc. **Rating** 96 **To** 2023 $60 CM ✪
The Esplanade Yarra Valley Pinot Noir 2015 Of the three '15 single vineyard releases, The Esplanade is the only one from the Lower Yarra Valley, and it exhibits its origins admirably. There is more power, intensity and structure. Deeply coloured; the bouquet is a brooding mix of plum, dark cherry, and a hint of smoky oak. The palate is equally flavoured, with a line of savoury tannins that go on and on. I expect this release to age incredibly well: could well need 10 years to begin to unfurl and strut its stuff. Screwcap. 13.5% alc. **Rating** 96 **To** 2035 $50 ✪
Deer Farm Vineyard Chardonnay 2015 This single vineyard release is sourced from the pioneering Deer Farm Vineyard in Gladysdale, planted '94. Barrel-fermented in a mixture of barriques and puncheons (50% new), it is a very modern example of Australian chardonnay. The fruit has a cool edge with white peach and fennel, backed by cedar and spice from the oak. The palate is still tightly wound and yet to fully express all that this wine has to offer, which is exactly as it should be. Tuck it away for 2–8 years before you take a second peek. Screwcap. 13% alc. **Rating** 95 **To** 2025 $40

Yarra Valley Pinot Noir 2015 With a track record dating back to the '80s, this is always a wine to look out for, and the '15 is no exception. The brightest crimson colour leads to a detailed and complex bouquet of plum, spice and cherry with a touch of rhubarb. The palate is equally detailed, silky, fine and with layers of flavour. It is the balance and harmony that drives this delicious pinot. Utterly drinkable now, it will age beautifully, and, if you can keep your hands off it, will easily pass 10+ years and be better for it. Screwcap. 13.5% alc. **Rating** 95 **To** 2028 $35 ✪

Yarra Valley Chardonnay 2015 Sourced from the Upper and Lower Yarra Valley, fermented in French barriques. This is a classy example of Yarra chardonnay. Melon, stone fruits, cashew and a hint of cedar, the palate flows seamlessly with bright mineral acid and a taut and fine finish. Screwcap. 13% alc. **Rating** 94 **To** 2023 $35

Deer Farm Vineyard Yarra Valley Pinot Gris 2015 Juicy little sucker. Elegant too. Pear, but mostly apple, with a fine, flavoursome, almost perfumed finish. Just the right texture and balance. Screwcap. 13% alc. **Rating** 94 **To** 2017 $33 CM

Hazeldene Vineyard Pinot Noir 2015 Exclusively from the Hazeldene Vineyard in the Upper Yarra, planted '96. Bright crimson; the bouquet is red-fruited and fragrant with redcurrant, raspberry and a lovely floral note. The palate is medium weight, silky, and with a lick of sappy tannins to close. Screwcap. 13.5% alc. **Rating** 94 **To** 2025 $50

🍷🍷🍷🍷 **Pinot Noir Chardonnay 2012** **Rating** 91 **To** 2022 $35 TS

Collector Wines ★★★★★

12 Bourke Street, Collector, NSW 2581 (postal) **Region** Canberra District
T (02) 6116 8722 **www**.collectorwines.com.au **Open** Not
Winemaker Alex McKay **Est.** 2007 **Dozens** 3000

Owner and winemaker Alex McKay makes exquisitely detailed wines, bending to the dictates of inclement weather on his doorstep, heading elsewhere if need be. He was part of a talented team at BRL Hardy's Kamberra Winery, and when it was closed down by Hardys' new owner CHAMP, decided to stay in the district, He is not known to speak much, and when he does, his voice is very quiet. So you have to remain alert to appreciate his unparalleled sense of humour. No such attention is needed for his wines, which are consistently excellent, their elegance appropriate for their maker. Exports to The Netherlands and Japan.

🍷🍷🍷🍷🍷 **Tiger Tiger Chardonnay 2014** I10V1 clone, the vineyard at 850m, hand-picked, whole bunch-pressed, fermented in French oak (30% new) full mlf, matured for 11 months. Rocket fuel power; ultimate intensity and focus, mlf was clearly essential; unsweetened grapefruit and zest plus some white peach and nutty oak. Screwcap. 12.9% alc. **Rating** 96 **To** 2025 $39 ✪

Reserve Shiraz 2014 40% whole bunches, the remainder whole berries, open wild ferment for 9 days, matured in French oak (40% new) for 14 months. This all about finesse and length, with a progressive build-up of complexity over the journey. Spice figures large, and the French oak is more visible, the process effortless. Screwcap. 13.2% alc. **Rating** 96 **To** 2044 $59 ✪

Marked Tree Red Shiraz 2014 25% whole bunches, the remainder whole berries, matured for 14 months in French oak (25% new). The usual movement and energy of Collector Wines, the intense bouquet full of exotic spices and black fruits, the palate opening with fine, sweet dark fruits rising to a crescendo of ripe tannins on the finish and aftertaste. Oh, and French oak too. Screwcap. 13.1% alc. **Rating** 95 **To** 2039 $28 ✪

Rose Red City Sangiovese 2014 92% sangiovese, 4% canaiolo nero and 2% each of colorino and mammolo; 10% whole bunches, the remainder whole berries, 7–14 days on skins, blended after fermentation, matured in French oak (15% new) for 14 months. Sangiovese (and friends) as only Alex McKay can make it: vibrant and juicy red fruits, tannins the seeing eye dog, strictly to help, not make trouble. Lovely wine. Screwcap. 13.2% alc. **Rating** 95 **To** 2029 $33 ✪

Colmar Estate

790 Pinnacle Road, Orange, NSW 2800 **Region** Orange
T 0419 977 270 **www**.colmarestate.com.au **Open** W'ends & public hols 10.30–5
Winemaker Chris Derrez, Lucy Maddox **Est.** 2013 **Dozens** 1200 **Vyds** 5.9ha
You don't have to look far for the inspiration behind the name when you find that owners Bill
Shrapnel and his wife Jane have long loved the wines of Alsace: Colmar is the main town in
that region. The Shrapnels realised a long-held ambition when they purchased an established,
high-altitude (980m) vineyard in May 2013. Everything they have done has turned to gold,
notably grafting cabernet sauvignon to pinot noir, merlot to chardonnay, and shiraz to pinot
gris. The plantings are now 1.51ha of pinot noir (clones 777, 115 and MV6), 1.25ha of
chardonnay (clones 95, 96 and P58), 1.22ha of sauvignon blanc and lesser quantities of riesling,
pinot gris and traminer.

ŶŶŶŶŶ **Orange Riesling 2015** Flavour and length. This cuts a fine figure but it's not too
slender; it has some body. Lime, bath salts, crisp green apple and spice notes. Don't
mind if I do. Trophies, Orange Wine Show '15 and NSW Wine Awards. Screwcap.
12.5% alc. **Rating** 95 **To** 2021 $28 CM ✪

ŶŶŶŶŶ **Single Vineyard Orange Riesling 2015** **Rating** 93 **To** 2016 $32 CM
Orange Pinot Noir 2014 **Rating** 93 **To** 2022 $32 CM
Orange Sauvignon Blanc 2015 **Rating** 92 **To** 2016 $24 CM ✪
Orange Pinot Rose 2015 **Rating** 92 **To** 2016 $26 CM

Colvin Wines

19 Boyle Street, Mosman, NSW 2088 (postal) **Region** Hunter Valley
T (02) 9908 7886 **www**.colvinwines.com.au **Open** Not
Winemaker Andrew Spinaze, Mark Richardson **Est.** 1999 **Dozens** 500 **Vyds** 5.2ha
In 1990 Sydney lawyer John Colvin and wife Robyn purchased the De Beyers Vineyard,
which has a history going back to the second half of the 19th century. By 1967, when a
syndicate bought 35ha of the original vineyard site, no vines remained. The syndicate planted
semillon on the alluvial soil of the creek flats and shiraz on the red clay hillsides. Up to 1998
all the grapes were sold to Tyrrell's, but since '99 quantities have been made for the Colvin
Wines label. These include Sangiovese, from a little over 1ha of vines planted by John in '96
because of his love of the wines of Tuscany.

ŶŶŶŶŶ **Museum Release Hunter Valley Semillon 2009** Brilliant green-straw; now
fully mature, with all its multifaceted lime and honey nuances on full display. It
will hold this quality for years to come, but will ultimately start to dry out and
decline in quality. Screwcap. 10.4% alc. **Rating** 95 **To** 2024 $49
Hunter Valley Semillon 2014 A very attractive semillon managing the transition
from youth to maturity with greater ease than most around 2–3yo. It is full of
citrus fruit, verging on lime. Screwcap. 11.5% alc. **Rating** 94 **To** 2029 $38

ŶŶŶŶŶ **Hunter Valley Sangiovese 2014** **Rating** 90 **To** 2021 $38

Condie Estate

480 Heathcote-Redesdale Road, Heathcote, Vic 3523 **Region** Heathcote
T 0404 480 422 **www**.condie.com.au **Open** W'ends & public hols 11–5
Winemaker Richie Condie **Est.** 2001 **Dozens** 1500 **Vyds** 6.8ha
Richie Condie worked as a corporate risk manager for a multinational company off the back
of a Bachelor of Commerce degree, but after establishing Condie Estate, completed several
viticulture and winemaking courses, including a diploma of winemaking at Dookie. Having
first established 2.4ha of shiraz, Richie and wife Rosanne followed with 2ha of sangiovese and
0.8ha of viognier. In 2010 they purchased a 1.6ha vineyard that had been planted in 1990,
where they have established a winery and cellar door. Richie says to anyone thinking of going
into wine production: 'Go and work in a small vineyard and winery for at least one year before
you start out for yourself. You need to understand how much hard physical work is involved
in planting a vineyard, looking after it, making the wine, and then selling it.' The proof of the
pudding is in the eating, with excellent wine quality.

🍷🍷🍷🍷🍷 **The Max Heathcote Shiraz 2013** 14 and 23yo vines, 75% PT23/25% Mount
Langi clones vinified separately, destemmed, open-fermented, cultured yeast,
8–10 days on skins, matured in French oak (25% new) for 24 months. There is
nothing in the vinification that is out of the ordinary, nor suggesting where the
power and complexity come from – it's all about the site and possibly the 25%
Mount Langi clone. There are spears of exhilarating jet-black fruits that run
through the centre of the palate; they also (unexpectedly) take the attention away
from the tannins. Screwcap. 14.7% alc. **Rating** 95 **To** 2038 $50

The Gwen Heathcote Shiraz 2014 14yo vines, 80% PT23/20% Mount Langi
clone, vinified separately, 60% whole berries, 40% destemmed, open-fermented,
cultured yeast, 8–10 days on skins, matured oak for 18 months (95% French, 20%
new, 5% in American). Heathcote has produced wines with high levels of alcohol
over the years, especially in drought years, Jasper Hill one of those affected in
years gone by. Theoretically this wine should light up on the finish like a furnace,
but it doesn't – instead it is simply rich and velvety, with no dead fruit characters.
Screwcap. 15.4% alc. **Rating** 94 **To** 2029 $30 ✪

Giarracca Heathcote Sangiovese 2015 Three clones, one ripening 9 days
later than the first two, hand-picked, destemmed, small batch open-fermented,
cultured yeast, 8–10 days on skins, 9 months maturation in used French oak.
Fascinating wine, with lavish amounts of bright red cherries and only a fine-spun
web of tannins; no problems at all for immediate consumption. It's almost too
good to be true, but there's not a false note that I can detect. Screwcap. 13% alc.
Rating 94 **To** 2025 $30 ✪

Conte Estate Wines   ★★★★

270 Sand Road, McLaren Flat, SA 5171 **Region** McLaren Vale
T (08) 8383 0183 **www.conteestatewines.com.au Open** By appt
Winemaker Danial Conte **Est.** 2003 **Dozens** 5000 **Vyds** 77ha
The Conte family has a large vineyard, predominantly established since 1960 but with 2.5ha
of shiraz planted 100 years earlier. The vineyard includes shiraz, grenache, cabernet sauvignon,
sauvignon blanc and chardonnay. While continuing to sell a large proportion of the production,
winemaking has become a larger part of the business. Exports to the US, Canada and China.

🍷🍷🍷🍷🍷 **Hunt Road McLaren Vale Cabernet Sauvignon 2012** Night-harvested,
semi-crushed and open-fermented for 10 days, matured in new and used French
barrels for 20 months. This has a lot to enjoy, with a clear expression of place (the
touch of black chocolate) and variety, cassis and cedar neatly joined, the tannins
fine and graceful. Cork. 14.5% alc. **Rating** 94 **To** 2027 $40

🍷🍷🍷🍷🍸 **Planted Circa 1880 Over The Hill Shiraz 2012 Rating** 93 **To** 2032 $75

Cooks Lot   ★★★★☆

Ferment, 87 Hill Street, Orange, NSW 2800 **Region** Orange
T (02) 9550 3228 **www.cookslot.com.au Open** Tues–Sat 11–5
Winemaker Duncan Cook **Est.** 2002 **Dozens** 4000
Duncan Cook began making wines for his eponymous brand in 2002, while undertaking his
oenology degree at CSU. He completed his degree in '10, and now works with a number of
small growers from Orange wishing to be part of the production of wines with distinctive
regional character. In '12 Duncan transferred his business from Mudgee to Orange, current
releases focusing on grapes grown in Orange. Exports to China.

🍷🍷🍷🍷🍷 **Allotment No. 3 Premium Range Orange Chardonnay 2013** Whole
bunch-pressed, free-run juice was wild yeast barrel-fermented with partial solids,
extended lees contact, mlf, matured in French oak for 18 months. A powerful
and complex wine; if there is any question about it, it lies with the quality of the
oak – it doesn't enchant. This to one side, the wine has a lot going for its white
peach, fig and cashew flavours. Screwcap. 13.5% alc. **Rating** 94 **To** 2020 $35

Allotment No. 8 Premium Range Orange Shiraz 2013 Wild yeast-fermented in open pots with some whole bunch inclusion, free-run ferment and pressings separately aged in French oak for 18 months before blending. This is an impressive wine, making its case quietly but insistently, red and black fruits juicy one moment, trimmed with superfine tannins the next. Screwcap. 13.5% alc. Rating 94 To 2030 $35

♥♥♥♥♡ **Allotment No. 333 Riesling 2015** Rating 92 To 2025 $22 ✪
Allotment No. 666 Pinot Gris 2015 Rating 90 To 2016 $22
Allotment No. 1111 Pinot Noir 2014 Rating 90 To 2019 $22

Coola Road   ★★★★★

Private Mail Bag 14, Mount Gambier, SA 5291 **Region** Mount Gambier
T 0487 700 422 **www**.coolaroad.com **Open** Not
Winemaker John Innes, Peter Douglas, Sue Bell **Est.** 2013 **Dozens** 1000 **Vyds** 103.5ha
Thomas and Sally Ellis are the current generation of the Ellis family, which has owned the Coola grazing property on which the vineyard is now established for over 160 years. They began planting the vineyard in the late 1990s with pinot noir, and have since extended the range to include sauvignon blanc, chardonnay, riesling and pinot gris. As the largest vineyard owner in the region, they decided they should have some of the grapes vinified to bring further recognition to the area. If global warming should recommence and increase significantly, the very cool region will stand to gain.

♥♥♥♥♥ **Single Vineyard Riesling 2015** Classic no-frills vinification. A totally delicious and equally striking wine awash with lime juice fruit balanced and lengthened by minerally acidity. A great left-field surprise, shades of Mosel Valley. Screwcap. 11% alc. Rating 95 To 2025 $20 ✪
Single Vineyard Pinot Gris 2015 This has a defiant, challenging attitude to those who say pinot gris is a girl's drink. It is brimful of spicy pear on the bouquet, with a soaring palate of Granny Smith apple flesh and skin, citrus juice and citrus pith, pear a calling card, crunchy/minerally acidity setting the length and breadth of a special pinot gris. Screwcap. 12% alc. Rating 95 To 2020 $20 ✪

♥♥♥♥♡ **Single Vineyard Mount Gambier Pinot Noir 2014** Rating 90 To 2019 $28

Coolangatta Estate   ★★★★★

1335 Bolong Road, Shoalhaven Heads, NSW 2535 **Region** Shoalhaven Coast
T (02) 4448 7131 **www**.coolangattaestate.com.au **Open** 7 days 10–5
Winemaker Tyrrell's **Est.** 1988 **Dozens** 5000 **Vyds** 10.5ha
Coolangatta Estate is part of a 150ha resort with accommodation, restaurants, golf course, etc; some of the oldest buildings were convict-built in 1822. The standard of viticulture is exceptionally high (immaculate Scott Henry trellising), and the contract winemaking is wholly professional. Coolangatta has a habit of bobbing up with medals at Sydney and Canberra wine shows with gold medals for its mature Semillons. In its own backyard, Coolangatta won the trophy for Best Wine of Show at the South Coast Wine Show for 13 consecutive years.

♥♥♥♥♥ **Individual Vineyard Wollstonecraft Semillon 2015** Light straw-green; a bright, lively and zesty wine with clear-cut mineral and citrus acidity sustaining it from start to finish; classic lemon/lemongrass flavours come through with utmost clarity. Screwcap. 10.9% alc. Rating 95 To 2030 $25 ✪
Aged Release Individual Vineyard Wollstonecraft Semillon 2011 Just moving into the mature phase of its life, and doing so with grace; a supple and balanced palate gains in intensity on the finish and aftertaste, as archetypal lemon citrus acidity flexes its muscles. Screwcap. 11% alc. Rating 95 To 2026 $35 ✪

♥♥♥♥♡ **Estate Grown Semillon 2015** Rating 92 To 2025 $25 ✪
Aged Release Estate Grown Semillon 2010 Rating 91 To 2018 $28 CM
Estate Grown Tannat 2014 Rating 91 To 2021 $30 CM

Coombe Farm

673–675 Maroondah Highway, Coldstream, Vic 3770 **Region** Yarra Valley
T (03) 9739 0173 **www**.coombeyarravalley.com.au **Open** 7 days 10–5 (Wed–Sun Jun–Aug)
Winemaker Nicole Esdaile **Est.** 1999 **Dozens** 10 000 **Vyds** 60ha

Once the Australian home of world-famous opera singer Dame Nellie Melba, The Melba Estate is now also the home of Coombe Farm Wines. The renovated motor house and stable block of the estate now house the cellar door as well as a providore, gallery and restaurant which overlooks the gardens. Tours of the gardens are also available. The quality of the estate-grown wines has been consistently good. Exports to the UK.

ΨΨΨΨΨ **Tribute Series Evelyn Yarra Valley Chardonnay 2014** You are left to wonder where the oak went even when you already know the answer. The fruit is very much in the grapefruit camp, the usual ally of white peach when the fruit is ripe, present and correct. Notwithstanding the price and breeding, this is a wine that is first and foremost refreshing. Screwcap. 13% alc. **Rating** 95 **To** 2034 $50
Yarra Valley Cabernet Merlot 2014 For obvious reasons, cabernet dominates from start to finish, merlot simply adding a touch of softer, fleshy fruit. All up, it is a most attractive juicy cassis-filled wine, the oak subtle, the tannins markedly fine and soft. Screwcap. 13% alc. **Rating** 94 **To** 2034 $35

ΨΨΨΨΨ **Yarra Valley Pinot Noir 2015 Rating** 93 **To** 2025 $37
Yarra Valley Chardonnay 2014 Rating 92 **To** 2029 $37

Cooper Burns

1 Golden Way, Nuriootpa, SA 5353 (postal) **Region** Barossa Valley
T (08) 8562 2865 **www**.cooperburns.com.au **Open** Not
Winemaker Mark Cooper, Russell Burns **Est.** 2004 **Dozens** 500

Cooper Burns is the winemaking partnership of Mark Cooper and Russell Burns. It is a virtual winery focusing on small batch, handmade wine from the Eden Valley and the northern end of the Barossa Valley. Production has been increased to add a Riesling and Grenache to the existing single vineyard Shiraz. Exports to the US and Hong Kong.

ΨΨΨΨΨ **The Bloody Valentine Shiraz 2012** Dark red, hints of brick red on the rim. This release is laden with dark, brooding fruits and that classic Barossa leather and earth. There is immediate appeal on the sumptuous palate, which is rich, rounded and almost slippery at the close. Diam. 15.2% alc. **Rating** 95 **To** 2032 $75
Eden Valley Riesling 2014 Pale mid-straw; classically proportioned Eden Valley riesling with lime, lemon and green apple; the palate is concentrated, balanced, the finish crystal clear. Partial barrel fermentation adds a lick of phenolics that drive the length and finish. Screwcap. 13.2% alc. **Rating** 94 **To** 2025 $22 **○**

ΨΨΨΨΨ **Barossa Valley Shiraz 2013 Rating** 93 **To** 2023 $35

Cooter & Cooter

82 Almond Grove Road, Whites Valley, SA 5172 **Region** McLaren Vale
T 0438 766 178 **www**.cooter.com.au **Open** Not
Winemaker James Cooter **Est.** 2012 **Dozens** 1200 **Vyds** 23ha

James and Kimberley Cooter have taken the slow road to establishing their business; the cursive script on the wine labels has been that of various Cooter businesses in South Australia since 1847. James came from a family with a modern history of more than 20 years in the wine industry. Kimberley is also a hands-on winemaker, having spent her early years with father Walter Clappis, a veteran McLaren Vale winemaker. In 2005 they headed for the US, working in California's Sonoma Valley, and returned to continue winemaking with Walter at The Hedonist. Now, with 20 vintages between them, she and James have established their own vineyard on the southern slopes of Whites Valley, with views to the coast. It has 18ha of shiraz and 3ha of cabernet sauvignon planted in 1996, and 2ha of old-vine grenache planted in the '50s. They also buy Clare Valley grapes to make (what else) Riesling.

¶¶¶¶♀ **McLaren Vale Shiraz 2014** A sweet, inviting blend of raspberry, blackberry and milk chocolate flavour, an age-old combination but forever a good one. Hints of licorice only add to its bold, soft-textured appeal. Drink it young. Screwcap. 14% alc. **Rating** 91 **To** 2021 $22 CM ✪
Watervale Riesling 2015 At the elegant end of the spectrum with talc and floral notes running ahead of lime and bath salt characters. Personality in a lightish package. Screwcap. 12% alc. **Rating** 90 **To** 2020 $22 CM

Cope-Williams ★★★★★

221 Ochiltrees Road, Romsey, Vic 3434 **Region** Macedon Ranges
T (03) 5429 5595 **www**.copewilliams.com.au **Open** By appt
Winemaker David Cowburn **Est.** 1977 **Dozens** 3000 **Vyds** 6.5ha
One of Macedon's pioneers, specialising in sparkling wines that are full-flavoured but also producing excellent Chardonnay and Pinot Noir table wines in warmer vintages. A traditional 'English Green'-type cricket ground and Real Tennis complex are available for hire and are booked out most days from spring through until autumn. The facilities have been leased to an independent operator, which Gordon Cope-Williams says will allow him to concentrate on the estate vineyards (3ha each of chardonnay and pinot noir and 0.5ha of cabernet sauvignon). Exports to Switzerland and NZ.

¶¶¶¶¶ **Chardonnay 2014** Hand-picked, whole bunch-pressed, two-thirds wild-fermented with solids in French barriques (15% new), one-third fermented in stainless steel with cultured yeast, 22% mlf, matured for 10 months. It vibrates with energy, reaching every corner of the mouth with intense fruit, every step worked out with care and clarity. Radically different from the '14 Curly Flat Chardonnay tasted at the same time, one of the keys much lower mlf, leaving the acidity as a major component. Screwcap. 12.5% alc. **Rating** 95 **To** 2024 $25 ✪
Pinot Noir 2014 Hand-picked, 30% whole bunches, 70% berries, wild-fermented, matured for 14 months in French barriques (18% new). Very good colour; fragrant spiced cherry aromas, with more of the same on the palate; David Cowburn has considerable experience ex contract winemaking for others. The wine has great poise and finesse. Screwcap. 12.5% alc. **Rating** 95 **To** 2023 $30 ✪

¶¶¶¶♀ **Romsey Willow NV Rating** 90 **To** 2018 $20 ✪

Coppabella of Tumbarumba ★★★★★

424 Tumbarumba Road, Tumbarumba, NSW 2653 (postal) **Region** Tumbarumba
T (02) 6382 7997 **www**.coppabella.com.au **Open** Not
Winemaker Jason Brown **Est.** 2011 **Dozens** 4000 **Vyds** 71.9ha
Coppabella is owned by Jason and Alecia Brown, best known as owners of the highly successful Moppity Vineyards in Hilltops. They became aware of the quality of Tumbarumba chardonnay and pinot noir, in particular the quality of the grapes from the 71ha Coppabella vineyard, when purchasing grapes for the Moppity Vineyards business. This was the second vineyard established (in 1993) by the region's founder, Ian Cowell, but frost and other problems led him to lease the vineyard to Southcorp, an arrangement that continued until 2007. The reversion of the management of the vineyard coincided with several failed vintages, and this precipitated a decision by the owner to close the vineyard and remove the vines. In October '11, at the last moment, the Browns purchased the vineyard, and have since invested heavily in it, rehabilitating the vines and grafting a number of blocks to the earlier-ripening Dijon clones of pinot noir and chardonnay. Coppabella is run as an entirely separate venture from Moppity, and it is already on the road to emulating the success of Moppity.

¶¶¶¶¶ **Sirius Single Vineyard Chardonnay 2014** Whole bunch-pressed to French oak (30% new) for fermentation and 11 months maturation. The complex bouquet constantly oscillates between stone fruit, citrus and oak, the palate a mirror image of all that, and adding greater texture and structure; the taste memory lingers for a seeming eternity. Screwcap. 12.5% alc. **Rating** 96 **To** 2025 $20 ✪

The Crest Chardonnay 2014 Shares the intensity and linearity of its less expensive sibling, but has more white peach on the mid-palate before a fanfare of pink grapefruit trumpets on the finish and aftertaste. You know the winemaking dials have been turned up, but the fruit (and bracing acidity) remain in command. Screwcap. 12.5% alc. **Rating** 95 **To** 2024 $32 ✪

Sirius Single Vineyard Pinot Noir 2014 Good depth and hue; a well-balanced, generously proportioned pinot with clear-cut varietal expression; fruit, oak and tannins have been precisely calibrated, the length all one could ask for, the future assured. Screwcap. 13.5% alc. **Rating** 95 **To** 2024 $60

Single Vineyard Chardonnay 2014 70% fermented in stainless steel, 30% whole bunch-pressed to used French oak, matured for 10 months. The focus on the varietal fruit pays tribute to an exceptional vineyard, the intensity of the stone fruit flavours quite remarkable for a chardonnay at this price. Screwcap. 13% alc. **Rating** 94 **To** 2022 $20

🍷🍷🍷🍷 **Single Vineyard Pinot Rose 2015** **Rating** 89 **To** 2016 $20
Single Vineyard Premier Cuvee 2013 **Rating** 89 **To** 2018 $20

Corduroy ★★★★

15 Bridge Terrace, Victor Harbour, SA 5211 (postal) **Region** Adelaide Hills
T 0405 123 272 **www**.corduroywines.com.au **Open** Not
Winemaker Phillip LeMessurier **Est.** 2009 **Dozens** 320

Phillip and Eliza LeMessurier have moved from the Hunter Valley to the Adelaide Hills, but are continuing the model they originally created in the Hunter under the tutelage of Andrew Thomas at Thomas Wines. In the new environment, they are matching place and variety to good effect.

🍷🍷🍷🍷🍷 **Adelaide Hills Shiraz 2014** Meaty shiraz with a deep core of blackberried fruit and spices flying hither and thither. We're looking at clove and woody, smoky notes in general but this is also a good example of how well-managed reduction can be a positive, especially in savoury-styled shiraz. Nutty aftertaste completes an impressive picture. Screwcap. 13% alc. **Rating** 94 **To** 2028 $34 CM

🍷🍷🍷🍷🍷 **Clare Valley Riesling 2015** **Rating** 92 **To** 2020 $22 CM ✪
Adelaide Hills Chardonnay 2015 **Rating** 92 **To** 2019 $28 CM
Piccadilly Pinot Noir 2015 **Rating** 92 **To** 2020 $28 CM

Coriole ★★★★★

Chaffeys Road, McLaren Vale, SA 5171 **Region** McLaren Vale
T (08) 8323 8305 **www**.coriole.com **Open** Mon–Fri 10–5, w'ends & public hols 11–5
Winemaker Alex Sherrah **Est.** 1967 **Dozens** 32 000 **Vyds** 48.5ha

While Coriole was not established until 1967, the cellar door and gardens date back to 1860, when the original farm houses that now constitute the cellar door were built. The oldest shiraz forming part of the estate plantings dates back to 1917, and since '85, Coriole has been an Australian pioneer of sangiovese and – more recently – the Italian white variety fiano. Shiraz has 65% of the plantings, and it is for this variety that Coriole is best known. Exports to all major markets.

🍷🍷🍷🍷🍷 **Lloyd Reserve McLaren Vale Shiraz 2013** 97yo vines, hand-picked, destemmed, open-fermented with cultured yeast, 12 days on skins, matured in French oak (20–30% new) for 20 months. What a treasure trove the McLaren Vale has, with vines/grapes/wines coming from ancient vines that signal all is well. The strength of the message is so powerful and clear you wonder why the Scarce Earth program occupies such effort and time, unfairly taking attention away from the glory of wines such as this. Screwcap. 14.5% alc. **Rating** 97 **To** 2049 $90 ✪

ŶŶŶŶŶ Scarce Earth Galaxidia Single Vineyard McLaren Vale Shiraz 2014 17yo
vines, machine-harvested, destemmed, open-fermented with cultured yeast, 12 days
on skins, oak-matured for 18 months. Excellent colour; a potent, full-bodied
celebration of variety and place, with inky black fruits, dark chocolate, licorice and
firm tannins. Screwcap. 14.5% alc. **Rating** 95 **To** 2039 $55
The Soloist Single Vineyard McLaren Vale Shiraz 2013 40yo vines, open-
fermented with cultured yeast, 10 days on skins, matured in French and American
oak for 20 months. The '13 vintage is powering along, refusing to cede any
territory to or recognition of the '12 and '14 vintages. This is a beautiful, medium
to full-bodied McLaren Vale shiraz, all the components of site, variety, fruit, oak
and tannins perfectly articulated. Screwcap. 14.7% alc. **Rating** 95 **To** 2043 $45
Estate Grown McLaren Vale Cabernet Sauvignon 2013 Matured for
18 months in French oak. Very good colour; a convincing demonstration of
the synergy between variety and region; the bouquet promises – and delivers –
cassis fruit, cedary oak, black olive and dried herb. Best of all is its airy elegance.
Screwcap. 14.5% alc. **Rating** 94 **To** 2028 $30 ●
McLaren Vale Sangiovese 2014 Planted 30 years ago by the pioneer of the
variety in this country, Mark Lloyd. I vividly remember struggling with it here in
Australia, but I've mellowed, and so have the vines (and Coriole). Good colour;
this has very good savoury dried and morello cherry fruits, the tannins firm but
correct. Every time I go back to this wine I like it more. Bring on the wild boar.
Screwcap. 14.5% alc. **Rating** 94 **To** 2029 $25 ●

ŶŶŶŶŶ Scarce Earth Old House Shiraz 2014 Rating 93 **To** 2034 $55
McLaren Vale Dancing Fig 2014 Rating 93 **To** 2029 $25 ●
McLaren Vale Picpoul 2015 Rating 91 **To** 2018 $25
Redstone McLaren Vale Shiraz 2014 Rating 90 **To** 2027 $20 ●

Costanzo & Sons ★★★★

602 Tames Road, Strathbogie, Vic 3666 **Region** Strathbogie Ranges
T 0447 740 055 **www.**costanzo.com.au **Open** By appt
Winemaker Ray Nadeson (Contract) **Est.** 2011 **Dozens** 500 **Vyds** 6ha
This is the venture of Joe Costanzo and Cindy Heath, Joe having grapegrowing in his DNA.
He was raised among his parents' 20ha vineyard in NSW on the Murray River, the family
business selling grapes to Brown Brothers, Seppelt, Bullers and Miranda Wines. By the age
of 17 he had decided to follow in their footsteps, working full-time in vineyards, and studied
viticulture for five years. He and Cindy searched for the perfect vineyard, and in 2011 finally
acquired one that had been planted between 1993 and '94 to 1.5ha each of sauvignon blanc
and chardonnay, and 3ha of pinot noir.

ŶŶŶŶŶ Single Vineyard Reserve Strathbogie Ranges Sauvignon Blanc 2014
100% barrel-fermented and matured in French barriques (30% new) for
10 months, 120 dozen made. A light year away from Marlborough, with positively
succulent fruit wrapped within swaddling clothes of oak, nonchalantly balanced by
the luscious fruit and crisp acidity. Screwcap. 13% alc. **Rating** 92 **To** 2016 $35

ŶŶŶŶ Singers La. Sauvignon Blanc 2014 Rating 89 **To** 2016 $17 ●
Methode Traditionelle Blanc de Noir 2013 Rating 89 **To** 2016 $32

Cowaramup Wines ★★★★☆

19 Tassel Road, Cowaramup, WA 6284 **Region** Margaret River
T (08) 9755 5195 **www.**cowaramupwines.com.au **Open** By appt
Winemaker Naturaliste Vintners (Bruce Dukes) **Est.** 1995 **Dozens** 5000 **Vyds** 17ha
Russell and Marilyn Reynolds run a biodynamic vineyard with the aid of sons Cameron
(viticulturist) and Anthony (assistant winemaker). Plantings began in 1996 and include merlot,
cabernet sauvignon, shiraz, semillon, chardonnay and sauvignon blanc. Notwithstanding low
yields and the discipline that biodynamic grapegrowing entails, wine prices are modest. Wines
are released under the Reserve, Clown Fish and New School labels.

♀♀♀♀♀ Reserve Limited Edition Semillon Sauvignon Blanc 2014 A 50/50% blend, machine-harvested at night, crushed and pressed, barrel-fermented with cultured yeast in French oak (33% new), matured in that oak for 10 months. This is a complex, layered wine with admirable balance between fruit, acidity and oak on the long, gently spicy, gently citrussy/grassy palate, tropical fruit nuances a backdrop. Screwcap. 12.5% alc. **Rating** 95 **To** 2022 $25 **○**

Clown Fish Sauvignon Blanc Semillon 2015 65/35%, machine-harvested at night, crushed and destemmed, cool-fermented with cultured yeast, 85% in stainless steel, 15% in new French oak, 4 months lees contact. Vibrantly fresh and tangy, green pea, cut grass, lemon juice and crunchy acidity. A Ferrari in a bottle. Screwcap. 13% alc. **Rating** 94 **To** 2018 $20 **○**

♀♀♀♀♀ Limited Edition Ellensbrook Cabernet 2014 Rating 91 **To** 2031 $30
Clown Fish Margaret River Chardonnay 2015 Rating 90 **To** 2022 $20 **○**

Crabtree Watervale Wines   ★★★★★

North Terrace, Watervale SA 5452 **Region** Clare Valley
T (08) 8843 0069 **www.**crabtreewines.com.au **Open** 7 days 10.30–4.30
Winemaker Kerri Thompson **Est.** 1979 **Dozens** 6000 **Vyds** 13.2ha
Crabtree is situated in the heart of the historic and iconic Watervale district, the tasting room and courtyard (set in the produce cellar of the original 1850s homestead) looking out over the estate vineyard. The winery was founded in 1984 by Robert Crabtree, who built a considerable reputation for medal-winning Riesling, Shiraz and Cabernet Sauvignon. In 2007 it was purchased by an independent group of wine enthusiasts, the winery firmly continuing in the established tradition of estate-grown premium wines (Robert remains a shareholder).

♀♀♀♀♀ Shiraz 2014 40yo vines, hand-picked and sorted, crushed, destemmed without rollers (for whole berries), open-fermented, 5 days cold soak, cultured yeast, 14 days on skin, matured in French oak (20% new) for 18 months. The first reaction is the texture ex the whole berry/near whole berry fermentation; then you go back to the very good colour and aromas, completing the circle with the excellent spicy/savoury embroidery on the pot pourri of black fruit flavours. Well above typical Clare Valley shiraz. Screwcap. 14% alc. **Rating** 95 **To** 2034 $30 **○**

Hilltop Vineyard Shiraz 2013 40yo vines, hand-picked and sorted, crushed, destemmed without rollers for whole berries), open-fermented, 5 days cold soak, cultured yeast, 14 days on skin, matured in French oak (20% new). Has the same structure and flavour profile as its '14 sibling, two peas from the same pod. It is fragrant, and all the fruit, oak and tannin components have bonded synergistically together. Exceptional bargain. Screwcap. 13.5% alc. **Rating** 94 **To** 2028 $22 **○**

♀♀♀♀♀ Cabernet Sauvignon 2014 Rating 93 **To** 2034 $30
Hilltop Vineyard Riesling 2015 Rating 90 **To** 2020 $22
Tempranillo 2014 Rating 90 **To** 2024 $26

cradle of hills   ★★★★☆

76 Rogers Road, Sellicks Hill, SA 5174 **Region** McLaren Vale
T (08) 8557 4023 **www.**cradle-of-hills.com.au **Open** By appt
Winemaker Paul Smith **Est.** 2009 **Dozens** 1000 **Vyds** 6.88ha
Paul Smith's introduction to wine was an unlikely one: the Royal Australian Navy, and in particular the wardroom cellar at the tender age of 19. A career change took Paul to the world of high-performance sports, and he met his horticulturist wife Tracy. From 2005 they travelled the world with their two children, spending a couple of years in Europe, working in and learning about the great wine regions, and how fine wine is made. Paul secured a winemaking diploma, and they now have almost 7ha of cabernet sauvignon and shiraz (roughly 50% each). They supplement the shiraz with grenache and mourvedre to make their Route de Bonheur (Road to Happiness) grenache mourvedre shiraz blend. Exports to Singapore.

ŶŶŶŶŶ **Row 23 McLaren Vale Shiraz 2014** 100 dozen. Splendid wine. Oak melted into fruit, spice splashed upon earth. Sparks, fires, a dry bed; it's all here, in the form of gun smoke and toast and a spice-shot stream of tannin. If it sounds overly intellectual it's not; there's plump fruit here, but it comes with all the trimmings. Screwcap. 14.5% alc. **Rating** 95 **To** 2030 $45 CM

ŶŶŶŶŶ **Wild Child Adelaide Hills Chardonnay 2015 Rating** 92 **To** 2020 $25 CM ✪
Old Rogues Shiraz Grenache 2014 Rating 91 **To** 2021 $22 CM ✪
Route du Bonheur McLaren Vale GMS 2013 Rating 91 **To** 2021 $27 CM

Craiglee ★★★★★

Sunbury Road, Sunbury, Vic 3429 **Region** Sunbury
T (03) 9744 4489 **www**.craiglee.com.au **Open** Sun & public hols 10–5
Winemaker Patrick Carmody **Est.** 1976 **Dozens** 2500 **Vyds** 9.5ha
A winery with a proud 19th-century record, Craiglee recommenced winemaking in 1976 after a prolonged hiatus. Produces one of the finest cool climate Shirazs in Australia, redolent of cherry, licorice and spice in the better (warmer) vintages, lighter-bodied in the cooler ones. Mature vines and improved viticulture have made the wines more consistent (except 2011) over the past 10 years or so. Exports to the UK, the US, Italy, Hong Kong and China. Wines were received too late for the book, but tasting notes can be found on www.winecompanion.com.au.

Craigow ★★★★★

528 Richmond Road, Cambridge, Tas 7170 **Region** Southern Tasmania
T (03) 6248 5379 **www**.craigow.com.au **Open** 7 days Xmas to Easter (except public hols)
Winemaker Frogmore Creek (Alain Rousseau) **Est.** 1989 **Dozens** 800 **Vyds** 8.75ha
Hobart surgeon Barry Edwards and wife Cathy have moved from being grapegrowers with only one wine to a portfolio of impressive wines, with long-lived Riesling of particular quality, closely attended by Pinot Noir, while continuing to sell most of their grapes.

ŶŶŶŶŶ **Pinot Noir 2015** Hand-picked, destemmed, wild fermented in open 1-tonne fermenter, pressed to French oak (20% new) for 8 months maturation. Tasmania meets Central Otago with the exceptional depth of crimson-purple colour and the power and concentration of black cherry, spices and liqueured plum flavours. Just when you think there is too much of a good thing, dusty/savoury tannins put the ship of state pointing in the right direction for a long voyage. Screwcap. 14% alc. **Rating** 95 **To** 2030 $45
Dessert Riesling 2015 Craigow and Pressing Matters provide the most striking Tasmanian freeze-concentrated rieslings – here intense Meyer lemon and lime juice fill the mouth with ricocheting flavours, acidity driving the finish. Screwcap. 8.6% alc. **Rating** 95 **To** 2025 $30 ✪
Sauvignon Blanc 2015 The very good vintage has helped, for this has more richness to the fruit on the bouquet and palate, the full spectrum of tropical fruits, a drizzle of blood orange juice, and a chord of Tasmanian acidity. Screwcap. 13% alc. **Rating** 94 **To** 2017 $30 ✪
Chardonnay 2015 Barrel-fermented in French oak (20% new). Complex barrel-ferment aromas start proceedings before the white peach, nectarine and grilled cashew flavours of the palate take control, leading into the final stanza of citrussy/ pink grapefruit acidity. Screwcap. 13% alc. **Rating** 94 **To** 2025 $35

ŶŶŶŶŶ **Rose 2015 Rating** 93 **To** 2017 $29
Riesling 2015 Rating 91 **To** 2025 $32

Crawford River Wines ★★★★★

741 Hotspur Upper Road, Condah, Vic 3303 **Region** Henty
T (03) 5578 2267 **www**.crawfordriverwines.com **Open** By appt
Winemaker John and Belinda Thomson **Est.** 1975 **Dozens** 3000 **Vyds** 10.5ha

Time flies, and it seems incredible that Crawford River celebrated its 40th birthday in 2015. Once a tiny outpost in a little-known wine region, Crawford River is a foremost producer of Riesling (and other excellent wines) thanks to the unremitting attention to detail and skill of its founder and winemaker, John Thomson (and moral support from wife Catherine). His talented elder daughter Belinda has returned part-time after completing her winemaking degree and working along the way in Marlborough (NZ), Bordeaux, Ribera del Duero (Spain), Bolgheri and Tuscany, and the Nahe (Germany), with Crawford River filling in the gaps. She continues working in Spain, effectively doing two vintages each year. Younger daughter Fiona is in charge of sales and marketing. Exports to the UK.

Riesling 2015 It's easy to marvel. The concentration here is stunning. It's a force of nature, literally. Flavour crashes in from the outset and then proceeds on a dominating path all the way through to the long, rock-strewn, chalk-splashed finish. Screwcap. 13.5% alc. **Rating** 97 **To** 2034 $45 CM ✪

Museum Release Riesling 2008 Has developed a great deal of complexity over time, with orange marmalade and passionfruit-like notes bouncing off the core of lime. Overall intensity is excellent, as is length. It has now entered its peak, and drinks like an exotic treat. Screwcap. 14% alc. **Rating** 95 **To** 2024 $70 CM
Nektar 2010 375ml. Serious intensity. Orange marmalade and lemon butter flavours imprint as much onto your memory as onto your palate. A touch of magic. Screwcap. 12% alc. **Rating** 95 **To** 2021 $55 CM
Young Vines Riesling 2015 Body of flavour but then a serious kick to the finish. Apple, lemon and lime with citrus rind and spice on that finish. Joyous riesling. Screwcap. 13.5% alc. **Rating** 94 **To** 2028 $32 CM
Rose 2015 Powerful wine with flavours and accents flying this way and that. Ample fruit but a twiggy, dusty savouriness rows hard for front position. Shows many a rose how it's done. Screwcap. 13.5% alc. **Rating** 94 **To** 2017 $28 CM ✪

Cabernet Merlot 2012 Rating 91 **To** 2026 $34 CM

Credaro Family Estate   ★★★★★

2175 Caves Road, Yallingup, WA 6282 **Region** Margaret River
T (08) 9756 6520 **www.**credarowines.com.au **Open** 7 days 10–5
Winemaker Dave Johnson **Est.** 1993 **Dozens** 10 000 **Vyds** 150ha
The Credaro family first settled in Margaret River in 1922, migrating from Northern Italy. Initially a few small plots of vines were planted to provide the family with wine in the European tradition. However, things began to change significantly in the '80s and '90s, and changes have continued through to 2015. The most recent has been the acquisition of a 40ha property, with 18ha of vineyard, in Wilyabrup (now called the Summus Vineyard) and the expansion of winery capacity to 1200 tonnes with 300 000 litres of additional tank space. Credaro now has seven separate vineyards (150ha in production), spread throughout the Margaret River: Credaro either owns or leases each property and grows/manages the vines with its own viticulture team. Exports to Thailand, Singapore and China.

1000 Crowns Chardonnay 2014 Hand-picked, whole bunch-pressed, free-run juice to French oak (30% new) for wild fermentation, SO₂ added post-fermentation to prevent mlf, but no acid or other additions, lees-stirred and matured for 9 months, four gold medals. This is natural wine at its zenith if you accept SO_2 can be used. It is beautifully focused and poised, with pink grapefruit the lead player on the palate, white-fleshed stone fruits following behind in close formation; the oak is positive, but knows its place. Screwcap. 13% alc. **Rating** 96 **To** 2022 $65 ✪
Kinship Chardonnay 2014 Hand-picked, whole bunch-pressed, free-run juice to French oak (30% new) for wild fermentation, SO₂ as for 1000 Crowns, lees-stirred. The difference between this and 1000 Crowns is in the fruit/barrel selection, but it's far from a gulf between the two wines. This, too, has elegance emblazoned on its breast pocket, the palate long and harmonious. Screwcap. 13% alc. **Rating** 95 **To** 2022 $32 ✪

Kinship Shiraz 2014 From the estate Carbunup Vineyard, whole-berry fermentation, part pressed to barrel to finish fermentation, part fermented dry in tank, matured for 14 months in French barriques (20% new). Very, very different from its Five Tails sibling, spice and powdery oak tannins present from the outset, the red and black fruits also having their tannins in play. Five Tails is raring to go, but this asks to be given more time, its quality and balance not in doubt. Screwcap. 14% alc. **Rating** 95 **To** 2034 $32 ✪

Kinship Cabernet Sauvignon 2014 From the Altus and Summus Vineyards, each with subtly different climates, one parcel destemmed to tank, inoculated with cultured yeast, on skins for 16 days and fermented to dryness, the second batch with 30 days on skins, both parcels matured for 18 months in French oak (25% new). A classically structured cabernet with tannins providing a fine gilt frame for the flavours of blackcurrant and bay leaf that fill the mid-palate, length a given. Screwcap. 14.5% alc. **Rating** 95 **To** 2034 $32 ✪

Five Tales Shiraz 2014 From the Summus, Cellar Door and Carbunup River Vineyards, whole-berry fermentation in with yeast ex the Côtes du Rhône, pumped over using the gentle Turbopigeur, 14 days on skins, matured for 10 months in French barriques (15% new). Vivid, full crimson-purple; a luscious combination of red, blue and purple fruits, perfectly supported by tannins and oak. Outstanding value. Screwcap. 14.5% alc. **Rating** 94 **To** 2029 $21 ✪

Kinship Cabernet Merlot 2014 Cabernet from the Carbunup River Vineyard, merlot from the Cellar Door Vineyard (Yallingup), crushed and destemmed with cultured (Bordeaux) yeast, pumped over with a Turbopigeur for 20 days, racked to French barriques (20% new) for mlf, matured for 15 months. A complex, medium to full-bodied wine with a chorus line of red and black fruits, rippling cedary oak linked with ripe tannins and a long finish. Its best is yet to come. Screwcap. 14.5% alc. **Rating** 94 **To** 2034 $32

Five Tales Margaret River 2014 Crushed and destemmed with cultured yeast, pumped over with a Turbopigeur for 14 days, matured in French barriques (10% new) for 10 months. Very good hue; oh to be able to make a cabernet as good as this for a price as low as this. It is literally flooded with cassis, the mouthfeel supple and feline, the length and aftertaste spot on. Screwcap. 14% alc. **Rating** 94 **To** 2029 $21 ✪

🍷🍷🍷🍷 **Kinship Sauvignon Blanc 2015** Rating 92 To 2017 $25 ✪
Kinship Semillon 2015 Rating 92 To 2019 $25 ✪
Five Tales Cabernet Merlot 2014 Rating 92 To 2029 $21 ✪
Five Tales Sauvignon Blanc Semillon 2015 Rating 90 To 2018 $21 ✪
Five Tales Merlot 2014 Rating 90 To 2024 $21 ✪

CRFT Wines ★★★★★

PO Box 197, Aldgate, SA 5154 **Region** Adelaide Hills
T 0413 475 485 **www**.crftwines.com.au **Open** Not
Winemaker Candice Helbig, Frewin Ries **Est.** 2012 **Dozens** 1200

Life and business partners NZ-born Frewin Ries and Barossa-born Candice Helbig crammed multiple wine lives into a relatively short period before giving up secure jobs and establishing CRFT in time for their inaugural 2013 vintage. Frewin started with four years at Cloudy Bay before heading to St Emilion, then to the iconic pinot noir maker in Sonoma, Williams Selyem, then four years with Kingston Estate, and subsequent years as a contract winemaker. Candice is a sixth-generation Barossan, trained as a laboratory technician. She spent eight years with Hardys, gaining her degree in oenology and viticulture from CSU, then to Boar's Rock and Mollydooker in '11, and now to CRFT. They say growth will come from additional single vineyards rather than by increasing the size of the make of any particular wine. They share the Lenswood Winery (the original Nepenthe Winery) with other kindred spirits. A shed-cum-cellar door is in the planning stage, as is the possibility of planting some gruner veltliner, a variety they find as fascinating as I find this duo. Exports to the UK and Singapore.

🍷🍷🍷🍷🍷 **Fechner Vineyard Moculta Eden Valley Shiraz 2014** Standard CRFT shiraz fermentation, except for the much later harvest date of 1 Mar and modest alcohol. Supple, yet complex; intense, yet rounded; savoury, yet deeply fruited. This has all the attributes of fine wine at its zenith. Yes, it's a great vineyard, and from the cooler Eden Valley, but Candice Helbig has coaxed every ounce of flavour from this medium-bodied wine, giving a sarcastic salute to those who think shiraz's life starts with 14.5% alcohol. Screwcap. 13.5% alc. **Rating** 97 **To** 2044 $65 ○

🍷🍷🍷🍷🍷 **Cemetery Vineyard Ebenezer Barossa Valley Shiraz 2014** Identical vinification to the Little Hill Vineyard, but picked 2 weeks later (7 Mar v 21 Feb), pressed to barrel between 2° and 4° baume, and taking around 3 weeks to complete mlf in barrel after racking off gross lees. The colour is excellent, the bouquet complexed by some oak nuances (even though the oak composition is much the same for all three Cemetery Shirazs), the medium-bodied palate with drive, depth and complexity. Screwcap. 14% alc. **Rating** 95 **To** 2034 $49

K1 Vineyard Kuitpo Gewurztraminer 2015 Cool, slow stainless steel fermentation followed by 3 months on lees for mouthfeel, bottled Jun, 95 dozen made. Magical winemaking has produced a vibrant, crisp wine that retains varietal expression on the long palate and lingering finish. Magical because there was nothing special in the fermentation process or subsequent maturation to achieve this result. Screwcap. 12% alc. **Rating** 94 **To** 2025 $27 ○

K1 Vineyard Kuitpo Adelaide Hills Gruner Veltliner 2015 Hand-picked, whole bunch-pressed, and cool, slow-fermented followed by lees contact, 129 dozen made. There is more white pepper on the bouquet than any of the other gruner veltliners I have tasted from this vineyard, and a deliciously fresh and crisp palate. For tonight. Screwcap. 12.5% alc. **Rating** 94 **To** 2016 $29 ○

Budenberg Vineyard Piccadilly Valley Adelaide Hills Pinot Noir 2014 Hand-picked 4 Apr and destemmed to open-top fermenter with 20% whole bunches, 5 days cold soak, pressed directly to French oak (30% new) for 10 months maturation, lees stirring first 2 months, bottled Feb '15, 92 dozen made. Good colour; blood plum fruit sits within a latticework of fine, persistent tannins. Needs more time than its siblings. Screwcap. 13.5% alc. **Rating** 94 **To** 2020 $39

Chapel Valley Vineyard Piccadilly Valley Adelaide Hills Pinot Noir 2014 Made in identical fashion to the Budenberg Vineyard Pinot Noir and with similar mix of clones 114 and 115, picked 3 Apr, except for one row of MV6 with the Budenberg wine, 94 dozen made. Fragrant spicy aromas are coupled with a touch of mint, the latter coming through on the palate as well. Paradoxically, this has the best mouthfeel and flavour of all three Pinots, albeit it is the lightest in body. Screwcap. 13.5% alc. **Rating** 94 **To** 2020 $39

Little Hill Vineyard Seppeltsfield Barossa Valley Shiraz 2014 Hand-picked, destemmed to an open fermenter, cultured yeast, thence directly to oak (60% French, 40% American, 20% new) for the last stages of primary ferment and mlf, 10 months in all. Given the similarity of vinification of the three CRFT '14 Shirazs, the price presumably reflects the input cost of the grapes. This has the lightest body of the trio, but has superb colour and is no namby pamby wine, elegance and length to the suite of black fruit flavours the name of the game. Screwcap. 14% alc. **Rating** 94 **To** 2029 $39

🍷🍷🍷🍷🍷 **Arranmore Vineyard Piccadilly Valley Adelaide Hills Pinot Noir 2014** **Rating** 93 **To** 2021 $39

Longview Vineyard Macclesfield Adelaide Hills Gruner Veltliner 2015 **Rating** 91 **To** 2017 $29

 **Cricket Flat**

Box 23, Penola, SA 5277 **Region** Coonawarra
T 0419 730 047 **www.cricketflat.com.au** **Open** Not
Winemaker Phil Lehmann **Est.** 1996 **Dozens** 300 **Vyds** 34ha

There is no cricket ground, nor (so far as I know) do owners Brett and Julianne Williams play cricket. But to begin at the beginning, the Williams family has lived and worked in Coonawarra for over three generations. Initially they established a mixed farming enterprise in the early 1970s, and it took another 20 years before they decided to plant the first vines on their 53ha property – 13ha of the Reynella Selection clone of cabernet sauvignon. Over the next 8 years they planted another 29ha of cabernet sauvignon and chardonnay. Between '99 and 2012 the grapes were sold to major players in the region, but in '13 Brett and Julianne decided to collaborate with their friend and well-known winemaker Phil Lehmann. In the early summer of '12 they noticed an abundance of crickets through the vineyard, which normally indicate a good growing season, and are a sign of good luck in many cultures, thus the name.

Crittenden Estate ★★★★★

25 Harrisons Road, Dromana, Vic 3936 **Region** Mornington Peninsula
T (03) 5981 8322 **www**.crittendenwines.com.au **Open** 7 days 10.30–4.30
Winemaker Rollo Crittenden **Est.** 1984 **Dozens** 8000 **Vyds** 4.8ha
Garry Crittenden was one of the pioneers on the Mornington Peninsula, establishing the family vineyard over 30 years ago, and introducing a number of avant garde pruning and canopy management techniques. In the manner of things, much has changed – and continues to change – in cool climate vineyard management. While pinot noir and chardonnay remain the principal focus, Garry's constant desire to push envelopes saw the establishment of a range of Italian varietals (Pinocchio) and Iberian Peninsula varieties (Los Hermanos). In 2015 winemaking returned to the family vineyard on the Mornington Peninsula in a newly built facility, with son Rollo Crittenden very much in charge. Exports to the UK and the US.

ΨΨΨΨΨ **The Zumma Pinot Noir 2014** Hand-picked clones MV6 and D5V12 from the home vineyard, 80% destemmed, 20% whole bunches, 5 days cold soak and wild-fermented in a large French oak fermenter, matured in French barriques (40% new) for 16 months. Good colour; clearly the most complex of the Crittenden '14 Pinots; the plum and black cherry fruit has not yielded to the French oak inputs, simply using them to gain momentum through to the long finish. Zumma indeed. Screwcap. 13.2% alc. **Rating** 95 **To** 2025 $57
Kangerong Pinot Noir 2014 Seven clones from the home vineyard planted in '82, hand-picked, chilled to 8°C, destemmed, 5 days cold soak, wild-fermented, hand-plunged, matured in French oak (20% new) for 15 months. Good hue; an expressive wild berry bouquet, a supple and smooth palate, everything in balance and in its due place. Needs a year or two to show its best. Screwcap. 13.2% alc. **Rating** 94 **To** 2023 $40

ΨΨΨΨΨ **Peninsula Pinot Noir 2014** **Rating** 93 **To** 2022 $35
The Zumma Chardonnay 2014 **Rating** 92 **To** 2023 $57
Peninsula Sauvignon Blanc Fume 2014 **Rating** 90 **To** 2021 $30
Kangerong Chardonnay 2014 **Rating** 90 **To** 2023 $40

Cullen Wines ★★★★★

4323 Caves Road, Wilyabrup, WA 6280 **Region** Margaret River
T (08) 9755 5277 **www**.cullenwines.com.au **Open** 7 days 10–4.30
Winemaker Vanya Cullen, Trevor Kent **Est.** 1971 **Dozens** 20 000 **Vyds** 49ha
One of the pioneers of Margaret River, and has always produced long-lived wines of highly individual style from the mature estate vineyards. The vineyard has progressed beyond organic to biodynamic certification and, subsequently, has become the first vineyard and winery in Australia to be certified carbon neutral. This requires the calculation of all of the carbon used and carbon dioxide emitted in the winery; the carbon is then offset by the planting of new trees. Winemaking is in the hands of Vanya Cullen, daughter of the founders; she is possessed of an extraordinarily good palate. It is impossible to single out any particular wine from the top echelon; all are superb. Exports to all major markets.

ŢŢŢŢŢ **Vanya Cabernet Sauvignon 2012** An extraordinary wine from the oldest ('71) estate plantings, matured for 19 months in French oak (47% new). Deeply coloured and highly fragrant, the palate takes you on a mesmerising ride with a mid-palate peak of pure, unalloyed cassis fruit, then a swish of integrated savoury tannins before rising again on the dark fruit line of the finish, thanks in part to 3% petit verdot. 388 dozen made. Screwcap. 13.5% alc. **Rating** 99 **To** 2057 $350
Diana Madeline 2014 89% cabernet sauvignon, 4% petit verdot, 3% merlot and 2% each of malbec and cabernet franc, blended after fermentation. Hand-picked and sorted, destemmed (66% whole berries), wild-fermented in stainless steel, average 23 days on skins, matured in French oak (69% new) for 18 months. Right in the slot of the style established (with some polishing and refining) over the years. The complexity of the texture and structure is second to none, led by the born-to-rule cabernet, the other varieties obviously of minor importance, but important nonetheless. The might of the tannins is the key to this great wine. Screwcap. 13.5% alc. **Rating** 98 **To** 2044 $125 ○

ŢŢŢŢŢ **Kevin John 2014** Hand-picked, whole bunch-pressed, wild-fermented in new French oak, matured for 8 months. The seemingly simple vinification has not resulted in a simple wine. There are multiple layers of fruit and oak (the percentage of new oak up to 100% from 30% in '13) ranging through white peach, nectarine, fig and then entering the world of wild fermentation in new oak path. The result is a complete wine of very high quality. Screwcap. 13.5% alc. **Rating** 96 **To** 2029 $105
Mangan Vineyard Margaret River Merlot Malbec Petit Verdot 2015 An 84/12/4% blend, hand-picked and sorted, destemmed (66% whole berries), wild-fermented, 21 days on skins, matured in French oak (42% new) for 7 months. Deep crimson-purple; this is merlot in all but name (1% more would do the trick), and by the length of the straight, the best in Australia, sold at a fraction of its intrinsic value. Gloriously supple blackcurrant fruit flows like a river of gold through the palate in the manner of the great vineyards of Bordeaux on the Right Bank. Screwcap. 14% alc. **Rating** 96 **To** 2040 $35 ○
Mangan Vineyard Margaret River Semillon Sauvignon Blanc 2015 58% semillon, 40% sauvignon blanc, 2% verdelho, wild-fermented, 22% of the blend aged in oak for 4 months. A three-dimensional fact sheet is needed to cover all the facets of this wine, but it all comes down to the way it has absorbed the oak, and having done so, how the synergy of the two main varieties totally blinds any attempt to work out exactly what either is contributing at any point. Harmony, balance and length is the take home lesson. Screwcap. 13% alc. **Rating** 95 **To** 2030 $29 ○
Mangan East Block 2014 72% petit verdot, 28% malbec blended after fermentation, hand-picked and sorted, destemmed (66% whole berries), wild-fermented in stainless steel, matured for 17 months in new French oak. This is naked, unbridled power resting on a Game of Tannins, which in turn trembles on the brink without going over. I will be interested in seeing how it develops – and when. Screwcap. 14% alc. **Rating** 94 **To** 2044 $55

Cultivar Wines   ★★★★

60 Spiller Road, Lethbridge, Vic 3222 **Region** Heathcote
T 0409 337 151 **www.**cultivar.com.au **Open** Not
Winemaker David Crawford **Est.** 2012 **Dozens** 750
Cultivar is the venture of industry veteran David Crawford and wife Meaghan, David with 25 years' experience across the entire Australian wine industry. The term 'cultivar' is technically a more appropriate word than 'variety' (according to Jancis Robinson), but is seldom used outside South Africa. For David, clones are in fact all-important, and, after a protracted search, he found a vineyard first planted in 1991 to clone PT23, with subsequent plantings of the well-known SA1654 clone and a mutated version of PT23, Mt Ida. David has leased the former Tarcoola Estate winery in conjunction with Bellbrae Estate, and this is where the Cultivar wines are made.

��♦♦♦ **Heathcote Shiraz 2014** It could be viewed as a fruit-bomb style but it's just so well done. It's a mouthful of sweet, ripe, dark berries, complemented by saltbush and just the right amount of sawdusty oak. Tannin is firm but tucked neatly into the fruit. Lovers of a hearty red will lap this up. Screwcap. 14.5% alc. **Rating** 94 **To** 2026 $32 CM

Cumulus Wines ★★★★

PO Box 41, Cudal, NSW 2864 **Region** Orange
T (02) 6390 7900 www.cumuluswines.com.au **Open** During Orange Food Week (Apr) and Wine Week (Oct)
Winemaker Debbie Lauritz, Matt Atallah **Est.** 2004 **Dozens** NFP **Vyds** 508ha
Cumulus Wines is majority owned by the Berardo Group of Portugal (which has numerous wine investments in Portugal, Canada and Madeira). Over 500ha of mature vineyards focus on shiraz, cabernet sauvignon, chardonnay and merlot. The wines are released under three brands: Rolling, from the Central Ranges Zone; Climbing, solely from Orange fruit; and Cumulus, super-premium from the best of the estate vineyard blocks. One of an increasing number of wineries to use lightweight bottles. The annual crush varies between 3000 and 6000 tonnes, and if all of the harvest were vinified it would result in between 210 000 and 420 000 dozens. In 2015 Cumulus merged with Beelgara (which also owns the Moss Bros, Riddoch Run and The Habitat brands). Exports to the UK, the US and other major markets.

♦♦♦♦♦ **Cumulus Orange Chardonnay 2014** Sunny but stylish. Peach and pear meet cedarwood and assorted spice. It has line and length all sewn up, but sheer drinkability is the clincher. Screwcap. 13.5% alc. **Rating** 94 **To** 2020 $35 CM

♦♦♦♦♀ **Rolling Central Ranges GSM 2014** Rating 93 To 2021 $19 CM ✪
Cumulus Orange Cabernet Sauvignon 2013 Rating 93 To 2028 $45 CM
Cumulus Orange Cabernet Sauvignon 2012 Rating 92 To 2027 $45 CM
Climbing Orange Pinot Gris 2014 Rating 90 To 2017 $24 CM
Cumulus Orange Shiraz 2013 Rating 90 To 2026 $45 CM

Cupitt's Winery ★★★★☆

58 Washburton Road, Ulladulla, NSW 2539 **Region** Shoalhaven Coast
T (02) 4455 7888 www.cupittwines.com.au **Open** Wed–Sun 10–5
Winemaker Rosie, Wally & Tom Cupitt **Est.** 2007 **Dozens** 3500 **Vyds** 4ha
Griff and Rosie Cupitt run a combined winery and restaurant complex, taking full advantage of the location on the south coast of NSW. Rosie studied oenology at CSU and has more than a decade of vintage experience, taking in France and Italy; she also happens to be the Shoalhaven representative for Slow Food International. The Cupitts have 4ha of vines centred on sauvignon blanc, cabernet franc and semillon, and also buy viognier and shiraz from Tumbarumba, shiraz, chardonnay and sauvignon blanc from the Southern Highlands, and verdelho from Canowindra (Cowra). Rosie has been joined in the winery by sons Wally and Tom.

♦♦♦♦♦ **Hilltops Nebbiolo 2014** Wild-fermented, very long post-ferment maceration, matured in French hogsheads (30% new). Exceptional crimson hue; similar bouquet and palate; red cherries and rose petals on the sweet side, tannins and a hint of tar on the savoury side no match for the cherries. Screwcap. 13.5% alc. **Rating** 95 **To** 2024 $36
Yarra Valley Chardonnay 2014 Well made; barrel fermentation has been well handled, simply framing Yarra Valley chardonnay in terms of flavour (ex 13% alcohol, white peach and grapefruit) and structure (excellent length). There was nothing second class about the grapes – Cupitt's reach is far and wide. Screwcap. 13% alc. **Rating** 94 **To** 2023 $32

♦♦♦♦♀ **The Pointer Tumbarumba Pinot Noir 2014** Rating 91 To 2020 $30
Southern Highlands Sauvignon Blanc 2015 Rating 90 To 2017 $24
Hilltops Viognier 2015 Rating 90 To 2018 $28
Rosie's Rose 2015 Rating 90 To 2016 $26
Hilltops Cabernet Sauvignon 2014 Rating 90 To 2025 $34

Curator Wine Company   ★★★★

28 Jenke Road, Marananga, SA 5355 **Region** Barossa Valley
T 0411 861 604 **www**.curatorwineco.com.au **Open** By appt
Winemaker Tom White **Est.** 2015 **Dozens** 600 **Vyds** 8ha
This business is owned by Tom and Bridget White, who have made a number of changes in direction over previous years, and have now decided to focus on Shiraz and Cabernet Sauvignon from the Barossa Valley.

ŸŸŸŸŸ **Marananga Barossa Valley Cabernet Sauvignon 2013** Dark red; dark fruits and a spicy note dominate the powerful and densely packed bouquet; the full-bodied palate has admirable texture and presence, the finish long and sweetly fruited. Diam. 15% alc. **Rating** 93 **To** 2020 $75
Marananga Barossa Valley Shiraz 2013 Wild-fermented, mlf finished in 100% new French oak, matured for 24 months. Dense, deep colour; the fruit, tannins and alcohol combine to make light work of the new French oak in this ultra full-bodied shiraz grown on two blocks with radically different soil profiles. Clearly poses the question 'would less mean more?' Diam. 15% alc. **Rating** 91 **To** 2033 $75

Curlewis Winery   ★★★★★

55 Navarre Road, Curlewis, Vic 3222 **Region** Geelong
T (03) 5250 4567 **www**.curlewiswinery.com.au **Open** By appt
Winemaker Rainer Breit, Stefano Marasco **Est.** 1998 **Dozens** 1300 **Vyds** 2.8ha
Rainer Breit and partner Wendy Oliver purchased their property in 1996 with 1.6ha of what were then 11-year-old pinot noir vines. Rainer, a self-taught winemaker, uses the full bag of pinot noir winemaking tricks: cold soaking, hot fermentation, post-ferment maceration, part inoculated and part wild yeast use, prolonged lees contact, and bottling the wine neither fined nor filtered. While self-confessed 'pinotphiles', they planted some chardonnay, supplemented by a little locally grown shiraz and chardonnay. Rainer and Wendy sold the business in May 2011 to Leesa Freyer and Stefano Marasco. Leesa and Stefano are devoted Pinot Noir drinkers, and also own and operate the Yarra Lounge in Yarraville, Melbourne. Exports to Canada, Sweden, the Maldives, Malaysia, Singapore and Hong Kong.

ŸŸŸŸŸ **Reserve Geelong Pinot Noir 2013** Hand-picked, hand-sorted at the destemmer, whole berry wild yeast-fermented in open tanks, hand-plunged 6–8 times daily, 14 days on skins, matured for 18 months in French barriques (15% new). The finest of the Curlewis '13 Pinots, with a lacy texture/mouthfeel. Will appeal to pinot aficionados more than to those who enjoy shiraz (even cool climate shiraz). Screwcap. 13% alc. **Rating** 95 **To** 2024 $65
Reserve Geelong Pinot Noir 2012 The colour development is within bounds; a complex wine with a meaty/charcuterie bouquet and a most attractive palate, spicy tannins folded within plum/cherry fruit. Now at the point where it is approaching a long plateau of maturity. Screwcap. 13% alc. **Rating** 95 **To** 2023 $60
Geelong Syrah 2013 Hand-picked, destemmed, whole berry wild fermentation, 14 days on skins, 18 months in French oak. Impressive full-bodied cool-grown shiraz, laden with black cherry, blackberry, licorice and pepper, French oak subtle but evident, the tannins likewise. All up, a seductive wine beckoning you to the glass. Screwcap. 13.5% alc. **Rating** 95 **To** 2028 $30 ✪
Geelong Pinot Noir 2013 Hand-picked, hand-sorted at the destemmer, whole berry wild yeast-fermented in open tanks, hand-plunged 6–8 times daily, 14 days on skins, matured for 18 months in French barriques (15% new). Good depth to the colour; fully (not over) ripe; dark cherry and plum fruit, excellent line, length and mouthfeel. Screwcap. 13% alc. **Rating** 94 **To** 2024 $45

ŸŸŸŸŸ **Bel Sel Geelong Chardonnay 2015** Rating 93 **To** 2021 $28
Bel Sel Geelong Pinot Noir 2013 Rating 92 **To** 2020 $28
Bel Sel Geelong Pinot Noir 2012 Rating 91 **To** 2019 $27

Curly Flat ★★★★★

263 Collivers Road, Lancefield, Vic 3435 **Region** Macedon Ranges
T (03) 5429 1956 **www.curlyflat.com Open** W'ends 12–5
Winemaker Phillip Moraghan, Matt Regan **Est.** 1991 **Dozens** 6000 **Vyds** 13ha
Phillip Moraghan and Jenifer Kolkka began developing Curly Flat in 1991, drawing in part
on Phillip's working experience in Switzerland in the late '80s, and with a passing nod to
Michael Leunig. With ceaseless help and guidance from the late Laurie Williams (and others),
they have painstakingly established an immaculately trained 8.5ha of pinot noir, 3.5ha of
chardonnay and 1ha of pinot gris, and a multi-level, gravity-flow winery. Exports to the UK,
Japan and Hong Kong.

ŸŸŸŸŸ **Chardonnay 2014** Hand-picked 26 Mar–14 Apr, whole bunch-pressed,
fermented 11–16 days in French oak (43% new), matured for 18 months, 50% mlf.
This is an exercise in lusciously layered complexity and power, taken only after
endless trials over previous vintages, but also respecting the integrity of the fruit.
Screwcap. 13.5% alc. **Rating** 96 **To** 2027 $50 ✪

Pinot Noir 2013 20 months in oak, 30% new. Characterised by its satiny
mouthfeel, though the swirls of sweet-sour cherries, cranberry, spice and cream
wage war on your senses. To excellent effect. Tannin, acidity, length; all march
imposingly through the mouth. Another beauty. Screwcap. 14% alc. **Rating** 96
To 2025 $56 CM ✪

The Curly Pinot Noir 2013 Dijon clones 114 and 115, 100% whole bunch
fermentation, 3 days cold soak, 15-day ferment, 21 days on skins, matured in
French oak (38% new) for 20 months. The colour is great, the palate abuzz
with energy and activity; red fruits, complex tannins, good acidity and obvious
French oak all compete for front of stage, but it's a case of one in, all in. In the
longer term, fruit will become the major player. Screwcap. 13.5% alc. **Rating** 95
To 2033 $64

Williams Crossing Pinot Noir 2014 Hand-picked, destemmed, 30% wild, 70%
cultured yeast, matured in French barriques (20% new) for 12 months. Impressive
second label, reflecting the fastidious approach of Curly Flat in the vineyard and
winery alike. The spicy bouquet has bright plum and red cherry fruit, oak and
tannins in serried support. Screwcap. 13.4% alc. **Rating** 94 **To** 2022 $27 ✪

ŸŸŸŸŸ **Williams Crossing Chardonnay 2014 Rating** 93 **To** 2021 $25 CM ✪
The Curly Chardonnay 2013 Rating 93 **To** 2019 $55
Pinot Gris 2015 Rating 93 **To** 2017 $34 CM
Macedon NV Rating 93 **To** 2018 $45 TS
White Pinot 2015 Rating 91 **To** 2017 $26 CM

Currency Creek Winery ★★★

Winery Road, Currency Creek, SA 5214 **Region** Currency Creek
T (08) 8555 4069 **www.currencycreekwinery.com.au Open** 7 days 10–5
Winemaker John Loxton, Phil Christenson, Graham Phillips **Est.** 1969 **Dozens** 1250
Vyds 12ha
For over 40 years this family-owned vineyard and relatively low-profile winery has produced
some outstanding wood-matured whites and pleasant, soft reds selling at attractive prices.
The vineyards have roughly equal plantings of shiraz, cabernet sauvignon, mourvedre and
chardonnay. It will be apparent from this that the essential part of the grape production is sold.
Graham Phillips and Jan Curzon purchased Currency Creek Winery in 2009. Exports to the
UK, the US and China.

ŸŸŸŸ **Reserve Brut Pinot Noir Chardonnay 2015** There's no suggestion of rose on
the label, but the colour is a glorious sunburst crimson. An almost equal blend of
pinot noir and chardonnay, it's the pinot that speaks most emphatically, filled with
candied strawberries, ripe raspberries and red cherries. A little sweetness on the
finish cleverly masks a touch of tannin grip. A bargain rose in the Charmat style
(second ferment in tank). Zork. 12% alc. **Rating** 88 **To** 2016 $17 TS ✪

Curtis Family Vineyards

514 Victor Harbor Road, McLaren Vale, SA 5171 **Region** McLaren Vale
T 0439 800 484 **www**.curtisfamilyvineyards.com **Open** Not
Winemaker Mark and Claudio Curtis **Est.** 1973 **Dozens** 10 000
The Curtis family traces its history back to 1499 when Paolo Curtis was appointed by
Cardinal de Medici to administer Papal lands in the area around Cervaro. (The name Curtis is
believed to derive from Curtius, a noble and wealthy Roman Empire family.) The family has
been growing grapes and making wine in McLaren Vale since 1973, having come to Australia
some years previously. Exports to the US, Canada, Thailand and China.

🍷🍷🍷🍷🍷 **Cavaliere McLaren Vale Shiraz 2013** Intense colour; wears the battle clothes
and armour of McLaren Vale with pride, dark, bitter chocolate wrapped around
black fruits, fine-grained tannins lancing the finish. It all works very well, the balance
and length of the palate hard to fault. Diam. 14% alc. **Rating** 94 **To** 2033 $70

🍷🍷🍷🍷🍷 **Limited Series McLaren Vale Grenache 2014 Rating** 92 **To** 2020 $100

Cuttaway Hill Wines

12587 Hume Highway, Sutton Forest, NSW 2577 **Region** Southern Highlands
T (02) 4858 1788 **www**.cuttawayhillwines.com.au **Open** 7 days 10.30–4.30
Winemaker Mark Bourne, Jeff Aston **Est.** 1998 **Dozens** 5000 **Vyds** 15ha
While the Bourne family did not acquire Cuttaway Hill from the founding O'Neil family
until 2011, Mark Bourne produced the region's first sparkling wines in '04 under the
Cuttaway Hill Laurence label. Until '11 Mark's principal focus was viticulture, and he was the
founding president of the Southern Highlands Vignerons Association, and chief organiser of
the Australian Highlands Wine Show. While he continues those involvements, he is now in
charge of all aspects of the Cuttaway Hill business. Exports to China.

🍷🍷🍷🍷 **Pinot Gris 2015** The grapes are grown using biodynamic principles, but the
wine is made in totally conventional fashion – and is good, thanks to the right
climate. Screwcap. 13.5% alc. **Rating** 89 **To** 2017 $28

d'Arenberg

Osborn Road, McLaren Vale, SA 5171 **Region** McLaren Vale
T (08) 8329 4888 **www**.darenberg.com.au **Open** 7 days 10–5
Winemaker Chester Osborn, Jack Walton **Est.** 1912 **Dozens** 270 000 **Vyds** 197.2ha
Nothing, they say, succeeds like success. Few operations in Australia fit this dictum better
than d'Arenberg, which has kept its almost 100-year-old heritage while moving into the 21st
century with flair and élan. At last count the d'Arenberg vineyards, at various locations, have
24 varieties planted, as well as 120 growers in McLaren Vale. There is no question that its past,
present and future revolve around its considerable portfolio of richly robed red wines, Shiraz,
Cabernet Sauvignon and Grenache being the cornerstones, but with over 20 varietal and/or
blend labels. The quality of the wines is unimpeachable, the prices logical and fair. Ridiculous
wine names the only downside. 44 wines tasted for this edition, possibly a record. It has a
profile in both the UK and the US that far larger companies would love to have. d'Arenberg
celebrated 100 years of family grapegrowing in '12 on the property that houses the winery,
cellar door and restaurant. A founding member of Australia's First Families of Wine. Exports
to all major markets.

🍷🍷🍷🍷🍷 **The Dry Dam Riesling 2008** Re-release. Extraordinary show career: 6 trophies
including Best Riesling in Adelaide Wine Show '15, and 15 gold medals, including
Perth, Sydney and two from the Canberra International Riesling Challenge. The
colour is green (amazing in itself), the palate perfectly balanced and still fresh as
a daisy, bursting with citrus/lime flavours, the length and balance impeccable. A
once in a lifetime McLaren Vale riesling offered at an absurdly low price. Screwcap.
11.5% alc. **Rating** 97 **To** 2023 $29 ✪

The Ironstone Pressings 2012 Not your average GSM blend. This release raises the stakes on the style. It's raked with tannin, shot with herbs, full of dust and dry spice notes, and also flush with succulent, fresh, blue- and black-berried fruit. Tannin is scintillatingly fine; length is a long-held note. One can only marvel. Screwcap. 14.4% alc. **Rating** 97 **To** 2030 $65 CM ✪

ΨΨΨΨΨ **The Dead Arm Shiraz 2012** Classic release. Meaty and substantial but poised. Blackberry, smoked herbs, crushed ants and earth. Sweet fruit rushes and fills; savoury notes sweep through the flanks. Firm but exuberant. Irrepressible. Screwcap. 14.6% alc. **Rating** 96 **To** 2030 $65 CM ✪

The Coppermine Road Cabernet Sauvignon 2012 Beautiful cabernet. Fresh at heart but fully franked with flavour. Boysenberry, asphalt, blackcurrant and assorted green and dry herbs. Perfect set. Waves of fine, dry, not-to-be-messed-with tannin. Kicks up dust as it leaves the mouth. Screwcap. 14.1% alc. **Rating** 96 **To** 2032 $65 CM ✪

The Dry Dam Riesling 2015 An utterly impressive wine from a winery best known for its flotilla of red wines; its fruit has the juicy flavour and mouthfeel of the kind expected of a dry Mosel Riesling; the intensity of the fruit is heightened by the crisp, crunchy acidity on the finish and aftertaste. The Dry Dam name is an anachronism. Screwcap. 10.7% alc. **Rating** 95 **To** 2025 $18 ✪

The Dead Arm Shiraz 2013 Crushed and destemmed, cultured yeast, open-fermented with heading down boards, followed by up to 18 months in French oak. Inky purple-crimson hue; a powerful, archetypal d'Arenberg Shiraz, swimming with black fruits of every description, dark chocolate and a generous helping of chewy tannins. Screwcap. 14.6% alc. **Rating** 95 **To** 2038 $29 ✪

The Love Grass Shiraz 2012 Shows the great '12 vintage to full advantage, my grumbles about the label notwithstanding. Comes as close to elegance as one can expect from the generous 'd'Arenberg Shirazs. There are spice and licorice notes to the finely pitched black fruits, dark chocolate in the background. Finely ground tannins provide a savoury farewell to a wine that could be enjoyed anywhere, anytime. Screwcap. 14.4% alc. **Rating** 95 **To** 2027 $25 ✪

The Laughing Magpie Shiraz Viognier 2012 Matured in 50/50% French and American oak (8% new) for 20 months. It's odd how the co-fermentation of viognier can appear to intensify the regional signature; it's certainly written large here, but there's a spark of fresh fruit with a different pitch to its note. An impressive example of this key wine in the d'Arenberg menagerie. Screwcap. 14.4% alc. **Rating** 95 **To** 2032 $29 ✪

The Derelict Vineyard Grenache 2012 Chester Osborn had the vision to acquire old, even derelict, vineyards when grenache was disregarded once its use in fortified wines had ended. The completion of fermentation in barrel has served very well: this is a grenache with macho attitude, red and blue fruits in a basket of integrated tannins and oak. Good as it is now, it will be best in another 10 years. Screwcap. 14.5% alc. **Rating** 95 **To** 2025 $29 ✪

The Athazagoraphobic Cat Sagrantino Cinsault 2011 A 95/5% blend; named after Audrey Hepburn, a cat who often followed Chester Osborn around the winery, terrified of being forgotten. The unusual but meritorious nature of the wine is likely to be lost in the hubbub of the labels of this and its $200 Old Bloke sibling. This is a seriously interesting wine, which clears the savoury/tannin bar with some ease, although you wouldn't think so at the first sip. The perfect match for food, because it will simply want to make you eat more, not drink more. Screwcap. 14.3% alc. **Rating** 95 **To** 2026 $200

The Wild Pixie Shiraz 2013 Matured in French oak (10% new) for 12 months. Bright crimson-purple, presumably ex co-fermentation with a small percentage of roussanne; an intense and complex wine with layers of black fruits, positive tannins and the oak infusion ex barrel ferment that I find so enjoyable. The net result is a spicy, medium to full-bodied wine with a long future. Screwcap. 14.6% alc. **Rating** 94 **To** 2033 $29 ✪

The Laughing Magpie Shiraz Viognier 2011 Has an unusually high percentage (10%) of co-fermented viognier, justified by the depth and complexity of the shiraz, and also by the unifying effect of completing the final third of the initial open fermentation in used French and American oak. It's a remarkable outcome for the vintage, shrugging off the impact of the rain. Screwcap. 14.2% alc. Rating 94 To 2021 $29 ✪

The Old Bloke & The Three Young Blondes Shiraz Roussanne Viognier Marsanne 2011 A 91/3/3/3% blend. I simply shake my head in wonder at the accusations of sexism generated by this clever label, and indeed wonder if it isn't a clever move by d'Arenberg designed to draw attention to the wine. For the record, as it were, there is a complex array of juicy red and black fruits with a crosscut of fine, leathery tannins. Screwcap. 14.2% alc. Rating 94 To 2031 $200

The Ironstone Pressings 2013 Matured in used French (81%) and American (19%) oak for 12 months. Deep crimson-purple, unmatched by virtually any Barossa Valley GSM; the alcohol, too, is strikingly low in GSM terms. Then there is the powerful array of red and black fruits. Good now, but will be better still in 2+ years. This is a unique style, patented – so it seems – by d'Arenberg. Screwcap. 14.3% alc. Rating 94 To 2025 $29 ✪

The Galvo Garage Adelaide Hills Cabernet Sauvignon Merlot Petit Verdot Cabernet Franc 2011 Made using the one-size fits all vinification method used by d'Arenberg, but stands apart from most of its siblings thanks to the charge of high quality tannins that provide structure for the black fruits led by cabernet and petit verdot. Impressive wine at any price, let alone this. Screwcap. 14.3% alc. Rating 94 To 2031 $29 ✪

ϙϙϙϙϙ The Broken Fishplate Sauvignon Blanc 2015 Rating 93 To 2017 $20 ✪
The Noble Mud Pie Viognier Arneis 2015 Rating 93 To 2021 $20 ✪
The Lucky Lizard Chardonnay 2014 Rating 92 To 2020 $25 ✪
The Love Grass Shiraz 2013 Rating 92 To 2028 $25 ✪
The Noble Wrinkled Riesling 2015 Rating 92 To 2020 $20 ✪
Stephanie the Gnome with Rose Tinted Glasses Shiraz Sangiovese 2015 Rating 91 To 2020 $18 ✪
The Wild Pixie Shiraz 2011 Rating 91 To 2021 $29
The Coppermine Road Cabernet 2013 Rating 91 To 2028 $29
The Sticks & Stones Tempranillo Grenache Tinta Cao Souzao 2011 Rating 91 To 2020 $29
The Noble Botryotinia Fuckeliana Adelaide Hills Semillon Sauvignon Blanc 2015 Rating 91 To 2020 $20 ✪
The Footbolt Shiraz 2013 Rating 90 To 2020 $18 ✪
d'Arry's Original Shiraz Grenache 2013 Rating 90 To 2025 $18 ✪
The High Trellis Cabernet Sauvignon 2013 Rating 90 To 2023 $18 ✪
The Conscious Biosphere McLaren Vale Aglianico Petit Sirah 2012 Rating 90 To 2020 $29

Dal Zotto Wines   ★★★★

Main Road, Whitfield, Vic 3733 **Region** King Valley
T (03) 5729 8321 **www.**dalzotto.com.au **Open** 7 days 10–5
Winemaker Michael Dal Zotto **Est.** 1987 **Dozens** 15 000 **Vyds** 48ha

The Dal Zotto family is a King Valley institution; ex-tobacco growers, then contract grapegrowers, they are now primarily focused on their Dal Zotto range. Led by Otto and Elena, and with sons Michael and Christian handling winemaking and sales/marketing respectively, the family is producing increasing amounts of wine of consistent quality from its substantial estate vineyard. The cellar door is in the centre of Whitfield, and is also home to their Trattoria (open weekends).

ϙϙϙϙϙ King Valley Pinot Grigio 2015 There's a bit of prettiness but there's good flavour too, mostly in the nashi pear, chalk and spice arena. Essentially refreshing, with substance. Screwcap. 12.5% alc. Rating 92 To 2017 $18 CM ✪

L'Immigrante Barbera 2013 Fresh and juicy, with enough tannin to give it some gravitas. Peppermint, chocolate and black cherry flavours flow attractively through the mouth, a flush of cranberry-flavoured acidity helping both its drinkability and its food-friendliness. Screwcap. 14% alc. **Rating** 92 **To** 2020 $60 CM

King Valley Riesling 2014 Fennel, lime, spice and apple. This delivers a deal of smooth-skinned flavour, and will find fans easily. Screwcap. 12.5% alc. **Rating** 90 **To** 2021 $19 CM ✪

🍷🍷🍷🍷 **L'Immigrante King Valley Prosecco 2014** **Rating** 89 **To** 2016 $36 TS

Dalfarras ★★★★☆

PO Box 123, Nagambie, Vic 3608 **Region** Nagambie Lakes
T (03) 5794 2637 **www**.tahbilk.com.au **Open** At Tahbilk
Winemaker Alister Purbrick, Alan George **Est.** 1991 **Dozens** 6400 **Vyds** 20.97ha

The personal project of Alister Purbrick and artist wife Rosa (née Dalfarra), whose paintings adorn the labels of the wines. Alister is best known as winemaker at Tahbilk (see separate entry), the family winery and home, but this range of wines is intended to (in Alister's words) 'allow me to expand my winemaking horizons and mould wines in styles different from Tahbilk'.

🍷🍷🍷🍷🍷 **Pinot Grigio 2015** From the King (80%) and Goulburn (20%) valleys, picked and crushed at night, different parcels undergoing different treatments: mlf, fermented and matured in French oak, or extended time on yeast lees. Distinct pink tinge; this is a tour de force of winemaking, producing a wine full of interest from the first whiff to the last sip. Two questions arise: why is it called grigio, not gris? And why is it so cheap? Screwcap. 12.5% alc. **Rating** 95 **To** 2017 $20 ✪

🍷🍷🍷🍷½ **Sangiovese 2014** **Rating** 90 **To** 2020 $18 ✪

Dalrymple ★★★★★

1337 Pipers Brook Road, Pipers Brook, Tas 7254 **Region** Northern Tasmania
T (03) 6382 7229 **www**.dalrymplevineyards.com.au **Open** Not
Winemaker Peter Caldwell **Est.** 1987 **Dozens** 4000 **Vyds** 17ha

Dalrymple was established many years ago by the Mitchell and Sundstrup families; the vineyard and brand were acquired by Hill-Smith Family Vineyards in late 2007. Plantings are split between pinot noir and sauvignon blanc, and the wines are made at Jansz Tasmania. In September 2010 Peter Caldwell was appointed as 'Vigneron', responsible for the vineyard, viticulture and winemaking. He brought with him 10 years' experience at Te Kairanga Wines (Martinborough, NZ), and 2 years with Josef Chromy Wines. His knowledge of pinot noir and chardonnay is obviously comprehensive. In Dec '12 Hill-Smith Family Vineyards acquired the 120ha property on which the original Frogmore Creek Vineyard was established; 10ha of that property is pinot noir specifically for Dalrymple.

🍷🍷🍷🍷🍷 **Single Site Swansea Pinot Noir 2014** Good depth and hue to the colour; Interesting wine; has the most supple mid-palate of the three Dalrymple Pinots, and also has a positive juicy finish and aftertaste of black cherry and plum. Screwcap. 13.5% alc. **Rating** 96 **To** 2027 $61 ✪

Single Site Coal River Pinot Noir 2014 Very good depth and hue; has the layered depth and power the Coal River Valley is able to bestow on most vineyards and varieties, perhaps due to a slightly drier climate than other parts of Tasmania. Screwcap. 13.5% alc. **Rating** 95 **To** 2027 $61

Cave Block Pipers River Chardonnay 2014 Has all the attitude, drive and precision that very good Tasmanian chardonnay can muster with deceptive ease; grapefruit and white peach are on equal terms, and provide balance in the face of quality oak, and the given of acidity. Screwcap. 12.5% alc. **Rating** 94 **To** 2024 $37

🍷🍷🍷🍷½ **Cottage Block Pinot Noir 2014** **Rating** 93 **To** 2024 $58
Pipers River Pinot Noir 2014 **Rating** 91 **To** 2020 $34

Dalwhinnie ★★★★★

448 Taltarni Road, Moonambel, Vic 3478 **Region** Pyrenees
T (03) 5467 2388 **www.**dalwhinnie.com.au **Open** 7 days 10–5
Winemaker David Jones, Rachel Gore **Est.** 1976 **Dozens** 4500 **Vyds** 26ha
David and Jenny Jones are making wines with tremendous depth of fruit flavour, reflecting the relatively low-yielding but very well maintained vineyards. The vineyards are dry-grown and managed organically, hence the low yield, but the quality more than compensates. A 50-tonne high-tech winery now allows the wines to be made onsite. Exports to the UK and other major markets.

🍷🍷🍷🍷🍷 **The Eagle Shiraz 2013** Deep purple-crimson; not just any eagle, but one with the grace and power of the wedgetail eagle, Australia's foremost avian symbol (emus don't fly). Juicy blackberry, anise and a mix of spice and pepper are wonderfully fresh and mouthwatering thanks to the controlled alcohol and acidity. Screwcap. 13.5% alc. **Rating** 97 **To** 2038 $165
Moonambel Cabernet 2013 Exceptionally dense crimson-purple showing through on the rim; blackcurrant/cassis fruit is perfectly matched with ripe, persistent tannins and quality oak. Virtually unchanged since first tasted Jan '15, and will surely be one of the great Dalwhinnie Cabernets as it slowly matures over the next 20+ years. Screwcap. 14% alc. **Rating** 97 **To** 2043 $55 ✪

🍷🍷🍷🍷🍷 **Moonambel Shiraz 2014** It is a masterclass in the use of French oak to amplify, not diminish, the fruit on the medium-bodied palate, with black cherry, plum and blackberry all in step; the tannins are no more than a gauze on the super-elegant finish. Screwcap. 13.5% alc. **Rating** 96 **To** 2039 $60 ✪
Moonambel Cabernet 2014 Deep, bright purple-crimson; as ever, a distinguished cabernet, perfectly groomed and perfectly balanced; the cassis fruit has a sprig of bay leaf, the tannins are firm but fine, and the French oak is both balanced and integrated. Screwcap. 13.5% alc. **Rating** 95 **To** 2034 $55

🍷🍷🍷🍷🍷 **Moonambel Chardonnay 2014 Rating** 93 **To** 2020 $45
Forest Hut Viognier 2015 Rating 93 **To** 2017 $45
The Hut Shiraz 2013 Rating 90 **To** 2023 $26

Dandelion Vineyards ★★★★★

PO Box 138, McLaren Vale, SA 5171 **Region** McLaren Vale
T (08) 8556 6099 **www.**dandelionvineyards.com.au **Open** Not
Winemaker Elena Brooks **Est.** 2007 **Dozens** NFP **Vyds** 124.2ha
This is a highly impressive partnership between Peggy and Carl Lindner (40%), Elena and Zar Brooks (40%), and Fiona and Brad Rey (20%). It brings together vineyards spread across the Adelaide Hills, Eden Valley, Langhorne Creek, McLaren Vale, Barossa Valley and Fleurieu Peninsula. Elena is not only the wife of industry dilettante Zar, but also a gifted winemaker. Exports to all major markets.

🍷🍷🍷🍷🍷 **Wonderland of the Eden Valley Riesling 2015** Hand-picked, whole bunch-pressed, cool-fermented, bottled without filtration or fining. Reflects 7.8g/l of acid and a very low pH of 2.8. This packs a punch that will always be part of a special riesling, bred and built to develop over a 20-year span, its minerally acidity wrapped around citrus fruit. Screwcap. 11.5% alc. **Rating** 95 **To** 2030 $60
Red Queen of the Eden Valley Shiraz 2013 Nonsense ersatz gold circles on the back label; one-third whole bunches in the bottom of open fermenters, two-thirds crushed on top, matured in 50% new/50% used French oak for 30 months. The full-on vinification was appropriate for the high quality fruit from 90yo vines. Screwcap. 14.5% alc. **Rating** 95 **To** 2033 $100
Lionheart of the Barossa Shiraz 2014 Has a string of overseas medals of various worth on the label, but no domestic awards. It is an interesting wine, with strong texture and structure, but no magic wand in the winery: hand-picked, crushed, open-fermented, 8 days on skins, 18 months maturation in predominantly

used French barriques. The mix of savoury spices is particularly interesting and attractive. Screwcap. 14.5% alc. **Rating** 94 **To** 2029 $27 **○**
Lion's Tooth of McLaren Vale Shiraz Riesling 2013 Wham bang; doesn't shout, even whimper, riesling, just McLaren Vale riding high on a broomstick of dark chocolate. Screwcap. 14.5% alc. **Rating** 94 **To** 2020 $27 **○**

ᵽᵽᵽᵽᵽ **Damsel of the Barossa Merlot 2014** Rating 91 To 2024 $27
Twilight of the Adelaide Hills Chardonnay 2014 Rating 90 To 2020 $27
Lioness of McLaren Vale Shiraz 2014 Rating 90 To 2025 $27

David Franz   ★★★★★

PO Box 677, Tanunda, SA 5352 **Region** Barossa Valley
T 0419 807 468 **www**.david-franz.com **Open** By appt
Winemaker David Franz Lehmann **Est.** 1998 **Dozens** 5000 **Vyds** 39.17ha
David Franz (Lehmann) is one of Margaret and Peter Lehmann's sons, and took a very circuitous path around the world before establishing his eponymous winery. Wife Nicki accompanied him on his odyssey and they, together with three children, two dogs, a mess of chickens and a surly shed cat, all happily live together in their house and winery. The utterly unique labels stem from (incomplete) university studies in graphic design; his degree in hospitality business management is less relevant, for visits to the winery, aka the shed, are strictly by appointment only. An extended family of five share the work in the vineyard and the shed. Exports to the UK, the US, Canada, Japan, Hong Kong and China.

ᵽᵽᵽᵽᵽ **Brother's Ilk Moskos' Birdwood Vineyard Adelaide Hills Chardonnay 2014** Much fuss in both the vineyard and winery has led to a low-fuss wine in the glass. This is tangy with apple, touched by brine, fennel and honeysuckle notes, and riven with citrus-shot peach. Give this another year in bottle and they'll be lining out the door for this; it's a wine of terrific potential. Screwcap. 12.2% alc. Rating 95 To 2021 $45 CM

ᵽᵽᵽᵽᵽ **Eden Valley Riesling 2014** Rating 93 To 2021 $25 CM **○**
Long Gully Ancient Vine Semillon 2014 Rating 93 To 2018 $22 CM **○**
General Practitioner Grenache Petit Verdot 2012 Rating 93 To 2023 $33
Deb Barossa Shiraz Cabernet Sauvignon Grenache Mataro Petit Verdot NV Rating 92 To 2020 $50 CM
Plane Turning Right Barossa Merlot Petit Verdot Cabernet Sauvignon 2012 Rating 92 To 2020 $25 CM **○**
Loan Vineyard Semillon 2014 Rating 91 To 2018 $35 CM
Eden Edge Riesling Semillon 2015 Rating 90 To 2019 $20 CM **○**

David Hook Wines   ★★★★★

Cnr Broke Road/Ekerts Road, Pokolbin, NSW 2320 **Region** Hunter Valley
T (02) 4998 7121 **www**.davidhookwines.com.au **Open** 7 days 10–4.30
Winemaker David Hook **Est.** 1984 **Dozens** 10000 **Vyds** 8ha
David Hook has over 25 years' experience as a winemaker for Tyrrell's and Lake's Folly, also doing the full Flying Winemaker bit with jobs in Bordeaux, the Rhône Valley, Spain, the US and Georgia. The estate-owned Pothana Vineyard has been in production for over 25 years, and the wines made from it are given the 'Old Vines' banner. This vineyard is planted on the Belford Dome, an ancient geological formation that provides red clay soils over limestone on the slopes, and sandy loams along the creek flats; the former for red wines, the latter for white.

ᵽᵽᵽᵽᵽ **Aged Release Old Vines Pothana Vineyard Belford Semillon 2011** This is dazzlingly fresh and vibrant, its lemon/lemongrass/crispy/crunchy acidity dancing wildly around the mouth, egged on by a faint touch of spritz. It will slowly develop over the next 10+ years without losing its mojo, and will excite you whenever you crack a bottle. Screwcap. 10.5% alc. **Rating** 97 **To** 2026 $50 **○**

ᵽᵽᵽᵽᵽ **Old Vines Pothana Vineyard Belford Shiraz 2014** Very good colour; an expressive and complex bouquet with black fruits, spice and sweet polished leather, the medium-bodied palate picking up where the bouquet leaves off, perfectly proportioned and balanced, black fruits and spices in abundance. Oh that I should live so long as to enjoy these wines as they move towards maturity 20+ years hence. Screwcap. 13.5% alc. **Rating** 96 **To** 2044 $40 **✪**

Reserve Central Ranges Nebbiolo 2014 The colour is very good for nebbiolo, and semaphores the right message: it has clear-cut varietal character with sour, morello and black cherries all contributing, and comfortably handling the tannins, especially on the back-palate. While I'm far from addicted to the variety, I'd happily share in a bottle of this the next time I'm eating Italian. Screwcap. 13.5% alc. **Rating** 95 **To** 2039 $38

Old Vines Pothana Vineyard Belford Semillon 2015 Pothana Semillons are noteworthy for their generosity, but in the best possible way, for they retain their line, length and profile, thus also responding well in the cellar. This dual release ('15 and '11) is a little skewed by the great white vintage of '11, but comparing the two is still a fascinating exercise. This wine has the generosity that means it's an each-way bet. Screwcap. 10.5% alc. **Rating** 94 **To** 2023 $25 **✪**

Reserve Central Ranges De Novo Rosso 2014 This is a decidedly convincing blend of barbera, nebbiolo and sangiovese. The colour is good, the aromas are a vase of red flowers with a background of spice, and the palate has good tension between red berries and savoury tannins. It is time to enjoy it now, but this could turn out to be a Cliff Young (despite Hook's short-term cellaring suggestion). Screwcap. 13% alc. **Rating** 94 **To** 2024 $30 **✪**

Reserve Central Ranges Barbera 2014 A useful partner to the De Novo Rosso and Nebbiolo. This is more supple and immediately welcoming, its red fruits bordering on outright juiciness. Barbera isn't meant to have so much character in Australia. Screwcap. 13.5% alc. **Rating** 94 **To** 2029 $30 **✪**

🍷🍷🍷🍷🍷 **Reserve Hunter Valley Sangiovese 2014** Rating 91 **To** 2024 $30

Dawson & James   ★★★★★

1240B Brookman Road, Dingabledinga, SA 5172 **Region** Southern Tasmania
T (08) 8556 7326 **www.**dawsonjames.com.au **Open** Not
Winemaker Peter Dawson, Tim James **Est.** 2010 **Dozens** 900
Peter Dawson and Tim James had long and highly successful careers as senior winemakers for Hardys/Accolade wines. Tim jumped ship first, becoming managing director of Wirra Wirra for seven years until 2007, while Peter stayed longer. Now both have multiple consulting roles. They have both long had a desire to grow and make wine in Tasmania, a desire which came to fruition in '10. The wines so far released have all been of the highest quality. Exports to the UK and Singapore.

🍷🍷🍷🍷🍷 **Pinot Noir 2014** Stunning pinot noir. Savoury and fruit-filled at once, its power obvious but so too its sophistication. You get your cake and the chance to eat it too. Smoky reduction, wood spice, cherry-plum, snapped twigs. The flavours ping, the quality sings. Screwcap. 13.5% alc. **Rating** 97 **To** 2024 $48 CM **✪**

🍷🍷🍷🍷🍷 **Chardonnay 2014** The flutter of silken fruit. This takes deliciousness to ridiculous levels. It drips with pear and preserved lemon, spice and cedary/milky oak. The flavours flow so well there's never any doubt they'll persist through the finish. Screwcap. 13.3% alc. **Rating** 96 **To** 2023 $48 CM **✪**

DCB Wine   ★★★★

505 Gembrook Road, Hoddles Creek, Vic 3139 **Region** Yarra Valley
T 0419 545 544 **www.**dcbwine.com.au **Open** Not
Winemaker Chris Bendle **Est.** 2013 **Dozens** NFP
DCB is a busman's holiday for Chris Bendle, currently a winemaker at Hoddles Creek Estate, where he has been since 2010. He has previously made wine in Tasmania, NZ and Oregon, thus he is the right person to provide wines that are elegant, affordable, and reward the pleasure

of drinking (Chris's aim). It should be said that the wines so far made have had sophisticated winemaking behind the wine in the glass.

ΨΨΨΨ♀ **Yarra Valley Chardonnay 2015** Elegant style and, most importantly, a ripping drink. Lemon curd, stone fruit, apple and spice notes sweep you off your feet and continue a good, fluid show all the way through to a steely/chalky finish. Screwcap. 12.9% alc. **Rating** 93 **To** 2021 $20 CM ✪
Yarra Valley Pinot Noir 2014 Value writ large. It's a pretty wine with attitude. Cherries, spices, stalks and blossomy notes. Lures you in but then gives you a torrid time. It can be both quaffed and contemplated. Screwcap. 13% alc. **Rating** 93 **To** 2022 $20 CM ✪
Yarra Valley Chardonnay 2014 Excellent follow-up to the inaugural '13 release. Intensity is down slightly but pure varietal character shines through unhindered. Kick of flavour to the finish emphasises the quality. Screwcap. 13% alc. **Rating** 92 **To** 2020 $20 CM ✪

ΨΨΨΨ **Yarra Valley Pinot Noir 2015 Rating** 89 **To** 2022 $20 CM

De Beaurepaire Wines ★★★★

182 Cudgegong Road, Rylstone, NSW 2849 **Region** Mudgee
T (02) 6379 1473 **www**.debeaurepairewines.com **Open** W'ends by appt
Winemaker Jacob Stein (Contract) **Est.** 1998 **Dozens** 1000 **Vyds** 52.3ha
The large De Beaurepaire vineyard was planted by Janet and Richard de Beaurepaire in 1998, and is situated on one of the oldest properties west of the Blue Mountains, at an altitude of 570–600m. The altitude, coupled with limestone soils, and with frontage to the Cudgegong River, provides grapes (and hence wines) very different from the normal Mudgee wines. The vineyard is planted to merlot, shiraz, cabernet sauvignon, pinot noir, petit verdot, viognier, chardonnay, semillon, verdelho and pinot gris; most of the grapes are sold.

ΨΨΨΨΨ **Victor Rylstone Mudgee Cabernet Sauvignon 2009** Machine-harvested, open-fermented, cultured yeast, 3 days cold soak, matured in French oak (20% new) for 14 months. Has retained remarkable depth and hue for its age; it is also attractively juicy, flooded with cassis to the fore, mint and a bouquet garni of wild herbs to the rear. Is still travelling well, with no end in sight for the plateau it is now entering. Screwcap. 14% alc. **Rating** 94 **To** 2029 $45

ΨΨΨΨ♀ **Leopold Rylstone Shiraz Viognier 2009 Rating** 93 **To** 2025 $45
Coeur d'Or Rylstone Botrytis Semillon 2013 Rating 93 **To** 2020 $35
Captain Starlight Cabernet Sauvignon 2011 Rating 91 **To** 2025 $25
Captain Starlight Merlot Cabernet Petit Verdot 2013 Rating 90 **To** 2025 $25

De Bortoli

De Bortoli Road, Bilbul, NSW 2680 **Region** Riverina
T (02) 6966 0100 **www**.debortoli.com.au **Open** Mon–Sat 9–5, Sun 9–4
Winemaker Darren De Bortoli, Julie Mortlock, John Coughlan **Est.** 1928 **Dozens** NFP
Vyds 311.5ha
Famous among the cognoscenti for its superb Noble One, which in fact accounts for only a minute part of its total production, this winery turns out low-priced varietal and generic wines that are invariably competently made. They come in part from estate vineyards, but also from contract-grown grapes. The rating is in part a reflection of the exceptional value for money offered across the range. In June 2012 De Bortoli received a $4.8 million grant from the Federal Government's Clean Technology Food and Foundries Investment Program. This grant supports an additional investment of $11 million by the De Bortoli family in their project called 'Re-engineering Our Future for a Carbon Economy'. De Bortoli is a founding member of Australia's First Families of Wine. Exports to all major markets.

♥♥♥♥♥ Noble One Botrytis Semillon 2013 De Bortoli remains the best Australian producer of this style, but the world has moved on from the glory days when critics raved about the wine, eagerly awaiting each release. This is still a luscious and perfectly balanced wine. 500ml. Screwcap. 10.5% alc. **Rating** 95 **To** 2016 $33 ✪

Black Noble NV Absolutely unique wine, with its own outlandish charm – and drinkability. Dark aged mahogany; an absolutely unique barrel-aged botrytis semillon (ex Noble One) with hyper-intense fruit cleansed by its volatile acidity – counterintuitive, of course. Overall, a sauvage note to its unique mouthfeel. 500ml. WAK screwcap. 17.5% alc. **Rating** 94 **To** 2016 $38

♥♥♥♥♡ Old Boys 21 Years Old Barrel Aged Tawny NV Rating 93 **To** 2016 $45
Deen Vat Series No 5 Botrytis Semillon 2011 Rating 92 **To** 2018 $14 ✪
8 Years Old Fine Tawny Port NV Rating 90 **To** 2017 $25

De Bortoli (Victoria)   ★★★★★

Pinnacle Lane, Dixons Creek, Vic 3775 **Region** Yarra Valley
T (03) 5965 2271 **www**.debortoliyarra.com.au **Open** 7 days 10–5
Winemaker Stephen Webber, Sarah Fagan, Andrew Bretherton **Est.** 1987
Dozens 350 000 **Vyds** 430ha
Arguably the most successful of all Yarra Valley wineries, not only in terms of the sheer volume of production, but also taking into account the quality of its wines. It is run by the husband and wife team of Leanne De Bortoli and Steve Webber, but owned by the De Bortoli family. The designated wines are released in three quality and price groups: at the top Single Vineyard, then Estate Grown, and in third place, Villages. Small volume labels also increase the offer with Riorret Single Vineyard Pinot Noir, Melba, La Bohème, an aromatic range of Yarra Valley wines, and Vinoque, enabling trials (at the commercial level) of new varieties and interesting blends in the Yarra. The BellaRiva Italian varietal wines are sourced from the King Valley, and Windy Peak from Vic regions, including the Yarra, King Valley and Heathcote. Finally, with effect from mid-2016, De Bortoli has purchased one of the most distinguished Upper Yarra vineyards, Lusatia Park. At the time of going to print, the family had not decided its long-range plans for the vineyard. Exports to all major markets. Unless otherwise stated, the wine is Yarra Valley.

♥♥♥♥♥ Melba Reserve Cabernet Sauvignon 2013 This is vice-regal stuff, bred in the purple. The bouquet is extremely expressive of the variety at its best, but it's the palate that works the magic, simultaneously elegant and intense, dripping with cassis, the tannins honed so fine they gently take your hand and lead you off into the night. Screwcap. 13.5% alc. **Rating** 97 **To** 2038 $45 ✪

♥♥♥♥♥ Riorret Balnarring Mornington Pinot Noir 2015 Deep colour; a luxuriant pinot, red-fleshed plum the primary flavour (flecks of spice and earth hidden within) that fill the mouth, yet leave the finish with a fresh upwards surge. Its future is writ large. Diam. 13.5% alc. **Rating** 95 **To** 2028 $42

Section A8 Syrah 2014 Planted in '71 by Graeme Miller, a visionary viticulturist, rated by De Bortoli as one of the finest vineyard sites in the Yarra Valley. This is a strikingly luscious wine with wonderfully responsive winemaking from the decision to pick through to the final taste of the wine in the glass, dripping with satsuma plum, blackberry fruit and exotic spices, the tannin and oak management faultless. Screwcap. 14% alc. **Rating** 95 **To** 2034 $52

Section A5 Chardonnay 2015 Produced from some of the Yarra Valley's oldest chardonnay vines, this is a wine to win you by degrees rather than brute force. Lowish alcohol sets the tone for an understated style, the varietal characters in a muted citrus and stone fruit vein, the oak influence almost subliminal but integral nonetheless. Screwcap. 12.7% alc. **Rating** 94 **To** 2025 $47

Villages Pinot Noir 2015 Released almost rudely young, but the quality is high. It's firm and structural with varietal fruit characters charging through its veins. Spice, cherry, spice and wood smoke. Life and lift. The price isn't quite laugh out loud, but it's not far off. Screwcap. 13% alc. **Rating** 94 **To** 2021 $22 CM ✪

Estate Grown Cabernet Sauvignon 2013 Dusty blackcurrant cabernet characters are meshed with toasty oak and leafy cool climate influence within a finely honed structure, the supple tannins adding the perfect finishing touch. Enjoyable now or later. Screwcap. 13.5% alc. **Rating** 94 **To** 2029 $25 ✪

Section D4 Nebbiolo 2013 Two clones planted in '05 and '06. This is swollen with potential as the vines become fully mature, however delicious it is now. Perfect colour, a perfumed rose petal and cherry blossom bouquet, then a juicy palate of red and black cherries, the tannins evident, of course, but refusing to grip no matter how long you hold the wine in your mouth. Screwcap. 13.5% alc. **Rating** 94 **To** 2028 $28 ✪

🍷🍷🍷🍷🍷 **Estate Grown Sauvignon 2015 Rating** 93 **To** 2020 $25 ✪
Estate Grown Chardonnay 2015 Rating 93 **To** 2022 $25 ✪
Vinoque Roundstone Vineyard Gamay Noir 2015 Rating 93 **To** 2017 $25 ✪
La Boheme Act Four Syrah Gamay 2015 Rating 93 **To** 2018 $20 ✪
Villages Chardonnay 2014 Rating 92 **To** 2021 $22 CM ✪
Estate Grown Pinot Noir 2015 Rating 92 **To** 2025 $25 ✪
Vinoque Art Martin Vineyard Sangiovese 2014 Rating 92 **To** 2020 $24 CM ✪
Section A7 Riesling 2015 Rating 90 **To** 2022 $30 CM
La Boheme Act Two Dry Pinot Noir Rose 2015 Rating 90 **To** 2017 $20 ✪
Windy Peak Heathcote Shiraz 2014 Rating 90 **To** 2026 $14 ✪
Villages Heathcote Shiraz Grenache 2014 Rating 90 **To** 2024 $20 ✪

De Iuliis   ★★★★★

1616 Broke Road, Pokolbin, NSW 2320 **Region** Hunter Valley
T (02) 4993 8000 **www.dewine.com.au Open** 7 days 10–5
Winemaker Michael De Iuliis **Est.** 1990 **Dozens** 10 000 **Vyds** 30ha
Three generations of the De Iuliis family have been involved in the establishment of their vineyard. The family acquired a property at Lovedale in 1986 and planted 18ha of vines in '90, selling the grapes from the first few vintages to Tyrrell's but retaining increasing amounts for release under the De Iuliis label. In '99 the land on Broke Road was purchased, where a winery and cellar door were built prior to the 2000 vintage. In '11 the business purchased 12ha of the long-established Steven Vineyard in Pokolbin. Winemaker Michael De Iuliis completed postgraduate studies in oenology at the Roseworthy campus of Adelaide University and was a Len Evans Tutorial scholar. He has lifted the quality of the wines into the highest echelon.

🍷🍷🍷🍷🍷 **Talga Road Vineyard Shiraz 2014** From a relatively new, but exciting vineyard. The flavours of this wine are of tsunami proportions, flooding the mouth with intense, but rounded, rolling balls of black fruits, polished leather, earthy tannins and yet more on the surge of the finish, where an unexpected flash of red fruits ignite. Magical value. Screwcap. 14.8% alc. **Rating** 97 **To** 2054 $40 ✪

Limited Release Shiraz 2013 Always limited to best-barrel selections from several sites to produce 250 dozen bottles. A precise rendition of the interaction between place and variety, the balance between fruit, oak and tannins is so perfect that it is hard to see where one finishes and the next starts. There's not an ounce of fat anywhere on the palate, just power and drive. Screwcap. 13.8% alc. **Rating** 97 **To** 2048 $70 ✪

🍷🍷🍷🍷🍷 **Wilderness Road Vineyard Semillon 2015** Grown on the sandy flats of Black Creek, famed for the quality of the grapes they produce. This marries elegance with intensity, starting with a lifted lemon/lime bouquet seamlessly moving onto a quite beautiful palate welding lemon, lemon zest, lime and acidity into a single stream of mouthwatering flavours. Screwcap. 10.5% alc. **Rating** 96 **To** 2035 $25 ✪

Steven Vineyard Shiraz 2014 The Steven Vineyard has always been known for the quality of its grapes, demand exceeding supply. The bouquet is very expressive, but it is the bottomless depth of the pools of varietal/regional flavours that provide the magic of this elegant, faultlessly balanced, medium-bodied shiraz. Screwcap. 14.2% alc. **Rating** 96 **To** 2039 $40 ✪

Semillon 2015 Has everything you could ask for in a young Hunter Valley semillon: bright straw-green hue, a lemongrass and citrus bouquet, then a long, intense palate built on the foundation of natural acidity. The whole life of the wine lies before it, as the citrus becomes honeyed, and finally some toasty nuances will appear. Screwcap. 10.5% alc. **Rating** 95 **To** 2030 $19

Aged Release Semillon 2009 Matured in temperature-controlled storage at the winery. It has the special conjunction of sparkling freshness and bite on the one hand, complex glacé lemon minus the sweetness (an oxymoron, I know), lemon zest, and a hint of honey on the other. Remarkable value for a wine over 6yo. Screwcap. 11% alc. **Rating** 95 **To** 2029 $30 ❂

LDR Vineyard Shiraz Touriga 2014 85/15% blend grown on the heavy clay soils of the family vineyard that (counterintuitively) gives rise to a light to medium-bodied wine that literally sparkles with its energy and vitality. The flavours are in a broad red-fruit spectrum, tannin and oak keeping a respectful distance, allowing the surge of fruit on the finish and aftertaste free play. Screwcap. 13.5% alc. **Rating** 95 **To** 2029 $40

Chardonnay 2014 Whole bunch-pressed, barrel-fermented in French oak – an expensive route for a $19 wine. The Hunter Valley is in a purple patch with chardonnays winning major trophies left, right and centre. This is right in the mix, with pure varietal expression (white peach and pink grapefruit) cosseted by impeccable oak. Screwcap. 13% alc. **Rating** 94 **To** 2020 $19 ❂

Shiraz 2014 There's a lot of everything from the moment the wine enters the mouth: alternating layers of red and black fruit, soft but persistent tannins, a lick of licorice and neatly judged oak. Long, too. Very much a wine of the vintage. Top value. Screwcap. 14.5% alc. **Rating** 94 **To** 2034 $25 ❂

De Salis Wines   ★★★★

Lofty Vineyard, 125 Mount Lofty Road, Nashdale, NSW 2800 **Region** Orange
T 0403 956 295 **www.desaliswines.com.au** **Open** 7 days 11–5
Winemaker Charles Svenson, Mitchell Svenson **Est.** 1999 **Dozens** 4000 **Vyds** 8.76ha
This is the venture of research scientist Charles (Charlie) Svenson and wife Loretta. Charlie became interested in winemaking when, aged 32, he returned to study microbiology and biochemistry at UNSW. His particular area of interest (for his PhD) was the yeast and bacterial fermentation of cellulosic waste to produce ethanol. In 2009, after a prolonged search, Charlie and Loretta purchased a vineyard first planted in 1993, then known as Wattleview and now as Lofty Vineyard. At 1050m, it is the highest vineyard in the Orange GI, with pinot noir (6 clones), chardonnay, merlot, pinot meunier and sauvignon blanc. In 2015 they purchased the Forest Edge Vineyard with pinot noir (2ha, including three clones), sauvignon blanc (2.5ha) and chardonnay (1.5ha). The majority of the fruit from this vineyard is sold to Brokenwood. For the record, at 1035m, it is the second-highest vineyard in Orange.

🍷🍷🍷🍷🍷 **Lofty Fume Blanc 2014** Similar handling to the Wild release but with the inclusion of some new oak. It hardly shows. This feels pristine and elegant with long, lilting length. It's more about finesse than power but it's fair to say it has all bases covered. Screwcap. 12.8% alc. **Rating** 94 **To** 2018 $45 CM

🍷🍷🍷🍷🍷 **Wild Fume Blanc 2014** **Rating** 93 **To** 2018 $35 CM
Lofty Cuvee 2010 **Rating** 92 **To** 2016 $65 TS
Wild Chardonnay 2014 **Rating** 91 **To** 2020 $38 CM
Lofty Pinot Noir 2013 **Rating** 91 **To** 2021 $85 CM
Lofty Cuvee 2011 **Rating** 91 **To** 2016 $65 TS
Chardonnay 2014 **Rating** 90 **To** 2019 $45 CM

Deakin Estate   ★★★☆

Kulkyne Way, via Red Cliffs, Vic 3496 **Region** Murray Darling
T (03) 5018 5555 **www.deakinestate.com.au** **Open** Not
Winemaker Frank Newman **Est.** 1980 **Dozens** 205 000 **Vyds** 350ha

This is owned by Freixenet of Spain, along with Katnook Estate. For over 10 years, Dr Phil Spillman steered the development of Deakin Estate, his rather large shoes to be filled by Frank Newman. Frank has had a long and varied career, starting at Penfolds working alongside Max Schubert, then Angove (for more than a decade) and BRL Hardy at Renmano. The very large production of Deakin Estate, with an enlarged range of brands, is only part of the story: with other labels produced at the estate, the annual crush of 2500 tonnes for Deakin is doubled, as is the production of bottled wines under those other labels. Exports to all major markets.

🍷🍷🍷 **La La Land Tempranillo 2014** Fermented and matured in tank with French and American oak chips for 3 months. Fresh and juicy; the crazy label and tapas bars will join with the wine as soul mates – it's got a lot happening at the price. Screwcap. 13.5% alc. **Rating** 88 **To** 2018 $18

Deep Woods Estate ★★★★★

889 Commonage Road, Yallingup, WA 6282 **Region** Margaret River
T (08) 9756 6066 **www**.deepwoods.com.au **Open** Wed–Sun 11–5, 7 days during hols
Winemaker Julian Langworthy, Dan Stocker **Est.** 1987 **Dozens** 30 000 **Vyds** 16ha
Owned by Perth businessman Peter Fogarty and family, who also own Lake's Folly in the Hunter Valley, and Millbrook in the Perth Hills. The 32ha property has 16ha of cabernet sauvignon, shiraz, merlot, cabernet franc, chardonnay, sauvignon blanc, semillon and verdelho. Exports to Germany, Malaysia, Singapore, Japan and China.

🍷🍷🍷🍷 **Grand Selection Wilyabrup Cabernet Sauvignon 2013** Open-fermented, with 12 days on skins. Matured for 18 months in French oak, with a selection of only five barrels, one new, then blended and bottled, with 2 years maturation prior to release. 110 dozen made. Just when you think the '14 Deep Woods Reserve could not be bettered, along comes this even more graceful and fluid wine, intensely perfumed with violets and cedar, the array of varietal fruit flavours gliding through the prodigious length of the palate. Sheer perfection. Screwcap. 14.1% alc. **Rating** 98 **To** 2043 $120 ✪

Reserve Block 7 Shiraz 2014 Partly from the estate Block 7, and partly from a mature adjacent Yallingup vineyard, it employs some whole bunch fermentation, cold soak and partial barrel fermentation of separate ferments, all then matured in new and used French barriques for 18 months. Deep crimson colour signals a full-bodied shiraz, redolent of black fruits of every description, spice and licorice sprinkled on top, and perfect oak and tannin management. Screwcap. 14.5% alc. **Rating** 97 **To** 2039 $45 ✪

Reserve Cabernet Sauvignon 2014 Elegance and purity personified. The varietal expression is pitch perfect, cassis standing proud, its handmaidens fine-grained tannins and cedary French oak. It is an effortless wine, no more than medium-bodied, and needs no further elaboration. Shades of Xanadu. Screwcap. 14% alc. **Rating** 97 **To** 2044 $60 ✪

🍷🍷🍷🍷 **Rose 2015** Tempranillo and shiraz with a small amount of vermentino, small parcels of oxidative-handled red fruit, the barrel-fermented lees-aged vermentino adding texture. Trophies Best Rose Margaret River Wine Show '15 and Qantas Wine Show of WA '15. Pale, bright pink; small wonder it has had such success, bringing texture and fruit depth into a seamless flow, finishing with a trumpet of savoury, mouthwatering finish and aftertaste. Screwcap. 12.5% alc. **Rating** 96 **To** 2018 $25 ✪

Hillside Chardonnay 2014 From the coolest sites accessed by Deep Woods in the region, wild-fermented in new and used oak. Grapefruit flavours ride high and wide on a palate with crunchy acidity and an afterthought of oak completing the picture. Value+. Screwcap. 13% alc. **Rating** 95 **To** 2022 $25 ✪

Reserve Chardonnay 2014 From two central Margaret River vineyards, whole bunch-pressed, wild yeast-fermented, matured in new and used French oak, kept separate until final blending and bottling. Richly robed and complex, yet doesn't allow things to get out of hand, particularly on its finely tuned finish and aftertaste. Screwcap. 13.5% alc. **Rating** 95 **To** 2024 $45

Sauvignon Blanc 2015 A mix of estate and contract-grown fruit from the south of Margaret River, a small percentage was barrel-fermented, with judicious lees stirring, part cool-fermented in stainless steel, gold medal Perth Wine Show '15. An exercise in pushing the envelope gently, the complexity engendered by the barrel ferment component is deliberately muted, the citrussy acidity on the back-palate and finish given maximum time and space; green pea/bean to lychee stuff. Screwcap. 12.5% alc. **Rating** 94 **To** 2017 $20 ✪

Shiraz et al 2014 The 'et al' is 10% malbec and 5% grenache, each parcel separately fermented, matured in large used oak barrels for 15 months. This is a compelling wine reflecting the quality of the grapes, the complexity from the 'et al' components and the winemaking skills of the team led by Julian Langworthy; it all adds up to opulence with trimmings of fine tannins. Extraordinary value. Screwcap. 14.5% alc. **Rating** 94 **To** 2034 $20 ✪

🍷🍷🍷🍷🍷 **Cabernet Sauvignon Merlot 2014** **Rating** 93 **To** 2029 $35
Chardonnay 2015 **Rating** 92 **To** 2023 $20 ✪
Harmony Rose 2015 **Rating** 92 **To** 2016 $15 CM ✪
Ivory Semillon Sauvignon Blanc 2015 **Rating** 91 **To** 2016 $15 CM ✪
Ebony Margaret River Cabernet Shiraz 2013 **Rating** 90 **To** 2023 $15 ✪

del Rios of Mt Anakie ★★★★☆

2320 Ballan Road, Anakie, Vic 3221 **Region** Geelong
T (03) 9497 4644 **www**.delrios.com.au **Open** W'ends 10–5
Winemaker John Durham, Gus del Rio **Est.** 1996 **Dozens** 3500 **Vyds** 17ha

Gus del Rio, of Spanish heritage, established a vineyard in 1996 on the slopes of Mt Anakie, northwest of Geelong (chardonnay, pinot noir, cabernet sauvignon, sauvignon blanc, shiraz, merlot and marsanne). The wines are made onsite in the fully equipped winery, which includes a bottling and labelling line able to process over 150 tonnes. The Hildegard Aura wines are a joint venture of Gus del Rio, John Durham and Doug Neal. Exports to China.

🍷🍷🍷🍷🍷 **Shiraz 2014** Hand-picked, 12% whole bunches, the remainder crushed and destemmed, 14 days on skins, pressed to French oak (33% new), after mlf, 50% racked and sulphured, the remainder left on lees for a further 12 months. Deeply coloured and deeply proportioned, its black fruits providing the playing field for the spices and licorice that are riddled through the core of the fruit; the left field winemaking has worked well. Screwcap. 13.8% alc. **Rating** 95 **To** 2034 $40

Sauvignon Blanc 2014 Wild-fermented in one new and two used barrels, matured for 8 months. An excellent sauvignon blanc with great length and focus, and an even more impressive finish; citrus, tropical and almond flavours play hide and seek with each other, but neither succeeds in entirely covering its tracks. Bright acidity has also had a major role. Screwcap. 13.2% alc. **Rating** 94 **To** 2018 $22 ✪

Chardonnay 2014 Barrel-fermented (30% new oak), matured for 10 months, a barrel selection. Rich and complex, hardly surprising given the very low yields, the decision to use mlf, the time spent in oak and the barrel selection. It's going too far to say this is an old-style chardonnay, but it certainly has depth to its multiple layers of flavour. Screwcap. 13.2% alc. **Rating** 94 **To** 2021 $28 ✪

Rose 2015 Hand-picked pinot noir, whole bunch-pressed, wild-fermented in tank at 18°C, matured on lees until end Aug. Attractive wine; a perfumed rose petal/red cherry/strawberry bouquet, then a fresh and crisp palate with a replay of the red fruits of the bouquet. Well made, the finish scintillatingly dry and long. Screwcap. 12.5% alc. **Rating** 94 **To** 2017 $20 ✪

🍷🍷🍷🍷 **Hildegard 2015** **Rating** 89 **To** 2020 $25
Geelong Pinot Noir 2014 **Rating** 88 **To** 2024 $35

Delamere Vineyard

Bridport Road, Pipers Brook, Tas 7254 **Region** Northern Tasmania
T (03) 6382 7190 **www**.delamerevineyards.com.au **Open** 7 days 10–5
Winemaker Shane Holloway, Fran Austin **Est.** 1983 **Dozens** 5000 **Vyds** 13.5ha
Delamere was one of the first vineyards planted in the Pipers Brook area. It was purchased by Shane Holloway and wife Fran Austin and their families in 2007. Shane and Fran are in charge of viticulture and winemaking. The vineyard has been expanded with 4ha of pinot noir and chardonnay. Exports to China.

Block 3 Chardonnay 2013 Whole bunch-pressed to 100% oak with fluffy solids, wild-fermented, matured for 12 months, released with 12 months bottle age. This is as fresh as the proverbial daisy, and you can see why it was held for a year before release. Fruit, acidity, alcohol and oak have been calculated down to the last microgram. It is flawless, and can be enjoyed to the fullest now or in 7 years time, especially if someone else is doing the honours. Diam. 13.2% alc. **Rating** 96 **To** 2023 $110

Chardonnay 2013 Wild yeast, a touch of mlf, a powerful hit of fruit flavour and the length to consummate it. This is an excellent wine to spend time with. On a bright line of acidity are hung quality fruit and oak. Screwcap. 13.5% alc. **Rating** 95 **To** 2023 $45 CM

Pinot Noir 2013 30yo estate vines, 50% whole bunches, wild yeast, open-fermented, 2–3 weeks on skins, matured in Burgundian oak. In terms of style, this stands halfway between its two vintage siblings, and in terms of price offers the best value. This is a complex pinot with a wicked jab to the solar plexus if you don't give it the respect it richly deserves. Delamere has the whole bunch approach in perfect control, adding a savoury/foresty dimension to the blood plum and cherry fruit, the palate long and composed. Screwcap. 13.5% alc. **Rating** 95 **To** 2025 $45

Block 8 Pinot Noir 2013 30% whole bunches, 5 days cold soak, 14 days on skins, matured for 10 months in French oak (50% new). Full-bodied, precariously balanced on the cusp of excess ripeness/alcohol, but (with food) will get away with it. It is very complex in both flavour (dark berries) and texture terms, and has time on its side to expand its wings. Diam. 13.9% alc. **Rating** 94 **To** 2028 $110

Rose 2015 Rating 93 **To** 2017 $20 ✪
Non Vintage Rose NV Rating 93 **To** 2017 $30 TS
Naissante Pinot Noir 2013 Rating 92 **To** 2021 $27
Cuvee 2012 Rating 92 **To** 2016 $45 TS
Non Vintage Cuvee NV Rating 92 **To** 2016 $30 TS

Delatite

26 High Street, Mansfield, Vic 3722 **Region** Upper Goulburn
T (03) 5775 2922 **www**.delatitewinery.com.au **Open** 7 days 11–5
Winemaker Andy Browning **Est.** 1982 **Dozens** 5000 **Vyds** 26ha
With its sweeping views across to the snow-clad Alps, this is uncompromising cool climate viticulture. Increasing vine age (many of the plantings are well over 30 years old), and the adoption of organic (and partial biodynamic) viticulture, seem also to have played a role in providing the red wines with more depth and texture; the white wines are as good as ever; all are wild yeast-fermented. In 2011 Vestey Holdings Limited, the international pastoral giant, acquired a majority holding in Delatite, and has said it represents one of 'what we hope will be a number of agricultural businesses here'. Exports to Denmark, China, Japan and Malaysia.

Donald's Block Reserve Cabernet Merlot 2012 Crushed and destemmed, wild yeast open-fermented, matured for 18 months in new French hogsheads. There is a background echo of Delatite mint, but also far more desirable characters, starting with the glorious crimson hue still in full plumage, the textured structure, the integration of French oak, and the perfectly groomed tannins. In short, it ticks all the boxes. Screwcap. 13.5% alc. **Rating** 95 **To** 2032 $60

Deadman's Hill Gewurztraminer 2015 Wild yeast-fermented and 'a little oak maturation'. Helped, perhaps, by a little residual sugar, the wine has more richness and depth than any previous Delatite gewurztraminer, as ready now as it will be later. Screwcap. 13% alc. **Rating** 94 **To** 2025 $24 **○**

ＹＹＹＹＹ **Riesling 2014 Rating** 93 **To** 2024 $25 **○**
Pinot Gris 2015 Rating 92 **To** 2020 $24 **○**
High Ground Roussanne 2015 Rating 92 **To** 2017 $17 **○**
High Ground Pinot Grigio 2015 Rating 90 **To** 2017 $17 **○**

Delinquente Wine Co   ★★★☆

36 Brooker Terrace, Richmond, SA 5033 **Region** Riverland
T 0437 876 407 **www**.delinquentewineco.com **Open** Not
Winemaker Various **Est.** 2013 **Dozens** 2000
A Hollywood actress was famous for saying 'I don't care what they say about me as long as they spell my name right.' Con-Greg Grigoriou might say 'I don't care how bad people think my wine labels are as long as they remember them.' They certainly set a new low-water mark in Australia. Con-Greg grew up on a vineyard in the Riverland, and spent a lot of time in wineries, with his father and grandfather, and has decided to concentrate on southern Italian grape varieties. It's a virtual winery operation, buying fruit from growers who share his vision and having the wine made wherever he is able to find a facility prepared to assist in the making of micro-quantities. Delinquente is getting a lot of airplay from the smart set, and it's no surprise to see production jump from 600 to 2000 dozen over the past year.

ＹＹＹＹＹ **The Bullet Dodger Riverland Montepulciano 2015** Good colour; a well-made wine hiding behind a particularly unpleasant version of the Delinquente label. There are red fruits and spices in abundance, and the tannins are a positive part of the wine. Screwcap. 13.5% alc. **Rating** 90 **To** 2018 $20 **○**

ＹＹＹＹ **Screaming Betty Riverland Vermentino 2015 Rating** 89 **To** 2017 $20

Dell'uva Wines   ★★★★★

194 Richards Road, Freeling, SA 5372 **Region** Barossa Valley
T (08) 8525 2245 **www**.delluvawines.com.au **Open** By appt
Winemaker Wayne Farquhar **Est.** 2014 **Dozens** 1500 **Vyds** 20ha
Owner and winemaker Wayne Farquhar moved from horticulture to viticultural, acquiring his first vineyard in 1979. His viticultural career was low-key for a number of years, but having tasted wines from all over the world over a decade of business travel, he decided to establish Dell'uva Wines off the back of his existing (conventional) vineyard on the western ridge of the Barossa Valley. In short order he established small plots of an A–Z of varieties: aglianico, albarino, ansonica, arinto, barbera, cabernet sauvignon, caniolo nero, carmenere, carnelian, chardonnay, dolcetto, durif, fiano, freisca, garnacha, graciano, grillo, lagrein, merlot, marsanne, mencia, montepulciano, moscato bianco, mourvedre, negroamaro, nero d'Avola, pinot blanc, pinot grigio, pinot noir, primitivo, roussanne, sagrantino, sangiovese, saperavi, shiraz, tannat, tempranillo, touriga nacional, verdejo, vermentino, verdicchio, viognier. With only 20ha available, the production of each wine is necessarily limited, the vinification as unconventional as the vineyard mix, utilising barrels, ceramic eggs, demijohns and tanks. The winemaking techniques have been chosen to throw maximum attention onto the inherent quality of the varieties, and this story has a long way to run.

ＹＹＹＹＹ **Tempranillo 2013** 10% whole bunches retained, the balance destemmed for whole berries, wild yeast, open-fermented with heading down boards, 2–3 days cold soak, matured for 23 months in French oak (20% new). Excellent colour; the bouquet is distinctive, with dusty, spicy nuances encircling plummy fruit parlaying into cherry on the gently lively palate, the modest alcohol doubtless playing a role. Screwcap. 13.5% alc. **Rating** 95 **To** 2034 $24 **○**
Touriga Nacional 2013 10% whole bunches, the balance destemmed for whole berries, wild yeast, open-fermented, matured for 23 months in French and

American oak. The distinctly fruity bouquet and juicy, medium-bodied palate sing from the same page, with layers of dark cherry/berry fruit resting on a foundation of soft, but persistent, tannins. A clear validation of the potential of the variety in the Barossa Valley. Screwcap. 14.5% alc. **Rating** 95 **To** 2025 $24 ○

Graciano 2013 Destemmed, wild-fermented; matured in used French oak for 23 months. Vibrant colour; a surprise packet, richer (bordering on luscious) than the relatively few 100% gracianos made in Australia; glossy black cherries fill the supple palate, with a last-minute savoury twist to the finish the icing on the cake. Screwcap. 14.5% alc. **Rating** 95 **To** 2038 $30 ○

Syrah 2013 Whole berries, wild yeast, open-fermented, 4 weeks post-ferment maceration, matured for 23 months in two-thirds new American and one-third used French oak. Attractive medium to full-bodied profile; blackberry and black cherry fruits have a fine-grained tannin support and structure; the oak is well integrated, the tannins soft. Screwcap. 14.5% alc. **Rating** 94 **To** 2033 $24 ○

Old Vine Grenache 2013 Remarkable colour; the vines were 90yo when the grapes were harvested, and this wine reflects that age; it is a celebration of red fruits without any distracting confectionery characters, the only caveat an aftertaste twitch of alcohol. Cork. 15% alc. **Rating** 94 **To** 2023 $40

Sangiovese 2013 Excellent colour; a fragrant and juicy wine with red, morello and black cherries sprinkled with spice; the normally prominent tannins have disappeared, allowing the wine – with its delicious aftertaste – to be drunk whenever you choose. Screwcap. 14% alc. **Rating** 94 **To** 2028 $30 ○

Mencia 2013 There's so much happening on the saturated fruits of the medium to full-bodied palate following the polished leather spice notes of the bouquet it's hard to pinpoint whether it is the blood plum, cherry or raspberry that leads the fruit charge, especially with the hints of spice and violets that linger on the finish. Sure to evolve, but how? A new arrival from Spain. Screwcap. 14.5% alc. **Rating** 94 **To** 2028 $45

♟♟♟♟♀ **Primitivo 2013** Rating 92 To 2025 $30
Aglianico 2013 Rating 92 To 2023 $24 ○
Saperavi 2013 Rating 92 To 2043 $40
Montepulciano 2013 Rating 91 To 2023 $30
Dolcetto 2013 Rating 90 To 2020 $24

Della Fay Wines   ★★★★☆

3276 Caves Road, Yallingup, WA 6284 **Region** Margaret River
T (08) 9755 2747 **www**.kellysvineyard.com.au **Open** By appt
Winemaker Michael Kelly **Est.** 1999 **Dozens** 3000 **Vyds** 8ha
This is the venture of the Kelly family, headed by district veteran Michael Kelly, who gained his degree in wine science from CSU before working at Seville Estate and Mount Mary in the Yarra Valley and Domaine Louis Chapuis in Burgundy, then coming back to WA working for Leeuwin Estate and Sandalford. From there he became the long-term winemaker at Fermoy Estate, but he and his family laid the ground for their own brand, buying prime viticultural land in Caves Road, Yallingup, in 1999. They planted 2ha each of cabernet sauvignon, nebbiolo and sauvignon blanc, and 1ha each of chardonnay and vermentino. Shiraz from the Geographe region also is included. 'Della Fay' honours the eponymous Kelly family matriarch. Exports to The Netherlands, South Korea, Singapore and China.

♟♟♟♟♟ **Margaret River Cabernet Sauvignon 2013** 15yo vines, machine-harvested, crushed/destemmed, open-fermented, cultured yeast, 15 days on skins, matured for 14–16 months in French oak (50% new). Abounds with blackcurrant, black olive and dried herb flavours, these in turn built on a medium-bodied foundation of ripe, but earthy, tannins. The overall balance is perfect, the longevity of the wine not in question. Screwcap. 14% alc. **Rating** 95 **To** 2038 $35 ○

♟♟♟♟♀ **Margaret River Vermentino 2014** Rating 93 To 2020 $18 ○
Geographe Shiraz 2013 Rating 90 To 2025 $30

Denton Viewhill Vineyard

160 Old Healesville Road, Yarra Glen, Vic 3775 **Region** Yarra Valley
T (03) 9012 3600 **www.**dentonwine.com **Open** By appt
Winemaker Luke Lambert **Est.** 1996 **Dozens** 2000 **Vyds** 31.3ha
Leading Melbourne architect John Denton and son Simon began the establishment of the vineyard with a first stage planting in 1997, completing the plantings in 2004. The conjunction of the name Viewhill derives from the fact that a granite plug 'was created 370 million years ago, sitting above the surrounding softer sandstones and silt of the valley'. This granite base is most unusual in the Yarra Valley, and, together with the natural amphitheatre that the plug created, has consistently produced exceptional grapes. The principal varieties planted are pinot noir, chardonnay and shiraz, with lesser quantities of nebbiolo, cabernet sauvignon, merlot, cabernet franc and petit verdot. Most of the grape production is sold, Coldstream Hills a major taker. DM stands for dead mouse. The much liked and respected Luke Lambert has joined Denton Viewhill as chief winemaker.

ŶŶŶŶŶ **DM Chardonnay 2014** Beauty is in the eye of the decanter. This is the kind of chardonnay to benefit greatly from a quick double-decant; it thereafter unfurls to reveal fleshy white peach, honeysuckle, lactose and spicy oak flavours of considerable dimension. It has enough power, enough flavour, majestic length and X-factor. Screwcap. 12.5% alc. **Rating** 96 **To** 2022 $43 CM ✪
DM Shiraz 2014 Standout. Expressive, savoury, peppery shiraz with nutty, cherried fruit blazing across the palate. Creamy, musky oak adds a certain flashiness. It's light on its feet but strong of will. Beautiful now and will age gorgeously. Screwcap. 13.5% alc. **Rating** 96 **To** 2028 $43 CM ✪

ŶŶŶŶŶ **DM Pinot Noir 2014** **Rating** 93 **To** 2022 $43 CM
DM Nebbiolo 2013 **Rating** 93 **To** 2026 $50 CM
Denton Shed Pinot Noir 2015 **Rating** 92 **To** 2017 $30 CM
Denton Shed Cabernet Franc 2015 **Rating** 91 **To** 2025 $30 CM
Denton Shed Chardonnay 2015 **Rating** 90 **To** 2020 $30 CM

Deonte Wines

15 Mary Street, Hawthorn, Vic 3122 **Region** Various
T (03) 9819 4890 **www.**deontewines.com.au **Open** By appt
Winemaker Benjamin Edwards, Jolian Segell **Est.** 2012 **Dozens** 10 000
This is the venture of Zhijun (George) Hu, who has started a virtual winery with the primary purpose of exporting to China and elsewhere in South-East Asia. The initial focus has been on the Yarra Valley, Coonawarra and the Barossa Valley, shiraz figuring prominently, either as a single variety, or as part of a blend with cabernet sauvignon. Having neither a vineyard nor a winery affords George maximum flexibility in purchasing grapes and/or bulk wine. Exports to China.

ŶŶŶŶŶ **Reserve 710 Barossa Valley Shiraz 2014** From old vines, matured in new and used French oak. The palate is luxuriantly full-bodied and velvety, with blackberry tart and dark cherry, the French oak neatly integrated, the tannins supple, and the finish long and layered. Screwcap. 14.3% alc. **Rating** 94 **To** 2029 $59

ŶŶŶŶŶ **Exceptional Barrels Coonawarra Cabernet Sauvignon 2014** **Rating** 93 **To** 2034 $59
Estate 512 Barossa Valley Cabernet Shiraz 2014 **Rating** 91 **To** 2029 $39

Derwent Estate

329 Lyell Highway, Granton, Tas 7070 **Region** Southern Tasmania
T (03) 6263 5802 **www.**derwentestate.com.au **Open** 7 days 10–4
Winemaker John Schuts **Est.** 1992 **Dozens** 2500 **Vyds** 10.08ha
Three generations of the Hanigan family are involved in the management of their historic Mt Nassau property, owned by the family since 1913. Given that over the last 100 years the

property has at various times been involved with sheep, cattle, vegetable production, quarrying and the production of lime, the addition of viticulture in '92 was not surprising. The vineyard has grown in stages, some of the grapes bound for Bay of Fires and Penfolds Yattarna. The grapes retained by Derwent Estate have produced consistently exceptional wines.

ΨΨΨΨΨ **Calcaire Chardonnay 2014** The slightly flinty bouquet sets the antennae waving. Utterly exceptional purity and great line, length and balance. It could come from anywhere, especially Chablis/White Burgundy. Beautiful. Trophies, including Best White Wine of Show, Tasmanian Wine Show '15. Screwcap. 12.8% alc. **Rating** 97 **To** 2024 $75 ✪
Late Harvest Riesling 2015 Hand-picked, cool-fermented, 60g/l residual sugar, 7.5gl acidity, top gold Tasmanian Wine Show '14. Beautifully balanced; blossom, nectar and lime juice define this exquisitely detailed wine. The Tasmanian climate is perfect for this style. Screwcap. 10% alc. **Rating** 97 **To** 2025 $25 ✪

ΨΨΨΨΨ **Chardonnay 2014** 22yo vines, the vineyard having supplied fruit for Penfolds Yattarna for most of that time. Whole bunch-pressed, fermented (plus mlf) and matured in French oak (25% new). Intense wine, with exemplary varietal expression balanced between grapefruit and white peach, the palate fine and long, the oak handling precise. Its great virtue is the way it stealthily, but inexorably, fills the mouth. Screwcap. 13.2% alc. **Rating** 95 **To** 2026 $37
Pinot Noir 2014 22yo vines, six clones, 85% destemmed, 15% whole bunches, open-fermented, wild and cultured yeast, hand-plunged, matured in French oak (25% new). Excellent colour; has all the power and depth that enables Tasmania to meet Central Otago on equal terms, both now ('14) and in the far distant future. Layers of lack cherry, satsuma plum and buckets of spice. Screwcap. 13.7% alc. **Rating** 95 **To** 2027 $37

ΨΨΨΨΨ **Pinot Gris 2015 Rating** 93 **To** 2017 $25 ✪
Riesling 2015 Rating 92 **To** 2020 $25 ✪

Deviation Road ★★★★★

207 Scott Creek Road, Longwood, SA 5153 **Region** Adelaide Hills
T (08) 8339 2633 **www**.deviationroad.com **Open** 7 days 10–5
Winemaker Kate and Hamish Laurie **Est.** 1999 **Dozens** 6000 **Vyds** 11.05ha
Deviation Road was created in 1998 by Hamish Laurie, great-great-grandson of Mary Laurie, SA's first female winemaker. He initially joined with father Dr Chris Laurie in '92 to help build the Hillstowe Wines business; the brand was sold in 2001, but the Laurie family retained the vineyard, which now supplies Deviation Road with its grapes. Wife Kate joined the business in '01, having studied winemaking and viticulture in Champagne, then spent four years at her family's Stone Bridge winery in Manjimup. It also has 3ha of pinot noir and shiraz at Longwood, where its cellar door is situated. Exports to the UK, the US and Hong Kong.

ΨΨΨΨΨ **Mary's Reserve Adelaide Hills Shiraz 2012** Matured for 2 years in French oak. The bouquet has a wealth of red and blue fruits, spices and cedary oak, the elegant medium-bodied palate giving no hint of the alcohol; supple and smooth, it is serenely cruising along. Screwcap. 14.5% alc. **Rating** 95 **To** 2027 $45
Beltana Adelaide Hills Blanc de Blancs 2011 The cool '11 season has charged Beltana with a lightning bolt of acidity, yet, crucially, with a ripeness that keeps its balance in check. Focused lemon and apple fruit are accented with fennel and fleeting nuances of struck flint reduction, underscored by the wonderful, mouthfilling texture of almost 5 years on lees. This is a vintage that promises exceptional endurance. Diam. 12% alc. **Rating** 95 **To** 2031 $85 TS
Adelaide Hills Pinot Gris 2015 80% stainless steel-fermented, 20% barrel-fermented in used oak with lees stirring. The approach works well; the wine has excellent supple texture, allowing the fruit to fully express itself while also finding a way to extend the length and finish. Screwcap. 12.5% alc. **Rating** 94 **To** 2017 $28 ✪

Top Note Block 4 Adelaide Hills Shiraz 2014 Peppermint-cream and black pepper fragrances introduce this pretty Adelaide Hills shiraz. It certainly boasts heightened aromatics. The palate is then all cherry-plum, violet and creamy oak. It's a quality crowd-pleaser. Screwcap. 13.5% alc. **Rating** 94 **To** 2025 $40 CM
Loftia Adelaide Hills Vintage Brut 2013 A magnificently elegant Adelaide Hills sparkling that sings with a more than two-thirds majority of chardonnay, charged with the energy of partial malic acidity and low dosage of 8g/l and softened by almost 3 years on lees. The result is effortlessly harmonious, confidently walking the high-wire between lively fruit expression and graceful restraint. Magnificently crafted. Diam. 12.5% alc. **Rating** 94 **To** 2021 $45 TS
Altair Adelaide Hills Brut Rose NV Gorgeous red cherry and strawberry fruit with pink pepper accents is framed in a lively salmon-pink guise with pinot noir playing a more prominent role than its 20% representation might suggest. The elegance of cool, high Adelaide Hills chardonnay predominantly from the '13 season takes the lead, with almost 3 years of lees age building seamless texture without diminishing youthful fruit expression. Diam. 12.5% alc. **Rating** 94 **To** 2017 $30 TS ✪

🍷🍷🍷🍷🍸 Adelaide Hills Sauvignon Blanc 2015 Rating 93 To 2017 $24 ✪
Top Note Adelaide Hills Noble Rose 2015 Rating 93 To 2019 $24 CM ✪
Adelaide Hills Pinot Noir 2013 Rating 90 To 2025 $45

Devil's Corner   ★★★★★

The Hazards Vineyard, Sherbourne Road, Apslawn, Tas 7190 **Region** East Coast Tasmania
T (03) 6257 8881 **www.**brownbrothers.com.au **Open** 7 days 10–5 (Nov–Apr)
Winemaker Tom Wallace **Est.** 1999 **Dozens** 70 000 **Vyds** 175ha
This is one of the separately managed operations of Brown Brothers' Tasmanian interests, taking The Hazards Vineyard as its chief source of supply. That vineyard is planted to pinot noir, chardonnay, sauvignon blanc, pinot gris, riesling, gewurztraminer and savagnin. The avant garde, striking and (for me) attractive labels mark a decided change from the past, and also distinguish Devil's Corner from the other Tasmanian activities of Brown Brothers.

🍷🍷🍷🍷🍷 Pinot Grigio 2015 Crystal white; citrus juice and zest gets in first, but pear takes hold of the mid-palate before citrus comes back to drive the finish; has energy and interest, doubtless why it was top gold in its class at the Tasmanian Wine Show '16. Screwcap. 12.5% alc. **Rating** 95 **To** 2017 $20 ✪
Resolution Pinot Noir 2014 Hand-picked, open-fermented. This wine has settled down in the way Devil's Corner Mt Amos still needs to achieve, but is nonetheless complex and powerful, inviting comparison to Central Otago pinots. Its colour, depth of flavour and length all promise a smooth transition into full maturity down the track. Screwcap. 13% alc. **Rating** 95 **To** 2029 $30 ✪

🍷🍷🍷🍷🍸 Mt Amos Pinot Noir 2014 Rating 90 To 2029 $65

Devil's Lair   ★★★★★

Rocky Road, Forest Grove via Margaret River, WA 6285 **Region** Margaret River
T 1300 651 650 **www.**devils-lair.com **Open** Not
Winemaker Luke Skeer **Est.** 1981 **Dozens** NFP
Having rapidly carved out a high reputation for itself through a combination of clever packaging and impressive wine quality, Devil's Lair was acquired by Southcorp in 1996. The estate vineyards have been substantially increased since, now with sauvignon blanc, semillon, chardonnay, cabernet sauvignon, merlot, shiraz, cabernet franc and petit verdot, supplemented by grapes purchased from contract growers. An exceptionally successful business; production has increased from 40 000 dozen to many times greater, in no small measure due to its Fifth Leg and Dance With the Devil wines. Exports to the UK, the US and other major markets.

🍷🍷🍷🍷🍷 Cabernet Sauvignon 2013 Highly fragrant; a lovely wine, everything precisely proportioned and placed, cassis fruit the standard bearer, closely followed by the supporting soldiers of immaculate oak and tannins. It is only medium-bodied, yet its purity gives the energy and drive unmatched by many full-bodied cabernets. Screwcap. 14% alc. **Rating** 96 **To** 2038 $50

Chardonnay 2014 A Margaret River classic, even if slightly off to one side with its purity; the winemaking is designed to throw the spotlight on the fruit, use new oak with discretion, and not push the envelope with the baume. Will mature with elegance. Screwcap. 13% alc. **Rating** 95 **To** 2024 $50

Cabernet Sauvignon 2012 A no-nonsense, full-bodied cabernet speaking with equal clarity about its variety and place of origin; tannins and French oak are woven through its intricately textured and structured palate, giving it balance that will ensure its long-term future beyond doubt. It is then (say 15 years) that it will sing loudest. Screwcap. 14.5% alc. **Rating** 95 **To** 2037 $50

♀♀♀♀♀ **The Hidden Cave Chardonnay 2015 Rating** 90 **To** 2019 $23

Dexter Wines   ★★★★★

210 Foxeys Road, Tuerong, Vic 3915 (postal) **Region** Mornington Peninsula
T (03) 5989 7007 **www.**dexterwines.com.au **Open** Not
Winemaker Tod Dexter **Est.** 2006 **Dozens** 1700 **Vyds** 7.1ha
Through a series of events, Tod Dexter arrived in the US with the intention of enjoying some skiing; having done that, he became an apprentice winemaker at Cakebread Cellars, a well-known Napa Valley winery. After seven years he returned to Australia and the Mornington Peninsula, and began the establishment of the vineyard in 1987, planted to pinot noir (4ha) and chardonnay (3.1ha). To keep the wolves from the door he became winemaker at Stonier, and leased his vineyard to Stonier. Having left Stonier to become Yabby Lake winemaker, and spurred on by turning 50 in 2006 (and at the urging of friends), he and wife Debbie established the Dexter label. Exports to the UK, the US, Denmark, Norway and the UAE.

♀♀♀♀♀ **Mornington Peninsula Chardonnay 2014** Essence of chardonnay. Simply glorious. White peach, grapefruit, chalk and spicy, cedary oak. It makes you sit straighter in your chair from the first sip; it's both powerful and complex; it then rockets out through the finish. Screwcap. 13% alc. **Rating** 97 **To** 2022 $40 CM

♀♀♀♀♀ **Mornington Peninsula Pinot Noir 2014** A wine of immediate impact and yet it's not overdone. It's perfumed, plum-rich, gently foresty and deliciously boysenberried. Smoky/spicy oak characters are entirely positive, if not downright seductive. Tobacco-like herb characters keep the sense of engrossing complexity rolling on. Screwcap. 13% alc. **Rating** 96 **To** 2024 $55 CM ⊘

Mornington Peninsula Chardonnay 2015 Such a tight, focused wine. Everything here feels hand-turned and considered. Grapefruit, candied lemon, smoky reduction, a slither of spicy oak; the flavours arc and reach, and ultimately linger. Will develop well. Screwcap. 13.5% alc. **Rating** 95 **To** 2022 $40 CM

Mornington Peninsula Pinot Noir 2015 It's introspective in its youth but it has quality characteristics. Cherry-plum, sure, but tangy cranberry, undergrowth and earth notes lend it a keen savoury edge. The long finish is threaded with fine, herb-flecked tannin. Screwcap. 13.5% alc. **Rating** 94 **To** 2024 $55 CM

di Lusso Estate   ★★★★

Eurunderee Lane, Mudgee, NSW 2850 **Region** Mudgee
T (02) 6373 3125 **www.**dilusso.com.au **Open** Wed–Sat 10–5, Sun 10–4, Mon 10–5
Winemaker Julia Conchie, Robert Paul (Consultant) **Est.** 1998 **Dozens** 5000 **Vyds** 6.5ha
Rob Fairall and partner Luanne Hill have brought to fruition their vision to establish an Italian 'enoteca' operation, offering Italian varietal wines and foods. When they began to plant their vineyard in 1998, the Italian varietal craze was yet to gain serious traction. They now have a thoroughly impressive range of barbera, sangiovese, vermentino, aleatico, lagrein, greco di tufo, picolit and nebbiolo. The estate also produces olives for olive oil and table olives, and the range of both wine and food will increase over the years. The decision to focus on Italian varieties has been a major success, the quality of the wines, however, the key to that success.

ΨΨΨΨ♀ **il Palio 2013** I think the blend of cabernet sauvignon, sangiovese, barbera and shiraz works, and works well with its currant/cherry flavour mix. But I'd like to know what the blend percentages are, if only as a matter of idle curiosity. Screwcap. 13.8% alc. **Rating** 93 **To** 2028 $26 **۞**
Sangiovese 2014 One can argue the toss endlessly about tannins in sangiovese. The problem is sangiovese can't be classified by a book of rules or analysis – and even if there was one, the interpretation would be argued over every bit as much. Is it ok here? Yes, it positively is. And there's bright colour, and lively red cherry fruits. Screwcap. 13.5% alc. **Rating** 92 **To** 2029 $23 **۞**
Cabernet Sauvignon 2014 The first vintage, grown on volcanic soil that faces the afternoon sun (ie west). It is deeply coloured, and very rich, with blackcurrant, plum and built-in tannins; somewhere along the way some dark chocolate has worked its way into the palate. Screwcap. 13% alc. **Rating** 91 **To** 2029 $35
Barbera 2015 Attractive wine; polished black cherry fruit, spice, fine tannins and acidity fit into the box neatly. Screwcap. 13.5% alc. **Rating** 91 **To** 2026 $26
Vermentino 2015 Plenty of aroma and flavour; a mix of dried lemon skin and a sea breeze. Good stuff. Screwcap. 12.9% alc. **Rating** 90 **To** 2018 $23

ΨΨΨΨ **Chardonnay 2015** **Rating** 89 **To** 2023 $26
Pinot Grigio 2015 **Rating** 89 **To** 2017 $26
Mudgee Picolit 2013 **Rating** 89 **To** 2022 $29

DiGiorgio Family Wines   ★★★★

Riddoch Highway, Coonawarra, SA 5263 **Region** Coonawarra
T (08) 8736 3222 **www**.digiorgio.com.au **Open** 7 days 10–5
Winemaker Peter Douglas **Est.** 1998 **Dozens** 25 000 **Vyds** 353.53ha
Stefano DiGiorgio emigrated from Abruzzo, Italy, in 1952. Over the years, he and his family gradually expanded their holdings at Lucindale. In '89 he began planting cabernet sauvignon (99ha), chardonnay (10ha), merlot (9ha), shiraz (6ha) and pinot noir (2ha). In 2002 the family purchased the historic Rouge Homme winery and its surrounding 13.5ha of vines, from Southcorp. Since that time the Coonawarra plantings have been increased to almost 230ha, the lion's share to cabernet sauvignon. The enterprise offers full winemaking services to vignerons in the Limestone Coast Zone. Exports to all major markets.

ΨΨΨΨΨ **Lucindale Limestone Coast Sauvignon Blanc 2015** Partial barrel fermentation in French oak. Clever winemaking had its rewards with a gold medal at the Adelaide Wine Show '15; its texture and structure are first class, allowing the passionfruit, gooseberry and grapefruit trifecta freedom to play without cloying the wine in any way. Screwcap. 12.5% alc. **Rating** 94 **To** 2017 $18 **۞**

ΨΨΨΨ♀ **Lucindale Cabernet Sauvignon 2013** **Rating** 92 **To** 2028 $20 **۞**

Dinny Goonan   ★★★★

880 Winchelsea-Deans Marsh Road, Bambra, Vic 3241 **Region** Geelong
T 0438 408 420 **www**.dinnygoonan.com.au **Open** 7 days Jan, w'ends & public hols Nov–Jun
Winemaker Dinny and Angus Goonan **Est.** 1990 **Dozens** 1500 **Vyds** 5.5ha
The establishment of Dinny Goonan dates back to 1988, when Dinny bought a 20ha property near Bambra, in the hinterland of the Otway Coast. Dinny had recently completed a viticulture diploma at CSU, and initially a wide range of varieties was planted in what is now known as the Nursery Block, to establish those best suited to the area. As these came into production Dinny headed back to CSU, where he completed a wine science degree. Production is focused on shiraz and riesling, with more extensive planting of these varieties.

ΨΨΨΨΨ **Single Vineyard Shiraz 2014** The spices and flavours come at you roly-poly, pell-mell, tumble-bumble. White pepper, twigs, leaves, stems, the lot. It's so full-on that it can be hard to see the fruit for the trees, though (ripe) fruit there certainly is. And ripe tannin too. Indeed, in its style, it's a hard wine to fault. Screwcap. 13% alc. **Rating** 94 **To** 2028 $30 CM **۞**

ŸŸŸŸ♀ Single Vineyard Riesling 2015 Rating 93 To 2022 $25 CM ✪
Museum Release Riesling 2008 Rating 92 To 2020 $25 CM ✪

Dionysus Winery ★★★★☆

1 Patemans Lane, Murrumbateman, NSW 2582 **Region** Canberra District
T (02) 6227 0208 **www**.dionysus-winery.com.au **Open** W'ends & public hols 10–5
Winemaker Michael O'Dea **Est.** 1998 **Dozens** 1000 **Vyds** 4ha
Michael and Wendy O'Dea founded the winery while they had parallel lives as public
servants in Canberra; they have now retired, and devote themselves full-time to Dionysus.
They purchased their property in 1996, and planted chardonnay, sauvignon blanc, riesling,
viognier, merlot, pinot noir, cabernet sauvignon and shiraz between '98 and 2001. Michael has
completed an associate degree in winemaking at CSU, and is responsible for viticulture and
winemaking; Wendy has completed various courses at the Canberra TAFE and is responsible
for wine marketing and (in their words) 'nagging Michael and being a general slushie'.

ŸŸŸŸŸ Canberra District Riesling 2015 Hand-picked, whole bunch-pressed with
cultured yeast, cool-fermented, matured for 3 months on lees in tank. A riesling
that immediately raises the stand and deliver sign with its racy lime juice core
surrounded by mouthwatering acidity. I really like the way it reinforces its message
on the aftertaste. Screwcap. 11.2% alc. **Rating** 95 To 2030 $20 ✪

ŸŸŸŸ♀ Canberra District Shiraz 2014 Rating 90 To 2029 $25

Dirty Three ★★★★★

150 Holgates Road, Leongatha South, Vic 3953 **Region** Gippsland
T 0413 547 932 **www**.dirtythreewines.com.au **Open** By appt
Winemaker Marcus Satchell **Est.** 2012 **Dozens** 500 **Vyds** 4ha
The three people in question are winemaker Marcus Satchell, sales and marketer Cameron
Mackenzie, and PR livewire Stuart Gregor. Each has a real-life job, this simply representing a
bit of (serious) fun. They have acquired a 4ha vineyard planted in 1998 to 3.1ha of pinot noir,
and a total of 0.9ha of riesling and chardonnay.

ŸŸŸŸŸ Holgates Road South Gippsland Pinot Noir 2014 Hand-picked, whole
berry wild-fermented in small open pots, matured for 12 months on lees in
French oak (20% new). Deeply coloured; has admirable depth and length without
any loss of varietal expression – plum and black cherry. Needs time, but will repay
it. Screwcap. 12.9% alc. **Rating** 95 To 2024 $48

Doc Adams ★★★★

2/41 High Street, Willunga, SA 5172 **Region** McLaren Vale
T (08) 8556 2111 **www**.docadamswines.com.au **Open** By appt
Winemaker Adam Jacobs **Est.** 2005 **Dozens** 5000 **Vyds** 27ha
Doc Adams is a partnership between viticulturist Adam Jacobs and orthopaedic surgeon Dr
Darren Waters (and their wives). Adam graduated from CSU with a degree in viticulture and
has had over 20 years' experience as a consultant viticulturist. Darren has grown low-yielding
shiraz vines in McLaren Vale since 1998. Exports to China.

ŸŸŸŸ♀ Grenache Shiraz Mourvedre 2014 Forget the price; the quality is clearly
above its station. There's a heart of licoricey flavour, but the edges are all bright
and raspberried and delicious. Spice notes keep it from seeming too simple. It's
mid-weight, but in the context of these blends it has excellent weight. Screwcap.
14.3% alc. **Rating** 92 To 2020 $16 CM ✪
Cabernet Sauvignon 2014 Varietal, well flavoured, splashed with dust and bay
leaf notes but well set with boysenberry and blackcurrant-like fruit. Hits the nail
on the head. Screwcap. 14.5% alc. **Rating** 90 To 2021 $16 CM ✪

ŸŸŸŸ McLaren Vale Shiraz 2014 Rating 89 To 2021 $25 CM

Dodgy Brothers   ★★★★

PO Box 655, McLaren Vale, SA 5171 **Region** McLaren Vale
T 0450 000 373 **www**.dodgybrotherswines.com **Open** Not
Winemaker Wes Pearson **Est.** 2010 **Dozens** 2000
This is a partnership between Canadian-born Flying Winemaker Wes Pearson, viticulturist
Peter Bolte and grapegrower Peter Sommerville. Wes graduated from the University of British
Columbia's biochemistry program in 2008, along the way working at wineries including
Chateau Leoville Las Cases in Bordeaux. In '08 he and his family moved to McLaren Vale,
and after working at several wineries, he took up a position at the Australian Wine Research
Institute as a sensory analyst. Peter Bolte has over 35 vintages in McLaren Vale under his
belt, and was the original Dodgy Brother. Peter Sommerville's vineyard provides cabernet
sauvignon, cabernet franc and petit verdot for the Dodgy Brothers Bordeaux blend. Exports
to Canada.

ΨΨΨΨΨ **Pinot Gris 2015** From Blewitt Springs, hand-picked, crushed, on skins for
4 hours, pressed, fermented with 30% solids in stainless steel, cold-matured in used
oak to prevent mlf. Pale blush-pink; all this has paid big dividends with a vibrant
gris showing the depth of varietal expression (spiced nashi pear) expected only
from far cooler climates. Screwcap. 12.9% alc. **Rating** 92 **To** 2018 $20 **✪**
DODG Sangiovese 2015 From Blewitt Springs, 35% whole bunches,
fermentation part wild, part cultured yeast, pressed to used puncheons, 160 dozen
made. The colour might well have come from the fermenter to the tasting table,
so vivid is it; the flavours are of cherry and raspberry, and – while intense – are
joyously devoid of obvious tannins. It will be drunk copiously if further bottles are
in reach. Screwcap. 12.5% alc. **Rating** 92 **To** 2018 $22 **✪**

ΨΨΨΨ **Grenache 2014 Rating** 89 **To** 2017 $20
Rose 2015 Rating 88 **To** 2017 $20

DogRidge Wine Company   ★★★★

129 Bagshaws Road, McLaren Flat, SA 5171 **Region** McLaren Vale
T (08) 8383 0140 **www**.dogridge.com.au **Open** 7 days 11–5
Winemaker Fred Howard **Est.** 1991 **Dozens** 10 000 **Vyds** 56ha
Dave and Jen Wright had a combined background of dentistry, art and a CSU viticultural
degree when they moved from Adelaide to McLaren Flat to become vignerons. They
inherited vines planted in the early 1940s as a source for Chateau Reynella fortified wines, and
their vineyards now range from 2001 plantings to some of the oldest vines in the immediate
district. At the McLaren Flat vineyards, DogRidge has 70+-year-old shiraz and grenache. Part
of the grape production is retained, part is sold. Quality at one end, value-packed at the other
end. Exports to the UK, the US and other major markets.

ΨΨΨΨΨ **Most Valuable Player Shiraz 2013** Right in the centre of mainstream
McLaren Vale shiraz from a very good vintage; a harmonious array of both red
and black fruits are cushioned by fine tannins and well-integrated oak, all in a
medium-bodied frame. Screwcap. 15% alc. **Rating** 93 **To** 2028 $65
All-Rounder Grenache 2014 From 75yo estate vines. The colour is light,
although bright, the bouquet and medium to full-bodied palate a pure reflection
of the variety and place; the red fruits at its core are polished by juicy acidity, and
framed by fine tannins. Screwcap. 14.5% alc. **Rating** 92 **To** 2029 $25 **✪**
Shirtfront Shiraz 2014 A deeply coloured, powerful, concentrated wine with
ripe tannins woven through blackberry fruit, licorice and a touch of bitter
chocolate. All up, has been well named – give it time to loosen its grip and you
will be rewarded. Screwcap. 14.5% alc. **Rating** 91 **To** 2034 $25
Grand Old Brand New Cabernet Sauvignon Shiraz Petit Verdot 2013
Vivid, deep crimson-purple; the cabernet and shiraz vines are 70yo, the petit
verdot 5yo, hence the name; it overflows with black fruits and tannins; I think
the balance is there, but the tannins are still dry and brutish. Time is of the
essence – a bare minimum of 5 years, preferably 10. Screwcap. 15% alc. **Rating** 91
To 2038 $40

The Pup Sauvignon Blanc 2015 A pretty smart sauvignon blanc for McLaren Vale, with bright tropical aromas and flavours, highlighted by juicy acidity. Another glass, please. Screwcap. 13% alc. **Rating** 90 To 2016 $18 ○

ŶŶŶŶ **The Pup Chardonnay 2013** Rating 89 To 2020 $18 ○
The Pup Shiraz 2014 Rating 89 To 2024 $18 ○
The Pup GSM 2014 Rating 89 To 2020 $18 ○
Canvas Shiraz Petit Verdot Grenache Cabernet 2013 Rating 88 To 2017 $10 ○
The Pup McLaren Vale Cabernet Merlot 2014 Rating 88 To 2017 $18

DogRock Winery ★★★★★

114 Degraves Road, Crowlands, Vic 3377 **Region** Pyrenees
T 0409 280 317 **www**.dogrock.com.au **Open** By appt
Winemaker Allen Hart **Est.** 1999 **Dozens** 500 **Vyds** 6.2ha
This is the micro-venture of Allen (now full-time winemaker) and Andrea (viticulturist) Hart. Having purchased the property in 1998, the planting of shiraz, riesling, tempranillo, grenache, chardonnay and marsanne began in 2000. Given Allen's former post as research scientist/winemaker with Foster's, the attitude taken to winemaking is unexpected. The estate-grown wines are made in a low-tech fashion, without gas cover or filtration, the Harts saying 'all wine will be sealed with a screwcap and no DogRock wine will ever be released under natural cork bark'. DogRock installed the first solar-powered irrigation system in Australia, capable of supplying water 365 days a year, even at night or in cloudy conditions.

ŶŶŶŶŶ **Pyrenees Shiraz 2013** Hand-picked, wild yeast open-fermented, 6–7 days on skins, basket-pressed, 14 months 60% new oak (85% French, 15% American). Exceptional deep crimson-purple colour; layer upon layer of blackberry, plum and licorice fruit on the medium to full-bodied palate; savoury tannins provide exactly the right response to the well of fruit. Cruising along, with little change over the past 10 months. Screwcap. 14% alc. **Rating** 95 To 2033 $25 ○
Degraves Road Pyrenees Chardonnay 2015 Hand-picked, wild yeast-fermented, matured on lees in French oak. A complex, well-balanced and full-flavoured palate with citrus, melon and white peach joined by nutty oak on a supple, creamy mouthfeel before acidity comes through on the finish. Likely best over the next few years. Screwcap. 12.5% alc. **Rating** 94 To 2020 $22 ○

ŶŶŶŶŶ **Pyrenees Riesling 2015** Rating 93 To 2025 $22 ○
Degraves Road Pyrenees Grenache 2014 Rating 93 To 2024 $35
Degraves Road Pyrenees Shiraz 2014 Rating 92 To 2034 $35
Pyrenees Shiraz 2014 Rating 91 To 2029 $25

Dolan Family Wines ★★★★

PO Box 500, Angaston, SA 5353 **Region** Barossa Valley
T 0438 816 034 **www**.dolanfamilywines.com.au **Open** Not
Winemaker Nigel and Timothy Dolan **Est.** 2007 **Dozens** 1000
Nigel is a fifth-generation member of the Dolan family, son Tim the sixth: truly, wine is in their blood. Nigel's father Bryan enrolled in the first oenology course offered by Roseworthy, graduating in 1949. His 30-year career at Saltram included the capture of the inaugural Jimmy Watson Trophy in '62. There was no nepotism involved when Nigel was appointed chief winemaker of Saltram in 1992, winning major accolades during his 15 years in that role. Currently he is a consulting winemaker as well as having principal responsibility for Dolan Family Wines. Nigel's son Tim is a graduate of the Adelaide University oenology course, and has worked internationally as well as in Australia. This is a virtual winery business for both, with neither vineyards nor winery – just lots of experience. Exports to Hong Kong.

ŶŶŶŶŶ **Barossa Valley Grenache Shiraz Mataro 2013** 45/40/15%, matured for 12 months in used French oak. A luscious, supple wine, replete with equal amounts of red and black fruits at play, tannin and oak extract precisely programmed in support. Great value, especially in the context of most Barossa Valley GSMs. Screwcap. 14.5% alc. **Rating** 91 **To** 2023 $25

ΨΨΨΨ **Barossa Shiraz 2013 Rating** 89 **To** 2023 $48
Rifleman's Clare Valley Riesling 2015 Rating 88 **To** 2020 $20

Domain Day ★★★★

24 Queen Street, Williamstown, SA 5351 **Region** Barossa Valley
T (08) 8524 6224 **www**.domainday.com.au **Open** 7 days 12–5
Winemaker Robin Day **Est.** 2000 **Dozens** 8000 **Vyds** 15.5ha
This is a classic case of an old dog learning new tricks, and doing so with panache. Robin Day had a long and distinguished career as chief winemaker and technical director of Orlando. He hastened slowly with the establishment of Domain Day, but there is nothing conservative about his approach in his vineyard at Mt Crawford, high in the hills (at 450m) of the southeastern extremity of the Barossa Valley, two sides of the vineyard bordering the Eden Valley. While the mainstream varieties are merlot, pinot noir and riesling, he has trawled Italy, France and Georgia for the other varieties: viognier, sangiovese, saperavi, lagrein, garganega, sagrantino and nebbiolo. Robin says, 'Years of writing descriptions for back labels have left me convinced that this energy is more gainfully employed in growing grapes and making wine.' Exports to Canada and China.

ΨΨΨΨΨ **One Serious Mt Crawford Riesling 2015** Other than three cultured yeasts to create greater complexity, standard cool fermentation in stainless steel. Crisp and lively, it has a classic lime/lemon/apple mix of fruits supported by crisp acidity, the palate bone dry. Screwcap. 12.8% alc. **Rating** 91 **To** 2015 $22 ❂
One Serious Mt Crawford Pinot Noir 2013 Seven clones; 30% whole bunches, Burgundian yeast (absorbs less colour/phenolics), matured in French hogsheads. An unusual bouquet and palate with pine needles and mint threaded through red fruits. Screwcap. 13.5% alc. **Rating** 90 **To** 2018 $35

Domaine A ★★★★★

105 Tea Tree Road, Campania, Tas 7026 **Region** Southern Tasmania
T (03) 6260 4174 **www**.domaine-a.com.au **Open** Mon–Fri 10–4
Winemaker Peter Althaus **Est.** 1973 **Dozens** 5000 **Vyds** 11ha
The striking black label of the premium Domaine A wine, dominated by the single multicoloured 'A', signified the change of ownership from George Park to Peter Althaus many years ago. The wines are made without compromise, and reflect the low yields from the immaculately tended vineyards. They represent aspects of both Old World and New World philosophies, techniques and styles. Exports to the UK, Canada, Denmark, Switzerland, Taiwan, Hong Kong, Singapore, Japan and China.

ΨΨΨΨΨ **Cabernet Sauvignon 2008** 90% cabernet sauvignon, 4% each of cabernet franc and merlot, 2% petit verdot; matured in new French barriques for 30 months. This seems to be going from strength to strength as the fruit, oak, and the tannins in particular, have welded together in a totally symbiotic fashion. It is still unique in the Australian context, but would fit seamlessly into the fabric of Bordeaux. Another point for its elegant maturity and reassuringly unmarked cork. 14% alc. **Rating** 96 **To** 2028 $120
Lady A Sauvignon Blanc 2014 Small batches from the 1h estate vineyard fermented in new French barriques, matured on fine lees for 12 months, and aged for 2 further years before release. Stands on its own in Australia with its weight and richness; this release is more tropical than prior years, and raises the question whether the fermentation proceeded to absolute dryness; the other possibility is sweetness from the high alcohol. Cork. 15% alc. **Rating** 94 **To** 2017 $60
Merlot 2010 Open-fermented, hand-plunged, matured in French barriques (50% new) for 24 months. Firm and savoury, but also with a generous helping of forest fruits; it is resolutely in Old World style, marching to the tune of its own (and Tasmania's) drum. Cork. 14% alc. **Rating** 94 **To** 2030 $85

Petit a 2010 The colour is exceptional for a 6yo wine, as is its freshness. A 60/35/4/1% blend of cabernet sauvignon, merlot, cabernet franc and petit verdot. The high percentage of merlot is intended to make this a quick-developing wine, although matured in used French barriques for 2 years, plus further time in the cellar until it is judged ready. Judged by normal standards, extremely full-bodied, but by those of Domain A, less so. And indeed the palate borders on outright juicy, with cassis, redcurrant, mulberry and spice. Cork. 14% alc. **Rating** 94 **To** 2025 $45

♀♀♀♀♀ Lady A Sauvignon Blanc 2012 Rating 93 To 2020 $60

Domaine Asmara

Gibb Road, Toolleen, Vic 3551 **Region** Heathcote
T (03) 5433 6133 **www**.domaineasmara.com **Open** 7 days 9–6.30
Winemaker Sanguine Estate **Est.** 2008 **Dozens** 2000 **Vyds** 12ha
Chemical engineer Andreas Greiving had a lifelong dream to own and operate a vineyard, and the opportunity came along with the global financial crisis. He was able to purchase a vineyard planted to shiraz (7ha), cabernet sauvignon (2ha), cabernet franc, durif and viognier (1ha each), and have the wines contract-made. The venture is co-managed by dentist wife Hennijati. Exports to the UK and China.

♀♀♀♀♀ Reserve Heathcote Cabernet Sauvignon 2014 Densely fruited and super-ripe but with just enough tannin to keep it from falling over itself. This is more for lovers of Big Reds than it is for cabernet lovers; it's more about volume than variety. The way it hits up with flavour, though, is certainly impressive. Cork. 14.7% alc. **Rating** 94 **To** 2024 $45 CM

♀♀♀♀♀ Infinity Shiraz 2014 Rating 93 To 2025 $75 CM
Private Collection Heathcote Shiraz 2014 Rating 93 To 2023 $35 CM
Reserve Heathcote Shiraz 2013 Rating 90 To 2024 $45 CM

 # Domaine Dawnelle ★★★★

PO Box 89, Claremont, Tas 7011 **Region** Southern Tasmania
T 0447 484 181 **www**.domainedawnelle.com **Open** Not
Winemaker Michael O'Brian **Est.** 2013 **Dozens** 200 **Vyds** 11ha
Domaine Dawnelle is a partnership between Michael O'Brien and Kylie Harrison. The name of the venture honours Michael's great-grandmother (and farm) in rural NSW. He studied at Charles Sturt University, and is a qualified viticulturalist and winemaker with 20 years experience in mainland Australia, abroad and, more recently, Tasmania. As well as planting 1.5ha of vineyard overlooking the Derwent River, he manages the Tinderbox Vineyard, providing the partnership with grapes until the estate vineyard comes into full bearing.

♀♀♀♀♀ Gloria Chardonnay 2015 Whole bunch-pressed, wild-fermented in oak, stirred until bottled. The age of the barriques isn't specified, but it's unlikely the percentage of new oak was high. Domaine Dawnelle is one of only a few using one-piece cork in chardonnay. Cork. 13.2% alc. **Rating** 94 **To** 2025 $46

♀♀♀♀♀ Chardonnay 2015 Rating 90 To 2023 $36

Domaine de Binet

469 Lovedale Road, Lovedale, NSW 2320 **Region** Hunter Valley
T 0418 211 378 **Open** Fri–Mon 10–4
Winemaker Daniel Binet **Est.** 2013 **Dozens** 2000
Domaine de Binet is the family label of Hunter Valley winemaker Daniel Binet. Daniel has been a winemaker for over 18 years in the region, and wine show judge domestically and internationally for the last 10 years. In 2008, Daniel became director for Ballabourneen Wine Co in partnership with Alex Stuart OAM of the former Stuart Bros Construction Company. His family label, Domaine de Binet, provides an opportunity to experiment with different wine varietals and alternative winemaking techniques.

♀♀♀♀♀ **Accidental Tourist Hunter Valley Grenache Barbera Nebbiolo 2014**
Harvested and fermented together. Essentially this is jubey and delicious but
it then turns peppery and tannic on the finish. Hello nebbiolo. It drinks like a
charm. Screwcap. 14% alc. **Rating** 92 **To** 2021 $25 CM ✪

Hunter Valley Petit Verdot 2014 Characterful. Let's call it that. It's reductive
and shot with plum/blackcurrant and redolent of hung game. It challenges as it
seduces. It's a brainteaser. Screwcap. 14.8% alc. **Rating** 91 **To** 2021 $25 CM

Hunter Valley Pinot Grigio 2015 Vivid colour, rose-esque. A slink of fruit
sweetness adds a roar to the strawberried fruit flavour, citrus and cranberry then
racing out through the finish. Moreish. Screwcap. 12% alc. **Rating** 90 **To** 2017
$25 CM

Hunter Valley Tempranillo 2014 Juicy red with added X-factor. Red berries
flood the palate with flavour and flesh, aided by anise and dried spice. It's the
subtle meatiness, though, giving it that extra edge. Screwcap. 13.5% alc. **Rating** 90
To 2020 $25 CM

♀♀♀♀ **Granite Belt Shiraz Cabernet 2014 Rating** 88 **To** 2019 $35 CM

Domaine Naturaliste   ★★★★★

Cnr Hairpin Road/Bussell Highway, Carbunup, WA 6280 **Region** Margaret River
T (08) 9755 1188 **www.**domainenaturaliste.com.au **Open** Not
Winemaker Bruce Dukes **Est.** 2012 **Dozens** 4000
Bruce Dukes' career dates back over 25 years, its foundations built around a degree
in agronomy from the University of WA, followed by a master's degree in viticulture and
agronomy from the University of California, Davis thence to a four-year stint at Francis Ford
Coppola's iconic Niebaum-Coppola winery in the Napa Valley. Back in WA he worked with
a consultancy and contract winemaking business in Margaret River in 2000. The winery was
set up to handle small and large amounts of fruit, but it was not until '12 that he moved to set
up his own winemaking business. Exports to the UK and Canada.

♀♀♀♀♀ **Morus Cabernet Sauvignon 2013** A wall of flavour abuts a wall of tannin. This
is a three-course dinner in liquid form, its density and architectural style both cut
from the finest of cloths and sprinkled with perfume. Naming blackcurrant, gravel,
cloves and dark chocolate doesn't do any kind of justice. We're much better off
simply calling it as it is: a brilliant wine. Cork. 13.5% alc. **Rating** 98 **To** 2045 $85
CM ✪

Morus Cabernet Sauvignon 2012 A full-bodied wine of remarkable intensity,
filling every crevice of the mouth with a pure stream of cassis and mulberry fruit,
oak and tannins dutifully lending support, but remaining in their place, simply
reinforcing the inherent elegance of the wine. ProCork. 13.5% alc. **Rating** 97
To 2032 $85 ✪

♀♀♀♀♀ **Artus Chardonnay 2014** Bright straw-green; it's far harder than it might seem
to combine complexity with purity and elegance; this has an entrancing lightness
of touch not commonly encountered in the normal profundity of Margaret River
chardonnay. This sits comfortably alongside the best of the region, and will be
unusually long-lived. Screwcap. 13% alc. **Rating** 96 **To** 2025 $47 ✪

Rachis Syrah 2014 It's medium weight and yet it announces its quality in
emphatic fashion. The filigreed tannin, the mix of savouriness and fruitiness, the
smoky sophistication of the finish. Value, all things considered, doesn't come much
better. Screwcap. 13.5% alc. **Rating** 96 **To** 2034 $29 CM ✪

Floris Chardonnay 2014 The focus is on varietal fruit, led by grapefruit,
then stone fruit; freshness comes vibrant acidity, and a tight control on the oak
contribution. Totally delicious now, but it will hold its form for the rest of the
decade (and beyond). Screwcap. 13.5% alc. **Rating** 95 **To** 2021 $30 ✪

Rebus Cabernet Sauvignon 2014 Medium weight tipping into full-bodied.
Blackberry, wood smoke, cassis, bay and gravel-like notes make a confident sweep
through the palate, taking grainy tannin in their stride. Screwcap. 13.8% alc.
Rating 95 **To** 2035 $33 CM ✪

Rebus Cabernet Sauvignon 2013 Bright colour; a winemaker's cabernet, with a fragrant cassis-accented bouquet, book-ended by persistent tannins typical of cabernet gliding elegantly along the medium-bodied palate between the book ends. Screwcap. 13.8% alc. **Rating** 95 **To** 2028 $34 **○**

Cabernet Sauvignon 2013 Incorporates some (less than 15%) malbec for red-fruit fragrance and fleshy tannins that have a disproportionate (but very good) influence on the overall flavour and mouthfeel of the wine. It has been so cleverly built that the price seems absurdly low – a gift horse with gold horseshoes. Screwcap. 14% alc. **Rating** 95 **To** 2023 $24 **○**

Sauvage Sauvignon Blanc Semillon 2014 Yes it has intensity and yes it persists beautifully through the finish, but it stakes its biggest quality claim on a less tangible arena: the shape of the wine as it passes through the mouth. It feels like the handiwork of someone with a keen eye for the design of flavours and textures. Screwcap. 13% alc. **Rating** 94 **To** 2018 $29 CM **○**

Purus Chardonnay 2014 It glows and glistens, seduces and satisfies. It's pure Margaret River chardonnay, done well, given some weight and some oak but ultimately allowed to flow smartly through a steely, sustained finish. Screwcap. 13% alc. **Rating** 94 **To** 2021 $43 CM

Domaine Rogha Crois Wines

73 Joe Rocks Road, Bungendore, NSW 2621 **Region** Canberra District
T 0411 228 839 **www.**drcwine.com.au **Open** By appt
Winemaker Malcolm Burdett, Andrew McEwin **Est.** 1998 **Dozens** 400 **Vyds** 2ha
David and Lyn Crossley purchased their property on the Lake George escarpment in 1998, planting clonally selected pinot noir, pinot gris, cabernet franc and merlot over the following 2 years, their inspiration the pioneering work done by Dr Edgar Riek. The vineyard is on a steep hillside at 800–840m, often snow-covered in winter, but protected from frosts by its slope. The small size of the vineyard facilitates micromanagement of the vines throughout the year. The name is Gaelic for 'quality cross'.

ΨΨΨΨΨ Barrel Select Pinot Noir 2013 10% whole bunches, 7 days cold soak, wild ferment to start then cultured yeast, 13 months in French barriques (50% new). Relatively delicate, it is remarkable how it has largely absorbed the new oak, leaving small red fruits at its heart. Screwcap. 13.9% alc. **Rating** 91 **To** 2020 $53

Domaines & Vineyards

PO Box 6096, Swanbourne, WA 6010 **Region** Western Australia
T (08) 6555 3280 **www.**dandv.com.au **Open** Not
Winemaker Robert Bowen **Est.** 2009 **Dozens** 10 000
One of the best-known winemakers in WA is Rob Bowen, with over 35 years' experience with several of WA's leading wineries, most recently Houghton. In 2009 he joined forces with a team of viticulturists (led by David Radomilijac) who collectively furnish the project with an extensive range of knowledge and expertise. The theme is to produce premium wines with a strong sense of place through a virtual winery exercise, all grapes to be hand-picked from the best available vineyards in the Margaret River and Pemberton regions. Two ranges of wines are produced: Robert Bowen (from Margaret River and Pemberton) and Pemberley (from the Pemberley Farms Vineyard owned by David). Exports to the UK, the US, China, Singapore and Hong Kong.

ΨΨΨΨΨ Robert Bowen Margaret River Chardonnay 2014 Whole bunch-pressed, wild-fermented in French barriques (50% new), matured for 10 months. A vibrant and intense palate with mouthwatering freshness. It has also effortlessly absorbed 50% new oak. A long and prosperous life lies ahead. Screwcap. 14% alc. **Rating** 95 **To** 2024 $60

Pemberley Pemberton Pinot Noir Rose 2015 Hand-picked, crushed and pressed, wild-fermented in used French barriques, 6 months on lees. Pale salmon; an unqualified success; a spicy, powdery rose hip/rose petal bouquet heralds a palate abounding with strawberry fruit and spices before finishing dry. Classic Provençale (at its best). Screwcap. 13% alc. **Rating** 95 **To** 2017 $25 ✪

Pemberley Pemberton Sauvignon Blanc 2015 90% crushed and pressed to tank for cultured yeast fermentation, 10% fermented in new Hungarian barriques. An attractive sauvignon, with passionfruit illuminating its bouquet and leading the palate, citrussy acidity falling in behind until it joins with acidity on the lively finish. Screwcap. 13% alc. **Rating** 94 **To** 2017 $25 ✪

 🍷🍷🍷🍷 **Robert Bowen Pemberton Pinot Noir 2014** Rating 89 To 2020 $45
Robert Bowen Swan Valley Shiraz 2014 Rating 88 To 2030 $45

Domaines Tatiarra ★★★★

2 Corrong Court, Eltham, Vic 3095 (postal) **Region** Heathcote
T 0428 628 420 **www**.tatiarra.com **Open** Not
Winemaker Ben Riggs **Est.** 1991 **Dozens** 5000 **Vyds** 13.4ha
Owned by a group of investors, Domaines Tatiarra's core asset is a 60ha property of Cambrian earth identified and developed by Bill Hepburn, who sold it to the investors in 1991. It produces only one varietal wine: shiraz. The majority of the wine comes from the Tatiarra (an Aboriginal word meaning 'beautiful country') property, but the Trademark Shiraz is an equal blend of McLaren Vale and Heathcote wine. The wines are made at the Scotchmans Hill winery in Geelong, with Ben Riggs commuting between there and McLaren Vale as required. Exports to the UK, the US, Canada, Denmark, Switzerland, Singapore and China.

🍷🍷🍷🍷🍷 **Cambrian Heathcote Shiraz 2013** The deep, dense colour heralds an uncompromisingly full-bodied wine, crammed with black fruits, graphite, bitter chocolate and tannins; oak adds its support to a wine with a very, very long future. Screwcap. 14.8% alc. **Rating** 93 **To** 2043 $32

Caravan of Dreams Heathcote Shiraz Pressings 2013 Matured in new American oak for 12 months. The inky purple-crimson colour is no surprise, nor is the unbridled power of the full-bodied palate; it has a problem of alcohol-induced warmth on the finish. This is, without question, the thumbprint of winemaker Ben Riggs. Screwcap. 15% alc. **Rating** 93 **To** 2043 $62

Culled Barrel Heathcote Shiraz 2013 Not for the first time, the Culled Barrel is the best value of the three '13 Tatiarra Shirazs. It has the same deep colour, opulent fruit, generous oak, abundant tannins and alcohol. If that (the alcohol) doesn't bother you, this is a super special. Screwcap. 15% alc. **Rating** 91 **To** 2033 $22 ✪

Dominique Portet ★★★★★

870–872 Maroondah Highway, Coldstream, Vic 3770 **Region** Yarra Valley
T (03) 5962 5760 **www**.dominiqueportet.com **Open** 7 days 10–5
Winemaker Ben Portet **Est.** 2000 **Dozens** 15 000 **Vyds** 4.3ha
Dominique Portet was bred in the purple. He spent his early years at Chateau Lafite (where his father was régisseur) and was one of the first Flying Winemakers, commuting to Clos du Val in the Napa Valley, where his brother was winemaker. He then spent over 20 years as managing director of Taltarni and Clover Hill. After retiring from Taltarni, he moved to the Yarra Valley, a region he had been closely observing since the mid-1980s. In 2001 he found the site he had long looked for and built his winery and cellar door, planting a quixotic mix of viognier, sauvignon blanc and merlot next to the winery. Son Ben is now executive winemaker, leaving Dominique with a roving role as de facto consultant and brand marketer. Ben (35) has a winemaking CV of awesome scope, covering all parts of France, South Africa, California and four vintages at Petaluma. Exports to the UK, Canada, Denmark, India, Dubai, Hong Kong, Singapore, Malaysia, China and Japan.

🍷🍷🍷🍷🍷 **Andre Pierre Yarra Valley Pyrenees Cabernet Sauvignon 2012** Destemmed and sorted by Oscillys, 4 weeks on skins, pressed and matured for 18 months in French oak (60% new). This richly deserved its trophy at the Yarra

Valley Wine Show. It is a superb wine, starting with the grapes I witnessed coming through the Oscillys, but never dreaming the perfect winemaking that would follow. Blackberry/cassis fruit has absorbed the French oak, and the tannins are magical, firm yet accommodating. The price reflects the quality of the wine. Cork. 13.9% alc. **Rating** 97 **To** 2047 $150 ✪

πππππ **Origine Yarra Valley Chardonnay 2014** Clear glass packaging is innovative, the move to secure grapes from mature vines in the Upper Yarra simply a smart one. A clearly articulated vision of the best of the Upper Yarra has resulted in a beautiful wine with intense varietal white peach, white flowers and grapefruit on the bouquet and palate; the length of the palate and clarity of the finish are exemplary, the price attractive. Screwcap. 13% alc. **Rating** 96 **To** 2022 $40 ✪
Yarra Valley Cabernet Sauvignon 2013 From two Yarra Valley vineyards with very different aspect and terroir, plus 5% merlot from the home block, hand-picked, and Oscillys berry-by-berry sorted, 3-day cold soak, 4-week fermentation/maceration, matured for 15 months in French oak (40% new). Trophy Yarra Valley Wine Show '15. Cool, elegant and intense, its black fruits shimmering with energy, and promising a great future. Cork. 14% alc. **Rating** 96 **To** 2038 $55 ✪
Heathcote Shiraz 2013 The cutting edge sorting gives the wine a flying start as it is fermented in stainless steel for 25 days before 15 months maturation in French oak (25% new). Cool winemaking has resulted in an elegant and supple wine, with a silky mouthfeel and marvellous length. Cork. 13.5% alc. **Rating** 95 **To** 2038 $48
Yarra Valley Brut Rose LD NV This is a traditional method 50% pinot noir, 30% chardonnay, 20% pinot meunier. Held on lees for 2 years prior to disgorgement and a light dosage. A totally delicious and elegantly poised wine, with fresh red fruits of every description dancing around on the bouquet and palate alike, the finish harmonious. Cork. 13% alc. **Rating** 94 **To** 2017 $28 ✪

πππππ **Fontaine Yarra Valley Rose 2015 Rating** 92 **To** 2017 $22 ✪
Yarra Valley Sauvignon Blanc 2015 Rating 90 **To** 2017 $28

Dorrien Estate   ★★★★★

Cnr Barossa Valley Way/Siegersdorf Road, Tanunda, SA 5352 **Region** Barossa Valley
T (08) 8561 2200 **www.**cellarmasters.com.au **Open** Not
Winemaker Corey Ryan (Chief) **Est.** 1982 **Dozens** 1 million
Dorrien Estate is the physical base of the vast Cellarmasters network that is the largest direct-sale outlet in Australia. It also makes wine for many producers across Australia at its modern winery, which has a capacity of 14.5 million litres in tank and barrel; however, a typical make of each wine will be little more than 1000 dozen. Most of the wines made for others are exclusively distributed by Cellarmasters. Acquired by Woolworths in May 2011.

πππππ **Mockingbird Hill Single Vineyard Skilly Block Clare Valley Riesling 2015** Slatey talcum powder and mineral, the classic template for Clare riesling, long and minerally. Will unfold generously over the next decade. Screwcap. 12.5% alc. **Rating** 95 **To** 2030 $38
Redemption Landmark Release Tumbarumba Chardonnay 2014 Grapefruit, melon and stone fruit all contribute on the bouquet; the medium-bodied palate is finely balanced and jammed with grapefruit and an almost lime-like acidity. Screwcap. 12.5% alc. **Rating** 94 **To** 2024 $42
Redemption Canberra District Shiraz 2014 A fragrant, spicy, pepper-infused and punchy bouquet, the palate replete with spice and grippy tannins. Lots of personality and drive. Screwcap. 13% alc. **Rating** 94 **To** 2024 $28 ✪
Krondorf Symmetry Barossa Shiraz 2013 The extremely deep colour leads to a black fruit-saturated bouquet, the palate plush and expansive with fine, but grippy, tannins to close. Screwcap. 14.5% alc. **Rating** 94 **To** 2033 $45

πππππ **Dorrien Estate Bin 1A Chardonnay 2014 Rating** 93 **To** 2020 $31
Yarra View Reserve Pinot Noir 2014 Rating 93 **To** 2024 $32

Mockingbird Hill MCR Block Shiraz 2014 Rating 93 To 2030 $64
Dorrien Estate Bin 1A Shiraz 2013 Rating 93 To 2032 $38
Black Wattle Vineyards Cabernet Sauvignon 2013 Rating 93 To 2028 $46

DOWIE DOOLE

276 California Road, McLaren Vale, SA 5171 **Region** McLaren Vale
T (08) 8323 8875 **www**.dowiedoole.com **Open** 7 days 10–5
Winemaker Chris Thomas **Est.** 1995 **Dozens** 25 000 **Vyds** 80ha
DOWIE DOOLE was founded in 1995 by Drew Dowie and Norm Doole. They had been
connected to the McLaren Vale community for many years and are renowned grapegrowers
in the region. In 2011 Brian Light passed the winemaking baton to his long-time protégé
Chris Thomas. Chris proudly continues the tradition of making outstanding wines from the
Dowie and Doole estate vineyards. Vineyard management is led by champions of sustainable
viticulture practices Dave Gartlemann and Drew Dowie. In May '16, with winemaker and
managing director Chris Thomas leading a group of like-minded investors, DOWIE DOOLE
acquired the 35ha of vines on the 53ha Conte Tatachilla Vineyard book-ended by 50-year-old
bushvine grenache and recently grafted ('12) vermentino, aglianico and lagrein. Exports to
all major markets.

🍷🍷🍷🍷🍷 **Reserve Shiraz 2013** A worthy follow-up to the excellent '12. The aromas are
classic McLaren Vale shiraz: plum, and a hint of spice wrapped in classy French oak.
The palate is a delicious melange of fruit, tannin and spice-laden oak; long and
well framed. Diam. 14.5% alc. **Rating** 95 To 2036 $80
Estate Shiraz 2014 Dark red; a purely fruited and aromatic bouquet, has plum
and dark fruits wrapped neatly in well-handled oak; fine, rounded and well
balanced, it admirably handles its concentrated fruit, and finishes long and fine.
Screwcap. 14% alc. **Rating** 94 To 2028 $25 ⊙
The Architect Blewitt Springs Shiraz 2013 From the Blewitt Springs district,
it is a distinctly individual expression. Spice, earth, dried herbs and hint of eucalypt
lead to a fine and silky palate that builds into a lithe and lengthy savoury finish.
Diam. 14.5% alc. **Rating** 94 To 2028 $66
The Teacher Willunga Foothills Shiraz 2013 Two contrasting expressions
of McLaren Vale shiraz. This release couldn't be any greater in flavour and size
than The Architect Blewitt Springs. Dark-fruited, saturated and powerful, it is
more classic McLaren Vale, The Architect lean, savoury and lithe. Diam. 14.5% alc.
Rating 94 To 2033 $66

🍷🍷🍷🍷🍷 **Tintookie Chenin Blanc 2012 Rating** 92 To 2022 $40
Blanc² 2015 Rating 92 To 2017 $35
G&T Grenache & Tempranillo 2015 Rating 92 To 2025 $25 ⊙

Drake

PO Box 417, Hamilton, NSW 2303 **Region** Yarra Valley
T 0417 670 655 **www**.drakesamson.com.au **Open** Not
Winemaker Mac Forbes, Matt Dunne **Est.** 2012 **Dozens** 600
Drake is a handshake business of Nicholas Crampton, winemaker Matt Dunne, and a friend
of Nicholas, Andrew Dunn. Mac Forbes is the executive winemaker for wines made in the
Yarra Valley, it being the intention to focus future activities on the Yarra. There will be further
wines made in NZ. Quality is uniformly high.

🍷🍷🍷🍷🍷 **Samson Yarra Valley Pinot Noir 2014** From Coldstream, Yarra Junction and
Seville, 10% whole bunches, 'foot stooping' (presumably foot stomping), matured
for 11 months in French oak (20% new). Striking label design. A highly fragrant
and expressive bouquet, then a palate with authority and class stamped all over
it; the rainbow of red fruits arcs over a hill of bramble and twigs. Lovely stuff.
Screwcap. 13% alc. **Rating** 96 To 2025 $35 ⊙

♀♀♀♀♀ Yarra Valley Chardonnay 2015 Rating 92 To 2026 $20 ✿
Strathbogie Ranges Pinot Noir 2015 Rating 91 To 2022 $20 ✿

Drayton's Family Wines   ★★★★☆

555 Oakey Creek Road, Cessnock, NSW 2321 **Region** Hunter Valley
T (02) 4998 7513 **www**.draytonswines.com.au **Open** Mon–Fri 8–5, w'ends 10–5
Winemaker Edgar Vales, Max and John Drayton **Est.** 1853 **Dozens** 40000 **Vyds** 72ha
This substantial Hunter Valley producer has suffered more than its share of misfortune over
the years, but has risen to the challenges. Edgar Vales is the chief winemaker after previous
experience as assistant winemaker with David Hook and First Creek Wines. His arrival
coincided with the release of a range of high quality wines. Exports to Ireland, Vietnam,
Singapore, Taiwan and China.

♀♀♀♀♀ Susanne Semillon 2011 Elevated, grassy aromatics introduce an intensely
textured and flavoured palate. Lemon pith, wax, hay and lemongrass flavours do
everything possible to both charm and impress. Screwcap. 11.5% alc. **Rating** 95
To 2022 $45 CM

♀♀♀♀♀ Vineyard Reserve Semillon 2011 Rating 93 To 2023 $30 CM
Vineyard Reserve Cabernet Sauvignon 2014 Rating 93 To 2040 $30 CM
Heritage Vines Shiraz 2011 Rating 92 To 2028 $60 CM
William Shiraz 2011 Rating 91 To 2025 $45 CM
Hunter Valley Semillon 2015 Rating 90 To 2020 $20 CM ✿
Bin 5555 Hunter Valley Shiraz 2013 Rating 90 To 2020 $20 CM ✿

Driftwood Estate   ★★★★★

3314 Caves Road, Wilyabrup, WA 6282 **Region** Margaret River
T (08) 9755 6323 **www**.driftwoodwines.com.au **Open** 7 days 10–5
Winemaker Eloise Jarvis, Paul Callaghan, Hugh Warren **Est.** 1989 **Dozens** 15000
Driftwood Estate is a well-established landmark on the Margaret River scene. Quite apart
from offering a brasserie restaurant capable of seating 200 people (open 7 days for lunch and
dinner) and a mock Greek open-air theatre, its wines feature striking and stylish packaging
and opulent flavours. The winery architecture is, it must be said, opulent rather than stylish.
Wines are released in three ranges: The Collection, Artifacts and Oceania. Exports to the UK,
Singapore and China.

♀♀♀♀♀ Artifacts Chardonnay 2015 Two vineyards, hand-picked, whole bunches, wild
yeast barrel-fermented (35% new), high solids, matured for 10 months. This is fast
out of the blocks, its highly attractive display of grapefruit and white peach on
the bouquet precisely reflected on the crisp, fruity palate. Clever winemaking was
rewarded. Screwcap. 13.2% alc. **Rating** 95 To 2023 $30 ✿
Artifacts Cabernet Sauvignon 2013 Includes 6.6% merlot and 4.1% petit
verdot, spending 11–19 months in barrel (40% new French). A delicious Bordeaux
blend, highly aromatic and flooded with juicy cassis, tannins and oak sufficient
to provide shape on the palate. Cabernet's answer to (high quality) Beaujolais.
Screwcap. 15% alc. **Rating** 95 To 2028 $30 ✿
Oceania Meritage 2013 41% cabernet sauvignon, 32% petit verdot,
17% merlot, 10% cabernet franc, matured in used European and American oak
for 7 months. Deep crimson-purple; given the intensely focused and powerful
palate, stacked with black and purple fruits. Incidentally, 'Meritage' was coined in
the Napa Valley for blends such as this. Screwcap. 14.8% alc. **Rating** 95 To 2033
$30 ✿
Artifacts Shiraz 2013 Matured for 18 months in oak (10% new French,
5% new Hungarian and 5% new American, 80% used), a best barrels selection.
Bright hue; a lively wine, the bouquet fragrant and expressive, red and black fruits
run in ballerina shoes across the medium-bodied palate, matched by crisp acidity
joining fine tannins on the finish. Screwcap. 14.8% alc. **Rating** 94 To 2033 $25 ✿

ŸŸŸŸŸ Artifacts 2015 Rating 92 To 2020 $25
The Collection Classic White 2015 Rating 91 To 2018 $21 ✪
The Collection Chardonnay 2015 Rating 90 To 2022 $30
The Collection Shiraz Cabernet 2013 Rating 90 To 2025 $21 ✪

Dromana Estate   ★★★★☆
555 Old Moorooduc Road, Tuerong, Vic 3933 **Region** Mornington Peninsula
T (03) 5974 4400 **www**.dromanaestate.com.au **Open** Not
Winemaker Peter Bauer **Est.** 1982 **Dozens** 30 000 **Vyds** 53.9ha
Since it was established over 30 years ago, Dromana Estate has undergone many changes, most notable the severance of involvement with the Crittenden family. It is owned by the investors of a publicly listed company, operating under the name of Mornington Winery Group Limited. It includes the Dromana Estate, Mornington Estate and David Traeger labels. Exports to the US, Canada and China.

ŸŸŸŸŸ Dromana Estate Pinot Noir 2014 MV6, hand-picked and sorted, destemmed,
30% whole bunches, open-fermented, wild yeast, matured in French oak. Has deeper colour, greater depth to the fruit on both bouquet and palate, and more structure than its Mornington Estate sibling. It has some savoury whole-bunch characters, but there's a matching wellspring of black cherry fruits, spices in the shallows. Screwcap. 13.5% alc. **Rating** 95 **To** 2029 $39

ŸŸŸŸŸ Mornington Estate Pinot Gris 2015 Rating 92 To 2017 $25 ✪
Mornington Estate Pinot Noir 2014 Rating 91 To 2020 $25
Mornington Estate Sauvignon Blanc 2014 Rating 90 To 2017 $25

Dudley Wines   ★★★★☆
1153 Willoughby Road, Penneshaw, Kangaroo Island, SA 5222 **Region** Kangaroo Island
T (08) 8553 1333 **www**.dudleywines.com.au **Open** 7 days 10–5
Winemaker Brodie Howard **Est.** 1994 **Dozens** 3500 **Vyds** 14ha
This is one of the most successful wineries on Kangaroo Island, owned by Jeff and Val Howard, with son Brodie as winemaker at the onsite winery. It has three vineyards on Dudley Peninsula: Porky Flat Vineyard, Hog Bay River and Sawyers. Two daughters and a daughter-in-law manage the cellar door sales, marketing and bookkeeping. Most of the wines are sold through licensed outlets on the Island.

ŸŸŸŸŸ Hog Bay Cabernet Sauvignon 2014 A wine that speaks clearly of the strongly
maritime climate of Kangaroo Island; it produces an elegant purity and intensity to the fruit flavours, which don't need new oak. This is truly a lovely medium-bodied cabernet, its balance ensuring a long future, however good it is now. Great value. Screwcap. 14% alc. **Rating** 95 **To** 2039 $36
Cape Hart Riesling 2015 Citrus blossom aromas lead off the tee, setting the path for the lime/lemon/grapefruit flavours to follow; glittering acidity drives the long, cleansing finish. Screwcap. 11.5% alc. **Rating** 94 **To** 2025 $22 ✪

ŸŸŸŸŸ Porky Flat Shiraz 2013 Rating 92 To 2028 $38

Duke's Vineyard   ★★★★★
Porongurup Road, Porongurup, WA 6324 **Region** Porongurup
T (08) 9853 1107 **www**.dukesvineyard.com **Open** 7 days 10–4.30
Winemaker Robert Diletti **Est.** 1998 **Dozens** 3500 **Vyds** 10ha
When Hilde and Ian (Duke) Ranson sold their clothing manufacturing business in 1998, they were able to fulfil a long-held dream of establishing a vineyard in the Porongurup subregion of Great Southern with the acquisition of a 65ha farm at the foot of the Porongurup Range. They planted shiraz and cabernet sauvignon (3ha each) and riesling (4ha). Hilde, a successful artist, designed the beautiful, scalloped, glass-walled cellar door sales area, with its mountain blue cladding. Great wines at great prices.

♟♟♟♟ **Magpie Hill Reserve Riesling 2015** This is Porongurup riesling at its best, its blossom-filled bouquet merely a short introduction to a wine that takes hold of the palate in an instant and refuses to let go, its potent, unsweetened array of lemon and lime flavours remorselessly building intensity from start to finish. Screwcap. 12.5% alc. **Rating** 97 **To** 2035 $30 ✪

Magpie Hill Reserve Riesling 2014 This is the essence of the special quality of Porongurup riesling, at once pure, yet sending the taste buds into overdrive, mapping the contest between citrus and electrifying acidity. All this, yet it has barely started on a journey that will build depth and richness for decades to come. Gold medal Qantas Wine Show WA '15. Screwcap. 11.5% alc. **Rating** 97 **To** 2035 $30 ✪

Magpie Hill Reserve Cabernet Sauvignon 2014 Hand-picked, matured in new French oak. The result of a great vineyard managed with maximum care on a great site, a top vintage, and super-skilled contract winemaking. Blackcurrant, bay leaf, black olive, cedary oak and finely tuned cabernet tannins are all in perfect balance. Screwcap. 13.5% alc. **Rating** 97 **To** 2049 $35 ✪

♟♟♟♟ **Magpie Hill Reserve Shiraz 2014** Deeply coloured; sings 'anything you can do, I can do better' to its lower-priced siblings, this with a touch more French oak and depth to its purple fruits, subtly weaving in plum behind dominant cherry fruit. Great balance ensures a long and prosperous future; a top vintage also helps. Screwcap. 13.8% alc. **Rating** 96 **To** 2044 $35 ✪

Single Vineyard Riesling 2015 Delicious stuff. The apple and lime blossom aromas are reflected in mirrored precision on the long, perfectly balanced and articulated palate. A classy riesling that is worth far more than $25. Screwcap. 12.2% alc. **Rating** 95 **To** 2030 $25 ✪

Single Vineyard Cabernet Sauvignon 2014 The same vinification as its Reserve sibling, except that French oak was mainly used. Deeply coloured; a striking, full-bodied cabernet; striking because, despite its weight and concentration, it is still immaculately balanced, with classic cabernet tannins in play, and exactly measured. Screwcap. 13.6% alc. **Rating** 95 **To** 2034 $26 ✪

Single Vineyard Shiraz 2014 Hand-picked, matured in French oak. A magical combination of intensity and finesse courtesy of an exceptionally long and finely structured palate, black cherry and spice Siamese twins, mouthwatering acidity another feature. Screwcap. 13.7% alc. **Rating** 94 **To** 2039 $26 ✪

♟♟♟♟ **Single Vineyard Autumn Riesling 2015** Rating 93 **To** 2027 $25 ✪
Single Vineyard Rose 2015 Rating 90 **To** 2017 $20 ✪

Dutschke Wines   ★★★★★

Lot 1 Gods Hill Road, Lyndoch, SA 5351 **Region** Barossa Valley
T (08) 8524 5485 **www.dutschkewines.com Open** By appt
Winemaker Wayne Dutschke **Est.** 1998 **Dozens** 6000 **Vyds** 15ha
Winemaker and owner Wayne Dutschke set up business with uncle (and grapegrower) Ken Semmler in 1990 to produce their first wine under the WillowBend label. The name was changed to Dutschke Wines in '98 when the opportunity came to export the wines to the US. Since then, Dutschke Wines has built its own small winery around the corner from Ken's vineyard, and the portfolio has steadily increased. While Wayne has now been making small batch wines for over 25 years, his use of whole berry ferments, open fermenters, basket presses and a quality oak regime have all remained the same. He was crowned Barossa Winemaker of the Year in 2010, inducted into the Barons of Barossa in '13, and is the author of a children's book about growing up in a winery called *My Dad has Purple Hands*. Exports to the US, Canada, Denmark, Germany, The Netherlands and Taiwan.

♟♟♟♟ **St Jakobi Single Vineyard Lyndoch Shiraz 2014** Destemmed, some whole berries, open-fermented, cultured yeast, 7–12 days on skins, basket-pressed, matured in 65% French and 35% American hogsheads (35% new) for 18 months. Black fruits block out all others, but neither the oak nor the tannins is compromised, both integral parts of the long, full-bodied palate, which carries its alcohol very well. Screwcap. 14.5% alc. **Rating** 95 **To** 2034 $40

Oscar Semmler St Jakobi Vineyard Shiraz 2013 38yo vines, open-fermented, cultured yeast, 12 days on skins, matured in 65% French and 35% American (30% new) for 18 months. While crammed full of black fruits, spices licorice and French oak, retains elegance and balance, the fine-grained tannins in keeping with this. Screwcap. 14.5% alc. **Rating** 95 **To** 2043 $68

GHR Neighbours Shiraz 2014 15–20yo vines from Max's Vineyard and Staker's Vineyard, 80–90yo vines from Wally's Block, open-fermented, cultured yeast, 7–24 days on skins, matured for 18 months in French and American oak (35% new). Deep crimson-purple; rich, ripe and full to the brim with blackberry and plum fruit; the American oak provides some mocha nuances to the full-bodied palate. Screwcap. 14.5% alc. **Rating** 94 **To** 2034 $32

♀♀♀♀♀ SAMI St Jakobi Vineyard Lyndoch Barossa Valley Cabernet Sauvignon **2014 Rating** 92 **To** 2039 $35

Eagles Rest Wines   ★★★★★

Lot 1, 534 Oakey Creek Road, Pokolbin, NSW 2320 **Region** Hunter Valley
T (02) 4998 6714 www.eaglesrestwines.com.au **Open** 7 days 10–5
Winemaker PJ Charteris, Jeff Byrne **Est.** 2007 **Dozens** 5000 **Vyds** 29ha
Eagles Rest has flown under the radar since its establishment in 2007, and still does. The estate is planted to 11ha of chardonnay, 10ha shiraz, 6ha semillon and 2ha verdelho.

♀♀♀♀♀ **Shed Block Shiraz 2011** From a cool Hunter vintage. It surges with predominantly red and purple fruits that appear first on the bouquet, then take control of the mid-palate, thence through to the finish and aftertaste. No more than medium-bodied, but will amaze future generations who taste it for the first time. Screwcap. 12.8% alc. **Rating** 96 **To** 2041 $69 ❍

Dam Block Semillon 2013 3 years young, not old. This is blue-blood aristocratic stuff with all the building blocks in place for a life measured in decades, not years. Its crisp, lemon, lemongrass and apple flavours (and consistent aromas) have a siren allure. Screwcap. 10% alc. **Rating** 95 **To** 2028 $35 ❍

♀♀♀♀♀ Maluna Block Hunter Valley Shiraz 2010 **Rating** 90 **To** 2025 $59

Eastern Peake   ★★★★★

67 Pickfords Road, Coghills Creek, Vic 3364 **Region** Ballarat
T (03) 5343 4245 www.easternpeake.com.au **Open** 7 days 11–5
Winemaker Owen Latta **Est.** 1983 **Dozens** 1200 **Vyds** 5.6ha
Norm Latta and Di Pym established Eastern Peake, 25km northeast of Ballarat on a high plateau overlooking the Creswick Valley, over 30 years ago. In the early years the grapes were sold, but the 5.6ha of vines are now dedicated to the production of Eastern Peake wines. Son Owen Latta has been responsible for the seismic increase in the quality of the wines, marking the 30th anniversary of the winery in fine style in 2013.

♀♀♀♀♀ **OB Terroir Pinot Noir 2013** 30yo vines, 10% whole bunches, wild yeast, 12 months in oak. The flavour, the feel, the firmness, the finish. Cherry and beetroot, plenty of tang, plenty of spice. It's appealing immediately, yet it's complex; it drinks well now, yet it will age. The finish is a fan of flavour; never a bad sign. Screwcap. 13% alc. **Rating** 96 **To** 2024 $60 CM ❍

Walsh Block Pinot Noir 2013 20yo vines, no whole bunches (50% used in '12). Intensity and fruit impact in a savoury landscape. This is beautifully composed and poised, an effect not hindered by long sinewy strings of herb-flecked tannin. Individual flavours are largely irrelevant; it's the form and style of it. Screwcap. 13% alc. **Rating** 95 **To** 2023 $40 CM

Walsh Block Syrah 2014 Savouriness writ large. It's almost hard to see the enjoyment for the trees and/or twigs. The fruit, though, is ripe, polished and certain of itself and the finish is tight, sound and impressive. It's off on its own adventure at the moment but it will mature into an excellent place. Screwcap. 13% alc. **Rating** 94 **To** 2030 $38 CM

Intrinsic Chardonnay 2013 Rating 93 **To** 2020 $38 CM
Pinot Tache Blanc du Noir 2014 Rating 93 **To** 2017 $28 CM
Project Zero SO2 Pinot Noir 2014 Rating 91 **To** 2018 $40 CM
Mount Block Pinot Noir 2013 Rating 91 **To** 2021 $40 CM

Echelon   ★★★★★

68 Anzac Street, Chullora, NSW 2190 **Region** Various
T (02) 9722 1200 **www.echelonwine.com.au Open** Not
Winemaker Various **Est.** 2009 **Dozens** NFP
Echelon is the brainchild of Nicholas Crampton, a wine marketer who understands wine (by no means a usual occurrence). He persuaded McWilliam's (Echelon's owner) to give free rein to his insights, and enlisted the aid of winemaker Corey Ryan. Brands under the Echelon umbrella are Last Horizon (single vineyard wines from Tasmania, made by Adrian Sparks), Partisan (from McLaren Vale), Armchair Critic and Under & Over (from established vineyards in the best regions) and Zeppelin (made by Corey Ryan and Kym Teusner, sourced from Barossa vineyards owned by Teusner or Sons of Eden, and often up to 80 years old).

Last Horizon Tamar Valley Pinot Noir 2014 20% whole bunches, 5 days cold soak, matured in used French oak for 10 months. Full, bright hue; a fragrant red-berry bouquet leads into a fleshy, comforting palate offering more generosity than the alcohol might suggest. Screwcap. 12.5% alc. **Rating** 94 **To** 2022 $31

Zeppelin Cellar Aged Riesling 2009 Rating 92 **To** 2020 $29
Last Horizon Tamar Valley Chardonnay 2014 Rating 92 **To** 2022 $37
Zeppelin Big Bertha Barossa Valley Shiraz 2014 Rating 90 **To** 2024 $18 ✪

Echo Hill Wines   ★★★☆

120 Adams Peak Road, Broke, NSW 2330 (postal) **Region** Hunter Valley
T 0439 462 651 **Open** Not
Winemaker Nick Paterson (Contract) **Est.** 1998 **Dozens** 1000 **Vyds** 4ha
The Day, Epper and Butler families respectively bring Australian, French and NZ background and heritage to Echo Hill. They retained local vigneron Andrew Margan, with 40 years' hands-on experience in growing and making wine, as a consultant in the early stages of the venture, including the selection of varieties and design of the vineyard blocks. They have also, very sensibly, started small, with only 2ha each of chardonnay and shiraz planted on the property, and virtually unlimited room for expansion. Next, they retained one of the best contract winemakers in the region, Nick Paterson, who guides the making of the wine from the grapes on the vine to wine in the bottle. Particularly for the Chinese market, the screwcaps provide far better protection during transport, warehousing, retail sale and maturation in bottle. Exports to China.

Hunter Valley Shiraz 2014 Mid-weight, low in oak influence and high in regional character. It's not hard to appreciate/enjoy this. Cherry-plum flavours with slips of dark earth and dry spice. Just a hint of choc. Juicy but firm. Screwcap. 13.5% alc. **Rating** 92 **To** 2028 $25 CM ✪

Eclectic Wines   ★★★★

687 Hermitage Road, Pokolbin, NSW 2320 (postal) **Region** Hunter Valley
T 0410 587 207 **www.eclecticwines.com.au Open** Fri–Mon
Winemaker First Creek Wines, Edgar Vales, Neil Pike **Est.** 2001 **Dozens** 3000
This is the venture of Paul and Kate Stuart, nominally based in the Hunter Valley, where they live and have a vineyard planted to shiraz and mourvedre; 'nominally', because Paul's 30+ years in the wine industry have given him the marketing knowledge to sustain the purchase of grapes from various regions, including Canberra and interstate. He balances the production

and sale of his own wines under the Eclectic label while also acting as an independent marketing and sales consultant to other producers, selling his clients' wine in different markets from those in which he sells his own. Exports to The Netherlands, Taiwan and China.

ＹＹＹＹＹ Hunter Valley Shiraz Merlot 2014 Plenty of fruit, plenty of tannin, and as a result a greater sense of 'grunt' than is normally associated with the reds of the region. This has definitely cashed in on the glory of the season. It's loaded with red and black-berried flavours and carries an attractive overlay of smoky oak. Screwcap. 14% alc. **Rating** 94 To 2028 $25 CM ❂

ＹＹＹＹＹ Pewter Label Clare Valley Riesling 2015 **Rating** 92 To 2022 $28 CM

Eddie McDougall Wines   ★★★☆

PO Box 2012, Hawthorn, Vic 3122 **Region** King Valley
T 0412 877 840 **www**.eddiemcdougall.com **Open** Not
Winemaker Eddie McDougall **Est.** 2007 **Dozens** 1000
Eddie McDougall's wine education began with part-time work in restaurants and bars while obtaining a Bachelor of International Business degree. The next step was a vineyard job at Shadowfax, then a postgraduate degree in wine technology and viticulture at the University of Melbourne. Next came Giant Steps, Clyde Park, O'Leary Walker, Wood Park and the top Barolo producer, Vietti. As a fascinating twist, he also spends part of the year making wines at 8th Estate Winery in Hong Kong, educating and sharing his philosophy of wine. Exports to China and Hong Kong.

ＹＹＹＹＹ Little Pig Rose 2015 Sangiovese, cool-fermented in stainless steel. Vivid, light puce; the bouquet and palate both speak of sangiovese, the red fruits with a finely judged twist of tannins. Screwcap. 13% alc. **Rating** 93 To 2018 $20 ❂

ＹＹＹＹ Classic King Valley Sangiovese 2014 **Rating** 89 To 2020 $25
King Valley Prosecco NV **Rating** 88 To 2016 $20 TS

Eden Hall   ★★★★☆

6 Washington Street, Angaston, SA 5353 **Region** Eden Valley
T 0400 991 968 **www**.edenhall.com.au **Open** 7 days 11–5
Winemaker Kym Teusner, Christa Deans **Est.** 2002 **Dozens** 4000 **Vyds** 32.3ha
David and Mardi Hall purchased the historic Avon Brae Estate in 1996. The 120ha property has been planted to cabernet sauvignon (the lion's share, with 13ha), riesling (9.25ha), shiraz (6ha) and smaller plantings of merlot, cabernet franc and viognier. The majority of the production is contracted to Yalumba, St Hallett and McGuigan Simeon, with 10% of the best grapes held back for the Eden Hall label. Exports to Canada and China.

ＹＹＹＹＹ Reserve Riesling 2015 Pale quartz-green; a beautifully delineated riesling, the gently flowery bouquet opening the curtains for a super-intense and finely structured palate driven by lime/lemon fruit, crisp acidity and a faint touch of CO_2. Screwcap. 11.3% alc. **Rating** 95 To 2035 $35 ❂
Riesling 2015 The bouquet is yet to develop, but the palate has abundant lime juice flavour backed by just the right amount of acidity. Its class comes with the finish and lingering aftertaste, easy to miss when you're speed dating or tasting. Screwcap. 11.5% alc. **Rating** 94 To 2028 $22 ❂
Block 4 Shiraz 2014 A selection of individual rows. Deep, healthy purple-crimson; black fruits and oak are intertwined rambling roses on the bouquet, the palate sending the same message, then fresh, mouthwatering tannins and acidity on the finish. A stylish shiraz. Screwcap. 14.5% alc. **Rating** 94 To 2034 $40
Block 3 Cabernet Sauvignon 2014 An impressive medium to full-bodied cabernet with a sinuous stream of pure cassis fruit coursing along the palate, the French oak evident, but (as it should) playing a support role through to the lingering finish. Screwcap. 14.5% alc. **Rating** 94 To 2034 $40

ＹＹＹＹＹ Gruner Veltliner 2015 **Rating** 92 To 2025 $35

Eden Road Wines ★★★★★

3182 Barton Highway, Murrumbateman, NSW 2582 **Region** Canberra District
T (02) 6226 8800 **www**.edenroadwines.com.au **Open** Wed–Sun 11–4
Winemaker Nick Spencer, Hamish Young **Est.** 2006 **Dozens** 9500 **Vyds** 3ha
The name of this business, now entirely based in the Canberra District, reflects an earlier stage of its development, when it also had a property in the Eden Valley. That has now been separated, and Eden Road's operations since 2008 centre on Hilltops, Canberra District and Tumbarumba. Eden Road has relocated to Murrumbateman, where it purchased the former Doonkuna winery and mature vineyard, marketing greatly assisted by winning the Jimmy Watson Trophy '09. Exports to the UK, the US, Maldives and Hong Kong.

🍷🍷🍷🍷🍷 **94 Block Syrah 2014** A medium-weight (almost lightweight) wine of personality and persistence. This will mature with the grace of magnificence. Mint, violets, cherry-plum, chicory and tiers of dried herbs. It's not a big wine by any stretch but it's gorgeously persistent, and has its arms loaded with charm. The finesse of the tannin here would do a watchmaker proud. Screwcap. 13% alc. **Rating** 96 **To** 2036 $100 CM
Canberra Syrah 2014 Medium-weight wine of beauty and length. Cherry-plum, peanuts, redcurrant and black pepper. Superfine tannin sets off succulent fruit. It zeroes in on perfection. Screwcap. 13% alc. **Rating** 95 **To** 2034 $60 CM

🍷🍷🍷🍷🍷 **Long Road Tumbarumba Chardonnay 2014 Rating** 93 **To** 2022 $27 CM ✪
Canberra Riesling 2015 Rating 92 **To** 2022 $30 CM
Long Road Tumbarumba Pinot Noir 2014 Rating 91 **To** 2020 $27 CM
Long Road Syrah 2014 Rating 91 **To** 2023 $28 CM
Gundagai Cabernet Sauvignon 2014 Rating 90 **To** 2024 $35 CM

Edenmae Estate Wines ★★★★☆

7 Miller Street, Springton, SA 5235 **Region** Eden Valley
T 0409 493 407 **www**.edenmae.com.au **Open** Fri–Sun 10–6
Winemaker Michelle Barr **Est.** 2007 **Dozens** 1800 **Vyds** 12ha
Owner/winemaker Michelle Barr runs Edenmae on a minimal intervention/organic viticulture basis. The vineyard is planted to riesling and shiraz (4ha each), pinot noir and cabernet sauvignon (2ha each), most around 40yo with some 10yo shiraz and 30yo pinot. Its boutique cellar door offers their full portfolio for tasting and platters. The rustic setting is also an ideal venue for private bookings (via email).

🍷🍷🍷🍷🍷 **Single Vineyard Eden Valley Riesling 2015** The flavour profile of most Eden Valley rieslings is different from that of the Clare Valley, Meyer lemon occupying centre stage in a pure stream that is less complex, but more refreshing, than the Clare Valley hallmark. Screwcap. 11.5% alc. **Rating** 95 **To** 2028 $18 ✪
Maluka Single Vineyard Shiraz 2012 Ticks all the boxes, each offering that bit extra over and above Jess. The fruit flavours are blackberry, black cherry and plum, each with an edgy/spicy note; the tannins are more evident, but strictly in balance; and the 2 years in French oak hasn't diminished the fruit one iota, but has helped soften and integrate the tannins. Screwcap. 14% alc. **Rating** 94 **To** 2032 $38

🍷🍷🍷🍷🍷 **Belle Single Vineyard Cabernet Sauvignon 2012 Rating** 92 **To** 2027 $32
Jess Single Vineyard Shiraz 2012 Rating 91 **To** 2025 $22 ✪
Methode Traditionnelle Pinot Noir 2012 Rating 91 **To** 2016 $38 TS

1847 | Yaldara Wines ★★★★

Chateau Yaldara, Hermann Thumm Drive, Lyndoch, SA 5351 **Region** Barossa Valley
T (08) 8524 5328 **www**.1847wines.com **Open** 7 days 9.30–5
Winemaker Alex Peel **Est.** 1996 **Dozens** 50 000 **Vyds** 53.9ha
1847 Wines is wholly owned by Treasure Valley Wines Pty Ltd, which is Chinese-owned. The year is when Barossa pioneer Johann Gramp planted his first vines in the region. There is in

fact no other connection between Gramp and his business, and 1847 Wines. 1847 Wines has 80ha of estate vineyards in the general vicinity of the original plantings by Johann Gramp. A 1000-tonne winery was built for the '14 vintage, handling the core production, destined to sell at $35 a bottle or more, together with new varieties and blends. This is underpinned by the acquisition of Chateau Yaldara in '14 providing a major retail outlet and massively enhanced production facilities. Exports to China.

ŢŢŢŢŢ **Yaldara 40 Years Old Tawny Port NV** Intensely syrupy, warm and soft with tar, malt, burnt sugar and mashed raisin flavours; it's delicious, and it lets you know it. Cork. 20% alc. **Rating** 94 **To** 2019 $175 CM

ŢŢŢŢŢ **Yaldara Ruban Barossa Valley Grenache 2014** **Rating** 93 **To** 2024 $25 ✪
1847 Pappy's Cabernet Sauvignon 2013 **Rating** 93 **To** 2028 $40
Yaldara Reserve Barossa Valley Shiraz 2013 **Rating** 92 **To** 2038 $35
Yaldara 30 Years Old Tawny Port NV **Rating** 92 **To** 2019 $100 CM
Yaldara Ruban Pinot Gris 2015 **Rating** 91 **To** 2016 $20 CM ✪
Yaldara Ruban McLaren Vale Shiraz 2014 **Rating** 91 **To** 2029 $25
Yaldara 20 Years Old Tawny Port NV **Rating** 91 **To** 2016 $50 CM

Ekhidna   ★★★★★

Main South Road, Wattle Flat, SA 5203 **Region** McLaren Vale
T (08) 8323 8496 **www**.ekhidnawines.com.au **Open** 7 days 11–5
Winemaker Matthew Rechner **Est.** 2001 **Dozens** 8000
Matt Rechner entered the wine industry in 1988, spending most of the years since at Tatachilla in McLaren Vale, starting as laboratory technician and finishing as operations manager. Frustrated by the constraints of large winery practice, he decided to initially strike out on his own in 2001 via the virtual winery option. The quality of the wines has been such that he has been able to build a winery and cellar door, the winery facilitating the use of various cutting-edge techniques. Production has risen from 3400 dozen in the '14 Wine Companion to its present level. Exports to the UK, Singapore and China.

ŢŢŢŢŢ **Linchpin Shiraz 2014** Matured in 20% new French and 80% used American oak for 24 months. McLaren Vale shiraz isn't born to be shy and retiring, and this is about as elegant as they come from the region. Savoury, spicy, peppery notes sprayed over the black fruits and neatly worked oak are all very impressive, the key words harmony and balance. Screwcap. 14.5% alc. **Rating** 95 **To** 2034 $40
Single Vineyard Shiraz 2012 Biodynamically grown grapes, matured for 24 months in French and American barriques (20% new). Whatever the vintage, and however old the wine is, the McLaren Vale regional stamp on shiraz is arguably the most distinctive in Australia, and I'm happy to lead the yes argument. I need hardly spell out the dark chocolate DNA that is so strong. But, of course, all the normal requirements of balance, depth, line and length have to be ticked off, as they are here. Screwcap. 14.5% alc. **Rating** 95 **To** 2037 $35 ✪
Rechner Shiraz 2012 20% matured in French oak, 80% in American oak for 36 months. Deliberately made in uncompromising full-bodied style, with savoury black fruits and oak blocking any inroad by dark chocolate, and none the worse for that. The density of the wine has not harmed its balance, and its end point is way down the track. Screwcap. 14.5% alc. **Rating** 95 **To** 2042 $60
Rechner McLaren Vale Shiraz 2010 The colour is still bright and deep, the fruit profile allowing some red nuances space to intrude, and there's a breath of regional chocolate peeping through. Screwcap. 14.5% alc. **Rating** 94 **To** 2030 $60

ŢŢŢŢŢ **McLaren Vale Grenache Shiraz 2013** **Rating** 92 **To** 2028 $22 ✪
Adelaide Hills Sauvignon Blanc 2015 **Rating** 90 **To** 2017 $20 ✪

Elderton

3–5 Tanunda Road, Nuriootpa, SA 5355 **Region** Barossa Valley
T (08) 8568 7878 **www**.eldertonwines.com.au **Open** Mon–Fri 10–5, w'ends, hols 11–4
Winemaker Richard Langford **Est.** 1982 **Dozens** 45 000 **Vyds** 75ha

The founding Ashmead family, with mother Lorraine supported by sons Allister and Cameron, continues to impress with their wines. The original source was 30ha of fully mature shiraz, cabernet sauvignon and merlot on the Barossa floor; subsequently 16ha of Eden Valley vineyards (shiraz, cabernet sauvignon, chardonnay, zinfandel, merlot and roussanne) were incorporated into the business. The Rohrlach Vineyard, with 75+-year-old shiraz, is under long-term lease and managed by the Ashmead family. Energetic promotion and marketing in Australia and overseas are paying dividends. Elegance and balance are the keys to these wines. Exports to all major markets.

ΨΨΨΨΨ **Neil Ashmead Grand Tourer Barossa Valley Shiraz 2014** A soaring star. Take this one straight to the pool room. It combines meatiness and savouriness with flair. It's an exquisite example of the beauty of a perfectly ripened medium-weight wine; it makes excess density look crass and unnecessary. Plums, cured meats, peppers and cloves. If you were listing it at a restaurant it would be as at home under the food heading as it is under wine. One out of the box. Screwcap. 14% alc. **Rating** 98 **To** 2030 $75 CM ✪

Command Single Vineyard Barossa Valley Shiraz 2013 Vineyard planted 1894, matured in French and American oak. The oak and the fruit have fast become inseparable. Rich blackberry, coal, earth and coffee-cream flavours cascade onto the palate and on out through the finish. Dry, filigreed tannin builds as the wine breathes; you only notice it once you're safe in its embrace. Both old school and new school at once; it's elegant and rich, unafraid of oak but blessed with pure, dark-berried fruit. Screwcap. 14.5% alc. **Rating** 97 **To** 2038 $110 CM ✪

ΨΨΨΨΨ **Western Ridge Barossa Valley Shiraz 2014** Elegance is in vogue at Elderton. We're talking poised, well-ripened, let-the-clubhead-do-the-work wines, where the fruit has time and space to display more than mere sweetness or, indeed, brute strength. This shows notes of coffee grounds, black pepper, blackberried fruit and cured meats, and closes the deal with a run of finely crafted tannin. Screwcap. 14.5% alc. **Rating** 96 **To** 2032 $55 CM ✪

Ashmead Single Vineyard Barossa Cabernet Sauvignon 2014 Vines planted '44. matured in French oak. Ripe fruits are rolled into a ball and the shutters haven't yet come up, but the tannin is firm, and everything seems trained to evolve slowly. Classy oak offers flavours of chocolate and sawdust; the fruit rings with blackcurrant and boysenberry. Performance will be excellent, given time. Screwcap. 14.5% alc. **Rating** 95 **To** 2035 $100 CM

Barossa Shiraz 2014 This would blow your hair back. It offers a whoosh of syrupy soft flavour. It's all plums and cloves and smoky oak; twist the top and the scents and flavours are at you at a rate of knots, as if they have pleasure to sell and the faster the deal is sealed, the better. It will cellar, but there's no need to. Screwcap. 14.5% alc. **Rating** 94 **To** 2026 $34 CM

Western Ridge Barossa Valley Grenache Carignan 2014 Light colour, bell-clear flavours, dried spice and redcurrant, tangy acidity that sits as one with the fruit and tannin. Oak is a minor player at most. Top-notch example of a lighter Barossan style. Screwcap. 14.5% alc. **Rating** 94 **To** 2022 $55 CM

Greenock Two Grenache Shiraz Mourvedre 2014 Lightish colour and distinctly mid-weight but the payoffs are elegance and nuance. This flows and slips and creates its own little word of flavour and feel; berries, cream and spices the conduits. A piece of Barossa craft. Screwcap. 14% alc. **Rating** 94 **To** 2022 $34 CM

Barossa Cabernet Sauvignon 2014 Claret style with a modern twist. Effortless flow of fruit and oak before sinewy, herb-strewn tannin pulls it all into line. It's not deep or heavy, but it has presence and length. And it feels beautifully well polished. Screwcap. 14.5% alc. **Rating** 94 **To** 2028 $34 CM

�socTTTTℚ Ode to Lorraine Barossa Cabernet Sauvignon Shiraz Merlot 2013
Rating 93 To 2030 $55 CM
Eden Valley Riesling 2015 Rating 92 To 2025 $24 CM ✪

Eldorado Road ★★★★★

46–48 Ford Street, Beechworth, Vic 3747 **Region** North East Victoria Zone
T (03) 5725 1698 **www**.eldoradoroad.com.au **Open** Fri–Sun 11–5
Winemaker Paul Dahlenburg, Lauretta Schulz **Est.** 2010 **Dozens** 700 **Vyds** 4ha
Paul Dahlenburg (nicknamed Bear), Lauretta Schulz (Laurie) and their children have leased
a 2ha block of shiraz planted in the 1890s with rootlings supplied from France (doubtless
grafted) in the wake of phylloxera's devastation of the Glenrowan and Rutherglen plantings.
Bear and Laurie knew about the origins of the vineyard, which was in a state of serious decline
after years of neglect. The owners of the vineyard were aware of its historic importance and
were more than happy to lease it. Four years of tireless work in the vineyard, reconstructing
the old vines, has finally resulted in tiny amounts of exceptionally good shiraz; they have also
planted a small area of nero d'Avola and durif.

TTTTT **Perseverance Old Vine Shiraz 2014** Vines planted in late 1800s, interplanted
with ugni blanc and co-fermented. Red and dark fruits interplay with an aromatic
and spicy undercurrent; superfine tannins and layers of red fruits and spice frame
a beautifully constructed wine; fine, juicy and vibrant, the impeccably balanced
palate goes on and on. Superb effort. Screwcap. 14.3% alc. **Rating** 96 **To** 2035
$60 ✪
Onyx Durif 2014 Dark red; laden with black and red fruits, there is a wonderful
fragrance and a lightness of touch here. The palate is vibrant, juicy and fine, poised,
long and earthy, but full of energy. Screwcap. 14.9% alc. **Rating** 95 **To** 2030 $35 ✪

TTTTℚ **Luminoso Rose 2015** Rating 90 To 2017 $23
Quasimodo Shiraz Durif Nero d'Avola 2013 Rating 90 To 2028 $28

Eldredge ★★★★

Spring Gully Road, Clare, SA 5453 **Region** Clare Valley
T (08) 8842 3086 **www**.eldredge.com.au **Open** 7 days 11–5
Winemaker Leigh Eldredge **Est.** 1993 **Dozens** 8000 **Vyds** 20.9ha
Leigh and Karen Eldredge have established their winery and cellar door in the Sevenhill
Ranges at an altitude of 500m above Watervale. The mature estate vineyard is planted to
shiraz, cabernet sauvignon, merlot, riesling, sangiovese and malbec. Exports to the UK, the
US, Canada, Singapore and China.

TTTTT **RL Clare Valley Cabernet Sauvignon 2013** Includes 7% each of merlot
and shiraz, matured in French and American oak. A workmanlike wine, with
notably fresh fruit flavours and mouthfeel; the merlot and shiraz support, rather
than detract from, the varietal expression; acidity and tannins are yet other pluses.
Surprise packet. Screwcap. 14.5% alc. **Rating** 94 **To** 2035 $35

TTTT **Kitty Clare Valley Rose 2015** Rating 89 To 2017 $20
Blue Chip Clare Valley Shiraz 2014 Rating 89 To 2034 $38
Clare Valley Semillon Sauvignon Blanc 2015 Rating 88 To 2017 $20
Boundary Clare Valley Shiraz Cabernet 2014 Rating 88 To 2029 $24

Eldridge Estate of Red Hill ★★★★★

120 Arthurs Seat Road, Red Hill, Vic 3937 **Region** Mornington Peninsula
T 0414 758 960 **www**.eldridge-estate.com.au **Open** Mon–Fri 12–4, w'ends & hols 11–5
Winemaker David Lloyd **Est.** 1985 **Dozens** 800 **Vyds** 2.8ha
The Eldridge Estate vineyard was purchased by David and (the late) Wendy Lloyd in 1995.
Major retrellising work has been undertaken, changing to Scott Henry, and all the wines
are estate-grown and made. David has also planted several Dijon-selected pinot noir clones

(114, 115 and 777), which have been contributing since 2004; likewise the Dijon chardonnay clone 96. Attention to detail permeates all he does in vineyard and winery. Exports to the US.

ΨΨΨΨΨ **Eldridge Clone 1 Pinot Noir 2014** Statuesque; powered by fruit, touched by smoky reduction, ripped with spice and stiffened by tannin. It's seductive and yet is not for suffering fools; it does things its own way, the right way, and you either get it or you don't. Screwcap. 14% alc. **Rating** 96 **To** 2024 $68 CM ✪

Chardonnay 2014 Primed with fruit and laced with winemaking complexity. The result: sheer pleasure. Oatmeal, nectarine, cedar wood, oak, some cream, some matches. Fireworks and fruit. Screwcap. 13% alc. **Rating** 95 **To** 2020 $40 CM

Wendy Chardonnay 2014 A tribute to Wendy Lloyd aka 'the queen of chardonnay'. It's a mighty fine tribute too. It's beautifully fruited, complex without being aggressive about it, and especially persistent. Purity. Finesse. A steely resolve. And a seamless flow from start to finish. Screwcap. 13% alc. **Rating** 95 **To** 2021 $50 CM

Pinot Noir 2014 It feels complete. The spice, the fruit, the perfume, the rolling hills of tannin, the stretch of flavour out towards the horizon. It combines macerated cherry (bass) with tang (treble); savouriness with a steady hand. It's all very nicely done. Screwcap. 14% alc. **Rating** 95 **To** 2022 $60 CM

Clonal Blend Pinot Noir 2014 From the outset it feels as though you're in safe hands. The various facets are neatly arranged: red and black cherried fruit, a thread of savouriness, perhaps some undergrowth, a tangy/twiggy burst to the finish. Oak is here but ever so well played. In the end, though, it's the form of tannin, like a perfectly folded shirt that confirms its quality completely. Screwcap. 14% alc. **Rating** 95 **To** 2022 $75 CM

Fume Blanc 2015 Passionfruit flavours here have the intensity of electricity. Whispers of lemongrass and smoky oak can just be heard, but the cut and burst of tropical fruit is terrific. Screwcap. 12.5% alc. **Rating** 94 **To** 2017 $29 CM ✪

Clonal Blend N Pinot Noir 2014 The bones here certainly don't lack flesh and yet overall you'd call this an elegant release. Black cherry, undergrowth and rounds of dried spice slip seductively through the palate, the finish then braided with flavour-infused tannin. Screwcap. 13.5% alc. **Rating** 94 **To** 2021 $68 CM

Single Clone Pinot Noir 2014 MV6. The flashy new clones grab all the attention but the old workhorse of Australian pinot noir has no intention of rolling over. This release has a fresh, complex drinkability, satiny to the touch and with beautifully integrated notes of garden herbs and wood spice. Tannin is all velvet. Beautifully done as a whole. Screwcap. 14% alc. **Rating** 94 **To** 2022 $68 CM

ΨΨΨΨΨ **Clonal Blend S Pinot Noir 2014** **Rating** 92 **To** 2021 $68 CM

Elgee Park   ★★★★★

24 Junction Road, Merricks North, Vic 3926 **Region** Mornington Peninsula
T (03) 5989 7338 **www.elgeeparkwines.com.au** **Open** At Merricks General Wine Store
Winemaker Geraldine McFaul (Contract) **Est.** 1972 **Dozens** 1600 **Vyds** 4.4ha
The pioneer of the Mornington Peninsula in its 20th-century rebirth, owned by Baillieu Myer and family. The vineyard is planted to riesling, chardonnay, viognier (some of the oldest vines in Australia), pinot gris, pinot noir, merlot and cabernet sauvignon. The vineyard is set in a picturesque natural amphitheatre with a northerly aspect looking out across Port Phillip Bay towards the Melbourne skyline.

ΨΨΨΨΨ **Mornington Peninsula Cabernet Merlot 2012** 100% destemmed, wild yeast open-fermented, 21 days on skins, 18 months in French oak (30% new). This has everything: bright colour, a fragrant and complex bouquet and a supple, silky palate with cassis and redcurrant in polite agreement with the integrated French oak, the tannins seen but not heard in an adults' playground. Screwcap. 13% alc. **Rating** 96 **To** 2032 $35 ✪

Mornington Peninsula Chardonnay 2014 Whole bunch-pressed direct to French barriques (25% new), cultured yeast, on lees for 10 months, 20% natural mlf. Bred in the purple, or gold, perhaps; strikes all the right notes, its white peach and grapefruit flavours resting within a precisely wrought cradle of bright acidity and subtle oak. Screwcap. 13.5% alc. **Rating** 95 **To** 2024 $50

🍷🍷🍷🍷🍷 **Mornington Peninsula Riesling 2015 Rating** 92 **To** 2021 $30 CM
Mornington Peninsula Pinot Gris 2015 Rating 90 **To** 2016 $35 CM
Mornington Peninsula Pinot Noir 2013 Rating 90 **To** 2020 $50

Ellis Wines   ★★★★

3025 Heathcote-Rochester Road, Colbinabbin, Vic 3559 (postal) **Region** Heathcote
T 0401 290 315 **www**.elliswines.com.au **Open** Not
Winemaker Guy Rathjen **Est.** 1998 **Dozens** 700 **Vyds** 54.6ha
Bryan and Joy Ellis own this family business, daughter Raylene Flanagan is the sales manager, and seven of the vineyard blocks are named after family members. For the first 10 years the Ellises were content to sell the grapes to a range of distinguished producers. However, since then a growing portion of the crop has been vinified.

🍷🍷🍷🍷🍷 **Premium Heathcote Shiraz 2013** Crushed and destemmed, once fermented, matured for 11 months in 100% new French oak. Great crimson-purple colour; the wine has some of the black fruits and spice more commonly found in the Grampians, firm tannins following the same path; the fruit is so powerful and intense it has taken the oak and folded it into a backdrop for the wine. A great future awaits. Screwcap. 14.7% alc. **Rating** 94 **To** 2038 $42

🍷🍷🍷🍷🍷 **Signature Label Heathcote Shiraz 2013 Rating** 93 **To** 2033 $34

Elmswood Estate   ★★★★★

75 Monbulk-Seville Road, Seville, Vic 3139 **Region** Yarra Valley
T (03) 5964 3015 **www**.elmswoodestate.com.au **Open** W'ends 12–5
Winemaker Han Tao Lau **Est.** 1981 **Dozens** 3000 **Vyds** 8.5ha
Planted to cabernet sauvignon, chardonnay, merlot, sauvignon blanc, pinot noir, shiraz and riesling on the red volcanic soils of the far southern side of the Yarra Valley. The cellar door operates from 'The Pavilion', a fully enclosed glass room situated on a ridge above the vineyard, with 180° views of the Upper Yarra Valley. It seats up to 110 guests, and is a popular wedding venue. Exports to Hong Kong and China.

🍷🍷🍷🍷🍷 **Chardonnay 2015** Hand-picked and sorted, whole bunch-pressed to French puncheons (17% new), 9 months on lees. The expressive bouquet is followed by an even more expressive palate, with white peach, grapefruit and a hint of passionfruit doing the heavy lifting, beautifully handled oak (it's barely a whisper) and acidity underwriting the length. Screwcap. 12.9% alc. **Rating** 95 **To** 2025 $33 ✪
Pinot Noir 2014 Hand-picked and sorted, destemmed, 10% whole bunches, matured for 10 months in French hogsheads (40% new). The very fragrant bouquet introduces a pinot with considerable life and movement, spice, strawberries, cherries (red, morello) all sliding sinuously across and along the palate. This doesn't ravish you with power, but with elegance and an unending stream of succulent flavours. Screwcap. 13.5% alc. **Rating** 95 **To** 2024 $38
Syrah 2014 Hand-picked, chilled overnight, hand-sorted, destemmed, 10% whole bunches, open-fermented, 2–4 weeks on skins, matured for 16 months in French oak (40% new). The very low yields of the '14 vintage required a careful approach in the winery, and this fragrant red-berried wine is a prime example; it treads lightly, yet decisively, its superfine tannins sewn through the fruit, a mouthwatering finish the result. Diam. 13.3% alc. **Rating** 95 **To** 2034 $35 ✪
Merlot 2014 Hand-picked, chilled overnight, hand-sorted, destemmed, open-fermented, 2–4 weeks on skins, matured for 17 months in French oak (37% new). Very good colour; this is an unusually full-bodied merlot resounding with

blackcurrant fruits on the intense palate and the tannins from the post-ferment maceration, augmented by oak. Will absolutely repay cellaring. Diam. 13.3% alc. **Rating** 94 **To** 2039 $32

Cabernet Sauvignon 2014 Hand-picked, chilled overnight, hand-sorted, destemmed, 10% whole bunches, open-fermented, 2–4 weeks on skins, matured for 16 months in French oak (40% new), 567 dozen made. A cabernet that is proud in its skin, making no apologies for its varietally firm tannins because there is cassis/blackcurrant in abundance. Its outstanding feature is its mouthwatering elegance and balance. Diam. 13.4% alc. **Rating** 94 **To** 2034 $35

♥♥♥♥♡ **Sauvignon Blanc 2015 Rating** 90 **To** 2017 $25

Eminence Wines ★★★★★

234 Burders Lane, Whitlands, Vic 3733 **Region** King Valley
T 0433 277 211 **www**.eminencewines.com.au **Open** Not
Winemaker Contract **Est.** 2008 **Dozens** 1000 **Vyds** 16ha

In 1998 David and Sharon Burder planted 8ha of chardonnay (clones I10V1 and 76), 5ha of pinot noir (clones 114, 115 and MV6), 2ha of pinot gris and 1ha of pinot meunier, backed by 5-year grape supply agreements with Yalumba and Brown Brothers. Daughter Clare began her wine life working in vineyards and cellar doors in the King Valley, thereafter in Melbourne at The Prince Wine Store. In 2008 she started Eminence and Tony Jordan has come on board to help Clare assemble the sparkling wines. At 870m, the vineyard is one of the higher vineyards in Australia, and wind and rain can wreak havoc. She has '12 and '13 maturing in bottle, and plans to release an NV Pinot Meunier Brut in the next 18 months. Further out, a cellar door and basic winery feature in a 5-year plan. As well as making the wines, she has been front and centre in distribution (now with Firebrand in Melbourne) and also teaches wine appreciation courses through her business, The Humble Tumbler (www.thehumbletumbler.com.au).

♥♥♥♥♥ **The Assembly Single Vineyard Sparkling 2010** From the genuinely very cool Whitlands plateau, a blend of 43% each of chardonnay and pinot noir and 14% pinot meunier, fermented in this bottle, with 42 months on lees, disgorged Jan '14, 200 dozen made. Pale straw-green, with persistent mousse, this has all the hallmarks of very fine sparkling wine, the fruit spanning apple, citrus and stone fruit with a dusting of spice and a memory of brioche. Will grow with further time in bottle. Crown seal. 11.9% alc. **Rating** 95 **To** 2020 $48

Eperosa ★★★★★

24 Maria Street, Tanunda, SA 5352 **Region** Barossa Valley
T 0428 111 121 **www**.eperosa.com.au **Open** By appt
Winemaker Brett Grocke **Est.** 2005 **Dozens** 800 **Vyds** 8.75ha

Eperosa owner Brett Grocke qualified as a viticulturist in 2001, and, through Grocke Viticulture, consults and provides technical services to over 200ha of vineyards spread across the Barossa Valley, Eden Valley, Adelaide Hills, Riverland, Langhorne Creek and Hindmarsh Valley. He is ideally placed to secure small parcels of organically managed grapes, hand-picked, whole bunch-fermented and foot-stomped, and neither filtered nor fined. The wines are of impeccable quality – the use of high quality, perfectly inserted, corks will allow the wines to reach their full maturity decades hence. Exports to the UK.

♥♥♥♥♥ **Elevation Eden Valley Shiraz 2014** Exceptionally well made. From three vineyards, the oldest dating back to 1858. Fragrant and purely fruited, its vibrancy and energy are the key to the captivating aromas. The palate is equally impressive; fine-grained, savoury tannins drive through the layers and layers of fruit, finishing poised and precise. Cork. 14.6% alc. **Rating** 97 **To** 2045 $45 **✪**

♥♥♥♥♥ **Elevation Barossa Valley Shiraz 2014** An impressively fragrant bouquet redolent with red and dark fruits, its vibrancy and purity captivating. The palate is equally impressive, vibrant and rich in flavour, the thread of fine-grained, savoury tannins driving the length and finish. Cork. 14.6% alc. **Rating** 96 **To** 2040 $45 **✪**

Stonegarden Eden Valley Grenache 2014 Organically grown on one of Australia's oldest vineyards (planted 1858–68), interplanted with small amounts of mataro and shiraz. This is another beautiful wine from Eperosa, the bouquet fine, perfumed and hauntingly fragrant, the palate detailed and precise finishing, with classic chalky old vine grenache tannins. Cork. 15.4% alc. **Rating** 96 **To** 2030 $80

Synthesis Barossa Valley Mataro Grenache Shiraz 2014 A four-vineyard 50/35/15% blend. It is complex, fragrant and finely poised. The balance and vibrancy in this wine are a testament to the care in the vineyards coupled with sensitive winemaking. Cork. 14.7% alc. **Rating** 96 **To** 2029 $32 ✪

Blanc Barossa Valley Semillon 2014 Deeply scented with an array of citrus, lemon curd, spice and lees, complexity derived from fermentation in used French hogsheads. An intense and full-flavoured palate with lovely pithy texture and remarkably well balanced acidity; long, rich and complex. Cork. 13.4% alc. **Rating** 95 **To** 2023 $32 ✪

L.R.C. Greenock Barossa Valley Shiraz 2014 From a single boundary row, wild open ferment, includes 1% riesling and 0.5% mataro, 21 dozen made. Beautifully poised, it completes the stunning releases from Eperosa. Cork. 13.7% alc. **Rating** 95 **To** 2045 $50

Eppalock Ridge ★★★★

6 Niemann Street, Bendigo, Vic 3550 (postal) **Region** Heathcote
T 0409 957 086 www.eppalockridge.com.au **Open** Not
Winemaker Don Lewis, Narelle King, Rod Hourigan **Est.** 1979 **Dozens** 3000
Sue and Rod Hourigan gave up their careers in fabric design and television production at the ABC in 1976 to chase their passion for fine wine. This took them first to McLaren Vale, with Sue working in the celebrated Barn Restaurant, and Rod starting at d'Arenberg; over the next three hectic years both worked vintages at Pirramimma and Coriole while undertaking the first short course for winemakers at CSU. They moved to Redesdale in '79 and established Eppalock Ridge on a basalt hilltop overlooking Lake Eppalock. The 10ha of shiraz, cabernet sauvignon, cabernet franc and merlot are capable of producing wines of high quality.

🍷🍷🍷🍷 **Shiraz 2014** 60% Goulburn, 40% Heathcote. Typical of Central Victorian shiraz when it is on song; the dark-berry fruits and licorice of the bouquet and palate hold sway until the finish, when even-tempered tannins make their pitch. Screwcap. 14.5% alc. **Rating** 93 **To** 2034 $30

Ernest Hill Wines ★★★★★

307 Wine Country Drive, Nulkaba, NSW 2325 **Region** Hunter Valley
T (02) 4991 4418 www.ernesthillwines.com.au **Open** 7 days 10–5
Winemaker Mark Woods **Est.** 1999 **Dozens** 6000 **Vyds** 12ha
This is part of a vineyard originally planted in the early 1970s by Harry Tulloch for Seppelt Wines; it was later renamed Pokolbin Creek Vineyard, and later still (in '99) the Wilson family purchased the upper (hill) part of the vineyard, and renamed it Ernest Hill. It is now planted to semillon, shiraz, chardonnay, verdelho, traminer, merlot, tempranillo and chambourcin. Exports to the US and China.

🍷🍷🍷🍷🍷 **William Henry Reserve Premium Hunter Shiraz 2014** Open-fermented, 15 days on skins, matured in 35% new oak for 15 months. The patriarch of a remarkable trio of shirazs; if these were the only three wines from the '14 vintage they could justify its celebration as the greatest vintage since '65. And don't think my 40-year drinking horizon is absurd – if the Diam does its duty, and the wine is property cellared, it will live far longer. 14.5% alc. **Rating** 97 **To** 2054 $60 ✪

🍷🍷🍷🍷🍷 **Shareholders Shiraz 2014** Open-fermented, cultured yeast, 14 days on skins, matured in 25% new oak for 14 months. Deep and bright colour; old vines produce fruit with a deceptive intensity; it is medium to full-bodied, but has perfect line, length and balance, the use of some new oak adding yet more to a classic Hunter Valley shiraz. Please leave some in the cellar for your children or grandchildren. Screwcap. 14.4% alc. **Rating** 95 **To** 2044 $30 **⊙**

Back Shed Shiraz 2014 Hand-picked, crushed/destemmed, open-fermented, cultured yeast, 14 days on skins, matured in used oak for 14 months. Flooded with blackberry and satsuma plum fruit on the medium to full-bodied bouquet and palate; in the mouth the tannins are simply an adjunct to the fruit, but will lend support in the decades ahead. Screwcap. 14.3% alc. **Rating** 94 **To** 2044 $25 **⊙**

🍷🍷🍷🍷🍷 **CEO Cabernet Sauvignon 2014** Rating 90 To 2029 $40
Andrew Watson Hunter Tempranillo 2014 Rating 90 To 2022 $40

Ernest Schuetz Estate Wines   ★★★★☆

Edgell Lane, Mudgee, NSW 2850 **Region** Mudgee
T 0402 326 612 **www.**ernestschuetzestate.com.au **Open** W'ends 10.30–4.30
Winemaker Jacob Stein, Robert Black **Est.** 2003 **Dozens** 4000 **Vyds** 4.1ha
Ernest Schuetz's involvement in the wine industry started in 1988 at the age of 21. Working in various liquor outlets and as a sales representative for Miranda Wines, McGuigan Simeon and, later, Watershed Wines, gave him an in-depth understanding of all aspects of the wine market. In 2003 he and wife Joanna purchased the Arronvale Vineyard (first planted in '91), at an altitude of 530m. When the Schuetzs acquired the vineyard it was planted to merlot, shiraz and cabernet sauvignon, and they have since grafted 1ha to riesling, pinot blanc, pinot gris, zinfandel and nebbiolo.

🍷🍷🍷🍷🍷 **Epica Amarone Method Mudgee Cabernet Shiraz 2013** 50% shiraz, 35% cabernet sauvignon, 15% merlot, hand-picked, air-dried on racks for 4 weeks, 50% whole bunches, 50% whole berries, hand-plunged/foot-stomped for 10 days, aged in two new French hogsheads for 21 months. This is a thoroughly impressive Amarone style, the density in flavour and in creamy texture terms blotting out any impact from the alcohol. Bravissimo. Screwcap. 16% alc. **Rating** 95 **To** 2043 $60
St Martin de Porres Unfiltered Mudgee Zinfandel Nebbiolo 2013 A 60/40% blend, 60% crushed and destemmed, 40% whole bunches, 24 hours cold soak, wild open ferment, matured for 21 months. This is a very easy wine to enjoy, its juicy fruits filling the mouth in a flash; I suppose the oak and tannins are there, but the fruit is more than a match for them. Screwcap. 14.5% alc. **Rating** 94 **To** 2033 $40

🍷🍷🍷🍷🍷 **Family Reserve Mudgee Black Syrah 2013** Rating 92 To 2038 $30
Terra X Off Dry Mudgee Rose 2015 Rating 90 To 2017 $19 **⊙**

Espier Estate   ★★★

Room 1208, 401 Docklands Drive, Docklands, Vic 3008 **Region** South Eastern Australia
T (03) 9670 4317 **www.**jnrwine.com **Open** Mon–Fri 9–5
Winemaker Sam Brewer **Est.** 2007 **Dozens** 25 000
This is the venture of Robert Luo and Jacky Lin. Sam Brewer has worked for Southcorp and De Bortoli, and in the US and China, and has been closely linked with the business since its establishment. The principal focus of the business is export to Asian countries, with China and Hong Kong the main areas. Much of the volume is linked to contract-made wines under the Espier Estate label, with prices ranging from entry level to those befitting premium regional styles. Exports to Asia.

🍷🍷🍷🍷 **Feel Reserve Heathcote Shiraz 2013** Good colour; a full-bodied wine rich in black fruits, the tannins soft, the oak in balance, but the alcohol warms the finish that bit too much. Very different from a tank sample tasted Mar '15. Cork. 14.5% alc. **Rating** 89 **To** 2025 $25

Estate 807

807 Scotsdale Road, Denmark, WA 6333 **Region** Denmark
T (08) 9840 9027 **www**.estate807.com.au **Open** Thurs–Sun 10–4
Winemaker James Kellie, Mike Garland **Est.** 1998 **Dozens** 1500 **Vyds** 4.2ha
Dr Stephen Junk and Ola Tylestam purchased Estate 807 in 2009. Stephen was a respected embryologist working in IVF, while Ola came from a financial background. They chose the property due to its good range of pinot noir and chardonnay clones (there are also plantings of cabernet sauvignon and sauvignon blanc). Farm animals are used in the vineyard: chickens and ducks eat the pests and sheep and alpacas provide manure and keep the vineyard neat and tidy.

♥♥♥♥♥ **Reserve Shiraz 2014** Matured in French oak. Strongly resonant of its cool climate. Spice, cracked pepper and mouthwatering acidity are all adjuncts to its black cherry and blueberry fruits, the tannins in their due place, French oak likewise. Screwcap. 14.5% alc. **Rating** 94 **To** 2029 $29 ✪

♥♥♥♥♀ **Mount Barker Riesling 2015 Rating** 92 **To** 2027 $25 ✪
Reserve Pinot Noir 2014 Rating 92 **To** 2024 $35
Sauvignon Blanc 2015 Rating 90 **To** 2017 $20 ✪

Evans & Tate

Cnr Metricup Road/Caves Road, Wilyabrup, WA 6280 **Region** Margaret River
T (08) 9755 6244 **www**.evansandtate.com.au **Open** 7 days 10.30–5
Winemaker Matthew Byrne, Lachlan McDonald **Est.** 1970 **Dozens** NFP **Vyds** 12.3ha
The 45-year history of Evans & Tate has been one of constant change and, for decades, expansion, acquiring large wineries in SA and NSW. For a series of reasons, nothing to do with the excellent quality of its Margaret River wines, the empire fell apart in 2005; McWilliam's finalised its acquisition of the Evans & Tate brand, cellar door and vineyards (and since a part share in the winery) in December '07. Wine quality was and continues to be maintained. Exports to all major markets.

♥♥♥♥♥ **Metricup Road Semillon Sauvignon Blanc 2015** Both semillon (wild yeast) and sauvignon blanc (part cultured, part wild) are fermented in French oak (part new), matured for 5 months. This fills the senses, both bouquet and palate, with a hectic profusion of tropical passionfruit and guava, citrus zest and juice, and spicy/toasty oak. The label design says it all: a ride in a frightening machine at a side show. You can't get much more than this. Screwcap. 12.5% alc. **Rating** 95 **To** 2018 $24 ✪
Redbrook Shiraz 2013 Margaret River at its elegant best, looking like a distinctly cool climate wine; it is fresh and lively, its medium body created by cherry and blackberry fruit surrounded by fine, savoury tannins and subtle, but firm, French oak. Screwcap. 14% alc. **Rating** 95 **To** 2038 $49

♥♥♥♥♀ **Redbrook Cabernet Sauvignon 2013 Rating** 93 **To** 2043 $49
Metricup Road Chardonnay 2015 Rating 91 **To** 2020 $24
Metricup Road Shiraz 2013 Rating 91 **To** 2033 $24

Evoi Wines

92 Dunsborough Lakes Drive, Dunsborough, WA 6281 **Region** Margaret River
T 0407 131 080 **www**.evoiwines.com **Open** By appt
Winemaker Nigel Ludlow **Est.** 2006 **Dozens** 5000
NZ-born Nigel Ludlow has a Bachelor of Science in human nutrition, but after a short career as a professional triathlete, he turned his attention to grapegrowing and winemaking, with a graduate diploma in oenology and viticulture from Lincoln University, NZ. Time at Selaks Drylands winery was a stepping stone to Flying Winemaking stints in Hungary, Spain and South Africa, before a return as senior winemaker at Nobilo. He thereafter moved to Vic, finally to Margaret River. It took time for Evoi to take shape, the first vintage of chardonnay being made in the lounge room of his house. By 2010 the barrels had been evicted to more

conventional storage, and since '14 the wines have been made in leased space at a commercial winery. Quality throughout has been exceptional. Exports to the UK and Hong Kong.

ŸŸŸŸŸ **art by Evoi Reserve Sauvignon Blanc Semillon 2015** Part wild-fermented in barriques, the remainder in tank. There is total synergy between the blend of varieties and the fermentation methods, opening with grass and green capsicum, then moving through to Meyer lemon, and finally to passionfruit – all tied together by a bow of acidity. Screwcap. 13% alc. **Rating** 95 To 2018 $18 ✪

Reserve Chardonnay 2014 Hand-picked, whole bunch-pressed to French oak (40% new) with 80% wild yeast and full solids, 20% mlf, matured for 12 months. Whereas Evoi's red wines are founded on layered complexity and power, the whites hunt for elegance. The flavours range from white peach to honeydew melon to fig, with a squeeze of fresh citrus on top; its length and balance are spot on. Screwcap. 13.5% alc. **Rating** 95 To 2024 $55

Cabernet Sauvignon 2014 Includes 3.5% petit verdot and 2% malbec. Open-fermented, a portion finished fermentation in barrel, 15 months maturation in French barriques (30% new). A full-bodied, majestic Margaret River cabernet with layers of blackcurrant fruit, bay leaf, plentiful ripe tannins and oak to match. Screwcap. 14.5% alc. **Rating** 95 To 2039 $32 ✪

The Satyr Reserve 2013 70% cabernet sauvignon, 16% petit verdot, 14% malbec. Crushed/destemmed, open-fermented, part finished fermentation in barrel, the balance going to barrel after post-ferment maceration, 16 months maturation in French barriques (30% new). This is an unequivocally imposing wine, still far from its best, but has the requisite balance to absolutely guarantee its long journey to its peak, all of its fruits in the black spectrum, its tattoo of tannins always there. Screwcap. 14.5% alc. **Rating** 95 To 2038 $55

Sauvignon Blanc Semillon 2015 Night-harvested, largely tank-fermented, with a small portion in French barriques, which is unexpectedly obvious on the bouquet, less so on the long and intensely focused palate. The blend percentages aren't specified, but the semillon has given the wine its minerally structure and drive. Screwcap. 13% alc. **Rating** 94 To 2017 $23 ✪

Chardonnay 2014 Hand-picked and whole bunch-pressed, fermented in 100l cubes and French barriques, partial wild and mlf. Screams Margaret River from the rooftops, with peaches and cream, tempered by segments of grapefruit and fruity acidity, even though I wonder whether mlf added to the palate. Screwcap. 13% alc. **Rating** 94 To 2020 $28 ✪

Faber Vineyard ★★★★☆

233 Haddrill Road, Baskerville, WA 6056 **Region** Swan Valley
T (08) 9296 0209 **www.fabervineyard.com.au Open** Fri–Sun 11–4
Winemaker John Griffiths **Est.** 1997 **Dozens** 2500 **Vyds** 4.5ha
John Griffiths, former Houghton winemaker, now university lecturer and consultant, teamed with wife Jane Micallef to found Faber Vineyard. They have established shiraz, verdelho (1.5ha each), brown muscat, chardonnay and petit verdot (0.5ha each). Says John, 'It may be somewhat quixotic, but I'm a great fan of traditional warm-area Australian wine styles, wines made in a relatively simple manner that reflect the concentrated ripe flavours one expects in these regions. And when one searches, some of these gems can be found from the Swan Valley.' Exports to Hong Kong and China.

ŸŸŸŸŸ **Reserve Swan Valley Shiraz 2013** X-factor. It's a raunchy, bold, oak- and fruit-laden wine, dark and muscular. And yet it's more than that. Earth, crushed ants, dry spice, coal, even raspberry. It's bright but brooding, thick but thoughtful. Something special. Cork. 14.5% alc. **Rating** 96 To 2032 $71 CM ✪

ŸŸŸŸŸ **Dwellingup Chardonnay 2014** Rating 93 To 2019 $30 CM
Petit Verdot 2014 Rating 93 To 2023 $29 CM
Dwellingup Malbec 2014 Rating 92 To 2024 $32 CM
Swan Verdelho 2015 Rating 91 To 2019 $20 CM ✪
Donnybrook Durif 2014 Rating 91 To 2024 $36 CM

Farr | Farr Rising   ★★★★★

27 Maddens Road, Bannockburn, Vic 3331 **Region** Geelong
T (03) 5281 1733 **www.byfarr.com.au Open** Not
Winemaker Nick Farr **Est.** 1994 **Dozens** 5500 **Vyds** 13.8ha

By Farr and Farr Rising continue to be separate brands from separate vineyards, the one major
change from previous years being that Nick Farr has assumed total responsibility for both
labels, leaving father Gary free to pursue the finer things in life without interruption. This has
in no way resulted in any diminution in the quality of the Pinot Noir, Chardonnay, Shiraz
and Viognier made. The vineyards are based on ancient river deposits within the Moorabool
Valley. There are six different soils spread across the Farr property, with the two main types
being rich, friable red and black volcanic loam, and limestone, which dominates the loam
in some areas. The other soils are quartz gravel through a red volcanic soil, ironstone (called
buckshot) in grey sandy loam with a heavy clay base, sandstone base and volcanic lava. The
soil's good drainage and low fertility are crucial in ensuring small yields of intensely flavoured
fruit. Exports to the UK, Canada, Denmark, Sweden, Hong Kong, Singapore, Taiwan, the
Maldives, China and Japan.

🍷🍷🍷🍷🍷 **Farrside by Farr Pinot Noir 2014** Clones 114, 115, 667 and MV6, hand-
picked and sorted, 60–70% destemmed, wild-fermented, matured for 18 months
in French oak (50–60% new). The bouquet, while complex, is the calm before
the storm of the palate, which strikes the second the wine enters the mouth, and
doesn't abate until long after the wine has gone from the glass. Its great character
is the fusion of plum/black cherry fruit with a savoury carpet of spices and sweet
earth. Quite simply, a very great pinot. Cork. 13.5% alc. **Rating** 98 **To** 2029
$83 ✪

Sangreal by Farr Pinot Noir 2014 Clones 114 and 115 planted '94, believed
to have mutated into a single 'Sangreal' clone. Always made with 60% whole
bunches, and 65% new oak maturation for 18 months. Typical bright, deep hue;
the bouquet exudes flowers (roses, violets), spices and a throbbing heartbeat of
gently savoury dark fruits; the palate magically twists all these characters into
a single silver-coated stream of red and blue fruits, the tannins no more than
background haze, oak a slender frame. A gorgeous pinot. Cork. 13% alc. **Rating** 97
To 2024 $83 ✪

Tout Pres by Farr Pinot Noir 2013 From a 1ha vineyard in an amphitheatre
with three different soil types, 6 clones mutated into a single Tout Pres clone
planted at 7300 vines per ha, normally 100% whole bunches in a single 5-tonne
open fermenter. An extra year may be part of the reason, the vintage another part,
for this being radically different from the other wines in the portfolio. The Farrs
would say it's the vineyard's unique terroir, including the ultra-close planting. It's
the most savoury of the five pinots, but not so savoury that it diminishes the dark
cherry/berry fruit and sweet spices at the heart of the wine. Cork. 13.5% alc.
Rating 97 **To** 2029 $110 ✪

🍷🍷🍷🍷🍷 **Farr Rising Pinot Noir 2014** MV6, 114 and 115 clones, open-fermented
with 60–70% destemmed, matured in Allier oak (25% new) for 18 months. The
bouquet immediately blares out the complexity the wine will bring to the palate,
and that it does in spades. The low yields of '14 and high ratio of skin to pulp
often brings darker fruits (compared to the '13) into play, and does so here; savoury
spicy also extend a fabulously long palate even further. Diam. 13% alc. **Rating** 96
To 2029 $48 ✪

By Farr Shiraz 2014 15+yo vines, 4% viognier co-fermented in open tanks,
20–22 days on skins, matured for 18 months in French oak (25% new). A very
elegant shiraz reflecting its modest alcohol, the moderating effect of viognier, and
gentle winemaking extraction. Spicy red fruits are already supple, and the balance
of oak and tannins can't be faulted. Shortly put, it could be drunk tomorrow.
Cork. 13% alc. **Rating** 96 **To** 2039 $64 ✪

By Farr Viognier 2014 Wild-fermented in used (5yo) French oak, matured for
11 months. Bright straw-green; it's fairly predictable, but this is a viognier that

breaks the rules (which don't apply to Yalumba) by having ample varietal character, no phenolics and a long palate. Simply don't cellar it for too long. Cork. 12.5% alc. **Rating** 95 **To** 2018 $64

Farr Rising Saignee 2015 Multiple pinot noir clones, wild-fermented in used (5yo) French oak, matured for 8 months. Salmon-pink; bled from fully ripe fruit; a great depth and intensity to the red fruit flavour profile, but runs a pure and linear passage through the long palate. One of the best barrel-fermented roses around. Diam. 14% alc. **Rating** 95 **To** 2018 $29 ✪

Farr Rising Gamay 2015 The Farrs are contemptuous of the average, indeed knowledgeable, consumers wondering about this new addition to the range, giving no clues on the minimalist labels. It opens with a trumpet of plummy fruit on the bouquet, following this with a palate of considerable texture and structure. Whatever else it may be, it's no lollipop style, and will hang in for several years yet. Diam. 13% alc. **Rating** 94 **To** 2021 $36

♟♟♟♟♟ **Farr Rising Shiraz 2014 Rating** 93 **To** 2030 $48
By Farr Chardonnay 2014 Rating 92 **To** 2019 $78

Feathertop Wines   ★★★★

Great Alpine Road, Porepunkah, Vic 3741 **Region** Alpine Valleys
T (03) 5756 2356 **www.**boynton.com.au **Open** 7 days 10–5
Winemaker Kel Boynton, Nick Toy **Est.** 1987 **Dozens** 10 000 **Vyds** 16ha
Kel Boynton has a beautiful vineyard, framed by Mt Feathertop rising above it. The initial very strong American oak input has been softened in more recent vintages to give a better fruit–oak balance. Kel has planted a spectacular array of 22 varieties, headed by savagnin, pinot gris, vermentino, sauvignon blanc, fiano, verdejo, riesling, friulano, pinot noir, tempranillo, sangiovese, merlot, shiraz, montepulciano and nebbiolo, with smaller plantings of prosecco, pinot meunier, dornfelder, durif, malbec, cabernet sauvignon and petit verdot. Exports to Austria.

♟♟♟♟♟ **Limited Release Riesling 2014** Mellifluous. Keen lime, apple and spice flavours burst deliciously through the palate. Musky, perfumed inflections to the finish and aftertaste. A wine a wide audience will enjoy. Screwcap. 11% alc. **Rating** 92 **To** 2023 $25 CM ✪

Alpine Valleys Savagnin 2015 It wears generosity on its sleeve. Abundant citrus, stone fruit and spice flavours carry through to a succulent, satisfying finish. Delicious. Screwcap. 12.5% alc. **Rating** 92 **To** 2016 $25 CM ✪

Limited Release Friulano 2014 What it does is combine floral, fruit-driven, pretty characters with dry, slatey, almost chalky aspects, and it does so seamlessly. Intensity is not a strong suit but it still has plenty going for it. Perfect for the lunch table. Screwcap. 12% alc. **Rating** 91 **To** 2016 $25 CM

Alpine Valleys Pinot Gris 2015 Spice, nashi pear and melon flavours wax on and wax off. Easygoing but with just enough to keep you interested. Screwcap. 13.5% alc. **Rating** 90 **To** 2016 $25 CM

Limited Release Pinots 2014 Interesting, savoury-styled blend of pinot noir and pinot meunier. Tangy red fruit meets herbs and assorted florals. It's attractive, food-friendly, slightly gamey and strung with lively acid. An extra year or two in bottle wouldn't hurt it. Screwcap. 12.5% alc. **Rating** 90 **To** 2022 $30 CM

Limited Release Tempranillo 2014 Well polished and presented with red cherry and modest plum flavours sluicing through the palate. Mouthwatering style, light but juicy, with tannin adding just enough chew to the finish. Screwcap. 14% alc. **Rating** 90 **To** 2021 $30 CM

♟♟♟♟ **Alpine Valleys Merlot 2013 Rating** 89 **To** 2022 $30 CM
Limited Release Sangiovese 2013 Rating 89 **To** 2023 $30 CM
Prosecco 2013 Rating 89 **To** 2017 $35 TS
Alpine Valleys Vermentino 2014 Rating 88 **To** 2017 $25 CM
Blanc de Blancs 2012 Rating 88 **To** 2032 $40 TS

Fermoy Estate ★★★★★

838 Metricup Road, Wilyabrup, WA 6280 **Region** Margaret River
T (08) 9755 6285 www.fermoy.com.au **Open** 7 days 10–5
Winemaker Jeremy Hodgson **Est.** 1985 **Dozens** 16 000 **Vyds** 47ha
A long-established winery with 17ha of semillon, sauvignon blanc, chardonnay, cabernet sauvignon and merlot. The Young family acquired Fermoy Estate in 2010, and built a new, larger cellar door which opened in '13, signalling the drive to increase domestic sales. Notwithstanding its significant production, it is happy to keep a relatively low profile, however difficult that may be given the quality of the wines. Jeremy Hodgson brings with him a first-class honours degree in oenology and viticulture, and a CV encompassing winemaking roles with Wise Wines, Cherubino Consultancy and, earlier, Plantagenet, Houghton and Goundrey Wines. Exports to Europe, Asia and China.

ŶŶŶŶŶ **Reserve Semillon 2015** Bright, energetic and piercing; the fruit and attendant acidity have swallowed whatever oak was used in its vinification; it has exceptional drive, its lemon/lemongrass/lemon curd flavours in perfect balance with its acidity. Screwcap. 12.5% alc. **Rating** 95 **To** 2025 $45
Sauvignon Blanc 2015 Partial barrel fermentation in new French oak adds a significant dimension to both the flavour and the mouthfeel of this wine, which wings its way from savoury herbal/snow pea to passionfruit and guava without missing a beat. Hard to argue with a wine such as this. Screwcap. 12.5% alc. **Rating** 95 **To** 2018 $25 ✪
Shiraz 2014 Estate-grown, matured for 18 months in a mix of French and American oak. A powerful and intense wine, with black fruits (berry and cherry), pepper, spice and licorice all on parade; has the tannin structure to sustain lengthy cellaring. Screwcap. 13.5% alc. **Rating** 95 **To** 2034 $25 ✪
Margaret River Shiraz 2013 Matured for 18 months in French and American oak. Has things in common with the '14, particularly the precision and intensity; here more red fruits are in evidence on a long palate, the oak precisely judged, the tannins firm but fine. Screwcap. 14.5% alc. **Rating** 94 **To** 2033 $25 ✪

ŶŶŶŶŶ **Reserve Chardonnay 2015** **Rating** 93 **To** 2022 $50
Semillon Sauvignon Blanc 2015 **Rating** 92 **To** 2017 $22 ✪
Geographe Rose 2015 **Rating** 92 **To** 2018 $22 ✪
Chardonnay 2015 **Rating** 91 **To** 2020 $30

Ferngrove ★★★★☆

276 Ferngrove Road, Frankland River, WA 6396 **Region** Frankland River
T (08) 9363 1300 www.ferngrove.com.au **Open** Mon–Sat 10–4
Winemaker Marco Pinares, Marelize Russouw **Est.** 1998 **Dozens** NFP **Vyds** 340ha
Known for producing consistent examples of cool climate wines across multiple price brackets, the Ferngrove stable includes the Stirlings, Orchid, Frankland River and Symbols ranges. Ferngrove Vineyards Pty Ltd enjoys the benefits of majority international ownership, but remains Australian-run. The success of the business is reflected in the increase in the estate vineyard area from 210ha to 340ha. Exports to all major markets.

ŶŶŶŶŶ **Cossack Frankland River Riesling 2015** From single block on the home vineyard, crushed and destemmed, pressed to stainless steel for a no-frills, cultured yeast cool ferment. The highly perfumed citrus blossom and lavender bouquet leads into an intense and complex palate, more than worthy of the reputation of this great site. Screwcap. 13% alc. **Rating** 96 **To** 2030 $23 ✪
Frankland River Chardonnay 2014 Machine-harvested, crushed and destemmed, fermented in French oak (30% new), matured for 9 months, gold medal Adelaide Wine Show '15. Zesty and lively, and no suggestion of sauvignon blanc, just fully ripened cool grown chardonnay. Like all Ferngrove wines, exceptional value. Screwcap. 13.5% alc. **Rating** 94 **To** 2024 $20 ✪

Limited Release Frankland River Malbec Rose 2015 Machine-harvested, destemmed/crushed, cool-fermented in stainless steel, gold medal National Cool Climate Wine Show '15. Vivid fuchsia-pink; clever winemaking; coats the mouth with flavours that are plummy one moment, spicy the next. Keeps you interested from start to finish. Screwcap. 13.7% alc. **Rating** 94 **To** 2017 $20 ✪

Limited Release Frankland River Cabernet Sauvignon 2014 Machine-harvested, destemmed, crushed, 14 days on skins, matured for 12 months in 100% new French oak. The bouquet and palate tell the same story: pure autocratic cabernet aroma, flavour and structure in a medium-bodied frame. The price makes no sense whatsoever. Screwcap. 13.5% alc. **Rating** 94 **To** 2039 $20 ✪

🍷🍷🍷🍷 **The Stirlings 2012** **Rating** 92 **To** 2037 $70
Limited Release Frankland River Malbec 2014 **Rating** 91 **To** 2029 $20 ✪
Frankland River Shiraz 2013 **Rating** 90 **To** 2023 $20 ✪

Fighting Gully Road ★★★★★

Kurrajong Way, Mayday Hill, Beechworth, Vic 3747 **Region** Beechworth
T (03) 5727 1434 **www**.fightinggully.com.au **Open** By appt
Winemaker Mark Walpole, Adrian Rodda **Est.** 1997 **Dozens** 3000 **Vyds** 8.3ha

Mark Walpole (who began his viticultural career with Brown Brothers in the late 1980s) and partner Carolyn De Poi found their elevated north-facing site to the south of Beechworth in 1995. They commenced planting the Aquila Audax Vineyard in 1997 with cabernet sauvignon and pinot noir, subsequently expanding with significant areas of sangiovese, tempranillo, shiraz, petit manseng and chardonnay. In 2009 they were fortunate to lease the oldest vineyard in the region, planted by the Smith family in 1978 to chardonnay and cabernet sauvignon – in fact Mark shares the Smith Family vineyard lease with long-term friend Adrian Rodda (see separate entry). Says Mark, 'We are now making wine in a building in the old and historic Mayday Hills Lunatic Asylum – a place that should be full of winemakers!'

🍷🍷🍷🍷🍷 **Shiraz 2013** Made in the same fashion as the '14. This has gorgeous medium-bodied mouthfeel, with spices and tannins waltzing around red cherry/berry fruits. It politely, but insistently, says drink me now, and tomorrow, and tomorrow… Screwcap. 13.8% alc. **Rating** 96 **To** 2028 $35 ✪

Shiraz 2014 Hand-picked and sorted, 30% whole bunches, wild open ferment, 21 days on skins, matured for 15 months in 30% new oak. This is a cool climate, medium-bodied shiraz full of spicy, tangy black cherry and plum fruit, the finish long and perfectly balanced. Screwcap. 13.5% alc. **Rating** 95 **To** 2029 $35 ✪

Tempranillo 2013 Lightly crushed, wild open ferment, 28 days on skins, matured in French oak (50% new) for 18 months. The spicy, cherry fragrance of the bouquet leads as straight as an arrow to the medium-bodied palate. The Rolls Royce treatment with 50% new French oak from the Bertranges forest was perfect. Screwcap. 13.5% alc. **Rating** 95 **To** 2028 $32 ✪

Pinot Noir 2014 Clone 114, 25% whole bunches (fermented separately), matured in French oak (40% new) for 9 months. It has been very well made, and it has equally good varietal fruit expression. It is among the very best pinots to have come from Beechworth, with no dry red characters at all. I shall watch future vintages with great interest. Screwcap. 13.5% alc. **Rating** 94 **To** 2020 $25 ✪

Sangiovese 2014 Crushed/destemmed, wild open ferment, 21 days on skins, matured in French oak (25% new) for 10 months, 5% colorino blended in. It's the ultimate compliment to sangiovese to absentmindedly roll it around your mouth after the first taste gives you the thumbs up; your concentration strays for a moment and you snap to, not because the tannins bite, but because you really enjoyed the wine. So go for it. Screwcap. 14% alc. **Rating** 94 **To** 2029 $28 ✪

🍷🍷🍷🍷 **Rose 2015** **Rating** 92 **To** 2018 $25 ✪
Aquila 2014 **Rating** 91 **To** 2024 $26
Tempranillo 2012 **Rating** 91 **To** 2025 $32

 # Fikkers Wine

1 Grandview Crescent, Healesville, Vic 3777 (postal) **Region** Yarra Valley
T 0437 142 078 **www.**fikkerswine.com.au **Open** Not
Winemaker Anthony Fikkers **Est.** 2010 **Dozens** 1300
Proprietor/winemaker Anthony Fikkers started his winemaking career in the Hunter Valley
before moving to settle permanently in the Yarra Valley. His modus operandi is to seek out
small parcels of wine in similar fashion to Mac Forbes, with whom he worked as assistant
winemaker. He certainly believes that variety is the spice of life, making the Two Bricks range,
the larger volume wines either unoaked or lightly oaked and a range of Single Vineyard
varietals, the vineyard sources changing from year to year reflecting availability, the make of
each wine typically around 70 dozen.

ΨΨΨΨΨ **Two Bricks Sauvignon Semillon 2015** 60% sauvignon blanc, 40% semillon, the
majority wild-fermented in French oak (15% new), 8% of the semillon fermented
on skins for 7 days, matured for 4 months. This is a powerful and complex fume
style that has delivered a high quality wine in a region with few such successes
(Out of Step one such). The semillon (and its treatment) is the secret weapon,
setting the framework for textures and flavours in the finished wine. Screwcap.
13% alc. **Rating** 95 **To** 2020 $26 ✪
Single Vineyard Chardonnay 2015 Whole bunch-pressed, wild-fermented in
French barriques (33% new), bottled Dec. Yet more proof of a winemaker able to
tick all the boxes, no matter where they are, nor how many. This wine has a razor-
sharp personality to its grapefruit/white peach duopoly, and trademark Yarra Valley
length. Screwcap. 13% alc. **Rating** 95 **To** 2023 $35 ✪

ΨΨΨΨΨ **Single Vineyard Pinot Noir 2015** **Rating** 93 **To** 2027 $35
Two Bricks Pinot Meunier 2015 **Rating** 92 **To** 2025 $26
Two Bricks Shiraz 2015 **Rating** 91 **To** 2026 $26
Two Bricks Sangiovese 2015 **Rating** 90 **To** 2022 $26

Fire Gully

Metricup Road, Wilyabrup, WA 6280 **Region** Margaret River
T (08) 9755 6220 **www.**firegully.com.au **Open** By appt
Winemaker Dr Michael Peterkin **Est.** 1988 **Dozens** 5000 **Vyds** 13.4ha
A 6ha lake created in a gully ravaged by bushfires gave the name. In 1998 Mike Peterkin of
Pierro purchased it, and manages the vineyard in conjunction with former owners Ellis and
Margaret Butcher. He regards the Fire Gully wines as entirely separate from those of Pierro:
the plantings are cabernet sauvignon, merlot, shiraz, semillon, sauvignon blanc, chardonnay,
viognier and chenin blanc. Exports to all major markets.

ΨΨΨΨΨ **Margaret River Sauvignon Blanc Semillon 2015** 50/50%, given additional
complexity by the fermentation of a small amount of sauvignon blanc in used
oak. The sheer volume of fruit, its power, focus and length, are all achievable in
Margaret River without the celebration expected if it had come from eastern
Australia. This is a singularly satisfying wine with no chinks in its armour.
Screwcap. 12.5% alc. **Rating** 95 **To** 2020 $24 ✪

ΨΨΨΨΨ **Margaret River Shiraz 2013** **Rating** 93 **To** 2028 $31
Margaret River Chardonnay 2014 **Rating** 91 **To** 2020 $31

First Creek Wines ★★★★★

600 McDonalds Road, Pokolbin, NSW 2320 **Region** Hunter Valley
T (02) 4998 7293 **www.**firstcreekwines.com.au **Open** 7 days 10–5
Winemaker Liz and Greg Silkman **Est.** 1984 **Dozens** 35 000
First Creek Wines is the brand of First Creek Winemaking Services, a major contract
winemaker (over 25 clients). Winemaker Liz Silkman (née Jackson) had an exceptional year
in 2011: she was a finalist in the Gourmet Traveller Winemaker of the Year awards, winner of

the Hunter Valley Winemaker of the Year, and won Best Red Wine of Show at the NSW Wine Awards for the Winemakers Reserve Shiraz 2010. Exports to the UK, Sweden and China.

🍷🍷🍷🍷🍷 **Winemaker's Reserve Semillon 2015** A pristine and complete Hunter semillon, it oozes its class from the outset; lemongrass and lime leaf lead to a beautifully shaped palate with texture, length and restraint; it has a pithy and long finish. Screwcap. 10.5% alc. **Rating** 96 **To** 2035 $50 ✪

Winemaker's Reserve Chardonnay 2015 Follows the all-conquering '14. In many ways not typical Hunter chardonnay, with struck match, grapefruit and lemon; has intense and powerful oak lined by taut acidity. Screwcap. **Rating** 96 **To** 2023 $60 ✪

Winemaker's Reserve Semillon 2010 At 6yo the complexity has begun to emerge, lime, wax and lemongrass leading to the unfurling and expansive palate, finishing long and limey. Screwcap. 11.5% alc. **Rating** 95 **To** 2020 $50

Winemaker's Reserve Shiraz 2014 Mulberry, blackberry and the trademark spice are here in spades. It is darkly coloured and plushly fruited, but underpinned by savoury and dusty tannins. Long, young and loads of potential. Screwcap. 14.5% alc. **Rating** 95 **To** 2028 $60

🍷🍷🍷🍷🍷 **Single Vineyard Black Cluster Semillon 2015** Rating 92 **To** 2025 $50
Semillon 2015 Rating 92 **To** 2025 $25 ✪

First Drop Wines ★★★★★

Beckwith Park, Barossa Valley Way, Nuriootpa, SA 5355 **Region** Barossa Valley
T (08) 8562 3324 **www.**firstdropwines.com **Open** Wed–Sat 10–4
Winemaker Matt Gant **Est.** 2005 **Dozens** 10000

The First Drop Wines of today has been transformed since its establishment in 2005. It now has a real winery, part of the old Penfolds winery at Nuriootpa, shared with Tim Smith Wines. The group of buildings is now called Beckwith Park, in honour of the man who did so much groundbreaking work for Penfolds (Ray Beckwith OAM, who died in 2012, but not before his 100th birthday; his other recognition came in the form of the Maurice O'Shea Award). Exports to the UK, the US, Canada, Denmark, Japan, Hong Kong, Singapore and NZ.

🍷🍷🍷🍷🍷 **Does Your Dog Bite Single Vineyard Wilton Eden Valley Syrah 2013** Hand-picked, open-fermented, 50% whole bunches, 50% crushed/destemmed, 10 days on skins, fermentation finished and matured for 18 months in French puncheons (33% new). It is very elegant, yet even more lively and intense, red fruits and spice joining the darker side of the spectrum. Stemmy tannins are the cream on the cake. Screwcap. 14% alc. **Rating** 96 **To** 2033 $50 ✪

Two Percent Barossa Shiraz 2014 Includes 2% moscatel, crushed/destemmed, static fermenters with 12 days on skins, fermentation finished in and matured for 20 months in French hogsheads (18% new) and American barriques. Deeply coloured; interesting use of moscatel for co-fermentation; the cadence of the palate ebbs and flows, alcohol showing one moment, unexpected elegance the next. Screwcap. 15% alc. **Rating** 95 **To** 2034 $38

Mother's Milk Barossa Shiraz 2014 Crushed/destemmed with cultured yeast in static fermenters, 8–12 days on skins, 12 months in French oak. Full-bodied and full-blooded; just when you think it's OTT, savoury tannins and a touch of oak pull back the plush, plummy fruit. Screwcap. 14.5% alc. **Rating** 94 **To** 2029 $25 ✪

Does Your Dog Bite Single Vineyard Moculta Eden Valley Syrah 2013 Crushed/destemmed, open-fermented, 10 days on skins, matured for 18 months in new French puncheons. Deep, dense colour, although brighter than the Craneford Syrah; this is similarly full-bodied, but allows a little more light into the dense fruit; the tannins are better balanced, and, tellingly, more savoury. Screwcap. 14.5% alc. **Rating** 94 **To** 2033 $50

Does Your Dog Bite Single Vineyard Craneford Eden Valley Syrah 2013 Crushed and destemmed, open-fermented with cultured yeast, 10 days on skins, fermentation finished in, and matured for 18 months in, French hogsheads

(45% new). Deep, dense colour; well and truly OTT. If everything in the wine was cut back by (say) 15%, it could be something special. The label is another (polarising) matter. Screwcap. 14.5% alc. **Rating** 94 To 2033 $50

McLaren Vale Touriga Nacional 2014 Destemmed, 8 days on skins, fermentation finished and matured in French hogsheads. Matt Gant must be keeping the label printers of Adelaide busy at work, the main instruction to the designers that no two labels can look even remotely the same. Regardless, this is an attractively juicy wine, its red fruity flavours with mouthwatering acidity. Excellent casual consumption wine. Screwcap. 13% alc. **Rating** 94 To 2022 $25 ✪

ㅏㅏㅏㅏㅏ **JR Gantos Quinta do sul McLaren Vale Cabernet Sauvignon Touriga Nacional 2012** Rating 93 To 2032 $38
Quinta do Sul 2013 Rating 93 To 2033 $30
Mother's Ruin Cabernet Sauvignon 2014 Rating 91 To 2020 $25
Vivo d'Adelaide Hills Arneis 2015 Rating 90 To 2017 $25
Half & Half Barossa Shiraz Monastrell 2014 Rating 90 To 2017 $25

Five Geese   ★★★★★

389 Chapel Hill Road, Blewitt Springs, SA 5171 (postal) **Region** McLaren Vale
T (08) 8383 0576 **www**.fivegeese.com.au **Open** Not
Winemaker Mike Farmilo **Est.** 1999 **Dozens** 5000 **Vyds** 28ha
Sue Trott is devoted to her Five Geese wines, which come from vines planted in 1927 and '65 (shiraz, cabernet sauvignon, grenache and mataro), nero d'Avola a more recent arrival. She sold the grapes for many years, but in '99 decided to create her own label and make a strictly limited amount of wine from the pick of the vineyards, which are run on organic principles. The quality of the wines, and their price, is exemplary. Exports to the UK, South Korea and Singapore.

ㅏㅏㅏㅏㅏ **The Pippali Old Vine Shiraz 2013** This Blewitt Springs vineyard was destroyed by a bushfire in '55, replanted '66, purchased by Sue Trott in '96. Fermented for 7 days on skins, matured for 20 months in new and 1yo French hogsheads. If the cork doesn't tell you this is destined for export, the expansive back label in German text seals the deal. From 47yo vines, and given significantly more oak, you might have expected a higher price. Regardless, it's got it all together. 14.5% alc. Rating 96 To 2035 $28 ✪
Indian File Old Vine Grenache 2014 Fermented with whole bunches and matured mostly in stainless steel. It still shows some signs of oak but it's mostly about fantastic fruit. Aniseed, raspberry and five-spice characters create a brilliant impression. Tannin then exerts discipline. Grenache for pinot noir lovers. Screwcap. 14.5% alc. Rating 95 To 2024 $28 CM ✪
Shiraz 2013 Crushed and destemmed, 7 days on skins, matured for 18 months in used hogsheads. Exceptional colour; these geese come right at you, wings waving, mouths agape, and all you've done is attempted to lift the glass. It's intense and long, with dark plum fruit wreathed in licorice, earth and persistent, but shapely, tannins. Screwcap. 14.5% alc. Rating 94 To 2033 $22 ✪
The Gander's Blend Old Vine Grenache Shiraz 2014 80/20%, the grenache from old bush vines, part whole-bunch fermentation on skins for 5 days, the shiraz on skins for 7 days, matured for 9 months in used oak. Marvellous colour for grenache (even with some shiraz), the vines 80yo and going strong; the bouquet is complex and truffly, the palate surging with life and strength. This will be a wine to behold in 10 years, for its balance is perfect, and that is only the beginning. Screwcap. 14.5% alc. Rating 94 To 2034 $28 ✪

ㅏㅏㅏㅏㅏ **La Volpe Nero d'Avola 2014** Rating 93 To 2021 $28 CM

Five Oaks Vineyard

60 Aitken Road, Seville, Vic 3139 **Region** Yarra Valley
T (03) 5964 3704 **www**.fiveoaks.com.au **Open** W'ends & public hols 11–5
Winemaker Wally Zuk **Est.** 1995 **Dozens** 1000 **Vyds** 3ha

Wally Zuk and wife Judy run all aspects of Five Oaks – far removed from Wally's background in nuclear physics. He has, however, completed the wine science degree at CSU, and is thus more than qualified to make the Five Oaks wines. The lion's share of the vineyard is planted to cabernet sauvignon (2.6ha), with 0.2ha each of riesling and merlot. Exports to Canada, Macau, Hong Kong and China.

Yarra Valley Cabernet Sauvignon 2014 Crushed, pressed, fermented in stainless steel with cultured yeast for 14 days, transferred to French oak (85% new) for completion of ferment and 18 months maturation. Vibrantly fresh; has made light work of all the new oak in which it was matured, dried herb and bay leaf contributing to its flavour spectrum. The tannins, on the other hand, are finer than usual. Screwcap. 13.8% alc. **Rating** 95 **To** 2029 $30 **○**

Flametree

Cnr Caves Road/Chain Avenue, Dunsborough, WA 6281 **Region** Margaret River
T (08) 9756 8577 **www**.flametreewines.com **Open** 7 days 10–5
Winemaker Cliff Royle, Julian Scott **Est.** 2007 **Dozens** 20 000

Flametree, owned by the Towner family (John, Liz, Rob and Annie), has had extraordinary success since its first vintage in 2007. The usual practice of planting a vineyard and then finding someone to make the wine was turned on its head: a state-of-the-art winery was built, and grape purchase agreements signed with growers in the region. Gold medal after gold medal and trophy after trophy followed, topped by the winning of the Jimmy Watson Trophy with its first red wine, the 2007 Cabernet Merlot. If all this were not enough, Flametree has since secured the services of former long-serving winemaker at Voyager Estate, Cliff Royle. Exports to the UK, Indonesia, Malaysia, the Philippines and Singapore.

S.R.S. Wilyabrup Cabernet Sauvignon 2013 Stamps its class from the outset. The berried juices flow, the leaves add a layer, the beat of gravelly tannin ensures it's all built on a firm foundation. Tea and dark chocolate notes trill at various points. Bankable quality. Screwcap. 14% alc. **Rating** 96 **To** 2033 $58 CM **○**

S.R.S. Wallcliffe Margaret River Chardonnay 2015 Gingin clone, hand-picked and whole bunch-pressed for wild yeast barrel ferment (100% new French oak); matured for 12 months. Margaret River chardonnay at its elegant best, with white peach, cashew and grapefruit standing clear and proud, the barrel-ferment inputs there, but relatively subtle. Screwcap. 13% alc. **Rating** 95 **To** 2022 $58

Margaret River Shiraz 2013 At the heartier end of the regional shiraz style and at the upper end of the quality scale too. This doesn't pull any punches. It's beefy with blackberry, licorice, dust and chicory notes and strings flavour-loaded tannin out through the finish. A bright but sturdy wine. The price is very attractive. Screwcap. 14% alc. **Rating** 95 **To** 2028 $27 CM **○**

Margaret River Pinot Rose 2015 Tasty. Very. Cherries and spices, strawberries, a bit of grip, a lot of drive. Clearly above average. Screwcap. 13% alc. **Rating** 94 **To** 2017 $25 CM **○**

Margaret River Cabernet Merlot 2013 Firm but fleshy. You can tuck into it now or tuck it away for 'ron. Blackcurrant, bay leaves, mulberry and undergrowthy/tobacco-like notes. It builds a good head of steam without overdoing it, and then finishes the job admirably through the finish. A picture of composure. Screwcap. 14% alc. **Rating** 94 **To** 2030 $33 CM

Margaret River 2015 Rating 93 **To** 2016 $24 CM **○**

Flaxman Wines

Lot 535 Flaxmans Valley Road, Angaston, SA 5353 **Region** Eden Valley
T 0411 668 949 **www.**flaxmanwines.com.au **Open** By appt
Winemaker Colin Sheppard **Est.** 2005 **Dozens** 1500 **Vyds** 2ha

After visiting the Barossa Valley for over a decade, Melbourne residents Colin Sheppard and wife Fi decided on a seachange, and in 2004 found a small, old vineyard overlooking Flaxmans Valley. It consists of 1ha of 60+ and 90-year-old riesling, 1ha of 65+ and 90-year-old shiraz and a 0.8ha of 60+-year-old semillon. The vines are dry-grown, hand-pruned and hand-picked, and treated – say the Sheppards – as their garden. Yields are restricted to under 4 tonnes per hectare, and exceptional parcels of locally grown grapes are also purchased. Colin has worked at various Barossa wineries for many years, and his attention to detail (and understanding of the process) is reflected in the consistently high quality of the wines. An onsite winery and cellar door are planned for the near future.

🍷🍷🍷🍷🍷 **Estate Eden Valley Shiraz 2013** Matured in one new French hogshead and two used French barriques for 24 months. Deep, dense purple-crimson, it is saturated with black fruits, spices galore and cracked pepper. The fruit has swallowed the new French oak, and the 80 dozen bottled will disappear like water into desert sand. Screwcap. 13.5% alc. **Rating** 96 **To** 2043 $55 ○
Eden Valley Riesling 2015 Cropped at 1 tonne/acre, making 190 dozen. Pure Eden Valley, pure Flaxman. Most will be drunk soon, and there's no sin in that, but if you don't hang on to a bottle or two you will never know what you have missed: a lime juice icy pole. Screwcap. 11.5% alc. **Rating** 95 **To** 2030 $27 ○

Flowstone Wines

11298 Bussell Highway, Forest Grove, WA 6286 **Region** Margaret River
T 0487 010 275 **www.**flowstonewines.com **Open** By appt
Winemaker Stuart Pym **Est.** 2013 **Dozens** 1000 **Vyds** 2.25ha

Flowstone is the venture of Stuart Pym and Phil Giglia. Stuart's involvement with wine commenced in 1983, when he moved to Margaret River to help his parents establish their vineyard and winery in Wilyabrup (since sold and now Hay Shed Hill). Lengthy winemaking careers at Voyager Estate (1991–2000), Devil's Lair ('00–08) and Stella Bella ('08–13), were rounded out with concurrent vintage work overseas. Phil is a self-confessed wine tragic, his fascination starting at the University of WA's Wine Club. The two met at a Margaret River Great Estates lunch in the late '90s, and hatched the idea of starting a small business, which took shape in '03 when the property was purchased. 0.5ha of chardonnay was planted the following year, the remainder in '09. Estate grapes are augmented by contract-grown grapes. The attention to detail of the venture is typified by the appeal of the label design, the labels themselves made from 81% limestone, the remainder bonding resin (there is no wood fibre or pulp).

🍷🍷🍷🍷🍷 **Sauvignon Blanc 2014** Whole bunch-pressed, fermented in used oak and demi-muids, matured for 11 months in oak, plus 15 months in bottle. The complex, vaguely smoky/charry bouquet shifts around radically on the super-intense and complex palate, with citrus and snow pea doing battle with ripe citrus and guava/lychee tropical fruits, the latter prevailing. Screwcap. 12.5% alc. **Rating** 97 **To** 2019 $32 ○
Queen of the Earth Chardonnay 2013 From the home vineyard at Forest Grove, planted in '04, hand-picked, whole bunch-pressed, fermented in French oak (50% new), mlf, matured for 18 months, plus a further 24 months in bottle. I'll bet every vine receives personal attention; as each year passes, the style of the Flowstone wines becomes more clearly marked. Here it is the depth and texture of the fruit, mlf and oak in measured support of each other that establishes the special quality the wine has. Screwcap. 13% alc. **Rating** 97 **To** 2023 $55 ○
Queen of the Earth Cabernet Sauvignon 2012 From a dry-grown Wilyabrup vineyard planted in the late '70s, hand-picked, open-fermented, 17 days on skins, matured in used French oak for 3 years. Excellent colour; a suave

Margaret River cabernet with all its bolshie cabernet tannins now in the role they will play long term; the bouquet has some elusive violets, the mouthfeel and overall structure picture perfect, the flavours of cassis and bay leaf enough to melt a pinot lover's heart. Screwcap. 14% alc. **Rating** 97 **To** 2037 $75 **○**

ΨΨΨΨΨ **Chardonnay 2013** From a single vineyard in Karridale, whole bunch-pressed, fermented in French oak (20% new), mlf, matured in oak for 11 months, plus 30 months in bottle. Karridale is in the coolest part of the Margaret River, but the youth of this wine is amazing – as it has been in prior vintages. No single fruit flavour dominates, nor is the oak particularly obvious, it's just a very good chardonnay. Screwcap. 13% alc. **Rating** 96 **To** 2023 $36 **○**
Queen of the Earth Chardonnay 2012 The second (1.3 tonnes) vintage from the home block, hand-picked, whole bunch-pressed, fermented in French barriques (50% new, 50% 1yo), matured for 18 months, plus a further 24 months in bottle. A beautifully detailed wine, all its components perfectly lined up, flowing seamlessly across the palate, stone fruit tempered by just-so citrussy acidity, the oak absorbed. Screwcap. 13% alc. **Rating** 96 **To** 2025 $55 **○**
Shiraz Grenache 2014 75/25%, the shiraz crushed and destemmed for open fermentation, the grenache whole bunch and foot-stomped for 3 weeks, thence to barrel; the shiraz was pressed mid-ferment to barrel to complete its fermentation and 7 months' maturation. Has an utterly enticing array of berry flavours, spices and wild herbs, the latter helping to lift and cleanse the palate. Screwcap. 14% alc. **Rating** 95 **To** 2024 $25 **○**

ΨΨΨΨΨ **Gewurztraminer 2014 Rating** 93 **To** 2020 $32
Cabernet Sauvignon Touriga 2012 Rating 91 **To** 2027 $36

Flying Fish Cove   ★★★★★
Caves Road, Wilyabrup, WA 6284 **Region** Margaret River
T (08) 9755 6600 **www**.flyingfishcove.com **Open** 7 days 11–5
Winemaker Simon Ding **Est.** 2000 **Dozens** 21 000 **Vyds** 25ha
Flying Fish Cove has two strings to its bow: contract winemaking for others, and the development of its own brand, partly based on 25ha of estate plantings. The long-serving winemakers both had a circuitous journey before falling prey to the lure of wine. Simon Ding finished an apprenticeship in metalwork in 1993. On returning to Australia in '96 he obtained a Bachelor of Science Degree and joined the Flying Fish Cove team in 2000. Damon Easthaugh has always lived in WA, spending seven years studying law at the University of Western Australia. Law did not have the same appeal as winemaking, and Damon became a founding member of the winery. Exports to the US and Malaysia.

ΨΨΨΨΨ **Prize Catch Cabernet Sauvignon 2014** From the estate vineyard in Wilyabrup, matured in new French barriques for 16 months. Its small volume means its show opportunities are few and far between, but its purity, elegance and length make it stand out in any company. The mix of cassis, mulberry, bay leaf and cedar is as classic as it is long. Screwcap. 14.5% alc. **Rating** 97 **To** 2039 $95 **○**

ΨΨΨΨΨ **The Wildberry Reserve Shiraz 2014** Crushed and destemmed into a static fermenter with cultured yeast, daily pump-overs, matured in French oak (33% new), 249 dozen made. Deep crimson-purple; very focused, intense and spicy, it has many of the characteristics of very cool climate shiraz. The style has great appeal for its freshness; how this came about with 14.5% alcohol is quirky, which adds even more appeal. Screwcap. **Rating** 95 **To** 2034 $40
The Wildberry Reserve Cabernet Sauvignon 2014 It is classic Margaret River: mulberry and cassis with a touch of bay leaf. The palate is fine, with gravelly tannins and silky, rounded texture, long and powerfully fruited. Will reward cellaring. Screwcap. 14.5% alc. **Rating** 95 **To** 2029 $40
Reserve Chardonnay 2014 Whole bunch-pressed direct French barriques (40% new) for wild fermentation. An altogether different style from the standard version, with lots of toasty/biscuity/nutty nuances (no mlf involved). An ex

tempore blend of the two wines on the tasting table produced the best result.
Screwcap. 13% alc. **Rating** 94 **To** 2024 $40

Prize Catch Chardonnay 2014 A micro-batch of only 54 dozen made
exclusively from free-run juice, fermented and aged in 100% new French oak.
It is intensely concentrated, loaded with tropical fruits and coupled with a fair
dose of spicy new oak. The palate is layered and powerful. A powerful and intense
experience. Screwcap. 13% alc. **Rating** 94 **To** 2020 $95

♀♀♀♀♀ **Shiraz 2014** Rating 93 To 2029 $22 **○**
        Chardonnay 2014 Rating 90 To 2020 $22

Flynns Wines   ★★★★★

Lot 5 Lewis Road, Heathcote, Vic 3523 **Region** Heathcote
T (03) 5433 6297 **www**.flynnswines.com **Open** Mon–Fri 11–4, w'ends 11.30–5
Winemaker Greg and Natala Flynn **Est.** 1999 **Dozens** 2000 **Vyds** 4.12ha
Greg and Natala Flynn spent 18 months searching for their property, which is 13km north of
Heathcote on red Cambrian soil. They have established shiraz, sangiovese, verdelho, cabernet
sauvignon and merlot. Greg is a Roseworthy marketing graduate, and has had over 25 years
working at the coal face of retail and wholesale businesses, interweaving 10 years of vineyard
and winemaking experience, supplemented by the two-year Bendigo TAFE winemaking
course. Just for good measure, wife Natala has joined in the vineyard and winery, and likewise
completed the TAFE course.

♀♀♀♀♀ **James Flynn Shiraz 2012** Hand-picked, destemmed and some whole berries,
        matured in new French and American barriques. Deep crimson-purple; seriously
        powerful and autocratic, with fruit, oak and tannins all in play from the first
        moment; blackberry with forest fruits, spice and licorice are some of the markers.
        Screwcap. 14.5% alc. **Rating** 96 **To** 2042 $70 **○**
        MC Shiraz 2013 Hand-picked, open-fermented, matured in American and
        French barriques (40% new) for 18 months. Spice, licorice, black cherry and oak
        define the parameters of the bouquet and the flavours of the medium-bodied
        palate, tannins the other noteworthy inclusion. This is the style that established
        Heathcote's reputation for generous, flavour-filled red wines. Screwcap. 14.9% alc.
        Rating 95 **To** 2033 $35 **○**

♀♀♀♀♀ **Heathcote Viognier 2015** Rating 93 To 2018 $28

Forbes & Forbes   ★★★★

30 Williamstown Road, Springton, SA 5235 **Region** Eden Valley
T (08) 8568 2709 **www**.forbeswine.com.au **Open** At Taste Eden Valley, Angaston
Winemaker Colin Forbes **Est.** 2008 **Dozens** 400 **Vyds** 5ha
This venture is owned by Colin and Robert Forbes, and their respective partners. Colin says,
'I have been in the industry for a "frightening" length of time', beginning with Thomas Hardy
& Sons in 1974. While Colin is particularly attached to riesling, the property owned by the
partners in Eden Valley has 2ha each of riesling and merlot, and 1ha of cabernet sauvignon.

♀♀♀♀♀ **Single Vineyard Eden Valley Riesling 2015** Has a citrus and apple blossom
        bouquet and a palate that precisely follows the path laid down by the bouquet.
        Its balance, intensity and length are all right on the money: a great each-way
        proposition at the right price. Screwcap. 12.8% alc. **Rating** 92 **To** 2025 $20 **○**

♀♀♀♀   **Fraternal Blend 2011** Rating 89 To 2019 $30 CM

Forest Hill Vineyard   ★★★★★

Cnr South Coast Highway/Myers Road, Denmark, WA 6333 **Region** Great Southern
T (08) 9848 2399 **www**.foresthillwines.com.au **Open** Thurs–Sun 10.30–4.30
Winemaker Liam Carmody, Guy Lyons **Est.** 1965 **Dozens** 12 000 **Vyds** 65ha

This family-owned business is one of the oldest 'new' winemaking operations in WA, and was the site of the first grape plantings in Great Southern in 1965. The Forest Hill brand became well known, aided by the fact that a '75 Riesling made by Sandalford from Forest Hill grapes won nine trophies. The quality of the wines made from the oldest vines (dry-grown) on the property is awesome (released under the numbered vineyard block labels). Exports to Taiwan, Hong Kong, Singapore and China.

ΨΨΨΨΨ **Block 1 Riesling 2015** Tick all the boxes for yardstick young Mount Barker riesling and then add another one for pure class – and tick that too. Scintillating aromas of lime and lemon with a lift of fragrant floral blossom. Tight and racy as expected on the palate, but with a more expansive feel and depth not so often seen at this early stage. Slatey, citrus, zinging acidity gathers on the finish and lingers almost indefinitely. Screwcap. 13% alc. **Rating** 97 **To** 2030 $40 ✪

Block 1 Riesling 2014 The fragrant bouquet is filled with citrus and apple blossom scents leading into the inexorably intense palate of lime/grapefruit flavours, sustained and lengthened by the full-on minerally grip to the finish. Gold medal Qantas Wine Show WA '15. Screwcap. 13% alc. **Rating** 97 **To** 2030 $40 ✪

Block 1 Riesling 2013 The complex, flowery bouquet has developed a hint of spice, and the palate is just starting to relax, with an expanding range of flavours and accompanying power. Its freshness, integrity, line and length are the hallmark of the continuity of the style of all the vintages of Block 1 so far made. Gold medal Qantas Wine Show WA '15. Screwcap. 13% alc. **Rating** 97 **To** 2033 $40 ✪

Block 1 Riesling 2012 The fragrant and flowery, talc and blossom-filled bouquet leads into a leisurely uncoiling palate of lime and lemon, with quite beautiful flavour, mouthfeel and balance. From the oldest riesling vines in WA. Still developing at a leisurely pace, and better than it was when first tasted in Mar '13. Screwcap. 11.5% alc. **Rating** 97 **To** 2027 $38 ✪

ΨΨΨΨΨ **Block 8 Chardonnay 2013** Chilled, free-run juice pressed to French oak (40% new) for fermentation and 10 months maturation. An ultra-elegant and fine chardonnay with grapefruit, melon and white peach fruit in a seamless stream running through the long, perfectly balanced palate, the oak having been effortlessly absorbed. Screwcap. 14% alc. **Rating** 96 **To** 2028 $45 ✪

Estate Chardonnay 2015 Pressed straight to French oak (30% new) for cool fermentation, partial mlf and 8 months maturation. A complex bouquet, with smoky/funky nuances ex solids fermentation, leads into a palate with great length, drive and precision. This has classic restraint, very different from Margaret River. Screwcap. 13% alc. **Rating** 95 **To** 2023 $30 ✪

Estate Shiraz 2014 Includes 4% shiraz and 1% cabernet sauvignon. Open-fermented, matured for 18 months in French oak (30% new). Superb colour; there's no argument here: take me or leave me. In best Mount Barker style, it has layer upon layer of black fruits interleaved with spice, black pepper and cedar; the balance is such that there's every reason to be patient for as long as the bank balance permits. Screwcap. 14% alc. **Rating** 95 **To** 2034 $30 ✪

Estate Cabernet Sauvignon 2014 Cool climate cabernet of great purity. Blackcurrant, graphite and tobacco all speak of the variety, and the cedary oak fits perfectly into the mix. Medium-bodied and elegant in style, the tannin is fine-grained and unobtrusive. Screwcap. 13.5% alc. **Rating** 95 **To** 2034 $32 ✪

Block 5 Cabernet Sauvignon 2013 Open-fermented, matured in French barriques (40% new) for 18 months. High quality cabernet, the flavours so intense they draw saliva to capture the blackcurrant, graphite and bay leaf flavours of the medium to full-bodied palate, tannins making extreme length a given, oak only a memory. Screwcap. 14% alc. **Rating** 95 **To** 2038 $60

Block 9 Shiraz 2013 Open-fermented, matured in French oak (35% new) for 18 months. French oak is a major contributor to the bouquet and palate of the wine (more than expected from 35% new), but there is a wealth of red and black cherry and blueberry fruit, and the texture and weight are impeccable, fresh acidity a further boon. Screwcap. 13.5% alc. **Rating** 94 **To** 2033 $60

♈♈♈♈♈ Estate Great Southern Riesling 2015 Rating 93 To 2030 $26 ✪
Estate Malbec 2014 Rating 93 To 2025 $28
Estate Great Southern Gewurztraminer 2015 Rating 92 To 2025 $26
Highbury Fields Cabernet Merlot 2013 Rating 91 To 2028 $22 ✪

Forester Estate   ★★★★★

1064 Wildwood Road, Yallingup, WA 6282 **Region** Margaret River
T (08) 9755 2788 **www.**foresterestate.com.au **Open** By appt
Winemaker Kevin McKay, Todd Payne **Est.** 2001 **Dozens** 25 000 **Vyds** 33.5ha
Forester Estate is owned by Kevin and Jenny McKay, with a 500-tonne winery, half devoted
to contract winemaking, the other half for the Forester label. Winemaker Todd Payne has
had a distinguished career, starting in the Great Southern, thereafter the Napa Valley, back to
Plantagenet, then Esk Valley in Hawke's Bay, plus two vintages in the Northern Rhône Valley,
one with esteemed producer Yves Cuilleron in 2008. His move back to WA completed the
circle. The estate vineyards are planted to sauvignon blanc, semillon, chardonnay, cabernet
sauvignon, shiraz, merlot, petit verdot, malbec and alicante bouschet. Exports to Japan.

♈♈♈♈♈ **Cabernet Sauvignon 2013** This has raw power, its sultry black fruits, no-sugar
black chocolate and tannins made to measure, all vaulting into the recesses of the
palate before you've had time to think. There's undoubtedly some oak buried in
the fruit and tannins, but it is totally hidden. Its clench-fisted balance tells you it's
well worth a 20+-year investment. Screwcap. 14% alc. **Rating** 96 **To** 2043 $38 ✪
Yelverton Reserve Cabernet 2013 93% cabernet sauvignon, 5% cabernet
franc, 2% petit verdot, matured for 22 months in French barriques (75% new). Has
swallowed up the new oak despite its medium body (and medium alcohol); it's a
highly animated wine, its fragrant bouquet and bright red fruit flavours inviting
intimate contact. If you accept, you'll leave fulfilled and happy. Screwcap. 13.5% alc.
Rating 96 **To** 2038 $62 ✪
Cabernet Merlot 2013 Small amounts of other Bordeaux varieties accompany
the cabernet and merlot. The colour is bright, as is the bouquet and the heart of
this lovely medium-bodied wine. There are rivulets of cassis fruit running through
the palate, the tannins arranged in precise support, oak incidental to the main
exercise. A now or whenever proposition, and super value. Screwcap. 14% alc.
Rating 95 **To** 2025 $24 ✪
Sauvignon Blanc 2015 Hand-picked, 54% fermented in stainless steel, the
remainder fermented and matured in French barriques (32% new), blended and
bottled Jul. It's all so easy, the outcome so convincing; the flavours range seamlessly
from capsicum and snow pea through wood spice, then to an equal mix of citrus
and tropical flavours. Screwcap. 13% alc. **Rating** 94 **To** 2017 $27 ✪
Semillon Sauvignon Blanc 2015 Oak neither used nor needed; snow pea,
grass, lemon and passionfruit insouciantly gambol through the bouquet and palate,
scattering pleasure as they do so. Delay if you must, but it's far from necessary.
Screwcap. 13% alc. **Rating** 94 **To** 2017 $24 ✪
Shiraz 2013 Another unique blend with 2% alicante bouschet (with red flesh
included), open-fermented, 50% matured in French barriques, 50% in tank,
blended and bottled after 20 months. The only contribution from the alicante
bouschet is the very good colour; what is striking is the successful split oak/
stainless steel maturation. This can lead to a break in the continuity of the palate –
but on the contrary, here it flows juicily and seductively across the palate. Screwcap.
14% alc. **Rating** 94 **To** 2028 $24 ✪
Cabernet Sauvignon Durif 2012 92/8%: just to underline the blend, some of
the juice has run off from the vat to increase the weight of the wine, matured for
22 months in French oak (45% new). Unsurprisingly, the fruits are as black as the
night sky, but they are most surprisingly round and polished, and the tannins are
so soft they are hidden within the folds of the fruit. It's only on retasting that the
power of the fruit becomes apparent. Screwcap. 13.5% alc. **Rating** 94 **To** 2032 $35

♈♈♈♈ Margaret River Chardonnay 2014 Rating 89 To 2020 $38

Forty Paces ★★★★

384 Montague Street, Albert Park, Vic 3206 (postal) **Region** Macedon Ranges
T 0418 424 785 **Open** Not
Winemaker Jason Peasley **Est.** 2001 **Dozens** 120 **Vyds** 0.5ha
Forty Paces has a tiny 0.6ha pinot noir vineyard with MV6, 114, 115 and 777 clones, planted by owner/winemaker Jason Peasley in 2001. Jason has no formal training, but was tutored on the job by Stuart Anderson at Epis in the Macedon Ranges. He names each year's wine with a word or words reflecting an aspect of the wine, the vintage or the climate for the year. He follows some organic and/or biodynamic practices in both the vineyard and the winery.

ΨΨΨΨΩ **Pinot Noir 2014** The Natural. Destemmed, open-fermented with 10% whole bunches, matured in French oak (20% new) for 16 months. Good colour; has considerable power and depth, varietal character not in question on the expressive bouquet or the layered, dark-berry palate. The low alcohol is a surprise, except for slightly savoury acidity on the long finish. Screwcap. 12.5% alc. **Rating** 92 **To** 2024 $36
Pinot Noir 2013 The Ascent. Destemmed, open-fermented with 10% whole bunches, matured in Sirugue barrels (20% new) for 15 months. A very powerful, ripe style with a sullen bouquet and a challenging, savoury finish to the palate. Was the extended maceration too long? Given the benefit of the doubt. Screwcap. 13.5% alc. **Rating** 90 **To** 2020 $36

Foster e Rocco ★★★★

PO Box 438, Heathcote, Vic 3523 **Region** Heathcote
T 0407 057 471 **www**.fostererocco.com.au **Open** Not
Winemaker Adam Foster, Lincoln Riley **Est.** 2008 **Dozens** 2500
Long-term sommeliers and friends Adam Foster and Lincoln Riley have established a business that has a very clear vision: food-friendly wine based on the versatility of sangiovese. They make their wine at Syrahmi, building it from the ground up, with fermentation in both stainless steel and a mixture of used French oak. Exports to the US, Japan and China.

ΨΨΨΨΨ **Nuovo Heathcote Sangiovese 2015** Light mid-red; sour cherry, spice and floral notes frame this purely fruited sangiovese. The palate is fine and juicy with a hint of savoury tannin at the finish. A lovely balanced wine that should be engaged with in its youth. Screwcap. 13.5% alc. **Rating** 94 **To** 2020 $25 ✪

ΨΨΨΨΩ **Heathcote Sangiovese Rose 2015 Rating** 90 **To** 2018 $25

Four Sisters ★★★☆

199 O'Dwyers Road, Tahbilk, Vic 3608 **Region** Central Victoria Zone
T (03) 5736 2400 **www**.foursisters.com.au **Open** Not
Winemaker Alan George, Jo Nash, Alister Purbrick **Est.** 1995 **Dozens** 45 000
The four sisters who inspired this venture were the daughters of the late Trevor Mast, a great winemaker who died before his time. Trevor had conceived the idea, and his eldest daughter Daiah, an emerging artist, designed the label. The business is owned by the Purbrick family (the owner of Tahbilk), one of Australia's great family-owned wineries. It orchestrates the purchase of the grapes for the brand, and also facilitates the winemaking. The production is wholly export-focused, with limited sales in Australia. It exports to 15 countries, including China, and that number may well diminish if Chinese distribution fulfils all its potential.

ΨΨΨΨΩ **Central Victoria Merlot 2014** A surprise packet, the colour bright, the bouquet appealing, the supple palate even more so. There are red fruits aplenty, the tannins are silky, the finish and aftertaste fresh and harmonious. A buy today, drink tonight proposition if ever there was one. Screwcap. 14.4% alc. **Rating** 90 **To** 2019 $16 ✪

ΨΨΨΨ **Central Victoria Shiraz 2014 Rating** 89 **To** 2020 $16 ✪
Central Victoria Cabernet Sauvignon 2014 Rating 89 **To** 2020 $16 ✪
Pinot Grigio 2015 Rating 88 **To** 2017 $14

Four Winds Vineyard ★★★★★

9 Patemans Lane, Murrumbateman, NSW 2582 **Region** Canberra District
T 0402 278 371 **www.**fourwindsvineyard.com.au **Open** W'ends 10–5
Winemaker Jaime and Bill Crowe **Est.** 1998 **Dozens** 2300 **Vyds** 11.9ha
Graeme and Suzanne Lunney conceived the idea for Four Winds in 1997, planting the first
vines in '98, moving to the property full-time in '99, and making the first vintage in 2000.
Daughter Sarah looks after promotions, and youngest daughter Jaime, complete with a degree
in forensic biology, has joined husband Bill in the winery. She brings with her several years'
experience with the former Kamberra winery, and three vintages in the Napa Valley.

🍷🍷🍷🍷🍷 **Canberra District Riesling 2015** One of many Canberra rieslings that attest
to the perfect climate of the region for the variety. Made in the usual fashion. It
has that mouthwatering edge to the fruit from a low pH, citrus flavours extending
to grapefruit, the length and precision faultless. Lovely wine. Screwcap. 11.2% alc.
Rating 95 **To** 2030 $25 ✪
Tom's Block Shiraz 2014 Nutty aromatics and flavours become meaty and
dark-cherried on the palate. Peppery characters play a role but not a dominating
one; so too cedary/smoky oak. The glory of the medium-weight red. Screwcap.
13.6% alc. **Rating** 95 **To** 2032 $55 CM

🍷🍷🍷🍷🍸 **Canberra District Shiraz 2014** **Rating** 93 **To** 2026 $30 CM

Fowles Wine ★★★★★

Cnr Hume Freeway/Lambing Gully Road, Avenel, Vic 3664 **Region** Strathbogie Ranges
T (03) 5796 2150 **www.**fowleswine.com **Open** 7 days 9–5
Winemaker Victor Nash, Lindsay Brown **Est.** 1968 **Dozens** 60 000 **Vyds** 145ha
This family-owned winery is led by Matt Fowles, with chief winemaker Victor Nash heading
the winemaking team. The large vineyard is primarily focused on riesling, chardonnay, shiraz
and cabernet sauvignon, and also includes sauvignon blanc, pinot noir, merlot, semillon,
viognier, gewurztraminer, savagnin, tempranillo, lagrein, arneis, vermentino, pinot gris and
sangiovese. Marketing is energetic, with the well-known Ladies Who Shoot Their Lunch label
available as large posters, the wines also available presented in a 6-bottle gun case. Exports to
the UK, the US, Canada and China.

🍷🍷🍷🍷🍷 **The Exception Cabernet Sauvignon 2013** This has the depth of its Stone
Dwellers sibling, but its power comes from finesse, cassis supplanting blackcurrant
as it effortlessly seduces your palate. Every way you look at it, from the front,
the back, the sides, it sings. Dial in a taste question and it will answer. Screwcap.
14.5% alc. **Rating** 97 **To** 2043 $50 ✪

🍷🍷🍷🍷🍷 **The Exception Strathbogie Ranges Cabernet Malbec 2012** 85/15%,
co-fermented, matured for 16 months in new French puncheons. Still very
youthful, but shows its class immediately; cabernet sauvignon is the master here,
elegantly disdainful of all else going on around is, be it malbec or its time in new
French oak. It has classic cabernet tannins, firm but not needing to seek to clamp
your jaws together. Screwcap. 13.7% alc. **Rating** 96 **To** 2037 $50 ✪
Stone Dwellers Riesling 2012 I made the following tasting note in Dec '12:
'The vital statistics for this wine might equally easily have been those of Tasmania
or the Rheingau: a pH of 2.93, t/a of 8.2 g/l and its low alcohol (especially low
since the palate is dry); it has excellent varietal definition, amplified by selected
yeasts and cool fermentation of clear juice, a cross between citrus and tropical fruit
held in check by those statistics.' The wine has more than fulfilled its promise, with
an extra layer of fruit. Screwcap. 11.8% alc. **Rating** 95 **To** 2022 $22 ✪
Stone Dwellers Riesling 2010 A trophy and two gold medals from the
Victorian Wines Show and Melbourne Wine Awards set the scene for a wine
still on the journey from primary to secondary flavours and mouthfeel. It has a
particularly fine and well-balanced palate, lime, apple and lemon all starting to gain
full momentum. Screwcap. 12% alc. **Rating** 95 **To** 2025 $22 ✪

The Rule Shiraz 2013 Open-fermented, the majority matured in 1yo French puncheons. Deep colour; a complex, full-bodied shiraz barely out of its swaddling clothes, a lifetime in front of it; blackberry, plum and warm spices run deep below the surface, sweet oak and supple tannins providing company. It's easy when you know how, but the knowledge has to be hard earned. Screwcap. 14.5% alc. **Rating** 95 **To** 2038 $50

Ladies who Shoot their Lunch Riesling 2015 Part was fermented in a used 4500l cask and kept on lees, part conventionally cool-fermented in stainless steel, 8% pinot gris (wild-fermented in French oak) was blended in. After nigh on a year, the wine is still quartz-white in (non) colour. The bouquet and palate are also still waking up, but they're made of the right stuff, particularly the crisp, crunchy palate. Patience will be rewarded. Screwcap. 12.5% alc. **Rating** 94 **To** 2027 $35

Ladies who Shoot their Lunch Wild Ferment Chardonnay 2014 Half wild-fermented, half cultured yeast, fermented and matured in French oak (30% new) of various sizes. Comes from a line of very successful wines of this lineage. The key to its style and quality is its inbuilt acidity, which provides the framework for all the other components to show their wares. Oak has also served the wine well, giving it longevity. Screwcap. 13.5% alc. **Rating** 94 **To** 2023 $35

Stone Dwellers Cabernet Sauvignon 2014 From three blocks at 448–501m, 80% matured for 6 months in new French and American oak, 20% in used French oak. A very appealing cabernet at this price, with crystal-clear cassis on a neatly focused medium-bodied palate, the polished tannins taking the curtain call. Screwcap. 14.5% alc. **Rating** 94 **To** 2029 $25 ✪

Stone Dwellers Cabernet Sauvignon 2013 The trick is to generate an impression of power without it looking as though you're trying too hard. This wine makes the trick look easy. It's built for the long haul, with callipers of tannin keeping everything firmly in place, but cassis, mint, chocolate and earthen/mineral characters still having plenty of space to make their voices heard. Screwcap. 14% alc. **Rating** 94 **To** 2033 $25 CM ✪

🍷🍷🍷🍷 **Stone Dwellers Riesling 2015** **Rating** 93 **To** 2030 $22 ✪
Ladies who Shoot their Lunch Shiraz 2013 **Rating** 93 **To** 2028 $35
490 metres Shiraz 2013 **Rating** 93 **To** 2028 $15 ✪
Upton Run Reserve Single Vineyard Strathbogie Ranges Riesling 2008 **Rating** 92 **To** 2020 $35
Farm to Table Pinot Noir 2013 **Rating** 90 **To** 2019 $15 ✪

Fox Creek Wines ★★★★★

140 Malpas Road, McLaren Vale, SA 5171 **Region** McLaren Vale
T (08) 8557 0000 **www**.foxcreekwines.com **Open** 7 days 10–5
Winemaker Scott Zrna, Ben Tanzer **Est.** 1995 **Dozens** 35 000 **Vyds** 21ha

Fox Creek has made a major impact since coming on-stream late in 1995. It is the venture of the extended Watts family, headed by Jim (a retired surgeon). Although Fox Creek is not certified organic, it uses sustainable vineyard practices, avoiding all systemic chemicals. In June 2015 Fox Creek announced a $500 000 winery expansion, developed in close collaboration with the winemaking team. Exports to all major markets.

🍷🍷🍷🍷🍷 **Reserve Shiraz 2014** Firm, muscular release with arms bulging with blackberried fruit. Coffeed oak licks at the seams, but the coal train of inky fruit powers on through, substantially unaffected, essentially pure and rich. You can certainly enjoy this now, but it has long-term written all over it. Screwcap. 14.5% alc. **Rating** 95 **To** 2034 $80 CM

Postmaster GSM 2014 The expressive, fragrant bouquet draws open the curtains of the palate, which bubbles with a swag of red fruits first up, then darker berry notes are sewn through the fine tannins on the back-palate and finish. It follows the usual practice of banning any new oak influence. Screwcap. 14.2% alc. **Rating** 95 **To** 2022 $23 ✪

Shiraz 2014 Right in the groove. Chocolate and blackberry, malt and licorice flavours. And lots of them all. It charges through the palate, but remains soft; it fills all corners but maintains an excellent sense of momentum. Fair to call this 'yum'. Screwcap. 14.5% alc. **Rating** 94 **To** 2025 $20 CM ✪

Old Vine Shiraz 2014 Deep purple-black colour and drenched in pure plummy flavour. Coffee-cream and spice notes add plenty, but the ooze of plum is the thing. Tannin is fine, and comes soaked in inky flavour. Despite its considerable arsenal it's not OTT; it remains drinkable (even young) and invitingly tactile. Screwcap. 14.5% alc. **Rating** 94 **To** 2030 $60 CM

🍷🍷🍷🍷🍷 **Vermentino 2015** Rating 93 To 2017 $23 CM ✪
Short Row Shiraz 2014 Rating 93 To 2027 $35 CM
JSM Shiraz Cabernet Sauvignon Cabernet Franc 2013 Rating 93 To 2023 $23 ✪
Jim's Script McLaren Vale Cabernet Sauvignon Merlot Cabernet Franc Petit Verdot 2013 Rating 91 To 2028 $23 ✪
McLaren Vale Merlot 2014 Rating 90 To 2023 $20 CM ✪

Fox Gordon

44 King William Road, Goodwood, SA 5034 **Region** Barossa Valley/Adelaide Hills
T (08) 8377 7707 www.foxgordon.com.au **Open** Not
Winemaker Natasha Mooney **Est.** 2000 **Dozens** 10 000
This is the venture of Sam and Rachel Atkins (née Fox) and winemaker Natasha (Tash) Mooney. Tash has had first-class experience in the Barossa Valley, particularly during her time as chief winemaker at Barossa Valley Estate. The partners initially produced only small quantities of high quality wine, allowing them time to look after their children; the venture was planned in the shade of the wisteria tree in Tash's back garden. The grapes come from dry-grown vineyards farmed under biodiversity principles. Classy packaging adds the final touch. Exports to the UK, Canada, Germany, India, Singapore, Hong Kong and China.

🍷🍷🍷🍷🍷 **Hannah's Swing Shiraz 2014** It is velvety and luscious, yet surges with intensity and vibrancy, red fruits in a titanic battle with black, tannins and oak clapping on ringside. Part of a growing band of vignerons who are challenging the Barossa Valley status quo of 14.5–16% alcohol required for full flavour. Screwcap. 13.7% alc. **Rating** 96 **To** 2044 $60 ✪
King Louis Barossa Valley Cabernet Sauvignon 2014 Fox Gordon has given this wine a flying start by keeping the alcohol under 14%, but the Barossa Valley is a very difficult region in which to grow cabernet with finesse/elegance. This cabernet overflows with flavour that is varietal, but falls short at the last hurdle. The cabernets of Great Southern provide a benchmark. Screwcap. 13.7% alc. **Rating** 94 **To** 2034 $60

🍷🍷🍷🍷🍷 **Sassy Adelaide Hills Sauvignon Blanc 2015** Rating 93 To 2016 $19 CM ✪
By George Barossa Valley Adelaide Hills Cabernet Tempranillo 2013 Rating 93 To 2033 $20 ✪
Charlotte's Web Pinot Grigio 2015 Rating 90 To 2016 $23 CM

Foxeys Hangout
★★★★★

795 White Hill Road, Red Hill, Vic 3937 **Region** Mornington Peninsula
T (03) 5989 2022 www.foxeys-hangout.com.au **Open** W'ends & public hols 11–5
Winemaker Tony and Michael Lee **Est.** 1998 **Dozens** 5000 **Vyds** 3.4ha
This is the venture of Tony Lee and journalist wife Cathy Gowdie. Cathy explains where it all began: 'We were not obvious candidates for a seachange. When we talked of moving to the country, friends pointed out that Tony and I were hardly back-to-nature types. "Do you own a single pair of shoes without heels?" asked a friend. At the end of a bleak winter, we bought an old farmhouse on 10 daffodil-dotted acres at Red Hill and planted a vineyard.' They planted pinot noir, chardonnay, pinot gris and shiraz on the north-facing slopes of the old farm.

ŶŶŶŶŶ **Shiraz 2014** Great colour; this is an exceptional shiraz by any standards, revelling in its cool climate and its affinity with the Northern Rhône Valley. It has intense black fruits, with a garland of spices and pepper, tannins part of the fabric, French oak the final touch. The time limits of the wine are unknowable. Bargain. Screwcap. 13.5% alc. **Rating** 97 **To** 2050 $45 **✪**

ŶŶŶŶŶ **Pinot Noir 2014** The clarity of the colour and the lifted vibrant bouquet set the scene for the delicious palate, where flavour and texture play hopscotch with each other, almost mesmerising in their agility; spice, dark cherry, truffle, and a hint of forest all flash continuously. Great value. Screwcap. 13.5% alc. **Rating** 96 **To** 2025 $35 **✪**

ŶŶŶŶŶ **Chardonnay 2014 Rating** 92 **To** 2020 $35
Rose 2015 Rating 92 **To** 2017 $25 **✪**
Kentucky Road 777 Pinot Noir 2014 Rating 92 **To** 2021 $75

Frankland Estate ★★★★★

Frankland Road, Frankland, WA 6396 **Region** Frankland River
T (08) 9855 1544 **www**.franklandestate.com.au **Open** Mon–Fri 10–4, public hols & w'ends by appt
Winemaker Hunter Smith, Brian Kent **Est.** 1988 **Dozens** 15000 **Vyds** 34.5ha
A significant operation, situated on a large sheep property owned by Barrie Smith and Judi Cullam. The vineyard has been established progressively since 1988; the introduction of an array of single vineyard Rieslings has been a highlight, driven by Judi's conviction that terroir is of utmost importance, and the soils are indeed different. The Isolation Ridge Vineyard is now organically grown. Frankland Estate has held important International Riesling tastings and seminars over the past decade. Exports to all major markets.

ŶŶŶŶŶ **Isolation Ridge Vineyard Riesling 2015** Detailed is the single-word essence of Isolation Ridge Riesling, with its citrus and wild flower blossom aromas and its compelling, perfectly balanced, ballerina-light imprint on the mouth. Is its own style. Screwcap. 12.5% alc. **Rating** 97 **To** 2030 $40 **✪**
Poison Hill Vineyard Riesling 2015 There is always (of course) a difference between the Poison Hill and Isolation Ridge, but seldom is it more obvious than this year. This is immediate and naked power, with a cascade of lime and grapefruit flavours rushing through the palate, finish and aftertaste. Ripe, to be sure, but how enjoyable. Screwcap. 12.5% alc. **Rating** 97 **To** 2030 $40 **✪**

ŶŶŶŶŶ **Smith Cullam Riesling 2015** Has well and truly established itself in the wine community; the finish is a magical blend of flint and fruit, the residual sugar perfectly balanced by titratable acidity; great length. Screwcap. 11.5% alc. **Rating** 96 **To** 2030 $55 **✪**
Isolation Ridge Vineyard Shiraz 2014 The sheer power of red and black cherry fruit, spice, bramble, earth, tannins, oak and a twinkle of acidity all demand your attention. Paradoxically, no one player captures the loud applause the wine generates. Screwcap. 13.5% alc. **Rating** 95 **To** 2039 $40
Isolation Ridge Vineyard Cabernet Sauvignon 2013 It's like watching the perfectly executed pass, the bolt towards the try-line thereafter inevitable. This attacks with blackberry/blackcurrant/dark chocolate flavour and then spreads and runs and swooshes in to a lengthy finish. Screwcap. 13.7% alc. **Rating** 95 **To** 2035 $28 CM **✪**
Olmo's Reward 2013 An estate blend, the major part cabernet franc and malbec, with a small portion of cabernet sauvignon. It has a phalanx of predominantly red-berry fruits on its bouquet and elegant, medium-bodied palate; the tannin and oak contribution is minor, albeit necessary. Screwcap. 13.5% alc. **Rating** 95 **To** 2028 $50
Rocky Gully Shiraz 2014 The power and intensity of Frankland River shiraz and a jab of viognier is on full display here, with an edgy quality to the black fruits,

spice and licorice that give this wine tension and interest; fine-grained tannins add a savoury note to the finish. Screwcap. 14.5% alc. **Rating** 94 **To** 2029 $20 ✪

🍷🍷🍷🍷♀ **Isolation Ridge Vineyard Shiraz 2013** **Rating** 91 **To** 2026 $40 CM
Mourvedre 2014 **Rating** 90 **To** 2021 $28 CM

Franklin Tate Estates   ★★★★☆

Gale Road, Kaloorup, WA 6280 **Region** Margaret River
T (08) 9267 8555 **www.**franklintateestates.com.au **Open** Not
Winemaker Rory Clifton-Parks **Est.** 2010 **Dozens** 30 000 **Vyds** 101.11ha
This is the second business established by Franklin and Heather Tate since the demise of Evans & Tate. In 2007 they came up with Miles From Nowhere (see separate entry), but this is a quite separate venture, with 101ha of vines (Miles From Nowhere has 47ha). The lion's share of the plantings go to sauvignon blanc and semillon (24ha each), chardonnay (22ha), shiraz (17ha) and cabernet sauvignon (8ha), with minor plantings of verdelho, petit verdot and viognier. Rory Clifton-Parks has been the winemaker for both incarnations. It's not surprising to see five Asian markets, and Canada, as the export focus.

🍷🍷🍷🍷 **Tate Sauvignon Blanc Semillon 2015** Delivers pretty much what one expects from this blend and this region. Snow pea, fresh asparagus, gooseberry and lemon. Rounded texture with just a hint of sweetness, and enough crispness on the finish to keep it all together. Screwcap. 12.5% alc. **Rating** 89 **To** 2018 $16 ✪
Tate Alexanders Vineyard Chardonnay 2014 Seems to lack the personality one might expect from a single vineyard chardonnay from a great chardonnay region. Shows peachy varietal fruit on the bouquet, and the palate is evenly balanced with ripe stone fruit flavours, but it's missing depth and drive. Pleasant enough drinking in its way, though. Screwcap. 13% alc. **Rating** 88 **To** 2019 $24

Fraser Gallop Estate   ★★★★★

493 Metricup Road, Wilyabrup, WA 6280 **Region** Margaret River
T (08) 9755 7553 **www.**frasergallopestate.com.au **Open** By appt
Winemaker Clive Otto, Kate Morgan **Est.** 1999 **Dozens** 11 000 **Vyds** 20ha
Nigel Gallop began the development of the vineyard in 1999, planting cabernet sauvignon, semillon, petit verdot, cabernet franc, malbec, merlot, sauvignon blanc and multi-clone chardonnay. The dry-grown vines have modest yields, followed by kid-glove treatment in the winery. With Clive Otto (formerly of Vasse Felix) on board, a 300-tonne winery was built, with highly qualified assistant winemaker Kate Morgan joining the team in 2008. The wines have had richly deserved success in wine shows and journalists' reviews. Exports to the UK, Canada, Switzerland, Germany, Indonesia, Singapore, Hong Kong and China.

🍷🍷🍷🍷🍷 **Parterre Wilyabrup Cabernet Sauvignon 2013** Still bright crimson-purple; a totally delicious and stylish Bordeaux blend; the bouquet is fragrant, the medium to full-bodied palate swoops high and low with cassis, spice, bay leaf, cedary oak and beautifully detailed tannins – and only 13.5% alcohol. Screwcap. **Rating** 97 **To** 2038 $45 ✪

🍷🍷🍷🍷🍷 **Parterre Semillon Sauvignon Blanc 2014** This wine has a siren blaring 'get out of my way', its flavours of lemon/lemon zest/bitter lemon ricocheting around the mouth, barrel-ferment inputs of minor consequence, as is the oak. A striking wine of high quality. Screwcap. 12.5% alc. **Rating** 96 **To** 2024 $35 ✪
Parterre Wilyabrup Chardonnay 2015 This wine never fails. It's probably the immaculate viticulture that is most responsible, but you also get the feeling the winemaking team don't push the envelope any further than they are totally comfortable with, the most obvious outcome the extreme purity the wine always has. Screwcap. 13% alc. **Rating** 96 **To** 2027 $39 ✪
Semillon Sauvignon Blanc 2015 In Fraser Gallop style, manages to pack more flavour – 100% authentic – into the wine than most others in this highly competitive bear pit. There is the full citrus range first up, with grapefruit obvious,

then the response (but not a challenge) of tropical fruits. You barely notice the absence of oak. Screwcap. 12.5% alc. **Rating** 95 **To** 2020 $24 **○**

Parterre Wilyabrup Chardonnay 2014 Wild-fermented in new and used French oak, 10 months maturation. The bright, light straw-green colour sends the right signal of an ultra-crisp chardonnay that races along the palate and into the lingering aftertaste, oak doing its duty and no more. Still developing, its best a couple of years away yet. Screwcap. 12.5% alc. **Rating** 95 **To** 2024 $39

Chardonnay 2015 This is your Margaret River captain speaking, through a complex bouquet with a reductive struck match note. The palate has an intense river pebble minerality and a Xmas stocking of grapefruit, lime and lemon fruit lightly kissed by oak. Screwcap. 13% alc. **Rating** 94 **To** 2025 $26 **○**

ΨΨΨΨΨ **Misceo 2014** Rating 93 **To** 2034 $30
Margaret River Cabernet Merlot 2014 Rating 92 **To** 2030 $26

Freeman Vineyards   ★★★★★
101 Prunevale Road, Prunevale, NSW 2587 **Region** Hilltops
T (02) 6384 4299 **www**.freemanvineyards.com.au **Open** By appt
Winemaker Dr Brian Freeman, Xanthe Freeman **Est.** 2000 **Dozens** 5000 **Vyds** 103ha
Dr Brian Freeman has spent much of his life in research and education, in the latter role as head of CSU's viticulture and oenology campus. In 2004 he purchased the 30-year-old vineyard previously known as Demondrille. He has also established a vineyard next door, and in all has 21 varieties that range from staples such as shiraz, cabernet sauvignon, semillon and riesling through to more exotic, trendy varieties such as tempranillo, and on to corvina, rondinella and harslevelu.

ΨΨΨΨΨ **Dolcino 2013** Totally botrytised, harvested on 2 May at 5am at −2.5°C, pressed immediately, wild-fermented slowly during 9 months in oak (50% new), Sweet Wine of the Year at the International Sweet Wine Challenge '15. Exceedingly complex, still pale and bright in colour, with an intriguing hay and musk bouquet, and sweetness that paints the tongue yet doesn't cloy. Screwcap. 12% alc. **Rating** 95 **To** 2030 $25 **○**

Altura Vineyard Nebbiolo 2014 Fermented with 21 days on skins, matured for 8 months in used French oak. Deeply coloured and unequivocally full-bodied, made in the old Piedmont style even though only 8 months in oak. The tannins 'liberal' (says Freeman), but not dry. Just get a large (1kg) flame-grilled bistecca and the world will be your oyster. Screwcap. 14.5% alc. **Rating** 94 **To** 2044 $35

Prosecco 2015 Another excellent release. Brian Freeman packs the flavour into his prosecco, without resorting to overt sweetness. This release is all citrus and bran, custard and cooked ripe pears. It builds and builds with flavour but then, ultimately, refreshes. Diam. 12.5% alc. **Rating** 94 **To** 2016 $23 CM **○**

ΨΨΨΨΨ **Rondo Rondinella Rose 2015** Rating 90 **To** 2016 $20 CM **○**

Freycinet   ★★★★★
15919 Tasman Highway via Bicheno, Tas 7215 **Region** East Coast Tasmania
T (03) 6257 8574 **www**.freycinetvineyard.com.au **Open** 7 days 10–4
Winemaker Claudio Radenti, Lindy Bull **Est.** 1980 **Dozens** 7000 **Vyds** 14.83ha
The Freycinet vineyards are situated on the sloping hillsides of a small valley. The soils are brown dermosol on top of Jurassic dolerite, and the combination of aspect, slope, soil and heat summation produces red grapes with unusual depth of colour and ripe flavours. One of the foremost producers of pinot noir, with an enviable track record of consistency – rare in such a temperamental variety. The Radenti (sparkling), Riesling and Chardonnay are also wines of the highest quality. In 2012 Freycinet acquired part of the neighbouring Coombend property from Brown Brothers. The 42ha property extends to the Tasman Highway, and includes a 5.75ha mature vineyard and a 4.2ha olive grove. Exports to the UK and Singapore.

♟♟♟♟♟ **Riesling 2015** The flowery, fragrant bouquet is stacked with lime, lemon and apple blossom, the palate following suit, allied with the usual Tasmanian acidity. In 5 or so years it will be an ambrosia of the gods. The hint of passionfruit may lead to its immediate consumption, but do keep a bottle aside for each one you drink now. Screwcap. 13.5% alc. **Rating** 96 **To** 2025 $30 ✪

Wineglass Bay Sauvignon Blanc 2015 Where did this come from? Tasmania isn't meant to make sauvignon blancs with this degree of flavour. Part fermented in used French oak and part in tank, it has the full display of tropical fruits led by passionfruit and gooseberry, lifted and cleansed on the very long finish by snap, crackle and pop acidity. Screwcap. 14% alc. **Rating** 96 **To** 2017 $29 ✪

Chardonnay 2014 Barrel-fermented in French oak with lees stirring. Marries elegance with intensity, the varietal fruit profile clearly articulated courtesy of pink grapefruit, stone fruit and zesty acidity; the length is outstanding. Screwcap. 13.5% alc. **Rating** 95 **To** 2021 $40

♟♟♟♟♟ **Cabernet Merlot 2012 Rating** 92 **To** 2025 $37

Frogmore Creek   ★★★★★

699 Richmond Road, Cambridge, Tas 7170 **Region** Southern Tasmania
T (03) 6248 4484 **www**.frogmorecreek.com.au **Open** 7 days 10–5
Winemaker Alain Rousseau, John Bown **Est.** 1997 **Dozens** 18000 **Vyds** 55ha
Frogmore Creek is a Pacific Rim joint venture, the owners being Tony Scherer of Tasmania and Jack Kidwiler of California. The business has grown very substantially, first establishing its own organically managed vineyard, and thereafter by a series of acquisitions. First was the purchase of the Hood/Wellington Wines business; next was the purchase of the large Roslyn Vineyard near Campania; and finally (in Oct 2010) the acquisition of Meadowbank Estate, where the cellar door is now located. In Dec '12 the original Frogmore Creek vineyard was sold to Hill-Smith Family Vineyards. Exports to the US, Japan, Indonesia and South Korea.

♟♟♟♟♟ **42 Degrees South Tasmania Premier Cuvee NV** A dynamic, refreshing and fruit-focused blend from across Tasmania that captures lemon and red-berry fruits of compelling purity, intricately crafted with beautifully ripe acidity and perfectly integrated dosage of 9g/l. Diam. 12% alc. **Rating** 91 **To** 2016 $28 TS

♟♟♟♟ **42°S Pinot Noir 2015 Rating** 88 **To** 2021 $28

Gaelic Cemetery Wines   ★★★★★

PO Box 54, Sevenhill, SA 5453 **Region** Clare Valley
T (08) 8843 4370 **www**.gaelic-cemeterywines.com **Open** Not
Winemaker Neil Pike, Steve Baraglia **Est.** 2005 **Dozens** 1500 **Vyds** 6.5ha
This is a joint venture between winemaker Neil Pike, viticulturist Andrew Pike and Adelaide retailers Mario and Ben Barletta. It hinges on a single vineyard owned by Grant Arnold, planted in 1996, adjacent to the historic cemetery of the region's Scottish pioneers. Situated in a secluded valley of the Clare hills, the low-cropping vineyard, say the partners, 'is always one of the earliest ripening shiraz vineyards in the region and mystifyingly produces fruit with both natural pH and acid analyses that can only be described as beautiful numbers'. The result is hands-off winemaking. Exports to the UK, the US, Canada, Germany, Singapore, Taiwan, Hong Kong and China.

♟♟♟♟♟ **Premium Riesling 2015** 4 trophies, 3 in riesling categories, and Best Wine of Show at the Clare Valley Wine Show '15. This starts where its gold medal-winning sibling finishes; it is awesome in the way it exerts its power, taking hold of the palate without any fuss, then tightening and lengthening its grip each time it is retasted. The rainbow of citrus fruits pays scant attention to the slatey acidity that is the bedrock of its long-term development. Screwcap. 12.5% alc. **Rating** 97 **To** 2035 $36 ✪

ŶŶŶŶŶ Cabernet Malbec 2012 Bold and ripe but firm. It establishes authority and
exercises it responsibly. Mint, coffee-cream, dark cakey blackberry and spicy/smoky
oak. Both powerful and precise. Cork. 14.5% alc. **Rating** 95 **To** 2032 $55 CM
Celtic Farm Clare Valley Riesling 2015 Made as a drink-now style for this
vintage, winning a gold medal at the Clare Valley Wine Show. Winning a gold
medal for riesling at this wine show is always particularly gratifying for the
winemaker, just as the Hunter Valley Wine Show is for semillon. While elegant,
balanced and clearly varietal, its strength is in the way the flavours gently coat the
mouth and then won't let go. Screwcap. 12.5% alc. **Rating** 94 **To** 2025 $23
Clare Valley Shiraz 2012 It's not the brightest card in the pack but it may well
be the blackest. This is a deep-set wine, crammed with asphalt, caramel and bay
leaf flavour, the finish grandly (and warmly) tannic. Heavy wine in a heavy bottle.
Cork. 14.5% alc. **Rating** 94 **To** 2025 $55 CM

Gala Estate   ★★★★★

14891 Tasman Highway, Cranbrook, Tas 7190 **Region** East Coast Tasmania
T 0408 681 014 **www**.galaestate.com.au **Open** 7 days 10–4 (closed winter)
Winemaker Greer Carland, Glen James **Est.** 2009 **Dozens** 3500 **Vyds** 11ha
This vineyard is situated on a 4000ha sheep station, with the sixth, seventh and eighth
generations headed by Robert and Patricia (Amos) Greenhill, custodians of the land granted
to Adam Amos in 1821; it is recognised as the second-oldest family business in Tasmania. The
11ha vineyard is heavily skewed to pinot noir (7ha), the remainder planted (in descending
order of area) to chardonnay, pinot gris, riesling, shiraz and sauvignon blanc. The main risk is
spring frost, and overhead spray irrigation serves two purposes: it provides adequate moisture
for early season growth, and frost protection at the end of the growing season. Wine show
success has finally come.

ŶŶŶŶŶ Constable Amos Pinot Noir 2013 Gold medal Hobart Wine Show '15,
and trophy for Best Red Wine of Show Tasmania Wine Show '16. A pinot of
exceptional power and intensity, yet retaining finesse, elegance and freshness; red
and black cherries and cedary oak fill the bouquet and are the drivers of the
palate in conjunction with high quality tannins, and a reprise of the French oak.
Screwcap. 13.5% alc. **Rating** 97 **To** 2024 $42

ŶŶŶŶŶ Late Harvest Riesling 2014 79g/l residual sugar, gold medals Hobart Wine
Show '15 and Tasmanian Wine Show '16. Absolutely, totally, seductively delicious.
Top-end Mosel Kabinett/Spatlese style, pure lime juice, the residual sugar/acid
balance perfect. Screwcap. 9.4% alc. **Rating** 96 **To** 2024 $32 ●

ŶŶŶŶŶ Riesling 2015 **Rating** 92 **To** 2025 $28
Pinot Noir 2015 **Rating** 92 **To** 2021 $28

Galafrey   ★★★★

Quangellup Road, Mount Barker, WA 6324 **Region** Mount Barker
T (08) 9851 2022 **www**.galafreywines.com.au **Open** 7 days 10–5
Winemaker Kim Tyrer **Est.** 1977 **Dozens** 4000 **Vyds** 13.1ha
The Galafrey story began when Ian and Linda Tyrer gave up high-profile jobs in the emerging
computer industry and arrived in Mount Barker to start growing grapes and making wine, the
vine-change partially prompted by their desire to bring up their children-to-be in a country
environment. The dry-grown vineyard they planted continues to be the turning point, the first
winery established in an ex-whaling building (long since replaced by a purpose-built winery).
The premature death of Ian at a time when the industry was buckling at the knees increased
the already considerable difficulties the family had to deal with, but deal with it they did.
Daughter Kim Tyrer is now CEO of the business, but Linda is still very much involved in the
day-to-day management of Galafrey. Exports to China.

ŶŶŶŶŶ Dry Grown Cabernet Sauvignon 2013 Stern and noticeably dry, but with
ample red/blackcurrant flavour and laces of dusty tannin. This is good now but it

will be better again given medium-term cellaring. Creamy oak has been artfully applied: it's little more than a whisper. Excellent example of an old-fashioned claret style. Screwcap. 14.5% alc. **Rating** 94 **To** 2025 $30 CM ✪

🍷🍷🍷🍷🍷 Dry Grown Reserve Riesling 2015 Rating 93 To 2025 $25 CM ✪
Dry Grown Vineyard Mount Barker Shiraz 2013 Rating 92 To 2020 $30

Galli Estate ★★★★★

1507 Melton Highway, Plumpton, Vic 3335 **Region** Sunbury
T (03) 9747 1444 **www.**galliestate.com.au **Open** 7 days 11–5
Winemaker Ben Ranken **Est.** 1997 **Dozens** 10 000 **Vyds** 160ha
Galli Estate has two vineyards: Heathcote, which produces the red wines (Shiraz, Sangiovese, Nebbiolo, Tempranillo, Grenache and Montepulciano), and the cooler climate vineyard at Plumpton, producing the whites (Chardonnay, Pinot Grigio, Sauvignon Blanc and Fiano). All wines are biodynamically estate-grown and made, with wine movements on the new moon. Exports to Canada, Singapore, China and Hong Kong.

🍷🍷🍷🍷🍷 Lorenzo 2014 Frost-affected vineyards resulted in very low yields (1t/acre). Shiraz, includes 2% viognier; wild ferment, matured for 18 months in French oak (30% new). The extra time in oak has opened up the texture and softened its tannins, but has in no way compromised its shiraz varietal expression or sense of place. Screwcap. 14% alc. **Rating** 96 **To** 2039 $55 ✪
Pamela 2014 Four Burgundy chardonnay clones; whole bunch-pressed to barrel (30% new); wild ferment. The slightly riper fruit and new oak (compared to Artigiano) changes the dynamics, with nectarine, white peach, fig and cashew the leaders, grapefruit bringing up the rear. Screwcap. 12.5% alc. **Rating** 95 **To** 2023 $55
Adele Syrah 2014 12.5% whole bunches, wild-fermented in large open oak vats, matured for 12 months in (25% new) oak. Great colour depth and hue. While full-bodied, this has more supple fruit than its Heathcote siblings, but shares the glossy black cherry and plum flavours. Long and well balanced, it has a very good future. Screwcap. 14% alc. **Rating** 95 **To** 2044 $38
Artigiano Sunbury Chardonnay 2014 Whole bunch-pressed to French oak (20% new), wild ferment, matured for 10 months. Hits all the right buttons, fruit and oak waltzing perfectly together towards the finish, where grapefruit leaps to the fore. Screwcap. 12.3% alc. **Rating** 94 **To** 2022 $30 ✪
Adele Fiano 2014 100% whole bunch-pressed, wild-fermented in barrel, matured for 10 months. Rides on its squeaky acidity and high-pitched flavours of lemon zest and crushed lime leaves. Screwcap. 11.5% alc. **Rating** 94 **To** 2020 $38
Riserva Sunbury Pinot Noir 2015 Hand-picked MV6 clone, 15% whole bunches, 85% whole berries, wild-fermented. A highly spiced and savoury bouquet is replicated on the long, persistent palate, forest floor characters intermingling with morello and red cherry fruits. Screwcap. 13% alc. **Rating** 94 **To** 2023 $55
Camelback Heathcote Shiraz 2015 Includes 2% viognier, six separate batches (different picking dates and clones), matured for 9 months in French oak (15% new). You get a lot of complexity and density for a $20 wine, indeed too much at this stage. The fruit crashes through on the finish like a wine with 15% alcohol, not 14%. Screwcap. 14% alc. **Rating** 94 **To** 2035 $20 ✪
Camelback Heathcote Shiraz 2014 Wild ferment, matured for 10 months in French oak (15% new). Has the lethal power of Galli Shirazs, but has far more spice to its make-up, which results in a more open-weave texture and overall accessibility – and is a grade A bargain. Screwcap. 14% alc. **Rating** 94 **To** 2029 $20 ✪

🍷🍷🍷🍷🍷 Tempranillo Grenache Mourvedre 2015 Rating 93 To 2025 $20 ✪
Camelback Sangiovese Cabernet Merlot 2015 Rating 93 To 2020 $20 ✪
Camelback Nebbiolo Rose 2015 Rating 92 To 2017 $20 ✪
Artigiano Sunbury Pinot Grigio 2015 Rating 90 To 2017 $20 ✪
Adele Pinot Grigio 2014 Rating 90 To 2017 $38

Gallows Wine Co

Lennox Road, Carbunup River, WA 6280 **Region** Margaret River
T (08) 9755 1060 **www**.gallows.com.au **Open** 7 days 10–5
Winemaker Charlie Maiolo, Neil Doddridge **Est.** 2008 **Dozens** 11 000 **Vyds** 27ha
This is the venture of the Maiolo family, headed by winemaker Charlie. The macabre name
is that of one of the most famous surf breaks on the Margaret River coast. The vineyard is
planted to semillon, sauvignon blanc, chardonnay, pinot noir, shiraz, merlot and cabernet
sauvignon. The site climate is strongly influenced by Geographe Bay, 5km to the north, and
facilitates the production of wines with a large spectrum of flavours and characteristics.

The Bommy Chardonnay 2014 The surf's right up with this wine. Somehow
bracing grapefruit and white peach, usually achieved at 13% alcohol, appears at
14%. Oak has barely raised its hand, so this is the vineyard speaking. Screwcap.
Rating 94 **To** 2024 $28 ○

The Bommy Semillon Sauvignon Blanc 2015 Rating 91 **To** 2018 $26

Gapsted ★★★★

3897 Great Alpine Road, Gapsted, Vic 3737 **Region** Alpine Valleys
T (03) 5751 1383 **www**.gapstedwines.com.au **Open** 7 days 10–5
Winemaker Michael Cope-Williams, Toni Pla Bou **Est.** 1997 **Dozens** 140 000
Vyds 256.1ha
Gapsted is the major brand of the Victorian Alps Winery, which started life (and continues) as
large-scale contract winemaking facilities. However, the quality of the wines made for its own
brand has led to the expansion of production not only under that label, but also under a raft of
cheaper, subsidiary labels. As well as the substantial estate plantings, Gapsted sources traditional
and alternative grape varieties from the King and Alpine Valleys. Exports to all major markets
except the US and Canada.

Tobacco Road King Valley Pinot Noir 2015 Dijon clones plus MV6, part
crushed and destemmed, part 12-day carbonic maceration, partial barrel ferment.
Rolls Royce vinification of the best clones, matured for 3 months in new French
oak. Brilliantly clear crimson; fresh and supple, purity is its watchword, worth $30,
not $16. Only one caveat: don't delay Screwcap. 14.2% alc. **Rating** 94 **To** 2018
$16 ○

Limited Release King Valley Viognier 2015 Rating 90 **To** 2017 $25
Sparkling Saperavi NV Rating 90 **To** 2017 $37 TS

Garagiste

4 Lawrey Street, Frankston, Vic 3199 (postal) **Region** Mornington Peninsula
T 0439 370 530 **www**.garagiste.com.au **Open** Not
Winemaker Barnaby Flanders **Est.** 2006 **Dozens** 2000 **Vyds** 3ha
Barnaby Flanders was a co-founder of Allies Wines (see separate entry) in 2003, with some
of the wines made under the Garagiste label. Allies has now gone its own way, and Barnaby
has a controlling interest in the Garagiste brand. The focus is on the Mornington Peninsula,
and in particular grapes from the sand-based soils of Tuerong and Moorooduc in the north,
the brown loam/red volcanic soils of Merricks and Merricks North in the middle, and the
red volcanic soils of Red Hill and Main Ridge in the most elevated southern sector. The
grapes are hand-sorted in the vineyard and again in the winery. Chardonnay is whole bunch-
pressed, barrel-fermented with wild yeast in new and used French oak, mlf variably used,
8–9 months on lees. Pinot noir is whole berry (destemmed) and/or whole bunches, wild-yeast
fermentation, 19–22 days on skins, 10 months maturation in French oak, mainly used, seldom
fined or filtered. Exports to Singapore, Hong Kong and China.

Le Stagiaire Chardonnay 2015 This is a vibrantly fresh and convincing
chardonnay with a bit of left-field whole bunch winemaking, and (it would seem)
no mlf; it's a very good outcome, the fruit spectrum all in the ripe zone, grapefruit

and white peach contesting bragging rights, oak an aid, not an end; it also steals some length from the Yarra Valley. Screwcap. 13% alc. **Rating** 97 **To** 2026 $30 ●

Merricks Chardonnay 2014 Usual vinification for a wine of unusual quality. There is a sleight of hand to the way these Garagiste Chardonnays are made that turns on the acidity of the wines and the use of 'partial mlf'. The wine has a brightness that is almost, but not quite, fierceness. A captivating style. Screwcap. 13% alc. **Rating** 97 **To** 2027 $45 ●

Le Stagiaire Chardonnay 2014 Shows the quality of the '14 vintage to full advantage, and also the willingness of Barney Flanders to throw the odd left-field play, here with 10% of the wine fermented as whole bunches. The wine has a mesmerising cut and thrust to its mouthfeel, and a grapefruit intensity to its fruit spectrum. Screwcap. 13% alc. **Rating** 97 **To** 2024 $30 ●

Terre de Feu Pinot Noir 2014 100% whole bunches, matured in 50% new French puncheons. An outstanding pinot; Barney Flanders has turned the very low yields across the Peninsula to his full advantage; the wine has a particular silky/slippery/savoury texture to the palate, adding significantly to its length, and paving the way for the plum and cherry fruits of the mid-palate, the new oak integrated. Screwcap. 13.5% alc. **Rating** 97 **To** 2028 $75 ●

ΨΨΨΨ **Tuerong Chardonnay 2014** Usual vinification. A slightly softer make-up than that of Merricks, but all things are relative; there is still great drive and complexity here, and a touch of fig. Screwcap. 13% alc. **Rating** 96 **To** 2025 $45 ●

Merricks Pinot Noir 2014 Usual winemaking protocol, except destemmed by gravity. A pinot of great power and authority that has absorbed the new oak and used the tannins to its own advantage; there are layers of blood and satsuma plum, and other purple fruits in abundance; has the mouthfeel and structure that typifies Garagiste Pinot. Screwcap. 13.5% alc. **Rating** 96 **To** 2026 $45 ●

Le Stagiaire Pinot Noir 2015 MV6, destemmed and crushed, wild-fermented in open fermenters. Youthful colour; the fragrant bouquet is filled with plum blossom and spice, the palate taking up the theme with enthusiasm; excellent length and a fresh, crisp finish. Will travel well in the future. Screwcap. 13.5% alc. **Rating** 95 **To** 2027 $30 ●

Le Stagiaire Pinot Noir 2014 Good colour; the impact of the MV6 clone is evident in all three Garagiste Pinots, likewise the increasing amount of new oak in the Merricks and Terre de Feu. This has depth to its dark berry/cherry/plum fruit and very good tannins. Screwcap. 13.5% alc. **Rating** 95 **To** 2025 $30 ●

ΨΨΨΨ♀ **Le Stagiaire Pinot Gris 2015** **Rating** 92 **To** 2017 $28
Le Stagiaire Rose 2015 **Rating** 92 **To** 2017 $25 ●

Garners Heritage Wine   ★★★★

54 Longwood-Mansfield Road, Longwood East, Vic 3666 **Region** Strathbogie Ranges
T (03) 5798 5513 **www**.garnerswine.com.au **Open** W'ends 11–4, 0410 649 030
Winemaker Lindsay Brown **Est.** 2005 **Dozens** 500 **Vyds** 1.8ha

Leon and Rosie Garner established Garners Heritage Wine in 2005, celebrating their tenth anniversary in '15. The 1.8ha boutique vineyard may be small, and the newest in the Strathbogie Ranges, but it has produced high class Shirazs. Although the region is classified as cool climate, the property is at the base of the mountain range, where the warm summers are ideal for growing shiraz. A very small amount is exported to Hong Kong.

ΨΨΨΨ **Strathbogie Ranges Shiraz 2014** Open-fermented, matured for 13 months in French and American oak (15% new). Right up there with the best Garners wines, with lively red berry fruits liberally garnished with spices. A model medium-bodied shiraz for immediate drinking, yet holding promise for the future. Screwcap. 14.3% alc. **Rating** 94 **To** 2029 $25 ●

ΨΨΨΨ♀ **Strathbogie Ranges Shiraz 2011** **Rating** 93 **To** 2021 $28
Strathbogie Ranges Shiraz 2009 **Rating** 93 **To** 2025 $28

Gartelmann Wines
★★★★☆

701 Lovedale Road, Lovedale, NSW 2321 **Region** Hunter Valley
T (02) 4930 7113 **www**.gartelmann.com.au **Open** Mon–Sat10–5, Sun 10–4
Winemaker Jorg Gartelmann, Liz Silkman **Est.** 1970 **Dozens** 7000
In 1996 Jan and Jorg Gartelmann purchased what was previously the George Hunter Estate – 16ha of mature vineyards, most established by Oliver Shaul in '70. In a change of emphasis, the vineyard was sold, and Gartelmann now sources its grapes from the Hunter Valley and other NSW regions, including the cool Rylstone area in Mudgee. Exports to the US, Germany, Singapore and China.

🍷🍷🍷🍷🍷 **Wilhelm Shiraz 2014** Medium weight but firm and insistent. There's no question over the quality of this. It's all cherry-plum, earth and spice, but the way it manages the respective loads of sweetness and savouriness feels so assured you'd describe it as compelling. Screwcap. 13.8% alc. **Rating** 95 **To** 2034 $25 CM ○
Diedrich Hunter Clare Valley Shiraz 2014 Excellent richness and length. One of those wines that combines (admirably) depth and prettiness. Dark berries, sweet and ripe, meet florals and spice. Perhaps some licorice too. Positively mouthfilling. Screwcap. 14.7% alc. **Rating** 94 **To** 2032 $45 CM
Jesse Mudgee Shiraz 2014 Bold blackberry and plum flavours meet a healthy dose of cedary/smoky oak. There's a creaminess to the texture and a firmness to the tannin; it lives for the present but the future is in its sights. Screwcap. 14.8% alc. **Rating** 94 **To** 2028 $40 CM

🍷🍷🍷🍷🍷 **Sarah Elizabeth Chardonnay 2015** Rating 92 **To** 2018 $30 CM
Mudgee Petit Verdot 2014 Rating 92 **To** 2023 $35 CM
Phillip Alexander 2014 Rating 91 **To** 2023 $25 CM

Gatt Wines
★★★★★

417 Boehms Springs Road, Flaxman Valley, SA 5235 **Region** Eden Valley
T (08) 8564 1166 **www**.gattwines.com **Open** Not
Winemaker David Norman **Est.** 1972 **Dozens** 8000 **Vyds** 53.35ha
When you read the hyperbole that sometimes accompanies the acquisition of an existing wine business, about transforming it into a world-class operation, it is easy to sigh and move on. When Ray Gatt acquired Eden Springs, he proceeded to translate words into deeds. As well as the 19.82ha Eden Springs Vineyard, he also acquired the historic Siegersdorf Vineyard (19.43ha) on the Barossa floor, and the neighbouring Graue Vineyard (11.4ha). The change of name from Eden Springs to Gatt Wines in 2011 was sensible. Exports to Denmark, Germany, South Korea, Japan, Macau, Hong Kong and China.

🍷🍷🍷🍷🍷 **Riesling 2015** Bright and lively, the perfumed bouquet a fireworks display of meadow and citrus flowers, the palate building on the great opening stanza with a shimmering array of lime/lemon, detailed acidity lengthening and cleansing the finish. Screwcap. 12% alc. **Rating** 96 **To** 2030 $30 ○
Pinot Gris 2015 A striking and voluminous bouquet of musk and poached pear is backed by the juicy palate; acidity plays an anchor role in this feast of plenty. As striking and delicious as pinot gris can be. Screwcap. 13.5% alc. **Rating** 95 **To** 2018 $30 ○
Eden Springs Cabernet Sauvignon 2010 A great vintage, and a well-made wine that collected 17 gold medals and two trophies in shows around the world over '12–13. Part of the success was due to the juicy cassis fruit, and part to controlled oak (French, 20% new). Screwcap. 13.5% alc. **Rating** 94 **To** 2025 $40

🍷🍷🍷🍷🍷 **High Eden Cabernet Sauvignon 2013** Rating 91 **To** 2028 $60
Barossa Valley Mataro 2014 Rating 91 **To** 2021 $100
Old Vine Barossa Valley Shiraz 2013 Rating 90 **To** 2038 $100
High Eden Shiraz 2013 Rating 90 **To** 2033 $60

Gembrook Hill

Launching Place Road, Gembrook, Vic 3783 **Region** Yarra Valley
T (03) 5968 1622 **www**.gembrookhill.com.au **Open** By appt
Winemaker Timo Mayer, Andrew Marks **Est.** 1983 **Dozens** 2500 **Vyds** 6ha
Ian and June Marks established Gembrook Hill, one of the oldest vineyards in the coolest part of the Upper Yarra Valley, and harvested some weeks later than the lower parts of the region. Son Andrew assists Timo Mayer on the winemaking front, each also having his own labels (see separate entries for The Wanderer and Mayer). The northeast-facing vineyard is in a natural amphitheatre; the low-yielding sauvignon blanc, chardonnay and pinot noir are not irrigated. The minimal approach to winemaking produces wines of a consistent style with finesse and elegance. Exports to the UK, Denmark, Japan and Malaysia. Table wines not submitted.

🍷🍷🍷🍷♀ **Blanc de Blancs 2011** The '11 vintage in this cool, high site has given birth to a blanc de blancs of high-tension acid drive and monumental longevity. 4 years on lees has built finesse and honed a fine, creamy bead, but it needs many years yet to tone that acidity. A touch of grassiness suggests underripeness, but it has the soft mouthfeel to handle it. Cork. 11.5% alc. **Rating** 90 **To** 2031 $56 TS

Gemtree Wines

167 Elliot Road, McLaren Flat, SA 5171 **Region** McLaren Vale
T (08) 8323 8199 **www**.gemtreewines.com **Open** 7 days 10–5
Winemaker Mike Brown, Joshua Waechter **Est.** 1998 **Dozens** 90 000 **Vyds** 138.47ha
Gemtree is a family-owned winery dedicated to growing better wine – naturally. Paul and Jill Buttery established the Gemtree vineyards in McLaren Vale in 1980. Now their son Andrew runs the business, their daughter Melissa Brown is the viticulturist and her husband Mike is the chief winemaker. Mike's philosophy is minimal intervention across all stages of the winemaking process to produce wines which are powerful and express the characteristics of each variety and the region. The vineyards are certified organic and farmed biodynamically, and the wine portfolio is of high quality. Exports to all major markets.

🍷🍷🍷🍷🍷 **Obsidian Shiraz 2013** After 24 months maturation, best barrel selection results in only 1% of Gemtree's shiraz production being selected for this wine. It announces itself with a roll of thunder with the darkest of black fruits and anise of the bouquet, the full-bodied palate with a dusting of bitter chocolate. Despite this naked power, the wine has remarkable balance, length a given. Screwcap. 14% alc. **Rating** 97 **To** 2048 $70 **✪**

🍷🍷🍷🍷🍷 **Scarce Earth Stage Six Shiraz 2014** It's all a question of degree with the Gemtree Shirazs, so loudly do they communicate place and variety. From a single sandy soil vineyard, this has an extra degree of finesse, coupled with mouthwatering acidity and great length. Screwcap. 14.5% alc. **Rating** 96 **To** 2034 $42 **✪**
Obsidian Shiraz 2014 The bouquet and palate take you into hidden chambers of McLaren Vale, so intense are the multilayered fruits; the remarkable character is the lack of any demarcation between fruit, oak and, above all else, tannins. Lay this down for your favourite grandchildren. Screwcap. 14% alc. **Rating** 96 **To** 2044 $75 **✪**
Ernest Allan McLaren Vale Shiraz 2014 Wild-fermented, matured in French barriques for 18 months. Inky purple-crimson, it is a distillation of all things McLaren Vale shiraz, jet-black fruits, spice, dark chocolate and generous, supple tannins and oak. Screwcap. 14.5% alc. **Rating** 95 **To** 2044 $42

🍷🍷🍷🍷♀ **Cinnabar GSM 2015 Rating** 93 **To** 2025 $25 **✪**
Bloodstone Shiraz 2014 Rating 90 **To** 2034 $20 **✪**
Uncut Shiraz 2014 Rating 90 **To** 2020 $25
Luna Temprana Tempranillo 2015 Rating 90 **To** 2018 $18 CM **✪**

Geoff Merrill Wines ★★★★★

291 Pimpala Road, Woodcroft, SA 5162 **Region** McLaren Vale
T (08) 8381 6877 **www**.geoffmerrillwines.com.au **Open** Mon–Fri 10–4.30, Sat 12–4.30
Winemaker Geoff Merrill, Scott Heidrich **Est.** 1980 **Dozens** 55 000 **Vyds** 45ha
If Geoff Merrill ever loses his impish sense of humour or his zest for life, high and not-so-high, we shall all be the poorer. The product range consists of three tiers: premium (varietal); Reserve, being the older wines, reflecting the desire for elegance and subtlety of this otherwise exuberant winemaker; and, at the top, Henley Shiraz. Exports to all major markets.

🍷🍷🍷🍷🍷 Henley McLaren Vale Shiraz 2007 Matured for 33 months in French hogsheads, bottled Oct '10. Has soared above the reputation for toughness the vintage has always had. It is positively juicy on the mid-palate with plum, sour cherry and black fruits, the oak and tannins sewn into the fabric of the wine. Cork. 14.5% alc. **Rating** 96 **To** 2030 $150

Henley Shiraz 2005 There was never any doubt about the balance and longevity of this wine, so its youth and power are no surprise. Black fruits, licorice, bitter chocolate and cedary tannins are all at one with each other. It is accessible now, but with a long life ahead. Cork. 14.5% alc. **Rating** 95 **To** 2020 $150

Bush Vine Grenache Rose 2015 Bright puce; has a fragrant, flowery bouquet of red cherry and raspberry, the palate with similar fruit flavours, but also unexpected texture that adds to the length and balance of a very good rose from a well-practised winemaker. Screwcap. 13.5% alc. **Rating** 94 **To** 2017 $21 ✪

🍷🍷🍷🍷 Reserve Cabernet Sauvignon 2009 **Rating** 93 **To** 2029 $45
Reserve McLaren Vale Shiraz 2009 **Rating** 90 **To** 2024 $55
Cilento 2011 **Rating** 90 **To** 2020 $24

Geoff Weaver ★★★★★

2 Gilpin Lane, Mitcham, SA 5062 (postal) **Region** Adelaide Hills
T (08) 8272 2105 **www**.geoffweaver.com.au **Open** Not
Winemaker Geoff Weaver **Est.** 1982 **Dozens** 3000 **Vyds** 12.3ha
This is the business of one-time Hardys chief winemaker Geoff Weaver. This Lenswood vineyard was established between 1982 and '88, and invariably produces immaculate Riesling and Sauvignon Blanc, a long-lived Chardonnays. The beauty of the labels ranks supreme. Exports to the UK, Hong Kong and Singapore.

🍷🍷🍷🍷🍷 Ferus Sauvignon Blanc 2014 Wild yeast-fermented in French barriques and aged on lees for 12 months. It offers a rare combination of elegance and complexity, the latter achieved without any funky/reductive characters, the former with a combination of citrus, white flowers and tropical flavours. Still cruising. Screwcap. 12% alc. **Rating** 97 **To** 2017 $40 ✪

🍷🍷🍷🍷🍷 Chardonnay 2013 Bunches were chilled to 5°C before being whole bunch-pressed to French barriques (50% new, 50% second use) for wild yeast fermentation, partial mlf, 12 months maturation. This, as they might say, is the cat's pyjamas, with its pyrotechnic display of grapefruit-driven fruit flavours, bright acidity and long finish. Is ambling surely along its development path. Screwcap. 13% alc. **Rating** 96 **To** 2023 $40 ✪

Sauvignon Blanc 2015 Hand-picked, but otherwise conventional cold fermentation in stainless steel. A picture-perfect display of all the tropical fruits (except durian) you've ever tasted; even a Dutch master couldn't display them on a single canvas. Despite this embarrassment of riches, the palate finishes fresh and crisp. Screwcap. 13.5% alc. **Rating** 95 **To** 2017 $25 ✪

Riesling 2015 Hand-picked and cold-fermented in stainless steel. It's a lady in waiting: the acidity of the vintage will prove its knight in shining armour as it approaches maturity, and all its perfume and high-toned citrus fruit will appear. Screwcap. 12.5% alc. **Rating** 94 **To** 2030 $25 ✪

🍷🍷🍷🍷 Pinot Noir 2013 **Rating** 93 **To** 2023 $40

Ghost Rock Vineyard   ★★★★☆

1055 Port Sorrell Road, Northdown, Tas 7307 **Region** Northern Tasmania
T (03) 6428 4005 **www.**ghostrock.com.au **Open** Wed–Sun & public hols 11–5
Winemaker Justin Arnold **Est.** 2001 **Dozens** 2800 **Vyds** 16ha
Cate and Colin Arnold purchased the former Patrick Creek Vineyard (planted exclusively to
pinot noir in 1989) in 2001. The vineyards, situated among the patchwork fields of Sassafras to
the south, and the white sands of the Port Sorell Peninsula to the north, now total 25ha: pinot
noir (14 clones) remains the bedrock of the plantings, other varieties including chardonnay,
pinot gris, riesling and sauvignon blanc. Son Justin has assumed winemaking responsibilities in
the new 100-tonne winery, having previously plied his trade in the Yarra Valley (Coldstream
Hills), Margaret River (Devil's Lair) and Napa Valley (Etude), and his wife Alicia runs the
cooking school and cellar door.

🍷🍷🍷🍷 **Riesling 2015** Ferment stopped with 8.7g/l of residual sugar and 8.8g/l of
acidity, lees-stirred for 6 months. Small wonder this is such a powerful and
demanding riesling, accurately described as a dance between sugar and acidity.
You see the residual sugar as fruit, lively laser beams of acidity weaving their way
through the length of the palate. Screwcap. 12.5% alc. **Rating** 97 To 2030 $29 ✪

🍷🍷🍷🍷 **Sauvignon Blanc 2015** Crushed, soaked for 6 hours in the press, 85% fermented
in tank with cultured yeast, 15% wild-fermented in new oak, both left on lees
for 4.5 months until bottling. This lifts the wine out of the ruck of the majority
of Tasmanian sauvignon blancs, with greater texture and overall enhanced fruit
flavours in a tropical spectrum. Screwcap. 13.5% alc. **Rating** 94 To 2017 $29 ✪

🍷🍷🍷🍷 **The Pinots 2015** Rating 93 To 2018 $26 ✪
Two Blocks Pinot Noir 2014 Rating 93 To 2021 $38
Catherine Sparkling 2013 Rating 93 To 2019 $49 TS
Chardonnay 2014 Rating 92 To 2020 $34
Pinot Gris 2015 Rating 90 To 2017 $29
Zoe Blush Sparkling 2013 Rating 90 To 2016 $38 TS

Giaconda   ★★★★★

30 McClay Road, Beechworth, Vic 3747 **Region** Beechworth
T (03) 5727 0246 **www.**giaconda.com.au **Open** By appt
Winemaker Rick Kinzbrunner **Est.** 1985 **Dozens** 3000 **Vyds** 5.5ha
These wines have a super-cult status and, given the small production, are extremely difficult
to find; they are sold chiefly through restaurants and via their website. All have a cosmopolitan
edge befitting Rick Kinzbrunner's international winemaking experience. The Chardonnay
is one of Australia's greatest, and is made and matured in the underground wine cellar hewn
out of granite. This permits gravity flow, and a year-round temperature range of 14–15°C,
promising even more for the future. Exports to the UK and the US.

🍷🍷🍷🍷 **Estate Vineyard Shiraz 2013** Made with ultimate skill and respect for the
strong sense of place this great wine invokes; Beechworth and shiraz are joined
at the hip to an extent equalled only by chardonnay and nebbiolo. The perfumed
bouquet of violets and white pepper leads into a supple, silky, medium-bodied
palate with fruit, oak and tannins in ultimate harmony. Cork. 13.5% alc. **Rating** 98
To 2038 $89 ✪

🍷🍷🍷🍷 **Warner Vineyard Shiraz 2013** Very different from the Estate Shiraz: more spicy
and savoury, more seeking to jump off the lead and head off into the unknown.
It's a high quality wine with loads of personality, but doesn't have the magisterial
presence of its sibling. Screwcap. 13.5% alc. **Rating** 96 To 2033 $79
Nebbiolo 2012 Light, but bright hue; this is an awesome nebbiolo, rearing up on
its hind legs and growling at anyone daring to open it before '20; its fragrance is
exceptional, which only serves to magnify the shock and awe of the palate; if you
see violets, good luck, but it won't change the palate. Cork. 14% alc. **Rating** 94
To 2037 $89

Giant Steps ★★★★★

336 Maroondah Highway, Healesville, Vic 3777 **Region** Yarra Valley
T (03) 5962 6111 **www**.giantstepswine.com.au **Open** 7 days 9 until late
Winemaker Phil Sexton, Steve Flamsteed, Julian Grounds **Est.** 1997 **Dozens** 10 000
Vyds 45ha

On 5 May 2016 the sale by Giant Steps of the Innocent Bystander brand and stock was completed. The former Innocent Bystander restaurant and shop has been substantially remodelled to put the focus on the high quality, single vineyard, single varietal wines in what is demonstrably a very distinguished portfolio. Its vineyard resources comprise the Sexton Vineyard (32ha) in the estate Lower Yarra and Applejack Vineyard (13ha) in the Upper Yarra, the Primavera Vineyard (8ha in the Upper Yarra, under long-term supervised contract) and Tarraford Vineyard (8.5ha in the Lower Yarra, under long-term lease). Exports to the UK, the US and other major markets.

♀♀♀♀♀ **Lusatia Park Vineyard Chardonnay 2015** A great Upper Yarra vineyard now owned by De Bortoli. Lifted fruit blossom aromas with a wraith of barrel ferment; the palate is exquisitely balanced, with the classic white peach/grapefruit duo filling the mouth without even trying. Screwcap. 13% alc. **Rating** 97 **To** 2029 $45 ✪

Tarraford Vineyard Chardonnay 2014 The bouquet is arresting in its complexity, with a faint echo of funk, but it is the palate that defines this wine, with its ripples and whirlpools of white peach, grapefruit and creamy cashew, all brought to a driving finish thanks to its natural acidity. Rolls Royce power, Yarra Valley length. Screwcap. 13.5% alc. **Rating** 97 **To** 2024 $45 ✪

Applejack Vineyard Pinot Noir 2015 Significantly deeper colour than prior vintages, likewise depth of fruit; the bouquet and palate are driven by black and red cherry fruit of exceptional generosity, but teasing with an unusual touch of dark chocolate. Small wonder Giant Steps says this is its best vintage yet. Screwcap. 13.5% alc. **Rating** 97 **To** 2027 $50 ✪

Lusatia Park Vineyard Pinot Noir 2015 Superb colour; the ultra-fragrant bouquet is picked up unceremoniously by the brilliant palate and despatched to the boundary. Takes the concept of elegant generosity onto another level with more movement in the chorus of red fruit flavours than you might think possible. This combines elegance with spicy, savoury intensity. Screwcap. 13% alc. **Rating** 97 **To** 2027 $50 ✪

Sexton Vineyard Pinot Noir 2015 Naturally, shares the superb colour of its siblings; here generosity takes the stage with richness and tannins woven into the superabundant red and black fruits by invisible mending. A brilliant wine by whatever standards you may choose, the lower Yarra Valley refusing to take a backwards step. Screwcap. 13.5% alc. **Rating** 97 **To** 2027 $50 ✪

♀♀♀♀♀ **Sexton Vineyard Chardonnay 2014** You can't make great wine by numbers, but the seamless balance of this wine stems from the perfect ripeness linked to its alcohol. Having taken on board the complex white flowers bouquet, it flows across the palate like a shower of confetti, dispensing stone fruit, grapefruit and splashes of balanced acidity. Screwcap. 13.5% alc. **Rating** 96 **To** 2024 $45 ✪

Primavera Vineyard Pinot Noir 2015 Another take on this great vintage, with savoury, spicy aromas and flavours surging over the bouquet and palate alike, putting whole bunch fermentation up in giant neon letters. The tangy, herbal, forest floor characters will always be the raison d'être of the wine, and I hope I'm around to see how this evolves over time. Screwcap. 13.8% alc. **Rating** 96 **To** 2027 $50 ✪

Sexton Vineyard Chardonnay 2015 A complex, multi-message bouquet hinting of the (relative) richness of the palate; unashamedly lower Yarra Valley with layers of grapefruit and white peach flesh and skin. Screwcap. 13.6% alc. **Rating** 95 **To** 2025 $45

Chardonnay 2015 An intense blend of grapefruit pith/zest/juice is coupled with shiny acidity on a palate that is a great example of the Yarra Valley's ace in the hole with chardonnay: extreme length. Screwcap. 13.5% alc. **Rating** 95 **To** 2025 $35 **۞**
Pinot Noir 2015 Matured in French oak (25% new) for 11 months. Bright, full colour; the wine progressively shifts and builds ground from the bouquet through to the palate, finish and – in particular – the aftertaste, by which time the sheer power of the dark red/purple fruits takes hold. Balance in a bottle. Screwcap. 13.8% alc. **Rating** 95 **To** 2025 $35 **۞**
Sexton Vineyard Pinot Noir 2014 Here the tannins are a little more evident, underpinning the savoury/spicy nuances to the fruits, oak less important. The strength of the wine is its length and balance. Screwcap. 13.5% alc. **Rating** 95 **To** 2030 $50
Applejack Vineyard Pinot Noir 2014 The relatively light colour and perfumed bouquet are typical of this Upper Yarra vineyard, as is the understated elegance and finesse of the palate, spicy/savoury red fruits and silky tannins in a back-up role. If 250 dozen had been made in 2012, not 245, it would have won the Jimmy Watson Trophy in '13. Screwcap. 13.5% alc. **Rating** 95 **To** 2027 $50
Sexton Vineyard Merlot 2014 Warmed for fermentation to start, once complete the fermenter sealed with water bags for 3 weeks maceration on skins, matured in French oak (40% new) for 17 months. This is near the very top of the merlot tree in Australia, needing no apology of any kind. Excellent colour, a come-hither bouquet and a palate alive with flowing cassis and plum fruit; the tannins are A-grade, the oak providing the frame for a perfect portrait of an oft-maligned variety. Screwcap. 14% alc. **Rating** 95 **To** 2034 $45
Harry's Monster 2014 50% merlot, 40% cabernet sauvignon, 10% petit verdot from the Sexton Vineyard, fermented separately, then treated à la Sexton Merlot, blended Jan '14 and matured in French oak (40% new) for 18 months. Pussyfooting with cabernet and merlot doesn't pay off, especially where you have the depth and varietal clarity of the grapes here, the petit verdot providing a rock solid bridge between the two varieties. Screwcap. 14% alc. **Rating** 95 **To** 2034 $55

Gibson   ★★★★★

190 Willows Road, Light Pass, SA 5355 **Region** Barossa Valley
T (08) 8562 3193 **www.**gibsonwines.com.au **Open** 7 days 11–5
Winemaker Rob Gibson **Est.** 1996 **Dozens** 10 000 **Vyds** 14.2ha
Rob Gibson spent much of his working life as a senior viticulturist for Penfolds, involved in research tracing the characters that particular parcels of grapes give to a wine, which left him with a passion for identifying and protecting what is left of the original vineyard plantings in Australia. He has a vineyard in the Barossa Valley at Light Pass (merlot), and one in the Eden Valley (shiraz and riesling), and also purchases grapes from McLaren Vale and the Adelaide Hills. Exports to Germany, Denmark, Hong Kong and China.

🍷🍷🍷🍷🍷 **Australian Old Vine Collection Eden Valley Shiraz 2010** The small production is from vines planted in the early 1900s. Great colour, still vibrant and deep; the wine enters the mouth in a seamless, deep flow of blackberry, plum and spice, then tightens on the back-palate courtesy of firm, but balanced tannins. A crease on the side of the cork let some wine escape and act as a glue, adhering the capsule to the bottle neck. 14.5% alc. **Rating** 96 **To** 2030 $100
Australian Old Vine Collection Barossa Shiraz 2010 The vines were planted between the mid-1800s and the early 1900s, hence the intensity and power of its precocious display of black fruits on the medium-bodied palate; precisely balanced firm, but ripe, tannins add to the length of an already long palate. The one issue is the wine travel along the sides of the cork. 14.5% alc. **Rating** 96 **To** 2030 $119
Eden Valley Riesling 2015 Fermented for 7 weeks and bottled early Jun. The impact and intensity of the wine are utterly remarkable, acidity a stainless-steel backbone taking the wine at breakneck speed across the palate and into the lingering finish. Screwcap. 10.5% alc. **Rating** 96 **To** 2030 $21 **۞**

Wilfreda 2014 Mataro, shiraz and grenache from old dry-grown, low-yielding vines. The low yield is obvious in the very good structure, often missing in action in Barossa Valley MSGs; the bouquet has attractive hints of pipe tobacco, moving towards spice, mocha and plum cake on the palate, gaining further from the gently savoury finish. Screwcap. 14.8% alc. Rating 94 To 2029 $27 ○

🍷🍷🍷🍷🍷 **The Dirtman Barossa Shiraz 2014** Rating 93 To 2034 $31
Discovery Road Zinfandel 2015 Rating 91 To 2018 $25
Discovery Road Fiano 2015 Rating 90 To 2018 $20 ○

🦢 Giggling Goose ★★★☆

PMB 72, Naracoorte, SA 5271 **Region** Padthaway
T 0438 656 012 **www**.gigglinggoose.com.au **Open** Not
Winemaker Leisha Munro, Grant Semmens **Est.** 2014 **Dozens** 1000 **Vyds** 70ha
Between 1997 and 2006, Sam and Fiona Ward planted the Giggling Goose vineyard to shiraz (30ha), cabernet sauvignon, viognier and chardonnay (9ha each), merlot (5ha), and sangiovese and sauvignon blanc (4ha each). Usually a little over half of the annual crush is sold as grapes, the remainder made into bulk and bottled wine (including Giggling Goose) by Limestone Coast Wines.

🍷🍷🍷🍷🍷 **Single Vineyard Padthaway Shiraz 2014** Matured in French oak and stainless steel for 12 months before bottling. Excellent crimson-purple colour, still vivid through to the rim; a voluptuously rich fore-palate before backing off slightly on the finish – no bad thing in the context of the wine. You get maximum flavour per dollar here. Coming ready or not. Screwcap. 14.5% alc. **Rating** 90 To 2024 $20 ✪

gilbert by Simon Gilbert | Gilbert + Gilbert ★★★★

PO Box 773, Mudgee, NSW 2850 **Region** Orange/Mudgee
T (02) 6373 1454 **www**.thegilbertsarecoming.com.au **Open** Not
Winemaker Simon and Will Gilbert **Est.** 2010 **Dozens** 3500 **Vyds** 25.81ha
For some time now Simon Gilbert has devoted himself to his consultancy and wine brokering business, Wineworks of Australia. As that business has grown, Simon has returned to the winery wearing his Wineworks of Australia hat, overseeing the winemaking of the estate-grown grapes, all exported. Separate from his consultancy business, he has established gilbert by Simon Gilbert, and also makes the wines for this label at the same winery. Distribution is limited to specialist wine retailers and restaurants. Fifth and sixth generations Simon, Will and Mark Gilbert have drawn on the family history (Joseph Gilbert was among the first to plant grapes in the Eden Valley in 1842, the property at Pewsey Vale remaining in the family until 1923) to produce Gilbert + Gilbert wines sourced from the Eden Valley. Exports to Hong Kong and China.

🍷🍷🍷🍷🍷 **Gilbert + Gilbert Museum Reserve Eden Valley Riesling 2010** A very elegant wine, still to reach its plateau – somewhere around the end of this decade. It is beautifully balanced, the residual sugar of 2.3g/l below the taste threshold, but not below texture level. Screwcap. 12.5% alc. **Rating** 95 To 2025 $38
gilbert by Simon Gilbert Sur Lie Orange Sauvignon Blanc 2015 Pale straw; a vibrant and complex aroma loaded with pear, apple and a herbal kick, barrel fermentation adding a touch of class. The palate has lovely intensity and drive, finishing long and precise. Screwcap. 13.5% alc. **Rating** 94 To 2022 $26 ○

🍷🍷🍷🍷🍷 **Gilbert + Gilbert Single Vineyard Eden Valley Riesling 2015** Rating 93 To 2024 $28
gilbert by Simon Gilbert Mudgee Orange Saignee Rose 2015 Rating 92 To 2017 $24 ○

Gioiello Estate

350 Molesworth-Dropmore Road, Molesworth, Vic 3718 **Region** Upper Goulburn
T 0437 240 502 **www**.gioiello.com.au **Open** Not
Winemaker Scott McCarthy (Contract) **Est.** 1987 **Dozens** 3500 **Vyds** 8.97ha
The Gioiello Estate vineyard was established by a Japanese company and originally known as
Daiwa Nar Darak. Planted between 1987 and '96, it accounts for just under 9ha on a 400ha
property of rolling hills, pastures, bushland, river flats, natural water springs and billabongs.
Now owned by the Schiavello family, the vineyard continues to produce high quality wines.

ÝÝÝÝÝ **Mt Concord Syrah 2013** Includes 2.5% co-fermented viognier, matured for
18 months in French barriques (66% new). Harmonious red cherry, plum and
blackberry fruits are framed by cedary French oak, the tannins fine, but playing an
important role. Still very youthful and will flourish with time in bottle. Screwcap.
14.2% alc. **Rating** 95 **To** 2033 $45
Reserve Chardonnay 2014 Hand-picked, whole bunch-pressed, wild yeast-
fermented in French barriques (25% new), matured for 10 months. Whereas its
sibling is loose, this is tight – or at least, tighter, counterintuitively with brighter
fruit, grapefruit joining stone fruit flavours; oak, too, is a positive contributor, with
no downside. Screwcap. 13% alc. **Rating** 94 **To** 2022 $40
Syrah 2013 2.5% co-fermented viognier, matured for 18 months in French
barriques (40% new). Bright crimson-purple hue; fresh spice and pepper nuances
to the juicy cherry and blackberry fruit, oak apparent but not intrusive, Marries
medium body with intensity in compelling fashion. Screwcap. 14.3% alc.
Rating 94 **To** 2028 $28 ✪

ÝÝÝÝÝ **Reserve Cabernet 2013** Rating 91 To 2023 $45

GISA

578 The Parade, Auldama, SA 5072 **Region** South Australia
T (08) 8338 2123 **www**.gisa.com.au **Open** Not
Winemaker Mat Henbest **Est.** 2006 **Dozens** 10 000
Mat and Lisa Henbest have chosen a clever name for their virtual winery – GISA stands
for Geographic Indication South Australia – neatly covering the fact that their wines come
variously from the Adelaide Hills (for Semillon, Sauvignon Blanc and Chardonnay), Clare
Valley (for Riesling), McLaren Vale (for Shiraz Viognier) and Barossa Valley (for Reserve
Shiraz). It in turn reflects Mat's long apprenticeship in the wine industry, working in retail
while he pursued tertiary qualifications, thereafter wholesaling wine to the retail and
restaurant trade. He then moved to Haselgrove, where he spent five years working closely with
the small winemaking team, refining his concept of style, and gaining experience on the other
side of the fence. Exports to China.

ÝÝÝÝÝ **Single Vineyard Polish Hill River Riesling 2015** Single vineyard. Lime leaf,
talc and green apple lead into a fine and precise palate, intense, taut, and just a baby.
Will develop nicely. Screwcap. 11% alc. **Rating** 94 **To** 2025 $25 ✪

ÝÝÝÝÝ **Piccadilly Chardonnay 2015** Rating 92 To 2020 $30
Round Barossa Valley Shiraz 2014 Rating 91 To 2024 $22 ✪

Gisborne Peak

69 Short Road, Gisborne South, Vic 3437 **Region** Macedon Ranges
T (03) 5428 2228 **www**.gisbornepeakwines.com.au **Open** 7 days 11–5
Winemaker John Ellis **Est.** 1978 **Dozens** 2000 **Vyds** 5.5ha
Bob Nixon began the development of Gisborne Peak way back in 1978, planting his dream
vineyard row by row. The tasting room has wide shaded verandahs, plenty of windows
and sweeping views. The vineyard is planted to pinot noir, chardonnay, semillon, riesling
and lagrein.

ΨΨΨΨΨ Riesling 2015 This cool grown riesling is a model of restraint; a lime, floral and talc bouquet leads to a tightly wound mineral palate that will require many years to unfold and flourish. Screwcap. 11.8% alc. **Rating** 94 **To** 2030 $32

ΨΨΨΨΨ Unwooded Chardonnay 2015 **Rating** 90 **To** 2018 $25
Foundation Block Pinot Noir 2013 **Rating** 90 **To** 2020 $32

Glaetzer Wines ★★★★★

PO Box 824 Tanunda, SA 5352 **Region** Barossa Valley
T (08) 8563 0947 **www**.glaetzer.com **Open** Not
Winemaker Ben Glaetzer **Est.** 1996 **Dozens** 15 000 **Vyds** 20ha
With a family history in the Barossa Valley dating back to 1888, Glaetzer Wines was established by Colin Glaetzer after 30 years of winemaking experience. Son Ben worked in the Hunter Valley and as a Flying Winemaker in many of the world's wine regions before returning to Glaetzer Wines and assuming the winemaking role. The wines are made with great skill and abundant personality. Exports to all major markets.

ΨΨΨΨΨ Bishop Shiraz 2014 Full, deep crimson-purple; revels in its multifaceted array of black fruits, led by blackberry, but with confit plum, earth, licorice, a hint of dark chocolate and spice to complete a high quality package. No heart-burning alcohol in sight. Screwcap. 14.5% alc. **Rating** 95 **To** 2034 $33 ✪
Wallace Shiraz Grenache 2014 78% 60–80yo shiraz from the Ebenezer district and 22% 80–110yo grenache. Definitely a cut above many Barossa Valley blends, and I like the back label description of 'decadent yet reserved, rich yet restrained'. I would simply add no confectionery notes, and wonder at the gift-horse price. Screwcap. 14.5% alc. **Rating** 95 **To** 2020 $23 ✪
Anaperenna 2014 76% shiraz, 24% cabernet sauvignon. Anaperenna is never about half-measures. This is warm with alcohol and high in oak influence, but the fruit is rich and boisterous and the tannin a wave worth watching. It's a wine of both concerns and copious compensations. Chocolate and blackberry, black earth and salted licorice. You get what you came for, and then some. Cork. 15% alc. **Rating** 94 **To** 2032 $52 CM

ΨΨΨΨΨ Amon-Ra Unfiltered Shiraz 2014 **Rating** 93 **To** 2026 $100 CM

Glaetzer-Dixon Family Winemakers ★★★★★

93 Brooker Avenue, Hobart, Tas 7000 **Region** Southern Tasmania
T 0417 852 287 **www**.gdfwinemakers.com **Open** By appt
Winemaker Nick Glaetzer **Est.** 2008 **Dozens** 2500
History does not relate what Nick Glaetzer's high-profile Barossa Valley winemaker relatives thought of his decision to move to Tasmania in 2005, to make cutting-edge cool climate styles. Obviously wife Sally approves. While his winemaking career began in the Barossa Valley, he reached into scattered parts of the New World and Old World alike, working successively in Languedoc, the Pfaltz, Margaret River, Riverland, Sunraysia, the Hunter Valley and Burgundy. Exports to the US, Canada, The Netherlands and Singapore.

ΨΨΨΨΨ Mon Pere Shiraz 2013 As remarkable as it sounds/seems, this label makes shiraz in Tasmania look easy. This is a top-notch wine in anyone's language. It's cool climate by nature but mostly it's exquisitely well polished. Peanuts, licorice, bright cherries, cloves and a wide assortments of spices. It all unfolds slowly, magically, inexorably. Mesmerising. Screwcap. 13.7% alc. **Rating** 96 **To** 2028 $50 CM ✪
Reveur Pinot Noir 2012 From four vineyards in the Coal Valley in southern Tasmania. 20 months in French oak, bottled unfiltered. It's rich but complex, with undergrowth influencing five-spice, black cherry and satsuma plum characters. Tannin is immaculate; so too oak integration and acid. Feels assured from start to finish. Screwcap. 13.7% alc. **Rating** 95 **To** 2023 $56 CM

ΨΨΨΨΨ Uberblanc Goldpunkt Riesling 2013 **Rating** 93 **To** 2023 $36 CM
Avance Pinot Noir 2014 **Rating** 93 **To** 2021 $30 CM
Uberblanc Riesling 2014 **Rating** 92 **To** 2021 $24 CM ✪

Glen Eldon Wines

143 Nitschke Road, Krondorf, SA 5352 **Region** Barossa Valley
T (08) 8568 2644 **www**.gleneldonwines.com.au **Open** By appt
Winemaker Richard Sheedy **Est.** 1997 **Dozens** 6000 **Vyds** 50ha
Owners Richard and Mary Sheedy (and their four children) have established the Glen Eldon
property in the Eden Valley. The shiraz and cabernet sauvignon come from their vineyards in
the Barossa Valley; viognier and merlot are contract-grown; the riesling is from the Eden Valley.
Exports to the US, Canada and China.

ŸŸŸŸŸ Old Vine Series Barossa Shiraz 2012 The colour is still deep and dense, the
bouquet and palate logical follow-ons. Perfectly ripened, savoury/spicy/licorice
nuances underlie layers of rounded, supple black fruits. The label alcohol seems
true to all aspects of the palate, giving the wine great longevity. A testament to a
great vintage. ProCork. 14.5% alc. **Rating** 97 **To** 2047 $100 ❂

ŸŸŸŸŸ Reserve Eden Valley Riesling 2015 Ratchets up intensity and length,
otherwise walking in the footsteps of its cheaper varietal sibling. Curiously, I'm
not sure its life will be longer: is the acidity lower, or is it partially masked by the
richness of the fruit flavours? Screwcap. 12% alc. **Rating** 96 **To** 2027 $30 ❂
Eden Valley Riesling 2015 The highly floral bouquet is followed by a palate of
purity and precision, with a palate feel unique to Glen Eldon, as if an artist had
delicately painted the tongue with fruit-sweet lime juice, the focus then shifting to
minerally acidity. Screwcap. 12% alc. **Rating** 95 **To** 2025 $30 ❂
Old Vine Series Barossa Shiraz Grenache 2012 Seems to have the black
cherry/blackberry of Eden Valley shiraz, and no confection has come through
ex the grenache. Dark, bitter chocolate also lurks in the background. ProCork.
14.5% alc. **Rating** 95 **To** 2027 $100
Old Vine Series Barossa Cabernet Sauvignon 2012 Dense black fruits and
ripe tannins of the full-bodied palate are exactly what the dark purple-crimson
colour and heady/earthy aromas lead you to expect. It has a mountain of extract
to feed off for decades to come. ProCork. 14.5% alc. **Rating** 95 **To** 2040 $100

ŸŸŸŸ Kicking Back Barossa Cabernet Shiraz 2013 Rating 88 **To** 2023 $18

Glenguin Estate

Milbrodale Road, Broke, NSW 2330 **Region** Hunter Valley
T (02) 6579 1009 **www**.glenguinestate.com.au **Open** 7 days 10–5
Winemaker Robin Tedder MW, Rhys Eather **Est.** 1993 **Dozens** 2000 **Vyds** 6ha
Glenguin Estate was established by the Tedder family, headed by Robin Tedder MW, close to
Broke and adjacent to Wollombi Brook. The backbone of the production comes from 20-year-
old plantings of semillon and shiraz. Tannat (1ha) and a new planting of grafted semillon, with
cuttings from Braemore/HVD, complete the picture. Vineyard manager Andrew Tedder,
who has considerable experience with organics and biodynamics, is overseeing the ongoing
development of Glenguin's organic program. Exports to NZ.

ŸŸŸŸŸ Aristea Shiraz 2014 30% whole bunches, matured in French puncheons
(50% new) for 14 months. A totally compelling wine with its multiplicity of
messages, half deriving from the terroir and vintage, half from the vinification.
It is at once savoury/earthy/leathery and brightly fruited, the fragrance superb,
the medium-bodied palate with drive to its predominantly red fruits. Screwcap.
13.5% alc. **Rating** 97 **To** 2054 $50 ❂
Schoolhouse Block Shiraz 2014 20% whole bunches, matured in French
hogsheads (25% new) for 12 months. Both the bouquet and palate have complex
elements deriving from the whole bunch component, but the wine shares the
medium-bodied freshness of its siblings, all three with the same modest alcohol.
Screwcap. 13.5% alc. **Rating** 97 **To** 2044 $35 ❂

ŸŸŸŸŸ Classic Aged Release Semillon 2006 Last tasted 4 years ago (95 points), and
has sailed serenely on, still fresh and vibrant, still with years to go. Lemon (in all its

forms) and pure acidity are the drivers, the length of the palate exceptional. Is it better than it was 4 years ago? Yes, it is. Is the wine worth the price? Absolutely – it should be twice that. Screwcap. 10% alc. **Rating** 96 **To** 2026 $30 ✪

Stonybroke Shiraz 2014 Includes 10% tannat, 10% whole bunches, finished in used French puncheons, matured for 12 months. Bright hue; has a striking juicy freshness to the array of red and black fruits; while only just medium-bodied, the palate has compelling length and freshness. Screwcap. 13.5% alc. **Rating** 95 **To** 2044 $25 ✪

Aged Release Aristea Shiraz 2007 30% whole bunches, matured for 14 months in French puncheons (50% new). Confidently holding its bright colour, and equally confidently all its quality markers since first tasted 3 years ago, my tasting note effectively unchanged. Black cherry, plum, cedar and a hint of spicy/earthy nuances are held within a web of fine tannins and quality oak. Screwcap. 14% alc. **Rating** 95 **To** 2037 $80

♥♥♥♥ **Semillon 2015 Rating** 88 **To** 2020 $20

Glenwillow Wines

Bendigo Pottery, 146 Midland Highway, Epsom, Vic 3551 **Region** Bendigo
T 0428 461 076 **www**.glenwillow.com.au **Open** W'ends 11–5
Winemaker Greg Dedman, Adam Marks **Est.** 1999 **Dozens** 750 **Vyds** 2.8ha
Peter and Cherryl Fyffe began their vineyard at Yandoit Creek, 10km south of Newstead, in 1999, planting 1.8ha of shiraz and 0.3ha of cabernet sauvignon, later branching out with 0.6ha of nebbiolo and 0.1ha of barbera. The vineyard, planted on a mixture of rich volcanic and clay loam interspersed with quartz and buckshot gravel, has an elevated north-facing aspect, which minimises the risk of frost.

♥♥♥♥♥ **Bendigo Cabernet Sauvignon 2013** Impressive from the outset. Full, firm and complex. Violet and mint notes head straight into sweet, luscious blackcurrant. Cedary oak plays a keen role. It tumbles over itself to impress but remains firm and tidy to close. Screwcap. 14% alc. **Rating** 95 **To** 2033 $28 CM ✪
Reserve Bendigo Shiraz 2013 It's soft to the point of easygoing, and yet the concentration of both fruit and tannin is striking. This is a reserve wine to utterly seduce. Plum, Xmas cake, cloves and smoky/creamy oak, with gum leaf characters present but well tamed. Oak plays a key role yet has not been overplayed. Full-bodied red, dressed in velvet. Screwcap. 14.4% alc. **Rating** 94 **To** 2030 $70 CM

♥♥♥♥♥ **Bendigo Shiraz 2013 Rating** 93 **To** 2025 $28 CM

Goaty Hill Wines

530 Auburn Road, Kayena, Tas 7270 **Region** Northern Tasmania
T 1300 819 997 **www**.goatyhill.com **Open** 7 days 11–5
Winemaker Jeremy Dineen (Contract) **Est.** 1998 **Dozens** 5000 **Vyds** 19.5ha
Kristine Grant, Markus Maislinger and Natasha and Tony Nieuwhof are close friends from two families who moved from Victoria to make wine in the pristine climate of the Tamar Valley. Most of the estate-grown grapes are now made into the Goaty Hill brand, although they still sell some of their premium fruit to Jansz Tasmania. There aren't any goats on the property, but there is, according to the owners, a friendly collection of children and dogs.

♥♥♥♥♥ **Riesling 2015** A lovely riesling with a glorious fusion of Bickford's lime juice and glinting acidity; the fruit is so intense it makes you wonder whether there is perceptible residual sugar, but there isn't (in chemical terms). The alcohol is a boon, not a bane. Screwcap. 12.9% alc. **Rating** 96 **To** 2035 $30 ✪
Chardonnay 2014 Mid-straw; white peach and melon with a distinct cool edge to the fruit characters. finely poised and driven by fine acids. It has lovely presence and balance, but lacks the length to complete the picture. Screwcap. 12.9% alc. **Rating** 94 **To** 2020 $36

♥♥♥♥♥ **Maia 2011 Rating** 90 **To** 2017 $42 TS

Golden Ball

1175 Beechworth Wangaratta Road, Beechworth, Vic 3747 **Region** Beechworth
T (03) 5727 0284 **www**.goldenball.com.au **Open** By appt
Winemaker James McLaurin **Est.** 1996 **Dozens** 850 **Vyds** 4ha
The vineyard is on one of the original land grants in the Beechworth region, planted by James and Janine McLaurin in 1996, mainly to shiraz, cabernet sauvignon, merlot and malbec, with lesser plantings of petit verdot, sagrantino and savagnin. The wines are aged in one-third new French oak, the remainder 2–3 years old. The low yields result in intensely flavoured wines, which are to be found in a Who's Who of Melbourne's best restaurants and a handful of local and Melbourne retailers. Exports to Singapore.

ŸŸŸŸŸ **là-bas Beechworth Chardonnay 2014** This is a haughty, aristocratic chardonnay of rare character and quality; it matches extreme flavour intensity with finesse on a prodigiously long palate. Pink grapefruit, almond kernel, bright, but not aggressive acidity, and an airbrush of oak mark a rare wine from the heart of Giaconda territory. Screwcap. 13.5% alc. **Rating** 98 **To** 2029 $55 ✪

ŸŸŸŸŸ **Saxon Beechworth Shiraz 2013** Wild-fermented, pressed to barrel for the last part of primary fermentation, matured for 18 months in French oak (33% new). A very complex, savoury ball of flavours with earth, spice, licorice and a hint of eucalypt surrounding the core of black fruits. The more it is tasted, the more it reveals its texture and length – truly remarkable given it only just gets over the medium-bodied line. Diam. 13.8% alc. **Rating** 95 **To** 2033 $55

ŸŸŸŸŸ **Cherish a la provencale 2015 Rating** 90 **To** 2017 $28

Golden Grove Estate

Sundown Road, Ballandean, Qld 4382 **Region** Granite Belt
T (07) 4684 1291 **www**.goldengroveestate.com.au **Open** 7 days 9–4
Winemaker Raymond Costanzo **Est.** 1993 **Dozens** 4000 **Vyds** 12.4ha
Golden Grove Estate was established by Mario and Sebastian Costanzo in 1946, producing stone fruits and table grapes. The first wine grapes (shiraz) were planted in '72, but it was not until '85, when ownership passed to son Sam and his wife Grace, that the use of the property began to change. In '93 chardonnay and merlot joined the shiraz, followed by cabernet sauvignon, sauvignon blanc and semillon. The baton has been passed down another generation to Ray Costanzo, who has lifted the quality of the wines remarkably, and has also planted tempranillo, durif, barbera, malbec, mourvedre, vermentino and nero d'Avola. Its consistent wine show success over recent years with alternative varieties is impressive.

ŸŸŸŸŸ **Vermentino 2015** 90% was wild-fermented, with a small component of barrel-fermented Granite Belt semillon to provide acid backbone. The skills of winemaker Ray Costanzo have made a wine humming like taut fencing wire, with citrus zest, green apple and lightning acidity lingering long in the mouth. Amazing. Screwcap. 12.5% alc. **Rating** 95 **To** 2018 $26 ✪
Joven Granite Belt Tempranillo 2014 Wild-ferment and 20% whole bunches are components of this vividly coloured wine; it has undoubtedly added a twist to the normally juicy-fruity Joven style, but no more than a twist, leaving the red fruits of tempranillo in firm control. Screwcap. 13.5% alc. **Rating** 95 **To** 2020 $24 ✪
Granite Belt Malbec 2013 If it is the first duty of malbec to taste of spiced plum, and it is, this wine fills the bill precisely. It does so without losing freshness or lightness of foot, all in all making bottle maturation redundant. In tried and true Golden Grove Estate style. Screwcap. 14.5% alc. **Rating** 95 **To** 2020 $28 ✪
Granite Belt Barbera 2014 Co-fermented with 10% durif. A fresh and juicy wine with red cherries and red fruits of all descriptions clambering over each other in an effort to please and gain maximum attention; the bright, crunchy acidity on the finish is typical of barbera. Screwcap. 13.5% alc. **Rating** 94 **To** 2022 $24 ✪

Granite Belt Nero d'Avola 2014 Estate-grown, matured in used French and American oak. Cherry blossom bursts from the glass when swirled, the juicy palate adding plum to the equation, but not without a touch of fine tannins. Screwcap. 13.4% alc. **Rating** 94 **To** 2020 $26 ○

🍷🍷🍷🍷♀ **Sauvignon Blanc Semillon 2015 Rating** 93 **To** 2020 $20 ○
Joven Tempranillo 2015 Rating 93 **To** 2023 $26 ○
Sauvignon Blanc 2015 Rating 92 **To** 2016 $26
Granite Belt Chardonnay 2014 Rating 92 **To** 2020 $26
Granite Belt Durif 2014 Rating 90 **To** 2024 $30

Golding Wines ★★★★

52 Western Branch Road, Lobethal, SA 5241 **Region** Adelaide Hills
T (08) 8389 5120 **www.**goldingwines.com.au **Open** 7 days 11–5
Winemaker Darren Golding, Brendon Keys, Natasha Mooney **Est.** 2002 **Dozens** 6000
Vyds 26.12ha

The Golding family story began in the Adelaide Hills three generations ago through market gardening and horticulture. Viticulture became part of the picture 26 years ago when their Western Branch Road vineyard was planted. Darren and Lucy Golding took over the helm in 2002, launching the Golding Wines brand. Viticultural holdings have increased recently with the purchase of more vineyard and new plantings of gamay and dornfelder added to existing pinot noir, shiraz, chardonnay, savagnin, pinot gris and sauvignon blanc. The cellar door within their rustic sandstone barn has recently been refurbished. Exports to the UK, the US, Canada, Hong Kong, the Philippines, Malaysia, Singapore and China.

🍷🍷🍷🍷🍷 **La Francesa Adelaide Hills Savagnin 2014** Made by Brendon Keys. Now this I like. Its colour is bright straw-green, the palate full of flavours in the broad traminer church; somehow Keys has coaxed out some complex phenolics that sit really well in the wine. Screwcap. 13.6% alc. **Rating** 94 **To** 2019 $30 ○
Francis John Pinot Noir 2014 Estate-grown in Lenswood, fermented in stainless steel, matured for 12 months in used French oak. Good wine is the first and last thought; it has excellent varietal character, and has been made to throw the searchlight on the fruit. Screwcap. 12.5% alc. **Rating** 94 **To** 2024 $40
Rocco Shiraz 2013 Matured for 12 months in used French oak, made by Michael Sykes. A fine example of fragrant Adelaide Hills shiraz, the climate cool enough to extend ripening, and giving the wine a savoury gene in its DNA. A disciplined hand on the winemaking tiller. Screwcap. 14.5% alc. **Rating** 94 **To** 2028 $40

🍷🍷🍷🍷♀ **The Handcart Adelaide Hills Shiraz 2013 Rating** 93 **To** 2030 $25 ○
The Local Adelaide Hills Sauvignon Blanc 2014 Rating 91 **To** 2017 $22 ○

Gomersal Wines ★★★☆

Lyndoch Road, Gomersal, SA 5352 **Region** Barossa Valley
T (08) 8563 3611 **www.**gomersalwines.com.au **Open** 7 days 10–5
Winemaker Barry White, Peter Pollard **Est.** 1887 **Dozens** 8500 **Vyds** 20ha

The 1887 establishment date has a degree of poetic licence. In 1887 Friedrich W Fromm planted the Wonganella Vineyards, following that with a winery on the edge of the Gomersal Creek in 1891; it remained in operation for 90 years, finally closing in 1983. In 2000 a group of friends 'with strong credentials in both the making and consumption end of the wine industry' bought the winery and re-established the vineyard, planting 17ha of shiraz, 2ha of mourvedre and 1ha of grenache via terraced bush vines. The Riesling comes from purchased grapes. Exports to The Netherlands, South Korea, Singapore and China.

🍷🍷🍷🍷 **Eden Valley Riesling 2015** An honest, no-tricks wine, with lime juice neatly framed by minerally acidity. We're a lucky lot in Australia with rieslings of this quality for a song. Screwcap. 12% alc. **Rating** 89 **To** 2023 $17 ○

Barossa Valley Grenache Shiraz Mataro 2013 Matured in new and used
American hogsheads for 10 months. Traditional Barossa Valley blend, a little blurred
around the edges, but you can't complain too much given its price. Screwcap.
14.5% alc. **Rating** 88 **To** 2020 $17

Goodman Wines   ★★★★☆

15 Symons Street, Healesville, Vic 3777 (postal) **Region** Yarra Valley
T 0447 030 011 **www**.goodmanwines.com.au **Open** Not
Winemaker Kate Goodman **Est.** 2012 **Dozens** 500
Kate Goodman started her winemaking career in McLaren Vale and the Clare Valley, thereafter
spending seven years winemaking at Seppelt in the Grampians. In 2000 she became chief
winemaker at Punt Road Wines, and remained there until '14, when she left to set up
Goodman Wines, leasing a winery together with fellow winemaker Caroline Mooney (the
latter of Bird on a Wire). Using some lead time planning, and with the knowledge and
approval of Punt Road's owners, she had made wines over the '12 and '13 vintages all from
mature Upper Yarra Valley vineyards.

 Yarra Valley Chardonnay 2014 From the Willowlake Vineyard, wild-fermented
on light lees in French oak (20% new). Lovely wine, showing the Yarra Valley to
best advantage, delicate white peach and cashew first up, grapefruity acidity to
finish. Screwcap. 12.5% alc. **Rating** 95 **To** 2023 $40
Yarra Valley Cabernet Sauvignon 2014 Open-fermented, pressed to French
oak (20% new). Well made; the fulcrum is bright cassis, achieved at the low end
of the range yet avoiding mint or wintergreen characters; the tannins are fine and
ripe, oak important. Screwcap. 13% alc. **Rating** 94 **To** 2030 $40

Yarra Valley Pinot Noir 2014 **Rating** 93 **To** 2024 $40
Pyrenees Shiraz 2014 **Rating** 93 **To** 2029 $35
Heathcote Vermentino 2015 **Rating** 92 **To** 2018 $30

Goona Warra Vineyard   ★★★☆

790 Sunbury Road, Sunbury, Vic 3429 **Region** Sunbury
T (03) 9740 7766 **www**.goonawarra.com.au **Open** By appt
Winemaker John Barnier, Emmett Andersen **Est.** 1863 **Dozens** 3000 **Vyds** 6.92ha
A historic stone winery, originally established under this name by a 19th-century Victorian
premier. Excellent tasting facilities, an outstanding venue for weddings and receptions. Exports
to Taiwan and China.

 Chairmans Reserve 2015 Fresh, bright and well presented but lacking on the
intensity front. Maturation in oak has added an attractive slinky smoothness to the
texture; pleasant compensation. Screwcap. 12.5% alc. **Rating** 89 **To** 2017 $20 CM
Chairmans Reserve Chardonnay 2015 Essentially attractive. For the most
part toffee, sweet apple and nectarine flavours swing amicably through the palate.
Screwcap. 14% alc. **Rating** 88 **To** 2017 $27 CM

Gooree Park Wines   ★★★

Gulgong Road, Mudgee, NSW 2850 **Region** Mudgee
T (02) 6378 1800 **www**.gooreepark.com.au **Open** Mon–Fri 10–5, w'ends 11–4
Winemaker Rueben Rodriguez **Est.** 2008 **Dozens** 3000 **Vyds** 546ha
Gooree Park Wines is part of a group of companies owned by Eduardo Cojuangco, other
companies including a thoroughbred horse stud and a pastoral enterprise and vineyards based
in Mudgee and Canowindra. Eduardo's interest in all forms of agriculture has resulted in the
planting of over 500ha of vines, starting with the Tullamour Vineyard in Mudgee in 1996,
Fords Creek in Mudgee in '97, and Mt Lewis Estate at Canowindra in '98.

ΨΨΨΨ **Shiraz Rose 2015** Estate-grown.Vivid, clear crimson-purple; fermented bone dry, so no disguising the alcohol, but cherry fruits do come to the rescue, plus crisp acidity on the finish. Screwcap. 13.9% alc. **Rating** 88 **To** 2017 $18
Crowned Glory Mudgee Shiraz 2014 Matured for 12 months in American and French oak. The American oak dominates proceedings with its vanillan and plum cake imprint; this to one side, a medium-bodied shiraz with soft tannins likely to develop quickly. Screwcap. 13.3% alc. **Rating** 88 **To** 2019 $32

Gossie & Co ★★★★☆

11 Bancroft Avenue, Roseville, NSW 2069 (postal) **Region** Hilltops/Pyrenees
T 0409 957 369 **Open** Not
Winemaker James Gosper **Est.** 2015 **Dozens** 250
In July 2014, James Gosper founded Gossie & Co, which provides advice on all aspects of production and wine marketing in Australia and globally. James' tertiary education at Charles Sturt University was followed by 10 years (1996–06) as Chief Winemaker and Operations Director at Domaine Chandon Australia. He then moved to Moet Hennessy USA as Brand Director for three years, then joined the Australian Wine & Brandy Corporation as Regional Director for North America (2009–11), returning to Australia for three years as General Manager Marketing, Wine Australia, retiring in June '14. This tiny branch of Gossie & Co may be the hair shirt to remind him of the challenges facing small wine producers in Australia.

ΨΨΨΨΨ **Pee Vee 2013** 100% petit verdot from the Mokhinui Vineyard in the Hilltops region, open-fermented and plunged, then pressed and matured for 12 months in French oak. Petit verdot is often an uncouth brawler, but is on its very best behaviour here, mixing red and blue fruits, spices and finely sieved tannins on the long palate. They don't come much better than this. Screwcap. 13% alc. **Rating** 95 **To** 2028 $27
Private Drop 2014 60% cabernet sauvignon, 40% shiraz, the cabernet sourced from the Mokhinui Vineyard in the Hilltops, the shiraz from the Malakoff Vineyard in the Pyrenees. The cabernet was given 3 months post-fermentation maceration before being pressed, then matured for 15 months in French oak. The shiraz component was part of the She Raz make, the components blended 15 May. Bright crimson; the bouquet has an ultra-fragrant spray of red and purple fruits, the palate following the path set for it without hesitation by the colour and bouquet. Delicious wine. Screwcap. 13.5% alc. **Rating** 94 **To** 2024 $27

ΨΨΨΨΨ **She Raz 2014** **Rating** 91 **To** 2029 $27

Gotham Wines ★★★☆

8 The Parade West, Kent Town, SA 5067 **Region** South Australia
T (08) 7324 3021 **www**.gothamwines.com.au **Open** Not
Winemaker Contract **Est.** 2004 **Dozens** 55000
In 2014 a group of wine enthusiasts, including former BRL Hardy CEO Stephen Millar, came together to purchase the Gotham Wine brands. The intention was (and is) to build on the existing domestic and export distribution of the wines, which include Wine Men of Gotham, Gotham, Stalking Horse and StepXStep brands, from Langhorne Creek, Clare Valley, Barossa Valley and McLaren Vale. Exports to Canada, Denmark, Malaysia, Thailand, Indonesia, Japan and NZ.

ΨΨΨΨΨ **Clare Valley Riesling 2015** A vibrant wine with bright minerally acidity spearing through intense lemon/lime fruit. If you want a cheap riesling to turn from frog to prince, this is the go. Screwcap. 12.5% alc. **Rating** 91 **To** 2025 $15

ΨΨΨΨ **Langhorne Creek Cabernet Sauvignon 2013** **Rating** 89 **To** 2020 $20
Langhorne Creek Shiraz 2014 **Rating** 88 **To** 2019 $20

Grace Farm

741 Cowaramup Bay Road, Gracetown, WA 6285 **Region** Margaret River
T (08) 9384 4995 **www**.gracefarm.com.au **Open** By appt
Winemaker Jonathan Mettam **Est.** 2006 **Dozens** 3000 **Vyds** 8.17ha
Situated in the Wilyabrup district, Grace Farm is the small, family-owned vineyard of Elizabeth and John Mair, taking its name from the nearby coastal hamlet of Gracetown. Situated beside picturesque natural forest, the vineyard is planted to cabernet sauvignon, chardonnay, sauvignon blanc and semillon. Viticulturist Tim Quinlan conducts tastings (by appointment), explaining Grace Farm's sustainable viticultural practices.

🍷🍷🍷🍷🍷 **Cabernet Sauvignon 2014** An exceptionally pure cabernet, its balance, texture, structure and length all in harmony. In the end, you come back to the perfume of the bouquet and the beautifully ripened cassis of the palate as the high points of a perfect cabernet, fine-grained tannins underwriting its ability to age with grace. Screwcap. 14.5% alc. **Rating** 96 **To** 2044 $30 ✪
Reserve Cabernet Sauvignon 2014 It's a long, sinewy, herb-splashed wine but the core of fruit is strong and authoritative. As a contender for the cellar, this mounts a convincing case. It carries both red and black currant flavours and feels dusty and smoky at various stages. From start to finish, immaculate. Screwcap. 14% alc. **Rating** 96 **To** 2034 $50 CM ✪

🍷🍷🍷🍷🍷 **Margaret River Sauvignon Blanc Semillon 2015 Rating** 92 **To** 2016 $21 ✪

Graillot

3–5 Harper Street, Abbotsford, Vic 3067 (postal) **Region** Heathcote
T 1300 610 919 **www**.graillotaustralia.com.au **Open** Not
Winemaker Alain Graillot, Luke Lambert **Est.** 2010 **Dozens** 900 **Vyds** 3.3ha
Graillot is owned by Robert Walters, well known for his role with Bibendum Wine Co., which (inter alia) imports fine wines from various parts of Europe, with France to the fore. He has imported the wines of Alain Graillot, one of the superstars of the northern Rhône Valley (in Crozes-Hermitage) for many years. The two become good friends during that time, and in 2010 that friendship took a new turn with the establishment of Graillot. Exports to Canada, France, The Netherlands, South Africa, Hong Kong and Japan.

🍷🍷🍷🍷🍷 **Heathcote Syrah 2014** From the top of the block, 50% whole bunches/50% whole berries, including small parcels of carbonic maceration. Has more texture to the palate than Project No. 2, and is more elegant. The dried herb/spice nuances add something No. 2 lacks, but that's not the end of the story. Two very different and accessible wines. Screwcap. 13% alc. **Rating** 96 **To** 2034 $46 ✪
Project Syrah No. 2 2014 From the top of the block, 40% whole bunches/60% whole berries, including small parcels of carbonic maceration. Powerful, yet supple and smooth, almost velvety, rates 100% on the hedonism scale. Don't open a bottle if you think you will only have a glass. Screwcap. 13% alc. **Rating** 95 **To** 2030 $32 ✪

Grampians Estate

1477 Western Highway, Great Western, Vic 3377 **Region** Grampians
T (03) 5354 6245 **www**.grampiansestate.com.au **Open** 7 days 10–5
Winemaker Andrew Davey, Tom Guthrie **Est.** 1989 **Dozens** 2000 **Vyds** 8ha
Graziers Sarah and Tom Guthrie began their diversification into wine in 1989, but their core business continues to be fat lamb and wool production. Both activities were ravaged by the 2006 bushfires, but each has recovered, that of their grapegrowing and winemaking rising like a phoenix from the ashes. They have acquired the Garden Gully winery at Great Western, giving them a cellar door and a vineyard with 2.4ha of 130-year-old shiraz and 3ha of 80-year-old riesling. Exports to Singapore and China.

ioooo Streeton Reserve Shiraz 2012 Matured in French oak for 2 years. It derives its
ultra-complex full body from its intense black fruits, graphite, tar, ripe tannins and
quality French oak. Will live for many decades. Screwcap. 13.5% alc. **Rating** 96
To 2042 $75 **☉**
Mafeking Shiraz 2013 Matured for 12 months in French and American oak.
The contrast with the Garden Gully Vineyard could not be greater; this has a
fragrant bouquet, and is positively cool in the mouth, with red fruits crowned by
spice, pepper and licorice, the tannins fine, the oak minimal. Screwcap. 13.5% alc.
Rating 95 To 2033 $25 **☉**

ioooo GST 2014 **Rating** 91 To 2020 $28
Garden Gully Vineyard Barrel Block Shiraz 2013 **Rating** 90 To 2033 $50

Granite Hills

1481 Burke and Wills Track, Baynton, Vic 3444 **Region** Macedon Ranges
T (03) 5423 7273 **www**.granitehills.com.au **Open** 7 days 11–6
Winemaker Llew Knight, Ian Gunter **Est.** 1970 **Dozens** 5000 **Vyds** 12.5ha
Granite Hills is one of the enduring classics, pioneering the successful growing of riesling
and shiraz in an uncompromisingly cool climate. It is based on riesling, chardonnay, shiraz,
cabernet sauvignon, cabernet franc, merlot and pinot noir (the last also used in its sparkling
wine). The Rieslings age superbly, the Shiraz the forerunner of the cool climate school
in Australia. Wines were received too late for the book, but tasting notes can be found on
www.winecompanion.com.au.

Grant Burge

279 Krondorf Road, Barossa Valley, SA 5352 **Region** Barossa Valley
T 1800 088 711 **www**.grantburgewines.com.au **Open** 7 days 10–5
Winemaker Craig Stansborough **Est.** 1988 **Dozens** 400 000
Grant and Helen Burge established the eponymous Grant Burge business in 1988. It grew
to being one of the largest family-owned wine businesses in the valley. In February 2015,
Accolade Wines announced it had acquired the Grant Burge brand, and the historic Krondorf
Winery. The 356ha of vineyards remain in family ownership, and will continue to supply
premium grapes to the Accolade-owned business.

ioooo Abednego 2012 Wondrously good GSM; the aromas verging on outright
perfume, and certainly spiced, but it is the palate that takes it into the highest
realm. There is an intricate pattern of predominantly cherry and blood plum,
raspberry and spice without the faintest hint of confection. Remarkably, all the
grapes come from vines over 100yo. Diam. 13.5% alc. **Rating** 97 To 2032 $76 **☉**

ioooo Meshach 2010 Still full of youthful power. It spent 2 years in oak, and was then
held for 3 years maturation in the Grant Burge cellars prior to release. This has
opened the door of a Barossa Valley shiraz of undeniable quality and longevity in
the realm of superabundant blackberry, licorice and spice. Diam. 14.5% alc. **Rating**
96 To 2035 $170
Filsell Old Vine Barossa Shiraz 2013 A powerful full-bodied shiraz with
blackberry, soused plum, licorice and a savoury bitter chocolate slice stolen from
McLaren Vale. Its depth and balance are augmented by firm, though ripe, tannins.
Screwcap. 14% alc. **Rating** 95 To 2033 $43
Cameron Vale Barossa Cabernet Sauvignon 2013 A decidedly elegant
wine, dripping with cassis/blackcurrant and cedary/earthy spices; its length and
balance can't be faulted. Screwcap. 14% alc. **Rating** 95 To 2038 $27 **☉**
Shadrach 2010 Dense colour; it's a full-bodied version of a full-bodied Shadrach.
It's not hard to guess why it hasn't been previously released, and even now it's
barely ready. But its blackcurrant fruit is varietal, the tannins are balanced, and the
oak is integrated. Diam. 13.5% alc. **Rating** 95 To 2030 $90
Barossa 20 Year Old Tawny NV Four *Decanter Magazine* (UK) trophies in
'04, '07, '10 and '12 are among a large list of gold medals this wine has achieved.

A solera system has served the wine well, with its average age of 20 years the rock of ages on which this seriously luscious tawny is built. Toffee, marmalade, spiced Barossan fruitcakes/breads, spice and chocolate are all there, and more. Cork. 19.5% alc. **Rating** 95 To 2017 $90

Balthasar Eden Valley Shiraz 2013 More elegant than you might expect. A combination of red and black berry flavours meet spice and leather, all tied together by an intricate web of tannin. Floral/citrus notes add to the lively impression. For now or later. Diam. 14% alc. **Rating** 94 To 2025 $43 CM

ŸŸŸŸŸ **5th Generation Barossa Shiraz 2014** Rating 93 To 2025 $20❂
Corryton Barossa Cabernet Sauvignon 2012 Rating 93 To 2025 $43 CM
Miamba Barossa Shiraz 2014 Rating 92 To 2034 $27
Helene Tasmania Grande Cuvee 2006 Rating 92 To 2017 $55 TS
Thorn Eden Valley Riesling 2015 Rating 90 To 2022 $25
5th Generation Pinot Gris 2015 Rating 90 To 2017 $20❂
East Argyle Adelaide Hills Pinot Gris 2015 Rating 90 To 2017 $25

Greedy Sheep

PO Box 530, Cowaramup, WA 6284 **Region** Margaret River
T (08) 9755 7428 www.greedysheep.com.au **Open** Not
Winemaker Dave Johnson **Est.** 2005 **Dozens** 4000 **Vyds** 6ha
When Bridget Allen purchased the Greedy Sheep property in 2004 it had been planted to cabernet sauvignon, merlot, cabernet franc and malbec in 1999. It pays to have a sense of humour, for in January '05 1000 sheep found their way into the vineyard, eating everything green within their reach, including unripe grapes, which must have challenged their digestion. Bridget also purchases fruit from her twin sister's vineyard, a mere 3km away.

ŸŸŸŸŸ **Single Vineyard Margaret River Cabernet Merlot 2013** Even-tempered and well ripened. Blackcurrant and mulberry flavours bring bay leaf and woody spice notes along for the ride. Beautifully balanced and, not unrelated, a joy to drink. Screwcap. 14.1% alc. **Rating** 93 To 2025 $30 CM

🍇 Green Door Wines

1112 Henty Road, Henty, WA 6236 **Region** Geographe
T 0439 511 652 www.greendoorwines.com.au **Open** Fri–Sun 11–4.30
Winemaker Ashley Keeffe, Jane Dunkley **Est.** 2007 **Dozens** 1000 **Vyds** 3.5ha
Ashley and Kathryn Keeffe purchased what was then a rundown vineyard in 2006. With a combination of new and pre-existing vines, there are now 0.75ha each of grenache, mourvedre, tempranillo and viano, and 0.25ha each of shiraz and verdelho. The wines are made in a small onsite winery (with the aid of consultant winemaker Jane Dunkley) using a range of winemaking methods, including the use of amphora pots.

ŸŸŸŸ **Flamenco Geographe Rose 2015** 60% grenache, 40% mourvedre, crushed, 3 days on skins. Bright colour; juicy red fruits fill the palate, finishing long, well balanced and dry. Screwcap. 12.5% alc. **Rating** 89 To 2017 $17❂
Spanish Steps Geographe Grenache Shiraz Mourvedre 2014 Hand-picked, basket-pressed, matured in French oak. Firm red and black fruits, fine tannins, good line, length and balance. Ready now, nothing to be gained from cellaring. Screwcap. 13.5% alc. **Rating** 89 To 2018 $19❂
El Toro Geographe Tempranillo 2014 Hand-picked, destemmed into open vats, basket-pressed at 4° baume to used oak for 12 months maturation. A complex wine, more black cherries/savoury tannins than usual, but the bundle of flavours do come together well. Has attitude, and will improve. Screwcap. 13.5% alc. **Rating** 89 To 2024 $25

 # Green Road Wines

170 Hutt Street, Adelaide, SA 5001 (postal) **Region** McLaren Vale
T 0411 434 393 **www**.greenroadwines.com.au **Open** Not
Winemaker Charlie Seppelt **Est.** 2012 **Dozens** 350 **Vyds** 0.9ha
Brothers Jake and Martin Greenrod are primarily restaurateurs with organic pizza restaurants in Adelaide. Way back, Jake studied oenology at Roseworthy for three years in the early 1990s, but didn't get around to completing the course. Nonetheless, it has certainly helped Green Road Wines. It has a 0.9ha vineyard planted to cabernet sauvignon. The wines are chiefly sold through their Hutt Street restaurant. Ian Hongell made the wines until 2015, and Charlie Seppelt took on the task from '16. And if the idea of organic gourmet pizzas presses your button, the Hahndorf spicy salami and the Barossa Valley double bacon causes the saliva to run.

Happy Days Shiraz Cabernet 2014 Plenty of words, but no facts on the back label, not even a claim of its McLaren Vale origin. However, a nicely modulated wine, fruit, oak and tannins all held in a medium-bodied frame. Drink now or much later. Screwcap. 14.5% alc. **Rating** 89 **To** 2028 $28

Shiraz Cabernet 2013 This comes rushing at you, eyes flashing, arms and legs going every which way, with a strongly savoury edge uncommon in McLaren Vale wines, the inclusion of whole bunches likewise uncommon yet possible. Patience needed. Screwcap. 14.5% alc. **Rating** 89 **To** 2028 $35

Greenstone Vineyards ★★★★★

179 Glenview Road, Yarra Glen, Vic 3775 **Region** Yarra Valley/Heathcote
T (03) 9730 1022 **www**.greenstonevineyards.com.au **Open** Thurs–Mon 10–5
Winemaker Travis Bush, Nathan Reeves **Est.** 2003 **Dozens** 7500 **Vyds** 45ha
In January 2015 events moved very quickly for what was then known as the Greenstone Vineyard, owned by three partners resident in the UK, Italy and Australia respectively. After protracted (but unpublicised) discussions the partners sold the property (a little over 20ha of vineyard and 20ha of bare land) to a private Chinese investor in late '14. It was, and is, a vineyard of very high quality, planted to shiraz (17ha), sangiovese (2.8ha), mataro (0.5ha) and colorino (0.1ha). Immediately ownership of the vineyard had changed, the investor purchased the former Sticks Winery (originally Yarra Ridge) and its surrounding estate vineyards, planted to chardonnay, cabernet sauvignon, pinot noir, sauvignon blanc, viognier, and merlot and petit verdot. Exports to China.

Heathcote Sangiovese 2013 This is serious stuff: layer upon layer of black cherry and bitter chocolate; it has a savoury profundity that takes you to the greatest names in Tuscany. Screwcap. 14% alc. **Rating** 97 **To** 2033 $60 ✪

Estate Series Yarra Valley Sauvignon Blanc 2015 Pressed to French hogsheads for a slow ferment (no mlf, no stirring or racking) for 8 months. If there were risks, none show; on the contrary, it has intensity and a tautness to the long, furiously focused finish. Screwcap. 12.5% alc. **Rating** 95 **To** 2020 $25 ✪

Heathcote Shiraz 2013 Classic Heathcote, succulent black and red fruits, tannins hand-stitched like an expensive Italian suit, custom cut to size. Screwcap. 13.5% alc. **Rating** 95 **To** 2033 $45

Estate Series Yarra Valley Chardonnay 2014 From the '83 estate planting. It has the effortless density that fully mature chardonnay can produce if given the chance. White peach, nectarine and pink grapefruit; French oak is subtle, the finish very good. Screwcap. 12% alc. **Rating** 94 **To** 2024 $30 ✪

Estate Series Yarra Valley Pinot Noir 2015 **Rating** 92 **To** 2028 $32

Estate Series Yarra Valley Methode Traditionnelle 2011 **Rating** 92 **To** 2019 $35 TS

Greg Cooley Wines

Lot 1 Main North Road, Clare, SA 5453 **Region** Clare Valley
T (08) 8843 4284 **www**.gregcooleywines.com.au **Open** 7 days 11–4
Winemaker Greg Cooley **Est.** 2002 **Dozens** 3000
Greg Cooley explains, 'All my wines are named after people who have been of influence to
me in my 45 years and their influence is as varied as the wine styles – from pizza shop owners,
to my greyhound's vet and South Australian author Monica McInerney.' I have to confess that
I am taken by Greg's path to glory, because my move through law to wine was punctuated by
the part-ownership of two greyhounds that always wanted to run in the opposite direction
from the rest of the field.

🍷🍷🍷🍷🍷 **Valerie Beh Single Vineyard Watervale Riesling 2015** Intensely floral and it
backs it up with a power of flavour. Lime, crushed spice and talc notes build to a
roar through the finish. Screwcap. 12.6% alc. **Rating** 94 **To** 2025 $23 CM **O**

🍷🍷🍷🍷🍷 **Winna and Toop Cabernet Merlot 2012** **Rating** 93 **To** 2025 $25 CM **O**
Dad & Meads Grenache Shiraz 2014 **Rating** 91 **To** 2021 $26 CM
Kalyi and Maura 10 Year Old Rutherglen Muscat NV **Rating** 90 **To** 2017
$30 CM

Grey Sands

6 Kerrisons Road, Glengarry, Tas 7275 **Region** Northern Tasmania
T (03) 6396 1167 **www**.greysands.com.au **Open** Sat–Mon 12–5 (mid-Nov–mid-Apr)
Winemaker Peter Dredge, Bob Richter **Est.** 1989 **Dozens** 1000 **Vyds** 3.5ha
Bob and Rita Richter began the establishment of Grey Sands in 1989, slowly increasing the
plantings to the present total. The ultra-high density of 8900 vines per hectare reflects the
experience gained by the Richters during a three-year stay in England, when they visited
many vineyards across Europe, as well as Bob's graduate diploma from Roseworthy College.
Plantings include pinot noir, merlot, pinot gris and malbec. Exports to Singapore.

🍷🍷🍷🍷🍷 **Pinot Noir 2010** Four clones, hand-picked, 20% whole bunches, 9 months
maturation. Very light colour, but amazingly bright and fresh hue; fresh, sweet red
cherry/berry fruits, fine tannins. A lovely pinot now, on a plateau of perfection it
will hold for some years yet. Diam. 13.8% alc. **Rating** 94 **To** 2020 $50
The Mattock 2013 60/30/10% merlot, malbec and cabernet franc. Its flavours
rest in a very nice place. Briar, chocolate, coffee and mulberry/blackcurrant notes.
Everything is well arranged, attractive, enjoyable now, but will repay patience.
Impeccable balance. Diam. 13.6% alc. **Rating** 94 **To** 2024 $35 CM

🍷🍷🍷🍷🍷 **Chardonnay Viognier 2010** **Rating** 92 **To** 2020 $35
Merlot 2008 **Rating** 91 **To** 2020 $40 CM

Groom

28 Langmeil Road, Tanunda, SA 5352 (postal) **Region** Barossa Valley
T (08) 8563 1101 **www**.groomwines.com **Open** Not
Winemaker Daryl Groom **Est.** 1997 **Dozens** 2300 **Vyds** 27.8ha
The full name of the business is Marschall Groom Cellars, a venture owned by David and
Jeanette Marschall and their six children, and Daryl and Lisa Groom and their four children.
Daryl was a highly regarded winemaker at Penfolds before he moved to Geyser Peak in
California. Years of discussion between the families resulted in the purchase of a 35ha block
of bare land adjacent to Penfolds' 130-year-old Kalimna Vineyard. Shiraz was planted in 1997,
giving its first vintage in '99. The next acquisition was an 8ha vineyard at Lenswood in the
Adelaide Hills, planted to sauvignon blanc. In 2000, 3.2ha of zinfandel was planted on the
Kalimna Bush Block. Exports to the US, Canada, Hong Kong, Taiwan and China.

🍷🍷🍷🍷🍷 **Barossa Valley Shiraz 2013** Matured for 20 months in 55% American and
45% French oak (30% new). Fabulous hue; makes and needs no apology for its
full-bodied palate of blackberry, satsuma plum, dark chocolate and licorice, toasty

oak adding another dimension, but not challenging the fruit, the ripe tannins equally courteous. Cork. 14.5% alc. **Rating** 95 **To** 2033 $49

ɽɽɽɽɿ **Adelaide Hills Sauvignon Blanc 2015 Rating** 92 **To** 2018 $24 **○**
Bush Block Barossa Valley Zinfandel 2014 Rating 90 **To** 2020 $30

Grosset ★★★★★

King Street, Auburn, SA 5451 **Region** Clare Valley
T (08) 8849 2175 **www.**grosset.com.au **Open** 10–5 Wed–Sun (spring)
Winemaker Jeffrey Grosset, Brent Treloar **Est.** 1981 **Dozens** 11 000 **Vyds** 22.2ha
Jeffrey Grosset has assumed the unchallenged mantle of Australia's foremost riesling maker in the wake of John Vickery stepping back to a consultancy role for Richmond Grove. Grosset's pre-eminence in riesling making is recognised both domestically and internationally; however, he merits equal recognition for the other wines in his portfolio: Semillon Sauvignon Blanc from Clare Valley/Adelaide Hills, Chardonnay and Pinot Noir from the Adelaide Hills and Gaia, a Bordeaux blend from the Clare Valley. These are all benchmarks. His quietly spoken manner conceals a steely will. Trial plantings (2ha) of fiano, aglianico, nero d'Avola and petit verdot (plus one or two more varieties planned) suggest some new wines may be gestating. Exports to all major markets.

ɽɽɽɽɽ **Springvale Riesling 2015** Takes life in its stride, feeling thoroughly unforced, yet its combination of prettiness, softness, and bursting flavour places it straight in tip-top territory. Blossomy citrus, chalk, fennel and steel notes convey the message, but its real class is in the wiring, the surge, the electricity it generates. Screwcap. 12.7% alc. **Rating** 97 **To** 2030 $40 CM **○**
Polish Hill Riesling 2015 The floral bouquet is still to fully open its wings and fly, but the palate makes you spring to attention, its natural acid structure providing a superb framework for the fruit to clamber all over. The purity and balance of the flavours shine brightly, the length and balance immaculate, lime, lemon and a hint of apple exactly pitched. It is a finer wine than the joyous Springvale. Screwcap. 12.7% alc. **Rating** 97 **To** 2030 $55 **○**

ɽɽɽɽɽ **Piccadilly Chardonnay 2014** Estate-grown, planted '82, fermented in French barriques (40% new) with partial mlf, 10 months in barrel. Chardonnay is putty in the hands of a master such as Jeffrey Grosset, everything in precise proportion and in its due place; white peach, a slice of green apple, a twist of grapefruit juice, and an airbrush of grilled cashew and cream, and you're there. Screwcap. 13% alc. **Rating** 96 **To** 2024 $67 **○**
Apiana 2015 Estate-grown fiano and semillon. Two keys: intensity and length. The way this wine carries on through the finish is like opening a door through to tomorrow. It's a textural wine, ripped with grapefruit, citrus and beeswax, but it's the thrust that really captures the attention. Screwcap. 12.7% alc. **Rating** 95 **To** 2017 $40 CM
Piccadilly Pinot Noir 2014 With two ferments, one conventional, the other whole bunch, pressed to French oak (60% new) for 12 months maturation. Shows the complexity Jeffrey Grosset was aiming to achieve; the structure ex whole bunches is filled out by a pot pourri of black cherry and plum fruit, the concentration of the small berry/small bunch vintage very evident. Screwcap. 13.5% alc. **Rating** 95 **To** 2025 $79
Gaia 2013 Cabernet sauvignon, cabernet franc, 800 dozen made. The bouquet has a haunting edge of fruit spice and French oak, the palate a very complex amalgam of juicy black fruits and gently etched tannins, a waft of Provence herbs on the aftertaste. Screwcap. 13.7% alc. **Rating** 95 **To** 2038 $80
Alea Clare Valley Riesling 2015 Edge of sweetness to a terrific burst of apple blossom and lime flavour. Deliciousness is rarely so powerful. Talc-like nuances of flavour and texture to the finish. Screwcap. 12.5% alc. **Rating** 95 **To** 2025 $36 CM

Clare Valley Adelaide Hills Semillon Sauvignon Blanc 2015 Simultaneously bright and complex. Gravelly, grassy notes come awash with succulent tutti-frutti flavour. Fleshy. Textural. Exuberant. Before an exhibition of controlled intensity through the finish. Screwcap. 12.7% alc. **Rating** 94 **To** 2019 $35 CM

Grove Estate Wines   ★★★★☆

4100 Murringo Road, Young, NSW 2594 **Region** Hilltops
T (02) 6382 6999 **www**.groveestate.com.au **Open** 7 days 10–5
Winemaker Brian Mullany **Est.** 1989 **Dozens** 4000 **Vyds** 46ha
The Grove Estate partners of the Mullany, Kirkwood and Flanders families purchased the then unplanted property situated on volcanic red soils at an elevation of 530m with the intention of producing premium cool climate wine grapes for sale to other winemakers. Over the ensuing years plantings included cabernet sauvignon, shiraz, merlot, zinfandel, barbera, sangiovese, petit verdot, chardonnay, semillon and nebbiolo. In 1997 a decision was taken to retain a small amount of cabernet sauvignon and have it vinified under the Grove Estate label, and the winemaking gathered pace thereafter. Exports to China.

♟♟♟♟♟ **The Cellar Block Hilltops Shiraz Viognier 2014** A vibrantly incisive medium-bodied wine with spice, licorice, black cherry and blackberry all in the action; it accelerates on the journey through the mouth, and leaves the footprint of its flavours long after it is ingested, strongly savoury notes an unqualified success – and pleasure. Screwcap. 13.5% alc. **Rating** 95 **To** 2029 $35 ❂
Sommita Hilltops Nebbiolo 2014 Of medium body; the bouquet is distinctly floral (rose petal, violet) and the lithe palate has red and purple fruits, cherries and blueberries, the tannins persistent but fine. Tasted alongside the Freeman nebbiolo, radically different in style, here New World to its core. Screwcap. 14% alc. **Rating** 94 **To** 2034 $45

♟♟♟♟♀ **Hilltops Zinfandel 2013** **Rating** 91 **To** 2020 $20 ❂

Gumpara Wines   ★★★★

410 Stockwell Road, Light Pass, SA 5355 **Region** Barossa Valley
T 0419 624 559 **www**.gumparawines.net.au **Open** By appt
Winemaker Mark Mader **Est.** 1999 **Dozens** 500 **Vyds** 21.53ha
In 1856 the Mader family left Silesia to settle in SA, acquiring a 25ha property at Light Pass. Over the generations, farming and fruit growing gave way to 100% grapegrowing; six generations later, in 2000, Mark Mader produced the first wine under the Gumpara label. After success with Shiraz, Mark branched out into Semillon made from a small parcel of almost 90-year-old estate vines. The portfolio may be small, but it's certainly diverse, with Vermentino and a range of fortified wines.

♟♟♟♟♟ **Mader Reserve Shiraz 2013** Midnight in the garden of Barossa shiraz. There's an inky blackness to this whopping red. It floods the mouth with blackberry, sweet warm coffee, black earth and toffeed oak flavour, the whole delivered in one giant seamless wave. If you hanker for a monster red you'd die happy. Cork. 15% alc. **Rating** 94 **To** 2030 $50 CM

♟♟♟♟♀ **Victor's Old Vine Shiraz 2014** **Rating** 93 **To** 2024 $25 CM ❂

Gundog Estate   ★★★★★

101 McDonalds Road, Pokolbin, NSW 2320 **Region** Hunter Valley
T (02) 4998 6873 **www**.gundogestate.com.au **Open** 7 days 10–5
Winemaker Matthew Burton **Est.** 2006 **Dozens** 8000 **Vyds** 5ha
Matt Burton makes four different Hunter Semillons and Shiraz from the Hunter Valley, Murrumbateman and Hilltops. He and wife Renee run the cellar door from the historic Pokolbin school house, next to the old Rosemount/Hungerford Hill building on McDonalds Road. They are also constructing a cellar door at the Gundaroo family property (in the

Canberra District) owned by parents Sharon and Geoff, which has 2.5ha each of chardonnay and cabernet sauvignon. The Burton McMahon wines are a joint collaboration between Matt Burton and Dylan McMahon of Seville Estate. Exports to the UK.

🍷🍷🍷🍷🍷 **Rare Game Hunter Valley Shiraz 2014** Matured for 16 months in French puncheons (40% new). This has the complexity, richness and power of a vintage that has been compared to '65. It fills every corner of the mouth without effort, and stays long after it has been swallowed. Despite all its manifest dark fruit richness, it also has freshness, reflected in its modest alcohol. Screwcap. 13.5% alc. Rating 97 To 2054 $50 ✪

🍷🍷🍷🍷🍷 **Canberra District Shiraz 2014** Has 3% viognier and 20% whole bunches, matured in French puncheons for 14 months (30% new). Glorious colour sets the scene for a wine of great elegance and (yet) intensity. This and its Rare Game sibling are both great wines, stylistically poles apart. Screwcap. 14.5% alc. Rating 96 To 2039 $40 ✪

The Chase Hunter Valley Semillon 2015 Matured on lees for 4 months, gold medals Queensland Wine Show and NSW Small Winemakers Show '15. A high quality semillon flooded with lemon, lemongrass and a twist of lime from the open stanza through to the grand finale and curtain call. Its natural acidity makes it a now or much later proposition. Screwcap. 10.5% alc. Rating 95 To 2025 $30 ✪

Indomitus Albus Hunter Valley Semillon 2015 Includes 2% gewurztraminer, cloudy juice wild-fermented on 25% skins, held on skins and lees for 6 months, bottled without fining, 100 dozen made. Natural wine addicts, get back in your hutch. This isn't yellow or orange, it is pale straw-green, it has no phenolics, and is as fresh as a daisy. There's a hint of spice on the bouquet, which may or may not be due to the gewurztraminer; other than this, it's lemon/lemongrass/citrussy acidity all the way to the bank. Screwcap. 10.5% alc. Rating 95 To 2025 $45

Burton McMahon George's Vineyard Chardonnay 2015 A zesty, zippy and mouthwatering chardonnay from the Upper Yarra, nectarine, white peach and grapefruit all in on the act, supported by some savoury barrel-ferment oak. Overall, slightly crisper than D'Aloisio's Vineyard. Screwcap. 13% alc. Rating 95 To 2022 $30 ✪

Burton McMahon D'Aloisio's Vineyard Chardonnay 2015 Upper Yarra Valley. Pleasant touches of reduction on the bouquet, the palate fine, long and well balanced; the flavour spectrum is of white peach coupled with some grapefruit and a touch of nutty oak. Screwcap. 13% alc. Rating 95 To 2022 $30 ✪

Hilltops Shiraz 2015 9 months in French oak (20% new). Strong colour; rich, peppery black fruits on the medium to full-bodied palate; oak and ripe tannins perfectly weighted and balanced. A lovely wine at any price, let alone this. Screwcap. 14% alc. Rating 95 To 2040 $25 ✪

Marksman's Canberra District Shiraz 2014 The combination of licoricey fruit and clovey/nutty oak is a winner here, particularly given the added presence of juicy (black) cherry and dry woody spice notes. It glistens with both fruitfulness and savouriness. Tannin is ultrafine. Acidity is lively. In short, it tosses class at every turn. Screwcap. 14.5% alc. Rating 95 To 2028 $60 CM

Canberra District Rose 2015 Cabernet sauvignon from the Gundaroo Vineyard, 24 hours' skin contact, then cool-fermented. Vivid, clear crimson, this is a boisterous rose, jumping with fountains of pure cassis fruit cut by a river bed of stony acidity and a twist of herb. Screwcap. 13% alc. Rating 94 To 2017 $25 ✪

Hunter's Shiraz 2015 Matured for 9 months in French puncheons (25% new). All the '15 Hunter shirazs have to stand in the shade of the '14s, but can claim regional identity as does this; red and black fruits, bramble, sweet leather and fine, but persistent tannins; classic savoury/earthy stuff. Screwcap. 14% alc. Rating 94 To 2035 $40

Smoking Barrel Red 2015 Canberra District (90%) and the Hunter Valley (10%). Rich, dark fruits, pepper and spice fill the bouquet, and the medium-bodied palate follows the road suggested by the bouquet. There's no question about the contribution of the Hunter Valley component, which adds adding a lighter, savoury touch. Screwcap. 13.5% alc. **Rating** 94 **To** 2035 $30 ○

ТТТТ♀ Hunter's Semillon 2015 Rating 91 To 2020 $25
Wild Hunter Valley Semillon 2015 Rating 91 To 2020 $30 CM
Indomitus Rutilus Canberra District Shiraz 2014 Rating 91 To 2019 $45

Guthrie Wines ★★★★★

661 Torrens Valley Road, Gumeracha, SA 5253 **Region** Adelaide Hills
T 0413 332 083 **www.**guthriewines.com.au **Open** Not
Winemaker Hugh Guthrie **Est.** 2012 **Dozens** 700
Growing up on his family's farm in the Adelaide Hills, Hugh Guthrie developed an early interest in the wines and vineyards of the region, completing a Masters of Oenology at the University of Adelaide before working in wineries around Australia and abroad. Most recently he was a winemaker at The Lane Vineyard, winner of many awards for its wines. Wife Sarah's interest has always been more in drinking than in making wine, and her work as an anaesthetist and mother is already a full-time job. Looking after the business side of Guthrie Wines mops up any of her spare time. In 2014 Hugh held his breath, jumped, quit his day job, and became full-time winemaker at Guthrie Wines.

ТТТТТ The Snare Syrah 2015 Matured in used French oak for 10 months. Bright hue; the bouquet is, needless to say, complex and spicy, as is the medium to full-bodied palate, which is all about fruit, not oak or even tannins. Black cherry is foremost, wild blackberry picked fresh from the vine next, spice, pepper and licorice all having their say. Screwcap. 13.4% alc. **Rating** 95 **To** 2030 $32 ○
The Wholebunch Syrah 2015 Whole bunch (minimalistic handling); available exclusively from the website. This is off the charts with its throbbing aromas and flavours, a red wine version of Tokaji Essenzia. It's all about the cascade of black fruits of every kind plus licorice, plus pepper; oak and tannins are irrelevant. You could give this wine any points, high or low – you can decide, and defend your position with ease. Diam. 13.4% alc. **Rating** 95 **To** 2040 $42

ТТТТ♀ The Little Things Sauvignon Blanc 2015 Rating 91 To 2017 $22 ○

Haan Wines ★★★★☆

148 Siegersdorf Road, Tanunda, SA 5352 **Region** Barossa Valley
T (08) 8562 4590 **www.**haanwines.com.au **Open** Not
Winemaker Sarah Siddons (Contract) **Est.** 1993 **Dozens** 3500 **Vyds** 16.3ha
Hans and Fransien Haan established their business in 1993 when they acquired a vineyard near Tanunda. The plantings are shiraz (5.3ha), merlot (3.4ha), cabernet sauvignon (3ha), viognier (2.4ha), cabernet franc (1ha) and malbec, petit verdot and semillon (0.4ha each). Oak undoubtedly plays a role in the shaping of the style of the Haan wines, but it is perfectly integrated, and the wines have the fruit weight to carry the oak. Exports to Switzerland, Czech Republic, China and other markets.

ТТТТТ Wilhelmus 2013 Cabernet sauvignon, merlot, cabernet franc, malbec and petit verdot. Time and again Haan produces a near-impossible outcome with this Bordeaux blend, one that only a handful of peers in the Barossa Valley seek to emulate (and none succeed). It is luscious and sweet, the conundrum of its alcohol unanswered, most likely unanswerable. Diam. 15% alc. **Rating** 95 **To** 2028 $65
Barossa Valley Shiraz Prestige 2013 Matured in French barriques. This has so much generosity I cannot imagine how it was necessary to leave it on the vine so long. The issue isn't the small taste when evaluating the wine, but how you would fare sharing a bottle with your partner, unless post-prandial enjoyment was the intention. Diam. 15% alc. **Rating** 94 **To** 2033 $65

ТТТТ♀ Barossa Valley Merlot Cabernet Franc 2014 Rating 92 To 2024 $25 ○

Hahndorf Hill Winery

38 Pain Road, Hahndorf, SA 5245 **Region** Adelaide Hills
T (08) 8388 7512 **www**.hahndorfhillwinery.com.au **Open** 7 days 10–5
Winemaker Larry Jacobs **Est.** 2002 **Dozens** 5000 **Vyds** 6.5ha

Larry Jacobs and Marc Dobson, both originally from South Africa, purchased Hahndorf Hill Winery in 2002. Larry gave up a career in intensive care medicine in 1988 when he bought an abandoned property in Stellenbosch, and established the near-iconic Mulderbosch Wines. When Mulderbosch was purchased at the end of '96, the pair migrated to Australia and eventually found their way to Hahndorf Hill. In '06, their investment in the winery and cellar door was rewarded by induction into the South Australian Great Tourism Hall of Fame. In '07 they began converting the vineyard to biodynamic status, and they were among the first movers in implementing a carbon offset program. Having successfully grown and made multi medal-winning blaufrankisch wines, they have successfully imported three clones of gruner veltliner from Austria, and their first vintage was made in '10. In '15 it won four trophies: the '13 Shiraz with Best Shiraz of Show at the Australian Cool Climate Show; the '15 Rose at the Adelaide Hills Wine Show; and the '15 Sauvignon Blanc and '15 White Mischief Gruner Veltliner at the Winewise Small Vignerons Awards. Exports to the UK, Singapore and China.

Sauvignon Blanc 2015 From two Adelaide Hills sites, one cooler, the other warmer. Fermented separately with different cultured yeasts. At the upper end of Adelaide Hills sauvignon quality, full of succulent tropical fruits, yet nimble-footed, its length, finish and aftertaste courtesy of refreshing acidity. Screwcap. 13% alc. **Rating** 95 **To** 2017 $23 ✪

GRU Gruner Veltliner 2015 Six clones hand-picked in four lots, each treated differently. If you understand 1yo semillon, marsanne or riesling, you will understand what the intensity and length of the palate promises given time to reveal the beauty within. This will provide an exciting ride over the next 10 years. Gold medal Adelaide Wine Show '15. Screwcap. 12.5% alc. **Rating** 95 **To** 2030 $28 ✪

White Mischief Gruner Veltliner 2015 Fermented in stainless steel and left on gross lees for an extended period prior to bottling. The wine shows its attitude and flexes its muscles right from the word go, although not so much in the classic white pepper mode of gruner veltliner, more in quietly luscious tropical fruits, spices and lemony acidity. Screwcap. 12.5% alc. **Rating** 95 **To** 2018 $23 ✪

Rose 2015 45% pinot noir, 28% merlot and 27% trollinger, hand-picked specifically for this rose. A restricted period of skin contact provided the light puce colour and the texture, which is a feature of the palate, and has undoubtedly contributed to its show success. The fresh, crisp acidity on the finish is also exemplary, balanced by sweet strawberry fruits, not residual sugar (there is none). Screwcap. 12.5% alc. **Rating** 95 **To** 2017 $23 ✪

Single Vineyard Shiraz 2013 Matured in used French barriques for 11 months. The joie de vivre of the pulsing palate obviously gained the judges' attention at the Cool Climate Wine Show; it is at once energetic, yet impeccably balanced, its spicy/peppery red fruits given context by superfine tannins. The decision not to use any new oak allowed the fruit to show its wares to best advantage. Screwcap. 14% alc. **Rating** 95 **To** 2028 $35 ✪

Compatriots 2014 80% shiraz, 10% cabernet sauvignon, 10% merlot. The components are made separately using the cold soak and maturation techniques adopted for the '13 Single Vineyard Shiraz. This is shiraz with the trimmings, highly fragrant and intense; the intensity is from the fruit, not the tannins, alcohol or oak: it comes from within. Screwcap. 14% alc. **Rating** 94 **To** 2034 $35

Pinot Grigio 2015 **Rating** 93 **To** 2017 $25 ✪
Zsa Zsa Adelaide Hills Zweigelt Rose 2015 **Rating** 93 **To** 2017 $25 ✪

 Haldon Estate Wines

59 Havelock Road, Beechworth, Vic 3747 **Region** Beechworth
T (03) 5728 2858 **www**.haldonestatewines.com.au **Open** W'ends 12–5 or by appt
Winemaker Tracey Richards **Est.** 2010 **Dozens** 400 **Vyds** 2.2ha

Tracey Richards and her partner Ranald (Ran) Currie still have day jobs to pay the bills, but have already had remarkable success with the wines they have made and marketed. Tracey has had a long love affair with wine, and studied oenology at CSU from 2000-05, graduating dux of her class. With an introduction from Rick Kinzbrunner's nephew, Peter Graham, she started working vintages at Giaconda from '03, and continued to do so each vintage until '12. They have planted 2.2ha of estate vines, which include chardonnay, riesling, semillon, sauvignon blanc, pinot noir, nebbiolo and cabernet sauvignon. For the time being they are sourcing some of the grapes from local vineyards. The house on the 3.8ha property is no ordinary abode, having been built in 1893. Tracey says they live in the house full-time 'and freeze most winters'. The vineyard established by the partners is in fact its third incarnation, the first dating back to the 1850s. Haldon has a little cellar door open most weekends in a farm outbuilding built circa 1900-30, thereafter a horse stable, and now (after it was gutted and restored) the cellar door.

ΨΨΨΨ⳨ Beechworth Shiraz 2013 Matured for 18 months in French barriques
(25% new), 100 dozen made. A complex wine with an à la mode winemaking
philosophy that works well. My only reservation is the degree of French oak
influence; every other aspect is well judged. Lots to like here. Screwcap. 13.1% alc.
Rating 92 **To** 2028 $35
The Piano Player Beechworth Rose 2014 The saignee (juice run-off) from
Cabernet Sauvignon (70%) and Shiraz, chilled and settled, wild-fermented in
used oak, matured on lees for 20 months. Salmon-pink; intense savoury, almost
citrus/herbal notes accompany the earthy bouquet. However, you can see the
blackcurrant cabernet fruit flavours, and the wine has attitude aplenty. Screwcap.
13.9% alc. **Rating** 90 **To** 2017 $22

ΨΨΨΨ   Beechworth Chardonnay 2013 Rating 89 **To** 2020 $39

Halls Gap Estate

4113 Ararat-Halls Gap Road, Halls Gap, Vic 3381 **Region** Grampians
T 0413 595 513 **www**.hallsgapestate.com.au **Open** Wed–Mon 10–5
Winemaker Duncan Buchanan **Est.** 1969 **Dozens** 2000 **Vyds** 10.5ha

I first visited this vineyard when it was known as Boroka Vineyard (having been established in 1969), and marvelled at the location in the wild country of Halls Gap. It wasn't wildly successful, but when Mount Langi Ghiran acquired it in 1998 it had already changed its name to The Gap Vineyard. It was a useful adjunct to Mount Langi Ghiran for a while, but by 2013 it had long outlived its original purpose. It was then that the opportunity arose for the Drummond family, led by Aaron, to purchase the somewhat rundown vineyard. They moved quickly; while the '13 vintage was made by Kate Petering at Mount Langi Ghiran, the blending, vineyard management and future vintages are all being controlled under contract by Circe Wines (Aaron Drummond's partnership business with Dan Buckle). At the start of '14 Dan and Aaron hired Duncan Buchanan (ex Dromana Estate viticulturist and winemaker), giving him the dual task of managing their Mornington Peninsula vineyards and spending all-important time at Halls Gap.

ΨΨΨΨΨ Fallen Giants Vineyard Riesling 2015 Quartz-white; a flowery/blossom-
filled bouquet with citrus to the fore; the palate fulfils the promise it implies, with
intense unsweetened lime juice on a bed of crackling rocky acidity. The Grampians
deserve to be on the roll call of some of Australia's best rieslings with limitless
potential. Screwcap. 11.5% alc. **Rating** 95 **To** 2030 $25 **☉**
Fallen Giants Vineyard Shiraz 2014 Follows with precision the footprints of
its '13 predecessor: come-hither colour, blackberry, and dark cherry fruits wreathed

by notes of spice, pepper and licorice, shaped by ultrafine, but persistent, tannins. A lovely cool grown wine. Screwcap. 14% alc. **Rating** 95 **To** 2039 $30 **☉**

Fallen Giants Vineyard Cabernet Sauvignon 2014 Cassis, rather than blackcurrant, comes through strongly on the bouquet and medium-bodied palate; the tannins are present, as they should be, but are so fine they are friendly, an uncommon trait with cabernet directing the traffic. It all adds up to a rare beast: a cabernet that leads you on, and does not turn you away. Screwcap. 14% alc. **Rating** 94 **To** 2034 $30 **☉**

Hamelin Bay   ★★★★

McDonald Road, Karridale, WA 6288 **Region** Margaret River
T (08) 9758 6779 **www.hbwines.com.au Open** 7 days 10–5
Winemaker Julian Scott **Est.** 1992 **Dozens** 10 000 **Vyds** 23.5ha
The Hamelin Bay vineyard was established by the Drake-Brockman family, pioneers of the region. Richard Drake-Brockman's great-grandmother, Grace Bussell, is famous for her courage when, in 1876, and aged 16, she rescued survivors of a shipwreck not far from the mouth of the Margaret River. Richard's great-grandfather Frederick, known for his exploration of the Kimberley, read about the feat in Perth's press and rode 300km on horseback to meet her – they married in 1882. Hamelin Bay's vineyard and winery is located within a few kilometres of Karridale, at the intersection of the Brockman and Bussell Highways, which were named in honour of both these pioneering families. Exports to the UK, Canada, Malaysia, Singapore and China.

🍷🍷🍷🍷🍷 **Five Ashes Reserve Chardonnay 2013** Wild-fermented, matured in French oak (40% new) for 9 months with stirring. Not an ostentatious style, but everything is placed where it should be; white peach, nectarine and grapefruit occupy centre stage, oak to one side, but not trashed. The high point of the palate comes on the finish, with its tangy citrussy acidity. Screwcap. 13.5% alc. **Rating** 94 **To** 2023 $49

🍷🍷🍷🍷 **Five Ashes Vineyard Sauvignon Blanc 2015 Rating** 89 **To** 2016 $25
Five Ashes Vineyard Chardonnay 2014 Rating 89 **To** 2018 $30
Rampant Red Shiraz Merlot Cabernet 2012 Rating 89 **To** 2020 $20

Hancock & Hancock   ★★★★

210 Chalk Hill Road, McLaren Vale, SA 5171 **Region** McLaren Vale
T 0417 291 708 **Open** Not
Winemaker Larry Cherubino, Mike Brown **Est.** 2007 **Dozens** 2400 **Vyds** 8.09ha
This is the venture of industry doyen Chris Hancock and brother John, who returned to their family roots when they purchased the McLaren Vale vineyard La Colline in 2007. Chris graduated as dux of the oenology degree at Roseworthy Agricultural College in 1963, taking up immediate employment with the Penfold family, working with Max Schubert, and thereafter in production and executive roles. In '76 he joined Rosemount Estate, and when it was acquired by Southcorp, stayed on with the business in the upper echelon of its management. When the late Bob Oatley re-entered the wine business, establishing what is now Robert Oatley Vineyards (ROV), Chris rejoined the family and is today Deputy Executive Chairman of ROV. It is with the blessing of the Oatley family that he founded Hancock & Hancock, the wines being distributed by Oatley Family Wine Merchants. Exports to the UK, Hong Kong and China.

🍷🍷🍷🍷🍷 **Home Vineyard Shiraz Grenache 2014** A 73/27% blend, matured in new and used French oak. Bright, full crimson-purple; this is a full-on, full-bodied blend, with shiraz taking control of proceedings from the outset with its blackberry, licorice fruit, grenache a red cherry bed head. Has plenty of miles under the bonnet to go. Screwcap. 14% alc. **Rating** 94 **To** 2034 $23 **☉**

🍷🍷🍷🍷🍷 **Home Vineyard Cabernet Touriga 2014 Rating** 92 **To** 2020 $23 **☉**

Handpicked Wines   ★★★★★

18/2 Park Street, Sydney, NSW 2000 (postal) **Region** Various
T (02) 9475 7888 **www.**handpickedwines.com **Open** By appt
Winemaker Gary Baldwin, Peter Dillon **Est.** 2001 **Dozens** 50 000 **Vyds** 63ha

Handpicked is part of DMG Fine Wines, a global wine business with its head office in Australia. Its roots go back over 50 years to the Taiwanese fish markets, and the vision of Ming Guang Dong, who built a successful broad-based business. His four children were educated in either the UK, Australia or Singapore, and today they are all involved in the business, with William Dong at the helm. Having worked with what became Handpicked Wines, he bought the business with the aim of creating great wines from great regions under one label. Today it makes wines in Italy, Chile, France and Spain, but the main arm is Australia, where Handpicked has 33ha in the Yarra Valley, 18ha in the Mornington Peninsula and 12ha in the Barossa Valley. It secured the services of Gary Baldwin as executive chief winemaker, and constructed a winery at the company's flagship Capella Vineyard at Bittern, on the Mornington Peninsula, destined to become the hospitality base for the business. In November 2014, Peter Dillon was successfully headhunted to assist Gary Baldwin; Dillon has established his credentials as a winemaker of the highest quality over the past 13 years. Exports to Italy, the Philippines, South Korea, Myanmar, Cambodia, Vietnam, Japan, Hong Kong and China.

ŸŸŸŸŸ **Collection Yarra Valley Chardonnay 2014** Whole bunch-pressed to French oak for fermentation and maturation. The emphasis is first and foremost on white and yellow peach and nectarine – no confusion with sauvignon blanc here. The barrel ferment has, as ever, integrated the oak, leaving hints of cashew to mark the way. Screwcap. 13.4% alc. **Rating** 95 **To** 2024 $45

Collection Tasmania Pinot Noir 2014 Matured for 11 months in French barriques (one-third new). Has an intense floral/red fruits bouquet, the palate picking up the pace further, with a powerful drive through to the finish and aftertaste offering a melange of dark and liqueur cherry to share the podium with the red fruits of the bouquet. Screwcap. 13.8% alc. **Rating** 95 **To** 2029 $60

Collection Yarra Valley Pinot Noir 2014 11 months maturation in French oak (one-third new). Light, but brilliant, purple-crimson hue; spicy, savoury characters are starting to build complexity, but with further to go, the cherry fruit with much left in the tank to take it forward for some years yet. Screwcap. 12.9% alc. **Rating** 95 **To** 2026 $60

Regional Selections Yarra Valley Rose 2015 Pinot noir, the majority fermented with skins from recently pressed marsanne, followed by a short maturation in French oak (75% new). Pink, with a touch of stem; a very complex savoury/smoky rose with unusual drive and texture, all the winemaking inputs controlled and complementary. Screwcap. 14.5% alc. **Rating** 94 **To** 2017 $29 ✪

Collection Barossa Valley Shiraz 2013 Matured for 18 months in new and used American, German and French hogsheads. An elegant, medium-bodied Barossa Valley shiraz, with blackberry and plum in the driver's seat, oak sitting alongside. I'm not convinced that the vanilla bean notes of American and/or German oak are the most appropriate, but the tannins do move the attention away from the oak. Screwcap. 14% alc. **Rating** 94 **To** 2033 $70

ŸŸŸŸŸ **Highbrow Hill Vineyard Chardonnay 2014** Rating 93 To 2022 $60 CM
Highbrow Hill Vineyard Marsanne 2014 Rating 93 To 2018 $60 CM
Regional Selections Pinot Noir 2015 Rating 93 To 2023 $29
Regional Selections Yarra Valley Merlot 2015 Rating 93 To 2029 $25 ✪
Regional Selections Coonawarra Cabernet Sauvignon 2013 Rating 92 To 2030 $25 ✪
Collection Coonawarra Cabernet Sauvignon 2013 Rating 90 To 2033 $70

Hanging Rock Winery   ★★★★★

88 Jim Road, Newham, Vic 3442 **Region** Macedon Ranges
T (03) 5427 0542 **www.**hangingrock.com.au **Open** 7 days 10–5
Winemaker Robert Ellis **Est.** 1983 **Dozens** 20 000 **Vyds** 14.5ha

The Macedon area has proved marginal in spots, and the Hanging Rock vineyards, with their lovely vista towards the Rock, are no exception. John Ellis thus elected to source additional grapes from various parts of Victoria to produce an interesting and diverse range of varietals at different price points. In 2011 John's children Ruth and Robert returned to the fold: Robert has an oenology degree from Adelaide University, since then working as a Flying Winemaker in Champagne, Burgundy, Oregon and Stellenbosch. More recently he worked as winemaker at Hewitson, before coming back to Hanging Rock to take over winemaking responsibilities from father John. Ruth has a degree in wine marketing from Adelaide University. Exports to the UK, the US and other major markets.

🍷🍷🍷🍷🍷 **Jim Jim Macedon Ranges Chardonnay 2013** Wild-fermented in French oak (30% new), matured for 10 months. Pale straw-green; the very cool site and low yields result in a wine with intensity built into every facet of its flavour and texture. In turn the wine will outlive all but a small handful of '13 Australian chardonnays. Screwcap. 13% alc. **Rating** 95 **To** 2030 $40

Heathcote Shiraz 2012 A wine with a distinguished track record, and had a ball in the '12 vintage. Full to the brim with luscious black cherry, blackberry and blueberry fruits, mouthfilling and succulent. Best of all is the finely articulated and fresh finish. Screwcap. 14.3% alc. **Rating** 95 **To** 2037 $75

Cambrian Rise Heathcote Shiraz 2013 Matured in used French and American oak (50/50%) for 18 months. The hue is still very youthful; spice and cracked pepper are first out of the blocks on the bouquet, the palate responding with savoury tannins wrapped around lively black fruits. Good stuff. Screwcap. 13.5% alc. **Rating** 94 **To** 2033 $30 **☉**

Macedon IX Late Disgorged Brut Cuvee NV A celebration of the power and complexity of the '97 base vintage and reserves spanning a decade, all aged in old oak, followed by 16 years on lees in bottle. It's predictably savoury, toasty and secondary, with remarkable spicy complexity and even Vegemite, culminating in a very long, dry finish laced with great lees texture. This is full-bodied Australian sparkling, ready for main course fare. Diam. 12% alc. **Rating** 94 **To** 2016 $115 TS

🍷🍷🍷🍷🍸 **Jim Jim Macedon Ranges Sauvignon Blanc 2015** **Rating** 93 **To** 2016 $30
Macedon Cuvee NV **Rating** 92 **To** 2016 $50 TS
Macedon Rose Brut NV **Rating** 92 **To** 2016 $39 TS
Macedon Ranges Pinot Noir 2014 **Rating** 91 **To** 2024 $35
Jim Jim Macedon Ranges Pinot Noir 2013 **Rating** 91 **To** 2023 $50

Happs ★★★★★

575 Commonage Road, Dunsborough, WA 6281 **Region** Margaret River
T (08) 9755 3300 **www**.happs.com.au **Open** 7 days 10–5
Winemaker Erl Happ, Mark Warren **Est.** 1978 **Dozens** 14 000 **Vyds** 35.2ha
One-time schoolteacher, potter and winemaker Erl Happ is the patriarch of a three-generation family. More than anything, Erl has been a creator and experimenter, building the self-designed winery from mudbrick, concrete form and timber, and making the first crusher. In 1994 he began an entirely new 30ha vineyard at Karridale, planted to no less than 28 varieties, including some of the earliest plantings in Australia of tempranillo. The Three Hills label is made from varieties grown at this vineyard. Erl passed on to son Myles a love of pottery, and Happs Pottery now has four potters, including Myles. Exports to the US, Denmark, The Netherlands, Malaysia, Hong Kong, China and Japan.

🍷🍷🍷🍷🍷 **Three Hills Eva Marie 2014** This is a semillon sauvignon blanc blend held back a year for release, and one of these fine days I'll find out whether barrel ferment has played a part in its breeding. In a sense it doesn't matter – this is a very good wine. Screwcap. 13% alc. **Rating** 95 **To** 2021 $30 **☉**

Three Hills Margaret River Chardonnay 2014 While built like Eva Marie, and with a similar ethos, this lifts the bar considerably with its far greater intensity. It doesn't bring anything new, but is just brighter and fuller. Can't be self-effacing like its sibling. Screwcap. 13% alc. **Rating** 95 **To** 2023 $45

Margaret River Shiraz 2014 Shows the cool climate of southern Margaret River with spice and pepper notes in the background of the savoury black fruits. This is crammed full of personality, a political cartoonist's manna from heaven. Don't get me wrong, this is a good wine powering towards full maturity 20 years hence. Screwcap. 14.5% alc. **Rating** 95 **To** 2039 $30 ○

ŢŢŢŢŢ **Chardonnay 2014 Rating** 91 **To** 2020 $24
Indigenous Series Semillon 2014 Rating 90 **To** 2018 $17 ○
Sauvignon Blanc Semillon 2015 Rating 90 **To** 2019 $24
Indigenous Series Merlot 2015 Rating 90 **To** 2022 $17 ○

Harcourt Valley Vineyards ★★★★★

3339 Calder Highway, Harcourt, Vic 3453 **Region** Bendigo
T (03) 5474 2223 **www.**harcourtvalley.com.au **Open** 7 days 11–5
Winemaker Quinn Livingstone **Est.** 1975 **Dozens** 2500 **Vyds** 4ha
Harcourt Valley Vineyards (planted 1975) has the oldest planting of vines in the Harcourt Valley. Using 100% estate-grown fruit Quinn Livingstone (second-generation winemaker) is making a number of small batch wines from the property. Minimal fruit handling is used in the winemaking process. A new tasting area overlooks the vines, with a large window that allows visitors to see the activity in the winery. Founder Barbara Broughton died in '12, aged 91, and Quinn's mother, Barbara Livingstone, has now retired. Exports to China.

ŢŢŢŢŢ **Single Vineyard Old Vine Bendigo Shiraz 2014** Matured in new French oak for 12 months. It has made light work of the oak, and the high percentage of whole bunches has joined with the low alcohol to give the wine uncommon vitality and freshness on the very long and finely structured palate. Screwcap. 13.2% alc. **Rating** 96 **To** 2034 $60 ○
Heathcote Rose 2015 Grenache, fermented in tank and barrel. Very pale pink; a highly perfumed bouquet, full of rose petals and spice, immediately grabs attention; the palate is crisp and bone dry, with savoury complexity snuggling up with the rose petals. Screwcap. 13.1% alc. **Rating** 95 **To** 2017 $20 ○
Barbara's Bendigo Shiraz 2014 30% whole bunches, matured in 70% French, 30% American oak (40% new) for 12 months. Good colour; the bouquet sets the scene with its purple and black fruits, spice and herb notes adding texture and structure. There's a lot still left in the locker here, including fresh acidity on the finish. Screwcap. 13.1% alc. **Rating** 94 **To** 2030 $25 ○
Mt Camel Range Heathcote Shiraz 2014 Because the flavours, texture and structure of Heathcote are softer than those of Bendigo, and include red berry as well as blackberry, no whole bunch was needed. This is a very attractive medium-bodied wine with a fragrant bouquet and a supple and soft come-hither palate. No need for patience here. Screwcap. 14.7% alc. **Rating** 94 **To** 2029 $25 ○

ŢŢŢŢŢ **Bendigo Cabernet Sauvignon 2014 Rating** 92 **To** 2029 $25 ○
Heathcote Bendigo GSM 2015 Rating 91 **To** 2018 $25

Hardys ★★★★★

202 Main Road, McLaren Vale, SA 5171 **Region** McLaren Vale
T (08) 8329 4124 **www.**hardyswine.com.au **Open** 7 days 10–4
Winemaker Paul Lapsley (Chief) **Est.** 1853 **Dozens** NFP
The 1992 merger of Thomas Hardy and the Berri Renmano group may have had some elements of a forced marriage, but the merged group prospered over the next 10 years. So successful was it that a further marriage followed in early 2003, with Constellation Wines of the US the groom, BRL Hardy the bride, creating the largest wine group in the world (the Australian arm was known as Constellation Wines Australia, or CWA); but it is now part of the Accolade Wines group. The Hardys wine brands are headed by Thomas Hardy Cabernet Sauvignon, Eileen Hardy Chardonnay, Pinot Noir and Shiraz; then the Sir James range of sparkling wines; next the HRB wines, the William Hardy quartet; then the expanded Oomoo range and the Nottage Hill wines. Exports to all major markets.

ŶŶŶŶŶ **Eileen Hardy McLaren Vale Shiraz 2013** The texture of this wine makes an instantaneous impression, which is exquisite, making the moderate alcohol seem even lower than it is. This is an old money aristocrat, elegantly unfurling layer after layer of red and black fruits, licorice and spice on the prodigiously long palate. The best Eileen since '71. Screwcap. 14.1% alc. **Rating** 98 **To** 2048 $130 **☉**

Eileen Hardy Tasmania Yarra Valley Chardonnay 2014 A wine with an impeccable pedigree, and synergy between Tasmania and Hardys' Upper Yarra Bastard Hill vineyard. It's not easy to identify the contributions of the respective regions, but I would guess the Yarra Valley adds fruit flesh to the minerally structure ex Tasmania. Screwcap. 13.5% alc. **Rating** 97 **To** 2024 $95 **☉**

Eileen Hardy McLaren Vale Shiraz 2012 Shiraz from 100+yo vines, matured in 70% new French oak. It proclaims its extreme class from the first whiff of blackberry, plum and licorice, but equally quickly disavows what might be characterised as a McLaren Vale cliche: overt dark chocolate. Instead spicy, savoury, beautifully structured tannins (and quality oak) add both textural and flavour complexity – all this with perfect line, length and balance. Screwcap. 14.5% alc. **Rating** 97 **To** 2042 $125 **☉**

Thomas Hardy Cabernet Sauvignon 2013 Margaret River/Coonawarra. Full red-purple; a potent, powerful cabernet, the focus on blackcurrant fruit, complexity provided by bay leaf/black olive/mint nuances; French oak is where is should be (on the shoulder of the fruit) and the tannins, while firm, hold no terrors. Screwcap. 14% alc. **Rating** 97 **To** 2043 $130 **☉**

ŶŶŶŶŶ **HRB Riesling 2015** D663. Clare Valley/Tasmania. Simply because the idea of the blend seems so logical doesn't assure its success, but Hardys went down the same path in '14 with the same outcome: a very complex riesling in terms of fruit flavours, texture, and structure. More to come down the track. Screwcap. 12.5% alc. **Rating** 96 **To** 2027 $30 **☉**

HRB Chardonnay 2014 Bin D660 Pemberton, Margaret River, Adelaide Hills. Only Hardys could bring such a regional blend together; barrel fermentation has provided part of the glue, but the sheer complexity and intensity of the fruit provides the major impact, with grapefruit and minerally acidity the drivers, nectarine also in the frame. Screwcap. 13.5% alc. **Rating** 95 **To** 2020 $30 **☉**

HRB Pinot Noir 2014 D661. You can blend many varieties across regions, but can you taunt the holy grail and pull it off with pinot noir? This is a blend of Tasmanian and Yarra Valley fruit, whole bunches wild fermented and given an 8 month stint in oak. The result is as perfumed as it is fine, the balance of sweet-sour fruit and minerally, twiggy tannin expertly judged. It appeals upfront but it finishes dry and herbal; it promotes an impression of integrity. Not difficult to herald it as a success. Screwcap. 13% alc. **Rating** 94 **To** 2021 $35 CM

Eileen Hardy Tasmania Pinot Noir 2014 Deep crimson-purple; competes with its sister Bay of Fires Pinot, and has a similar throbbing power behind the deep colour of its robes. It is still impossibly young and trenchantly demands time for its texture to open up and its spicy black cherry/plum to supply the mouthfeel. Screwcap. 13.4% alc. **Rating** 94 **To** 2029 $95

ŶŶŶŶŶ **Tintara McLaren Vale Shiraz 2014 Rating** 93 **To** 2029 $28
Tintara McLaren Vale Cabernet Sauvignon 2014 Rating 93 **To** 2030 $28
Sir James Vintage Pinot Noir Chardonnay 2009 Rating 93 **To** 2017 $28
HRB Pinot Gris 2014 Rating 91 **To** 2016 $30
Starve Dog Lane Adelaide Hills Pinot Gris 2014 Rating 91 **To** 2017 $19**☉**
William Hardy McLaren Vale Shiraz 2014 Rating 91 **To** 2025 $18**☉**
Starve Dog Lane Clare Valley Shiraz 2013 Rating 90 **To** 2023 $19**☉**

Hare's Chase ★★★★★

PO Box 46, Melrose Park, SA 5039 **Region** Barossa Valley
T (08) 8277 3506 **www.**hareschase.com **Open** Not
Winemaker Peter Taylor **Est.** 1998 **Dozens** 5000 **Vyds** 16.8ha

Hare's Chase is the creation of two families, headed respectively by Peter Taylor as winemaker, and Mike de la Haye as general manager; they own a 100-year-old vineyard in the Marananga Valley area of the Barossa Valley. The simple, functional winery sits at the top of a rocky hill in the centre of the vineyard, which has some of the best red soil available for dry-grown viticulture. The winemaking arm of the partnership is provided by Peter Taylor, TWE director of wine production, with over 30 vintages' experience. In 2016 Peter and Mike say 'After 15 years of developing Hare's Chase, we are starting to believe we may one day give up our day jobs.' Exports to the US, Canada, Switzerland, Singapore, Hong Kong, Malaysia and China.

ΥΥΥΥΥ **Lepus 2013** The second vintage (the first '10) of this flagship wine from the best-performing vines of the vineyard, matured in French oak (75% new), racked by gravity using a syphon. This is an outstanding shiraz, making its mark from the first whiff of the bouquet (and colour). Black fruits, fine tannins and oak move tightly together on a choreographed dance that weaves its way across a palate which miraculously is no more than medium-bodied. To say the wine is graceful does it scant justice. Screwcap. 14% alc. **Rating** 98 **To** 2053 $130 ✪

ΥΥΥΥΥ **Ironscraper Barossa Valley Shiraz 2013** Dark, brooding colour and a palate to match. This is thick and grunty with asphalt, tar and liquid (dark) chocolate oozing slowly through the mouth. So chunky with flavour, you could carve it. It's well done, too. Screwcap. 14% alc. **Rating** 94 **To** 2028 $35 CM

ΥΥΥΥ **Barossa Valley Tempranillo 2014 Rating** 88 **To** 2022 $25 CM

Harewood Estate ★★★★★

Scotsdale Road, Denmark, WA 6333 **Region** Denmark
T (08) 9840 9078 **www**.harewood.com.au **Open** Fri–Mon 10–4, 7 days school hols
Winemaker James Kellie, Paul Nelson **Est.** 1988 **Dozens** 20 000 **Vyds** 19.2ha
In 2003 James Kellie, responsible for the contract making of Harewood's wines since 1998, purchased the estate with his father and sister as partners. A 300-tonne winery was constructed, offering both contract winemaking services for the Great Southern region and the ability to expand the Harewood range to include subregional wines. In January 2010 James, together with wife Careena, purchased his father's and sister's shares to become 100% owners. Exports to the UK, the US, Denmark, Switzerland, Indonesia, Hong Kong, Malaysia, Macau, Singapore, China and Japan.

ΥΥΥΥΥ **Denmark Riesling 2015** The sheer intensity of this wine is almost painful, the aftertaste endlessly repeating the message of the palate. Small wonder it won a gold medal at the Qantas Wine Show of WA, a larger wonder which other wine deprived it of the trophy. Screwcap. 12% alc. **Rating** 96 **To** 2027 $21 ✪
Porongurup Riesling 2015 It only takes a millisecond for the elfin finesse of utterly seamless fruit and acidity to turn on the neon lights saying 'Welcome to Porongurup'. It is radically different in style from its Denmark sibling, but the two wines are sublime. Screwcap. 12% alc. **Rating** 96 **To** 2030 $25 ✪
Frankland River Riesling 2015 The delicate, flowery bouquet leads into a juicy citrussy wold of lime, lemon, grapefruit and a wisp of mandarin. Riesling seldom says 'hello sailor', but this does – and more than just says hello. Screwcap. 12% alc. **Rating** 95 **To** 2025 $21 ✪
Museum Release Great Southern Riesling 2008 The magic of aged riesling. 8yo and just getting into stride. Classic aromas of toast, honey and hay announce this wine. You see those components again on the palate with the added dimension of the slatey, limey acidity which has a character of its own, and in a way is the defining element. Screwcap. 12% alc. **Rating** 95 **To** 2028 $40
Great Southern Cabernet Sauvignon 2014 Matured for 18 months in French oak (20% new). From the first whiff and first taste through to the finish and aftertaste, this wine languidly says 'I am pure cabernet, take me or leave me, no arguments, no questions.' It is austere, its precision absolute, bay leaf, dried herbs enmeshed into its cabernet DNA. Screwcap. 14.5% alc. **Rating** 95 **To** 2039 $21 ✪

Mount Barker Riesling 2015 Takes a little while to gain traction and speed, but gets there in the end. One of the four Harewood Rieslings had to fall a step behind the others, and this is it. On any other day it would look a million dollars, and perhaps its day will come. Screwcap. 12% alc. **Rating** 94 **To** 2023 **$21** ✪
Reserve Great Southern Semillon Sauvignon Blanc 2015 A 56/44% blend, crushed/destemmed, fermented in new French puncheons, 10 months maturation. The first thought is why is the price differential between this and the standard version so small, this more expensive to make? The next thought is how well the fruit has soaked up a large helping of new oak. This is an impressive wine that has a real cellaring future. Screwcap. 13% alc. **Rating** 94 **To** 2021 **$25** ✪
Museum Release C Block Pinot Noir 2001 7 days cold soak, matured for 10 months in French oak (20% new). This has to be judged/assessed on a one-off basis, and enjoyed with – for example – wild mushroom and quail risotto. The forest floor and spice elements are its pillars, holding up the remaining red fruits of the pinot. A really good example of fully aged pinot for those who have not tasted such a wine. Screwcap. 14.5% alc. **Rating** 94 **To** 2018 **$45**
Reserve Great Southern Shiraz 2013 Matured for 30 months in French barriques (40% new). This very complex wine has had the treatment in the winery, with maximum flavour, texture, extract and structure the result. Because it has balance, it will go the journey, but how long that is is anyone's guess. Screwcap. 14.5% alc. **Rating** 94 **To** 2043 **$34**
Reserve Great Southern Cabernet Sauvignon 2013 Matured for 30 months in French oak (40% new). Despite the vintage shift, and the much increased impact of French oak, this comes out of the same crucible as the Estate '14 (non Reserve). It needs more time than the Estate, the oak needing to be assimilated. Screwcap. 14.5% alc. **Rating** 94 **To** 2048 **$34**

🍷🍷🍷🍷🍷 **Great Southern Chardonnay 2015** **Rating** 93 **To** 2022 **$25** ✪
Reserve Great Southern Chardonnay 2014 **Rating** 93 **To** 2022 **$34**
Reserve Denmark Pinot Noir 2014 **Rating** 92 **To** 2023 **$45**
Great Southern Shiraz Cabernet 2014 **Rating** 92 **To** 2029 **$21** ✪
Great Southern Cabernet Merlot 2014 **Rating** 91 **To** 2029 **$21** ✪

Harkham Winery ★★★★☆

266 De Beyers Road, Pokolbin, NSW 2321 **Region** Hunter Valley
T (02) 4998 7648 **www**.harkhamwine.com **Open** W'ends 10–5, Mon–Fri by appt
Winemaker Richard Harkham **Est.** 1985 **Dozens** 1500 **Vyds** 3ha
In 2005 Terry, Efrem and Richard Harkham acquired Windarra estate from the founding Andresen family. They manage the vineyard organically, and practise minimal intervention in the winery, reaching its zenith with the preservative-free Aziza's Shiraz, and the Old Vines Shiraz. Exports to the US, France and Hong Kong.

🍷🍷🍷🍷🍷 **Old Vines Shiraz 2011** From 70yo vines, one portion whole bunch wild-fermented, a second portion open-fermented with cultured yeast, both pressed to French oak (35% new) for 12 months maturation. A classic full-bodied Hunter Valley shiraz from a very good vintage; has succulent depth and power to its parade of black fruits, earth and bramble, the tannins soft and life sustaining. Diam. 14% alc. **Rating** 95 **To** 2041 **$40**

🍷🍷🍷🍷🍷 **Harkhamtage 2011** **Rating** 92 **To** 2031 **$32**

Hart & Hunter ★★★★★

Gabriel's Paddock, 463 Deasys Road, Pokolbin, NSW 2325 **Region** Hunter Valley
T 0401 605 219 **www**.hartandhunter.com.au **Open** Thurs–Sun 10–4
Winemaker Damien Stevens, Jodie Belleville **Est.** 2009 **Dozens** 2500
This is the venture of winemaking couple Damien Stevens and Jodie Belleville, with partners Daniel and Elle Hart. The grapes are purchased from highly regarded growers within the Hunter, with the emphasis on single vineyard wines and small batch processing. Continuing

success for the venture led to the opening of a cellar door in late 2015, offering not only the three best-known Hunter varieties, but experimental wines and alternative varieties. Success in wine shows was underlined at the '15 Hunter Valley Boutique Wine Show where the '15 Oakey Creek Semillon, the '14 26 Rows Chardonnay and the '14 The Hill Shiraz all won trophies. Exports to the UK.

🍷🍷🍷🍷🍷 **Oakey Creek Semillon 2011** Still pale straw-green, the wine likewise having barely changed since its youth. This can be an issue for some wines that fade away without ever opening their petals, but there's no risk of that here. The first honeyed notes have joined vibrant citrus, the acidity seeming less obvious. Lovely wine. Screwcap. 10.5% alc. **Rating** 96 **To** 2026 $55 ○
The Hill Shiraz 2014 Deeper colour than Ablington, but equally bright; the wine from which this four-best-barrel selection came was also from Ablington, but considered the best part of the vineyard. The black and purple fruits are more overtly powerful and complex than those of its sibling, but both came out of the same crucible. An outstanding wine from a once-in-a-lifetime vintage. Screwcap. 13.8% alc. **Rating** 96 **To** 2044 $75 ○
The Remparts Semillon 2015 This has some things in common with Oakey Creek (hardly surprising) but there are more very different things. Here an exceptionally juicy palate of Meyer lemon is a direct reflection of the blossom-filled bouquet before racy acidity takes complete control of the vibrantly fresh palate. Screwcap. 11% alc. **Rating** 95 **To** 2035 $30 ○
Single Vineyard Series Oakey Creek Semillon 2015 Comparing semillons vintaged elsewhere in Australia to Hunter Valley semillons always brings you to attention, the drive of these wines in a different category. Here a shimmering blaze of lemongrass, fresh herbs and lemon juice is catapulted by the acidity into the far distance. Screwcap. 10.5% alc. **Rating** 95 **To** 2030 $30 ○
Single Vineyard Series Ablington Shiraz 2014 Vivid crimson-purple; a vibrant, lively and elegant wine, the fragrant chocolate and berry-filled bouquet making way for the juicy and graceful medium-bodied palate, red fruits and spices coupling with cedary French oak and fine tannins that draw out the long finish. Hart & Hunter nailed this vintage, albeit with a different philosophy from others. Screwcap. 13.5% alc. **Rating** 95 **To** 2029 $47

🍷🍷🍷🍷🍸 **Dr B's Fiano 2015 Rating** 90 **To** 2018 $28

Hart of the Barossa   ★★★★☆

Cnr Vine Vale Road/Light Pass Road, Tanunda, SA 5352 **Region** Barossa Valley
T 0412 586 006 **www.**hartofthebarossa.com.au **Open** By appt
Winemaker Michael and Alisa Hart, Troy Kalleske (Consultant) **Est.** 2007 **Dozens** 2200
Vyds 6.5ha
The ancestors of Michael and Alisa Hart arrived in SA in 1845, their first address (with seven children) a hollow tree on the banks of the North Para River. Michael and Alisa personally tend the vineyard, which is the oldest certified organic vineyard in the Barossa Valley, and includes a patch of 110-year-old shiraz. The quality of the wines coming from these vines is exceptional; unfortunately, there is only enough to fill two hogsheads a year (66 dozen bottles). The other wines made are also impressive, particularly given their prices. Exports to Germany, Hong Kong, Taiwan and China.

🍷🍷🍷🍷🍷 **The Faithful Limited Release Old Vine Shiraz 2013** Quite glorious. Intense blackberried fruit comes stitched with dried herbs and particularly earthen notes; toasty oak both sweetens and extends the flavours; and then the finest, classiest tannin pulls it all through to an ultra-persistent finish. A class. Screwcap. 14.5% alc. **Rating** 96 **To** 2040 $79 CM
The Brave Limited Release Shiraz 2013 Inky plum, violet and blackcurrant flavours rush headlong into resiny vanillan oak. Has all guns blazing but the aim is sure, the whole complete. Screwcap. 14.5% alc. **Rating** 94 **To** 2028 $28 CM ○

🍷🍷🍷🍷🍸 **The Blesing Limited Release Cabernet Sauvignon 2013 Rating** 93 **To** 2030 $32 CM

Haselgrove Wines

187 Sand Road, McLaren Vale, SA 5171 **Region** McLaren Vale
T (08) 8323 8706 **www.**haselgrove.com.au **Open** By appt
Winemaker Greg Clack, Matthew Copping **Est.** 1981 **Dozens** 40 000 **Vyds** 9.7ha
Italian-Australian industry veterans Don Totino, Don Luca, Tony Carrocci and Steve Maglieri decided to purchase Haselgrove 'over a game of cards and couple of hearty reds' in 2008. They have completely changed the product range, its price and its presentation: the Legend Series $75 to $150, the Origin Series at $35, and First Cut at $18. Then there is the very large custom crush facility which provides all-important cash flow. Exports to Canada, Malaysia, South Korea, Hong Kong, China and NZ.

♥♥♥♥♥ **The Lear Single Vineyard Shiraz 2014** Big of frame, soft at heart. In most respects this is a powerhouse wine, though its supple nature makes it easy to be around. A lake of blackberried flavour, a mountain of tannin, a field of violets, roads of asphalt leading through. A vast vista of flavour. You get the idea. Screwcap. 14.5% alc. **Rating** 95 **To** 2040 $90 CM
Col Cross Single Vineyard Shiraz 2014 This floods the mouth with sweet blackberried fruit, but in many ways it's more characterised by its distinctive earthen edges. Creamy/cedary/nutty oak plays a positive, but fully integrated role. It fits clearly into the hedonistic category and yet it's neat, clean and well managed. Diam. 14.5% alc. **Rating** 95 **To** 2035 $90 CM
Switch GSM Grenache Shiraz Mourvedre 2014 A full-bodied blend in archetypal McLaren Vale style, awash with satsuma plum, dark small-berry fruits, spice and a powerful framework of ripe tannins and oak to guide its long path to the future. Screwcap. 14.5% alc. **Rating** 95 **To** 2039 $40
Catkin Shiraz 2014 Pressed before dryness to barrels (new and used) to complete fermentation, matured for 15 months. Full-bodied, this is McLaren Vale in full stride, black fruits, dark chocolate, tannins and oak all present in abundance. You either drink the wine soonish or leave it alone for a casual decade or two. Screwcap. 14.5% alc. **Rating** 94 **To** 2035 $40
Catkin Shiraz 2013 Deep colour; full to the gunnels with black fruits, licorice, dark chocolate and French oak, tannins submerged by the fruit, but doubtless present; full-bodied, but balanced, and pleading for at least 5 years' maturation. Screwcap. 14.5% alc. **Rating** 94 **To** 2043 $40

♥♥♥♥♡ **Scarce Earth The Ambassador Shiraz 2014** Rating 93 To 2030 $85 CM
Staff Adelaide Hills Chardonnay 2015 Rating 91 To 2020 $25 CM

Hastwell & Lightfoot   ★★★★☆

204 Foggos Road, McLaren Vale, SA 5171 **Region** McLaren Vale
T (08) 8323 8692 **www.**hastwellandlightfoot.com.au **Open** Fri–Sun 11–5
Winemaker James Hastwell **Est.** 1988 **Dozens** 4500 **Vyds** 16ha
Established in 1988 by Mark and Wendy Hastwell and Martin and Jill Lightfoot. Having initially sold much of the production, they have made a significant commitment to the Hastwell & Lightfoot brand, producing wines from estate-grown varieties. The vines are grafted onto devigorating rootstocks that restrain the development of dead fruit characters in warmer seasons. James Hastwell, son of Mark and Wendy, has his winery just 2km from the vineyard. Exports to the UK, Canada, Denmark, Norway, Germany, Malaysia, Taiwan, Singapore and China.

♥♥♥♥♥ **38 Days 2013** Cabernet shiraz. Step into a lake of tannin and be enveloped by full-bodied depth of flavour. Blackcurrant, saltbush, ground coffee, juicy blackberry. It's well integrated, big on power, mouth-puckering and lengthy. A long future is assured. Screwcap. 14% alc. **Rating** 95 **To** 2040 $40 CM
Sands of Time Single Vineyard McLaren Vale Shiraz 2013 Vanillan oak plays a key role but the fruit doesn't shy away at all. This is an attractive package. Firm blackberry and spice with a soft layer of dark chocolate and that vanillan croon. Screwcap. 14% alc. **Rating** 94 **To** 2033 $30 CM ✪

McLaren Vale Cabernet Sauvignon 2013 Powerhouse style, well done. Plum, asphalt, inky blackberry, cloves, a touch of campfire; it pours on the flavour but gives you something to think about at the same time, and has both the length and the scaffolding to make sure that it matures well (long term) as well. Value plus. Screwcap. 14.5% alc. **Rating** 94 **To** 2033 $23 CM ✪

🍷🍷🍷🍷🍸 **McLaren Vale Vermentino 2015 Rating** 90 **To** 2017 $21 CM ✪

Hay Shed Hill Wines ★★★★★

511 Harmans Mill Road, Wilyabrup, WA 6280 **Region** Margaret River
T (08) 9755 6046 **www**.hayshedhill.com.au **Open** 7 days 9–5
Winemaker Michael Kerrigan **Est.** 1987 **Dozens** 24000 **Vyds** 18.55ha
Mike Kerrigan, former winemaker at Howard Park, acquired the business in late 2006 (with co-ownership by the West Cape Howe syndicate) and is now the full-time winemaker. He had every confidence that he could dramatically lift the quality of the wines, which is precisely what he has done. The five wines in the Vineyard, White Label and Block series are all made from estate-grown grapes. The Block series are the ultimate site-specific wines, made from separate blocks within the vineyard. They consist of Block 1 Semillon Sauvignon Blanc, Block 6 Chardonnay, Block 8 Cabernet Franc and Block 2 Cabernet Sauvignon. The Pitchfork wines are made from contract-grown grapes in the region. Exports to the UK, the US, Denmark, Singapore, Malaysia, Japan, Hong Kong and China.

🍷🍷🍷🍷🍷 **Block 1 Semillon Sauvignon Blanc 2015** Subtle use of barrel fermentation. It's a superb effort: it's not a rock concert, but a symphony, intelligent and nuanced, long and superbly balanced. Screwcap. 12% alc. **Rating** 96 **To** 2025 $28 ✪
Block 6 Chardonnay 2015 The progression of Margaret River chardonnay continues unabated. Exceptionally fine and poised, it is laden with white peach, nectarine and a hint of complex leesy oak. Superbly fine and poised, long and energetic. Screwcap. 12.5% alc. **Rating** 96 **To** 2025 $40 ✪
Block 8 Cabernet Franc 2014 It's rare to find a 100% cabernet franc, and this demonstrates that there should be more. Lifted florals and berry fruit lead to a finely poised palate, superfine and with substantial length. It builds and builds, its finish full of energy. Screwcap. 14% alc. **Rating** 95 **To** 2026 $40
Cabernet Sauvignon 2014 Wines like this can certainly be cellared but you're always left to wonder: why wait? Balance, flavour and texture are in such good form now that there's no good reason to deny yourself. Screwcap. 14% alc. **Rating** 94 **To** 2030 $28 CM ✪
Malbec 2014 It feels effortless and firm simultaneously, no mean feat. This is a 'thinking person's red', in the best sense of the words. Long chains of integrated tannin, smoke and ferrous nuances, berried fruits, herbs. It cuts its own path, and it's a rewarding one. Screwcap. 14% alc. **Rating** 94 **To** 2028 $30 CM ✪

🍷🍷🍷🍷🍸 **Shiraz Tempranillo 2014 Rating** 93 **To** 2020 $22 CM ✪
Merlot 2014 Rating 93 **To** 2026 $30 CM
Cabernet Merlot 2014 Rating 93 **To** 2025 $22 CM ✪
Nebbiolo 2015 Rating 93 **To** 2028 $30 CM
G40 Mount Barker Riesling 2015 Rating 93 **To** 2022 $25 ✪
Sauvignon Blanc Semillon 2015 Rating 92 **To** 2017 $22 CM ✪
Pitchfork Pink 2015 Rating 92 **To** 2016 $17 ✪
Tempranillo 2014 Rating 92 **To** 2021 $30 CM
Pitchfork Margaret River Chardonnay 2015 Rating 90 **To** 2018 $17 ✪
Grenache 2014 Rating 90 **To** 2020 $30 CM

Hazyblur Wines ★★★

Lot 5 Angle Vale Road, Virginia, SA 5120 **Region** Kangaroo Island
T (08) 8380 9307 **www**.hazyblur.com **Open** By appt
Winemaker Ross Trimboli, Andrew Jachmann **Est.** 1998 **Dozens** 4000 **Vyds** 6ha

Robyne and Ross Trimboli hit the jackpot with their 2000 vintage red wines, sourced from various regions in SA, including one described by Robert Parker Jr as 'Barotta, the most northerly region in SA' (it is in fact Baroota, and is not the most northerly), with Parker points ranging between 91 and 95. One of the wines was a Late Harvest Shiraz, tipping the scales at 17% alcohol, and contract-grown at Kangaroo Island. It is here that the Trimbolis have established their own vineyard, planted to cabernet sauvignon, shiraz, pinot noir and pinot gris. Exports to Asia.

♥♥♥♥   **Cabernet Sauvignon 2014** Blackcurrant, tobacco and loam characters combine to create a distinctive flavour profile. It never really gets out of third gear but it's steady all the way through to a sustained finish. Screwcap. 14.5% alc. **Rating** 89 To 2021 $25 CM
Pinot Gris 2015 Just fractionally on the slight side but ripe tutti-frutti flavours certainly make for enjoyable no-fuss drinking. Screwcap. 13.5% alc. **Rating** 88 To 2017 $20 CM
Basket Press Shiraz 2014 Plum, dried herb and blackcurrant flavours of good dimension and appeal come to a slightly awkward conclusion. Screwcap. 14.5% alc. **Rating** 88 To 2021 $25 CM

Head in the Clouds

36 Neate Avenue, Belair, SA 5052 **Region** Adelaide Hills
T 0404 440 298 **www.**headinthecloudswines.com **Open** Not
Winemaker Tom Robinson, Ashley Coats **Est.** 2008 **Dozens** 260
This is the part-time business of winemaker Tom Robinson and sales manager Ashley Coats. In a potential demarcation dispute, Tom Robinson won the *Gourmet Traveller Wine* magazine New Wine Writer Award '12, and holds a Masters degree in French literature. Each of them has a part-time teaching job at Mercedes College, Tom lecturing in French, Ashley head of the Arts Faculty. Tom's journey through wine is a prodigious one, covering the US for many years, and more recently, Australia. With a production of around 250 dozen, they had travelled below the Halliday radar, but have been making wines under the Head in the Clouds banner since 2008.

♥♥♥♥   **Adelaide Hills Pinot Grigio 2015** Attractive style, with an abundance of citrus, pear and white peach flavours, given line and freshness by crisp acidity. Screwcap. 12.8% alc. **Rating** 89 To 2017 $18 ○

Head Wines

Lot 1 Stonewell Road, Stonewell, SA 5352 **Region** Barossa Valley
T 0413 114 233 **www.**headwines.com.au **Open** By appt Feb–Apr
Winemaker Alex Head **Est.** 2006 **Dozens** 5000 **Vyds** 7.5ha
Head Wines is the intriguing and highly focused venture of Alex Head, who came into the wine industry in 1997 with a degree in biochemistry from Sydney University. Experience in fine wine retail stores, wholesale importers and an auction house was followed by vintage work at wineries he particularly admired: Tyrrell's, Torbreck, Laughing Jack and Cirillo Estate. The naming of the wines reflects his fascination with Côte-Rôtie in the Northern Rhône Valley. The two facing slopes in Côte-Rôtie are known as Côte Blonde and Côte Brune, sometimes combining grapes from the two slopes as Côte Brune et Blonde. Head's Blonde comes from an east-facing slope in the Stone Well area, while The Brunette comes from a very low-yielding vineyard in the Moppa area. In each case, open fermentation (with whole bunches included) and basket-pressing precedes maturation in French oak. Exports to Denmark, The Netherlands and Japan.

♥♥♥♥♥   **The Brunette Moppa Barossa Valley Shiraz 2014** From a vineyard at the top of Moppa Hill (380m), matured for 12 months in French barriques (one-third new). Deep colour; marries deep, rich, velvety black fruits with perfect balance, so much that the full-bodied nature of the wine passes you by. The tannins, in particular, are as smooth as silk, as are the precisely engineered wheels that glide the palate through and along its prodigious length. Screwcap. 14.3% alc. **Rating** 97 To 2054 $55 ○

ΨΨΨΨΨ The Blonde Stone Well Barossa Valley Shiraz 2014 From the Stone Well parish with red clay soils and a deep limestone base providing riper, sweeter fruit than surrounding vineyards, good acidity due to the limestone content; matured in French hogsheads for 12 months (one-third new). Like all the Head Shirazs, has excellent deep crimson-purple colour; this is a wine full of perfectly ripened sweet fruit embroidered with fine, ripe tannins and integrated oak. Screwcap. 14.1% alc. **Rating** 96 **To** 2044 $45 ✪

Ancestor Vine Springton Eden Valley Grenache 2014 From a 155yo vineyard in Springton, 30% whole bunches wild-fermented in a wooden vat twice for three weeks, matured for 12 months in a used 600l demi-muid. There is a classic pot pourri of red fruit aromas and flavours ranging from poached strawberries and spice through to raspberry and ultimately red cherry; there is also a striking purity to the cadence of these flavours thanks to a whisper of sweet tannins holding the flavours in flight pattern. Screwcap. 14.5% alc. **Rating** 97 **To** 2024 $100

Barossa Valley Grenache Rose 2015 Cool-fermented to dryness, wild yeast, 10% barrel-fermented viognier added for texture and perceived sweetness. Trophy Best Rose, Melbourne Wine Awards '15. Pale salmon-pink; the fragrant, flowery bouquet and light palate with wild strawberries to the fore, spice and the undefinable finish (underwritten by the viognier) all attest to the skills and lateral thinking of Alex Head. Screwcap. 13% alc. **Rating** 95 **To** 2017 $25 ✪

Springton Eden Valley Riesling 2015 The exceptional retention of acidity in '15 sees this with 7.9g/l. It has a Germanic classicism, Rheingau not Mosel. The bouquet reaches high out of the glass, the superfine, elegant palate wandering on a path of crunchy acidity among the citrus hedgerows on either side. A butterfly's kiss promises more to come. Screwcap. 11.5% alc. **Rating** 94 **To** 2030 $22 ✪

The Contrarian Marananga Barossa Valley Shiraz 2014 A cool, long fermentation incorporating whole bunches, matured for 12 months in French demi-muids (50% new). An exciting, challenging wine with cracked black pepper, spice and anise all crowding on the bouquet, but with control; the palate is very intense and long, demanding time, and making you wonder whether a light egg white fining would have taken some of the savoury/bolshie attitude of the tannins down a peg or two. Screwcap. 14.2% alc. **Rating** 94 **To** 2034 $32

Old Vine Krondorf Barossa Valley Grenache 2014 From a 72yo vineyard, half hand-picked at 14°, half at 15° baume, 15% whole bunches, matured for 12 months in a very old 2500l foudre, a small percentage of mourvedre added. Especially in Barossa Valley terms, this is a grenache with attitude; red berries, touches of nougat and fruit spice, and a convincing continuity through the length of its elegant palate. Screwcap. 14.5% alc. **Rating** 94 **To** 2024 $35

ΨΨΨΨΨ Head Red Barossa Valley Shiraz 2014 Rating 93 To 2034 $25 ✪
Head Red Barossa Valley GSM 2014 Rating 91 To 2020 $25

Heafod Glen Winery ★★★★

8691 West Swan Road, Henley Brook, WA 6055 **Region** Swan Valley
T (08) 9296 3444 **www**.heafodglenwine.com.au **Open** Wed–Sun 10–5
Winemaker Liam Clarke **Est.** 1999 **Dozens** 2500 **Vyds** 3ha
A combined vineyard and restaurant business, each set on outdoing the other, each with major accolades. Founder Neil Head taught himself winemaking, but in 2007 employed Liam Clarke (with a degree in viticulture and oenology), and a string of significant show successes for Verdelho, Viognier and Reserve Chardonnay has followed. Chesters Restaurant has received many awards over the years. Exports to Japan.

ΨΨΨΨΨ HB2 Vineyard Semillon 2015 Estate-grown, fermented and matured for 4 weeks in new French oak. Cleverly thought out and implemented winemaking has had the desired effect, giving the wine texture and flavour complexity without unwanted phenolics. This has room to grow in the manner Australian semillon makers understand. Screwcap. 11.5% alc. **Rating** 94 **To** 2025 $27 ✪

ΨΨΨΨΩ HB2 Vineyard Viognier 2015 Rating 92 To 2016 $29
HB2 Vineyard Cabernet Sauvignon 2012 Rating 92 To 2027 $35

Heartland Wines ★★★★

The Winehouse, Wellington Road, Langhorne Creek, SA 5255 **Region** Langhorne Creek
T (08) 8333 1363 **www**.heartlandwines.com.au **Open** 7 days 10–5
Winemaker Ben Glaetzer **Est.** 2001 **Dozens** 50000 **Vyds** 200ha
A joint venture of industry veterans: winemakers Ben Glaetzer and Scott Collett, and wine
industry management specialist Grant Tilbrook. Heartland focuses on cabernet sauvignon and
shiraz from Langhorne Creek, John Glaetzer (head winemaker at Wolf Blass for over 30 years,
and Ben's uncle) liaising with growers and vineyards he has known for over three decades,
the wines made by Ben at Barossa Vintners. Director's Cut is the flagship release. Exports to
all major markets.

ΨΨΨΨΩ Directors' Cut Shiraz 2013 Matured in new French and American oak for
14 months. Full crimson–purple; supple, mouthfilling and hedonistic, with that
velvety softness Langhorne Creek provides without sacrificing shape or focus;
blackberry jelly beans and licorice strap are the flavours, even if they sound naff.
Screwcap. 14.5% alc. **Rating** 93 To 2033 $32
Directors' Cut Cabernet Sauvignon 2013 Matured for 14 months in
new French and American hogsheads. A wine that will please most, but not all;
Langhorne Creek cabernet's soft tannins mean discretion where oak is needed,
saving money while making an even better wine. Screwcap. 15% alc. **Rating** 91
To 2028 $33
One 2013 61% cabernet sauvignon, 39% shiraz, matured in new French and
American oak for 14 months. Very rich and powerful, following in the footsteps of
the Wolf Blass Black Label of years gone by. Everything is spelt out in large letters:
alcohol, fruit and oak. Drinking more than a small glass would need SAS training.
Screwcap. 15.5% alc. **Rating** 90 To 2033 $79

Heathcote Estate ★★★★★

98 High Street, Heathcote, Vic 3523 **Region** Heathcote
T (03) 5433 2488 **www**.yabbylake.com **Open** 7 days 10–5
Winemaker Tom Carson, Chris Forge **Est.** 1998 **Dozens** 5000 **Vyds** 34ha
Heathcote Estate and Yabby Lake Vineyards are owned by the Kirby family, of Village
Roadshow Ltd. They purchased a prime piece of Heathcote red Cambrian soil in 1999,
planting shiraz (30ha) and grenache (4ha), the latter an interesting variant on viognier. The
wines are matured exclusively in French oak (50% new). The arrival of the hugely talented
Tom Carson as Group Winemaker has added lustre to the winery and its wines. The cellar
door, situated in an old bakery in the Heathcote township, provides a relaxed dining area.
Exports to the US, the UK, Canada, Sweden, Singapore, Hong Kong and China.

ΨΨΨΨΨ Single Vineyard Shiraz 2014 Matured in French oak (20% new). Deep
crimson; a regal wine demanding attention to its array of black and blue fruits,
licorice and black pepper; it has the mouthfeel of cool grown shiraz, amplified by
its controlled alcohol. Its length is a strong point, as is the texture and structure
of its tannins. Screwcap. 13.5% alc. **Rating** 95 To 2039 $45

ΨΨΨΨΩ Grenache Noir 2013 Rating 92 To 2023 $28

Heathcote Winery ★★★★

183–185 High Street, Heathcote, Vic 3523 **Region** Heathcote
T (03) 5433 2595 **www**.heathcotewinery.com.au **Open** 7 days 10–5
Winemaker David Main **Est.** 1978 **Dozens** 8000 **Vyds** 15.25ha

The cellar door of Heathcote Winery is situated in the main street of Heathcote, housed in a restored miner's cottage built by Thomas Craven in 1854 to cater for the huge influx of goldminers. The winery is immediately behind the cellar door, and processed the first vintage in 1983, following the planting of the vineyards in '78. Stephen Wilkins is the principal shareholder, supported by Colin Gaetjens and Carol Russo, Stephen commenting, 'The reality is we are family owned.' Shiraz and Shiraz Viognier account for 90% of the production.

Mail Coach Shiraz 2014 Warm, hearty and complete. This is an excellent release. Cloves, smoky oak, oodles of blackberried fruit, perhaps a lick of ironstone. Coffeed flavour, most likely from oak, is part of the tapestry. Tannin ripples from the mid-palate onwards. Essence of Heathcote shiraz. Screwcap. 14.5% alc. **Rating** 94 **To** 2028 $35 CM

Cravens Place Shiraz 2014 Rating 90 **To** 2020 $22 CM

Hedberg Hill
701 The Escort Way, Orange, NSW 2800 **Region** Orange
T 0429 694 051 **www.**hedberghill.com.au **Open** W'ends 10–5
Winemaker Chris Derez, Lucy Maddox **Est.** 1998 **Dozens** 500 **Vyds** 5.6ha
Peter and Lee Hedberg have established their hilltop vineyard (880m altitude) 4km west of Orange, with 0.8ha each of cabernet sauvignon, merlot, tempranillo, chardonnay, viognier, sauvignon blanc and riesling. The cellar door has great views of the surrounding valleys.

Peter's Riesling 2015 Attractive upfront and the flavours continue all the way through to a satisfying finish. Lime, spice and candied orange. Delicious. Screwcap. 11.2% alc. **Rating** 91 **To** 2022 $20 CM ✪
Rose 2015 Cabernet sauvignon and merlot. Dust, briar and blackcurrant aromas lead to a juicy-but-dry palate of good length and composure. Decidedly savoury, in a good way. Screwcap. 13% alc. **Rating** 91 **To** 2017 $20 CM ✪
Claudia's Viognier 2015 Keeps itself nice and at the same time, offers a decent serve of stone fruit and spice flavour. Clearly varietal, and well managed. Screwcap. 13% alc. **Rating** 90 **To** 2017 $24 CM

Guy's Sauvignon Blanc 2015 Rating 89 **To** 2017 $20 CM
Lara's Chardonnay 2015 Rating 89 **To** 2020 $24 CM

Heemskerk
660 Blessington Road, White Hills, Tas 7258 (postal) **Region** Tasmania
T 1300 651 650 **www.**heemskerk.com.au **Open** Not
Winemaker Peter Munro **Est.** 1975 **Dozens** NFP
The Heemskerk brand established by Graham Wiltshire when he planted the first vines in 1965 (in the Pipers River region) is a very different business these days. It is part of TWE, and sources its grapes from vineyards including the Riversdale Vineyard in the Coal River Valley for riesling; the Lowestoft Vineyard in the Derwent Valley for pinot noir; and the Tolpuddle Vineyard in the Coal River Valley for chardonnay.

Coal River Valley Chardonnay 2015 An intense citrus-driven bouquet with notes of grapefruit, lemon and a background of spicy, mealy oak. The palate is mineral-driven and poised, the layers of flavour matching the mineral intensity that drives the finish on and on. Screwcap. 13% alc. **Rating** 96 **To** 2030 $50 ✪
Coal River Valley Riesling 2015 Intensity and elegance form a crown on a purple cushion, for royalty is at hand here. How this failed to excite the judges at the Tasmanian Wine Show '16 is beyond me. Perhaps it was due to the severity/autocracy of the citrus flavours. Screwcap. 12% alc. **Rating** 95 **To** 2025 $45
Southern Tasmania Chardonnay 2014 Matured in new and used French oak. This is all about purity and grace, the fragrant bouquet of citrus and apple blossom, the lacy palate with white stone fruit and grapefruit, oak an obedient servant. Screwcap. 12.5% alc. **Rating** 95 **To** 2024 $50

Southern Tasmanian Pinot Noir 2015 Clones MV6 and Davis (D Series), pressed to French oak (35% new). Very powerful and concentrated, with tannins threaded through the palate in tandem with French oak. All the building blocks are there and in balance, but the wine needs years for its secondary savoury/spicy characters to emerge. Screwcap. 13.5% alc. **Rating** 95 **To** 2024 $50

ŶŶŶŶŶ **Abel's Tempest Chardonnay 2014** Rating 93 To 2019 $25 ✪
Georg Jensen Hallmark Cuvee NV Rating 91 To 2017 $40

Heggies Vineyard ★★★★

Heggies Range Road, Eden Valley, SA 5235 **Region** Eden Valley
T (08) 8561 3200 **www.**heggiesvineyard.com **Open** By appt
Winemaker Peter Gambetta **Est.** 1971 **Dozens** 15 000 **Vyds** 62ha
Heggies was the second of the high-altitude (570m) vineyards established by the Hill-Smith family. Plantings on the 120ha former grazing property began in 1973; the principal varieties are riesling, chardonnay, viognier and merlot. There are then two special plantings: a 1.1ha reserve chardonnay block, and 27ha of various clonal trials. Exports to all major markets.

ŶŶŶŶŶ **Botrytis Riesling 2015** Luscious lime juice, sustained and balanced by fine, cleansing acidity. 375ml. Screwcap. 11% alc. **Rating** 94 **To** 2025 $27 ✪

ŶŶŶŶŶ **Riesling 2015** Rating 93 To 2025 $24 ✪
Chardonnay 2014 Rating 90 To 2018 $31

Heidenreich Estate ★★★★☆

PO Box 99, Tanunda, SA 5352 **Region** Barossa Valley
T (08) 8563 2644 **www.**heidenreichvineyards.com.au **Open** By appt
Winemaker Noel Heidenreich, Sarah Siddons **Est.** 1998 **Dozens** 2000 **Vyds** 47.3ha
The Heidenreich family arrived in the Barossa in 1857, with successive generations growing grapes ever since. It is now owned and run by Noel and Cheryl Heidenreich who, having changed the vineyard plantings and done much work on the soil, were content to sell the grapes from their 45ha (at three different sites) of shiraz, cabernet sauvignon, cabernet franc, viognier and chardonnay until 1998, when they and friends crushed a tonne in total of shiraz, cabernet sauvignon and cabernet franc. Since that time, production has soared; much is exported to San Diego (US), and a little sold locally, the remainder exported to Hong Kong and China.

ŶŶŶŶŶ **The Old School Principals Barossa Valley Shiraz 2014** Heavily influenced by custardy, vanillan oak but simultaneously flooded with pure, ripe, intense dark-berried flavour. This is arrestingly rich and quite perfectly structured. You have to enjoy the taste of oak, but if you do this is a belter of a wine. Screwcap. 14.5% alc. **Rating** 95 **To** 2035 $30 CM ✪

Heifer Station ★★★★

PO Box 5082, Orange, NSW 2800 **Region** Orange
T 0407 621 150 **www.**heiferstation.com **Open** Not
Winemaker Daniel Shaw, Charles Svenson **Est.** 1999 **Dozens** 1500 **Vyds** 24.3ha
Founders Phillip and Michelle Stivens both grew up on the land, but spent over 25 years in the corporate world, Phillip as owner-operator of real estate offices in Parkes and Orange, Michelle working in the Attorney-General's Department. When their five adult children left the nest, they decided to retire to the land and grow fat cattle, and when Heifer Station, a property Phillip had admired for years, came onto the market they did not hesitate to purchase it. There was an existing 25ha vineyard, planted in 1998, barely visible through the blackberries, and their intention was to remove the vines. But locals argued they should not do so, pointing to the ideal soils: red loam over limestone. After much contemplation, they agreed to give the vineyard a chance to prove its worth. It has indeed proved its worth, and a cellar door is planned.

♟♟♟♟♟ **Orange Shiraz 2014** Matured for 14 months in French oak (33% new). Very deep colour; wholly convincing cool grown shiraz, with attractive spice, pepper and licorice notes permeating the black cherry and blackberry fruit, oak and tannin management spot on. Screwcap. 13.5% alc. **Rating** 94 To 2034 $30 ✪

♟♟♟♟♟ **Orange Pinot Noir 2014 Rating** 91 To 2022 $28

Heirloom Vineyards   ★★★★★

Salopian Inn, Cnr Main Rd/McMurtrie Road, McLaren Vale, SA 5171
Region McLaren Vale
T (08) 8556 6099 **www.**heirloomvineyards.com.au **Open** 7 days 10–5
Winemaker Elena Brooks **Est.** 2004 **Dozens** NFP
This is (yet another) venture for Zar Brooks and his wife Elena. They met during the 2000 vintage, and one thing led to another, as they say. Dandelion Vineyards and Zonte's Footstep came along first, and continue, but other partners are involved in those ventures (they are also co-owners of the Salopian Inn, with the cellar door in the restaurant). The lofty aims here are 'to preserve the best of tradition, the unique old vineyards of SA, and to champion the best clones of each variety, embracing organic and biodynamic farming'. I don't doubt for one moment the sincerity of the underlying sentiments, but there's a fair degree of Brooksian marketing spin involved. Exports to all major markets.

♟♟♟♟♟ **Eden Valley Riesling 2015** Laden with lime and lemongrass; the tightly wound and focused palate drives on to a pristine finish that persists and reverberates with piercing intensity. Screwcap. 11.5% alc. **Rating** 95 To 2028 $30 ✪
Barossa Shiraz 2014 A beautifully and finely balanced wine is lusciously fruited, but retains its elegance through finely grained tannins and a torrent of black and red fruits. It is drinkable in the short term, but will improve as each year passes. Screwcap. 14.5% alc. **Rating** 95 To 2030 $40
Eden Valley Shiraz 2013 It is the structure, texture and precise finish of this wine that sees you coming back for more. Blackberry, licorice, anise, a touch of tar and dried herbs – the palate sings with myriad flavours and fine, savoury tannins driving the length. Screwcap. 14.5% alc. **Rating** 95 To 2033 $80
Adelaide Hills Sauvignon Blanc 2015 Pristine and crystal-clear sauvignon blanc, apple, passionfruit and a hint of capsicum, the palate finely tuned and perfectly balanced. Screwcap. 12% alc. **Rating** 94 To 2017 $30 ✪
Adelaide Hills Pinot Noir 2015 Mid-red, good depth; this spicy, red fruit-scented pinot is juicy, fine and full of fine-grained tannins, the silky finish and kick of eucalypt typical. Screwcap. 13.5% alc. **Rating** 94 To 2025 $40

Helen & Joey Estate   ★★★★☆

12–14 Spring Lane, Gruyere, Vic 3770 **Region** Yarra Valley
T (03) 9728 1574 **www.**hjestate.com.au **Open** Mon & Fri 11–5, w'ends 11–5
Winemaker Stuart Dudine **Est.** 2011 **Dozens** 11000 **Vyds** 35ha
This is the venture of Helen Xu, who purchased the large Fernando Vineyard on Spring Lane (next to Yeringberg) in 2010. It is planted to pinot noir, cabernet sauvignon, merlot, chardonnay, pinot gris, shiraz and sauvignon blanc. Helen's background is quite varied. She has a Masters degree in analytical chemistry, and was a QA manager for Nestlé for several years. She now owns a business in Shanghai, working with textile ink development together with husband Joey, and they currently split their time between China and Australia. They work closely with Wine Australia, and are active members of the Yarra Valley Winegrowers Association. Exports to Singapore, Japan and China.

♟♟♟♟♟ **Alena Single Vineyard Yarra Valley Chardonnay 2014** Exceptional. This is excellence as a force of nature. It has a robust swagger. It tastes of grapefruit, toast, fennel and peach but it's the mouthfeel, the all-encompassing power, the sizzling length. One sip and you're onto a beauty. Screwcap. 13% alc. **Rating** 96 To 2021 $40 CM ✪

ŸŸŸŸŸ Layla Single Vineyard Pinot Noir 2014 Rating 93 To 2020 $29 CM
Alena Single Vineyard Shiraz 2014 Rating 93 To 2026 $40 CM
Inara Rose 2015 Rating 92 To 2017 $19 CM ○
Layla Single Vineyard Cabernet Sauvignon Merlot 2014 Rating 92
To 2025 $29 CM
Alena Single Vineyard Cabernet Sauvignon Merlot 2014 Rating 92
To 2026 $40 CM
Layla Single Vineyard Cabernet Sauvignon 2014 Rating 92 To 2025
$29 CM
Layla Yarra Valley Chardonnay 2015 Rating 91 To 2020 $29 CM
Alena Single Vineyard Cabernet Sauvignon 2014 Rating 91 To 2026
$40 CM
Inara Pinot Gris 2015 Rating 90 To 2016 $19 CM ○
Inara Merlot 2014 Rating 90 To 2021 $19 CM ○

Helen's Hill Estate

16 Ingram Road, Lilydale, Vic 3140 **Region** Yarra Valley
T (03) 9739 1573 **www.**helenshill.com.au **Open** 7 days 10–5
Winemaker Scott McCarthy **Est.** 1984 **Dozens** 15 000 **Vyds** 53ha
Helen's Hill Estate is named after the previous owner of the property, Helen Fraser. Venture
partners Andrew and Robyn McIntosh and Roma and Allan Nalder combined childhood
farming experience with more recent careers in medicine and finance to establish and
manage the day-to-day operations of the estate. It produces two labels: Helen's Hill Estate
and Ingram Rd, both labels made onsite. Scott McCarthy started his career early by working
vintages during school holidays before gaining diverse and extensive experience in the Barossa
and Yarra valleys, Napa Valley, Languedoc, the Loire Valley and Marlborough. The winery, cellar
door complex and elegant 140-seat restaurant command some of the best views in the valley.
Exports to Hong Kong, the Maldives and China.

ŸŸŸŸŸ Old Block Reserve Yarra Valley Pinot Noir 2013 MV6 clone, hand-picked
and sorted, matured for 14 months in French barriques (40% new). Bright, clear
crimson; a highly expressive bouquet with gently spiced red fruit and flower
aromas; superfine, elegant and long, red cherry to the fore, it has made light work
of the new oak, the lingering finish mouthwatering and fresh. This is Volnay, silky,
supple and seductive. Screwcap. 12.8% alc. **Rating** 96 **To** 2023 $60 ○
Range View Reserve Pinot Noir 2013 Pommard clone (D4V5), matured for
14 months in French barriques (40% new). Dark berry and plum aromas flow
seamlessly into a perfectly proportioned palate, fruit, oak and fine-grained tannins
all making a contribution to a complex pinot batting well above its 12.8% alc.
Screwcap. **Rating** 96 **To** 2023 $60 ○
Breachley Block Single Vineyard Yarra Valley Chardonnay 2015
Predominantly from P58 and Mendoza clones. Has the hallmark length of flavour
on the palate (and aftertaste) firmly stamped on it, but not at the expense of
complexity. The classic white peach, grapefruit and oak-derived cashew are tightly
woven together by flinty acidity on the finish. Screwcap. 12.8% alc. **Rating** 95
To 2023 $35 ○
Old Orchard Single Vineyard Yarra Valley Cabernets 2013 Cabernet
sauvignon, merlot, cabernet franc, malbec and petit verdot. Deep colour; a
distinguished, full-bodied Bordeaux blend with blackcurrant, mulberry, black olive,
briar and French oak all in play. Has the length and balance to repay extended
cellaring. Screwcap. 13.7% alc. **Rating** 95 **To** 2038 $40
Long Walk Single Vineyard Yarra Valley Pinot Noir 2014 The alcohol
reading would suggest that it's light, and in appearance it is. In the mouth, though,
it has real get up and go, with herb and cherry-plum notes striking decisively
towards a firm but long finish. Textbook shape; the aftertaste is the scene of the
main action. Screwcap. 12.8% alc. **Rating** 94 **To** 2024 $35 CM

ŸŸŸŸỴ̈ Ingram Rd Cabernet Merlot 2013 Rating 92 To 2033 $20 ✪
Ingram Rd Pinot Grigio 2015 Rating 91 To 2016 $20 CM ✪
Ingram Rd Pinot Noir 2014 Rating 91 To 2020 $20 CM ✪
Ingram Road Single Vineyard Chardonnay 2015 Rating 90 To 2019 $20 ✪

Helm   ★★★★★

19 Butt's Road, Murrumbateman, NSW 2582 **Region** Canberra District
T (02) 6227 5953 **www**.helmwines.com.au **Open** Thurs–Mon 10–5
Winemaker Ken and Stephanie Helm **Est.** 1973 **Dozens** 5000 **Vyds** 17ha
Ken Helm celebrated his 40th vintage in 2016. Over the years he has achieved many things
through dogged persistence on the one hand, vision on the other. Riesling has been an all-
consuming interest for him, ultimately rewarded with rieslings of consistently high quality.
He has also given much to the broader wine community, extending from the narrow focus
of the Canberra District to the broad canvas of the international world of riesling: in '00 he
established the Canberra International Riesling Challenge. In '14 his youngest child Stephanie
(and husband Ben Osborne, Helm's vineyard manager) purchased Yass Valley Wines, rebranding
it as 'The Vintner's Daughter', and he persuaded Stephanie to join him as winemaker at Helm.
Exports to Macau and Hong Kong.

ŸŸŸŸŸ Premium Canberra District Riesling 2015 The Helm Classic Dry sibling is a
very good wine, but this is on another level, its power and length awesome. Slatey
acidity is the foundation, allowing the trifecta of lime, lemon and apple to build
layer upon layer of fruit flavour, aping some of the new-generation German dry
rieslings from the Rheinhessen. Screwcap. 11.3% alc. **Rating** 97 **To** 2035 $48 ✪

ŸŸŸŸŸ Classic Dry Canberra District Riesling 2015 An outstanding vintage, on a
par with '08 and '13 – and the biggest crush on record (40 tonnes). This is right
up with the best rieslings from Helm, with a highly floral bouquet of citrus and
apple blossom; the palate builds on what is already a superb varietal display, lime
juice, a hint of green apple, and perfect tension between minerally acidity and fruit.
Screwcap. 11.8% alc. **Rating** 96 **To** 2028 $35 ✪
Tumbarumba Riesling 2015 From a high elevation (630m) in the vineyard, and
has all the hallmarks of a very cool grown wine; made with a deft touch by Ken
Helm. The bouquet is still shy, but the palate has exceptional energy and drive to
its lime and green apple fruit. Gold medal Canberra Wine Show '15. Screwcap.
11% alc. **Rating** 95 **To** 2025 $28 ✪

ŸŸŸŸỴ̈ Half Dry Canberra District Riesling 2015 Rating 93 To 2028 $28

Hemera Estate   ★★★★★

1516 Barossa Valley Way, Lyndoch, SA 5351 **Region** Barossa Valley
T (08) 8524 4033 **www**.hemeraestate.com.au **Open** 7 days 10–5
Winemaker Alex MacClelland **Est.** 1999 **Dozens** 15 000 **Vyds** 44ha
Hemera Estate was originally founded by Darius and Pauline Ross in 1999 as Ross Estate
Wines. The name change came about in 2012 after the business was sold to Winston Wine.
This purchase also saw renewed investment in the winery, vineyard and tasting room, with a
focus on consistently producing high quality wines. Running very much on an estate basis,
the winery and tasting room are located on the 44ha vineyard in the southern Barossa Valley,
planted to 11 varieties, including shiraz, cabernet sauvignon, cabernet franc, tempranillo,
mataro and marsanne, with blocks of old vine grenache (105yo) and riesling (48yo). Exports
to the UK, the US and China.

ŸŸŸŸŸ Tier 1 Barossa Shiraz Cabernet Sauvignon 2012 68/32%. Matured for
20 months in new French and American oak. The oak is powerful, but so is
the fruit, and a truce is quickly declared, the sheer intensity of the components
brooking no dissent. The seamless nature of the wine guarantees an exceptionally
long and distinguished life. Screwcap. 14.5% alc. **Rating** 97 **To** 2052 $125 ✪

ၯၯၯၯၯ JDR Barossa Shiraz 2012 The colour is still deep and youthful, the bouquet very complex, with a whirl of black fruits, licorice, spice and quality oak, promising more each time you return to it. The bouquet attaches itself seamlessly to the remarkably intense and long palate, balance and length its greatest assets. Screwcap. 14.5% alc. **Rating** 96 **To** 2042 $80
Single Vineyard Cabernet Sauvignon 2014 Matured for 18 months in French oak. The intensity and freshness of the cassis fruit at the core of the palate has unusual grace, part derived from the moderate alcohol. Screwcap. 14% alc. **Rating** 95 **To** 2040 $40

ၯၯၯၯၯ **Shiraz 2014** Rating 93 **To** 2034 $40
Aurora Limited Release Shiraz 2013 Rating 92 **To** 2023 $65
Single Vineyard Riesling 2015 Rating 90 **To** 2025 $25

Henry's Drive Vignerons ★★★★
41 Hodgson Road, Padthaway, SA 5271 **Region** Padthaway
T (08) 8765 5251 www.henrysdrive.com **Open** 7 days 10–4
Winemaker Kim Jackson **Est.** 1998 **Dozens** 65 000 **Vyds** 94.9ha
Named after the proprietor of the 19th-century mail coach service that once ran through their property, Henry's Drive Vignerons is the wine operation established by Kim Longbottom and her late husband Mark. Kim is continuing to build the family tradition of winemaking, with brands such as Henry's Drive, Parson's Flat, The Trial of John Montford, Dead Letter Office, Pillar Box, Morse Code and The Postmistress. Exports to the UK, the US, Canada, Denmark, Singapore, China and NZ.

ၯၯၯၯၯ **H Syrah 2014** Fermented with 10% whole bunches included, and matured for 10 months in new to 3yo French puncheons. Vivid purple-crimson, it is stacked to the rafters with black and purple fruits, the tannins soft, the oak very evident. Plenty of promise. Screwcap. 14.5% alc. **Rating** 91 **To** 2034 $25

ၯၯၯၯ **H Chardonnay 2014** Rating 89 **To** 2017 $25
Pillar Box Shiraz 2013 Rating 89 **To** 2025 $20
Pillar Box Red Shiraz Cabernet 2013 Rating 89 **To** 2020 $16 CM ✪
Pillar Box Cabernet Sauvignon 2013 Rating 89 **To** 2023 $20

Henschke ★★★★★
1428 Keyneton Road, Keyneton, SA 5353 **Region** Eden Valley
T (08) 8564 8223 www.henschke.com.au **Open** Mon–Fri 9–4.30, Sat 9–12
Winemaker Stephen Henschke **Est.** 1868 **Dozens** 30 000 **Vyds** 121.72ha
Regarded as the best medium-sized red wine producer in Australia, Henschke has gone from strength to strength over the past three decades under the guidance of winemaker Stephen and viticulturist Prue Henschke. The red wines fully capitalise on the very old, low-yielding, high quality vines and are superbly made with sensitive but positive use of new small oak: Hill of Grace is second only to Penfolds Grange as Australia's red wine icon (since 2005 sold with a screwcap). A founding member of Australia's First Families of Wine. Exports to all major markets.

ၯၯၯၯၯ **Hill Of Grace 2010** From a very good vintage. The colour shows no sign of age, the bouquet and palate reminiscent of a Beethoven symphony, throbbing with power, its black fruits in a web of fine, ripe tannins, building inexorably to the last movement, constantly revisiting and rephrasing all that has gone before. Vino-Lok. 14.5% alc. **Rating** 99 **To** 2050 $699
Hill Of Grace 2006 Excellent colour; this is living up to the promise it had when first tasted in Mar '10; this is still incredibly youthful, its black fruits heightened rather than threatened by the firm tannins on the finish. With the advantage of hindsight, the initial drink-to date of '26 can be taken out to '46. The screwcap was a game changer from the outset, but has particular importance for great vintages like this. Sold with the '05 in a Museum Release Collector's Box for $1795. Screwcap. 14.5% alc. **Rating** 98 **To** 2046

Julius Eden Valley Riesling 2015 A celebration of Eden Valley riesling, starting with the fragrant, perfumed flowery bouquet, finishing with mouthwatering acidity. In between, lemon, lime and green apple make a flavour mosaic, its patterns never-ending, all joining seamlessly. Prodigious length. Great value. Screwcap. 11.5% alc. **Rating** 97 **To** 2030 $33 ✪

The Alan Adelaide Hills Pinot Noir 2012 This is a quite beautiful pinot, its spicy black cherry fruit filling the bouquet, and at every point along the way to – and through – the aftertaste. The balance of the fruit, plus savoury nuances allied with acidity, will confer exceptional longevity. Vino-Lok. 13.5% alc. **Rating** 97 **To** 2027 $93 ✪

Marble Angel Vineyard Cabernet Sauvignon 2012 From a 40yo vineyard in the Light Pass district of the Barossa Valley, matured in French hogsheads (40% new) for 18 months. Pays homage to the sculpture skills of Julius Henschke, often using marble from a quarry near Angaston for headstones and angels in the Gnadenberg cemetery. This is a striking cabernet reflecting the great vintage and what must be a very special vineyard, for its varietal expression is bell clear, and juicily seductive. Vino-Lok. 14.5% alc. **Rating** 97 **To** 2042 $84 ✪

Cyril Henschke 2012 79% cabernet sauvignon, 15% cabernet franc, 7% merlot, vinified separately, matured in French hogsheads (38% new) for 18 months. This is one of Australia's greatest cabernets, staring down Coonawarra and Margaret River (just for starters). The argument evaporates when you admit – as you must – that those wines are in such different styles it's an apples and oranges comparison. This has a purity and elegance that puts it in a class of its own. Screwcap. 14% alc. **Rating** 97 **To** 2039 $155

🍷🍷🍷🍷🍷 **Tappa Pass Vineyard Selection Eden Valley Shiraz 2013** 100yo shiraz from the Eden and Barossa valleys, matured in French hogsheads (61% new) for 18 months. Vibrant crimson-purple; highly perfumed red berries, spice and pepper bouquet; a silky, supple medium-bodied palate, the oak integrated, the tannins fine. Vino-Lok. 14.5% alc. **Rating** 96 **To** 2038 $100

Hill Of Grace 2005 Very good retention of hue; the bouquet is now moving into secondary mode, with a seamless fusion of the black fruits, oak and tannins. There are highways and byways to explore, but you always come back to the point of departure. Along the way nuances of red fruits have joined in, and the spices previously locked away are now great contributors to the wine. Whereas the '06 still needs time, this is open for business, and will likely be at its best over the next 9–10 years. Sold with the '06 in a Museum Release Collector's Box for $1795. Screwcap. 14.5% alc. **Rating** 96 **To** 2025

Green's Hill Adelaide Hills Riesling 2015 A totally delicious wine, enough to win the hearts and minds of the most ardent supporters of those far inferior wines made of pinot gris or sauvignon blanc. The flavours fill the mouth with an exultant display of all things citrus, the finish polished and freshened by the effortless natural acidity. Screwcap. 12.5% alc. **Rating** 95 **To** 2028 $26 ✪

Keyneton Euphonium 2013 A blend of shiraz, cabernet sauvignon, merlot and cabernet franc which says more about the vineyard and the Henschke winemaking expertise than the fruit composition. All the flavours are, as usual, fused together, oak and tannins providing context. Screwcap. 14% alc. **Rating** 95 **To** 2033 $56

Johann's Garden 2014 70% grenache, 24% mataro, 6% shiraz vinified separately, matured in used French oak for 10 months. This is arguably the most delicious wine in the Henschke stable; it's got a pinot noir-like note to its texture and mouthfeel. Screwcap. 14.5% alc. **Rating** 95 **To** 2029 $56

Croft Adelaide Hills Chardonnay 2014 Bright straw-green; I hesitate to use the word 'traditional', but the fully ripened stone fruit flavour profile and faintly creamy/nutty notes of the mid-palate have immediate appeal; while there is no want of acidity, this is no wannabe sauvignon blanc style, and the wine will have a fiercely loyal band of supporters. Screwcap. 13.5% alc. **Rating** 94 **To** 2021 $40

Innes Vineyard Littlehampton Adelaide Hills Pinot Gris 2015 Henschke was an early mover with pinot gris, and has been able to get that little bit more out of it each vintage. Screwcap. 13.5% alc. **Rating** 94 **To** 2022 $36

Eden Valley Noble Rot Semillon 2015 Tropical and citrus flavours fight it out; has the all-important balance between residual sugar and titratable acidity; succulent and juicy, but doesn't cloy. Screwcap. 10.5% alc. **Rating** 94 **To** 2020 $40

Hentley Farm Wines

Cnr Jenke Road/Gerald Roberts Road, Seppeltsfield, SA 5355 **Region** Barossa Valley
T (08) 8562 8427 **www.**hentleyfarm.com.au **Open** 7 days 11–5
Winemaker Andrew Quin **Est.** 1999 **Dozens** 15 000 **Vyds** 38.21ha
Keith and Alison Hentschke purchased Hentley Farm in 1997, as an old vineyard and mixed farming property. Keith has thoroughly impressive credentials, having studied agricultural science at Roseworthy, graduating with the Gramp Hardy Smith Memorial Prize for Most Outstanding Student, later adding an MBA. During the 1990s he had a senior production role with Orlando, before moving on to manage Fabal, one of Australia's largest vineyard management companies. A total of 38.2ha were planted between 1999 and 2005. In '04 an adjoining 6.5ha vineyard, christened Clos Otto, was acquired. Shiraz dominates the plantings, with 32.5ha. Situated on the banks of Greenock Creek, the vineyard has red clay loam soils overlaying shattered limestone, lightly rocked slopes and little topsoil. Joining Keith in the vineyard and winery are Greg Mader as viticulturist, and Andrew Quin as winemaker, both with very impressive CVs. 2015 *Wine Companion* Winery of the Year. Exports to the US and other major markets.

ŸŸŸŸŸ **The Beast Barossa Valley Shiraz 2014** The road to intensity is littered with blackberries. This is where wine meets bitumen meets fruit meets oak. It's colossal in its breadth, depth and reach. It's like some prehistoric creature; it will take an awful lot for its magnificence to ever be dimmed; it will live on for as long as you want it to. Screwcap. 14.8% alc. **Rating** 97 **To** 2045 $95 CM ✪

The Quintessential Barossa Valley Shiraz Cabernet 2014 It doesn't flow, it oozes. It's smooth, rich, dark, powerfully built and yet soft. It draws you straight in and keeps you there. Musky oak, sweet cedar wood, blackcurrant, asphalt, ripe-but-fresh plums. Quintessential, indeed. It is, simply, an outstanding wine. Screwcap. 14.6% alc. **Rating** 97 **To** 2036 $65 CM ✪

H Block Shiraz Cabernet 2014 70/30% blend. Immaculately conceived and executed. Pure blackcurrant and blackberry; elements of mint and dark earth; a tail swish of cedary/chocolatey oak. It impresses all the way along the palate but the finish is quite superb. Cork. 14.7% alc. **Rating** 97 **To** 2040 $175 CM

ŸŸŸŸŸ **The Creation Barossa Valley Shiraz 2014** It's not a brooding beast; the quality meets every mark. Most surprising is its elegance. It tastes of earth, aniseed, jubey blackberry and sweet/dried spices, but it's the fresh friskiness of it that sets its character. Tannin then curls through the finish like a perfectly aimed outswinger. Cork. 14.8% alc. **Rating** 96 **To** 2040 $175 CM

The Stray Mongrel 2015 Crackerjack blend of grenache, shiraz and zinfandel. Pure licorice and raspberry, ribbons of spice, charcuterie and dark chocolate. Coffee grounds too perhaps. It takes deliciousness and wraps both arms around it. And yet it's firm with tannin too. A complete package. Screwcap. 14.7% alc. **Rating** 96 **To** 2023 $29 CM ✪

Barossa Valley Shiraz 2015 Concentration of flavour and overall form and poise are quite incredible given that this isn't among the top-of-the-tree releases from the estate. This is where the wine drinker really is the winner. It's thick with flavour but remains buoyant, even jolly, with life. Tannin too shirks no issues whatsoever. Screwcap. 14.8% alc. **Rating** 95 **To** 2030 $29 CM ✪

Clos Otto Barossa Valley Shiraz 2014 Full-bodied in every sense. Rich, thick, powerful, its muscles bulging with sweet, blackberried, jam-stuffed fruit, its limbs of licorice and coffeed oak rippling with chunky ropes of tannin. You could moor ships to this. Its flavours reach into deep, inky pools; the finish pulls it all safely into harbour. Cork. 14.8% alc. **Rating** 95 **To** 2040 **$190** CM

The Beauty Barossa Valley Shiraz 2014 Size, shape, power and length; there's a lot crammed into this package, and yet at no point does it suggest being overdone. It's a fresh, vigorous red with anise, raspberry, squishy blackberries and wood spice notes ramping the appeal up high. It'll age but there's no real reason to wait. Screwcap. 14% alc. **Rating** 95 **To** 2032 **$65** CM

The Old Legend Grenache 2015 Light in colour but rich in presence and impact. This is a glorious grenache. It's all red fruits and earth, dried herbs and smoky oak, with licorice root rising through the aftertaste. But best of all, it has length and X-factor in spades. Screwcap. 14% alc. **Rating** 95 **To** 2025 **$65** CM

Barossa Valley Cabernet Sauvignon 2015 Inky and rich. Dark berry and coal flavours power through the palate. Tannin pulls on the reins but the fruit charges on. A mouthful of gorgeousness. Screwcap. 14.4% alc. **Rating** 95 **To** 2032 **$29** CM ✪

von Kasper Barossa Valley Cabernet Sauvignon 2014 Certainly at the big (and warm) end of the spectrum but grainy, dusty tannin keeps varietal character intact. Chocolate and blackcurrant flavours run the show for the most part. Long life ahead. Cork. 14.5% alc. **Rating** 94 **To** 2036 **$95** CM

🍷🍷🍷🍷🍷 **The Rogue Barossa Field Blend 2015** **Rating** 93 **To** 2023 **$24** CM ✪
The Marl Barossa Valley Grenache 2015 **Rating** 93 **To** 2020 **$21** CM ✪
The Quatro 2014 **Rating** 93 **To** 2030 **$40** CM
Eden Valley Riesling 2015 **Rating** 91 **To** 2020 **$25**
Poppy Barossa Valley Field Blend 2015 **Rating** 91 **To** 2018 **$25** CM
Barossa Valley Rose 2015 **Rating** 91 **To** 2017 **$22** ✪
Dirty Bliss Grenache Shiraz Mourvedre 2014 **Rating** 91 **To** 2021 **$22** CM ✪
The Marl Cabernet Sauvignon 2014 **Rating** 91 **To** 2021 **$21** CM ✪
Vintage Blanc de Noir 2015 **Rating** 91 **To** 2017 **$29** TS
The Marl Barossa Valley Shiraz 2014 **Rating** 90 **To** 2020 **$21** CM ✪
Black Beauty Sparkling Shiraz NV **Rating** 90 **To** 2025 **$65** TS

Henty Estate ★★★★★

657 Hensley Park Road, Hamilton, Vic 3300 (postal) **Region** Henty
T (03) 5572 4446 **www**.henty-estate.com.au **Open** Not
Winemaker Peter Dixon **Est.** 1991 **Dozens** 1400 **Vyds** 7ha

Peter and Glenys Dixon have hastened slowly with Henty Estate. In 1991 they began the planting of 4.5ha of shiraz, 1ha each of cabernet sauvignon and chardonnay, and 0.5ha of riesling. In their words, 'we avoided the temptation to make wine until the vineyard was mature', establishing the winery in 2003. Encouraged by neighbour John Thomson, they have limited the yield to 3–4 tonnes per hectare on the VSP-trained, dry grown vineyard.

🍷🍷🍷🍷🍷 **Riesling 2015** After the citrus-filled bouquet, the palate moves with alacrity, taking control with its pungent blend of electric acidity woven through Meyer lemon and green lime fruit. The energy created is akin to a lemon sorbet devoured on a blazing hot day. Screwcap. 12.8% alc. **Rating** 96 **To** 2027 **$22** ✪

Chardonnay 2015 A minuscule yield of 1t/ha, hand-picked, fermented in stainless steel to 4° baume, then transferred to French oak (Vosges) to complete fermentation and 6 months maturation, no mlf. Given the cost of growing the grapes and the French oak, and the quality of the wine, the price borders on the unbelievable. It is classic ultra-cool-grown style, pink grapefruit the key. Screwcap. 12.6% alc. **Rating** 95 **To** 2025 **$24** ✪

Cabernet Sauvignon 2014 This should be mission impossible, but Crawford River has chosen to accept it. It is full of blackcurrant/cassis backed by fine tannins, both unequivocally ripe, and defining the quality. Oak comes in simply to achieve an extra point. Screwcap. 13.4% alc. **Rating** 95 **To** 2034 **$26** ✪

ŢŢŢŢŢ Edward Shiraz 2013 Rating 93 To 2033 $35
Shiraz 2014 Rating 92 To 2029 $26

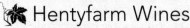

Hentyfarm Wines ★★★★★

250 Wattletree Road, Holgate, NSW 2250 **Region** Henty
T 0423 029 200 **www**.hentyfarm.com.au **Open** Not
Winemaker Justin Purser **Est.** 2009 **Dozens** 1500
Dr John Gladstones names the Henty GI the coolest climate in Australia, cooler than Tasmania. This is both bane and blessing, for when it's cold, it's bitterly so. The other fact of life it has to contend with is its remoteness, lurking just inside the SA/Vic border. The rest is all good news, for this region is capable of producing riesling, chardonnay and pinot noir of the highest quality. Seppelt's Drumborg Vineyard focuses on riesling, pinot noir and chardonnay, Crawford River on riesling, both adding lustre to the region. In 2009 Jonathan (Jono) Mogg and partner Belinda Low made several weekend trips in the company of (then) Best's winemaker Adam Wadewitz and his partner Nikki. They were able to buy grapes from renowned Henty grower Alastair Taylor, and the first vintage of Chardonnay was made in '09. In '11 a Pinot Noir was added to the portfolio, followed by Pinot Gris in '13. This was grown by 'biological grape farmers' Jack and Lois Doevan. The wines are made under contract by Justin Purser at Best's Wines, with a final extension of Riesling and Pinot Meunier from Alastair Taylor's vineyard coming up soon. Exports to China.

ŢŢŢŢŢ **Pinot Noir 2013** Has kept its hue well; the fragrant bouquet leaves no doubt about the quality of the wine and its varietal expression with a complex mix of red cherry, strawberry and plum aromas, the palate possessed of Burgundian-like tannins. The result is an intense, long palate perfectly balancing fruit and forest floor. Screwcap. 12% alc. **Rating** 96 To 2023 $35 ○
Riesling 2015 Restraint and ultimate precision are the markers of a lovely riesling still in its swaddling clothes. But there are already seductive hints of lime and green apple on the palate, with crystalline acidity lined up in support on the endless finish. Screwcap. 11.5% alc. **Rating** 95 To 2035 $25 ○
Chardonnay 2013 Henty produces super long-lived chardonnays (as well as rieslings), and this wine is right in the mainstream. Its length and persistence are prodigious, with grapefruit and white peach fruit tightly embraced by acidity, oak little more than a squeak. Screwcap. 12.8% alc. **Rating** 95 To 2030 $35 ○

ŢŢŢŢŢ **Pinot Gris 2015** Rating 93 To 2018 $25 ○

Herbert Vineyard ★★★☆

Bishop Road, Mount Gambier, SA 5290 **Region** Mount Gambier
T 0408 849 080 **www**.herbertvineyard.com.au **Open** By appt
Winemaker David Herbert **Est.** 1996 **Dozens** 450 **Vyds** 2.4ha
David and Trudy Herbert have planted 1.9ha of pinot noir, and a total of 0.5ha of cabernet sauvignon, merlot and pinot gris (the majority of the pinot noir is sold for sparkling wine). They have built a two-level (mini) winery overlooking a 1300-square metre maze, which is reflected in the label logo.

ŢŢŢŢŢ **Square Mile Pinot Noir 2014** Fresh and cranberried with spice notes smattered across the finish. The overall profile has an attractive, tangy sweet-sourness. It's light, but drinkability and interest levels are good. Screwcap. 13% alc. **Rating** 90 To 2021 $26 CM

ŢŢŢŢ **Barrel Number 1 Pinot Noir 2013** Rating 89 To 2019 $37 CM

Heritage Estate ★★★★☆

Granite Belt Drive, Cottonvale, Qld 4375 **Region** Granite Belt
T (07) 4685 2197 **www**.heritagewines.com.au **Open** 7 days 9–5
Winemaker John Handy **Est.** 1992 **Dozens** 5000 **Vyds** 10ha

Heritage Estate (owned by Bryce and Paddy Kassulke) has two estate vineyards in the Granite Belt, one at Cottonvale (north) at an altitude of 960m, where it grows white varieties, and the other at Ballandean, a slightly warmer site where red varieties and marsanne are planted. Heritage Estate has been a prolific award-winner in various Qld wine shows and (I am pleased to report) it has invested in a new bottling line, enabling it to use screwcaps. After a series of difficult vintages, with the Cottonvale vineyard hit by hail in 2013, Heritage Estate has bounced back impressively, taking full advantage of the excellent '14 vintage. A winery to watch.

ΨΨΨΨΨ Old Vine Reserve Granite Belt Shiraz 2014 Dark red; a lovely pure-fruited and fragrant bouquet, redolent with spice and red fruits; the palate has restraint and a lovely coating of fruit and tannin; it is impeccably balanced, and represents the continual refinement in the wines from Heritage Estate. Screwcap. 14.5% alc. **Rating** 94 **To** 2030 $30 ✪

ΨΨΨΨΨ Granite Belt Fiano 2015 Rating 93 **To** 2022 $25 ✪
Wild Ferment Granite Belt Marsanne 2014 Rating 92 **To** 2018 $25 ✪
Reserve Granite Belt Tempranillo 2015 Rating 90 **To** 2020 $28

Heritage Wines   ★★★☆

399 Seppeltsfield Road, Marananga, SA 5355 **Region** Barossa Valley
T (08) 8562 2880 **www**.heritagewinery.com.au **Open** Mon–Fri 10–5, w'ends 11–5
Winemaker Stephen Hoff **Est.** 1984 **Dozens** 4000 **Vyds** 8.3ha
A little-known winery that deserves a wider audience, for veteran owner/winemaker Stephen Hoff is apt to produce some startlingly good wines. At various times the Riesling (from old Clare Valley vines), Cabernet Sauvignon and Shiraz (now the flag-bearer) have all excelled. The vineyard is planted to shiraz (5.5ha), cabernet sauvignon (2.5ha) and malbec (0.3ha). Exports to the UK, the US, Thailand, Hong Kong, Malaysia and Singapore.

ΨΨΨΨΨ Rossco's Shiraz 2013 Matured for 12 months in used American barriques followed by 6 months in new American barriques. Dense, deep crimson-purple, the rim bright; a powerful, full-bodied wine with deep rivers of blackberry and licorice running through the length of the palate. I'm not quite so pleased by the oak choice/management, but it's a relatively minor matter in the overall context of the wine. Cork. 14.5% alc. **Rating** 94 **To** 2038 $50

ΨΨΨΨ Barossa Semillon 2015 Rating 89 **To** 2020 $15 ✪

Hesketh Wine Company   ★★★★

28 The Parade, Norwood, SA 5067 **Region** Various
T (08) 8232 8622 **www**.heskethwinecompany.com.au **Open** Not
Winemaker Phil Lehmann **Est.** 2006 **Dozens** 20000
Headed by Jonathon Hesketh, this is part of WD Wines Pty Ltd, which also owns Parker Coonawarra Estate and St John's Road in the Barossa Valley. Jonathon spent 7 years as the Global Sales & Marketing Manager of Wirra Wirra, two and a half years as General Manager of Distinguished Vineyards in NZ. He also happens to be the son of Robert Hesketh, one of the key players in the development of many facets of the SA wine industry.

ΨΨΨΨΨ Regional Selection Barossa Valley Shiraz 2014 Beautifully put together. The fruit loads, the tannin rolls, oak slides into general contention and throughout everything remains bright, attractive, satisfying. Plums, earth, violets, cloves. Excellent buying. Screwcap. 14.5% alc. **Rating** 92 **To** 2021 $18 CM ✪
Regional Selection Adelaide Hills Sauvignon Blanc 2015 Awash with tropical fruit flavour. Sprightly from go to whoa. Apple and passionfruit with bursts of citrus. Gentle rub of sweet pea. Rushes up to meet you with a bright smile on its face. Screwcap. 12.5% alc. **Rating** 91 **To** 2016 $18 CM ✪
Regional Selection Clare Valley Riesling 2014 Grown in the Polish Hill River and Watervale districts. It's lively with talc and lime flavours and edged

with spice. It's dry. It has enough penetration to satisfy but also the flavour and accessibility to woo now. Screwcap. 11.5% alc. **Rating** 90 **To** 2020 $18 CM **✪**

Lost Weekend Chardonnay 2014 20% fermented and briefly matured in new French barriques, the remainder in stainless steel. A surprise packet, with more intensity and focus than the region normally provides at any price, let alone this. Screwcap. 13% alc. **Rating** 90 **To** 2017 $12 **✪**

Mezzo Tatiara District Shiraz 2015 Purple-coloured and plush with sweet, ripe, berried fruit. Crowd-pleaser, done well. Has an air of generosity. Screwcap. 14.5% alc. **Rating** 90 **To** 2019 $18 CM **✪**

Mezzo Tatiara District Shiraz Mataro 2015 Mouthfilling red with leather, licorice and blackberry flavours building plenty of body. Indeed there's excellent weight of flavour here. Screwcap. 14.5% alc. **Rating** 90 **To** 2020 $18 CM **✪**

Regional Selection Coonawarra Cabernet Sauvignon 2013 Market times are tough when a Coonawarra cabernet of this quality has a price of $19. It is on the full side of medium-bodied, with cassis fruit to the fore, a hint of bay leaf and unusually soft tannins. Arguably at its best now, but won't fall over quickly. Screwcap. 14.5% alc. **Rating** 90 **To** 2020 $19 **✪**

Barossa Valley Montepulciano 2014 Aged for 18 months in all-French oak, none of it new. There are almost no oak flavours to be seen, allowing the fruit to roam into clear open space. The effect is delicious. Tar, cherries, plums and floral aspects. Sweet, sour and savoury. Earthen tannin ties it all together neatly. Screwcap. 13.5% alc. **Rating** 90 **To** 2020 $25 CM

Heslop Wines ★★★

PO Box 93, Mudgee, NSW 2850 **Region** Mudgee
T (02) 6372 3903 **www.**heslopwines.com.au **Open** Not
Winemaker Robert Heslop **Est.** 2011 **Dozens** 250 **Vyds** 4ha
This is the venture of Bob and Julie Heslop, who returned to Mudgee (where Julie was born) in 1984, purchasing a property across the road from Julie's father's vineyard; the vendor was Ferdie Roth, a member of the famous Mudgee wine family, who had planted the muscat hamburg vines still on the property. Bob's winemaking career began at Kay Bros in McLaren Vale, while undertaking oenology studies at CSU. Using sustainable viticulture practices, they have planted 4ha to a Joseph's Coat of 11 varieties. A winery was built in 2011.

♀♀♀♀ **Mudgee Chardonnay 2014** Interesting wine: the colour is good, as are the bouquet and entry into the mouth; a strongly flavoured mid-palate turns distinctly sweet on the finish and aftertaste. Will appeal to some for that very reason. Screwcap. 14% alc. **Rating** 88 **To** 2017 $25

Hewitson

66 Seppeltsfield Road, Nuriootpa, SA 5355 **Region** Adelaide Zone
T (08) 8212 6233 **www.**hewitson.com.au **Open** 7 days 9–5
Winemaker Dean Hewitson **Est.** 1996 **Dozens** 25 000 **Vyds** 4.5ha
Dean Hewitson was a winemaker at Petaluma for 10 years, during which time he managed to do three vintages in France and one in Oregon as well as undertaking his Masters at the University of California, Davis. It is hardly surprising that the wines are immaculately made from a technical viewpoint. Dean sources 30-year-old riesling from the Eden Valley and 70-year-old shiraz from McLaren Vale; he also makes a Barossa Valley Mourvedre from vines planted in 1853 at Rowland Flat, and Barossa Valley Shiraz and Grenache from 60-year-old vines at Tanunda. Exports to the UK, the US and other major markets.

♀♀♀♀♀ **Old Garden Barossa Valley Mourvedre 2012** The vineyard was planted in 1853, and simply has to be the oldest in the world. Don't be fooled by the relatively light colour, or its first signs of development; literally dances with its roundabout of spicy, savoury fruits that percolate through the bouquet and palate with equal persistence and intensity, the savoury finish emphatic, yet light-footed. Screwcap. 14% alc. **Rating** 96 **To** 2027 $88

Gun Metal Eden Valley Riesling 2015 Refreshing and elegant, fruit and acid happy to remain in their due place in a way similar to Porongurup. Drink it now for its zest, or in a decade for the layers of fruit and honey it will have by then. Screwcap. 12% alc. **Rating** 95 **To** 2019 $23 ❂

LuLu Adelaide Hills Sauvignon Blanc 2015 Has admirable purity and intensity of varietal character; kiwi fruit, lychee, passionfruit, white peach and citrus are all on parade; the crisp natural acidity is sufficient to provide structure and length but doesn't distract. Screwcap. 12% alc. **Rating** 95 **To** 2016 $23 ❂

Ned & Henry's Barossa Valley Shiraz 2014 Cracking quality. Draws you in. Red and black berries, aniseed, wood spice, fresh leather. Delights as it dances along your tongue. Plentiful but then smoky and controlled through the finish. Compelling value. Screwcap. 14% alc. **Rating** 95 **To** 2028 $28 CM ❂

Miss Harry Barossa Valley Grenache Mourvedre Shiraz Cinsault Carignan 2013 50% grenache, 23% mourvedre, 22% shiraz with 5% of cinsault and carignan, 15% whole bunches, matured in used French oak for 16 months. There are no other Barossa Valley Rhône blends with this composition and sheer elegance. It is willowy and savoury, with mouth-cleansing acidity, yet also with a garland of diverse red fruit flavours, all fresh, none sticky or jubey. Simply lovely. Screwcap. 14% alc. **Rating** 95 **To** 2023 $28 ❂

Baby Bush Barossa Valley Mourvedre 2013 Dean Hewitson notes that the oldest Baby Bush vines are now 18yo, 'so not quite babies anymore'. This release included 15% whole bunches in the ferment. It hasn't hurt the wine's sense of self. It edges towards completeness. Rakes of tannin, drives of acid, imposing fruit, leather and spice. Most impressive. A good option for the medium-term cellar. Screwcap. 14% alc. **Rating** 94 **To** 2025 $27 CM ❂

Heydon Estate ★★★★★

325 Tom Cullity Drive, Wilyabrup, WA 6280 **Region** Margaret River
T (08) 9755 6995 **www**.heydonestate.com.au **Open** 7 days 10–5
Winemaker Mark Messenger **Est.** 1988 **Dozens** 1800 **Vyds** 10ha
Margaret River dentist and cricket tragic George Heydon and wife Mary have been involved in the region's wine industry since 1995. They became 50% partners in Arlewood, and when that partnership was dissolved in 2004 they retained the property and the precious 2ha of cabernet sauvignon and 2.5ha of Gingin clone chardonnay planted in '88. Additional plantings from '95 include Dijon chardonnay clones, sauvignon blanc, semillon, shiraz and petit verdot. The estate is now biodynamic, near neighbour Vanya Cullen having inspired the decision. Exports to the UK, Singapore and Hong Kong.

🍷🍷🍷🍷🍷 **W.G. Grace Single Vineyard Cabernet Sauvignon 2010** A complete powerhouse. It's firm and controlled but every ripple suggests quality and depth. Blackcurrant, gravel, violet and bay leaf notes drive forcefully from start to finish. The finish is firm, fine and exceptionally long. Screwcap. 14% alc. **Rating** 97 **To** 2040 $75 CM ❂

🍷🍷🍷🍷🍷 **The Willow Single Vineyard Chardonnay 2012** It recognises all the quality prerequisites and then slots them in one by one. Richness, firmness, length, an array of flavours and a clear impression of generosity. It bursts with flavour; it's a class act. Screwcap. 13.5% alc. **Rating** 95 **To** 2021 $50 CM

The Sledge Single Vineyard Margaret River Shiraz 2013 A power of dark chocolate matched to firm, ripe blackberried/black cherried fruit. This is an impressive mouthful of red wine. Clove and dried spice notes add a sense of 'extra'. A fine future awaits. Screwcap. 14.5% alc. **Rating** 95 **To** 2035 $40 CM

 HG Vintners ★★★☆

362 Pipers Creek-Pastoria Road, Pipers Creek, Vic 3444 **Region** Macedon Ranges
T 0407 821 049 **www**.hgvintners.com.au **Open** W'ends 12–5
Winemaker Brian Martin **Est.** 2015 **Dozens** 500 **Vyds** 5ha

In late 2015 winemaker Brian Martin purchased a vineyard which has passed through a number of ownerships since its establishment in 1999. It was first known as Loxley Vineyard, and later Harmony Row. The vineyard has a long-established cellar door, and offers Shiraz, Pinot Noir, Riesling and Chardonay (and a couple of sparkling wines) under the Hunter Gatherer label. Alternative varieties are marketed under the Marvio label, the first two wines a Sangiovese and a Sangiovese Rose.

♀♀♀♀♀ **Hunter-Gatherer Heathcote Shiraz 2012** Good colour; black fruits, spice, mocha/fruitcake and licorice drive the bouquet and medium to full-bodied palate, the tannins and oak integrated. Screwcap. 13.5% alc. **Rating** 90 **To** 2022 $35

♀♀♀♀ **Hunter-Gatherer Macedon Chardonnay 2013 Rating** 89 **To** 2018 $30
Marvio Heathcote Sangiovese Rose 2015 Rating 89 **To** 2017 $25
Hunter-Gatherer Heathcote Riesling 2015 Rating 88 **To** 2020 $25

Hickinbotham Clarendon Vineyard   ★★★★★

92 Brooks Road, Clarendon, SA 5157 **Region** McLaren Vale
T (08) 8383 7504 **www.**hickinbothamwines.com.au **Open** By appt
Winemaker Charlie Seppelt, Chris Carpenter **Est.** 2012 **Dozens** 5000 **Vyds** 68.8ha
Alan Hickinbotham established the vineyard bearing his name in 1971 when he planted dry grown cabernet sauvignon and shiraz in contoured rows on the sloping site. He was a very successful builder, this his first venture into wine, but his father Alan Robb Hickinbotham had a long and distinguished career, co-founding the oenology diploma at Roseworthy in '36. In 2012 Clarendon, and the stately sandstone house on the property, was purchased by Jackson Family Wines, and is run as a separate business from Yangarra Estate Vineyard, with different winemaking teams and wines. Exports to all major markets.

♀♀♀♀♀ **The Peake Cabernet Shiraz 2013** 57/43% from blocks planted in '71 and '01, separately fermented. The silky Rolls Royce power and intensity tells of painstaking fruit and barrel selection, the result a flawless wine of rare quality and complexity in a mirror-calm sea of black fruits. Screwcap. 14% alc. **Rating** 98 **To** 2053 $150 ✪
Shiraz 2013 From estate blocks planted in '71, matured for 15 months in Burgundy-coopered barrels. The vivid crimson-purple colour bodes well, and the medium-bodied palate does not disappoint, the texture and structure outstanding, fruit, oak and tannins seamlessly woven together, the finish absolutely compelling. Do give it time. Screwcap. 14.5% alc. **Rating** 97 **To** 2048 $75 ✪

♀♀♀♀♀ **Brooks Road Shiraz 2014** Deep crimson-purple; a very complex wine, all the components handled with the skill of a circus juggler, keeping all in the air. Its extreme fragrance and intensity on the palate have a lightness to their touch, with spiced red and black fruits, licorice and fine tannins, oak the (almost) unseen hand. Screwcap. 14% alc. **Rating** 96 **To** 2039 $75 ✪
The Revivalist Merlot 2013 'Revivalist' refers to extensive vineyard work on vines planted in '76; matured for 15 months in Bordeaux-coopered barrels. The bouquet is fragrant and very expressive, the palate opening with an elegant fusion of cassis and French oak, but leaving it to the finish and aftertaste to show its ultimate class, fine-grained tannins adding another dimension. Screwcap. 14.5% alc. **Rating** 96 **To** 2043 $75 ✪
The Peake Cabernet Shiraz 2014 Exceptionally potent and powerful, initially giving the (false) impression that its alcohol is more than 14%. Retasting brings it back into perspective, the two varieties bonded, yet each preserving its varietal integrity and structural architecture. A wine of exceptional quality, destined to outlive most who taste it. Screwcap. 14% alc. **Rating** 96 **To** 2049 $150
The Revivalist Merlot 2014 Matured for 15 months in French oak. Shows that serious merlot can be made in McLaren Vale (or the Clarendon Hills sector thereof). The bouquet is fragrant and accurately signals the gently savoury/dried herb undergrowth of the cassis and plum that sits firmly on top. Good tannins tie the knot. Screwcap. 14% alc. **Rating** 95 **To** 2034 $75

Cabernet Sauvignon 2013 Matured for 15 months in Bordeaux oak. The epitome of top quality McLaren Vale cabernet in its inimitable style: generous, yet firmly structured, cassis, choc-mint, ripe tannins and integrated oak of high quality. Screwcap. 13.5% alc. **Rating** 95 **To** 2038 $75

Trueman Cabernet Sauvignon 2014 A juicy cassis-driven cabernet of purity and typicity, oak and tannins a means to an end, and doing precisely what they should. Screwcap. 14% alc. **Rating** 94 **To** 2039 $75

Higher Plane ★★★★★

98 Tom Cullity Drive, Cowaramup, WA 6284 **Region** Margaret River
T (08) 9755 9000 **www.**higherplanewines.com.au **Open** At Juniper Estate, 7 days 10–5
Winemaker Mark Messenger **Est.** 1996 **Dozens** 2500 **Vyds** 14.55ha

In late 2006 Higher Plane was purchased by the late Roger Hill and Gillian Anderson (of Juniper Estate), but kept as a stand-alone brand, with different distributors, etc. The Higher Plane vineyards are planted to all the key varieties: chardonnay and sauvignon blanc are foremost, with cabernet sauvignon, merlot, tempranillo, fiano, semillon, cabernet franc, malbec and petit verdot making up the rest of the plantings. Exports to Hong Kong.

🍷🍷🍷🍷🍷 **Chardonnay 2013** Mendoza clone, matured for 10 months in French barriques (40% new), a best barrels selection. It has the purity of line of the '14, but the Mendoza clone and extra 12 months in bottle have increased its intensity and complexity. This is the better wine. Screwcap. 13.5% alc. **Rating** 95 **To** 2021 $35 ✪

The Messenger 2012 50% cabernet sauvignon, 24% malbec, 12% merlot, 10% cabernet franc, 4% petit verdot, matured in French barriques (50% new) for 18 months. While full-bodied, this has already got its house in order, its cascade of red and black fruits refusing to lets the ample tannins dominate, oak adding to the discussion, but not taking sides. Screwcap. 14% alc. **Rating** 95 **To** 2037 $65

Semillon Sauvignon Blanc 2015 50/50%, fermented in stainless steel with some months lees contact. It's a zesty combination of Meyer lemon and lemongrass from the semillon, and guava and lychee from the sauvignon blanc; acidity is the glue that binds. Screwcap. 12.5% alc. **Rating** 94 **To** 2020 $22✪

Forest Grove Chardonnay 2014 Mendoza and French clones, fermented in French oak (25% new), 10 months on lees. An utterly seductive chardonnay, its delicacy not for those looking for bombastic chardonnays that can be fashioned in Margaret River; the accent is on supple fruit, the mouthfeel almost milky in its impact, yet fresh as a daisy. Screwcap. 13% alc. **Rating** 94 **To** 2024 $25 ✪

Cabernet Sauvignon 2012 Includes 7% cabernet franc, 5% malbec and 1% petit verdot; matured for 18 months in French barriques (45% new). An energetic wine with drive and clarity to its varietal fruit expression; as yet the oak and tannins are standoffish, but they will come to the party. Screwcap. 14% alc. **Rating** 94 **To** 2032 $50

Highland Heritage Estate ★★★★☆

4698 Mitchell Highway, Orange, NSW 2800 **Region** Orange
T (02) 6363 5602 **www.**daquinogroup.com.au **Open** 7 days 9–5
Winemaker John Hordern, Rex D'Aquino **Est.** 1984 **Dozens** 5000 **Vyds** 15ha

Owned and operated by the D'Aquino family, the vineyard, restaurant and cellar door are located on 125ha 3km east of the city of Orange. The vineyard is planted to 15ha of chardonnay, sauvignon blanc, riesling, pinot noir, merlot and shiraz. At an elevation of 900m, on deep alluvial and rich basalt soils, the cool to cold climate and long growing season produce elegant reds and crisp, clean whites. Exports to all major markets.

🍷🍷🍷🍷 **Rose 2014** Made with shiraz. It's dry and herbal, with redcurrant-like fruit flavours and a grippy finish. Food style. Screwcap. 12% alc. **Rating** 89 **To** 2017 $25 CM

Shiraz 2013 A medium-bodied mix of cherry-plum fruit and creamy oak, the latter generously applied. Spice notes expand the offer; tannin reins it in. Needs a few years to show its best. Screwcap. 14% alc. **Rating** 89 **To** 2024 $25 CM
Nikki D Riesling 2012 Orange and lime flavours bounce straight onto a well-flavoured palate before gradually running out of momentum through the finish. Screwcap. 8.5% alc. **Rating** 89 **To** 2021 $22 CM

Hill-Smith Estate ★★★★★

Flaxmans Valley Road, Eden Valley, SA 5235 **Region** Various
T (08) 8561 3200 **www**.hillsmithestate.com **Open** By appt
Winemaker Teresa Heuzenroeder **Est.** 1979 **Dozens** 5000 **Vyds** 12ha
The Eden Valley vineyard sits at an altitude of 510m, providing a cool climate that extends the growing season; rocky, acidic soil, coupled with winter rainfall and dry summers, results in modest crops. As an added bonus, the vineyard is surrounded by conservation park. Other white wines otherwise lacking a home have been put under the Hill-Smith Estate umbrella.

🍷🍷🍷🍷🍷 **Parish Vineyard Tasmania Coal River Valley Riesling 2015** Fascinating wine. Striking. Grapefruit, lemon pith, the juice of citrus. It's powerful in both fruit and personality, and has the length to match. Screwcap. 12.5% alc. **Rating** 96 **To** 2030 $30 CM ✪
Adelaide Hills Chardonnay 2014 Who said you can't have it all? This has the fruit, the flair, the winemaking, the spirit of summer. It tastes of grapefruit, principally, though toasty oak and stone fruit flavours help drive it powerfully along. If you sank a mine into this it would strike pure chardonnay pleasure. Screwcap. 13.5% alc. **Rating** 95 **To** 2020 $30 CM ✪

🍷🍷🍷🍷🍷 **Eden Valley Sauvignon Blanc 2015** Rating 93 **To** 2017 $22 CM ✪
Eden Valley Chardonnay 2014 Rating 91 **To** 2019 $24 CM

Hillbillé ★★★★

Blackwood Valley Estate, Balingup Road, Nannup, WA 6275 **Region** Blackwood Valley
T (08) 9481 0888 **www**.hillbille.com **Open** By appt
Winemaker Naturaliste Vintners (Bruce Dukes) **Est.** 1998 **Dozens** 5000 **Vyds** 18ha
Gary and Rai Bettridge have planted chardonnay, shiraz, cabernet sauvignon, merlot, semillon, sauvignon blanc and viognier on their 75ha family property. The vineyard is situated in the Blackwood Valley between Balingup and Nannup, which the RAC describes as 'the most scenic drive in the southwest of WA'. Part of the grape production is sold to other makers, the remainder vinified for Hillbillé. Exports to Japan, Singapore, Hong Kong and China.

🍷🍷🍷🍷🍷 **Estate Shiraz 2014** Good hue; has an aromatic, fruit-driven bouquet with glazed/preserved fruit aromas, then a more conventional red cherry and blueberry palate framed by good tannins and minerally acidity. Screwcap. 14.2% alc. **Rating** 91 **To** 2029 $18 ✪
Estate 2015 The semillon plays a prominent role in creating the aromas and flavours of the blend, with lemon blossom and zest coupled with crunchy acidity. A very neat wine at the price. Screwcap. 12.9% alc. **Rating** 90 **To** 2017 $18 ✪

Hillbrook Wines ★★★★

Cnr Hillbrook Road/Wheatley Coast Road, Quinninup, WA 6258 **Region** Pemberton
T (08) 9776 7202 **www**.hillbrookwines.com.au **Open** Fri–Sun & public hols 11–5
Winemaker Rob Diletti (Castle Rock Estate) **Est.** 1996 **Dozens** NFP **Vyds** 8ha
When Brian Ede and partner Anne Walsh left Alice Springs in 1996 to move to Pemberton, they made (in their words) the ultimate tree change. As well as establishing sauvignon blanc (3.4ha), merlot (2ha), semillon (1.2ha), pinot noir (0.8ha) and a smattering of chardonnay, they have 600 olive trees. A substantial portion of the estate-produced grapes are sold, only part vinified for the Hillbrook label.

ŶŶŶŶŶ **Chardonnay 2014** Clones 95 and 96, fermented in French oak (30% new) then matured for 10 months. Gleaming straw-green; this wine is almost too perfect, too unruffled as its white peach and grapefruit flavours flow across the mouth in precisely the way suggested by the bouquet. Then comes the price: again, dangerously perfect. Screwcap. 12.5% alc. **Rating** 94 **To** 2020 $26 **❂**

ŶŶŶŶŶ **Merlot 2012 Rating** 91 **To** 2022 $26

Hillcrest Vineyard ★★★★★

31 Phillip Road, Woori Yallock, Vic 3139 h**Region** Yarra Valley
T (03) 5964 6689 **www.**hillcrestvineyard.com.au **Open** By appt
Winemaker David and Tanya Bryant **Est.** 1970 **Dozens** 500 **Vyds** 8.1ha
The small, effectively dry grown vineyard was established by Graeme and Joy Sweet, who ultimately sold it to David and Tanya Bryant. The pinot noir, chardonnay, merlot and cabernet sauvignon grown on the property have always been of the highest quality and, when Coldstream Hills was in its infancy, were particularly important resources for it. For some years the wines were made by Phillip Jones (Bass Phillip), but the winemaking is now carried out onsite by David and Tanya. Exports to Singapore.

ŶŶŶŶŶ **Village Yarra Valley Pinot Noir 2014** Meat, spice, perfume, intrigue; apart from anything else, this is enormous value for money. Stem, plum and wood smoke flavours tang and seduce their way through the palate, firm tannin then bringing all the various flings and fancies home. Nothing here has been dumbed down. Diam. 13.9% alc. **Rating** 95 **To** 2022 $25 CM **❂**

ŶŶŶŶ **Village Chardonnay 2014 Rating** 89 **To** 2019 $25 CM
Premium Cabernet Sauvignon 2014 Rating 89 **To** 2028 $70 CM

Hither & Yon ★★★★

17 High Street, Willunga, SA 5172 **Region** McLaren Vale
T (08) 8556 2082 **www.**hitherandyon.com.au **Open** 7 days 11–4
Winemaker Richard Leask **Est.** 2012 **Dozens** 5000 **Vyds** 90ha
Brothers Richard and Malcolm Leask arrived as youngsters in McLaren Vale in the 1970s, following a family move from the Hunter Valley. Since father Ian Leask established the first family vineyard in '80, a further six sites spread across McLaren Vale have been added. Currently 13 varieties are planted over 90ha, with more plantings planned. In 2011 Richard and Malcolm started the Hither & Yon label, focusing on small single vineyard parcels, which change each year depending on the vintage and site. Richard manages all the vineyards and makes the wines, Malcolm handles production, sales and the historic cellar door. The labels feature the brand's ampersand, created by a different artist for each wine.

ŶŶŶŶŶ **Grenache Mataro 2015** 60% grenache, 40% mataro. Still somewhat callow, with a touch of reduction showing. Behind that the aromas and flavours are both savoury and sweet-fruited with raspberry, chocolate, and mulchy notes in the mix. Well-integrated tannin and acid keeps things fresh and in order. Screwcap. 14.2% alc. **Rating** 92 **To** 2022 $24 **❂**
Cabernet Sauvignon 2014 Definitive cabernet aromas hold sway, regional influence playing its part and oak chiming in. Evenly flavoured on the palate, the typically firm cabernet structure in good balance with the typical McLaren Vale generosity. Screwcap. 14% alc. **Rating** 91 **To** 2024 $24
McLaren Vale Shiraz Cabernet 2014 70/30%. Wow. McLaren Vale dark chocolate completely encases the fruit, tannin and oak of the wine – an extreme manifestation of the region, which can't be described as a fault. Some will love it, others will scratch their heads. Screwcap. 14.5% alc. **Rating** 90 **To** 2024 $38
Nero d'Avola 2015 Pressed to tank, bottled Jun '15. Attractive juicy red berry flavours; the wine doesn't need any oak amelioration; good length. Screwcap. 14.5% alc. **Rating** 90 **To** 2020 $29

Hobbs of Barossa Ranges

550 Flaxman's Valley Road, Angaston, SA 5353 **Region** Barossa Valley
T 0427 177 740 **www**.hobbsvintners.com.au **Open** At Artisans of Barossa
Winemaker Pete Schell, Chris Ringland (Consultant) **Est.** 1998 **Dozens** 1100 **Vyds** 6ha
Hobbs of Barossa Ranges is the high-profile, if somewhat challenging, venture of Greg and Allison Hobbs. The estate vineyards revolve around 1ha of shiraz planted in 1908, 1ha planted in '88, 1ha planted in '97 and 1.82ha planted in 2004. In '09 0.4ha of old white frontignac was removed, giving space for another small planting of shiraz. The viticultural portfolio is completed with 0.6ha of semillon planted in the 1960s, and an inspired 0.6ha of viognier ('88). All the wines, made by Peter Schell (at Spinifex), push the envelope. The only conventionally made wine is the Shiraz Viognier, with a production of 130 dozen. Gregor, an Amarone-style Shiraz in full-blooded table wine mode, and a quartet of dessert wines, are produced by cane cutting followed by further desiccation on racks. The Grenache comes from a Barossa floor vineyard, the Semillon, Viognier and White Frontignac from estate-grown grapes. Exports to the US, Denmark, Singapore, Taiwan and China.

🍷🍷🍷🍷🍷 **Gregor Shiraz 2013** Thick with blacked-fruited flavour. Warm with alcohol. Pulled with flavour-drenched tannin. It's a thunderstorm in a glass, rolling thunder and all. The power and length of it cannot be denied. Cork. 16% alc. **Rating** 95 To 2030 $140 CM

🍷🍷🍷🍷🍷 **1905 Shiraz 2013** Rating 93 To 2030 $130 CM
Tango Shiraz Viognier 2013 Rating 93 To 2028 $120 CM
Tin Lids Shiraz Cabernet Sauvignon 2013 Rating 93 To 2028 $50 CM

Hochkirch Wines

Hamilton Highway, Tarrington, Vic 3301 **Region** Henty
T (03) 5573 5200 **Open** 11–5 by appt
Winemaker John Nagorcka **Est.** 1997 **Dozens** 4000 **Vyds** 8ha
Jennifer and John Nagorcka have developed Hochkirch in response to the very cool climate: growing season temperatures are similar to those in Burgundy. A high-density planting pattern was implemented, with a low fruiting wire taking advantage of soil warmth in the growing season, and the focus was placed on pinot noir (5ha), with lesser quantities of riesling, chardonnay, semillon and shiraz. The Nagorckas have moved to certified biodynamic viticulture and the vines are not irrigated. Exports to Japan.

🍷🍷🍷🍷🍷 **Tarrington Vineyards Chardonnay 2015** I can't understand why a metal screwcap is any different from a glass bottle – neither is natural, both are machine-made. So why compromise the ability of the wine to mature with grace by using cork? 13% alc. **Rating** 90 To 2018 $50

🍷🍷🍷🍷 **Riesling 2015** Rating 89 To 2020 $35
Villages Pinot Noir 2014 Rating 89 To 2018 $32

Hoddles Creek Estate ★★★★★

505 Gembrook Road, Hoddles Creek, Vic 3139 **Region** Yarra Valley
T (03) 5967 4692 **www**.hoddlescreekestate.com.au **Open** By appt
Winemaker Franco D'Anna, Chris Bendle **Est.** 1997 **Dozens** 20 000 **Vyds** 33.3ha
The D'Anna family has established a vineyard on the property that has been in the family since 1960. The vineyards (chardonnay, pinot noir, sauvignon blanc, cabernet sauvignon, pinot gris, merlot and pinot blanc) are hand-pruned and hand-harvested, and a 300-tonne, split-level winery was built in 2003. Son Franco is the viticulturist and inspired winemaker; he started to work in the family liquor store at 13, graduating to chief wine buyer by the time he was 21, then completed a Bachelor of Commerce degree at Melbourne University before studying viticulture at CSU. A vintage at Coldstream Hills, then two years' vintage experience with Peter Dredge at Witchmount, and Mario Marson (ex Mount Mary) as mentor in the '03 vintage, has put an old head on young shoulders. The Wickhams Rd label uses grapes from

an estate vineyard in Gippsland, and purchased grapes from the Yarra Valley and Mornington Peninsula. Best Value Winery Wine Companion Awards '15. Exports to The Netherlands, Dubai, Singapore, Japan and China.

⚆⚆⚆⚆⚆ **1ᵉʳ Chardonnay 2014** Matured for 12 months in French barriques (30% new). Is Yarra Valley chardonnay to its bootstraps as you travel the almost unending path to the finish and aftertaste, grapefruit, nectarine and white peach the mile posts, grilled nuts here and there and acidity running precisely along the middle of the path. Screwcap. 13.2% alc. **Rating** 96 **To** 2025 $45 ✪

1ᵉʳ Yarra Valley Pinot Noir 2014 Matured in French barriques (35% new) for 12 months. Stylish and convincing, red and purple fruits on the bouquet taking immediate control of the vibrant palate which swirls around the tip of the tongue, building layers as it progresses through to the tangy, lively finish. The whole bunch tannins are the touchstone of the wine. Screwcap. 13.2% alc. **Rating** 96 **To** 2024 $45 ✪

Yarra Valley Chardonnay 2014 'Estate-grown, no additions' is a cryptic note on the back label. It has phenomenal power and drive, a pure rendition of grapes from an immaculately tended vineyard. Natural acidity gives a special quality to the wine's shimmer of grapefruit and white peach, French oak merely an observer. Screwcap. 13.2% alc. **Rating** 95 **To** 2020 $20 ✪

Yarra Valley Pinot Gris 2015 Says Franco D'Anna, 'I was fed up making the same boring wine.' All that has now changed. 70% goes to (old) barrels, and 30% spends time on skins. 'Essentially we are treating this like a red wine.' It tastes of apple and slate, spice and almonds. It has mouthfeel. Screwcap. 12.5% alc. **Rating** 95 **To** 2016 $22 CM ✪

Syberia Yarra Valley Chardonnay 2013 It unfurls slowly, its white peach and crunchy apple flavours kissed by notes of almond, cream, toast and oatmeal. The finish is minerally and long, but elegant. It doesn't try too hard which, much like watching Mark Waugh at the crease in days gone by, has you wondering whether it tries quite hard enough. Screwcap. 12.7% alc. **Rating** 94 **To** 2023 $60 CM

Yarra Valley Pinot Blanc 2015 No matter how it's cut or diced, this variety just seems to love the Hoddles Creek lifestyle. This release feels soft in the mouth but has a quartz-like, mineral cut to the finish. It's pale in colour but offers plenty to wrap your lips around. It's absolutely worth seeking out – at an extremely attractive price. Screwcap. 12.5% alc. **Rating** 94 **To** 2020 $22 CM ✪

⚆⚆⚆⚆⚆ **Wickhams Road Chardonnay 2015** **Rating** 93 **To** 2021 $18 CM ✪
Wickhams Road Pinot Noir 2015 **Rating** 93 **To** 2024 $18 CM ✪
Yarra Valley Pinot Noir 2014 **Rating** 93 **To** 2024 $20 ✪
Wickhams Road Gippsland Chardonnay 2015 **Rating** 92 **To** 2021 $18 CM ✪
Wickhams Road Gippsland Pinot Noir 2015 **Rating** 91 **To** 2022 $18 CM ✪

Hollick

★★★★☆

Riddoch Highway, Coonawarra, SA 5263 **Region** Coonawarra
T (08) 8737 2318 **www**.hollick.com **Open** Mon–Fri 9–5, w'ends & public hols 10–5
Winemaker Ian Hollick, Joe Cory **Est.** 1983 **Dozens** 40 000 **Vyds** 87ha
In April 2014 the Hollick family announced that a major investment had been made in their business by the large Chinese group Hong Kong Yingda Investment Co. Ltd. Involved in hospitality and tourism in China, part of its business involves vineyard and winery operations. The Hollick family continues to own a part of the business, and continues to manage it in the same way as usual. Major benefits to Hollick are working capital and access to the Chinese market; and Hong Kong Yingda Investment Co. Ltd will gain expertise from the Hollick family. Exports to most major markets.

⚆⚆⚆⚆⚆ **Ravenswood Cabernet Sauvignon 2013** Velvet glove and the power to match. Blackcurrant, leather, bay leaves and toasty oak characters pour on the flavour before tannin gives the finish a bit of rumble. Screwcap. 14% alc. **Rating** 95 **To** 2030 $77 CM

🍷🍷🍷🍷🍷 The Nectar 2015 Rating 93 To 2021 $25 CM ○
Wilgha Shiraz 2013 Rating 92 To 2020 $54 CM
Neilson's Block Merlot 2013 Rating 92 To 2026 $54 CM
The Gondolier Barbera 2014 Rating 92 To 2020 $29 CM
The Bard Shiraz 2014 Rating 91 To 2021 $24 CM
Tannery Block Cabernet Sauvignon Merlot 2013 Rating 90 To 2025
$25 CM

Hollydene Estate   ★★★★

3483 Golden Highway, Jerrys Plains, NSW 2330 **Region** Hunter Valley
T (02) 6576 4021 **www**.hollydeneestate.com **Open** 7 days 9–5
Winemaker Matt Burton **Est.** 1965 **Dozens** 2000 **Vyds** 40ha
Karen Williams has three vineyards and associated properties, all established in the 1960s.
They are Hollydene Estate, Wybong Estate and Arrowfield, the latter one of the original
vinous landmarks in the Upper Hunter. The three vineyards produce grapes for the Juul and
Hollydene Estate labels. Exports to Indonesia and China.

🍷🍷🍷🍷🍷 Juul Blanc de Blancs 2008 A refreshingly pale straw hue announces a
scintillatingly youthful blanc de blancs that rejoices in the lemon and apple
freshness of Mornington Peninsula chardonnay and tones it impeccably with
a light dosage of 6g/l. 6 years on lees. More than a year in bottle (Dec '14
disgorgement) has done nothing to interrupt graceful, primary fruit purity, while
enhancing integration and texture. Great potential yet. Diam. 12.5% alc. **Rating** 94
To 2023 $50 TS

🍷🍷🍷🍷🍷 Estate Upper Hunter Valley Semillon 2014 Rating 90 To 2020 $22

Holm Oak   ★★★★★

11 West Bay Road, Rowella, Tas 7270 **Region** Northern Tasmania
T (03) 6394 7577 **www**.holmoakvineyards.com.au **Open** 7 days 11–5
Winemaker Rebecca Duffy **Est.** 1983 **Dozens** 10 000 **Vyds** 11.62ha
Holm Oak takes its name from its grove of oak trees, planted around the beginning of the 20th
century and originally intended for the making of tennis racquets. Winemaker Rebecca Duffy,
daughter of owners Ian and Robyn Wilson, has extensive winemaking experience in Australia
and California, and husband Tim, a viticultural agronomist, manages the vineyard (pinot noir,
cabernet sauvignon, chardonnay, riesling, sauvignon blanc and pinot gris, with small amounts
of merlot, cabernet franc and arneis). Exports to the US, Canada, Norway and Japan.

🍷🍷🍷🍷🍷 The Wizard Pinot Noir 2014 Mainly selected from six rows of the oldest vines,
the balance from newer plantings of clones MV6 and D4V2, matured in French
oak for over 12 months (50% new, 40% 1yo). This is a profound pinot with a
voluptuous array of plum and black cherry fruit. The new oak is evident, but
integrated and balanced. Screwcap. 13.5% alc. **Rating** 96 **To** 2029 $60 ○
Pinot Noir 2014 Matured for 9 months in French oak (20% new). Red cherry,
strawberry and plum aromas and lush red fruits fill the palate, balanced by fine
tannins and quality oak. Screwcap. 13% alc. **Rating** 95 **To** 2024 $32 ○
Hot Shot Pinot Noir 2014 Only two barrels selected, one fermented with
50% whole bunches/50% whole berries, the other 100% whole bunches. A
very complex savoury style with lots on offer from the bouquet and palate
alike; satsuma plum, dark cherry and spice flavours fire the first shot, texture and
structure the next, the long, lingering finish and aftertaste the coup de grace.
Screwcap. 13.5% alc. **Rating** 95 **To** 2027 $130
Pinot Gris 2015 20% was wild-fermented in used oak barrels, the remainder
cool-fermented in tank. This approach has paid big dividends, with a fragrant and
flowery pear and jasmine bouquet, the palate with pear and a hint of star anise.
Screwcap. 13.5% alc. **Rating** 94 **To** 2017 $25 ○

ŸŸŸŸ♀ **Arneis 2015** Rating 93 To 2018 $25 **◐**
The Wizard Chardonnay 2014 Rating 91 To 2020 $60
Riesling 2015 Rating 90 To 2018 $25
Sauvignon Blanc 2015 Rating 90 To 2017 $25

Home Hill ★★★★★

38 Nairn Street, Ranelagh, Tas 7109 **Region** Southern Tasmania
T (03) 6264 1200 **www.**homehillwines.com.au **Open** 7 days 10–5
Winemaker Gilli and Paul Lipscombe **Est.** 1994 **Dozens** 2000 **Vyds** 5ha
Terry and Rosemary Bennett planted their first 0.5ha of vines in 1994 on gentle slopes
in the beautiful Huon Valley. Between '94 and '99 the plantings were increased to 3ha of
pinot noir, 1.5ha of chardonnay and 0.5ha of sylvaner. Home Hill has had great success with
its exemplary Pinot Noirs, consistent multi-trophy and gold medal winners in the ultra-
competitive Tasmanian Wine Show. Impressive enough, but pale into insignificance in the
wake of winning the Jimmy Watson Trophy at the Melbourne Wine Awards '15.

ŸŸŸŸŸ **Kelly's Reserve Pinot Noir 2014** 10 months in French oak (40% new).
Takes Home Hill's Estate Pinot onto another level of intensity and length, an
object lesson in combining power with finesse thanks to its perfect balance and
mouthfeel. Red and black cherry fruits dance in lockstep with superb tannins; a
waft of cedary French oak adds another dimension. Winner of the Jimmy Watson
Trophy '15. Screwcap. 13.8% alc. **Rating** 97 To 2029 $75 **◐**

ŸŸŸŸŸ **Estate Pinot Noir 2013** 10 months in French oak (20% new). Stood out even
as a young wine for the power and impact of its black cherries, savoury spices
and persistent tannins, its impressively long palate in the heartland of the long-
lived Home Hill style. Top gold Class 40 Melbourne Wine Awards '15. Screwcap.
13.9% alc. **Rating** 96 To 2025 $36 **◐**
Estate Pinot Noir 2014 10 months in oak (20% new). Faultless colour; the
bouquet and palate fill the senses with perfumed red cherry and blueberry fruits,
delicately yet firmly encased in a film of fine tannins that provide both balance and
utterly convincing length. Screwcap. 13.5% alc. **Rating** 95 To 2025 $38

Horner Wines ★★★☆

12 Shedden Street, Cessnock, NSW 2325 **Region** Hunter Valley
T 0427 201 391 **www.**nakedwines.com.au **Open** Not
Winemaker Ashley Horner **Est.** 2013 **Dozens** 6500 **Vyds** 12ha
Horner Wines is the family venture of Ashley and Lauren Horner, with viticultural input
from Glen and Josephine Horner. It began when verdelho, chardonnay, viognier and shiraz
were planted; the vineyard is now fully certified organic. Grapes are also sourced from organic
vineyards in Orange and Cowra. Ashley had a 14-year career working at Rosemount Estate,
Penfolds, Kamberra Estate, Saint Clair (NZ) and Mount Pleasant, ultimately becoming
winemaker at Tamburlaine and completing a Diploma in Wine Technology at Dookie
College. Lauren has a degree in hospitality/tourism, and is now involved in the running of
Horner Wines. The move from grapegrowing to winemaking was precipitated by the fall in
demand for grapes, and they sell the wines through www.nakedwines.com.au

ŸŸŸŸ **Family Reserve Chardonnay 2015** Light in flavour but it has personality.
Lactose, chalk and hay-like characters play around a core of zesty stone fruit.
Screwcap. 12.5% alc. **Rating** 89 To 2019 $24 CM
Family Reserve Viognier 2015 Barrel-fermented. It's a soft, almost easygoing
white with sweet pear, stone fruit and citrus flavours cruising through the palate.
Not hard to enjoy. Screwcap. 12% alc. **Rating** 89 To 2017 $23 CM
Little Jack Organic Riesling 2015 Apple, lemon sorbet and blossomy flavours/
aromas make for delicious, accessible drinking. It's not intense, or long, but it
certainly is enjoyable. Screwcap. 12.4% alc. **Rating** 88 To 2019 $17 CM **◐**

Little Jack Organic Sauvignon Blanc 2015 Packed with sweet fruit of various description. Just lacks a bit of finish. Screwcap. 12.4% alc. **Rating** 88 **To** 2016 $17 CM ✪

Houghton ★★★★★

148 Dale Road, Middle Swan, WA 6065 **Region** Swan Valley
T (08) 9274 9540 **www**.houghton-wines.com.au **Open** 7 days 10–5
Winemaker Ross Pamment **Est.** 1836 **Dozens** NFP

Houghton's reputation was once largely dependent on its (then) White Burgundy, equally good when young or 5 years old. In the last 20 years its portfolio has changed out of all recognition, with a kaleidoscopic range of high quality wines from the Margaret River, Frankland River, Great Southern and Pemberton regions to the fore. The Jack Mann and Gladstones red wines stand at the forefront, the Wisdom range covering all varietal bases in great style. Nor should the value-for-money Stripe brand be ignored. To borrow a saying of the late Jack Mann, 'There are no bad wines here.' With a history of 180 years, its future now lies in the hands of Accolade Wines. Exports to the UK and Asia.

🍷🍷🍷🍷🍷 **Gladstones Margaret River Cabernet Sauvignon 2013** A fitting tribute to Margaret River's father, Dr John Gladstones. A Cirque du Soleil wine, immensely complex, yet feline and sure-footed as it plays with fresh cassis fruit, fine-grained sandy tannins and French oak of the highest quality, rearranging these components again and again. Screwcap. 13.5% alc. **Rating** 97 **To** 2048 $85 ✪

Jack Mann Cabernet Sauvignon 2013 The most powerful and concentrated of all the deluxe/icon wines in the Houghton range, a distillation of blackcurrant, black olive, bay leaf and cedary oak, the tannins lined up in a haughty (sorry for the pun) support. No compromise here – the wine would have pleased Jack Mann enormously. Screwcap. 14% alc. **Rating** 97 **To** 2050 $115 ✪

🍷🍷🍷🍷🍷 **Gladstones Margaret River Cabernet Sauvignon 2014** It thrives in its moderate alcohol, which in turn serves to emphasise the cassis/blackcurrant and black olive fruit; the tannins, too, are precisely weighted. However, the new French oak, while correct for the medium and long term, still needs time to fully integrate. Screwcap. 13.5% alc. **Rating** 96 **To** 2049 $85

CW Ferguson Great Southern Cabernet Malbec 2013 The bouquet offers blackcurrant, plum, tobacco and cedar, the gloriously juicy fruit flavours slipping down the palate and into the finish without any threatening move from the tannins (ripe and well behaved), and the oak (generous, but high quality). Screwcap. 14% alc. **Rating** 96 **To** 2039 $60 ✪

The Bandit Frankland River Shiraz 2014 Fluid, supple red with anise, blackberry and plum notes delivered in delicious style. Earth/mineral and pepper notes play a secondary but important role. The glory of the medium-weight red. Winner of the Stodart Trophy at the Qld Wine Show. Screwcap. 13.5% alc. **Rating** 94 **To** 2025 $20 CM ✪

Crofters Frankland River Cabernet Sauvignon 2014 The bouquet has that elevated aroma unique to Frankland River, a purity of dark/cassis fruit, the palate following suit with one major exception: the powdery, persistent tannins on the finish. All this is encompassed in a perfectly balanced medium-bodied framework, guaranteeing a multi-decade life. Screwcap. 13.5% alc. **Rating** 94 **To** 2034 $19 ✪

House of Arras ★★★★★

Bay of Fires, 40 Baxters Road, Pipers River, Tas 7252 **Region** Northern Tasmania
T (03) 6362 7622 **www**.houseofarras.com.au **Open** 7 days 10–5
Winemaker Ed Carr **Est.** 1995 **Dozens** NFP

The rise and rise of the fortunes of the House of Arras has been due to two things: first, the exceptional skills of winemaker Ed Carr, and second, its access to high quality Tasmanian chardonnay and pinot noir. While there have been distinguished sparkling wines made in Tasmania for many years, none has so consistently scaled the heights of Arras. The complexity, texture and structure of the wines are akin to that of Bollinger RD and Krug; the connection stems from the 7–15+ years the wines spend on lees prior to disgorgement.

YYYYY **Blanc de Blancs 2005** Fermentation and 100% mlf take place on faintly cloudy juice. The wine then spent 8 years on yeast lees before disgorgement in early '15, the dosage 8.4g/l. Gleaming yellow-gold, it is everything you could wish for, with luscious grapefruit and nectarine fruits balanced to perfection by the brioche/biscuit flavours and creamy mouthfeel from the long time on lees. Cork. 12.5% alc. **Rating** 97 **To** 2017 $80 ✪

YYYYY **Grand Vintage 2006** 67% chardonnay, 33% pinot noir. On tirage for over 7 years, it has the ultrafine bead that only comes with such age; the complex bouquet of toast and nougat leads into a palate with exceptional structure and freshness, the latter derived partly from the use of some new oak with the base wines. Cork. 12.5% alc. **Rating** 96 **To** 2018 $70 ✪

Blanc de Blancs 2006 The delightfully toasty/nutty/honey personality of mature chardonnay has emerged with clarity and jubilation, backed by impeccably focused and enduring acidity, perfectly balanced with a low dosage of less than 6g/l. Cork. 12.5% alc. **Rating** 96 **To** 2021 $80 TS

20th Anniversary Late Disgorged 2003 This Late Disgorged is one of Ed Carr's greatest achievements. This is a cuvee of breathtaking energy, propelling the primary lemon and white peach of an almost two-thirds majority of chardonnay with a laser line of enduring acidity. Nutty, bready, lees-derived complexity harmonises impeccably with a core of fruit integrity. Cork. 12.9% alc. **Rating** 96 **To** 2023 $150 TS

20th Anniversary Late Disgorged 1998 Released for the third time, here after a glorious 16 years on lees, this is a cuvee that rejoices in the grand tertiary characters of green olive and warm hearth. Textural grip sits comfortably in its warm, glowing, succulent secondary fruit, lingering with enduring persistence. Cork. 12.5% alc. **Rating** 96 **To** 2017 $350 TS

Rose 2005 75% pinot noir, 25% chardonnay. Salmon-bronze hued, it has grip and length, bright and clear strawberries (from the addition of pinot table wine) and a potent spice and truffle tapestry of flavours. Over 6 years on tirage, and over 6 months on cork (which Carr believes is invaluable). 12.5% alc. **Rating** 96 **To** 2018 $80

Grand Vintage 2007 75% chardonnay; has exciting fruit energy of lemons, apples and white stone fruits. The reductive tendency of chardonnay has been captured in grilled toast and struck flint nuances. A low dosage of just 6g/l is all it needs. Wonderfully fine, lees-derived mouthfeel and outstanding persistence confirm a true Grand Vintage. Cork. 12.5% alc. **Rating** 95 **To** 2019 $70 TS

Brut Elite NV Cuvee 801. Built on the outstanding '08 harvest with elegantly fine lemon and apple fruit layered around wonderful texture and fine-tuned almond meal lees complexity, and compelling nuances of struck flint reduction. Cork. 12.5% alc. **Rating** 94 **To** 2020 $50 TS

YYYYY **A by Arras Premium Cuvee NV Rating** 93 **To** 2017 $25 TS ✪

House of Cards ★★★★★

3220 Caves Road, Yallingup, WA 6282 **Region** Margaret River
T (08) 9755 2583 **www**.houseofcardswine.com.au **Open** 7 days 10–5
Winemaker Travis Wray **Est.** 2011 **Dozens** 4000 **Vyds** 12ha
House of Cards is owned and operated by Elizabeth and Travis Wray, Travis managing the vineyard and making the wines, Elizabeth managing sales and marketing. The name of the winery is a reflection of the gamble that all viticulturists and winemakers face every vintage: 'You have to play the hand you are dealt by Mother Nature.' They are involved in every aspect of the business, from growing the grapes to marketing and sales. They only use estate-grown grapes, open-top fermentation, hand-plunging and manual basket-pressing. It's certainly doing it the hard way, but it must seem all worthwhile when they produce wines of such quality.

ΨΨΨΨΨ Jack Single Vineyard Malbec 2014 Matured for 18 months in French oak (40% new). It is soft and voluptuous now but the finish wears a serious face of tannin; this is best left alone in a cool, dark place awhile. Leather, blackberry, violets and studs of dried herbs, even tobacco. It's a brute, in a good way. Cork. 14.5% alc. Rating 96 To 2040 $48 CM ✪
Limited Release Ace of Spades 2014 Cabernet malbec. Stick it straight in the cellar. It shows substantial flavours of dark chocolate, cassis, bay leaves, leather and earth, but the curls of tannin and the long reverberations of flavour suggest that this is going to mature like a dream. Cork. 14.7% alc. Rating 95 To 2035 $65 CM

ΨΨΨΨΨ The Royals Single Vineyard Chardonnay 2015 Rating 93 To 2021 $32 CM
The Joker Single Vineyard Semillon Blanc 2015 Rating 92 To 2017 $21 CM ✪
The Joker Single Vineyard Merlot 2014 Rating 92 To 2026 $24 CM ✪
The Royals Single Vineyard Cabernet 2014 Rating 92 To 2027 $44 CM
The Joker Rose 2015 Rating 91 To 2017 $21 CM ✪
The Joker Single Vineyard Shiraz 2014 Rating 91 To 2025 $24 CM

Howard Vineyard   ★★★★☆

53 Bald Hills Road, Nairne, SA 5252 **Region** Adelaide Hills
T (08) 8188 0203 **www.howardvineyard.com** **Open** Fri–Sun 10–5
Winemaker Tom Northcott **Est.** 2005 **Dozens** 6000 **Vyds** 60ha
This dates back to the late 1990s, with the establishment of two vineyards at different locations in the Adelaide Hills. The Schoenthal Vineyard, near Lobethal, at an elevation of 440–500m, is planted primarily to sauvignon blanc and chardonnay, with smaller amounts of pinot noir and pinot gris. The Howard Vineyard is at a lower elevation, and the slightly warmer site has been planted to sauvignon blanc, chardonnay, semillon, cabernet sauvignon, shiraz, viognier and cabernet franc. The grapes not required for the Howard Vineyard label are sold to other winemakers. Tom Northcott graduated with a Bachelor of Viticulture and Oenology from Adelaide University, having completed vintages in Languedoc (France) and with Grant Burge, Peter Lehmann, Houghton and Bay of Fires. Exports to Hong Kong and China.

ΨΨΨΨΨ Amos Adelaide Hills Chardonnay 2015 Dijon clones 76 and 95, matured for 9 months in French oak (33% new). These are two outstanding clones, and the winemaking has brought out the best in them: picked at the right time, whole bunch-pressing, yeast and oak handling beyond reproach. A lovely, elegant, fruit-filled wine. Screwcap. 13% alc. Rating 96 To 2025 $35 ✪
Clover Adelaide Hills 2015 Flavour and mouthfeel. There's a lot to hang your hat on here. Sweet pea, tropical fruit, gravel, spice. Concentration of flavour is up there too. Screwcap. 13.2% alc. Rating 94 To 2016 $25 CM ✪
Picnic Adelaide Hills Rose 2015 On the money, and then some, once again. Rose to be reckoned with. Dry and spicy but jubey and floral as well. Foot in many camps but all of them placed with care. Made with 100% cabernet franc. Just right. Ditto value. Screwcap. 13.2% alc. Rating 94 To 2017 $19 CM ✪

ΨΨΨΨΨ Picnic Adelaide Hills Sauvignon Blanc 2015 Rating 92 To 2016 $19 CM ✪
Clover Riesling 2015 Rating 91 To 2022 $25 CM
Clover Adelaide Hills Pinot Gris 2015 Rating 91 To 2017 $25 CM
Clover Adelaide Hills Pinot Chardonnay NV Rating 90 To 2017 $25 CM

Hugh Hamilton Wines   ★★★★★

94 McMurtrie Road, McLaren Vale, SA 5171 **Region** McLaren Vale
T (08) 8323 8689 **www.hughhamiltonwines.com.au** **Open** 7 days 11–5
Winemaker Peter Leske **Est.** 1991 **Dozens** 20 000 **Vyds** 21.14ha
In 2014, fifth-generation family member Hugh Hamilton handed over the reins to daughter Mary, the sixth generation of the family. It was she who developed the irreverent black sheep packaging. But it's more than simply marketing: the business will continue to embrace both mainstream and alternative varieties, its 85-year-old shiraz and 65-year-old cabernet

sauvignon at its Blewitt Springs vineyard providing the ability to develop the Pure Black label. This reflects changes in the way the vines are trellised, picking and fermenting in small open fermenters, using gravity for wine movements, and maturation in high quality French oak. The cellar door is lined with the original jarrah from Vat 15 of the historic Hamilton's Ewell winery, the largest wooden vat ever built in the southern hemisphere. Exports to the UK, the US, Canada, Sweden, Finland, Malaysia and China.

ㅇㅇㅇㅇㅇ **Black Blood III Black Sheep Vineyard Shiraz 2014** From the light, sandy soils of Blewitt Springs. The finest and purest of the trio, with some red fruit notes among the black; more spicy and fragrant, and a long, lively finish and aftertaste; the tannins are particularly fine. Screwcap. 14.6% alc. **Rating** 96 **To** 2034 $79

Black Blood II Church Vineyard Shiraz 2014 Black Blood II has loose dark alluvial soils over deep clay. Very good texture and structure, generous without going OTT; shares the blackberry core common to all three Black Blood wines. There is a lift to the back palate that provides light and shade in the texture, the juicy finish long and particularly compelling. Screwcap. 14.6% alc. **Rating** 95 **To** 2034 $79

Tonnellerie Damy Single Barrel Cellar Vineyard Shiraz 2014 Sequential barrel maturation for 20 months, 8 months new, then 12 months used. 24 dozen made. Deep crimson-purple; this has extraordinary power and thrust, part inky black fruits, part tannins, part distinctly toasty oak, licorice and a dab of dark chocolate. Screwcap. 14.5% alc. **Rating** 95 **To** 2039 $50

Tonnellerie Francois Freres Single Barrel Cellar Vineyard Shiraz 2014 The same sequential barrel maturation for 20 months as Damy, 24 dozen made. Less powerful, the reverse of expectations, the Francois Freres oak tamed by the power of McLaren Vale shiraz, espresso notes on the bouquet and palate. Screwcap. 14.5% alc. **Rating** 94 **To** 2030 $50

Tonnellerie Remond Single Barrel Cellar Vineyard McLaren Vale Shiraz 2014 The same sequential barrel maturation for 20 months, 24 dozen made. A highly fragrant spicy/charry/aniseed bouquet, the black fruits and persistent, but ripe, tannins running through the long, full-bodied palate. Screwcap. 14.5% alc. **Rating** 94 **To** 2034 $50

Shearer's Cut Shiraz 2014 From bush vines planted in 1910, 120 dozen made. Elegant and lively, the fruit almost sweet, the bouquet perfumed, the tannins fine – yet it is intense and ready for a long life. Screwcap. 14.5% alc. **Rating** 94 **To** 2034 $24 ✪

ㅇㅇㅇㅇㅇ **Black Blood I Cellar Vineyard Shiraz 2014** Rating 93 To 2034 $79
Jekyll & Hyde McLaren Vale Shiraz Viognier 2014 Rating 93 To 2034 $50
The Rascal McLaren Vale Shiraz 2014 Rating 92 To 2030 $29
Black Ops McLaren Vale Shiraz Saperavi 2014 Rating 91 To 2030 $32
Oddball McLaren Vale Saperavi 2014 Rating 90 To 2024 $50

Hugo ★★★★☆

246 Elliott Road, McLaren Flat, SA 5171 **Region** McLaren Vale
T (08) 8383 0098 **www**.hugowines.com.au **Open** Mon–Fri 10–5, Sat 12–5, Sun 10.30–5
Winemaker John Hugo **Est.** 1982 **Dozens** 7000 **Vyds** 25ha
Came from relative obscurity to prominence in the late 1980s with some lovely ripe, sweet reds, which, while strongly American oak-influenced, were quite outstanding. It picked up the pace again after a dull period in the mid-'90s, and has made the most of the recent run of good vintages. The estate plantings include shiraz, cabernet sauvignon, chardonnay, grenache and sauvignon blanc, with part of the grape production sold to others. Exports to the UK and Canada.

ㅇㅇㅇㅇㅇ **Reserve McLaren Vale Shiraz 2013** Substantial red in all respects: oak, fruit and tannin. This is a tiptop example of the old (but never out of) fashioned blood and thunder style. Thick blackberry, coffee grounds, bitumen and ground, clovey

spice. It's all there, in excellent fettle, thoroughly unapologetic. Screwcap. 14.5% alc.
Rating 95 To 2030 $55 CM

 McLaren Vale Shiraz 2013 Rating 92 To 2022 $25 CM ◐

Hungerford Hill ★★★★★

2450 Broke Road, Pokolbin, NSW 2320 **Region** Hunter Valley
T (02) 4998 0710 **www**.hungerfordhill.com.au **Open** Sun–Thurs 10–5, Fri–Sat 10–6
Winemaker Adrian Lockhart **Est.** 1967 **Dozens** 17 000 **Vyds** 5ha
Since acquiring Hungerford Hill a decade ago, the Kirby family has sought to build on the
Hungerford Hill story that began over 40 years ago. James Kirby was involved in his family's
engineering business during its growth to become one of Australia's leading automotive
refrigeration and air-conditioning manufacturers. The winemaking team continues to make
wines from the Hunter Valley and from the cool climate regions of Hilltops and Tumbarumba.
Exports to all major markets.

♥♥♥♥♥ Cote D'Or Hunter Valley Shiraz 2014 Super complexity and, more
importantly, drinkability. This cashes in on the vintage. Coffee-cream characters,
plenty of earth and spice, and an oozing shift of cherry-plum flavour. It's right
in the groove of what you'd expect of Hunter shiraz, but the revs are higher, the
finish longer. Screwcap. 13.5% alc. **Rating** 96 To 2038 $65 CM ◐
Blackberry Vineyard Hunter Valley Semillon 2011 Quite the looker. This
is perfumed and intense and beguiling as a result. It's at a beautiful stage of its
life; fresh but attractively (and gently) wizened. Worthy of a large-bowled glass.
Screwcap. 10% alc. **Rating** 95 To 2021 $55 CM
Gundagai Shiraz 2014 The road to Gundagai is littered with broken shiraz, but
this isn't one of them. This is good tucker. Full of fruit but boxed by savouriness.
Splashed with coffeed oak. Meaty, but as no more than a nuance. If you see it, buy.
Screwcap. 13.5% alc. **Rating** 95 To 2027 $30 CM ◐
Hilltops Cabernet Sauvignon 2014 Just enough lusciousness to sink you
straight into its world. Plums, fleshy blackcurrant, musk and vanilla, all delivered
with sheer exuberance. Both oak and fruit are allowed to let rip, to excellent effect.
Screwcap. 13.2% alc. **Rating** 95 To 2030 $36 CM
Tumbarumba Pinot Meunier 2014 Sweet, sour and savoury at once, a little
reductive too, and – if you hadn't already twigged – chockablock with interest.
Desperately light in colour but there's more than one way to skin a cat; this is a
wine of presence. Screwcap. 12.4% alc. **Rating** 94 To 2022 $36 CM

♥♥♥♥♡ Hunter Valley Shiraz 2014 Rating 93 To 2032 $36 CM
Tumbarumba Pinot Gris 2015 Rating 92 To 2016 $27 CM
Tumbarumba Pinot Noir 2014 Rating 91 To 2020 $36 CM
Hunter Valley Semillon 2015 Rating 90 To 2025 $27 CM

Huntington Estate ★★★★★

Ulan Road, Mudgee, NSW 2850 **Region** Mudgee
T 1800 995 931 **www**.huntingtonestate.com.au **Open** Mon–Sat 10–5, Sun 10–4
Winemaker Tim Stevens **Est.** 1969 **Dozens** 15 000 **Vyds** 43.8ha
Since taking ownership of Huntington Estate from the founding Roberts family, Tim Stevens
has sensibly refrained from making major changes. The policy of having older vintage wines
available is continuing, making the cellar door a first port of call for visitors to Mudgee. On
the other side, the Music Festival suffers only one problem: there are not enough tickets to
satisfy the demand. It really has a well-deserved life of its own, and will do so for years to
come. Exports to China.

♥♥♥♥♥ Special Reserve Mudgee Shiraz 2013 Deep colour; there are enthusiastic
contributions of fruit, oak and tannins; because these are all in balance, the Reserve
classification makes eminent sense, underwritten by lovely, glossy black cherry and

blackberry flavours running through the length of the palate. Screwcap. 14.3% alc. Rating 95 To 2033 $40

🍷🍷🍷🍷🍷 Mudgee Semillon 2015 Rating 93 To 2029 $22○
Block 3 Mudgee Cabernet Sauvignon 2013 Rating 92 To 2028 $70

Hurley Vineyard ★★★★★

101 Balnarring Road, Balnarring, Vic 3926 **Region** Mornington Peninsula
T (03) 5931 3000 **www.**hurleyvineyard.com.au **Open** 1st w'end each month 11–5
Winemaker Kevin Bell **Est.** 1998 **Dozens** 1000 **Vyds** 3.5ha
It's never as easy as it seems. Despite leading busy city lives, Kevin Bell and wife Tricia Byrnes have done most of the hard work in establishing Hurley Vineyard themselves, with family and friends. Most conspicuously, Kevin has completed the Applied Science (Wine Science) degree at CSU, drawing on Nat White for consultancy advice, and occasionally from Phillip Jones of Bass Phillip and Domaine Fourrier in Gevrey Chambertin. He has not allowed a significant heart issue to prevent him continuing with his first love.

🍷🍷🍷🍷🍷 Garamond Mornington Peninsula Pinot Noir 2014 All three Hurley Pinots are vinified the same way, the difference the clones, here 100% MV6: a total of 21 days on skins, all spend 18 months in Troncais French oak (33% new) without any disturbance, each assembled and classified barrel by barrel. This wine is slightly more advanced in colour than its siblings, but the bouquet is highly expressive, with red fruits (cherry/strawberry) to the fore and a foundation of savoury/earthy tannins and oak. This is the most densely packed of the trio. Diam. 13.5% alc. Rating 96 To 2026 $80
Lodestone Mornington Peninsula Pinot Noir 2014 33% each MV6 and 114, 16.5% each of 115 and 77 clones. The clonal mix is the most complex, and Burgundian makers would incline towards this wine simply because of that fact. It certainly gains velocity on the back-palate and finish, and is the most seductive of the trio. Diam. 13.4% alc. Rating 95 To 2024 $70
Hommage Mornington Peninsula Pinot Noir 2014 90% G5V16, 10% MV6 clones. A perfumed bouquet abounding with red fruits sets the scene for a lively, juicy palate seamlessly woven with gently foresty tannins; the ultra-tight low-toast oak can be seen clearly. Plum joins the red fruits, the mouthfeel silky and smooth through the mid-palate, picking up some sous bois on the finish. Diam. 13.6% alc. Rating 94 To 2021 $70

Hutton Vale Farm ★★★★★

Stone Jar Road, Angaston, SA 5353 **Region** Eden Valley
T (08) 8564 8270 **www.**huttonvale.com **Open** By appt
Winemaker Kym Teusner **Est.** 1960 **Dozens** 600 **Vyds** 27ha
John Howard Angas arrived in SA in 1843, and inter alia gave his name to Angaston, purchasing and developing significant farming property close to the still embryonic town. He named part of this Hutton Vale, and it is this property that is now owned and occupied by his great-great-grandson John and wife Jan Angas. In 2012, the Angas family and Teusner Wines shook hands on a new partnership arrangement, under which the Angases grow the grapes, and Kym Teusner is responsible for the winemaking, sales and marketing of Hutton Vale wines. The vineyards in question first caught Kym's attention when he was at Torbreck, and he fulfilled a long-term ambition with the new agreement. Just when the future seemed assured, the vineyards were badly affected by a grass fire in August '14. While much of the vineyard will ultimately be regenerated, some of the oldest grenache vines were completely destroyed, as were 55 of the magnificent 500yo gum trees that are part of the striking landscape of Hutton Vale. Small quantities of its wines are exported to China.

🍷🍷🍷🍷🍷 Shiraz 2012 Matured for 2 years in French puncheons (5% new). A very, very distinguished Eden Valley shiraz; the intense black fruits/licorice/spice fruit has absorbed the French oak and largely dismissed the tannins, the latter providing a distant drum beat on the exceptionally long finish and aftertaste. Screwcap. 15% alc. **Rating** 98 **To** 2052 $80

ŢŢŢŢŢ **Riesling 2015** A wine that supports the notion that you can never have too much of a good thing. The aromas and flavour of lemon fruit are insistent, indeed bold, but have perfect weight and length. A gold-plated each-way bet, now or in decades to come. Screwcap. 12% alc. **Rating** 95 **To** 2030 $29
Shiraz 2013 This is steeped in black fruits, and carries its alcohol with aplomb. This will give pleasure to at least two more generations of the Angas family. Screwcap. 15% alc. **Rating** 95 **To** 2043 $75
Cabernet Sauvignon 2012 Matured 50% new/50% used French hogsheads for 24 months. Deeply coloured, with a dusty cabernet bouquet, it manages to circumvent the burden of its alcohol, but you have to wonder how good it might have been at 14% – however, that might have left the 50% new oak exposed, where here it isn't. Screwcap. 15% alc. **Rating** 95 **To** 2042 $80
Grenache Mataro 2012 Matured in French puncheons (20% new) for 2 years. The bouquet is evocative, with notes of spice, brush fence and plum, the palate equally complex, putting the lie to the idea that these varieties won't ripen in the Eden Valley. A long life ahead. Screwcap. 15% alc. **Rating** 94 **To** 2027 $80

ŢŢŢŢ Eden Valley Cabernet Sauvignon 2013 Rating 88 To 2023 $75

Idavue Estate ★★★★

470 Northern Highway, Heathcote, Vic 3523 **Region** Heathcote
T 0429 617 287 **www**.idavueestate.com **Open** W'ends 10.30–5
Winemaker Andrew and Sandra Whytcross **Est.** 2000 **Dozens** 600 **Vyds** 5.7ha
Owners and winemakers Andrew and Sandra Whytcross both undertook a two-year winemaking course through the Bendigo TAFE; with assistance from son Marty, they also look after the vineyard, which is planted to shiraz (3ha), cabernet sauvignon (1.9ha), and semillon and chardonnay (0.4ha each). The red wines are made in typical small batch fashion with hand-picked fruit, hand-plunged fermenters and a basket press.

ŢŢŢŢŢ Heathcote Cabernet Sauvignon 2012 Matured for 24 months in French oak (30% new). A rich wine, cassis and tannins both seeking to assert their primacy, both failing to gain the upper hand. If you like generous cabernet sauvignons, this should appeal. Screwcap. 14% alc. **Rating** 93 **To** 2032 $30
Blue Note Heathcote Shiraz 2013 The full-bodied palate has polished black fruits, integrated tannins and oak, all generating a lush richness. Screwcap. 14% alc. **Rating** 92 **To** 2043 $39
Heathcote Shiraz 2013 Very different from Blue Note, with a spicy/savoury cast to its medium-bodied palate; it is interesting that both wines have the same alcohol, showing once again that statistics can be damned. Drink this, cellar Blue Note. Screwcap. 14% alc. **Rating** 91 **To** 2028 $35

In Dreams ★★★★★

179 Glenview Road, Yarra Glen, Vic 3775 **Region** Yarra Valley
T (03) 8413 8379 **www**.indreams.com.au **Open** Not
Winemaker Nina Stocker **Est.** 2013 **Dozens** 3000
In Dreams is well named, because it is a project that has been 'fizzing away' for nearly eight years. It is the venture of Nina Stocker (daughter of eminent wine scientist Dr John Stocker) and Callie Jemmeson. Their combined winemaking experience has been gained in the Yarra Valley, Rhône Valley, Barolo, Emilia Romana, California, Alentejo, Central Otago and Marlborough. The wines predominantly come from Upper Yarra Valley fruit. Winemaking takes place in a micro-winery within the framework of a larger winery in Yarra Glen.

ŢŢŢŢŢ Yarra Valley Chardonnay 2014 This is a marvellous expression of Yarra Valley chardonnay, packed with grapefruit and white peach on its bouquet and very long palate, the barrel-ferment oak inputs just so. It will probably be at its best over the next 5 years. Screwcap. 13.5% alc. **Rating** 95 **To** 2020 $23

Yarra Valley Pinot Noir 2013 As striking a label as I've seen for years, and a very interesting story behind the label. This is a seriously good young pinot, with a seriously good future. It is flooded with all manner of red fruits, but retains supple, elegant mouthfeel; its length and balance are the foundation stones of its future. Screwcap. 13.5% alc. **Rating** 95 **To** 2025 $28 ◐

Indigo Vineyard ★★★★★

1221 Beechworth-Wangaratta Road, Everton Upper, Vic 3678 **Region** Beechworth
T (03) 5727 0233 www.indigovineyard.com.au **Open** Wed–Sun 11–4
Winemaker Stuart Hordern, Marc Scalzo **Est.** 1999 **Dozens** 3300 **Vyds** 46.15ha
Indigo Vineyard has a little over 46ha of vineyards planted to 11 varieties, including the top French and Italian grapes. The business was and is primarily directed to growing grapes for sale to Brokenwood, but since 2004 increasing amounts have been vinified for the Indigo label. The somewhat incestuous nature of the whole business sees the Indigo wines being made at Brokenwood (Marc Scalzo makes the Pinot Grigio).

🍷🍷🍷🍷🍷 **Alpine Valleys Beechworth Pinot Grigio 2015** Highly aromatic. Invites you in with a hug and a smile. Pear, barley, spice and apple flavours. Above-average intensity. Above-average charm. Well worth tracking down. Screwcap. 13.5% alc. **Rating** 94 **To** 2016 $25 CM ◐
Beechworth Pinot Noir 2015 Dry and spicy but with enough fruit to carry the style. This is fast becoming one of the standout pinot noirs of the region. Deli meat, wood smoke and boysenberry flavours build an anthem of impressive flavour. Screwcap. 13.3% alc. **Rating** 94 **To** 2024 $35 CM
Beechworth Sangiovese 2015 Beautifully formed. Light to medium-weight but the mix of berried fruits and smoky, peppery, clovey characters is a winner. Fleshy tannin does just enough to give the wine shape. Terrific drinkability. Screwcap. 13.9% alc. **Rating** 94 **To** 2021 $35 CM

🍷🍷🍷🍷🍷 **Secret Village Beechworth Chardonnay 2015** **Rating** 93 **To** 2021 $50 CM
Beechworth Shiraz 2014 **Rating** 93 **To** 2023 $35 CM
McNamara Chardonnay 2015 **Rating** 92 **To** 2019 $35 CM
Secret Village Beechworth Viognier 2014 **Rating** 92 **To** 2017 $35 CM
Alpine Valleys Beechworth Chardonnay 2015 **Rating** 91 **To** 2021 $35 CM
Cabernet Sauvignon 2013 **Rating** 90 **To** 2021 $25 CM

Ingoldby ★★★★

GPO Box 753, Melbourne, Vic 3001 **Region** McLaren Vale
T 1300 651 650 www.ingoldby.com.au **Open** Not
Winemaker Kate Hongell **Est.** 1983 **Dozens** 48000 **Vyds** 37ha
Part of TWE, with the wines now having a sole McLaren Vale source. Over the years Ingoldby has produced some excellent wines, which can provide great value for money.

🍷🍷🍷🍷🍷 **McLaren Vale Cabernet Sauvignon 2013** A mix of dark-berry fruit and leaf, hallmarks of classic McLaren Vale cabernet. The palate is poised and fine, and impeccably balanced. At this price, one to look out for – you can enjoy now, but it will age admirably. Screwcap. 14.5% alc. **Rating** 94 **To** 2022 $20 ◐

🍷🍷🍷🍷🍷 **McLaren Vale Shiraz 2014** **Rating** 92 **To** 2022 $19 CM ◐
McLaren Vale Cabernet Shiraz Merlot 2013 **Rating** 91 **To** 2019 $19 CM ◐

Inkwell ★★★★☆

PO Box 33, Sellicks Beach, SA 5174 **Region** McLaren Vale
T 0430 050 115 www.inkwellwines.com **Open** By appt
Winemaker Dudley Brown **Est.** 2003 **Dozens** 800 **Vyds** 12ha
Inkwell was born in 2003 when Dudley Brown returned to Australia from California and bought a rundown vineyard on the serendipitously named California Road. He inherited 5ha

of neglected shiraz, and planted an additional 7ha to viognier (2.5ha), zinfandel (2.5ha) and heritage shiraz clones (2ha). The five-year restoration of the old vines and establishment of the new reads like the ultimate handbook for aspiring vignerons, particularly those who are prepared to work non-stop. The reward has been rich. Dudley is adamant that the production will be capped at 1000 dozen; almost all the grapes are sold. Exports to the US and Canada.

🍷🍷🍷🍷🍷 **Dub Style No 2 Grenache 2014** 88yo dry grown bush vines. 100% whole bunches. All neutral oak. Smashing wine. Complex, characterful, long and sinewy. It's hard not to keep coming back for more and more. Herbs, spices and red and black berries. Opens the door to greet you and is still going as the final guests leave. Screwcap. 14.4% alc. **Rating** 96 **To** 2023 $35 CM ✪

🍷🍷🍷🍷🍷 **Blonde on Blonde Viognier 2015 Rating** 93 **To** 2016 $26 CM ✪
    Road to Joy Shiraz Primitivo 2013 Rating 93 **To** 2024 $26 CM ✪
    Reckoner Cabernet Shiraz 2013 Rating 93 **To** 2026 $30 CM
    Black and Blue Fortified Zinfandel 2013 Rating 93 **To** 2021 $35 CM
    I&I Shiraz 2013 Rating 92 **To** 2024 $30 CM
    Dub Style No 1 Red Mix 2013 Rating 91 **To** 2020 $20 CM ✪
    Infidels McLaren Vale Primitivo 2014 Rating 91 **To** 2021 $30 CM

Innocent Bystander ★★★★★

314 Maroondah Highway, Healesville, Vic 3777 **Region** Yarra Valley
T (03) 5720 5500 **www.**innocentbystander.com.au **Open** By appt
Winemaker Wendy Cameron, Joel Tilbrook, Cate Looney, Geoff Alexander, Chloe Earl
Est. 1997 **Dozens** 49 000 **Vyds** 45ha
On 5 April 2016 Brown Brothers and Giant Steps announced that the Innocent Bystander brand (including Mea Culpa) and stock had been sold to Brown Brothers, the acquisition completed by 5 May 2016. As part of the acquisition, Brown Brothers purchased the White Rabbit Brewery site adjacent to Giant Steps, and this has become the cellar door home of Innocent Bystander. Its business is in two completely different wine categories, both fitting neatly with Brown Brothers. On the one hand is the big volume (confidential) of vintage moscato, the grapes coming from the King Valley, and non vintage prosecco, similarly sourced. Thus Brown Brothers was better able to meet the needs of those big-volume products than was Innocent Bystander. The other side of the business is the premium, high quality Yarra Valley single varietal wines, with substantial brand value. Exports to the UK, the US and other major markets.

🍷🍷🍷🍷🍷 **Mea Culpa Yarra Valley Syrah 2013** Matured for 14 months in new and used French puncheons. Vibrant crimson-purple; a fragrant, almost perfumed bouquet with exotic spice and pepper notes is taken to another level by the silk and velvet of the dark fruits of the palate, trimmed by fine-grained, savoury tannins on the finish. Screwcap. 13.5% alc. **Rating** 97 **To** 2033 $60 ✪

🍷🍷🍷🍷🍷 **Mea Culpa Yarra Valley Syrah 2014** Trevor Mast Trophy for Best Shiraz, Melbourne Wine Awards '15. Matured for 14 months in new and used French oak. Lifted, fragrant sweet spice and pepper leap from the glass, with whole-bunch and mulberry-like aromas forcing their way through with a swirl. The palate is a flood of dark fruit with leafy undergrowth elements. Oak is unobtrusively wound in with the acidity and tannin providing admirable length and definition to the finish. Screwcap. 13.5% alc. **Rating** 96 **To** 2030 $60 ✪
    Yarra Valley Chardonnay 2015 Wild-fermented in new and used French barriques, matured for 9 months. White peach blossom is first out of the blocks on the bouquet and the palate alike, then it gets interesting as other white fruits shimmy with grapefruit, almond kernel and cashew also craving attention. It is a chardonnay that floats airily over, not in, the glass. Screwcap. 13% alc. **Rating** 95 **To** 2026 $25 ✪
    Yarra Valley Pinot Noir 2014 40% matured in stainless steel, the remainder in new and used French barriques for 9 months. Spun like a silk scarf from Rajasthan, the colours shifting endlessly, the cloth as light as a feather, yet warm

on a cold night. Artistic skill of the highest order – and a steal. Screwcap. 13.5% alc.
Rating 95 **To** 2027 $25 ○
Known Pleasures Shiraz 2014 The very low yield in the Yarra Valley in '14 led
Innocent Bystander to cast its net far and wide, here to the Gateway biodynamic
vineyard in McLaren Vale. This is a no-holds-barred full-bodied shiraz in imperious
regional style; its flavours, texture and structure all point in a single direction: the
cellar for at least 5 years, with an unknowable life thereafter. Screwcap. 14.5% alc.
Rating 95 **To** 2045 $60
Yarra Valley Syrah 2014 Matured in French oak for 12 months, gold medal
Melbourne Wine Awards '15, trophy Best Shiraz Yarra Valley Wine Show '15.
Made in that trademark will o' the wisp style patented by Innocent Bystander, red
and black fruits, fine sesame tannins, spices of all kinds, and a kiss of textural oak.
Obvious drop-dead bargain. Screwcap. 13.8% alc. **Rating** 95 **To** 2025 $25 ○

Iron Cloud Wines   ★★★★

Suite 16, 18 Stirling Highway, Nedlands, WA 6009 (postal) **Region** Geographe
T 0401 860 891 **www**.pepperilly.com **Open** Not
Winemaker Damian Hutton **Est.** 1999 **Dozens** 5000 **Vyds** 11ha
Partners Geoff and Karyn Cross, and Warwick Lavis, planted their vineyard in 1991 with 2ha
each of cabernet sauvignon, shiraz and sauvignon blanc, and 1ha each of semillon, viognier,
chardonnay, mourvedre and grenache. The vineyard has views across the Ferguson Valley to
the ocean, with sea breezes providing good ventilation. Exports to China.

ΨΨΨΨΨ **Ferguson Valley Shiraz 2014** Matured in French and American oak. A wine
abuzz with a slew of aromas, flavours, textures and structure; seek and ye shall
find. Red and black fruits, coffee, fruitcake and spice; you simply don't notice the
alcohol, just the fine tannins on the finish. Screwcap. 15% alc. **Rating** 93 **To** 2029
$22 ○
Ferguson Valley Cabernet Malbec 2014 Matured for 12 months in new and
used French oak. The malbec has introduced a fair lashing of plum into the blend,
cabernet providing the structure it always has – and that malbec so often lacks. The
result is an attractive wine with a chorus of dark fruits, soft tannins and enough
oak. Screwcap. 14.5% alc. **Rating** 92 **To** 2029 $24 ○
Ferguson Valley GSM 2014 50/37/10% plus 3% touriga, matured in French
oak. Is its own master, not to be compared with SA blends; spiced plum and red
cherry fruit have been dipped into a bowl of warm spices blended with fine
tannins. Screwcap. 14.5% alc. **Rating** 91 **To** 2024 $24

ΨΨΨΨ   **Ferguson Valley Chardonnay 2014** **Rating** 89 **To** 2017 $28
Ferguson Valley Rose 2015 **Rating** 89 **To** 2017 $18 ○
Ferguson Valley Cabernet Shiraz 2014 **Rating** 89 **To** 2025 $18 ○

Ironwood Estate   ★★★★

2191 Porongurup Road, Porongurup, WA 6234 **Region** Porongurup
T (08) 9853 1126 **www**.ironwoodestatewines.com.au **Open** Wed–Mon 11–5
Winemaker Wignalls Wines (Michael Perkins) **Est.** 1996 **Dozens** 2500 **Vyds** 5ha
Ironwood Estate was established in 1996 under the ownership of Mary and Eugene Harma.
An estate vineyard planted to riesling, sauvignon blanc, chardonnay, shiraz, merlot and
cabernet sauvignon (in more or less equal amounts) was established on a northern slope of
the Porongurup Range. Exports to Japan and Singapore.

ΨΨΨΨΨ **Reserve Porongurup Chardonnay 2014** No one's going to complain about
a shortage of flavour. Straw-green in colour and with peach aplenty, the swing of
cedary oak simply takes the volume control and gives it a gentle nudge. Screwcap.
14.8% alc. **Rating** 92 **To** 2019 $25 CM ○
Porongurup Merlot 2013 Black and red berries add bass and treble notes. A
general earthiness contributes more weight, as does grunty tannin. You'd bet that
this has a future ahead of it. Screwcap. 14.7% alc. **Rating** 92 **To** 2025 $25 CM ○

ŶŶŶŶ   **Porongurup Cabernet Sauvignon 2013** Rating 89 To 2020 $20 CM
Rocky Rose 2015 Rating 88 To 2017 $18 CM

Irvine ★★★★

PO Box 308, Angaston, SA 5353 **Region** Eden Valley
T (08) 8564 1046 **www**.irvinewines.com.au **Open** At Taste Eden Valley, Angaston
Winemaker Kirk Lambert **Est.** 1983 **Dozens** 8000 **Vyds** 80ha
When James (Jim) Irvine established his eponymous winery, he chose a singularly difficult
focus for the business: the production of great merlot from the Eden Valley. Throughout the
years of establishment, and indeed thereafter, he was a much-in-demand consultant, bobbing
up in all sorts of places. Yet when he decided to sell the business in 2014, its potential was
greatly increased with the dowry provided by the purchasing Wade and Miles families. In 1867
Henry Winter Miles planted 0.8ha of shiraz, next door to what will be the cellar door (due to
open Nov '16). Successive generations of the Miles family had added to the vineyard portfolio
from 1967, both acquiring existing vineyards and planting others (Bens Block vineyard at
Penrice is home to 120yo vines). Henry's great-grandson Peter Miles and partner John Wade
collectively own 160ha spread through the Barossa and Eden valleys although only 80ha fall
within the new Irvine partnership. Exports to the UK, Switzerland, the UAE, Singapore,
Taiwan, Hong Kong and China.

ŶŶŶŶ   **Springhill Pinot Gris 2015** A distinct light pink tinge reflecting some skin
contact. A no-frills style, with nashi pear, apple and white peach aromas and
flavours; good acid balance. Screwcap. 13.5% alc. Rating 89 To 2016 $19 ✪
The Estate Barossa Shiraz 2014 Matured for 18 months in French oak
(30% new). Big, powerful and rich, the alcohol seeming to be significantly
higher than 14.5%, but I'm not arguing about its authenticity, just the mouthfeel.
Screwcap. Rating 89 To 2024 $25
The Estate Eden Valley Cabernet Merlot Cabernet Franc 2014 An
80/15/5% blend, matured in French oak (20% new) for 18 months. Medium to
full-bodied, it does have cassis/blackcurrant as its dominant flavours, but needs
more time to open its wings. Screwcap. 14% alc. Rating 89 To 2030 $25

Island Brook Estate ★★★☆

7388 Bussell Highway, Metricup, WA 6280 **Region** Margaret River
T (08) 9755 7501 **www**.islandbrook.com.au **Open** Fri–Mon 10–4, 7 days school hols
Winemaker Evan Haywood, Josephine Perry **Est.** 1985 **Dozens** 1000 **Vyds** 7ha
Major changes have taken place at Island Brook Estate since December 2011 when it was
leased from the Zorzi family. It is now operated by Evan and Vanessa Haywood. It draws on
7ha of estate vineyards planted to semillon, chardonnay, verdelho, cabernet sauvignon and
merlot. Luxurious chalet accommodation continues to be available, and the quality of the
wines has been immeasurably improved.

ŶŶŶŶŶ   **Margaret River Chardonnay 2014** Matured in new and used French oak,
bottled 7 Sept. This has all the structure and intensity missing from some of the
other Island Brook wines; it was returned to tank after some months in oak, and
hasn't been ruffled. Grapefruit aromas and (deliciously) edgy flavours lift the wine,
as does its natural acidity. Screwcap. 13% alc. Rating 94 To 2019 $24 ✪

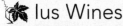 # Ius Wines ★★★★

Mary Street, Coonawarra, SA 5263 **Region** South Australia
T 0488 771 046 **www**.ius.com.au **Open** Not
Winemaker Sam Brand **Est.** 2012 **Dozens** 10 000
This is a virtual winery, with neither vineyards nor winery of its own. In physical terms,
however, it is linked to the Brand Wine Group, with Sam Brand the winemaker and one of
its two directors. The other is Tom Cosgrove, a seventh-generation Australian with a 25-year
track record with sales and distribution of fresh foods and wine. China is the major market.

ŶŶŶŶŶ **Hinterland Coonawarra Cabernet Sauvignon 2012** Excellent hue for a 4yo cabernet, and the wine lives up to the promise of the colour; blackcurrant, black olive and bay leaf flavours are intertwined with cedary oak, the tannins nodding in approval. Hard to fault. Screwcap. 14% alc. **Rating** 94 **To** 2027 $40

Ivanhoe Wines

525 Marrowbone Road, Pokolbin, NSW 2320 **Region** Hunter Valley
T (02) 4998 7325 **www.**ivanhoewines.com.au **Open** 7 days 10–5
Winemaker Stephen Drayton, Gary Reed **Est.** 1995 **Dozens** 8000 **Vyds** 19.1ha
Stephen Drayton is the son of the late Reg Drayton and, with wife Tracy, is the third branch of the family to be actively involved in winemaking in the Hunter Valley. The property on which the vineyard is situated has been called Ivanhoe for over 140 years, and 40+-year-old vines provide high quality fruit for the label. The award-winning cellar door is a replica of the old homestead (burnt down, along with much of the winery, in the 1968 bushfires).

ŶŶŶŶ **Hunter Valley Verdelho 2014** A perfectly pleasant and correct verdelho – but no more. Screwcap. 14.5% alc. **Rating** 88 **To** 2016 $28

J&J Wines

Lot 115 Rivers Lane, McLaren Vale, SA 5172 **Region** McLaren Vale
T (08) 8339 9330 **www.**jjvineyards.com.au **Open** Third Thurs each month 10.30–5.30
Winemaker Winescope (Scott Rawlinson) **Est.** 1998 **Dozens** 5000 **Vyds** 5.5ha
J&J is owned and operated by three generations of the Mason family. The estate vineyards are organically managed, but are significantly supplemented by contract-grown grapes. It has come a long way since 2004, the first year when some of the estate grapes were not purchased but were vinified to make wine for the private use of the family. Exports to Hong Kong.

ŶŶŶŶŶ **Eminence McLaren Vale Shiraz 2013** Plump fruit, lavish oak, ropes of tannin and X-factor. It's a compelling combination. The way this builds and firms and then ripples out through the finish, all black fruit, leather and cream-smothered mocha, is really quite something. Diam. 14% alc. **Rating** 95 **To** 2030 $50 CM

ŶŶŶŶŶ **Eminence McLaren Vale Shiraz 2012** **Rating** 93 **To** 2027 $50 CM
Eminence McLaren Vale Shiraz 2010 **Rating** 90 **To** 2022 $50 CM

Jack Rabbit Vineyard

85 McAdams Lane, Bellarine, Vic 3221 **Region** Geelong
T (03) 5251 2223 **www.**jackrabbitvineyard.com.au **Open** 7 days 10–5
Winemaker Nyall Condon **Est.** 1989 **Dozens** 8000 **Vyds** 2ha
Jack Rabbit vineyard is owned by David and Lyndsay Sharp of Leura Park Estate. Its 2ha of vineyards (planted equally to pinot noir and cabernet sauvignon), take second place to its Restaurant at Jack Rabbit, plus the House of Jack Rabbit tasting room, cellar door and café (open 7 days for lunch, Fri–Sat for dinner). The estate vineyards are supplemented by contract-grown fruit.

ŶŶŶŶŶ **Bellarine Peninsula Pinot Noir 2014** Pinot noir in a Bordeaux bottle. Fragrant sweet-sour cherry aromas/flavours come laced with snapped twig and dried herb notes. Forget the bottle, this is pinot noir to its back teeth. The finish is dry and slightly gamey but there's a wealth of pleasure to be had here. Screwcap. 13% alc. **Rating** 92 **To** 2021 $30 CM
Bellarine Peninsula Pinot Grigio 2015 Halway house between gris and grigio in style. Full-bodied but not OTT. Apple and citrus with inflections of spice. Dry finish. Screwcap. 13% alc. **Rating** 90 **To** 2016 $30 CM

ŶŶŶŶ **Bellarine Peninsula Riesling 2015** **Rating** 89 **To** 2021 $30 CM
Bellarine Peninsula Sauvignon Blanc 2015 **Rating** 88 **To** 2017 $30 CM
Bellarine Peninsula Cabernet Shiraz 2014 **Rating** 88 **To** 2020 $30 CM

Jacob's Creek

Barossa Valley Way, Rowland Flat, SA 5352 **Region** Barossa Valley
T (08) 8521 3000 **www**.jacobscreek.com **Open** 7 days 10–5
Winemaker Ben Bryant **Est.** 1973 **Dozens** NFP **Vyds** 1600ha
Jacob's Creek is one of the largest-selling brands in the world, and the global success of the
base range has had the perverse effect of prejudicing many critics and wine writers who fail
(so it seems) to objectively look behind the label and taste what is in fact in the glass. Jacob's
Creek has multiple ranges, and all the wines have a connection, direct or indirect, with Johann
Gramp, who built his tiny stone winery on the banks of the creek in 1847. The ranges include
Heritage (Johann Shiraz Cabernet, Steingarten Riesling, Reeves Point Chardonnay and
Centenary Hill Barossa Shiraz); then St Hugo; Reserve (all major varietals); and Classic (ditto).
Exports to the UK, the US, Canada and China, and other major markets.

99999 **St Hugo Coonawarra Barossa Cabernet Sauvignon Shiraz 2013** A full-
bodied wine that has better line and structure than its siblings, although it has
(very properly) some years yet in which to come together; it has depth to its
blackcurrant/blackberry fruit, and to its very good tannin structure. Screwcap.
14.5% alc. **Rating** 94 **To** 2033 $55

99999 **Double Barrel Barossa Shiraz 2013 Rating** 92 **To** 2019 $25 CM **◐**
St Hugo Coonawarra Cabernet Sauvignon 2012 Rating 92 **To** 2032 $55
St Hugo Barossa Shiraz 2013 Rating 91 **To** 2033 $55
Classic Riesling 2015 Rating 90 **To** 2017 $12 **◐**
Reserve Barossa Riesling 2015 Rating 90 **To** 2018 $18 **◐**
Classic Riesling 2014 Rating 90 **To** 2024 $12 **◐**

James & Co. Wines

359 Cornishtown Road, Rutherglen, Vic 3685 **Region** Beechworth
T (02) 6032 7556 **www**.jamesandcowines.com.au **Open** Not
Winemaker Ricky James **Est.** 2011 **Dozens** 450
Ricky and Georgie James intended to buy land in Beechworth and establish a vineyard
planted primarily to sangiovese. They say, 'Serendipity led us to Mark Walpole, and we were
given the chance to purchase fruit from his Fighting Gully Road Vineyard.' In the meantime,
they had set up their home in Rutherglen, and intend to float between the two regions – in
their words, 'James & Co. is a winery with a vineyard of no fixed address.' The underlying aim
is to produce a lighter-bodied red wine than is usually found in Rutherglen.

99999 **Beechworth Sangiovese 2013** Generous fruit and oak in a medium-
weight context. Tobacco, black cherry, anise and cedary vanillan flavours tell an
entertaining story. Screwcap. 14% alc. **Rating** 92 **To** 2021 $35 CM
Beechworth Sangiovese Rose 2015 Pale salmon-crimson. Aromatic and
juicy but with texture, some of it aided by alcohol, to boot. Flings of red cherry,
cranberry and various dry spices. More impact than its colour might suggest.
Screwcap. 14% alc. **Rating** 91 **To** 2016 $20 CM **◐**

Jamiesons Run

58 Queensbridge Street, Southbank, Vic 3006 **Region** Coonawarra
T 1300 651 650 **www**.jamiesonsrun.com.au **Open** Not
Winemaker Andrew Hales **Est.** 1987 **Dozens** NFP
The wheel has turned full circle for Jamiesons Run. It started out as a single-label, mid-market,
high-volume brand developed by Ray King during his time as CEO of Mildara. It grew and
grew until Mildara, having many years since been merged with Wolf Blass, decided to rename
the Mildara Coonawarra winery Jamiesons Run, with the Mildara label just one of a number
falling under the Jamiesons Run umbrella. Now the Jamiesons Run winery is no more –
Foster's sold it, but retained the brand. Exports to Asia.

♟♟♟♟ Limestone Coast Cabernet Sauvignon 2014 They've put a bit of shape back into this wine. It tastes of blackcurrant and herbs, but importantly it's not too loose or sweet; it holds itself well through the palate. There's even a lick of vanillan oak here. It's not bad at all. Screwcap. 14% alc. **Rating** 88 **To** 2020 $15 CM ❍

Jane Brook Estate Wines ★★★★

229 Toodyay Road, Middle Swan, WA 6056 **Region** Swan Valley
T (08) 9274 1432 www.janebrook.com.au **Open** 7 days 10–5
Winemaker Mark Baird **Est.** 1972 **Dozens** 20 000 **Vyds** 18.2ha
Beverley and David Atkinson have worked tirelessly to build up the Jane Brook Estate wine business over the past 40 years. All wines are produced from the estate vineyards in Swan Valley (6.5ha) and Margaret River (11.7ha). Exports to China.

♟♟♟♟♟ Shovelgate Vineyard Margaret River Chardonnay 2013 Fermented and matured in French oak (10% new), no mlf. Bright and crisp, it has the usual white flesh stone fruit and grapefruit framed by subtle oak. Screwcap. 12.5% alc. **Rating** 92 **To** 2021 $35
Shovelgate Vineyard Margaret River Sauvignon Blanc 2015 Tropical fruits are rampant; those who enjoy the fruity side of sauvignon blanc will be in seventh heaven. Screwcap. 12.2% alc. **Rating** 90 **To** 2017 $23

♟♟♟♟ Atkinson Family Reserve Shiraz 2014 **Rating** 89 **To** 2024 $50
Shovelgate Vineyard Margaret River Malbec 2014 **Rating** 89 **To** 2024 $35

Jansz Tasmania ★★★★★

1216b Pipers Brook Road, Pipers Brook, Tas 7254 **Region** Northern Tasmania
T (03) 6382 7066 www.jansztas.com **Open** 7 days 10–4.30
Winemaker Louisa Rose **Est.** 1985 **Dozens** 38 000 **Vyds** 30ha
Jansz is part of Hill-Smith Family Vineyards, and was one of the early sparkling wine labels in Tasmania, stemming from a short-lived relationship between Heemskerk and Louis Roederer. Its 15ha of chardonnay, 12ha of pinot noir and 3ha of pinot meunier correspond almost exactly to the blend composition of the Jansz wines. It is the only Tasmanian winery entirely devoted to the production of sparkling wine (although the small amount of Dalrymple Estate wines is also made here), and is of high quality. Part of the former Frogmore Creek Vineyard purchased by Hill-Smith Family Vineyards in Dec 2012 is dedicated to the needs of Jansz Tasmania. Exports to all major markets.

♟♟♟♟♟ Single Vineyard Vintage Chardonnay 2009 The grapes were whole bunch-pressed, and only free-run juice retained, fermented in French barriques, then 5½ years on lees before disgorgement, 100 dozen bottles made. It really scores with its balance and freshness, acidity and white peach/citrus fruit in lockstep; wonderful length and an outright bargain. Cork. 12% alc. **Rating** 96 **To** 2019 $65 ❍

♟♟♟♟♟ Premium Cuvee 2010 The juxtaposition of the fresh lemon and apple fruit of this cool vineyard and the toasty, spicy, honeyed, ginger theatrics of barrel fermentation (50%) and 4.5 years lees age has attained a crescendo here. It's finely textured, magnificently persistent and driven by a scintillating acid line. One of the greats from this exceptional vineyard. Cork. 12.5% alc. **Rating** 95 **To** 2020 $47 TS
Late Disgorged 2007 This has attained its prime, upholding the crunchy lemon and red apple fruits of youth and building to wonderful, pronounced layers of honey on toast, brioche, even hints of wood smoke and iodine. Extended lees age has built wonderfully creamy texture, impeccable line and enduring persistence. Outstanding. Cork. 12% alc. **Rating** 95 **To** 2017 $56 TS
Rose NV This declares its greatness in its delicate restraint, and the latest release is as pale and elegant as ever. The faintest salmon blush tint subtly coaxes out dainty red berry and red cherry fruits, but the theme here is more about mouthfilling

lees-derived texture and cool, energetic Tasmanian acidity than it is about overt flavour. Cork. 12% alc. **Rating** 94 **To** 2016 $32 TS

ŸŸŸŸŸ **Vintage Rose 2012 Rating** 93 **To** 2022 $53 TS
Premium Cuvee NV Rating 91 **To** 2017 $32 TS

Jarrah Ridge Winery ★★★☆

651 Great Northern Highway, Herne Hill, WA 6056 **Region** Swan Valley
T (08) 9296 6337 **www**.jarrahridge.com **Open** Fri–Sun 10–5
Winemaker Mark Morton, Michael Ng, John Griffiths **Est.** 1998 **Dozens** 10 000
Vyds 20.5ha
Following the death of founder Syd Pond, Mark Morton and Jimmy Wong have acquired Jarrah Ridge Winery, with the principal focus the development of the brand in China, a country in which the pair has worked since 2008. The employment of a number of contract winemakers gives them the flexibility to increase the volume and range of the portfolio in response to rapidly changing market dynamics. Exports to Canada, Singapore, Hong Kong and China.

ŸŸŸŸŸ **Reserve Manjimup Cabernet Sauvignon 2013** Machine-harvested, cultured yeast, 5 days cold soak, matured in French oak (35% new) for 15 months. Deep crimson-purple; pushes full-bodied to the edge of the envelope, but stops short of tearing it; laden with blackcurrant, black olive and bay leaf; the tannins are firm but not the least bit dry or abrasive. Deserves 5+ years, but won't bite if you want to drink it now. Cork. 14.5% alc. **Rating** 93 **To** 2033 $35

ŸŸŸŸ **Late Harvest 2012 Rating** 89 **To** 2022 $16 ❂
Reserve Swan Valley Shiraz 2014 Rating 88 **To** 2030 $35

Jasper Hill ★★★★★

Drummonds Lane, Heathcote, Vic 3523 **Region** Heathcote
T (03) 5433 2528 **www**.jasperhill.com **Open** By appt
Winemaker Ron Laughton, Emily McNally **Est.** 1979 **Dozens** 2500 **Vyds** 26.5ha
The red wines of Jasper Hill are highly regarded and much sought after. Over the past decade drought has caused some variation in style and weight, but as long as vintage conditions allow, these are wonderfully rich and full-flavoured wines. The vineyards are dry grown and are managed organically. No wines were received for this edition. Exports to the UK, the US, Canada, France, Denmark, Hong Kong and Singapore.

jb Wines ★★★

PO Box 530, Tanunda, SA 5352 **Region** Barossa Valley
T 0408 794 389 **www**.jbwines.com **Open** By appt
Winemaker Joe Barritt **Est.** 2005 **Dozens** 700 **Vyds** 18ha
The Barritt family has been growing grapes in the Barossa since the 1850s, but this particular venture was established in 2005 by Lenore, Joe and Greg Barritt. It is based on shiraz, cabernet sauvignon and chardonnay (with tiny amounts of zinfandel, pinot blanc and clairette) planted between 1972 and '03. Greg runs the vineyard operations; Joe, with a Bachelor of Agricultural Science degree from Adelaide University, followed by 10 years of winemaking in Australia, France and the US, is now the winemaker. Exports to Hong Kong.

ŸŸŸŸ **Sobels Barossa Valley Cabernet Sauvignon 2012** Big, bold fruit is at the far extreme for cabernet sauvignon; the lack of aggressive tannins is a plus for the mouthfeel, the alcohol wobbling around in the mouth. Screwcap. 14.8% alc. **Rating** 89 **To** 2019 $30
Joseph's Barossa Valley Zinfandel 2012 Zinfandel demands high baume, and hence high alcohol, to achieve ripeness. That is the case here, and just when you think all is well, a flash of heat comes on the aftertaste. Not much can be done about it. Screwcap. 15.2% alc. **Rating** 88 **To** 2020 $50

Jeanneret Wines

Jeanneret Road, Sevenhill, SA 5453 **Region** Clare Valley
T (08) 8843 4308 **www.**jeanneretwines.com **Open** Mon–Fri 9–5, w'ends 10–5
Winemaker Ben Jeanneret, Harry Dickinson **Est.** 1992 **Dozens** 12000 **Vyds** 6ha
Ben Jeanneret has progressively built the range and quantity of wines he makes at the onsite winery. In addition to the estate vineyards, Jeanneret has grape purchase contracts with owners of an additional 20ha spread throughout the Clare Valley. Exports to the US, Canada and Japan.

ΨΨΨΨΨ **Single Vineyard Sevenhill Riesling 2015** Has considerable power, drive and intensity, lime/citrus leading the way, but allowing crisp, crunchy apple to also help. Its balance is such that you can drink it now with food, not just as a simple glass on a sunny day. Screwcap. 13% alc. **Rating** 95 **To** 2028 $25 **O**
Single Vineyard Sevenhill Riesling 2014 A fragrant and fresh, flowery blossom-filled bouquet, then a palate with the poise of a ballerina; lemon and apple perform a pas de deux, crisp acidity pushing the flavours on relentlessly, building complexity as it goes. Screwcap. 12.8% alc. **Rating** 95 **To** 2024 $25 **O**
Sideways Clare Valley Riesling 2015 Bright straw-green; not so much sideways as the dead centre of Clare Valley riesling style, and a particularly fine example at that. Lime, lemon and a hint of apple guide the perfumed bouquet and palate alike, the length, line and balance impeccable. Screwcap. 13.5% alc. **Rating** 94 **To** 2030 $18 **O**

ΨΨΨΨφ **Rank and File Clare Valley Shiraz 2013** **Rating** 93 **To** 2028 $23 **O**
Single Vineyard Watervale Riesling 2014 **Rating** 91 **To** 2029 $25
Moon Dance Clare Valley Malbec 2014 **Rating** 90 **To** 2024 $20 **O**

Jericho Wines

13 Seacombe Cresecent, Seacombe Heights, SA 5047 (postal) **Region** Adelaide Hills/McLaren Vale
T 0499 013 554 **www.**jerichowines.com.au **Open** Not
Winemaker Neil and Andrew Jericho **Est.** 2012 **Dozens** 1500
Neil Jericho made wine for over 35 years in Victoria, mainly in the Rutherglen and King Valley regions, interspersed with stints in Portugal. In this venture the whole family is in play, with wife Kaye a 'vintage widow'; eldest daughter Sally has obtained marketing and accounting degrees from the University of Adelaide; and son Andrew, who obtained his Bachelor of Oenology from the University of Adelaide (in 2003), having worked for 10 years in McLaren Vale.

ΨΨΨΨΨ **Single Vineyard Adelaide Hills Fume Blanc 2015** Fermented in French oak. It is powerful, yet soft; entirely the intention, you'd expect. Lemongrass and lime with highlights of rind and gravel. Honed finish. Excellent package for the asking price. Screwcap. 13.3% alc. **Rating** 94 **To** 2019 $25 CM **O**
Single Vineyard Adelaide Hills Tempranillo 2015 Drink-now tempranillo, done to perfection. Spicy, sweet, savoury and floral. Quite masterfully put together. Cherry, plum, anise and dried spice notes. Clips of cedary oak. Almost impossible to stop at one glass. Screwcap. 13.4% alc. **Rating** 94 **To** 2020 $25 CM **O**

ΨΨΨΨφ **Single Vineyard Adelaide Hills Fiano 2015** **Rating** 93 **To** 2017 $25 CM **O**

Jim Barry Wines

33 Craigs Hill Road, Clare, SA 5453 **Region** Clare Valley
T (08) 8842 2261 **www.**jimbarry.com **Open** Mon–Fri 9–5, w'ends, hols 9–4
Winemaker Peter Barry, Tom Barry, Derrick Quinton **Est.** 1959 **Dozens** 80 000
Vyds 249ha
The patriarch of this highly successful wine business, Jim Barry, died in 2004, but the business continues under the active management of several of his many children, led by the irrepressible Peter Barry. The ultra-premium release is The Armagh Shiraz, with the McCrae Wood red

wines not far behind. Jim Barry Wines is able to draw upon mature Clare Valley vineyards, plus a small holding in Coonawarra. After studying and travelling, third-generation winemaker Tom and commercial manager Sam Barry have joined the business, launching The Barry Bros label, Tom celebrating by winning the Gourmet Traveller Wine Young Winemaker of the Year '13. A founding member of Australia's First Families of Wine. Exports to all major markets.

ΤΤΤΤΤ **The Armagh Shiraz 2010** Matured for 14 months in 67% French, 33% American oak, 70% new. A deeply woven bouquet of blackberry, blackcurrant and plum flows through into the rich, multilayered palate; while oak and ripe tannins are also plentiful, the balance and harmony of the wine mean it is not the least ponderous. Screwcap. 14.5% alc. **Rating** 97 **To** 2040 $300

ΤΤΤΤΤ **The Florita Clare Valley Riesling 2015** Pale, pristine and intense. This is where fruit meets beauty. It hits, it holds, it runs, it prevails. Lime and everything after. Clare Valley riesling in all its youthful glory. Screwcap. 12.3% alc. **Rating** 96 **To** 2034 $45 CM ✪

The Armagh Shiraz 2013 A powerhouse release. It rips, it churns, it impresses and most of all, it gets on with business. Dense black-berried fruits of various persuasions, coffee-cream oak, sprinkles of dried herbs and a surge of flavour and tannin to close. It's like admiring a big sea; the power complete with the glory. Screwcap. 14.1% alc. **Rating** 96 **To** 2040 $270 CM

Cellar Release The Florita Clare Valley Riesling 2007 Gleaming green-straw; graceful mature riesling with the quadrella of lime, toast, honey and acidity all in unison. Will sing loud and long with the appropriate food. Screwcap. 13% alc. **Rating** 95 **To** 2020 $50

First Eleven Coonawarra Cabernet Sauvignon 2013 A well-mannered wine of size and volume. Tarzan in a dinner suit. Dense plum and blackcurrant with a jellied sweetness to the edges. Just a suggestion of herbs. A silty lake of tannin. Now or a long time later; it will swing in and deliver. Screwcap. 14% alc. **Rating** 95 **To** 2035 $60 CM

First Eleven Coonawarra Cabernet Sauvignon 2012 Very elegant and sophisticated packaging, totally appropriate in the context of a significantly complex cabernet; blackcurrant fruit has a savoury amalgam of Coonawarra earth, tannins and prominent, but high quality, oak – all giving the wine excellent length. Screwcap. 13.5% alc. **Rating** 95 **To** 2032 $60

The Lodge Hill Riesling 2015 Bright and chalky at once. Glitters in the glass. Scintillating lemon and bath salt flavours hit, run, and keep on going. Rindy, almost smoky, characters play through the finish. Intensity impresses throughout. Screwcap. 12.3% alc. **Rating** 94 **To** 2026 $22 CM ✪

The Veto Clare Valley Riesling 2015 10% barrel-fermented in used French oak, all held on lees for 6 weeks. Cruises along on the supple palate until the finish, when it grows another leg. Has time to grow a fourth leg. Screwcap. 12.5% alc. **Rating** 94 **To** 2030 $35

Cellar Release The Florita Clare Valley Riesling 2010 Developing steadily and well. Full straw colour. Honeysuckle, orange and lime flavours come accompanied by spice and lanolin. Entering its peak now. Screwcap. 12.5% alc. **Rating** 94 **To** 2024 $50 CM

The Veto Clare Valley Shiraz 2013 It takes brutality and covers it in cotton wool. The core is strong, intense, all saturated plum and coffee grounds. But the edges are softer, spicier, creamier, even fractionally leafy. The core will keep it going for many a year; the edges make it attractive now. Screwcap. 14% alc. **Rating** 94 **To** 2028 $35 CM

The McRae Wood Clare Valley Shiraz 2013 Firm with tannin and alive with promise. It's not the brightest spark but deep pools of blackberried fruit and swirls of firm coffeed tannin make it a monty for sound future development. Screwcap. 14% alc. **Rating** 94 **To** 2034 $55 CM

The Armagh Shiraz 2012 Truffle, leather and heightened blackcurrant aromas/flavours dominate all the initial impressions, marking complexity as a main driver at the expense of pure fruit power. This isn't the blockbuster you might imagine;

the flavour profile too is exotic, if not downright quirky. It will fascinate fields of drinkers for many years. Screwcap. 13.7% alc. **Rating** 94 **To** 2035 $270 CM
PB Shiraz Cabernet Sauvignon 2013 More elegant than powerful, but there's plenty of fruit flavour. Leather, spice, black cherry and blackberry, with bay leaf and coffee grounds on back-up vocals. It will mature reliably well. Screwcap. 13.5% alc. **Rating** 94 **To** 2028 $60 CM
PB Shiraz Cabernet Sauvignon 2012 Blackberry and blackcurrant comes with a melt of dark chocolate draped seductively over the top. There are saltbush and herb notes here but they are second stringers to the main game of fruit and oak. Tannin has a strength to it. Screwcap. 14% alc. **Rating** 94 **To** 2028 $60 CM
The Veto Coonawarra Cabernet Sauvignon 2013 A well-oiled machine. The flavour streams through the mouth, all power and control, its notes of earth, mint and blackcurrant kept in place by belts of leathery tannin. No doubting its quality. Screwcap. 14% alc. **Rating** 94 **To** 2030 $35 CM

ᵧᵧᵧᵧᵧ **The Veto Clare Valley Shiraz 2014** Rating 93 To 2030 $35 CM
The Veto Coonawarra Cabernet 2014 Rating 92 To 2026 $35 CM
Watervale Riesling 2015 Rating 91 To 2021 $18 CM ✪
The Benbournie Cabernet Sauvignon 2012 Rating 91 To 2026 $70 CM
The Barry Bros 2014 Rating 90 To 2024 $19 ✪

Jim Brand Wines ★★★★

PO Box 18, Coonawarra, SA 5263 **Region** Coonawarra
T (08) 8736 3252 www.jimbrandwines.com.au **Open** Not
Winemaker Brand family, Bruce Gregory (Consultant) **Est.** 2000 **Dozens** 3000 **Vyds** 9ha
The Brand family story starts with the arrival of Eric Brand in Coonawarra in 1950. He married Nancy Redman and purchased a 24ha block from the Redman family, relinquishing his job as a baker and becoming a grapegrower. It was not until '66 that the first Brand's Laira wine was made. The family sold 50% of the Brand's Laira winery in '94 to McWilliam's, Jim Brand staying on as chief winemaker until he died in 2005, after a long battle with cancer, unable to fulfil his ambition to make quality wine under his name. Sam Brand is the fourth generation of this family, which has played a major role in Coonawarra for over 50 years. Exports to Fiji, Hong Kong and China.

ᵧᵧᵧᵧᵧ **Single Vineyard Glenroy Shiraz 2013** Pressed to French oak (50% new) to complete fermentation, matured for 18 months. Classy wine; the oak (and barrel ferment) is obvious, but so are the red/black cherry and blackberry fruit and supple tannins. Screwcap. 14.5% alc. **Rating** 94 **To** 2038 $70

ᵧᵧᵧᵧᵧ **Silent Partner Cabernet Sauvignon 2013** Rating 93 To 2033 $36

Jinks Creek Winery ★★★★

Tonimbuk Road, Tonimbuk, Vic 3815 **Region** Gippsland
T (03) 5629 8502 www.jinkscreekwinery.com.au **Open** Sun 12–5
Winemaker Andrew Clarke **Est.** 1981 **Dozens** 2000 **Vyds** 3.52ha
Planting of the Jinks Creek vineyard antedated the building of the winery by 11 years, and the wines are made from estate-grown grapes. Perched above the vineyard with an uninterrupted view of the Bunyip State Forest and Black Snake Ranges, a refurbished 100-year-old wool shed has been renovated to house a restaurant, art gallery and cellar door. This venue is constructed entirely from recycled materials sourced from Gippsland, including old lining boards, a kauri pine dance floor and a perfectly preserved pressed-tin ceiling. Exports to the US.

ᵧᵧᵧᵧᵧ **Yarra Valley Merlot Shiraz 2014** Bright crimson-purple; a thoroughly left-field blend wherever you may be; this is certainly the first for the Yarra Valley. There is some real synergy as the red fruits of both components (rather than dark or black) mesh neatly together. Screwcap. 14.3% alc. **Rating** 92 **To** 2024 $30
Pinot Noir 2014 Seven clones matured in French oak for 12 months. Light colour, but there are attractive red berry/cherry flavours, and no attempt at

over-extraction. A pretty wine, interesting for its clonal mix, which of itself is not the golden key to pinot's heart. Screwcap. 14% alc. **Rating** 91 **To** 2024 $30

🍷🍷🍷🍷 **Sauvignon Blanc 2014** **Rating** 89 **To** 2017 $25
Gippsland Sparkling Rose 2010 **Rating** 88 **To** 2017 $30 TS

Jirra Wines at Jeir Station ★★★☆

Jeir Station, 2443 Barton Highway, Yass, NSW 2582 **Region** Canberra District
T (02) 6227 5671 **www**.jirrawines.com.au **Open** Not
Winemaker Canberra Winemakers **Est.** 2007 **Dozens** 1500 **Vyds** 4ha

The present-day Jeir Station, while a substantial 120ha, was once part of a 6500ha grazing property owned by the Johnston family between 1825 and 1918. The old homestead was built around 1835 by convict labour, and still stands today. In 2000 present owners Colin and Kay Andrews planted shiraz, cabernet sauvignon, chardonnay, viognier and sangiovese, and have the wines contract-made by Rob Howell and Greg Gallagher of Canberra Winemakers.

🍷🍷🍷🍷 **Canberra District Sangiovese 2010** Obvious colour development, but still bright; likewise the bouquet and palate; interesting wine; the tannins are no more, but the dark cherry fruit is very much alive, with a pleasing lift of savoury dark cherry on the finish. A double bargain, for both its history and its price. Screwcap. 13% alc. **Rating** 89 **To** 2020 $16 ✪

Canberra District Fresco Riesling 2015 This must have been very early picked, for the residual sugar in this off-dry wine (relative to its acidity) is low. It's breezy, bright and minerally. Screwcap. 10.1% alc. **Rating** 89 **To** 2018 $14 ✪

John Duval Wines ★★★★★

PO Box 622, Tanunda, SA 5352 **Region** Barossa Valley
T (08) 8562 2266 **www**.johnduvalwines.com **Open** At Artisans of Barossa
Winemaker John Duval **Est.** 2003 **Dozens** 7000

John Duval is an internationally recognised winemaker, having been the custodian of Penfolds Grange for almost 30 years as part of his role as chief red winemaker at Penfolds. In 2003 he established his eponymous brand; he continues to provide consultancy services to clients all over the world. While his main focus is on old-vine shiraz, he has extended his portfolio with other Rhône varieties. Exports to all major markets.

🍷🍷🍷🍷🍷 **Eligo The Barossa Shiraz 2013** Represents the best wine of the vintage, sourced from the Barossa and Eden valleys, matured for 20 months in French hogsheads (75% new). The aim is a structured (achieved in spades) and elegant (give it 10 years) expression of Barossa shiraz. My query on elegance is due to the obvious French oak: it simply needs a Grange-like decade to come into balance. Cork. 14.5% alc. **Rating** 97 **To** 2048 $120 ✪

🍷🍷🍷🍷🍷 **Entity Barossa Shiraz 2014** Matured for 15 months in French oak (35% new). Succulent, rich and powerful, with predominantly black fruits and some spice. The hallmarks are its supple mouthfeel and effortless balance. Screwcap. 14.5% alc. **Rating** 96 **To** 2044 $50 ✪

Plexus Barossa Valley Shiraz Grenache Mourvedre 2014 A 47/32/21% blend drawn from old vineyards, matured in French hogsheads (10% new). As is appropriate, complex, but largely fruit-driven, with red cherries/berries and plums to the fore, oak and (particularly) tannins taking a back seat. Screwcap. 14.5% alc. **Rating** 94 **To** 2026 $40

John Gehrig Wines ★★★★

Oxley-Milawa Road, Oxley, Vic 3678 **Region** King Valley
T (03) 5727 3395 **www**.johngehrigwines.com.au **Open** 7 days 10–5
Winemaker Ross Gehrig **Est.** 1976 **Dozens** 5600 **Vyds** 85ha

The Gehrig family has been making wine for five generations in Rutherglen, but in August 2011 the shape and size of the business increased rapidly. The purchase of an 80ha vineyard from Rutherglen Winemakers saw estate plantings rise from 6ha to 85ha; the vineyard purchased by Gehrig has a rich history, with an 1870 building known as Snarts Winery operating until the 1940s. Heritage listed, it has been restored and now operates as the cellar door. Work continues to rehabilitate the vineyard; part is used for the significantly increased John Gehrig production, the remainder of the grapes are sold.

🍷🍷🍷🍷🍷 **King Valley Sparkling Merlot NV** All the best things about merlot are captured in this sparkling style: fragrance, dark berry fruits, well-defined acidity and finely textured tannins. It's impeccably crafted and singly redefines what sparkling merlot can achieve, doing so with both enticing appeal and promising longevity. A surprise worth discovering. Crown seal. 14% alc. **Rating** 93 **To** 2019 $35 TS
King Valley Liqueur Muscat NV John Gehrig does not use the 4-tier classification system, but if he did, this would have approached Grand. There is a style difference, however, this wine more luscious, but with less rancio, and overall good balance. 375ml. Screwcap. 18% alc. **Rating** 93 **To** 2018 $55
RG King Valley Pinot Noir 2012 Has retained remarkably fresh hue, and the bouquet and palate are no less impressive, with elegant red fruits foremost; it does introduce some briary/savoury notes on the aftertaste, and I would tend to strike while the (fruit) iron is hot. Screwcap. 14.3% alc. **Rating** 92 **To** 2018 $55
King Valley Cremant de Gamay 2006 The soft tannins of gamay lend themselves well to a sparkling style, here upholding impressive primary black fruit integrity at a full decade of age. With great length and seamless integration, this is a versatile and food-friendly sparkling alternative. Crown seal. 13.5% alc. **Rating** 92 **To** 2021 $40 TS
Fox Liqueur NV A potent liqueur style, way beyond the ordinary idea of tawny; much more luscious and rich, venturing into muscat country; presumably a solera. No change since '14. 375ml. 'You may ask why the name Fox ...Well that was John's nickname when he was playing sport, as he was cunning and sly as a fox.' Screwcap. 18% alc. **Rating** 91 **To** 2018 $55
Grand Tawny NV A solero blended tawny using 10yo material as its base from old sherry hogsheads. Very complex, but in old-fashioned, high-baume style, a light year away from (say) Seppeltsfield. Will no doubt make cellar door visitors happy. No change since '14. 500ml. Screwcap. 18% alc. **Rating** 90 **To** 2018 $32
Muscat NV Obviously younger and fresher than the Liqueur Muscat, but with strong raisin/Christmas pudding varietal flavours, and still with a viscous texture. 500ml. Screwcap. 18% alc. **Rating** 90 **To** 2018 $32

John Kosovich Wines ★★★★★

Cnr Memorial Ave/Great Northern Hwy, Baskerville, WA 6056 **Region** Swan Valley
T (08) 9296 4356 **www**.johnkosovichwines.com.au **Open** 7 days 10–5.30
Winemaker Anthony Kosovich **Est.** 1922 **Dozens** 3000 **Vyds** 10.9ha
John Kosovich Wines operated as Westfield Wines until 2003, when it changed its name to honour John's 50th vintage. The name change did not signify any change in either philosophy or direction for this much-admired producer of gloriously complex Rare Muscats. The 7.4ha of old vines in the Swan Valley accompany 3.5ha established in Pemberton in 1989. Son Anthony joined his father in 1994.

🍷🍷🍷🍷🍷 **Rare Muscat NV** Base material from '50 is blended with vintages from '74–'96. The intensity here has to be seen/tasted to be believed. It oozes up and down the glass as you sip at it, its flavours of burnt toffee and intense raisin licked at by notes of fresh, black, sweet coffee. Quite staggering, really. It's like stepping into a whole new world. 375ml. Diam. 19% alc. **Rating** 97 **To** 2017 $95 CM ❂

🍷🍷🍷🍷🍷 **Bottle Aged Reserve Swan Valley Chenin Blanc 2011** In the zone. Drinking beautifully. Apple, citrus, spice and assorted exotica. It feels textural and yet there's no oak involved. Drink now. Screwcap. 12.5% alc. **Rating** 95 **To** 2020 $32 CM ✪

ỶỶỶỶỸ **Reserve Pemberton Cabernet Malbec 2014 Rating** 93 **To** 2025 $45 CM

John's Blend ★★★★★

18 Neil Avenue, Nuriootpa, SA 5355 (postal) **Region** Langhorne Creek
T (08) 8562 1820 **www**.johnsblend.com.au **Open** At The Winehouse, Langhorne Creek
Winemaker John Glaetzer **Est.** 1974 **Dozens** 2200 **Vyds** 23ha
John Glaetzer was Wolf Blass's right-hand man almost from the word go, the power behind the throne of the three Jimmy Watson trophies awarded to Wolf Blass Wines ('74, '75, '76) and the small matter of 11 Montgomery trophies for the Best Red Wine at the Adelaide Wine Show. This has always been a personal venture on the side, as it were, of John and wife Margarete, officially sanctioned, of course, and needing little marketing effort. Exports to Canada, Switzerland, Indonesia, Singapore and Japan.

ỶỶỶỶỶ **Individual Selection Langhorne Creek Cabernet Sauvignon 2012**
Fermentation was completed in new French hogsheads with 35 months maturation. With the great '12 vintage to help, this is in the heroic style that one expects from John Glaetzer, full of every ingredient: luscious cassis fruit dripping from every bough, cubic metres of new French oak and St Bernard-sized tannins all built to live together for decades. Cork. 14.5% alc. **Rating** 96 **To** 2042 $35 ✪
Margarete's Langhorne Creek Shiraz 2013 The same vinification and maturation as John's Blend. You know exactly what you will get from John Glaetzer: luscious fruits interwoven with high quality oak and soft, fluffy tannins, all exuding come-hither charm. Cork. 14.5% alc. **Rating** 95 **To** 2028 $35 ✪

Jones Road ★★★★★

2 Godings Road, Moorooduc, Vic 3933 **Region** Mornington Peninsula
T (03) 5978 8080 **www**.jonesroad.com.au **Open** W'ends 11–5
Winemaker Travis Bush **Est.** 1998 **Dozens** 7500 **Vyds** 26.5ha
It's a long story, but after establishing a very large and very successful herb-producing business in the UK, Rob Frewer and family migrated to Australia in 1997. By a circuitous route they ended up with a property on the Mornington Peninsula, planting pinot noir and chardonnay, then pinot gris, sauvignon blanc and merlot; they have since leased another vineyard at Mt Eliza, and purchased Ermes Estate in 2007.

ỶỶỶỶỶ **Nepean Chardonnay 2014** Various slings and arrows of fruit and spice combine to create a sense of magic. Ginger, oatmeal, grapefruit and white peach characters slip into gloves of fresh fennel and smoky oak. At risk of stating the bleeding obvious, this is a beautiful white wine. Screwcap. 12.5% alc. **Rating** 96 **To** 2021 $60 CM ✪
Chardonnay 2014 One sniff and sip and it's abundantly clear that this wine is at the top of its game. It has a seamless grace; it combines stone fruits, steel, spice and wood as if they'd all been grown as one. Screwcap. 12.5% alc. **Rating** 95 **To** 2021 $32 CM ✪
Pinot Noir 2014 Fragrant and then firm; flavoursome and then fine. This has the prettiness to catch your eye and the substance to make you want to stay. Macerated cherry-plum, mineral, wood spice and twigs. It's not at all sweet but there's more than enough fruit, and ample length. Time will be kind. Screwcap. 12.5% alc. **Rating** 94 **To** 2023 $38 CM
Nepean Pinot Noir 2014 It sizzles with savouriness. Wood spice and tangy cherry, smoky oak and orange rind characters lend this both an exotic feel and a lively disposition. Bass notes come via charcuterie and stewy plums. Tannin, it has plenty. It shows all the signs that it will develop very well. Screwcap. 12.8% alc. **Rating** 94 **To** 2023 $60 CM

Jones Winery & Vineyard   ★★★★

Jones Road, Rutherglen, Vic 3685 **Region** Rutherglen
T (02) 6032 8496 **www**.joneswinery.com **Open** Mon, Thurs, Fri 10–4, w'ends 10–5
Winemaker Mandy Jones **Est.** 1860 **Dozens** 2000 **Vyds** 9.8ha

Jones Winery & Vineyard was established in 1860 and stands testament to a rich winemaking tradition. Since 1927, the winery has been owned and operated by the Jones family. Two blocks of old vines have been preserved (including 1.69ha of shiraz), supported by further blocks progressively planted between '75 and 2008. Today, Jones Winery & Vineyard is jointly operated by winemaker Mandy Jones, who brings 14 years of experience working at Château Carsin in Bordeaux, France, and her brother Arthur Jones. Together they produce a small range of boutique wines.

ㅜㅜㅜㅜㅜ **Rutherglen Malbec 2013** Matured for 18 months in French oak (20% new). A surprise packet, with fresh, supple black fruits, fine tannins and neatly controlled French oak. The wine lays a strong claim to recognition of its elegance. Screwcap. 12.7% alc. **Rating** 94 **To** 2028 $35

ㅜㅜㅜㅜㅜ **Classic Rutherglen Muscat NV Rating** 93 **To** 2017 $30
Rutherglen Marsanne 2015 Rating 91 **To** 2023 $25
Rutherglen Fiano 2015 Rating 90 **To** 2019 $25
LJ 2013 Rating 90 **To** 2038 $65
Rutherglen Shiraz 2013 Rating 90 **To** 2038 $32
Rutherglen Durif 2013 Rating 90 **To** 2030 $38

Josef Chromy Wines   ★★★★★

370 Relbia Road, Relbia, Tas 7258 **Region** Northern Tasmania
T (03) 6335 8700 **www**.josefchromy.com.au **Open** 7 days 10–5
Winemaker Jeremy Dineen **Est.** 2004 **Dozens** 30 000 **Vyds** 60ha

Joe Chromy just refuses to lie down and admit that the wine industry in Tasmania is akin to a financial black hole in space. After escaping from Czechoslovakia in 1950, establishing Blue Ribbon Meats, using the proceeds of that sale to buy Rochecombe and Heemskerk vineyards, then selling those and establishing Tamar Ridge before it, too, was sold, Joe is at it again; this time he's invested $40 million in a wine-based business. If this were not remarkable enough, Joe is in his 80s, and has recovered from a major stroke. The foundation of the new wine business is the Old Stornoway Vineyard, with 60ha of mature vines, the lion's share to pinot noir and chardonnay. Chromy's grandson, Dean Cocker, is business manager of the restaurant, function and wine centre, which has spectacular views over White Hills to Ben Lomond, the vineyard and the lakes. The homestead is now a dedicated wine centre and cellar door, offering WSET (Wine & Spirit Education Trust) courses. Exports to all major markets.

ㅜㅜㅜㅜㅜ **ZDAR Riesling 2012** Quartz-green, this is 50% about place, 50% about variety (or vice versa); it wings its way on pure Cape Grim acidity that serves to amplify citrus and apple fruit flavours, yet continues to remind you of its presence. As fresh as the day it was bottled. Screwcap. 12.7% alc. **Rating** 95 **To** 2037 $42
ZDAR Vintage 2005 An entire French patisserie of wonderful complexity has slowly unravelled during 9 years on lees, producing a beautifully silky, creamy and enticing style. Pinot noir and chardonnay leave their impression in secondary red berry, stone fruit and citrus, polished with a light dosage of 6.5g/l. It's long, seamless and dreamy. Diam. 12.2% alc. **Rating** 95 **To** 2017 $105 TS
Botrytis 2015 Riesling. Tasmania does these wines so well it must give any German winemakers who taste them a shiver down their spine. This has 170g/l of residual sugar, but it also has intense lime juice fruit and electric acidity and more complexity down the track. Screwcap. 9.5% alc. **Rating** 95 **To** 2025 $28 ✪
Riesling 2015 Taut and linear. Slate, mineral and citrus, in that order of impact. Juicy finish. Hit of lime rind to the aftertaste. Elegant but not at all lacking. Don't leave it at the altar. Screwcap. 13% alc. **Rating** 94 **To** 2026 $28 CM ✪
Sauvignon Blanc 2015 Estate-grown on the Relbia Vineyard, cold-settled clear juice cool-fermented dry in stainless steel, immediately clarified and stabilised for

early bottling. The interplay of tropical guava, herbaceous notes, pronounced citrus flavours and crisp acidity give the illusion of lees or oak texture when there is none. Screwcap. 13.9% alc. **Rating** 94 **To** 2017 $28 ✪

Pinot Gris 2015 This is full to the gunnels with attitude – and a richly textured, verging on opulent, palate of poached pears trimmed by firm acidity before it breaks free again on the aftertaste. Screwcap. 14.5% alc. **Rating** 94 **To** 2018 $28 ✪

Pinot Noir 2014 Holding its youthful, although light, hue; a fruit-driven style with an array of red cherry and raspberry fruits, and a hint of strawberry. This is one of those pinots you are happy to drink, not deconstruct. Screwcap. 13.6% alc. **Rating** 94 **To** 2024 $38

🍷🍷🍷🍷🍷 ZDAR Pinot Noir 2011 **Rating** 93 **To** 2026 $55
PEPIK Chardonnay 2015 **Rating** 91 **To** 2020 $25
PEPIK Sekt NV **Rating** 90 **To** 2021 $32 TS
DELIKAT SGR Riesling 2015 **Rating** 90 **To** 2022 $28

Journey Wines   ★★★★★

1a/29 Hunter Road, Healesville, Vic 3777 (postal) **Region** Yarra Valley
T 0427 298 098 **www**.journeywines.com.au **Open** Not
Winemaker Damian North **Est.** 2011 **Dozens** 2500
The name chosen by Damian North for his brand is particularly appropriate given the winding path he has taken before starting (with his wife and three youngish children) his own label. Originally a sommelier at Tetsuya's when it was still at Rozelle, he was inspired to enrol in the oenology course at CSU, gaining his first practical winemaking experience as assistant winemaker at Tarrawarra Estate for several years. Then, with family in tow, he moved to Oregon's Benton-Lane Winery to make pinot noir for several years, before returning to become winemaker at Leeuwin Estate for five years, indulging in his other vinous passion, chardonnay. The wheel has turned full circle as the family has returned to the Yarra Valley, securing 2ha of chardonnay, 2.5ha of pinot noir and 2ha of shiraz under contract arrangements, and making the wines at Medhurst. Exports to the UK, Singapore and Thailand.

🍷🍷🍷🍷🍷 Heathcote Shiraz 2014 Spice, cedary oak and a plum/blackberry melange start the journey on the bouquet; the palate is intense and focused on the same path, with highlights of licorice and spice. Despite its intensity it is elegant and medium-bodied. Screwcap. 13.5% alc. **Rating** 96 **To** 2044 $40 ✪

Yarra Valley Chardonnay 2014 25% fermented in new puncheons, the balance in used puncheons and barriques; matured for 10 months. This is a powerful chardonnay with layers of white peach fruit interleaved with grapefruit. It carries this off with panache. Screwcap. 13% alc. **Rating** 95 **To** 2026 $34 ✪

Yarra Valley Pinot Noir 2014 The hue is bright and full, the red plum fruit aromas gaining considerable pace and drive on the impressively long palate; the whole bunch component has given the wine a savoury dressing that is a perfect foil for the fruit and spice to come with more age. I really like this. Screwcap. 12.5% alc. **Rating** 95 **To** 2028 $34 ✪

Juniper Estate   ★★★★★

98 Tom Cullity Drive, Cowaramup, WA 6284 **Region** Margaret River
T (08) 9755 9000 **www**.juniperestate.com.au **Open** 7 days 10–5
Winemaker Mark Messenger **Est.** 1973 **Dozens** 12 000 **Vyds** 19.5ha
When Roger Hill and Gillian Anderson purchased the Wrights' vineyard in 1998, the 10ha vineyard was already 25 years old, but in need of retrellising and a certain amount of nursing to bring it back to health. All of that has happened, along with the planting of additional shiraz and cabernet sauvignon. The Juniper Crossing wines use a mix of estate-grown grapes and grapes from other Margaret River vineyards, while the Juniper Estate releases are made only from the estate plantings. Since Roger's accidental death in '13, Gillian has continued running Juniper Estate and Higher Plane. Exports to the UK, the US, Ireland, Canada, Hong Kong, the Philippines, Singapore and NZ.

ŶŶŶŶŶ **Aquitaine Blanc 2014** Pours it on like a steam train. It's a seamless display of fruit and oak, its sweet pea and gravel characters tucked neatly into grapefruit, passionfruit and wood smoke. It feels velvety on the tongue, and finishes confidently. Screwcap. 13.5% alc. **Rating** 95 **To** 2019 $30 CM ☻

Chardonnay 2014 Richness is the first impression but it turns on the class through the finish. White peach, grapefruit, chalk and sweet oak are powerful but elegant, the finish lengthy. Screwcap. 13% alc. **Rating** 94 **To** 2021 $38 CM

Juniper Crossing Cabernet Merlot 2013 Juniper Crossing is in the top league of value for money in the cabernet merlot category. It is only medium-bodied, but there's terrific tension between the blackcurrant/red berry fruit flavours and the texture of the dusty tannins, the tension creating the length. Screwcap. 14% alc. **Rating** 94 **To** 2030 $20 ☻

Cabernet Sauvignon 2012 The picture is still unfolding but it's clear this is a powerful cabernet presented in an elegant frame. Mulberry and cassis, game and chicory, bay leaves and a slide of cedary oak. It's so neat it feels freshly ironed. Screwcap. 14% alc. **Rating** 94 **To** 2032 $65 CM

Aquitaine Rouge 2013 Full Bordeaux blend. Made to cellar. No compromise to 'early drinking'. Strung with tannin and dried herbs but with ample fruit lying in reserve. A wine with a clear plan and purpose in life. Time is the last piece in the puzzle. Screwcap. 14% alc. **Rating** 94 **To** 2032 $38 CM

ŶŶŶŶŶ **Semillon 2014 Rating** 93 **To** 2018 $30 CM

Juniper Crossing Chardonnay 2015 Rating 93 **To** 2020 $22 CM ☻

Juniper Crossing Shiraz 2014 Rating 93 **To** 2025 $22 CM ☻

Margaret River Shiraz 2013 Rating 93 **To** 2028 $38 CM

Juniper Crossing Tempranillo 2014 Rating 92 **To** 2020 $22 CM ☻

Juniper Crossing 2015 Rating 90 **To** 2018 $20 ☻

Just Red Wines ★★★★

2370 Eukey Road, Ballandean, Qld 4382 **Region** Granite Belt
T (07) 4684 1322 www.justred.com.au **Open** W'ends & public hols 10–5
Winemaker Michael Hassall **Est.** 1998 **Dozens** 1500 **Vyds** 2.6ha
Tony, Julia and Michael Hassall have planted shiraz and merlot (plus cabernet sauvignon, tannat and viognier not yet in production) at an altitude of just under 900m. They minimise the use of chemicals wherever possible, but do not hesitate to protect the grapes if weather conditions threaten an outbreak of mildew or botrytis. The Hassalls' daughter, Nikki, was very much involved in the creation of the vineyard, and was driving back from university to be there for the first day of picking. In the ultimate cruel finger of fate, the car crashed and she was killed. After a pause, wine production has been resumed.

ŶŶŶŶŶ **Granite Belt Merlot 2014** Matured in French oak (40% new) for 12 months. Vivid crimson-purple; the Granite Belt can produce elegant merlot with clear varietal character, proof positive in this wine; its light to medium body adds to its appeal, fresh cassis/red berry fruit supported by fine, savoury tannins. An outrageous bargain. Screwcap. 13.4% alc. **Rating** 92 **To** 2020 $19 ☻

Granite Belt Tannat 2015 Hand-picked, crushed, destemmed, open-fermented, 7 days on skins, matured for 6 months in French oak (50% new). Vivid, deep colour; an exotic vulcanised rubber/earth/tar bouquet; has those sharp-edged tannins tannat is famous for, which led to the invention of micro-oxygenation in France. Screwcap. 14.2% alc. **Rating** 91 **To** 2022 $29

Kaesler Wines ★★★★★

Barossa Valley Way, Nuriootpa, SA 5355 **Region** Barossa Valley
T (08) 8562 4488 www.kaesler.com.au **Open** 7 days 11–5
Winemaker Reid Bosward **Est.** 1990 **Dozens** 20 000 **Vyds** 50ha
The first members of the Kaesler family settled in the Barossa Valley in 1845. The vineyards date back to 1893, but the Kaesler family ownership ended in 1968. After several changes, the

present (much-expanded) Kaesler Wines was acquired by a small group of investment bankers (who have since acquired Yarra Yering), in conjunction with former Flying Winemaker Reid Bosward and wife Bindy. Reid's experience shows through in the wines, which now come from estate vineyards, 40ha adjacent to the winery, and 10ha in the Marananga area. The latter includes shiraz planted in 1899, with both blocks seeing plantings in the 1930s, '60s, then each decade through to the present. Wines were received too late for the book, but tasting notes can be found on www.winecompanion.com.au. Exports to all major markets.

Kalleske ★★★★★
6 Murray Street, Greenock, SA 5360 **Region** Barossa Valley
T (08) 8563 4000 **www**.kalleske.com **Open** 7 days 10–5
Winemaker Troy Kalleske **Est.** 1999 **Dozens** 15 000 **Vyds** 48ha
The Kalleske family has been growing and selling grapes on a mixed farming property at Greenock for 140 years. Sixth-generation Troy Kalleske, with brother Tony, established the winery and created the Kalleske label in 1999. The vineyard is planted to shiraz (27ha), grenache (6ha), mataro (2ha), chenin blanc, durif, viognier, zinfandel, petit verdot, semillon and tempranillo (1ha each). The vines vary in age, with the oldest dating back to 1875; the overall average age is around 50 years. All are grown biodynamically and organically. Exports to all major markets.

🍷🍷🍷🍷🍷 **Johann Georg Old Vine Single Vineyard Barossa Valley Shiraz 2013** This vineyard was planted in 1875. This wine is literally painful with the intensity and complexity of its unbridled black-fruited assault on the palate. You could write 100 words describing the aromas and flavours, the next person writing the same length, equally valid, but having nothing in common with the first description. Kalleske offers 13 specific flavour descriptors threaded through different, more general, observations. Screwcap. 14.5% alc. **Rating** 97 **To** 2063 $120 ❂

🍷🍷🍷🍷🍷 **Flower Biodynamic Barrel Project Shiraz 2014** Far and away the best of the trio. Lifted, lively, deep and confident, all at once. Blackberry and florals, saucy-sweet oak and a pop of cherry pie. It is, simply, a beautiful wine. For now or later. Screwcap. 14.5% alc. **Rating** 95 **To** 2030 $50 CM
Greenock Single Vineyard Barossa Valley Shiraz 2014 Matured for 18 months in American and French hogsheads (30% new). Interesting wine; while very complex, with a multitude of dark fruit aromas and flavours, the overall impression is of a cool vineyard – which it isn't, of course. Nor does the American oak intrude. I like it. Screwcap. 14.5% alc. **Rating** 95 **To** 2034 $40
JMK Barossa Valley Shiraz VP 2015 Clean, pure, complex and compelling. The spice, the fruitcake, the boldness of blackberry, the wonderful purity of it. Worth every cent of the asking price, and then some. 375ml. Screwcap. 18.5% alc. **Rating** 95 **To** 2030 $23 CM ❂
Moppa Barossa Valley Shiraz 2014 The wine contains some co-fermented viognier (5%) and back-blended petit verdot (10%). Matured in French, American and Hungarian oak (25% new) for 14 months. Dense purple-crimson, it launches an Exocet missile of the blackest of black fruits, dark chocolate and strong tannins. Screwcap. 14% alc. **Rating** 94 **To** 2034 $28 ❂
Eduard Old Vine Barossa Valley Shiraz 2013 Pressed to French and American hogsheads for the final stages of fermentation; matured for 2 years. It is powerful, and unequivocally full-bodied, black fruits totally dominant, so much so that the tannins seem mild. Its best days are far into the future. Screwcap. 14.5% alc. **Rating** 94 **To** 2043 $85
Clarry's Barossa Valley GSM 2015 The quality keeps rolling along. Cherries, spices, plums, candied citrus, licorice allsorts; there's plenty going on and it's all welcome. Firm but velvety tannin ties it neatly together. Bonza. Screwcap. 14% alc. **Rating** 94 **To** 2021 $21 CM ❂

🍷🍷🍷🍷🍷 **Buckboard Single Vineyard Durif 2014 Rating** 93 **To** 2025 $24 ❂
Merchant Single Vineyard Barossa Valley Cabernet Sauvignon 2014 **Rating** 91 **To** 2029 $28

Plenarius Barossa Valley Viognier 2015 Rating 90 To 2016 $26 CM
Fruit Biodynamic Barrel Project Shiraz 2014 Rating 90 To 2024 $50 CM

Kangarilla Road Vineyard ★★★★★

Kangarilla Road, McLaren Vale, SA 5171 **Region** McLaren Vale
T (08) 8383 0533 www.kangarillaroad.com.au **Open** Mon–Fri 9–5, w'ends 11–5
Winemaker Kevin O'Brien **Est.** 1997 **Dozens** 65 000 **Vyds** 14ha
In Jan 2013 Kangarilla Road founders Kevin O'Brien and wife Helen succeeded in breaking
the mould for a winery sale, and crafted a remarkable win–win outcome. They sold their
winery and surrounding vineyard to Gemtree Vineyards, which has had its wine made at
Kangarilla Road since '01 under the watchful eye of Kevin. The O'Briens have retained their
adjacent JOBS Vineyard and the Kangarilla Road wines continue to be made by Kevin at
the winery. Luck of the Irish, perhaps. Exports to the UK, the US and other major markets.

🍷🍷🍷🍷🍷 **Alluvial Fans Shiraz 2014** Matured in old oak to keep the focus on the terroir/
soil. It is the essence of McLaren Vale, with sumptuous black fruits, dark chocolate
and firm tannins providing abundant structure. The overall savoury impact works
well. Screwcap. 14.5% alc. **Rating** 95 **To** 2039 $45
Blanche Point Formation McLaren Vale Shiraz 2014 Deeper colour than
Alluvial Fans; the mouthfeel and flavour are distinctly different. The dark berry
fruits are rounder and more supple, filling the mouth, and displacing the dark
chocolate. Chacun à son gout. Screwcap. 14.5% alc. **Rating** 95 **To** 2039 $45
Shiraz 2014 There's a lot of wine here. It's much more than just the mid-palate
of Australia; it's the start and finish too. It's thick with blackberried flavour, carries
highlights of raspberry, and laces toasty/creamy/clovey oak seductively throughout.
It's the quintessentially mouthfilling red. Screwcap. 14.5% alc. **Rating** 94 **To** 2025
$25 CM ❂

🍷🍷🍷🍷🍸 **Black St Peters Zinfandel 2014** Rating 92 To 2035 $70
Cabernet Sauvignon 2014 Rating 90 To 2029 $28

Karatta Wines ★★★★

292 Clay Wells Road, Robe, SA 5276 **Region** Robe
T (08) 8735 7255 www.karattawines.com.au **Open** W'ends & hols 11–4
Winemaker Chris Gray **Est.** 1994 **Dozens** 4000 **Vyds** 39.6ha
Owned by David and Peg Woods, Karatta Wines is named after Karatta House, one of Robe's
well-known heritage-listed icons. Built in 1858, Karatta House was occupied by the South
Australian Governor, Sir James Fergusson, during the summers of 1868 to '71. Vineyards
include the 12 Mile Vineyard and Tenison Vineyard, both in the Robe region.

🍷🍷🍷🍷🍸 **Robe Shiraz 2013** Matured in French barriques (40% new). Brilliant crimson-
purple; flush with black cherry and blackberry on the supple, medium to full-
bodied palate, it eats, breathes and sleeps value for money. If you are looking for
a $20 wine to lay down for someone's year of birth, this does the trick. Screwcap.
13.8% alc. **Rating** 94 **To** 2034 $20 ❂

🍷🍷🍷🍷🍸 **Robe Cabernet Sauvignon 2013** Rating 93 To 2028 $20 ❂

Karrawatta ★★★★☆

818 Greenhills Road, Meadows, SA 5201 **Region** Adelaide Hills/Langhorne Creek
T (08) 8537 0511 www.karrawatta.com.au **Open** By appt
Winemaker Mark Gilbert **Est.** 1996 **Dozens** 990 **Vyds** 46.6ha
Mark Gilbert is the great-great-great-grandson of Joseph Gilbert, who established the Pewsey
Vale vineyard (and winery) in 1847. What is not generally known is that Joseph Gilbert had
named the property Karrawatta, a name already in use for another property. The right to use
the name was decided on the toss of a coin in a local SA pub, forcing Gilbert (who lost) to
relinquish the Karrawatta name and adopt Pewsey Vale instead. The Karrawatta of today is not
in the Barossa Ranges, but the Adelaide Hills; there is a neat coincidence here, because in 1847

Pewsey Vale was the highest vineyard planting in SA, and Mark Gilbert's Karrawatta is one of the highest plantings in the Adelaide Hills. It is true he only has 13.8ha of vines here, and 32.8ha in Langhorne Creek, but never let the facts get in the way of a good story.

ΨΨΨΨΨ **Limited Edition Christo's Paddock Langhorne Creek Cabernet Sauvignon 2014** Substance is its middle name. It loads blackcurrant, tar, mint and dark chocolate flavours in the barrel and fires them at you with great and accurate force; it feels controlled throughout, in equal part satisfying and impressive. Screwcap. 14.5% alc. **Rating** 95 **To** 2034 $54 CM

Limited Edition Dairy Block Adelaide Hills Shiraz 2014 Light to medium-bodied and with complex twists at every turn. Nuts, herbs and deli meat characters sing through cherry-plum fruit. There's a succulence to this, a lightness on its feet. It certainly fits the 'Burgundian shiraz' genre. And the tannin, well, it's quite perfect. Screwcap. 14.5% alc. **Rating** 94 **To** 2026 $38 CM

Limited Edition Joseph Langhorne Creek Shiraz 2014 It knows when to push and when to ease off. The intensity levels of licorice, blackberry and saltbush-like flavour are dramatic in an in-your-face way, but the seductive slips of coffee-cream oak and red-berried flavour are delivered at just the right moments. Tannin helps fuse the components. It's big, and it's (very) good. Screwcap. 14.5% alc. **Rating** 94 **To** 2032 $57 CM

ΨΨΨΨΨ **Sophie's Hill Pinot Grigio 2015** Rating 93 **To** 2017 $26 CM ✪
Anna's Adelaide Hills Sauvignon Blanc 2015 Rating 91 **To** 2017 $26 CM

KarriBindi ★★★★☆

111 Scott Road, Karridale, WA 6288 (postal) **Region** Margaret River
T (08) 9758 5570 **www**.karribindi.com.au **Open** Not
Winemaker Kris Wealand **Est.** 1997 **Dozens** 2500 **Vyds** 32.05ha
KarriBindi is owned by Kevin, Yvonne and Kris Wealand. The name is derived from Karridale and the surrounding karri forests, and from Bindi, the home town of one of the members of the Wealand family. In Nyoongar, 'karri' means strong, special, spiritual, tall tree and 'bindi' means butterfly, hence the label's picture of a butterfly soaring through karri trees. The Wealands have established sauvignon blanc (15ha), chardonnay (6.25ha), cabernet sauvignon (4ha), plus smaller plantings of semillon, shiraz and merlot. KarriBindi supplies a number of high-profile Margaret River wineries, reserving approximately 20% for its own label. Exports to Singapore and China.

ΨΨΨΨΨ **Semillon Sauvignon Blanc 2015** It hits, it runs, it persists. This is beautifully flavoured and textured and then has that extra bit of carry through the finish. Excellent value. Screwcap. 12.5% alc. **Rating** 94 **To** 2018 $20 CM ✪

ΨΨΨΨΨ **Margaret River Chardonnay 2014** Rating 93 **To** 2021 $30 CM
Margaret River Sauvignon Blanc 2015 Rating 91 **To** 2017 $20 CM ✪

Katnook Coonawarra ★★★★★

Riddoch Highway, Coonawarra, SA 5263 **Region** Coonawarra
T (08) 8737 0300 **www**.katnookestate.com.au **Open** Mon–Sat 10–5, Sun 11–5
Winemaker Wayne Stehbens **Est.** 1979 **Dozens** 90 000 **Vyds** 198ha
Second in size (in the region) to Wynns Coonawarra Estate, Katnook has made significant strides since its acquisition by Freixenet, the Spanish Cava producer; at one time selling most of its grapes, it now sells a maximum of 10%. The historic stone woolshed in which the second vintage in Coonawarra (1896) was made, and which has served Katnook since 1980, has been restored. Likewise, the former office of John Riddoch has been fully restored and is now the cellar door, and the former stables now serve as a function area. Well over half the total estate plantings are cabernet sauvignon and shiraz, with the Odyssey Cabernet Sauvignon and Prodigy Shiraz the icon duo at the top of a multitiered production. Exports to all major markets.

🍷🍷🍷🍷🍷 **Prodigy Shiraz 2012** Matured for 25 months in 43% French (21% new) and 57% American barriques (27% new). Has retained very good hue; Prodigy marches to the tune of its own drum, and practice has long since made perfect. Despite all the winemaking, and in particular the time spent in oak, it has retained balance, emerging at the end of the process as elegant, the tannins supple, the wine fresh. Cork. 14.5% alc. **Rating** 96 **To** 2037 $100

Amara Vineyard Cabernet Sauvignon 2013 Its maturation for 16 months in French barriques (50% new) simply confirms what the palate already says: this is made in the Baroque (significantly oaked) style established by Odyssey and Prodigy. But as with the two big guns, there's also a power of fruit from the 40yo vines. Screwcap. 14% alc. **Rating** 95 **To** 2038 $50

Odyssey Cabernet Sauvignon 2012 Matured for 24 months in 90% French (46% new) and 10% used American oak. Hyper-intense, full-bodied cabernet varietal fruit is beyond the normal Odyssey style, but none the worse for that; blackcurrant and bay leaf, plus notes of tar, race along the palate, barely checking their momentum on the finish and aftertaste. Cork. 14.5% alc. **Rating** 95 **To** 2037 $100

The Caledonian Cabernet Shiraz 2013 55% cabernet sauvignon, 35% shiraz, 5% each of petit verdot and tannat, matured for 14 months in American oak (35% new). Good colour; an opulent, medium to full-bodied blend with a cascade of blackcurrant, blackberry, cherry, tannins and vanillan oak all sweeping along the palate. Screwcap. 14% alc. **Rating** 94 **To** 2038 $50

🍷🍷🍷🍷🍷 **Estate Chardonnay 2014 Rating** 90 **To** 2020 $28
Estate Merlot 2013 Rating 90 **To** 2028 $40
Founder's Block Sparkling Shiraz 2013 Rating 90 **To** 2020 $23 CM

Kay Brothers Amery Vineyards ★★★★★

57 Kays Road, McLaren Vale, SA 5171 **Region** McLaren Vale
T (08) 8323 8211 www.kaybrothersamerywines.com **Open** Mon–Fri 9–5, w'ends & public hols 11–5
Winemaker Colin Kay, Duncan Kennedy **Est.** 1890 **Dozens** 10000 **Vyds** 22ha
A traditional winery with a rich history and just over 20ha of priceless old vines; while the white wines have been variable, the red wines and fortified wines can be very good. Of particular interest is Block 6 Shiraz, made from 100-year-old vines; both vines and wines are going from strength to strength. Celebrated its 125th anniversary in 2015. Exports to the US, Canada, Switzerland, Germany, Malaysia, Hong Kong, Singapore, South Korea and China.

🍷🍷🍷🍷🍷 **Block 6 Shiraz 2013** From 121yo estate vines, matured for 19 months in French oak (33% new). An extremely complex wine, juicy fruits of every colour and description engaged in an Indian arm wrestle with briary/spicy/savoury tannins, French oak the timekeeper, not engaged in the wrestle. Screwcap. 14.5% alc. **Rating** 96 **To** 2038 $80

Hillside Shiraz 2013 Matured for 18 months in American and Balkan oak. This is a distillation of all things McLaren Vale shiraz, a poached plum, blackberry and dark chocolate ragout, softly, but insistently, painting every corner of the mouth, the masterstroke the mouthwatering tannins simultaneously freshening and lengthening the finish. Screwcap. 14% alc. **Rating** 95 **To** 2033 $45

Basket Pressed Shiraz 2014 An incredibly dense and luxuriant palate grabs all the attention; how this has been achieved with 14% alcohol is anyone's guess, but I'm not disposed to argue, because the outcome is a totally serendipitous, supple, full-bodied shiraz replete with dark Swiss chocolate wrapped around luscious black fruits. Screwcap. **Rating** 94 **To** 2034 $25 ❂

125th Anniversary Sparkling Shiraz NV Packed with all the depth and intrigue of Kay's still reds, this first release sparkling is built primarily around '08 shiraz aged in old oak for more than 5 years, subtly dosed with Kay's Old Tawny. It's packed with wonderful layers of black fruits, licorice and dark chocolate, framed in well-handled, finely structured tannins that bring great promise in the cellar. Crown seal. 14% alc. **Rating** 94 **To** 2031 $45 TS

ŢŢŢŢ¶ **Basket Pressed McLaren Vale Grenache 2014** Rating 93 To 2022 $25 **☉**

Keith Tulloch Wine ★★★★★

Hermitage Road, Pokolbin, NSW 2320 **Region** Hunter Valley
T (02) 4998 7500 **www.**keithtullochwine.com.au **Open** 7 days 10–5
Winemaker Keith Tulloch, Joel Carey **Est.** 1997 **Dozens** 10 000 **Vyds** 7.4ha
Keith Tulloch is, of course, a member of the Tulloch family, which has played a leading role in the Hunter Valley for over a century. Formerly a winemaker at Lindemans and Rothbury Estate, he developed his own label in 1997. There is the same almost obsessive attention to detail, the same almost ascetic intellectual approach, the same refusal to accept anything but the best as that of Jeffrey Grosset. Exports to the UK, the US, Canada, Sweden and Hong Kong.

ŢŢŢŢŢ **Museum Release Semillon 2009** 41yo vines on the estate vineyard planted on alluvial sand. A freakishly youthful straw-green hue sets the scene for a glorious 7yo semillon, its balance immaculate, racy lemon citrus now riding astride the acidity, and will effortlessly do the same for years, indeed decades, ahead. Screwcap. 11% alc. **Rating** 97 **To** 2024 $45 **☉**

ŢŢŢŢŢ **The Kester Shiraz 2014** From 85yo vines, includes 2% viognier, matured for 18 months in French oak (50% new). Keith Tulloch has thrown the book at this wine, knowing how special the year was, and how much extract it could handle. The result is a wine built for the ages, the oak and tannins very powerful, but an integral part of a great wine. Screwcap. 14.5% alc. **Rating** 96 **To** 2049 $70 **☉**
Shiraz Viognier 2014 95% shiraz from 40yo vines, 5% viognier, co-fermented, matured for 15 months in French oak (30% new). Bright colour as expected; a firm, medium-bodied shiraz, still to welcome the light of day, but that will come; firm tannins are part of the reason, the rest simply fruit concentration. Screwcap. 14% alc. **Rating** 95 **To** 2044 $35 **☉**
Semillon 2015 A semillon already offering lemon, lime and grapefruit flavours in abundance, sustained by the guy ropes of acidity keeping it firmly anchored in place for future development. If you obtain a bottle of the '09 you will not hesitate to buy and cellar this. Screwcap. 11% alc. **Rating** 94 **To** 2030 $28 **☉**
Gairn Vineyard Tumbarumba Chardonnay 2015 Fermented in French oak (30% new) with various yeast inputs, 50% mlf, matured on lees for 10 months. Elegant wine, very fresh and perfectly balanced; pink grapefruit leads the citrus component, but there are also pear and apple in the background; the oak and mlf have also been well managed. Screwcap. 13% alc. **Rating** 94 **To** 2022 $40
Tawarri Vineyard Shiraz 2014 From 25yo vines at 460m on the eastern slopes of the Great Dividing Range within the fringe of the Hunter Valley, matured in French oak (40% new) for 18 months. Intense, deep crimson-purple; a no-nonsense full-bodied shiraz with a range of sombre, brooding black fruits and pepper attesting to the very different (and cooler) climate; the formidable tannins do need time to resolve. Screwcap. 14.5% alc. **Rating** 94 **To** 2039 $48
The Wife Shiraz 2014 86% shiraz from 80yo vines, 14% viognier, co-fermented, matured in used French oak for 18 months. The unusually high percentage of viognier hasn't diluted the colour; in fact it has added more purple to the hue, but it has softened and sweetened the flavour spectrum, and softened the tannin extract. It is the wine to drink while you wait for the other Keith Tulloch Shiraz Viognier (and the '14s generally) to soften. Screwcap. 14% alc. **Rating** 94 **To** 2039 $60

ŢŢŢŢ¶ **Chardonnay 2015** Rating 92 To 2021 $32
Epogee Winemakers Selection Viogner Marsanne Roussanne 2015 Rating 91 To 2020 $40

Kellermeister

Barossa Valley Highway, Lyndoch, SA 5351 **Region** Barossa Valley
T (08) 8524 4303 **www**.kellermeister.com.au **Open** 7 days 9.30–5.30
Winemaker Mark Pearce **Est.** 1976 **Dozens** 30 000 **Vyds** 20ha

Since joining Kellermeister from Wirra Wirra in 2009, Mark Pearce has successfully worked through challenging times to ensure the survival of the winery and its brands; and upon the retirement of founders Ralph and Val Jones in late '12, the Pearce family acquired the business. Surrounded by a young, close-knit team, Mark is committed to continuing to build on the legacy that the founders began almost 40 years ago. His winemaking focus is on continuing to preserve Kellermeister's best wines, while introducing new wines, made with the intention of expressing the purity of the provenance of the Barossa. Exports to the US, Canada, Switzerland, Denmark, Israel, Taiwan, China and Japan.

🍷🍷🍷🍷🍷 **Black Sash Shiraz 2013** From 100yo vines in the Ebenezer district and one other site. A majestic wine combining elegance with full-bodied power, blackberry fruit shading out other flavours that you can sense without deconstruction. The palate has extreme length and excellent balance, the oak hidden somewhere in the folds of the wine. A standout bargain. Screwcap. 14.5% alc. **Rating** 97 **To** 2048 $65 **○**

Wild Witch Barossa Shiraz 2013 Vines 26–100yo from Ebenezer, Lyndoch and Eden Valley, vinified and matured separately with 30 months in French oak (50% new). The only question about this label is whether it will be very good indeed or outstanding. This vintage it's in the latter camp, with fabulous colour for a 3yo, a velvet-smooth palate of exceptional complexity and harmony. Underneath that velvety smoothness there are flavours of blackberry, licorice, tannin and French oak chasing each other energetically. Screwcap. 14.7% alc. **Rating** 97 **To** 2053 $85 **○**

🍷🍷🍷🍷🍷 **The Wombat General Hand Picked Eden Valley Riesling 2015** From the Fechner Vineyard, family-owned for six generations, hand-picked, whole bunch-pressed and only 450l per tonne free-run juice. A striking combination of mouthwatering lime juice and crisp acidity, as pure as the driven snow, and prodigiously long in the mouth. Screwcap. 12.5% alc. **Rating** 95 **To** 2030 $22 **○**

🍷🍷🍷🍷🍷 **Threefold Farm Missy Moo Single Vineyard Mataro 2013** Rating 91 To 2023 $45

The Rambling Ruins Eden Valley Pinot Gris 2015 Rating 90 To 2017 $22
Threefold Farm Whiskers Single Vineyard Grenache 2014 Rating 90 To 2020 $45
Threefold Farm Whiskers Single Vineyard Grenache 2013 Rating 90 To 2019 $45

Kellybrook

Fulford Road, Wonga Park, Vic 3115 **Region** Yarra Valley
T (03) 9722 1304 **www**.kellybrookwinery.com.au **Open** 7 days 11–5
Winemaker Philip and Darren Kelly **Est.** 1962 **Dozens** 3000 **Vyds** 8.5ha

The vineyard is at Wonga Park, one of the gateways to the Yarra Valley, and has a picnic area and a full-scale restaurant. A very competent producer of both cider and apple brandy (in Calvados style) as well as table wine. When it received its winery licence in 1970, it became the first winery in the Yarra Valley to open its doors in the 20th century, a distinction often ignored or forgotten (by this author as well as others).

🍷🍷🍷🍷🍷 **Estate Shiraz 2014** A very distinguished Yarra Valley shiraz born of a cool vintage, intense but not extractive, complex but clearly varietal, all within the compass of the cool climate. For the record, black and blue fruits dominate, but not to the exclusion of red fruit notes, with the tannins precisely managed. Diam. 13.5% alc. **Rating** 95 **To** 2034 $40

Chardonnay 2014 Certainly gets well past wannabe sauvignon blanc territory with ripe stone fruits to the fore, citrus/grapefruit lined to acidity on the finish;

the oak has been restrained, befitting the elegant nature of the wine. Screwcap. 12.7% alc. **Rating** 94 **To** 2025 $24

Rose 2015 Early-picked cabernet. Pink tinged with salmon; the colour, bouquet and palate all point to barrel fermentation in used French oak; while bone dry, it has texture verging on viscosity, the bright red berry flavours and notes of spice all adding up to a very, very good rose – one that can be drunk now or later. Screwcap. 12% alc. **Rating** 94 **To** 2020 $18 ⊙

𝍢𝍢𝍢𝍢𝍢 **Riesling 2015 Rating** 91 **To** 2022 $19 ⊙

Kelman Vineyard   ★★★☆

2 Oakey Creek Road, Pokolbin, NSW 2320 **Region** Hunter Valley
T (02) 4991 5456 **www.**kelmanvineyard.com.au **Open** 7 days 10–4
Winemaker Jeff Byrne **Est.** 1999 **Dozens** 1600 **Vyds** 9.3ha
Kelman Vineyard is a California-type development: a 40ha property has been subdivided into 80 residential development lots, with vines wending between the lots, which are under common ownership. Part of the chardonnay was grafted to shiraz before coming into full production, and the vineyard has the potential to produce 8000 dozen bottles per year.

𝍢𝍢𝍢𝍢 **Moscato 2015** This is a lot to pay for a half-bottle of moscato, but it is a good one, with a pretty pale salmon hue, clean and bright flavours of lemon, strawberries, musk and ginger and plenty of sweetness (93g/l). Screwcap. 6% alc. **Rating** 88 **To** 2016 $18 TS

Kennedy   ★★★★

Maple Park, 224 Wallenjoe Road, Corop, Vic 3559 (postal) **Region** Heathcote
T (03) 5484 8293 **www.**kennedyvintners.com.au **Open** Not
Winemaker Sandro Mosele (Contract) **Est.** 2002 **Dozens** 1000 **Vyds** 29.2ha
Having been farmers in the Colbinabbin area of Heathcote for 27 years, John and Patricia Kennedy were on the spot when a prime piece of red Cambrian soil on the east-facing slope of Mt Camel Range became available for purchase. They planted 20ha of shiraz in 2002. As they gained knowledge of the intricate differences within the site, and worked with contract winemaker Sandro Mosele, further plantings of shiraz, tempranillo and mourvedre followed in '07. The Shiraz is made in small open fermenters, using indigenous yeasts and gentle pigeage before being taken to French oak (20% new) for 12 months' maturation prior to bottling.

𝍢𝍢𝍢𝍢𝍢 **Cambria Heathcote Shiraz 2013** Heathcote has suffered from intermittent excessive alcohol over the past 10+ years, part beyond control in the all too numerous drought years, part due to acceptance of the new normal, a sad state of affairs. This shows that all the flavour needed, and then some, can come from moderate alcohol. Blackberry, satsuma plum, spice and pepper are all here before you meet up with the tannin and oak contributions. Diam. 13.5% alc. **Rating** 92 **To** 2030 $32

Pink Hills 2015 Estate-grown mataro. Pale salmon-pink; a perfumed bouquet leads into an initially juicy palate that changes stride towards the finish with pleasingly dry, chalky notes. Has the X-factor. Screwcap. 13.5% alc. **Rating** 90 **To** 2017 $20 ⊙

𝍢𝍢𝍢𝍢 **Heathcote Shiraz 2013 Rating** 88 **To** 2023 $25

🍇 Kensington Wines   ★★★★

1590 Highlands Road, Whiteheads Creek, Vic 3660 **Region** Upper Goulburn
T (03) 5796 9155 **www.**kensingtonwines.com.au **Open** Sun 11–5
Winemaker Nina Stocker, Frank Bonic **Est.** 2010 **Dozens** 20 000 **Vyds** 4ha
This is the venture of husband and wife Anddy and Kandy Xu, born and raised in China, but now resident in Australia, who have built up Kensington Wines over the past six years. They have created a broad portfolio of wines by sourcing grapes and wines, mostly from

regions across Vic, but also SA. While the primary market is China (and other Asian countries), the wines have not been made with residual sugar sweetness, and are also sold in Australia. Kandy and Anddy's purchase of the Rocky Passes Vineyard (and cellar door) in the Upper Goulburn region in 2015 was a significant development in terms of their commitment to quality Australian wine, as was securing the services of winemaker Nina Stocker, daughter of Dr John Stocker, former chairman of the Grape and Wine Research & Development Corporation. Kandy has broadened her experience and wine qualifications by completing the WSET Diploma, and undertaking a vintage at Brown Brothers. She was co-founder of the Chinese Wine Association of Australia and continues as the chair of that Association. She has also translated the First Families of Wine book into Mandarin, and likewise translated my Top 100 Wineries of Australia into Mandarin. Exports to China and other Asia countries.

ΨΨΨΨΩ **Benella Vineyard Shiraz 2014** Matured in French oak (30% new) for 12–18 months. Good colour; a well-made wine, black cherry and plum fruit providing both the aromas of the bouquet and the flavours on the palate; French oak and tannins contribute to texture and structure. Screwcap. 14.5% alc. **Rating** 93 **To** 2034 $35

Heathcote Shiraz 2014 Matured in tank with staves, 70% in used French and American barrels for 12 months. Excellent colour; intense fruit and oak fill the full-bodied palate; the tannins are ripe and sit well with the fruit, giving the wine balance as well as length. Will develop well for decades, but can also be enjoyed as a younger wine. Screwcap. 14.5% alc. **Rating** 93 **To** 2034 $35

Traditional Method Mornington Peninsula Chardonnay Pinot Noir 2004 Well made, with very good white flowers/white peach notes leading on the bouquet and palate. The dosage has been precisely calculated, leaving the palate fresh, and seeking the next glass. It will develop further with another year or two in bottle. Diam. 12.5% alc. **Rating** 93 **To** 2018 $45

Nagambie Vineyard Goulburn Valley Shiraz 2013 Matured in French oak (50% new) for 18 months. Good colour; full-bodied, very rich, with an array of luscious black fruits, satsuma plum, dark spices and cedary oak. Will develop very well. Screwcap. 14.8% alc. **Rating** 92 **To** 2033 $45

Archduke Great Stone Coonawarra Cabernet Sauvignon 2013 50% matured in 1yo French oak for 12 months, 50% in used barrels with new French oak staves. Very good colour; professionally made, with medium to full-bodied layers of blackcurrant/cassis fruit, plum and cedary oak. The balance is good, as is the length, but it needs some years to slim down. Cork. 14% alc. **Rating** 91 **To** 2028 $35

Archduke Moppity Vineyards Hilltops Cabernet Sauvignon 2010 From an exceptional vineyard in the region with unlimited potential. Is now ready for enjoyment, its tannins softened, oak integrated and secondary/earthy/spicy flavours matched alongside supple cassis fruit. Cork. 12.9% alc. **Rating** 91 **To** 2020 $30

Brave Goose Vineyard Goulburn Valley Cabernet Shiraz 2014 Matured in French oak (35% new) for 12 months. Very good colour; an attractive, expressive bouquet of red fruits, the light to medium-bodied palate elegant and fresh, with good length and balance, subtle oak and light tannins. Cork. 13.8% alc. **Rating** 91 **To** 2024 $65

Estate Edition Limestone Coast Riesling 2013 Attractive development, with soft lime citrus fruit perfectly balanced by crisp acidity on the long palate; it has a dry finish, and will continue to gain flavour over the next 3 years. Screwcap. 12% alc. **Rating** 90 **To** 2020 $15 ✪

ΨΨΨΨ **Marquis Shiraz 2012 Rating** 89 **To** 2020 $25
Archduke Yarra Valley Trio Allegro 2010 Rating 89 **To** 2020 $35
Archduke Politini Vineyard King Valley Cabernet Sauvignon 2013 **Rating** 88 **To** 2020 $35

Kerrigan + Berry ★★★★★

PO Box 221, Cowaramup, WA 6284 **Region** South West Australia Zone
T (08) 9755 6046 **www.**kerriganandberry.com.au **Open** At Hay Shed Hill
Winemaker Michael Kerrigan, Gavin Berry **Est.** 2007 **Dozens** 1200
Owners Michael Kerrigan and Gavin Berry have been making wine in WA for a combined period of over 40 years, and say they have been most closely associated with the two varieties that in their opinion define WA: riesling and cabernet sauvignon. This is strictly a weekend and after-hours venture, separate from their respective roles as chief winemakers at Hay Shed Hill and West Cape Howe. They have focused on what is important, and explain, 'We have spent a total of zero hours on marketing research, and no consultants have been injured in the making of these wines.' Exports to the UK, the US, Singapore and China.

ΨΨΨΨΨ **Mt Barker Great Southern Frankland River Shiraz 2014** Fragrant black fruits, multi spices, licorice and a subnote of tar presage a totally distinguished and focused cool palate–cool in the sense of grapes that have been cool grown and picked at optimal ripeness, reflected by its sheer intensity. Screwcap. 14% alc. Rating 97 To 2044

ΨΨΨΨΨ **Mt Barker Great Southern Riesling 2015** Lemon and lime notes spider their way through to a biting, dramatic finish. Frisson meets pure white wine. Talc and mineral characters add to the landscape. Scintillating. Screwcap. 12% alc. **Rating** 95 To 2028 $30 CM ○
Mt Barker Margaret River Cabernet Sauvignon 2012 A complex wine, the colour excellent, the bouquet and palate both intense and focused; there is some new French oak, but the firm tannins need a few years to soften. Screwcap. 14% alc. **Rating** 95 To 2030 $70

Kersbrook Hill ★★★★

1498 South Para Road, Kersbrook, SA 5231 **Region** Adelaide Hills
T (08) 8389 3301 **www.**kersbrookhill.com.au **Open** 7 days 10–5.30
Winemaker Simon Greenleaf, Peter Schell, Ryan Haynes **Est.** 1998 **Dozens** 8000
Vyds 11ha
Paul and Mary Clark purchased what is now the Kersbrook Hill property, then grazing land, in 1997, planting 0.4ha of shiraz on a reality-check basis. Encouraged by the results, they increased the plantings to 3ha of shiraz and 1ha of riesling two years later. Yet further expansion of the vineyards has seen the area under vine increased to 11ha, cabernet sauvignon (with 6ha) the somewhat unusual frontrunner. Mark Whisson is consultant viticulturist (Mark has been growing grapes in the Adelaide Hills for over 20 years). Exports to the US, Singapore, Hong Kong and China.

ΨΨΨΨΨ **The Craftsman 2012** Deep straw-green; a most unusual riesling, matured for 2 years in second-use French oak. It results in an attractive cross between lime/citrus and peach/stone fruit, still with a gentle spine of acidity. A special wine that withstood the bushfire in Jan '15. Screwcap. 12% alc. **Rating** 94 To 2020 $60

ΨΨΨΨΨ **Grace Louise Cabernet Sauvignon 2012** Rating 93 To 2032 $80
Ripasso Shiraz 2011 Rating 92 To 2020 $40
Cabernet Sauvignon 2012 Rating 92 To 2022 $25 ○
Strange Bedfellows 2013 Rating 92 To 2028 $25 ○
Shiraz 2012 Rating 91 To 2032 $25
Riesling 2014 Rating 90 To 2020 $25

Kidman Wines ★★★★

13713 Riddoch Highway, Coonawarra, SA 5263 **Region** Coonawarra
T (08) 8736 5071 **www.**kidmanwines.com.au **Open** 7 days 10–5
Winemaker Sid Kidman **Est.** 1984 **Dozens** 6000 **Vyds** 17.2ha

Sid Kidman planted the first vines on the property in 1971, and has been managing the vineyard ever since. Over the years it has grown to include cabernet sauvignon, shiraz, riesling and sauvignon blanc. The cellar door is housed in the old stables on the property; they were built in 1859 and are a great link with the district's history. Susie and Sid have recently been joined by their son George, who becomes the fourth generation of the Kidman family to be involved with the property. Exports to Malaysia and China.

ŶŶŶŶ꒭ Riesling 2015 The crunch of apple and the sear of citrus. This has both flavour and acidity and as a result, satisfying length. It drinks well. Screwcap. 11.5% alc. **Rating** 90 **To** 2021 $16 CM ⊙

Shiraz 2013 Rich with fruit, oak and alcohol warmth; combined, they create a wine which, just, works. Plum and black cherry with gum leaf and toasty/malty oak over the top. Screwcap. 14% alc. **Rating** 90 **To** 2022 $22 CM

Kies Family Wines   ★★★★☆

Lot 2 Barossa Valley Way, Lyndoch, SA 5381 **Region** Barossa Valley
T (08) 8524 4110 **www.**kieswines.com.au **Open** 7 days 9–4
Winemaker Joanne Irvine **Est.** 1969 **Dozens** 5000 **Vyds** 30ha
The Kies family has been resident in the Barossa Valley since 1857; the present generation of winemakers is the fifth. Until 1969 the family sold almost all their grapes, but in that year they launched their own brand, Karrawirra. The coexistence of Killawarra forced a name change in '83 to Redgum Vineyard; this business was subsequently sold. Later still, Kies Family Wines opened for business, drawing upon vineyards (up to 100 years old) that had remained in the family throughout the changes, offering a wide range of wines through the 1880 cellar door. Exports to Singapore, Hong Kong and China.

ŶŶŶŶŶ Dedication Shiraz 2014 Has a bit of swagger to it. The fruit struts, the tannin crashes, the flavours curl on and out through the finish. We're talking red and black berries, licorice, smoky/cedary oak and and drills of graphite. It's a substantial wine, the premium price entirely warranted. Cork. 14.5% alc. **Rating** 95 **To** 2030 $45 CM

ŶŶŶŶ꒭ Generations Tawny Port NV **Rating** 92 **To** 2017 $65 CM
Chaff Mill Cabernet Sauvignon 2012 **Rating** 91 **To** 2025 $30 CM

Kilikanoon   ★★★★★

Penna Lane, Penwortham, SA 5453 **Region** Clare Valley
T (08) 8843 4206 **www.**kilikanoon.com.au **Open** 7 days 11–5
Winemaker Kevin Mitchell, Barry Kooij **Est.** 1997 **Dozens** 80000 **Vyds** 330ha
Kilikanoon has travelled in the fast lane since winemaker Kevin Mitchell established it in 1997 on the foundation of 6ha of vines he owns with father Mort. With the aid of investors, its 80000-dozen production comes from over 300ha of estate-owned vineyards, and access to the best grapes from a total of 2266ha across SA. Between 2013 and early '14 all links between Kilikanoon and Seppeltsfield were ended; the sale of Kilikanoon's share in Seppeltsfield, together with the sale of Kilikanoon's Crowhurst Vineyard in the Barossa Valley, led to the purchase by Kilikanoon of the winery which it had previously leased, and purchase of the Mount Surmon Vineyard. Exports to most major markets.

ŶŶŶŶŶ Attunga 1865 Clare Valley Shiraz 2012 Deep, but vivid, crimson-purple; a great Australian full-bodied shiraz, 150yo vines planted on terra rossa and limestone soil, and given kid gloves in the winery. The rich and velvety array of black fruits are framed by quality oak and tannins that the French might say are à point: definitely there, but unobtrusive. It will amble through the next 50 years. Screwcap. 14.5% alc. **Rating** 97 **To** 2062 $250

ŶŶŶŶŶ Mort's Reserve Clare Valley Riesling 2015 Hand-picked from the Khileyre and Mort's Block Vineyards. Takes up where the worthy Killerman's Run Riesling leaves off; the floral bouquet leads into a torrent of lemon, lime and grapefruit flavours bound together by natural acidity on the exceptionally long palate and aftertaste. Screwcap. 12.5% alc. **Rating** 96 **To** 2035 $35 ❂

Attunga Clare Valley Mataro 2013 The bouquet is complex; savoury notes of black olive, tar and cured meat with red fruit, mint and charry oak. The fruit wins through on the palate, with the flavours of dark cherry prominent, the savoury elements chiming in, the depth, length and persistent finish of fine tannin outstanding. Screwcap. 14.5% alc. **Rating** 96 **To** 2033 $44 ❂

Exodus Barossa Valley Shiraz 2014 I really like this wine: its open weave, medium body and freshness all come together on an expressive bouquet and long, lingering palate. The fruit/oak/tannin balance couldn't be improved on, making it an ace in the hole for consumption at any time you need a classy wine that won't take over the conversation. Screwcap. 14.5% alc. **Rating** 95 **To** 2034 $40

Baudinet Blend Clare Valley Grenache Shiraz Mataro 2013 50% grenache, 40% shiraz, 10% mataro, matured for 15 months in French oak (10% new). A Clare Valley GSM with deeper colour, greater structure, more dark fruits and all-up attitude than most – doubly surprising given that grenache, not shiraz, is the senior partner. Screwcap. 14.5% alc. **Rating** 95 **To** 2023 $55

Mort's Block Clare Valley Riesling 2015 Low-yielding, hand-picked vines from Watervale provide the fruit and dictate the style; this is Clare riesling in a stern frame of mind. The bouquet is all about lemon and grapefruit rather than blossom and talc, and the palate is austere and minerally. Slatey acidity is the backbone and the lasting impression on the finish. Lock it up in the cellar and hide the key. Screwcap. 12.5% alc. **Rating** 94 **To** 2035 $25 ❂

Killerman's Run Clare Valley Riesling 2015 Its bouquet is good, but it's the palate that gets all the antennae wagging, with its ravishing lemon/lime citrus fruit curling through to the long finish. Screwcap. 12.5% alc. **Rating** 94 **To** 2030 $20 ❂

Prophecy Barossa Valley Shiraz 2014 Matured in French oak (30% new) for 18 months. The bouquet comes at you in a rush of black fruits and cedary oak, but any apprehension of excessive extract disappears on the palate. While full-bodied, it is very well balanced. Screwcap. 14.5% alc. **Rating** 94 **To** 2039 $44

Miracle Hill McLaren Vale Shiraz 2012 If you want a full-boded shiraz to match a flame-grilled Bistecca Fiorentino this is your wine, and you can do without any side dishes. It is full to the brim with savoury blackberry fruit, and tannins that strike hard as the wine enters the mouth but, having made their point, retract their claws. Screwcap. 14.5% alc. **Rating** 94 **To** 2042 $80

Mort's Cut Watervale Riesling 2013 Dessert style but with no obvious botrytis. Clearly riesling on the bouquet, showing some toasty development and richness of aroma. Lime juice and honey flavours dance across the palate, with impeccably fine acidity the perfect counterweight to the relatively moderate sweetness. Quite lovely. 375ml. Screwcap. 11% alc. **Rating** 94 **To** 2025 $30 ❂

♟♟♟♟♀ **Killerman's Run Clare Valley Shiraz 2014** Rating 93 To 2022 $20 ❂
Tregea Reserve Clare Valley Cabernet Sauvignon 2012 Rating 93 To 2032 $80
Covenant Clare Valley Shiraz 2013 Rating 92 To 2030 $40
Duke Reserve Clare Valley Grenache 2013 Rating 92 To 2023 $80

Killerby   ★★★★☆

4259 Caves Road, Wilyabrup, WA 6280 **Region** Margaret River
T (08) 9755 5983 **www.**killerby.com.au **Open** 7 days 10–5
Winemaker Marco Pinares, Marelize Russouw **Est.** 1973 **Dozens** NFP **Vyds** 4ha
Owned by Ferngrove Vineyards Pty Ltd since 2008, Killerby has relaunched, opening its architect-designed 'Cellar Store' (with one of the longest tasting benches in Australia) in 2013. With a variety of local produce available, it pays homage to the history of the Killerby family (in the late 1930s, Benjamin George Lee Killerby established a general store to supply the pioneers of the region, with grandson Dr Benjamin Barry Killerby planting one of the first vineyards in Geographe in '73). Exports to the UK.

ΨΨΨΨΨ **Chardonnay 2014** Matured in French oak, two-thirds new, one-third 1yo. Unusually fine and elegant in the context of Margaret River, rather than rich and complex; its length and balance are immaculate. Six gold medals '15. Screwcap. 13.5% alc. **Rating** 96 **To** 2026 $30 ✪

Shiraz 2013 Spent 14 months in 100% new French oak, an expensive way to make a $32 wine. The oak manages to integrate with the fruit, finishing its fermentation in barrel having been a great help. The fruits are all black, blackberry to the fore, and the tannins are fine-grained and ripe. Screwcap. 14.5% alc. **Rating** 94 **To** 2038

Cabernet Sauvignon 2014 Matured in new French oak for 14 months. Bright crimson-purple; it's a toss-up deciding between the length or the depth as the most impressive part of the wine. It has that layered complexity of the region that is sometimes soft, as it is here, but tannins are still very evident (as they should be). Screwcap. 14% alc. **Rating** 94 **To** 2034 $32

Killibinbin   ★★★★

PO Box 10, Langhorne Creek, SA 5255 **Region** Langhorne Creek
T (08) 8537 3382 **www.**killibinbin.com.au **Open** Not
Winemaker Jim Urlwin **Est.** 1997 **Dozens** 3500 **Vyds** 10ha
In late 2010 Guy and Liz Adams (of Metala Vineyards fame) acquired the Killibinbin brand. The wines continue to be sourced solely from the Metala Vineyards (10ha are dedicated to Killibinbin: 5ha each of shiraz and cabernet sauvignon). Exports to the UK, the US, Canada, Sweden, Denmark, Ukraine, South Korea and Taiwan.

ΨΨΨΨΨ **Scream Langhorne Creek Shiraz 2013** Matured for 18 months in 20% new American barriques and 80% used French and American barriques. Deep colour; a full-bodied, rich wine in typical Killibinbin style; the decision to cut back on new oak was correct, the omelette of fruit, tannins and oak on maximum settings. Screwcap. 14.5% alc. **Rating** 91 **To** 2028 $27

ΨΨΨΨ **Scaredy Cat Langhorne Creek Cabernet Sauvignon Shiraz 2013** **Rating** 89 **To** 2023 $19 ✪

Killiecrankie Wines   ★★★★

103 Soldier Road, Ravenswood, Vic 3453 **Region** Bendigo
T (03) 5435 3155 **www.**killiecrankiewines.com **Open** W'ends 11–6
Winemaker John Monteath **Est.** 2000 **Dozens** 400 **Vyds** 1ha
John Monteath moved to the Bendigo region in 1999 to pursue his interest in viticulture and winemaking, and while helping to establish the vineyard from which the grapes are sourced, gained experience at Water Wheel, Heathcote Estate, Balgownie and Blackjack. The vineyard is planted to four shiraz clones, and is the backbone of the Bendigo wine. The small crop is hand-picked, with the resultant wines made in true garagiste style. Small parcels of premium fruit are also sourced from meticulously tended vineyards in Bendigo and Heathcote.

ΨΨΨΨΨ **Crankie Pearl 2015** Viognier. Heady version thereof but it makes it work. Rich with warm spice, fennel, stone fruit and slate. Lingers well. Impressive. Screwcap. 13.5% alc. **Rating** 93 **To** 2016 $25 CM ✪

Bendigo Shiraz 2013 Strong with oak. Ripe plum and mint flavours come swamped by vanillan. It's smooth and generally attractive, but it's always a concern when both the first and last impression come from the barrel rather than the vineyard. Screwcap. 14% alc. **Rating** 90 **To** 2025 $40 CM

ΨΨΨΨ **Montspear Heathcote Shiraz 2014** **Rating** 89 **To** 2020 $20 CM
Ruby Shiraz 2014 **Rating** 88 **To** 2019 $23 CM
Lola Montez Tempranillo 2015 **Rating** 88 **To** 2019 $25 CM

Kiltynane Estate

Cnr School Lane/Yarra Glen-Healesville Road, Tarrawarra, Vic 3775 **Region** Yarra Valley
T 0418 339 555 **www**.kiltynane.com.au **Open** W'ends 11–4
Winemaker Kate Kirkhope **Est.** 2000 **Dozens** 500

Kate Kirkhope sold her Yarra Valley vineyard and moved to the Bellarine Peninsula. The brand name Kiltynane Estate has been retained, the grapes coming partly from the Yarra Valley and partly from Swan Bay. Back vintages of Kiltynane's Yarra Valley-grown and made wines are also still available. Exports to Denmark.

🍷🍷🍷🍷 **Bellarine Peninsula Pinot Noir 2013** 12 months in French oak (new and used). Incredibly deep colour for a pinot, and the palate lives up to the colour, with black cherry and plum relentlessly filling the mouth. What it was like when taken from the barrel I can't imagine, any more than I can be sure where the wine is headed. Screwcap. 13% alc. **Rating** 90 **To** 2033 $50

Kimbolton Wines

The Winehouse Cellar Door, 1509 Langhorne Creek Road, Langhorne Creek, SA 5255
Region Langhorne Creek
T (08) 8537 3359 **www**.kimboltonwines.com.au **Open** 7 days 10–5
Winemaker Contract **Est.** 1998 **Dozens** 1500 **Vyds** 55.4ha

The Kimbolton property originally formed part of the Potts Bleasdale estate; in 1946 it was acquired by Henry and Thelma Case, parents of current owner, Len Case. The grapes from the vineyard plantings (cabernet sauvignon, shiraz, chardonnay, carignan and montepulciano) are sold to leading wineries, with small amounts retained for the Kimbolton label. The name comes from a medieval town in Bedfordshire, UK, from which some of Len's wife Judy's ancestors emigrated.

🍷🍷🍷🍷 **The Rifleman Langhorne Creek Shiraz 2012** There's a lot to admire in this medium to full-bodied shiraz: its colour, black fruit and earthy/foresty bouquet and its full-on savoury palate with licorice and chocolate adding to the impact. Screwcap. 14.8% alc. **Rating** 93 **To** 2027 $50
Special Release Brad's Block Langhorne Creek Montepulciano 2014 A lively fusion of springtime red flowers and fruits with a few violets poking their noses through; positively delicate mouthfeel is most attractive. Don't let the horse get out of the stable. Screwcap. 13.5% alc. **Rating** 93 **To** 2020 $30
Fig Tree Langhorne Creek Cabernet Sauvignon 2013 Deep, bright crimson-purple; has luscious fruits with clear varietal expression, here putting cassis upfront on the stage, the orchestra in the pit in front providing plush texture and structure. Screwcap. 14.4% alc. **Rating** 91 **To** 2028 $24

King River Estate

3556 Wangaratta-Whitfield Road, Wangaratta, Vic 3678 **Region** King Valley
T (03) 5729 3689 **www**.kingriverestate.com.au **Open** 7 days 11–5
Winemaker Trevor Knaggs **Est.** 1996 **Dozens** 3000 **Vyds** 13ha

Trevor Knaggs, with assistance from father Colin, began the establishment of King River Estate in 1990, making the first wines in '96. The initial plantings of chardonnay and cabernet sauvignon were followed by merlot and shiraz. More recent plantings have extended the varietal range to include verdelho, viognier, barbera and sangiovese. Biodynamic practices are used in the vineyard. Exports to China and Singapore.

🍷🍷🍷 **King Valley Saperavi 2014** Inky colour. Ripped with tannin, but there's (just) enough fruit to make you think this style could work, given time. Screwcap. 14.5% alc. **Rating** 88 **To** 2023 $35 CM

Kingston Estate Wines ★★★★

Sturt Highway, Kingston-on-Murray, SA 5331 **Region** South Australia
T (08) 8243 3700 **www.**kingstonestatewines.com **Open** Not
Winemaker Bill Moularadellis, Brett Duffin, Helen Foggo, Donna Hartwig **Est.** 1979
Dozens 100 000 **Vyds** 1000ha

Kingston Estate, under the direction of Bill Moularadellis, has its production roots in the Riverland region, but also has long-term purchase contracts with growers in the Clare Valley, the Adelaide Hills, Coonawarra, Langhorne Creek and Mount Benson. It has also spread its net to take in a wide range of varietals, mainstream and exotic, under a number of brands at various price points. Exports to all major markets.

🍷🍷🍷🍷🍷 **Echelon Shiraz 2012** Medium-bodied but with ample flavour. Blackberry, ground coffee, bitter choc and perhaps some earth-like notes. It fills the mouth and satisfies; tannin has been well massaged into the boot. Screwcap. 14.5% alc. **Rating** 92 **To** 2021 $29 CM
Adelaide Hills Sauvignon Blanc 2015 Well put together. Clean, frisky citrus and passionfruit flavours come with just enough intensity, and just enough deftness of touch. Value. Screwcap. 12% alc. **Rating** 91 **To** 2016 $16 CM ○
Shiraz 2014 Clare Valley, Mount Benson. Depth of flavour is very good. Mint, earth, choc and blackberry. No argument over its mouthfilling delivery of flavour. Just enough length. Screwcap. 14.5% alc. **Rating** 90 **To** 2020 $16 CM ○
Merlot 2014 Mount Benson, Clare Valley. Sweet berried fruit with a light dusting of dried herbs. Emphasis on red berries more than black. It works. Screwcap. 13.5% alc. **Rating** 90 **To** 2020 $16 CM ○

🍷🍷🍷🍷 **Padthaway Chardonnay 2015** **Rating** 88 **To** 2017 $16 CM ○
Adelaide Hills Pinot Gris 2015 **Rating** 88 **To** 2017 $16 CM ○

Kirrihill Wines ★★★★

12 Main North Road, Clare, SA 5453 **Region** Clare Valley
T (08) 8842 4087 **www.**kirrihillwines.com.au **Open** 7 days 10–4
Winemaker Hamish Seabrook **Est.** 1998 **Dozens** 30 000

Kirrihill was founded in 1998 in the picturesque Clare Valley. Grapes are sourced from specially selected parcels of Kirrihill's 600ha of managed vineyards, as well as the Edwards and Stanway families' properties in the region. The Regional Range comprises blends from across the region, while the Vineyard Selection Series aims to elicit a sense of place from the chosen vineyards. The Alternative range features Fiano, Vermentino, Montepulciano, Nebbiolo, Tempranillo and Sangiovese. Exports to all major markets.

🍷🍷🍷🍷🍷 **Vineyard Selection Series Watervale Riesling 2015** Citrus girded with steel. Long slatey finish, studded with lime rind/pith characters. Impressive. Screwcap. 12.6% alc. **Rating** 94 **To** 2025 $20 CM ○
Vineyard Selection Series Tullymore Vineyard Clare Valley Cabernet Sauvignon 2013 Inky black-purple in colour. Brooding varietal aromas of dense blackcurrant, blackberry, dried herb and mint. Oak sits in the background but quietly makes its presence felt. Richly and deeply flavoured with the elements of the bouquet taking their place again on the palate. Overall a substantial and convincing style which will evolve over many years without doubt. Screwcap. 14.8% alc. **Rating** 94 **To** 2035 $25 ○

🍷🍷🍷🍷🍷 **Tullymore Vineyard Shiraz 2013** **Rating** 93 **To** 2024 $20 CM ○
Mount Lofty Montepulciano 2014 **Rating** 93 **To** 2034 $28
Regional Range Clare Valley Riesling 2015 **Rating** 91 **To** 2021 $16 CM ○
Regional Range Clare Valley Shiraz 2014 **Rating** 91 **To** 2029 $18 ○
Regional Range Clare Valley Cabernet Sauvignon 2014 **Rating** 91 **To** 2039 $18 ○
Adelaide Hills Arneis 2014 **Rating** 90 **To** 2018 $25
Clare Valley Sangiovese 2014 **Rating** 90 **To** 2020 $28

KJB Wine Group

2 Acri Street, Prestons, NSW (postal) **Region** McLaren Vale
T 0409 570 694 **Open** Not
Winemaker Kurt Brill **Est.** 2008 **Dozens** 550
KJB Wine Group (formerly Oenotria Vintners) is the venture of Kurt Brill, who began his involvement in the wine industry in 2003, largely through the encouragement of his wife Gillian. He commenced the wine marketing course at the University of Adelaide, but ultimately switched from that to the winemaking degree at CSU. His main business is the distribution company Grace James Fine Wines, but he also runs a virtual winery operation, purchasing cabernet sauvignon and shiraz from vineyards in McLaren Vale. Exports to the UK and The Netherlands.

PPPPP Land of the Vines Cabernets 2013 Cabernet sauvignon and cabernet franc, two-thirds in the former's favour. This announces both its quality and its value from the outset. Substantial core of blackberried flavour comes offset by dried grass, bitter choc and mint-like notes. Earth and undergrowth aspects add to the complex show. Assertive tannin brings yet more flavour with it. Warm with alcohol, but quite stunning. Screwcap. 15% alc. **Rating** 95 **To** 2026 $23 CM ✪

PPPP Land of the Vines Cabernet Sauvignon 2013 Rating 88 **To** 2020 $23 CM

Knappstein

2 Pioneer Avenue, Clare, SA 5453 **Region** Clare Valley
T (08) 8841 2100 **www.**knappstein.com.au **Open** Mon–Fri 9–5, w'ends 11–4
Winemaker Glenn Barry **Est.** 1969 **Dozens** 40 000 **Vyds** 114ha
Knappstein's full name is Knappstein Enterprise Winery & Brewery, reflecting its history before being acquired by Petaluma, and since then part of Lion Nathan's stable. The substantial mature estate vineyards in prime locations supply grapes both for the Knappstein brand and for wider Petaluma use. Exports to all major markets.

PPPPP The Insider Limited Release Clare Valley Shiraz Malbec 2014 A 60/40% blend, 100% whole bunches, hand-plunged, all gravity flows, no mention of oak at any stage, nor evident in the freshness and precision of its red fruit finish. As ready now as it will ever be. Screwcap. 12% alc. **Rating** 90 **To** 2018 $28

PPPP The Insider Riesling 2014 Rating 89 **To** 2024 $28

Knee Deep Wines

160 Johnson Road, Wilyabrup, WA 6280 **Region** Margaret River
T (08) 9755 6776 **www.**kneedeepwines.com.au **Open** 7 days 10–5
Winemaker Bruce Dukes **Est.** 2000 **Dozens** 7500 **Vyds** 20. ha
Perth surgeon and veteran yachtsman Phil Childs and wife Sue have planted their property in Wilyabrup to chardonnay (3.2ha), sauvignon blanc (4ha), semillon (1.48ha), chenin blanc (4ha), cabernet sauvignon (6.34ha) and shiraz (1.24ha). The name, Knee Deep Wines, was inspired by the passion and commitment needed to produce premium wine and as a tongue-in-cheek acknowledgement of jumping in 'boots and all' during a testing time in the wine industry, the grape glut building more or less in tune with the venture. Exports to Germany.

PPPPP Kim's Limited Release Margaret River Chardonnay 2013 Whole bunch-pressed, free-run juice fermented in French oak (33–40% new), 20–30% spontaneous mlf, matured on lees for 10 months. A seriously good chardonnay, beautifully made. The fruit definition is perfect – racy grapefruit and juicy white peach – the oak integration and balance likewise, the finish compelling. Still exceptionally youthful. Screwcap. 13.5% alc. **Rating** 96 **To** 2023 $45 ✪
Hayley's Limited Release Margaret River Shiraz 2014 Whole-berry ferment 10–14 days, matured in French oak (33–40% new) for 10–14 months with occasional lees stirring. Bright, clear colour; cherry and spice aromas on the bouquet lead into a fresh, lively medium-bodied palate, red fruits to the fore, the

juicy flavours given context by fine, yet savoury, tannins. All up, perfect balance and length. Screwcap. 14% alc. **Rating** 95 **To** 2029 $65

Kelsea's Limited Release Margaret River Cabernet Sauvignon 2012 Fermented on skins 12–18 days, pressed to French oak (40–50% new) for 10–18 months. A full-bodied, complex cabernet that has had all the winemaking dials turned up to maximum, but in tune with each other, and in balance. The primary blackcurrant fruit is hedged by black olive, the tannins positive but fine, the oak obvious but not excessive. Screwcap. 14.5% alc. **Rating** 95 **To** 2037 $65

🍷🍷🍷🍷🍷 Margaret River Sauvignon Blanc Semillon 2015 **Rating** 91 **To** 2020 $18 ○
Margaret River Sauvignon Blanc 2015 **Rating** 90 **To** 2018 $22

Knotting Hill Estate Vineyard   ★★★★

247 Carter Road, Wilyabrup WA 6280 **Region** Margaret River
T (08) 9755 7733 www.knottinghill.com.au **Open** 7 days 11–5
Winemaker Flying Fish Cove (Simon Ding) **Est.** 1997 **Dozens** 3500 **Vyds** 37.5ha
The Gould family has been farming in WA since 1907, and still owns the land grant taken up on their arrival from Scotland. In '97 two generations of the family decided to diversify, and acquired Knotting Hill, their Wilyabrup property. In '98, using their extensive farming background, they propagated 56 000 cuttings in an onsite nursery, supervised plantings, created a 5.5ha lake, and built the 45m bridge entry to the local limestone cellar door. In 2002 they leased the wheat farm, and have since devoted all their time to Knotting Hill. The spectacular vineyard setting is established within a natural amphitheatre, with the lake at the bottom.

🍷🍷🍷🍷🍷 Jack Gordon Margaret River Cabernet Sauvignon 2013 Dark colour and flavour. Blackcurrant, gravel, eucalypt and chocolate flavours fill the palate and extend faithfully out through the finish. Tannin throws a lasso around it all. Promising future ahead. Screwcap. 13.5% alc. **Rating** 94 **To** 2028 $48 CM

🍷🍷🍷🍷🍷 Michael Thomas Margaret River Malbec 2014 **Rating** 90 **To** 2020 $48 CM

Koonara   ★★★★★

44 Main Street, Penola, SA 5277 **Region** Coonawarra
T (08) 8737 3222 www.koonara.com **Open** 7 days 10–6
Winemaker Peter Douglas **Est.** 1988 **Dozens** 8000 **Vyds** 9ha
Koonara is a sister, or, more appropriately, a brother company to Reschke Wines. The latter is run by Burke Reschke, Koonara by his brother Dru. Both are sons of Trevor Reschke, who planted the first vines on the Koonara property in 1988. Peter Douglas, formerly Wynns' chief winemaker before moving overseas for some years, has returned to the district and is consultant winemaker. Since 2013 Koonara have leased and managed the Kongorong Partnership Vineyard in Mount Gambier, which had previously sold its grapes to Koonara. Exports to Canada, Singapore and China.

🍷🍷🍷🍷🍷 A Song for Alice Mount Gambier Riesling 2015 A perfumed, flowery bouquet paves the way for an extremely intense palate with electric acidity underwriting the lime/lemon/apple palate which has 5–10 years of body building in front of it. Screwcap. 12% alc. **Rating** 95 **To** 2030 $20 ○

Angel's Peak Coonawarra Shiraz 2013 Relatively light colour, but there is an abundance of fruit neatly balanced between sweet berries and more spicy/savoury notes, undoubtedly assisted by the moderate alcohol. The more you taste this wine, the more it impresses. Screwcap. 14% alc. **Rating** 95 **To** 2038 $22 ○

Cape Banks Mount Gambier Chardonnay 2015 The incisive cut and thrust of the wine is the direct result of the ultra-cool climate, not dissimilar to that of Henty. Grapefruit, white peach and nectarine are bound together by acidity, so tightly there is little room for oak to express itself. Screwcap. 13.7% alc. **Rating** 94 **To** 2024 $25 ○

🍷🍷🍷🍷🍷 Ambriel's Gift Family Reserve Coonawarra Cabernet Sauvignon 2013 **Rating** 93 **To** 2043 $45

Cape Banks Mount Gambier Pinot Noir 2013 Rating 92 To 2020 $25 ✪
The Guardian Angel Pinot Chardonnay 2015 Rating 90 To 2017 $25 TS

Koonowla Wines ★★★★

18 Koonowla Road, Auburn, SA 5451 **Region** Clare Valley
T (08) 8849 2270 **www.**koonowla.com **Open** W'ends & public hols 10–5
Winemaker O'Leary Walker Wines **Est.** 1997 **Dozens** 5000 **Vyds** 48.77ha
Koonowla is a historic Clare Valley property; situated just east of Auburn, it was first planted with vines in the 1890s, and by the early 1900s was producing 60 000 litres of wine annually. A disastrous fire in '26 destroyed the winery and wine stocks, and the property was converted to grain and wool production. Replanting of vines began in '85, and accelerated after Andrew and Booie Michael purchased the property in '91; there are now almost 50ha of cabernet sauvignon, riesling, shiraz, merlot and semillon. In an all-too-familiar story, the grapes were sold until falling prices forced a change in strategy; now a major part of the grapes is vinified by the infinitely experienced David O'Leary and Nick Walker. Exports to the UK, the US, Scandinavia, Malaysia, China and NZ.

🍷🍷🍷🍷🍷 **The AJM Reserve Clare Valley Shiraz 2013** From a single estate block of red loam over chalky limestone, and a barrel (French) selection of the best. Counterintuitively, it hides its high alcohol (its siblings 14.5%) behind a veil of fresh fruit and acidity, not oak or tannins. That limestone must surely have played a role. Screwcap. 15% alc. **Rating** 94 To 2030 $40

🍷🍷🍷🍷🍷 **Clare Valley Shiraz 2013** Rating 93 To 2028 $22 ✪
Clare Valley Cabernet Sauvignon 2013 Rating 90 To 2028 $22

Kooyong ★★★★★

PO Box 153, Red Hill South, Vic 3937 **Region** Mornington Peninsula
T (03) 5989 4444 **www.**kooyongwines.com.au **Open** At Port Phillip Estate
Winemaker Glen Hayley **Est.** 1996 **Dozens** 13 000 **Vyds** 40ha
Kooyong, owned by Giorgio and Dianne Gjergja, released its first wines in 2001. The vineyard is planted to pinot noir (20ha), chardonnay (10.4ha) and, more recently, pinot gris (3ha). In July '15, following the departure of Sandro Mosele, his assistant of six years, Glen Hayley, was appointed to take his place. The Kooyong wines are made at the state-of-the-art winery of Port Phillip Estate, also owned by the Gjergjas. Exports to the UK, the US, Canada, Sweden, Norway, Singapore, Hong Kong, Japan and China.

🍷🍷🍷🍷🍷 **Single Vineyard Selection Haven Pinot Noir 2014** It rises to power on the back of meaty, weighty, black cherried fruit flavour, though notes of dried spice, smoky oak and tangy cranberry certainly contribute to the ascension. Ropes of tannin are the parliament in which the flavour cavorts. The outstanding form of this wine continues. Screwcap. 13% alc. **Rating** 96 To 2024 $75 CM ✪
Single Vineyard Selection Meres Pinot Noir 2014 This turns the screws on quality. It's firm and varietally rich with meat, spice, black cherry and volleys of undergrowth and assorted earth notes. It's as if it's been borne up out of the ground. It's savoury, smoky and sweet-fruited, but in the end it's nothing but itself. Screwcap. 13% alc. **Rating** 96 To 2024 $75 CM ✪
Single Vineyard Selection Ferrous Pinot Noir 2014 Super tight and structural with gun smoke, flint, dry cherry and sinewy herb notes striking a distinctive pose through the palate. Controlled reduction is a key part of the wine's make-up. So too tannin and acid. So too a charm of its own design. Screwcap. 12.5% alc. **Rating** 96 To 2024 $75 CM ✪
Clonale Mornington Peninsula Chardonnay 2015 About as delicious as chardonnay gets. Beautiful white peach and pear fruit, pure and sunny, angles slowly down to a sustained, toasty, mealy finish. A joy to drink. Screwcap. 13% alc. **Rating** 95 To 2020 $33 CM ✪
Massale Mornington Peninsula Pinot Noir 2014 A prototype of the modern drinking red. Complex, charming, mid-weight without being lacking, fragrant,

lengthy. Sweet fruit meets smoky reduction meets wood meets savoury herbs. Shine a light into any of its nooks and you'll find something fascinating. Don't hesitate: drink it now. Screwcap. 13% alc. **Rating** 95 **To** 2022 $33 CM ✪
Estate Mornington Peninsula Pinot Noir 2014 Emphasis on bright fruit is steadily taking a back seat at Kooyong as the murkier depths of the forest floor are rummaged through. This is stewy and earthen with woody spice and tangello notes pinging out in front. Dry tannin exerts a force on the wine; there's almost an Italianate feel here. Screwcap. 13% alc. **Rating** 94 **To** 2023 $53 CM

ŢŢŢŢŢ **Beurrot Pinot Gris 2015 Rating** 93 **To** 2017 $33 CM

Krinklewood Biodynamic Vineyard ★★★★☆

712 Wollombi Road, Broke, NSW 2330 **Region** Hunter Valley
T (02) 6579 1322 **www**.krinklewood.com **Open** Fri–Sun 10–5
Winemaker Rod Windrim **Est.** 1981 **Dozens** 8000 **Vyds** 19.9ha
Krinklewood is a family-owned certified biodynamic organic winery. Every aspect of the property is managed in a holistic and sustainable way, Rod Windrim's extensive herb crops, native grasses and farm animals all contributing to biodynamic preparations to maintain healthy soil biology. The small winery is home to a Vaslin Bucher basket press and two Nomblot French fermentation eggs, a natural approach to winemaking.

ŢŢŢŢŢ **Semillon 2015** Crushed and pressed free-run juice cool-fermented in stainless steel. Its engine cranks up slowly at first, but then increases speed on the mid-palate, and crashes through the sound barrier on the finish and aftertaste. Unsweetened lemon juice, lemon pith and rind, and high-tensile acidity take no prisoners. Screwcap. 10% alc. **Rating** 95 **To** 2035 $24 ✪
Basket Press Shiraz 2014 I suppose it's from the Hunter Valley, but it makes no specific claim of that on the label; mind you, the wine in the glass goes as far as an inanimate substance can to communicate with humans: it's elegant, spicy and savoury on one side, brimming with plum and dark berry fruit on the other, tannins and oak where they should be. Screwcap. 13.5% alc. **Rating** 94 **To** 2044 $45

ŢŢŢŢŢ **Francesca Rose 2015 Rating** 92 **To** 2017 $25 ✪

Kurrajong Downs ★★★☆

Casino Road, Tenterfield, NSW 2372 **Region** New England
T (02) 6736 4590 **www**.kurrajongdownswines.com **Open** Thurs–Mon 9–4
Winemaker Symphony Hill (Mike Hayes) **Est.** 2000 **Dozens** 2000 **Vyds** 4.4ha
Jonus Rhodes arrived at Tenterfield in 1858, lured by the gold he mined for the next 40 years, until his death in '98. He was evidently successful, for the family now runs a 2800ha cattle-grazing property, on which Lynton and Sue Rhodes began the development of their vineyard, at an altitude of 850m, in 1996. Plantings include pinot noir, shiraz, cabernet sauvignon, chardonnay, semillon, gewurztraminer and tempranillo.

ŢŢŢŢŢ **Black Duck Tenterfield Shiraz 2014** Mint, violets, garden herbs, black pepper; there's a fair bit going on here, if you listen hard enough; the volume isn't set too high but such attractive characters are there adorning the core of black cherried fruit. Screwcap. 14.5% alc. **Rating** 90 **To** 2022 $38 CM

ŢŢŢŢ **All Nations Tenterfield Pinot Noir 2014 Rating** 88 **To** 2019 $29 CM

Kurtz Family Vineyards ★★★★

731 Light Pass Road, Angaston, SA, 5353 **Region** Barossa Valley
T 0418 810 982 **www**.kurtzfamilyvineyards.com.au **Open** By appt
Winemaker Steve Kurtz **Est.** 1996 **Dozens** 1800 **Vyds** 15.04ha
The Kurtz family vineyard is at Light Pass, with 9ha of shiraz, the remainder planted to chardonnay, cabernet sauvignon, semillon, sauvignon blanc, petit verdot, grenache, mataro and malbec. Steve Kurtz has followed in the footsteps of his great-grandfather Ben Kurtz, who first

grew grapes at Light Pass in the 1930s. During a career working first at Saltram, and then at Foster's until 2006, Steve gained invaluable experience from Nigel Dolan, Caroline Dunn and John Glaetzer, among others. Exports to the US, Canada, Macau and China.

🍷🍷🍷🍷🍷 **Schmick Cabernet Sauvignon 2012** This is clearly the best wine in the Kurtz cellar, with rich cassis fruit in expensive new French oak for 27 months. Its Achilles heel is the linked problems of high alcohol and tannins that still make straight for the inside of the upper lip. There's a lot to enjoy if you have a very large helping of steak in front of you. Screwcap. 15% alc. **Rating** 94 **To** 2037 $80

🍷🍷🍷🍷🍷 **Seven Sleepers Barossa Cabernet Sauvignon Petit Verdot Shiraz Malbec 2013 Rating** 90 **To** 2020 $18 ✪

Kyneton Ridge Estate

90 Blackhill School Road, Kyneton, Vic 3444 **Region** Macedon Ranges
T (03) 5422 7377 **www.**kynetonridge.com.au **Open** W'ends & public hols 10–5
Winemaker John and Luke Boucher **Est.** 1997 **Dozens** 1000 **Vyds** 4ha
Established by John Boucher and partner Pauline Russell in the shadow of Black Mountain, an ideal environment for pinot noir and chardonnay vines. With five generations of winemaking behind them, John and Luke Boucher continue the quest for quality and refinement. They maintain the traditional hand-making processes that complement the character of the wines; new facilities have recently been introduced to enhance the production process for the sparkling wines. The additional production capacity gives the opportunity to source additional suitable quality parcels of shiraz and cabernet sauvignon from Macedon and Heathcote.

🍷🍷🍷🍷🍷 **Aged Release Premium Macedon Ranges Pinot Noir 2012** Estate-grown, hand-plunged, basket-pressed. Developing slowly as expected; still the big end of town. Same points and longevity. Screwcap. 13% alc. **Rating** 94 **To** 2022 $52

🍷🍷🍷🍷🍷 **The John Boucher Aged Release 2011 Rating** 92 **To** 2021 $32 TS
The John Boucher Aged Release 2009 Rating 90 **To** 2018 $45 TS

 # L.A.S. Vino

PO Box 361, Cowaramup, WA 6284 **Region** Margaret River
www.lasvino.com **Open** Not
Winemaker Nic Peterkin **Est.** 2013 **Dozens** 800
Nic Peterkin, owner of this newly established business, is the grandson of the late Diana Cullen (Cullen Wines) and the son of Mike Peterkin (Pierro). After graduating from Adelaide University with a Masters Degree in oenology, and travelling the world as a Flying Winemaker, he came back to roost in Margaret River with the ambition of making wines that are a little bit different, but also within the bounds of conventional oenological science. The intention is to keep the project small, and thus make only 200 dozen of each of Chardonnay, Chenin Blanc, Pinot Noir (Albino Pinot) and Touriga Nacional (Pirate Blend). Exports to the UK, Singapore and Japan.

🍷🍷🍷🍷🍷 **Margaret River Portuguese Pirate Blend 2013** 55/35/10% touriga nacional, tinta cao and sousao from 40yo vines lurking in the north of Margaret River, hand-picked in separate batches 2 weeks apart, with both bunch and berry sorting, wild fermented, matured in used oak for 18 months. An appropriately exotic mix of a plethora of spices, raspberry and red cherry, with fine-grained savoury tannins on the long finish. ProCork. 14% alc. **Rating** 94 **To** 2023 $63

🍷🍷🍷🍷🍷 **Wild Ferment Margaret River Chardonnay 2013 Rating** 90 **To** 2018 $46

 # L'Enologa Wines

2 Chard Court, Red Cliffs, Vic 3496 **Region** Murray Darling
T 0429 099 193 **www.**lenologa.com.au **Open** Not
Winemaker Elizabeth Marwood **Est.** 2015 **Dozens** 150

Elizabeth Marwood was born in Western Australia, and after 15 years' winemaking experience, moved to the Murray Darling in 2009. The move was triggered by completion of a year-long Masters degree in Italy at the University of Gastronomic Sciences. After working in a commercial winery for a few years, an opportunity arose to purchase alternative Italian varieties from the Chalmers Merbein Vineyard, and make small batch wines under the L'Enologa Wines label, L'Enologa being the Italian feminine form of winemaker. The ethos behind the brand is the selection of the correct varieties for the climate where they are grown.

ŸŸŸŸŸ **Aglianico 2015** Hand-picked, bunch-sorted, crushed, destemmed, some whole bunches, seed removal, wild open ferment, 14 days on skins, matured for 5 months in used oak. Strong tobacco and rose petal aromas, then a super-zesty, fresh palate; some red berries. Screwcap. 13% alc. **Rating** 90 **To** 2018 $30

ŸŸŸŸ **Fiano 2015 Rating** 89 **To** 2017 $25
Sangiovese Rosato 2015 Rating 89 **To** 2017 $25

La Bise   ★★★★
PO Box 918, Williamstown, SA 5351 **Region** Adelaide Hills/Southern Flinders
T 0439 823 251 **www.**labisewines.com.au **Open** Not
Winemaker Natasha Mooney **Est.** 2006 **Dozens** 1500
This is a reasonably significant busman's holiday for Natasha Mooney, a well-known and highly regarded winemaker whose 'day job' (her term) is to provide winemaking consultancy services for some of SA's larger wineries. This allows her to find small, unique parcels of grapes that might otherwise be blended into large-volume brands. She manages the arrangements so that there is no conflict of interest, making wines that are about fruit and vineyard expression. She aims for mouthfeel and drinkability without high alcohol, and for that she should be loudly applauded.

ŸŸŸŸŸ **Adelaide Hills Shiraz 2014** 12yo vines in the north of the Adelaide Hills at 330m. Full crimson-purple; a fragrant bouquet and a fresh, vibrant palate looking more like 13% than 14% alcohol; red cherry, spice and blood plum flavours are anchored on a bed of fine tannins. Screwcap. **Rating** 93 **To** 2029 $22 ✪
Adelaide Hills Pinot Gris 2015 From Gumeracha, hand-picked, whole bunch-pressed, tank-fermented with lees stirring before and after fermentation. Pink-bronze; given the no-frills vinification, the grapes have an X-factor – unless, of course, it's the lees stirring; there is an extra degree of mouthfeel. Screwcap. 13% alc. **Rating** 91 **To** 2017 $22 ✪
Adelaide Hills Arneis 2015 From 11yo vines at Kersbrook. Has edgy citrus/apple skin flavours that poke their noses up from time to time. It's a person of interest, as the police say. Screwcap. 13.2% alc. **Rating** 90 **To** 2018 $22
Le Petite Frais Adelaide Hills Rose 2015 Sangiovese, tempranillo and shiraz. The fragrant bouquet is akin to sitting in a strawberry field, the palate like picking strawberries that are still firm and fresh. Screwcap. 13.2% alc. **Rating** 90 **To** 2017 $22
Adelaide Hills Tempranillo 2014 Decidedly savoury nooks and crannies, and a good call of bruised tomato leaf aroma from Natasha Mooney. Barely medium-bodied, it looks as if it will develop earlier than some other tempranillos. Screwcap. 14% alc. **Rating** 90 **To** 2020 $22

La Linea   ★★★★
36 Shipsters Road, Kensington Park, SA 5068 (postal) **Region** Adelaide Hills
T (08) 8431 3556 **www.**lalinea.com.au **Open** Not
Winemaker Peter Leske **Est.** 2007 **Dozens** 3500 **Vyds** 9.5ha
La Linea is a partnership of several experienced wine industry professionals, including Peter Leske and David LeMire MW. Peter was among the first to recognise the potential of tempranillo in Australia, and his knowledge of it is reflected in the three wine styles made from the variety: Tempranillo Rose, Tempranillo blended from several Adelaide Hills vineyards, and Norteno, from a single vineyard at the northern end of the Hills. Two Rieslings are produced

under the Vertigo label: TRKN (short for trocken), and the off-dry 25GR (25g/l residual sugar). Exports to the UK.

ΨΨΨΨΨ **Norteno Adelaide Hills Tempranillo 2013** Mid-red, a touch of brick on the rim; dark fruits, spice and a hint of rose petal frame the brooding bouquet; fine-grained tannins with a savoury edge drive the palate firmly and assertively, finishing somewhat dry. Screwcap. 13.5% alc. **Rating** 91 **To** 2020 $35

ΨΨΨΨ **Vertigo 25GR Adelaide Hills Riesling 2015 Rating** 88 **To** 2016 $24

Lake Barrington Vineyard ★★★★☆

1133–1136 West Kentish Road, West Kentish, Tas 7306 **Region** Northern Tasmania
T (03) 6491 1249 **www**.lbv.com.au **Open** Wed–Sun 11–4 (Jan–Feb), w'ends 11–4 (Nov–Mar)
Winemaker Frogmore Creek (Alain Rousseau), White Rock, Julian Alcorso **Est.** 1986
Dozens 450 **Vyds** 1ha
Charles and Jill Macek purchased the vineyard from founder Maree Tayler in 2005. Charles is a distinguished company director (Telstra, Wesfarmers). Lake Barrington's primary focus is on high quality sparkling wine, and it has won many trophies and gold medals over the years at the Tasmanian Wine Show; it makes lesser quantities of chardonnay and pinot noir.

ΨΨΨΨ **Alexandra 2007** With no less than 8 years on lees, this is a cuvee layered with the nutty, toasty nuances of maturity, sustained by cool Tasmanian acidity. Well crafted by Alain Rousseau at Frogmore Creek, with integrated dosage supporting a long and linear finish, interrupted by phenolic grip. Diam. 12.5% alc. **Rating** 89 **To** 2017 $45 TS

Lake Breeze Wines ★★★★★

Step Road, Langhorne Creek, SA 5255 **Region** Langhorne Creek
T (08) 8537 3017 **www**.lakebreeze.com.au **Open** 7 days 10–5
Winemaker Greg Follett **Est.** 1987 **Dozens** 20000 **Vyds** 90ha
The Folletts have been farmers at Langhorne Creek since 1880, and grapegrowers since the 1930s. Part of the grape production is sold, but the quality of the Lake Breeze wines is exemplary, with the red wines particularly appealing. Lake Breeze also owns and makes the False Cape wines from Kangaroo Island. Exports to the UK, Switzerland, Denmark, Germany, Peru, Vietnam, Singapore, Hong Kong, Japan and China.

ΨΨΨΨΨ **False Cape The Captain Kangaroo Island Cabernet Sauvignon 2013**
The bouquet signals serious intent, and it's no bluff: this is a very good full-bodied cabernet, replete with a deep stream of blackcurrant fruit and the tannins and oak are right on the money. Screwcap. 14% alc. **Rating** 95 **To** 2030 $30 ✪
Arthur's Reserve Langhorne Creek Cabernet Sauvignon Petit Verdot Malbec 2013 90% cabernet sauvignon, 5% each petit verdot and malbec. A wine that pays homage to Arthur John Follett, who planted the first vines on the property in the 1880s, and to the ability of Langhorne Creek to produce very high quality cabernet. This wine effortlessly lays out the road map for great cabernet in the making to follow, luscious, yet firmly structured and well balanced. Screwcap. 14% alc. **Rating** 95 **To** 2033 $38
Winemaker's Selection Langhorne Creek Shiraz 2014 A wine that fills all the senses, with a complex bouquet of charcuterie and jet black fruits leading into a palate that opens with some fleeting red fruit notes before a savoury swell of black fruits takes command. Screwcap. 14.5% alc. **Rating** 94 **To** 2034 $38
Section 54 Langhorne Creek Shiraz 2014 Matured in French oak for 18 months. Full-flavoured rather than full-bodied, a rainbow of fruits rather than a bulwark of tannins, and supremely unconcerned whether it's consumed now or later. In a word, delicious. Screwcap. 14.5% alc. **Rating** 94 **To** 2029 $25 ✪

ΨΨΨΨΨ **The Drake Cabernet Sauvignon Shiraz 2012 Rating** 91 **To** 2042 $70

Lake Cooper Estate

1608 Midland Highway, Corop, Vic 316 **Region** Heathcote
T (03) 9387 7657 **www**.lakecooperestate.com.au **Open** W'ends & public hols 11–5
Winemaker Donald Risstrom, Sam Brewer **Est.** 1998 **Dozens** 7800 **Vyds** 29.8ha
Lake Cooper Estate is a substantial venture in the burgeoning Heathcote region, set on the side of Mt Camel Range with panoramic views of Lake Cooper, Greens Lake and the Corop township. Planting began in 1998 with 12ha of shiraz, subsequently extended to 18ha of shiraz and 9.5ha of cabernet sauvignon. Small amounts of merlot, chardonnay, sauvignon blanc and verdelho have since been planted. Exports to China.

🍷🍷🍷🍷🍷 **Well Bin 1962 Heathcote Shiraz 2013** Good colour; fragrant pepper and spice bouquet, then a medium-bodied palate with lively interaction between the spicy/peppery/licorice notes of the jet black fruits and the savoury tannins. Good tension. Cork. 14.5% alc. **Rating** 93 **To** 2030 $38
Pang Ler Heathcote Cabernet Sauvignon 2014 Good, bright colour; flooded with cassis, to the virtual exclusion of any other fruit flavours on the palate. Has a flavour bank here that will stand it in good stead for another decade as it gains more complexity. Cork. 14.5% alc. **Rating** 90 **To** 2029 $29

Lake George Winery ★★★★☆

Old Federal Highway, Lake George, NSW 2581 **Region** Canberra District
T (02) 9948 4676 **www**.lakegeorgewinery.com.au **Open** Wed–Sun 10–4.30
Winemaker Nick O'Leary **Est.** 1971 **Dozens** 3000 **Vyds** 20ha
Lake George Winery was established by legend-in-his-own-lifetime Dr Edgar Riek, who has contributed so much to the Canberra District and the Australian wine industry. It has now passed into good hands, and the plantings of 40-year-old chardonnay, pinot noir, cabernet sauvignon, semillon and merlot have been joined by shiraz, tempranillo, pinot gris, viognier, pinot noir and malbec. The winemaking techniques include basket-pressing and small batch barrel maturation under the expert eye of Nick O'Leary. Exports to China.

🍷🍷🍷🍷🍷 **Giannoula Riesling 2015** The vintage was ideal for Canberra District riesling, all of the wines with attitude, bordering on outright exuberance. Bickford's lime juice cordial on the finish is accompanied by acidity present through the length of the palate. Screwcap. 11.5% alc. **Rating** 92 **To** 2025 $25 ✪
Pinot Gris 2015 Cool-fermented and early-bottled. Quartz-white; emphatic, fresh and lively pear and citrus flavours. No-frills winemaking has been its own reward. Screwcap. 12% alc. **Rating** 92 **To** 2017 $25 ✪
Rose 2015 Shiraz, destemmed and crushed, 15 hours skin contact, fermented in stainless steel. Bright, light crimson-pink; red cherries and wild strawberries drive the bouquet and palate alike, with a twist of lemony acidity on the fresh finish. Plenty to enjoy here. Screwcap. 12% alc. **Rating** 90 **To** 2017 $18 ✪

🍷🍷🍷🍷 **Cabernet Merlot 2015 Rating** 89 **To** 2020 $20

Lake's Folly ★★★★★

2416 Broke Road, Pokolbin, NSW 2320 **Region** Hunter Valley
T (02) 4998 7507 **www**.lakesfolly.com.au **Open** 7 days 10–4 while wine available
Winemaker Rodney Kempe **Est.** 1963 **Dozens** 4500 **Vyds** 12.2ha
The first of the weekend wineries to produce wines for commercial sale, long revered for its Cabernet Sauvignon and nowadays its Chardonnay. Very properly, terroir and climate produce a distinct regional influence and thus a distinctive wine style. Lake's Folly no longer has any connection with the Lake family, having been acquired some years ago by Perth businessman Peter Fogarty. Peter's family company previously established the Millbrook Winery in the Perth Hills and has since acquired Deep Woods Estate in Margaret River, so is no stranger to the joys and agonies of running a small winery. Wines were received too late for the book, but tasting notes can be found on www.winecompanion.com.au.

Lambert Vineyards

810 Norton Road, Wamboin, NSW 2620 **Region** Canberra District
T (02) 6238 3866 **www**.lambertvineyards.com.au **Open** By appt
Winemaker Steve and Ruth Lambert **Est.** 1998 **Dozens** 2200 **Vyds** 10ha
Ruth and Steve Lambert have established riesling (2.5ha), pinot noir (1.8ha), chardonnay (1.6ha), pinot gris (1.4ha), merlot (1.2ha), cabernet sauvignon and shiraz (0.2ha each). Steve makes the many wines onsite, and does so with skill and sensitivity.

Riesling 2014 Bursting with apple and lime flavours. Impressive straight out of the blocks, and more or less holds its power all the way through to the finish. Drinking well now. Screwcap. 12.2% alc. **Rating** 94 To 2022 $18 CM ❂

Pinot Gris 2014 Rating 92 To 2016 $20 CM ❂
Shiraz 2013 Rating 92 To 2026 $25 CM ❂
Union 2013 Rating 90 To 2024 $25 CM

Lambrook Wines

6 Coorara Avenue, Payneham South, SA 5070 **Region** Adelaide Hills
T 0437 672 651 **www**.lambrook.com.au **Open** By appt
Winemaker Adam Lampit, Michael Sykes **Est.** 2008 **Dozens** 5000
This is a virtual winery created by husband and wife team Adam and Brooke Lampit. With almost two decades of industry experience between them, they began purchasing sauvignon blanc, shiraz and pinot noir (for sparkling) in 2008. Adam's experience has come through working with Stonehaven, Norfolk Rise and Bird in Hand.

Adelaide Hills Shiraz 2013 Open-fermented and matured in French oak for 15 months. Bright crimson-purple, this is an intriguing wine, with spice, black pepper, licorice and tar all present on the bouquet, the palate presenting an immediate replay, and managing to carry its alcohol without undue hardship. Screwcap. 14.5% alc. **Rating** 92 To 2028 $25 ❂
Adelaide Hills Chardonnay 2014 A no-nonsense chardonnay, with depth and integrity to its upfront stone fruit and cashew flavours, complexity coming courtesy of the citrus and mineral-accented acidity on the finish. Screwcap. 13% alc. **Rating** 90 To 2020 $30
Adelaide Hills Rose 2015 60% shiraz, 40% pinot noir. Vivid pink; lively, fresh and flavoursome, with cherry/strawberry/raspberry engaged in an even battle for supremacy; the crisp finish tightens things up nicely. Screwcap. 12% alc. **Rating** 90 To 2017 $20 ❂

Adelaide Hills Sauvignon Blanc 2015 Rating 89 To 2017 $20

Lamont's Winery

85 Bisdee Road, Millendon, WA 6056 **Region** Swan Valley
T (08) 9296 4485 **www**.lamonts.com.au **Open** Thurs–Sun 10–5
Winemaker Digby Leddin **Est.** 1978 **Dozens** 7000 **Vyds** 2ha
Corin Lamont is the daughter of the late Jack Mann, and oversees the making of wines in a style that would have pleased her father. Lamont's also boasts a superb restaurant run by granddaughter Kate Lamont. The wines are going from strength to strength, utilising both estate-grown and contract-grown (from southern regions) grapes. Lamont's restaurant in Perth, open for lunch and dinner Mon–Fri, offers food of the highest quality, and is superbly situated. The Margaret River cellar door is open 7 days 11–5 for wine tasting, sales and lunch.

Chardonnay 2014 From a vineyard at Donnybrook. It's an open display of sunny, varietal fruit with sweet, sawdusty oak woven through. Balance is impeccable. Screwcap. 13.5% alc. **Rating** 93 To 2020 $35 CM
Black Monster 2013 Made with malbec grown at Donnybrook. All French oak. Dark in colour but not quite black. Leather, earth and blackberried fruit turns

gravelly and tannic through the finish. Chocolatey oak adds a bit extra. It works. Screwcap. 14.5% alc. **Rating** 92 **To** 2025 $55 CM

White Monster 2014 No region or variety shown on the bottle (but it's chardonnay from Margaret River), except to say that it's barrel-fermented and allowed to go through mlf. A fully worked style, rich with butterscotch, cedar wood and sweet fuzzy peach flavour. It goes for broke, but the finish is, thankfully, filled with fresh juicy fruit. Screwcap. 13.1% alc. **Rating** 91 **To** 2019 $45 CM

Margaret River Viognier 2014 Oak-matured, and obviously. Creamy wood-spice notes introduce stone fruit and ginger. It's luscious in the mouth, seductively so. Screwcap. 14.5% alc. **Rating** 91 **To** 2017 $35 CM

Family Reserve 2014 Shiraz, cabernet sauvignon and malbec. Dark berried fruit flavours sashay through the palate, pleasing as they go. This has weight, balance and poise on its side. Gravelly gum nut characters with earth and blackcurrant. Tasty. Screwcap. 14.3% alc. **Rating** 91 **To** 2024 $30 CM

Landaire ★★★★

PO Box 14, Padthaway, SA 5271 **Region** Padthaway
T 0417 408 147 **www**.landaire.com.au **Open** Not
Winemaker Pete Bissell **Est.** 2012 **Dozens** 2000 **Vyds** 200ha
David and Carolyn Brown have been major grapegrowers in Padthaway over the past 18 years, David having had a vineyard and farming background, Carolyn with a background in science. Landaire has evolved from a desire after many years of growing grapes at their Glendon Vineyard to select small quantities of the best grapes and have them vinified by Pete Bissell, chief winemaker at Balnaves. It has proved a sure-fire recipe for success. Exports to the UK.

ΨΨΨΨΩ **Chardonnay 2014** It makes every post a winner. The fruit is rich, but taut; the oak is assertive but tucked in; the finish desperate to break free and run loose but ultimately disciplined and long. It won't makes old bones, but over the next few years it will put on an excellent display. Screwcap. 12.5% alc. **Rating** 93 **To** 2019 $28 CM

Shiraz 2013 Plenty of dark fruit and with both fineness and finesse. Landaire has certainly burst from the blocks. Bitter chocolate, cloves, blackberry and sweet, smooth plums. There's oak but not too much; it's at the upper reaches of ripeness but it doesn't overstep the mark. Tannin, integrated, keeps the package tidy. Screwcap. 14.5% alc. **Rating** 93 **To** 2026 $32 CM

Tempranillo 2015 Ever so delicious. Bright, perfumed, lively, satisfying. Cherries, plums, cola, dried spice, a slip of anise. It drinks beautifully. Screwcap. 13.5% alc. **Rating** 92 **To** 2020 $26 CM

Vermentino 2015 Significant spritz. Powerful wine, mostly brine and grapefruit but with swings of bath salts and citrus, the finish then gravelly, almost smoky. Much going on, in some cases too much but for the most part it's hard not to admire/enjoy its character. Screwcap. 13.5% alc. **Rating** 91 **To** 2018 $26 CM

Landhaus Estate ★★★★★

PO Box 2135, Bethany SA 5352 **Region** Barossa Valley
T (08) 8353 8442 **www**.landhauswines.com.au **Open** Not
Winemaker Kane Jaunutis **Est.** 2002 **Dozens** 10 000 **Vyds** 1ha
John, Barbara and son Kane Jaunutis purchased Landhaus Estate in 2002, followed by 'The Landhaus' cottage and 1ha vineyard at Bethany. Bethany is the oldest German-established town in the Barossa (1842) and the cottage was one of the first to be built. Kane has worked vintages for Mitolo and Kellermeister, as well as managing East End Cellars, one of Australia's leading fine wine retailers, while John brings decades of owner/management experience and Barbara 20 years in sales and marketing. Rehabilitation of the estate plantings and establishing a grower network have paid handsome dividends. Exports to Canada, Singapore and China.

ΨΨΨΨΨ **Rare Barossa Valley Shiraz 2012** From the Hoffman Vineyard at Ebenezer, only 1 (new French) puncheon was made, fermented and matured for 36 months on full lees. The lees contact is a powerful antioxidant, and is a factor in the

freshness of what is a remarkable wine of great length. Screwcap. 14.3% alc.
Rating 97 **To** 2047 $120 **○**

♥♥♥♥♥ **Classics Barossa Valley Shiraz 2013** Very good colour; rich, full-bodied and full-flavoured; the only question is whether 18 months maturation in 100% new French oak was too much of a good thing. Because the wine still has balance, and the black fruits are still well and truly on display, it gets the benefit of the minor doubt. Screwcap. 14.1% alc. **Rating** 95 **To** 2038 $50
Classics Barossa Valley Shiraz Mourvedre 2013 A 50/50% blend, matured for 20 months in French oak (50% new). I have to say I'm thoroughly impressed with these Landhaus '13 releases, and with the 'only $29' price tag of this very good medium-bodied wine. It has great balance, and there is a striking juiciness to the palate that lifts on the finish. The tension engendered by the contrast of the sweet fruit and savoury tannins is the deal-maker. Screwcap. 14% alc. **Rating** 95 **To** 2033 $29 **○**
Classics Barossa Valley Shiraz Cabernet Sauvignon 2013 A 60/40% blend. It is 100% correct to comment on the chocolate component on the bouquet and palate (à la McLaren Vale), although the lively assemblage of blackberry, cassis and cedary oak draws attention away from the chocolate. Another winner. Screwcap. 14% alc. **Rating** 94 **To** 2035 $39
Classics Barossa Valley Grenache Shiraz Mourvedre 2013 A 43/39/18% blend from low-yielding vineyards average 60yo, open-fermented separately, completing primary fermentation and mlf in French oak (20% new), matured for 20 months. Exceptional retention of hue; powerful fruit, very well balanced and constructed, with black as well as the predominantly red fruits; the oak treatment pays particular dividends. Screwcap. 14% alc. **Rating** 94 **To** 2023 $29 **○**

♥♥♥♥♡ **Classics Barossa Valley Grenache 2013** **Rating** 93 **To** 2023 $27 **○**
Classics Barossa Valley Cabernet Sauvignon 2013 **Rating** 91 **To** 2028 $60

Lane's End Vineyard ★★★★★

885 Mount William Road, Lancefield, Vic 3435 **Region** Macedon Ranges
T (03) 5429 1760 **www**.lanesend.com.au **Open** By appt
Winemaker Howard Matthews, Kilchurn Wines **Est.** 1985 **Dozens** 500 **Vyds** 2ha
Pharmacist Howard Matthews and family purchased the former Woodend Winery in 2000, with 1.8ha of chardonnay and pinot noir (and a small amount of cabernet franc) dating back to the mid-1980s. The cabernet franc has been grafted over to pinot noir (with a mix of four clones), and the chardonnay now totals 1ha. Howard has been making the wines for over a decade.

♥♥♥♥♥ **Macedon Ranges Chardonnay 2014** Power aplenty but it uses it wisely. White peach, apple, lime and grapefruit get plenty of runs on the board but lactose and spicy oak play important roles too. Pour this into a large-bowled glass and marvel as it unfurls and breathes. Screwcap. 12.8% alc. **Rating** 95 **To** 2022 $35 CM **○**
Cottage Macedon Ranges Chardonnay 2015 Exotic and intense with lime, cider apple and spice flavours exploding through the palate. Makes its presence felt and then some. Terrific value and, naturally, drinking. Screwcap. 13.5% alc. **Rating** 94 **To** 2019 $23 CM **○**

Lange's Frankland Wines ★★★

633 Frankland-Cranbrook Road, Frankland River, WA 6396 **Region** Frankland River
T 0438 511 828 **www**.langesfranklandwines.com.au **Open** Not
Winemaker James Kellie **Est.** 1997 **Dozens** 65 **Vyds** 20ha
This venture involves three generations of this branch of the Lange family, with Don and Maxine grandparents, son Kim and wife Chelsea the second generation, and their children Jack, Ella and Dylan the third generation. The first vines were planted in 1997, on an elevated site called Lange's Place. Until 2011 the grapes were sold, but in that year the first Shiraz was made, and is in fact the only Shiraz so far released, with five subsequent vintages in various stages of maturation.

🍷🍷🍷🍷 **Frankland River Shiraz 2011** Machine-harvested, crushed and destemmed, 3 days cold soak, open-fermented, cultured yeast, 4 weeks on skins, matured in French oak (25% new) for 30 months. The long time in French oak has had a major impact on the wine; it's good oak and it's good fruit, but the marriage should have ended earlier than it did. Screwcap. 14.5% alc. **Rating** 89 **To** 2021 $35

Langmeil Winery ★★★★★

Cnr Para Road/Langmeil Road, Tanunda, SA 5352 **Region** Barossa Valley
T (08) 8563 2595 **www**.langmeilwinery.com.au **Open** 7 days 10.30–4.30
Winemaker Paul Lindner, Tyson Bitter **Est.** 1996 **Dozens** 35 000 **Vyds** 31.4ha
Vines were first planted at Langmeil (which possesses the oldest block of shiraz in Australia) in the 1840s, and the first winery on the site, known as Paradale Wines, opened in 1932. In '96, cousins Carl and Richard Lindner with brother-in-law Chris Bitter formed a partnership to acquire and refurbish the winery and its 5ha vineyard (planted to shiraz, and including 2ha planted in 1843). Another vineyard was acquired in '98, which included cabernet sauvignon and grenache. In late 2012 the Lindner family put a succession plan into action: Richard and Shirley Lindner, and their sons Paul and James, have acquired 100% ownership of the business. In terms of management, little changes: Paul has been chief winemaker and James the sales and marketing manager since the winery began in '96. Exports to all major markets.

🍷🍷🍷🍷🍷 **The Freedom 1843 Barossa Shiraz 2013** The accent of the fruit is as different from that of its Eden Valley sibling as one should expect, with a smoked meat/charcuterie element behind the blackberry and plum fruit; the tannins are good, as is the oak. My points are not justified on wine quality (the alcohol issue), but are given because of history. Screwcap. 15% alc. **Rating** 95 **To** 2033 $125
Orphan Bank Barossa Shiraz 2013 68% Barossa Valley (picked 13 Feb), 32% Eden Valley (picked 20 Mar), matured for 24 months in French hogsheads (56% new). A lively, medium-bodied shiraz, light on its feet, the Eden Valley playing an important role; the fruit flavours span both red and dark, but are in no way extractive, the savoury tannins on the finish giving the wine its very good texture and structure. Screwcap. 14.5% alc. **Rating** 95 **To** 2038 $55

🍷🍷🍷🍷🍷 **Valley Floor Barossa Shiraz 2013** **Rating** 93 **To** 2028 $30
Pure Eden Barossa Shiraz 2013 **Rating** 91 **To** 2033 $125

Lanz Vineyards ★★★★☆

220 Scenic Road, Lyndoch, SA 5351 **Region** Barossa Valley
T 0417 858 967 **www**.lanzvineyards.com **Open** By appt
Winemaker Michael Paxton **Est.** 1998 **Dozens** 800 **Vyds** 16ha
The major part of the grape production is sold to premium producers in the Barossa Valley. However, Marianne and Thomas Lanz take enough of the grapes to make their Shiraz and Grenache Shiraz Mourvedre. Their choice of Michael Paxton as winemaker is no accident; he is a committed biodynamic grower (as is his father, David) and the Lanzs are aiming at the 'three L' wine style: Lower alcohol, Lower intervention, and Lower carbon footprint. Exports to Switzerland, Germany and Singapore.

🍷🍷🍷🍷🍷 **Scenic Road Single Vineyard Barossa Valley Shiraz 2014** While a single vineyard, separate fermentation and maturation of portions over 6 months, blended and returned to oak (used French barriques) for a further 6 months. Deep crimson-purple; this is an unashamedly full-bodied shiraz, yet is well balanced and supple, its black fruits fresh and firm, tannins in a pure support role. Those black fruits have a spicy complexity that only appears the second or third time you taste the wine. Value+. Screwcap. 13.5% alc. **Rating** 94 **To** 2034 $25 ✪

🍷🍷🍷🍷🍷 **The Club GSM 2014** **Rating** 93 **To** 2029 $20 ✪

Lark Hill

521 Bungendore Road, Bungendore, NSW 2621 **Region** Canberra District
T (02) 6238 1393 **www.**larkhillwine.com.au **Open** Wed–Mon 10–5
Winemaker Dr David, Sue and Chris Carpenter **Est.** 1978 **Dozens** 4000 **Vyds** 10.5ha
The Lark Hill vineyard is situated at an altitude of 860m, offering splendid views of the
Lake George escarpment. The Carpenters have made wines of real quality, style and elegance
from the start, but have defied all the odds (and conventional thinking) with the quality of
their Pinot Noirs in favourable vintages. Significant changes have come in the wake of son
Christopher gaining three degrees, including a double in wine science and viticulture through
CSU, and the biodynamic certification of the vineyard. They have also planted 1ha of gruner
veltliner; it is hard to understand why there have been so few plantings of this high quality
Austrian variety. In 2011 Lark Hill purchased one of the two Ravensworth vineyards from
Bryan Martin, with plantings of sangiovese, shiraz, viognier, roussanne and marsanne; they
will also be converting it (renamed Dark Horse) to biodynamic farming. Exports to the UK.

♀♀♀♀♀ **Exaltation 2013** One-third each sangiovese, shiraz and merlot, separately
fermented and matured, assessed Dec '13, the best components blended and given
1 year of further maturation. While I wasn't expecting much from this thoroughly
left-field blend, it actually works well, both in terms of its deep-seated red fruit
flavours and its texture and structure. Screwcap. 13.5% alc. **Rating** 93 **To** 2028 $65
Canberra District Riesling 2015 An elegant biodynamic wine typical of the
Canberra District's ability to bring out the best in the variety; its crux is the zesty,
bright acidity that serves to amplify, rather than diminish, the essentially light citrus
fruit. Screwcap. 11.5% alc. **Rating** 92 **To** 2025 $35
Canberra District Gruner Veltliner 2015 The growing maturity (relatively
speaking) of the vines seems to be reflected in some recent vintages, especially
here. There are pepper nuances to the bouquet, and there is mouthfeel. Age in
bottle will add to its stature. Screwcap. 12.5% alc. **Rating** 92 **To** 2024 $45
Canberra District Viognier 2015 Part wild-fermented in used oak. Has all
the hallmarks, good and bad, of viognier in general, and the curate's egg in this
instance comes down on the good side, with some apricot and ginger, and no
excess phenolics. Screwcap. 11.5% alc. **Rating** 91 **To** 2018 $25
Canberra District Chardonnay 2015 Estate-grown, wild-fermented in
French oak, matured on lees for 9 months. Delicate stone fruit, honeydew melon
and grapefruit flavours are supported by creamy cashew ex the oak; balance, not
intensity is its strength. Screwcap. 12.5% alc. **Rating** 90 **To** 2022 $45

♀♀♀♀ **Canberra District Pinot Noir 2015 Rating** 89 **To** 2020 $45

Larry Cherubino Wines

15 York Street, Subiaco, WA 6008 **Region** Western Australia
T (08) 9382 2379 **www.**larrycherubino.com **Open** Not
Winemaker Larry Cherubino, Andrew Siddell **Est.** 2005 **Dozens** 8000 **Vyds** 120ha
Larry Cherubino has had a particularly distinguished winemaking career, first at Hardys
Tintara, then Houghton, and thereafter as consultant/Flying Winemaker in Australia, NZ,
South Africa, the US and Italy. He has developed three ranges: at the top is Cherubino
(Riesling, Sauvignon Blanc, Shiraz and Cabernet Sauvignon); next The Yard, single vineyard
wines from WA; and at the bottom the Ad Hoc label, all single region wines. The range and
quality of his wines is extraordinary, the prices irresistible. The runaway success of the business
has seen the accumulation of 120ha of vineyards, the appointment of an additional winemaker,
and Larry's own appointment as Director of Winemaking at Robert Oatley Vineyards. Exports
to the UK, the US, Canada, Ireland, Switzerland, Hong Kong, South Korea, Singapore, China
and NZ.

♀♀♀♀♀ **Cherubino Margaret River Cabernet Sauvignon 2013** This autocratic
cabernet forestalls even a hint of criticism, its blue-blood breeding oozing from
every pore. Indeed, so harmonious is it, so perfectly balanced, so long, that there
isn't much to say. Blackcurrant, bay leaf and bejewelled tannins are framed by a

fine filigree of oak. A great wine from a top vintage. Screwcap. 14% alc. **Rating** 97 To 2048 $75 ✪

🍷🍷🍷🍷🍷 **Cherubino Great Southern Riesling 2015** The impact of this wine is immediate: unsweetened lemon/lemon zest and mouthgripping acidity. And before I continue, let me assure you, it's all good stuff. It has a fabulous future, and would be my cellaring pick of the four Cherubino '15 Rieslings. Screwcap. 12.5% alc. **Rating** 96 **To** 2035 $35 ✪

Cherubino Porongurup Riesling 2015 Bright straw-green; a picture-perfect riesling at the start of a long and prosperous life; the bouquet is as yet reticent, but the palate is ready to do business on Porongurup's terms. Citrus, pear and apple are the spearhead, crunchy acidity the defence at the rear. To be left for as long as you possibly can. Screwcap. 12.5% alc. **Rating** 96 **To** 2030 $40 ✪

Cherubino Pemberton Sauvignon Blanc 2015 Some colour development heralds a complex bouquet, with wild yeast fermentation in new French oak on one side of the net, rich gooseberry, kiwi fruit and passionfruit on the other side, neither with any ascendancy over the other. A satisfying sauvignon blanc in a particular style. Screwcap. 13% alc. **Rating** 96 **To** 2017 $35 ✪

Cherubino Margaret River Chardonnay 2015 A beautifully composed chardonnay, everything in the right place, and everything balanced. The fruit flavours span white stone fruit and pink grapefruit, none overt, and the acidity is neatly tucked in behind. Screwcap. 12.3% alc. **Rating** 96 **To** 2026 $49 ✪

Cherubino Laissez Faire Syrah 2014 Hand-picked, hand-sorted, wild-fermented, no acid addition. The colour beckons, as does the bouquet, but the palate has an amber light flashing. This is stacked with the black fruits of the region, plus bitter chocolate, licorice and tannins that are ripe and of the appropriate proportion. Screwcap. 13.5% alc. **Rating** 96 **To** 2039 $39 ✪

Cherubino Frankland River Shiraz 2014 Has the power and the glory of Frankland River, Larry Cherubino has kept it under control to the point of elegance, no mean achievement. Black fruits, licorice, bitter chocolate and inbuilt tannins are all there, as is some new oak bobbing around in the background. The question does have to be asked: would the wine have been even better with another 6–12 months in barrel? Screwcap. 14% alc. **Rating** 96 **To** 2039 $55 ✪

Cherubino Laissez Faire Syrah Grenache 2014 It is 100% Frankland River, a region that always produces effortless power, depth and integrity in its red wines, not a whit diminished by the grenache, which simply adds a juicy elegance. The balance is perfect, as is the now or whenever style. Screwcap. 14.5% alc. **Rating** 96 **To** 2029 $25 ✪

Pedestal Margaret River Cabernet Merlot 2013 The volume and quality of the flavours of this wine make a complete mockery of the price. The colour is deep and vibrant, the palate overflowing with luscious red and black fruits, ripe tannins and high quality oak. It's no sin to drink now (with a large piece of beef ex a charcoal grill), but it will still be firing on all cylinders when I'm pushing up daisies. Screwcap. 14% alc. **Rating** 96 **To** 2045 $25 ✪

Cherubino Frankland River Cabernet Sauvignon 2014 Deep crimson-purple; this is cabernet as only Frankland River can do it. Autocratic blackcurrant fruit, black olive and bay leaf, fine tannins and great length. Screwcap. 13.7% alc. **Rating** 96 **To** 2039 $110

Cherubino Laissez Faire Riesling 2015 It has a singular juicy quality, the flavour straight from Bickford's lime juice, the acidity just where it should be. Its exuberance is a little strange for the normally shy and reserved Porongurup riesling, but for most this will simply be a plus. Screwcap. 12.3% alc. **Rating** 95 **To** 2025 $29 ✪

The Yard Channybearup Pemberton Sauvignon Blanc 2015 Hand-picked and sorted, part fermented in and matured in French oak for 3 months. This has triggered the straw tinge to the colour, and also provided texture and structure, with an emphatic cleansing finish, aided by crunchy acidity. Top value. Screwcap. 13% alc. **Rating** 95 **To** 2017 $25 ✪

Ad Hoc Straw Man Margaret River Sauvignon Blanc Semillon 2015
The normally delphic Larry Cherubino bursts into voluble info on the back
label, declaring 'Reminds me of dried summer straw and fresh cut grass'. Whether
that says it all about the bouquet and fore-palate is a moot point, but it certainly
undersells the deliciously lively lemon sherbet/tropical mix of the finish and
aftertaste. Screwcap. 12.5% alc. **Rating** 95 **To** 2018 $21 ○

Pedestal Margaret River Semillon Sauvignon Blanc 2015 An 80/20%
blend, matured in French oak for 3 months. It has so much power and drive it
leaves most (not all) others wallowing in its wake; capsicum, redcurrant, citrus and
guava are all erected on a scaffold of acidity on the long palate. Screwcap. 13% alc.
Rating 95 **To** 2018 $25 ○

The Yard Justin Frankland River Shiraz 2014 You suspect this vineyard may
have provided all or some of the grapes for the top of the range wine, this being
a wine of great quality, but less intense and powerful – which makes it so much
easier to understand and enjoy now (preferably a minimum of 5 years from now).
Screwcap. 14.3% alc. **Rating** 95 **To** 2034 $35 ○

The Yard Riversdale Frankland River Cabernet Sauvignon 2014 Open-
fermented in small pots, moderate extraction through 28 days on skins, matured
for 8 months in new and 1yo oak. The bouquet is highly expressive, with cassis
beating the drum long and hard, the tannins fine but important, as is the oak.
Screwcap. 14% alc. **Rating** 95 **To** 2030 $35 ○

Cherubino Margaret River Cabernet Sauvignon 2014 Hand-picked, cooled
overnight, sorted, crushed/destemmed, 6 weeks fermentation and post-ferment
maceration, matured for 18 months in French oak. Vivid purple-crimson; the
bouquet has cassis/blackcurrant/redcurrant fruit, with black olive and bay leaf, the
tannins round and soft. Screwcap. 13.1% alc. **Rating** 95 **To** 2034 $75

Ad Hoc Wallflower Great Southern Riesling 2015 Marries freshness and
finesse with plentiful varietal fruit expression; wherever you look in the five
subregions of Great Southern, riesling of high quality is on offer – here at a
bargain basement price. Will reward patience. Gold medals Perth and National
Wine Shows '15. Screwcap. 12.5% alc. **Rating** 94 **To** 2025 $21 ○

Pedestal Margaret River Chardonnay 2015 Hand-picked, whole bunch-
pressed, wild-fermented in new and 1yo French oak, bottled Dec '15. Interesting:
the first note on the bouquet is preserved lemon, then both white peach and
nectarine, characters that expand progressively through to the finish and aftertaste.
Screwcap. 13% alc. **Rating** 94 **To** 2022 $25 ○

Cherubino Laissez Faire Chardonnay 2015 From Porongurup, and the
analysis reflects the cool climate. Hand-picked, whole bunch-pressed, naturally
settled juice wild-fermented. Chabliesque in its intensity, the absence of oak far
from obvious. Great drive to the grapefruit flavour extends the aftertaste to a near
unbelievable length. Screwcap. 13% alc. **Rating** 94 **To** 2025 $39

Pedestal Margaret River Chardonnay 2014 Unsurprisingly, the very model
of Margaret River chardonnay in a sub-$30 field, and offers exceptional value.
It doesn't have a hair out of place, varietal fruit, oak and acidity precisely where
they should be. The outcome is a wine ready when you are. Screwcap. 13.5% alc.
Rating 94 **To** 2020 $25 ○

Cherubino Laissez Faire Fiano 2015 From Frankland River, hand-picked
and sorted, wild-fermented with no significant additions during fermentation
and/or prior to early bottling. Other than Bremerton's '14 Fiano, it has far more
weight and richness to its palate than any other fiano so far made in Australia, with
nashi pear, apple skin and citrus. Backed up by zesty acidity. Screwcap. 13.5% alc.
Rating 94 **To** 2019 $29 ○

Cherubino Laissez Faire Field Blend 2015 An exotic dry grown blend of
pinot gris, gewurztraminer, sauvignon gris and riesling, a vinous exocet missile, its
rainbow of flavours starting immediately, continuing without any break through to
the finish of the long palate. Remarkable. Screwcap. 12% alc. **Rating** 94 **To** 2022
$25 ○

The Yard Acacia Frankland River Shiraz 2014 The Acacia Vineyard was planted in '97. True to the region and Larry Cherubino's interpretation of it, but less awesome in its power, and hence more approachable; sultry black fruits remain the order of the day, with attendant briary tannins marauding on the finish. Screwcap. 14% alc. **Rating** 94 **To** 2044 $35

Ad Hoc Middle of Everywhere Frankland River Shiraz 2014 A neat introduction to Larry Cherubino's exploration of Frankland River, a subregion he has put his proverbial house on. It has the black fruits – the blackest of black indeed – licorice and sturdy tannins to sustain the wine now (with a barbecued ox) or much later. Screwcap. 14% alc. **Rating** 94 **To** 2034 $21 ○

The Yard Riversdale Frankland River Shiraz 2014 The Riversdale Vineyard was established '97 on the red stony soils of the banks of the Frankland River. The components of potent black fruits, tannins, oak and acidity are all in play, but are yet to come together and speak in unison. Screwcap. 14% alc. **Rating** 94 **To** 2034 $35

ҮҮҮҮ̨ **Ad Hoc Nitty Gritty Pemberton Pinot Grigio 2015** Rating 93 To 2018 $21 ○
Cherubino Laissez Faire Grenache 2014 Rating 93 To 2024 $29
Pedestal Margaret River Cabernet Merlot 2014 Rating 93 To 2029 $25 ○
Ad Hoc Avant Gardening Frankland Cabernet Sauvignon Malbec 2014 Rating 93 To 2024 $21 ○
Ad Hoc Hen & Chicken Pemberton Chardonnay 2015 Rating 92 To 2020 $21 ○
LC Pannoo Vineyard Porongurup Sauvignon Blanc 2015 Rating 91 To 2016 $20 ○
LC Channybearup Vineyard Pemberton Chardonnay 2015 Rating 91 To 2018 $20 ○
Cherubino Laissez Faire Pinot Noir 2015 Rating 90 To 2023 $39
LC Pusey Road Vineyard Wilyabrup Margaret River Cabernet Sauvignon 2014 Rating 90 To 2024 $20 ○

Latitude 34 Wine Co   ★★★★

St Johns Brook, 283 Yelverton North Road, Yelverton, WA 6281 **Region** Margaret River **T** (08) 9417 5633 **www**.latitude34wineco.com **Open** By appt
Winemaker Mark Thompson, Giulio Corbellani **Est.** 1997 **Dozens** 70 000 **Vyds** 120ha
Latitude 34 is the parent company of wine brands Optimus, St Johns Brook, The Blackwood and Barwick Estates (www.barwickwines.com). Margaret River is the physical base of the business, the winery being St Johns Brook. The 120ha of vineyards is made up of 37ha in Margaret River, and 83ha in the Blackwood Valley, the Pemberton vineyards (68ha) having been sold in 2015. Exports to the UK, the US and other major markets.

ҮҮҮҮҮ **St Johns Brook Single Vineyard Margaret River Sauvignon Blanc Semillon 2015** Machine-harvested, crushed/destemmed, cultured yeast, matured in tank and French oak (10% new) for 12 months. The considerable winemaking inputs have produced a crisp, crunchy wine; needed more mid-palate fruit for higher points, but does have good length. Screwcap. 12.2% alc. **Rating** 90 **To** 2017 $24

The Blackwood Sir Henry Shiraz 2014 20+yo vines, machine-harvested, destemmed and crushed, fermented in tank with cultured yeast, 10–16 days post-ferment maceration, matured in used French oak for 12 months. Good colour; a medium to full-bodied shiraz with red and black cherry fruits coupled with spice, pepper and licorice, tannins and oak under control. Has time to go. Screwcap. 14.5% alc. **Rating** 90 **To** 2034 $50

Optimus The Terraces Block 2 Shiraz 2013 20+yo vines from the Blackwood Valley, matured for 12 months in new American oak. Very good colour; this is very full-bodied, all the dials of power, fruit, tannins and oak turned up to maximum, the saving grace the (relatively) lower alcohol in this wine compared

to the 15.3% of its '14 sibling. Biggest is a long way short of best. Screwcap.
14.6% alc. **Rating** 90 **To** 2028 $72

**Barwick Estates Black Label Margaret River Cabernet Sauvignon
2014** Crushed/destemmed, 10–16 days post-ferment maceration, matured for
12 months in French oak (50% new). The wine is only just medium-bodied, and
the new oak is obvious. With a few more years in bottle, the oak should integrate.
Double-gold China Wine & Spirits Competition '14 (curious timing), bronze
medal Melbourne Wine Awards '15. Screwcap. 13.3% alc. **Rating** 90 **To** 2024 $32

ŶŶŶŶ **The Blackwood Captain James Cabernet 2014** Rating 89 To 2020 $45
Optimus The Terraces Block 3 Cabernet 2014 Rating 89 To 2034 $85
The Blackwood El Toro Rojo Tempranillo 2014 Rating 89 To 2018 $40
The Blackwood Rushy Creek Rose 2015 Rating 88 To 2017 $15 ✪

Latta ★★★★

67 Pickfords Road, Coghills Creek, Vic 3364 **Region** Macedon Ranges
T 0408 594 454 **www.**lattavino.com.au **Open** By appt
Winemaker Owen Latta **Est.** 2012 **Dozens** 1500
This is the culmination of a long-standing desire of Owen Latta to make wines from small
plantings in the Pyrenees, Grampians and Macedon regions. Eastern Peake, owned by the
Latta family, makes wine from the Ballarat region, and the rationale was to avoid confusing the
nature of the two operations. He says he has empathy with the growers he works with from
when he and his father were themselves contract grapegrowers for others. The degree of that
empathy is fortified by the fact that the growers have been known to the Latta family for over
15 years. The wines are, to put it mildly, unconventional.

ŶŶŶŶŶ **Young Skin No. 1 Pyrenees Nebbiolo 2014** Light in colour but high in
aroma. It leads you straight in. Licorice allsorts, dried herbs and leather flavours
then carry you to the terminal of tannin waiting for you on the finish. It's a
charismatic wine, but it's best summed up with: if nebbiolo is your varietal idol,
then this should be on your shopping list. Screwcap. 13% alc. **Rating** 93 **To** 2024
$35 CM
Shays Flat Pyrenees Sangiovese 2013 It takes time to open up, but the
complexity and texture of the wine feel classy from the outset. We're looking at
jubey red cherries, wood spice and anise, firm tannin and a suede-like softness.
There's perfume and sweetness to the fruit, but there's an attractive dryness to the
finish. It deserves a large-bowled glass. Screwcap. 13% alc. **Rating** 92 **To** 2021
$35 CM
Malakoff Pyrenees Shiraz 2013 Light to medium weight with cherry-plum
flavours leading into pencil and earth. It has a free-flowing freshness to it, a joie de
vivre. Screwcap. 14.5% alc. **Rating** 90 **To** 2020 $30 CM
Moonambel Pyrenees Cabernet Sauvignon 2012 30yo vines. Its appeal is
immediate. Redcurrant and blackberry with hints of mint and game. Dry tannin.
Herbs. Lots going on. Succulent, but it firms considerably as it closes. Screwcap.
13% alc. **Rating** 90 **To** 2022 $35 CM

ŶŶŶŶ **Malakoff Pyrenees Viognier 2015** Rating 88 To 2017 $25 CM

Laughing Jack ★★★★★

194 Stonewell Road, Marananga, SA 5355 **Region** Barossa Valley
T (08) 8562 3878 **www.**laughingjackwines.com.au **Open** By appt
Winemaker Shawn Kalleske **Est.** 1999 **Dozens** 3000 **Vyds** 38.88ha
The Kalleske family has many branches in the Barossa Valley. Laughing Jack is owned by
Shawn, Nathan, Ian and Carol Kalleske, and Linda Schroeter. The lion's share of the vineyard
is planted to shiraz, with lesser amounts of semillon and grenache. Vine age varies considerably,
with old dry-grown shiraz the jewel in the crown. A small part of the grape production is
taken for the Laughing Jack Shiraz. As any Australian knows, the kookaburra is also called the

laughing jackass, and there is a resident flock of kookaburras in the stands of blue and red gums surrounding the vineyards. Exports to Malaysia, Hong Kong and China.

🍷🍷🍷🍷🍷 **Moppa Hill Block 6 Barossa Valley Shiraz 2014** Hand-picked twice over 7 days, 40% whole berries, 60% crushed, open-fermented, 75% matured in used French puncheons, 25% in new French barriques for 17 months. Spectacularly rich and vibrant, with midnight black fruits, licorice and tar, oak and tannins securely stowed in the nest. Screwcap. 14.5% alc. **Rating** 96 **To** 2039 $35 ⭕
Moppa Block Barossa Valley Shiraz 2013 Only 140 dozen produced due to the ultra-low yield, crushed/destemmed, open-fermented, 14 days on skins, matured for 20 months in French oak (62% new with very tight grain). Intense, deep black fruit flavours are illuminated by an unexpected and delicious silver stream of red fruits. Cork. 14.5% alc. **Rating** 95 **To** 2043 $95
Greenock Barossa Valley Shiraz 2013 The estate yield of 0.65t/a was no laughing matter; destemmed and crushed, fermented and macerated for 21 days, matured for 24 months in French and American hogsheads. Vibrates power, depth and brooding saturnine complexity. Despite this, it has balance, and will mature into an exciting wine. Screwcap. 14.5% alc. **Rating** 94 **To** 2043 $45

🍷🍷🍷🍷🍷 **Jack's Shiraz 2014 Rating** 93 **To** 2034 $23 ⭕
Jack's Grenache Shiraz Mourvedre 2014 Rating 92 **To** 2025 $23 ⭕

Laurance of Margaret River   ★★★★★

3518 Caves Road, Wilyabrup, WA 6280 **Region** Margaret River
T (08) 9755 6199 **www.**laurancewines.com **Open** 7 days 11–5
Winemaker Naturaliste Vintners (Bruce Dukes) **Est.** 2001 **Dozens** 8000 **Vyds** 23ha
Founder and chairwoman Dianne Laurance is the driving force behind this family-owned business. The 100ha property has vines (planted in 1996 to three clones of chardonnay, plus sauvignon blanc, shiraz, cabernet sauvignon, semillon and merlot), beautiful gardens, artwork and sculptures. The quality of the wines can be lost behind the unusual bottles, reminiscent of Perrier-Jouët's Belle Epoque deluxe Champagne. Exports to Singapore, Hong Kong, Malaysia, Thailand and China.

🍷🍷🍷🍷🍷 **Chardonnay 2013** Estate-grown, fermented and matured in French oak for 10 months. Very well made, and the fruit has been the springboard, intense, zesty and long, with grapefruit and white peach to the fore. Screwcap. 13.8% alc. **Rating** 96 **To** 2023 $30 ⭕
Semillon Sauvignon Blanc 2015 50/50%, fermented separately in stainless steel, gold medal Margaret River Wine Show '15. The structure and flavour intensity build progressively as the wine moves through to the finish, where lemongrass and gooseberry lock horns, the flavours lingering long after the wine has left the mouth. Screwcap. 13% alc. **Rating** 95 **To** 2020 $20 ⭕
Rose 2015 100% estate-grown grenache. Vivid, light puce; it is easy to see why the wine was given a gold medal at Melbourne: its red fruits are sheathed in vibrant acidity, the mouthfeel and length well beyond the norm, and opening a vista for grenache in the Margaret River. Screwcap. 13% alc. **Rating** 95 **To** 2017 $29 ⭕
Shiraz 2013 20yo vines, includes 1.8% viognier, open-fermented together with some whole bunches, cultured yeast, 12 days on skins, matured in French oak (25% new) for 15 months. A wine with attitude and complexity to burn; black cherry, blackberry and surprisingly firm (although ripe and balanced) tannins have a cool(er)-climate intensity. Screwcap. 14% alc. **Rating** 95 **To** 2038 $27 ⭕
Red 2012 60% cabernet sauvignon, 27% merlot, 13% malbec, machine-harvested, matured for 18 months in French oak (40% new). Good colour; has more substance and structure than the disarmingly simple name would suggest; excellent colour, oak and tannins also add a dimension to the wine. Screwcap. 14% alc. **Rating** 95 **To** 2032 $30 ⭕

Icon Cabernet 2012 Machine-harvested, 40 days on skins, pressed, matured in French oak (50% new) for 18 months. Deep crimson-purple; densely structured and textured, no surprise given the vinification. Simply not ready anytime soon, but does have balance, and the patient will be handsomely rewarded. Screwcap. 14% alc. **Rating** 95 **To** 2047 $48

♀♀♀♀♀ **Merlot 2013 Rating** 93 **To** 2028 $32

Laurel Bank   ★★★☆

130 Black Snake Lane, Granton, Tas 7030 **Region** Southern Tasmania
T (03) 6263 5977 **www**.laurelbankwines.com.au **Open** By appt
Winemaker Winemaking Tasmania **Est.** 1987 **Dozens** 1500 **Vyds** 3.5ha
Laurel (hence Laurel Bank) and Kerry Carland's north-facing vineyard, overlooking the Derwent River, is planted to sauvignon blanc, riesling, pinot noir, cabernet sauvignon and merlot. They delayed the first release of their wines for some years and (by virtue of the number of entries they were able to make) won the trophy for Most Successful Exhibitor at the Hobart Wine Show '95. Things have settled down since; wine quality is reliable.

♀♀♀♀♀ **Sauvignon Blanc 2015** Pure, essence-like passionfruit and mango flavours run juicily along a most appealing palate. Delicious. Screwcap. 12.7% alc. **Rating** 90 **To** 2017 $22 CM

Leaning Church Vineyard   ★★★★

76 Brooks Road, Lalla, Tas 7267 **Region** Northern Tasmania
T (03) 6395 4447 **www**.leaningchurch.com.au **Open** 7 days 10–5 (Oct–Apr)
Winemaker Jeremy Dineen **Est.** 1991 **Dozens** 2000 **Vyds** 6.3ha
In 2011 Mark and Sarah Hirst purchased the then 20-year-old Lalla Gully Vineyard from long-term owner Taltarni. Sarah has a background in journalism, media, event management and wine marketing; Mark has years of experience in agriculture, accounting and business management. It's difficult not to describe that as a match made in heaven.

♀♀♀♀♀ **Sauvignon Blanc 2015** Sweet grassy aromatics before a medium-intense, succulent palate. It's not hard to enjoy this. Tropical fruit cut with apple, gravel and pure passionfruit pulp. Lingers nicely too. Screwcap. 13.1% alc. **Rating** 91 **To** 2016 $30 CM
Sweet Riesling 2015 Simple and straightforward at first but then it slings through the finish with gusto. Mandarin, apple and lime. Watch out, this is seriously delicious. Screwcap. 7.3% alc. **Rating** 91 **To** 2020 $28 CM

♀♀♀♀ **Pinot Noir 2013 Rating** 89 **To** 2020 $35 CM

Leasingham   ★★★★★

PO Box 57, Clare, SA 5453 **Region** Clare Valley
T 1800 088 711 **www**.leasingham-wines.com.au **Open** Not
Winemaker Paul Lapsley **Est.** 1893 **Dozens** NFP
Leasingham has experienced death by a thousand cuts. First, its then owner, CWA, sold its Rogers Vineyard to Tim Adams in 2009, and unsuccessfully endeavoured to separately sell the winemaking equipment and cellar door, while retaining the winery. In January '11 Tim Adams purchased the winery, cellar door and winemaking equipment, making the once-proud Leasingham a virtual winery (or brand). The quality of the wines has not suffered. Exports to the UK and Canada.

♀♀♀♀♀ **Classic Clare Provis Vineyard Shiraz 2010** This is a mighty, mouthfilling full-bodied shiraz, with a medley of succulent black fruit flavours and a touch of McLaren Vale-like dark chocolate lurking in the shadows. Its greatest attribute is its savoury complexity on the finish, balancing the opulence of the mid-palate fruit. Compelling value. First tasted 2 years ago, the tasting note then and now identical. Screwcap. 14% alc. **Rating** 96 **To** 2043 $60 ✪

Provis Vineyard Classic Clare Cabernet Sauvignon 2013 The deep colour heralds a Clare Valley cabernet of rare distinction and identity. Its blackcurrant fruit strides out confidently like the Pied Piper of Hamelin, with very positive cedary oak and savoury tannins following in perfect step. Other than Wendouree, this has to be at the top of the cabernet tree in Clare. Screwcap. 14% alc. **Rating** 96 **To** 2048 $60 ○

Classic Clare Riesling 2009 Has been gallivanting around wine shows in Asia and the UK, but hasn't previously crossed my palate. An attractive wine, ready now, but not pulling any price punches. Screwcap. 12% alc. **Rating** 95 **To** 2019 $50

Classic Clare Sparkling Shiraz 2006 An impressively deep yet vibrant purple hue at a decade of age announces a sparkling shiraz of towering fruit integrity, grand maturity and masterful structure. There is depth and intensity here of black fruits of all kinds, with the most subtle nuances of sweet leather and game just beginning to emerge. Tannins are at once fine and integrated yet confident and enduring, promising an exciting future. Cork. 14% alc. **Rating** 94 **To** 2031 $68 TS

ΨΨΨΨ♀ **Bin 7 Clare Valley Riesling 2014** Rating 91 To 2021 $20 ○
Bin 61 Clare Valley Shiraz 2013 Rating 91 To 2035 $27
Bin 56 Clare Valley Cabernet Malbec 2013 Rating 91 To 2030 $27

Leconfield   ★★★★☆

Riddoch Highway, Coonawarra, SA 5263 **Region** Coonawarra
T (08) 8737 2326 **www**.leconfieldwines.com **Open** Mon–Fri 11–4.30, w'ends 11–4
Winemaker Paul Gordon, Tim Bailey **Est.** 1974 **Dozens** 25 000 **Vyds** 43.7ha
Sydney Hamilton purchased the unplanted property that was to become Leconfield in 1974, having worked in the family wine business for over 30 years until his retirement in the mid-'50s. When he acquired the property and set about planting it, he was 76, and reluctantly bowed to family pressure to sell Leconfield to nephew Richard in '81. Richard has progressively increased the vineyards to their present level, over 75% to cabernet sauvignon, for long the winery's specialty. For reasons outside the *Wine Companion*'s control, not all the current releases were available for tasting for this edition. Exports to the UK, Canada, Denmark, Switzerland, Belgium, Japan, Malaysia, Hong Kong, Singapore, the Philippines, Vietnam, China and NZ.

ΨΨΨΨΨ **Cabernet Merlot 2013** This 77/23% blend may not be everyone's cup of tea, because the black olive notes are very much to the fore of a savoury wine. For my part, this brings back memories of Bordeaux pre-Parkerisation, a proper Englishman's claret. Screwcap. 14% alc. **Rating** 94 **To** 2028 $25 ○

ΨΨΨΨ♀ **Cabernet Sauvignon 2014** Rating 93 To 2030 $34

Leeuwin Estate   ★★★★★

Stevens Road, Margaret River, WA 6285 **Region** Margaret River
T (08) 9759 0000 **www**.leeuwinestate.com.au **Open** 7 days 10–5
Winemaker Paul Atwood, Tim Lovett **Est.** 1974 **Dozens** 50 000 **Vyds** 121ha
This outstanding winery and vineyard is owned by the Horgan family, founded by Denis and Tricia, who continue their involvement, with son Justin Horgan and daughter Simone Furlong joint chief executives. The Art Series Chardonnay is, in my opinion, Australia's finest example, based on the wines of the last 30 vintages. The move to screwcap brought a large smile to the faces of those who understand just how superbly the wine ages. The large estate plantings, coupled with strategic purchases of grapes from other growers, provide the base for high quality Art Series Cabernet Sauvignon and Shiraz; the hugely successful, quick-selling Art Series Riesling and Sauvignon Blanc; and lesser-priced Prelude and Siblings wines. Exports to all major markets.

ΨΨΨΨΨ **Art Series Margaret River Chardonnay 2013** 55% machine-picked at night, 45% hand-picked, 64% cultured yeast, 36% wild yeast, fermented in and matured for 11 months in new French oak. Supremely elegant and finely balanced, and has absorbed the new oak in a manner worthy of a Grand Cru White Burgundy, leaving the fragrant bouquet and finely structured palate of startling length to occupy centre stage. Screwcap. 13.5% alc. **Rating** 98 **To** 2033 $96 ✪

Art Series Margaret River Chardonnay 2012 A very youthful bright green-quartz colour sets the scene for a riveting wine of exquisite purity and finesse. It almost floats in the mouth, so effortless is its invocation of all things chardonnay: white flowers, white stone fruits and immaculately balanced acidity. Oak? Well, yes it's there, but rendered mute by the fruit. Has greater staying power than any other Australian chardonnay. Screwcap. 14% alc. **Rating** 98 **To** 2032 $99 ✪

♟♟♟♟♟ **Art Series Margaret River Shiraz 2013** 75% machine-harvested, 25% hand-picked, destemmed and whole bunch-fermented respectively with cultured yeast, matured for 18 months in French oak (53% new). Leeuwin took time to come to terms with its Shirazs, but is now master of its destiny. It has black cherry and plum flavours in superabundance, plus finely tuned tannins; its modest alcohol is the key. Screwcap. 13.5% alc. **Rating** 96 **To** 2038 $38 ✪

Art Series Margaret River Cabernet Sauvignon 2012 Destemmed, cultured yeast, matured for 21 months in French oak (40% new). The headline, the main text and the footnotes all say one thing and one thing only: purity. And I suppose I should add elegance. They simply don't come better in this mode. Screwcap. 13.5% alc. **Rating** 96 **To** 2042 $68 ✪

Siblings Margaret River Sauvignon Blanc Semillon 2015 A 66/34% blend, fermented with cultured yeast in used French oak, matured in oak for 3 months, then 7 months in tank. Bred in the purple, with snow pea to start, next a parade of tropical fruits, striking citrus to finish, the oak influence evident in texture, not in flavour. Screwcap. 13.5% alc. **Rating** 94 **To** 2018 $23 ✪

Prelude Vineyards Margaret River Chardonnay 2014 Most chardonnay vignerons would give their eye teeth to have a wine as good as this as their entry point. Light, bright colour, and a juicy array of nectarine, white peach and gentle citrus fruit have distracted all attention from the oak. A lovely wine. Screwcap. 13.5% alc. **Rating** 94 **To** 2029 $34

Prelude Vineyards Margaret River Cabernet Merlot 2012 The bright hue sets the scene for the bright cassis and redcurrant fruit of the palate, which has miraculously put the oak into its back pocket. Screwcap. 14% alc. **Rating** 94 **To** 2037 $28 ✪

♟♟♟♟♙ **Art Series Margaret River Riesling 2015** Rating 93 **To** 2025 $23 ✪
Siblings Margaret River Shiraz 2013 Rating 92 **To** 2025 $23 ✪

Lenton Brae Wines ★★★★★

3887 Caves Road, Margaret River, WA 6285 **Region** Margaret River
T (08) 9755 6255 **www**.lentonbrae.com **Open** 7 days 10–6
Winemaker Edward Tomlinson **Est.** 1982 **Dozens** NFP **Vyds** 9ha
The late architect Bruce Tomlinson built a strikingly beautiful winery (heritage-listed by the Shire of Busselton), now in the hands of winemaker son Edward (Ed), who consistently makes elegant wines in classic Margaret River style. A midwinter (French time) trip to Pomerol in Bordeaux to research merlot is an indication of his commitment. Exports to Indonesia, Singapore and China.

♟♟♟♟♟ **Southside Margaret River Chardonnay 2015** Vines planted in '82, fermented and matured in new and used French oak. Initially a delicate bouquet and palate, but the flavours build rapidly in the mouth; the wine has great attack (a word often used by French tasters), with grapefruit flesh and zest to the fore of a long and distinguished palate. Screwcap. 13.5% alc. **Rating** 95 **To** 2025 $26 ✪

Margaret River Cabernet Merlot 2014 65% cabernet sauvignon, 32% merlot, 3% petit verdot. In fine Margaret River style, cassis ex the merlot beats the drum of flavour, cabernet providing elegant structure, and petit verdot violets on the way in on the bouquet. Screwcap. 14.5% alc. **Rating** 95 **To** 2034 $26 ✪

Wilyabrup Semillon Sauvignon Blanc 2013 Has abundant energy and drive, semillon contributing to both the structure and flavour, the grip on the finish extending the length of the palate. The individual flavours have been welded into a coherent whole that will give pleasure for years to come. Screwcap. 11.5% alc. Rating 94 To 2021 $60

Wilyabrup Margaret River Chardonnay 2013 Light straw-green; a wine all about effortless elegance – Brideshead Revisited stuff, and on a slow road to maturity. If you lift the sheets, there is surprising strength in the grapefruit-accented acidity, and it is on this that the wine will build in the years ahead. Screwcap. 14% alc. Rating 94 To 2025 $60

ΨΨΨΨ℥ By the Horns Sauvignon Blanc 2015 Rating 90 To 2020 $22

Leo Buring   ★★★★★

Sturt Highway, Nuriootpa, SA 5355 **Region** Eden Valley/Clare Valley
T 1300 651 650 **Open** Not
Winemaker Peter Munro **Est.** 1934 **Dozens** NFP
Between 1965 and 2000, Leo Buring was Australia's foremost producer of Rieslings, with a rich legacy left by former winemaker John Vickery. After veering away from its core business with other varietal wines, it has now been refocused as a specialist Riesling producer. Top of the range are the Leopold Derwent Valley and the Leonay Eden Valley Rieslings, under a changing DW bin no. (DWR for '14, DWS for '15 etc), supported by Clare Valley and Eden Valley Rieslings at significantly lower prices, and expanding its wings to Tasmania and WA.

ΨΨΨΨΨ Leopold Tasmania Riesling 2015 DW S20. Labelled as Tasmania but it's from the White Hills Vineyard in the Tamar. It's a striking wine, bristling with chalk, talc and brilliant lemon-lime, its concentration and focus pitch perfect. Screwcap. 12.5% alc. Rating 96 To 2030 $40 CM ✪

Leonay Riesling 2015 DW S17. You might call it austere to begin with but the finish is a brilliant beam of light. It pulls out the rapier and allows the sun to glimmer from its edges. Florals, citrus and bath salts, perhaps some fennel. Quality nailed to the mast. Screwcap. 11.5% alc. Rating 96 To 2028 $40 CM ✪

ΨΨΨΨ℥ Medium Sweet Eden Valley Riesling 2015 Rating 92 To 2025 $20 CM ✪

Leogate Estate Wines   ★★★★★

1693 Broke Road, Pokolbin, NSW 2320 **Region** Hunter Valley
T (02) 4998 7499 **www**.leogate.com.au **Open** 7 days 10–5
Winemaker Mark Woods **Est.** 2009 **Dozens** 14 000 **Vyds** 66ha
Since purchasing the substantial Brokenback Vineyard in 2009 (a key part of the original Rothbury Estate, with vines over 40 years old), Bill and Vicki Widin have wasted no time. Initially the Widins leased the Tempus Two winery, but prior to the '13 vintage they completed the construction of their own winery and cellar door. They have also expanded the range of varieties, supplementing the long-established 30ha of shiraz, 25ha of chardonnay and 3ha of semillon with between 0.5 and 2ha of each of verdelho, viognier, gewurztraminer, pinot gris and tempranillo. They have had a string of wine show successes for their very impressive portfolio. Exports to Hong Kong.

ΨΨΨΨΨ The Basin Reserve Shiraz 2014 Deep, intensely bright hue; the bouquet is complex and multilayered, with classic Hunter characters: plum, earth, spice and layers of dark and red fruits. The palate flows magnificently, with a precise and intense line of fruit and tannin that goes on and on. Screwcap. 14.5% alc. Rating 97 To 2039 $115 ✪

Museum Release The Basin Reserve Shiraz 2011 When I tasted this wine in Jan '13 I gave it 96 points and a drink-to date of '50 because of its full-bodied opulence and (indirect) style link to the '65 Lindemans Bin 3100 and 3110 Shirazs. I stand by my descriptions and comments, even with the hindsight of the '14 vintage, but I am impressed with Leogate's chutzpah in raising the price of this museum release by 600%. Screwcap. 14% alc. Rating 97 To 2050 $325

ㅜㅜㅜㅜㅜ **Museum Release Reserve Semillon 2010** Pale straw-green; still exceptionally youthful, with fresh lemongrass, lemon and the promise of even more fruit in the years to come. Given 95 points when first tasted 5 years ago, and a drink-to date of 2025. Screwcap. 11.4% alc. **Rating** 96 **To** 2025 $40
Western Slopes Reserve Shiraz 2014 From west-facing vines on a small plot of the Brokenback Vineyard planted in the early '70s. Dark crimson-purple, beautifully deep and intensely bright; it has a layered and spicy bouquet with hints of dried herbs setting it apart from the other '14 Shirazs. It is firmer and the tannins more present, but the finish no less intense and long. Screwcap. 14.5% alc. **Rating** 95 **To** 2046 $115
Malabar Reserve Shiraz 2014 Dark crimson-purple; there is a purity and intensity that runs through the Leogate '14 Shirazs; intense plum, earth and spicy oak lead to a tightly wound, but exceptionally fine-grained, palate; long, savoury, and particularly intense. Screwcap. 14% alc. **Rating** 95 **To** 2035 $80

ㅜㅜㅜㅜ♀ **Creek Bed Reserve Semillon 2015 Rating** 93 **To** 2025 $30
H10 Block Reserve Chardonnay 2014 Rating 92 **To** 2020 $38

Lerida Estate ★★★★★

The Vineyards, Old Federal Highway, Lake George, NSW 2581 **Region** Canberra District
T (02) 6295 6640 **www**.leridaestate.com.au **Open** 7 days 10–5
Winemaker Malcolm Burdett **Est.** 1997 **Dozens** 6000 **Vyds** 7.93ha
Lerida Estate, owned by Jim Lumbers and Anne Caine, owes a great deal to the inspiration of Dr Edgar Riek, planted as it is immediately to the south of his former Lake George vineyard, and also planted mainly to pinot noir (there are smaller plantings of pinot gris, chardonnay, shiraz, merlot, cabernet franc and viognier). The Glenn Murcutt-designed winery, barrel room, cellar door and café complex has spectacular views over Lake George. Exports to China.

ㅜㅜㅜㅜㅜ **Lake George Canberra District Chardonnay 2014** Hand-picked, destemmed, fermented in used French barriques, matured for 11 months. Very good for Canberra District chardonnay, with focus, drive and precision, grapefruit, white peach and high-strung acidity dominating, the oak imparting texture and structure. Screwcap. 12.7% alc. **Rating** 95 **To** 2022 $24
Canberra District Botrytis Pinot Gris 2015 Hand-picked with substantial botrytis, stainless steel-fermented, retaining 180g/l residual sugar and acidity of 9.45g/l. The impressive numbers are simply a sign of what is a very good wine that is far harder to get right than most people realise, and that many also downgrade because it's pinot gris and very sweet. It's worth every cent of the price. Screwcap. 11.2% alc. **Rating** 95 **To** 2020 $39

ㅜㅜㅜㅜ♀ **Josephine Canberra District Pinot Noir 2013 Rating** 91 **To** 2020 $65
Canberra District Pinot Grigio 2015 Rating 90 **To** 2018 $24
Canberra District Shiraz Viognier 2014 Rating 90 **To** 2024 $80

Lethbridge Wines ★★★★★

74 Burrows Road, Lethbridge, Vic 3222 **Region** Geelong
T (03) 5281 7279 **www**.lethbridgewines.com **Open** Mon–Fri, and 1st & 3rd w'end of month 10.30–5
Winemaker Ray Nadeson, Maree Collis, Alexander Byrne **Est.** 1996 **Dozens** 5000 **Vyds** 7ha
Lethbridge was founded by scientists Ray Nadeson, Maree Collis and Adrian Thomas. In Ray's words, 'Our belief is that the best wines express the unique character of special places.' As well as understanding the importance of terroir, the partners have built a unique straw-bale winery, designed to recreate the controlled environment of cellars and caves in Europe. Winemaking is no less ecological: hand-picking, indigenous yeast fermentation, small open fermenters, pigeage (foot-stomping) and minimal handling of the wines throughout the maturation process are all part and parcel of the highly successful Lethbridge approach.

Ray also has a distinctive approach to full-blown chardonnay and pinot noir. There is also a contract winemaking limb to the business. Exports to the UK.

🍷🍷🍷🍷🍷 **Pinot Meunier 2014** Hand-picked, destemmed, 7-day cold soak, wild yeast-fermented in open vats, hand-plunged, pressed straight to French barrels, 9 months maturation. A forthright pinot meunier, with an evocative bouquet, and a palate with potent plum fruit offset by savoury, polished leather, spice and earth nuances. A lot to muse over as you drink it. Screwcap. 13.5% alc. **Rating** 95 **To** 2027 $42

Serendipity Great Western Shiraz 2014 From Doug Smith's Hyde Park Vineyard. A concentrated and powerful wine, very much in the Lethbridge style, oozing ripe blackberry fruits from every pore; savoury tannins and French oak complete the picture of a full-bodied, balanced and long-lived wine. Screwcap. 14.5% alc. **Rating** 95 **To** 2049 $42

Indra 2013 A lengthy apology on the label for the use of varying amounts of whole bunches paves the way for the disclosure of 80% in this shiraz. It is more elegant than the '14 wines, albeit with the particular savoury/stemmy nuances of whole bunches, something that will polarise opinions – they have a mouthwatering impact. Screwcap. 14% alc. **Rating** 95 **To** 2033 $95

Great Western Shiraz 2014 Wild yeast-fermented, matured in large-format used oak with low levels of SO_2. The fragrant spicy black fruits bouquet leads into a spicy, savoury palate filled with red and black fruits, finishing with fine, earthy tannins. Screwcap. 14.5% alc. **Rating** 94 **To** 2034 $30 ✪

Malakoff Vineyard Shiraz 2014 Fruit thinning every year brings the yield down to 5t/ha. The dense purple-crimson colour reflects this discipline, the theme picked up by the ultra-powerful palate overflowing with black fruits and licorice flavours, the indisputable tannins pushed into second place. Cries out for a decade in bottle, then another two. Screwcap. 14.5% alc. **Rating** 94 **To** 2044 $42

Leura Park Estate   ★★★★★

1400 Portarlington Road, Curlewis, Vic 3222 **Region** Geelong
T (03) 5253 3180 **www.leuraparkestate.com.au** **Open** W'ends 10.30–5, 7 days Jan
Winemaker Darren Burke **Est.** 1995 **Dozens** 5000 **Vyds** 15.94ha
Leura Park Estate's vineyard is planted to chardonnay (50%), pinot noir, pinot gris, sauvignon blanc, riesling and shiraz. Owners David and Lyndsay Sharp are committed to minimal interference in the vineyard, and have expanded the estate-grown wine range (Sauvignon Blanc, Pinot Gris, Chardonnay, Pinot Noir and Shiraz) to include Vintage Grande Cuvee. The next step was the erection of a winery for the 2010 vintage, leading to increased production and ongoing wine show success. Exports to South Korea and Singapore.

🍷🍷🍷🍷🍷 **Limited Release Block 1 Reserve Chardonnay 2013** Hand-picked, whole bunch-pressed, wild-fermented in new and used French oak, partial mlf, matured for 10 months. This has all the line, focus and freshness of many '14 chardonnays; it also has finesse, with the flavours poised between citrus and stone fruit, the oak integrated, and the finish long. Screwcap. 13.7% alc. **Rating** 95 **To** 2025 $45

Bellarine Peninsula Pinot Noir 2014 Hand-picked, cold soak, whole bunches, wild yeast, foot-stomped, post-ferment maceration, matured for 10 months in new and used French oak. The whole-berry character, which I like, comes through strongly on the palate, with a carpet of spice and forest; over and above this, the wine has great energy and lift on the palate and finish. Screwcap. 12% alc. **Rating** 95 **To** 2024 $33 ✪

Bellarine Peninsula Shiraz 2014 Two trophies Best Shiraz and Best Wine of Show Geelong Wine Show '15, trophy Best Shiraz, bronze medal Melbourne Wine Awards '15. Elegance, rather than depth or power, is the strength of this wine; it has a genuine flavour of the northern Rhône Valley, spicy and long, I'll go with the '15 Geelong Wine Show multiple trophies. Screwcap. 13% alc. **Rating** 95 **To** 2024 $35 ✪

🍷🍷🍷🍷🍷 **Bellarine Peninsula Chardonnay 2014** **Rating** 91 **To** 2020 $25

Levantine Hill Estate

Level 1, 461 Bourke Street, Melbourne, Vic 3000 **Region** Yarra Valley
T (03) 8602 0831 **www**.levantinehill.com.au **Open** Not
Winemaker Paul Bridgeman **Est.** 2009 **Dozens** 4400 **Vyds** 23.6ha
This is the most ambitious project in the Yarra Valley since the establishment of Domaine Chandon a quarter of a century ago. It is the venture of Lebanese-born Elias (Eli) Jreissati and wife Colleen, Eli having amassed a fortune as a property developer, that business continuing apace. Levantine Hill has two vineyards, the larger and older established by Soo & Son in 1995, and purchased by Levantine Hill in 2010. It not only has 18ha of productive vines, but also has a frontage to the Maroondah Highway, and – at the bottom of a very steep hill – to the Yarra River. The second vineyard fronts Hill Road with a little over 5ha of young vines. All the major varieties of the Yarra Valley are planted on one or other of the two vineyards, but the Soo & Son vineyard is the more important from a business viewpoint. It has provided space for a cellar door, restaurant and winery designed by Fender Katsalidis, who created Hobart's avant garde, and technically awesomely challenging MONA (Museum of Old and New Art), and the Eureka Tower in Melbourne. The ground-hugging, futuristic buildings, their roof line reminiscent of a stealth bomber, are visible from the Maroondah Highway, and easily accessed via Hill Road.

TTTTT **Yarra Valley Chardonnay 2014** From the steep east-facing slope of the 'old' vineyard, hand-picked and fermented in French oak. Given its modest alcohol, this is a particularly complex wine, with excellent texture to its mix of ripe fruit, melon, cashew and toasty oak flavours. Screwcap. 13% alc. **Rating** 95 **To** 2020 $80
Katherine's Paddock Yarra Valley Chardonnay 2014 Hand-picked, sorted, whole bunch-pressed, fermented in French barrels (25% new) with a mix of wild and cultured yeast, aged on lees for 10 months, select barrels undergoing mlf, blended and aged on fine lees in tank for a further 4 months. A powerful and complex chardonnay reflecting the thought and experience lying behind the multifaceted winemaking approach. The small harvest and its Yarra origin were also important. Screwcap. 13.5% alc. **Rating** 95 **To** 2025 $125
Yarra Valley Rose 2015 71% cabernet sauvignon, 24% pinot noir, 4% merlot, 1% petit verdot. Salmon-pink; a deadly serious rose, very complex in terms of both texture and flavour; exotic spices underpin red and purple fruits. It is a mosaic, with every piece fitting neatly. One of the best roses around. Screwcap. 13.5% alc. **Rating** 95 **To** 2017 $35 ✪
Melissa's Paddock Yarra Valley Syrah 2014 Shades of grey in a red wine glass. There is so much going on here, yet no single flavour or texture stands out: fruit, spice, oak, tannins all flit silently in and out of view. There is nothing tawdry about the wine, which breaks free on its finish and aftertaste. Cork. 13% alc. **Rating** 95 **To** 2034 $200
Samantha's Paddock Yarra Valley Melange Traditionnel 2013 81% cabernet sauvignon, 16% merlot, 2% cabernet franc, 1% petit verdot, the varieties fermented and matured separately. At the start of a long journey, although I wish the colour was a little deeper. This to one side, it is complex, long and well balanced. Others will comment on the prices of these wines, and whether they are sustainable in the long term. Cork. 12.5% alc. **Rating** 95 **To** 2028 $125
Colleen's Paddock Yarra Valley Pinot Noir 2014 The gushing back label is best left unread. Complex winemaking is reflected in this wine, which says different things along the way to its finish, where the lift is reminiscent of Burgundy – but not Grand Cru. Cork. 13% alc. **Rating** 94 **To** 2024

TTTT **Yarra Valley Sauvignon Blanc Semillon 2015 Rating** 88 **To** 2017 $35
Yarra Valley Melange Traditionnel Blanc 2014 Rating 88 **To** 2017 $80

Liebich Wein

Steingarten Road, Rowland Flat, SA 5352 **Region** Barossa Valley
T (08) 8524 4543 **www.**liebichwein.com.au **Open** Wed–Mon 11–5
Winemaker Ron Liebich **Est.** 1992 **Dozens** 2500 **Vyds** 28.2ha

The Liebich family have been grapegrowers and winemakers at Rowland Flat since 1919, with CW 'Darkie' Liebich one of the great local characters. His nephew Ron began making wine in '69, but it was not until '92 that he and wife Janet began selling wine under the Liebich Wein label. The business has grown surely but steadily, with a new warehouse commissioned in 2008 vastly improving storage and handling capacity. Exports to the UK, Denmark, Germany, Switzerland, Singapore and China.

ΨΨΨΨΨ Rare Barossa Valley Tawny NV The tawny hue (no red hints) and viscosity attest to the age of the wine, drawn from a solera started in 1919; it has good rancio, and no volatile acidity. 250ml. Cork. 18.5% alc. **Rating** 94 **To** 2017 $50

ΨΨΨΨ The Potter's Barossa Valley Merlot 2010 Rating 88 **To** 2020 $25

Lightfoot & Sons

Myrtle Point Vineyard, 717 Calulu Road, Bairnsdale, Vic 3875 **Region** Gippsland
T (03) 5156 9205 **www.**lightfootwines.com **Open** Not
Winemaker Alastair Butt, Tom Lightfoot **Est.** 1995 **Dozens** 8000 **Vyds** 29.3ha

Brian and Helen Lightfoot have established pinot noir, shiraz, chardonnay, cabernet sauvignon and merlot, the lion's share to pinot noir and shiraz. The soil is very similar to that of Coonawarra, with terra rossa over limestone. Most of the grapes are sold (as originally planned) to other Vic winemakers. With the arrival of Alastair Butt (formerly of Brokenwood and Seville Estate), and supported by son Tom, production has increased, and may well rise further. Second son Rob has also come on board, bringing 10 years' experience in sales and marketing.

ΨΨΨΨΨ Myrtle Point Single Vineyard Gippsland Lakes Chardonnay 2015
Pale mid-straw; citrus, spice and white peach are in play with a background of complexity derived from barrel fermentation and partial mlf. The palate is beautifully poised, with driving mineral acids and layers of texture and flavour. It is powerful, long and impressive. Screwcap. 13.2% alc. **Rating** 95 **To** 2024 $26 ◐
Myrtle Point Single Vineyard Gippsland Lakes Pinot Noir 2015
MV6, 20% of the total was whole bunches, but individual batches ranged from zero to 75%, matured in French oak (15% new). An elegant mid-weight pinot, primarily with red fruits providing the flavour, supported by fine-grained tannins and integrated oak. It's clear the Gippsland Lakes enjoyed the same ideal conditions as regions further west in Vic. Screwcap. 13% alc. **Rating** 95 **To** 2028 $28 ◐

Lillian

Box 174, Pemberton, WA 6260 **Region** Pemberton
T (08) 9776 0193 **Open** Not
Winemaker John Brocksopp **Est.** 1993 **Dozens** 320 **Vyds** 3.2ha

Long-serving (and continuing consultant) viticulturist to Leeuwin Estate John Brocksopp has established 2.8ha of the Rhône trio of marsanne, roussanne and viognier, and 0.4ha of shiraz. He is also purchasing grapes from other growers in Pemberton. Exports to Japan.

ΨΨΨΨΨ Lefroy Brook Pemberton Pinot Noir 2014 Wild-fermented, 18 days on skins, matured in French oak (33% new) for 15 months. Bright crimson hue; very attractive red cherry fruit that, like the palate, has purity; this has not ruled out complexity ex vinification and oak. All up, has greater concentration than any previous Lillian Pinot. Screwcap. 13.7% alc. **Rating** 94 **To** 2024 $26 ◐

ΨΨΨΨΨ Lefroy Brook Pemberton Chardonnay 2013 Rating 92 **To** 2019 $26

Lillypilly Estate ★★★★★

47 Lillypilly Road, Leeton, NSW 2705 **Region** Riverina
T (02) 6953 4069 **www**.lillypilly.com **Open** Mon–Sat 10–5.30, Sun by appt
Winemaker Robert Fiumara **Est.** 1982 **Dozens** 10000 **Vyds** 27.9ha
Botrytised white wines are by far the best offering from Lillypilly, with the Noble Muscat of Alexandria unique to the winery; these wines have both style and intensity of flavour and can age well. Table wine quality is always steady – a prime example of not fixing what is not broken. Exports to the UK, the US, Canada and China.

🍷🍷🍷🍷🍷 **Family Reserve Noble Harvest 2012** More developed hue than the '08 Reserve Noble Blend, into full gold; apricot/cumquat backed by lime and lemon; obvious botrytis; a touch of fresh ginger. 375ml. Screwcap. 11% alc. **Rating** 95 To 2022 $40

Museum Release Family Reserve Noble Blend 2002 Burnished orange-bronze; obvious botrytis, very complex fruit, starting to dry out a fraction. Double-gold Sydney International Wine Competition '06 and '11. 375ml. Screwcap. 12.5% alc. **Rating** 95 To 2020 $65

Sweet Harvest 2015 Pale straw-green; lively and juicy, citrus to the fore. At the start of its life, but has very good balance to support its development. 375ml. Screwcap. 10% alc. **Rating** 94 To 2025 $16 ❂

Show Reserve Noble Blend 2008 Yellow-gold, still bright; intensely sweet, less obvious botrytis than the '12 Reserve Noble Harvest. Double-gold Sydney International Wine Competition '11. 375ml. Screwcap. 11% alc. **Rating** 94 To 2018 $58

Lindeman's (Coonawarra) ★★★★★

58 Queensbridge Street, Southbank, Vic 3006 **Region** Coonawarra
T 1300 651 650 **www**.lindemans.com **Open** Not
Winemaker Brett Sharpe **Est.** 1965 **Dozens** NFP
Lindeman's Coonawarra vineyards have assumed a greater importance than ever thanks to the move towards single region wines. The Coonawarra Trio of Limestone Ridge Vineyard Shiraz Cabernet, St George Vineyard Cabernet Sauvignon and Pyrus Cabernet Sauvignon Merlot Cabernet Franc are all of exemplary quality.

🍷🍷🍷🍷🍷 **Coonawarra Trio St George Vineyard Cabernet Sauvignon 2014** Enough to restore one's faith in Coonawarra. This is a lovely wine, supple, medium-bodied, long and perfectly balanced. The cassis, redcurrant and mulberry flavours flow in a juicy stream, uninterrupted by egregious oak or tannins. Screwcap. 13.5% alc. **Rating** 97 To 2039 $70 ❂

🍷🍷🍷🍷🍷 **Coonawarra Trio Limestone Ridge Vineyard Shiraz Cabernet 2014** I am as guilty as anyone in forgetting the Trio in discussion of the state of play in Coonawarra. This is a lovely Coonawarra shiraz cabernet combining an umbrella of elegance over a complex fusion of blackcurrant, mulberry, earth and oak. Worth every dollar. Screwcap. 14% alc. **Rating** 96 To 2039 $70 ❂

Coonawarra Trio Pyrus Cabernet Sauvignon Merlot Malbec 2014 An 82/12/6% blend. There are striking aromas of rolled tobacco and spice underpinning a wealth of cassis and plum; the tannins are exemplary, firm but not aggressive, and the French oak is likewise balanced. Screwcap. 13.5% alc. **Rating** 95 To 2039 $70

Lindeman's (Hunter Valley) ★★★★

McDonalds Road, Pokolbin, NSW 2320 **Region** Hunter Valley
T (02) 4993 3700 **www**.lindemans.com **Open** 7 days 10–5
Winemaker Wayne Falkenberg, Brett Sharpe **Est.** 1843 **Dozens** NFP
Just when I expected it least, Lindeman's has produced some seriously good wines from the Hunter Valley, and one half of the Lindeman's winemaking or marketing side (without talking

to the other half) has exhumed some of the Bin number systems that were used in the glory days of the 1960s, admittedly without total consistency. Thus for white wines, 50 or 55 were the last two digits used for what was named Riesling, 70 for what was named White Burgundy, and 75 for what was called Chablis; with the shiraz-based wines, the last two digits were 00, 03 or 10. The most famous were the 1965 Claret and Burgundy releases Bin 3100 and Bin 3110, the most famous Chablis 1967 Bin 3475. Exports to all major markets.

ŢŢŢŢŢ **Limited Release Reserve Ben Ean Vineyard Hunter Valley Shiraz 2014** Bin 1400. Smart new label retains just enough of the past. A classic medium-bodied Hunter shiraz with spicy/earthy/leathery nuances to the mix of red (cherry) and black (cherry and berry) fruits. I'm not convinced that this fully used the potential of the site and the vintage, but it's still a very useful wine with a long future. Screwcap. 14.5% alc. **Rating** 94 **To** 2039 $30 ✪

Lindenderry at Red Hill ★★★★★

142 Arthurs Seat Road, Red Hill, Vic 3937 **Region** Mornington Peninsula
T (03) 5989 2933 **www.**lindenderry.com.au **Open** W'ends 11–5
Winemaker Barnaby Flanders **Est.** 1999 **Dozens** 1000 **Vyds** 3.35ha
Lindenderry at Red Hill is a sister operation to Lancemore Hill in the Macedon Ranges and Lindenwarrah at Milawa. It has a five-star country house hotel, conference facilities, a function area, day spa and restaurant on 16ha of gardens, but also has a little over 3ha of vineyards, planted equally to pinot noir and chardonnay over 15 years ago. Notwithstanding the reputation of the previous contract winemakers for Lindenderry, the wines now being made by Barney Flanders are the best yet. He has made the most of the estate-grown grapes in Mornington Peninsula and Macedon, adding cream to the cake by sourcing some excellent Grampians shiraz.

ŢŢŢŢŢ **Reserve Mornington Peninsula Chardonnay 2014** Hand-sorted in the vineyard, whole bunch-pressed, wild-fermented in a 1yo François Frères puncheon, partial mlf, matured on lees for 10 months. There must have been fruit selection in the first place, the best parcel used for this, although the alcohol is identical to the standard wine. So how partial was partial mlf? And how much did it ameliorate the acidity? Screwcap. 13% alc. **Rating** 95 **To** 2022 $60
Grampians Shiraz 2014 Destemmed to small open fermenters, wild yeast, 40 days on skins, matured in French hogsheads (15% new) for 14 months. A medium to full-bodied wine, very much in Grampians style; blackberry and plum are interwoven, and if the long time on skins post-ferment was designed to soften the tannins, it achieved that handsomely. The restraint in the use of new oak has also paid dividends. Screwcap. 13.5% alc. **Rating** 95 **To** 2034 $35 ✪
Mornington Peninsula Chardonnay 2014 P58 clone from the home vineyard at Red Hill, whole bunch-pressed, wild-fermented and matured on lees in new and used French oak for 9 months. If, as appears to be the case from both the taste of the wine and vinification details supplied, no mlf was used, it makes a case for the reduced use of mlf across the region. It certainly gets your attention, and lingers. Screwcap. 13% alc. **Rating** 94 **To** 2020 $40

ŢŢŢŢŢ **Mornington Peninsula Pinot Noir 2014** Rating 93 **To** 2024 $45
Macedon Ranges Pinot Gris 2015 Rating 92 **To** 2018 $35
Macedon Ranges Pinot Noir 2014 Rating 91 **To** 2020 $40

Lindenton Wines ★★★★

102 High Street, Heathcote, Vic 3523 **Region** Heathcote
T (03) 5433 3246 **Open** 7 days 10–4 by appt
Winemaker Phil Meehan **Est.** 2003 **Dozens** 1000 **Vyds** 4ha
Jim Harrison's Lindenton Wines is a semi-retirement occupation. His business plan is based on the purchase of grapes from smaller growers in the region who do not have access to winemaking facilities or outlets for their fruit. From the word go there has been an extensive range of wines available, running through Verdelho, Chardonnay, Viognier, Marsanne, Merlot,

Shiraz, Shiraz Viognier and top-of-the-tree Melange. Jim's longer-range plan is to make the wines himself.

ΥΥΥΥΥ **Limited Release Reserve Shiraz 2013** Matured in French oak for 18 months. Excellent colour for age; a stylish wine that ticks all the boxes; the predominantly black fruits are supple, but there are complex notes in both the flavour and texture profiles of the medium-bodied palate; best is the way the savoury background yields to the dark fruits that glide through on the finish and aftertaste. Screwcap. 14.5% alc. **Rating** 94 **To** 2038 $30 ✪

ΥΥΥΥΥ **Limited Release Cabernet Sauvignon 2013 Rating** 92 **To** 2028 $30

Linfield Road Wines

65 Victoria Terrace, Williamstown, SA 5351 **Region** Barossa Valley
T (08) 8524 7355 **www.**linfieldroadwines.com **Open** Thurs–Sun 10–5
Winemaker Daniel Wilson, Steve Wilson **Est.** 2002 **Dozens** 2500 **Vyds** 19ha
Linfield Road produces small batches of single vineyard wines from the Wilson family vineyard at Williamstown. The story began in 1860 when Edmund Major Wilson planted the first vines on the outskirts of Williamstown. Since Edmund's first plantings, the Wilsons have fostered a viticulture tradition that now spans five generations; three generations of the family currently live and work on the property, located at the very southern edge of the Barossa. It is situated high above the valley floor, with cooler nights and longer ripening periods. Exports to Canada, Malaysia, Singapore, Japan and China.

ΥΥΥΥΥ **The Stubborn Patriarch Barossa Shiraz 2014** Blackberry, black forest, lots of black fruits flow effortlessly through the plush and richly fruited palate. Screwcap. 14.5% alc. **Rating** 93 **To** 2028 $28
The Black Hammer Barossa Cabernet Sauvignon 2014 Dark fruits backed by leafy cabernet fruit. It is rich and powerful, finishing with savoury tannins and a curranty fruit character. Screwcap. 15% alc. **Rating** 92 **To** 2030 $26

ΥΥΥΥ **The Steam Maker Riesling 2015 Rating** 88 **To** 2018 $20 CM

Lino Ramble

2 Hall St, McLaren Vale, SA 5171 (postal) **Region** McLaren Vale
T 0409 553 448 **www.**linoramble.com.au **Open** Not
Winemaker Andy Coppard **Est.** 2012 **Dozens** 700
After 20 years of working for other wine companies, big and small, interstate and internationally, the last 7 years with Kay Brothers, Andy Coppard yearned for the opportunity to start his own business. However, he needed a partner, and found her at Kay Brothers, where she (Angela Townsend) was business manager; she is now Lino Ramble's first employee. They say, 'We've climbed on top of the dog kennel, tied a cape around our necks, held our breaths, and jumped.' Their first vintage was 2012, with 350 dozen bottles, a similar volume was made in '13, and they doubled that for the '14 vintage. And if you are curious about the name (as I was), the story has overtones of James Joyce's stream of consciousness mental rambles.

ΥΥΥΥΥ **Treadlie McLaren Vale Grenache Shiraz Mataro 2014** It's sweet and savoury, finely tannic and yet succulent all at once. It drinks beautifully. The combination of light and shade is beguiling. Screwcap. 14.5% alc. **Rating** 95 **To** 2020 $30 CM ✪

ΥΥΥΥΥ **Tom Bowler McLaren Vale Nero d'Avola 2014 Rating** 92 **To** 2021 $30 CM

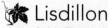 Lisdillon ★★★

11264 Tasman Highway, Swansea, Tas 7190 **Region** East Coast Tasmania
T (03) 6257 7567 **www.**lisdillon.com.au **Open** Not
Winemaker Winemaking Tasmania **Est.** 2008 **Dozens** 275 **Vyds** 1.5ha
The Cotton family has been farming on the east coast of Tasmania for almost 200 years, over six generations. The property was first surveyed by first-generation Francis Cotton in 1830.

Skipping 178 years, sheepfarmer Crispin Cotton decided to plant vines on the property in 2008, choosing pinot noir (1ha) and sauvignon blanc (0.5ha). Lisdillon is a very beautiful part of a beautiful island, and when Crispin passed away in April '14, his widow Jane and daughter Katherine took over management of the vineyard. Further plantings are planned.

Little Brampton Wines   ★★★★

PO Box 61, Clare, SA 5453 **Region** Clare Valley
T (08) 8843 4201 **www.**littlebramptonwines.com.au **Open** At The Little Red Grape, Sevenhill
Winemaker Contract **Est.** 2001 **Dozens** 400 **Vyds** 10ha
Little Brampton Wines is a boutique, family-owned business operated by Alan and Pamela Schwarz. They purchased their 24ha property in the heart of the Clare Valley in the early 1990s (Alan had graduated from Roseworthy in '81). The property had produced grapes since the 1860s, but the vineyard had been removed during the Vine Pull Scheme of the 1980s. The Schwarzs have replanted riesling (2ha), shiraz and cabernet sauvignon (4ha each) on northwest slopes at 520m. Exports to the UK and Singapore.

ΨΨΨΨΨ **Flagpole Clare Valley Riesling 2015** Pale quartz-green; restraint and elegance are the hallmark of this classy young riesling, its best years still to come. Lime, green apple and slatey acidity have all the requisite length and balance for a long life. Screwcap. 12.5% alc. **Rating** 94 **To** 2030 $24 ✪
Gateway Clare Valley Shiraz 2013 The dense colour sends a message that this is an intense, full-bodied shiraz, full to the brim with black cherries, blackberries and spice, reflecting its location on the western ridge of the Valley, one of its highest points. Despite its full-bodied structure and generous oak, it is very well balanced. Screwcap. 14.5% alc. **Rating** 94 **To** 2033 $30 ✪

Little Cathedral   ★★★★

PO Box 218, Clifton Hill, Vic 3068 **Region** Upper Goulburn
T 0412 581 912 **www.**littlecathedral.com.au **Open** Not
Winemaker Dave McIntosh **Est.** 1996 **Dozens** 300 **Vyds** 3.25ha
The vineyard was planted in 1996 under the lee of the striking Cathedral Ranges at Taggerty. It has been established on a gentle north-facing slope at an altitude of 280m, and should irrigation be required, it comes from the gin-clear Little River, a mountain stream that originates deep within the forest that the vineyard backs onto. Since Madge Alexandra and Anna Pickworth acquired the property in 2006, it has been a sharp learning curve about the challenges of nature. Happily, they have surmounted the hurdles of inclement weather and bushfires. The ability of the vineyard to produce good Pinot Noir is beyond doubt.

ΨΨΨΨΨ **Pinot Noir 2014** MV6, hand-picked and sorted, destemmed, 20% whole bunches, open-fermented, wild yeast, 25 days on skins, matured in French oak for 10 months. There's a big tug of war between small red and black fruits on the one hand, earthy/savoury/briary notes on the other. It's not generous, but does have potential to (pleasantly) surprise. Screwcap. 13% alc. **Rating** 90 **To** 2022 $30
Pinot Noir 2012 Very good retention of hue; for better or worse, very typical of Little Cathedral's Pinots, with a tightly furled umbrella of red and blue fruits over slightly hard acidity. Food is the saviour for the style. Screwcap. 12.9% alc. **Rating** 90 **To** 2018 $25

ΨΨΨΨ **Pinot Noir Rose 2015 Rating** 89 **To** 2017 $24
Pinot Noir 2015 Rating 89 **To** 2023 $30

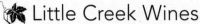 Little Creek Wines   ★★★★☆

15 Grantley Avenue, Victor Harbor, SA 5211 (postal) **Region** McLaren Vale
T 0415 047 719 **www.**littlecreekwines.com **Open** Not
Winemaker Duane Coates **Est.** 2014 **Dozens** 60

This is a partnership between Sam Gibson and brother-in-law Patrick Coghlan. Their real jobs are an archery wholesale business (Pats Archery) situated on the Fleurieu Peninsula. Pat is the leading compound archer in Australia and Sam is the manager of the business, importing and distributing all types of archery equipment. Sam is the one with wine in his veins; his father, Rob Gibson, owns the 5 red star Gibson Wines, and Sam's brother Abel Gibson has his own label, Ruggabellus. For many years Sam and Pat became (archery) friends with Duane Coates, which ultimately led to the creation of this micro-business, with Duane the winemaker. The grapes come from premium growers, and the partners have no intention of establishing/ purchasing vineyards or increasing the amount of the wine at the present time.

Shiraz Cabernet 2014 Inaugural release. 55% Langhorne Creek cabernet/45% Blewitt Springs shiraz. Rich with blackberry, redcurrant and milk chocolate flavour. It generally presents as seamless and smooth until the finish, where grainy tannin enters the fray. It's perhaps most characterised by its admirable combination of both inky depth and general brightness. Screwcap. 14% alc. **Rating** 95 **To** 2028 $30 CM ❂

Little Yarra Wines

PO Box 2311, Richmond South, Vic 3121 **Region** Yarra Valley
T 0401 228 196 **www.**littleyarra.com.au **Open** Not
Winemaker Dylan McMahon **Est.** 2013 **Dozens** 450 **Vyds** 1.2ha
Little Yarra Wines is a family partnership between Ian, Pip and Matt Pattison and Pip's sister Mary Padbury. The Pattisons previously operated a vineyard and winery in the Macedon Ranges (Metcalfe Valley Wines), but could not resist buying the Little Yarra Wines property and its plantings of 0.6ha each of pinot noir and chardonnay. The quality of the grapes also allowed them to secure Dylan McMahon as winemaker, with input from Matt Pattison.

Chardonnay 2015 A stunning chardonnay that takes all that the Upper Yarra climate and terroir has to offer. It's almost painfully energetic and lively, with grapefruit just pipping white peach at the finishing post after a mad dash up the straight. It gets an extra point thanks to its finish and aftertaste. Screwcap. 13.2% alc. **Rating** 97 **To** 2026 $35 ❂

Pinot Noir 2015 Excellent colour. It is a neat match with the chardonnay: an expressive bouquet and an energetic palate with red and black cherry fruit lighting the way; long finish and aftertaste. Screwcap. 13.3% alc. **Rating** 95 **To** 2024 $35 ❂

Livewire Wines ★★★★

PO Box 369, Portarlington, Vic 3223 **Region** Geelong
T 0439 024 007 **www.**livewirewines.com.au **Open** Not
Winemaker Anthony Brain **Est.** 2011 **Dozens** 1000
Anthony Brain started working life as a chef, but in the late 1990s 'took a slight bend into the wine industry'. He started gathering experience in the Yarra Valley, and simultaneously started oenology studies at CSU. Margaret River followed, as did time in SA before returning to the Yarra, working at De Bortoli from 2003 to '07 (undertaking vintages in the Hunter, King and Yarra valleys). Five vintages as winemaker at Bellarine Estate followed, giving him 'a platform and understanding of the Geelong region and the opportunity to learn more about sites, viticulture and winemaking decisions'.

Sauvignon 2015 A complex barrel-fermented wine, all about texture and structure, not about fruit flavours, Old World, not New World. Has a decent jab of acidity to keep the mind focused and register the length of the wine. Screwcap. 12.3% alc. **Rating** 94 **To** 2019 $28 ❂

Bellarine Peninsula Pinot Noir 2015 Rating 93 To 2023 $32
Whole Bunch Love Grampians Shiraz 2015 Rating 93 To 2028 $30
Ballanclea Field Blend 2015 Rating 92 To 2017 $28
The Swanno Tempranillo 2015 Rating 92 To 2028 $32

Lloyd Brothers

34 Warners Road, McLaren Vale, SA 5171 **Region** McLaren Vale
T (08) 8323 8792 **www**.lloydbrothers.com.au **Open** 7 days 11–5
Winemaker Ross Durbidge **Est.** 2002 **Dozens** 5000 **Vyds** 38ha
Lloyd Brothers Wine and Olive Company is owned and operated by David and Matthew
Lloyd, third-generation McLaren Vale vignerons. Their 25ha estate overlooks the township,
and is planted to 12ha shiraz, 0.8ha bushvine grenache and 0.4ha bushvine mataro (plus
sauvignon blanc, chardonnay, pinot gris and shiraz in the Adelaide Hills). The shiraz planting
allows the creation of a full range of styles, including Rose, Sparkling Shiraz, Fortified Shiraz
and Estate Shiraz, along with the White Chalk Shiraz, so named because of the white chalk
used to mark each barrel during the classification process. Exports to the UK.

🍷🍷🍷🍷🍷 **McLaren Vale Grenache 2014** Hand-picked, 80% crushed and destemmed,
20% whole bunches, 10% juice run-off, 7 days cold soak, 18 days fermentation and
maceration, matured for 18 months in French oak (20% new). A lot of thought
and work have gone into this, and have largely succeeded; if it has an Achilles heel,
it is the whole bunch inclusion. Screwcap. 14.5% alc. **Rating** 92 **To** 2021 $30
Adelaide Hills Syrah 2014 Crushed and destemmed, wild yeast open-
fermented with 5 days cold soak, matured in French and American oak for
14 months. Were it not for the decision to pick early, this would have gone
completely OTT; as it is, the winemaker's thumbprints are all over the wine,
particularly the soft, furry tannins. Screwcap. 13% alc. **Rating** 90 **To** 2034 $30

🍷🍷🍷🍷 **McLaren Vale Mataro 2014 Rating** 88 **To** 2024 $30

Lobethal Road Wines

2254 Onkaparinga Valley Road, Mount Torrens, SA 5244 **Region** Adelaide Hills
T (08) 8389 4595 **www**.lobethalroad.com **Open** W'ends & public hols 11–5
Winemaker Michael Sykes (Contract) **Est.** 1998 **Dozens** 5500 **Vyds** 5.1ha
Dave Neyle and Inga Lidums bring diverse, but very relevant, experience to the Lobethal
Road vineyard, the lion's share planted to shiraz (3.1ha), with smaller amounts of chardonnay,
tempranillo, sauvignon blanc and graciano. Dave has been in vineyard development and
management in SA and Tasmania since 1990. Inga has 25+ years' experience in marketing and
graphic design in Australia and overseas, with a focus on the wine and food industries. The
property is managed with minimal chemical input.

🍷🍷🍷🍷🍷 **Adelaide Hills Tempranillo Graciano 2014** An estate-grown 92/8% blend,
matured in used French oak for 10 months. The cool climate sets the varieties
up nicely, with spicy undertones to the red fruits of tempranillo and the more
savoury notes of the graciano; the alcohol is neatly judged, the overall effect fresh.
Screwcap. 14% alc. **Rating** 93 **To** 2024 $25 ✪
Adelaide Hills Chardonnay 2015 Despite its intensity and complexity, it is (or
seems to be) unoaked, its considerable presence deriving from its fruit trifecta of
white peach, almond and grapefruit. Lees contact and partial mlf are both possible
contributors. Screwcap. 12.8% alc. **Rating** 92 **To** 2021 $25 ✪
Adelaide Hills Shiraz 2014 Bright, zesty, lively and crunchy red fruits with a
web of spices that are quick to please, then cheekily throw a line to you suggesting
there is more to be found on the back-palate and finish – which there is.
Screwcap. 14% alc. **Rating** 92 **To** 2024 $25 ✪
Maja Blanc de Blancs 2012 An even and appealing expression of the cool
citrus and apple fruit of Adelaide Hills chardonnay, comfortably supported by the
subtle nutty nuances of 3 years on lees, neatly completed with an elegant dosage
of 5g/l. It finishes with sour acidity and reasonable persistence. Diam. 12% alc.
Rating 91 **To** 2017 $35 TS
Adelaide Hills Sauvignon Blanc 2015 From a single site, made in the usual
no-frills fashion of giving voice to the rich, tropical fruits with an added burst of
grapefruity acidity on the finish. Screwcap. 12.2% alc. **Rating** 90 **To** 2016 $22

Lofty Valley Wines

100 Collins Road, Summertown, SA 5141 **Region** Adelaide Hills
T 0400 930 818 **www.**loftyvalleywines.com.au **Open** Sat by appt
Winemaker Various **Est.** 2004 **Dozens** 400 **Vyds** 3ha
Medical practitioner Brian Gilbert began collecting wine when he was 19, flirting with the
idea of becoming a winemaker before being headed firmly in the direction of medicine by his
parents. Thirty or so years later he purchased a blackberry and gorse-infested 12ha property in
the Adelaide Hills, eventually obtaining permission to establish a vineyard. Chardonnay (2ha)
was planted in 2004, and 1ha of pinot noir in '07, both on steep slopes.

ΨΨΨΨΨ **Steeped Single Vineyard Pinot Noir 2014** The remainder of the pinot
vintage (ie excluding the Collins Class III). Excellent colour and clarity; fragrant
red fruits and a finely structured and textured palate, fruit, oak and tannins all on
the same page. Harmony is the key. Screwcap. 13% alc. **Rating** 95 **To** 2026 $39

ΨΨΨΨΨ **Steeper Single Vineyard Pinot Noir 2015 Rating** 93 **To** 2025 $39
Collins Class III Pinot Noir 2014 Rating 93 **To** 2026 $49

Logan Wines

Castlereagh Highway, Apple Tree Flat, Mudgee, NSW 2850 **Region** Mudgee
T (02) 6373 1333 **www.**loganwines.com.au **Open** 7 days 10–5
Winemaker Peter Logan **Est.** 1997 **Dozens** 45 000
Logan is a family-owned and operated business with emphasis on cool climate wines from
Orange and Mudgee. The business is run by husband and wife team Peter (winemaker)
and Hannah (sales and marketing). Peter majored in biology and chemistry at Macquarie
University, moving into the pharmaceutical world working as a process chemist. In a reversal
of the usual roles, his father encouraged him to change careers, and Peter obtained a graduate
diploma of oenology from the University of Adelaide in 1996. The winery and tasting room
are situated on the Mudgee vineyard, but the best wines are all made from grapes grown in
the Orange region. Exports to the EU, Japan and other major markets.

ΨΨΨΨΨ **Orange Sauvignon Blanc 2015** Lick-your-lips intensity. This almost veers
into the profound, at least in terms of depth. Gravel, passionfruit pulp, herbs,
assorted tropical fruits. It strikes and then runs for all it's worth. Screwcap. 13% alc.
Rating 95 **To** 2016 $23 CM ❂
Ridge of Tears Orange Shiraz 2013 Cool climate writ large. In a good and
positive way. Pepper, leaves, black cherries and graphite. Slight dusting of chocolate.
Firm. Feels as though it won't take no for an answer. Good way for a wine to feel.
Commands attention. Screwcap. 14% alc. **Rating** 95 **To** 2028 $45 CM
Ridge of Tears Mudgee Shiraz 2013 This has a fresh, savoury, peppery
outlook on life. Its face sits on a well-proportioned frame, complete with cherry-
plum fruit of good concentration and dimension, aided by fennel and wood
smoke. Freshness, complexity, fruit accessibility and the structure to age: it's quite a
killer combination. Screwcap. 14% alc. **Rating** 94 **To** 2026 $45 CM

ΨΨΨΨΨ **Hannah Orange Rose 2015 Rating** 92 **To** 2017 $23 CM ❂
Weemala Orange Riesling 2015 Rating 91 **To** 2020 $20 CM ❂
Orange Pinot Noir 2014 Rating 91 **To** 2022 $30
Vintage M Orange Cuvee 2012 Rating 90 **To** 2018 $35 CM

🍇 Lonely Shore

18 Bavin Street, Denmark, WA 6333 (postal) **Region** Denmark
T 0418 907 594 **www.**lonelyshore.com.au **Open** Not
Winemaker Liam Carmody **Est.** 2014 **Dozens** 200 **Vyds** 2ha
Liam Carmody's grandmother (Freda Vines) was the author of an historical novel published
in 1958, telling the story of early settlement on the south coast of WA. Liam graduated
from Curtin University in 2003, since working in Sonoma, California, NZ, France, South
Africa and the Mornington Peninsula before settling in Denmark and taking up a full-time

winemaking role at Forest Hill. Thus Lonely Shore is very much a busman's holiday. The grapes come from the dry-grown DeiTos Vineyard near Manjimup.

🍷🍷🍷🍷🍷 **DeiTos Vineyard Pinot Noir 2015** 10% whole bunches, 90% crushed/destemmed, 8 days cold soak, open-fermented, hand-plunged, basket-pressed, matured for 9 months in French barriques (20% new). A transparent pinot precisely reflecting all the inputs in the winery; red fruits with spicy/savoury nuances in a light-bodied framework. Screwcap. 13.5% alc. **Rating** 90 **To** 2020 $44

Lonely Vineyard ★★★★

61 Emmett Road, Crafers West, SA 5152 (postal) **Region** Eden Valley
T 0413 481 163 **www**.lonelyvineyard.com.au **Open** Not
Winemaker Michael Schreurs **Est.** 2008 **Dozens** 400 **Vyds** 1.5ha
This is the venture of winemaker Michael Schreurs and Karina Ouwens, a commercial lawyer from Adelaide. Daughter Amalia Schreurs can 'hoover a box of sultanas in record time' while Meesh, the family cat, 'treats Karina and Amalia well, and Michael with the contempt he deserves. As cats do.' One or other of the partners (perhaps both) has a great sense of humour. Michael's winemaking career began with Seppelt Great Western winery for three years, followed by six years at Henschke, and, more recently, The Lane Vineyard in the Adelaide Hills, backed up by stints in Burgundy, the Rhône Valley, the US and Spain. Exports to the UK.

🍷🍷🍷🍷🍷 **Eden Valley Riesling 2015** From the Cactus Vineyard, 73yo vines at 460m, hand-picked and sorted, whole bunch-pressed, cool-fermented in stainless steel. Quartz-white; a very pure and delicate wine, its provenance and its mouthfeel a one-way sign pointing to your cellar: this is a gold-plated certainty to develop with extreme finesse and grace in the years and decades to come. Screwcap. 12.5% alc. **Rating** 92 **To** 2030 $26
Eden Valley Montepulciano 2014 Montepulciano clone SAVI01 grafted onto riesling on the Horseshoe Vineyard at 440m, hand-picked, small batch-fermented on skins for up to 17 days, basket-pressed, matured in used French puncheons for 14 months. Attractive spicy/flowery/red blossom bouquet roughly translates into a medium-bodied palate. Screwcap. 13.5% alc. **Rating** 91 **To** 2019 $36

Long Rail Gully Wines ★★★★

161 Long Rail Gully Road, Murrumbateman, NSW 2582 **Region** Canberra District
T (02) 6226 8115 **www**.longrailgully.com.au **Open** W'ends & hols 11–5
Winemaker Richard Parker **Est.** 1998 **Dozens** 15000 **Vyds** 24ha
Long Rail Gully is operated by the Parker family, headed by Barbara and Garry Parker, who began the planting of the 24ha vineyard in 1998. The plantings comprise shiraz (8ha), cabernet sauvignon (4ha), merlot, riesling and pinot gris (3.5ha each) and pinot noir (1.5ha). Winemaker son Richard studied winemaking at CSU, and was responsible for selecting the natural amphitheatre site for the vineyard, designing the layout, and supervising the planting. He also operates a successful contract winemaking business for wineries situated in Orange, Hilltops, Cowra and locally. Exports to China.

🍷🍷🍷🍷🍷 **Murrumbateman Shiraz 2014** A most attractive wine. One of those mid-weight reds that just gets the proportions right. Oak, cherry-plum fruit, (black) pepper, spice, nuts. It's all strung on a taut line of acidity, and it's all kept firm by dry, spice-shot tannin. Value plus. Screwcap. 13.8% alc. **Rating** 94 **To** 2027 $25 CM ✪

🍷🍷🍷🍷🍷 **Murrumbateman Riesling 2015 Rating** 90 **To** 2023 $22 CM
Murrumbateman Pinot Noir 2014 Rating 90 **To** 2021 $35 CM

Longleat Wines ★★★★

105 Old Weir Road, Murchison, Vic 3610 **Region** Goulburn Valley
T (03) 5826 2294 **www**.murchisonwines.com.au **Open** W'ends & most public hols 10–5
Winemaker Guido Vazzoler **Est.** 1975 **Dozens** 4000 **Vyds** 8.1ha

Sandra (ex-kindergarten teacher turned cheesemaker) and Guido Vazzoler (ex-Brown Brothers) acquired the long-established Murchison Estate vineyard in 2003 (renaming it Longleat Wines), after living on the property (as tenants) for some years. The mature vineyard has 3.2ha of shiraz, 2.3ha of cabernet sauvignon, 0.8ha each of semillon, sauvignon blanc and chardonnay, and 0.2ha of petit verdot. Exports to Hong Kong and China.

ŶŶŶŶŶ **Murchison Shiraz 2014** Fresh and flavoursome with ground coffee, chocolate and blackberry flavours running tidily through the palate. Nicely done. Screwcap. 14.5% alc. **Rating** 92 **To** 2023 $22 CM ✪
Ragazzone 2013 Cane-cut petit verdot. It's almost candied in its fruit-and-oak sweetness, the flavours of musk, raspberry and red licorice given a juicy tweak by orange-choc notes on the finish. Alcohol doesn't rear; lively flavour holds sway. Cork. 15.1% alc. **Rating** 91 **To** 2021 $45 CM

Longline Wines   ★★★★☆
PO Box 28, Old Noarlunga, SA 5168 **Region** McLaren Vale/Adelaide Hills
T 0415 244 124 **www.**longlinewines.com.au **Open** Not
Winemaker Paul Carpenter **Est.** 2013 **Dozens** 900
The name reflects the changing nature of the Carpenter family's activities. Over 40 years ago Bob Carpenter gave up his job as a bank manager, becoming a longline fisherman at Goolwa; this was in turn replaced by a move to McLaren Vale for farming activities. Son Paul graduated from Adelaide University and began his professional life as a cereal researcher for the university, but a vintage job at Geoff Merrill Wines at the end of his university studies led to the decision to switch to winemaking. Over the next 20 years he worked both locally and internationally, in the Rhône Valley and Beaujolais, and at Archery Summit in Oregon. Back in Australia he worked for Hardys, and is currently a winemaker at Wirra Wirra. Together with partner Martine, he secures small parcels of outstanding grapes from four grower vineyards of grenache and shiraz (three vineyards in McLaren Vale, the fourth in the Adelaide Hills).

ŶŶŶŶŶ **Bimini Twist Grenache Rose 2015** Vivid crimson, with scents of red flowers followed by a red berry-filled palate, soft and slurpy, but with no hint of residual sugar. A rose for all seasons. Screwcap. 13% alc. **Rating** 90 **To** 2017 $20 ✪
Albright Grenache 2014 Light, bright hue; the fragrant red berry bouquet tells you all is well in the grenache world, the palate likewise. Screwcap. 14.5% alc. **Rating** 90 **To** 2020 $26

ŶŶŶŶ **Blood Knot Adelaide Hills Shiraz 2014** **Rating** 89 **To** 2021 $26

Lost Buoy Wines   ★★★★
PO Box 156, Aldinga Beach, SA 5173 **Region** McLaren Vale
T 0400 505 043 **www.**lostbuoywines.com.au **Open** Not
Winemaker Phil Christiansen **Est.** 2010 **Dozens** 1500 **Vyds** 18.5ha
Originally called Lion Point Wines, the name change forced by Lion Nathan. Seeking a new name for the 3.2ha of grenache and 2.8ha of shiraz planted at the turn of the century, and saved from property developers when the local Kelley family stepped in, the Lost Buoy name stems from the coastal location of the estate vineyard, perched high on the cliff top at Port Willunga's Lion Point. The wines are released at two price levels: the entry point Lost at Sea range (The Edge Shiraz and Gulf View Sauvignon Blanc) are made from grapes purchased from other growers, the Preserver range of Cliff Block Grenache and Lion Point Shiraz from the estate vineyard. Winemaker Phil Christiansen has long experience in the region. Exports to Canada and Singapore.

ŶŶŶŶŶ **Lion Point Shiraz 2014** Creamy vanillan oak coats a medium-weight serving of blackberry and blueberry fruit. Straightforward but smooth and inviting. Screwcap. 14.7% alc. **Rating** 92 **To** 2024 $30 CM
The Edge Shiraz 2014 Balanced, well fruited, kissed only lightly (but well) with oak and sound/satisfying through the finish. Admirable quality and value. Screwcap. 13.5% alc. **Rating** 91 **To** 2020 $18 CM ✪

Cliff Block Grenache 2014 Sweet and tangy with orange and spice notes liberally spread across raspberried fruit. Well balanced and made, if a little oddball in its flavour profile. Screwcap. 14.9% alc. **Rating** 91 **To** 2020 $30 CM

Lou Miranda Estate ★★★★

1876 Barossa Valley Way, Rowland Flat, SA 5352 **Region** Barossa Valley
T (08) 8524 4537 **www.**loumirandaestate.com.au **Open** Mon–Fri 10–4.30, w'ends 11–4
Winemaker Lou Miranda, Janelle Zerk **Est.** 2005 **Dozens** 20 000 **Vyds** 23.29ha
Lou Miranda's daughters Lisa and Victoria are the driving force behind the estate, albeit with continuing hands-on involvement from Lou. The jewels in the crown of the estate plantings are 0.5ha of mourvedre planted in 1897 and 1.5ha of shiraz planted in 1907. The remaining vines have been planted gradually since '95, the varietal choice widened by cabernet sauvignon, merlot, chardonnay and pinot grigio. Exports to the UK, the US, and other major markets.

🍷🍷🍷🍷🍷 **Leone Barossa Valley Pinot Grigio 2015** Astonishing (until you taste it) that a Barossa Valley pinot grigio should win gold medals at the Australian Small Winemakers and Adelaide Wine Shows '15, sheer serendipity, given the no-frills winemaking approach from start to finish. The reason is the sheer distillation of nashi pear fruit, with a faint textural layer, possibly ex brief pre-fermentation skin contact and some lees contact in tank; the balance and length are good, not driven by residual sugar. Screwcap. 12% alc. **Rating** 94 **To** 2017 $22 ✪

🍷🍷🍷🍷🍷 **Old Vine Barossa Valley Shiraz 2012** **Rating** 91 **To** 2032 $42

Lowe Wines ★★★★☆

Tinja Lane, Mudgee, NSW 2850 **Region** Mudgee
T (02) 6372 0800 **www.**lowewine.com.au **Open** 7 days 10–5
Winemaker David Lowe, Liam Heslop **Est.** 1987 **Dozens** 17 000 **Vyds** 41.3ha
Lowe Wines has undergone a number of changes in recent years, the most recent the acquisition of Louee and its two vineyards. The first is at Rylstone, led by shiraz, cabernet sauvignon, petit verdot and merlot, with chardonnay, cabernet franc, verdelho and viognier making up the balance. The second is on Nullo Mountain, bordered by the Wollemi National Park, at an altitude of 1100m, high by any standards, and often the coolest location in Australia. Lowe Wines continues with its organic profile. The Tinja property has been in the Lowe family ownership for five generations. Exports to the UK and Japan.

🍷🍷🍷🍷🍷 **Louee Museum Release Nullo Mountain Rylstone Late Picked Riesling 2010** Excellent, bright colour; a very interesting wine, with lime, honeycomb, beeswax. The intense finish and aftertaste reflect the acidity conferred by the very cool, high-altitude site. Screwcap. 12% alc. **Rating** 95 **To** 2020 $50
Nullo Mountain Sauvignon Blanc 2014 Wild-fermented and matured on lees in new French puncheons. Tropical fruits, coupled with delicate but persistent acidity, have absorbed the oak flavours into the fabric of what is still a very nice sauvignon blanc. Screwcap. 11.4% alc. **Rating** 94 **To** 2017 $30 ✪

🍷🍷🍷🍷🍷 **Nullo Mountain Riesling 2013** **Rating** 93 **To** 2023 $50

Lyons Will Estate ★★★★

60 Whalans Track, Lancefield, Vic 3435 **Region** Macedon Ranges
T 0405 006 771 **www.**lyonswillestate.com.au **Open** By appt
Winemaker Llew Knight (Contract) **Est.** 1996 **Dozens** 300 **Vyds** 4.2ha
Oliver Rapson (with a background in digital advertising) and Renata Morello (a physiotherapist with a PhD in public health) believe the Macedon Ranges has the best of both worlds: less than an hour's drive to Melbourne, ideal for pinot and chardonnay, and still sparsely settled. The property had 2ha of vines planted in '96 (pinot noir clones D5V12, D4v2 and 115 and chardonnay), and they have extended the pinot noir to 1.2 ha, increasing the 115 and introducing MV6, and planted 1ha each of riesling and gamay. A new winery was completed

for the 2016 vintage, and they also have visions of planting a further 0.8ha of chardonnay in '16. It's a fair assumption that if their winery eventuates as planned, the local knowledge of Llew Knight, and of course his vast winemaking experience, will prove to be very useful.

ΨΨΨΨΨ **Macedon Ranges Chardonnay 2014** From the 1ha estate vineyard with the traditional I10V1 and I10V5 clones, hand-picked at 1.7t/a, fermented in French barriques (38% new), matured for 15 months. An unambiguously good chardonnay, perfectly ripe, with ripe peach, honeydew melon and grapefruit all having their say on the long, well-balanced palate, oak merely a conveyance. ProCork. 13.5% alc. **Rating** 94 **To** 2022 $34

ΨΨΨΨ **Macedon Ranges Pinot Noir 2014** Rating 90 To 2018 $31

M. Chapoutier Australia ★★★★☆

141–143 High Street, Heathcote, Vic 3523 **Region** Pyrenees/Heathcote
T (03) 5433 2411 **www.**mchapoutieraustralia.com **Open** 7 days 10–5
Winemaker Michel Chapoutier **Est.** 1998 **Dozens** 10 000 **Vyds** 50ha
M. Chapoutier Australia is the eponymous offshoot of the famous Rhône Valley producer. The business focuses on vineyards in the Pyrenees, Heathcote and Beechworth, with collaboration from Ron Laughton of Jasper Hill and Rick Kinzbrunner of Giaconda. After first establishing a vineyard in Heathcote adjacent to Jasper Hill (see La Pleiade), Chapoutier purchased the Malakoff Vineyard in the Pyrenees to create Domaine Terlato & Chapoutier (the Terlato & Chapoutier joint venture was established in 2000; Terlato still owns 50% of the Malakoff Vineyard). In 2009 Michel Chapoutier purchased two neighbouring vineyards, Landsborough Valley and Shays Flat; all these are now fully owned by Domaine Tournon. (Domaine Tournon consists of Landsborough and Shays Flat Estates in the Pyrenees and Lady's Lane Estate in Heathcote.) Exports to all major markets.

ΨΨΨΨΨ **Domaine Terlato & Chapoutier Shiraz Viognier 2013** 95/5%. The colour attests to the co-fermentation, and indirectly to the contrasting juicy and fleshy display of red and black cherry fruits, pepper and spice. Zero expenditure on oak partly explains the price, and you can't have it both ways – but how good might it have been with oak. Screwcap. 14.5% alc. **Rating** 91 **To** 2025 $18 **✪**

ΨΨΨΨ **Domaine Terlato & Chapoutier Lieu-dit Malakoff Pyrenees Shiraz 2013** Rating 89 To 2028 $40

Mac Forbes ★★★★★

Graceburn Wine Room, 11a Green Street, Healesville, Vic 3777 **Region** Yarra Valley
T (03) 9818 8099 **www.**macforbes.com **Open** Thurs–Sat 11–7, Sun 11–5
Winemaker Mac Forbes, Austin Black **Est.** 2004 **Dozens** 4500
Mac Forbes cut his vinous teeth at Mount Mary, where he was winemaker for several years before heading overseas in 2002. He spent two years in London working for Southcorp in a marketing liaison role, then travelled to Portugal and Austria to gain further winemaking experience. He returned to the Yarra Valley prior to the '05 vintage, purchasing grapes for the two-tier portfolio: first, the Victorian range (employing unusual varieties or unusual winemaking techniques); and second, the Yarra Valley range of multiple terroir-based offerings of Chardonnay and Pinot Noir. Exports to the UK, the US, Spain, Sweden and Norway.

ΨΨΨΨΨ **Woori Yallock Pinot Noir 2014** From MV6 clones planted in '95, hand-picked, wild yeast-fermented, matured for 11 months in new and used French oak. The bouquet is expressive, but quickly forgotten once the exceptional drive and intensity of the very long palate take control of proceedings; black cherry and plum fruit have excellent texture thanks to fine-grained, pleasantly savoury, tannins. ArdeaSeal. 12.7% alc. **Rating** 96 **To** 2024 $70 **✪**
Hoddles Creek Chardonnay 2014 A scintillating wine. An example of precision engineering in some ways though there's a freedom to the fruit, a joie de vivre. Grapefruit, apple, pear and flint characters cavort through the palate before

curtains of chalk draw down on the close. Screwcap. 13% alc. **Rating** 95 **To** 2022 $50 CM

Coldstream Pinot Noir 2014 Stringy, perfumed, ashen and jam-packed with spice. It has savouriness leaching through its pores, and yet plump accessible fruit is at its core. Nervy acidity completes a captivating picture. ArdeaSeal. 12.4% alc. **Rating** 95 **To** 2025 $50 CM

Woori Yallock Chardonnay 2014 Mouthwatering style. A frisky chardonnay with the juice of apple and citrus dripping through pear and stone fruit. Incredibly pure. Almost riesling-esque. Cork. 12.6% alc. **Rating** 94 **To** 2023 $50 CM

Wesburn Pinot Noir 2014 Light, perfumed, finely woven pinot noir. It takes some getting accustomed to. It's reminiscent of nebbiolo in the gravelly pour of tannin through the back palate, the gamey/earthen hit at the front, the way it takes time and patience for the perfume and fruit to be properly revealed. Needs a sleep in a cool, dark place. Cork. 11.6% alc. **Rating** 94 **To** 2026 $70 CM

Yarra Junction Pinot Noir 2014 Light but compelling. Perfumed red berries meet violets, woody spice, pepper and undergrowth. It all rolls along, it doesn't coagulate; the flavours seem more water-based than alcohol-based, and have a lilting flow as a result. ArdeaSeal. 12% alc. **Rating** 94 **To** 2024 $50 CM

RS29 Riesling 2015 Pure but complex. This has 29g/l residual sugar, though it remains racy and fresh; indeed it's bursting with life. Citrus, gun smoke, orange peel, red apple. Acidity drives the sweetness and flavour seamlessly on. Screwcap. 10% alc. **Rating** 94 **To** 2024 $40 CM

🍷🍷🍷🍷🍷 **RS56 Riesling 2015 Rating** 93 **To** 2021 $40 CM
RS10 Riesling 2015 Rating 91 **To** 2021 $35 CM
Spring Riesling 2015 Rating 91 **To** 2019 $25 CM

Macedon Ridge Wines ★★★★

PO Box 35, Mount Macedon, Vic 3441 **Region** Macedon Ranges
T (03) 5427 0047 **Open** Not
Winemaker Scott Ireland, Andrew Koerner **Est.** 1985 **Dozens** 1500 **Vyds** 3ha
The Macedon Ridge vineyard was established in 1984 on the northern slopes of Mt Macedon. Right from the outset the aim was to produce sparkling wines, and with this in mind, 1.5ha each of chardonnay and 1ha of pinot noir were established. Owners Geoff and Leesa Mackay are responsible for the meticulous management of the vines.

🍷🍷🍷🍷🍷 **Morgen 2010** Methode Traditionelle, 100% estate-grown pinot noir, with 4 years on lees. Pale salmon-pink; a delicate style, with wild strawberry and spice flavours; the balance and length are excellent. Cork. 12% alc. **Rating** 93 **To** 2020 $50

McGlashan's Wallington Estate ★★★★★

225 Swan Bay Road, Wallington, Vic 3221 **Region** Geelong
T (03) 5250 5760 **www**.mcglashans.com.au **Open** Thurs–Sun 11–5, 7 days in Jan
Winemaker Robin Brockett (Contract) **Est.** 1996 **Dozens** 1500 **Vyds** 12ha
Russell and Jan McGlashan began the establishment of their vineyard in 1996. Chardonnay (6ha) and pinot noir (4ha) make up the bulk of the plantings, the remainder shiraz and pinot gris (1ha each); the wines are made by Robin Brockett, with his usual skill and attention to detail. The newly opened cellar door offers food and music, and will see an increase in direct sales.

🍷🍷🍷🍷🍷 **Bellarine Peninsula Chardonnay 2014** Part hand, part machine-picked, matured in French oak for 12 months. A lively, indeed piercing, stream of grapefruit and white peach sets the scene for what is to follow, oak well off centre stage. This is the vineyard speaking, pure and uninterrupted. Screwcap. 14% alc. **Rating** 95 **To** 2022 $30 ✪

Bellarine Peninsula Shiraz 2014 Hand-picked, some whole bunches, otherwise crushed and destemmed, matured in French oak for 12 months, American for 8. This has attitude oozing from every pore, with drive and focus to the palate, where spice, pepper, black cherry, blackberry and fine, but firm, tannins coalesce, the alcohol nowhere to be seen. Screwcap. 14.5% alc. **Rating** 95 **To** 2029 $35 **○**

♀♀♀♀♀ Bellarine Peninsula Pinot Noir 2013 Rating 92 To 2020 $30
Bellarine Peninsula Shiraz 2013 Rating 90 To 2023 $35

McGuigan Wines   ★★★★★

Cnr Broke Road/McDonalds Road, Pokolbin, NSW 2321 **Region** Hunter Valley
T (02) 4998 7400 **www.**mcguiganwines.com.au **Open** 7 days 9.30–5
Winemaker Peter Hall, James Evers **Est.** 1992 **Dozens** 1.5 million
McGuigan Wines is an Australian wine brand operating under parent company Australian Vintage Ltd. McGuigan represents four generations of Australian winemaking, and while its roots are firmly planted in the Hunter Valley, its vine holdings extend across SA, from the Barossa Valley to the Adelaide Hills and the Eden and Clare valleys, into Victoria and NSW. McGuigan Wines' processing facilities operate out of three core regions: the Hunter Valley, Sunraysia and the Barossa Valley. Exports to all major markets.

♀♀♀♀♀ The Shortlist Hunter Valley Semillon 2015 This has all the intensity, race and breed Bin 9000 used to have; lemongrass, lanolin, lemon zest and minerally acidity cascade over the very long palate, with zero sugar sorbet-like flavours, and a long future. Screwcap. 11% alc. **Rating** 96 **To** 2030 $29 **○**
Personal Reserve Bainton Vineyard Hunter Valley Shiraz 2014 This is a died in the wool classic from the '14 vintage. The grapes were picked at precisely the right time, resulting in great generosity, the mouthfeel velvety yet fresh, the plum, blackberry and spice fruit a long way away from the savoury/earthy notes that will develop with age. At every point along the journey there will be pleasure. Diam. 13.5% alc. **Rating** 96 **To** 2054 $50 **○**
The Shortlist Eden Valley Riesling 2015 This wine is raring to go, with lime leaves, lime juice and spice flying in all directions, which is no doubt why it won three trophies. It has a spine of acidity that will stand it in good stead over the next 5–10 years. Screwcap. 12% alc. **Rating** 95 **To** 2025 $29 **○**
The Philosophy Cabernet Shiraz 2012 It's not the monster you might expect. It throws tangy herbs through cranberry, blackberry and plum notes then builds through the back palate. It seduces slowly. Chocolatey oak is well integrated; it sits in the back row. Tannin is fine, almost filigreed. It's not the deepest of wines but it has a long future ahead. Diam. 14% alc. **Rating** 95 **To** 2032 $150 CM
Personal Reserve Hunter Valley Chardonnay 2015 In with a band of Hunter Valley winemakers doing exceptional things with chardonnay, taking it beyond pleasantly fruity and mouthfilling by introducing edges ex careful picking maturity (the capricious Hunter Valley weather permitting) and fermentation manipulation to introduce some reduction and struck match notes, and using oak as a method, not an end. Diam. 13% alc. **Rating** 94 **To** 2023 $35

♀♀♀♀♀ The Shortlist Adelaide Hills Chardonnay 2014 Rating 92 To 2019 $29
Cellar Select Barossa Valley Grenache 2014 Rating 91 To 2022 $29
The Shortlist Barossa Valley Shiraz 2013 Rating 90 To 2030 $29
The Shortlist Barossa Valley Montepulciano 2014 Rating 90 To 2021 $29

McHenry Hohnen Vintners   ★★★★★

5962 Caves Road, Margaret River, WA 6285 **Region** Margaret River
T (08) 9757 7600 **www.**mchenryhohnen.com.au **Open** 7 days 10.30–4.30
Winemaker Trent Carroll **Est.** 2004 **Dozens** 10 000 **Vyds** 56ha
McHenry Hohnen is owned by the McHenry and Hohnen families, sourcing grapes from four vineyards owned by various members of the families. Vines have been established on the McHenry, Calgardup Brook, Rocky Road and McLeod Creek properties. A significant part of the grape production is sold to others (including Cape Mentelle). The family members with direct executive responsibilities are leading Perth retailer Murray McHenry and Cape

Mentelle founder and former long-term winemaker David Hohnen. Exports to the UK, Ireland, Sweden, Indonesia, Japan, Singapore, Hong Kong and NZ.

🍷🍷🍷🍷🍷 **Rocky Road Margaret River Semillon Sauvignon Blanc 2015** 69% semillon, 31% sauvignon blanc, partial wild fermentation, 10% skin-contact fermentation, 20% fermented in barrel, 70% cool-fermented in stainless steel. A very complex wine, in terms of both the layered flavours and the texture. A giveaway price for what is a high quality wine – which has pushed the envelope hard, but stopped before tearing it. Screwcap. 12.8% alc. **Rating** 95 **To** 2020 $20 ✪

Calgardup Brook Vineyard Margaret River Chardonnay 2014 Hand-picked, whole bunch-pressed to French oak (20% new), wild-fermented, no mlf, aged on lees. Lemon meringue is a great call for the bouquet, some spice also in the action; elegant white peach flavours give way to bouncy grapefruit zest on the well-balanced and long finish. Screwcap. 13.5% alc. **Rating** 95 **To** 2025 $40

Burnside Vineyard Margaret River Chardonnay 2014 Hand-picked, whole bunch-pressed to French oak (20% new), wild-fermented, no mlf, aged on lees. The bouquet is complex and welcoming, then an early change of pace gives an energetic palate with nectarine and peach supported by citrus-tinged acidity. Screwcap. 13.5% alc. **Rating** 95 **To** 2025 $40

Amigos Marsanne Chardonnay Roussanne 2012 A 62/24/14% blend, whole bunch-pressed, wild-fermented, 50/50% stone fermenters and barrel, partial mlf, aged on lees. The glorious straw-green colour is worth the price alone; served blind you might pick it as riesling as much as chardonnay; it has length, drive and balance, and I'll bet it will grow more legs yet with another 5 years in bottle. Screwcap. 13.5% alc. **Rating** 95 **To** 2022 $27 ✪

Hazel's Vineyard Margaret River Cabernet Sauvignon 2013 15% whole bunches, matured for 14 months in French oak (20% new). A high quality cabernet with attitude and individuality; blackcurrant fruit is fused with black olive and dried herbs, the earthy tannins supple/silky in texture; the cedary oak infusion is the cat's whiskers. Screwcap. 14.5% alc. **Rating** 95 **To** 2038 $49

Hazel's Vineyard Margaret River Chardonnay 2014 Hand-picked, whole bunch-pressed to French oak (20% new), wild-fermented, no mlf, aged on lees. White peach and nougat on the bouquet and palate are followed by lightly spiced apple before minerally acidity cleanses the finish. Screwcap. 13.5% alc. **Rating** 94 **To** 2023 $40

Rolling Stone 2013 37% cabernet sauvignon, 25% each of malbec and merlot, 13% petit verdot, matured for 15 months in French oak (30% new). A complex, medium-bodied wine carefully groomed at every point along the way, with layers of flavours ex the fruit and oak. On the face of it, that oak shouldn't be excessive, but it certainly has a lot to say. Time will tell the tale. Screwcap. 14.7% alc. **Rating** 94 **To** 2033 $90

McKellar Ridge Wines   ★★★★

2 Euroka Avenue, Murrumbateman, NSW 2582 **Region** Canberra District **T** 0409 789 861 **www**.mckellarridgewines.com.au **Open** Sun 12–5 Sept–Jun **Winemaker** Dr Brian Johnston **Est.** 2000 **Dozens** 600 **Vyds** 5.5ha

Dr Brian Johnston has completed a postgraduate diploma in science at CSU, focusing on wine science and wine production techniques. The wines come from low-yielding mature vines (shiraz, cabernet sauvignon, chardonnay, merlot and viognier), and are said to be made using 'a combination of traditional and new winemaking techniques, the emphasis on fruit-driven styles'. I am yet to understand what this oft-used statement actually means – I strongly suspect it is empty of meaning.

🍷🍷🍷🍷🍷 **Canberra District Pinot Noir 2014** Mid-crimson; some fragrant red fruits with a quite nuanced and detailed bouquet. The palate is superfine and elegant with surprisingly fine, savoury tannins. Weighing in at 12.6% alcohol, it's a delicious glass of pinot. Screwcap. **Rating** 93 **To** 2020 $30

Trio Cabernet Sauvignon Merlot Cabernet Franc 2014 A particularly leafy and red fruit-dominant nose lead to a medium-bodied and finely poised palate, red fruits to close. Screwcap. 13.7% alc. **Rating** 92 **To** 2020 $30

ŸŸŸŸ **Canberra District Riesling 2015 Rating** 89 **To** 2022 $22
Canberra District Merlot Shiraz Rose 2015 Rating 89 **To** 2017 $20
Canberra District Shiraz Viognier 2014 Rating 89 **To** 2020 $32

McLaren Vale III Associates ★★★★☆

309 Foggo Road, McLaren Vale, SA 5171 **Region** McLaren Vale
T 1800 501 513 **www**.mclarenvaleiiiassociates.com.au **Open** Mon–Fri 9–5, w'ends 11–5
Winemaker Brian Light, Campbell Greer **Est.** 1999 **Dozens** 12000 **Vyds** 34ha
McLaren Vale III Associates is a very successful boutique winery. Mary Greer, Managing Director, Reg Wymond, Director, and Brian Light, Winemaker, have over 80 years' total experience in the wine industry. An impressive portfolio of estate-grown wines allows them control over quality and consistency, and thus success in Australian and international wine shows. Its signature wine is Giant Squid Ink Shiraz. Exports to the US, Canada, Indonesia, Hong Kong, Singapore, South Korea, Japan and China.

ŸŸŸŸŸ **Four Score Grenache 2014** The name reflects the 86yo vines; partial whole bunch inclusion, open-fermented, matured for 20 months in used American and French oak. McLaren Vale regularly comes up with greater intensity and length, better colour and fresher red fruit flavours than the Barossa Valley. This is a bargain in grenache terms. Screwcap. 14.5% alc. **Rating** 95 **To** 2029 $35 ○
Squid Ink Reserve Shiraz 2013 Matured for 18 months in new French-coopered American oak. The sheer volume of the oak to one side, this is a very good McLaren Vale shiraz, with all the black fruits, dark chocolate, licorice and ripe tannins one has come to expect. Screwcap. 14.5% alc. **Rating** 94 **To** 2033 $55

ŸŸŸŸŸ **Giant Squid Ink Reserve Shiraz 2012 Rating** 92 **To** 2032 $150
The Descendant of Squid Ink Shiraz 2014 Rating 90 **To** 2029 $35

McLeish Estate ★★★★☆

462 De Beyers Road, Pokolbin, NSW 2320 **Region** Hunter Valley
T (02) 4998 7754 **www**.mcleishhunterwines.com.au **Open** 7 days 10–5
Winemaker Andrew Thomas (Contract) **Est.** 1985 **Dozens** 8000 **Vyds** 17.3ha
Bob and Maryanne McLeish have established a particularly successful business, based on estate plantings. The wines are of consistently high quality, and more than a few have accumulated show records leading to gold medal-encrusted labels. The quality of the grapes is part of the equation, the other the skills of winemaker Andrew Thomas. 2015 marked McLeish Estate's 30th vintage. Over the years, there have been 30 trophies, 76 gold, 66 silver, and 80 bronze medals, the majority won in the Hunter Valley Wine Show and Sydney Wine Show. Exports to the UK, the US and Asia.

ŸŸŸŸŸ **Hunter Valley Semillon 2015** The flavour spectrum here borrows bits from sauvignon blanc and chardonnay to tack on to its mainframe of lemon, lemongrass and lime. A tough vintage, but challenges create opportunities; life-giving acidity has been left intact. Screwcap. 10.5% alc. **Rating** 95 **To** 2025 $25 ○

ŸŸŸŸŸ **Semillon Sauvignon Blanc 2015 Rating** 93 **To** 2018 $18 ○
Hunter Valley Shiraz 2014 Rating 93 **To** 2024 $25 ○
Reserve Hunter Valley Shiraz 2013 Rating 93 **To** 2026 $65 CM
Hunter Valley Cabernet Sauvignon Shiraz 2014 Rating 93 **To** 2034 $25 ○
Hunter Valley Semillon Chardonnay 2014 Rating 91 **To** 2019 $20 CM ○
Hunter Valley Verdelho 2015 Rating 91 **To** 2017 $18 ○
Jessica's Hunter Valley Botrytis Semillon 2013 Rating 91 **To** 2019 $25 CM

McPherson Wines

6 Expo Court, Mount Waverley, Vic 3149 **Region** Nagambie Lakes
T (03) 9263 0200 **www.**mcphersonwines.com.au **Open** Not
Winemaker Jo Nash **Est.** 1993 **Dozens** 450 000 **Vyds** 262ha
McPherson Wines is, by any standards, a substantial business. Its wines are largely produced for the export market, with enough sales in Australia to gain some measure of recognition here. Made at various locations from the estate vineyards and contract-grown grapes, they represent very good value. McPherson Wines is a joint venture between Andrew McPherson and Alister Purbrick (Tahbilk), both of whom have had a lifetime of experience in the industry. Quality is unfailingly good. Exports to all major markets.

🍷🍷🍷🍷🍷 **Don't tell Gary 2014** Grampians shiraz, open-fermented, wild yeast, hand-plunged, matured in French puncheons (80% new) for 12 months. Gary is the CFO of McPherson Wines, and would indeed be intrigued by the (low) price. This elegant, light to medium-bodied shiraz laughs in the face of its 14.5% alcohol; it has that perfumed purity that is the hallmark of Grampians shiraz, and has quite literally swallowed up the new oak. Gold medal Victorian Wines Show '16. Screwcap. 14.5% alc. **Rating** 95 **To** 2029 $24 ✪

🍷🍷🍷🍷🍷 **Chapter Three Strathbogie Ranges Shiraz 2014** **Rating** 93 **To** 2034 $25 ✪
Basilisk Central Victoria Shiraz Mourvedre 2014 **Rating** 91 **To** 2029 $18 ✪
MWC Pinot Gris 2015 **Rating** 90 **To** 2017 $19 ✪
MWC Shiraz Mourvedre 2014 **Rating** 90 **To** 2020 $19 ✪

McWilliam's

Jack McWilliam Road, Hanwood, NSW 2680 **Region** Riverina
T (02) 6963 3400 **www.**mcwilliams.com.au **Open** Wed–Sat 10–4
Winemaker Bryan Currie, Russell Cody **Est.** 1916 **Dozens** NFP **Vyds** 455.7ha
The best wines to emanate from the Hanwood winery are in whole or part from other regions, notably the Hilltops, Coonawarra, Yarra Valley, Tumbarumba, Margaret River and Eden Valley. As McWilliam's viticultural resources have expanded, it has been able to produce regional blends from across Australia of startlingly good value. The winery rating is strongly reliant on the exceptional value for money of the Hanwood Estate and Inheritance brands. The value of Mount Pleasant (Hunter Valley), Barwang (Hilltops) and Evans & Tate (Margaret River) will become ever more apparent as the ability of these brands to deliver world-class wines at appropriate prices is leveraged by group chief winemaker Jim Chatto. A founding member of Australia's First Families of Wine, 100 per cent owned by the McWilliam family. Exports to all major markets.

🍷🍷🍷🍷🍷 **1877 Hilltops Shiraz 2014** The icon wine of the large vineyard in Hilltops. Elegant and medium-bodied, its freshness and vibrant red and black fruits are couched in quality oak and finely detailed tannins. Its balance means it can be enjoyed young, mature or aged. Screwcap. 13.5% alc. **Rating** 96 **To** 2040 $80
Wildling Limited Release Signature Reserve Winemaker's Red Blend 2009 This shiraz and cabernet is (presumably) a regional blend and successfully hunted for trophies in the Riverina and Rutherglen Wine Shows, the Adelaide Show with more credibility. The wine is full-bodied, but not bulky, with a most appealing blend of blackcurrant, blackberry, ripe tannins as important as the French oak. Screwcap. 14.5% alc. **Rating** 96 **To** 2039 $50 ✪
842 Tumbarumba Chardonnay 2014 Pale straw-green; an aristocratic chardonnay, if there can be such a thing; complex, yet fruit-driven with bright acidity; enviable length and purity. Screwcap. 13% alc. **Rating** 95 **To** 2021 $70
Single Vineyard Tumbarumba Chardonnay 2013 A wine of youth and integrity; the flavours feel as if they have been carved from the fruit by a surgeon with a fine scalpel and no pressure. The oak is entirely sympathetic to the fruit, the acidity likewise. Screwcap. 13.5% alc. **Rating** 94 **To** 2025 $40
Single Vineyard Hilltops Shiraz 2014 The deep colour signals a wine with power and complexity; the bouquet is both spicy and savoury, black fruits dripping

from every bower of the tree, precision-shaped tannins and quality oak perfectly matched. Screwcap. 13.5% alc. **Rating** 94 **To** 2039 $40

Tightrope Walker Heathcote Shiraz 2012 From Colbinabbin in the north of the Heathcote region. It's in rude good health, brimful of blackberry and plum with sandalwood and clove notes as appropriate foils. Supple tannin keeps it all from getting unruly. Screwcap. 14% alc. **Rating** 94 **To** 2026 $39 CM

ŶŶŶŶŶ **Appellation Series Tumbarumba Pinot Noir 2014** Rating 93 To 2019 $24 ✪

Appellation Series Hilltops Shiraz 2014 Rating 93 To 2029 $25 ✪
Cool Climate Shiraz 2013 Rating 91 To 2020 $13 CM ✪
Hanwood Estate Chardonnay 2014 Rating 90 To 2018 $14 ✪
Tightrope Walker Yarra Valley Chardonnay 2014 Rating 90 To 2019 $25
Tightrope Walker Yarra Valley Pinot Noir 2015 Rating 90 To 2020 $25

Maglieri of McLaren Vale ★★★

GPO Box 753, Melbourne, Vic 3001 **Region** McLaren Vale
T 1300 651 650 **Open** Not
Winemaker Kate Hongell **Est.** 1972 **Dozens** 4000 **Vyds** 10ha
This was one of the better-kept secrets among the wine cognoscenti, but not among the many customers who drank thousands of cases of white and red Lambrusco every year; an example of niche marketing at its profitable best. It was a formula that proved irresistible to Beringer Blass, which acquired Maglieri in 1999. Unfortunately, it is no longer possible to make Lambrusco from grapes other than true lambrusco, and there are only a few hectares planted in Australia.

ŶŶŶŶ **Cabernet Sauvignon 2013** Red-fruited expression of cabernet. Bright and juicy with gravelly/bay leaf notes as trace elements to the finish. Strings of integrated tannin. Not a beefy, robust wine, but a good one, and none the worse for that. Screwcap. 14.5% alc. **Rating** 89 **To** 2021 $22 CM

Magpie Estate ★★★★

PO Box 126, Tanunda, SA 5352 **Region** Barossa Valley
T (08) 8562 3300 **www.**magpieestate.com **Open** Not
Winemaker Rolf Binder, Noel Young **Est.** 1993 **Dozens** 7000
This is a partnership between Rolf Binder and Cambridge (UK) wine merchant Noel Young. Conceived in the early 1990s when grenache and mourvedre were largely forgotten varieties, the two Rhône-philes have adopted that great larrikin of the Australian sky – the magpie – as their mascot for the brand. Fruit is sourced from around 15 growers, each batch kept separate, enabling many blend options; the winemaking approach is minimal intervention, with little new oak. Rolf and Noel say they have a lot of fun making the wines, but are also serious about quality and delivering value for money. Exports to the UK, Canada, Denmark, Poland, Finland, Hong Kong and Singapore.

ŶŶŶŶŶ **The Sack Barossa Valley Shiraz 2013** Bold and black but well controlled. This is impressive. Toasty oak nestles into blackberried fruit, earth and gun smoke notes adding extra layers of complexity. Screwcap. 14.5% alc. **Rating** 94 **To** 2026 $30 CM ✪

The Gomersal Barossa Valley Grenache 2013 Sweet and spicy but with plenty of dry, authoritative tannin and keen length. There is no question of this wine's quality. Screwcap. 14.5% alc. **Rating** 94 **To** 2024 $45 CM

ŶŶŶŶŶ **Rag & Bones Eden Valley Riesling 2015** Rating 92 To 2025 $22 CM ✪

Main Ridge Estate ★★★★★

80 William Road, Red Hill, Vic 3937 **Region** Mornington Peninsula
T (03) 5989 2686 **www**.mre.com.au **Open** Mon–Fri 12–4, w'ends 12–5
Winemaker James Sexton, Linda Hodges, Nat White (Consultant) **Est.** 1975
Dozens 1200 **Vyds** 2.8ha

Quietly spoken and charming Nat and Rosalie White founded the first commercial winery on the Mornington Peninsula, with an immaculately maintained vineyard and equally meticulously run winery. In December 2015, ownership of Main Ridge Estate passed to the Sexton family, following the retirement of Nat and Rosalie after 40 years. Tim and Libby Sexton have an extensive background in large-scale hospitality, first in the UK, then with Zinc at Federation Square Melbourne, and the MCG. Son James Sexton completed the Bachelor of Wine Science degree at CSU in 2015. Nat will continue as a consultant to Main Ridge.

♥♥♥♥♥ **Mornington Peninsula Chardonnay 2014** 12 hours skin contact, barrel-
fermented with wild yeast and mlf, matured for 11 months in new and 1yo
French barriques. Has the characteristic richness of Margaret River, mlf (and skin
contact) giving an extra layer of complexity without compromising length or
poise. Screwcap. 13.5% alc. **Rating** 95 **To** 2022 $65
The Acre Mornington Peninsula Pinot Noir 2014 Identical vinification to
Half Acre. A warmly spiced bouquet, with controlled yet pulsating complexity on
the palate as dark red and purple fruits circle around each other; the length and
aftertaste are most impressive. Screwcap. 13.5% alc. **Rating** 95 **To** 2023 $75
Half Acre Mornington Peninsula Pinot Noir 2014 Open-fermented, wild-
fermented, 18 days on skins, matured for 18 months in new and used French
barriques. Full crimson–purple, no obvious difference from The Acre; red and
black cherry fruit has insistence and focus that are restrained; but these are twins,
even if not identical. Screwcap. 13.5% alc. **Rating** 95 **To** 2024 $85

Majella ★★★★★

Lynn Road, Coonawarra, SA 5263 **Region** Coonawarra
T (08) 8736 3055 **www**.majellawines.com.au **Open** 7 days 10–4.30
Winemaker Bruce Gregory **Est.** 1969 **Dozens** 25 000 **Vyds** 55ha

Majella is one of the foremost grapegrowers in Coonawarra, with important vineyards, principally shiraz and cabernet sauvignon, plus a little riesling and merlot. The Malleea is one of Coonawarra's classics, The Musician one of Australia's most outstanding red wines selling for less than $20 (since '04 The Musician has won seven trophies and 72 medals). Exports to the UK, Canada and other major markets.

♥♥♥♥♥ **Cabernet Sauvignon 2013** Bright, deep crimson; there is nothing half-hearted
about this wine; rather it is a pure evocation of cool grown cabernet, its texture
and structure allowing cassis and mulberry fruit, and contrasting touches of black
olive, free play, tannin and oak in the backdrop. Seriously attractive. Screwcap.
14.5% alc. **Rating** 95 **To** 2033 $35 ✪
The Malleea 2012 55% cabernet sauvignon, 45% shiraz from the oldest blocks,
matured in new French hogsheads for 18 months. It is holding its youthful colour
without any change; a very good medium-bodied wine from a very good vintage,
supple and long in the mouth, with black fruits led by blackberry and blackcurrant
in synergistic union. Diam. 14.5% alc. **Rating** 95 **To** 2032 $80
Shiraz 2013 Good colour; a fresh and vibrant bouquet and palate both send the
same pure message of delicious red berry fruits, spice and a faint hint of licorice,
the savoury tannins providing both context and the necessary structure. Screwcap.
14.5% alc. **Rating** 94 **To** 2028 $30 ✪
Merlot 2014 A merlot worthy of the name, the colour good, the bouquet with
cassis uppermost, the medium-bodied palate seamlessly picking up the message,
and adding redcurrant framed by French oak. Supple tannins underline the quality
of the wine. Screwcap. 14% alc. **Rating** 94 **To** 2029 $30 ✪

🍷🍷🍷🍷🍷 The Musician Cabernet Shiraz 2014 Rating 91 To 2024 $18 ✪
Merlot 2013 Rating 90 To 2020 $30
Sparkling Shiraz 2009 Rating 90 To 2019 $30 TS

Malcolm Creek Vineyard   ★★★★

33 Bonython Road, Kersbrook, SA 5231 **Region** Adelaide Hills
T (08) 8389 3619 www.malcolmcreekwines.com.au **Open** By appt
Winemaker Peter Leske, Michael Sykes **Est.** 1982 **Dozens** 800 **Vyds** 2ha
Malcolm Creek was the retirement venture of Reg Tolley, who decided to upgrade his
retirement by selling the venture to Bitten and Karsten Pedersen in 2007. The wines are
invariably well made and develop gracefully; they are worth seeking out, and are usually
available with some extra bottle age at a very modest price. However, a series of natural
disasters have decimated Malcolm Creek's production in recent years: '11 cabernet sauvignon
not harvested due to continuous rain; '14 chardonnay not produced because of microscopic
yield following rain and wind at flowering; and the '15 vintage truncated by bushfire and
smoke taint. The rating has been retained. Exports to the UK, the US, Denmark, Malaysia
and China.

🍷🍷🍷🍷 **Adelaide Hills Sauvignon Blanc 2015** A mix of hand and machine harvesting,
crushed/destemmed, airbag-pressed, cultured yeast, and a slow, cool fermentation.
The bouquet has more tropical fruits than the Adelaide Hills usually provides,
and the palate follows on in precisely the same path. Will greatly appeal to some.
Screwcap. 13% alc. **Rating** 89 **To** 2016 $20

Mandala   ★★★★★

1568 Melba Highway, Dixons Creek, Vic 3775 **Region** Yarra Valley
T (03) 5965 2016 www.mandalawines.com.au **Open** Mon–Fri 10–4, w'ends 10–5
Winemaker Scott McCarthy, Andrew Santarossa, Charles Smedley **Est.** 2007
Dozens 8000 **Vyds** 29ha
Mandala is owned by Charles Smedley, who acquired the established vineyard in 2007. The
vineyard has vines up to 20 years old, but the spectacular restaurant and cellar door complex
is a more recent addition. The vineyards are primarily at the home base, Dixons Creek, with
chardonnay (8ha), cabernet sauvignon (6ha), sauvignon blanc and pinot noir (4ha each), shiraz
(2ha) and merlot (1ha). There is a separate 4ha vineyard planted entirely to pinot noir with an
impressive clonal mix at Yarra Junction. Exports to China.

🍷🍷🍷🍷🍷 **The Compass Yarra Valley Chardonnay 2013** Completely different style
from Mandala's standard chardonnay. This is lean and long, with honeysuckle,
condensed milk and general lactose characters adding spunk to cool, citrussy, white
peach-like fruit. It's refreshing, chalky and slippery smooth at once. Screwcap.
12.5% alc. **Rating** 94 **To** 2022 $50 CM

🍷🍷🍷🍷🍷 The Prophet Yarra Valley Pinot Noir 2014 Rating 92 To 2020 $50 CM
Yarra Valley Cabernet Sauvignon 2014 Rating 92 To 2025 $30 CM
Yarra Valley Chardonnay 2014 Rating 91 To 2018 $30 CM
Yarra Valley Shiraz 2014 Rating 90 To 2023 $30 CM
Butterfly Cabernet Sauvignon 2013 Rating 90 To 2027 $50 CM
Yarra Valley Blanc de Blancs 2012 Rating 90 To 2016 $35 CM

Mandalay Estate   ★★★★

Mandalay Road, Glen Mervyn via Donnybrook, WA 6239 **Region** Geographe
T (08) 9732 2006 www.mandalayroad.com.au **Open** 7 days 11–5
Winemaker Peter Stanlake, John Griffiths **Est.** 1997 **Dozens** 600 **Vyds** 4.2ha
Tony and Bernice O'Connell left careers in science and education to establish plantings of
shiraz, chardonnay, zinfandel, cabernet sauvignon on their property in 1997 (followed by
durif). A hands-on approach with low yields has brought out the best characteristics of the
grape varieties and the region. Exports to Taiwan.

🍷🍷🍷🍷🍷 **Mandalay Road Sauvignon Blanc Semillon 2015** A 52/48% blend, gold medal Blackwood Valley Wine Show and Boutique Winemakers Show '15. Has considerable drive and focus, semillon contributing the framework for the gently tropical fruit of the bouquet and palate; the overall balance and length is very good, the wine a bargain. Screwcap. 13.1% alc. **Rating** 92 **To** 2018 $20 ✪
Mandalay Road Stump Block Geographe Shiraz 2015 Machine-harvested, open-fermented with wild yeast to start, cultured yeast added after 9 days on skins, matured in French oak (40% new). The oak is obvious on the bouquet, and carries through the palate where spicy blackberry fruit takes over the running, finishing strongly, the tannins neatly folded in the back pocket of the fruit. Screwcap. 14.4% alc. **Rating** 92 **To** 2027 $30
Mandalay Road Geographe Durif 2014 Dark red; dark fruits, plum and blackberry dominate the concentrated profile. The palate delivers all the richness one could expect from the aromas. Powerful and textured, it retains its balance. Screwcap. 13.6% alc. **Rating** 91 **To** 2025 $30

🍷🍷🍷🍷 **Mandalay Road Geographe Chardonnay 2015 Rating** 89 **To** 2027 $25 ✪

Mandoon Estate

★★★★★

10 Harris Road, Caversham, WA 6055 **Region** Swan District
T (08) 6279 0500 **www.**mandoonestate.com.au **Open** Mon–Thurs 10–5, Fri 10–late, Sat 7.30–late, Sun 7.30–5
Winemaker Ryan Sudano **Est.** 2009 **Dozens** 10 000 **Vyds** 10ha
Mandoon Estate, headed by Allan Erceg, has made a considerable impression with its wines in a very short time. In 2008 the family purchased a 13.2ha site in Caversham in the Swan Valley, on a property that had been in the hands of the Roe family since its initial settlement in the 1840s. Construction of the winery was completed in time for the first vintage, in '10. Winemaker Ryan Sudano has metaphorically laid waste to Australian Wine shows with the quality of the wines he has made. In '15 Mandoon collected 14 trophies and 31 gold medals; included in the trophies were Most Successful Exhibitor (under 300t) at the Perth Royal Show, for the third consecutive year, the Most Successful Exhibitor (under 250t) at the Qantas Wine Show of WA, for the fourth consecutive time, and Most Successful Exhibitor at the WA Boutique Wine Show, following last year's trophy.

🍷🍷🍷🍷🍷 **Reserve Research Station Margaret River Cabernet Sauvignon 2012** The grapes come from a small 38yo planting of cabernet sauvignon by the State Government as part of the Research Station's experiments to ascertain the varieties best suited to the region. The Bramley Vineyard (as it was known) has been restored by Mandoon, and the old vines have given us this beautifully structured and utterly pure evocation of cabernet sauvignon, blackcurrant fruit to the fore, tannins and oak lined up in magisterial support. Has cruised effortlessly over the past year, barely changed. Screwcap. 14.5% alc. **Rating** 97 **To** 2042 $79 ✪

🍷🍷🍷🍷🍷 **Margaret River Cabernet Merlot 2014** A highly fragrant and intensely flavoured, yet elegant, blend, the tannins unusually silky and fine. Cassis, redcurrant and cedar are the go-to flavours in a wine that may seem ready now (and in a way it is), but will still be ready and waiting 30 years down the track. Screwcap. 14% alc. **Rating** 96 **To** 2044 $30 ✪
Margaret River Sauvignon Blanc 2015 Early picking has picked the wine up by the scruff of its neck, creating intensity and drive in a framework of lively, mouthwatering acidity; the oak can be sensed more than tasted, but is a definite contributor. Serious value. Screwcap. 12.5% alc. **Rating** 95 **To** 2017 $23 ✪
Swan Valley Verdelho 2015 One of the blocks that provided the grapes was planted 120 years ago, highly likely to be the oldest in the world. It is intense and pure, its multi-fruit base wreathed in crunchy acidity, the finish long and dry. Screwcap. 13% alc. **Rating** 94 **To** 2019 $23 ✪

🍷🍷🍷🍷🍷 **Old Vine Shiraz 2014 Rating** 93 **To** 2029 $30
Old Vine Grenache 2014 Rating 90 **To** 2019 $26
Surveyors Red 2014 Rating 90 **To** 2029 $23

Mansfield Wines

201 Eurunderee Lane, Mudgee, NSW 2850 **Region** Mudgee
T (02) 6373 3871 **www**.mansfieldwines.com.au **Open** Thurs–Tues & public hols 10–5
Winemaker Bob Heslop, Ian McLellan **Est.** 1975 **Dozens** 1500 **Vyds** 5.5ha
Ian McLellan and family purchased Mansfield Wines from his cousin Peter Mansfield in
late 1997. The original plantings, which included chardonnay, frontignac, sauvignon blanc,
cabernet sauvignon, merlot and shiraz, were removed, to be replaced by a Joseph's coat
patchwork of savagnin, vermentino, petit manseng, parellada, tempranillo, touriga, zinfandel
and tinta cao, supported by grenache, mourvedre and pedro ximinez. Souzao and carignan
are more recent arrivals.

🍷🍷🍷🍷🍷 **Late Harvest Petit Manseng 2013** It's a wild ride, starting with its burnished
gold hue, then spicy crystallised orange peel fruit, finishing with a burst of fresh
ginger cleansing the finish. For sweet wine nerds. 375ml. Screwcap. 13% alc.
Rating 92 **To** 2018 $20 ⊙
Touriga Nacional 2014 Open-fermented, hand-plunged, basket-pressed,
matured in American oak (30% new) for 22 months. No issues here, the planets
of fruit, oak and tannins all aligned; poached plum and star anise flavours lead the
supple, medium-bodied palate. Diam. 13% alc. **Rating** 90 **To** 2020 $23

Marchand & Burch

241 Scotsdale Road, Denmark, WA 6333 **Region** Great Southern
T (08) 9848 2345 **www**.burchfamilywines.com.au **Open** 7 days 10–4
Winemaker Janice McDonald, Pascal Marchand **Est.** 2006 **Dozens** 1100 **Vyds** 8.46ha
A joint venture between Canadian-born and Burgundian-trained Pascal Marchand and
Burch Family Wines. Grapes are sourced from single vineyards, and in most cases, from single
blocks within those vineyards (4.51ha of chardonnay and 3.95ha of pinot noir, in each case
variously situated in Mount Barker and Porongurup). Biodynamic practices underpin the
viticulture in the Australian and French vineyards, and Burgundian viticultural techniques
have been adopted in the Australian vineyards (eg narrow rows and high-density plantings,
Guyot pruning, vertical shoot positioning, and leaf and lateral shoot removal). Exports to the
UK, the US and other major markets.

🍷🍷🍷🍷🍷 **Porongurup Chardonnay 2015** A magical combination of finesse and
elegance; grapefruit zest and white peach fruit have made short work of the new
oak component. A stylish, high quality wine with tremendous length. Screwcap.
13% alc. **Rating** 96 **To** 2025 $73 ⊙
Porongurup Chardonnay 2014 Whole bunch-pressed to French oak
(40% new) for 10 months' maturation, stirred weekly, partial mlf. This might have
resulted in a broad palate, but instead it is beautifully fresh and linear, leaving the
mouth as fresh as a daisy, the mix of white stone fruit and grapefruit perfectly
gauged, oak playing a pure support role. Screwcap. 13% alc. **Rating** 96 **To** 2025
$73 ⊙
Mount Barrow Pinot Noir 2014 Two individual blocks from a single estate
vineyard with high-density planting of Dijon clones, 10 months in French
barriques (45% new). A most impressive wine, in terms of structure, texture and
flavour; it borders on full-bodied, the poached red and black fruits taking no
prisoners. Demands patience. Screwcap. 13.5% alc. **Rating** 95 **To** 2024 $50

🍷🍷🍷🍷🍷 **Mount Barrow Mount Barker Pinot Noir 2015** **Rating** 91 **To** 2025 $60

Margan Family

1238 Milbrodale Road, Broke, NSW 2330 **Region** Hunter Valley
T (02) 6579 1317 **www**.margan.com.au **Open** 7 days 10–5
Winemaker Andrew Margan **Est.** 1997 **Dozens** 30 000 **Vyds** 98ha
Andrew Margan, following in his late father's footsteps, entered the wine industry over
20 years ago, working as a Flying Winemaker in Europe, then for Tyrrell's. The growth of the

Margan Family business over the next 20 years is the result of unremitting hard work and a keen understanding of the opportunities Australia's most visited wine region provides. They have won innumerable awards in the tourism sector, against competition in the Hunter Valley, across NSW, and Australia-wide. The next generation will be able to cover all bases when their parents retire. Eldest son Ollie is finishing a double degree in winemaking and viticultural science at the University of Adelaide; daughter Alessa is studying communications at UTS while working in wine and food PR, and younger son James is enrolled in economics at Sydney University. Andrew has continued to push the envelope in the range of wines being made, without losing focus on the varieties that have made the Hunter famous. He began the development with barbera in 1998, and since then has progressively planted mourvedre, albarino, tempranillo and graciano. Exports to the UK, Germany, Norway, Indonesia, Malaysia, Vietnam, Hong Kong and China.

♀♀♀♀♀ **Hunter Valley Semillon 2015** Has everything you could ask for in a young Hunter Valley semillon: bright straw-green hue, a lemongrass and citrus bouquet, then a long, intense palate built on the foundation of natural acidity. There is ample flavour now, but the whole life of the wine lies before it, as the citrus becomes honeyed, and finally some toasty nuances will appear. Screwcap. 12.5% alc. **Rating** 95 **To** 2030 $15 ✪

Limited Release Semillon 2015 Intense lemongrass and citrus flavours give this body, complexity and drive. It has an exciting future ahead. Screwcap. 12.5% alc. **Rating** 95 **To** 2028 $30 CM ✪

Aged Release Semillon 2011 Highly textural. The mouthfeel has a chubbiness to it, an apt foil for the cut of lemon and lemongrass flavour running the length of the palate. There are some developed flavours, but it still feels tight; it's a year or so from really entering the groove. Screwcap. 11.5% alc. **Rating** 94 **To** 2026 $50 CM

Hunter Valley Shiraz 2014 From 40yo vines on the estate's red volcanic soil. There is an overarching freshness to the varietal expression on the bouquet and palate, doubtless stemming from the controlled alcohol in a vintage where the perfect weather might have led to a decision to delay harvest. It is only medium-bodied, but its balance of both flavour and structure guarantees a very long life for its gently earthy dark fruits. Screwcap. 13.5% alc. **Rating** 94 **To** 2034 $20 ✪

Aged Release Shiraz 2011 From 40+yo vines of the Timbervines Vineyard. The oak is giving the fruit a run for its money, and will likely do so over the coming years, but without coming to blows. Remember the high quality of Hunter Valley shiraz from this vintage. Screwcap. 13.5% alc. **Rating** 94 **To** 2031 $100

Shiraz Mourvedre 2014 Depth of fruit, complexity of flavour, fineness (and firmness) of tannin. This is an excellent red, its berried flavours given breadth by ample notes of leather, saltbush and spice. Oak is present but a bit player at most. A fine future awaits. Screwcap. 14.5% alc. **Rating** 94 **To** 2028 $40 CM

♀♀♀♀♀ **Limited Release Chardonnay 2015 Rating** 93 **To** 2020 $40 CM
Hunter Valley Cabernet Sauvignon 2014 Rating 92 **To** 2024 $25 ✪
Tempranillo Graciano Shiraz 2014 Rating 91 **To** 2020 $40 CM
Hunter Valley Chardonnay 2015 Rating 90 **To** 2019 $15 ✪

Margaret Hill Vineyard   ★★★★★

18 Northcote Avenue, Balwyn, Vic 3103 (postal) **Region** Heathcote
T (03) 9836 2168 **www.**guangtiangroup.com.au **Open** Not
Winemaker Ben Portet **Est.** 1996 **Dozens** 1100 **Vyds** 12.5ha
Formerly known as Toolleen Vineyard, the name Margaret Hill Vineyard was chosen by owner Linchun Bao (and wife Chunye Qiu) after they acquired the business from the Huang family in 2010. They have upgraded the vineyard equipment and irrigation system, and are restoring full health and vigour to the vineyard, which is equally split between cabernet sauvignon and shiraz. Wines are released under the Margaret Hill and Kudo labels. The quality of the vineyard, and the skill of contract winemaker Ben Portet, have together been responsible for the high quality of the wines. Exports to China.

🍷🍷🍷🍷🍷 **Kudo Heathcote Shiraz 2014** 100% Bests Old (1866) Clone, hand-picked, berry-sorted by Oscilly machine, matured for 14 months in French oak (20% new). Deep crimson-purple; a truly beautiful Heathcote shiraz with exceptional black cherry/berry varietal fruit, utterly compelling mouthfeel/texture (including superb, fine-ground tannins) and great length. A privilege to taste it. Cork. 13.5% alc. **Rating** 98 **To** 2039

🍷🍷🍷🍷🍷 **Kudo Heathcote Cabernet Sauvignon 2014** The timing of the decision to pick totally correct, and has a lot to do with the quality of the wine (along with Ben Portet's skill). Bright crimson-purple; this has exceptionally juicy and fine cassis fruit steaming alongside fine tannins and integrated oak. Elegance and intensity walk hand in hand. Cork. 13.5% alc. **Rating** 96 **To** 2039

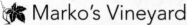

Marko's Vineyard ★★★☆

PO Box 7518, Brisbane, Qld 4169 **Region** Adelaide Hills
T 0418 783 456 **www**.markosvineyard.com.au **Open** Not
Winemaker Darryl Catlin **Est.** 2014 **Dozens** 4200 **Vyds** 27ha
This is the reincarnation of the former Shaw + Smith M3 Vineyard, established in 1994 by Mark, Margie, Matthew and Michael Hill Smith, collectively owners of 70%, and Shaw + Smith, 30%. The split ownership wasn't generally understood, and in September 2014 Matthew Hill Smith and daughter Christobel purchased the shares hitherto owned by Margie Hill Smith, Michael Hill Smith and Shaw + Smith. In a parallel sale, Matthew Hill Smith sold his shares in Shaw + Smith and Tolpuddle Wines. The M3 Vineyard is a registered trademark of Shaw + Smith, hence the renaming. What does not change is the planting of 27ha of sauvignon blanc, chardonnay and shiraz. 2016 will see the release of '15 Shiraz and, in due course, a premium barrel-fermented chardonnay.

🍷🍷🍷🍷🍷 **Adelaide Hills Sauvignon Blanc 2015** A pleasant, competently made sauvignon with a gentle mix of kiwi fruit and some citrus notes. Ready now, but the acidity will steer it safely through to the end of '16. Screwcap. 13% alc. **Rating** 90 **To** 2016 $27

🍷🍷🍷🍷 **Adelaide Hills Oakless Chardonnay 2015 Rating** 89 **To** 2018 $27

Marq Wines ★★★★★

PO Box 1415, Dunsborough, WA 6281 **Region** Margaret River
T 0411 122 662 **www**.marqwines.com.au **Open** Not
Winemaker Mark Warren **Est.** 2011 **Dozens** 2000
Mark Warren has a degree in wine science from CSU and a science degree from the University of WA; to complete the circle, he is currently lecturing in wine science and wine sensory processes at Curtin University, Margaret River. He also has 26 years' experience in both the Swan Valley and Margaret River, and his current major commercial role is producing the extensive Happs range as well as wines under contract for several other Margaret River brands. When all of this is added up, he is responsible for 60 to 70 individual wines each year, now including wines under his own Marq Wines label. A quick look at the list of Vermentino, Fiano, Wild & Worked Sauvignon Blanc Semillon, Wild Ferment Chardonnay, Rose, Gamay, Tempranillo, Malbec, and Cut & Dry Shiraz (Amarone style) points to the underlying philosophy: an exploration of the potential of alternative varieties and unusual winemaking methods by someone with an undoubted technical understanding of the processes involved.

🍷🍷🍷🍷🍷 **Wild and Worked Margaret River Sauvignon Blanc Semillon 2015** 56% sauvignon blanc, 37% semillon, 7% muscadelle; crushed, destemmed, the sauvignon blanc spent 4 days on skins and was wild-fermented and matured for 8 months in used French oak. As rich and complex as its vinification suggests, with layers of tropical fruits tempered by the lemony fruit and acidity of the semillon. Screwcap. 12.7% alc. **Rating** 95 **To** 2018 $25 ✪
Margaret River Vermentino 2015 Quartz-white; has great intensity and drive, taking it past the fiano without a second glance. Its core of wiry acidity, with

nuances of unsweetened green lemon, could be intensified by serving it ice cold as a pick-me-up the morning after. Screwcap. 11.2% alc. **Rating** 95 **To** 2030 $25 ○

Wild Ferment Margaret River Chardonnay 2014 It's not in-your-face with its funkiness but there's just enough complexity to keep things interesting; you don't get bored, but it's not hard work either. The fruit is powerful, the texture pleasing, the length satisfying. Screwcap. 13% alc. **Rating** 94 **To** 2021 $30 CM ○

Margaret River Fiano 2015 Has the energy and bustle of good fiano, with fruit zest and pith combined with crunchy acidity. While light-bodied, it has the ability to cover a wide range of dishes. Screwcap. 12.9% alc. **Rating** 94 **To** 2029 $25 ○

Serious Margaret River Rose 2015 Its length is what really sets it apart. It's flavoursome and dry and even a little textural, in a tangy-but-satiny way, but the carry on of flavour as you swallow is what makes you sit up and take notice. Screwcap. 12.7% alc. **Rating** 94 **To** 2017 $25 CM ○

Margaret River Malbec 2014 Hearty but well balanced. A thick slice of flashy/creamy oak rests on a bed of plum-shot fruit. Spice notes stroll throughout. Assertive tannin cracks through the latter third of the wine. Substantial from every angle. Screwcap. 14.8% alc. **Rating** 94 **To** 2026 $30 CM ○

♟♟♟♟♟ **Margaret River Gamay 2014** Rating 93 **To** 2020 $25 CM ○

Massena Vineyards   ★★★★★

PO Box 643, Angaston, SA 5353 **Region** Barossa Valley
T (08) 8564 3037 **www**.massena.com.au **Open** At Artisans of Barossa
Winemaker Jaysen Collins **Est.** 2000 **Dozens** 3000 **Vyds** 4ha
Massena Vineyards draws upon 1ha each of mataro, saperavi, petite syrah and tannat at Nuriootpa, also purchasing grapes from other growers. It is an export-oriented business, although the wines can also be purchased by mail order, which, given both the quality and innovative nature of the wines, seems more than ordinarily worthwhile. Exports to the US, Switzerland, Denmark, South Korea, Hong Kong and China.

♟♟♟♟♟ **The Moonlight Run 2014** 58% mataro, 22% grenache, 20% shiraz. It is intense and powerful, yet supple, its fragrant bouquet replicated by the rippling cascade of spices, cherry, raspberry and delicately balanced tannins that help extend the long palate. An object lesson in containing the alcohol. Screwcap. 14% alc. **Rating** 96 **To** 2024 $32 ○

The Howling Dog 2014 A deeply coloured, ultra-exotic blend (72% saperavi, 16% petite sirah (durif), 12% tannat) that has all the qualities its varietal parentage promises; it is infinitely powerful and compact, a vinous black hole in space, yet retains sufficient balance to guide it through decades of change. Screwcap. 14.5% alc. **Rating** 95 **To** 2044 $36

The Eleventh Hour 2014 Has the best of both worlds: the lush black fruits of Barossa shiraz plus freshness and poise. Makes its point quietly, not with a sledge hammer. Screwcap. 14% alc. **Rating** 94 **To** 2029 $40

♟♟♟♟♟ **The Surly Muse 2015** Rating 92 **To** 2019 $23 CM ○
The Twilight Path 2014 Rating 91 **To** 2020 $28

Massoni   ★★★★☆

30 Brasser Avenue, Dromana, Vic 3936 **Region** Pyrenees/Mornington Peninsula
T (03) 5981 0711 **www**.massoniwines.com **Open** By appt 10–4.30
Winemaker Fred Ursini, Robert Paul **Est.** 1984 **Dozens** 25 000 **Vyds** 277.5ha
Massoni is a substantial business owned by the Pellegrino and Ursini families, and is a venture with two completely distinct arms. In terms of vineyard and land size, by far the larger is the GlenKara vineyard in the Pyrenees (269ha). It also has 8.5ha on the Mornington Peninsula where Massoni started, and where it gained its reputation. In 2012 Massoni purchased the former Tucks Ridge/Red Hill winemaking facility at Dromana. Exports to China.

♀♀♀♀♀ **Pyrenees Ranges Shiraz 2012** From the Glenkara estate vineyard, matured in French and American hogsheads for 14 months. It is awesomely full-bodied with black fruits, bitter chocolate and ripe tannins playing tag with each other, and not becoming tired. Where does the $25 price tag come from? Screwcap. 14.5% alc. Rating 95 To 2042 $25 ✪

♀♀♀♀ **Mornington Peninsula Pinot Noir 2013** Rating 89 To 2023 $30

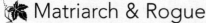

Matriarch & Rogue

PO Box 6752, Clare, SA 5453 **Region** Clare Valley
T 0419 901 892 **www**.matriarchandrogue.com.au **Open** Not
Winemaker Marnie Roberts **Est.** 2014 **Dozens** 800
The catchy name is based on five sisters who are the third generation of the Byrne family, with a history going back to the family's home in Ireland. The sisters are known as the Patrick Byrne girls, and the wines are a tribute to the strong women of the family, and the rogues they married. Winemaker/proprietor Marnie Roberts (also Claymore winemaker) is, one assumes, one of the strong women.

♀♀♀♀♀ **Alice Clare Valley Shiraz 2014** Full colour; a supple medium to full-bodied shiraz with vanillan oak and chocolate sharing the stage with plum and blackberry fruit, the tannins standing to one side as the fruit flavours argue about equal rights. Screwcap. 14% alc. Rating 91 To 2029 $25

♀♀♀♀ **Mary Clare Valley Tempranillo 2014** Rating 89 To 2019 $25

Maverick Wines ★★★★★

981 Light Pass Road, Vine Vale, Moorooroo, SA 5352 **Region** Barossa Valley
T (08) 8563 3551 **www**.maverickwines.com.au **Open** Mon–Tues 1.30–4.30 or by appt
Winemaker Ronald Brown **Est.** 2004 **Dozens** 12 000 **Vyds** 61.7ha
This is the business established by the then already highly experienced vigneron Ronald Brown. It has evolved with the transition of the seven vineyards it now owns across the Barossa and Eden Valleys into biodynamic grape production. The vines range from 40 to over 140 years old, underpinning the consistency of the quality wines produced under the Maverick label. Exports to the UK, the US and other major markets.

♀♀♀♀♀ **Museum Release Trial Hill Eden Valley Riesling 2008** Deep, glowing green-gold. Who said screwcaps wouldn't allow a wine to develop? This has, and is now nearing the end of its upwards path. Compelling at its price, with lime, toast, honey and acidity all as one. Screwcap. 12.5% alc. Rating 95 To 2018 $25 ✪
Greenock Rise Barossa Valley Shiraz 2013 A big serve of blackberried flavour and a firm framework of tannin. The alcohol reading is (very) high but you wouldn't know it; there's nothing fierce or hot about it, but it does pour on the flavour as if there's no tomorrow. Cork. 15.5% alc. Rating 95 To 2030 $70 CM
Silk Road Old Ben Vineyard Eden Valley Riesling 2014 A generous, well-balanced wine utterly typical of the Eden Valley; Meyer lemon is the fruit base, but will be joined by honey (and possibly toast) over the next few years, making it even more appealing than it is now. Screwcap. 11% alc. Rating 94 To 2024 $35
Twins Barossa Grenache Shiraz Mourvedre 2014 Well balanced and impressively well powered. It doesn't put a foot wrong but, more than that, it intrigues. The blend of red/black-berried fruit and earth, spice and wild herb notes is delicious and delightful. Screwcap. 14.5% alc. Rating 94 To 2024 $27 CM ✪
Twins Barossa Grenache Shiraz Mourvedre 2013 Immaculately presented. Red and black-berried fruit, anise, spice, all of it delivered juicily and well. The finish is firm but not too much so; fruit carries the day. Impossible not to admire it. Screwcap. 14.9% alc. Rating 94 To 2023 $27 CM ✪

♀♀♀♀♀ **Trial Hill Eden Valley Riesling 2015** Rating 93 To 2024 $30 CM
Twins Barossa Shiraz 2013 Rating 93 To 2023 $27 CM ✪

Barossa Valley Cabernet Sauvignon Merlot Petit Verdot Cabernet Franc
2013 Rating 93 To 2024 $27 CM ✪
Trial Hill Eden Valley Riesling 2014 Rating 91 To 2021 $30 CM
Maverick Billich The Red Barossa Shiraz Grenache Mourvedre 2013
Rating 90 To 2021 $50 CM

Maxwell Wines   ★★★★★

Olivers Road, McLaren Vale, SA 5171 **Region** McLaren Vale
T (08) 8323 8200 **www**.maxwellwines.com.au **Open** 7 days 10–5
Winemaker Andrew Jericho, Mark Maxwell **Est.** 1979 **Dozens** 24 000 **Vyds** 40ha
Maxwell Wines has carved out a reputation as a premium producer in McLaren Vale. The
brand has produced some excellent red wines in recent years. The majority of the vines on the
estate were planted in 1972, and include 19 rows of the highly regarded Reynella Selection
cabernet sauvignon. The Ellen Street shiraz block in front of the winery was planted in '53.
During vintage, visitors to the elevated cellar door can watch the gravity-flow operations in
the winery. Owned and operated by Mark Maxwell. Exports to all major markets.

ŶŶŶŶŶ **Eocene Ancient Earth McLaren Vale Shiraz 2013** Vines planted in '74 on
34–56 million-year-old grey-brown loam over limestone; matured for 20 months
in French hogsheads (20% new). Unalloyed full-bodied shiraz, laden with black
fruits, licorice and ripe, savoury tannins. Despite its size and weight, it has agility,
and leaves the mouth content. Screwcap. 14.8% alc. **Rating** 95 **To** 2048 $55
Ellen Street McLaren Vale Shiraz 2013 Deep colour; the bouquet has
attractive sooty blackberry aromas that swell on the classy palate as satsuma plum,
blackberry, bitter (70%) chocolate and finely pitched tannins join the party.
Most impressive is the agility of a wine that is a whisker away from full-bodied.
Screwcap. 14.5% alc. **Rating** 95 **To** 2033 $40
Silver Hammer McLaren Vale Shiraz 2014 Full-bodied and robust; licorice,
dark chocolate, savoury/tarry nuances and firm, but ripe tannins are the
architecture for the blackberry and plum fruit, positive oak the icing on the cake.
Terrific value. Screwcap. 14.5% alc. **Rating** 94 **To** 2034 $20 ✪
Lime Cave McLaren Vale Cabernet Sauvignon 2013 Great colour heralds a
cabernet with all the power and drive you could wish for, with layered cassis fruit,
dried herb, impressive tannins and good oak balance and integration. The maritime
climate of McLaren Vale is well suited to cabernet. Screwcap. 14.5% alc. **Rating** 94
To 2033 $40

ŶŶŶŶ♀ **Four Roads Old Vine Grenache 2014** Rating 93 To 2021 $28 CM
Barrel Fermented McLaren Vale Verdelho 2015 Rating 90 To 2018 $24

Mayer   ★★★★★

66 Miller Road, Healesville, Vic 3777 **Region** Yarra Valley
T (03) 5967 3779 **www**.timomayer.com.au **Open** By appt
Winemaker Timo Mayer **Est.** 1999 **Dozens** 1000 **Vyds** 2.4ha
Timo Mayer, also winemaker at Gembrook Hill Vineyard, teamed with partner Rhonda
Ferguson to establish Mayer on the slopes of Mt Toolebewong, 8km south of Healesville. The
steepness of those slopes is presumably 'celebrated' in the name given to the wines (Bloody
Hill). Pinot noir has the lion's share of the high-density vineyard, with smaller amounts of
shiraz and chardonnay. Mayer's winemaking credo is minimal interference and handling, and
no filtration. Exports to the UK, Germany, Denmark, Singapore and Japan.

ŶŶŶŶŶ **Yarra Valley Pinot Noir 2014** Although the colour shows no sign of this, it is
made with 100% whole bunches, and the stalk influence is more obvious on the
back-palate than it is on entry to the mouth; the pinot fruit expression is appealing
and pretty, albeit light. Diam. 13% alc. **Rating** 95 **To** 2025 $55
Dr Mayer Yarra Valley Pinot Noir 2014 While in the elegant, light-bodied
style of all the Mayer Pinots, this has more red fruit at its centre, and a clearer,

more direct expression; the tannins are silky, the length and balance good. Diam. 13% alc. **Rating** 95 **To** 2023 $55

Yarra Valley Syrah 2014 Made with 100% whole bunches, a brave approach in the Yarra Valley, but made in the context of fully ripe fruit. Yes, there are some stemmy nuances, but they are totally at home in the silky, medium-bodied palate, which has red fruits and spices ready for the long haul. Diam. 14% alc. **Rating** 95 **To** 2024 $55

Yarra Valley Cabernet 2014 Only Timo Mayer would dare to pick cabernet at 13° baume and whole-bunch ferment it – but then again, only Timo could make all this work as well as it does. The hue is bright but light (typical of whole bunches), the flavours bright and juicy, the tannins surprisingly good. Diam. 12.8% alc. **Rating** 94 **To** 2029 $55

Mayfield Vineyard ★★★★☆

954 Icely Road, Orange, NSW 2800 **Region** Orange
T (02) 6365 9292 **www**.mayfieldvineyard.com **Open** W'ends 10–4
Winemaker Antonio D'Onise, Simon Gilbert **Est.** 1998 **Dozens** 12 000 **Vyds** 20.3ha

The property – including the house in which owners Richard and Kathy Thomas now live – has a rich history as a leading Suffolk sheep stud, founded upon the vast fortune accumulated by the Crawford family via its biscuit business in the UK. The estate vineyard has 7.9ha of sauvignon blanc, 3.8ha of pinot noir, 3.4ha each of cabernet sauvignon and merlot, and slightly less than 1ha each of sangiovese and chardonnay. Exports to the UK and Asia.

🍷🍷🍷🍷🍷 **Single Vineyard Orange Pinot Noir 2015** Mayfields Pinots are from the same vineyard (same climate, same yield), and given the same oak treatment in the winery (used French oak). The difference? This is MV6 clone. Brighter and clearer crimson than its sibling, the aromas intense and in the red fruit spectrum; the palate opens with the same high-toned red cherry/spicy flavours through to the mid-palate, then moves in a different direction with its savoury tannins before coming back to its beautiful red fruits on the finish and aftertaste. Screwcap. 13% alc. **Rating** 95 **To** 2025 $35 ✪

🍷🍷🍷🍷 **M Series Orange Pinot Noir 2015** **Rating** 92 **To** 2022 $35

Mayford Wines ★★★★☆

6815 Great Alpine Road, Porepunkah, Vic 3740 **Region** Alpine Valleys
T (03) 5756 2528 **www**.mayfordwines.com **Open** By appt
Winemaker Eleana Anderson **Est.** 1995 **Dozens** 800 **Vyds** 3ha

The roots of Mayford go back to 1995, when forester Brian Nicholson planted a small amount of shiraz, since extended to 0.8ha, chardonnay (1.6ha) and tempranillo (0.6ha). In their words, 'in-house winemaking commenced shortly after he selected his seasoned winemaker bride in '02'. Wife and co-owner Eleana Anderson became a Flying Winemaker, working four vintages in Germany while completing her wine science degree at CSU (having much earlier obtained an arts degree). Vintages in Australia included one at Boynton's Feathertop (also at Porepunkah), where she met her husband-to-be. Initially, she was unenthusiastic about the potential of tempranillo, which Brian had planted after consultation with Mark Walpole, Brown Brothers' viticulturist, but since making the first vintage in '06 she has been thoroughly enamoured of the variety. Eleana practises minimalist winemaking, declining to use enzymes, cultured yeasts, tannins and/or copper. Exports to Singapore.

🍷🍷🍷🍷🍷 **Tempranillo 2014** This was the wine that brought Mayford into the public gaze with the sheer quality of its first release, and it hasn't lost ground since then. This is a prime example, with the structure and depth to rival its Spanish brethren, dark cherry fruit the flag bearer, oak and tannins marching proudly behind. Screwcap. 14% alc. **Rating** 95 **To** 2029 $36

Chardonnay 2014 An elegant and clear rendition of chardonnay from a region usually more noted for quantity than quality, and there is indeed a slight crack in the armour on that score. Eleana Anderson has made the most of what she has been given, without trying to overcompensate; this is a fresh and juicy wine. Screwcap. 14% alc. **Rating** 94 **To** 2022 $36

🍷🍷🍷🍷♀ Shiraz 2013 **Rating** 91 **To** 2023 $40

Maygars Hill Winery

53 Longwood-Mansfield Road, Longwood, Vic 3665 **Region** Strathbogie Ranges
T 0402 136 448 **www**.maygarshill.com.au **Open** By appt
Winemaker Contract **Est.** 1997 **Dozens** 900 **Vyds** 3.2ha

Jenny Houghton purchased this 8ha property in 1994, planting shiraz (1.9ha) and cabernet sauvignon (1.3ha). The name comes from Lieutenant Colonel Maygar, who fought with outstanding bravery in the Boer War in South Africa in 1901, and was awarded the Victoria Cross. In World War I he rose to command the 8th Light Horse Regiment, winning yet further medals for bravery. Exports to Fiji and China.

🍷🍷🍷🍷🍷 Shiraz 2014 A gloriously elegant medium-bodied wine, with exceptional balance, line and length; the perfumed purity of the bouquet is played out on the almost delicate, and totally seductive, palate, the handling of oak and tannins deliberately throwing all the emphasis on the predominantly red fruit flavours. Gold medal Victorian Wine Show '15, but in my opinion deserved the trophy for Best Shiraz. Screwcap. 14% alc. **Rating** 96 **To** 2034 $28 ✪

Reserve Shiraz 2014 You'd almost call this brooding and yet it also has an open-faced drinkability. It's the girl-next-door with a PhD in the gravitational pull of grape matter. Blackberry, gum leaf, rich plums, black pepper. It's quite some wine. Screwcap. 14.5% alc. **Rating** 95 **To** 2032 $38 CM

Cabernet Sauvignon 2014 This is cool-grown cabernet, its acidity one of the cornerstones, fine tannins being the other. Not a normal show style, the Victorian Wine Show '15 judges to be commended on awarding it a gold medal. Screwcap. 14% alc. **Rating** 95 **To** 2030 $28 ✪

Mayhem & Co

49 Collingrove Avenue, Broadview, SA 5083 **Region** Adelaide Hills
T 0468 384 817 **www**.mayhemandcowine.com.au **Open** Not
Winemaker Brendon Keys, Andrew Hill **Est.** 2009 **Dozens** 1400

Mayhem & Co. is owned by Andrew Hill. Andrew worked vintages at Wirra Wirra and Chapel Hill before taking on senior sales and marketing roles with Koonara, Tomich Hill and Reschke Wines. The wines are made from grapes purchased from various growers in the Adelaide Hills, Eden Valley and McLaren Vale.

🍷🍷🍷🍷♀ Hipster Eden Valley Riesling 2015 Hand-picked and whole bunch-pressed with a single cultured yeast, 2 months lees contact prior to bottling. Well made from a good vintage; there's not a hair out of place, and – counterintuitively – that's what is lacking in the mirror calm of the wine. A bit of mayhem needed. Screwcap. 12.6% alc. **Rating** 91 **To** 2025 $30

Mazza Wines

PO Box 480, Donnybrook, WA 6239 **Region** Geographe
T (08) 9201 1114 **www**.mazza.com.au **Open** Not
Winemaker Contract **Est.** 2002 **Dozens** 1000 **Vyds** 4ha

David and Anne Mazza were inspired by the great wines of Rioja and the Douro Valley, and continue a long-standing family tradition of making wine. They have planted the key varieties of those two regions: tempranillo, graciano, bastardo, souzao, tinta cao and touriga nacional. They believe they were the first Australian vineyard to present this collection of varieties on a single site, and I am reasonably certain they are correct in this belief. Whether it is still true is a matter of conjecture – it's a fast-moving scene in Australia these days. Exports to the UK.

ΨΨΨΨΨ **Geographe Touriga Nacional 2012** The most juicy, spicy and freshest; light to medium-bodied but has poise and length, fine tannins providing structure. Enjoyable on any terms. Screwcap. 15% alc. **Rating** 93 **To** 2023 $38
Geographe Tinta Cao 2012 14yo vines, hand-picked and sorted, destemmed, open-fermented with cultured yeast, 5 days cold soak, matured in used oak for 20 months. Very lively; juicy red fruits; balanced tannins; medium-bodied; good line and length. Screwcap. 14% alc. **Rating** 92 **To** 2020 $32
Geographe Graciano 2012 14yo vines, hand-picked and sorted, destemmed, open-fermented with cultured yeast, 5 days cold soak, matured in used oak for 20 months. Purple and blue fruits; fine tannins; good line, length and balance. Screwcap. 15% alc. **Rating** 91 **To** 2022 $32
Geographe Bastardo Rose 2015 7yo vines, hand-picked and sorted, crushed, tank-fermented with cultured yeast, 24 hours on skins. Salmon-pink; a fragrant, spicy bouquet, juicy mouthfeel, spice and red fruits, good length. Screwcap. 14% alc. **Rating** 90 **To** 2017 $19 ✪
Geographe Tempranillo 2012 14yo vines, destemmed, open-fermented with cultured yeast, 5 days cold soak, 10 days post-ferment maceration, matured in used oak for 20 months. Dark cherry fruits; spicy edge to the tannins is attractive; still youthful; good length. Screwcap. 14% alc. **Rating** 90 **To** 2020 $28

Medhurst ★★★★★

24–26 Medhurst Road, Gruyere, Vic 3770 **Region** Yarra Valley
T (03) 5964 9022 www.medhurstwines.com.au **Open** Thurs–Mon & public hols 11–5
Winemaker Simon Steel **Est.** 2000 **Dozens** 4200 **Vyds** 12.21ha
The wheel has come full circle for Ross and Robyn Wilson. In the course of a very distinguished corporate career, Ross was CEO of Southcorp when it brought the Penfolds, Lindemans and Wynns businesses under the Southcorp banner. Robyn spent her childhood in the Yarra Valley, her parents living less than a kilometre away from Medhurst. The vineyard is planted to sauvignon blanc, chardonnay, pinot noir, cabernet sauvignon and shiraz, all running on a low-yield basis. A large winery was built in 2011; it focuses on small batch production, and also provides contract winemaking services. The visual impact of the winery has been minimised by recessing the building into the slope of land and locating the barrel room underground. The winery was recognised for its architectural excellence at the Victorian Architecture Awards '12. Exports to Hong Kong and China.

ΨΨΨΨΨ **Reserve Yarra Valley Chardonnay 2013** Whole bunch-pressed, wild-fermented in a single 1yo French puncheon, no stirring or mlf, bottled Feb '14, 50 dozen made. Certainly deserves its Reserve status: super-intense, long and focused. Just wait for the '14 Reserve. Screwcap. 13% alc. **Rating** 96 **To** 2024 $60 ✪
Reserve Yarra Valley Pinot Noir 2013 MV6, wild-fermented, 15% whole bunches, matured in a single new French puncheon. Bright, clear colour; ticks each and very box with precision. A lovely pinot, equally expressive of place and variety, not relying on any left-field look-at-me-aren't-I-clever tricks. Screwcap. 13% alc. **Rating** 96 **To** 2025 $60 ✪
Reserve Yarra Valley Cabernet 2013 Estate-grown, matured for 18 months in French oak. Bright crimson-purple; a powerful, autocratic cabernet making it clear you take it on its terms or not at all. Powerful blackcurrant fruit has a crown of tannins and bay leaves, cedary French oak also playing an important role. Screwcap. 13.5% alc. **Rating** 96 **To** 2033 $60 ✪
Yarra Valley Chardonnay 2014 Hand-picked, whole bunch-pressed 'dirty juice' run to French oak for wild fermentation and 7 months maturation (with lees stirring). There is a gently savoury edge ex the cloudy juice fermentation that lees stirring hasn't diminished; has very good line, length and balance, all reflecting the great chardonnay vintage. Screwcap. 13.4% alc. **Rating** 95 **To** 2024 $33 ✪
Yarra Valley Shiraz 2013 A low-yielding vintage open-fermented variously with 25–100% whole bunches and whole berries, matured in new and used French oak. A very elegant medium-bodied shiraz that has repaid the winemaking

inputs with supple red and blue berry fruits, superfine tannins and integrated oak. Screwcap. 13.4% alc. **Rating** 95 **To** 2028 $33 ❂

YRB 2015 55% pinot noir, 45% shiraz, a tribute to Maurice O'Shea, hand-picked, destemmed, open fermenters, no pigeage/pump-overs after wild fermentation initiated, matured in a used French puncheon. Vivid crimson-purple; remarkable synergy of its red cherry fruits. Screwcap. 13% alc. **Rating** 94 **To** 2020 $30 ❂

♀♀♀♀♀ Yarra Valley Cabernet 2013 Rating 93 To 2029 $33
Yarra Valley Sauvignon Blanc 2015 Rating 92 To 2018 $25 ❂
Steel's Hill Yarra Valley Pinot Noir 2015 Rating 92 To 2025 $28

Meehan Vineyard   ★★★★

4536 McIvor Highway, Heathcote, Vic 3523 **Region** Heathcote
T 0407 058 432 **www**.meehanvineyard.com **Open** W'ends & public hols 10–5
Winemaker Phil Meehan **Est.** 2003 **Dozens** 1200 **Vyds** 2ha

In 1999, after their children had left the nest, Phil and Judy Meehan decided to return to the country and grow grapes for sale to wineries. In that year they took the first step, planting a small pinot noir vineyard at Bannockburn. It then took until April 2003 to find a near-perfect site, just within the Heathcote town boundary, its northeast-facing gentle slope on the famous Cambrian soil. Phil graduated with a Diploma of Winemaking and a Diploma of Viticulture in '05, saying, 'After a mere six years of study I only learned, after all that time, just how much more to winemaking there was to learn.' Exports to Malaysia and Hong Kong.

♀♀♀♀♀ William Heathcote Shiraz 2014 Dark inky red; a very densely packed bouquet with loads of ripe dark fruits, brambly notes backed by eucalypt and an earthy complexity; full-flavoured, with succulent and densely packed fruit; long and powerful. Screwcap. 14.8% alc. **Rating** 93 **To** 2026 $50
Heathcote Shiraz 2014 Dark red; a intensely ripe and concentrated plummy, dark-fruited bouquet leads to an intense, rounded and full-throttle shiraz Screwcap. 14.5% alc. **Rating** 92 **To** 2026 $28

Meerea Park   ★★★★★

Pavilion B, 2144 Broke Road, Pokolbin, NSW 2320 **Region** Hunter Valley
T (02) 4998 7474 **www**.meereapark.com.au **Open** 7 days 10–5
Winemaker Rhys Eather **Est.** 1991 **Dozens** 11 000

This is the project of Rhys and Garth Eather, whose great-great-grandfather, Alexander Munro, established a famous vineyard in the 19th century, known as Bebeah. While the range of wines chiefly focuses on semillon and shiraz, it extends to other varieties (including chardonnay), and also into other regions. Meerea Park has moved its cellar door to the striking Tempus Two winery now owned by the Roche family, situated on the corner of Broke Road/McDonald Road. Other tenants of the building include the Smelly Cheese Shop, Oishi Restaurant, Goldfish bar and cocktail lounge, The Barrel Room, and Tempus Two's own cellar door. It hardly need be said that the quality of the wines, especially with 5 years' cellaring, is outstanding. Exports to the US, Ireland, Singapore and China.

♀♀♀♀♀ Alexander Munro Individual Vineyard Hunter Valley Shiraz 2014 From the Black Cluster Vineyard, fermented in a new 3500l foudre, transferred to French barriques (55% new) for 18 months maturation. While only medium-bodied, this is a wine for future generations to glory in; the fruits are predominantly in the red berry range, the tannins and oak line up in support with military precision and immacluate balance. Screwcap. 14% alc. **Rating** 97 **To** 2049 $100 ❂

♀♀♀♀♀ Alexander Munro Individual Vineyard Hunter Valley Shiraz 2011 From the Ivanhoe Vineyard, 50% whole bunches, matured for 20 months in French barriques (45% new). The fruit flavours are red, but there are exotic aromas and flavours within that broad category, not the least the spicy, savoury tannins with that defining Hunter Valley mark of fresh earth. One of those wines that gets better each time it is retasted. Screwcap. 13.5% alc. **Rating** 96 **To** 2041 $85

Terracotta Individual Vineyard Hunter Valley Semillon 2011 Has completed its 5-year apprenticeship, and it now shows what you can expect from semillon at the start of its adult life. Lemongrass, mineral and the first display of toast are all in balance, and will saunter through the next decade arm in arm, adding yet more flesh and flavours. Screwcap. 11% alc. **Rating** 95 **To** 2026 $35 ✪

XYZ Hunter Valley Shiraz 2014 Complexity is rarely so delicious. This is spot on. Plum and cherry liqueur fruit, smoke, licorice, cloves and meaty, spicy aspects galore. Firm but exuberant. There's plenty to think on here but even more to simply tuck into and enjoy. Screwcap. 14% alc. **Rating** 95 **To** 2027 $25 CM ✪

The Aunts Individual Vineyard Hunter Valley Shiraz 2014 Open-fermented, matured in French oak. Utterly different from the other Meerea Park '14 Shirazs. Here tannins and extract are the drivers at this stage, but there are enough black fruits to justify the tannins and give balance to the long palate. Offers much pleasure in the years ahead. Screwcap. 14% alc. **Rating** 95 **To** 2039 $30 ✪

BLACK Hunter Valley Shiraz 2014 This is all about line, length and persistence, not about depth or power in the conventional sense. Its problem – if it be that – is that it is so silky and juicy it could be enjoyed today, long before any secondary aromas and flavours are given a chance to add the complexity that undoubtedly lies in wait. Screwcap. 13.5% alc. **Rating** 95 **To** 2049 $225

Indie Individual Vineyard Hunter Valley Shiraz Pinot 2014 65/35% co-fermented in open vats, matured for 17 months in French puncheons (50% new). Light colour points to the pinot, but there's no deficiency in the bright red fruit aromas and flavours or the length of the palate. Obviously a look back to O'Shea. The most remarkable aspect is the way the French oak has been taken into the fabric of the wine. Fascinating. Screwcap. 13.5% alc. **Rating** 95 **To** 2040 $40

Alexander Munro Individual Vineyard Hunter Valley Semillon 2011 Hand-picked from the celebrated Braemore Vineyard, whole bunch-pressed, cultured yeast, left on heavy lees for 4 months. The only obvious sign of age is the green colour; everything else is largely locked up. Screwcap. 11% alc. **Rating** 94 **To** 2026 $45

Aged Release Alexander Munro Individual Vineyard Hunter Valley Semillon 2006 Gleaming straw-green; 10 years young, with unsweetened lemon juice, pith and zest resting on a bed of firm minerals, still to rise from its slumber. Screwcap. 11% alc. **Rating** 94 **To** 2026 $75

Hell Hole Hunter Valley Shiraz 2014 I'll never get the point of the front and back labels of this wine, seemingly praising the at-times hellish heat of the Hunter Valley. This is a potent wine, taking no prisoners, resting its attack on lifted red fruits more than tannins or extract. I'm in two minds about it, and am effectively suspending judgement. Screwcap. 14% alc. **Rating** 94 **To** 2034 $60

Terracotta Individual Vineyard Hunter Valley Syrah 2014 98% old vine shiraz, with 2% viognier co-fermented. Deep colour, grading to bright crimson on the rim; classic Hunter Valley shiraz with notes of earth, bramble and polished leather woven through the strikingly long medium-bodied palate. It has devoured the oak and taken the tannins prisoner. High quality now, but the decades to come will lift its profile further still. Screwcap. 14% alc. **Rating** 94 **To** 2044 $70

♟♟♟♟♟ **Bebeah Hunter Valley Shiraz 2014** Rating 93 To 2044 $30
Bebeah Hunter Valley Semillon 2015 Rating 91 To 2030 $30
Hell Hole Hunter Valley Semillon 2015 Rating 91 To 2025 $25

🍇 Mercuri Estate   ★★★☆

9484 Horrocks Highway, Clare, SA 5453 **Region** Clare Valley
T (08) 8842 3081 **www**.mercuriestate.com **Open** By appt
Winemaker Hamish Seabrook **Est.** 2015 **Dozens** 5000
This is the venture of Ennio Mercuri, whose family has had a 50-year history in the manufacturing industry. It's been a staged development, which gained massively with the

acquisition of the 52.6ha Cardinham Estate vineyard, with a history of wines made from St Clare vineyards at Leasingham, and pinot grigio sourced from the Adelaide Hills. This will give rise to a number of ranges of wines in the future, along with the planned opening of a cellar door. Exports to China

♥♥♥♥♀ Ryder Watervale Riesling 2014 The Greek gods would unleash thunderbolts at the idiots who couldn't realise that this wine leaves all but the very best pinot grigios (an oxymoron?) in its wake. What's more, it will get better and better over the next 5 years, a prospect no pinot gris/grigio could claim. This is flooded with lime juice and excellent balancing acidity – delicious now or later. Screwcap. 12.5% alc. **Rating** 93 **To** 2022 $14 ✪

♥♥♥♥ Ryder Clare Valley Cabernet Sauvignon 2013 Rating 89 To 2018 $14 ✪
Settebello Bastoni Cabernet Sauvignon 2013 Rating 89 To 2038 $25
Settebello Spade Watervale Riesling 2015 Rating 88 To 2020 $19
Ryder Clare Valley Shiraz 2013 Rating 88 To 2023 $14 CM ✪

Merindoc Vintners   ★★★★☆

2905 Lancefield-Tooborac Road, Tooborac, Vic 3522 **Region** Heathcote
T (03) 5433 5188 **www**.merindoc.com.au **Open** W'ends 10–4
Winemaker Steve Webber, Sergio Carlei **Est.** 1994 **Dozens** 2500 **Vyds** 60ha
Stephen Shelmerdine has been a major figure in the wine industry for over 25 years, like his family (who founded Mitchelton Winery) before him, and has been honoured for his many services to the industry. Substantial quantities of the grapes produced are sold to others; a small amount of high quality wine is contract-made. The Merindoc and Willoughby Bridge wines are produced from the two eponymous estate vineyards in Heathcote. Exports to China.

♥♥♥♥♥ Willoughby Bridge Rose 2015 Beautiful dry rose. Textural, spicy, brushed with cranberried/raspberried fruit, and succulent through the finish. One can ask for little more. Screwcap. 13.7% alc. **Rating** 95 **To** 2017 $24 CM ✪
Willoughby Bridge Syrah Grenache Mourvedre 2014 A picture of good (wine) health. Oomph, complexity, a syrupy smoothness and oodles of seductive length. Plums, earth and cloves. Great drinking. It will mature well but there's really no need to wait. Screwcap. 14% alc. **Rating** 94 **To** 2024 $24 CM ✪
Heathcote Sparkling Shiraz 2013 A delightfully elegant sparkling shiraz that captures the spicy, peppery fruit profile and the granitic ironstone texture of Heathcote geology. Black cherry and blackberry fruits have been impeccably upheld with depth, tang and bright definition. Masterfully crafted and delightfully captivating for an inaugural release. Diam. 13.7% alc. **Rating** 94 **To** 2023 $35 TS

♥♥♥♥♀ Merindoc Heathcote Riesling 2015 Rating 92 To 2022 $24 CM ✪
Shelmerdine Heathcote Shiraz 2013 Rating 90 To 2025 $68 CM

Mermerus Vineyard   ★★★★

60 Soho Road, Drysdale, Vic 3222 **Region** Geelong
T (03) 5253 2718 **www**.mermerus.com.au **Open** Sun 11–4
Winemaker Paul Champion **Est.** 2000 **Dozens** 500 **Vyds** 2.5ha
Paul Champion has established pinot noir, chardonnay and riesling at Mermerus. The wines are made from the small but very neat winery on the property, with small batch handling and wild yeast fermentation playing a major part in the winemaking, oak taking a back seat. Paul also acts as contract winemaker for small growers in the region.

♥♥♥♥♀ Bellarine Peninsula Chardonnay 2015 Hand-picked, crushed, basket-pressed with stems, fermented in French oak (25% new), a small portion wild-fermented and mlf, matured for 10 months. The stems are used to assist drainage from the basket press, not to impart any flavour. White-fleshed stone fruit and some toasty/nutty notes ex the oak drive the palate, with a little citrussy acidity in the background. Screwcap. 13.5% alc. **Rating** 93 **To** 2020 $25 ✪

Bellarine Peninsula Pinot Noir 2014 Good hue and depth; fragrant, gently spicy nuances add a dimension to the flavours of red and black cherry, plum also in the mix. A satisfying pinot with good varietal expression. Screwcap. 13.5% alc. **Rating** 91 **To** 2020 $35

Bellarine Peninsula Shiraz 2014 Good colour; oak plays a major role here, even though none of the oak was new; the bouquet has spice, pepper and cedar aromas linked to the black cherry fruit of the light to medium-bodied palate. With the caveat of the oak, a nice cool grown shiraz. Screwcap. 14% alc. **Rating** 90 **To** 2023 $25

♥♥♥♥ **Bellarine Peninsula Rose 2015** **Rating** 88 **To** 2017 $20

Merricks Estate ★★★★☆

Thompsons Lane, Merricks, Vic 3916 **Region** Mornington Peninsula
T (03) 5989 8416 **www**.merricksestate.com.au **Open** 1st w'end of month
Winemaker Paul Evans, Alex White **Est.** 1977 **Dozens** 2500 **Vyds** 4ha
Melbourne solicitor George Kefford, with wife Jacky, runs Merricks Estate as a weekend and holiday enterprise. It produces distinctive, spicy, cool climate Shiraz, which has accumulated an impressive array of show trophies and gold medals. As the current tasting notes comprehensively demonstrate, the fully mature vineyard and skilled contract winemaking are producing top-class wines. Exports to Hong Kong.

♥♥♥♥♥ **Thompson's Lane Shiraz 2012** This is a complete bargain at $24. From the highly regarded '12 vintage, it has now settled down, and provides a total counterpoint to the big end of shiraz town. Spice, pepper, red and brambly fruits lead to a delicious palate backed by layers of detail. Only 12.5% alcohol. Screwcap. 12.5% alc. **Rating** 96 **To** 2022 $24 ❂

♥♥♥♥♡ **Mornington Peninsula Pinot Noir 2013** **Rating** 93 **To** 2020 $40
Thompson's Lane Rose 2015 **Rating** 91 **To** 2017 $25

Merum Estate ★★★★☆

PO Box 840, Denmark, WA 6333 **Region** Pemberton
T (08) 9848 3443 **www**.merumestate.com.au **Open** Not
Winemaker Harewood Estate (James Kellie) **Est.** 1996 **Dozens** 4000 **Vyds** 10ha
Merum Estate stirred from slumber after morphing from grower and winemaker to pure grapegrowing after the 2006 vintage. Viticulturist Mike Melsom is the link with the past, for it was he and partner Julie Roberts who were responsible for the extremely good wines made in '05 and '06. The wines are released at three levels, headed by the Premium Reserve range.

♥♥♥♥♥ **Premium Reserve Single Vineyard Pemberton Semillon 2014** As ever, fermented and matured in French oak. Lively, zest, lemon curd, lemongrass and lemony acidity all stand proud amid the oak, its contribution the textural framework, and adding to the length. Screwcap. 13% alc. **Rating** 95 **To** 2021 $29 ❂
Premium Reserve Single Vineyard Pemberton Chardonnay 2014 Similar to its less expensive sibling, except that there's more of everything; the flavour spectrum is almost a carbon copy – strange there's not more grapefruit. Screwcap. 14% alc. **Rating** 94 **To** 2024 $29 ❂

♥♥♥♥♡ **Pemberton Semillon Sauvignon Blanc 2014** **Rating** 93 **To** 2020 $20 ❂
Pemberton Shiraz 2012 **Rating** 93 **To** 2027 $20 ❂
Premium Reserve Pemberton Shiraz 2013 **Rating** 92 **To** 2038 $29
Pemberton Chardonnay 2014 **Rating** 91 **To** 2020 $20 ❂

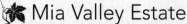 Mia Valley Estate ★★★☆

203 Daniels Lane, Mia Mia, Vic 3444 **Region** Heathcote
T (03) 5425 5515 **www**.miavalleyestate.com.au **Open** 7 days 10–5
Winemaker Norbert & Pamela Baumgartner **Est.** 1999 **Dozens** 1000 **Vyds** 3.2ha

Norbert and Pamela Baumgartner both had indirect connections with wine, plus a direct interest in drinking it. In the early 1980s, based in Melbourne, they began a search for suitable vineyard land. However, it proved too difficult to find what they wanted, and the plans were put on hold. It took until '98 for them to discover their property: 40ha with softly undulating land and the Mia Mia (pronounced mya-mya) Creek running through it. They planted 1.6ha of shiraz and in 2002 produced their first vintage. It encouraged them to plant another 1.6ha. Along the way Norbert completed winemaking and viticulture courses, and worked with David Anderson of Wild Duck Creek, and Peter Beckingham. They made their wines for the '02 to '05 vintages in their air-conditioned garage in Melbourne. In '05 they converted the vineyard shed into a mini-winery, expanding it in '06 to a winery and temporary accommodation, commuting on weekends from Melbourne until '09. They then ran into the '09 bushfires, the '11 rains, floods and disease, a '12 vintage more than they could handle, '14 decimated by frosts, late '15 and '16 severe drought. Are they giving up? No sign of it so far. Exports to the UK, the US and China.

ŶŶŶŶŶ **Reserve Heathcote Shiraz 2013** Super-ripe fruit, sweet chocolatey oak and a lift of mint. It's simple, substantial and effective, with firm tannin the finishing touch. Diam. 14.2% alc. **Rating** 93 **To** 2025 $30 CM

ŶŶŶŶ **Reserve Heathcote Shiraz 2011 Rating** 88 **To** 2020 $35 CM
Mia Mia Heathcote Shiraz Cabernet 2013 Rating 88 **To** 2021 $35 CM

Miceli   ★★★★

60 Main Creek Road, Arthurs Seat, Vic 3936 **Region** Mornington Peninsula
T (03) 5989 2755 **www.**miceli.com.au **Open** W'ends 12–5, public hols by appt
Winemaker Anthony Miceli **Est.** 1991 **Dozens** 4000 **Vyds** 5.5ha
This may be a part-time labour of love for general practitioner Dr Anthony Miceli, but that hasn't prevented him taking the venture very seriously. He acquired the property in 1989 specifically to establish a vineyard, planting 1.8ha in '91. Subsequent plantings have brought it to its present size, with pinot gris, chardonnay and pinot noir the varieties grown. Between '91 and '97 Dr Miceli completed the wine science course at CSU; he now manages both vineyard and winery. One of the top producers of sparkling wine on the Peninsula.

ŶŶŶŶŶ **Olivia's Mornington Peninsula Chardonnay 2012** Plenty going on. Hay, earth and malt-like characters introduce ripe peachy fruit. It's both full-bodied and funky, with struck match notes littering the (dry) finish. Characterful. Screwcap. 13.5% alc. **Rating** 92 **To** 2019 $30 CM
Iolanda Mornington Peninsula Pinot Grigio 2014 A bit of flesh, a lot of race. This darts through the mouth but it doesn't forget to deliver on a bit of flavour. It's a good option. Screwcap. 13% alc. **Rating** 92 **To** 2017 $24 CM **O**
Lucy's Choice Mornington Peninsula Pinot Noir 2014 Spiced, macerated cherry flavours power through the palate, a clip of cedary oak helping things along. Screwcap. 13.5% alc. **Rating** 91 **To** 2021 $35 CM

Michael Hall Wines   ★★★★★

10 George Street, Tanunda, SA 5352 (postal) **Region** Mount Lofty Ranges Zone
T 0419 126 290 **www.**michaelhallwines.com **Open** Not
Winemaker Michael Hall **Est.** 2008 **Dozens** 1800
For reasons no longer relevant (however interesting), Michael Hall was once a jewellery valuer for Sotheby's in Switzerland. He came to Australia in 2001 to pursue winemaking, a lifelong interest, and undertook the wine science degree at CSU, graduating as dux in '05. His vintage work in Australia and France is a veritable who's who: in Australia with Cullen, Giaconda, Henschke, Shaw + Smith, Coldstream Hills and Veritas; in France with Domaine Leflaive, Meo-Camuzet, Vieux Telegraphe and Trevallon. He is now involved full-time with his eponymous brand, and does some teaching at the Nuriootpa TAFE. The wines are as impressive as his CV suggests they should be. Exports to the UK.

ŶŶŶŶŶ Flaxman Valley Eden Valley Syrah 2014 Very small fruit set and crop, destemmed, 25% fermented in puncheons, 75% open-fermented, matured for 20 months in French oak (25% new). Rich and opulent, with a brocade of red and black berry fruits garnished with spice and a little pepper; oak and finely ground tannins join in on the finish. Screwcap. 13.9% alc. **Rating** 96 **To** 2044 $50 ✪

Piccadilly and Verdun Adelaide Hills Chardonnay 2014 Low yields and the vintage were always destined to produce wines with concentration and depth, but it is the length of the palate that sets this wine apart; white peach and nectarine flavours have not been challenged by oak, and partial mlf has added a creamy textural note alongside citrussy acidity. Screwcap. 13.3% alc. **Rating** 95 **To** 2021 $50

Piccadilly and Balhannah Adelaide Hills Pinot Noir 2014 10% whole bunches, 15% on skins for 72 days, matured for 17 months in French oak (27% new), 200 dozen made. The complex vinification achieved its objectives; while rich and (in pinot terms) full-bodied, it has all the makings of an outstanding wine in 3–4 years' time, when all of the fruits and tannins open their wings and soar skywards. Screwcap. 13.6% alc. **Rating** 95 **To** 2025 $44

Sang de Pigeon Barossa Valley Shiraz 2014 Includes 10% Adelaide Hills shiraz. Richly plumed and textured, ripe tannins and accented oak jumping in with the fruit right from the outset and providing an almost creamy mouthfeel. Screwcap. 14.2% alc. **Rating** 95 **To** 2039 $30 ✪

Flaxman Valley Eden Valley Syrah 2013 Wild-fermented (10% in barrel), and a portion with long maceration, total time in French oak (30% new) 19 months. A rich and complex wine was the result, with vibrant red and blue fruits framed by persistent, but welcome, tannins. Opens a conversation now that will continue for years to come. Screwcap. 14.1% alc. **Rating** 95 **To** 2038 $48

Piccadilly Adelaide Hills Chardonnay 2014 Inviting, come-hither style boasting cream, peach and grapefruit flavours/textures. Generosity has its own power. The finish then turns rocky, dry, minerally; the gem on its finger. Screwcap. 13.3% alc. **Rating** 94 **To** 2019 $50 CM

Stone Well Barossa Valley Shiraz 2013 No one could want greater body or flavour than this at 14.1% alcohol, so why make wine at 15% or above? Reverse osmosis was not used here, by the way. The flavours are typical, well balanced, and range from blackberry to soused plum, the tannins ripe. Screwcap. 14.1% alc. **Rating** 94 **To** 2035 $44

ŶŶŶŶŶ Adelaide Hills Sauvignon Blanc 2015 **Rating** 92 **To** 2017 $35
Greenock Barossa Valley Roussanne 2015 **Rating** 90 **To** 2025 $38

Michelini Wines ★★★☆

Great Alpine Road, Myrtleford, Vic 3737 **Region** Alpine Valleys
T (03) 5751 1990 **www**.micheliniwines.com.au **Open** 7 days 10–5
Winemaker Federico Zagami **Est.** 1982 **Dozens** 10 000 **Vyds** 34.5ha
The Michelini family are among the best-known grapegrowers in the Buckland Valley of North East Victoria. Having migrated from Italy in 1949, they originally grew tobacco, diversifying into vineyards in '82. The main vineyard (16.8ha), on terra rossa soil, is at an altitude of 300m, mostly with frontage to the Buckland River. The Devils Creek Vineyard (17.7ha) was planted in '91 on grafted rootstocks, merlot and chardonnay taking the lion's share. Exports to China.

ŶŶŶŶŶ Italian Selection Pinot Grigio 2015 Plenty of drive. Sweet pear and apple flavours with hints of honeysuckle. Attractive. Generous. Screwcap. 12.5% alc. **Rating** 90 **To** 2016 $20 CM ✪

ŶŶŶŶ Italian Selection Vermentino 2015 **Rating** 88 **To** 2016 $25 CM

Mike Press Wines

PO Box 224, Lobethal, SA 5241 **Region** Adelaide Hills
T (08) 8389 5546 **www.**mikepresswines.com.au **Open** Not
Winemaker Mike Press **Est.** 1998 **Dozens** 12 000 **Vyds** 22.7ha

Mike and Judy Press established their Kenton Valley Vineyards in 1998, when they purchased 34ha of land in the Adelaide Hills at an elevation of 500m. They planted mainstream cool climate varieties (merlot, shiraz, cabernet sauvignon, sauvignon blanc, chardonnay and pinot noir), intending to sell the grapes to other wine producers. Even an illustrious 43-year career in the wine industry did not prepare Mike for the downturn in grape prices that followed, and that led to the development of the Mike Press wine label. They produce high quality Sauvignon Blanc, Chardonnay, Pinot Noir, Merlot, Shiraz, Cabernet Merlot and Cabernet Sauvignon, which are sold at mouth-wateringly low prices. I've decided to give this winery/maker proprietary five stars because there is no other producer offering estate-grown and made wines at prices to compete with these.

ΨΨΨΨΨ **Sauvignon Blanc 2015** The awesome power and intensity of this wine will catch many by surprise; the bouquet is correct and varietal, but by the time it reaches the mid-palate you can sense the express train loaded with citrus, green pea and sparks of tropical fruits blazing through the finish and cleansing aftertaste of mouthwatering acidity. Screwcap. 12.7% alc. **Rating** 94 **To** 2016 $13 ✪

ΨΨΨΨΨ **Single Vineyard Cabernet Sauvignon 2014 Rating** 93 **To** 2029 $14 ✪
Single Vineyard Chardonnay 2015 Rating 90 **To** 2016 $13 ✪

Miles from Nowhere

PO Box 197, Belmont, WA 6984 **Region** Margaret River
T (08) 9267 8555 **www.**milesfromnowhere.com.au **Open** Not
Winemaker Rory Clifton-Parks **Est.** 2007 **Dozens** 18 000 **Vyds** 46.9ha

Miles from Nowhere is one of the born-again wineries of Franklin (Frank) and Heather Tate; Frank was CEO of Evans & Tate for many years. The demise of Evans & Tate has been well chronicled, but has not prevented the Tates from doing what they know best. The plantings of petit verdot, chardonnay, shiraz, sauvignon blanc, semillon, viognier, cabernet sauvignon and merlot are scattered across the Margaret River region – miles from nowhere. Exports to the UK, Canada, Sweden and Thailand.

ΨΨΨΨΨ **Best Blocks Margaret River Chardonnay 2014** A well-tailored combination of high quality fruit and oak. Aromas of cashew and smoky barrel-ferment mesh comfortably with the varietal citrus and stone fruit on the bouquet, the palate likewise in good balance, the flavours all in order. Sitting in a sweet spot for drinking now. Screwcap. 13.2% alc. **Rating** 93 **To** 2018 $32
Best Blocks Margaret River Semillon Sauvignon Blanc 2015 Only 10% of this 50/50 blend is fermented in oak, but it has some influence. Essentially a textural wine, the fruit characters of snow pea, lemon and gooseberry are subtle, the minerally, flinty elements playing their part in the style. Length of flavour and persistence on the finish are positives, although the tart acidity is perhaps a little too pronounced. Screwcap. 12.8% alc. **Rating** 92 **To** 2018 $32
Best Blocks Margaret River Shiraz 2014 First impression on the bouquet is peppermint; unusual for Margaret River. Things settle down to a more predictable theme, with red fruit and gamey notes emerging, supported by a dollop of oak. Flavours of dark plum, dark chocolate and sweet spice are threaded through the palate, which is supple and long, the astringency of tannin/acid quite pronounced on the finish. Needs a little time. Screwcap. 14.6% alc. **Rating** 92 **To** 2024 $32
Margaret River Cabernet Merlot 2014 Pretty much all the elements you expect to find are here. Aromas of blackcurrant, mint, a touch of leafiness and distinctive regional character. Glides through the palate with fresh, buoyant flavours expressing the varieties in a harmonious and well-mannered style. Good value obvious. Screwcap. 14.2% alc. **Rating** 92 **To** 2022 $18 ✪

Margaret River Shiraz 2014 Good varietal expression on the bouquet, with red fruit, spice, and a dusting of white pepper. Medium-bodied, the flavours fresh and bright with the red-fruited theme continuing, astringency just a touch obtrusive at this stage. A little more time in bottle should make for a more complete wine. Screwcap. 14.4% alc. **Rating** 91 **To** 2022 $18 ✪

ΨΨΨΨ **Best Blocks Cabernet Sauvignon 2014 Rating** 89 **To** 2030 $32
Margaret River Sauvignon Blanc Semillon 2015 Rating 88 **To** 2016 $18
Margaret River Chardonnay 2015 Rating 88 **To** 2018 $18

Millbrook Winery   ★★★★★

Old Chestnut Lane, Jarrahdale, WA 6124 **Region** Perth Hills
T (08) 9525 5796 **www**.millbrookwinery.com.au **Open** Wed–Sun 10–5
Winemaker Damian Hutton **Est.** 1996 **Dozens** 15 000 **Vyds** 7.8ha
The strikingly situated Millbrook Winery is owned by highly successful Perth-based entrepreneur Peter Fogarty and wife Lee. They also own Lake's Folly in the Hunter Valley, Smithbrook in Pemberton and Deep Woods Estate in Margaret River. Millbrook draws on vineyards in the Perth Hills planted to sauvignon blanc, semillon, chardonnay, viognier, cabernet sauvignon, merlot, shiraz and petit verdot. The wines are of consistently high quality. Exports to Germany, Malaysia, Hong Kong, Singapore, China and Japan.

ΨΨΨΨΨ **Pemberton Arneis 2014** This is a top-flight example of the variety in Australia. There is what I can only describe as a grainy quality to the bouquet and palate, with a mix of pear skin, almond, green apple and lively lemony acidity. Screwcap. 13% alc. **Rating** 95 **To** 2017 $28 ✪
LR Chardonnay 2014 Minerally finish but the palate is aflame with sweet, ripe fruit. You can pretty much guarantee that all who drink this will enjoy it. White peach, grapefruit and sweet, saucy oak. Integration of the various components is a feature. Fantastic finish/aftertaste. Screwcap. 14% alc. **Rating** 95 **To** 2021 $45 CM
LR Durif 2014 Hulking wine. Thick with tannin but also with flavour. Serve this and it will command the room. Intense blackberry. fresh leather, boot polish, vanillan. You can't help but be impressed by both its power and its length. Screwcap. 15% alc. **Rating** 95 **To** 2035 $45 CM
Estate Shiraz Viognier 2013 It's on the front foot from the outset, shooting plum and blackberry fruit flavours straight at you, leaf matter, pepper, florals and spice racing enthusiastically in to support. It's both strong and pretty at once, and therefore seductive. Screwcap. 14.5% alc. **Rating** 94 **To** 2028 $35 CM
Geographe Grenache Shiraz Mourvedre 2015 Fundamentally delicious. Turbo-charged with dry spice, sweet and savoury, with gun smoke and black cherry flavours as the sweet-running motor. Web of tannin completes a most attractive picture. Screwcap. 14.5% alc. **Rating** 94 **To** 2022 $22 CM ✪
Petit Verdot 2014 It curls with tannin and hits with dark, berried fruit. Violet, resiny oak, blackcurrant; there's a lot of flavour here, and it's well prosecuted too. Screwcap. 14.5% alc. **Rating** 94 **To** 2030 $28 CM ✪

ΨΨΨΨΨ **Pemberton Arneis 2015 Rating** 93 **To** 2017 $28 CM
Margaret River Sauvignon Blanc 2015 Rating 92 **To** 2016 $20 CM ✪
Barking Owl SSB 2015 Rating 92 **To** 2018 $18 ✪
Geographe Tempranillo 2014 Rating 92 **To** 2023 $22 CM ✪
Barking Owl Shiraz 2013 Rating 91 **To** 2021 $18 CM ✪
Geographe Sangiovese 2014 Rating 91 **To** 2021 $20 CM ✪
PX Pedro Ximenes NV Rating 91 **To** 2017 $60 CM
Estate Viognier 2015 Rating 90 **To** 2017 $35 CM
Perth Hills Viognier 2014 Rating 90 **To** 2017 $22 CM

Milton Vineyard ★★★★★

14635 Tasman Highway, Cranbrook, Tas 7190 **Region** East Coast Tasmania
T (03) 6257 8298 **www**.miltonvineyard.com.au **Open** 7 days 10–5
Winemaker Winemaking Tasmania (Julian Alcorso) **Est.** 1992 **Dozens** 6000 **Vyds** 13ha
Michael and Kerry Dunbabin have one of the most historic properties in Tasmania, dating
back to 1826. The property is 1800ha, meaning the vineyard (5ha of pinot noir, 1.45a each of
riesling and pinot gris, 1.5ha each of chardonnay and gewurztraminer, plus 10 rows of shiraz)
has plenty of room for expansion.

ŸŸŸŸŸ **Riesling 2015** If you are in the right place, nothing much except care is
needed in the winery, and Milton Vineyard is definitely in the right place. This
is a precisely shaped and formed riesling, lime and grapefruit seamlessly welded
to minerally acidity on the very long palate. This will flourish for many years to
come. Screwcap. 12.5% alc. **Rating** 95 **To** 2030 $25 ✪
Pinot Noir 2014 Bright crimson hue; the bouquet sets the antennae waving,
the gently savoury black cherry, plum and licorice fruit flavours show no sign of
overripeness. In best pinot fashion, makes its presence felt in no uncertain fashion
on the finish and aftertaste. Gold medal Tasmanian Wine Show '15. Screwcap.
14% alc. **Rating** 95 **To** 2021 $35 ✪

ŸŸŸŸŸ **Pinot Gris 2015 Rating** 93 **To** 2017 $25 ✪
Gewurztraminer 2015 Rating 91 **To** 2025 $25
Iced Riesling 2014 Rating 91 **To** 2020 $30

Ministry of Clouds ★★★★★

39a Wakefield Street, Kent Town, SA 5067 **Region** Various
T 0417 864 615 **www**.ministryofclouds.com.au **Open** Not
Winemaker Julian Forwood, Bernice Ong, Tim Geddes **Est.** 2012 **Dozens** 2500
Bernice Ong and Julian Forwood say, 'The name Ministry of Clouds symbolises the
relinquishing of our past security and structure (ministry) for the beguiling freedom,
independence and adventure (clouds) inherent in our own venture.' I doubt whether there are
two partners in a young wine business with such extraordinary depth in sales and marketing of
wine, stretching back well over 20 years. Trying to pick out highlights is futile, simply because
there are so many of them. They bypassed owning vineyards or building wineries, instead
headhunting key winemakers in the Clare Valley and Tasmania for riesling and chardonnay
respectively, and the assistance of Tim Geddes at his winery in McLaren Vale, where they make
the red wines in conjunction with Tim. Exports to Singapore and Hong Kong.

ŸŸŸŸŸ **Tasmania Chardonnay 2014** This is a Tasmanian chardonnay of the highest
quality, with a sea breeze of crisp, bright fruit on the fore-palate, then a southerly
buster with the power and length that drives the back-palate and finish. Screwcap.
12.9% alc. **Rating** 96 **To** 2025 $48 ✪
McLaren Vale Shiraz 2014 Terrific colour and intensity at every point along the
way. A storm of black fruits and tannins breaks out from the first sip, and continues
relentlessly until you arrive at the back-palate, finish and aftertaste, when the
skies clear and the clarity of the pure black fruits is revealed. Screwcap. 14.1% alc.
Rating 96 **To** 2044 $30 ✪
Single Vineyard Blewitt Springs Shiraz 2014 5% whole bunches,
95% (genuine) whole berries, given extended post-ferment maceration, matured
for 18 months in French barriques. Elegance at the level of this wine is seldom
encountered in McLaren Vale, doubly so given its intensity and length. A lovely,
savoury/earthy aftertaste. Screwcap. 14.5% alc. **Rating** 96 **To** 2039 $58 ✪
McLaren Vale Mataro 2014 From two vineyards, one early-ripening bushvine
block at Sellicks, and a cooler Blewitt Springs site ripening 2 weeks later.
Destemmed, not crushed, wild open ferment, matured in used oak for 19 months.
Works brilliantly. Screwcap. 14% alc. **Rating** 96 **To** 2034 $38 ✪
Tasmania Chardonnay 2015 Hand-picked, whole bunch-pressed direct to
barrel, keeping the free-run and pressings stages separate for blending options,

wild-fermented, matured in used oak for 9 months, stirred for 3 months, no mlf. Cleverly conceived and executed. Fiercely bright and energetic, it will flourish for 10 years, live for 20. Screwcap. 12.9% alc. **Rating** 95 **To** 2035 $48

Minko Wines ★★★★

13 High Street, Willunga, SA 5172 **Region** Southern Fleurieu
T (08) 8556 4987 **www**.minkowines.com **Open** Wed–Fri, Sun 11–5, Sat 9.30–5
Winemaker James Hastwell, Linda Domas **Est.** 1997 **Dozens** 1800 **Vyds** 15.8ha
Mike Boerema (veterinarian) and Margo Kellet (ceramic artist) established the Minko vineyard on their cattle property at Mt Compass. The vineyard, which uses biodynamic methods, is planted to pinot noir, merlot, cabernet sauvignon, chardonnay, pinot gris and savagnin; 60ha of the 160ha property is heritage-listed. Exports to the UK.

♀♀♀♀♀ **Cabernet Sauvignon 2013** Grown on the Mt Compass estate vineyard. Bright colour; the elegant medium-bodied palate has a classic cool grown varietal mix of cassis, dried herb and black olive backed by typical cabernet tannins, oak the largely unseen partner. Screwcap. 14.2% alc. **Rating** 93 **To** 2028 $24 ○
Pinot Grigio 2015 A grigio with attitude and flavour, a haunting hint of strawberry behind the dominant nashi pear and fresh ginger of the bouquet and palate. Gives grigio status. Screwcap. 13.4% alc. **Rating** 90 **To** 2017 $20 ○
Merlot 2013 Interesting wine, with a suite of aromas and flavours suggestive of a merlot with lower alcohol. There are notes of stem, green olive and mint intermingled with red berry fruits and fine tannins on the medium–bodied palate. Screwcap. 14.2% alc. **Rating** 90 **To** 2020 $24
Methode Traditionelle Blanc de Blancs 2012 Chardonnay from Minko's Mount Compass Vineyard on the Fleurieu Peninsula. It has good balance, good length, and no shortage of zesty grapefruit flavours along with just a hint of brioche. Crown seal. 11.5% alc. **Rating** 90 **To** 2018 $35

♀♀♀♀ **Pinot Noir Savagnin Rose 2015 Rating** 89 **To** 2016 $20
Pinot Noir 2013 Rating 89 **To** 2020 $28

Minnow Creek ★★★★☆

5 Hillside Road, Blackwood, SA 5051 (postal) **Region** McLaren Vale
T 0404 288 108 **www**.minnowcreekwines.com.au **Open** Not
Winemaker Tony Walker **Est.** 2005 **Dozens** 1800
Former Fox Creek winemaker Tony Walker has set up Minnow Creek in partnership with William Neubauer; the grapes are grown by Don Lopresti at vineyards just west of Willunga. The name of the venture reflects the intention of the partners to keep the business focused on quality rather than quantity. Exports to the US, Canada and Germany.

♀♀♀♀♀ **The Black Minnow 2014** 74% sangiovese, 17% cabernet, 5% tempranillo and 4% merlot, matured in used 50/50% French and American oak for 16 months. Bright colour; deliciously juicy, with red cherry, sour cherry and a hint of cassis running the flavour flags; the tannins verge on silky. This is quite a wine at the price. Screwcap. 13% alc. **Rating** 94 **To** 2024 $20 ○

Mistletoe Wines ★★★★★

771 Hermitage Road, Pokolbin, NSW 2320 **Region** Hunter Valley
T (02) 4998 7770 **www**.mistletoewines.com.au **Open** 7 days 10–6
Winemaker Nick Paterson, Scott Stephens **Est.** 1989 **Dozens** 5000 **Vyds** 5.5ha
Mistletoe Wines, owned by Ken and Gwen Sloan, can trace its history back to 1909, when a vineyard was planted on what was then called Mistletoe Farm. The Mistletoe Farm brand made a brief appearance in the late '70s. The wines are made onsite by Nick Paterson, who has had significant experience in the Hunter Valley. The quality and consistency of these wines is irreproachable, as is their price.

ΨΨΨΨΨ Reserve Hunter Valley Semillon 2005 Bright straw-green, still pale; the initial fresh delivery is the calm before the storm as the wine expands, then races over every taste bud in the mouth. It has the flavours of cut grass (sneered at by some Hunter Valley semillon makers), lemongrass, green pea and overarching lemon citrus. Screwcap. 10% alc. **Rating** 96 **To** 2022 $22 ✪

Grand Reserve Hunter Valley Shiraz 2014 Matured in French puncheons for 15 months. Undoubtedly the most savoury and complex Mistletoe wine from the vintage; there is a combination of black, purple and red fruits (blackberry, plum and cherry) flowing through to the long finish. Screwcap. 13.8% alc. **Rating** 96 **To** 2049 $75 ✪

Reserve Hunter Valley Shiraz 2014 Has all the complexity and depth of its siblings, but is exceptionally supple and elegant; well and truly into blackberry territory, with exceptional length and balance. Screwcap. 13.8% alc. **Rating** 96 **To** 2054 $50 ✪

Reserve Hunter Valley Semillon 2015 Hand-picked, whole bunch-pressed, extended post-ferment on cold gross lees. Impressive flavour and intensity; how much is due to the lees contact we'll never know, and it really doesn't matter at the end of the day. Lemongrass, citrus and crisp acidity run through to the finish of a long palate. Screwcap. 10.7% alc. **Rating** 95 **To** 2027 $25 ✪

Home Vineyard Hunter Valley Shiraz 2014 Matured in French oak for 16 months. Attractive medium-bodied wine, perfect ripeness; plum dominant, allied with blackberry, earthy notes merely a background whisper; the tannins are exceptionally good, giving the wine a velvety texture. Screwcap. 13.5% alc. **Rating** 95 **To** 2040 $40

Reserve Hunter Valley Shiraz 2005 The third release (the first two '07 and '10) from one of the best vintages of the first decade of the new millennium, and still mooching along quietly. The colour is good, the bouquet a complex offering of black fruits, earth and leather faithfully reproduced by the medium-bodied palate. Gets an extra point to celebrate its age. Screwcap. 13% alc. **Rating** 95 **To** 2025 $75

Hilltops Shiraz Viognier 2014 97/3%, whole bunch viognier co-fermented, 15 days on skins, matured for 14 months in French (70%) and American oak. A prime example of the generosity and balance of Hilltops shiraz, the rich flavours cruising along and through the medium-bodied palate; tannins and oak are also part of the impressive picture. A seriously attractive wine, at a seriously attractive price. Screwcap. 13.8% alc. **Rating** 95 **To** 2029 $25 ✪

ΨΨΨΨΨ Hunter Shiraz 2014 Rating 93 To 2034 $30
Home Vineyard Hunter Valley Semillon 2015 Rating 93 To 2025 $22 ✪
Reserve Hunter Valley Chardonnay 2014 Rating 92 To 2033 $32
Barrel Fermented Hunter Valley Rose 2015 Rating 90 To 2020 $22

Mitchell   ★★★★★

Hughes Park Road, Sevenhill via Clare, SA 5453 **Region** Clare Valley
T (08) 8843 4258 **www**.mitchellwines.com **Open** 7 days 10–4
Winemaker Andrew Mitchell **Est.** 1975 **Dozens** 30 000 **Vyds** 75ha
One of the stalwarts of the Clare Valley, established by Jane and Andrew Mitchell, producing long-lived rieslings and cabernet sauvignons in classic regional style. The range now includes very creditable semillon, grenache and shiraz. A lovely old stone apple shed provides the cellar door and upper section of the upgraded winery. Children Angus and Edwina are now working in the business, heralding generational changes. Over the years the Mitchells have established or acquired 75ha of vineyards on four excellent sites, some vines over 50 years old; all are managed organically, with the use of biodynamic composts for over a decade. Exports to the UK, the US, Canada, Singapore, Hong Kong, China and NZ.

ΨΨΨΨΨ McNicol Clare Valley Riesling 2008 Mid-gold-green hue, no colour shift in the last 3½ years, and no sign of its unusual alcohol (a function of the vintage).

Breaks all the rules, but does so with real verve and style. Screwcap. 14% alc. **Rating** 96 **To** 2025 $35 ✪

Sevenhill Vineyard Cabernet Sauvignon 2012 Rich, firm and showing excellent persistence. There are no queries over the wine's complexity either. Dust, herbs, a juicy flow of blackcurrant, earthen notes, tobacco characters. Toasty oak is a subtle influence at most. Eucalypt characters are there, as rising agents, without ever threatening to dominate. And tannin is a solid, majestic swirl through the back half of the wine. Screwcap. 14.5% alc. **Rating** 95 **To** 2027 $30 CM ✪

Watervale Riesling 2015 Plenty of flesh and drive and, frankly, appeal. This looks the goods right now, though history as much as anything suggests it has plenty up its sleeve. Citrus and talc on a straight line of acidity. No-brainer. Screwcap. 13.5% alc. **Rating** 94 **To** 2025 $24 CM ✪

ⓎⓎⓎⓎⓎ **Peppertree Vineyard Clare Valley Shiraz 2013** Rating 93 **To** 2032 $28 CM
McNicol Clare Valley Shiraz 2008 Rating 92 **To** 2024 $45 CM
Clare Valley Semillon 2014 Rating 91 **To** 2019 $24 CM

Mitchell Harris Wines   ★★★★★

38 Doveton Street North, Ballarat, Vic 3350 **Region** Pyrenees
T 0417 566 025 **www**.mitchellharris.com.au **Open** Sun–Tues 11–6, Wed 11–9, Thurs–Sat 11–11
Winemaker John Harris **Est.** 2008 **Dozens** 1800
Mitchell Harris Wines is a partnership between Alicia and Craig Mitchell and Shannyn and John Harris, the latter winemaker for this eponymous producer. John began his career at Mount Avoca, then spent eight years as winemaker at Domaine Chandon in the Yarra Valley, cramming in northern hemisphere vintages in California and Oregon. The Mitchells grew up in the Ballarat area, and have an affinity for the Macedon and Pyrenees districts. While the total make is not large, a lot of thought has gone into the creation of each of the wines. In 2012 a multipurpose space was created in an 1880s brick workshop and warehouse, the renovation providing a cellar door and education facility.

ⓎⓎⓎⓎⓎ **Major by Mitchell Harris 2014** 60% cabernet sauvignon, 40% shiraz. The blend certainly doesn't lose its birthright. How John came up with the blend I don't know; was it pre-planned? It seems to grow the weight of the two components, yet retain the elegance. Diam. 13.5% alc. **Rating** 97 **To** 2044 $65 ✪

ⓎⓎⓎⓎⓎ **Pyrenees Shiraz 2014** Co-fermented with 2% viognier,. A strange business when you swear you can smell the elegance in the bouquet, but I did/do here. The vibrant red fruits, fine-grained tannins and silky smooth medium-bodied palate all deliver the goods. Screwcap. 13.5% alc. **Rating** 96 **To** 2029 $35 ✪

Pyrenees Cabernet Sauvignon 2014 The elegance I detected with the bouquet of the Shiraz came through with utmost clarity here; likewise the palate is effortless, despite the complex vinification, and despite the fact that cabernet is expected to inflict a certain amount of pain, here the dual faces of the variety are at peace with each other. Screwcap. 13% alc. **Rating** 96 **To** 2039 $30 ✪

Pyrenees Sauvignon Blanc Fume 2015 A powerful and complex wine thanks to the low yield in the vineyard; while it underwent partial mlf, wild fermentation of solids juice and spent 6 months on lees, it still ended up light on its feet, cleansed by a long, savoury finish. Screwcap. 13.3% alc. **Rating** 95 **To** 2018 $27 ✪

Pyrenees Sangiovese 2014 Bright hue, moderate depth, exactly what you expect from good sangiovese. The bright bowl of cherries (red and black) flows over, plus spice, plus chocolate – this is an Italian gelattoria. The twist of tannins on the finish brings it back into the real world in the best fashion. Value. Screwcap. 12.8% alc. **Rating** 95 **To** 2029 $30 ✪

ⓎⓎⓎⓎⓎ **Sabre 2012** Rating 90 **To** 2019 $42 TS

Mitolo Wines

PO Box 520, Virginia, SA 5120 **Region** McLaren Vale
T (08) 8282 9012 **www**.mitolowines.com.au **Open** Not
Winemaker Ben Glaetzer **Est.** 1999 **Dozens** 30 000
Mitolo had a meteoric rise once Frank Mitolo decided to turn a winemaking hobby into a business. In 2000 he took the plunge into the commercial end of the business, inviting Ben Glaetzer to make the wines. Split between the Jester range and single vineyard wines, Mitolo began life as a red wine-dominant brand, but now also produces Rose and Vermentino. Exports to all major markets.

ᵽᵽᵽᵽᵽ 7th Son 2014 48% grenache, 45% shiraz, 7% sagrantino. No one will go breaking the heart of cherry-plum flavour, the flash of herbs, the whispers of smoky oak here; tannin simply won't allow it. There are big ropes of the stuff wrapped firm around the hull of fruit. It's certainly not a wine for everyone, but there's an argument to say that it is quite monumental. Screwcap. 14.5% alc. **Rating** 96 To 2034 $35 CM ✪
Savitar McLaren Vale Shiraz 2013 Inky colour and flavour. Coconut oak nestles into blackberried fruit, the result intense in a cuddly way. That there is the main appeal, but it's not a one-trick pony: smoky, almost woody tones play along the background, aided by sweet roasted nut characters. Upper echelon without question. Screwcap. 14.5% alc. **Rating** 95 To 2032 $80 CM

ᵽᵽᵽᵽᵽ Angela McLaren Vale Shiraz 2014 Rating 93 To 2026 $35 CM
Jester McLaren Vale Shiraz 2014 Rating 93 To 2024 $25 CM ✪
Jester McLaren Vale Sangiovese Rose 2015 Rating 91 To 2017 $22 ✪
G.A.M. McLaren Vale Shiraz 2013 Rating 91 To 2026 $58 CM
The Nessus McLaren Vale Malbec 2014 Rating 91 To 2021 $15 CM ✪
Jester Cabernet Sauvignon 2014 Rating 90 To 2024 $25 CM

MoFro Wines

6 Dumfries Court, Moama, NSW 2731 (postal) **Region** Perricoota
T 0408 993 182 **www**.mofrowines.com.au **Open** Not
Winemaker Trent Eacott **Est.** 2014 **Dozens** 370 **Vyds** 7ha
This is the business of the Eacott family, father Alan and mother Susan the vignerons, son Trent the winemaker. It is situated on the northern banks of the Murray River. Most of the grapes from the 20yo plantings of cabernet sauvignon and shiraz are sold to other wineries, but a small amount is held back for the MoFro label.

Molly Morgan Vineyard

496 Talga Road, Rothbury, NSW 2320 **Region** Hunter Valley
T (02) 4930 7695 **www**.mollymorgan.com **Open** Not
Winemaker Rhys Eather **Est.** 1963 **Dozens** 2000 **Vyds** 7.65ha
Established by the Roberts family in 1963, later acquired by a syndicate headed by Andrew Simons from Camperdown Cellars, Molly Morgan focuses on estate-grown wines from vines now over 40 years old. The vineyard is named after an English beauty whose colourful life of theft, arson, cattle rustling and sly grog running led to her being transported as convict twice. Her generous financial support of the local community earned her the title of 'Queen of the Hunter'.

ᵽᵽᵽᵽᵽ MoMo Premium Reserve Shiraz 2014 Has all the attributes of its highly regional sibling, but with the intensity dialled up several notches. It was matured 'in a blend of French oak'. The slight astringency on the finish will be as much friend as foe in the years ahead. Screwcap. 14% alc. **Rating** 90 To 2034 $40

ᵽᵽᵽᵽ MoMo Semillon 2012 Rating 88 To 2022 $22
MoMo Shiraz 2014 Rating 88 To 2022 $30

Mon Tout

129 Brooks Road, Margaret River, WA 6285 **Region** Margaret River
T 0408 845 583 **www**.montout.com.au **Open** Not
Winemaker Richard Burch, Janice McDonald **Est.** 2014 **Dozens** NFP **Vyds** 28ha
This is the venture of second-generation vintner Richard Burch, son of Jeff and Amy
Burch. Between 2003 and '12 he managed to spend two years at Curtin University studying
viticulture and oenology, before deciding this wasn't his thing. He then had a gap year,
travelling through Europe and Asia with friends, before homing pigeon-like returning to
Perth to enrol in a three-degree wine marketing course at Edith Cowan University. Mon Tout
is a small separate venture from his position as brand manager for the east coast of Australia for
Burch Family Wines. The wines reflect Janice McDonald's exceptional experience and skill.

🍷🍷🍷🍷 **Biodynamic Margaret River Chardonnay 2015** Hand-picked from a
biodynamic vineyard in southern Margaret River, wild-fermented, matured in
French oak. An interesting mouthfeel and flavour profile; peach, fig and cashew
roll along the succulent palate, acidity enough to cleanse the finish, but no more.
Screwcap. 13% alc. **Rating** 94 **To** 2025 $30 ❂

🍷🍷🍷🍷 **Biodynamic Margaret River Rose 2015 Rating** 93 **To** 2016 $30 CM

Mons Rubra

Cheveley Road, Woodend North, Vic 3442 **Region** Macedon Ranges
T 0457 777 202 **www**.monsrubra.com **Open** Not
Winemaker Passing Clouds (Cameron Leith) **Est.** 2004 **Dozens** 400 **Vyds** 1ha
Mons Rubra has been developed by Max and Susan Haverfield. With a broad-based interest
in wine, and after some research, they purchased their property in the Macedon Ranges; it
is situated in the 600–700m elevation range, with friable volcanic soils. They settled on the
most widely propagated clone of pinot noir in Australia, MV6, which seems to perform well
wherever it is planted. Initially the wine was made by John Ellis at Hanging Rock (2004 to
'10), but it is now being made by the Leith family at their Passing Clouds winery at Musk.

🍷🍷🍷🍷 **Macedon Ranges Pinot Noir 2014** Five-day cold soak, cultured yeast
fermentation, pressed to French oak (35% new) for 12 months maturation.
A complex wine pointing to varied vinification methods. It has the depth and
stature of fully, but not over, ripe pinot, with savoury characters along with dark
plum and cherry fruit; the oak, too, has been well handled. A good outcome from
a vintage with some challenges. Screwcap. 13% alc. **Rating** 94 **To** 2022 $39

Montalto ★★★★★

33 Shoreham Road, Red Hill South, Vic 3937 **Region** Mornington Peninsula
T (03) 5989 8412 **www**.montalto.com.au **Open** 7 days 11–5
Winemaker Simon Black **Est.** 1998 **Dozens** 13 000 **Vyds** 46.9ha
John Mitchell and family established Montalto in 1998, but the core of the vineyard goes
back to '86. Ther vineyard is planted to pinot noir, chardonnay, pinot gris, riesling, shiraz,
tempranillo and sauvignon blanc. Intensive vineyard work opens up the canopy, with yields
ranging between 3.7 and 6.1 tonnes per hectare. Wines are released in three ranges, the flagship
Single Vineyard, Montalto and Pennon Hill. Montalto leases several vineyards that span the
Peninsula, giving vastly greater diversity of pinot noir sources, and greater insurance against
weather extremes. There is also a broad range of clones adding to that diversity. Montalto has
hit new heights with its wines from these blocks. Exports to China.

🍷🍷🍷🍷 **Single Vineyard Main Ridge Block Mornington Peninsula Pinot Noir
2014** Multiple trophy winner. It's not hard to see why. It's firm but bright, stern
but immediately attractive. It throws gorgeous scents of rosewater and strawberry
and pulls herbs, earth and dark cherry into the arena on the palate. It has the
bases covered and quite a bit extra. Indeed it's a humdinger. Screwcap. 13.7% alc.
Rating 97 **To** 2025 $70 CM ❂

ŸŸŸŸŸ **Estate Mornington Peninsula Shiraz 2014** Expressive, well flavoured, well structured and lengthy; but most of all, entrancing. Pepper and spice, star anise and black cherry, smoked meats and nuts, the whole kit and caboodle. But cohesive. Ask it over for dinner and you'll never want it to leave. Screwcap. 14.1% alc. **Rating** 96 To 2030 $50 CM ❂

Estate Mornington Peninsula Chardonnay 2014 It feels breezy and nonchalant, and yet its class is clear. The weight of stone fruit flavour is just so; the application of cedary/creamy oak likewise; and the chalky/citrussy length impressive, to say the least. It grows beautifully in the glass too; no matter how you serve it, it comes up trumps. Screwcap. 13% alc. **Rating** 95 To 2021 $42 CM

Estate Mornington Peninsula Pinot Gris 2015 Texture and flavour combine to create a rare beast of fearful symmetry; this is a wine of impact and drive and yet it slips and slides creamily as it travels through your mouth. Pleasure and finesse in one. Screwcap. 13.4% alc. **Rating** 95 To 2017 $36 CM

Single Vineyard Tuerong Block Mornington Peninsula Pinot Noir 2014 Fruit whistling through a forest of twigs and leaves and wood smoke. This is simultaneously characterful and pleasurable. Black cherries and strawberries lay the groundwork but various savoury/minerally inputs fly here and there. Screwcap. 13% alc. **Rating** 95 To 2021 $70 CM

Pennon Hill Mornington Peninsula Pinot Noir 2014 Announces itself with a blare of herb, spice and varietal fruit fragrance. You know you're onto something from the outset. The palate continues the show, all tang, herb, wood and sweet-sour fruit, a dry rake of tannin keeping undergrowth and herb notes well tilled. It's very tight; it needs time to relax. But it's also very good. Screwcap. 13% alc. **Rating** 95 To 2023 $50 CM

Single Vineyard The Eleven Mornington Peninsula Chardonnay 2014 As a wine it's like a bed of feathers. It's so soft and mellifluous it's almost ridiculous. It's all white peach and almonds, citrus and toasty oak. It slides through your mouth like a dream. Screwcap. 12.9% alc. **Rating** 94 To 2022 $60 CM

Pennon Hill Chardonnay 2014 If you met it at a party you'd be hoping it'd come home with you. It's affable, well mannered, has a bit of fun about it, and dips its lid to sophistication. One could ask or hope for little more. It lingers majestically through the finish; you can build your drinking life around wines like this. Screwcap. 13.1% alc. **Rating** 94 To 2020 $28 CM ❂

Pennon Hill Pinot Grigio 2015 It takes time to open up, not often said of pinot grigio, its complexities slowly revealed as its taut persona relaxes with air. Grapefruit, spice and citrus are the drivers, but it's the intensity of flavour and the honed length that really impress. A step beyond the norm. Screwcap. 13.3% alc. **Rating** 94 To 2017 $25 CM ❂

Pennon Hill Shiraz 2014 No mistaking its cool climate origin. Black pepper and snapped twig notes show through clearly, though the bloom of black cherry and plum flavour is the star of the show. Tannin is ripe and anise pokes its head above the parapet. The longer you sit with this wine, the more impressed you become. Screwcap. 13.6% alc. **Rating** 94 To 2016 $32 CM

ŸŸŸŸŸ **Estate Mornington Peninsula Riesling 2015** **Rating** 93 To 2020 $25 CM ❂
Merricks Block Pinot Noir 2014 **Rating** 93 To 2020 $70 CM
Pennon Hill Mornington Peninsula Sauvignon Blanc 2015 **Rating** 92 To 2017 $25 CM ❂
Pennon Hill Rose 2015 **Rating** 91 To 2017 $25 CM
Pennon Hill Tempranillo 2014 **Rating** 91 To 2021 $32 CM

Montara   ★★★★★

76 Chalambar Road, Ararat, Vic 3377 **Region** Grampians
T (03) 5352 3868 **www.**montarawines.com.au **Open** Fri–Sun 11–4
Winemaker Leigh Clarnette **Est.** 1970 **Dozens** 3000 **Vyds** 19.2ha
Gained considerable attention for its pinot noirs during the 1980s, and continues to produce wines of distinctive style under the ownership of no less than six siblings of the Stapleton

family. As I can attest from several visits over the years, the view from the cellar door is one of the best in the Grampians region. Exports to Canada, South Korea and China.

ŶŶŶŶŶ **Grampians Riesling 2015** A striking wine given its youth; already full to the gunnels with delicious Bickford's lime juice. It has the length and balance to see it safely through some years to come, but it will never be more enjoyable than it is now. Gold medal Victorian Wine Show '15. Screwcap. 11.5% alc. **Rating** 95 To 2019 $23 ✪

Chalambar Road Grampians Shiraz 2013 Chalambar Road is the address of Montara, the vineyards on slopes draining cold air at night. This full-bodied shiraz speaks eloquently of the cool climate, with spice, pepper, graphite and tar all embedded in the untold depths of the fruit. Cork. 14% alc. **Rating** 95 To 2043 $70

Gold Rush Grampians Riesling 2015 Light straw-green; positively glows with its display of lime, lemon and pink grapefruit flavours. Odds on to be gulped down long before it achieves its destiny, but arguably there's no harm in that. Screwcap. 11.5% alc. **Rating** 94 To 2025 $23 ✪

Gold Rush Grampians Chardonnay 2014 Two clones picked separately, fermented and matured in French oak (35% new) for 11 months. This is well made, with a flinty/minerally nuance running through the juicy cool-grown, grapefruit-dominant, palate. Screwcap. 13% alc. **Rating** 94 To 2023 $23 ✪

Chalambar Road Grampians Cabernet Sauvignon 2013 The juicy fruit of Montara's red wines comes through strongly, 40yo vines certainly contributing to the flavour and layered mouthfeel. It's not often a cabernet flashes a come-hither sign, but this does. Screwcap. 14% alc. **Rating** 94 To 2030 $70

ŶŶŶŶŶ **Gold Rush Grampians Cabernet Sauvignon 2013** Rating 90 To 2023 $25

Montgomery's Hill ★★★★☆

South Coast Highway, Upper Kalgan, Albany, WA 6330 **Region** Albany
T (08) 9844 3715 **www**.montgomeryshill.com.au **Open** 7 days 11–5 (Jun–Aug 12–4)
Winemaker Plantagenet, Castle Rock **Est.** 1996 **Dozens** 6000
Montgomery's Hill is 16km northeast of Albany on a north-facing slope on the banks of the Kalgan River. Previously an apple orchard, it is a diversification for the third generation of the Montgomery family, Pamela and Murray. Chardonnay, cabernet sauvignon, cabernet franc, sauvignon blanc, shiraz and merlot were planted in 1996–97. The elegant wines are made with a gentle touch, and offer excellent value.

ŶŶŶŶŶ **Albany Cabernet Sauvignon 2014** Excellent colour; a very intense, full-bodied cabernet of striking purity and integrity, blackcurrant/cassis, graphite, bay leaf and built-in tannins all doing what comes naturally, cedary oak almost an accidental bystander. Will be phenomenally long-lived. Screwcap. 13.5% alc. Rating 95 To 2044 $25 ✪

Albany Sauvignon Blanc 2015 Paints the entire canvas with snow pea, grass and wild herb through to passionfruit, guava and lychee fruit, a sturdy frame provided by lingering acidity keeping the canvas tight. Screwcap. 13% alc. Rating 94 To 2017

Albany Merlot 2014 A merlot of rare power and conviction, full of blackcurrant fruit, spice and a splash of plum; the tannins are there, but are sheathed, and oak is likewise consigned to a support role. Its balance is excellent, guaranteeing future development. Screwcap. 13.5% alc. **Rating** 94 To 2030

ŶŶŶŶŶ **Albany Shiraz 2014** Rating 92 To 2029 $28
Albany Cabernet Merlot 2014 Rating 92 To 2034

Montvalley   ★★★★

150 Mitchells Road, Mount View, NSW 2325 (postal) **Region** Hunter Valley
T (02) 4991 7993 **www.**montvalley.com.au **Open** Not
Winemaker Daniel Binet **Est.** 1998 **Dozens** 2000 **Vyds** 5.7ha
Having looked at dozens of properties over the previous decade, John and Deirdre Colvin
purchased their 80ha property in 1998. They chose the name Montvalley in part because
it reflects the beautiful valley in the Brokenback Ranges of which the property forms part,
and in part because the name Colvin originates from France, 'col' meaning valley and 'vin'
meaning vines. They have planted almost 6ha of vines, the lion's share to shiraz, with lesser
amounts of chardonnay and semillon.

♥♥♥♥♥ **Hunter Valley Shiraz 2014** Matured for 13 months in used French and
American oak. It has a fragrant array of red fruits that play out on the juicy palate.
Another take on the '14 vintage: unusual, but utterly convincing, silky tannins
providing context. Screwcap. 13.5% alc. **Rating** 94 To 2034 $30 ✪

♥♥♥♥♡ **Hunter Valley Chardonnay 2014** Rating 93 To 2024 $27 ✪
Hunter Valley Semillon 2014 Rating 91 To 2034 $30
Lightly Oaked Hunter Valley Chardonnay 2014 Rating 90 To 2024 $27

Moombaki Wines   ★★★★★

341 Parker Road, Kentdale via Denmark, WA 6333 **Region** Denmark
T (08) 9840 8006 **www.**moombaki.com **Open** 7 days 11–5
Winemaker Harewood Estate (James Kellie) **Est.** 1997 **Dozens** 900 **Vyds** 2.4ha
David Britten and Melissa Boughey established vines on a north-facing gravel hillside with
picturesque Kent River frontage. Not content with establishing the vineyard (cabernet
sauvignon, shiraz, cabernet franc, malbec and chardonnay), they put in significant mixed tree
plantings to increase wildlife habitats. They chose Moombaki as their vineyard name: it is a
local Aboriginal word meaning 'where the river meets the sky'.

♥♥♥♥♥ **Chardonnay 2014** It's easier said than done to preserve elegance while satisfying
the need for ample varietal fruit expression. All of which is a roundabout way of
saying that this has white peach and pink grapefruit aromas and flavours on a long,
fluid and graceful palate. Screwcap. 13.5% alc. **Rating** 95 To 2021 $39
Shiraz 2013 A finely detailed, light to medium-bodied shiraz, parading its
cool climate origins, picked before it lost any of its natural acidity; the result is a
delicious wine, spicy/peppery notes tucked in the pockets of red fruits, adding
another mile or two to the length of the finish. Screwcap. 13% alc. **Rating** 95
To 2028 $39
Museum Release Reserve 2005 Little change over the past 18 months,
the tannins are in balance: still holding its colour very well; an elegant blend of
cabernet sauvignon, shiraz, cabernet franc and malbec, now with cedary/cigar
box flavours joining black fruits, hallmark savoury tannins doing no more than
providing a platform for and extending the finish of a complex wine, time still on
its side. 840 numbered bottles. Screwcap. 14% alc. **Rating** 95 To 2025 $105
Cabernet Sauvignon Cabernet Franc Malbec 2013 50/27/23%. The
savoury tannins of Moombaki are part of every one of its red wines, young or old,
doubtless extracted by the long post-ferment maceration. It's a question of degree,
however: the '05 Museum Release shows the fruit can live longer than the tannins,
and here there is a cornucopia of blackcurrant/cassis, redcurrant and mulberry all
confronting the tannins. Screwcap. 14% alc. **Rating** 94 To 2028 $39

♥♥♥♥♡ **Museum Release Shiraz 2008** Rating 90 To 2020 $75

Moondah Brook   ★★★

Dale Road, Middle Swan, WA 6056 **Region** Swan Valley
T 1800 088 711 **www.**moondahbrook.com.au **Open** Not
Winemaker Garth Cliff **Est.** 1968 **Dozens** NFP

Part of Accolade Wines, Moondah Brook has its own special character, as it draws part of its fruit from the large Gingin vineyard, 70km north of the Swan Valley, and part from Margaret River and Great Southern. From time to time it has exceeded its own reputation for reliability with some quite lovely wines, in particular honeyed Chenin Blanc, generous Shiraz and finely structured Cabernet Sauvignon. But not this year. Exports to Asia.

♥♥♥♥ **Cabernet Sauvignon 2012** Is still youthful, and has strong blackcurrant fruit, but the oak is in your face and needs to settle down. Screwcap. 13.5% alc. Rating 88 To 2020 $16 ✪

Moores Hill Estate   ★★★★☆

3343 West Tamar Highway, Sidmouth, Tas 7270 **Region** Northern Tasmania
T (03) 6394 7649 **www**.mooreshill.com.au **Open** 7 days 10–5
Winemaker Julian Allport **Est.** 1997 **Dozens** 4000 **Vyds** 4.5ha
The Moores Hill Estate vineyard (jointly owned by winemaker Julian Allport with Fiona and Lance Weller) consists of pinot noir, chardonnay and riesling, with a very small amount of cabernet sauvignon and merlot. The vines are located on a northeast-facing hillside, 5km from the Tamar River and 30km from Bass Strait.

♥♥♥♥♥ **Riesling 2015** Gorgeous flavour and persistence. Lemon and lime sorbet. It's not complex but it doesn't need to be. Screwcap. 12.4% alc. Rating 94 To 2028 $32 CM

Pinot Gris 2015 Soft and flowing but with plenty of kick to the flavour. One of those 'more please, if you insist' wines; not something you often say of gris. Honeysuckle, fresh pear and citrus flavour. Feels beautiful in the mouth. Screwcap. 13.9% alc. Rating 94 To 2017 $30 CM ✪

Pinot Noir 2014 The road to flavour is covered in satin. Foresty plum notes come layered with wood spice and bright red cherry. Texture and length though are the keys to the wine's indisputable quality. Screwcap. 13.2% alc. Rating 94 To 2023 $40 CM

CGR Late Harvest Riesling 2015 Intensity is very good to excellent but it's the zing of flavour-filled acidity that really elevates it. A grapey ripeness, penetrating lime, apple and spice; captivatingly clean and lively. Screwcap. 8.8% alc. Rating 94 To 2018 $35 CM

♥♥♥♥♡ **Tasmania Blanc de Blancs NV** Rating 91 To 2018 $45 TS

Moorilla Estate   ★★★★★

655 Main Road, Berriedale, Tas 7011 **Region** Southern Tasmania
T (03) 6277 9900 **www**.moorilla.com.au **Open** Wed–Mon 9.30–5
Winemaker Conor van der Reest **Est.** 1958 **Dozens** 9400 **Vyds** 15.36ha
Moorilla Estate was the second winery to be established in Tasmania in the 20th century, Jean Miguet's La Provence beating it to the punch by two years. However, through much of the history of Moorilla Estate, it was the most important winery in the state, if not in size but as the icon. Magnificently situated on a mini-isthmus reaching into the Derwent River, it has always been a must-visit for wine lovers and tourists. Production is around 90 tonnes per year, sourced entirely from the vineyards around Moorilla and its St Matthias Vineyard (Tamar Valley). The winery is part of an overall development said by observers (not Moorilla) to have cost upwards of $150 million. Its raison d'être is the establishment of an art gallery (MONA) that has the highest atmospheric environment accreditation of any gallery in the southern hemisphere, housing both the extraordinary ancient and contemporary art collection assembled by Moorilla's owner, David Walsh, and visiting exhibitions from major art museums around the world. Exports to the UK and Hong Kong.

♥♥♥♥♥ **Muse Pinot Noir 2013** From five parts of the vineyard on the west bank of the Derwent River, an exceedingly complex choice of winemaking techniques A deadset serious pinot, not to be undertaken lightly. The bouquet sets the scene, posing all manner of questions, the palate doubling the volume of the

Q&A process. Violets, spice, cedar, warm earth, black and red cherry, persistent, fine tannins and a legitimate sword of oak. Screwcap. 13.8% alc. **Rating** 96 **To** 2028 $55 **○**

Muse St Matthias Vineyard Chardonnay 2014 Incredibly complex vinification with each barrel treated as a separate ferment with some wild, some cultured yeast and numerous other permutations and combinations. It is quite possible for confusion to reign supreme as each contribution cancels the other out, but here the message is fragrantly bright and clear grapefruit juice, zest and pith in one stream, white peach and cashew in another, all in the thrall of quite beautiful acidity. Screwcap. 13.6% alc. **Rating** 95 **To** 2022 $45

Cloth Label White 2013 21% sauvignon blanc, 19% each chardonnay and gewurztraminer, 16% riesling, 13% pinot gris and 12% pinot noir, each fermented for a short time on skins, matured in French oak for 14 months. This is in a class all of its own, succeeding where the Cloth Label Red failed, textured and balanced, with a field of flowers in its flavour spectrum. I'm not persuaded by the price, but I can visualise a likely market target that happily will be. Go north, young man. Screwcap. 12.7% alc. **Rating** 95 **To** 2023 $110

Praxis St Matthias Vineyard Pinot Noir 2014 Light, but bright hue; winemaker Conor van der Reest was a wild child winemaker when he arrived at Moorilla in '09, but now has impressive control over the untold complexities of sculpting each wine he makes. This is a fine example: while light-bodied, it is very complex, with a thrilling tension between its red fruits and savoury side lights. Drink now or later – it's up to you. Screwcap. 13.5% alc. **Rating** 95 **To** 2023 $32 **○**

Muse St Matthias Vineyard Syrah 2013 Ok, this is a very cool climate in which to be playing with shiraz, not unlike Germany. But Conor van der Reest has matured exceptionally well as a winemaker, now with an enviable accumulation of knowledge. This is perfumed, elegant, and absolutely flavour-ripe. Screwcap. 13.6% alc. **Rating** 95 **To** 2028 $65

Muse Extra Brut Rose Methode Traditionelle 2010 Ten per cent blended pinot noir red wine delivers a pale salmon hue and draws out elegant red cherry and red berry fruits. 4+ years on lees has built a mouthfilling texture. Gold medal at the Tasmanian Wine Show '15. Diam. 11.9% alc. **Rating** 95 **To** 2022 $49

Muse St Matthias Vineyard Pinot Gris 2015 Has a distinct pink tinge, most likely ex the stainless steel destemmed portion. In best Moorilla Estate tradition, this doesn't leave anything on the floor; a complex whirl of fresh and poached clove-spiced pear, then a crisp finish. Screwcap. 13.4% alc. **Rating** 94 **To** 2017 $32

🍷🍷🍷🍷🍷 **Praxis Sauvignon Blanc 2015 Rating** 91 **To** 2017 $25
Muse Sauvignon 2014 Rating 91 **To** 2017 $30
Praxis Chardonnay Musque 2015 Rating 90 **To** 2021 $28

Moorooduc Estate ★★★★★

501 Derril Road, Moorooduc, Vic 3936 **Region** Mornington Peninsula
T (03) 5971 8506 **www**.moorooducestate.com.au **Open** 7 days 11–5
Winemaker Dr Richard McIntyre **Est.** 1983 **Dozens** 5000 **Vyds** 6.5ha

Richard McIntyre has taken Moorooduc Estate to new heights, having completely mastered the difficult art of gaining maximum results from wild yeast fermentations. Starting with the 2010 vintage, there was a complete revamp of grape sources, and hence changes to the tiered structure of the releases. These changes were driven by the simple fact that the estate vineyards had no possibility of providing the 5000–6000 dozen bottles of wine sold each year. The entry point wines under the Devil Bend Creek label remain, as before, principally sourced from the Osborn Vineyard. The mid-priced Chardonnay and Pinot Noir are no longer single-estate vineyard wines, and are now simply labelled by vintage and variety. Next come the Robinson Vineyard Pinot Noir and Chardonnay, elevated to reserve wine status, priced a little below the ultimate 'Ducs' (The Moorooduc McIntyre). Exports to the UK, the US, Canada, Hong Kong and Singapore.

ΨΨΨΨΨ **The Moorooduc McIntyre Pinot Noir 2014** The colour gives no clue about
the velvety richness and depth of the aromas and tastes of this wine. It's far from
the big end of town, but it's smooth and sophisticated, blood plum, satsuma
plum, spiced plum; a beautifully crafted, fine and fresh finish. Screwcap. 14% alc.
Rating 97 **To** 2026 $65 ✪
The Moorooduc McIntyre Pinot Noir 2013 Deep, bright colour, with a
haunting array of aromas ranging through spiced plums to hints of forest floor and
truffles, the palate nonchalantly picking up the thread and amplifying it. This has
far more weight and vinosity than most from the region, with even greater things
to come over the next 10 years. Screwcap. 14% alc. **Rating** 97 **To** 2028 $65 ✪

ΨΨΨΨΨ **The Moorooduc McIntyre Chardonnay 2014** The deeper, though still bright,
colour of this chardonnay sends a very accurate message of grilled cashew, fig,
white peach and nectarine arriving all at once on the palate. Hedonism lives.
Screwcap. 12.5% alc. **Rating** 96 **To** 2025 $65 ✪
Robinson Vineyard Chardonnay 2014 Fresh, lively and crisp is take 1; take
2 is the intense squeaky acidity that appears without warning; take 3 is the blend
of stone and citrus fruits; and take 4 the nutty/creamy notes ex mlf and oak.
Screwcap. 12% alc. **Rating** 95 **To** 2024 $55
Robinson Vineyard Pinot Noir 2014 The fragrant, savoury, spicy bouquet is
alluring, its cherry blossom bouquet giving a big come-on to anyone caring to
look twice; the palate, while fresh and juicy, introduces a gentle savoury back-
palate and finish. Screwcap. 14% alc. **Rating** 95 **To** 2028 $55

Moortangi Estate ★★★★

120 Wills Road, Dixons Creek, Vic 3775 **Region** Yarra Valley
T (03) 9600 4001 **www**.moortangiestate.com.au **Open** Not
Winemaker Sergio Carlei **Est.** 2002 **Dozens** NA **Vyds** 5.75ha
Paul and Pamela Hyland purchased a beautiful grazing property at Dixons Creek already
christened 'Moortangi'. They planted the north-facing paddocks with shiraz (4ha), cabernet
sauvignon (0.9ha), merlot (0.5ha) and viognier (0.35ha), and while waiting for the vines
to mature purchased shiraz from Heathcote for their first vintage. They have continued to
make the Old Vine Heathcote Shiraz from vines planted in the 1950s in grey loam soils, the
Cambrian Shiraz from red soils. By 2009 the vines were flourishing and they anticipated their
first vintage, but the Black Saturday bushfires devastated the property, destroying the majority
of their vines. In 2010 they saw shoots on their main planting of shiraz, and they have since
laboriously resurrected the vineyard on a vine-by-vine basis, and now oversee what they
regard as an exceptional vineyard. They say their love of wine brought them to this place, and
has been sorely tested, but ultimately fulfilled.

ΨΨΨΨΨ **Cambrian Shiraz 2010** Open-fermented in large wooden vats, matured for
18 months in new and used French oak. A full-bodied and complex wine; satsuma
plum, blackberry and spice have a heavy-duty foundation of tannins and oak that
will sustain it for years. Diam. 13.5% alc. **Rating** 92 **To** 2030 $35

Moppity Vineyards ★★★★★

Moppity Road, Young, NSW 2594 (postal) **Region** Hilltops
T (02) 6382 6222 **www**.moppity.com.au **Open** Not
Winemaker Jason Brown **Est.** 1973 **Dozens** 30 000 **Vyds** 73ha
Jason Brown and wife Alecia, with backgrounds in fine wine retail and accounting, purchased
Moppity Vineyards in 2004 when it was already 31 years old. Initially they were content to
sell the grapes to other makers, but that changed with the release of the '06 Shiraz, which
won top gold in its class at the London International Wine & Spirit Competition. In Nov
'09 the '08 Eden Road Long Road Hilltops Shiraz, made from Moppity Vineyards grapes,
won the Jimmy Watson Trophy. These awards are among a cascade of golds for its Shirazs,
Riesling, Tumbarumba Chardonnay and Cabernet Sauvignon. Production (and sales) have
soared, and all of the grapes from the estate are now used for the Moppity Vineyards brand.

The Lock & Key range provides exceptional value for money. Moppity has also established Coppabella, a separate venture, in Tumbarumba. Exports to the UK and China.

🍷🍷🍷🍷🍷 **Reserve Hilltops Shiraz 2014** The colour is perfect, the bouquet full of black fruit promise, but it is the immediacy and intensity of the attack of the fruit on the palate that leaves no doubt that the winemaking team was given full discretion on the cut-off point for inclusion under this label. Super-intense and spicy/pepper fruit, high quality oak and firmly focused tannins make an unforgettable taste experience. Screwcap. 13.9% alc. **Rating** 97 **To** 2045 $70 ✪

🍷🍷🍷🍷🍷 **Reserve Hilltops Cabernet Sauvignon 2014** Produced from old vines yielding only 1 tonne per acre. The deep crimson-purple colour is matched by the intensity of the cassis, black olive and dried herb fruit; high quality oak and ripe, gravelly tannins complete a wine of undoubted excellence. Screwcap. 13.9% alc. **Rating** 96 **To** 2044 $70 ✪

Estate Hilltops Cabernet Sauvignon 2014 An ultra-expressive bouquet, cassis, with a handmaiden of oak. Nigh-on the perfect expression of cool grown cabernet, cassis, gossamer tannins and cedary oak a silken cord without end. One trophy and seven gold medals. Screwcap. 14% alc. **Rating** 96 **To** 2040 $32 ✪

Estate Tumbarumba Chardonnay 2014 A fragrant, flowery bouquet leads (logically) into a zesty palate with both focus and length to its display of grapefruit and white stone fruit wreathed in mouthwatering acidity, French oak precisely positioned and weighted. Two trophies Australian Small Winemakers Show '15. Screwcap. 13% alc. **Rating** 95 **To** 2022 $32 ✪

Estate Hilltops Shiraz 2014 High quality shiraz, with everything just where it should be, and sending all the right messages. The firm blackberry and plum fruit carries the oak with nonchalance, and welcomes the textural support of the ripe tannins. Length. Balance. From the right side of the tracks. Screwcap. 14% alc. **Rating** 95 **To** 2034 $32 ✪

Estate Hilltops Merlot 2014 This looks towards Pomerol, Bordeaux for its inspiration. Plum doesn't feature in its make-up, ousted by a blend of vibrant fruit, bay leaf and persistent, fine-grained tannins; cedary oak also makes a contribution. Screwcap. 13.9% alc. **Rating** 95 **To** 2029 $32 ✪

Reserve Hilltops Cabernet Sauvignon 2013 A very elegant cabernet, little more than medium-bodied, but with plenty to say about its place and variety. Cassis drives the bouquet, hand in glove with quality French oak, black olive and bay leaf joining the ripe tannins that embroider the palate and its long finish. Screwcap. 13.9% alc. **Rating** 95 **To** 2033 $70

Atticus 2013 Shades of Harper Lee and *Go Set a Watchman*? From small parcels of the oldest vines on the vineyard, Moppity's standard-bearer. Its colour isn't particularly deep, but the fragrance of its black fruits (tinged with red) and the length of its medium-bodied, sinuous palate are most attractive. Screwcap. 13% alc. **Rating** 95 **To** 2028 $70

Lock & Key Chardonnay 2014 Bright straw-green; classic grapefruit and white peach aromas and flavours; particularly good length, likewise oak balance and integration, finishes with crisp acidity. Exceptional bargain. Screwcap. 12.5% alc. **Rating** 94 **To** 2020 $20 ✪

Lock & Key Shiraz 2014 Good hue and depth to the colour; a prime example of cool grown shiraz, its quality conferred by the 40yo estate vineyard and skilled winemaking. Blackberry and plum fruit drives the bouquet and medium to full-bodied palate, with a touch of choc-mint adding to the flavour parcel, ripe tannins to the structure. Screwcap. 14% alc. **Rating** 94 **To** 2034 $20 ✪

Lock & Key Reserve Shiraz 2014 Matured in used ('passive') French oak. The hue is excellent crimson-purple, sending the right message for a wine that, while ready for business tonight, can be confidently cellared. Red fruits, soft tannins and somewhat more oak influence than the back label suggests, albeit tending to mocha. Very nice wine. Screwcap. 14% alc. **Rating** 94 **To** 2025 $27 ✪

Lock & Key Reserve Tempranillo 2014 Good hue, although not especially deep, sends an ambivalent message that is immediately swept to one side by the layered richness of the red and black cherry fruits; oak and tannin management has also been exemplary. Screwcap. 13.5% alc. **Rating** 94 **To** 2029 $27 ●

ＹＹＹＹＹ **Lock & Key Merlot 2014 Rating** 93 **To** 2024 $20 ●
Lock & Key Rose 2015 Rating 92 **To** 2017 $20 ●
Lock & Key Reserve Cabernet Sauvignon 2014 Rating 91 **To** 2029 $27

Morambro Creek Wines ★★★★☆

PMB 98, Naracoorte, SA 5271 (postal) **Region** Padthaway
T (08) 8765 6043 **www**.morambrocreek.com.au **Open** Not
Winemaker Ben Riggs **Est.** 1994 **Dozens** 30 000 **Vyds** 178.5ha
The Bryson family has been involved in agriculture for more than a century, moving to Padthaway in 1955 as farmers and graziers. Since the '90s, they have progressively established large plantings of shiraz (88.5ha), cabernet sauvignon (47.5ha), chardonnay (34.5ha) and sauvignon blanc (8ha). The Morambro Creek and Mt Monster wines have been consistent winners of wine show medals, but the current releases take the wines onto a level not previously achieved. Exports to the UK, the US and other major markets.

ＹＹＹＹＹ **The Bryson Barrel Select 2013** 55% shiraz and 45% cabernet sauvignon. Intense purple-crimson colour, and a notably complex array of fruit aromas and flavours augmented by 18 months in new and used French and American oak. Plum cake, dark chocolate and gently chewy tannins are all part of a complex jigsaw puzzle. Screwcap. 14.5% alc. **Rating** 94 **To** 2028 $55

ＹＹＹＹＹ **Padthaway Shiraz 2013 Rating** 92 **To** 2033 $35
Jip Jip Rocks Padthaway Shiraz 2014 Rating 91 **To** 2029 $21 ●
Jip Jip Rocks Padthaway Sauvignon Blanc 2015 Rating 90 **To** 2016 $21 ●

Morgan Simpson ★★★

PO Box 39, Kensington Park, SA 5068 **Region** McLaren Vale
T 0417 843 118 **www**.morgansimpson.com.au **Open** Not
Winemaker Richard Simpson **Est.** 1998 **Dozens** 1200 **Vyds** 20.9ha
Morgan Simpson was founded by SA businessman George Morgan (since retired) and winemaker Richard Simpson, who is a graduate of CSU. The grapes are sourced from the Clos Robert Vineyard (where the wine is made), planted to shiraz (10.8ha), cabernet sauvignon (3.8ha), mourvedre (3.5ha) and chardonnay (1.8ha), established by Robert Allen Simpson in 1972. Most of the grapes are sold, the remainder used to provide the reasonably priced, drinkable wines for which Morgan Simpson has become well known.

Morgan Vineyards ★★★★

30 Davross Court, Seville, Vic 3139 **Region** Yarra Valley
T 0422 396 356 **www**.morganvineyards.net.au **Open** Thurs–Sun 11–5
Winemaker Andy Matthews **Est.** 1971 **Dozens** 1200 **Vyds** 4.8ha
Founder Roger Morgan planted cabernet sauvignon and pinot noir in 1971, extending those plantings over '89–'91, adding merlot in the same year, and chardonnay two years later. The property was purchased by Simon and Michele Gunther in 2009. They have since done considerable work in rejuvenating the vineyard and surrounding land.

ＹＹＹＹＹ **Yarra Valley Merlot 2014** Very foresty/savoury/herbal/black olive, but all within the range of cool grown merlot flavours, especially when its plentiful blackcurrant fruit is factored in. Definitely looks to Bordeaux rather than to warm grown Napa Valley or Australian merlot. Gold medal Melbourne Wine Awards '15. Screwcap. 13.6% alc. **Rating** 95 **To** 2029 $35 ●

ＹＹＹＹ **Yarra Valley Pinot Noir 2014 Rating** 89 **To** 2025 $35
Yarra Valley Cabernet Sauvignon 2013 Rating 88 **To** 2028 $35

Morningside Vineyard

711 Middle Tea Tree Road, Tea Tree, Tas 7017 **Region** Southern Tasmania
T (03) 6268 1748 **Open** By appt
Winemaker Peter Bosworth **Est.** 1980 **Dozens** 600 **Vyds** 2.8ha
The name 'Morningside' was given to the old property on which the vineyard stands because it gets the morning sun first; the property on the other side of the valley was known as Eveningside. Consistent with the observation of the early settlers, the Morningside grapes achieve full maturity with good colour and varietal flavour. Production will increase as the vineyard matures; recent additions of clonally selected pinot noir (including 8104, 115 and 777) are now in bearing. The Bosworth family, headed by Peter and wife Brenda, do all the vineyard and winery work, with conspicuous attention to detail.

ŸŸŸŸŸ **Pinot Noir 2013** All class; the stars of colour, bouquet and palate are all in alignment; wafts of spice and forest intermingle with red cherries and black, the savoury, complex palate seamlessly picking up the theme, extending it through to the long finish. Screwcap. 13.7% alc. **Rating** 95 **To** 2023 $35 ✪

ŸŸŸŸŸ **Riesling 2015 Rating** 93 **To** 2024 $25 CM ✪

Morris

Mia Mia Road, Rutherglen, Vic 3685 **Region** Rutherglen
T (02) 6026 7303 **www**.morriswines.com.au **Open** Mon–Sat 9–5, Sun 10–5
Winemaker David Morris **Est.** 1859 **Dozens** 100 000 **Vyds** 96ha
One of the greatest of the fortified winemakers, ranking with Chambers Rosewood. Morris has changed the labelling system for its sublime fortified wines, with a higher-than-average entry point for the (Classic) Liqueur Muscat; Tokay and the ultra-premium wines are being released under the Old Premium Liqueur (Rare) label. The art of these wines lies in the blending of very old and much younger material. They have no equivalent in any other part of the world.

ŸŸŸŸŸ **Old Premium Rare Liqueur Muscat NV** Deep olive-brown, coating the sides of the glass briefly when it is swirled; needless to say, is exceptionally rich and luscious, but – even more – complex, with a dense array of oriental sweet spices, dried raisins, and (for me) childhood memories of mother's Christmas pudding laced with brandy. And, yes, this really does go with dark, bitter chocolate in any form. 500ml. Cork. 17.5% alc. **Rating** 98 **To** 2018 $50 ✪

ŸŸŸŸŸ **Cellar Reserve Grand Tawny NV** Medium depth to the colour, true tawny and not liqueur; a vibrant palate, with rich and luscious fruit, then extreme rancio providing perfect balance, the acidity neither biting nor volatile. Great texture. 500ml. Cork. 18% alc. **Rating** 96 **To** 2013 $50 ✪
Old Premium Rare Liqueur Topaque NV Mahogany, with an olive rim; aromas of Christmas cake and tea; incredibly viscous and rich, with layer upon layer of flavours ranging through ginger snap, burnt butterscotch, and every imaginable spice, the length and depth of the palate as extraordinary as is that of the aftertaste. Released in tiny quantities each year, maintaining the extreme average age of each release. 500ml. Screwcap. 18% alc. **Rating** 96 **To** 2018 $75 ✪
Cellar One Classic Liqueur Rutherglen Topaque NV Great topaque and muscat are made with the young wines as the starting point, and they have to be good. This wine is that and then some, with full-on butterscotch, tea leaf, cup cake and crème brûlée flavours, reaching a peak on the back-palate before drying out nicely on the finish, leaving the mouth fresh and looking for the next sip. 500ml. Screwcap. 17.5% alc. **Rating** 94 **To** 2018 $35

ŸŸŸŸŸ **Classic Liqueur Topaque NV Rating** 93 **To** 2013 $21 ✪
Classic Liqueur Muscat NV Rating 93 **To** 2018 $21 ✪

Mosquito Hill Wines

18 Trinity Street, College Park, SA 5069 (postal) **Region** Southern Fleurieu
T 0411 661 149 **www**.mosquitohillwines.com.au **Open** Not
Winemaker Glyn Jamieson **Est.** 2004 **Dozens** 1700 **Vyds** 4.2ha
This is the venture of Glyn Jamieson, who happens to be the prestigious Dorothy Mortlock
Professor and Chairman of the Department of Surgery of the University of Adelaide. His
interest in wine dates back decades, and in 1994 he commenced the part-time (distance)
degree at CSU: he says that while he never failed an exam, it did take him 11 years to
complete the course. A year in France directed him to Burgundy, rather than Bordeaux,
hence the planting of chardonnay, pinot blanc and savagnin on the slopes of Mt Jagged on the
Magpies Song Vineyard and pinot noir (clones 114 and MV6) on the Hawthorns Vineyard. He
built a small onsite winery for the first vintage in 2011. Exports to Hong Kong.

ŸŸŸŸŸ **Chardonnay 2015** Whole bunch-pressed to French barriques (30% new). This
is a chardonnay with attitude, complexity and varietal character all on immediate
display, so much so I think the window of opportunity will be wide open for the
next 3 years. Screwcap. 12.9% alc. **Rating** 94 **To** 2019 $24 ❸

ŸŸŸŸŸ **Pinot Blanc 2015 Rating** 90 **To** 2018 $24
Pinot Noir 2014 Rating 90 **To** 2019 $33
Seven Barrels Pinot Noir 2012 Rating 90 **To** 2019 $55

Moss Wood

★★★★★

926 Metricup Road, Wilyabrup, WA 6284 **Region** Margaret River
T (08) 9755 6266 **www**.mosswood.com.au **Open** By appt
Winemaker Clare and Keith Mugford **Est.** 1969 **Dozens** 14 000 **Vyds** 18.14ha
Widely regarded as one of the best wineries in the region, producing glorious Chardonnay,
power-laden Semillon and elegant Cabernet Sauvignon that lives for decades. Moss Wood also
owns the Ribbon Vale Estate, the wines treated as vineyard-designated within the Moss Wood
umbrella. The current releases are of exceptionally high quality. Exports to all major markets.

ŸŸŸŸŸ **Wilyabrup Margaret River Cabernet Sauvignon 2012** The high quality
vintage shines through this wine, illuminating its intricate multifaceted complexity;
almost, but not quite, juicy cassis fruit is swathed in perfectly balanced French
oak and gently ripe tannins. The only problem will be keeping your hands off it.
Screwcap. 14% alc. **Rating** 98 **To** 2042 $125 ❸
Ribbon Vale Vineyard Wilyabrup Margaret River Merlot 2013
92% merlot, 8% cabernet franc, matured in French oak for 30 months. If
there's a better merlot in Australia, please get its maker to send a bottle for
tasting. The bouquet is perfumed, and multifaceted, red fruits, spice and French
oak all competing for space, the palate an object lesson in terms of flavours
(predominantly red fruits), texture (supple) and structure (superfine tannins). The
oak? Well, yes, it's there. Screwcap. 13.5% alc. **Rating** 97 **To** 2038 $60 ❸
Wilyabrup Margaret River Cabernet Sauvignon 2013 Matured for
28 months in French barriques (30% new). A powerful, full-bodied cabernet that
still manages to achieve finesse thanks to the perfect balance of fruit, oak and
tannins. An autocratic portrait of cabernet, and of photographic reality. Screwcap.
14% alc. **Rating** 97 **To** 2043 $125 ❸

ŸŸŸŸŸ **Ribbon Vale Vineyard Wilyabrup Margaret River Sauvignon Blanc
Semillon 2015** 74/26%. All the stars are in alignment here, a realisation imposing
itself sternly on the finish and – in particular – the aftertaste, where the intensity
of the flavours causes you to gasp, the best remedy another glass (and gasp). Lemon
rind and zest, unsweetened juice and razor-sharp minerally acidity all hit the high
spots. Screwcap. 13% alc. **Rating** 96 **To** 2020 $32 ❸
Ribbon Vale Vineyard Margaret River Cabernet Sauvignon Merlot 2012
Deep crimson-purple; a rich, complex, medium+-bodied wine, the bouquet
and palate saturated with cassis, redcurrant and plum; exemplary tannin and oak

management, better balanced (the tannins in particular) than the '11. Will develop superbly over many years to come. Still terrific, fresh and vibrant. Screwcap. 14% alc. **Rating** 96 **To** 2032 $50 ○

Wilyabrup Margaret River Semillon 2015 Hand-picked, destemmed and crushed, chilled juice, then standard no-frills vinification. A wine with a juicy intensity to its power that runs through to an emphatic, lingering aftertaste. On a different page from Hunter Valley semillon, but a good one. Screwcap. 14% alc. **Rating** 95 **To** 2030 $38

Margaret River Chardonnay 2014 Hand-picked, whole bunch-pressed to tank for initiation of fermentation with cultured yeast, transferred to French barriques (43% new), full mlf, with adjustment of tartaric acid and SO_2, 20 months maturation. Diminishing acidity (by mlf) and then adjusting it is an uncommon approach. It's hard to find fault with the wine; it has an incisive edge to the mouthfeel, the fruit flavours precisely placed on the tipping point between citrus and stone fruit, benefiting from both, but not at the expense of either. Screwcap. 14% alc. **Rating** 95 **To** 2025 $65

Amy's 2014 Cabernet, merlot, petit verdot and malbec overflowing with a rainbow of cassis/blackcurrant redcurrant, plum and mulberry on the bouquet and palate alike. So great is the impact of the fruit that it buries the tannins, but allows the French oak to add yet another flavour. Why not tonight? Screwcap. 14% alc. **Rating** 95 **To** 2029 $35 ○

Wilyabrup Margaret River Pinot Noir 2013 I cannot remember a Moss Wood Pinot with as much varietal character as this wine. Global warming? This canary in the coal mine is hopping about brightly, whistling loud and clear. It would be fascinating to secrete it in a blind tasting of pinots from Australia's top regions, and throw in a handful of Burgundies and Central Otagos. Screwcap. 14% alc. **Rating** 94 **To** 2027 $60

Ribbon Vale Vineyard Wilyabrup Margaret River Cabernet Sauvignon 2013 92% cabernet sauvignon, plus 4% each of cabernet franc and merlot. A forthright cabernet, medium to full-bodied, with fruit, oak and tannins all making significant contributions. It is easy to see why the wine was given such a lengthy stay in oak – it must have been a handful when young. Even now it is chock-full of blackcurrant fruit and bay leaf. Screwcap. 14% alc. **Rating** 94 **To** 2048 $60

Mount Avoca   ★★★★★

Moates Lane, Avoca, Vic 3467 **Region** Pyrenees
T (03) 5465 3282 **www**.mountavoca.com **Open** 7 days 10–5
Winemaker Dominic Bosch **Est.** 1970 **Dozens** 10 000 **Vyds** 23.46ha
A winery that has long been one of the stalwarts of the Pyrenees region, owned by Matthew and Lisa Barry. The estate vineyards (shiraz, sauvignon blanc, cabernet sauvignon, chardonnay, merlot, cabernet franc and semillon) are organically managed. The Moates Lane wines are partly or wholly made from contract-grown grapes, but other releases are estate-grown. Newly installed winemaker Dominic Bosch has winemaking degrees from his native Spain and a Masters in Oenology from the University of Adelaide, plus extensive experience in Australia, California, New Zealand France and Spain. Exports to China.

ＹＹＹＹＹ Old Vine Pyrenees Shiraz 2013 Co-fermented with viognier, the source of the slashing crimson-purple colour. Fills the mouth with opulent black cherry and plum fruit, immaculately balanced oak and tannin support. This is a really lovely wine that will welcome you with open arms whenever you pop the question. Screwcap. 13.5% alc. **Rating** 96 **To** 2038 $40 ○

Estate Range Pyrenees Cabernet Sauvignon 2013 Good retention of youthful hue; a graceful cabernet, retaining shape, intensity, length and varietal character; the French oak has been well handled, the tannins even more so. Screwcap. 13.5% alc. **Rating** 95 **To** 2030 $33 ○

Limited Release Pyrenees Nebbiolo 2015 If you believe the first duty of nebbiolo is to inflict a degree of pain courtesy of tannins, the more fearsome the better, this wine won't impress you. Vinous bondage isn't my game, and I really like this juicy nebbiolo with its cherry/crabapple/plum trio of flavours, lively acidity drawing out the long finish, cedary oak also in the game. My drink-to date may be way short of the mark. Screwcap. 13.5% alc. **Rating** 95 **To** 2025 $50

Back Block Pyrenees Shiraz 2014 Good colour; the complex bouquet of blood plum, multi-spice and licorice is faithfully reproduced on the medium-bodied palate, with the benefit of supple tannins and good oak integration. Neatly composed and then some. Screwcap. 14.5% alc. **Rating** 94 **To** 2029 $38

Malakoff Pyrenees Shiraz 2013 From the distinguished eponymous vineyard, it has greater depth than the Estate Shiraz, the fruit focus on black and purple berries, the tannins likewise more sturdy. Approachable now, but deserves more time. Screwcap. 13.5% alc. **Rating** 94 **To** 2033 $40

ＴＴＴＴＴ **Pyrenees Limited Release Sangiovese 2015** Rating 92 To 2025 $40
Jack Barry Pyrenees Sparkling Shiraz NV Rating 92 To 2020 $40 TS
Estate Range Pyrenees Shiraz 2013 Rating 91 To 2029 $33
Back Block Pyrenees Cabernet Merlot 2014 Rating 91 To 2022 $38
Limited Release Pyrenees Fume Blanc 2014 Rating 90 To 2017 $29
Estate Range Pyrenees Chardonnay 2015 Rating 90 To 2020 $29
Limited Release Pyrenees Viognier 2014 Rating 90 To 2018 $29
Moates Lane Shiraz 2013 Rating 90 To 2023 $15 ✪
Estate Range Pyrenees Merlot 2015 Rating 90 To 2025 $33

Mount Cathedral Vineyards ★★★★

125 Knafl Road, Taggerty, Vic 3714 **Region** Upper Goulburn
T 0409 354 069 **www**.mtcathedralvineyards.com **Open** By appt
Winemaker Oscar Rosa, Nick Arena **Est.** 1995 **Dozens** 950 **Vyds** 5ha
The Rosa and Arena families established Mount Cathedral Vineyards in 1995, at an elevation of 300m on the north face of Mt Cathedral. The first plantings were 1.2ha of merlot and 0.8ha of chardonnay, followed by 2.5ha of cabernet sauvignon and 0.5ha of cabernet franc in 1996. No pesticides or systemic chemicals are used in the vineyard. Oscar Rosa, chief winemaker, has a Bachelor of Wine Science from CSU, and gained practical experience working at Yering Station in the late '90s. Exports to Singapore.

ＴＴＴＴＴ **Reserve Cabernet Sauvignon 2013** Vividly coloured, with legs streaming down the sides of the glass, cassis and finely structured cabernet tannins intertwined on the full-bodied, but balanced, palate. This is the best of the Mount Cathedral wines. Cork. 13% alc. **Rating** 94 **To** 2043 $42

ＴＴＴＴＴ **Cabernet Merlot 2013** Rating 90 To 2030 $26

Mount Charlie Winery ★★★

228 Mount Charlie Road, Riddells Creek, Vic 3431 **Region** Macedon Ranges
T (03) 5428 6946 **www**.mountcharlie.com.au **Open** Thurs–Sun 10–5
Winemaker Trefor Morgan **Est.** 1991 **Dozens** 700 **Vyds** 3ha
Mount Charlie's wines are sold principally by mail order and through selected restaurants. A futures program encourages mailing-list sales, with a substantial discount to the eventual release price. Owner/winemaker Trefor Morgan is perhaps better known as Professor of Physiology at Melbourne University. The vineyard is planted to 0.5ha each of chardonnay, sauvignon blanc, tempranillo, merlot, malbec and shiraz.

ＴＴＴＴ **Sauvignon Blanc 2015** Whole bunch-pressed, no-frills cool fermentation in stainless steel. Has considerable power and complexity, and some colour pickup; the flavours extend into tropical, and there is a thump on the finish that may or may not be a touch of sweetness. Screwcap. 13% alc. **Rating** 89 **To** 2017 $20

Mount Coghill Vineyard

Cnr Pickfords Road/Coghills Creek Road, Coghills Creek, Vic 3364 **Region** Ballarat
T (03) 5343 4329 **www.**ballaratwineries.com/mtcoghill.htm **Open** W'ends 10–5
Winemaker Owen Latta **Est.** 1993 **Dozens** 300 **Vyds** 0.7ha
Ian and Margaret Pym began planting their tiny vineyard in 1995 with 1280 pinot noir
rootlings, adding 450 chardonnay rootlings the next year. Wine has been made and released
under the Mount Coghill Vineyard label since 2001. Ian is an award-winning photographer,
and his photographs are on display at the cellar door.

Ballarat Chardonnay 2014 Straw-yellow colour. Ginger and apple cider
flavours flow into grapefruit and spiced apple. Somewhat unusual flavour profile
but it finishes well. Screwcap. 12.5% alc. **Rating** 91 **To** 2020 $25 CM
Ballarat Pinot Noir 2014 Fresh, frisky and with an array of flavours to tuck into.
Tangerine, red cherry, a touch of leather, splashes of herbs. It's a succulent wine,
the flavours rolling sweetly out through the finish. Screwcap. 13% alc. **Rating** 91
To 2021 $25 CM

Mount Eyre Vineyards

173 Gillards Road, Pokolbin, NSW 2320 **Region** Hunter Valley
T 0438 683 973 **www.**mounteyre.com **Open** At Garden Cellars, Hunter Valley Gardens
Winemaker Andrew Spinaze, Mark Richardson, Michael McManus **Est.** 1970
Dozens 3000 **Vyds** 45.5ha
This is the venture of two families whose involvement in wine extends back several centuries
in an unbroken line: the Tsironis family in the Peleponnese, Greece, and the Iannuzzi family in
Vallo della Lucania, Italy. Their largest vineyard is at Broke, with a smaller vineyard at Pokolbin.
The three principal varieties planted are chardonnay, shiraz and semillon, with small amounts
of merlot, viognier, chambourcin, verdelho, negro amaro, fiano and nero d'Avola. Exports to
Canada, the Cook Islands, Vanuatu, Hong Kong and China.

Three Ponds Holman Hunter Valley Shiraz 2014 Bold in Hunter shiraz
terms and with firm, striking tannin to match. This a wine worth pulling the
decanter out for; it takes time to coax it from its shell. Jubey cherry and earth with
a slick of sweet, cedary oak. Will develop well. Screwcap. 13.4% alc. **Rating** 93
To 2027 $55 CM
Three Ponds Hunter Valley Verdelho 2014 Flows with juicy fruit flavour but
has just enough finesse through the finish to elevate it. Well-mannered wine; better
suited to the dinner table than to the after (or before) party. Screwcap. 13% alc.
Rating 90 **To** 2017 $23 CM

Three Ponds Hunter Valley Verdelho 2015 Rating 89 **To** 2016 $23 CM
Three Ponds Hunter Valley Fiano 2015 Rating 89 **To** 2017 $25 CM
Three Ponds Hunter Valley Shiraz 2014 Rating 89 **To** 2029 $30
Three Ponds Hunter Valley Merlot 2014 Rating 88 **To** 2021 $25 CM

Mount Horrocks

The Old Railway Station, Curling Street, Auburn, SA 5451 **Region** Clare Valley
T (08) 8849 2243 **www.**mounthorrocks.com **Open** W'ends & public hols 10–5
Winemaker Stephanie Toole **Est.** 1982 **Dozens** 3500 **Vyds** 9.4ha
Owner/winemaker Stephanie Toole has never deviated from the pursuit of excellence in
the vineyard and winery. She has three vineyard sites in the Clare Valley, each managed using
natural farming and organic practices. The attention to detail and refusal to cut corners is
obvious in all of her wines. The cellar door is in the old, but renovated, Auburn railway station.
Exports to the UK, the US and other major markets.

Watervale Riesling 2015 The best Mount Horrocks Riesling so far tasted. It has
a blossom-filled bouquet, but best of all, an exquisitely poised palate, juicy lime/
lemon fruit in a filigree of bright acidity, leaving the mouth at peace with the
world. Screwcap. 12.5% alc. **Rating** 97 **To** 2030 $33 ✪

ŸŸŸŸŸ **Clare Valley Shiraz 2013** The evocative bouquet semaphores the satsuma plum and blackberry fruits at the heart of the wine, surrounded and supported by fine-grained tannins building authority to the finish of the immaculately balanced medium-bodied palate; the oak is totally integrated. Screwcap. 14% alc. **Rating** 96 To 2033 $40 **○**

Clare Valley Semillon 2015 Creamy oak, intense stone fruit and citrus, sizzling length. Style, flavour and the finishing touches of quality. A bright, clear beauty. Screwcap. 13% alc. **Rating** 95 **To** 2023 $32 CM **○**

Clare Valley Shiraz 2014 A complex array of flavours, textures and tangs. Everything is beautifully integrated and yet you can feel and appreciate the positive effect of whole bunches, oak and spice-shot tannin. This isn't your standard fare. It's measured, composed, lively and exquisitely well balanced. Screwcap. 14% alc. **Rating** 95 **To** 2030 $44 CM

Clare Valley Cabernet Sauvignon 2014 The purity of fruit here is something quite special. The flavours flush through the mouth in cleansing fashion, offering cassis, fresh mint, assorted garden herbs and a velvety lick of oak. Medium-bodied; vital; complex; polished; and not at all 'big' or overdone. The word 'exemplary' comes to mind. Screwcap. 14% alc. **Rating** 95 **To** 2035 $44 CM

Clare Valley Cabernet Sauvignon 2013 Matured for 18 months in French barriques (40% new). Served blind, I would never have picked its Clare Valley origin. It is a beautifully crafted cabernet, with a fruit purity seldom seen in Clare cabernet, its cassis folded within fine-grained tannins and quality French oak, length and balance all one could hope for. Screwcap. 14% alc. **Rating** 95 To 2033 $40

Watervale Nero d'Avola 2013 Light, bright crimson; a spring festival of red fruits on the fragrant bouquet and a supple, medium-bodied palate that has a quasi pinot noir finish, lifting and expanding on the aftertaste. Screwcap. 14% alc. **Rating** 95 To 2023 $37

Clare Valley Semillon 2014 As always, 100% barrel-fermented and matured. It is a semillon that is all about layered richness and texture, with some toasty notes awaiting the little butter destined to appear in a couple of years. Acidity provides cleansing balance and length. Screwcap. 13% alc. **Rating** 94 **To** 2025 $31

ŸŸŸŸ♀ **Watervale Nero d'Avola 2014 Rating** 93 To 2022 $37 CM
Cordon Cut Clare Valley Riesling 2015 Rating 92 To 2019 $37 CM

Mount Langi Ghiran ★★★★★

Warrak Road, Buangor, Vic 3375 **Region** Grampians
T (03) 5354 3207 **www**.langi.com.au **Open** Mon–Fri 9–5, w'ends 10–5
Winemaker Ben Haines **Est.** 1969 **Dozens** 60000 **Vyds** 86ha
A maker of outstanding cool climate peppery Shiraz, crammed with flavour and vinosity, and very good Cabernet Sauvignon. The Shiraz has long pointed the way for cool climate examples of the variety. The business was acquired by the Rathbone family group in 2002, and the marketing integrated with the Yering Station and Xanadu Estate wines, a synergistic mix with no overlap. Wine quality is exemplary. Exports to all major markets.

ŸŸŸŸŸ **Langi Grampians Shiraz 2014** From the Langi Old Block planted in '63, matured in French oak (35% new) for 16 months. While full-bodied, this has exceptional poise and elegance, the circus elephant standing on a ball. Intense red, purple and black fruits, ripe tannins and cedary oak are members of an orchestra playing Beethoven. Screwcap. 14% alc. **Rating** 98 **To** 2039 $120 **○**

Mast Grampians Shiraz 2014 25yo vines, matured in French oak (35% new) for 16 months. Each of the '14 Langi Shirazs has its own personality and presence, very different from the others. This is medium to full-bodied, with power and drive to its dark fruits, ripe tannins and oak. It is a mouthwatering wine of great quality and style. Wine for Mozart. Screwcap. 14% alc. **Rating** 97 **To** 2039 $60 **○**

ŶŶŶŶŶ **Cliff Edge Grampians Shiraz 2014** Small batches variously open-fermented, matured in French oak (20% new) for 15 months. An immaculately balanced and structured wine, effortless in its medium-bodied guise, delivering juicy red fruits, cedar and spice on a bed of feathery tannins. J.S. Bach harpsichord. Screwcap. 13.8% alc. **Rating** 95 **To** 2029 $30 ✪

Bradach Vineyard Pinot Noir 2013 32yo vines (cuttings from Best's old vines); matured in used French oak for 10 months. Very light colour; this is pinot to its bootstraps, with a highly fragrant small red fruits bouquet, and a palate that follows on seamlessly, the red fruits also picking up some elements of forest floor to increase the complexity. Screwcap. 13.2% alc. **Rating** 94 **To** 2025 $35

Cliff Edge Grampians Cabernet Sauvignon 2014 Bright hue; elegance is the motto of this lovely wine; everything is present and in its due place, nothing is distracting. Fragrant cassis with plumes of spice, violets and earth define the fruit of the bouquet and palate, feather-light tannins and whispering cedar oak providing all the structure needed. Screwcap. 13.2% alc. **Rating** 94 **To** 2029 $30 ✪

ŶŶŶŶŶ **The Divide Shiraz 2013** Rating 92 To 2023 $23 ✪

Mt Lofty Ranges Vineyard ★★★★★

Harris Road, Lenswood, SA 5240 **Region** Adelaide Hills
T (08) 8389 8339 www.mtloftyrangesvineyard.com.au **Open** Fri–Sun 11–5
Winemaker Peter Leske, Taras Ochota **Est.** 1992 **Dozens** 3000 **Vyds** 4.6ha
Mt Lofty Ranges is owned and operated by Sharon Pearson and Garry Sweeney. Nestled high in the Lenswood subregion of the Adelaide Hills at an altitude of 500m, the very steep north-facing vineyard (pinot noir, sauvignon blanc, chardonnay and riesling) is hand-pruned and hand-picked. The soil is sandy clay loam with a rock base of white quartz and ironstone, and irrigation is kept to a minimum to allow the wines to display vintage characteristics.

ŶŶŶŶŶ **S&G Shiraz 2014** Savoury, meaty, gently reductive and awash with roasted nut flavours. You get the picture. It's a well-established style and the most important factor is always execution. This has a slinky smooth texture, has the balance just right, and pulses appreciably through the finish. It should mature magically. Screwcap. 13.2% alc. **Rating** 95 **To** 2027 $85 CM

S&G Chardonnay 2014 600 bottles only. A meditation on elegance. White peach and citrus with highlights of oak-spice, but as with the S&G Pinot Noir, there are no jaunts or edges; it's a slipstream of satiny flavour. Beautiful. Screwcap. 12.4% alc. **Rating** 94 **To** 2021 $85 CM

Old Pump Shed Pinot Noir 2014 Structure, expressed in both tannin and acid, is a principal concern of the wine but there's ample fruit applied to the frame. Any missteps here go unnoticed; this is in excellent shape, with a future. Screwcap. 13% alc. **Rating** 94 **To** 2023 $30 CM ✪

S&G Pinot Noir 2014 600 bottles only. Pure silk in the mouth. Cherries and plums with flashes of coffee and spice, but essentially seamless. Tannin continues the fully integrated theme. 'Sleek' is a good word for it. Screwcap. 13.2% alc. **Rating** 94 **To** 2021 $85 CM

ŶŶŶŶŶ **Adelaide Hills Shiraz 2014** Rating 93 To 2026 $30 CM
Old Apple Block Chardonnay 2014 Rating 92 To 2020 $30 CM
Pinot Noir Chardonnay 2012 Rating 92 To 2020 $40 TS
Hand Picked Riesling 2015 Rating 91 To 2024 $27 CM
Old Cherry Block Sauvignon Blanc 2015 Rating 91 To 2017 $20 CM ✪

Mount Majura Vineyard ★★★★★

88 Lime Kiln Road, Majura, ACT 2609 **Region** Canberra District
T (02) 6262 3070 www.mountmajura.com.au **Open** Thurs–Mon 10–5
Winemaker Dr Frank van de Loo **Est.** 1988 **Dozens** 4000 **Vyds** 9.3ha
Vines were first planted in 1988 by Dinny Killen on a site on her family property that had been especially recommended by Dr Edgar Riek; its attractions were red soil of volcanic

origin over limestone, with reasonably steep east and northeast slopes providing an element of frost protection. The tiny vineyard has been significantly expanded since it was purchased in '99. Blocks of pinot noir and chardonnay have been joined by pinot gris, shiraz, tempranillo, riesling, graciano, mondeuse, cabernet franc and touriga. In addition, there has been an active planting program for the pinot noir, introducing Dijon clones 114, 155 and 777. All the grapes used come from these estate plantings. One of the star performers in the Canberra District.

🍷🍷🍷🍷🍷 **TSG Canberra District Tempranillo Shiraz Graciano 2015** Mount Majura has a distinguished track record with this blend, and this is yet another extremely good example. What puts it at the front of its class is the balance, texture and synergy, and I shouldn't forget the structure, possibly its best feature. It isn't some spare parts cobbled together because they're Iberian or Italian or whatever: everything sings in perfect harmony. Screwcap. 13.5% alc. **Rating** 96 **To** 2030 $34 ✪

Canberra District Tempranillo 2015 Another wine for which Mount Majura is rightly regarded as a master. The bouquet is highly perfumed, the palate flooded with exotic velvety fruits before becoming more savoury and textured on the finish, leaving the mouth alert, like a pointer in the duck season. Screwcap. 14% alc. **Rating** 95 **To** 2028 $45

Canberra District Riesling 2015 Light straw-green; charged with lime juice flavours, given texture and structure by the acidity needed to give balance and freshness. Arguably, just a little too much of a good thing, but time may make me eat, better still drink, my words. The value remains unchallenged. Screwcap. 12% alc. **Rating** 94 **To** 2022 $29 ✪

Dry Spur 2015 Tempranillo. The texture and flavours are different, particularly on the finish; there are brightly framed highlights, both red and black, and a juicy finish. Screwcap. 14% alc. **Rating** 94 **To** 2028 $45

🍷🍷🍷🍷🍷 **Rock Block 2015** Rating 93 To 2028 $45
Little Dam 2015 Rating 93 To 2028 $45
Canberra District Noble Pinot Gris 2015 Rating 93 To 2020 $22 ✪
Canberra District Shiraz 2014 Rating 91 To 2027 $34
Canberra District Touriga 2015 Rating 90 To 2023 $29

Mount Mary ★★★★★

Coldstream West Road, Lilydale, Vic 3140 **Region** Yarra Valley
T (03) 9739 1761 **www.**mountmary.com.au **Open** Not
Winemaker Sam Middleton **Est.** 1971 **Dozens** 4000 **Vyds** 12ha
Superbly refined, elegant and intense Cabernets and usually outstanding and long-lived Pinot Noirs fully justify Mount Mary's exalted reputation. The Triolet blend is very good; more recent vintages of Chardonnay are even better. Founder and long-term winemaker, the late Dr John Middleton, was one of the great, and truly original, figures in the Australian wine industry. He liked nothing more than to tilt at windmills, and would do so with passion. His annual newsletter grew longer as each year passed, although the paper size did not. The only change necessary was a reduction in font size, and ultimately very strong light or a magnifying glass (or both) was needed to fully appreciate the barbed wit and incisive mind of this great character. The determination of the family to continue the business is simply wonderful. Grandson Sam is protecting the Mount Mary legacy, and doing so with open-minded charm, not afraid to consider ways to make great wines even greater. Exports to the UK, the US, Denmark, Hong Kong, Singapore, South Korea and China.

🍷🍷🍷🍷🍷 **Yarra Valley Chardonnay 2014** Gleaming straw-green; a patrician of barrel-fermented chardonnays that has long since stood proud in the Mount Mary pantheon; fruit, oak and acidity are fused so tightly together deconstruction isn't possible and, in any event, would be irrelevant. Great Yarra Valley chardonnay, great length. Screwcap. 13.3% alc. **Rating** 97 **To** 2030 $105 ✪

Yarra Valley Quintet 2014 While there wasn't a lot of wine made in the Yarra Valley in '14 (wind and rain during flowering), some wine of very high quality was made – witness this. Mount Mary has shown over the decades that Quintet develops superbly, and this complex dark berry-flavoured Bordeaux blend will do just that. Cork. 13% alc. **Rating** 97 **To** 2039 $145 ✪

🍷🍷🍷🍷🍷 Yarra Valley Pinot Noir 2014 Deep colour by any pinot standards, especially those of Mount Mary. Shows the small-berry, small bunch genesis of this low-yielding year; plum leads, with black cherry close behind, the balance and length nigh-on perfect. If ever a Mount Mary Pinot was built for the cellar, this is it. Cork. 12.8% alc. **Rating** 95 **To** 2029 $130

Mount Monument Winery ★★★★☆

1399 Romsey Road, Romsey, Vic 3434 **Region** Macedon Ranges
T (03) 9261 1800 **www**.mountmonumentwines.com **Open** By appt
Winemaker Ben Rankin **Est.** 2008 **Dozens** 1000 **Vyds** 2.3ha
Mount Monument nestles into the shoulder of Mount Macedon, one of Australia's coolest wine regions. At 600m the volcanic silica soils are host to the chardonnay, pinot noir and riesling planted many years prior to its acquisition by Nonda Katsalidis. Under viticulturist John Heitmann, the vineyard is managed with minimal chemical intervention, and utilises organic and biodynamic inputs.

🍷🍷🍷🍷🍷 Riesling 2015 Hand-picked, destemmed, pressed, wild-fermented, a short time on lees post ferment. Reflects the cool climate of Mount Macedon at every step along the way with its ultra-pure lime and lemon fruit and its bracelet of bright acidity. Knight Granite Hills Riesling shows just how well Macedon Ranges rieslings develop over time. Screwcap. 12.3% alc. **Rating** 95 **To** 2030 $30 ✪

🍷🍷🍷🍷 Pinot Noir 2013 **Rating** 90 **To** 2020 $30

Mount Pleasant ★★★★★

401 Marrowbone Road, Pokolbin, NSW 2320 **Region** Hunter Valley
T (02) 4998 7505 **www**.mountpleasantwines.com.au **Open** 7 days 10–4
Winemaker Jim Chatto, Adrian Sparks **Est.** 1921 **Dozens** NFP **Vyds** 88.2ha
McWilliam's Elizabeth and the glorious Lovedale Semillon were generally commercially available with four to five years of bottle age; they were treasures with a consistently superb show record. The individual vineyard wines, together with the Maurice O'Shea memorial wines, add to the lustre of this proud name. However, the appointment of Jim Chatto as group chief winemaker in 2013, and the '14 vintage, the best since 1965, has lifted the range and quality of the red wines back to the glory days of Maurice O'Shea in the 1930s and '40s. Henceforth it will be known as Mount Pleasant, severing the (name) connection with McWilliam's. With seven shirazs scoring between 97 and 99 points, supported by three semillons scoring more than 95 points, it was the only possible choice as Winery of the Year in this *Wine Companion*. Exports to all major markets.

🍷🍷🍷🍷🍷 Maurice O'Shea Shiraz 2014 'Arguably, one of the greatest red vintages in living memory,' says Mount Pleasant. The flagship wine. Has the gently throbbing power of a Rolls Royce; superb, deep crimson-purple hue, itself rare in the Hunter Valley. Countless layers of black fruits have absorbed the oak and put the undoubted tannins into limbo land. O'Shea would have died a happy man had this been his last wine. Dissecting it now is an academic exercise at best, so great is its future. This is as close to a 100-year potential as you are ever likely to find. Screwcap. 14% alc. **Rating** 99 **To** 2064 $250 ✪

Lovedale Hunter Valley Semillon 2009 Won its first trophy in Melbourne in '12, the next six in Queensland in '14 and '15. In other words, is only now hitting its straps, and doing so in brilliant fashion, initially delicately delicious, literally taking off on the back-palate and aftertaste. Worth every cent of the price. Screwcap. 10.5% alc. **Rating** 98 **To** 2030 $70 ✪

Old Paddock & Old Hill Hunter Valley Shiraz 2014 Enthralling, intense finesse, a juicy, vibrant mouthfeel and flavour delivery that is quite exceptional.

If you don't want to partake of vinocide, leave the O'Shea alone and drink this – or better still – the Rosehill. Seldom has terroir spoken with such eloquence in Australia. Screwcap. 14% alc. **Rating** 98 **To** 2054 $50 ✪

Mountain A Medium Bodied Dry Red 2011 Mountain A was one of Maurice O'Shea's greatest wines. Bright hue; this is even better than it was in Mar '15, the pure bouquet flooded with red fruits parlayed into a palate with utterly perfect mouthfeel/texture thanks to its tannins woven through the fruit. I have bought some hoping I will be around in 10 years time. Screwcap. 13.5% alc. **Rating** 98 **To** 2041 $75 ✪

Lovedale Hunter Valley Semillon 2010 Still as fresh as a daisy, its freshness accentuated by a touch of CO_2 spritz deliberately left in the wine; the result is an unusual conjunction of delicacy and intensity, the explanation lying in its purity. It is truly difficult to visualise the end point of a semillon such as this. Seven gold medals. Screwcap. 10% alc. **Rating** 97 **To** 2035 $64 ✪

1880 Vines Old Hill Vineyard Hunter Valley Shiraz 2014 From the oldest vines in the Block range, and the lightest colour; ultra-classic Hunter Valley shiraz with savoury/earthy/spicy undertones to the medium-bodied blue and black fruits of the palate, contributing as much to the structure and texture of the wine as to the flavour. Screwcap. 14% alc. **Rating** 97 **To** 2054 $135 ✪

1921 Vines Old Paddock Vineyard Hunter Valley Shiraz 2014 A powerful, but immaculately balanced shiraz, blackberry fruit within a gauze of ripe, positive tannins. The breed and lineage of the wine is razor sharp, the length and balance impeccable. Like its siblings, it's easy to say the flavours have some savoury characters, much harder to condense and describe their unique nature. Screwcap. 14% alc. **Rating** 97 **To** 2054 $135 ✪

1946 Vines Rosehill Vineyard Hunter Valley Shiraz 2014 In a very different metier from its Old Hill and Old Paddock siblings, here the juicy red fruits of the bouquet set the scene for the palate, silky and suave, but with wonderful length and persistence. Screwcap. 14% alc. **Rating** 97 **To** 2049 $135 ✪

Mountain C Light Bodied Dry Red 2014 This is light-bodied in comparison to Mountain A, and has a deceptive O'Shea feel to it – in other words, in strict terminology it is closer to medium-bodied in the wider world. It has red fruits as well as black, and the tannins, while plentiful, are very fine and supple, meshing perfectly with the fruit. Will drink well throughout its life. Screwcap. 13% alc. **Rating** 97 **To** 2039 $75 ✪

ƎƎƎƎƎ **Mothervine Hunter Valley Pinot Noir 2014** This is a seriously interesting wine. Story of the vines aside, the wine in the glass screams character and quality. It's medium weight but it leaves a deep impression. Sprays of twiggy tannin, rushes of boysenberry and black cherry, both a sweetness and a sourness, and an entrancing earthen-pepperiness. It's a wine of both individuality and length. It would make a champion choice for any cellar. Screwcap. 13% alc. **Rating** 96 **To** 2030 $48 CM ✪

1965 Vines Rosehill Vineyard Hunter Valley Shiraz 2014 The impact of this wine is immediate, and very different from the high-strung elegance of its siblings. It's not a question of tannins, but the intensity and depth of the dark fruits. There's no question this wine will take longer than most of its siblings to reach its peak 30 years hence, and go on from there. Screwcap. 14% alc. **Rating** 96 **To** 2054 $135

Rosehill Vineyard Hunter Valley Shiraz 2014 A very high quality '14 Hunter Valley shiraz that would stand tall above others were it not for its OP&OH and O'Shea siblings. A full-bodied wine in a different idiom from its siblings, Hunter earth and leather (relatively speaking) more obvious. A great future. Screwcap. 14% alc. **Rating** 96 **To** 2044 $50 ✪

Mountain A Medium Bodied Dry Red 2014 I'll start to nitpick: this is in full-bodied territory, not medium-bodied; the colour is deep purple-crimson, un-Hunter-like in a normal vintage, but '14 has turned everything upside down. This is charged with blackberry, tar and leather, plus foresty/earthy tannins.

Impossible to give a drink-to date – whatever you pick it will keep pushing it out as the years go by. Screwcap. 13.5% alc. **Rating** 96 **To** 2049 $75 **✪**

Museum Release Rosehill Vineyard Hunter Valley Shiraz 2009 Its future is starting to peep through the curtains as the unity of place and variety takes shape. Hunter Valley earth, polished leather, spices and tannins are the pillars supporting the amalgam of plum and red berries and fruits. It is no more than medium-bodied, but has a long future. Screwcap. 14% alc. **Rating** 96 **To** 2029 $60 **✪**

Elizabeth Hunter Valley Semillon 2015 Very pale colour no surprise; as fresh and as crisp as they come, with citrus, lemongrass and lanolin all playing a role. Drink now, in 5, 10, or even 20 years with total confidence. Screwcap. 10% alc. **Rating** 95 **To** 2020 $24 **✪**

Elizabeth Hunter Valley Semillon 2007 Cellar-aged. Gleaming yellow-gold; eight gold medals between '07 and '13 speak for themselves. It is now near its plateau, acidity its best friend, the fruit a mix of lemongrass and dried grass. It will develop even greater depth, so don't look this remarkable gift horse in the mouth right now. Screwcap. 11% alc. **Rating** 94 **To** 2022 $19 **✪**

Leontine Hunter Valley Chardonnay 2014 When all the right levers are pulled at all the right times, the Hunter Valley has proven again and again that it can produce chardonnays with the finesse of this wine without losing varietal expression. Screwcap. 13% alc. **Rating** 94 **To** 2022 $35

B-Side Airport Block Lovedale Vineyard Field Blend 2015 A blend of semillon and verdelho interplanted on the Lovedale Vineyard. Semillon rides shotgun, keeping the verdelho with its head down in the midst of a potent lemongrass/citrus/mineral play. Screwcap. 10.5% alc. **Rating** 94 **To** 2027 $27 **✪**

Mountain D Full Bodied Dry Red 2013 Hand-picked, cold-soaked, open-fermented, 8 days on skins, matured in French oak for 15 months (35% new). Archetypal Hunter Valley shiraz, with black fruits, earth, leather, tar and persistent, but not blocky, tannins providing the goal posts for the playing field of flavours. Screwcap. 14% alc. **Rating** 94 **To** 2043 $75

🍷🍷🍷🍷🍷 **Limited Release Aged Liqueur Verdelho NV** Rating 93 **To** 2017 $90
Mount Henry Shiraz Pinot Noir 2013 Rating 90 **To** 2023 $45

Mount Stapylton Wines   ★★★★

14 Cleeve Court, Toorak, Vic 3142 (postal) **Region** Grampians
T 0425 713 044 **www**.mts-wines.com **Open** Not
Winemaker Don McRae, Caroline Mooney **Est.** 2002 **Dozens** 600 **Vyds** 2.2ha
Mount Stapylton Vineyard is planted on the historic Goonwinnow Homestead farming property at Laharum, on the northwest side of the Grampians in front of Mt Stapylton. In 2010 founders Howard and Samantha Staehr sold the homestead property, but leased back the vineyard. The Little Yarra Station Vineyard (1.2ha planted in '09) in the Yarra Valley provides the grapes for the Pamela Chardonnay and the Victoria Pinot Noir. The wines are listed with several iconic restaurants in Sydney and Melbourne.

🍷🍷🍷🍷🍷 **Ivan Grampians Shiraz 2014** Sweet boysenberry and cherry flavours draw you in from the outset but it's the burst of candied orange and cranberry on the finish that really locks you in its favour. It's not the deepest of reds, and there's plenty of tangy acidity, but it rushes up to greet you and remains friendly throughout. Screwcap. 14.5% alc. **Rating** 92 **To** 2024 $50 CM

Mount Terrible   ★★★★★

289 Licola Road, Jamieson, Vic 3723 **Region** Central Victoria Zone
T (03) 5777 0703 **www**.mountterriblewines.com.au **Open** By appt
Winemaker John Eason **Est.** 2001 **Dozens** 350 **Vyds** 2ha
John Eason and wife Janene Ridley began the long, slow (and at times very painful) business of establishing their vineyard just north of Mt Terrible in 1992 – hence the choice of name. In 2001 they planted 2ha of pinot noir (MV6, 115, 114 and 777 clones) on a gently sloping, north-facing river terrace adjacent to the Jamieson River. DIY trials persuaded John to have

the first commercial vintage in '06 contract-made, but he has since made the wines himself in a fireproof winery built on top of an underground wine cellar. John has a sense of humour second to none, but must wonder what he has done to provoke the weather gods, alternating in their provision of fire, storm and tempest. The '12 and '13 vintages have provided some well earned relief. Exports to the UK.

♥♥♥♥♥ **Jamieson Pinot Noir 2013** From estate-grown 115, 777 and MV6 clones, 10% whole bunch inclusion, post-ferment maceration followed by 18 months maturation in one-third each new, 1yo and 2yo French barriques. A powerful, impeccably balanced pinot, flush with red and black cherry fruit, and a gold-plated future. Screwcap. 13.5% alc. **Rating** 95 **To** 2025 $42
Jamieson Pinot Noir 2012 Provides a clear picture of the future of the '13 with flowery, spicy aromatics and a clean-shaven palate of dark cherry and plum fruits bedecked with fine savoury/foresty tannins, and a very long, expansive finish. Screwcap. 13.5% alc. **Rating** 95 **To** 2022 $42

Mount Trio Vineyard   ★★★★☆

2534 Porongurup Road, Mount Barker WA 6324 **Region** Porongurup
T (08) 9853 1136 **www**.mounttriowines.com.au **Open** By appt
Winemaker Gavin Berry, Andrew Vesey **Est.** 1989 **Dozens** 3000 **Vyds** 8.8ha
Mount Trio was established by Gavin Berry and wife Gill Graham (plus partners) shortly after they moved to the Mount Barker area in late 1988, Gavin to take up the position of chief winemaker at Plantagenet, which he held until 2004, when he and partners acquired the now very successful and much larger West Cape Howe. They have slowly built up the business, increasing estate plantings with riesling (2.7ha), shiraz (2.4ha), sauvignon blanc (2ha) and pinot noir (1.7ha). Exports to the UK, the US, Denmark and China.

♥♥♥♥♥ **Home Block Porongurup Pinot Noir 2014** A selection of the best four French barriques, it is the best Porongurup pinot made to date. While powerful, the varietal character is bell clear, with red and black cherries the motor that drives the long palate and its excellent texture; the savoury, but fine, tannins guarantee the future. Screwcap. 13.5% alc. **Rating** 95 **To** 2025 $32 ○

♥♥♥♥♡ **Great Southern Sauvignon Blanc 2015** Rating 92 To 2016 $17 ○
Porongurup Riesling 2015 Rating 91 To 2023 $21 ○
Porongurup Shiraz 2014 Rating 90 To 2024 $21 ○

Mount View Estate   ★★★★★

Mount View Road, Mount View, NSW 2325 **Region** Hunter Valley
T (02) 4990 3307 **www**.mtviewestate.com.au **Open** Mon–Sat 10–5, Sun 10–4
Winemaker Scott Stephens **Est.** 1971 **Dozens** 4000 **Vyds** 16ha
Mount View Estate's vineyard was planted by the very knowledgeable Harry Tulloch 45 years ago; he recognised the quality of the red basalt volcanic soils of the very attractive hillside vineyard. Prior owners John and Polly Burgess purchased the adjoining Limestone Creek Vineyard in 2004 (planted in 1982), which fits seamlessly into Mount View Estate's production. The quality of the wines is outstanding. The business changed hands in '16, now owned by a Chinese national, but no further details are available.

♥♥♥♥♥ **Museum Release Reserve Hunter Valley Semillon 2006** Lime, lemon and honey get a rapturous reception from the palate; the balance between fruit and acidity is perfect. When released as a yearling, Mount View suggested cellaring for 4–5 years would see it develop into a classic toasty semillon. They got that one wrong, didn't they? Screwcap. 10.3% alc. **Rating** 96 **To** 2021 $50 ○
Flagship Hunter Valley Shiraz 2014 This has greater depth of colour than the Reserve, but paradoxically, is more elegant. The French oak (33% new versus 20% new in the Reserve) is another point of difference, but both wines are superb. Screwcap. 13.5% alc. **Rating** 96 **To** 2044 $70 ○
Reserve Hunter Valley Shiraz 2014 The sheer power and length of the palate are intimidating, as is the complexity, picking (at will) characters from cool climates

as well as the (very) warm Hunter Valley. The fruits are predominantly black, but there are also red flashes, and the tannins intertwine with the earthy nuances and the oak. Screwcap. 13.5% alc. **Rating** 95 **To** 2044 $40

Reserve Hunter Valley Semillon 2015 Has the special squeaky acidity, a tactile mouthfeel that catches parts of the mouth as it moves around, highlighting the lemon/lemongrass flavours and prolonging the length. Newborn, but destined for greatness (taste the '06). Screwcap. 11.5% alc. **Rating** 94 **To** 2026 $35

Reserve Hunter Valley Chardonnay 2015 Typical of the chardonnay style that has proliferated in the Hunter Valley over the past 5+ years. It has a bracing edgy/pithy character to the citrus/stone fruit fusion at the heart of the wine, and you don't really notice the oak. Screwcap. 13% alc. **Rating** 94 **To** 2028 $35

Reserve Hunter Valley Cabernet Sauvignon 2014 My, my! Even cabernet flourished in '14. This is fleshy and luscious, but not the least cooked; it has dried herbs and Hunter Valley earth to give texture and structure, the length and balance faultless. Clever winemaking. Screwcap. 13.5% alc. **Rating** 94 **To** 2034 $40

Mount William Winery   ★★★

890 Mount William Road, Tantaraboo, Vic 3764 **Region** Macedon Ranges
T (03) 5429 1595 **www**.mtwilliamwinery.com.au **Open** W'ends 11–5
Winemaker David Cowburn, Murray Cousins **Est.** 1985 **Dozens** 1500 **Vyds** 7.5ha
Adrienne and Murray Cousins purchased a 220ha grazing property in 1985; the sheep and Angus cattle remain the principal part of the general farming program, but between '87 and '99 they established pinot noir, chardonnay, cabernet franc and merlot. The quality of the wines has been consistently good, and they are sold through a stone cellar door, as well as at a number of fine wine retailers around Melbourne.

♟♟♟♟ **Jorja-Alexis Pinot Noir Rose 2010** After a full 5 years on lees, this unites the understated strawberry hull and red cherry fruit of pinot noir with savoury, biscuity notes of extended lees age. Low dosage balances lively Macedon acidity, with a little phenolic bitterness disrupting the finish. Diam. 13% alc. **Rating** 89 **To** 2020 $35 TS

Mountadam   ★★★★☆

High Eden Road, Eden Valley, SA 5235 **Region** Eden Valley
T (08) 8564 1900 **www**.mountadam.com.au **Open** By appt
Winemaker Helen McCarthy **Est.** 1972 **Dozens** 35 000 **Vyds** 80ha
Founded by the late David Wynn for the benefit of winemaker son Adam, Mountadam was (somewhat surprisingly) purchased by Cape Mentelle (doubtless under the direction of Möet Hennessy Wine Estates) in 2000. Rather less surprising was its sale in '05 to Adelaide businessman David Brown, who has extensive interests in the Padthaway region. This acquisition was of the vineyard on the western side of the High Eden Road. In '07 David purchased a parcel of land on the opposite (eastern) side of the road, which was unplanted, and in '15 acquired the large vineyard on the eastern side of the road from TWE, thus reassembling all of the land originally purchased by David Wynn in the late '60s. The Brown family has decided that henceforth the original vineyard will be known as 'Mountadam West', and the newly acquired vineyard as 'Mountadam East'. Exports to the UK, France, Switzerland, Poland and Hong Kong.

♟♟♟♟♟ **Barossa Chardonnay 2014** Bright straw-green; there's no doubt Mountadam has been the foremost producer of chardonnay in the Eden Valley over the past two decades. This isn't particularly complex, but it has an appealing mix of ripe citrus (Meyer lemon), white peach and melon, oak restrained. Likely a very low yield. Screwcap. 14% alc. **Rating** 95 **To** 2022 $18 ✪

♟♟♟♟♟ **Eden Valley Riesling 2015** Rating 93 **To** 2025 $25 ✪

Barossa Shiraz 2014 Rating 93 **To** 2029 $18 ✪
High Eden Estate Chardonnay 2015 Rating 92 **To** 2021 $35
Eden Valley Pinot Gris 2015 Rating 90 **To** 2016 $25

Mr Barval Fine Wines

182 Stevens Road, Margaret River, WA 6285 **Region** Margaret River
T 0481 453 038 **www**.mrbarval.com **Open** Not
Winemaker Robert Gherardi **Est.** 2015 **Dozens** 510

Robert Gherardi was born with wine in his blood, as a small boy going to Margaret River to pick grapes with three generations of his extended Italian family. The grapes were taken to his grandmother's suburban backyard to begin the fermentation, followed by a big lunch or dinner to celebrate the arrival of the new vintage-to-be. Nonetheless, his first degree was in marine science and biotechnology; while completing the course he worked in an independent wine store in Perth. Having tasted his way around the world in the bottle, and aged 25, he enrolled in the full oenology and viticulture degree. This led to employment at Moss Wood for four years, then Brown Hill Estate as assistant winemaker, and finally to Cullen for three years. Vanya Cullen encouraged him to travel to Barolo and work with Elio Altare for three harvests over a five-year period. This included moving to Barolo with his wife and children to experience the full four seasons of viticulture and winemaking. He returns to Italy each year for his boutique travel business with customised tours of Barolo, Valtellina and further north. And so he arrived at the name for his winery: M(argaret) R(iver), Bar(olo) and Val(tellina).

♀♀♀♀♀ **Margaret River Chardonnay 2015** Whole bunch-pressed direct to barrel, wild fermentation, matured for 10 months in French barriques (14% new). A lovely chardonnay with the drive and focus of grapefruit and crunchy acidity ex Karridale contributing the most, Wilyabrup providing the peachy flesh of the mid-palate. Screwcap. 13.7% alc. **Rating** 95 **To** 2024 $35 ✿

♀♀♀♀♀ **Nebbia 2015 Rating** 93 **To** 2030 $25 ✿

Mr Mick

7 Dominic Street, Clare, SA 5453 **Region** Clare Valley
T (08) 8842 2555 **www**.mrmick.com.au **Open** 7 days 10–5
Winemaker Tim Adams, Brett Schutz **Est.** 2011 **Dozens** 25 000

This is the venture of Tim Adams and wife Pam Goldsack, the name chosen to honour KH (Mick) Knappstein, a legend in the Clare Valley and the broader Australian wine community. Tim worked at Leasingham Wines with Mick between 1975 and '86, and knew him well. When Tim and Pam acquired the Leasingham winery in January 2011, together with its historic buildings, it brought the wheel full circle. Various commentators (including myself) have used Mick's great one-liner, 'There are only two types of people in the world: those who were born in Clare, and those who wish they had been.' Exports to China and NZ.

♀♀♀♀ **Clare Valley Vermentino 2015** Chalk, brine but mostly citrus flavours race through the mouth. Musk-like lift adds an extra layer. Attractive. Screwcap. 12% alc. **Rating** 89 **To** 2016 $17 CM ✿
Novo Clare Valley Sangiovese 2015 Young, fruit-driven, cherried red with just enough chewy tannin to keep it tidy. Has pizza written all over it. Screwcap. 13% alc. **Rating** 89 **To** 2019 $17 CM ✿
Limestone Coast Pinot Grigio 2015 Grippy grigio with refreshing citrus driving through the palate. Screwcap. 11.5% alc. **Rating** 88 **To** 2015 $17 CM ✿

Mr Riggs Wine Company

55 Main Road, McLaren Flat, SA 5171 **Region** McLaren Vale
T (08) 8383 2055 **www**.mrriggs.com.au **Open** Fri 12–4, Sat 10–4, Sun 12–4
Winemaker Ben Riggs **Est.** 2001 **Dozens** 20 000 **Vyds** 7.5ha

With over a quarter of a century of winemaking experience, Ben Riggs is well established under his own banner. Ben sources the best fruit from individual vineyards in McLaren Vale, Clare Valley, Adelaide Hills, Langhorne Creek, Coonawarra, and from his own Piebald Gully Vineyard (shiraz and viognier). Each wine is intended to express the essence of not only the vineyard, but also the region's terroir. The vision of the Mr Riggs brand is unpretentious and personal: 'to make the wines I love to drink'. He drinks very well. Exports to the US, Canada, China and other major markets.

ɣɣɣɣɣ Montepulciano d'Adelaide Hills 2014 Deep crimson hue; offers a pot pourri of spiced red cherry, black cherry and satsuma plum on the bouquet and palate alike, but wait, there's more to come: the texture ex the cedary/spicy tannins is utterly seductive, and carries the flavours along with it onto the finish and aftertaste. Screwcap. 14% alc. **Rating** 96 **To** 2024 $27 ✪

Piebald Adelaide Syrah 2013 The Adelaide GI encompasses McLaren Vale and Adelaide Hills, the McLaren Vale from the Clarendon district, itself close to the Adelaide Hills. It results in a more elegant and fragrant array of red fruits than the normal Mr Riggs Shirazs, the finish delightfully fresh, the tannins silky and the oak submissive. Screwcap. 14.5% alc. **Rating** 95 **To** 2025 $27 ✪

Scarce Earth McLaren Vale Shiraz 2013 This is a seriously good McLaren Vale shiraz from the Piebald Gully Vineyard. Despite the intensity and depth on offer, there is no heat or cooked fruit from the alcohol, just black fruits, a little dark chocolate and savoury tannins. Diam. 15% alc. **Rating** 95 **To** 2028 $50

McLaren Vale Shiraz 2013 Dense crimson-purple; this is a rich and profound wine, firmly ticking every box with a broad-tipped marker pen. It is full of black fruits, with studs of red cherry and chocolate illuminating the core of dark fruits; the tannins are plentiful, but ripe and integrated, the oak precisely judged. Diam. 14.5% alc. **Rating** 95 **To** 2043 $50

Generation Series The Elder McLaren Vale Fortified Shiraz 2013 The heady scents of blackberry, pollen and cornflour recall the great 'vintage ports' of Chateau Reynella, a nice memory for those old enough to have it. On the palate it's a little more contemporary, the fruit sweet and supple, the tannin already in balance. It will age long and effortlessly, but don't be deterred from drinking it now; there is plenty to like. 500ml. Screwcap. 18% alc. **Rating** 94 **To** 2035 $30 ✪

ɣɣɣɣɣ Watervale Riesling 2015 Rating 93 To 2030 $24 ✪
Watervale Riesling 2014 Rating 93 To 2024 $22 ✪
Outpost Coonawarra Cabernet 2014 Rating 93 To 2029 $24 ✪
Battle Axe McLaren Vale Sparkling Shiraz NV Rating 93 To 2020 $24 ✪
Generation Series Sticky End Riesling 2013 Rating 93 To 2019 $24 ✪
The Gaffer McLaren Vale Shiraz 2014 Rating 91 To 2024 $22 ✪
Mrs McLaren Vale Viognier 2015 Rating 90 To 2018 $24
Castro's Ligador Master Blender McLaren Vale Shiraz Mataro 2013 Rating 90 To 2023 $18 ✪
Yacca Paddock Adelaide Hills Tempranillo 2014 Rating 90 To 2025 $30

Munari Wines   ★★★★☆

Ladys Creek Vineyard, 1129 Northern Highway, Heathcote, Vic 3523 **Region** Heathcote
T (03) 5433 3366 **www.**munariwines.com **Open** Tues–Sun 11–5
Winemaker Adrian Munari **Est.** 1993 **Dozens** 3000 **Vyds** 6.9ha
Established on one of the original Heathcote farming properties, Ladys Creek Vineyard is situated on the narrow Cambrian strip 11km north of the town. Adrian Munari has harnessed traditional winemaking practices to New World innovation to produce complex, fruit-driven wines that marry concentration and elegance. They are produced from estate plantings of shiraz, cabernet sauvignon, merlot, cabernet franc and malbec. Exports to France, Denmark, Taiwan and China.

ɣɣɣɣɣ Ladys Pass Heathcote Shiraz 2013 Mid-deep red; distinctly spicy and fragrant, with underlying tar and black fruits; the palate is remarkably fine and silky at first, but the tannins build admirably, finishing taut and focused. Screwcap. 14% alc. **Rating** 94 **To** 2030 $40

The Ridge Upper Goulburn Shiraz 2013 From Broadford in the Upper Goulburn, a lovely example of cool grown shiraz, red fruits, spice and a hint of pepper leading to a silky and finely balanced palate. Everything is in order, in this fruit-driven shiraz. Screwcap. 14% alc. **Rating** 94 **To** 2023 $30 ✪

ŸŸŸŸ♀ Schoolhouse Red Heathcote Shiraz Viognier 2014 Rating 92 To 2022 $45
Heathcote Cabernet Sauvignon 2013 Rating 92 To 2023 $30
The Beauregard Heathcote Shiraz 2013 Rating 91 To 2023 $30

Murdoch Hill   ★★★★★

260 Mappinga Road, Woodside, SA 5244 **Region** Adelaide Hills
T (08) 8389 7081 **www**.murdochhill.com.au **Open** By appt
Winemaker Michael Downer **Est.** 1998 **Dozens** 4000 **Vyds** 20.48ha
A little over 20ha of vines have been established on the undulating, gum-studded countryside
of Charlie and Julie Downer's 60-year-old Erika property, 4km east of Oakbank. In descending
order of importance, the varieties planted are sauvignon blanc, shiraz, cabernet sauvignon and
chardonnay. Son Michael, with a Bachelor of Oenology degree from Adelaide University, is
winemaker. Exports to the UK and China.

ŸŸŸŸŸ The Landau Single Vineyard Oakbank Adelaide Hills Syrah 2015 Another
notch up the ladder from Cronberry Block. It is made with the same attention
to detail, black fruits of every description on parade, laced with spice, pepper,
leather and licorice, oak and tannins circling the palate from start to finish. Diam.
13.5% alc. **Rating** 96 To 2030 $46 ✪
The Tilbury Single Vineyard Piccadilly Valley Chardonnay 2015 I have
to out myself by revealing I'm acid tolerant, so the concern of Michael Downer
about the acidity of the Champagne clone G9V7 wouldn't have worried me as
much, and my comments on the Murdoch Hill standard Chardonnay apply here.
That said, this is the better wine, with more grip and presence. Diam. 13% alc.
Rating 95 To 2025 $46
The Phaeton Single Vineyard Piccadilly Valley Pinot Noir 2015 Clones
114, 115 and MV6, 38% whole bunches. Like all the Murdoch Hill pinots, the hue
is bright and clear; the aromas are of cherry and allspice, the palate bringing both
cherry and plum into play. The most conventional of the pinots, squeaking home
in front of Ridley. Diam. 13% alc. **Rating** 95 To 2029 $46
Cronberry Block Adelaide Hills Syrah 2015 Deep crimson-purple; Michael
Downer's infinitely patient attention to detail has been rewarded with a very
complex medium to full-bodied palate, the flavours of blackberry, blackcurrant and
satsuma plum laced with cracked black pepper, licorice and tar. The only question
is the amount of new oak. Screwcap. 13.5% alc. **Rating** 95 To 2035 $28 ✪
Cronberry Block Adelaide Hills Syrah 2014 Fragrant, spiced black cherry
and a twitch of French oak soar from the bouquet, the palate building on a
similar array of flavours. Excellent fine tannins (part fruit, part oak) put this wine
into a must-buy category for drinking now or much later. Screwcap. 13.5% alc.
Rating 95 To 2029 $28 ✪
Single Vineyard Adelaide Hills Sauvignon Blanc 2015 What the Adelaide
Hills is able to do better than any other region in the eastern half of Australia:
produce fragrant, juicy sauvignon blanc that covers a full range of varietal
fruits while retaining fresh, natural acidity on the finish and aftertaste – and no
unfermented sugar. Screwcap. 12.5% alc. **Rating** 94 To 2016 $22 ✪
Adelaide Hills Chardonnay 2015 Made to measure like an Italian suit, even if
actually made in China; the key partial mlf. Not being able to see the before and
after story, I can't be sure, but I wonder whether less, or better still none, might
have left the wine with a bit more bite, even at the cost of a wrinkle here and
there. Screwcap. 13% alc. **Rating** 94 To 2022 $28 ✪
Ridley Adelaide Hills Pinot X Two 2015 Fragrant, lively forest floor rustles
through the bouquet and palate, red fruits making an early entrance and refusing
to lie down. One of a handful of such wines in Australia. A surprise packet here
for quality and rarity. A blend of pinots noir and meunier. Screwcap. 13% alc.
Rating 94 To 2025 $36

ŸŸŸŸ♀ Adelaide Hills Red Blend 2015 Rating 92 To 2025 $28

Murrindindi Vineyards

30 Cummins Lane, Murrindindi, Vic 3717 **Region** Upper Goulburn
T 0438 305 314 **www**.murrindindivineyards.com **Open** Not
Winemaker Hugh Cuthbertson **Est.** 1979 **Dozens** 6000 **Vyds** 16ha
This small winery is owned and run by Hugh Cuthbertson, established by parents Alan and
Jan (now retired) as a minor diversification from their cattle property. Hugh, himself with a
long and high-profile wine career, has overseen the marketing of the wines, including the
Family Reserve and Don't Tell Dad brands. Exports to the UK, the US, Finland and China.

Family Reserve Yea Valley Shiraz 2014 This is a delicious shiraz, showing
the climate (halfway between cool and warm) to best advantage. The colour is
excellent, the medium-bodied palate flush with black and red cherry fruit; spice
and pepper are also in the game, oak and tannins off in the wings. Makes its point
with elegance. Screwcap. 13.2% alc. **Rating** 95 To 2030 $30 ✪

Mr Hugh McLaren Vale Shiraz 2014 **Rating** 93 To 2039 $50

Murrumbateman Winery

Cnr Barton Highway/McIntosh Circuit, Murrumbateman, NSW 2582
Region Canberra District
T (02) 6227 5584 **www**.murrumbatemanwinery.com.au **Open** Fri–Sun 10–5
Winemaker Bobbie Makin **Est.** 1972 **Dozens** 1000 **Vyds** 4ha
Draws upon 4ha of estate-grown sauvignon blanc and shiraz. It also incorporates an à la carte
restaurant and function room, together with picnic and barbecue areas.

Muster Wines

c/- 60 Sheffield Street, Malvern, SA 5061 **Region** Barossa Valley
T 0430 360 350 **www**.musterwineco.com.au **Open** By appt
Winemaker David Muster **Est.** 2007 **Dozens** 2500
Gottfried Muster arrived from Europe with his young family in 1859, settling in the Barossa
Valley. Thus direct descendent David Muster was born and bred in the wine purple. This is
a virtual winery business; David Muster has been buying and selling wine since 2007. He
forages for small batches of wines in the Barossa and Clare valleys, and clearly has developed
some very useful contacts, allowing the release of relatively small amounts under each label,
sometimes offering very good value. Exports to the US.

Polish Hill River Riesling 2014 From a single vineyard in the Polish Hill
district, lightly pressed. A lovely riesling that caresses the mouth; elegant, yet with
juicy lime and green apple flavours running through the long palate; the pale
straw-green colour is another indicator of the quality and longevity of the wine.
Exceptional value. Screwcap. 12.2% alc. **Rating** 95 To 2030 $20 ✪
Eden Valley Riesling 2013 From old vines grown at an elevation of 400m,
very high in the Eden Valley. Bright quartz-green; a vibrant bouquet with citrus
blossom to the fore, but taking the impact of the wine even further on the palate,
where juicy lime fruit dances with minerally acidity on an exceptionally long
palate. Screwcap. 12% alc. **Rating** 95 To 2028 $21 ✪
Polish Hill River Riesling 2015 Includes 3% co-fermented gewurztraminer. It is
flooded with Bickford's lime juice flavours, so much so there is no need for – and
little point in – waiting. Screwcap. 11.5% alc. **Rating** 94 To 2025 $22 ✪
Barossa Muster Shiraz 2012 Improbably, this wine is (as suggested by David
Muster) a case of 'Barossa meets northern Rhône'. It is aromatic and elegant, with
Côte Rôtie-like spice and charcuterie flavours to the long, medium-bodied palate.
Excellent value. Screwcap. 13.7% alc. **Rating** 94 To 2025 $25 ✪

Mars Needs Merlot 2014 **Rating** 89 To 2029 $81
Rare Tawny 1980 **Rating** 89 To 2017 $48
Mars Needs Clare Valley Shiraz 2013 **Rating** 88 To 2023 $18
Barossa Mourvedre 2010 **Rating** 88 To 2020 $25

Myrtaceae ★★★★

53 Main Creek Road, Main Ridge, Vic 3928 **Region** Mornington Peninsula
T (03) 5989 2045 **www**.myrtaceae.com.au **Open** W'ends & public hols 12–5
Winemaker Julie Trueman **Est.** 1985 **Dozens** 300 **Vyds** 1ha
Owners John Trueman (viticulturist) and wife Julie (winemaker) began the planting of
Myrtaceae in 1985, intending to make a Bordeaux-style red blend. It became evident that
these late-ripening varieties were not well suited to the site, so the vineyard was converted to
chardonnay (0.6ha) and pinot noir (0.4ha) in '98. Part of the property is devoted to the Land
for Wildlife Scheme; the integrated Australian garden is a particular feature.

🍷🍷🍷🍷 **Selwyns Fault Mornington Peninsula Rose 2015** Pinot noir, crushed,
        9 hours cold soak, pressed to tank with cultured yeast, after 3 days transferred to
        French oak for completion of fermentation and 6 months maturation. Wonderfully
        fragrant red flowers/berries; crisp, bright and juicy red fruits; dry but fruity finish.
        Lovely rose. Screwcap. 13.5% alc. **Rating** 94 **To** 2017 $23 **O**

🍷🍷🍷🍷 **Mornington Peninsula Pinot Noir 2013 Rating** 90 **To** 2019 $40

Naked Run Wines ★★★★★

36 Parawae Road, Salisbury Plain, SA 5109 (postal) **Region** Clare Valley/Barossa Valley
T 0408 807 655 **www**.nakedrunwines.com.au **Open** Not
Winemaker Steven Baraglia **Est.** 2005 **Dozens** 1200
Naked Run is the virtual winery of Jayme Wood, Bradley Currie and Steven Baraglia, their
skills ranging from viticulture through to production, and also to the all-important sales and
marketing (and not to be confused with Naked Wines). The riesling is sourced from Clare
Valley, grenache from the Williamstown area of the Barossa Valley, and shiraz from Greenock.
The price/quality ratio is utterly exceptional.

🍷🍷🍷🍷 **The First Clare Valley Riesling 2015** A wine all about its place. Trophy for
        Best Single Vineyard White Wine, National Wine Show '15; gold medal and part
        of the Provenance class trio at the Clare Valley Wine Show, gold medal Adelaide
        Wine Show '15. The quality of the wine is built on the scaffold of its structure
        and texture, which hold delicious citrus and apple flavours in a gentle embrace.
        this is a classic Clare riesling of the highest quality, dangerously addictive. Screwcap.
        12% alc. **Rating** 97 **To** 2035 $22 **O**

🍷🍷🍷🍷 **Place in Time Sevenhill Clare Valley Riesling 2010** Full green-gold. The
        wine has developed very well indeed over the years, with a delicious honeyed
        overlay to its lime/citrus base, acidity providing the framework. Screwcap.
        12.5% alc. **Rating** 95 **To** 2020 $35 **O**
        BWC Barossa Valley Shiraz 2014 It is focused on plum, red and dark fruits
        and a deft lick of oak; the palate is seamless and rounded, finishing with a hint of
        spice; richly flavoured and extremely drinkable. Screwcap. 14.5% alc. **Rating** 94
        To 2024

🍷🍷🍷🍷 **Place in Time Greenock Shiraz 2010 Rating** 93 **To** 2030 $65
        Hill 5 Clare Valley Shiraz Cabernet 2014 Rating 92 **To** 2024
        The Aldo Old Vine Grenache Shiraz 2014 Rating 91 **To** 2024 $22 **O**

Nannup Ridge Estate ★★★★☆

PO Box 2, Nannup, WA 6275 **Region** Blackwood Valley
T (08) 9286 2202 **www**.nannupridge.com.au **Open** Not
Winemaker Bruce Dukes, Coby Ladwig **Est.** 1998 **Dozens** 5500 **Vyds** 31ha
The business is owned by the Blizard and Fitzgerald families, who purchased the then
unplanted property from the family that had farmed it since the early 1900s. Mark and Alison
Blizard had in fact moved to the region in the early '90s and established a small vineyard
on the banks of the beautiful Donnelly River. The partners established 31ha of mainstream
varieties (and 1ha of tempranillo) backed by a (then) grape sale agreement with Constellation.

They still regard themselves as grapegrowers, but have successful wines skilfully contract-made from the estate production. Terrific value is par for the course. Exports to China.

ŶŶŶŶŶ **Firetower Sauvignon Blanc 2015** Dials up to maximum firepower at high speed. The flavours are so complex and intense you wonder whether some barrel ferment has been used, but it hasn't; highly fragrant and floral, the palate running through snow pea to gooseberry, thence lemongrass/lemon curd and a final blast of grapefruit and lime. Screwcap. 12.4% alc. **Rating** 95 **To** 2017 $21 **❂**

ŶŶŶŶŶ **Rolling Hills Cabernet Sauvignon 2014 Rating** 92 **To** 2029 $28
Rolling Hills Shiraz 2014 Rating 91 **To** 2029 $28

Narkoojee   ★★★★★

170 Francis Road, Glengarry, Vic 3854 **Region** Gippsland
T (03) 5192 4257 **www**.narkoojee.com **Open** 7 days 10.30–4.30
Winemaker Harry and Axel Friend **Est.** 1981 **Dozens** 6000 **Vyds** 10.3ha
Narkoojee Vineyard (originally a dairy farm owned by the Friend family) is near the old gold-mining town of Walhalla and looks out over the Strzelecki Ranges. The wines are produced from a little over 10ha of estate vineyards, with chardonnay accounting for half the total. Former lecturer in civil engineering and extremely successful amateur winemaker Harry Friend changed horses in 1994 to take joint control, with son Axel, of the family vineyard and winery, and hasn't missed a beat since; their skills show through with all the wines, none more so than the Chardonnay. Exports to Canada, Japan and China.

ŶŶŶŶŶ **Valerie Gippsland Shiraz 2014** Mid-dark crimson; an immediately complex and alluring bouquet with pepper, spice, red and dark fruits supported by cedary oak. Supple, powerful and multifaceted, the palate is fine and deliciously proportioned. Screwcap. 14% alc. **Rating** 95 **To** 2025 $60
Reserve Maxwell Gippsland Cabernet 2014 This is an impressive cabernet from Gippsland. Briary and brambly fruit, coupled with an omnipresent dose of new oak, leads to a brambly and focused palate that builds tannin and length as it opens. Screwcap. 13.5% alc. **Rating** 95 **To** 2034 $38
Valerie Gippsland Pinot Noir 2014 Dark red; the aromas are darkly fruited, spicy and framed by new oak; the palate is equally impressive, densely packed and concentrated, spice, dark fruits and chewy tannins driving the length. Screwcap. 14% alc. **Rating** 94 **To** 2025 $60

ŶŶŶŶŶ **Valerie Gippsland Chardonnay 2014 Rating** 91 **To** 2020 $60

Nazaaray   ★★★☆

266 Meakins Road, Flinders, Vic 3929 **Region** Mornington Peninsula
T (03) 5989 0126 **www**.nazaaray.com.au **Open** 1st w'end of month
Winemaker Paramdeep Ghumman **Est.** 1996 **Dozens** 800 **Vyds** 2.28ha
Paramdeep Ghumman is, as far as I am aware, the only Indian-born winery proprietor in Australia. He and his wife purchased the Nazaaray vineyard property in 1991. An initial trial planting of 400 vines in '96 was gradually expanded to the present level of 1.6ha of pinot noir, 0.44ha of pinot gris and 0.12ha each of sauvignon blanc and shiraz. Notwithstanding the micro size of the estate, all the wines are made and bottled onsite.

ŶŶŶŶŶ **Mornington Peninsula Chardonnay 2015** Only 3 barrels made, fermented (including mlf) in new and used French oak. The oak is subtle, and the very fresh stone fruit flavours leave little doubt the mlf was necessary. Well handled from go to whoa. Screwcap. 14% alc. **Rating** 94 **To** 2022 $45

ŶŶŶŶŶ **Mornington Peninsula Pinot Gris 2015 Rating** 92 **To** 2019 $30

Nepenthe ★★★★

Jones Road, Balhannah, SA 5242 **Region** Adelaide Hills
T (08) 8398 8888 **www**.nepenthe.com.au **Open** 7 days 10–4
Winemaker Alex Trescowthick **Est.** 1994 **Dozens** 40 000 **Vyds** 108.68ha

Nepenthe quickly established its reputation as a producer of high quality wines, but founder Ed Tweddell died unexpectedly in 2006, and the business was purchased by Australian Vintage Limited the following year. The winery was closed in '09, and winemaking operations transferred to McGuigan Wines (Barossa Valley). The Nepenthe winery has since been purchased by Peter Leske and Mark Kozned, and provides contract winemaking services via their Revenir venture. Nepenthe has over 100ha of close-planted vines spread over four vineyards in the Adelaide Hills, with an exotic array of varieties. Exports to the UK, the US and other major markets.

ΨΨΨΨΨ **Pinnacle Ithaca Adelaide Hills Chardonnay 2014** Ripe yellow stone fruit and bacony oak, both laid on thick. This is a full-bodied style but at no point does it run away with itself and/or lose its disciplined feel. No mean feat. Screwcap. 13% alc. **Rating** 93 **To** 2020 $36 CM
Winemaker's Selection Adelaide Hills Arneis 2015 Crunchy white with brine, chalk and ripe melon flavours cracking out across the palate. Clean and brisk for now, but character lurks. Screwcap. 13% alc. **Rating** 92 **To** 2017 $20 CM ✪
Adelaide Hills Tempranillo 2014 Another good release. Juicy raspberry and black cherry with infusions of charcuterie. You could just about drink this anywhere, anytime. Screwcap. 14% alc. **Rating** 92 **To** 2020 $20 CM ✪
Adelaide Hills Sauvignon Blanc 2015 It's a grassy, gravelly, almost smoky style with passionfruit pulp and apple-like flavours providing the flesh and cut. Lots of complex flavour. Screwcap. 12.5% alc. **Rating** 91 **To** 2017 $20 CM ✪
Adelaide Hills Pinot Gris 2015 Element of coiled power to this. It has weight, texture and length in its back pocket and yet it feels tight. It's clearly aiming high. Screwcap. 14% alc. **Rating** 91 **To** 2017 $20 CM ✪
Pinnacle Gate Block Adelaide Hills Shiraz 2013 Weight and indeed complexity, but it's not overly endowed with vigour and/or life. Black cherries, tips of raspberry, a hint of tar and then dry, spicy, foresty notes. Screwcap. 14% alc. **Rating** 91 **To** 2028 $36 CM
Adelaide Hills Chardonnay 2015 Compact and well presented, with stone fruit, chalk and spice notes building more than enough flavour to latch onto. Whispers of cream are an attractive finishing touch. Screwcap. 14% alc. **Rating** 90 **To** 2018 $20 CM ✪
Winemaker's Selection Adelaide Hills Gruner Veltliner 2015 The left hand doesn't quite know what the right hand is up to but it certainly delivers volume of flavour. Pepper, citrus and rosewater with lychee-like inputs. It tries to be pretty and savoury at once. Screwcap. 13.5% alc. **Rating** 90 **To** 2017 $20 CM ✪
Pinnacle The Good Doctor Adelaide Hills Pinot Noir 2014 Sizeable in varietal terms and boasted a stewy heart of flavour. Various spices and woods add complexity, but not spark. Screwcap. 13.5% alc. **Rating** 90 **To** 2023 $36 CM
Adelaide Hills Pinot Noir 2014 Grunty pinot noir with reductive wood smoke stitched into dark, plummy flavour. Sour cherry notes to the edges give a varietal wink. Hefty but silken. Screwcap. 14% alc. **Rating** 90 **To** 2021 $20 CM ✪

ΨΨΨΨ **Winemaker's Selection Viognier 2015 Rating** 89 **To** 2017 $20 CM
Adelaide Hills Shiraz 2013 Rating 89 **To** 2022 $20 CM

New Era Vineyards ★★★★

PO Box 391, Woodside SA 5244 **Region** Adelaide Hills
T 0413 544 246 **www**.neweravineyards.com.au **Open** Not
Winemaker Robert and Iain Baxter **Est.** 1988 **Dozens** 500 **Vyds** 13ha

The New Era vineyard is situated over a gold reef that was mined for 60 years until all recoverable gold had been extracted (mining ceased in 1940). The vineyard was originally planted to chardonnay, shiraz, cabernet sauvignon, merlot and sauvignon, mostly contracted to Foster's. Recently 2ha of cabernet sauvignon and 1.1ha of merlot have been grafted over to sauvignon blanc. Much of the production is sold to other winemakers in the region. The small amount of wine made has been the subject of favourable reviews.

ΥΥΥΥΥ **Basket Pressed Barrel Select Adelaide Hills Shiraz 2013** A best-barrel selection from the total make, the choice made not long prior to bottling. The wine is superior to the base wine, but doesn't introduce anything new or exceptional. Screwcap. 13.5% alc. **Rating** 93 **To** 2020 $45

Basket Pressed Adelaide Hills Shiraz 2013 The bouquet is a fragrant revolving wheel of spice, licorice, black cherry and French oak, the palate ramping up the intensity of those characters, tannins also surreptitiously entering the game. Screwcap. 13.5% alc. **Rating** 92 **To** 2028 $25 ✪

Basket Pressed Langhorne Creek Adelaide Hills Cabernet Sauvignon 2014 The Langhorne Creek component does most of the talking with its typical supple, laidback mouthfeel encouraging the second glass. There is cassis to burn, and darker berry inputs from the Adelaide Hills portion. All up, great value. Screwcap. 14% alc. **Rating** 92 **To** 2029 $25 ✪

Adelaide Hills Syrah Rose 2015 Full fuchsia-crimson; crisp and lively, with spicy dark cherry fruits on the bouquet, then running through the length of the palate. Seamless. Screwcap. 13% alc. **Rating** 90 **To** 2018 $18 ✪

ΥΥΥΥ **Adelaide Hills Sauvignon Blanc 2015 Rating** 89 **To** 2017 $18 ✪
Basket Pressed Adelaide Hills Pinot Noir 2015 Rating 88 **To** 2020 $30

Newtons Ridge Estate ★★★★

1170 Cooriemungle Road, Timboon, Vic 3268 **Region** Geelong
T (03) 5598 7394 **www.**newtonsridgeestate.com.au **Open** Thurs–Mon 11–4 Oct–Easter
Winemaker David Falk **Est.** 1998 **Dozens** 850 **Vyds** 5ha
David and Carla Falk have operated a real estate and livestock agency in since 1989, the property 'just a couple of ridges away' from Newtons Ridge Estate. When they heard that founder David Newton was contemplating pulling out the vines, they purchased the vineyard, in 2012, completing a circle that began in the 1880s when Carla's family were among the first vignerons in Geelong – they produce wine in Switzerland to this day.

ΥΥΥΥΥ **Shiraz 2014** From the Grampians, open-fermented, matured in French oak. A potent, full-bodied wine with spice and pepper sprinkled generously through blackberry and blackcurrant fruit, but are not as prominent as the tannins. The good news is that they (the tannins) are of high quality, and will settle into their life's mission: to provide protection and longevity for the wine over many years to come. Screwcap. 14.1% alc. **Rating** 94 **To** 2040 $35

ΥΥΥΥΥ **Sparkling Tache 2010 Rating** 92 **To** 2019 $35
Chardonnay 2014 Rating 91 **To** 2020 $50

Ngeringa ★★★★★

119 Williams Road, Mount Barker, SA 5251 **Region** Adelaide Hills
T (08) 8398 2867 **www.**ngeringa.com **Open** Last Sun month 11–5 or by appt
Winemaker Erinn Klein **Est.** 2001 **Dozens** 2000 **Vyds** 5ha
Erinn and Janet Klein say, 'As fervent practitioners of biodynamic wine growing, we respect biodynamics as a sensitivity to the rhythms of nature, the health of the soil and the connection between plant, animal and cosmos. It is a pragmatic solution to farming without the use of chemicals and a necessary acknowledgement that the farm unit is part of a great whole.' It is not an easy solution, and the Kleins have increased the immensity of the challenge by using ultra-close vine spacing of 1.5m × 1m, necessitating a large amount of hand-training of the vines plus the use of a tiny crawler tractor. Lest it be thought they have stumbled onto biodynamic growing without understanding wine science, they teamed up while studying at Adelaide University in 2000 (Erinn – oenology, Janet – viticulture/wine marketing), and then spent time looking at the great viticultural regions of the Old World, with a particular emphasis on biodynamics. The JE label is used for the basic wines, Ngeringa only for the very

best (NASAA Certified Biodynamic Cert No. 5184). Exports to the US, Canada, Austria, Belgium, Norway, Japan, Taiwan, Hong Kong and China.

PPPPP **Adelaide Hills Syrah 2012** The quality of the vintage, the site, the ultra-close planting and the grapes all combine to provide a wine with energy, intensity and elegance, an uncommon trio. Red fruits, led by cherry, spice, pepper and licorice are all in play; quality oak and fine-grained tannins complete the picture. Screwcap. 13.5% alc. **Rating** 95 **To** 2027 $55

Altus 2010 Made in the same fashion as Tuscan Vin Santo, hand-harvested at low baume and dehydrated on racks for 4 weeks, pressed to a single old French barrique for wild fermentation, matured for 5 years; has worked very well. Indeed cumquat, sweet Middle Eastern spices and perfect acidity bounce off each other like New Year's Eve fireworks. 375ml. Screwcap. 9% alc. **Rating** 95 **To** 2022 $40

Elliptic Adelaide Hills Chardonnay 2013 This is a good wine by any standards, with the energy proponents of biodynamics expect to achieve. The flavours are of white peach, honeydew melon and pear, the acidity good and the oak integrated. Screwcap. 13.5% alc. **Rating** 94 **To** 2021 $40

PPPPP **Adelaide Hills Nebbiolo 2014** Rating 93 **To** 2024 $35
Adelaide Hills Rose 2014 Rating 92 **To** 2016 $28
Adelaide Hills Chardonnay 2013 Rating 91 **To** 2020 $40
Eclat Adelaide Hills Brut NV Rating 90 **To** 2017 $40

Nicholson River ★★★★

57 Liddells Road, Nicholson, Vic 3882 **Region** Gippsland
T (03) 5156 8241 **www**.nicholsonriverwinery.com.au **Open** 7 days 10–5 during hols
Winemaker Ken Eckersley **Est.** 1978 **Dozens** 1000 **Vyds** 8ha

Nicholson River's fierce commitment to quality in the face of the temperamental Gippsland climate and frustratingly small production has been handsomely repaid by some massive Chardonnays and impressive red wines. Ken Eckersley refers to his Chardonnays not as white wines but as gold wines, and lists them accordingly in his newsletter.

PPPPP **Chardonnay 2014** Glowing straw yellow. Peach and malt flavours are given relief by fresh, juicy apple. It's rich to start but as it works its way along the palate it becomes finer and mealier. Indeed the final impression is one of sophistication. Screwcap. 12.6% alc. **Rating** 92 **To** 2020 $45 CM

PPPP **Sangiovese 2014** Rating 89 **To** 2020 $35 CM

Nick Haselgrove Wines ★★★★

281 Tatachilla Road, McLaren Vale, SA 5171 **Region** Adelaide Zone
T (08) 8323 6124 **www**.nhwines.com.au **Open** By appt
Winemaker Nick Haselgrove **Est.** 2010 **Dozens** 10 000

After various sales, amalgamations and disposals of particular brands, Nick Haselgrove now owns The Old Faithful (see separate entry), Blackbilly, Clarence Hill, James Haselgrove, Tir na N'Og, and Wishing Tree brands. Exports to the US and other major markets.

PPPPP **James Haselgrove Futures McLaren Vale Shiraz 2011** The '11 vintage has imprinted this wine with the trademark cool-edged fruit and spicy herbal lift. The palate is medium-bodied and plushly fruited. Drinking very nicely now. Diam. 14.5% alc. **Rating** 93 **To** 2020 $40

Blackbilly Adelaide Chardonnay 2014 Generously flavoured, with melon, peach and a hint of pineapple. The palate is equally generous and rounded, finishing long. Screwcap. 13% alc. **Rating** 91 **To** 2018 $23 ✪

James Haselgrove Futures McLaren Vale Shiraz 2012 A Reserve release from '12, it is a wine saturated in black fruits and substantial extract, firm, grippy and powerful. Not for the faint-hearted. Diam. 14.5% alc. **Rating** 91 **To** 2040 $40

PPPP **Clarence Hill Reserve McLaren Vale Shiraz 2012** Rating 89 **To** 2030 $32

Nick O'Leary Wines ★★★★★

129 Donnelly Lane, Bungendore, NSW 2621 **Region** Canberra District
T (02) 6161 8739 **www**.nickolearywines.com.au **Open** By appt
Winemaker Nick O'Leary **Est.** 2007 **Dozens** 6000

At the ripe old age of 28, Nick O'Leary had been involved in the wine industry for over a decade, working variously in retail, wholesale, viticulture and winemaking. Two years earlier he had laid the foundation for Nick O'Leary Wines, purchasing shiraz from local vignerons (commencing in 2006); riesling following in '08. His wines have had extraordinarily consistent success in local wine shows and competitions since the first vintages, and are building on that early success in spectacular fashion. At the NSW Wine Awards '15, the 2014 Shiraz was awarded the NSW Wine of the Year Trophy exactly as the 2013 Shiraz had in the prior year – the first time any winery had won the award in consecutive years.

ŸŸŸŸŸ Riesling 2015 Wow. This is an IED (improvised explosive device), with quite amazing fruit taking a millisecond to explode into every recess in the mouth, with a distillation of diamond-pure lime juice. For good measure, these lime flavours are unique to this wine. When to drink? Any time you wish to shed the sorrows and worries of this world, so buy heaps. Screwcap. 12% alc. **Rating** 97 **To** 2035 $25 ◑

ŸŸŸŸŸ White Rocks Riesling 2015 The vines were planted in '73 on the old shoreline of Lake George; hand-picked, whole bunch-pressed, cool-fermented. Of exceptional intensity, with intense lime/lemon/grapefruit flavours; great now, better still in 5+ years. Screwcap. 12% alc. **Rating** 96 **To** 2030 $37 ◑
Seven Gates Tempranillo 2014 Open-fermented, 10% whole bunches, 90% whole berries, matured in French puncheons (10% new) for 12 months. A tempranillo with unusual texture and savoury notes, neither easily explained by vinification. A challenging wine. Screwcap. 13.5% alc. **Rating** 94 **To** 2029 $35

ŸŸŸŸŸ Rose 2015 **Rating** 93 **To** 2017 $21 ◑

Night Harvest ★★★★★

PO Box 921, Busselton, WA 6280 **Region** Margaret River
T (08) 9755 1521 **www**.nightharvest.com.au **Open** Not
Winemaker Bruce Dukes **Est.** 2005 **Dozens** 40 000 **Vyds** 300ha

Andy and Mandy Ferreira arrived in Margaret River in 1986 as newly married young migrants. They soon became involved in the construction and establishment of new vineyards, as well as growing vegetables for the local and export markets. Their vineyard-contracting business expanded quickly when the region experienced its rapid growth in the late '90s, so the vegetable business was closed, and they put all their focus into wine. They were involved in the establishment of about 300ha of Margaret River vineyards, many of which they continue to manage today (Woodside Valley Estate and Chapman Grove are among the 16 estates that fall into this category.) As their fortunes grew, they purchased their own property and produced their first wines in 2005. Harvesting is a key part of their business, and currently they harvest fruit from over 100 sites. Hence the Night Harvest brand was born, and Butler Crest was added as a premium label. Exports to the UK, the US, Thailand, Hong Kong and China.

ŸŸŸŸŸ Butler Crest Margaret River Cabernet Sauvignon 2014 Estate-grown, matured in French oak. Offers very good varietal and regional expression, with ample blackcurrant/cassis fruit, balanced tannins and subtle French oak on the medium to full-bodied palate. Sure-fire development ahead. Gold medal WA Wine Show '15. Screwcap. 14.4% alc. **Rating** 95 **To** 2029 $25 ◑
John George Cabernet Sauvignon 2014 Red fruits have as much to say as black in a palate that is, and always will be, only medium-bodied, fine-grained tannins gracefully retracting where needed, French oak one of the few constants. Its sub-14% alcohol has much to do with this, but all the innumerable moving parts are under the control of ringmaster and winemaker Bruce Dukes. Screwcap. 13.8% alc. **Rating** 95 **To** 2034 $40

John George Shiraz 2014 Excellent colour; cigar box/cedary oak is the first out of the blocks on a medium-bodied palate; the fruit is relatively delicate, but its red berries are inviting, as are the freshness and length of the palate. Give it a year or two and the oak will back off somewhat. Screwcap. 13.6% alc. **Rating** 94 **To** 2030 $40

ΨΨΨΨΨ **Margaret River Cabernet Sauvignon 2014** Rating 90 To 2029 $25

Nine Fingers

PO Box 212, Lobethal, SA 5241 **Region** Adelaide Hills
T (08) 8389 6049 **Open** By appt
Winemaker Michael Sykes (Contract) **Est.** 1999 **Dozens** 300 **Vyds** 1ha
Simon and Penny Cox established their sauvignon blanc vineyard after encouragement from local winemaker Robb Cootes of Leland Estate. The small vineyard has meant that they do all the viticultural work, and meticulously tend the vines. They obviously have a sense of humour, which may not be shared by their youngest daughter Olivia. In 2002, 2-year-old Olivia's efforts to point out bunches that needed to be thinned resulted in Penny's secateurs cutting off the end of Olivia's finger. A race to hospital and successful microsurgery resulted in the full restoration of the finger; strangely, Olivia has shown little interest in viticulture since. Exports to Singapore.

ΨΨΨΨΨ **Sauvignon Blanc 2015** While the bouquet and fore-palate don't have much to say, the palate certainly does, with citrus and passionfruit foremost on the stage, building to a climax on the finish. A bronze medal from the Adelaide Hills Wine Show seems parsimonious. Screwcap. 13.2% alc. **Rating** 90 **To** 2016 $20 ✪

916

916 Steels Creek Road, Steels Creek, Vic 3775 (postal) **Region** Yarra Valley
T (03) 5965 2124 **www**.916.com.au **Open** Not
Winemaker Ben Haines **Est.** 2008 **Dozens** 210 **Vyds** 2ha
916, established by John Brand and Erin-Marie O'Neill, is one of three wineries in the *Wine Companion* using three digits as their name, others being 919 and 201. A year after they acquired their 8ha property, bushfires destroyed their home and all their possessions, but they rebuilt their lives and home, reinvesting in wine and vineyard alike. Viticulturist John Evans, formerly at Yering Station and now at Rochford Wines, became involved with the vineyard in 1996. No '14 was made due to unacceptably low yield; the next release will be the '15. They chose their viticulturist well, and they have a highly gifted winemaker in the form of Ben Haines. Exports to the US, China and Singapore.

ΨΨΨΨΨ **Yarra Valley Pinot Noir 2013** From MV6 clone vines. Bright crimson-purple; a very expressive bouquet with a deep pinot and allspice aroma is replayed on the full, but well-balanced palate, plum, spice and positive oak all contributing. Sure to develop well. Diam. 13.5% alc. **Rating** 94 **To** 2023 $90

919 Wines ★★★★

39 Hodges Road, Berri, SA 5343 **Region** Riverland
T 0408 855 272 **www**.919wines.com.au **Open** Wed–Sun & public hols 10–5
Winemaker Eric and Jenny Semmler **Est.** 2002 **Dozens** 2000 **Vyds** 17ha
Eric and Jenny Semmler have been involved in the wine industry since 1986, and have a special interest in fortified wines. Eric previously made fortified wines for Hardys, and worked at Brown Brothers. Jenny has worked for Strathbogie Vineyards, Pennyweight Wines and St Huberts. They have planted micro-quantities of varieties for fortified wines: palomino, durif, tempranillo, muscat à petits grains, tinta cao, shiraz, tokay and touriga nacional. They use minimal water application, deliberately reducing the crop levels, practising organic and biodynamic techniques. In 2011 they purchased the 12.3ha property at Loxton they now call Ella Semmler's Vineyard.

♟♟♟♟♀ **Shiraz 2015** The prettiness of violet and vanilla; the work of dense, ripe, inky plum; the foundation of firm, grainy tannin. It's a well-built house, fitted and decorated, both ready to be enjoyed now and built to last. Screwcap. 14.5% alc. **Rating** 93 **To** 2027 $47 CM

Vermentino 2015 Quite extraordinary texture and character. It falls squarely into the 'love or loathe' category. It's dry and oystery with citrus rind and grapefruit pith notes; it's not of great use unless you serve it alongside food, and then it beams at you. Screwcap. 13.5% alc. **Rating** 92 **To** 2017 $26 CM

Tempranillo 2013 Strong oak but equally strong fruit. It's a muscle-bound tempranillo with darker cherry flavours tending towards licorice. Rivers of toast and malt usher the fruit across the tannic grooves of the finish. It's not going anywhere in a hurry. Screwcap. 14.5% alc. **Rating** 92 **To** 2024 $42 CM

Sangiovese 2015 Seductive fruit-and-wood scents lead to a palate well endowed with both fruit sweetness and spice-driven savouriness. Quite lovely to drink. Screwcap. 13.5% alc. **Rating** 91 **To** 2019 $32 CM

♟♟♟♟ **Durif 2013 Rating** 88 **To** 2020 $42 CM
Touriga Nacional 2015 Rating 88 **To** 2024 $42 CM
Classic Muscat NV Rating 88 **To** 2017 $40 CM

Nintingbool   ★★★★☆

56 Wongerer Lane, Smythes Creek, Vic 3351 (postal) **Region** Ballarat
T (03) 5342 4393 **www**.nintingbool.com **Open** Not
Winemaker Peter Bothe **Est.** 1998 **Dozens** 460 **Vyds** 2ha
Peter and Jill Bothe purchased the Nintingbool property in 1982 and built their home in '84, using bluestone dating back to the goldrush period. They established an extensive Australian native garden and home orchard, but in '98 diversified by planting pinot noir, a further planting the following year lifting the total to 2ha. This is one of the coolest mainland regions, and demands absolute attention to detail (and a warm growing season) for success.

♟♟♟♟♟ **Smythes Creek Shiraz 2014** This is spicy, perfumed, complex and thoroughly delicious. Sit back and let it entertain you. Cherry-plum, redcurrant, anise and dried spices thrown by the fistful. Immaculate tannin structure. Indeed pitch-perfect all over. Screwcap. 14.1% alc. **Rating** 95 **To** 2032 $27 CM

♟♟♟♟♀ **Smythes Creek Pinot Noir 2013 Rating** 93 **To** 2024 $35 CM

Noble Red   ★★★☆

18 Brennan Avenue, Upper Beaconsfield, Vic 3808 (postal) **Region** Heathcote
T 0400 594 440 **www**.nobleredwines.com **Open** Not
Winemaker Roman Sobiesiak, Osicka Wines **Est.** 2002 **Dozens** 700 **Vyds** 6ha
Roman and Margaret Sobiesiak acquired their property in 2002. There was 0.25ha of shiraz planted in the 1970s, and a progressive planting program has seen the area increase to 6ha, shiraz (3.6ha) accounting for the lion's share, the remainder equally split to tempranillo, mourvedre, merlot and cabernet sauvignon. They adopted a dry-grown approach, which meant slow development during the prolonged drought, but their commitment remains undimmed. Indeed, visiting many wine regions around the world and working within the industry locally has increased their determination. Exports to China.

♟♟♟♟♀ **Heathcote Shiraz 2014** Excellent colour; a full-bodied shiraz built around ripe fruit and sandy tannins that appear immediately the wine is tasted, and won't go away. I'm in two minds about the oak, and in particular whether it will come into better balance with age. Screwcap. 14.8% alc. **Rating** 90 **To** 2022 $25

Nocton Vineyard   ★★★★

373 Colebrook Road, Richmond, Tas 7025 **Region** Southern Tasmania
T 0418 645 807 **www**.noctonwine.com.au **Open** By appt
Winemaker Winemaking Tasmania **Est.** 1998 **Dozens** 10000 **Vyds** 34ha

Nocton Vineyard is the reincarnation of Nocton Park. After years of inactivity (other than the ongoing sale of the grapes from what is a first-class vineyard) it largely disappeared from sight. There are two labels: N1 for the premium range, almost entirely made from estate-grown grapes, and the Coal River label at a lower price. The quality across the two labels is very good. Exports to China.

♥♥♥♥♀ **Coal River Valley Chardonnay 2015** Sweet peachy fruit with slips of cedary oak. Simple appeal at this early stage but generous to a fault. Screwcap. 13.5% alc. **Rating** 90 **To** 2018 $28 CM

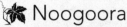 # Noogoora ★★★

13 Marla Crescent, Noarlunga Downs, SA 5168 (postal) **Region** McLaren Vale
T 0429 672 858 **www**.noogoora.com.au **Open** Not
Winemaker Pieter Breugem, Celeste Roberts **Est.** 2015 **Dozens** 2000
Just so you know, Noogoora is a drought-resistant plant, despised by graziers as a weed, but, say Noogoora's owners, it 'thrives in good times and survives the lean periods. This fits with our lifestyle. It's all about family, friends and flourishing in the good times.' Owners Martin Kay, Celeste Roberts and Pieter Breugem have worked together for many years at a winery (not Noogoora), Celeste and Pieter husband and wife winemakers, Martin the marketer. This is seen by the trio as fun, but there's real purpose to overseeing the making the Noogoora wine.

♥♥♥♥ **Short Rib McLaren Vale Shiraz 2013** Crushed and destemmed, 5 days cold soak, open-fermented, wild yeast-initiated fermentation, then cultured yeast added, matured in American hogsheads for 14 months. The colour and bouquet are good, the medium to full-bodied palate taking the baton with ease, fruit, oak and tannins all in sync; it's berry-driven, with dark chocolate not on the roster – that's not a criticism. Screwcap. 14.5% alc. **Rating** 89 **To** 2028 $20

Norfolk Rise Vineyard

Limestone Coast Road, Mount Benson, SA 5265 **Region** Mount Benson
T (08) 8768 5080 **www**.norfolkrise.com.au **Open** Not
Winemaker Daniel Berrigan **Est.** 2000 **Dozens** 20 000 **Vyds** 130ha
This is by far the largest and most important development in the Mount Benson region. It is ultimately owned by a privately held Belgian company, G & C Kreglinger, established in 1797. In early 2002 Kreglinger acquired Pipers Brook Vineyard; it has maintained the separate brands of the two ventures. There are 46 blocks of sauvignon blanc, pinot gris, pinot noir, shiraz, merlot and cabernet sauvignon, allowing a range of options in making the six single-variety wines in the portfolio. The business has moved away from the export of bulk wine to bottled wine, with significantly better returns to the winery. Exports to Europe and Asia.

♥♥♥♥ **Mount Benson Pinot Grigio 2015** Estate-grown, avoided juice oxidation, a standard long, cool fermentation. The flavours are typical sotto voce (this is grigio), but the wine surprises with a lift in the intensity on the finish. Screwcap. 12.5% alc. **Rating** 89 **To** 2016 $16 ✪
Mt Benson Barossa Valley Shiraz 2014 Part estate-grown, part contract-grown, fermented in small batches, the normal skin contact 7–10 days, but extended maceration for part of the fruit, matured in predominantly French barriques for 12 months. A unique blend of these two regions which works well, black cherry and plum fruit to the fore; despite the low yield, it is not over-extracted, simply emphatic in its flavour and texture profile. A bargain, with improvement still in store. Screwcap. 14% alc. **Rating** 89 **To** 2024 $16 ✪

Norton Estate

758 Plush Hannans Road, Lower Norton, Vic 3401 **Region** Western Victoria Zone
T (03) 5384 8235 **www**.nortonestate.com.au **Open** Fri–Sun & public hols 11–4
Winemaker Best's Wines **Est.** 1997 **Dozens** 1000 **Vyds** 4.66ha

In 1996 the Spence family purchased a rundown farm at Lower Norton and, rather than looking to the traditional wool, meat and wheat markets, trusted their instincts and planted vines on the elevated, frost-free, buckshot rises. The surprising vigour of the initial planting of shiraz prompted further plantings of shiraz, cabernet sauvignon and sauvignon blanc, plus a small planting of the American variety 'Norton'. The vineyard is halfway between the Grampians and Mt Arapiles, 6km northwest of the Grampians region, and has to be content with the Western Victoria Zone, but the wines show regional Grampians character and style.

🍷🍷🍷🍷🍷 **Wendy's Block Shiraz 2014** Made from a tiny block of 600 vines, the best on the estate, named in honour of Wendy Spence, founder of the estate. It has excellent colour, and has a quiet depth to the supple, medium-bodied palate; blackberry, black cherry and plum all contribute to the perfect balance and mouthfeel, oak and tannins pushed into the background. Screwcap. 13.5% alc. **Rating** 95 **To** 2034 $65

🍷🍷🍷🍷🍷 **Arapiles Run Shiraz 2014 Rating** 93 **To** 2029 $36
Sauvignon Blanc 2015 Rating 91 **To** 2017 $18 ✪

Nova Vita Wines ★★★★
11 Woodlands Road, Kenton Valley, SA 5235 **Region** Adelaide Hills
T (08) 8356 0454 **www.**novavitawines.com.au **Open** Not
Winemaker Mark Kozned **Est.** 2005 **Dozens** 10 000 **Vyds** 46ha
Mark and Jo Kozned's 30ha Woodlands Ridge Vineyard is planted to chardonnay, sauvignon blanc, pinot gris and shiraz. They have subsequently established the Tunnel Hill Vineyard, with 16ha planted to pinot noir, shiraz, cabernet sauvignon, sauvignon blanc, semillon, verdelho, merlot and sangiovese. The name Nova Vita reflects the beginning of the Kozneds' new life, the firebird on the label coming from their Russian ancestry. It is a Russian myth that only a happy or lucky person may see the bird or hear its song. The Kozneds have joined forces with Peter Leske to form Revenir, a contract winemaking business that has purchased the former Nepenthe winery. Exports to Thailand, Singapore and China.

🍷🍷🍷🍷🍷 **Firebird Shiraz 2013** Beefy red with blackberry, saltbush and red/black cherry fruit flavours talking up a big game. Meat, spice and (dark) chocolatey oak notes add to the conversation. Tannin pulls the strings tight. Big end of town for the region, but done well. Screwcap. 13.5% alc. **Rating** 94 **To** 2027 $35 CM

🍷🍷🍷🍷🍷 **Firebird Gruner Veltliner 2015 Rating** 93 **To** 2017 $25 CM ✪
Reserve Shiraz 2013 Rating 90 **To** 2035 $100 CM
George Kozned Fortitude Shiraz 2013 Rating 90 **To** 2025 $30 CM
George Kozned Aspiration NV Rating 90 **To** 2017 $20 TS ✪

Nugan Estate ★★★★
Kidman Way, Wilbriggie, NSW 2680 **Region** Riverina
T (02) 9362 9993 **www.**nuganestate.com.au **Open** Mon–Fri 9–5
Winemaker Daren Owers **Est.** 1999 **Dozens** 500 000 **Vyds** 491ha
Nugan Estate arrived on the scene like a whirlwind. It is an offshoot of the Nugan Group headed by Michelle Nugan (until her retirement in Feb 2013), inter alia the recipient of an Export Hero Award in '00. In the mid-1990s the company began developing vineyards, and it is now a veritable giant, with five vineyards: Cookoothama (335ha), Manuka Grove (46ha) in the Riverina, Frasca's Lane (100ha) in the King Valley and McLaren Parish (10ha) in McLaren Vale. The wine business is now in the energetic hands of Matthew and Tiffany Nugan, Michelle's children. Exports to the UK, the US and other major markets.

🍷🍷🍷🍷🍷 **Cookoothama Limited Release Darlington Point Botrytis Semillon 2010** Yellow-gold; for those who don't know, botrytis semillon is a world apart from cane cut – this (botrytis) has fruit complexity with a textural edge as well as lusciously sweet fruit; length rather than a dead-end street; crystallised cumquat and cream flavours. Screwcap. 11% alc. **Rating** 93 **To** 2018 $21 ✪

McLaren Parish Vineyard McLaren Vale Shiraz 2014 A well-made full-bodied shiraz that could only have come from McLaren Vale. Black fruits have a forest of powdery tannins, but the fruit (and dark chocolate) does assert itself on the finish and aftertaste. Screwcap. 14.5% alc. **Rating** 92 **To** 2034 $23 **○**

Alcira Vineyard Coonawarra Cabernet Sauvignon 2014 Medium-dark red; the aromas have Coonawarra written all over them, mint, cassis, mulberry with a briary background. Firm and slightly chunky tannins drive the length of the wine. Screwcap. 14% alc. **Rating** 92 **To** 2020 $23 **○**

Manuka Grove Vineyard Durif 2013 Big and inky colour leads to a deeply concentrated and spicy bouquet. The palate is similarly proportioned, offering loads of flavour and texture. Screwcap. 15% alc. **Rating** 92 **To** 2025 $23 **○**

♥♥♥♥ **Frasca's Lane Vineyard Chardonnay 2015 Rating** 89 **To** 2017 $20

O'Leary Walker Wines ★★★★★

Horrocks Highway, Leasingham, SA 5452 **Region** Clare Valley
T (08) 8843 0022 **www**.olearywalkerwines.com **Open** Mon–Sat 10–4, Sun 11–4
Winemaker David O'Leary, Nick Walker, Keeda Zilm **Est.** 2001 **Dozens** 20 000
Vyds 35ha
David O'Leary and Nick Walker together had more than 30 years' experience as winemakers working for some of the biggest Australian wine groups when they took the plunge in 2001 and backed themselves to establish their own winery and brand. Initially the principal focus was on the Clare Valley, with 10ha of riesling, shiraz, cabernet sauvignon and semillon the main plantings; thereafter attention swung to the Adelaide Hills, where they now have 25ha of chardonnay, cabernet sauvignon, pinot noir, shiraz, sauvignon blanc and merlot. Exports to the UK, Ireland and Asia.

♥♥♥♥♥ **Polish Hill River Riesling 2015** Gleaming straw-green; celebrates the vintage and the subregion; there are layers of lime-accented fruit and a hint of crushed lime leaves, given balance by slatey acidity. Exceptional value. Screwcap. 12% alc. **Rating** 95 **To** 2027 $22 **○**

The Lucky Punter Adelaide Hills Sauvignon Blanc 2015 A swirl of cut grass, green pea, citrus zest, kiwi fruit and gooseberry wrapped in the embrace of minerally acidity that takes no prisoners. This is a sauvignon blanc that flaunts its wares, and has no intention of backing off on the lingering finish. Should appeal to a broad church. Screwcap. 11.5% alc. **Rating** 95 **To** 2017 $18 **○**

♥♥♥♥♡ **The Bookies' Bag Pinot Noir 2014 Rating** 93 **To** 2025 $25 **○**
Watervale Riesling 2015 Rating 92 **To** 2030 $19 **○**
Final Instructions Adelaide Hills Shiraz 2014 Rating 92 **To** 2024 $35
Clare Valley Cabernet Malbec 2013 Rating 92 **To** 2023 $22 **○**
Clare Valley Shiraz 2013 Rating 91 **To** 2028 $22 **○**

Oakdene ★★★★★

255 Grubb Road, Wallington, Vic 3221 **Region** Geelong
T (03) 5256 3886 **www**.oakdene.com.au **Open** 7 days 10–4
Winemaker Robin Brockett, Marcus Holt **Est.** 2001 **Dozens** 7000 **Vyds** 12ha
Bernard and Elizabeth Hooley purchased Oakdene in 2001. Bernard focused on planting the vineyard (shiraz, pinot gris, sauvignon blanc, pinot noir, chardonnay, merlot, cabernet franc and cabernet sauvignon), while Elizabeth worked to restore the 1920s homestead. Much of the wine is sold through the award-winning Oakdene Restaurant and cellar door. The quality is exemplary, as is the consistency of that quality; Robin Brockett's skills are on full display.

♥♥♥♥♥ **William Shiraz 2014** In beautiful form. Meat and spice notes galore but with plush, ripe, generous fruit as a flood of seductive power. Tannin is smoky, filigreed, and deceptively firm. The longer you spend with this wine the more it impresses. It's stellar. Screwcap. 14.1% alc. **Rating** 96 **To** 2030 $42 CM **○**

Jessica Sauvignon 2015 Barrel-fermented, and hasn't it worked a treat. This is a wine that seems entirely sure of its self. Ripped with flavour, fruit and oak; textural; lengthy. Importantly, it remains fresh and fruit-driven as you swallow; the drive of fruit has not been sedated. Screwcap. 12.8% alc. **Rating** 95 To 2017 $28 CM ○

▼▼▼▼▽ **Liz's Chardonnay 2014 Rating** 93 To 2020 $35 CM
Peta's Pinot Noir 2014 Rating 93 To 2021 $42 CM
Ly Ly Pinot Gris 2015 Rating 92 To 2016 $28 CM
Sauvignon Blanc 2015 Rating 91 To 2016 $21 ○
Pinot Grigio 2015 Rating 90 To 2016 $23
Pinot Noir 2014 Rating 90 To 2019 $24 CM
Bernard's Cabernets 2014 Rating 90 To 2025 $30 CM
Late Harvest Riesling 2015 Rating 90 To 2017 $23 CM

Oakridge Wines   ★★★★★

864 Maroondah Highway, Coldstream, Vic 3770 **Region** Yarra Valley
T (03) 9738 9900 **www**.oakridgewines.com.au **Open** 7 days 10–5
Winemaker David Bicknell **Est.** 1978 **Dozens** 24 000 **Vyds** 22.3ha
Winemaker and CEO David Bicknell has proved his worth time and again as an extremely talented winemaker. At the top of the brand tier is 864, all Yarra Valley vineyard selections, only released in the best years (Chardonnay, Pinot Noir, Shiraz, Cabernet Sauvignon, Riesling); next is the Oakridge Local Vineyard Series (the Chardonnay, Pinot Noir and Sauvignon Blanc come from the cooler Upper Yarra Valley; the Shiraz, Cabernet Sauvignon and Viognier from the Lower Yarra); and the Over the Shoulder range, drawn from all of the sources available to Oakridge (Sauvignon Blanc, Pinot Grigio, Pinot Noir, Shiraz Viognier, Cabernet Sauvignon). The two estate vineyards are at 864 Maroondah Highway (9.8ha) and 200 Hazeldene Road, Gladysdale (12.5ha). Exports to the UK, the US, Sweden, The Netherlands, Norway, Fiji, Papua New Guinea, Singapore, Hong Kong and China.

▼▼▼▼▼ **Local Vineyard Series Willowlake Vineyard Yarra Valley Chardonnay 2014** From the heart of the Upper Yarra (and its oldest vineyard), this has unequalled finesse and brightness to its fruit profile, ranging through grapefruit and white peach on the bouquet and palate alike. Screwcap. 13.4% alc. **Rating** 97 To 2024 $36 ○
864 Single Block Release B-Block Lusatia Park Vineyard Yarra Valley Pinot Noir 2014 A beautiful wine from a great vineyard, purchased by De Bortoli in '15. It instantaneously catches you in a silken web of a multitude of red berry and plum flavours; you know the tannins are there, like children to be seen but not heard, oak likewise. One of the most beautiful Yarra Valley pinots from the vintage. Screwcap. 13.8% alc. **Rating** 97 To 2026 $77 ○

▼▼▼▼▼ **Local Vineyard Series Lusatia Park Vineyard Chardonnay 2014** There is a fragrant, bordering on perfume, bouquet joining hands with the riveting freshness of the long, vibrant palate. Not from the highest vineyard in the Upper Yarra Valley, but there's no questioning its place, with a seamless mix of white peach and grapefruit. Screwcap. 13.7% alc. **Rating** 96 To 2024 $36 ○
Local Vineyard Series Willowlake Vineyard Pinot Noir 2014 Willowlake is the oldest Upper Yarra vineyard, and always has that little bit extra in fruit complexity – both red and black fruits, even if red is still the leader – fine tannins and oak totally in balance. Screwcap. 13.4% alc. **Rating** 96 To 2029 $36 ○
Local Vineyard Series Barkala Ridge Vineyard Chardonnay 2015 Complex and seductive at once. Grapefruit, flint, chalk and nashi pear flavours get the mouth watering; stone fruit and smoky oak characters bring it all home. Minerally finish fixes the quality in stone. Screwcap. 13.5% alc. **Rating** 95 To 2024 $38 CM
Local Vineyard Series Lusatia Park Vineyard Yarra Valley Pinot Noir 2014 Vivid crystal-clear colour; pinot speaking of variety and place with no winemaking ego getting in the way; red cherry/berry fruits have a bracing by fine

tannins; the oak is well integrated, with only a judicious amount new. Screwcap. 13.5% alc. **Rating** 95 To 2024 $36

864 Single Block Release Winery Block Oakridge Vineyard Yarra Valley Syrah 2013 Superb clear crimson; a Yarra Valley shiraz built for the ages; the fruit flavours cruise between black and red, picking up nuances of whatever takes your fancy while doing so, but it's the structure created out of the whole bunch fermentation that creates the future. Screwcap. 13.4% alc. **Rating** 95 To 2038 $77

Local Vineyard Series Blanc de Blancs 2011 A perfect vintage for Yarra Valley Blanc de Blancs (aka chardonnay); fine, long and penetrating, with white peach to the fore, a dusting of brioche and cream, then an emphatic finish thanks to perfectly weighted acidity. Diam. 12.5% alc. **Rating** 95 To 2021 $40

864 Single Block Release Drive Block Funder & Diamond Vineyard Yarra Valley Chardonnay 2014 A particularly fine and elegant chardonnay still evolving in bottle, and needing yet more time as at Feb '16. A late bloomer that will make it given time. Screwcap. 13.5% alc. **Rating** 94 To 2026 $77

Over the Shoulder Yarra Valley Pinot Grigio 2014 A low-crop year has produced a high-intensity result. It boasts a particularly acute burst of grapefruit and smoke-like flavour through the finish; it's a simple affair to that point but then it launches, and you'd swear, after you've swallowed, that the flavours echo like a gun shot. The asking price suggests this effect was easily achieved; it wasn't. Screwcap. 12% alc. **Rating** 94 To 2016 $22 CM ●

Local Vineyard Series Murrummong Vineyard Yarra Valley Arneis 2014 Beautiful example of the variety. Direct and lengthy but along the way notes of honeysuckle, pear, barley sugar and lime are showcased quite deliciously. Screwcap. 13% alc. **Rating** 94 To 2017 $26 CM ●

Meunier 2015 Good colour for the usually pale meunier; red and black cherries tussle for supremacy on the bouquet and palate, giving rise to positive texture and structure, ghostly tannins walking the ramparts. A truly intriguing wine with intense juicy/spicy flavours. Screwcap. 13.7% alc. **Rating** 94 To 2017 $26 ●

Local Vineyard Series Oakridge Vineyard Yarra Valley Shiraz 2014 A largely sotto voce style that creeps up on you, progressively building black cherry/spice/oak aromas and flavours, but without dragging tannins along for the journey. Screwcap. 13.8% alc. **Rating** 94 To 2034 $37

Local Vineyard Series Oakridge Vineyard Yarra Valley Cabernet Sauvignon 2013 It is very fresh, bright and lively, cassis providing the wherewithal for both the bouquet and the medium-bodied palate, oak and tannins sitting neatly in the rear seat. Screwcap. 12.9% alc. **Rating** 94 To 2028 $36

♟♟♟♟♟ **Local Vineyard Series Willowlake Vineyard Yarra Valley Sauvignon Blanc 2014** Rating 93 To 2019 $32 CM
Over the Shoulder Pinot Grigio 2015 Rating 93 To 2017 $23 CM ●
Over the Shoulder Chardonnay 2014 Rating 92 To 2020 $22 ●
Over the Shoulder Pinot Noir 2014 Rating 91 To 2020 $22 ●
Baton Rouge 2013 Rating 91 To 2024 $28 CM
Baton Rouge Rose 2015 Rating 90 To 2016 $21 CM ●

Oceans Estate   ★★★★

290 Courtney Road, Karridale, WA 6288 (postal) **Region** Margaret River
T (08) 9758 2240 **www.tomasiwines.com.au Open** Not
Winemaker Frank Kittler **Est.** 1999 **Dozens** 1500 **Vyds** 6.4ha
Oceans Estate was purchased by the Tomasi family (headed by Frank and Attilia) in 1995, and has 4ha of sauvignon blanc, 1ha each of pinot noir and merlot and 0.4ha of semillon. The wines are made onsite. Exports to Singapore.

♟♟♟♟♟ **Tomasi Cabernet Sauvignon 2014** Mid-brick-red; cooler grown, from the southeast part of Margaret River, it shows typical bay leaf, mulberry and darker berry fruit; medium-bodied and fleshy, soft tannins. It is enjoyable now. Screwcap. 14% alc. **Rating** 92 To 2020 $30

Tomasi Chardonnay 2014 Mid-straw; this is a ripe and powerful expression of Margaret River chardonnay, tropical fruits with ample texture and flavour. Plenty of wine for the price. Screwcap. 13% alc. **Rating** 91 **To** 2017 $25

♀♀♀♀ **Lashings Semillon Sauvignon Blanc 2015 Rating** 89 **To** 2017 $16 ✪
Tomasi Margaret River Merlot 2014 Rating 89 **To** 2022 $30

Ochota Barrels   ★★★★★

Merchants Road, Basket Range, SA 5138 **Region** Adelaide Hills
T 0400 798 818 **www**.ochotabarrels.com **Open** Not
Winemaker Taras Ochota **Est.** 2008 **Dozens** 900 **Vyds** 0.5ha
Taras Ochota has had an incredibly varied career as a winemaker after completing his oenology degree at Adelaide University. He has not only made wine for top-end Australian producers, but has had a Flying Winemaker role in many parts of the world, most recently as consultant winemaker for one of Sweden's largest wine-importing companies, working on Italian wines from Puglia and Sicily made specifically for Oenoforos. Wife Amber has accompanied him to many places, working in a multiplicity of technical and marketing roles. Exports to the UK, the US, Canada Denmark, Norway and Japan.

♀♀♀♀♀ **The Shellac Vineyard Syrah 2015** 30% whole bunches, 6 days cold soak, hand-plunged for 69 days on skins, basket-pressed to used French oak for 7 months maturation. Despite relatively early picking, has awesome, relentless power, concentration and drive emanating from the very heart of the jet black fruits rather than tannins and/or oak. Will live forever. Screwcap. 13.2% alc. **Rating** 97 **To** 2045 $60 ✪

♀♀♀♀♀ **+5V0V Chardonnay 2015** A biodynamic vineyard producing only 399 bottles. It has an impressive and complex aroma, with nectarine, lemon and an intriguing spicy note. The palate is equally impressive, poised and long, the pithy texture and mineral drive going on and on. Screwcap. 12.8% alc. **Rating** 95 **To** 2020 $60
The Green Room Grenache Syrah 2015 From a single vineyard in McLaren Vale planted in '46 to 82% grenache and 18% syrah. This is a vibrantly pretty wine awash with a garden of red flowers, blossoms and an elusive scatter of spices; its freshness is wonderful to behold. Screwcap. 13.3% alc. **Rating** 95 **To** 2025 $35 ✪

♀♀♀♀♀ **Surfer Rosa Garnacha 2015 Rating** 93 **To** 2017 $25 ✪
The Price of Silence Gamay 2015 Rating 93 **To** 2022 $40
Texture Like Sun Sector Red 2015 Rating 93 **To** 2025 $35
Weird Berries in the Woods Gewurztraminer 2015 Rating 92 **To** 2022 $35
I am the Owl Syrah 2015 Rating 91 **To** 2030 $40
A Sense of Compression Grenache 2014 Rating 91 **To** 2019 $80
Impeccable Disorder Pinot Noir 2015 Rating 90 **To** 2025 $80

Oddfellows Wines   ★★★☆

523 Chapel Road, Langhorne Creek, SA 5255 **Region** Langhorne Creek
T (08) 8537 3326 **www**.oddfellowswines.com.au **Open** Not
Winemaker David Knight **Est.** 1997 **Dozens** 2500 **Vyds** 46.1ha
Oddfellows is the name taken by a group of five individuals who decided to put their expertise, energy and investments into making premium wine. Langhorne Creek vignerons David and Cathy Knight were two of the original members, and in 2007 took over ownership and running of the venture. David worked with Greg Follett from Lake Breeze to produce the wines, gradually taking over more responsibility, and is now both winemaker and viticulturist. Exports to the UK, the US, Canada, Singapore, Indonesia, Hong Kong and China.

♀♀♀♀♀ **Langhorne Creek Cabernet Sauvignon 2014** Varietal character. A good spread and volume of flavour. A sound, dusty, curranty finish. This has a raft of quality markers in placer, and adds a creamy smoothness for good measure. Screwcap. 14.5% alc. **Rating** 93 **To** 2025 $25 CM ✪

Old Kent River Wines ★★★★☆

1114 Turpin Road, Rocky Gully, WA 6397 **Region** Frankland River
T (08) 9855 1589 **www.**oldkentriverwines.com.au **Open** Wed–Sun 11–4
Winemaker Rockcliffe (Coby Ladwig) **Est.** 1985 **Dozens** 800 **Vyds** 17ha
Mark and Debbie Noack have earned much respect from their neighbours and from the other producers to whom they sell more than half the production from the vineyard on their sheep property. The quality of their wines has gone from strength to strength, Mark having worked particularly hard with his Pinot Noir. The Noacks have added a 2ha vineyard at Denmark to their much older 15ha vineyard at Rocky Gully. Cellar door sales are located in a traditional old dance hall, halfway between Denmark and Walpole.

ŸŸŸŸŸ **Frankland River Shiraz 2013** Attractive shiraz from a region made to measure; this wine's crunchy blackberry, black cherry and spice fruit has finely wrought tannins and integrated French oak. An exercise in power and finesse. Screwcap. 13.5% alc. **Rating** 95 **To** 2028 $24 ✪
Frankland River Chardonnay 2014 Bright straw-green; the bouquet is distinctly complex, with some (deliberate) struck match funk; the palate is similarly tight and locked in, but enough juicy pink grapefruit is on show to make it an each-way bet, now or later. Screwcap. 13% alc. **Rating** 94 **To** 2024 $29 ✪
Frankland River Pinot Noir 2013 The lower alcohol (than the '14) invests this wine with more freedom to move; it is fresh, elegant and poised, its array of small red berries the centre of attention, oak and tannins just where they should be, building its length. Screwcap. 13.5% alc. **Rating** 94 **To** 2023 $35

ŸŸŸŸ♀ **Frankland River Sauvignon Blanc 2014 Rating** 93 **To** 2017 $24 ✪
Frankland River Pinot Noir 2014 Rating 92 **To** 2025 $35

Old Oval Estate ★★★★

18 Sand Road, McLaren Vale, SA 5171 **Region** McLaren Vale
T (08) 8323 9100 **www.**oldovalestate.com.au **Open** Fri–Sun 11–5
Winemaker Phil Christiensen, Matt Wenke **Est.** 1998 **Dozens** 1000 **Vyds** 6ha
Joan Rowley purchased an 8ha allotment in the heart of McLaren Vale, where she built a new family home for herself and her three children. Ben Paxton (Paxton Wines) was working at Hardys at the time, and arranged a 10-year grape supply contract if she were to plant vines on the property. When the contract came to an end in 2007, Joan recruited local winemaker Phil Christiensen to make the wines. Joan had established the gardens and grounds at the Old Oval Estate for a weddings/functions business, with sales of the wines. This led to a cellar door. Daughter Patrisse Caddle (with a bed & breakfast in McLaren Vale) assists with the marketing and strategy of Old Oval. Son Cameron has purchased a vineyard in Whiting's Road to contribute to the supply of grapes, and yet another daughter, Amanda, works in the cellar door on weekends, and does the bookkeeping. Grandchildren are all already in Joan's sights to work at the cellar door while they undertake their university studies.

ŸŸŸŸŸ **Fork in the Road Reserve McLaren Vale Shiraz 2014** Scarce Earth. Onto an altogether different plane, yet leaving a trail back to the starting point that Blind Freddie couldn't lose. Supple but intense black fruits, a blast of oak and ripe, firm tannins. Screwcap. 14.5% alc. **Rating** 94 **To** 2034 $35
Fork in the Road McLaren Vale Shiraz 2012 Only 64 dozen made from a single vineyard, in keeping with the Scarce Earth program; only used American hogsheads were used for the 18 months maturation. It is a medium-bodied shiraz that is strongly regional. The tannins are soft. Screwcap. 14.5% alc. **Rating** 94 **To** 2032 $29 ✪

ŸŸŸŸ♀ **Fork in the Road McLaren Vale Shiraz 2011 Rating** 90 **To** 2021 $20 ✪

Old Plains

71 High Street, Grange, SA 5023 (postal) **Region** Adelaide Plains
T 0407 605 601 **www**.oldplains.com **Open** Not
Winemaker Domenic Torzi, Tim Freeland **Est.** 2003 **Dozens** 4000 **Vyds** 14ha
Old Plains is a partnership between Tim Freeland and Domenic Torzi, who have acquired small parcels of old vine shiraz (3ha), grenache (1ha) and cabernet sauvignon (4ha) in the Adelaide Plains region. A portion of the wines, sold under the Old Plains and Longhop labels, is exported to the US, Denmark, Hong Kong, Singapore and China.

Power of One Old Vine Shiraz 2013 Squishy red and black berries, cut with spice and dry earth. There's obviously quality fruit at play here but more obvious is its deliciousness. Sweet, ripe, and flooded with flavour, but not at all flaccid. Screwcap. 14% alc. **Rating** 92 **To** 2023 $30 CM
Longhop Mount Lofty Ranges Cabernet Sauvignon 2014 Structural integrity, sure, but it's the fruit purity that draws you in. Boysenberry, blackcurrant and mint characters keep a hearty conversation going all the way through to a satisfying finish. Screwcap. 14.5% alc. **Rating** 91 **To** 2022 $18 CM ✪
Longhop Adelaide Hills Pinot Gris 2015 Pink tinge. Plenty of nashi pear and spice flavours with a hit of zesty lemon to the finish. Won't leave anyone disappointed. Screwcap. 13% alc. **Rating** 90 **To** 2017 $18 CM ✪
Longhop Mount Lofty Ranges Shiraz 2014 A generous release. Plenty of dark berried fruit and lifted bay leaf/mint notes. A raspberried sweetness comes forward given time to breathe. Not hard to take. Screwcap. 14.5% alc. **Rating** 90 **To** 2020 $18 CM ✪

Longhop Old Vine Grenache 2013 **Rating** 89 **To** 2020 $18 CM ✪

Olivers Taranga Vineyards

246 Seaview Road, McLaren Vale, SA 5171 **Region** McLaren Vale
T (08) 8323 8498 **www**.oliverstaranga.com **Open** 7 days 10–4
Winemaker Corrina Wright **Est.** 1841 **Dozens** 8000 **Vyds** 85.42ha
William and Elizabeth Oliver arrived from Scotland in 1839 to settle at McLaren Vale. Six generations later, members of the family are still living on the Whitehill and Taranga farms. The Taranga property has 15 varieties planted (the lion's share to shiraz and cabernet sauvignon, with lesser quantities of chardonnay, chenin blanc, durif, fiano, grenache, mataro, merlot, petit verdot, sagrantino, semillon, tempranillo, viognier and white frontignac). Corrina Wright (the Oliver family's first winemaker) makes the wines and in 2011 the family celebrated 170 years of grapegrowing. Exports to Canada, Hong Kong and China.

Small Batch McLaren Vale Fiano 2015 A slashing serve of ripe grapefruit rushes to a net of fine chalk-and-spice notes. It's a powerful wine, complete with struck match aromatics and a whisper of honeysuckle. Not easily dismissed. Screwcap. 12.8% alc. **Rating** 92 **To** 2017 $24 CM ✪
Small Batch McLaren Vale Grenache 2013 Silky smooth with milk chocolate and suede characters adding pure seduction to the raspberried/earthen/dried spice fruit notes. Medium-bodied and sweet-accented. Classy frame of tannin suggests it will age but the flavour profile implores you to hook in right now. Screwcap. 13% alc. **Rating** 92 **To** 2028 $30 CM
YarnBomb by Corrina Wright McLaren Vale Cabernet Sauvignon 2013 Warm with alcohol but rich in flavour. Dusty bitumen on a road of blackberry. Mouthfilling. Kicks again with more fruit/dust/saltbush through the finish. Screwcap. 15% alc. **Rating** 91 **To** 2024 $22 CM ✪
Small Batch McLaren Vale Vermentino 2015 Light to medium-bodied, with grapefruit, citrus and spice notes leading to a gently grippy finish. Dry and textural. Works pretty well. Screwcap. 12.5% alc. **Rating** 90 **To** 2016 $24 CM

YarnBomb by Corrina Wright McLaren Vale Shiraz 2013 Earth, plum and fire. This offers a big mouthful of red wine. Asphalt, burnt coal, chocolate, dirt, intense plum and warm alcohol. It's an attacking wine; it gives you all it's got. Screwcap. 15% alc. **Rating** 90 To 2022 $22 CM

Onannon ★★★★★

PO Box 190, Flinders, Vic 3929 **Region** Mornington Peninsula
T 0409 698 111 **www**.onannon.com.au **Open** Not
Winemaker Sam Middleton, Kaspar Hermann, Will Byron **Est.** 2008 **Dozens** 1450
Vyds 3ha
Sam Middleton, Kaspar Hermann and Will Byron have donated the last two or three letters of their surnames to come up with Onannon. They have many things in common, not the least working vintages at Coldstream Hills, Will for six years, Sam for two (before ultimately returning to the family's winery, Mount Mary) and Kaspar for one. Since then they have bounced between vintages in Burgundy and Australia. Strictly speaking, I should disqualify myself from making any comment about them or their wine, but you would have to go a long way to find three more open-hearted and utterly committed winemakers; the world is their oyster, their ambitions unlimited. For the past 7 years they have taken over the lease and full management of the Red Hill site and its 3ha of pinot noir. Exports to the UK.

♥♥♥♥♥ Mornington Peninsula Pinot Noir 2015 Good colour; has the power, line and length of its sibling, and adds a dimension from its plummy fruit. This has all the requisites for a 10+-year future. Screwcap. 14% alc. **Rating** 96 To 2027 $46 ✪
Gippsland Chardonnay 2015 A stylish chardonnay with the abundant flavour East Gippsland can provide, protected in this instance by the exclusion of mlf. As it is, the flavour spectrum is firmly stone fruit/melon/fig, acidity the key in keeping the fruit under control, and simultaneously providing length. Screwcap. 13.5% alc. **Rating** 95 To 2021 $41
Gippsland Pinot Noir 2015 6 days cold soak, open-fermented, matured in French oak. The light, but bright, colour gives no hint of the intensity and length of the savoury/foresty base to the red fruits of the long, finely structured palate. A wine of considerable finesse. Screwcap. 13.5% alc. **Rating** 95 To 2025 $41

♥♥♥♥♡ Yarra Valley Rose 2015 **Rating** 93 To 2017 $27 ✪
Mornington Peninsula Pinot Noir 2014 **Rating** 93 To 2025 $46
Mornington Peninsula Pinot Gris 2015 **Rating** 90 To 2017 $31

One 4 One Estate ★★★★

141 Killara Road, Gruyere, Vic 3770 (postal) **Region** Yarra Valley
T 0409 113 677 **www**.one4oneestate.com.au **Open** Not
Winemaker Lisa Marino and consultants **Est.** 2010 **Dozens** 200 **Vyds** 1.2ha
Lisa and Joe Marino purchased the property in 2010 after falling in love with the views. Two acres of merlot had been planted in '06, and a little under 1 acre of pinot noir was close-planted in '11 by the Marinos. In April 2016 the property was sold; at the time of going to print the long-term plans for the estate were unknown.

♥♥♥♥♡ Limited Release Merlot 2013 Foot-stomped after a day in the fermenter; matured for 13 months in French barriques (50% new). Has flourished over the past year, the red fruits neatly balanced by tannins and integrated oak, the finish dry and long. Screwcap. 12.8% alc. **Rating** 90 To 2023 $44

Orange Mountain Wines ★★★★☆

10 Radnedge Lane, Orange, NSW 2800 **Region** Orange
T (02) 6365 2626 **www**.orangemountain.com.au **Open** Wed–Fri 9–3, w'ends 9–5
Winemaker Terry Dolle **Est.** 1997 **Dozens** 2000 **Vyds** 1ha
Having established the business back in 1997, Terry Dolle made the decision to sell the Manildra vineyard in 2009. He now makes wine from small parcels of hand-picked fruit,

using an old basket press and barrel maturation. These are in principle all single vineyard wines reflecting the terroir of Orange. Severe hail damage savagely reduced both the '14 and '15 vintage crops, but the previous winery rating has been kept. He has retained 1ha of chardonnay and pinot noir, which he manages along with the winemaking. Exports to China.

ΨΨΨΨΨ **Limited Release Viognier 2014** Now this really is the exception that proves the rule: a viognier with crystal-clear varietal characters of apricot coupled with nuances of fresh ginger and a splash of citrus, yet finishing as fresh and crisp as a spring day. Nonetheless, I wouldn't be tempted to cellar it for more than a year or two. Screwcap. 14% alc. **Rating** 95 **To** 2017 $25 ✪

ΨΨΨΨΨ **1397 Shiraz Viognier 2013 Rating** 90 **To** 2023 $42

Oranje Tractor

198 Link Road, Albany, WA 6330 **Region** Albany
T (08) 9842 5175 **www**.oranjetractor.com **Open** Sat–Mon 11–5 (Sat–Thurs school hols)
Winemaker Rob Diletti **Est.** 1998 **Dozens** 12 000 **Vyds** 2.9ha
The name celebrates the 1964 vintage orange-coloured Fiat tractor acquired when Murray Gomm and Pamela Lincoln began the establishment of the vineyard. Murray was born next door, but moved to Perth to work in physical education and health promotion. Here he met nutritionist Pamela, who completed the wine science degree at CSU in 2000, before being awarded a Churchill Fellowship to study organic grape and wine production in the US and Europe. When the partners established their vineyard, they went down the organic path.

ΨΨΨΨΨ **Albany Sauvignon Blanc 2015** Feels and tastes good. Pear and assorted tropical fruits get the palate up and running before sweet pea notes add an extra layer to the back half. Screwcap. 12.5% alc. **Rating** 90 **To** 2017 $34 CM

ΨΨΨΨ **Top Paddock Shiraz 2014 Rating** 89 **To** 2021 $35 CM

Orlando

Barossa Valley Way, Rowland Flat, SA 5352 **Region** Barossa Valley
T (08) 8521 3111 **www**.pernod-ricard-winemakers.com **Open** Not
Winemaker Ben Bryant **Est.** 1847 **Dozens** NFP **Vyds** 1600ha
Orlando is the parent who has been divorced by its child, Jacob's Creek (see separate entry). While Orlando is over 165 years old, Jacob's Creek is little more than 40 years old. For what are doubtless sound marketing reasons, Orlando aided and abetted the divorce, but the average consumer is unlikely to understand the logic, and – if truth be known – will care about it even less. The vineyard holding is for all brands (notably Jacob's Creek) and for all regions across SA, Vic and NSW; it will likely be less in coming years.

ΨΨΨΨΨ **St Helga Eden Valley Riesling 2015** Once a revered label with a substantial price, St Helga is now back in the tightly contested ruck of under $20 – but the quality remains inviolate. An airy delicacy to its lime and lemon aromas and flavours, yet draws saliva from the mouth with crisp acidity that drives through on the finish and aftertaste. Screwcap. 11.5% alc. **Rating** 93 **To** 2025 $20 ✪

🌿 Oscuro Wines

PO Box 87, Lilydale, Vic 3140 **Region** Yarra Valley
T 0402 084 514 **www**.oscurowines.com.au **Open** Not
Winemaker Nick D'Aloisio, Sergio Carlei **Est.** 2015 **Dozens** 110
Nick D'Aloisio grew up in the Yarra Valley, and has worked in the wine business from a very young age. He's been involved in many areas of the industry, culminating in the creating of Oscuro Wines in 2015. He had earlier set in train Oscuro's business, purchasing shiraz from the Yarraland Vineyard in '12, making the wine with the help of Sergio Carlei. It was bottled and released in late '15. The brand will focus on single vineyard, hand-picked fruit with minimal intervention winemaking.

🍷🍷🍷🍷🍷 Il Principe Yarra Valley Syrah 2012 Hand-picked, small batch, whole bunches, extended maturation in French oak. A juicy, medium-bodied cool-grown shiraz from a very good vintage. Much to enjoy as long as you like lots of French oak. Cork. 13.8% alc. **Rating** 90 **To** 2020 $40

Ottelia ★★★★

2280 V&A Lane, Coonawarra, SA 5263 **Region** Coonawarra
T 0409 836 298 **www**.ottelia.com.au **Open** Thurs–Mon 10–4
Winemaker John Innes **Est.** 2001 **Dozens** 5000 **Vyds** 9ha
John and Melissa Innes moved to Coonawarra intending, in John's words, to 'stay a little while'. The first sign of a change of heart was the purchase of a property ringed by red gums, and with a natural wetland dotted with *Ottelia ovalifolia*, a native water lily. They still live in the house they built there, John having worked as winemaker at Rymill Coonawarra while Melissa established a restaurant. After 20 years at Rymill, John left to focus on consultancy work throughout the Limestone Coast, and to establish and run Ottelia.

🍷🍷🍷🍷🍷 Pinot Gris 2015 The intensity is there, the composure, the drinkability and the length. This takes crunchy apple and pear flavours and presents them on a perfectly arranged platter. Screwcap. 12.2% alc. **Rating** 94 **To** 2017 $22 CM **☉**

🍷🍷🍷🍷🍷 Mount Gambier Riesling 2015 **Rating** 93 **To** 2026 $22 CM **☉**
Mount Gambier Sauvignon Blanc 2015 **Rating** 91 **To** 2018 $22 CM **☉**

Ouse River Wines ★★★★☆

PO Box 40, Ouse, Tas 7140 **Region** Southern Tasmania
T (03) 6287 1309 **www**.ouseriverwines.com **Open** Not
Winemaker Peter Dredge, David Calvert, Alain Rousseau (Contract) **Est.** 2002
Dozens 200 **Vyds** 8.3ha
Ouse River Wines is one of the most interesting developments in Tasmania. Bernard and Margaret Brain own a 1000ha property north of Ouse at the top end of the Derwent Valley, on the edge of the central highlands. They run nine enterprises on the property, including the vineyard the furthest inland in Tasmania, with a continental climate, and diurnal temperature range during ripening of 7°C more than the areas surrounding Hobart. In the early 1990s Bernard and Margaret attended wine-tasting classes run by Phil Laing, which prompted the planting of a trial area of six varieties to see whether they would ripen. In 2002 they approached Ray Guerin to see what he thought: the answer was a contract for 10 years with Hardys. The first planting of 1ha in late '02 was followed by an extra hectare planted each year until '06; a further 2ha was planted in '09, and 1.25ha in '11, with an end total of 4.7ha of pinot noir and 3.6ha of chardonnay. The pinot was incorporated in Arras from the second vintage, and in every vintage it has been made since. After the Hardys contract ended, 95% of the fruit was sold, mainly for use in sparkling wine, but enough going to table wine to excite considerable interest. They asked the purchasers whether they would buy additional grapes, and the answer was 110 tonnes, which will drive substantial new plantings with ample suitable land.

🍷🍷🍷🍷🍷 Pinot Noir 2013 Bright, clear crimson; a lively mix of fragrant red fruits and bramble on the bouquet; the palate has real elegance, with very good length and finish. Screwcap. 13.5% alc. **Rating** 92 **To** 2020 $25 **☉**

Out of Step ★★★★★

6 McKenzie Avenue, Healesville, Vic 3777 (postal) **Region** Yarra Valley
T 0419 681 577 **www**.outofstepwineco.com **Open** Not
Winemaker David Chatfield, Nathan Reeves **Est.** 2012 **Dozens** 1000
Out of Step is the micro virtual winery of David Chatfield and Nathan Reeves. David explains, 'I worked in the music industry for a long time promoting tours for international acts, so I'm very familiar with financial risk.' Nathan works full-time as a cellar hand at Greenstone Vineyards, David full-time at Out of Step. Both are getting close to finishing their winemaking

degrees, but are increasingly distracted by actually making the wines. Along the way they have variously chalked up experience at Stella Bella (Margaret River), Lusatia Park Vineyard, Sticks (Yarra Valley) and Vinify (California). Their initial foray with a Sauvignon Blanc sourced from Lusatia Park was spectacular; they also have a Chardonnay from the celebrated Syme on Yarra Vineyard, and a Nebbiolo from the Malakoff Vineyard in the Pyrenees.

🍷🍷🍷🍷🍷 **Lusatia Park Vineyard Yarra Valley Sauvignon Blanc 2014** Gleaming straw-green; follows in the footsteps of the two prior vintages, lifting sauvignon blanc way out of the ruck, yielding nothing to the Adelaide Hills or Margaret River, demanding you drink it without moderation; it is at once luscious, yet fine, filling the senses with its array of perfectly ripened and formed fruit, its sauvignon blanc DNA largely irrelevant. Shades of Didier Dageneau. Screwcap. 13% alc. **Rating** 96 **To** 2017 $26 **❂**

Willowlake Vineyard Yarra Valley Sauvignon Blanc 2015 This is the oldest Upper Yarra vineyard (established in '79) and is relatively large, consistently growing and selling high quality grapes to many purchasers. The bouquet is complex (reductive, or burnt match), the palate with layers of flavours somewhere between savoury and tropical. Screwcap. 13% alc. **Rating** 95 **To** 2016 $27 **❂**

Lusatia Park Vineyard Yarra Valley Sauvignon Blanc 2015 This exceptional vineyard was purchased by De Bortoli prior to the '16 vintage, and Lusatia's many clients (including Out of Step) will no longer have access to it. The wine has a positively flowery element within the complexity of the bouquet, an uncommon combination for the variety, but part of the magic Out of Step brings to its Sauvignon Blancs. Screwcap. 13% alc. **Rating** 95 **To** 2017 $27 **❂**

Lone Star Creek Yarra Valley Sauvignon Blanc 2014 By chance, across the road from Lusatia Park. When I tasted this for the first time last year I wrote, 'This picks Yarra Valley sauvignon blanc up by the scruff of its neck and invests it with the character so often missing in action. You actually want to drink this wine.' Screwcap. 13% alc. **Rating** 95 **To** 2017

Syme on Yarra Chardonnay 2014 From a single block of P58 clone planted in '98. The bouquet is very complex, with some Burgundian funk, the palate intense, lively and long with a core of grapefruit and white peach. Its best years are still in front of it. Screwcap. 12% alc. **Rating** 95 **To** 2024 $30 **❂**

Syme on Yarra Shiraz 2014 The crimson hue and spicy, smoked meat bouquet set the playing field for the palate, where whole bunch/stem nuances chase juicy fruits and fine tannins. Those who don't enjoy whole bunch flavours will hate it, but I love it. Screwcap. 13.5% alc. **Rating** 95 **To** 2029 $30 **❂**

🍷🍷🍷🍷 **Malakoff Estate Vineyard Nebbiolo 2014** **Rating** 88 **To** 2017 $30

Oxenbury Vineyard   ★★★☆

PO Box 533, Beechworth, Vic 3747 **Region** Beechworth
T 0411 249 704 **Open** Not
Winemaker Andrew Doyle **Est.** 2001 **Dozens** 700 **Vyds** 8ha
Andrew Doyle has developed his Oxenbury Vineyard with nebbiolo (2ha), viognier (1ha) and other whites (1ha) on very steep mudstone, slate and shale soils. The wines are available at the Ox and Hound Bistro, 42 Ford Street, Beechworth Mon–Fri from 6 pm. Andrew also purchases grapes from others in the Beechworth region for the Cow Hill wines.

🍷🍷🍷🍷🍷 **The Amphitheatre Beechworth Marsanne Roussanne Viognier 2014** One-third of each variety. Mid-straw; honeysuckle and spiced pears, with an apricot/ginger note from the viognier; the palate continues with similar flavours, coupled with the anticipated textural interplay of the three varieties. It is an admirable effort, retaining delicacy, but not sacrificing flavour or length. Cork. 13% alc. **Rating** 93 **To** 2022 $28

Oxford Landing Estates

Pipeline Road, Nuriootpa, SA 5355 **Region** Riverland
T (08) 8561 3200 **www**.oxfordlanding.com.au **Open** By appt
Winemaker Andrew La Nauze **Est.** 1958 **Dozens** NFP **Vyds** 250ha
Oxford Landing Estate is, so the website tells us, 'A real place, a real vineyard. A place distinguished by clear blue skies, rich red soil and an abundance of golden sunshine.' In the 50+ years since the vineyard was planted, the brand has grown to reach all corners of the world. Success has been due to over-delivery against expectations at its price points, and it has largely escaped the scorn of the UK wine press. In 2008 a five-year experiment began to determine whether a block of vines could survive and produce an annual crop with only 10% of the normal irrigation. The result showed that the vines could survive, but with a crop production of between 40% and 65%. There is also 1ha of native vegetation for every 1ha of vineyard. Exports to the UK, the US and NZ.

🍷🍷🍷🍷 **Sauvignon Blanc 2015** Thumbs up. Juicy and fresh with just enough volume to satisfy. Sweet tropical fruit cut with gravel, grass and lime. Chill it down and enjoy. Screwcap. 10.5% alc. **Rating** 88 **To** 2016 $9 CM ✪
Cabernet Sauvignon Shiraz 2014 Light colour, but solid enough flavour. This will keep many folks happy. Berried fruit with a slight (attractive) dustiness. Screwcap. 13.5% alc. **Rating** 88 **To** 2019 $9 CM ✪

pacha mama

PO Box 2208, Sunbury, Vic 3429 **Region** Various Vic
T 0432 021 668 **www**.pachamamawines.com.au **Open** Not
Winemaker Callie Jemmeson, Nina Stocker **Est.** 2010 **Dozens** 5000 **Vyds** 14ha
When David Jemmeson established pacha mama in 2010, he had already worked in the wine community for 30 years, his experience crossing the Tasman, and also businesses such as Riedel. He also found time to travel to the Andean mountains, and says the liveliness, colour and vibrancy of South American culture was the inspiration for the brand (pacha mama is the Inca earth goddess). David also has a long history of interconnection with Don Lewis, dating back to their working together and developing the Mitchelton, Blackwood Park and Preece brands. The vineyard is planted to pinot gris, riesling and shiraz.

🍷🍷🍷🍷🍷 **Central Victoria Pinot Gris 2015** Short skin contact, cultured yeast, 80% fermented and matured in French oak for 3 months, 20% cool-fermented in stainless steel. Some pale pink hue possibly ex the stainless steel portion (autosuggestion is a marvellous thing): there's a distinct touch of strawberry behind the nashi pear. Screwcap. 13.8% alc. **Rating** 90 **To** 2017 $21 ✪

Pacific Vintners

98 Henley Beach Road, Mile End, SA 5031 **Region** South Australia
T 0401 389 295 **www**.pacificvintners.com.au **Open** Not
Winemaker Romain Duvernay **Est.** 2015 **Dozens** 150 000
This business has been established with exports to China as the main focus. Romain Duvernay graduated from the Institute of Oenology in Bordeaux in 1995, and spent several years working in the Lauguedoc Roussillon region. He began winemaking in Australia in 2014, and is responsible for the logisitical aspects of acquiring the very large amount of wine passing through the hands of Pacific Vintners. It does not have a winery, nor any vineyards. Exports to France, Spain and China.

Palmarium

395B Belmore Road, Balwyn, Vic 3103 (postal) **Region** Various
T 0422 546 825 **www**.palmarium.com.au **Open** Not
Winemaker John Ellis, Kym Teusner **Est.** 2010 **Dozens** 650
This virtual winery was established by Peter Mornement. His philosophy (and business plan) was simple: to develop a portfolio of high quality, high value shiraz from six premium

shiraz-producing regions. Each wine would be made by a winemaker in that region with an established reputation, and a simple instruction from Peter: buy the best fruit you can, and use the new oak of your choice. The quantity of each wine made will be 650 dozen bottles. He has joined forces with John Ellis (of Hanging Rock) for Heathcote and Kym Teusner for Barossa Valley wines. Exports to China.

🍷🍷🍷🍷🍷 **Exemplar Barossa Valley Shiraz 2011** From low-yielding old vines in Gomersal, matured for 2 years in new oak, 80% French, 20% American, made by Kim Teusner. It's fascinating how the '11 vintage wines are appearing out of the woodwork, often with strange stories. The very idea of 2 years in new oak for an '11 vintage single vineyard wine is strange. The modest alcohol is another surprise (a very good one). Yet the wine has exceptional colour for its age, and the fruits have a symbiotic bond with the oak. Screwcap. 14% alc. **Rating** 95 **To** 2030 $85

Palmer Wines   ★★★★★

1271 Caves Road, Dunsborough, WA 6281 **Region** Margaret River
T (08) 9756 7024 **www**.palmerwines.com.au **Open** 7 days 10–5
Winemaker Mark Warren, Bruce Jukes **Est.** 1977 **Dozens** 6000 **Vyds** 51.39ha
Steve and Helen Palmer have mature plantings of cabernet sauvignon, sauvignon blanc, shiraz, merlot, chardonnay and semillon, with smaller amounts of malbec and cabernet franc. Recent vintages have had major success in WA and national wine shows. Exports to Indonesia, Hong Kong and China.

🍷🍷🍷🍷🍷 **Purebred Sauvignon Blanc Semillon 2015** A 50/50% blend fermented in French oak (30% new), matured for 10 months. The contribution of the semillon is less obvious than expected, the reason being the seamless union of fruit, oak and acidity achieved with this seriously good wine. What's more, it will thrive over the next couple of years. Screwcap. 12.5% alc. **Rating** 95 **To** 2020 $30 ✪
Reserve Chardonnay 2014 Gin Gin clone, hand-picked, whole bunch-pressed, fermented and matured for 10 months in French oak (40% new). Delicious chardonnay with bounteous white peach and nectarine fruit does all the heavy lifting on the long palate, which has eagerly sopped up the new oak. Screwcap. 13.4% alc. **Rating** 95 **To** 2028 $35 ✪
Purebred Cabernet Blend 2014 79% cabernet sauvignon, 16% merlot, 3% malbec, 2% cabernet franc. Layered, rich and opulent, flooded with cassis and black olive on the bouquet and palate, with French oak adding yet more flavour, tannins ripe and balanced. Screwcap. 14.6% alc. **Rating** 95 **To** 2034 $37
Reserve Cabernets The Grandee 2014 75% cabernet sauvignon, 15% merlot, 8% malbec, 2% cabernet franc. This has more obvious tannins and more dried herb/earth/briar notes (although still opulent) than the Purebred Cabernet Blend: a style, not a quality, difference. Screwcap. 14.6% alc. **Rating** 95 **To** 2040 $37
Sauvignon Blanc 2015 Ranges through herbal, snow pea aromas to an intense and persistent palate continuing the path set by the bouquet, but embellishing it with guava and green pineapple fruit, finishing with Meyer lemon acidity. Screwcap. 12.7% alc. **Rating** 94 **To** 2018 $25 ✪
Merlot 2011 A luscious full-bodied merlot (bordering an oxymoron) that stays within the confines of the desirable varietal expression, even if French oak and tannins drive the palate every bit as much as the sensuous display of cassis/ blackcurrant fruit. A long life ahead. Screwcap. 14.9% alc. **Rating** 94 **To** 2031 $30 ✪

🍷🍷🍷🍷 **Malbec 2014** **Rating** 93 **To** 2034 $35
Sauvignon Blanc Semillon 2015 **Rating** 92 **To** 2019 $25 ✪
Krackerjack Bin 1 2014 **Rating** 92 **To** 2017 $20 ✪
Merlot 2014 **Rating** 92 **To** 2029 $25 ✪
Reserve Shiraz 2014 **Rating** 91 **To** 2029 $35

Pankhurst

'Old Woodgrove', Woodgrove Road, Hall, NSW 2618 **Region** Canberra District
T (02) 6230 2592 **www**.pankhurstwines.com.au **Open** W'ends & public hols
Winemaker Brian Sinclair, Malcolm Burnett **Est.** 1986 **Dozens** 2000 **Vyds** 5ha
Agricultural scientist and consultant Allan Pankhurst and wife Christine (with a degree in pharmaceutical science) have established a split-canopy vineyard (pinot noir, chardonnay, cabernet sauvignon, merlot, sangiovese, tempranillo, semillon and sauvignon blanc). Pankhurst has had success with Pinot Noir, Chardonnay and Cabernet Merlot. Exports to China.

ዮዮዮዮዮ **Canberra District Chardonnay 2013** Attractive mix of yellow stone fruit, darts of grapefruit and honeysuckle flavours. Beautifully ripened. Ready to go now. Screwcap. 13.5% alc. **Rating** 91 **To** 2018 $20 CM ✪

ዮዮዮዮ **Canberra District Cabernet Merlot 2013 Rating** 88 **To** 2023 $25 CM

Panther's Patch Wines

1827 The Escort Way, Borenore, NSW 2800 **Region** Orange
T (02) 6360 1639/0411 242 545 **Open** By appt
Winemaker Chris Derrez, Lucy Maddox **Est.** 2015 **Dozens** 350 **Vyds** 2.2ha
Hakan and Virginia Holm acquired the 10ha property and its abandoned vineyard in 2009 as a country retirement retreat. Little did they know about the effort required to rehabilitate the vineyard and look after the rest of the property, they confess. 2012 saw the first vintage, and they decided to enter the wine in the Orange Wine Show, where they were awarded a silver medal, each and every successive vintage winning some award. They named the vineyard after the 5-week-old black barb kelpie puppy dropped on their doorstep shortly after acquiring the vineyard. Panther keeps the place clear of rabbits, foxes, cockatoos, etc, with most of the vineyard work done by Hakan and Virginia (the exception is vintage, when a contractor transports the grapes to the highly experienced Madrez Wine Services).

ዮዮዮዮዮ **Orange Sauvignon Blanc 2015** Gold and trophy National Cool Climate Wine Show '15 and Orange Wine Show '15 is an impressive achievement, and there's no question the wine has good varietal character, but for the life of me, I can't see the intensity or X-factor that the judges at those shows obviously found. I simply have to be wrong, but there it is. Screwcap. 12.5% alc. **Rating** 92 **To** 2016 $22 ✪
Orange Cabernet Sauvignon 2013 Bright crimson-purple; fragrant cassis aromas are matched by juicy cassis on the supple, medium-bodied palate; cabernet isn't easy at an altitude of 700m, but Madrez made light work of it with this wine. Screwcap. 13.5% alc. **Rating** 91 **To** 2023 $22 ✪

Paracombe Wines

294b Paracombe Road, Paracombe, SA 5132 **Region** Adelaide Hills
T (08) 8380 5058 **www**.paracombewines.com **Open** By appt
Winemaker Paul Drogemuller, James Barry **Est.** 1983 **Dozens** 12500 **Vyds** 22.1ha
Paul and Kathy Drogemuller established Paracombe Wines in 1983 in the wake of the devastating Ash Wednesday bushfires. The winery is located high on a plateau at Paracombe, looking out over the Mount Lofty Ranges, the vineyard run with minimal irrigation and hand-pruning to keep yields low. The wines are made onsite, with every part of the production process through to distribution handled from there. Exports to the UK, Canada, Denmark, Sweden, Poland, Indonesia, Singapore, Taiwan, Hong Kong, Malaysia, Japan and China.

ዮዮዮዮዮ **The Reuben 2012** A time-honoured 57/19/13/9/2% blend of cabernet sauvignon, merlot, cabernet franc, malbec and shiraz that has paid handsome dividends this year with its beguiling display of gently spicy cassis fruits and a comfortingly savoury finish. Screwcap. 14.5% alc. **Rating** 93 **To** 2027 $23 ✪
Holland Creek Riesling 2015 Deliciousness writ large. Sweet red apples, floral elements, good intensity and body. Satisfying length. Gentle sweetness matched to excellent fruit. Screwcap. 12.5% alc. **Rating** 92 **To** 2021 $20 CM ✪

The Reuben 2013 57/19/13/9/2% cabernet sauvignon, cabernet franc, merlot, malbec and shiraz. Ripe rich flavour. Black berries and dark chocolate, dried herbs and tobacco. Packs a punch, but remains controlled, though muscular tannin could do with a stint in a cool, dark place to mellow. Screwcap. 14.5% alc. **Rating** 91 **To** 2023 $23 CM ✪
Pinot Gris 2015 Attractive delivery of flavour. Spice, brine, dry pear and crunchy apple notes. Good food style. Works well. Screwcap. 13% alc. **Rating** 90 **To** 2016 $20 CM ✪

🍷🍷🍷🍷 **Malbec 2013** **Rating** 89 **To** 2022 $27 CM
Chardonnay 2015 **Rating** 88 **To** 2017 $21 CM

Paradigm Hill ★★★★★

26 Merricks Road, Merricks, Vic 3916 **Region** Mornington Peninsula
T (03) 5989 9000 **www**.paradigmhill.com.au **Open** W'ends 12–5
Winemaker Dr George Mihaly **Est.** 1999 **Dozens** 1200 **Vyds** 4.2ha

Dr George Mihaly (with a background in medical research, biotechnology and pharmaceutical industries) and wife Ruth (a former chef and caterer) realised a 30-year dream of establishing their own vineyard and winery, abandoning their previous careers to do so. George had all the necessary scientific qualifications, and built on those by making the 2001 Merricks Creek wines, moving to home base at Paradigm Hill in '02, all along receiving guidance and advice from Nat White of Main Ridge Estate. The vineyard, under Ruth's control with advice from Shane Strange, is planted to 2.1ha of pinot noir, 0.9ha of shiraz, 0.82ha of riesling and 0.38ha of pinot gris. Exports to The Netherlands, Singapore and China.

🍷🍷🍷🍷🍷 **Les Cinq Pinot Noir 2014** Class written all over it. Powerfully fruited, and structured, yet satiny to the touch. Foresty black cherries, strings of herbs, sinewy tannin. Intense in both fruit and disposition. It needs time but everything is firmly set in place. Screwcap. 12.8% alc. **Rating** 96 **To** 2025 $79 CM
L'ami Sage Pinot Noir 2013 The 19 separate facts on the back label include resveratrol (4.6mg/l) and (for example) pH and titratable acidity both at picking and at bottling. Pure and beautifully balanced, red and black cherry fruit gently framed by oak and fine-grained tannins. Cruising serenely since first tasted in Dec '14. 658 dozen made. Screwcap. 13.5% alc. **Rating** 96 **To** 2025 $66 ✪
Col's Block Shiraz 2014 The life, the spice, the lift, the length. This is cool climate shiraz done extremely well. The flavours are familiar: red/black cherry, white pepper, cloves and dry leaf matter. The oak too: all cedary and smoky. But the succulence, power and length are out of the ordinary. Screwcap. 12.4% alc. **Rating** 95 **To** 2028 $48 CM
Transition Rose 2015 Shiraz, fermented in oak and kept there for 6 months. It's a pale wine that says adios to wimpiness. It's stern with cranberry, strawberry and red cherry, its kicks of both spice and tannin adding to the impression of strength. Character, flavour, tang and form; all work in the wine's favour. Screwcap. 12% alc. **Rating** 94 **To** 2018 $38 CM

🍷🍷🍷🍷½ **Pinot Gris 2015** **Rating** 93 **To** 2018 $55 CM
L'ami Sage Pinot Noir 2014 **Rating** 93 **To** 2024 $66 CM
Riesling 2015 **Rating** 90 **To** 2023 $38 CM

Paradise IV ★★★★★

45 Dog Rocks Road, Batesford, Vic 3213 (postal) **Region** Geelong
T (03) 5276 1536 **www**.paradiseivwines.com.au **Open** Not
Winemaker Douglas Neal **Est.** 1988 **Dozens** 800 **Vyds** 3.1ha

The former Moorabool Estate has been renamed Paradise IV for the very good reason that it is the site of the original Paradise IV Vineyard, planted in 1848 by Swiss vigneron Jean-Henri Dardel. It is owned by Ruth and Graham Bonney. The winery has an underground barrel room, and the winemaking turns around wild yeast fermentation, natural mlf, gravity movement of the wine and so forth. Exports to China.

ŢŢŢŢŢ The Dardel 2014 100% shiraz wild-fermented in open vats, 5 days cold soak, 10% whole bunches, 40% whole berries, 50% crushed and destemmed, matured on lees in French oak (25% new). Bright crimson; the gently spiced bouquet leads into a supple, elegant, medium-bodied palate, with as much red fruit as black in play. A stylish wine. Screwcap. 13.5% alc. **Rating** 95 **To** 2034 $60
Chaumont 2014 85% cabernet sauvignon and 15% shiraz, cabernet franc and merlot, destemmed and crushed, wild-fermented, with 5 days cold soak, matured for 12 months in French oak (50% new). Bright, full hue; this is a delicious wine with cassis fruit flowing along the supple, medium-bodied palate, the tannins and oak influences judged to perfection. Screwcap. 13.5% alc. **Rating** 95 **To** 2034 $50

ŢŢŢŢŢ Geelong Chardonnay 2014 **Rating** 90 **To** 2018 $50

Paramoor Wines

439 Three Chain Road, Carlsruhe via Woodend, Vic 3442 **Region** Macedon Ranges
T (03) 5427 1057 **www**.paramoor.com.au **Open** Fri–Mon 10–5
Winemaker William Fraser **Est.** 2003 **Dozens** 1200 **Vyds** 1.5ha
Paramoor Wines is the retirement venture of Will Fraser, formerly Managing Director of Kodak Australasia. To be strictly correct, he is Dr William Fraser, armed with a PhD in chemistry from Adelaide University. Much later he added a diploma of wine technology from the University of Melbourne (Dookie campus). Paramoor is set on 17ha of beautiful country not far from Hanging Rock; it was originally a Clydesdale horse farm, with a magnificent heritage-style barn now used for cellar door sales and functions. Will has planted 0.5ha each of pinot noir, pinot gris and riesling, and leases 2.6ha of vines in the lower Goulburn Valley (shiraz, cabernet sauvignon, merlot). He also receives regular supplies of pinot noir and chardonnay from another Macedon Ranges vineyard owned by friends.

ŢŢŢŢŢ Winifred Pinot Gris 2015 Whole bunch-pressed, cold-fermented. Has integrity and presence. A complete wine; strong varietal expression, with nashi pear to the fore, extended by long citrus-accented acidity on the finish. Deserved its gold medal at the Victorian Wines Show '15. Screwcap. 13.5% alc. **Rating** 95 **To** 2017 $24 ✪
Uncle Fred Cabernet Sauvignon 2014 Lovely wine, cassis to the fore; line, length and balance; tannins and oak precisely calibrated; excellent varietal expression. Gold medal Victorian Wines Show '15. Diam. 12.7% alc. **Rating** 95 **To** 2029 $28 ✪

Paringa Estate

44 Paringa Road, Red Hill South, Vic 3937 **Region** Mornington Peninsula
T (03) 5989 2669 **www**.paringaestate.com.au **Open** 7 days 11–5
Winemaker Lindsay McCall **Est.** 1985 **Dozens** 15 000 **Vyds** 24.7ha
Schoolteacher-turned-winemaker Lindsay McCall has shown an absolutely exceptional gift for winemaking across a range of styles, but with immensely complex Pinot Noir and Shiraz leading the way. The wines have an unmatched level of success in the wine shows and competitions Paringa Estate is able to enter, the limitation being the relatively small production of the top wines in the portfolio. His skills are no less evident in contract winemaking for others. Exports to the UK, Canada, Denmark, Ukraine, Singapore, Hong Kong, China and Japan.

ŢŢŢŢŢ Estate Mornington Peninsula Pinot Noir 2014 Exceptional retention of crimson-purple hue; in classic Paringa style, offering that extra dimension of varietal fruit, with no hint of over-extraction, even less 'dry reddish'. Supple and mouthfilling, it offers a fail-safe journey into secondary aromas and flavours in the years ahead. Screwcap. 13.5% alc. **Rating** 96 **To** 2027 $60 ✪
Estate Chardonnay 2014 Lindsay McCall seems able to invest his Chardonnays with a greater clarity of line and purpose than many of his Mornington Peninsula peers, something obvious in this wine. It has a purity The Paringa can't match, its

white peach, grapefruit and cashew all from the same page. Screwcap. 13.5% alc. **Rating** 95 **To** 2022 $35 ✪

The Paringa Single Vineyard Mornington Peninsula Pinot Noir 2013 Outside the normal Paringa Estate style, more elegant and fine with red fruits dominant; in part it reflects the vintage, which made southern Vic pinots notably elegant, with excellent line and length. I suspect they will also surprise with their tenacity over the years ahead. You would never guess this has 14.5% alcohol. Screwcap. **Rating** 95 **To** 2025 $90

Estate Mornington Peninsula Shiraz 2013 Matured for 18 months in French barriques (25% new). The fragrant, fruit-driven bouquet leads into a medium-bodied palate that manages to be both juicy and firm, the latter reflecting the polished tannins that provide structure. Screwcap. 14% alc. **Rating** 95 **To** 2033 $50

Estate Pinot Gris 2014 Two-thirds cultured yeast cool-fermented in stainless steel, one-third wild-fermented in used French oak. A resounding success with the best of both worlds, fresh-cut pear and apple ex the tank portion, tangy/minerally notes from the barrel ferment. Overall, finishes fresh, the price a joy to behold. Screwcap. 13.5% alc. **Rating** 94 **To** 2017 $20 ✪

Peninsula Pinot Noir 2014 In the heartland of Paringa Estate style: generous, mouthfilling and satisfying, but if you look a little deeper, complexity is there in spades; cherry and plum are framed by notes of forest/forest floor and whole bunches. Will age very well. Screwcap. 13.5% alc. **Rating** 94 **To** 2026 $27 ✪

Peninsula Shiraz 2014 Despite the depth and intensity of the flavour spectrum, the wine has a quicksilver mouthfeel and chemistry, the systems warned by the fragrant and sensuous bouquet of bright red and purple fruits. Fine tannins and integrated French oak complete the picture. Screwcap. 14% alc. **Rating** 94 **To** 2029 $27 ✪

The Paringa Single Vineyard Shiraz 2013 The medium to full-bodied palate is led by blackberry, plum, licorice and spice flavours that are rounded up by tannins uninterested in hearing any discussion about their powerful grip. A wine that absolutely demands patience, but will repay it. Screwcap. 14% alc. **Rating** 94 **To** 2043 $80

🍷🍷🍷🍷 **The Paringa Single Vineyard Chardonnay 2014** **Rating** 93 **To** 2020 $50
Peninsula Chardonnay 2014 **Rating** 90 **To** 2020 $25

Parker Coonawarra Estate ★★★★★

1568 Riddoch Highway, Penola, SA 5277 **Region** Coonawarra
T (08) 8737 3525 **www**.parkercoonawarraestate.com.au **Open** 7 days 10–4
Winemaker Phil Lehmann **Est.** 1985 **Dozens** 30 000 **Vyds** 20ha

Parker Coonawarra Estate is at the southern end of Coonawarra, on rich terra rossa soil over limestone. Cabernet sauvignon is the dominant variety (17.45ha), with minor plantings of merlot and petit verdot. It is now part of WD Wines Pty Ltd, which also owns Hesketh Wine Company and St John's Road in the Barossa Valley. Production has risen substantially since the change of ownership. Exports to all major markets.

🍷🍷🍷🍷🍷 **First Growth 2012** A classic cabernet that pulls no punches in its formation, starting in the vineyard and running through to the finish of the palate. Blackcurrant and cedary oak drive the bouquet, the medium to full-bodied palate following suit. There is a flood of fruit, then the tannins wash ashore as the wave of fruit recedes, oak floating on the whims of the palate; the length and balance are exceptional. Screwcap. 14% alc. **Rating** 97 **To** 2042 $110 ✪

🍷🍷🍷🍷🍷 **Terra Rossa Cabernet Sauvignon 2013** Part of the wine spent 30 days on skins to underwrite a long life; matured for 21 months in oak. An exceptional wine, flush with cassis and bay leaf fruit, and perfectly balanced tannins on a long, perfectly balanced finish. Screwcap. 14.5% alc. **Rating** 96 **To** 2043 $34 ✪

First Growth 2010 Fermentation and skin maceration took 35 days; matured in new French thick-staved Chateau barrels, held for 3 years in temperature-controlled storage. It is a monumental wine, still a decade or more away from its best, flooded with regional mulberry, cassis and a faint hint of mint, the tannins in shape, the cedary oak in balance. Screwcap. 14.5% alc. **Rating** 96 **To** 2050 $110

Terra Rossa Shiraz 2014 Incredibly fine and smooth. It's as if everything has been turned to high gloss. Peppermint, chocolate and ripe plum flavours flood the palate before extending comfortably out through the finish. Ripe, bright and substantial, it also has just enough underlying complexity to keep it from ever seeming simple. Screwcap. 14.5% alc. **Rating** 95 **To** 2032 $34 CM ✪

Terra Rossa Shiraz 2013 The colour is healthy and deep, the bouquet and medium-bodied palate with a flourish of forest berry fruits, blackberry to the fore, and of cedary oak, the ripe tannins providing the glue for the balance and length. Screwcap. 14.5% alc. **Rating** 95 **To** 2038 $34 ✪

Terra Rossa Cabernet Sauvignon 2014 A flood of cassis, a rush of mint, the odd trick of tobacco and a pure integrated ooze of dark chocolate. This is the power of cabernet in race mode, all sleek and svelte. Yes, it's good. Screwcap. 14.5% alc. **Rating** 95 **To** 2034 $34 CM ✪

95 Block 2013 Sweet with oak but beautifully structured and fruited. A long life awaits. A mix of blackcurrant and redcurrant streams through a forest of cedar wood, tobacco leaf and milk chocolate. There's a whiff of hedonism to this; a spirit of seduction. 78.5% cabernet sauvignon; 21.5% petit verdot. Screwcap. 14.5% alc. **Rating** 95 **To** 2033 $65 CM

♥♥♥♥♀ **Terra Rossa Merlot 2014** Rating 92 To 2026 $34 CM
Shiraz 2014 Rating 91 To 2022 $24 CM
Terra Rossa Merlot 2013 Rating 91 To 2033 $34
Chardonnay 2015 Rating 90 To 2019 $24 CM

Parous ★★★★☆

1 Gomersal Road, Tanunda, SA 5352 **Region** Barossa Valley
T 0437 159 858 **www.**parous.com.au **Open** Not
Winemaker Matt Head **Est.** 2010 **Dozens** 2500
Winemaker/proprietor Matt Head worked in the Hunter Valley, California and Margaret River for more than 15 years before making his home in the Barossa Valley and establishing Parous. It is focused on small batch wines made from grapes sourced from the Barossa Valley and McLaren Vale. Exports to China.

♥♥♥♥♀ **McLaren Vale Shiraz Mataro 2014** 60/40%, crushed/destemmed, open-fermented, matured for 12 months in French oak (40% new). Strongly regional, dark chocolate wrapped around the rich core of black fruits and tannins; there is a juicy quality that pleases. Screwcap. 14.5% alc. **Rating** 93 **To** 2034 $35

Passing Clouds ★★★★☆

30 Roddas Lane, Musk, Vic 3461 **Region** Macedon Ranges
T (03) 5348 5550 **www.**passingclouds.com.au **Open** 7 days 11–5
Winemaker Cameron Leith **Est.** 1974 **Dozens** 3500 **Vyds** 9.8ha
Graeme Leith and son Cameron undertook a monumental vine change when they moved the entire operation that started way back in 1974 in Bendigo to its new location at Musk, near Daylesford. The vines at the original vineyard had been disabled by ongoing drought and all manner of pestilence, and it was no longer feasible to continue the business there. The emphasis has moved to elegant Pinot Noir and Chardonnay, with a foot still in Bendigo courtesy of their friends, the Adams at Riola. Satisfied with his work, Graeme Leith has now left the winemaking in the hands of Cameron, and is using his formidable skills as a writer. Exports to all major markets.

♥♥♥♥♥ **Bendigo Shiraz 2014** Hand-picked from 27 Feb to 22 Mar, small batches, 35% 4 weeks post-ferment maceration, matured for 12 months in French oak (25% new). Excellent depth and hue; the astonishing length of the harvest, and maceration post fermentation have paid major dividends for a wine with equal

amounts of power and elegance, and 100% varietal expression. Screwcap. 14.5% alc.
Rating 94 **To** 2039 $31
Graeme's Blend Shiraz Cabernet 2014 55/45% from two very different
sites, open-fermented, matured in French oak (25% new). The blend is seamless,
blackberry, blackcurrant, plum, oak and tannins all joined at the hip. While
integrated, the flavour of the oak needs to recede a little, which it will do.
Screwcap. 14% alc. **Rating** 94 **To** 2034 $31

♀♀♀♀♀ **The Angel 2014 Rating** 93 **To** 2029 $47
Macedon Ranges Syrah 2014 Rating 92 **To** 2029 $47

Patina   ★★★★★
109 Summerhill Lane, Orange, NSW 2800 **Region** Orange
T (02) 6362 8336 **www**.patinawines.com.au **Open** W'ends 11–5
Winemaker Gerald Naef **Est.** 1999 **Dozens** 3000 **Vyds** 3ha
Gerald Naef's home in Woodbridge in California was surrounded by the vast vineyard and
winery operations of Gallo and Robert Mondavi. It would be hard to imagine a more different
environment than that provided by Orange. Gerald and wife Angie left California in 1981,
initially establishing an irrigation farm in the northwest of NSW; 20 years later they moved
to Orange, and by 2006 Gerald was a final-year student of wine science at CSU. He set up a
micro-winery at the Orange Cool Stores, his first wine the trophy-winning '03 Chardonnay.

♀♀♀♀♀ **Reserve Orange Chardonnay 2013** The flavours swing and slide and linger.
Grapefruit and white peach come creamed with cashewy goodness. It's rich
but lengthy, powerful but classily turned out. Gorgeous. Screwcap. 12.7% alc.
Rating 96 **To** 2021 $45 CM ✪
Orange Chardonnay 2012 Glittering prize of a wine. It oozes mid-palate
flavour, and complexity, but it then it brings in the quartz and rumbles the finish
with rocky, stony flavour. Oak, yes, malty and toasty both, but the impact comes
via other means. Screwcap. 12.7% alc. **Rating** 95 **To** 2021 $30 CM ✪
Orange Chardonnay 2013 Lowish alcohol but there's a body of flavour to
be enjoyed here. Peach, malt, bran and grapefruit flavours unleash on the mid-
palate in particular. A wine that simply refuses to be denied. Screwcap. 12.9% alc.
Rating 94 **To** 2019 $30 CM ✪
Reserve Orange Chardonnay 2011 Roasted nuts, popcorn, melon and spice;
the context is mellow and mature but there's a lot going on here. Intensity and
length are on song too. It sits in a very good drinking place right now. Screwcap.
12.1% alc. **Rating** 94 **To** 2019 $45 CM

♀♀♀♀♀ **Orange Chardonnay 2011 Rating** 91 **To** 2018 $30 CM
Orange Riesling 2015 Rating 90 **To** 2021 $30 CM

Patrick of Coonawarra   ★★★★★
Cnr Ravenswood Lane/Riddoch Highway, Coonawarra, SA 5263 **Region** Coonawarra
T (08) 8737 3687 **www**.patrickofcoonawarra.com.au **Open** 7 days 10–5
Winemaker Luke Tocaciu **Est.** 2004 **Dozens** 5000 **Vyds** 79.5ha
Patrick Tocaciu (who died in 2013) was a district veteran, with prior careers at Heathfield
Ridge Winery and Hollick Wines. Wrattonbully plantings (41ha) cover all the major varieties,
while the Coonawarra plantings (38.5ha) give rise to the Home Block Cabernet Sauvignon.
Patrick of Coonawarra also carries out contract winemaking for others. Son Luke, with a
degree in oenology from Adelaide University and vintage experience in Australia and the US,
has taken over in the winery.

♀♀♀♀♀ **Estate Grown Mount Gambier Pinot Noir 2014** Superb crimson colour
promises much, and the wine duly delivers; it is succulent one moment, structured
the next, velvet and mineral, yet impeccably balanced, with harmonious new oak
wrapping up the parcel. Mount Gambier is already showing its ability to produce
top-class pinot. Screwcap. 12.8% alc. **Rating** 96 **To** 2029 $29 ✪

Aged Coonawarra Riesling 2011 Light straw-green; has started on an unhurried journey to full maturity, the engine of crunchy, crisp acidity carrying the green apple and citrus fruit, lightly buttered and browned toast in the shadows of the finish. Drink now if you wish, but another 3–5 years should see it close to its peak. Screwcap. 10.5% alc. **Rating** 95 **To** 2021 $39

Estate Grown Fume Blanc 2014 Fermented and matured in French puncheons. A complex wine, with skilled use of oak to enhance the fruit profile, not obliterate it. Sauvignon blanc is often reluctant to speak in Coonawarra, but here there are distinct tropical/guava/passionfruit notes in a gentle embrace of oak and acidity. Hop right into it. Screwcap. 11.5% alc. **Rating** 94 **To** 2016 $25 ✪

Estate Grown Cabernet Sauvignon 2013 Estate-grown, matured in 60% American and 40% French barriques. Intense cabernet varietal expression with cassis to the fore, and a nice twist of bay leaf before precisely fined tannins provide the structure and length for today and the decades ahead; oak doesn't intrude, but nor is it absent. Screwcap. 13.8% alc. **Rating** 94 **To** 2033 $29 ✪

Grande Reserve Cabernet Sauvignon 2010 40 months maturation in new French oak plus 4 years in bottle doesn't add up as at Jan '16. The estate-grown fruit for this wine must have been superb. It was a great vintage, and it comes from 12ha of old vines surrounding the Tocaciu house. It is a beautifully crafted wine with striking cassis fruit, but would it have been better with 30 months in oak? Or even 24? Oak is the anteater that has transferred its attention to the wine. Cork. 13.8% alc. **Rating** 94 **To** 2030 $125

🍷🍷🍷🍷⚲ **Estate Grown Riesling 2015** **Rating** 93 **To** 2023 $25 ✪

Patritti Wines ★★★★★

13–23 Clacton Road, Dover Gardens, SA 5048 **Region** Adelaide Zone
T (08) 8296 8261 **www.**patritti.com.au **Open** Mon–Sat 9–5 (7 days Dec)
Winemaker James Mungall, Ben Heide **Est.** 1926 **Dozens** 160 000 **Vyds** 16ha
A family-owned business offering wines at modest prices, but with impressive vineyard holdings of 10ha of shiraz in Blewitt Springs and 6ha of grenache at Aldinga North. The surging production points to success in export markets, and also to the utilisation of contract-grown grapes as well as estate-grown. Patritti is currently releasing wines of very high quality at enticing prices, and a range of lesser-quality wines at unfathomably low prices. The JPB Single Vineyard celebrates the arrival of Giovanni Patritti in Australia in 1925; he sold his wines under the 'John Patritti Brighton' label. Exports to the US and other major markets.

🍷🍷🍷🍷🍷 **JPB Single Vineyard Shiraz 2014** The sheer power of this wine is awesome, all of the parts of the bouquet and palate locked into place by an unseen hand, the logic of the progression of the aromas and flavours brooking no argument. The most amazing feature is the wine's transparency, superfine tannins invisibly mended into the brilliant fabric of the red, purple and black fruits, sweetness and bitterness (in the best sense) engaged in a battle neither one will ever win. Cork. 14.5% alc. **Rating** 97 **To** 2054 $60 ✪

🍷🍷🍷🍷🍷 **Marion Vineyard Limited Release Adelaide Grenache Shiraz 2013** This wine lives up to the track record of the 105yo vineyard, medium to full-bodied with black fruits leading, the red berries also contributing. The price is absurdly low. If Patritti were to use a screwcap I would be prepared to say the wine will live to 2107 – marking the 200th birthday of the vineyard – so perfect is the balance. Cork. 14.5% alc. **Rating** 96 **To** 2043 $28 ✪

Lot Three Single Vineyard McLaren Vale Shiraz 2014 This is the chip off the shoulder of JPB; it is a thoroughly intriguing example of Blewitt Spring's ability to imbue its wines with a savoury/foresty character that other parts of McLaren Vale could only seek to emulate by early picking/whole bunches, and even then would be a pale shadow of this wine's drive and extreme length. Commands respect. Quality cork. 14% alc. **Rating** 95 **To** 2039 $35 ✪

Blewitt Springs Estate McLaren Vale Cabernet Shiraz 2013 The four cornerstones – elegance, balance, length and purity – of this wine are set in the sandy terroir of Blewitt Springs, and its refreshing breezes. Given the freakish power of the top three-priced releases, and the freakishly low price of this wine, it's a case of vive la différence. Cork. 13.5% alc. **Rating** 94 **To** 2033 $18 **☉**

ᵀᵀᵀᵀ᮫ **Blewitt Springs Estate Cabernet 2014** Rating 92 **To** 2034 $18 **☉**
Blewitt Springs Estate Cabernet Petit Verdot Merlot 2014 Rating 90
To 2029 $18 **☉**

Paul Conti Wines ★★★★

529 Wanneroo Road, Woodvale, WA 6026 **Region** Greater Perth Zone
T (08) 9409 9160 **www**.paulcontiwines.com.au **Open** Mon–Sat 10–5, Sun by appt
Winemaker Paul and Jason Conti **Est.** 1948 **Dozens** 4000 **Vyds** 14ha
Third-generation winemaker Jason Conti has assumed control of winemaking, although father Paul (who succeeded his own father in 1968) remains involved in the business. Over the years Paul challenged and redefined industry perceptions and standards; the challenge for Jason is to achieve the same degree of success in a relentlessly and increasingly competitive market environment, and he is doing just that. Plantings at the Carabooda Vineyard have been expanded with tempranillo, petit verdot and viognier, and pinot noir and chardonnay are purchased from Pemberton. In a further extension, a property has been acquired at Cowaramup in Margaret River, with sauvignon blanc, shiraz, cabernet sauvignon, semillon, muscat and malbec. Jason is a firm believer in organics, and the Swan Valley and Manjimup vineyards will soon join the family's Cowaramup organic vineyard. The original 2ha vineyard (shiraz) of the Mariginiup Vineyard remains the cornerstone. Exports to the UK, Malaysia, China and Japan.

ᵀᵀᵀᵀᵀ **Margaret River Cabernet Sauvignon 2014** It has the heft, the style, the
length. It tastes of blackcurrant, dark chocolate and bay leaves and feels powerful throughout. Finesse is not one of its strong points, but there's a whole lot else it offers. Screwcap. 14% alc. **Rating** 92 **To** 2026 $20 CM **☉**
Pemberton Pinot Noir 2014 Tang, perfume, varietal character and a bit of interest; this hits the sweet spot from a range of angles. It doesn't have the length of the best pinots but it has just about everything else. Well worth a try. Screwcap. 14% alc. **Rating** 91 **To** 2021 $25 CM

ᵀᵀᵀᵀ **Margaret River Chardonnay 2014** Rating 89 **To** 2019 $20 CM
Roccella Grenache Shiraz 2014 Rating 89 **To** 2020 $18 CM **☉**
Tuart Block Chenin Blanc 2015 Rating 88 **To** 2020 $18 CM

Paul Nelson Wines ★★★★

14 Roberts Road, Denmark, WA 6333 (postal) **Region** Great Southern
T 0406 495 066 **www**.paulnelsonwines.com.au **Open** Not
Winemaker Paul Nelson **Est.** 2009 **Dozens** 700
Paul Nelson started making wine with one foot in the Swan Valley, the other in the Great Southern, while completing a bachelor's degree in viticulture and oenology at Curtin University. He then worked successively at Houghton in the Swan Valley, Goundrey in Mount Barker, Santa Ynez in California, South Africa (for four vintages), hemisphere hopping to the Rheinhessen, three vintages in Cyprus, then moving to a large Indian winemaker in Mumbai before returning to work for Houghton. He has since moved on from Houghton and (in partnership with wife Bianca) makes small quantities of table wines.

ᵀᵀᵀᵀ **Riesling 2015** 60% from Frankland River, 40% Mount Barker; 10% barrel-
fermented. It certainly succeeds in pushing the envelope, the impact of the barrel-fermented portion obvious, but not over the top. It imparts some phenolic characters, akin to Alsace or Austria. Difference is the spice of life. Screwcap. 11% alc. **Rating** 91 **To** 2025 $28

Great Southern Fume Blanc 2015 Mid-straw; tropical fruits dominate with a touch of smoky complexity. A rich and full-flavoured sauvignon with loads of concentrated fruit and slippery texture. Screwcap. 13% alc. **Rating** 91 **To** 2020 $30

Paul Osicka ★★★★★

Majors Creek Vineyard at Graytown, Vic 3608 **Region** Heathcote
T (03) 5794 9235 **Open** By appt
Winemaker Paul and Simon Osicka **Est.** 1955 **Dozens** NFP **Vyds** 13ha
The Osicka family arrived in Australia from Czechoslovakia in the early 1950s. Vignerons in their own country, their vineyard was the first new venture in Central and Southern Victoria for over half a century. With the return of Simon Osicka to the family business, there have been substantial changes. Simon had senior winemaking positions at Houghton, Leasingham, and as group red winemaker for Constellation Wines Australia, interleaved with vintages in Italy, Canada, Germany and France, working at the prestigious Domaine J.L. Chave in Hermitage for the '10 vintage. The fermentation of the red wines has been changed from static to open fermenters, and French oak has replaced American oak. 2015 marked the 60th anniversary of the planting of the vineyard. Exports to Denmark.

ŶŶŶŶŶ **Moormbool Reserve Shiraz 2014** Only made in the best vintages, matured in French hogsheads for 14 months, the two best barrels selected for this wine. Excellent crimson rim to the full colour; the fruit aromas are multifaceted, predominantly dark, the flavours that fill the full-bodied palate more savoury than those of its sibling, with serious (ripe) tannins for the long haul – exactly what this wine needs. Screwcap. 14.5% alc. **Rating** 95 **To** 2039 $48
Majors Creek Vineyard Shiraz 2014 Strong colour; a highly complex bouquet is mirrored by the palate, with the gamut of black cherry, blackberry, licorice, pepper and cedary oak flavours; the texture borders on thick, needing to shed its puppy fat of fruit and oak tannins. Screwcap. 14.5% alc. **Rating** 95 **To** 2034 $35 ✪

ŶŶŶŶŶ **Majors Creek Vineyard Heathcote Cabernet Sauvignon 2014 Rating** 93 **To** 2039 $30

Paulett ★★★★★

Polish Hill Road, Polish Hill River, SA 5453 **Region** Clare Valley
T (08) 8843 4328 **www**.paulettwines.com.au **Open** 7 days 10–5
Winemaker Neil Paulett, Kelvin Budarick **Est.** 1983 **Dozens** 15 000 **Vyds** 41.9ha
The Paulett story is a saga of Australian perseverance, commencing with the 1982 purchase of a property with 1ha of vines and a house, promptly destroyed by the terrible Ash Wednesday bushfires the following year. Son Matthew joined Neil and Alison Paulett as a partner in the business some years ago; he is responsible for viticulture on the property holding, much expanded following the purchase of a large vineyard at Watervale. The winery and cellar door have wonderful views over the Polish Hill River region, the memories of the bushfires long gone. Exports to the UK, Singapore, Malaysia, China and NZ.

ŶŶŶŶŶ **Antonina Polish Hill River Riesling 2015** It's hard to imagine a more distinctive riesling. There's a softness to its texture and a smokiness to its flavour profile, and yet it's also so drastically pure in its presentation of citrus and grapefruit-like flavour. You don't just drink this wine; you engage in a staring contest with it. It's incredibly dry and yet it drips with flavour. It's enough to make you marvel. Screwcap. 12.5% alc. **Rating** 96 **To** 2032 $50 CM ✪
Andreas Polish Hill River Shiraz 2012 Interesting wine from 100yo vines. It's very intense, and the question is what are the respective contributions of fruit, oak and tannins? I am absolutely satisfied that the sultry black fruits are the leaders of the pack, oak and tannins playing roughly equal support roles for a wine with a long and prosperous future, sitting comfortably in the Andreas tradition established since '01. Screwcap. 12.5% alc. **Rating** 95 **To** 2032 $50
47/74 Hand Crafted Malbec Cabernet 2010 60/40%. Heavy with gamey tannin and rich with blackberried fruit, earthen notes motoring away in the

background. This is the polar opposite of a shrinking violet. It's so thick with flavour it's hard to find a way in, though eucalypt and redcurrant notes help. It has 'long termer' written all over it. Screwcap. 14.5% alc. **Rating** 95 To 2040 $90 CM
Polish Hill River Riesling 2015 It has power and flavour but it also has a lovely lilt to it. It's like listening to someone with a pleasing accent; the words are the same but you just enjoy the inflections. Lemon, lime, spice and talc flavours here; all familiar, but all so beautifully turned out. Screwcap. 12.5% alc. **Rating** 94 To 2028 $23 CM ✪

🍷🍷🍷🍷🍷 **Polish Hill River Shiraz 2013** Rating 92 To 2024 $25 CM ✪
Polish Hill River Cabernet Merlot 2012 Rating 91 To 2024 $25 CM

Paulmara Estates   ★★★

47 Park Avenue, Rosslyn Park, SA 5072 (postal) **Region** Barossa Valley
T 0417 895 138 **www.**paulmara.com.au **Open** Not
Winemaker Paul Georgiadis, Neil Pike **Est.** 1999 **Dozens** 275 **Vyds** 12.8ha
Born to an immigrant Greek family, Paul Georgiadis grew up in Waikerie, where his family had vineyards and orchards. His parents worked sufficiently hard to send him first to St Peters College in Adelaide and then to Adelaide University to do a marketing degree. He became the whirlwind grower-relations manager for Southcorp, and one of the best-known faces in the Barossa Valley. Paul and wife Mara established a vineyard in 1995, planted to semillon, shiraz, sangiovese, merlot and cabernet sauvignon. Part of the production is sold, and the best shiraz makes the Syna Shiraz ('syna' being Greek for together).

🍷🍷🍷🍷 **The Melee Grenache Nero d'Avola Shiraz Malbec 2014** The nero d'Avola is estate-grown and hand-picked, the remainder contract-grown, crushed, 10 days on skins before 6–7 months in used French oak. The bouquet and palate are complex, spicy on the bouquet, more savoury on the palate, red fruits the raft to carry the spice and savoury intrusions. Screwcap. 14.5% alc. **Rating** 89 To 2018 $20

Paxton   ★★★★★

68 Wheaton Road, McLaren Vale, SA 5171 **Region** McLaren Vale
T (08) 8323 9131 **www.**paxtonvineyards.com **Open** 7 days 10–5
Winemaker Richard Freebairn **Est.** 1979 **Dozens** 23 500 **Vyds** 82.7ha
David Paxton is of one Australia's most successful and well-respected viticulturists, with a career spanning more than 30 years. He started his successful premium grower business in 1979 and has been involved with planting and managing some of the most prestigious vineyards in McLaren Vale, Barossa, Yarra Valley, Margaret River and Adelaide Hills for top global wineries. There are six vineyards in the family holdings in McLaren Vale; Thomas Block (28ha), Jones Block (22ha), Quandong Farm (19ha), Landcross Farm (2ha), Maslin (3.5ha) and 19th (12.5ha). All are certified organic and biodynamic, making Paxton one of the largest biodynamic producers in Australia. The vineyards have some of the region's oldest vines including the 125-year-old EJ shiraz. His principal focus is on his own operations in McLaren Vale with Paxton Wines, established in '98 as a premium Shiraz, Grenache and Cabernet producer. Winemaker Richard Freebairn joined Paxton Wines as head winemaker in 2014 with the '15 vintage being his first. The cellar door sits on Landcross Farm, a historic 1860s sheep farm in the original village consisting of limestone houses and shearing shed. Exports to the UK, the US and other major markets.

🍷🍷🍷🍷🍷 **Jones Block Single Vineyard McLaren Vale Shiraz 2013** This one looks the goods. It's thick with blackberried fruit flavour but there are rounds of earthen, coffeed complexity; it doesn't taste simple and yet it doesn't invoke a headache in its attempt to impress. The finish is long and well framed; it will live a long life. Screwcap. 14.5% alc. **Rating** 96 To 2038 $40 CM ✪
Quandong Farm Single Vineyard McLaren Vale Shiraz 2014 20% whole bunches placed in small batch fermenters, the remaining 80% destemmed on top; matured in French oak for 12 months. The perfumed and supple medium-bodied

palate is the polar opposite of the MV Shiraz; it is deceptively long, with a fresh finish. Screwcap. 13.5% alc. **Rating** 95 **To** 2024 $30 **○**
Elizabeth Jean 100 Year McLaren Vale Shiraz 2012 Spearmint, lavender, redcurrant and leather, with creamy oak smoothing over the top. It's bold, balanced, elegant and familiar, and yet it feels individual at the same time. Sappy herb notes are part of this impression; so too touches of game. Clearly this has many years ahead of it. Screwcap. 14.5% alc. **Rating** 95 **To** 2030 $90 CM
Thomas Block Single Vineyard McLaren Vale Chardonnay 2014 This is a very smart McLaren Vale chardonnay, of which there aren't many. It is lively and fresh, with white peach to the fore, the palate with very good length and balance. Can't really ask more from the Vale at any price, let alone this. Screwcap. 13% alc. **Rating** 94 **To** 2020 $25 **○**

🍷🍷🍷🍷🍷 **MV McLaren Vale Shiraz 2014** **Rating** 93 **To** 2034 $20 **○**
Cracker Barrels Shiraz Cabernet 2013 **Rating** 93 **To** 2028 $55 CM
AAA McLaren Vale Shiraz Grenache 2013 **Rating** 93 **To** 2023 $22 **○**
Organic McLaren Vale Tempranillo 2015 **Rating** 93 **To** 2020 $25 CM **○**
Thomas Block Chardonnay 2015 **Rating** 92 **To** 2019 $27 CM
AAA McLaren Vale Shiraz Grenache 2014 **Rating** 92 **To** 2022 $22 CM **○**
McLaren Vale Grenache 2015 **Rating** 92 **To** 2021 $35 CM
MV Cabernet Sauvignon 2013 **Rating** 92 **To** 2025 $22 CM **○**
Biodynamic McLaren Vale Graciano 2014 **Rating** 92 **To** 2020 $30 CM
Organic McLaren Vale Shiraz Rose 2015 **Rating** 91 **To** 2016 $19 **○**
Biodynamic McLaren Vale Tempranillo 2014 **Rating** 91 **To** 2020 $25 CM
The Guesser Red 2013 **Rating** 90 **To** 2023 $18 **○**
Organic McLaren Vale Graciano 2015 **Rating** 90 **To** 2018 $30 CM

Payne's Rise   ★★★★☆

10 Paynes Road, Seville, Vic 3139 **Region** Yarra Valley
T (03) 5964 2504 **www**.paynesrise.com.au **Open** Thurs–Sun 11–5
Winemaker Franco D'Anna (Contract) **Est.** 1998 **Dozens** 1500 **Vyds** 5ha
Tim and Narelle Cullen have progressively established 5ha of cabernet sauvignon, shiraz, pinot noir, chardonnay and sauvignon blanc since 1998, new plantings continuing on a small scale, including several clones of chardonnay in 2014. They carry out all the vineyard work; Tim is also a viticulturist for a local agribusiness, and Narelle is responsible for sales and marketing. The contract-made wines have won both gold medals and trophies at the Yarra Valley Wine Show since '10, echoed by success at the Victorian Wines Show.

🍷🍷🍷🍷🍷 **Yarra Valley Chardonnay 2015** The wine has the urgency and energy that is a hallmark of the Seville district, and makes the chardonnays often rise to the top in wine tastings and shows. It's certainly here, but the wine also has the length of the greater Yarra region. Beautifully orchestrated by Franco D'Anna. Screwcap. 13% alc. **Rating** 95 **To** 2023 $25 **○**

🍷🍷🍷🍷🍷 **Mr Jed Yarra Valley Pinot Noir 2015** **Rating** 93 **To** 2025 $30
Mr Jed Yarra Valley Pinot Noir 2014 **Rating** 93 **To** 2020 $30
Redlands Yarra Valley Shiraz 2014 **Rating** 93 **To** 2019 $30
Yarra Valley Chardonnay 2014 **Rating** 90 **To** 2020 $25 CM
Yarra Valley Cabernet Sauvignon 2014 **Rating** 90 **To** 2024 $30

Peccavi Wines   ★★★★★

1121 Wildwood Road, Yallingup Siding, WA 6282 **Region** Margaret River
T 0423 958 255 **www**.peccavi-wines.com **Open** By appt
Winemaker Brian Fletcher **Est.** 1996 **Dozens** 2500 **Vyds** 16ha
Jeremy Muller was introduced to the great wines of the world by his father when he was young, and says he spent years searching New and Old World wine regions (even looking at the sites of ancient Roman vineyards in England), but did not find what he was looking for until one holiday in Margaret River. There he found a vineyard in Yallingup that was

available for sale, and he did not hesitate. He quickly put together an impressive contract winemaking team, and appointed Colin Bell as viticulturist. The wines are released under two labels: Peccavi, for 100% estate-grown fruit (all hand-picked) and No Regrets, for wines with contract-grown grapes and estate material. The quality of the wines is very good, reflecting the skills and experience of Brian Fletcher. Exports to the UAE, Singapore, Hong Kong and China.

ŸŸŸŸŸ Margaret River Chardonnay 2013 Light straw-green; has the length and intensity of top-class Yarra Valley chardonnay, and the depth of Margaret River; the best of two worlds is heady stuff, as is the pure class of this wine. Screwcap. 12.5% alc. **Rating** 97 **To** 2025 $58 ✪

ŸŸŸŸŸ Margaret River Shiraz 2012 Good colour; revels in its power and complexity, knowing that most will recognise the allure of the spicy, peppery black fruits; is the type of flavour more commonly encountered in very cool climates, but there's no distortion of the palate. Screwcap. 14% alc. **Rating** 95 **To** 2042 $52
Margaret River Cabernet Sauvignon 2012 Has the Peccavi signature of laidback intensity, or elegant precision, no added extras such as warmed seats. The anomaly of cabernet sauvignon has been exposed by a master surgeon, the cassis almost crisp. Screwcap. 14.5% alc. **Rating** 95 **To** 2032 $68

ŸŸŸŸ No Regrets Cabernet Merlot 2012 **Rating** 89 **To** 2020 $26

Peel Estate   ★★★★☆
290 Fletcher Road, Karnup, WA 6176 **Region** Peel
T (08) 9524 1221 **www**.peelwine.com.au **Open** 7 days 10–5
Winemaker Will Nairn, Mark Morton **Est.** 1974 **Dozens** 4000 **Vyds** 16ha
Peel's icon wine is the Shiraz, a wine of considerable finesse and with a remarkably consistent track record. Every year Will Nairn holds a Great Shiraz Tasting for six-year-old Australian Shirazs, and pits Peel Estate (in a blind tasting attended by 100 or so people) against Australia's best; it is never disgraced. The wood-matured Chenin Blanc is another winery specialty. Exports to the UK, Ireland, China and Japan.

ŸŸŸŸŸ Chardonnay 2014 Partial fermentation in French puncheons and extended lees contact has turned this into a major surprise packet, vibrant with grapefruit and nectarine, and with a hawser line of great acidity pulling the wine across the palate in fine style. My, my, oh the penny has just dropped – the grapes aren't from Peel, but Margaret River. But nothing changes. Screwcap. 14.5% alc. **Rating** 95 **To** 2021 $25 ✪

ŸŸŸŸŸ Wood Matured Chenin Blanc 2012 **Rating** 90 **To** 2020 $25

Penfolds   ★★★★★
30 Tanunda Road, Nuriootpa, SA 5355 **Region** Barossa Valley
T (08) 8568 8408 **www**.penfolds.com **Open** 7 days 10–5
Winemaker Peter Gago **Est.** 1844 **Dozens** NFP
Penfolds is the star in the crown of Treasury Wine Estates (TWE), but its history predates the formation of TWE by close on 170 years. Its shape has changed in terms of its vineyards, its management, its passing parade of great winemakers, and its wines. There is no other single winery brand in the New, or the Old, World with the depth and breadth of Penfolds. Retail prices range from less than $20 to $785 for Grange, which is the cornerstone, produced every year, albeit with the volume determined by the quality of the vintage, not by cash flow. There is now a range of regional wines of single varieties, and the Bin Range of wines that include both regional blends and (in some instances) varietal blends. Despite the very successful Yattarna and Reserve Bin A Chardonnays, and some impressive Rieslings, this remains a red wine producer at heart. Exports to all major markets.

ŸŸŸŸŸ The Max Schubert Commemorative Release Barossa Valley Coonawarra Cabernet Shiraz 2012 Wow. A 61/39% blend of Barossa shiraz and Coonawarra cabernet led to 1962 Bin 60A, Max Schubert's single greatest wine. This inherits Bin 60A's regional and varietal blend, its extreme longevity and its impeccable balance of fruit, oak and tannins. All it needs is lots of time. Screwcap. 14% alc. **Rating** 98 **To** 2052 $450

Great Grandfather Limited Release Rare Tawny NV Bottle no. 0807 of 4200 from the Series 16 selection. Light golden brown; arguably the best of all Australian tawnies, with more luscious fruit than Seppelt DP90 (the other contender); luscious it may be, but it is also wonderfully elegant, with rancio and Christmas cake and toffee flavours on the mid-palate, moving to a spicy, dry and ultimately fresh finish. Cork. 19.4% alc. **Rating** 98 **To** 2018 $350

Reserve Bin A Adelaide Hills Chardonnay 2014 Pressed straight to French barriques (82% new) for wild fermentation and 9 months maturation. The impact of the bouquet is immediate and multifaceted, with a perfectly judged touch of struck match/flint. The palate takes the wine onto another plane altogether, with imperious drive and tenacity to its unsweetened grapefruit and white peach flavours. Screwcap. 12.5% alc. **Rating** 97 **To** 2024 $100 ✪

Cellar Reserve Coonawarra Cabernet Sauvignon 2012 This is a Coonawarra cabernet as only Penfolds can create it, the bouquet's instant communication of class and style. Cassis, black olive and cedary oak are the foundations for a wine with perfect dimensions; you are well into the tasting note before you realise you haven't even thought about the tannins, so skilfully have they been handled from the moment the grapes began fermenting. And then you realise the superb French oak hasn't even been mentioned. Screwcap. 14.5% alc. **Rating** 97 **To** 2052 $200

Grandfather Rare Tawny NV Seriously powerful; the very complex bouquet has gingerbread, spice and singed toffee aromas cut by the rancio that comes through on the long, intense, yet elegantly structured and balanced palate. A skilled blending of some younger wine has had the desired effect. Incredibly long, intense and complex. Cork. 20% alc. **Rating** 97 **To** 2018 $100 ✪

♟♟♟♟♟ **Bin 51 Eden Valley Riesling 2015** Highly floral; has a definite touch of lavender on the bouquet along with notes of herb and the more usual citrus. Fascinating – the low pH gives the palate the minerally structure to carry the apple skin and lemon/citrus zest and pith. A vibrantly fresh wine bred to stay. And to think there was a time not so long ago when Penfolds had L-plates on its white winemaking. Screwcap. 11.5% alc. **Rating** 96 **To** 2025 $30 ✪

Yattarna Chardonnay 2013 From the Coal and Derwent valleys (Tas) and the Adelaide Hills, pressed to French barriques (62% new, 38% 1yo) for 8 months. The wine is so precise and tightly wound it is hard to imagine it went through 100% mlf but, at the same time, the decision to limit the amount of new oak falls neatly into place. It is developing at such a leisurely pace it is hard to visualise an end point. Gun flint, wet stone, green apple and grapefruit are among the contributors to the seamless flavour stream. Screwcap. 12.5% alc. **Rating** 96 **To** 2023 $150

RWT Barossa Valley Shiraz 2013 17 months in French hogsheads (57% new). Excellent depth and hue to the colour; French oak is a point of difference, not simply for the sake of difference, but as part of the superstructure of a very complex wine. The tannins could trick you into believing it is cabernet, not shiraz, as does the crossover of blackberry and blackcurrant. Its chemical analysis does not point to above-average acidity, but here, too, there is an exclamation mark. This is a serious wine of the kind one might expect from the northern end of the Rhône Valley. Screwcap. 14.5% alc. **Rating** 96 **To** 2043 $175

Bin 150 Marananga Shiraz 2013 I've been a believer in the exceptional quality and style of this wine from the first vintage, and this simply builds on that belief. Spends 12 months in a cocktail of new and used French and American oak (50/50%), and is a powerful testimony to the generations of knowledge accumulated by the Penfolds team guiding the positive use of oak without in any way diminishing the fruit. The allure of the bouquet is immediate, as are the deliciously grainy texture of the mouthfeel and the almost decadent well of black fruit flavours. Screwcap. 14.4% alc. **Rating** 96 **To** 2043 $80

St Henri Shiraz 2012 3% cabernet to accompany the shiraz, the grapes from the Barossa Valley, McLaren Vale, Adelaide Hills, Robe and the Clare Valley. In the manner of all St Henris, matured for 13 months in 50yo oak vats (1460I). This is an exercise on a chequerboard of savoury/smoky black fruits with firm, but polished, tannins. A great St Henri that will come into its own in a bare minimum of 10 years, and live long thereafter. Screwcap. 14.5% alc. **Rating** 96 **To** 2047 $100

Bin 169 Coonawarra Cabernet Sauvignon 2013 What can one say? This is a Ferrari in drag, the power enveloped in a steely body, the rumble of the engine barely heard. Blackcurrant, dried herb and black olive fruit have swallowed up the 16 months the wine spent in 100% new French hogsheads, making any comment on the tannins irrelevant, however powerful they are. Cork. 14.5% alc. **Rating** 96 **To** 2043 $350

Cellar Reserve Adelaide Hills Chardonnay 2014 From a single vineyard near Gumeracha. It has a very complex bouquet, almost certainly reflecting wild yeast fermentation, its final acidity natural, but possibly diminished by some mlf. Considered oak use has gone hand in glove with the stone fruit flavours. Screwcap. 12% alc. **Rating** 95 **To** 2024 $55

Bin 128 Coonawarra Shiraz 2013 Deep, dense wine, matured in 100% French oak. This is one of the richest, most dense Bin 128s I can recollect, its long-term future assured – just remember the Woodley Treasure Chest series or Wynns Shiraz from the '50s and '60s. Velvety black fruits are magically captured in a rich, round, mouthfilling burst of flavour. Screwcap. 14.5% alc. **Rating** 95 **To** 2038 $40

Max's Shiraz Cabernet 2013 76/24% from McLaren Vale, Barossa Valley, Wrattonbully and Robe, matured for 12 months in American oak (5% new). Excellent colour introduces a complex, yet seamless and balanced, medium to full-bodied wine. There is a savoury/earthy backdrop to the blackberry, blackcurrant and plum fruit; both tannins and oak are fused with the fruit flavours, making this a poor man's Bin 389. How the world turns full circle. Screwcap. 14.5% alc. **Rating** 95 **To** 2033 $35 ✪

Bin 707 Cabernet Sauvignon 2013 From the Adelaide Hills, Barossa Valley, Wrattonbully and Coonawarra, 16 months in 100% new American hogsheads. This is at the other end of the universe compared to Bin 169, quintessentially Penfolds, dangerously drinkable, cassis riding high with a shotgun of black olive at its side. American oak has no business finding compatibility with cabernet, but hey, this is Penfolds at work with a super-complex regional base. Cork. 14.5% alc. **Rating** 95 **To** 2048 $500

Bin 389 Cabernet Shiraz 2013 51/49% from the Barossa Valley, McLaren Vale, Padthaway, Wrattonbully and Coonawarra that spent 12 months in American hogsheads (88% new and 1yo, 12% 2yo). The 'don't mess with me' message is immediate, the bouquet a shower of dark, savoury, earthy aromas, the palate trenchantly full-bodied – yet balanced and utterly persuasive. It needs 5 years to settle down and be friendly, but will handsomely repay patience. Screwcap. 14.5% alc. **Rating** 95 **To** 2043 $80

Cellar Reserve Northern Tasmania Traminer 2014 Delicious feather-light traminer with clear-cut varietal character freshened by Tasmanian acidity. There are no tricks to the winemaking; the magic is in the fruit. It doesn't need food, but there's every reason why you should take it to your favourite Chinese BYO restaurant. Screwcap. 13.5% alc. **Rating** 94 **To** 2022 $55

Bin 28 Kalimna Shiraz 2013 From the Barossa Valley, McLaren Vale, Padthaway and Langhorne Creek, matured for 12 months in used American hogsheads handed down from prior duties with Grange, Bin 389 and so forth. Healthy and deep colour, with a rich bouquet of licorice, spice, dark chocolate and blackberry all in unison. Good stuff indeed, with the savoury/inky/graphite impact of the very long, balanced medium to full-bodied palate. This could well evolve into one of the best Bin 28s. Screwcap. 14.5% alc. **Rating** 94 **To** 2033 $40

Bin 407 Cabernet Sauvignon 2013 An interesting regional blend from McLaren Vale, Padthaway, Coonawarra, Wrattonbully and the Barossa Valley, it spent 12 months in 26% new French hogsheads, the remainder in new (12%) and used American hogsheads. Like all the '13 Penfolds red releases, has very good colour, and unquestioned varietal character from the first whiff through to the finish and aftertaste. It has elegance, balance and a restrained medium-bodied persona. It fully reflects the long arm Penfolds has with its fruit sourcing. Screwcap. 14.5% alc. **Rating** 94 **To** 2033 $80

♀♀♀♀♀ **Bin 311 Tumbarumba Chardonnay 2014 Rating** 93 **To** 2020 $40
Max's Shiraz 2013 Rating 93 **To** 2028 $35
Grange 2011 Rating 93 **To** 2026 $785
Father Grand Tawny NV Rating 93 **To** 2018 $40
Bin 2 Shiraz Mataro 2013 Rating 92 **To** 2028
Koonunga Hill Seventy Six Shiraz Cabernet 2014 Rating 91 **To** 2029 $25

Penfolds Magill Estate ★★★★★
78 Penfold Road, Magill, SA 5072 **Region** Adelaide Zone
T (08) 8301 5569 **www**.penfolds.com **Open** 7 days 9–6
Winemaker Peter Gago **Est.** 1844 **Dozens** NFP **Vyds** 5.2ha
This is the birthplace of Penfolds, established by Dr Christopher Rawson Penfold in 1844; his house is still part of the immaculately maintained property. It includes 5.2ha of precious shiraz used to make Magill Estate Shiraz; and the original and subsequent winery buildings, most still in operation or in museum condition. In May 2015, Penfolds unveiled the redevelopment of Magill Estate with the opening of a new cellar door (where visitors can taste Grange by the glass) and Magill Estate Kitchen, a casual dining environment with a grazing menu built on local and fresh ingredients for sharing. The much-awarded Magill Estate Restaurant, with its panoramic views of the city, remains a temple for sublime food and wine matching. Exports to al major markets.

♀♀♀♀♀ **Magill Estate Shiraz 2013** Simplicity itself: 100% shiraz, 100% Magill Estate and matured for 14 months in 95% new oak (71% French, 24% American). Sometimes shy and retiring, this is a Magill Estate with a plenitude of attitude, singing a long chorus of utterly impressive black fruits, rising to an operatic fanfare on its finish. I cannot remember a better Magill Estate, even though Penfolds is not especially proud of the wine: 'a solid Magill Estate'. Cork. 14.4% alc. **Rating** 95 **To** 2033 $130

Penley Estate ★★★★★
McLeans Road, Coonawarra, SA 5263 **Region** Coonawarra
T (08) 8736 3211 **www**.penley.com.au **Open** Mon–Fri 10–4, w'ends 11–5
Winemaker Kym Tolley, Greg Foster **Est.** 1988 **Dozens** 35 000 **Vyds** 111ha
Owner Kym Tolley describes himself as a fifth-generation winemaker, the family tree involving both the Penfolds and the Tolleys. He worked in the industry for 17 years before establishing Penley Estate and has made every post a winner since, producing a succession of rich, complex wines, especially Cabernet Sauvignons with a degree of elegance. Wines were received too late for the book, but tasting notes can be found on www.winecompanion.com.au. Exports to all major markets.

Penmara
Unit 19, 75 Pacific Highway, Waitara, NSW 2077 (postal) **Region** Hunter Valley/Orange
T 0410 403 143 **www**.penmarawines.com.au **Open** Not
Winemaker Hunter Wine Services **Est.** 2000 **Dozens** 25 000 **Vyds** 120ha
Penmara, with its banner 'Five Families: One Vision', was formed when five family-owned vineyards joined together to create a new venture with a focus on export markets. Based in the Hunter Valley, with vineyards also in Orange and other surrounding areas, Penmara has access

to 120ha of shiraz, chardonnay, cabernet sauvignon, semillon, verdelho and merlot. Exports to the US, Canada, South Korea, Malaysia, Singapore and China.

🍷🍷🍷🍷🍷 **Reserve Orange Shiraz 2013** Grapes crushed and destemmed to static fermenters with pump-overs, mainly matured in used French and American oak for 12 months. Light, but bright, colour; it has an immediate clarion call of cool grown shiraz, light-bodied, yet fragrantly spicy and bright cherry-fruited. Probably best now or soonish. Screwcap. 13.5% alc. **Rating** 90 **To** 2019 $20 ✪

🍷🍷🍷🍷 **The White Ribbon Hunter Valley Classic Dry White Semillon 2015** **Rating** 89 **To** 2030 $15 ✪

Penna Lane Wines ★★★★

Lot 51 Penna Lane, Penwortham via Clare, SA 5453 **Region** Clare Valley
T 0403 462 431 **www.**pennalanewines.com.au **Open** Fri–Sun 11–5
Winemaker Peter Treloar, Chris Proud **Est.** 1998 **Dozens** 4500 **Vyds** 4.37ha
Penna Lane is located in the beautiful Skilly Valley, 10km south of Clare. The estate vineyard (shiraz, cabernet sauvignon and semillon) is planted at an elevation of 450m, which allows a long, slow ripening period, usually resulting in wines with intense varietal fruit flavours. Exports to Hong Kong, South Korea, Fiji, Vietnam, Thailand, China and Japan.

🍷🍷🍷🍷🍷 **Skilly Valley Riesling 2015** The vineyard is at 450m, and the climate has a significant – and beneficial – impact on the wine, giving it finesse built on a framework of taut, minerally acidity. There is citrus to be had from its free-run juice, but I would unhesitatingly cellar this while drinking its less expensive sibling. Screwcap. 12.5% alc. **Rating** 94 **To** 2028 $25 ✪

🍷🍷🍷🍷🍷 **Clare Valley Shiraz 2014 Rating** 92 **To** 2034 $25 ✪
Watervale Riesling 2015 Rating 91 **To** 2020 $20 ✪

Penny's Hill ★★★★★

281 Main Road, McLaren Vale, SA 5171 **Region** McLaren Vale
T (08) 8557 0800 **www.**pennyshill.com.au **Open** 7 days 10–5
Winemaker Alexia Roberts **Est.** 1988 **Dozens** 85 000 **Vyds** 44ha
Founded in 1988 by Tony and Susie Parkinson, Penny's Hill produces high quality Shiraz (Footprint and The Skeleton Key) from its close-planted McLaren Vale estate, also the source of the Edwards Road Cabernet Sauvignon and The Experiment Grenache. Malpas Road and Goss Corner Vineyards complete the estate holdings, providing fruit for Cracking Black Shiraz and Malpas Road Merlot. White wines (The Agreement Sauvignon Blanc and The Minimalist Chardonnay) are sourced from 'estates of mates' in the Adelaide Hills. Also includes the Black Chook and Thomas Goss Brands. Penny's Hill cellars are located at the historic Ingleburne Farm, which also houses the award-winning The Kitchen Door restaurant and Red Dot Gallery. Noted for its distinctive 'red dot' packaging. Exports to all major markets.

🍷🍷🍷🍷🍷 **Footprint McLaren Vale Shiraz 2014** Seamless presentation of blackberry and blackcurrant fruit flavour, well complemented by tips of mint, musk and coffee-cream. Tannin is velvety but firm enough. In short, it's in terrific form. Screwcap. 14.5% alc. **Rating** 96 **To** 2034 $65 CM ✪
Footprint McLaren Vale Shiraz 2013 Pretty as a picture. Robust too. This smiles at you as it crushes your hand. Violet, vanilla, velvety plum and asphalt. A current of undergrowthy character too. This is a force to be reckoned with, a booming drive hit straight down the fairway. Screwcap. 14.5% alc. **Rating** 96 **To** 2035 $65 CM ✪
The Agreement Adelaide Hills Sauvignon Blanc 2015 Another Adelaide Hills sauvignon blanc from '15 to show well above average intensity and a high level of natural acidity, but has admirable balance courtesy of a seamless mix of fresh citrus and tropical fruits. A worthy successor to the high quality '14. Screwcap. 12.5% alc. **Rating** 95 **To** 2016 $20 ✪

Skeleton Key McLaren Vale Shiraz 2014 Some wines just float perfectly into place. This is one of them. It tastes of milk chocolate, blackberry and earth, and has clear ferrous attributes. There's a gentle creaminess to the oak but the fruit sweeps it amiably along. It takes full-bodied drinkability and hits it right on the knocker. Screwcap. 14.5% alc. **Rating** 95 **To** 2030 $35 CM **☉**

Cracking Black McLaren Vale Shiraz 2014 Neat and composed and yet with all the power you could ever need or want. Dark chocolate, dates, fresh blackberry and licorice notes run proudly through the palate, aided and abetted by cords of tannin. Screwcap. 14.5% alc. **Rating** 95 **To** 2030 $25 CM **☉**

Skeleton Key McLaren Vale Shiraz 2013 Beating heart of flavour. Blackberry and dark chocolate with bitumen characters adding to the grunt. Tannin is present and dangerous but comes swaddled in ripe, berried, juicy fruit. Hard wine to fault/easy wine to enjoy, and the pleasure won't be short-lived either. Screwcap. 14.5% alc. **Rating** 94 **To** 2028 $35 CM

The Experiment McLaren Vale Grenache 2014 It feels velvety as it rolls across the tongue and offers plenty of licorice and dark-berried flavours. It's a crowd-pleaser with integrity, and deserves to be lapped up as a result. Screwcap. 14.5% alc. **Rating** 94 **To** 2022 $35 CM

ᵀᵀᵀᵀᵀ Edwards Road McLaren Vale Cabernet Sauvignon 2014 Rating 93 To 2030 $25 CM **☉**
The Specialized McLaren Vale Shiraz Cabernet Merlot 2014 Rating 92 To 2026 $25 CM **☉**

Peos Estate ★★★★☆

Graphite Road, Manjimup, WA 6258 **Region** Manjimup
T (08) 9772 1378 **www.peosestate.com.au Open** Not
Winemaker Coby Ladwig, Michael Ng **Est.** 1996 **Dozens** 12 000 **Vyds** 36.8ha
The Peos family has farmed the West Manjimup district for over 50 years, the third generation of four brothers commencing the development of the vineyard in 1996. There is a little over 34ha of vines, including shiraz (10ha), merlot (6.8ha), chardonnay (6.7ha), cabernet sauvignon (4ha), sauvignon blanc (3ha), and pinot noir and verdelho (2ha each). Exports to China.

ᵀᵀᵀᵀᵀ Four Kings Single Vineyard Manjimup Cabernet Sauvignon 2014
A medium to full-bodied cabernet that shouts its varietal base from the rooftops, stacked with cassis and bay leaf, and the cabernet tannins to match that fruit; the oak is from high class coopers Damy and Seguin Moreau. This is the real deal, the full hand. Screwcap. 14.5% alc. **Rating** 95 **To** 2034 $25 **☉**

ᵀᵀᵀᵀᵀ Four Kings Shiraz 2014 Rating 93 To 2034 $25 **☉**
Four Aces Chardonnay 2014 Rating 92 To 2018 $35
Four Kings Cabernet Merlot 2014 Rating 92 To 2030 $25 **☉**

Pepper Tree Wines ★★★★★

Halls Road, Pokolbin, NSW 2320 **Region** Hunter Valley
T (02) 4909 7100 **www.peppertreewines.com.au Open** Mon–Fri 9–5, w'ends 9.30–5
Winemaker Gwyn Olsen **Est.** 1991 **Dozens** 50 000 **Vyds** 172.1ha
Pepper Tree is part of a complex that also contains The Convent guest house and Circa 1876 Restaurant. It is owned by a company controlled by Dr John Davis, who owns 50% of Briar Ridge. It sources the majority of its Hunter Valley fruit from its Tallavera Grove vineyard at Mt View, but also has premium vineyards at Orange, Coonawarra and Wrattonbully. Self-evidently, the wines are exceptional value for money. The highly credentialled Gwyn Olsen ('12 Dux, Advanced Wine Assessment course, AWRI; '14 Young Winemaker of the Year, Gourmet Traveller Wine; '15 Rising Star of the Year, Hunter Valley Legends Awards; and '15 Len Evans Tutorial Scholar) was appointed winemaker in '15. Exports to the UK, Denmark, Singapore and China.

ŸŸŸŸŸ **Single Vineyard Reserve Tallawanta Hunter Valley Shiraz 2013** The bouquet has it all, the palate ascending the very heights of Hunter Valley shiraz, with exceptional intensity and depth to its black fruits (cherry, blackberry) overlain with a web of gently savoury/earthy tannins in best regional fashion; the oak adds even more to the package. This is a full-bodied 50-year wine. Screwcap. 14.5% alc. **Rating** 98 **To** 2060 $140 ✪

Single Vineyard Venus Block Orange Chardonnay 2014 Barrel-fermented and matured, it has quite beautiful fruit flavour and definition as it flows evenly across the palate, fulfilling the promise of the bouquet, and lingering long after it is swallowed; white peach, pink grapefruit and cashew all intermingle. From the top of the Orange quality tree for chardonnay. Screwcap. 12.5% alc. **Rating** 97 **To** 2025 $35 ✪

ŸŸŸŸŸ **Single Vineyard Premium Reserve Alluvius Hunter Valley Semillon 2015** Light straw-green; this is a classic Hunter Valley semillon of the highest quality, staring down the challenge of botrytis with its purity, line and length; the bouquet and palate offer a magical balance of intensity and elegance, lemongrass, lemon zest and vibrant acidity all contributing. Screwcap. 10.5% alc. **Rating** 96 **To** 2035 $35 ✪

Limited Release Tallavera Hunter Valley Shiraz 2014 From the red volcanic soil over crumbly limestone of Mt View. Black cherry and mulberry aromas are joined by distinct earthy, spicy characters on the long, energetic palate and lingering aftertaste, with cedary oak and tannins the subtle drum beat. Screwcap. 14% alc. **Rating** 96 **To** 2039 $45 ✪

Limited Release CF Block Hunter Valley Shiraz 2014 From Claude Ferraris' vineyard on Hermitage Road. Bright hued, its complex black and red cherries are framed by balanced oak on the bouquet, which is tied to the palate by an umbilical cord adding a dimension of classy oak and fruit tannins, but not changing the trajectory of flavours. Screwcap. 14% alc. **Rating** 96 **To** 2039 $45 ✪

Single Vineyard Reserve Coquun Hunter Valley Shiraz 2014 It's a wine of balance, power and length, the pirouette of savoury-spicy-cherried flavours anchored by fine-set tannin and ripe cherry-leather fruit. Exquisite integration of oak. Screwcap. 14.2% alc. **Rating** 95 **To** 2035 $90 CM

Single Vineyard Reserve Block 21A Wrattonbully Cabernet Sauvignon 2014 Vivid, full crimson-purple; a full-bodied, immaculately balanced cabernet, chock-full of mulberry, blueberry and – above all else – cassis fruit; then there are the ripe but implacable tannins, oak waving its hand to speak, but not given a hearing. Patience needed. Screwcap. 14% alc. **Rating** 95 **To** 2049 $60

Limited Release Hunter Valley Semillon 2015 Hand-picked, whole bunch-pressed, cultured yeast, cool-fermented in stainless steel. Classic young semillon, but with that little bit extra now making it an each-way bet – and a sure winner. Screwcap. 10.5% alc. **Rating** 94 **To** 2030 $22 ✪

Single Vineyard Limited Release Orange Chardonnay 2014 This differentiates itself from its Hunter Valley sibling by its greater intensity, and greater focus on the grapefruit end of the spectrum; French oak provides a seamless structure and adds to the length. Will develop with assurance over this decade and into the next. Screwcap. 12.2% alc. **Rating** 94 **To** 2024 $22 ✪

Limited Release Hunter Valley Shiraz 2014 It is in every sense a substantial medium to full-bodied shiraz reflecting not only place, but also the great Hunter vintage. The flavours range through red and black cherry, blackberry and plum, each speaking with clarity rather than in a jumble. It's a pretty cool price for a wine that will grow and grow in the bottle for decades to come. Screwcap. 14% alc. **Rating** 94 **To** 2044 $35

Single Vineyard Reserve 8R Wrattonbully Merlot 2014 Regional choc-mint announces itself on the bouquet, the varietal aromas of mulberry fruit and leaf more subtle. Generous and fleshy on the palate, quality French oak underpins the flavours of berry and mint with supple tannin providing structure and length. Screwcap. 14% alc. **Rating** 94 **To** 2028 $60

Single Vineyard Reserve Elderslee Road Wrattonbully Cabernet Sauvignon 2014 A classy cabernet, and an adequate alternative for those unwilling to buy Block 21A at $60, even if the value for money is much the same in each case. This has brilliant colour, a fragrant bouquet, abundant juicy cassis and fine tannins throughout the palate. Screwcap. 14.2% alc. **Rating** 94 **To** 2034 $42

♀♀♀♀♀ **Semillon Sauvignon Blanc 2015 Rating** 93 **To** 2018 $19 ○
Venus Block Orange Chardonnay 2015 Rating 93 **To** 2022 $35
Limited Release Hunter Valley Chardonnay 2014 Rating 92 **To** 2018 $22 ○
The Gravels Wrattonbully Shiraz Viognier 2014 Rating 92 **To** 2025 $42

Petaluma   ★★★★★

254 Pfeiffer Road, Woodside, SA 5244 **Region** Adelaide Hills
T (08) 8339 9300 **www**.petaluma.com.au **Open** Fri–Mon 10–4
Winemaker Andrew Hardy, Mike Mudge **Est.** 1976 **Dozens** 60 000 **Vyds** 240ha
The Petaluma range has been expanded beyond the core group of Croser Sparkling, Clare Valley Riesling, Piccadilly Chardonnay and Coonawarra (Cabernet Sauvignon/Merlot). Newer arrivals of note include Adelaide Hills Viognier and Adelaide Hills Shiraz. The SA plantings in the Clare Valley, Coonawarra and Adelaide Hills provide a more than sufficient source of estate-grown grapes for the wines. A new winery and cellar door were opened in 2015 on a greenfield site with views of Mt Lofty. Exports to all major markets.

♀♀♀♀♀ **Tiers Piccadilly Valley Chardonnay 2013** This pioneering vineyard in Piccadilly delivers the trademark precision and minerality that provide an exceptional length of palate. Wrapped in a generous robe of oak, the wine will continue to unfurl over the next decade. Screwcap. 13.5% alc. **Rating** 96 **To** 2020 $115
Evans Vineyard Coonawarra 2012 A finely detailed portrait of Coonawarra cabernet framed by the contribution of the merlot and (a little) shiraz. It is only medium-bodied, but its precision and length are utterly convincing, helped no doubt by the great vintage. Screwcap. 14.5% alc. **Rating** 96 **To** 2032 $60 ○
Hanlin Hill Clare Valley Riesling 2015 From vines planted in '68, this single vineyard Clare riesling has an enviable track record, and the '15 follows admirably. Classic Clare lime blossom, flowing effortlessly to the mineral-laden and powerful finish. Screwcap. 13.5% alc. **Rating** 95 **To** 2030 $28 ○
Piccadilly Valley Chardonnay 2014 The much reduced harvest (a wet and windy spring) was carried out over 19 days, fermented and matured in French oak (60% new). It's a very concentrated chardonnay, with white peach and nectarine tightly embraced by flinty, minerally acidity. Needs a few years for that embrace to relax. Screwcap. 13.5% alc. **Rating** 95 **To** 2024 $40
Adelaide Hills Shiraz 2013 From the eastern edge of the Adelaide Hills, hand-picked, cold-soaked for 14 days, transferred to a percentage of new oak, which raises its hand on the bouquet, but the palate is an array of black fruits, licorice and pepper with fine and chalky tannins. Screwcap. 15% alc. **Rating** 95 **To** 2028 $45
White Adelaide Hills Pinot Gris 2015 Hand-picked, whole bunch-pressed, fermented in used French oak. The effort has been worthwhile; as the wine nears the finish, it begins to show the power it has picked up via barrel fermentation; the aftertaste is particularly powerful and lingering. Screwcap. 13.5% alc. **Rating** 94 **To** 2018 $22 ○
Croser Late Disgorged 2003 A minuscule production of just 744 bottles delivers all the exuberance of 80% pinot noir, full barrel fermentation and 11 years on yeast lees. It's filled with grilled pineapple, glacé fig, toast, toffee and nutmeg, lingering long with enticing, golden lusciousness. Such generosity makes zero dosage all it needs. Drink now. Diam. 13% alc. **Rating** 94 **To** 2016 $55 TS

♀♀♀♀♀ **Croser 2012 Rating** 93 **To** 2022 $35 TS
White Adelaide Hills Sauvignon Blanc 2015 Rating 92 **To** 2017 $22 ○

Peter Drayton Wines

Ironbark Hill Vineyard, 694 Hermitage Road, Pokolbin, NSW 2321 **Region** Hunter Valley
T (02) 6574 7085 **www.**pdwines.com.au **Open** 7 days 10–5
Winemaker Liz Jackson, Keith Tulloch **Est.** 2001 **Dozens** 10000 **Vyds** 16.5ha
Owned by Peter and Leesa Drayton. Peter's father, Max Drayton, and brothers John and
Greg, run Drayton's Family Wines. The estate plantings include shiraz, chardonnay, semillon,
cabernet sauvignon, tempranillo, merlot, verdelho and tyrian. Peter is a commercial/industrial
builder, so constructing the cellar door was a busman's holiday. The vineyard features an
atmospheric function venue and wedding chapel set among the vines, with events organised
and catered for by Café Enzo. Exports to Vietnam, Hong Kong and China.

ŶŶŶŶŶ **Premium Release Semillon 2013** Yes. This is lovely. Aromatically it's particularly
pretty. Oyster shells and honeysuckle, lemon and hay. Texturally it almost feels
supple. A delight. Screwcap. 11% alc. **Rating** 95 **To** 2021 $25 CM ✪
Premium Release Semillon 2015 Clear, clean lines. A slender but well-
proportioned body of flavour. And a ringing, persistent finish. Tick, tick and tick.
Screwcap. 11% alc. **Rating** 94 **To** 2025 $25 CM ✪
Premium Release Shiraz 2014 It gets its retro on but the power of the vintage
sweeps the flavours up and out through the finish. Leather, caramel, tar and spice
flavours rumble through the palate before setting the finish aflame. Screwcap.
14.8% alc. **Rating** 94 **To** 2030 $36 CM

ŶŶŶŶŶ **Premium Release Merlot 2014 Rating** 93 **To** 2026 $36 CM
Heritage Reserve Chardonnay 2015 Rating 92 **To** 2019 $25 CM ✪
Premium Release Chardonnay 2015 Rating 92 **To** 2019 $25 CM ✪
TJD Reserve Museum Release Verdelho 2015 Rating 92 **To** 2019 $45 CM
Semillon Verdelho 2015 Rating 90 **To** 2018 $22 CM

Peter Lehmann

Para Road, Tanunda, SA 5352 **Region** Barossa Valley
T (08) 8565 9555 **www.**peterlehmannwines.com **Open** Mon–Fri 9.30–5, w'ends &
public hols 10.30–4.30
Winemaker Ian Hongell, Peter Kelly, Tim Dolan **Est.** 1979 **Dozens** 750000
The seemingly indestructible Peter Lehmann (the person) died in June 2013, laying the seeds
for what became the last step in the sale of the minority Lehmann family ownership in the
company. The Hess Group of California had acquired control in '03 (leaving part of the capital
with the Lehmann family), but a decade later it became apparent that Hess wished to quit its
holding. Various suitors put their case forward, but Margaret Lehmann (Peter's widow) wanted
ongoing family, not corporate, ownership. Casella thus was able to make the successful bid in
November '14, followed by the acquisition of Brand's Laira in December '15. Exports to all
major markets.

ŶŶŶŶŶ **VSV 1885 Barossa Valley Shiraz 2014** It defies conventional thinking, but
this wine from 129yo vines is less powerful than Carey (17yo) and Valley View
Road (15yo) vines. But it's the most elegant, and I'm bemused by the pricing,
this the bargain. Supple red and black fruits have just the right amount of French
oak back-up, and the svelte tannins are all-important in the creation of the wine.
Screwcap. 14% alc. **Rating** 97 **To** 2044 $60 ✪

ŶŶŶŶŶ **Wigan Eden Valley Riesling 2011** Standard cool fermentation in stainless steel,
the magic coming from the quality of the grapes and the time spent in bottle. Pale,
bright straw-green, it is still in short pants, and needs another 5 years to approach
full maturity, when it could be one of the great Wigans. Fantastic each-way odds
for a song. Screwcap. 11% alc. **Rating** 96 **To** 2031 $32 ✪
Black Queen Sparkling Shiraz 2010 After conventional fermentation, the
wine spent 2 years in used French oak before bottle fermentation and 2 years on
lees. It has very good shiraz varietal character, dark brooding fruits layered with

spice and licorice, the tannins admirably fine and supple; excellent balance/dosage. Cork. 14% alc. **Rating** 96 **To** 2038 $42 ✪

Margaret Barossa Semillon 2010 Led the revolution in the approach to Barossa Valley semillon vinification around the turn of the century, and hasn't tried to reinvent the wheel. Access to old vines, attention to detail in the winery, and early bottling produce the same old magic. Screwcap. 11% alc. **Rating** 95 **To** 2020 $32 ✪

VSV Valley View Road Barossa Valley Shiraz 2014 This is particularly well balanced. And medium-bodied; the flavours are split between red and black, the latter with the major contribution; the tannins are ripe and supple, the finish continuing the smooth flow across the length of the palate. Emerges as the shiraz most obviously ready, albeit with a long future. Screwcap. 14.5% alc. **Rating** 95 **To** 2034 $60

Stonewell Barossa Shiraz 2011 Only two vineyards provided grapes of Stonewell standard, hence a small make. Has excellent flavour and balance, dismissing the challenge of the vintage. You would never pick the vintage in an options game, its black fruits perfectly ripe. Screwcap. 14.5% alc. **Rating** 95 **To** 2031 $100

Futures Barossa Shiraz Cabernet 2012 It is quite likely that the Eden Valley has contributed to what is a lovely wine, reflecting the quality of this great vintage. The bouquet and palate are as one, blackcurrant and blackberry joined by spicy plum nuances, the tannins fine, the oak having done its job very well. Screwcap. 14.5% alc. **Rating** 95 **To** 2027 $26 ✪

VSV Carey Barossa Valley Shiraz 2014 This has the fullest body and most powerful tannins of the VSV Shirazs, the flavours of blackberry, plum, anise and tar. Screwcap. 14.5% alc. **Rating** 94 **To** 2044 $60

♟♟♟♟ **Black Queen Sparkling Shiraz 2011** Rating 89 To 2026 $42 TS

Pewsey Vale   ★★★★★

Eden Valley Road, Eden Valley, SA 5353 **Region** Eden Valley
T (08) 8561 3200 **www**.pewseyvale.com **Open** By appt
Winemaker Louisa Rose **Est.** 1847 **Dozens** 20 000 **Vyds** 65ha

Pewsey Vale was a famous vineyard established in 1847 by Joseph Gilbert, and it was appropriate that when the Hill-Smith family began the renaissance of the Eden Valley plantings in 1961, it should do so by purchasing Pewsey Vale and establishing 50ha of riesling. The Riesling also finally benefited from being the first wine to be bottled with a Stelvin screwcap, in '77. While public reaction forced the abandonment of the initiative for almost 20 years, Pewsey Vale never lost faith in the technical advantages of the closure. A quick taste (or better, a share of a bottle) of five to seven-year-old Contours Riesling will tell you why. Exports to all major markets.

♟♟♟♟♟ **Single Vineyard Eden Valley Riesling 2015** Acquired and planted in the '60s; in its day the '69 was a celebrated wine. It is tightly knit, its citrus and apple flavours anchored on a bedrock of minerally acidity. On a hot summer's day this will shine, but it also has plenty in reserve for the next 5 years. Screwcap. 12% alc. Rating 95 To 2030 $25 ✪

The Contours Museum Reserve Single Vineyard Estate Eden Valley Riesling 2011 The mid-palate is almost plump with flavour but the finish shoots out long and impressive. This has arrived at a good place; it's a good reason for the Museum Release program. Volleys of lime, spice and toast-like flavour; all with powerful serves. Screwcap. 11.5% alc. **Rating** 95 **To** 2022 $34 CM ✪

Prima Eden Valley Riesling 2015 The fermentation was stopped with 23.6g/l of residual sugar, and acidity of 8.5g/l. Obviously, picked early, and the acidity is the driving force, allied with the expected lime/lemon sherbet flavours. Now or in a decade. Screwcap. 9.5% alc. **Rating** 94 **To** 2025 $26 ✪

Pfeiffer Wines ★★★★★

167 Distillery Road, Wahgunyah, Vic 3687 **Region** Rutherglen
T (02) 6033 2805 **www**.pfeifferwines.com.au **Open** Mon–Sat 9–5, Sun 10–5
Winemaker Chris and Jen Pfeiffer **Est.** 1984 **Dozens** 20 000 **Vyds** 32ha

Family-owned and run, Pfeiffer Wines occupies one of the historic wineries (built in 1880) that abound in North East Victoria, and which is worth a visit on this score alone. In 2012 Chris Pfeiffer was awarded an Order of Australia Medal (OAM) for his services to the wine industry. Both hitherto and into the future, Pfeiffer's Muscats, Topaques and other fortified wines are a key part of the business. The arrival of daughter Jen, by a somewhat circuitous and initially unplanned route, has dramatically lifted the quality of the table wines, led by the reds. Chris Pfeiffer celebrated his 40th vintage in '13, having well and truly set the scene for supremely gifted daughter Jen to assume the chief winemaking role in due course. Exports to the UK, the US, Canada, Belgium, Malaysia, Singapore and China.

♀♀♀♀♀ **Rare Rutherglen Muscat NV** Average age 25 years. Similar depth to the colour of the Grand, but more olive/mahogany; a wonderful bouquet, of raisins and spices in a blender mix, the palate of exceptional lusciousness (different from and more than just sweetness), the flavours running through Christmas pudding, raisins and burnt toffee, distinct rancio cleansing the finish. 500ml. Screwcap. 17.5% alc. **Rating** 98 **To** 2018 $123 ❂

Rare Rutherglen Topaque NV Average age 25 years. Deep, but clear burnt amber colour, grading to olive on the rim; unbridled power and complexity, no calm moments here, its flavours intense and mouthgripping, yet not sweet in conventional terms. Has exceptional length, with flavours of tea leaf, honey, cake and exotic spices. 500ml. Screwcap. 17.5% alc. **Rating** 97 **To** 2018 $123 ❂

♀♀♀♀♀ **Grand Rutherglen Topaque NV** Muscadelle, average age 18 years. Mid-mahogany colour; a perfumed and rich bouquet, the lift of the rancio providing extra complexity and feeding through into the palate; here burnt toffee, Christmas cake and malt provide a luscious and complex, yet not heavy, finish. Is very much in the Pfeiffer style, intensity with lightness of foot. 500ml. Screwcap. 17.5% alc. **Rating** 96 **To** 2018 $83

Grand Rutherglen Muscat NV Average age 23 years. Deep colour; muscat to its back teeth, with glorious Arabian spice and raisin interplay interwoven with touches of toffee and bitter chocolate; the length and balance are perfect, as is the rancio. In the Pfeiffer style, intensity with elegance. 500ml. Screwcap. 17.5% alc. **Rating** 96 **To** 2018 $83

Gamay 2015 Estate 'young' (15+yo) and old (40+yo) vines, hand-picked bunches placed in airtight bins with cultured yeast, fermentation taking place within the berries, pigeage over 3 days, pressed to stainless steel, bottled mid-May. Beaujolais gamay has to be the model. Singularly well made, full of red cherry fruits, yet remains so light on its feet, the acidity sweet (!) and tantalising. Something quite special. Screwcap. 13.5% alc. **Rating** 95 **To** 2020 $18 ❂

Classic Rutherglen Topaque NV Bright gold-amber; it is radically different from, and more complex than, its lesser sibling, with sweet honey, malt and cake flavours balanced by the rancio, which also extends the finish. 500ml. Screwcap. 17.5% alc. **Rating** 95 **To** 2018 $29 ❂

Shiraz 2014 Deep crimson-purple hue; jam-packed with fruit and ripe tannins, oak singing loudly in the background, plum, blackberry and black cherry clamouring for space in the foreground. Good now, better still in the future. Screwcap. 14.5% alc. **Rating** 94 **To** 2034 $25 ❂

Merlot 2014 Bright crimson-purple; Jen Pfeiffer is a very thoughtful and skilled winemaker, each step she's taken has paid big dividends. This is a serious merlot, with a classic bay leaf/dried herb/cassis/blackcurrant assemblage of flavours on the medium-bodied palate, its balance underwriting its longevity. Screwcap. 13.5% alc. **Rating** 94 **To** 2029 $25 ❂

Cabernet Sauvignon 2014 Excellent colour; a winemaker at the top of her game, conjuring a cabernet of this quality from these two regions; blackcurrant fruit, bay leaf, tannins and oak are all in perfect sync. Screwcap. 13.5% alc. Rating 94 To 2034 $25 ✪

Tempranillo 2014 Good depth; rich flavours of black and red cherry, with bits and pieces of plum and blackberry, all come together on the long, complex palate. Screwcap. 14.5% alc. **Rating** 94 **To** 2029 $24 ✪

Durif 2014 Dense, inky purple-crimson; deliberately and unashamedly full-bodied, made for the long haul, or for winter by a fireside, or a beach night bbq. When to drink (in years)? Now, that's the question. It's as close as a table wine can go to being timeless – now or in 1000 days. Screwcap. 14.5% alc. **Rating** 94 **To** 2040 $32

Seriously Nutty NV Complex and intense, this is the next development phase (in cask) of the Seriously Fine. It is more complex and intense, similar to a dry amontillado in style. Takes after its nutty name, and adds dried orange peel and the clean finish of a spring day. Screwcap. 21.5% alc. **Rating** 94 **To** 2018 $50

Christopher's VP 2013 Very much in the new-generation mode: much drier and closer to Portuguese vintage style. Dark, black fruits, chocolate and spices are left intact by the high quality fortifying spirit. Given its screwcap, it could well cruise through several decades. Screwcap. 18.5% alc. **Rating** 94 **To** 2035 $30 ✪

Rutherglen Topaque NV Bright golden-amber; has aromas and flavours of tea leaf, spices, candied fruit and honey, the finish cleansing and dry – dry by comparison with the mid-palate, that is. 500ml. Screwcap. 17.5% alc. **Rating** 94 **To** 2018 $20 ✪

Classic Rutherglen Muscat NV Average age 11–12 years. Very little difference in hue from that of the entry point Rutherglen Muscat, but greater focus and intensity to the raisin/plum pudding fruit; excellent rancio and cut to the long finish. Screwcap. 17.5% alc. **Rating** 94 **To** 2018 $29 ✪

🍷🍷🍷🍷🍷 Seriously Fine NV Rating 93 To 2018 $29
Classic Rutherglen Tawny NV Rating 93 To 2018 $20 ✪
Rutherglen Muscat NV Rating 93 To 2018 $20 ✪
Chardonnay 2015 Rating 90 To 2020 $20 ✪
Carlyle Shiraz 2014 Rating 90 To 2029 $18 ✪
Carlyle Cabernet Merlot 2014 Rating 90 To 2029 $18 ✪

Phaedrus Estate   ★★★★☆

220 Mornington-Tyabb Road, Moorooduc, Vic 3933 **Region** Mornington Peninsula
T (03) 5978 8134 **www.phaedrus.com.au Open** W'ends & public hols 11–5
Winemaker Ewan Campbell, Maitena Zantvoort **Est.** 1997 **Dozens** 2000 **Vyds** 2.5ha
Since Maitena Zantvoort and Ewan Campbell established Phaedrus Estate, they have gained a reputation for producing premium cool climate wines. Their winemaking philosophy brings art and science together to produce wines showing regional and varietal character with minimal winemaking interference. The vineyard includes 1ha of pinot noir and 0.5ha each of pinot gris, chardonnay and shiraz. Exports to Hong Kong.

🍷🍷🍷🍷🍷 Single Vineyard Reserve Mornington Peninsula Pinot Noir 2014 Varietal character is in no way sacrificed and yet it has extra grunt, extra volume of savoury, stemmy complexity, and a more forceful push through the finish. Every now and then you pick up a wine and instantly think: they nailed it. This is one such. Screwcap. 13.9% alc. **Rating** 96 **To** 2025 $45 CM ✪

Mornington Peninsula Pinot Noir 2014 Depth and reach. Macerated cherry and plum flavours come thoroughly infused with sweet, woody spice notes. It sets up the drama and then methodically resolves all the various plot points through the back half of the wine. Long finish is the icing. Screwcap. 13.7% alc. **Rating** 94 **To** 2023 $26 CM ✪

🍷🍷🍷🍷🍷 Mornington Peninsula Chardonnay 2015 Rating 91 To 2020 $26 CM
Mister Wolf Sauvignon Blanc 2015 Rating 90 To 2017 $19 CM ✪

PHI ★★★★★

Lusatia Park Vineyard, Owens Road, Woori Yallock, Vic 3139 **Region** Yarra Valley/Heathcote
T (03) 5964 6070 **www**.phiwines.com **Open** By appt
Winemaker Steve Webber **Est.** 2005 **Dozens** 1700 **Vyds** 15ha

This was a joint venture between two very influential wine families: De Bortoli and Shelmerdine. The key executives are Stephen Shelmerdine and Steve Webber (and wives Kate and Leanne). It rests upon the selection and management of specific blocks of vines without regard to cost. The wines are made from the 7.5ha Lusatia Park Vineyard in the Yarra Valley, and the estate-owned 7.5ha vineyard in Heathcote. The vineyard was acquired by De Bortoli in November '15, effective after the '16 harvest. At the time of going to print, no further details were available.

Lusatia Park Vineyard Pinot Noir 2014 MV6 planted in '85, hand-picked and sorted, open-fermented, 20% whole bunches, matured in French barriques (35% new) for 8 months. The fragrant red berry sets the ball rolling in the right direction, and the elegant, savoury palate continues the story, with spicy red and purple berry fruits, fine tannins and integrated French oak; already offering an open window into its future. Screwcap. 13.5% alc. **Rating** 95 **To** 2024 **$55**

Heathcote Syrah Grenache Mourvedre 2014 **Rating** 93 **To** 2034 **$26** ✪
Lusatia Park Vineyard Chardonnay 2014 **Rating** 91 **To** 2022 **$45**

Philip Shaw Wines ★★★★★

Koomooloo Vineyard, Caldwell Lane, Orange, NSW 2800 **Region** Orange
T (02) 6365 2334 **www**.philipshaw.com.au **Open** 7 days 11–5
Winemaker Philip and Daniel Shaw **Est.** 1989 **Dozens** 25 000 **Vyds** 47ha

Philip Shaw, former chief winemaker of Rosemount Estate and then Southcorp, first became interested in the Orange region in 1985. In '88 he purchased the Koomooloo Vineyard and began extensive plantings, the varieties including shiraz, merlot, pinot noir, sauvignon blanc, cabernet franc, cabernet sauvignon and viognier. Son Daniel has joined Philip in the winery, at a time when the quality of the portfolio of wines is going from strength to strength. Exports to the UK, the US and other major markets.

No. 11 Orange Chardonnay 2014 Whole bunch-pressed, wild-fermented in French oak (30% new), 12 months maturation. Bright straw-green; a seriously good chardonnay, 30+ years practice making perfect; a very long palate, making light of the very low alcohol. Screwcap. 11.5% alc. **Rating** 95 **To** 2020 **$35** ✪

No. 5 Orange Cabernet Sauvignon 2012 From the Koomooloo Vineyard, hand-picked and sorted, destemmed and crushed, wild open ferment, matured for 20 months in French oak (60% new). Has a strong savoury, cool grown print on its personality, the tannins superfine, but an essential part of a very elegant Old World wine. Screwcap. 13.5% alc. **Rating** 95 **To** 2037 **$75**

The Wire Walker Orange Pinot Noir 2015 **Rating** 91 **To** 2022 **$22** ✪
No. 8 Orange Pinot Noir 2014 **Rating** 91 **To** 2019 **$40**
No. 19 Orange Sauvignon Blanc 2014 **Rating** 90 **To** 2017 **$25**
The Architect Orange Chardonnay 2014 **Rating** 90 **To** 2018 **$22**
No. 11 Orange Chardonnay 2013 **Rating** 90 **To** 2020 **$35**
The Wire Walker Orange Pinot Noir 2014 **Rating** 90 **To** 2021 **$22**
No. 89 Orange Shiraz 2013 **Rating** 90 **To** 2025 **$50**

Philip's Frolic ★★★☆

Aura Rose, Collina de Re, 5126 Mansfield-Whitfield Rd, Whitlands, Vic 3678
Region King Valley/Southern Highlands
T 1300 883 787 **www**.philipsfrolic.com.au **Open** Not
Winemaker Adrian Lockhard, Garry Wall **Est.** 2010 **Dozens** 20 000 **Vyds** 2ha

Philip Madden has set himself a challenge: to make shiraz with the elegance, spice and style to rival the best of the Rhône from a 2ha vineyard on the western edge of the Southern Highlands in NSW. Not content with that challenge, he has decided to produce a rose as a tribute to Provence using pinot meunier grown on the Collina de Re vineyard in the King Valley. In this endeavour he is joined by Joanna Prettyman and John Love. The masterplan is to sell large quantities to China, and to release the wines on the Australian market at bargain prices thereafter. Exports to China.

ŶŶŶŶ♀ Aura King Valley Rose 2015 Pale transparent pink; a pinot meunier with six people having roles in its production, very like the credits for a film (short or long) or a TV soapie, with three co-producers, including Philip Madden. It comes from John Love's Collina del Re Vineyard at the very top of the King Valley, and its crisp, incisive varietal character stands out like a beacon: super-spicy, super-dry and super-long on the finish and aftertaste. Screwcap. 13.1% alc. **Rating** 92 **To** 2017 $28

Piano Piano

852 Beechworth-Wangaratta Road, Everton Upper, Vic 3678 **Region** Beechworth
T (03) 5727 0382 **www**.pianopiano.com.au **Open** By appt
Winemaker Marc Scalzo **Est.** 2001 **Dozens** 1500 **Vyds** 4.6ha
'Piano piano' means 'slowly slowly' in Italian, and this is how Marc Scalzo and wife Lisa Hernan have approached the development of their business. Marc has a degree in oenology from CSU and many years' practical experience as a winemaker with Brown Brothers, and vintage experience with Giaconda, John Gehrig, and in NZ with Seresin Estate and Delegat's. In 1997 they planted 2.6ha of merlot, cabernet sauvignon, tempranillo and touriga nacional on their Brangie Vineyard in the King Valley; they followed up with 1.2ha of chardonnay ('06) and 0.8ha of shiraz ('08) on their Beechworth property.

ŶŶŶŶŶ Sophie's Block Beechworth Chardonnay 2013 Wild-fermented in French oak (35% new), matured for 10 months. Elegant and wonderfully fresh for a 3yo chardonnay, and no hint of unripe fruit. The new oak has been drawn inwards into the heart of the wine, giving its fragrance and delicate flavours free play. Makes your heart skip a beat. Screwcap. 13% alc. **Rating** 95 **To** 2023 $35 **✪**
Henry's Block Beechworth Shiraz 2013 Matured for 20 months in French oak (50% new). This is a wine that makes you sit up and pay attention, its finish all class, but plenty happening along the way with its dark cherry fruit impregnated with black pepper, spice and licorice. The tannin and oak management is impressive, particularly the latter, for the wine has absorbed all the new oak. Screwcap. 13.5% alc. **Rating** 95 **To** 2033 $35 **✪**

ŶŶŶŶ♀ Mario's Blend Tempranillo Touriga 2013 Rating 91 **To** 2023 $22 **✪**

Pierrepoint Wines

271 Pierrepoint Road, Tarrington, Vic 3300 **Region** Henty
T (03) 5572 5553 **www**.pierrepointwines.com.au **Open** Most days 11–6
Winemaker Scott Ireland (Contract) **Est.** 1998 **Dozens** 450 **Vyds** 5ha
Pierrepoint was established by Andrew and Jennifer Lacey on the foothills of Mt Pierrepoint between Hamilton and Tarrington at an altitude of 200m. The predominantly red buckshot soils of the vineyard are derived from ancient volcanic basalt, rich in minerals and free-draining. Two hectares each of pinot noir and pinot gris, and 1ha of chardonnay are planted on an ideal north-facing slope.

ŶŶŶŶŶ Alexandra Chardonnay 2013 The very cool Henty climate, low yields and high quality winemaking join hands in producing a chardonnay that has exceptional intensity and length, yet is light on its feet, with a fused mix of grapefruit and white peach. Screwcap. 12.5% alc. **Rating** 95 **To** 2023 $35 **✪**
Pinot Noir 2012 Estate-grown with very low yield of 2.5t/ha; 12 months maturation in French oak. Deeply coloured, its flavours are in the dark fruit

spectrum, with black cherries and savoury plum flavours. A pinot that will live and evolve for more than a decade. Screwcap. 13% alc. **Rating** 94 **To** 2025 $39

Pierro   ★★★★★

Caves Road, Wilyabrup via Cowaramup, WA 6284 **Region** Margaret River
T (08) 9755 6220 **www.**pierro.com.au **Open** 7 days 10–5
Winemaker Dr Michael Peterkin **Est.** 1979 **Dozens** 10 000 **Vyds** 7.85ha
Dr Michael Peterkin is another of the legion of Margaret River medical practitioner-vignerons; for good measure, he married into the Cullen family. Pierro is renowned for its stylish white wines, which often exhibit tremendous complexity; the Chardonnay can be monumental in its weight and texture. That said, its red wines from good vintages can be every bit as good. Exports to the UK, Denmark, Belgium, Russia, Malaysia, Indonesia, Hong Kong, Singapore and Japan.

♀♀♀♀♀ **Margaret River Chardonnay 2014** Picked over 1 month, hand-sorted, chilled to 5°C, whole bunch-pressed, 90% cultured yeast, 10% wild, primary fermentation and mlf in French oak (50% new) with 12 months maturation and stirring. One of the Margaret River princes of chardonnay, with perfect balance and length, the suite of flavours so complex they border on savoury; the length is remarkable. Screwcap. 14% alc. **Rating** 96 **To** 2023 $82
Reserve Margaret River Cabernet Sauvignon Merlot 2012 70% cabernet sauvignon, 24% merlot, the remainder cabernet franc, petit verdot and malbec, 18 months in French barriques (60% new). Bright, clear colour; a remarkably elegant, juicy red and black berry fruit-filled wine, neither oak or tannins seeking to interfere with the fruit. One of those rare wines to be drunk now or in 20+ years. Screwcap. 14% alc. **Rating** 96 **To** 2035 $77
L.T.C. 2015 SSB with a little touch of chardonnay. Vibrantly crisp and intense, it also has a little touch of CO_2, giving a sparkle to the finish. Screwcap. 13.5% alc. **Rating** 95 **To** 2018 $34 **☉**
Margaret River Cabernet Sauvignon Merlot L.T.Cf. 2013 55% cabernet sauvignon, 31% merlot, 9% cabernet franc, 3% malbec, 2% petit verdot. Doesn't quite have the same purity and freshness as the Reserve Cabernet Sauvignon Merlot, but is arguably more complex and certainly has length to burn; redcurrant, blackcurrant and dried herbs are all in play. Screwcap. 14% alc. **Rating** 94 **To** 2033 $40

♀♀♀♀ **Margaret River Pino's 2014 Rating** 89 **To** 2024 $53

Pig in the House   ★★★

Balcombe Road, Billimari, NSW 2804 **Region** Cowra
T 0427 443 598 **www.**piginthehouse.com.au **Open** Fri–Sun 11–5 by appt
Winemaker Antonio D'Onise **Est.** 2002 **Dozens** 1500 **Vyds** 25ha
Jason and Rebecca O'Dea established their vineyard (7ha shiraz, 6ha cabernet sauvignon, 5ha merlot, 4.5ha chardonnay and 2.5ha sauvignon blanc) on a block of land formerly used as home for 20 free-range pigs – making any explanation about the name of the business totally unnecessary. Given its prior use, one would imagine the vines would grow lustily, and it is no surprise that organic certification has been given by Biological Farmers of Australia. The O'Deas have in fact taken the process several steps further, using biodynamic preparations and significantly reducing all sprays. The wines made are good advertisements for organic/biodynamic farming. Exports to Japan and China.

♀♀♀♀ **Certified Organic Shiraz 2014** In good shape. A sweet ball of berried flavour rolls through the palate, brightened by notes of port wine jelly and violet. Will please most red drinkers. Screwcap. 14% alc. **Rating** 89 **To** 2020 $25 CM
Certified Organic Sauvignon Blanc 2014 Tutti-frutti style in general though it slashes through the finish with a race of citrus. It's like a funny joke with a message that cuts. Screwcap. 12.5% alc. **Rating** 88 **To** 2017 $25 CM

Pike & Joyce ★★★★★

730 Mawson Road, Lenswood, SA 5240 **Region** Adelaide Hills
T (08) 8389 8102 **www.**pikeandjoyce.com.au **Open** Not
Winemaker Neil Pike, John Trotter **Est.** 1998 **Dozens** 5000 **Vyds** 18.5ha
This is a partnership between the Pike family (of Clare Valley fame) and the Joyce family, related to Andrew Pike's wife, Cathy. The Joyce family have been orchardists at Lenswood for over 100 years, and also have extensive operations in the Riverland. Together with Andrew they have established a vineyard planted to sauvignon blanc (5.9ha), pinot noir (5.73ha), pinot gris (3.22ha), chardonnay (3.18ha) and semillon (0.47ha). The wines are made at the Pikes' Clare Valley winery. Exports to the UK, China and other major markets.

🍷🍷🍷🍷🍷 **The Bleedings Pinot Noir Rose 2015** Reductive and spicy but it feels velvety and is far more compelling than your average rose. In short, it's light and dry with plenty going on. Screwcap. 13.5% alc. **Rating** 94 **To** 2017 $18 CM ✪

🍷🍷🍷🍷🍷 **Sirocco Chardonnay 2015 Rating** 93 **To** 2020 $35 CM
Beurre Bosc Pinot Gris 2015 Rating 93 **To** 2020 $24 ✪
Descente Sauvignon Blanc 2015 Rating 91 **To** 2017 $24
Vue du Nord Pinot Noir 2015 Rating 91 **To** 2021 $38
Separe Gruner Veltliner 2015 Rating 90 **To** 2019 $28
Rapide Pinot Noir 2015 Rating 90 **To** 2019 $22 CM

Pikes ★★★★★

Polish Hill River Road, Sevenhill, SA 5453 **Region** Clare Valley
T (08) 8843 4370 **www.**pikeswines.com.au **Open** 7 days 10–4
Winemaker Neil Pike, Steve Baraglia **Est.** 1984 **Dozens** 35 000 **Vyds** 73ha
Owned by the Pike brothers: Andrew was for many years the senior viticulturist with Southcorp, Neil was a winemaker at Mitchell. Pikes now has its own winery, with Neil presiding. In most vintages its white wines, led by Riesling, are the most impressive. Planting of the vineyards has been an ongoing affair, with a panoply of varietals, new and traditional. The Merle is Pikes' limited-production flagship Riesling. Exports to the UK, the US, China, and other major markets.

🍷🍷🍷🍷🍷 **The Merle Clare Valley Riesling 2015** Made for the long haul. The quality of the fruit establishes itself in a millisecond, swooping and gliding across and along the palate; this is the lime equivalent of Meyer lemon, deliciously juicy and fresh, fruit (not sugar) sweet. Screwcap. 12.5% alc. **Rating** 96 **To** 2030 $45 ✪
The E.W.P. Clare Valley Shiraz 2013 Coffee-cream meets peppermint and sweet, ripe blackberry and black cherry. Undergrowth and clove-like notes add extra gears of flavour. The thing that (perhaps) surprises is how juicy this is; it's not a blockbuster; it builds power as much by revs as by force. Screwcap. 13.5% alc. **Rating** 95 **To** 2026 $65 CM
Traditionale Clare Valley Riesling 2015 From Polish Hill River, Watervale, Leasingham and Sevenhill. A generous and immediately enjoyable wine, filling the mouth with lime, lemon and apple flavours, perfectly braced by acidity. Screwcap. 12% alc. **Rating** 94 **To** 2025 $27 ✪

🍷🍷🍷🍷🍷 **Impostores Clare Valley Savignan 2015 Rating** 92 **To** 2017 $20 CM ✪
Luccio Clare Valley Fiano 2015 Rating 91 **To** 2017 $19 CM ✪
Luccio Clare Valley Sangiovese Rose 2015 Rating 91 **To** 2017 $19 CM ✪
Los Campaneros Shiraz Tempranillo 2013 Rating 90 **To** 2020 $20 CM ✪
The Hill Block Clare Valley Cabernet 2013 Rating 90 **To** 2030 $65 CM

Pimpernel Vineyards ★★★★★

6 Hill Road, Coldstream, Vic 3770 **Region** Yarra Valley
T 0457 326 436 **www.**pimpernelvineyards.com.au **Open** W'ends & public hols 11–5
Winemaker Damien Archibald, Mark Horrigan **Est.** 2001 **Dozens** 2000 **Vyds** 6ha

Lilydale-based cardiologist Mark Horrigan's love affair with wine started long before he had heard about either the Yarra Valley or his family's links, centuries ago, to Condrieu, France. He is a direct descendant of the Chapuis family, his ultimate ancestors buried in the Church of St Etienne in 1377. In a cosmopolitan twist, his father came from a Welsh mining village, but made his way to university and found many things to enjoy, not the least wine. When the family moved to Australia in 1959, wine remained part of everyday life and, as Mark grew up in the '70s, the obsession passed from father to son. In 2001 he and wife Fiona purchased a property in the Yarra Valley on which they have built a (second) house, planted a vineyard, and erected a capacious winery designed by WA architect Peter Moran. In the course of doing so they became good friends of near-neighbour the late Dr Bailey Carrodus; some of the delphic labelling of Pimpernel's wines is pure Carrodus.

ΨΨΨΨΨ **GSM2 2014** There's a band of Rhône devotees who are making some delicious wines, this one of the best. It has all the multi-spice aromas in the book, the palate revelling in the unconstrained juicy fruit flavours. Length isn't always a feature of these wines, but it certainly is here. Diam. **Rating** 96 **To** 2030 $45 **○**
Pinot Noir Two 2014 Has the brightest hue of the '14 Pimpernel Pinots; the bouquet of spiced plum is a rehearsal for the medium-bodied palate that follows. This has the most finesse and deft handling of dry extract. Diam. 13.7% alc. **Rating** 95 **To** 2029 $45
Grouch 2014 Immediately establishes its power and complexity, flaunting its array of jet black fruits, tannins and oak all singing from the same page, honouring the Yarra Yering Dry Red No. 2 made by the late Bailey Carrodus. As belies its name, this needs 5 years before it will unreservedly welcome visitors. Shiraz. Diam. **Rating** 95 **To** 2030 $80
Pinot Noir Three 2014 Deeper colour than One; a complex bouquet with a spicy overlay to dark berry fruit; the palate is powerful, but briary/stemmy, these characters especially obvious on the aftertaste. The hope is that time will help soften the impact. Diam. **Rating** 94 **To** 2029 $80
Shiraz 2014 Bright hue, although not especially deep; the palate is medium-bodied and supple, the flavours obviously spicy and varietal, with a mix of red and blackberry fruits. Needs a touch more power. Diam. **Rating** 94 **To** 2030 $50

ΨΨΨΨΨ **Pinot Noir One 2014 Rating** 93 **To** 2027 $45
Marsanne Viognier 2014 Rating 92 **To** 2018 $50
Viognier 2014 Rating 90 **To** 2018 $50

Pindarie   ★★★★☆

946 Rosedale Road, Gomersal, SA 5352 **Region** Barossa Valley
T (08) 8524 9019 **www.**pindarie.com.au **Open** Mon–Fri 11–4, w'ends 11–5
Winemaker Peter Leske **Est.** 2005 **Dozens** 5000 **Vyds** 32.4ha
Owners Tony Brooks and Wendy Allan met at Roseworthy College in 1985. Tony was the sixth generation of farmers in SA and WA, and was studying agriculture; NZ-born Wendy was studying viticulture. On graduation Tony worked overseas managing sheep feedlots in Saudi Arabia, Turkey and Jordan, while Wendy worked for the next 12 years with Penfolds, commencing as a grower liaison officer and working her way up to become a senior viticulturist. She also found time to study viticulture in California, Israel, Italy, Germany, France, Portugal, Spain and Chile, working vintages and assessing vineyards for wine projects. In 2001 she completed a graduate diploma in wine business. The cellar door and café (which won a major tourism award in '12) has panoramic views. Exports to China.

ΨΨΨΨΨ **Schoff's Hill Cabernet Sauvignon 2014** A major surprise, with a juicy cassis stream of flavour outside the usual for the Barossa Valley; really surprises with its overall elegance on the back-palate and finish. Tannins? Yes, they are there, but don't seek to upset the boat. Screwcap. 14% alc. **Rating** 95 **To** 2034 $26 **○**

ΨΨΨΨΨ **Western Ridge Barossa Valley Shiraz 2014 Rating** 93 **To** 2034 $26 **○**
The Risk Taker Barossa Valley Tempranillo 2015 Rating 90 **To** 2022 $26

Pinelli Wines

30 Bennett Street, Caversham, WA 6055 **Region** Swan District
T (08) 9279 6818 **www**.pinelliwines.com.au **Open** Mon–Sat 9–5, Sun 10–5
Winemaker Robert and Daniel Pinelli **Est.** 1980 **Dozens** 17000 **Vyds** 9.78ha
Domenic and Iolanda Pinelli emigrated from Italy in the mid-1950s, and it was not long before Domenic was employed by Waldeck Wines, then one of the Swan Valley's more important wineries. With the benefit of 20 years' experience gained with Waldeck, in '80 he purchased a 2.8ha vineyard that had been established many years previously. It became the site of the Pinelli family winery, cellar door and home vineyard, subsequently significantly expanded, with cabernet sauvignon, colombard, merlot and shiraz. Son Robert graduated with a degree in oenology from Roseworthy in 1987, and has been the winemaker at Pinelli for over 20 years. His brother Daniel obtained a degree in civil engineering from the University of WA in '94, but eventually the lure of the family winery became too strong, so he joined his brother in '02, and obtained his oenology degree from CSU in '07. He graduated with distinction, and was awarded the Domaine Chandon Sparkling Wine Award for best sparkling wine production student.

ŶŶŶŶŶ Reserve Durif 2014 Burly, surly, brooding red with coal, leather, blackberry and resiny vanilla flavours oozing through the mouth. It comes with tannin, thick and dry; indeed it comes with all the attributes required for a long, healthy life. Screwcap. 14.5% alc. **Rating** 95 **To** 2030 $35 CM ❂

ŶŶŶŶŶ Reserve Shiraz 2014 Rating 91 **To** 2026 $28 CM

Pinnaroo Estate Wines

16 Jubilee Avenue, Warriewood, NSW 2804 (postal) **Region** Cowra
T (02) 9999 2525 **www**.pinnaroowines.com.au **Open** Not
Winemaker Madrez Wine Services **Est.** 2003 **Dozens** 1500 **Vyds** 120ha
This substantial venture is situated in the Canowindra district on the banks of the Belubula River. The original land owner was John Grant, a convict transported to NSW in 1811, pardoned in 1821. He became a well-known and respected farmer, leaving behind 12 children and 30000 acres of grazing land on the Belubula and Lachlan Rivers. It was divided into two in 1909, and 1620ha became Pinnaroo. It is now owned by a group of eight families, five of whom are farmers, who have planted 120ha of vines with the intention of simply growing grapes for sale to others. Initially a small amount was kept to produce wines for personal consumption, but 200–400 dozen of each wine in its portfolio are made for sale to restaurants and function centres.

ŶŶŶŶŶ Partners Reserve Orange Shiraz 2013 A closed stainless-steel fermenter, 72 hours cold soak, cultured yeast, 10 days on skins, regular delestage, matured for 12 months in French oak. Abundant black and red cherry fruit with a liberal sprinkling of spice and pepper play out on both the bouquet and the medium-bodied palate. This is a wholly seductive shiraz, ready now or whenever. Bargain. Screwcap. 14% alc. **Rating** 94 **To** 2033 $25

Pipers Brook Vineyard

1216 Pipers Brook Road, Pipers Brook, Tas 7254 **Region** Northern Tasmania
T (03) 6382 7527 **www**.pipersbrook.com.au **Open** 7 days 10–5
Winemaker Bryan Widstrand **Est.** 1974 **Dozens** 70000 **Vyds** 194ha
The Pipers Brook empire has almost 200ha of vineyard supporting the Pipers Brook and Ninth Island labels, with the major focus, of course, being on Pipers Brook. Fastidious viticulture and winemaking, immaculate packaging and enterprising marketing create a potent and effective blend. Pipers Brook operates two cellar door outlets, one at headquarters, the other at Strathlyn. Pipers Brook is owned by Belgian-owned sheepskin business Kreglinger, which has also established the large Norfolk Island winery and vineyard at Mount Benson in SA (see separate entry). Exports to the UK, the US and other major markets.

ŢŢŢŢŢ **Chardonnay 2014** This is a lovely chardonnay; its bouquet provides gently funky complexity, and the wine glides across the palate as if it had ball bearing moccasins on its feet. The fruit/oak balance is perfect, the fruit flavours equally split between stone fruit, apple and citrus. Screwcap. 13% alc. **Rating** 97 **To** 2025 $34 ✪

ŢŢŢŢŢ **Kreglinger Vintage Brut de Blanc 2003** Fermentation entirely in old French oak barriques, followed by a full 11 years on lees, has produced a wonderfully creamy texture and layers of toasty/nutty/bready complexity. Charged by a core of cool acidity, it is yet only part way through its evolution and may go down as one of Australia's most enduring sparkling wines. Cork. 12.5% alc. **Rating** 95 **To** 2033 $65 TS
Estate Riesling 2015 Crackles with spice and slate, includes highlights of rosewater and citrus blossom, and sings melodically out through the finish. In good form. Screwcap. 13% alc. **Rating** 94 **To** 2026 $34 CM
Kreglinger Brut Rose 2005 This is a gorgeously pale salmon rose of layered complexity. Partial fermentation in old French oak and almost 6 years on lees in bottle has produced palate grip and texture that underline secondary strawberry and red cherry flavours. Delicately youthful even at 11yo, it carries long and restrained through the finish. Cork. 12.5% alc. **Rating** 94 **To** 2018 $65 TS
Pirie Traditional Method NV The bright energy and endurance of northern Tasmanian chardonnay and pinot noir are elegantly framed in gorgeous lees-derived complexity, making for a cuvee that is vibrant and fresh and at the same time deeply textural and complex. The accord is captivating, and line and length are outstanding. The finest Pirie NV yet and one of the best value sparklings on the shelves. Cork. 12.5% alc. **Rating** 94 **To** 2018 $32 TS

ŢŢŢŢŢ **Gewurztraminer 2015** Rating 92 **To** 2019 $34
Sparkling 2009 Rating 92 **To** 2024 $37 TS
Ninth Island Tasmania Traditional Method NV Rating 91 **To** 2017 $30 TS
Pinot Gris 2014 Rating 90 **To** 2017 $34

Pirramimma   ★★★★★

Johnston Road, McLaren Vale, SA 5171 **Region** McLaren Vale
T (08) 8323 8205 **www**.pirramimma.com.au **Open** Mon–Fri 10–4.30, w'ends & public hols 10.30–5
Winemaker Geoff Johnston **Est.** 1892 **Dozens** 50 000 **Vyds** 91.5ha
A long-established family-owned company with outstanding vineyard resources. It is using those resources to full effect, with a series of intense old-vine varietals including Semillon, Sauvignon Blanc, Chardonnay, Shiraz, Grenache, Cabernet Sauvignon and Petit Verdot, all fashioned without over-embellishment. Wines are released under several ranges: Pirramimma, Stock's Hill, Pirra, Gilden Lily, Eight Carat, Wattle Park, Vineyard Select, Katunga and Lion's Gate. Exports to all major markets.

ŢŢŢŢŢ **McLaren Vale Petit Verdot 2013** Pirramimma was among the first to plant petit verdot in SA, and was the first to win a gold medal at the Adelaide Wine Show. This really is a seductive wine, the maritime climate of McLaren Vale warm enough to soften the hard impact petit verdot can have in cooler climates when presented unblended. Screwcap. 14.5% alc. **Rating** 95 **To** 2030 $30 ✪
Ironstone Petit Verdot 2013 Hulking red with dry tannin ricocheting to all corners of the mouth, (thankfully) backed by a substantial volume of both curranty fruit and toasty/coffeed oak. The epitome of the 'cellaring style'. It needs to be left alone for some years. Cork. 14.9% alc. **Rating** 95 **To** 2040 $50 CM

ŢŢŢŢŢ **303 Watervale Riesling 2015** Rating 93 **To** 2024 $25 CM ✪
Vineyard Select McLaren Vale Cabernet Sauvignon 2012 Rating 93 **To** 2028 $35 CM
Vineyard Select Petit Verdot 2012 Rating 93 **To** 2026 $35 CM
McLaren Vale Shiraz 2013 Rating 92 **To** 2028 $30 CM
Wattle Park Adelaide Hills Shiraz 2013 Rating 92 **To** 2025 $20 CM ✪

Vineyard Select Petit Verdot Shiraz 2013 Rating 92 To 2028 $25 ✪
Vineyard Select McLaren Vale Shiraz 2013 Rating 91 To 2028 $25
Vineyard Select McLaren Vale Petit Verdot 2013 Rating 91 To 2025 $25
Stock's Hill Cabernet Petit Verdot Merlot 2013 Rating 90 To 2022 $20 CM ✪
Eight Carat Petit Verdot 2013 Rating 90 To 2021 $18 CM ✪

Pizzini ★★★★

175 King Valley Road, Whitfield, Vic 3768 **Region** King Valley
T (03) 5729 8278 **www**.pizzini.com.au **Open** 7 days 10–5
Winemaker Joel Pizzini **Est.** 1980 **Dozens** 40 000 **Vyds** 48.7ha
Fred and Katrina Pizzini have been grapegrowers in the King Valley for over 30 years, with a substantial vineyard. Originally much of the grape production was sold, but today 80% is retained for the Pizzini brand, and the focus is on winemaking, which has been particularly successful. Their wines rank high among the many King Valley producers. It is not surprising that their wines should span both Italian and traditional varieties, and I can personally vouch for their Italian cooking skills. Katrina's A tavola! cooking school gives lessons in antipasti, gnocchi, risotto, cakes and desserts, and of course, pasta. Exports to the UK and Japan.

♥♥♥♥♥ King Valley Rosetta 2015 Pale pink; a very well made sangiovese rose; a perfumed bouquet and crystal-pure palate of small red fruits/berries; bone dry, with crisp acidity sewn through the length of the palate, all adding up to inviting freshness – and that second glass. Screwcap. 12% alc. Rating 94 To 2017 $19 ✪

♥♥♥♥♡ King Valley Arneis 2015 Rating 93 To 2020 $24 ✪
Pietra Rossa King Valley Sangiovese 2014 Rating 93 To 2024 $28
Il Barone 2013 Rating 92 To 2023 $45
King Valley Riesling 2015 Rating 91 To 2025 $18 ✪

Plan B ★★★★

679 Calgardup Road, Forest Grove, WA 6286 **Region** Great Southern/Margaret River
T 0413 759 030 **www**.planbwines.com **Open** Not
Winemaker Bill Crappsley **Est.** 2005 **Dozens** 40 000 **Vyds** 20ha
Plan B is a joint venture between Terry Chellappah, wine consultant, Bill Crappsley, a veteran winemaker/consultant, and Andrew Blythe. The Shiraz is sourced from Bill's Calgardup Vineyard, the remaining wines from Arlewood, and all are single vineyard releases. It has been a notably successful Plan B under Terry's management, with significant increases in production. In 2014 Bill Crappsley was awarded the Jack Mann Memorial Medal for significant services to the WA Wine Industry, coinciding with his 50 years in winemaking in WA. He has also won the Di Cullen Award (in '07), and the George Mulgrue Award (in 1999), both recognising his services to the industry. Exports include the UK, Canada, China.

♥♥♥♥♥ ST Frankland River Shiraz 2013 Includes 5% tempranillo. Excellent hue; it is powerful and very long in the mouth; the fruits are all black, with some blackcurrant having crept in along with the dominant blackberry, the finesse of the tannins providing a pressure-valve release for the somewhat elevated alcohol. Screwcap. 14.8% alc. Rating 94 To 2035 $20 ✪

♥♥♥♥♡ Margaret River Chardonnay 2014 Rating 93 To 2020 $27 ✪
OD Frankland River Riesling 2015 Rating 91 To 2025 $20 ✪
TV Geographe Tempranillo Viognier 2014 Rating 90 To 2022 $26

Plantagenet ★★★★★

Albany Highway, Mount Barker, WA 6324 **Region** Mount Barker
T (08) 9851 3111 **www**.plantagenetwines.com **Open** 7 days 10–4.30
Winemaker Luke Eckersley, Chris Murtha **Est.** 1974 **Dozens** 25 000 **Vyds** 130ha
Plantagenet was established by Tony Smith, who continues to be involved in its management over 40 years later, notwithstanding that it has been owned by Lionel Samson & Son for

many years. He established five vineyards: Bouverie in 1968, Wyjup in '71, Rocky Horror I in '88, Rocky Horror 2 in '97 and Rosetta in '99. These vineyards are the cornerstone of the substantial production of the consistently high quality wines that have always been the mark of Plantagenet: highly aromatic Riesling, tangy citrus-tinged Chardonnay, glorious Rhône-style Shiraz and ultra-stylish Cabernet Sauvignon. Exports to the UK, the US, Canada, China and Japan.

🍷🍷🍷🍷🍷 **Great Southern Riesling 2015** A classic wine, and ever reliable; it has a particular delicacy, yet has pure lime juice flavours, purity heightened by the natural acidity. Good now, even better in 5+ years. Great value. Screwcap. 12% alc. **Rating** 95 **To** 2030 $25 ✪

Great Southern Chardonnay 2014 Plantagenet was one of the pioneers of chardonnay in the Great Southern, and its experience shows through with the combination of elegance and intensity of the varietal fruit, oak in respectful support, as is bright acidity. Screwcap. 13.5% alc. **Rating** 95 **To** 2024 $30 ✪

Great Southern Shiraz 2013 An infusion of ultra-fragrant spice, pepper and licorice opens proceedings, the vibrant red cherry and blood plum fruit unfazed by that, if only because it is in no way threatened by tannins or French oak. Classic cool climate style. Screwcap. 13.5% alc. **Rating** 95 **To** 2033 $45

Great Southern Cabernet Sauvignon 2013 True blue cabernet style, savoury dried herbs immediately asserting their place alongside the cassis fruit, cabernet tannins doing exactly what is expected of them as they simultaneously dry off and lengthen the finish. Screwcap. 14% alc. **Rating** 94 **To** 2028 $45

🍷🍷🍷🍷🍷 **Omrah Great Southern Chardonnay 2014 Rating** 90 **To** 2018 $19 ✪

Poacher's Ridge Vineyard ★★★★★

1630 Spencer Road, Narrikup, WA 6326 **Region** Mount Barker
T (08) 9857 6066 **www.**poachersridge.com.au **Open** Fri–Sun 10–4
Winemaker Robert Diletti (Contract) **Est.** 2000 **Dozens** 1000 **Vyds** 6.9ha
Alex and Janet Taylor purchased the Poacher's Ridge property in 1999. It had previously been used for cattle grazing. The vineyard includes shiraz, cabernet sauvignon, merlot, riesling, marsanne and viognier. Winning the Tri Nations '07 merlot class against the might of Australia, NZ and South Africa with its '05 Louis' Block Great Southern Merlot was a dream come true. Nor was it a one-time success: Poacher's Ridge Merlot is always at, or near, the top of the tree.

🍷🍷🍷🍷🍷 **Louis' Block Great Southern Riesling 2015** The bouquet is yet to unfurl its wings, but the palate is jumping with a range of lime, lemon and green apple flavours, minerally acidity woven throughout. Each sip reveals more complexity and greater intensity, the flavours lingering long after the wine has left the mouth. A great riesling. Screwcap. 12% alc. **Rating** 96 **To** 2030 $24 ✪

Sophie's Yard Great Southern Shiraz 2014 The deep, vivid crimson-purple colour semaphores the epic array of blackberry, blackcurrant, black cherry, licorice, spice and pepper that fill the bouquet and medium to full-bodied palate alike. This is a wine made in the vineyard, and Rob Diletti's role was to act as a quality control officer, doing as little as possible. The length of the future of the wine is unknowable. Screwcap. 14.1% alc. **Rating** 96 **To** 2054 $28 ✪

Louis' Block Great Southern Merlot 2014 Savoury aromas of truffle and lanolin jostle for attention on the bouquet with the more expected varietal characters of plum and mulberry. Sleek and silky on the palate, the flavours of the grape mesh seamlessly with the French oak; the tannin is fine and in perfect harmony. Polished and pleasurable to drink now or later. Screwcap. 13.5% alc. **Rating** 94 **To** 2025 $28 ✪

🍷🍷🍷🍷🍷 **Louis' Block Cabernet Sauvignon 2014 Rating** 91 **To** 2030 $28

Pokolbin Estate

McDonalds Road, Pokolbin, NSW 2321 **Region** Hunter Valley
T (02) 4998 7524 **www**.pokolbinestate.com.au **Open** 7 days 9–5
Winemaker Andrew Thomas (Contract) **Est.** 1980 **Dozens** 4000 **Vyds** 15.7ha
Pokolbin Estate has a very unusual, but very good, multi-varietal, multi-vintage array of wines
available for sale at any one time. The Riesling is true Riesling, not misnamed Semillon,
the latter being one of their best wines, and wines under screwcap going back six or seven
vintages, and single vineyard offerings to boot, are available.

Phil Swannell Semillon 2015 Has ultra-classic drive and intensity to its display
of all things lemon – grass, zest, pith, curd – braced by crystalline acidity. Screwcap.
10% alc. **Rating** 95 **To** 2030 $25 **◐**
Limited Release Reserve Hunter Valley Shiraz 2014 Excellent crimson-
purple hue; dark berry/cherry fruit provides the core of the bouquet and
medium-bodied palate alike. There is a striking purity to the wine, tannins and oak
relegated to the sidelines, leaving the finish bright and clear. Another affirmation of
the quality of the '14 Hunter Valley shiraz vintage. Screwcap. 14% alc. **Rating** 95
To 2039 $60

Hunter Valley Riesling 2015 Rating 89 **To** 2025 $25

Pondalowie Vineyards

123 View Street, Bendigo, Vic 3550 **Region** Bendigo
T 0439 373 366 **www**.pondalowie.com.au **Open** W'ends 12–5
Winemaker Dominic Morris, Krystina Morris **Est.** 1997 **Dozens** 3000 **Vyds** 10ha
Dominic and Krystina Morris both have strong winemaking backgrounds gained in Australia,
Portugal and France. Dominic worked alternate vintages in Australia and Portugal from 1995
to 2012, and Krystina has also worked at St Hallett and Boar's Rock. They have established
5.5ha of shiraz, 2ha each of tempranillo and cabernet sauvignon, and a little malbec.
Incidentally, the illustration on the Pondalowie label is not a piece of barbed wire, but a very
abstract representation of the winery kelpie dog. Exports to Hong Kong and Japan.

Reserve Heathcote Shiraz 2013 Matured in French and American oak. A
vintage that Pondalowie rates as a standout for shiraz; a magisterial exercise in
perfectly weighted power; juicy black fruits are framed by oak (still to back off a
little) and ripe tannins; its overarching supple mouthfeel and length are the keys.
Screwcap. 14% alc. **Rating** 95 **To** 2033 $40
Heathcote Shiraz 2015 Bright colour; a complex wine with a fragrant bouquet
of dark fruits and oak suggesting the texture and flavour spectrum that the palate
duly delivers, with fine-grained fruit and oak tannins providing the framework for
the light to medium-bodied dark cherry fruits; the lower alcohol invests the wine
with elegance. Screwcap. 13.5% alc. **Rating** 94 **To** 2030 $20 **◐**
Special Release Shiraz 2013 Hand-picked multi-clone shiraz, open-fermented,
matured in French oak for 18 months. This comes at you like a tsunami with
a surge of black fruits, forest, licorice, roast coffee and bitter chocolate locked
together by as yet unrelenting tannins; the balance protects the future. Screwcap.
14.5% alc. **Rating** 94 **To** 2038 $60
MT+ Tempranillo 2015 The bouquet is voluminous, with exotic spices flying
out of the glass carrying the message of saturated satsuma plum on the medium-
bodied palate, a savoury flourish on the finish, partly from American and French
oak. Screwcap. 13.5% alc. **Rating** 94 **To** 2025 $30 **◐**

Vineyard Blend 2015 Rating 91 **To** 2023 $20 **◐**

Pooley Wines ★★★★★

1431 Richmond Road, Richmond, Tas 7025 **Region** Southern Tasmania
T (03) 6260 2895 **www**.pooleywines.com.au **Open** 7 days 10–5
Winemaker Anna Pooley **Est.** 1985 **Dozens** 5000 **Vyds** 16ha

Three generations of the Pooley family have been involved in the development of Pooley Wines, although the winery was previously known as Cooinda Vale. Plantings have now reached over 12ha in a region that is warmer and drier than most people realise. In 2003 the family planted pinot noir and pinot grigio (with more recent plantings of pinot noir and chardonnay) at Belmont Vineyard, a heritage property with an 1830s Georgian home and a (second) cellar door in the old sandstone barn and stables.

ŢŢŢŢŢ **Riesling 2015** From two vineyards (Coal River Valley, Tamar Valley), the first picked 23 Mar, the second 9 Apr, cool-fermented, 980 dozen made. This is an outstanding Tasmanian riesling, elegant, yet loaded with lime and apple juice set within a crown of acidity. Great now, great 10 or more years hence. Screwcap. 12.5% alc. **Rating** 96 **To** 2035 $32 ✪

Butchers Hill Pinot Noir 2014 Perfumed steamroller. It lures you in and then hits you up with all manner or spices, fruits, perfumes and textures. Cherry-plum, twigs, spearmint and violet, with fresh cedary oak and plenty of stemmy herbs. There's nothing ambivalent; it's a 'definitely' wine. Screwcap. 13% alc. **Rating** 96 **To** 2025 $50 CM ✪

Gewurztraminer 2015 Scintillating. Brimful of musk but riven with citrus and stone fruit. It both struts and runs. An experience. Screwcap. 13.8% alc. **Rating** 95 **To** 2019 $36 CM

Margaret Pooley Tribute Riesling 2015 Consummate ease. The flavours flow across the tongue, as pure as they feel sure. Lemon, slate and spice. Time is all that is required. Screwcap. 12.3% alc. **Rating** 94 **To** 2030 $50 CM

Pinot Noir 2014 Bright and tangy with just enough undergrowthy character to promote a sense of complexity. Fine, light, tight style complete with steely/minerally tannin. Reaches out impressively through the finish. Screwcap. 13% alc. **Rating** 94 **To** 2024 $36 CM

ŢŢŢŢ¶ **Pinot Grigio 2015 Rating** 93 **To** 2019 $28 CM

Poonawatta ★★★★★

1227 Eden Valley Road, Flaxman Valley, SA 5235 **Region** Eden Valley
T (08) 8565 3248 **www**.poonawatta.com **Open** By appt
Winemaker Reid Bosward, Andrew Holt **Est.** 1880 **Dozens** 1800 **Vyds** 3.6ha

The Poonawatta story is complex, stemming from 0.8ha of shiraz planted in 1880. When Andrew Holt's parents purchased the Poonawatta property, the vineyard had suffered decades of neglect, and the slow process of restoration began. While that was underway, the strongest canes available from the winter pruning of the 1880 block were slowly and progressively dug into the stony soil of the site. It took seven years to establish the 0.8ha Cuttings Block, and the yield is even lower than that of the 1880 Block. Second label, Monties Block, sits underneath The Cuttings (from the 'new' vines) and, at the top, is The 1880. The Riesling is produced from a single vineyard of 2ha hand-planted by the Holt family in the 1970s. Exports to Canada, France, Denmark, Taiwan, Hong Kong and China.

ŢŢŢŢŢ **Museum Release Eden Valley Riesling 2011** It bursts with fresh lime and spice, the slightest semblance of honeysuckle just starting to appear. Fair to say this is developing beautifully. Screwcap. 11.6% alc. **Rating** 95 **To** 2026 $30 CM ✪

The 1880 Eden Valley Shiraz 2012 Density of flavour but not at the expense of freshness. Abundant tannin, but melted into the fruit. Spice, plenty of it, but the wine is essentially floral and fruity. This is a wine of folds and layers, the full extent of which will only be revealed with the passing of time. Cork. 14.7% alc. **Rating** 95 **To** 2035 $90 CM

The Eden Riesling 2015 Saves its best for last. It opens with attractive floral and lime flavours, but it's the kick of quartz, chalk and lime rind on the finish that really quickens the pulse. Beautiful linger of flavour as you swallow. Screwcap. 12% alc. **Rating** 94 **To** 2027 $26 CM ○

♟♟♟♟♟ **The Cuttings Eden Valley Shiraz 2012 Rating** 92 **To** 2026 $49 CM

Port Phillip Estate ★★★★★

263 Red Hill Road, Red Hill, Vic 3937 **Region** Mornington Peninsula
T (03) 5989 4444 **www**.portphillipestate.com.au **Open** 7 days 11–5
Winemaker Glen Hayley **Est.** 1987 **Dozens** 7000 **Vyds** 9.3ha
Port Phillip Estate has been owned by Giorgio and Dianne Gjergja since 2000. The ability of the site to produce outstanding Syrah, Pinot Noir and Chardonnay, and very good Sauvignon Blanc, is something special. In July '15, following the departure of Sandro Mosele, his assistant of six years, Glen Hayley, was appointed to take his place. Whence climate change? Quite possibly the estate may have answers for decades to come. The futuristic, multimillion-dollar restaurant, cellar door and winery complex, designed by award-winning Wood/Marsh Architecture, overlooks the vineyards and Westernport Bay. Exports to the UK, Canada, Singapore and China.

♟♟♟♟♟ **Single Site Red Hill Chardonnay 2014** An exercise in elegance and seamless harmony from start to finish; the complex bouquet stands slightly to one side (a hint of intended reduction), the palate as smooth as silk, the patterns of white peach, gentle acidity and subtle oak leaving the mouth fresh and yearning for more. Screwcap. 13% alc. **Rating** 96 **To** 2024 $35 ○
Serenne Single Vineyard Selection Mornington Peninsula Shiraz 2014 Matured in used French oak for 16 months. Moderately light colour; the fragrant bouquet focuses on red and black cherries, the lissom palate gently reinforcing the message. It is the epitome of elegance, and could easily be missed. Screwcap. 13% alc. **Rating** 95 **To** 2029 $50
Sauvignon 2015 Hand-picked, whole bunch-pressed, wild yeast, two-thirds fermented in a concrete tank, one-third in French oak, matured for 6 months. Lively and fresh; gooseberry, passionfruit, orange blossom and natty acidity all roll around the palate, progressively reinforcing the flavour (and pleasure) of the wine as they do so. Screwcap. 13.5% alc. **Rating** 94 **To** 2017 $26 ○
Single Site Red Hill Mornington Peninsula Pinot Noir 2014 Matured in French oak (20% new) for 11 months, not fined or filtered. Good hue, clear purple-crimson; has a tangy brightness to the cherry-accented fruit flavours, the palate long and particularly well balanced; a juicy, fresh finish, oak no more than a whisper. Screwcap. 13% alc. **Rating** 94 **To** 2024 $40

♟♟♟♟♟ **Quartier Pinot Gris 2015 Rating** 92 **To** 2016 $26 CM
Salasso Mornington Peninsula Rose 2015 Rating 92 **To** 2017 $24 CM ○
Single Site Balnarring Pinot Noir 2014 Rating 90 **To** 2022 $40

Possums Vineyard ★★★★☆

88 Adams Road, Blewitt Springs, SA 5171 **Region** McLaren Vale
T (08) 8272 3406 **www**.possumswines.com.au **Open** By appt
Winemaker Pieter Breugem **Est.** 2000 **Dozens** 8000 **Vyds** 44.8ha
Possums Vineyard is owned by Dr John Possingham and Carol Summers. They have two vineyards in McLaren Vale – one at Blewitt Springs, the other at Willunga – covering shiraz (20a), cabernet sauvignon (16ha) and chardonnay (14ha), with lesser plantings of pinot gris, viognier and malbec. Winemaker Pieter Breugem has come from South Africa via the US and Constellation Wines. Exports to the UK, Denmark, Germany, Hong Kong and China.

♟♟♟♟♟ **Possingham & Summers Signature McLaren Vale Shiraz 2012** From estate vines up to 70yo, matured in French hogsheads for 32 months. Contrary to expectations, the fruit has absorbed the oak with consummate ease, cedar and cigar box just part of a matrix of blackberry, satsuma plum, dark chocolate and fine-grained tannins on a medium to full-bodied palate with excellent length and balance. Screwcap. 14.5% alc. **Rating** 96 **To** 2042 $45 ○

ŸŸŸŸŸ Reserve McLaren Vale Shiraz 2012 Rating 93 To 2025 $45 CM
Dr John's Willunga Shiraz 2013 Rating 92 To 2022 $25 CM ○
Possingham & Summers Shiraz 2012 Rating 92 To 2032 $18 ○
Possingham & Summers Signature Cabernet Sauvignon 2012 Rating 91
To 2027 $45

Prancing Horse Estate ★★★★

39 Paringa Road, Red Hill South, Vic 3937 **Region** Mornington Peninsula
T (03) 5989 2602 **www**.prancinghorseestate.com **Open** Sat 12–5, Sun by appt
Winemaker Sergio Carlei, Pascal Marchand, Patrick Piuze **Est.** 1990 **Dozens** 1500
Vyds 6.5ha
Anthony and Catherine Hancy acquired the Lavender Bay Vineyard in early 2002, renaming
it Prancing Horse Estate and embarking on increasing the estate vineyards, with 2ha each of
chardonnay and pinot noir, and 0.5ha of pinot gris. The vineyard moved to organic farming
in '03, progressing to biodynamic in '07. They appointed Sergio Carlei as winemaker, and
the following year became joint owners with Sergio in Carlei Wines. An additional property
150m west of the existing vineyard was purchased, and 2ha of vines planted. Prancing Horse
has become one of a small group of Australian wineries having wines made for them in
Burgundy. Pascal Marchand makes an annual release of Morey-St-Denis Clos des Ormes
Premier Cru and Meursault Premier Cru Blagny, while Patrick Piuze makes four Chablis
appellation wines. Exports to the UK, the US, France and Sweden.

ŸŸŸŸŸ **The Pony Mornington Peninsula Chardonnay 2014** I10V1 clone, hand-
picked, destemmed and crushed, wild yeast-fermented in French oak (30% new),
matured for 16 months. Very vibrant and juicy, the question is how much is citrus,
how much is stone fruit? Screwcap. 12.5% alc. **Rating** 90 **To** 2020 $30

ŸŸŸŸ Mornington Peninsula Chardonnay 2013 Rating 89 To 2018 $55

Precipice Wines ★★★★

67 Fairview Avenue, Croydon North, Vic 3136 (postal) **Region** Yarra Valley
T 0403 665 980 **Open** Not
Winemaker Marty Singh **Est.** 2011 **Dozens** 500
Marty Singh says that after 20 years of selling, tasting, drinking and making wine the
temptation to start his own brand was just too strong, although the production means that it
is still very much a part-time job. His practical skills were learned over a decade of working
alongside winemakers such as David Bicknell and Adrian Rodda. The first vintage, in 2012,
was of a Shiraz grown on the Hyde Park Vineyard in the Coldstream area; it was backed up
by the '13 production of the same wine, coupled with Chardonnay from the Willow Lake
Vineyard in the Upper Yarra Valley.

ŸŸŸŸŸ Hyde Park Vineyard Yarra Valley Syrah 2013 Vivid crimson purple; a juicy
wine with an avalanche of red and black fruits, fine tannins and oak. Screwcap.
13% alc. **Rating** 90 **To** 2028 $38

Pressing Matters ★★★★★

665 Middle Tea Tree Road, Tea Tree, Tas 7017 **Region** Southern Tasmania
T (03) 6268 1947 **www**.pressingmatters.com.au **Open** By appt 0408 126 668
Winemaker Winemaking Tasmania, Paul Smart **Est.** 2002 **Dozens** 1300 **Vyds** 7.1ha
Greg Melick simultaneously wears more hats than most people manage in a lifetime. He is
a top-level barrister (Senior Counsel), a Major General (the highest rank in the Australian
Army Reserve) and has presided over a number of headline special commissions and enquiries
into subjects as diverse as cricket match-fixing allegations and the Beaconsfield mine collapse.
More recently he has become Deputy President of the Administrative Appeals Tribunal and
Chief Commissioner of the Tasmanian Integrity Commission. Yet, if asked, he would probably
nominate wine as his major focus in life. Having built up an exceptional cellar of the great
wines of Europe, he has turned his attention to grapegrowing and winemaking, planting 2.9ha

of riesling at his vineyard in the Coal River Valley. It is a perfect north-facing slope, and the Mosel-style Rieslings are sweeping all before them. His multi-clone 4.2ha pinot noir block is also striking gold. Exports to the US and Singapore.

ΨΨΨΨΨ **R0 Riesling 2015** It has flavour, texture and searing acidity. It's hard to imagine that this will do anything other than mature very well. Exquisite balance. Lime, slate and mineral. Everything in fine order. Screwcap. 11.5% alc. **Rating** 95 To 2027 $33 CM **✪**

R9 Riesling 2015 It feels complete. There's sweetness here, but the swing of acidity and gentle textural elements have the wine slinging both deliciously and long through the palate. Irresistible is the word. Screwcap. 11.9% alc. **Rating** 95 To 2023 $33 CM **✪**

R139 Riesling 2015 Exquisite flavour. More than enough complexity tucked up its sleeve but the run of sweet citrussy flavour and the carry of it through the finish are top notch. 375ml. Screwcap. 10.1% alc. **Rating** 95 To 2022 $30 CM **✪**

Coal River Valley Pinot Noir 2014 There's quite a bit of sulphur-stink, especially on opening, but the wine's lines of acidity and tannin have no trouble pulling cherry-plum flavours through to a long finish. Foresty notes add another dimension. Screwcap. 13.7% alc. **Rating** 94 To 2026 $56 CM

R69 Riesling 2015 Soft and semi-intense but with excellent line and length. Oranges. Fresh picked and cut. With squeezes of lemon, even grapefruit. Simply, lovely. Screwcap. 10.4% alc. **Rating** 94 To 2022 $33 CM

Primo Estate ★★★★★

McMurtrie Road, McLaren Vale, SA 5171 **Region** McLaren Vale
T (08) 8323 6800 **www.**primoestate.com.au **Open** 7 days 11–4
Winemaker Joseph Grilli, Daniel Zuzolo **Est.** 1979 **Dozens** 30 000 **Vyds** 34ha
Joe Grilli has always produced innovative and excellent wines. The biennial release of the Joseph Sparkling Red (in its tall Italian glass bottle) is eagerly awaited, the wine immediately selling out. Also highly regarded are the vintage-dated extra-virgin olive oils. However, the core lies with the La Biondina, the Il Briccone Shiraz Sangiovese and the Joseph Moda Cabernet Merlot. The business has expanded to take in both McLaren Vale and Clarendon, with plantings of colombard, shiraz, cabernet sauvignon, riesling, merlot, sauvignon blanc, chardonnay, pinot gris, sangiovese, nebbiolo and merlot. Exports to all major markets.

ΨΨΨΨΨ **Joseph Moda McLaren Vale Cabernet Sauvignon Merlot 2013** 80/20%, partially dried grapes (in Amarone style). A deep crimson colour and stunning depth of velvety flavours ranging through blackcurrant compote, dark chocolate, allspice and soused plum, contemptuously brushing away the alcohol. One of the best from the long line of this wine. Screwcap. 15% alc. **Rating** 96 To 2038 $80

Joseph Sparkling Red NV Full purple yet still vibrant, the latest disgorgement of this iconic sparkling red captures all the mystery and the theatrics of a blend of every vintage since the late '80s and some from the early '60s and '70s. McLaren Vale shiraz brings its back-fruit depth and cabernet and merlot their bright blackcurrant crunch and fine tannin grip. The finish explodes into an endless panoply of dark chocolate, black olives, exotic spice, dried fruits and coal dust. Masterful. Cork. 13.5% alc. **Rating** 96 To 2020 $80 TS

Il Briccone McLaren Vale Shiraz Sangiovese 2014 85% shiraz from Primo's Angel Gully Vineyard in the Clarendon district, 15% sangiovese from a local grower. A most attractive medium-bodied blend with maximum synergy; the finish and aftertaste have an interchanging array of spice, red and black fruits, the tannins fine. Screwcap. 14.5% alc. **Rating** 95 To 2024 $25 **✪**

Joseph Angel Gully Clarendon Shiraz 2013 Deep colour; a powerful, complex, full-bodied wine made from dry grown vines planted on shallow rocky soils that always provide deep, intense black fruit flavours and abundant tannins; add the generous oak influence and you have a wine for the ages, but that is reluctant to let you fully enjoy it now – you will in a decade or so. Screwcap. 14.5% alc. **Rating** 94 To 2043 $80

Zamberlan McLaren Vale Cabernet Sauvignon Sangiovese 2014 The sangiovese component is fermented with the skins left from a prior cabernet sauvignon ferment, matured in oak for 12 months. The crimson–purple colour is excellent, the palate full-bodied, with blackcurrant, cherry and dark chocolate tightly held together by the tannins. Good now, better in 5 years, better again in 10. Screwcap. 14% alc. **Rating** 94 **To** 2034 $35

ΥΥΥΥΥ **Joseph d'Elena Adelaide Pinot Grigio 2015** Rating 93 To 2017 $30
Shale Stone McLaren Vale Shiraz 2014 Rating 93 To 2039 $32
La Biondina Colombard 2015 Rating 90 To 2016 $16 ✪

Principia

★★★★☆

139 Main Creek Road, Red Hill, Vic 3937 (postal) **Region** Mornington Peninsula
T (03) 5931 0010 **www**.principiawines.com.au **Open** By appt
Winemaker Darrin Gaffy **Est.** 1995 **Dozens** 600 **Vyds** 3.5ha
Darrin Gaffy's guiding philosophy for Principia is minimal interference, thus the vines (2.7ha of pinot noir and 0.8ha of chardonnay) are not irrigated, yields are restricted to 3.75 tonnes per hectare or less, and all wine movements are by gravity or by gas pressure, which in turn means there is no filtration, and both primary and secondary fermentation are by wild yeast. 'Principia' comes from the word 'beginnings' in Latin: the *Principia* was Sir Isaac Newton's famous scientific work that incorporated his theory of gravitation and the laws of motion.

ΥΥΥΥΥ **Mornington Peninsula Chardonnay 2014** There's a candied or crystallised fruit aspect to this and yet it also darts with tangy, citrussy flavour: it feels as if you have a piece of exotica in your glass. It tastes of figs, lime, grapefruit and nectarine, and it swings both effortlessly and confidently through the finish. A 'bravo' wine. Screwcap. 13.3% alc. **Rating** 95 **To** 2021 $45 CM

ΥΥΥΥΥ **Mornington Peninsula Pinot Noir 2014** Rating 93 To 2022 $45 CM

Printhie Wines

★★★★★

489 Yuranigh Road, Molong, NSW 2866 **Region** Orange
T (02) 6366 8422 **www**.printhiewines.com.au **Open** Mon–Sat 10–4
Winemaker Drew Tuckwell **Est.** 1996 **Dozens** 20 000 **Vyds** 33.1ha
Owned by the Swift family, and the next generation Edward and David have taken over (from Ed Swift) the reins to guide the business into its next era. In 2016 Printhie 'clocked up' 10 years of commercial wine production, and the vineyards are now reaching a good level of maturity at 20 years. The 30ha of estate vineyards are planted at lower elevations and supply all the red varieties and the pinot gris, other varieties purchased from other growers in the region. Winemaker Drew Tuckwell has been at Printhie for nearly a decade, and has over 20 years of winemaking experience in Australia and Europe.

ΥΥΥΥΥ **Super Duper Orange Syrah 2012** Good hue, although not deep; a perfumed bouquet of red and purple fruits, spice and pepper; the palate is only light to medium-bodied at best, but it's a pocket rocket within that context, with red fruits, fine-grained tannins and positive oak in utterly perfect balance and length. On the empty glass test with other good reds, this would be the first one finished. Screwcap. 13.1% alc. **Rating** 95 **To** 2032 $85
MCC Chardonnay 2014 Shows oak influence, but the melon, peach and citrus fruit won't be denied. Rich and flavoursome without going too far, its cool climate origins and varietal expression are the defining characters, winemaking adding a layer of complexity. Screwcap. 12.5% alc. **Rating** 94 **To** 2022 $35

ΥΥΥΥΥ **Super Duper Orange Chardonnay 2013** Rating 93 To 2023 $85
MCC Orange Shiraz 2014 Rating 93 To 2025 $35
Mountain Range Orange Sauvignon Blanc 2015 Rating 92 To 2017 $18 ✪
Mountain Range Orange Shiraz 2014 Rating 92 To 2020 $18 ✪
Mountain Range Orange Chardonnay 2015 Rating 90 To 2020 $18 ✪
Swift Cuvee Brut NV Rating 90 To 2019 $40 TS

Project Wine

83 Pioneer Road, Angas Plains, SA 5255 **Region** South Australia
T (08) 73424 3031 **www**.projectwine.com.au **Open** Not
Winemaker Peter Pollard **Est.** 2001 **Dozens** 120 000
Project Wine is a large winery, established in 2001 by a group of Adelaide business people. Originally designed as a contract winemaking facility, the business has developed a sales and distribution arm that has rapidly developed markets, both domestically and overseas. The winery is located in Langhorne Creek, and sources fruit from most key SA wine regions, including McLaren Vale, Barossa Valley and Adelaide Hills. The diversity of grape sourcing allows the winery to produce a wide range of products under the Tail Spin, Pioneer Road, Parson's Paddock and Bird's Eye View labels. Exports to the UK, Canada, Japan and China.

ŸŸŸŸ **Parson's Paddock Langhorne Creek Sauvignon Blanc 2015** Crushed, pressed, cool-fermented in stainless steel, 5 months on lees. Crystal white; a major surprise, full of flavour on the long palate, unsweetened citrus and crackling acidity the recurrent messages. It wouldn't appear that there is any residual sugar either. Sensational value. Screwcap. 12.5% alc. **Rating** 89 **To** 2017 $13 ✪

Provenance Wines   ★★★★★

870 Steiglitz Road, Sutherlands Creek, Vic 3331 **Region** Geelong
T (03) 5281 2230 **www**.provenancewines.com.au **Open** By appt
Winemaker Scott Ireland, Sam Vogel **Est.** 1997 **Dozens** 2000 **Vyds** 5ha
Scott Ireland and partner Jen Lilburn established Provenance Wines in 1997 as a natural extension of Scott's years of winemaking experience, both here and abroad. Located in the Moorabool Valley, the winery team focuses on the classics in a cool climate sense – Pinot Gris, Chardonnay and Pinot Noir in particular, as well as Shiraz. Fruit is sourced from both within the Geelong region and further afield (when the fruit warrants selection). The future of Provenance will be influenced by its 2012 acquisition of 30ha property with red volcanic soil and a spring-fed dam; 1.5ha of pinot noir was planted in '12. They are also major players in contract making for the Geelong region.

ŸŸŸŸŸ **Golden Plains Chardonnay 2014** 58% Geelong, 36% Henty, 16% Ballarat. You can easily see the diamond-cut fruit from the ultra-cool Ballarat and Henty regions, with its livewire acidity balanced and complexed by the richer stone fruit flavours ex Geelong. Works brilliantly. Screwcap. 13.5% alc. **Rating** 95 **To** 2025 $29 ✪
Golden Plains Pinot Noir 2014 73% Geelong, 17% Henty, 10% Ballarat. Deeply coloured, this full, complex wine has a rainbow of spice, earth, black fruits (plum, cherry), and fine-grained tannins on the long finish. A just reward for what must have been a logistical nightmare – and a bargain. Screwcap. 12.8% alc. **Rating** 95 **To** 2027 $29 ✪
Regional Selection Geelong Pinot Noir 2013 58% retained as whole bunches, matured in French barriques (33% new). Good retention of colour; despite the whole bunch imprint, red and black cherries trace a fluid line, caressing the palate through to a long, perfectly balanced finish. Screwcap. 13% alc. **Rating** 95 **To** 2023 $47
Geelong Shiraz 2014 73% matured in used puncheons, 27% in concrete eggs. This is unexpectedly full-bodied, concentrated and powerful, with black cherry, blackberry, pepper and spice in a cradle of ripe, but insistent, tannins and (inexplicably) some oak. Balance is the key, but cellar it as long as you can. Screwcap. 13.5% alc. **Rating** 95 **To** 2049 $32 ✪

ŸŸŸŸŸ **The Griesling 2015 Rating** 93 **To** 2016 $25 CM ✪
Long Night Rose 2015 Rating 90 **To** 2016 $35 CM

Punch ★★★★★

2130 Kinglake Road, St Andrews, Vic 3761 (postal) **Region** Yarra Valley
T (03) 9710 1155 **www**.punched.com.au **Open** Not
Winemaker James Lance **Est.** 2004 **Dozens** 800 **Vyds** 3.45ha

In the wake of Graeme Rathbone taking over the brand (but not the real estate) of Diamond Valley, the Lances' son James and his wife Claire leased the vineyard and winery from David and Catherine Lance, including the 0.25ha block of close-planted pinot noir. In all, Punch has 2.25ha of pinot noir (including the close-planted), 0.8ha of chardonnay and 0.4ha of cabernet sauvignon. When the 2009 Black Saturday bushfires destroyed the crop, various grapegrowers wrote offering assistance, which led to the purchase of the grapes used for that dire year, and the beginning of the 'Friends of Punch' wines.

ŸŸŸŸŸ Lance's Vineyard Close Planted Pinot Noir 2014 That extra flourish. That something that only certain special wines only ever manage to attain. This has it. This is it. This is the pinot noir fanatics far and wide dream of growing, and caressing into bottle. Screwcap. 13.5% alc. **Rating** 97 **To** 2027 $90 CM ✪

ŸŸŸŸŸ Lance's Vineyard Pinot Noir 2014 There's a focus to this that would do a sniper proud. It's as if it's been fussed over and over until it's exactly right. It broods on macerated cherry, red and black, and runs earth, undergrowth, mint and wood spice characters through its veins. The finish kicks again – with flavour, not with alcohol. It has a superb future ahead. Screwcap. 13% alc. **Rating** 96 **To** 2026 $55 CM ✪

Lance's Vineyard Chardonnay 2014 Cramful of deliciousness. The flavour here is so intense it almost hurts. It's flush with grapefruit, barley, lime and cedar-spiced oak, said flavours bell clear and yet delivered in soft, creamy style. Screwcap. 13% alc. **Rating** 95 **To** 2022 $45 CM

Friends of Punch Queenstown Vineyards Shiraz 2014 It's a spicy affair with a heart of meaty, foresty darkness. It's a complex form of seduction, but once you're in there's little escape. The lures: nuts, stems, black cherries, wood smoke. It's beautifully put together, it must be said. Screwcap. 13.5% alc. **Rating** 94 **To** 2026 $32 CM

ŸŸŸŸ Lance's Vineyard Cabernet 2014 **Rating** 89 **To** 2025 $45 CM

Punt Road ★★★★★

10 St Huberts Road, Coldstream, Vic 3770 **Region** Yarra Valley
T (03) 9739 0666 **www**.puntroadwines.com.au **Open** 7 days 10–5
Winemaker Tim Shand **Est.** 2000 **Dozens** 20 000 **Vyds** 65.61ha

Punt Road is owned by the Napoleone family. All the wines are produced from vineyards owned by the family; this has resulted in the introduction of the Airlie Bank range, a mostly sub-$20 Yarra Valley range made in a fruit-driven, lightly oaked style to complement the successful Punt Road range at the premium end of their offerings. There is also more focus on small-production single vineyard wines under the Punt Road label. Exports to the US, Canada, Singapore, Hong Kong, Japan, China and other major markets.

ŸŸŸŸŸ Napoleone Vineyard Block 3 Yarra Valley Cabernet Sauvignon 2014 Hand-picked, prolonged cold soak, cultured yeast, matured in French barriques (25% new). The yields were low across the Valley, with small berries, but this wine is perfectly balanced and extracted, the mouthfeel supple, the flavours of cassis and briar completing an impressive work of wine. Screwcap. 13.5% alc. **Rating** 95 **To** 2034 $29 ✪

Napoleone Vineyard Yarra Valley Chardonnay 2014 Bright straw-green; encapsulates the style of Yarra Valley chardonnay to perfection: a seamless blend of white peach, nectarine and pink grapefruit that creates the foundation of the length of the palate, acidity extending that length further. Oak is there, but simply provides context. Screwcap. 12.5% alc. **Rating** 94 **To** 2024 $25 ✪

ԾԾԾԾԾ Napoleone Vineyard Block 2 Yarra Valley Chardonnay 2015 Rating 93
To 2022 $28
Yarra Valley Napoleone Vineyard 2011 Rating 92 To 2017 $32 TS
Napoleone Vineyard Pinot Gris 2015 Rating 91 To 2017 $23 ✪
Napoleone Vineyard Yarra Valley Pinot Noir 2015 Rating 90 To 2020 $29
Airlie Bank Yarra Valley Noir 2015 Rating 90 To 2023 $22
Airlie Bank Yarra Valley Franc 2015 Rating 90 To 2019 $22

Pure Vision | Nature's Step Organic Wines ★★★

PO Box 258, Virginia, SA 5120 **Region** Adelaide Plains
T 0412 800 875 **www**.lightsviewgroup.com.au **Open** Not
Winemaker Joanne Irvine, Ken Carypidis **Est.** 2001 **Dozens** 9000 **Vyds** 55ha
The Carypidis family runs two brands: Pure Vision (15ha of certified organically grown
grapes), and Nature's Step. Growing grapes under a certified organic regime is much easier
if the region is warm to hot and dry, conditions unsuitable for botrytis and downy mildew.
You are still left with weed growth (no herbicides are allowed) and powdery mildew (sulphur
sprays are permitted) but the overall task is much simpler. The Adelaide Plains, where Pure
Vision's vineyard is situated, is such a region, and Ken Carypidis has been clever enough to
secure the services of Joanne Irvine as co-winemaker. Exports to the US, Canada, Taiwan,
Hong Kong and China.

ԾԾԾԾ Pure Vision Organic Cabernet Sauvignon 2014 This comes through as if
an enterprising winemaker had found a way to put the flavour of two bottles
into one – and of course organic/biodynamic vignerons would give me a pitying
stare and say 'of course that's what we do the whole time. Get a life.' Screwcap.
14.5% alc. **Rating** 89 To 2022 $15 ✪

Purple Hands Wines   ★★★★★

32 Brandreth Street, Tusmore, SA 5065 (postal) **Region** Barossa Valley
T 0401 988 185 **www**.purplehandswines.com.au **Open** Not
Winemaker Craig Stansborough **Est.** 2006 **Dozens** 2500 **Vyds** 14ha
This is a partnership between Craig Stansborough, who provides the winemaking know-how
and an 8ha vineyard of shiraz, northwest of Williamstown in a cooler corner of the southern
Barossa, and Mark Slade, who provides the passion. Don't ask me how this works – I don't
know, but I do know they are producing outstanding single vineyard wines (the grenache is
contract-grown) of quite remarkable elegance. The wines are made at Grant Burge, where
Craig is chief winemaker. Exports to the Philippines and Singapore.

ԾԾԾԾԾ Planta Circa Ancient Vine Barossa Valley Cabernet Sauvignon 2014
63 dozen. Made from a tiny patch of cabernet vines planted 133 years ago. It
combines monumental power with monumental restraint: the result, pure class. It's
like old money; nothing too flashy; endurance is its middle name; it starts with the
word 'classic' in clear script on the tip of your tongue and doesn't let the pen lift
until long into the aftertaste. If a big company made this, it would be $500. Diam.
14% alc. **Rating** 98 To 2040 $70 CM ✪

ԾԾԾԾԾ Barossa Valley Shiraz 2014 Firm hands of tannin deliver dark-berried flavours
in pristine, perfectly ripened condition. There's definition to the muscle; there's
juice racing beneath the skin. You can't help but be impressed. Screwcap. 14% alc.
Rating 95 To 2030 $30 CM ✪
Barossa Valley Mataro Grenache Shiraz 2015 61/20/19. The flavours float
on folds of silk. We're talking redcurrant, plum, earth and woody spice, and while
there's a whisper of licorice this is not a deep or heavy wine. It offers plenty, but
it doesn't step into the lost lands of the overblown. Another big tick. Screwcap.
14% alc. **Rating** 94 To 2023 $30 CM ✪

ԾԾԾԾԾ Old Vine Barossa Valley Grenache 2015 Rating 93 To 2021 $30 CM
Adelaide Hills Pinot Gris 2015 Rating 91 To 2017 $22 CM ✪

Quarisa Wines

743 Slopes Road, Tharbogang, NSW 2680 (postal) **Region** South Australia
T (02) 6963 6222 **www**.quarisa.com.au **Open** Not
Winemaker John Quarisa **Est.** 2005 **Dozens** NFP

John Quarisa has had a distinguished career as a winemaker spanning over 20 years, working for some of Australia's largest wineries, including McWilliam's, Casella and Nugan Estate. He was also chiefly responsible in 2004 for winning the Jimmy Watson Trophy (Melbourne) and the Stodart Trophy (Adelaide). John and Josephine Quarisa have set up a very successful family business using grapes from various parts of NSW and SA, made in leased space. Production has risen in leaps and bounds, doubtless sustained by the exceptional value for money provided by the wines. Exports include the UK, Canada, Denmark, Sweden, Malaysia, Indonesia, Hong Kong, Japan and NZ.

ŸŸŸŸ? **Johnny Q Shiraz 2014** From Coonawarra and Padthaway. Quarisa has done it all before, and will (hopefully do it again and again. Poured blind, you'd work out the Limestone Coast origin, but not the $12 price tag. This is a very impressive medium-bodied shiraz – decant and pour for royalty. Screwcap. 14.5% alc.
Rating 90 **To** 2020 **$12 ✪**
Treasures Coonawarra Cabernet Sauvignon 2014 Night-harvested, a combination of rotary and open fermenters with heading down boards, completing fermentation in new and used French and American oak, matured for 16 months. Here the question becomes 'what's the trap?' No one else can make a Coonawarra cabernet using these vinification protocols and afford to sell if for $15. Screwcap. 14% alc. **Rating** 90 **To** 2024 **$15 ✪**

ŸŸŸŸ **Caravan Durif 2015 Rating** 89 **To** 2025 **$13 ✪**
Treasures Adelaide Hills Chardonnay 2015 Rating 88 **To** 2017 **$15 ✪**

Quartz Hill Vineyard

65 Lillicur West Road, Lamplough, Vic 3352 (postal) **Region** Pyrenees
T (03) 5465 3670 **www**.quartzhillwines.com.au **Open** Not
Winemaker Darrin Gaffy, John Durham **Est.** 1995 **Dozens** 400 **Vyds** 3.6ha

Quartz Hill was established in 1995, with Shane and Michelle Mead relocating from Melbourne to run their vineyard in '99. After growing grapes for other wine labels for many years, the first Quartz Hill wine came onto the market in '09. Winemaking is a family effort, with brother Darrin Gaffy from Principia on the Mornington Peninsula (see separate entry) as winemaker, and all winemaking processes performed traditionally, by hand. Shane and Michelle grow their own shiraz and viognier, and, when available, purchase select parcels of fruit from other Pyrenees growers.

ŸŸŸŸŸ **Pyrenees Shiraz 2014** A medium-bodied shiraz of considerable finesse and length, with some Grampians-like character in its make-up. Spice and cracked pepper on the bouquet also come through on the red and black fruits of the palate; the measurement of the tannins is truly bespoke, the oak also perfectly integrated. Screwcap. 13.8% alc. **Rating** 94 **To** 2034 $35

ŸŸŸŸ? **Pyrenees Viognier 2014 Rating** 92 **To** 2017 $35

Quattro Mano ★★★★

PO Box 189, Hahndorf, SA 5245 **Region** Barossa Valley
T 0430 647 470 **www**.quattromano.com.au **Open** By appt
Winemaker Anthony Carapetis, Christopher Taylor, Philippe Morin **Est.** 2006
Dozens 2500 **Vyds** 3.8ha

Anthony Carapetis, Philippe Morin and Chris Taylor have collective experience of over 50 years working in various facets of the wine industry, Philippe as a leading sommelier for over 25 years, and presently as Director of French Oak Cooperage, Anthony and Chris as winemakers. The dream of Quattro Mano began in the mid-1990s, but only became a reality in 2006 (I'm still not sure how three equals four). They produce an eclectic range of wines, Tempranillo the cornerstone. It's an impressive, albeit small, business. Exports to the US and Japan.

🍷🍷🍷🍷🍷 **La Gracia 2014** It's a poised, well-controlled shiraz with boysenberry, violet, garden mint and smoky oak flavours cruising through the palate. There's then an undergrowthy, foresty aspect to the finish. It doesn't have massive intensity, but it's full-bodied in a succulent way. Cork. 13.9% alc. **Rating** 94 **To** 2030 $60 CM

🍷🍷🍷🍷🍷 **La Gracia Barossa Valley Tempranillo 2013 Rating** 93 **To** 2023 $50 CM

Quealy Winemakers ★★★★☆

62 Bittern-Dromana Road, Balnarring, Vic 3926 **Region** Mornington Peninsula
T (03) 5983 2483 **www**.quealy.com.au **Open** 7 days 11–5
Winemaker Kathleen Quealy, Kevin McCarthy **Est.** 1982 **Dozens** 8000 **Vyds** 8ha
Kathleen Quealy and Kevin McCarthy were among the early waves of winemakers on Mornington Peninsula. They challenged the status quo – most publicly by introducing Mornington Peninsula pinot gris/grigio (with great success). Behind this was improvement and diversification in site selection, plus viticulture and winemaking techniques that allowed their business to grow significantly. The estate plantings are 2ha each of pinot noir, pinot gris and friulano as well as smaller plots of riesling, chardonnay and moscato giallo. Pobblebonk is Kathleen's field blend from their own property, prescient in terms of the natural wine movement. Their leased vineyards are established on what Kathleen and Kevin consider to be premium sites for pinot gris and pinot noir, and are now single vineyard wines: Musk Creek and the newer Tussie Mussie Vineyard. Kathleen and Kevin are assisted by winemaker Dan Calvert, who has worked with Quealy for 7 years. Their son Tom has joined the business with a particular focus on natural wine, Turbul Friulano his first such wine. Exports to the UK and France.

🍷🍷🍷🍷🍷 **Musk Creek Pinot Gris 2015** 22yo vines, extended whole bunch-pressing, wild-fermented in stainless steel. The multiple layers that Kathleen Quealy has been able to achieve are startling, particularly given stainless steel fermentation – must be something to do with extended whole bunch-pressing. Screwcap. 14.5% alc. **Rating** 95 **To** 2017 $30 ✪
Seventeen Rows Pinot Noir 2014 From the oldest MV6 vines on the Peninsula, planted in '82. I like Kathleen Quealy's description of the wine as visceral and brooding; it's very intense, with all sorts of hidden corners along the journey through the palate. The vines are a great asset, delivering a very complex, savoury pinot that, by virtue of its provenance and its maker, simply has to respond to time in bottle. Screwcap. 13.5% alc. **Rating** 94 **To** 2023 $60

🍷🍷🍷🍷🍷 **Tussie Mussie Pinot Gris 2015 Rating** 91 **To** 2017 $30
Friulano Amphora 2015 Rating 90 **To** 2017 $28
Mornington Peninsula Pinot Noir 2014 Rating 90 **To** 2024 $30

Quilty Wines ★★★★

16 Inglis Street, Mudgee, NSW 2850 (postal) **Region** Mudgee
T 0419 936 233 **www**.quiltywines.com.au **Open** Not
Winemaker Des Quilty, Jacob Stein **Est.** 2008 **Dozens** 600
Owner Des Quilty grew up in the Hunter Valley and studied agriculture at the University of New England. To support himself while at university, he drifted into viticulture, his first job after graduation at Tyrrell's as assistant vineyard manager. He was soon promoted and formed part of the Tyrrell's management team in the first half of the 1990s. Over the latter half of the '90s he worked for a rural outlet supplying products to Hunter Valley grape and wine producers, before moving to Mudgee as a viticulturist around 2000. While his focus remains on that region, he has also been involved in vineyards in Orange and Young. He ventured into small-scale winemaking in '08, relying on the depth of his experience to secure small parcels of top quality grapes to make top quality wines.

♟♟♟♟♟ **Black Thimble Mudgee Shiraz 2013** 183 dozen. Smoky vanillan oak adds a polished veneer to ripe, cherry-plum fruit. It boasts both a firmness and a fleshiness and feels sure of itself through the finish. Highly accomplished. Screwcap. 14% alc. **Rating** 93 To 2027 $28 CM
Black Thimble Single Vineyard Apple Tree Flat Mudgee Shiraz 2014 It's a medium-bodied wine offering an attractive mix of sweetness and savouriness. Vanillan oak, plum-shot fruit, wood smoke and dried spice notes give plenty of character; indeed it has a bit of spunk about it. Overall balance is good too, as is texture. Most will enjoy. Screwcap. 14.5% alc. **Rating** 92 To 2024 $28 CM

♟♟♟♟ **Running Stitch Single Vineyard Apple Tree Flat Mudgee Cabernet Sauvignon 2014 Rating** 88 To 2022 $28 CM
Patchwork Mudgee Cabernet Sauvignon Petit Verdot 2014 Rating 88 To 2020 $28 CM

 # R. Paulazzo Wines   ★★★★★
852 Oakes Road, Yoogali, NSW 2680 **Region** Riverina
T 0412 969 002 **www.**rpaulazzo.com.au **Open** By appt
Winemaker Rob Paulazzo **Est.** 2013 **Dozens** NFP **Vyds** 12ha
Rob Paulazzo began winemaking in 1977, and has covered a lot of ground before establishing his eponymous Riverina business. In Australia he worked for McWilliam's and Orlando, and Giesen in NZ, also completing four vintages in Burgundy, plus vintages in Tuscany, the Napa Valley, Niagara Peninsula (Canada), and Marlborough. In addition to the family's vineyard, established over 80 years ago, Rob is also sourcing fruit from Hilltops, Tumbarumba, Orange and Canberra District.

♟♟♟♟♟ **G-0501 Hilltops Shiraz 2014** Hand-picked, crushed/destemmed, 15% whole bunches, 3 days cold soak, cultured yeast, 12 days on skins, matured for 12 months in French oak (20% new). A seriously good wine with admirable texture and structure; spicy, peppery and lively black cherry/blackberry fruits fill the medium-bodied palate and long finish. Screwcap. 14% alc. **Rating** 96 To 2034 $28 ✪
M-2305 Tumbarumba Chardonnay 2015 Hand-picked, whole bunch-pressed, fermented with full solids in French oak (20 new), matured on lees with stirring, no mlf, a barrel selection. A striking wine with the thrust and crunchy acidity of Tumbarumba to go alongside (or through) the grapefruit, melon and white peach fruit. Screwcap. 13% alc. **Rating** 95 To 2022 $28 ✪
F-1833 Riverina Botrytis Semillon 2013 Very complex and luscious, with highly spiced marmalade and a long drying finish hinged on good acidity. 375ml. Screwcap. 12% alc. **Rating** 94 To 2018 $28 ✪

♟♟♟♟♟ **K-1707 Tumbarumba Pinot Noir 2015 Rating** 90 To 2022 $28

Radford Wines   ★★★★★
RSD 355, Eden Valley, SA 5235 (postal) **Region** Eden Valley
T (08) 8565 3256 **www.**radfordwines.com **Open** Not
Winemaker Gill and Ben Radford **Est.** 2003 **Dozens** 2000 **Vyds** 4.2ha
I first met Ben Radford when he was working as a head winemaker at the Longridge/ Winecorp group in Stellenbosch, South Africa. A bevy of international journalists grilled Ben, a French winemaker and a South African about the wines they were producing for the group. The others refused to admit that there were any shortcomings in the wines they had made (there were), but Ben took the opposite tack, criticising his own wines even though they were clearly the best. He and wife Gill are now the proud owners of a vineyard in the Eden Valley, with 1.2ha of riesling planted in 1930, another 1.1ha planted in '70, 1.7ha of shiraz planted in 2000 and 0.2ha of mataro planted in '10. Following Ben's appointment as winemaker at Rockford in '07, executive winemaking responsibilities are now Gill's. Exports to the UK, the US, Canada, Denmark and South Africa.

ŶŶŶŶŶ **Quartz Garden Eden Valley Riesling 2014** Lime/lemon fruit dances with crisp, minerally acidity, the pace of the dance reaching fever pitch on the finish and aftertaste. From the same old Eden Valley vineyard that has been supplying Radford for years. Great value. Screwcap. 12% alc. **Rating** 95 **To** 2030 $25
Spice Bush Eden Valley Shiraz 2012 The hue is fine, and there is a power of fruit; black fruits start, then there is a sunburst of spice and a twist of licorice, oak and tannins voicing their support – all this in a medium-bodied wine of considerable elegance. Screwcap. 13.8% alc. **Rating** 95 **To** 2042 $45

Raidis Estate   ★★★★

147 Church Street, Penola, SA 5277 **Region** Coonawarra
T (08) 8737 2966 **www**.raidis.com.au **Open** Thurs–Sun 12–6
Winemaker Steven Raidis **Est.** 2006 **Dozens** 4500 **Vyds** 24.29ha
The Raidis family has lived and worked in Coonawarra for over 40 years. Chris Raidis was only three years old when he arrived in Australia with his parents, who were market gardeners in Greece before coming here. In 1994 he planted just under 5ha of cabernet sauvignon; son Steven significantly expanded the vineyard in 2003 with sauvignon blanc, riesling, pinot gris, merlot and shiraz. The cellar door was opened by then Deputy Prime Minister Julia Gillard in Nov '09, an impressive example of pulling power.

ŶŶŶŶŶ **The Kid Coonawarra Riesling 2015** Lime, apple and slate flavours lend this a keen sense of intensity. A dry, satisfying finish seals the deal. A good 'un. Screwcap. 11.5% alc. **Rating** 91 **To** 2021 $20 CM
Cheeky Coonawarra Pinot Gris 2015 Pale copper. Twiggy spice meets crunchy apple and nashi pear. Has a bit of spunk, a bit of interest. Dry finish. Eminently food-friendly, in the best sense of the words. Screwcap. 13.9% alc. **Rating** 91 **To** 2017 $20 CM ●

Ravens Croft Wines   ★★★★

274 Spring Creek Road, Stanthorpe, Qld 4380 **Region** Granite Belt
T (07) 4683 3252 **www**.ravenscroftwines.com.au **Open** Fri–Sun 10.30–4.30
Winemaker Mark Ravenscroft **Est.** 2002 **Dozens** 800 **Vyds** 1.2ha
Mark Ravenscroft was born in South Africa and studied oenology there. He moved to Australia in the early 1990s, and in '94 became an Australian citizen. His wines come from estate plantings of verdelho and pinotage, supplemented by contract-grown grapes from other vineyards in the region. The wines are made onsite.

ŶŶŶŶŶ **Granite Belt Chardonnay 2015** It certainly keeps itself nice with barley sugar, pear, white peach and spicy oak flavours lending the wine both race and punch. Delicious. Screwcap. 13% alc. **Rating** 92 **To** 2020 $40 CM
Granite Belt Pinot Grigio 2015 Hand-picked, destemmed and crushed, free-run and first light-pressed juice cold-fermented. A grigio with greater attitude than many of its peers; nashi pear is the leader of the pack, peach and quince also appearing as part of the equation. Screwcap. 12% alc. **Rating** 90 **To** 2017 $25

ŶŶŶŶ **Granite Belt Verdelho 2015** **Rating** 89 **To** 2017 $25
Granite Belt Tempranillo 2015 **Rating** 89 **To** 2019 $28 CM
Granite Belt Pinotage 2014 **Rating** 88 **To** 2019 $40 CM

Ravensworth   ★★★★★

312 Patemans Lane, Murrumbateman, ACT 2582 **Region** Canberra District
T (02) 6226 8368 **www**.ravensworthwines.com.au **Open** Not
Winemaker Bryan Martin **Est.** 2000 **Dozens** 2000
Winemaker, vineyard manager and partner Bryan Martin (with dual wine science and wine growing degrees from CSU) has a background in wine retail, and food and beverage work in the hospitality industry, and teaches part-time. He is also assistant winemaker to Tim Kirk at Clonakilla, after seven years at Jeir Creek. Judging at wine shows is another string to his bow.

Ravensworth has two vineyards: Rosehill (cabernet sauvignon, merlot and sauvignon blanc) and Martin Block (shiraz, viognier, marsanne and sangiovese).

ŸŸŸŸŸ Canberra District Sangiovese 2014 No pause for thought: this is gloriously delicious sangiovese. Then I find out that five vineyards have provided grapes for the wine, which explains how the layers of red fruits, headed by cherry, have been built into the wine; even more remarkable is its freshness, reflected in the very modest alcohol. On top of all this there are fine, savoury tannins giving texture and structure that will underwrite the medium-term cellaring of the wine. Screwcap. 13% alc. **Rating** 97 **To** 2025 $25 ✪

ŸŸŸŸŸ Riesling 2014 A quite beautiful riesling, underlining the bond between region and variety, whole bunch-pressing and (counterintuitively) some barrel fermentation have resulted in a flowery/spicy (talc) bouquet, then a palate that floats lightly, but infinitely seductively, in the mouth, the aftertaste exceptional. All class at a bargain basement price. Screwcap. 12% alc. **Rating** 96 **To** 2029 $25 ✪

Charlie-Foxtrot Gamay Noir 2015 Bright, light crimson-purple; the bouquet is intensely perfumed, and the flavours are carbon-copy images: if anything, even more intense and exotic. No gamay equal to this has previously been made in Australia. Tumbarumba delivers the gladioli. Screwcap. 12.5% alc. **Rating** 96 **To** 2020 $32 ✪

Murrumbateman Shiraz Viognier 2015 Not content with his workplace at Clonakilla, Bryan Martin makes wine at home as well. Completely obsessed with Canberra Shiraz Viognier, his latest effort from '15 is a blinder, mid-dark red colour, complex and deeply scented, the palate seamless, powerful and graceful. Screwcap. 13.5% alc. **Rating** 96 **To** 2030 $36 ✪

Hilltops Nebbiolo 2014 Builds on the '13, Bryan Martin's first vintage of the variety. It is a stealth bomber, its flavours flooding the senses before you realise the intensity and power of the mouthfeel. This has a virtually unlimited future, but 5 years might see it at the start of a long plateau. Screwcap. 14% alc. **Rating** 96 **To** 2020 $35 ✪

Riesling 2015 Made in two batches, the largest whole bunch-pressed to cool (15°C) ferment in stainless steel, the second to ceramic eggs (16–18°C). A bold, but totally successful approach, the untold story pH of 3, 8.7g/l titratable acidity and 5g/l residual sugar. These figures explain the power, depth and balance of the wine. Screwcap. 12% alc. **Rating** 95 **To** 2029 $25 ✪

Hilltops Nebbiolo 2015 Deeper colour than most nebbiolos, with intense crimson; rose petals, spice, earth and a lick of tar and dried herbs lead to a generous and relatively rounded palate, the trademark savoury tannins building and driving the length. Screwcap. 13.5% alc. **Rating** 95 **To** 2030

Canberra District Sangiovese 2015 Includes 6% cabernet sauvignon, wild open-fermented in five batches, matured in used French oak. Light, bright colour; the bowl of cherries on the bouquet becomes more complex on the medium-bodied, very long, savoury/spicy palate; almost painfully pure, but give it a year and you'll be very happy. Screwcap. 13% alc. **Rating** 94 **To** 2030 $25 ✪

ŸŸŸŸŸ Canberra District Pinot Gris 2014 Rating 93 To 2016 $25 ✪
The Grainery 2015 Rating 93 To 2022 $32
Murrumbateman Shiraz Viognier 2014 Rating 92 To 2025 $35
Garnacha Tinta y Cinq-Sao 2015 Rating 91 To 2022 $32
Seven Months 2015 Rating 90 To 2023 $32

Red Art | Rojomoma   ★★★★

16 Sturt Road, Nuriootpa, SA 5355 **Region** Barossa Valley
T 0421 272 336 **www**.rojomoma.com.au **Open** By appt
Winemaker Bernadette Kaeding, Sam Kurtz **Est.** 2004 **Dozens** 400 **Vyds** 5.4ha
2015 was a momentous year for the Red Art | Rojomoma business, when winemaker and life partner of Bernadette Kaeding, Sam Kurtz, left his position as chief winemaker within the

Orlando group, where he had worked for over 20 years. He had in fact helped Bernadette with the care of Red Art since 1996, when Bernadette purchased the nucleus of the vineyard. It had 1.49ha of 80-year-old dry grown grenache; the remaining 3.95ha were planted over several years with shiraz, cabernet sauvignon, petit verdot and tempranillo. Until 2004 the grapes from the old and new plantings were sold to Rockford, Chateau Tanunda, Spinifex and David Franz. In that year she decided to make a small batch of wine (with advice from Sam) and continued to accumulate wine until '11, when she began selling wines under the Red Art label. With Sam coming onboard full-time it seems likely that all the grapes will be henceforth used in making the Red Art wines.

ŶŶŶŶŶ **Red Art Single Vineyard Barossa Valley Shiraz 2012** Hand-picked, open-fermented, partial whole bunch fermentation, matured in new and used oak. This is more nimble on its feet than the Raj's Pick, with glossy black cherry fruits, fine tannins and balanced oak. Good now, better still in 5+ years. Screwcap. 13.5% alc. **Rating** 92 **To** 2027 $30

Cellar Release Red Art Single Vineyard Barossa Valley Petit Verdot 2004 15 days on skins, 8 months in new French oak, then 6 months in used American oak, 34 dozen made. This shows the tenacity of petit verdot in a good vintage; the wine is very much alive, with both red and black fruits aplenty, and the tannins are under control, the overall balance good. Screwcap. 13.4% alc. **Rating** 92 **To** 2024 $55

Raj's Pick Single Vineyard Barossa Valley Shiraz 2012 Made from the best bunches from the oldest rows of the northern part of the vineyard, everything done by hand, including making and applying the linen-like labels. It's a powerful, chewy wine with some dried fruit flavours that are not unattractive, tannins and oak also contributing. Screwcap. 14% alc. **Rating** 91 **To** 2030 $75

Cellar Release Red Art Single Vineyard Barossa Valley Shiraz 2004 Made in a shed attached to the home with an old crusher that took one bunch at a time, 2 weeks on skins, matured in French and American oak (20% new) for 12 months. Still very much alive and kicking, with ripe fruit flavours, mainly black, ripe tannins and good balance. Screwcap. 14.3% alc. **Rating** 90 **To** 2024 $55

ŶŶŶŶ **Cellar Release Red Art Single Vineyard Barossa Valley Grenache Shiraz 2006 Rating** 89 **To** 2020 $55

Red Deer Station ★★★☆

Lot 511 Barossa Valley Way, Tanunda, SA 5352 **Region** Barossa Valley/Riverland
T 0439 894 571 **www**.reddeerstation.com.au **Open** By appt
Winemaker James-Paul Marin **Est.** 1991 **Dozens** 10 000 **Vyds** 0.5ha
Red Deer Station is owned by winemaker James-Paul Marin, with a small 0.5ha vineyard in Tanunda. With a 15-year background in the wine community, James-Paul has drawn mainly on supplies from the Riverland and Southeast Australia, the latter which may or may not have the Riverina as an additional source of wine. The focus of the business is on exports, with sustainability one of its selling points, via a tree-planting program in Kenya linked to sales of wines. Exports to Canada, Sweden, Singapore, China and NZ.

ŶŶŶŶŶ **Antiquities Shiraz 2013** Matured in American oak for 2 years, plus a further 2 years bottle age. An essence of Barossa Valley shiraz, unctuous and velvety, carrying its alcohol without complaint. Needs many years in its super-weight bottle, but you get a lot of wine for the price. Cork. 15% alc. **Rating** 93 **To** 2038 $69

ŶŶŶŶ **Royal Reserve Cabernet Sauvignon 2013 Rating** 89 **To** 2023 $150
Barossa Valley Vineyards GSM 2012 Rating 88 **To** 2022 $35

Red Edge ★★★★☆

Golden Gully Road, Heathcote, Vic 3523 **Region** Heathcote
T 0407 422 067 **www**.rededgewine.com.au **Open** By appt
Winemaker Peter Dredge **Est.** 1971 **Dozens** 1500 **Vyds** 14ha

Red Edge's vineyard dates back to 1971 and the renaissance of the Victorian wine industry. In the early '80s it produced the wonderful wines of Flynn & Williams, and was rehabilitated by Peter and Judy Dredge, producing two quite lovely wines in their inaugural vintage and continuing that form in succeeding years. Exports to the US, Canada and China.

♥♥♥♥♥ 71 Block Heathcote Shiraz 2013 Solely from the '71 block, wild yeast-fermented and matured for 30 months in four new French barriques. Distinctively deeply coloured, the wine offers a passing parade of luscious black fruits, cedary oak and fine tannins. Destined for a very long and prosperous life thanks to its impeccable balance. Screwcap. 15% alc. **Rating** 96 **To** 2048 $60 **○**
Heathcote Shiraz 2013 Primarily from the estate 15yo Jackson's Lane Vineyard, some from the '71 block vines, 25% whole bunches, matured for 2 years in French oak (30% new). A complex wine reflecting all the winemaker inputs; well balanced and harmonious, with obvious oak and some savoury tannins that are carried by dark fruits. Screwcap. 14.8% alc. **Rating** 94 **To** 2028 $40

♥♥♥♥♀ VP 2008 Rating 92 **To** 2017 $35
Heathcote Cabernet Sauvignon 2013 Rating 90 **To** 2023 $30

Red Feet Wines

49 Cemetery Lane, King Valley, Vic 3678 **Region** King Valley
T (03) 5729 3535 **www.**redfeet.com.au **Open** Not
Winemaker Damien Star **Est.** 2010 **Dozens** 450 **Vyds** 1ha
Red Feet is the venture of Damien and sister Megan Star, he the winemaker and viticulturist, she the business manager. Damien graduated with a wine science degree from CSU in 2001, and worked in the Riverina and Riverland before heading to Germany, Fingerlakes in the US, and finally Kamberra in the ACT. The most valuable three years of Damien's career were spent at Kamberra with Alex McKay (and indirectly the Hardys winemaking team, headed by Paul Lapsley); this came to an abrupt end when Constellation Wines (the then Hardys owner) mothballed the winery in 2006. Megan grew up on a farm with Damien, and understands the importance of quality and value-adding, obtaining a Bachelor Degree in Agricultural Economics and a PhD in Natural Resource Management. Damien found his way to the King Valley, working for several local wineries before he and Megan purchased a 33ha property in the King Valley which had a house, a dilapidated vineyard and a farm shed. They replanted the 1ha vineyard split between sangiovese, nebbiolo, montepulciano and zinfandel. The shed, with its earth floor, became a de facto winery, its pride and joy a 300kg hand-operated basket press. The vineyard produced its first vintage in 2015.

♥♥♥♥♥ King Valley Tempranillo 2014 From a low-yielding vineyard at Cheshunt on red loam soil; foot-stomped by Red Feet Wine Club members, matured in used French oak. Has all you could ask for: texture and structure, plus clear-cut multi-cherry fruits. Screwcap. 13.6% alc. **Rating** 94 **To** 2022 $35

♥♥♥♥♀ King Valley Syrah 2013 Rating 93 **To** 2038 $35
King Valley Pinot Gris 2015 Rating 91 **To** 2017 $25
King Valley Sangiovese 2014 Rating 90 **To** 2024 $35

Red Hill Estate

53 Shoreham Road, Red Hill South, Vic 3937 **Region** Mornington Peninsula
T (03) 5989 2838 **www.**redhillestate.com.au **Open** 7 days 11–5
Winemaker Donna Stephens **Est.** 1989 **Dozens** 25 000 **Vyds** 72.2ha
Red Hill Estate was established by the late Sir Peter Derham and wife Lady Derham. It has undergone a number of changes of ownership since the Derhams sold the business in 2007, but its acquisition by China's Fullshare Group in April '16 will bring stability. The controlling shareholder of Fullshare is Hong Kong real estate billionare Ji Changqun, listed by Forbes as the 73rd richest man in China. Exports to the US, Canada, Ireland, Poland, Sweden, Singapore, Japan and Hong Kong.

ҮҮҮҮҮ Merricks Grove Mornington Peninsula Chardonnay 2013 The flavours
stride through the palate as if they're on a mission. It makes for compelling
drinking. Nectarine, white peach, chalk and toast/spicy oak. Long, dry-but-juicy
finish. Gorgeous. Screwcap. 13.5% alc. **Rating** 96 **To** 2021 $37 CM ✪
Merricks Grove Mornington Peninsula Pinot Noir 2013 It all revolves
around the finish. Chalky, spicy tannin seems to gather up the sweet-sour-savoury
fruit flavours and pull them out through the finish in strict, ordered file. We have
poise. We have power. Screwcap. 14.5% alc. **Rating** 95 **To** 2022 $37 CM
P&Q Mornington Peninsula Chardonnay 2013 The silk of creamed cashews.
The sweetness of estery banana and ripe peaches. A flare of wood smoke. This
tastes of chardonnay and money; accordingly, it's seductive. Screwcap. 14% alc.
Rating 94 **To** 2020 $60 CM
Single Vineyard Mornington Peninsula Pinot Noir 2014 You like spice?
This has it. A core of sweet fruit? That too. Some tang but not too much? Yep.
Length? Sure. A bit of force to the tannin? Plenty of it and well integrated too.
Indeed, across all parameters this wine performs admirably, if not quite hitting the
absolute heights. Screwcap. 14% alc. **Rating** 94 **To** 2022 $60 CM
M&N Mornington Peninsula Pinot Noir 2013 Step through the savoury
forest into a field of cranberry and red, twiggy cherry. It's a challenging wine,
twisted with dried herbs and various savoury elements, of clear quality but also,
clearly, in need of a little time. Screwcap. 14% alc. **Rating** 94 **To** 2024 $60 CM

ҮҮҮҮҮ Cellar Door Pinot Noir 2014 **Rating** 93 **To** 2021 $28 CM
Cellar Door Chardonnay 2013 **Rating** 92 **To** 2020 $28 CM
Mossolini Mornington Peninsula Shiraz 2013 **Rating** 92 **To** 2025 $60 CM
Cool Climate Pinot Grigio 2015 **Rating** 91 **To** 2016 $25 CM
Cool Climate Pinot Noir 2014 **Rating** 91 **To** 2019 $25 CM

Redbank   ★★★★

Whitfield Road, King Valley, Vic 3678 **Region** King Valley
T 0411 404 296 **www.**redbankwines.com **Open** Not
Winemaker Nick Dry **Est.** 2005 **Dozens** 33 000 **Vyds** 15ha
The Redbank brand was for decades the umbrella for Neill and Sally Robb's Sally's Paddock.
In 2005 Hill-Smith Family Vineyards acquired the Redbank brand from the Robbs, leaving
them with the winery, surrounding vineyard and the Sally's Paddock label. Redbank purchases
grapes from the King Valley, Whitlands, Beechworth and the Ovens Valley (among other
vineyard sources). Exports to all major markets.

ҮҮҮҮҮ King Valley Prosecco 2015 Prosecco in all its youthful, crunchy, fruit-focused
glory, charged with the tang of the cool, high King Valley, delivering nashi pear,
fennel and lemon with a hint of pepper. It finishes refreshingly dry and lively,
lingering with a well-poised acid line and compelling persistence. Screwcap.
11% alc. **Rating** 91 **To** 2016 $22 TS ✪
King Valley Fiano 2014 There is a volume of support around the traps for this
variety; here the lemony varietal character ranges across fresh, mouth-puckering
lemon, Meyer lemon and finally a hint of crystallised lemon. Screwcap. 13% alc.
Rating 90 **To** 2016 $22

ҮҮҮҮ Ellora King Valley Vintage Chardonnay Pinot Noir Brut Cuvee 2012
Rating 89 **To** 2019 $24 TS
Emily Chardonnay Pinot Noir NV **Rating** 88 **To** 2017 $15 TS ✪

Redden Bridge Wines   ★★★

PO Box 1223, Naracoorte, SA 5271 **Region** Wrattonbully
T (08) 8762 1588 **www.**reddenbridge.com **Open** Not
Winemaker Robin Moody (Contract) **Est.** 2002 **Dozens** 1900 **Vyds** 28ha
This is the venture of Greg and Emma Koch, Greg with a quarter-century of viticultural
experience, first in Coonawarra (17 years) and thereafter turning his attention to Wrattonbully,

buying land there in 1995 and setting up Terra Rossa Viticultural Management to assist growers across the Limestone Coast. Greg and Emma now have 23ha of cabernet sauvignon and 5ha of pinot gris, and retain the services of the immensely experienced Robin Moody to oversee the making of the Redden Bridge wines at Cape Jaffa Estate.

????? **O Organic Pinot Grigio 2015** Cool-fermented in stainless steel, then cross-flow filtration, generally agreed to be the most effective method developed to date, but not often linked to organic, biodynamic and biological practices (I personally see no conflict). Has more stone fruit and citrus – almost into verdelho – than most pinot grigios. Perhaps this is organic/biodynamics at work. Screwcap. 12% alc. **Rating** 88 **To** 2016 $20

Redesdale Estate Wines   ★★★★

46 Gibbards Lane, Redesdale, Vic 3444 **Region** Heathcote
T (03) 5425 3236 **www**.redesdale.com **Open** By appt
Winemaker Alan Cooper **Est.** 1982 **Dozens** 800 **Vyds** 4ha
Planting of the Redesdale Estate vines began in 1982 on the northeast slopes of a 25ha grazing property fronting the Campaspe River on one side. The rocky quartz and granite soil meant the vines had to struggle, and when Peter Williams and wife Suzanne Arnall-Williams purchased the property in '88 the vineyard was in a state of disrepair. They have rejuvenated it, planted an olive grove, and, more recently, erected a two-storey house surrounded by a garden which is part of the Victorian Open Garden Scheme.

????? **Heathcote Shiraz 2013** Hand-picked, wild-fermented, whole bunches, open vats, 12 months in new and used French oak, not fined or filtered. A rich and powerful full-bodied shiraz, still in primary mode; densely textured, but no bitter extract or rough tannins. Screwcap. 14.4% alc. **Rating** 91 **To** 2028 $37
La Scassatina 2014 65% cabernet sauvignon and cabernet franc, 35% shiraz, hand-picked and sorted, whole-berry wild open ferment, 20 days on skins, matured in French oak (20% new) for 14 months. Bright and juicy first up with some red fruits, but more black, then the tannin cavalry rides through the finish. Screwcap. 14% alc. **Rating** 90 **To** 2024 $39

???? **Heathcote Cabernet Sauvignon Cabernet Franc 2012** Rating 89
To 2020 $37

Redgate   ★★★★★

659 Boodjidup Road, Margaret River, WA 6285 **Region** Margaret River
T (08) 9757 6488 **www**.redgatewines.com.au **Open** 7 days 10–4.30
Winemaker Joel Page **Est.** 1977 **Dozens** 6000 **Vyds** 18ha
Founder and owner of Redgate, the late Bill Ullinger, chose the name not simply because of the nearby eponymous beach, but also because – so it is said – a local farmer (with a prominent red gate at his property) had run an illegal spirit-still 100 or so years ago, and its patrons would come to the property and ask whether there was any 'red gate' available. True or not, Redgate was one of the early movers in the Margaret River, now with close to 20ha of mature estate plantings (the majority to sauvignon blanc, semillon, cabernet sauvignon, cabernet franc, shiraz and chardonnay, with smaller plantings of chenin blanc and merlot). Exports to Denmark, Switzerland, Singapore, Japan and China.

????? **Margaret River Cabernet Sauvignon 2014** Destemmed and crushed, cultured yeast, 6 days on skins, matured for 18 months in French barriques (25% new). An imperious, full-bodied Margaret River cabernet, blackcurrant, black olive, bay leaf and tar all on parade on the bouquet and palate alike, oak merely an adjunct. Its fruit purity is excellent. Screwcap. 14.1% alc. **Rating** 95 **To** 2034 $38
Ullinger Reserve Margaret River Cabernet Sauvignon 2014 Matured for 18 months in French barriques (35% new). The extra 10% of new French oak (compared to its sibling) makes a surprising difference considering the full-bodied

nature of both wines. This is as far up the scale as one can go without over-extraction. Screwcap. 14.2% alc. **Rating** 95 **To** 2039 $65

WW Ullinger Reserve Margaret River Chardonnay 2014 Whole bunch-pressed, 70% cultured yeast, 30% wild-fermented in French oak (25% new), matured for 8 months. The variables are riper fruit, more wild ferment and more new oak than its junior sibling. Small wonder, then, that this is more complex, with greater power and length. Screwcap. 14.2% alc. **Rating** 94 **To** 2025 $60

ŸŸŸŸŸ Margaret River Cabernet Franc 2014 Rating 93 To 2029 $40
Margaret River Sauvignon Blanc Semillon 2015 Rating 91 To 2020 $22 ✪
Margaret River Chardonnay 2014 Rating 91 To 2024 $35
Margaret River Bin 588 2014 Rating 91 To 2029 $24
Margaret River Chenin Blanc 2015 Rating 90 To 2018 $21 ✪
Margaret River Shiraz 2014 Rating 90 To 2040 $33

Redheads Studios ★★★★

733b Light Pass Road, Angaston, SA 5353 **Region** South Australia
T 0457 073 347 **www**.redheadswine.com **Open** By appt
Winemaker Dan Graham **Est.** 2003 **Dozens** 10 000
Redheads was established by Tony Laithwaite and wife Barbara in McLaren Vale. The aim was to allow young winemakers working under corporate banners to do some moonlighting, producing small batch wines for Tony to sell throughout the world. Justin Lane, Adam Hooper, Nat McMurtie and Andrew Pieri were part of the early team; the winery evolved under the guidance of Steve Grimley, with some of the original members still involved, together with a fresh batch of younger, eager winemakers. A major change followed when the winery moved to Angaston, with Dan Graham heading the winemaking team and now sourcing fruit from all over SA. While the scale of production has changed, the aim of making wines from new varieties and/or with new styles continues.

ŸŸŸŸŸ Le Batard Barossa Rose 2015 Grenache destemmed into open pots with some marsanne skins, plunged every 3–4 hours, after 24 hours pressed and fermented in stainless steel and oak, then half in stainless steel, half in oak for 4 months, 100% mlf. Very complex and savoury style, full of attitude, and trenchantly demanding food. Good stuff. Screwcap. 12.5% alc. **Rating** 92 **To** 2017 $20 ✪

Redman ★★★★☆

Main Road, Coonawarra, SA 5263 **Region** Coonawarra
T (08) 8736 3331 **www**.redman.com.au **Open** Mon–Fri 9–5, w'ends 10–4
Winemaker Bruce, Malcolm and Daniel Redman **Est.** 1966 **Dozens** 18 000 **Vyds** 34ha
In March 2008 the Redman family celebrated 100 years of winemaking in Coonawarra. The '08 vintage also marked the arrival of Daniel, fourth-generation Redman winemaker. Daniel gained winemaking experience in Central Victoria, the Barossa Valley and the US before taking up his new position. It was felicitous timing, for the '04 Cabernet Sauvignon and '04 Cabernet Merlot were each awarded a gold medal from the national wine show circuit in '07, the first such accolades for a considerable time. A major vineyard rejuvenation program is underway, but there will be no change to the portfolio of wines. The quality has stabilised at a level in keeping with the long-term history of the winery and its mature vines.

ŸŸŸŸŸ Coonawarra Cabernet Sauvignon 2010 Won two trophies at the National Wine Show, including Best Dry Red Wine and seven gold medals, all in '12, then retired undefeated. It was matured in French oak (33% new) for 12–18 months, and is a beautifully supple and smooth cabernet of great purity and elegance. The enigma is why the 50yo vineyard has not produced wine of this quality year in, year out. Cork. 14.4% alc. **Rating** 96 **To** 2040 $40 ✪

ŸŸŸŸŸ Coonawarra Shiraz 2012 Rating 92 To 2025 $23 CM ✪
Coonawarra Cabernet Sauvignon 2013 Rating 92 To 2033 $28
Coonawarra Shiraz 2013 Rating 90 To 2028 $22

Reillys Wines   ★★★★☆

Cnr Leasingham Road/Hill Street, Mintaro, SA 5415 **Region** Clare Valley
T (08) 8843 9013 **www**.reillyswines.com.au **Open** 7 days 10–4
Winemaker Justin Ardill **Est.** 1994 **Dozens** 25 000 **Vyds** 115ha
This has been a very successful venture for Adelaide cardiologist Justin Ardill and wife Julie,
beginning as a hobby in 1994, but growing significantly over the intervening years. They now
have vineyards at Watervale, Leasingham and Mintaro, growing riesling, cabernet sauvignon,
shiraz, grenache, tempranillo and merlot. The cellar door and restaurant were built between
1856 and 1866 by Irish immigrant Hugh Reilly; 140 years later they were restored by the
Ardills, distant relatives of Reilly who have been making wines in the Clare Valley for a mere
20 years or so. Exports to the US, Canada, Ireland, Malaysia, China and Singapore.

♀♀♀♀♀ **Watervale Riesling 2015** From the Smyth's Block and St Clare Vineyards.
100% free-run juice, gold medals Clare Valley and Adelaide Wine Shows '15.
This is a delicate, but perfectly proportioned and balanced wine, purity its calling
card. Oozes potential for those who give it 5 years, better still 10 years, for the
development of a cavalcade of lime, honey and lightly browned toast. Screwcap.
12.5% alc. **Rating** 95 **To** 2030 $22 ○

♀♀♀♀♀ **Dry Land Clare Valley Tempranillo 2013 Rating** 92 **To** 2023 $25 ○

Relbia Estate   ★★★★

1 Bridge Road, Launceston, Tas 7250 **Region** Northern Tasmania
T (03) 6332 1000 **www**.relbiaestate.com.au **Open** Mon–Thurs 10–5, Fri–Sat 10–11
Winemaker Ockie Myburgh **Est.** 2011 **Dozens** 2350
Dean Cocker is the grandson of Josef Chromy, and managing director of Josef Chromy Wines,
and has worn two hats: one as a commercial lawyer in Melbourne and Sydney, the other with
personal involvement in the Tasmanian wine industry since 1994. He has retained Ockie
Myburgh as winemaker, stating the obvious in revealing Ockie South African heritage and
first winemaking degree, complemented by a Bachelor in Winemaking from the University of
Western Sydney in 2005. Ockie has made wine in many parts of Australia, the most important
and most recent as assistant winemaker at Bay of Fires in Tasmania. Exports to the UK.

♀♀♀♀♀ **Sauvignon Blanc 2015** Machine-harvested, 10% fermented in new French oak,
matured for 2 months. That little bit of barrel ferment has had a disproportionate
effect on what was in any event a sauvignon blanc with more tropical fruit than
usual for Tasmania – or perhaps I should say 'was usual', for the winds of change
are blowing in the right direction. Screwcap. 14% alc. **Rating** 94 **To** 2018 $27 ○

♀♀♀♀♀ **Riesling 2015 Rating** 93 **To** 2025 $27 ○
Pinot Grigio 2015 Rating 92 **To** 2018 $27

Renards Folly   ★★★★

PO Box 499, McLaren Vale, SA 5171 **Region** McLaren Vale
T (08) 8556 2404 **www**.renardsfolly.com **Open** Not
Winemaker Tony Walker **Est.** 2005 **Dozens** 3000
The dancing foxes on the label, one with a red tail, give a subliminal hint that this is a virtual
winery, owned by Linda Kemp. Aided by friend and winemaker Tony Walker, they source
grapes from McLaren Vale, and allow the Vale to express itself without too much elaboration,
the alcohol nicely controlled. Exports to the US, Canada, Germany and Singapore.

♀♀♀♀♀ **Fighting Fox McLaren Vale Shiraz 2014** Gutsy red with tar and plum flavours
laid on. Plenty of tannin too. Unsubtle, but it sure packs a punch. Screwcap.
14% alc. **Rating** 91 **To** 2021 CM
McLaren Vale Shiraz 2014 This is exactly the kind of smooth red so many
are on the lookout for; it's generous in both (dark berried) fruit and oak and it's
generally well done. Screwcap. 14% alc. **Rating** 90 **To** 2019 CM

Renzaglia Wines

38 Bosworth Falls Road, O'Connell, NSW 2795 **Region** Central Ranges Zone
T (02) 6337 5756 **www**.renzagliawines.com.au **Open** By appt
Winemaker Mark Renzaglia **Est.** 2011 **Dozens** 2000 **Vyds** 5ha
The eponymous winery of Mark and Sandy Renzaglia. Mark is a second-generation vigneron, his father growing vines in southern Illinois, US. Mark and Sandy planted their first vineyard in 1997 (1ha of chardonnay, cabernet sauvignon and merlot), Mark making wine in small quantities while working as a grapegrower/winemaker at Winburndale Wines for 11 years. In 2011 he left Winburndale and, with Sandy, started their own business. He also manages a vineyard in the middle of the famous Mt Panorama race circuit, and has access to the grapes from the 4ha Mount Panorama Estate (Brokenwood purchased chardonnay from that vineyard for some years). This gives him access to shiraz, semillon, cabernet sauvignon and chardonnay. He also purchases grapes from other local growers. Exports to the US.

Mount Panorama Estate Chardonnay 2014 The flavours are similar to its Dog's Day sibling (in the grapefruit spectrum), but there is an additional layer to the mouthfeel and flavour. Unambiguously good wine. Screwcap. 12.5% alc. **Rating** 92 **To** 2020 $28

Mount Panorama Estate Shiraz 2013 This is no shrinking violet, but the overall balance can't be faulted, the bright crimson colour an appropriate signal of the inherent quality of the wine, resulting from a best-barrel selection – 87 dozen made. A surprise packet. Screwcap. 14% alc. **Rating** 91 **To** 2028 $30

Dog's Day Chardonnay 2014 The vineyard has long proven its ability to produce good chardonnay (Brokenwood made some for several vintages), with fresh acidity a feature underpinning both the flavour (grapefruit) and length; the relative absence of oak is a positive. Screwcap. 12.5% alc. **Rating** 90 **To** 2018 $20 ♻

Sauvignon Blanc 2015 Rating 89 To 2016 $22
Bella Luna Chardonnay 2013 Rating 89 To 2017 $28
Shiraz 2013 Rating 89 To 2023 $20
Cabernet Sauvignon 2014 Rating 88 To 2024 $20
Mount Panorama Estate Cabernet 2014 Rating 88 To 2027 $30

Reschke Wines

Level 1, 183 Melbourne Street, North Adelaide, SA 5006 (postal) **Region** Coonawarra
T (08) 8239 0500 **www**.reschke.com.au **Open** Not
Winemaker Peter Douglas (Contract) **Est.** 1998 **Dozens** 25 000 **Vyds** 155ha
The Reschke family has been a landowner in Coonawarra for 100 years, with a large holding that is part terra rossa, part woodland. Cabernet sauvignon (with 120ha) takes the lion's share of the plantings, with merlot, shiraz and petit verdot making up the balance. Exports to the UK, Canada, Germany, Malaysia, Japan, Hong Kong and China.

Empyrean Coonawarra Cabernet Sauvignon 2008 Estate-grown, matured in 100% new French barriques for 3 years. The cork looks newly inserted (Dec '15), leaving a gap of 4 years in the history of the wine, although we do know it was picked 25 Mar in the middle of the celebrated (for the wrong reasons) heatwave. It is not cooked, and the freshness is admirable. Perhaps it was held in tank for 3 years before going to oak, or was moved back and forth. 14% alc. **Rating** 93 **To** 2025 $150

Resolution Vineyard

4 Glen Street, South Hobart, Tas 7004 **Region** Southern Tasmania
T (03) 6224 9497 **www**.theresolutionvineyard.com **Open** By appt
Winemaker Frogmore Creek **Est.** 2003 **Dozens** 250 **Vyds** 0.8ha
Owners Charles and Alison Hewitt live in England and entrust the care of the property and vineyard to Alison's father Peter Brown, with support from former Parks & Wildlife

ranger Val Dell. A love of red burgundy and fishing was sufficient for Charles to establish the vineyard, planted to three clones of pinot noir, in Tasmania, where Alison had spent most of her formative years. The vineyard is on a north-facing slope overlooking the D'Entrecasteaux Channel. Exports to the UK.

♟♟♟♟♀ **Pinot Noir 2014** Flighty acidity, twiggy herbs, wood smoke, cherry-plum. It doesn't all (yet) hang together but there's plenty here, and every indication that it will knit attractively together given time. Screwcap. 13% alc. **Rating** 91 **To** 2024 $30 CM

Reynella   ★★★★★
Reynell Road, Reynella, SA 5161 **Region** McLaren Vale/Fleurieu Peninsula
T 1800 088 711 **www.**reynellawines.com.au **Open** Mon–Tues 11–5, Wed–Fri 10–5
Winemaker Paul Carpenter **Est.** 1838 **Dozens** NFP
John Reynell laid the foundations for Chateau Reynella in 1838; over the next 100 years the stone buildings, winery and underground cellars, with attractive gardens, were constructed. Thomas Hardy's first job in SA was with Reynella; he noted in his diary that he would be able to better himself soon. He did just that, becoming by far the largest producer in SA by the end of the 19th century; 150 or so years after Chateau Reynella's foundation, CWA (now Accolade Wines) completed the circle by acquiring it and making it corporate headquarters, while preserving the integrity of the Reynella brand in no uncertain fashion. Exports to all major markets.

♟♟♟♟♟ **Basket Pressed McLaren Vale Shiraz 2014** This is Rolls Royce stuff from a big company, made exactly as it might be by a small producer. It's open-fermented with precise plunging automated by the winemakers with the push of a button, and then put in 100% new French oak for 15 months. Lead me to Hermitage in the Rhône Valley and I'll find its brother. Screwcap. 14.5% alc. **Rating** 96 **To** 2044 $64 **○**

Rhythm Stick Wines   ★★★★
89 Campbell Road, Penwortham, SA 5453 **Region** Clare Valley
T (08) 8843 4325 **www.**rhythmstickwines.com.au **Open** By appt
Winemaker Tim Adams **Est.** 2007 **Dozens** 1060 **Vyds** 1.62ha
Rhythm Stick has come a long way in a short time, and with a small vineyard. It is owned by Ron and Jeanette Ely, who in 1997 purchased a 3.2ha property at Penwortham. The couple had already decided that in the future they would plant a vineyard, and simply to obtain experience they planted 135 cabernet sauvignon cuttings from Waninga Vineyards in four short rows. They produced a few dozen bottles of Cabernet a year, sharing it with friends. In '02 they planted riesling, and the first harvest followed in '06, the grapes from this and the ensuing two vintages sold to Clare Valley winemakers. Prior to the '09 harvest they were advised that due to the GFC no grapes would be required, which advanced Ron's planned retirement after 40 years in electrical engineering consulting and management.

♟♟♟♟♀ **Red Robin Single Vineyard Clare Valley Riesling 2015** Pure lime, perfumed and expressive, turns to slatey spice as it concludes. Just enough intensity to impress. Screwcap. 12.5% alc. **Rating** 90 **To** 2021 $19 CM **○**

Richard Hamilton   ★★★★
Cnr Main Road/Johnston Road, McLaren Vale, SA 5171 **Region** McLaren Vale
T (08) 8323 8830 **www.**leconfieldwines.com **Open** Mon–Fri 10–5, w'ends 11–5
Winemaker Paul Gordon, Tim Bailey **Est.** 1972 **Dozens** 25 000 **Vyds** 71.6ha
Richard Hamilton has outstanding estate vineyards, some of great age, all fully mature. An experienced and skilled winemaking team has allowed the full potential of those vineyards to be realised. The quality, style and consistency of both red and white wines has reached a new

level; being able to keep only the best parcels for the Richard Hamilton brand is an enormous advantage. For reasons outside the *Wine Companion's* control, not all the current releases were available for tasting for this edition. Exports to the UK, the US, Canada, Denmark, Sweden, Germany, Belgium, Malaysia, Vietnam, Hong Kong, Singapore, Japan, China and NZ.

ŸŸŸŸ **McLaren Vale Shiraz 2014** From estate vines 15–50yo, pressed before dryness, part finishing fermentation in barrel, matured for 16 months in predominantly French oak, the remainder American. The underplay of dark chocolate provides the regional anchor for a pleasant, medium-bodied shiraz. Neatly priced. Screwcap. 14% alc. **Rating** 89 **To** 2020 $21
Adelaide Hills Sauvignon Blanc 2015 Cold-fermented in stainless steel, one month lees contact post-ferment. Mainstream tropical fruits are enlivened on the finish by citrussy acidity. Nice wine for (the usual) immediate consumption. Screwcap. 12.5% alc. **Rating** 88 **To** 2016 $20
The Hills Adelaide Hills Pinot Gris 2015 Crisp and fruity with red apple and spice notes to the fore. Straightforward and refreshing. Screwcap. 12.5% alc. **Rating** 88 **To** 2016 $20 CM

Richard Meyman Wines   ★★★★
PO Box 173, Franklin, Tas 7113 **Region** Southern Tasmania
T 0417 492 835 **www.**richardmeymanwines.com.au **Open** Not
Winemaker Winemaking Tasmania **Est.** 2010 **Dozens** 400
Richard Meyman had accumulated many years in the wine trade as grower, owner and manager before returning to Tasmania to resurrect and run the important Nocton Park vineyard in the Richmond/Coal River area. Few would dispute the primacy of pinot noir as Tasmania's finest grape variety, and its multifaceted riesling is in the same quality league. So it is that Richard has chosen those two varieties, and put them in the hands of Tasmania's leading contract winemaker.

ŸŸŸŸŸ **Waseca Minnesotta Riesling 2015** Standard no-frills winemaking. The resounding Tasmanian acidity, 'only 7.52g/l', wakes you up in a hurry if your concentration has for any reason wandered. Whether made in Germany or Australia, there is an implacable direction of flavour, the only defence being the inclusion of some residual sugar. Screwcap. 13.2% alc. **Rating** 94 **To** 2025 $24 ✪
Colebrook Road Pinot Noir 2014 Deeply coloured, it is Tasmania's battle cry to Central Otago: anything you can do, I can do better. Intensely flavoured and built (and strongly aromatic), it is pure pinot, with black cherry, a touch of plum and incipient spice. Given enough time (5+ years), this will surely hum with energy and complexity. Screwcap. 13.5% alc. **Rating** 94 **To** 2029 $27 ✪

Richmond Grove   ★★★★
Para Road, Tanunda, SA 5352 **Region** Barossa Valley
T (08) 8563 7303 **www.**richmondgrovewines.com **Open** Not
Winemaker Stephen Cook **Est.** 1983 **Dozens** NFP
Richmond Grove draws its grapes from diverse sources. The Barossa Valley and Watervale Rieslings, a legacy of master winemaker John Vickery, represent excellent value for money year in, year out. The Coonawarra Cabernet Sauvignon is not as incongruous as it may seem, for John Vickery was transferred to Coonawarra for a couple of years in the latter stages of his career at Leo Buring, until sanity prevailed and he returned to the Barossa Valley to continue making Riesling, thereafter moving to Richmond Grove prior to his retirement in 2009.

ŸŸŸŸŸ **Limited Release Watervale Vineyards Riesling 2015** Crisp, lively natural acidity and intense lime juice flavours are pluses; the fact that the '00 vintage was one of the reasons why the Clare Valley winemakers moved en masse to screwcap largely lost in the mists of time. Screwcap. 12.6% alc. **Rating** 93 **To** 2025 $23 ✪

Ridgemill Estate

218 Donges Road, Severnlea, Qld 4352 **Region** Granite Belt
T (07) 4683 5211 **www**.ridgemillestate.com **Open** Fri–Mon 10–5, Sun 10–3
Winemaker Martin Cooper, Peter McGlashan **Est.** 1998 **Dozens** 900 **Vyds** 2.1ha
Martin Cooper and Dianne Maddison acquired what was then known as Emerald Hill
Winery in 2004. In '05 they reshaped the vineyards, which now have plantings of chardonnay,
tempranillo, shiraz, merlot, cabernet sauvignon, saperavi, verdelho and viognier, setting a
course down the alternative variety road. The quite spectacular winery and cellar door facility
also operates self-contained cabins in the vineyard.

♀♀♀♀♀ **Granite Belt Merlot 2013** Good colour and depth; poached blackcurrant
on the bouquet changes its spots on the far more savoury, cabernet-like, dark
berries and dried herbs of the palate. A real wine from merlot. Screwcap. 13% alc.
Rating 92 **To** 2023 $30
Hungry Horse MTG 2013 70/15/15% tempranillo, monastrell and grenache,
matured for 12–14 months in used oak. The colour is bright and clear, the light-
bodied palate fresh and vibrant, full of red cherry fruit, the finish crisp and juicy.
Screwcap. 13.5% alc. **Rating** 91 **To** 2020 $30
The Lincoln Granite Belt Shiraz Viognier 2013 The bright colour attests to
the co-fermentation with viognier, although presumably another 3% was added
to the wine (a minimum of 5% is required for it to be mentioned on the label).
Crisp, lively and juicy, no need for cellaring. Screwcap. 12.5% alc. **Rating** 90
To 2020 $30

RidgeView Wines

273 Sweetwater Road, Pokolbin, NSW 2320 **Region** Hunter Valley
T (02) 6574 7332 **www**.ridgeview.com.au **Open** Wed–Sun 10–5
Winemaker Darren Scott, Gary MacLean **Est.** 2000 **Dozens** 5000 **Vyds** 9ha
Darren and Tracey Scott have transformed a 40ha timbered farm into a vineyard, together
with self-contained accommodation and a cellar door. The lion's share of the plantings are
4.5ha of shiraz, with cabernet sauvignon, chambourcin, merlot, pinot gris, viognier and
traminer making up a somewhat eclectic selection of other varieties. Exports to Japan.

♀♀♀♀♀ **Generations Single Vineyard Reserve Hunter Valley Semillon 2015**
Impeccable. Clear, bright, racy and long. Has its arrow pointed at the future, and
little else. Screwcap. 10% alc. **Rating** 94 **To** 2028 $25 CM ✪

♀♀♀♀♀ **Impressions Hunter Valley Chardonnay 2013 Rating** 93 **To** 2021 $30 CM
Impressions Hunter Valley Shiraz 2013 Rating 93 **To** 2025 $35 CM
Generations Museum Release Hunter Valley Shiraz 2007 Rating 92
To 2021 $50 CM
Museum Release Cabernet 2007 Rating 90 **To** 2018 $50 CM

Rieslingfreak

8 Roenfeldt Drive, Tanunda, SA 5352 **Region** Clare Valley
T (08) 8563 3963 **www**.rieslingfreak.com **Open** By appt
Winemaker John Hughes **Est.** 2009 **Dozens** 5000 **Vyds** 35ha
The name of John Hughes' winery leaves no doubt about his long-term ambition: to explore
every avenue of riesling, whether bone-dry or sweet, coming from regions across the wine
world, albeit with a strong focus on Australia. The wines made from his Clare Valley vineyard
offer dry (No. 2, No. 3 and No. 4) and off-dry (No. 5 and No. 8) styles. Exports to Canada,
Norway, Hong Kong and NZ.

♀♀♀♀♀ **No. 4 Riesling 2015** Cold-fermented, bottled Jun, 2.8g/l residual sugar.
This does a puzzling U-turn, with excellent crystal-clear lemon and lime fruit,
inexplicable if you simply look at the residual sugar, still below the level of
detection. The answer is simple: this is from the Eden Valley, and what has to be a
very good vineyard. Screwcap. 11.5% alc. **Rating** 95 **To** 2030 $23 ✪

No. 2 Riesling 2015 Cold-fermented, bottled Jun, 1.2 g/l residual sugar. Takes things calmly, with a relaxed run-up before releasing the ball, which in turn swings away late in its trajectory; it is here that the intensity of its citrus/grapefruit and river pebble acidity explode into full perspective and length. Screwcap. 10.5% alc. Rating 95 To 2030 $35 ✪

No. 6 Riesling 2009 This is from the Clare Valley, and was not released until '14. John Hughes thinks there is potential for more (positive) development and I share that view. There is a rivulet of fine acidity on the finish, tinkling alongside the banks of gentle lime and toast. Screwcap. 11.5% alc. Rating 94 To 2024 $35

♟♟♟♟♙ **No. 5 Riesling 2015** Rating 93 To 2025 $23 ✪

Rileys of Eden Valley ★★★★☆

PO Box 71, Eden Valley, SA 5235 **Region** Eden Valley
T (08) 8564 1029 **www**.rileysofedenvalley.com.au **Open** Not
Winemaker Peter Riley, Jo Irvine (Consultant) **Est.** 2006 **Dozens** 2000 **Vyds** 12.37ha
Rileys of Eden Valley is owned by Terry and Jan Riley with son Peter, who, way back in 1982, purchased 32ha of a grazing property that they believed had potential for quality grape production. The first vines were planted in that year and now extend to over 12ha. In '98 Terry retired from his position (Professor of Mechanical Engineering) at the University of SA, allowing him to concentrate on the vineyard, and, more recently, winemaking activities, but the whole family (including granddaughter Maddy) have been involved in the development of the property. It had always been intended that the grapes would be sold, but when not all the grapes were contracted in '06, the Rileys decided to produce some wine (even though they ended up with buyers for all the production that year).

♟♟♟♟♟ **Family Riesling 2015** Fermented in tank, cultured yeast, 2 months lees contact. A very attractive Eden Valley riesling, Meyer lemon and apple blossom to the fore; has excellent length and persistence, lime joining lemon (and acidity) on the finish. Screwcap. 12% alc. Rating 94 To 2030 $20 ✪

♟♟♟♟♙ **Jump Ship Shiraz 2013** Rating 93 To 2020 $25 ✪

Riposte ★★★★★

PO Box 256, Lobethal, SA 5241 **Region** Adelaide Hills
T (08) 8389 8149 **www**.timknappstein.com.au **Open** Not
Winemaker Tim Knappstein **Est.** 2006 **Dozens** 10500
It's never too late to teach an old dog new tricks when the old dog in question is Tim Knappstein. With 50+ years of winemaking and more than 500 wine show awards under his belt, Tim started yet another new wine life in 2006 with Riposte, a subtle response to the various vicissitudes he has suffered over the years. While having no continuing financial interest in Lenswood Vineyards, established many years ago, Tim is able to source grapes from it and also from other prime sites in surrounding areas. The prices for almost all the wines are astonishingly low. Exports to the UK, the US, Switzerland, Denmark, Indonesia and China.

♟♟♟♟♟ **The Sabre Adelaide Hills Pinot Noir 2014** This has utterly convincing varietal character, spiced black cherries allied with touches of charcuterie, the texture/mouthfeel with enough complexity to take it into the top echelon. Other than Ashton Hills, this is as good as it gets in this neck of the woods. Screwcap. 13.5% alc. Rating 96 To 2027 $38 ✪

The Scimitar Clare Valley Riesling 2015 There's so much to get stuck into right now, there's a good argument not to waste cellar space by holding on to some. (The better solution is to build a bigger cellar.) Lime and Meyer lemon flood the mouth, acidity a friend. Screwcap. 12.5% alc. Rating 95 To 2025 $20 ✪

The Dagger Adelaide Hills Pinot Noir 2015 Full crimson-purple hue; a fine web of earth and spice is wound through the dark cherry and damson plum fruit of the bouquet and palate alike, providing an extra measure of texture and structure. Still in its infancy, but promises much for the future – and an enticing price. Screwcap. 13% alc. Rating 94 To 2025 $20 ✪

The Cutlass Adelaide Hills Shiraz 2013 The hue is bright and clear, the fragrant bouquet offers a mix of plum and dark cherry fruit, with gentle touches of spice and licorice; there is a heartbeat of freshness in the wine that lifts it into top quality. Screwcap. 14% alc. **Rating** 94 **To** 2028 $25 ✪

ㅇㅇㅇㅇㅇ **The Stiletto Adelaide Hills Pinot Gris 2014 Rating** 93 **To** 2017 $20 ✪
The Foil Adelaide Hills Sauvignon Blanc 2015 Rating 92 **To** 2016 $20 ✪

Rise Vineyards   ★★★★

PO Box 7336, Adelaide, SA 5000 **Region** Clare Valley
T 0419 844 238 **www**.risevineyards.com.au **Open** Not
Winemaker Matthew McCulloch **Est.** 2009 **Dozens** 1500
Rise is very much a busman's holiday for owners Grant Norman and Matthew McCulloch. The two are a close-knit team, with Grant looking after the business and Matt the wine. Matt spent more than a decade in the UK wine trade. In 2006 Matt and wife Gina moved to the Clare Valley, where he was responsible for sales and marketing at Kirrihill Wines, of which Grant, an Australian wine industry veteran, was general manager. The move to Clare enabled Matt and Gina to realise a long-held dream of owning their own vineyard, growing the grapes and making the wine, with the help of Grant and his wife Alice. Having spent 11 years on the road working with more than 70 winemakers in 13 countries, Matt was convinced the focus of Rise should be on making small-scale, terroir-driven Riesling, Cabernet Sauvignon Grenache and Shiraz, reflecting the unique vineyard sites from which they come.

ㅇㅇㅇㅇㅇ **Single Vineyard Watervale Riesling 2015** From a high altitude (460m) organically farmed vineyard in Watervale. Lime, lemongrass and orange blossom lead to a typically tightly wound and steely finish. Needs time to show its best. Screwcap. 11.5% alc. **Rating** 94 **To** 2025 $20 ✪

ㅇㅇㅇㅇㅇ **Single Vineyard Clare Valley Grenache 2014 Rating** 92 **To** 2024 $25 ✪

 # Risky Business Wines   ★★★★

PO Box 6015, East Perth, WA 6892 **Region** Various
T 0457 482 957 **www**.riskybusinesswines.com.au **Open** Not
Winemaker Michael Kerrigan, Andrew Vesey, Gavin Berry **Est.** 2013 **Dozens** 3500
The name Risky Business is decidedly tongue-in-cheek, for the partnership headed by Rob Quenby has neatly sidestepped any semblance of risk. First up, the grapes come from vineyards in Great Southern and Margaret River that are managed by Quenby Viticultural Services. Since the batches of wine are very small (150–800 dozen), the partnership is able to preselect grapes specifically suited to the wine style and price. So there is no capital tied up in vineyards, nor in a winery – the wines are contract-made. Exports to the Pacific Rim, Japan.

ㅇㅇㅇㅇㅇ **Pinot Noir Rose 2015** The grapes come from the Pemberton region, well suited to rose. The perfumed, spiced red fruit bouquet is followed by a long, dry, savoury palate, strawberry fruit breaking free on the faintly sweet finish and aftertaste. Everyone's friend. Screwcap. 12.5% alc. **Rating** 94 **To** 2017 $25 ✪
Margaret River Cabernet Sauvignon 2014 There are some very smart parcels of cabernet from several blocks; it positively hums with its sweet cassis fruit built on a base of ripe tannins, oak functional rather than decorative. Good value. Screwcap. 14.5% alc. **Rating** 94 **To** 2034 $25 ✪

ㅇㅇㅇㅇㅇ **Fume Blanc 2014 Rating** 93 **To** 2017 $25 ✪
White Knuckle Chardonnay 2014 Rating 93 **To** 2023 $25 ✪
Shiraz Tempranillo Grenache 2014 Rating 93 **To** 2034 $25 ✪
Cabernet Sauvignon 2013 Rating 93 **To** 2033 $25 ✪
Malbec 2014 Rating 91 **To** 2029 $25

Riversdale Estate

222 Denholms Road, Cambridge, Tas 7170 **Region** Southern Tasmania
T (03) 6248 5666 **www.**riversdaleestate.com.au **Open** 7 days 10–5
Winemaker Nick Badrice **Est.** 1991 **Dozens** 9000 **Vyds** 37ha
Ian Roberts purchased the Riversdale property in 1980 while a university student, and says
he paid a record price for the district. The unique feature of the property is its frontage to the
Pittwater waterfront, which acts as a buffer against frost, and also moderates the climate during
the ripening phase. It is a large property, with 37ha of vines, and one of the largest olive groves
in Tasmania, producing 50 olive-based products. Five families live permanently on the estate,
providing all the labour for the various operations, which also include four 5-star French
Provincial cottages overlooking the vines. A new cellar door and French bistro opened in Jan
'16. Wine quality is consistently good, and can be outstanding.

ΨΨΨΨΨ **Roaring 40s Riesling 2015** Wow, the impact of this riesling is extraordinary; the
intensity of the essence of lime juice fruit is almost painful, the aftertaste lingering
for minutes. Not entered in the Tasmanian Wine Show, which is a pity. Buy 2
dozen bottles, one for now, one for your roaring 40s if it's not too late. Diam.
11.5% alc. **Rating** 97 **To** 2030 $22 ✪

ΨΨΨΨΨ **Centaurus Pinot Noir 2014** Creeps up on you; the colour is ok, the bouquet
pleasantly spicy, and it's not until the second take on the palate – like a trout
returning for a fly on the water it missed the first time – that the dark plum skin
flavours take hold, and linger long. Screwcap. 14% alc. **Rating** 94 **To** 2025 $48

ΨΨΨΨΨ **Roaring 40s Pinot Noir 2015** **Rating** 93 **To** 2021 $24 ✪
Roaring 40s Pinot Grigio 2015 **Rating** 90 **To** 2017 $22

Rob Dolan Wines

21–23 Delaneys Road, South Warrandyte, Vic 3134 **Region** Yarra Valley
T (03) 9876 5885 **www.**robdolanwines.com.au **Open** 7 days 10–5
Winemaker Rob Dolan, Mark Nikolich **Est.** 2010 **Dozens** 20 000 **Vyds** 20ha
Rob Dolan has been making wine in the Yarra Valley for over 20 years, and knows every
nook and cranny there. In 2011 he was able to purchase the Hardys Yarra Burn winery at
an enticing price. It is singularly well equipped, and as well as making the excellent Rob
Dolan wines, he carries on an extensive contract winemaking business. Business is booming,
production having doubled, with exports driving much of the increase. Exports to the UK,
the US, Canada, Malaysia, Singapore, Hong Kong and China.

ΨΨΨΨΨ **Yarra Valley Cabernet Sauvignon 2014** Essence of Yarra Valley cabernet.
Medium-bodied, curranty, fresh with acidity, laced with dried herbs and with a
keen future ahead. Deceptive tannin; it's there but it remains discreet. It doesn't
announce itself but the patient will be rewarded. Screwcap. 13% alc. **Rating** 94
To 2028 $35 CM

ΨΨΨΨΨ **Yarra Valley Chardonnay 2015** **Rating** 93 **To** 2020 $30 CM
True Colours Yarra Valley Dry Rose 2015 **Rating** 93 **To** 2017 $24 CM ✪
True Colours Yarra Valley Chardonnay 2015 **Rating** 92 **To** 2020 $24 CM ✪
Yarra Valley Pinot Noir 2015 **Rating** 92 **To** 2020 $35 CM
Yarra Valley Shiraz 2014 **Rating** 92 **To** 2025 $35 CM
Yarra Valley Pinot Gris 2014 **Rating** 91 **To** 2016 $30 CM
True Colours Yarra Valley Field Blend 2015 **Rating** 90 **To** 2017 $24 CM

Rob Hall Wines

157 Pine Avenue, Healesville, Vic 3777 (postal) **Region** Yarra Valley
T 0448 224 003 **www.**robhallwine.com.au **Open** Not
Winemaker Rob Hall **Est.** 2013 **Dozens** 2000 **Vyds** 3ha
Rob Hall has had considerable experience in making Yarra Valley chardonnay and pinot noir,
previously at Mount Mary, and thereafter at Kellybrook Winery. His business took several steps

forward in 2015. First, he acquired the 3ha vineyard on the property where he grew up. It was planted in 1996 by his parents (in particular, mother Harriet, hence Harriet's Vineyard). Next, from Jan '15 he leased the Limbic winery at Pakenham Upper. It has an underground barrel room, making it ideal for maturation, and also enabling much cellar work to be conducted using gravity. It is well equipped with a sorting table, Bucher crusher/destemmer, and a Bucher press.

ŸŸŸŸŸ **Harriet's Vineyard Yarra Valley Chardonnay 2015** 90% whole bunch-pressed to barrel with full solids, 10% destemmed and fermented on skins, 80% cultured yeast, matured in used French oak, bottled Nov. He who dares … Rob Hall has made a stunning chardonnay, complexity not for its own sake, but because it really works. Layers of fruit multiply, each adding another skin to the body. Edgy and racy. Powerful and seductive. Screwcap. 12.5% alc. **Rating** 96 **To** 2025 $38 ✪
Harriet's Vineyard Yarra Valley Pinot Noir 2015 Very good colour; the bouquet would have a truffle hound quivering in its harness, so complex is it: the more you delve, the more you find. The same blend of red/blue fruits and savoury/foresty notes (possibly ex extended maceration) greets you on the palate. Screwcap. 13% alc. **Rating** 95 **To** 2025 $45
Yarra Valley Chardonnay 2015 From vineyards at Healesville, Gladysdale and Dixon's Creek, small batches, 60% whole bunch-pressed, 30% destemmed with 24 hours skin contact, 10% destemmed and fermented on skins, 60% cultured yeast, matured in French oak (5% new). You can't criticise the end result, but it does have some elements of the puppy with a new toy, not sure what to do with it, but not happy to let go. Whole bunch-pressed one moment, 24 hours skin contact next, and then some fruit fermented on skins. The danger was that they would all cancel each other out, but that didn't happen. And the crazy time and money costs saved by only 5% new oak. Screwcap. 12.5% alc. **Rating** 94 **To** 2023 $25 ✪
Yarra Valley Petit Verdot 2015 Deep, intense crimson-purple; luxuriant flavours and structure, but with near-hidden notes of black olive and charred meat. It is a variety I would have an each-way bet on if I were planting a vineyard tomorrow. Screwcap. 13.8% alc. **Rating** 94 **To** 2030 $30 ✪

ŸŸŸŸ♀ **Yarra Valley Pinot Noir 2015** Rating 93 **To** 2024 $25 ✪

Robert Channon Wines   ★★★★

32 Bradley Lane, Amiens, Qld 4352 **Region** Granite Belt
T (07) 4683 3260 **www**.robertchannonwines.com **Open** Mon, Tues & Fri 11–4, w'ends 10–5
Winemaker Paola Cabezas **Est.** 1998 **Dozens** 2000 **Vyds** 8ha
Peggy and Robert Channon have established verdelho, chardonnay, pinot gris, shiraz, cabernet sauvignon and pinot noir under permanent bird protection netting. The initial cost of installing permanent netting is high, but in the long term it is well worth it: it excludes birds and protects the grapes against hail damage. Also, there is no pressure to pick the grapes before they are fully ripe.

ŸŸŸŸŸ **Granite Belt Verdelho 2015** Champion White Wine trophy Queensland Wine Awards '15. Robert Channon has long been a master of the dark arts of verdelho; at least part can be attributed to his permanent high-span netting covering the entire vineyard. Screwcap. 13.5% alc. **Rating** 94 **To** 2017 $28 ✪

ŸŸŸŸ♀ **Reserve Chardonnay 2015** Rating 91 **To** 2022 $30
Wild Ferment Chardonnay 2015 Rating 90 **To** 2020 $55

Robert Johnson Vineyards   ★★★★★

Old Woollen Mill, Lobethal, SA 5241 **Region** Eden Valley
T (08) 8359 2600 **www**.robertjohnsonvineyards.com.au **Open** W'ends and 11–5
Winemaker Robert Johnson **Est.** 1997 **Dozens** 3000 **Vyds** 3.86ha

The home base for Robert Johnson is a 12ha vineyard and olive grove purchased in 1996, with 0.4ha of merlot and 5ha of olive trees. The olive grove has been rehabilitated, and 2.1ha of shiraz, 1.2ha of merlot and a small patch of viognier have been established. Wines made from estate-grown grapes are released under the Robert Johnson label; these are supplemented by Alan & Veitch wines made from grapes purchased from the Sam Virgara vineyard in the Adelaide Hills, and named after Robert Johnson's parents. Exports to the US and Poland.

♥♥♥♥♥ Eden Valley Viognier 2014 A bold decision to take the bull by its horns has paid off; wild-fermented on full solids in a mix of 1yo and older French oak, plus 7 months' maturation has given texture and structure, yet allowed the varietal character of viognier free play. Altogether impressive – and a major surprise. Screwcap. 13.5% alc. **Rating** 95 **To** 2017 $32 **☺**
Adelaide Hills Pinot Noir 2013 100% clone 777, wild-fermented with extended maceration and 17 months maturation in used French oak. Lays out its elegance and purity of red berry fruits the moment it enters the mouth, and doesn't falter at any point through to the finish and aftertaste; the superfine tannins are a feature. Screwcap. 13% alc. **Rating** 95 **To** 2023 $30 **☺**
Adelaide Hills Chardonnay 2014 A quality chardonnay that speaks loud and clear about its place of origin; crisp white peach has a squeeze of grapefruit juice mouthfeel, bright acidity more important than oak in shaping the mouthfeel. Will go on from here. Screwcap. 13% alc. **Rating** 94 **To** 2021 $26 **☺**

♥♥♥♥♀ il Dittico 2013 Rating 93 To 2023 $30
Alan & Veitch Gruner Veltliner 2015 Rating 91 To 2020 $24

Robert Oatley Vineyards ★★★★★

Craigmoor Road, Mudgee, NSW 2850 **Region** Mudgee
T (02) 6372 2208 **www.**robertoatley.com.au **Open** 7 days 10–4
Winemaker Larry Cherubino, Marc Udy **Est.** 2006 **Dozens** NFP **Vyds** 440ha
Robert Oatley Vineyards is the venture of the Oatley family, previously best known as the owners of Rosemount Estate until it was sold to Southcorp. Sandy Oatley is chairman following the death of father Bob in 2016. Wild Oats, as anyone with the remotest interest in yachting and the Sydney–Hobart Yacht Race will know, has been the name of Bob's racing yachts. The family has long owned vineyards in Mudgee, but the new business was rapidly expanded by the acquisition of the Montrose winery and the Craigmoor cellar door and restaurant. The recruitment of Larry Cherubino as a winemaker has been a major factor in the radical reshaping of the overall business, with most the best wines now coming coming from WA. While there is a plethora of wines, the portfolio is easy to understand: at the bottom, Pocketwatch; next Wild Oats; Robert Oatley Signature Series; Robert Oatley Finisterre; and at the top, Robert Oatley The Pennant. Exports to the UK, the US and other major markets (including China).

♥♥♥♥♥ Robert Oatley The Pennant Great Southern Cabernet Sauvignon 2011
Matured for 12 months in new and 1yo French oak, before a best-barrels selection. A fragrant bouquet, cedar and cigar box to the fore; then an intense medium-bodied palate, with blackcurrant, cedar and fine tannins underwriting the extreme length of a glorious cabernet. Screwcap. 14% alc. **Rating** 97 **To** 2041 $80 **☺**

♥♥♥♥♥ Montrose Black Mudgee Shiraz 2014 Deep purple-crimson; there's a hive of activity going on here, and it's all pointing in the right direction. Black and blue fruits have shot-silk tannins that fall through the palate well before you arrive at the many-splendoured finish. This is a special Montrose Shiraz. Screwcap. 13.5% alc. **Rating** 96 **To** 2039 $35 **☺**
Robert Oatley Finisterre Margaret River Cabernet Sauvignon 2013
Matured for 15 months in new and used French oak. This really has echoes of Bordeaux, particularly on the back palate and finish, when the ripe, but firm, tannins mesh with the blackcurrant fruit so much that you're not sure where one stops to allow the other a chance to speak. Then throw in the French oak, and

you simply have to let it all wash over you: relax and enjoy it. Screwcap. 13.5% alc.
Rating 96 To 2043 $40 ✪

Robert Oatley Finisterre Margaret River Cabernet Sauvignon 2012
Ultra-typical Margaret River cabernet, with dusty/earthy nuances to the gently
ripe blackcurrant and bay leaf varietal fruit; the tannin structure is particularly
good, drawing out the complexity of the long, lingering finish. Screwcap. 14% alc.
Rating 96 To 2027 $40 ✪

Robert Oatley Finisterre Margaret River Chardonnay 2015 A
deliberately restrained style, all the components balanced, which is the reason why
deconstruction or pointing to one aspect of the wine is a waste of time. Its future
will be bright. Screwcap. 12.5% alc. Rating 94 To 2023 $37

Robert Oatley Finisterre Margaret River Chardonnay 2013 The bouquet
has elements of grapefruit/citrus blossom which flow through to the opening
of the seamless palate, which brings white peach and cashew into play before
precisely balanced citrussy acidity takes hold of the long finish. Trophy Best Wine
of Show Hobart '14, but the '14 Finisterre Margaret River is an even better wine.
Screwcap. 13% alc. Rating 94 To 2020 $37

Four in Hand Barossa Shiraz 2014 Trophy Best Blended Red Sydney
International Wine Competition '16. Vivid, deep crimson-purple; it is very supple,
and distributes its dark berry and mocha fruit evenly across the length and breadth
of the medium to full-bodied palate; the tannins come out of an identical crucible,
being soft and pliable. Screwcap. 14% alc. Rating 94 To 2029 $27 ✪

Robert Oatley Finisterre Great Southern Syrah 2013 Matured for
12 months in new and used French oak. The introduction is the fragrant spicy
berry bouquet, this taken on board in the medium-bodied palate without batting
an eyelid; supple tannins flesh out the elegant finish of an attractive wine. Screwcap.
13.5% alc. Rating 94 To 2033 $40

Robert Oatley GSM McLaren Vale Grenache Shiraz Mourvedre 2015
A 47/46/7% blend, machine-harvested, open-fermented, cultured yeast, 6 months
in new and used French oak. This is a really attractive GSM, with bright red juicy
fruits that sweep you along to a fresh and lively finish. A touch of earth adds a
sense of place. Screwcap. 14% alc. Rating 94 To 2025 $23 ✪

🍷🍷🍷🍷🍷 **Wild Oats Sauvignon Blanc 2015** Rating 93 To 2017 $18 ✪
Robert Oatley Margaret River Sauvignon 2015 Rating 93 To 2019 $23 ✪
Robert Oatley McLaren Vale Shiraz 2014 Rating 93 To 2030 $23 ✪
Robert Oatley Margaret River Cabernet Sauvignon 2014 Rating 93
To 2029 $23 ✪
Wild Oats Mudgee Pinot Grigio 2015 Rating 92 To 2017 $18 ✪
Robert Oatley Heathcote Shiraz 2014 Rating 92 To 2029 $23 ✪
Robert Oatley Finisterre Mornington Peninsula Pinot Noir 2013
Rating 91 To 2022 $37
Montrose Stony Creek Chardonnay 2014 Rating 90 To 2019 $23
Robert Oatley Yarra Valley Pinot Noir 2014 Rating 90 To 2020 $23

Robert Stein Vineyard   ★★★★★

Pipeclay Lane, Mudgee, NSW 2850 **Region** Mudgee
T (02) 6373 3991 **www.**robertstein.com.au **Open** 7 days 10–4.30
Winemaker Jacob Stein **Est.** 1976 **Dozens** 20 000 **Vyds** 18.67ha
While three generations of the family have been involved since Robert (Bob) Stein began
the establishment of the vineyard, the chain stretches even further back, going to Bob's great-
great-grandfather, Johann Stein, who was brought to Australia in 1838 by the Macarthur
family to supervise the planting of the Camden Park Vineyard. Bob's son Drew and grandson
Jacob have now taken over winemaking responsibilities. Jacob worked vintages in Italy,
Canada, Margaret River and Avoca, and, more particularly, in the Rheingau and Rheinhessen
regions of Germany. Since his return one success has followed another. Exports to Germany,
Hong Kong, Singapore and China.

ŶŶŶŶŶ **Museum Release Mudgee Riesling 2008** Stormed the show ring in '08 with two trophies and a top 10 place in the Canberra International Riesling Challenge. Bright, gleaming straw-green; it is packed with flavour, but is still as fresh as a daisy thanks to a faint tickle of CO_2 and feathery acidity. The way the palate builds the flavour profile progressively through to the finish and aftertaste is doubly impressive. Screwcap. 11.5% alc. **Rating** 96 **To** 2023 $70 ✪
Mudgee Riesling 2015 Part was fermented on skins, no doubt the reason for the complexity and depth of the wine, à la Alsace. Truly fascinating, and I have little or no idea how it will develop with age. Screwcap. 13% alc. **Rating** 95 **To** 2025 $25 ✪
Half Dry Mudgee Riesling 2015 Wine of Show at the Mudgee Wine Show. It's aromatic, textural and unusual; it's a wine that stands out. 20% of the wine was wild-fermented on skins, and then matured in older French oak. As a result it's yeasty and floral and rich, the sweetness adding volume but not poking out. It almost feels dry, as there's a volume to the flavour. Different, definitely, in a positive way. Screwcap. 12% alc. **Rating** 95 **To** 2024 $40 CM
Reserve Mudgee Shiraz 2013 There's a very large amount of energy tied up in this complex bundle of dark fruits, a caravan of spices, integrated oak and ripe tannins. Its greatest attribute is its balance, a long-term insurance policy. Screwcap. 13.5% alc. **Rating** 94 **To** 2030 $50
Mudgee Shiraz Viognier 2013 4% viognier, co-fermented, 30% whole bunches, matured for 14 months in French and American hogsheads (15% new). Yes, every box has been ticked by a through and through professional, daring anyone to say how it could have been improved on. And the price is right. Screwcap. 13.5% alc. **Rating** 94 **To** 2030 $25 ✪

ŶŶŶŶŶ **Reserve Mudgee Chardonnay 2014** Rating 93 **To** 2021 $40
Mudgee Semillon 2015 Rating 92 **To** 2025 $25 ✪
Reserve Mudgee Cabernet Sauvignon 2013 Rating 90 **To** 2025 $50
SRG Semillon Riesling Gewurztraminer 2015 Rating 90 **To** 2018 $15 ✪

Robertson of Clare ★★★★

PO Box 149, Killara, NSW 2071 **Region** Clare Valley
T (02) 9499 6002 www.rocwines.com.au **Open** Not
Winemaker Leigh Eldredge, Biagio Famularo **Est.** 2004 **Dozens** NFP
This is the highly unusual venture of Bryan Robertson, initially producing a single wine: MAXV. The Bordeaux varieties that go to produce MAXV are all grown in the Clare Valley, and individual varietal parcels are matured in 19 variations of 100% new French oak barrels. The primary fermentation takes place in barrel using what is called 'vinification integrale'. MAXV has been joined by the Block 6 Shiraz. Exports to Singapore, Hong Kong and China.

ŶŶŶŶŶ **Block 6 Gentle Press Shiraz 2014** Tannin, fruit, acid and oak aren't entirely on the same page but time will bring them closer together. Taken part by part the quality is clear; dense dark berried fruit, strong arms of tannin and flashes of clovey cedar wood all have a bit of class about them. Will reward the patient. Screwcap. 14.5% alc. **Rating** 93 **To** 2030 $25 CM ✪

Rochford Wines ★★★★★

878–880 Maroondah Highway, Coldstream, Vic 3770 **Region** Yarra Valley
T (03) 5957 3333 www.rochfordwines.com.au **Open** 7 days 9–5
Winemaker Marc Lunt **Est.** 1988 **Dozens** 16 000 **Vyds** 23.2ha
This Yarra Valley property was purchased by Helmut Konecsny in 2002; he had already established a reputation for Pinot Noir and Chardonnay from the family-owned Romsey Park vineyard in the Macedon Ranges. Since '10, Helmut has focused on his Yarra Valley winery and vineyards. Winemaker Marc Lunt had a stellar career as a Flying Winemaker over a six-year period in Bordeaux and Burgundy; in the latter region he worked at Armand Rousseau and Domaine de la Romanée-Conti. The property also has a large restaurant and café, cellar

door, retail shop, expansive natural amphitheatre and observation tower. It is a showpiece in the region, hosting a series of popular summer concerts. Exports to China.

♟♟♟♟♟ **Premier Yarra Valley Pinot Noir 2015** Fragrant flowery rose petals and sweet red berry fruits; the palate explodes under your feet with its sheer intensity and complexity, its tannins ex whole bunches up in Grand Cru territory; there is a choir of red and purple fruits, and an orchestra of spices behind those fruits. Wholly remarkable. Screwcap. 13.5% alc. **Rating** 98 **To** 2030 $80 ✪
Terre Yarra Valley Chardonnay 2015 From the Swallowfield Vineyard at Gembrook, hand-picked, crushed, wild-fermented in French oak, matured for 10 months. A wine of exceptional power and concentration, yet perfectly balanced in every way. The grapefruit-accented palate has extraordinary precision on the very long finish. Screwcap. 13.5% alc. **Rating** 97 **To** 2027 $54 ✪

♟♟♟♟♟ **Yarra Valley Pinot Noir 2015** Hand-picked 18 Mar, 50% whole bunches, cold soak, 23 days on skins, 10 months in French oak (20% new). Bright, clear crimson-purple; perfumed Parisian boudoir stuff; the palate ends all the nonsense with its breed and class, being perfectly structured, with a wealth of red fruits and contrasting filigreed tannins. Screwcap. 13.5% alc. **Rating** 96 **To** 2029 $38 ✪
Yarra Valley Chardonnay 2015 From two vineyard sites, hand-picked, crushed and pressed, wild-fermented in French oak (30% new), stirred as needed, 10 months in oak. Combines some melon as well as white peach and grapefruit on the lively, crisp finish. Screwcap. 13.5% alc. **Rating** 95 **To** 2035 $34 ✪
Yarra Valley Rose 2015 67% shiraz, 33% cabernet sauvignon, hand-picked, whole bunch-pressed, 50% fermented in stainless steel, 50% wild-fermented in used puncheons. A seriously good rose with a savoury intensity to its mouthwatering, tangy red fruits. Winemaking of a high order. Screwcap. 12.9% alc. **Rating** 95 **To** 2022 $27 ✪
L'Enfant Unique Yarra Valley Pinot Noir 2015 Hand-picked, 50% whole bunches, 23 days on skins, 10 months maturation in French oak (20% new). Bright, clear crimson; a very attractive bouquet of dark cherry and plum; the mouthfeel and length are exemplary; fruit, oak and pinot tannins all have their stars aligned. Screwcap. 13.8% alc. **Rating** 95 **To** 2025 $68
Latitude Yarra Valley Chardonnay 2015 Vibrant grapefruit/white peach fruit, with the length typical of good Yarra Valley chardonnay, and this certainly is that and more. A bargain to challenge Hoddles Creek. Screwcap. 13% alc. **Rating** 94 **To** 2023 $20 ✪
Dans les Bois Yarra Valley Pinot Noir 2015 Very pale to red rose-like colour; the intense bouquet will come as a shock, the long, savoury forest floor carpet for the red berry diamonds likewise. Only true pinot noir aficionados will buy the wine having seen the colour. Screwcap. 12.9% alc. **Rating** 94 **To** 2025 $54

♟♟♟♟♟ **Yarra Valley Syrah 2014 Rating** 92 **To** 2029 $33

RockBare | Mojo ★★★★

102 Main St, Hahndorf, SA 5245 **Region** McLaren Vale
T (08) 8388 7155 **www**.rockbare.com.au **Open** 7 days 11–5
Winemaker Marty O'Flaherty **Est.** 2000 **Dozens** 13 000 **Vyds** 29ha
RockBare Wines completed its first vintage in 2000. At the helm is winemaker Marty O'Flaherty, who was born and raised in the Western District of Victoria. He had a successful career as a chef, culminating in an award-winning term in charge at the acclaimed Stefano's in Mildura. While there he had his vinous epiphany and duly headed off to Charles Sturt University on his winemaking odyssey, holding various winemaking positions before finally landing at the helm of RockBare in 2009. The RockBare cellar door is located in the main street of Hahndorf, the Mojo wines available from www.mojowine.com.au. Exports to all major markets.

♟♟♟♟♟ **Mojo Sauvignon Blanc 2014** From the Adelaide Hills, with the wine given left-field treatment: part fermented on skins, part barrel-fermented, and given some lees stirring. Very clever winemaking has produced a sauvignon blanc with more structure and texture than usual, but leaving the fresh varietal fruit free play. A great result. Screwcap. 12.5% alc. **Rating** 93 **To** 2016 $20 ❂

RockBare McLaren Vale Shiraz 2014 Mainstream traditional McLaren Vale style, full to the brim with warm, verging on jammy, purple fruits. Would come into its own on a cold winter's night with a large piece of steak cooked over the coals of the fire. Screwcap. 15% alc. **Rating** 93 **To** 2030 $25 ❂

RockBare Barossa Babe Shiraz 2013 Matured for 2 years in new French oak. How it evades the impact of the alcohol on the finish eludes me, but it does. Obviously it's full-bodied, for the fruit has absorbed the oak, weaving it through the trifecta of plum, blackberry and chocolate. Amazing. Screwcap. 15.5% alc. **Rating** 91 **To** 2033 $45

RockBare The Clare Valley Riesling 2015 A well-made wine with clearly expressed varietal character, its line, length and balance its strong points, reflecting the excellent vintage. Screwcap. 12.5% alc. **Rating** 90 **To** 2025 $22

Rockcliffe ★★★★★

18 Hamilton Road, Denmark, WA 6333 **Region** Denmark
T (08) 9848 2622 **www.rockcliffe.com.au Open** 7 days 11–5
Winemaker Coby Ladwig, Brenden Smith **Est.** 1990 **Dozens** 10 000 **Vyds** 10ha
The Rockcliffe winery and vineyard business, formerly known as Matilda's Estate, is owned by citizen of the world Steve Hall. As part of the name change of the business, the wine ranges echo local surf place names, headed by Rockcliffe itself, but extending to Third Reef, Forty Foot Drop and Quarram Rocks. Over the years, Rockcliffe has won more than its fair share of trophies, gold and silver medals in wine shows. Exports to Canada and China.

ŶŶŶŶŶ **Single Site Denmark Chardonnay 2014** The highly fragrant and expressive bouquet has a knife edge of reduction adding another degree of complexity, but doesn't prepare you for the explosive power of the racy palate, built around unsweetened grapefruit and minerally acidity. You want to rise from your chair to salute the wine. Screwcap. 14% alc. **Rating** 97 **To** 2025 $45 ❂

Single Site Denmark Pinot Noir 2015 Very good purple-crimson hue; the cool climate of Denmark should always have produced quality pinot noir; perhaps young vines and limited winemaking experience were responsible. Whatever, this is a lovely pinot, full of cherry and plum fruit, spice and integrated oak. It is great now, and will be dispatched quick smart, but will be superb in a few years. Screwcap. 14% alc. **Rating** 97 **To** 2028 $45 ❂

ŶŶŶŶŶ **Single Site Frankland Shiraz 2013** Shows the ability of Frankland River to produce cool climate shiraz with an admirable mix of full body and elegance; black cherry and blackberry are shot through with spice and pepper, quality oak bringing up the rear; has impeccable length and balance, and will richly reward patience. Screwcap. 14.5% alc. **Rating** 96 **To** 2043 $45 ❂

Third Reef Great Southern Shiraz 2014 Machine-harvested, destemmed and crushed to small open fermenters, extended post-ferment maceration, pressed to French oak (40% new) for 15 months maturation. You can immediately recognise the maceration, which has laid a mosaic of powdery tannins without in any way detracting from the truly delicious black and red cherry fruits, cedary French oak adding a burnish to the mosaic. Screwcap. 14% alc. **Rating** 95 **To** 2039 $30 ❂

Third Reef Great Southern Cabernet Sauvignon 2014 Excellent colour; unequivocally cabernet from go to whoa. Blackcurrant, black olive, bay leaf and lanolin. Great structure; supple and sweet-fruited but the tannin of grape and oak keep a strict line. A brilliant example of how good this variety can be in this region. Screwcap. 14.5% alc. **Rating** 95 **To** 2034 $30 ❂

Single Site Mount Barker Riesling 2015 It crashes lime and flowery apple flavour across your tongue. It's intense but eager to ensure that its message is understood; its flavours are essentially open and ready to be tucked into. Screwcap. 11.5% alc. **Rating** 94 **To** 2025 $28 CM ❂

Third Reef Great Southern Pinot Noir 2015 Immediately appealing, the aromas of cherry jam, blue plums and a green/herbal scent jumping from the glass. Bright and breezy flavours of youth will no doubt develop into something more complex with time, the light but firm astringency keeping the structure tight and trim. No issue with drinking now, and well worth a stint in the cellar. Screwcap. 14% alc. **Rating** 94 **To** 2023 $30 ❍

Quarram Rocks Great Southern Shiraz Cabernet 2014 75/25%. Matured for for 15 months in French oak (30% new). A bold, rich and complex blend, seemingly operating way below its expected price range; it's flush with blackberry, blackcurrant, plum and licorice, even the contribution of French oak pushed backstage. The price is embarrassingly low. Screwcap. 14.5% alc. **Rating** 94 **To** 2039 $21 ❍

Single Site Mount Barker Cabernet Sauvignon 2013 Deep colour; matured in French oak, which has certainly left its mark, adding a cedary/chocolatey note to the abundant plush cassis fruit, the savoury dried herb providing balance; the tannins are plentiful, but soft. Screwcap. 14% alc. **Rating** 94 **To** 2033 $45

🍷🍷🍷🍷🍷 **Third Reef Great Southern Chardonnay 2015** Rating 93 To 2023 $30
Quarram Rocks SBS 2015 Rating 92 To 2019 $21 ❍
Third Reef Great Southern Riesling 2015 Rating 91 To 2023 $22 CM ❍

Rockford ★★★★★

131 Krondorf Road, Tanunda, SA 5352 **Region** Barossa Valley
T (08) 8563 2720 **www**.rockfordwines.com.au **Open** 7 days 11–5
Winemaker Robert O'Callaghan, Ben Radford **Est.** 1984 **Dozens** NFP
Rockford can only be described as an icon, no matter how overused that word may be. It has a devoted band of customers who buy most of the wine through the cellar door or mail order (Rocky O'Callaghan's entrancing annual newsletter is like no other). Some wine is sold through restaurants, and there are two retailers in Sydney, and one each in Melbourne, Brisbane and Perth. Whether they will have the Basket Press Shiraz available is another matter; it is as scarce as Henschke Hill of Grace (but less expensive). Ben Radford, whom I first met in South Africa some years ago, has been entrenched as Rocky's right-hand man, and is destined to take over responsibility for winemaking when the time comes for Rocky to step back from an active role. Exports to the UK, Canada, Switzerland, Russia, Vietnam, South Korea, Singapore, Japan, Hong Kong, China and NZ.

🍷🍷🍷🍷🍷 **Basket Press Barossa Shiraz 2012** A great classic from a great vintage. At the end of the day, it's all about the grapes that come from loyal growers who shook hands with Rocky O'Callaghan many years ago. There are no magic tricks in the winery, just attention to detail. Cork. 14.2% alc. **Rating** 96 **To** 2047 $61 ❍
Black Shiraz NV Spanning a magnificent depth of maturity, the iconic Rockford Black is as multifaceted as ever, delivering the deep black fruits and pepper of Barossa shiraz, set against a backdrop of dark chocolate, licorice, game and even a hint of Christmas cake and orange rind. Impeccably handled tannins are softly integrated while promising great potential over the coming decade. Aug '15 disgorgement. Cork. 13.5% alc. **Rating** 95 **To** 2025 $63 TS

🍷🍷🍷🍷🍷 **Rod & Spur Barossa Valley Shiraz Cabernet 2013** Rating 91 To 2038 $35
Barossa Valley White Frontignac 2015 Rating 91 To 2020 $19 ❍
Moppa Springs Barossa Valley Grenache Mataro Shiraz 2012 Rating 90 To 2022 $28
Rifle Range Cabernet Sauvignon 2013 Rating 90 To 2030 $43

Rockridge Estate ★★★☆

PO Box 374, Kent Town, SA 5071 **Region** Clare Valley
T (08) 8358 0480 **www**.rockridgewines.com.au **Open** Not
Winemaker Justin Ardill (red), Peter Leske (white) **Est.** 2007 **Dozens** 5000 **Vyds** 40ha

In the Vine Pull Scheme of the 1980s, the 120ha Leasingham Wines vineyard in the hills immediately above the hamlet of Leasingham was removed. Partially replanted in '99, this precious block of terra rossa over deep limestone produces outstanding grapes. In 2007 owners Andrew Miller, Richard Yeend and Justin Ardill decided to retain a significant part of the crop to produce Riesling, Shiraz and Sparkling Riesling, purchasing sauvignon blanc from premium cool climate regions. The Rockridge range is produced exclusively for Independent Brands Australian (IBA) for sale in Cellarbrations, Bottle-O and IGA stores.

ΨΨΨΨΨ **Clare Valley Shiraz 2014** This is an extraordinary wine; sure it is full-bodied++, but it also has balance, even elegance, to its flood of black, blue and red fruits. Whether on a quality measure, or weight for age, it has to be one of the best value reds around. The Rockridge Shirazs vividly remind me of the '54 and '58 Baileys Shirazs I brought at the cellar door in '68. Screwcap. 14.5% alc. **Rating** 91 To 2040 $15 ❂

ΨΨΨΨ **Cellar Selection Watervale Shiraz 2014 Rating** 89 To 2100 $18 ❂
Watervale Riesling 2015 Rating 88 To 2020 $15 ❂

Rogers & Rufus ★★★

PO Box 10, Angaston, SA 5353 **Region** Barossa Valley
T (08) 8561 5200 **www.**rogersandrufus.com **Open** Not
Winemaker Andrew La Nauze **Est.** 2009 **Dozens** NFP
This is a decidedly under the bedcover partnership between Robert Hill-Smith and his immediate family, and Rupert and Jo Clevely, Rupert the former Veuve Clicquot director in Australia, but now running gastro pub group Geronimo Inns in London. Late in 2008 the Hill-Smiths and Clevelys decided (in their words) 'to do something fun together with a serious dip at Euro styled dry and savoury delicate rose using three site specific, old, low-yielding, dry-grown grenache sites from the Barossa floor'. Most of the production is sold in the US, with a small allocation marketed in Australia by Samuel Smith & Son.

ΨΨΨΨ **Barossa Grenache Rose 2015** Pale colour with a hint of spritz. Attractive mix of raspberried fruit and twiggier, spicier, more earthen influences. Finishes fresh. Screwcap. 12% alc. **Rating** 89 To 2016 $23 CM

Rolf Binder ★★★★★

Cnr Seppeltsfield Road/Stelzer Road, Tanunda, SA 5352 **Region** Barossa Valley
T (08) 8562 3300 **www.**rolfbinder.com **Open** Mon–Sat 10–4.30, Sun on long weekends
Winemaker Rolf Binder, Christa Deans **Est.** 1955 **Dozens** 39 500 **Vyds** 110ha
Rolf Binder, formerly known as Veritas, was established in the Barossa Valley in 1955 by Rolf Heinrich Binder. Today second-generation winemakers Rolf Binder and sister Christa Deans produce an extensive range of highly acclaimed wines from the estate and premium Barossa and Eden Valley vineyards. The Hahn family were among the original Barossa Valley settlers, and were heavily involved with grapegrowing from 1845. The JJ Hahn brand was created in 1997 as a joint venture between sixth-generation Barossans James and Jacqui Hahn and Rolf Binder. Since their retirement, Rolf has assumed ownership of the brand. Exports to all major markets.

ΨΨΨΨΨ **Heysen Barossa Valley Shiraz 2013** Deep, vivid colour; a complex and enticing bouquet has licorice, spice, black fruits and oak all competing for space, a battle of epic proportions on the palate. A full-bodied shiraz of the highest quality, thanks to not only its power, but also its balance and harmony, oak and tannins precisely weighted. Screwcap. 14.5% alc. **Rating** 97 To 2048 $70 ❂

ΨΨΨΨ **Hanisch Barossa Valley Shiraz 2013** A great example of the very best traditional style of Barossa Valley shiraz, precisely filled to the brim with black fruits, licorice, fine, but persistent, tannins and quality oak. It makes its point calmly, and won't brook any dissent. Cork. 14.5% alc. **Rating** 96 To 2048 $110

Eden Valley Riesling 2015 One of those wines stating the case for the Eden Valley to be rated/appreciated/preferred to the Clare Valley. But it's a specific case which doesn't of itself prove a general rule. Its special quality is the purity of the mouth-caressing lime juice, from one perspective powerful, from another delicate. Screwcap. 12.5% alc. **Rating** 95 **To** 2030 $25 ◐

JJ Hahn Western Ridge 1975 Planting Barossa Valley Shiraz 2013 This has some of the characters of its Heysen sibling, but in a lower key and intensity – which should come as no surprise given the price differential. The licorice/spice/black fruit triptych still stands proud, as does its intensity and length. 41yo vines at work. Screwcap. 14% alc. **Rating** 94 **To** 2033 $25 ◐

ɪɪɪɪ9 **Barossa Valley Shiraz 2014** Rating 92 To 2024 $22 ◐
Veritas Shiraz Malbec 2013 Rating 92 To 2038 $25 ◐
Rolf Binder's Bulls Blood Barossa Valley Shiraz Mataro Pressings 2013 Rating 92 To 2033 $50
Halliwell Barossa Valley Shiraz Grenache 2013 Rating 92 To 2023 $25 ◐
Heinrich Shiraz Mataro Grenache 2013 Rating 92 To 2028 $40
Eden Valley Montepulciano 2014 Rating 92 To 2027 $35
Rolf Binder's Bulls Blood Barossa Valley Shiraz Mataro Pressings 2012 Rating 91 To 2032 $50
Hales Barossa Valley Shiraz 2014 Rating 90 To 2024 $25
Selection Barossa Valley Shiraz 2014 Rating 90 To 2029 $18 ◐
Silvern a Greenock Shiraz 2014 Rating 90 To 2024 $18 ◐
Cabernet Sauvignon Merlot 2014 Rating 90 To 2021 $20 ◐

Romney Park Wines   ★★★★★

116 Johnsons Road, Balhannah, SA 5242 **Region** Adelaide Hills
T (08) 8398 0698 **www.**romneyparkwines.com.au **Open** By appt
Winemaker Rod and Rachel Short **Est.** 1997 **Dozens** 500 **Vyds** 2.8ha
Rod and Rachel Short planted chardonnay, shiraz and pinot noir in 1997. Yields are limited to 3.7–5 tonnes per hectare for the red wines, and 2–3 tonnes for the chardonnay. The vineyard is managed organically, with guinea fowl cleaning up the insects, all vines hand-picked and hand-pruned. In every way (including the wines) has the beauty of a hand-painted miniature. Exports to China.

ɪɪɪɪ9 **Adelaide Hills Pinot Noir 2013** Estate-grown, matured for 6 months in new and used French barriques. The bouquet is fragrant and welcoming, the palate with savoury, earthy complexity; a pinot all about texture and structure, not primary fruit. Diam. 13.8% alc. **Rating** 91 **To** 2020 $48

Ros Ritchie Wines   ★★★★☆

1974 Long Lane, Barwite, Vic 3722 **Region** Upper Goulburn
T 0448 900 541 **www.**rosritchiewines.com **Open** By appt
Winemaker Ros Ritchie **Est.** 2008 **Dozens** 2000 **Vyds** 5ha
Ros Ritchie was winemaker at the Ritchie family's Delatite winery from 1981 to 2006, but moved on to establish her own winery with husband John in '08. They lease a vineyard (merlot and cabernet sauvignon) close to Mansfield and source their white wines from growers who work in tandem with them to provide high quality grapes. Foremost are Gumbleton, Retief and Baxendale Vineyards, the last planted by the very experienced viticulturist Jim Baxendale (and wife Ruth) high above the King River Valley. All the vineyards are managed with minimal spray regimes. Exports to Hong Kong and China.

ɪɪɪɪɪ **Dead Man's Hill Vineyard Gewurztraminer 2015** A beautiful white wine. It seduces by balance, texture, flavour and length, though in the end it enchants by its own design. Chalk, crisp apple, lychee, rosewater and spice. It's distinct, it's defined, it has edge and yet it flows. Snap, crackle and glycerol pop. Absolutely a wine to covet. Screwcap. 13.5% alc. **Rating** 96 **To** 2025 $25 CM ◐

ŶŶŶŶŶ Barwite Vineyards Riesling 2015 Rating 93 To 2024 $25 CM ○
ŶŶŶŶŶ Barwite Vineyards Pinot Noir Rose 2015 Rating 90 To 2017 $20 CM ○

Rosabrook Margaret River Wine ★★★★★

1390 Rosa Brook Road, Rosabrook, WA 6285 **Region** Margaret River
T (08) 9368 4555 **www**.rosabrook.com.au **Open** Not
Winemaker Brian Fletcher **Est.** 1980 **Dozens** 12000 **Vyds** 25ha
The original Rosabrook estate vineyards were established between 1984 and '96. In 2007 Rosabrook relocated its vineyard to the northwestern end of the Margaret River wine region, overlooking Geographe Bay and the Indian Ocean. The warm days and cool nights, influenced by the ocean, result in slow, mild-ripening conditions. Exports to the UK, Sweden, Dubai, Hong Kong and China.

ŶŶŶŶŶ Single Vineyard Estate Chardonnay 2014 A brilliantly incisive and energetic chardonnay, with a complex smoky bouquet and exceptional drive to the palate, the colour still undeveloped; grapefruit and minerally acidity are intertwined, and the wine cries out for another 2–3 years in bottle to show its full majesty. Screwcap. 13% alc. **Rating** 96 **To** 2025 $45 ○
Single Vineyard Estate Cabernet Sauvignon 2013 Margaret River continues to throw down the gauntlet to Coonawarra, seeking to make Australia's best cabernets. This has all the autocratic cadences and flavours of pretenders to the Bordeaux throne: blackcurrant, cedar, earth and black olive flavours, with seamless, but persistent, tannins underpinning both the quality and length of the full-bodied palate. Screwcap. 14.5% alc. **Rating** 96 **To** 2043 $45 ○

ŶŶŶŶŶ Single Vineyard Estate Cabernet Sauvignon 2014 Rating 93 To 2034 $45
Single Vineyard Estate Tempranillo 2014 Rating 92 To 2029 $65
Cabernet Sauvignon 2014 Rating 90 To 2025 $25

 # Rosalie House Vineyard ★★★

135 Lavenders Road, Lilyvale, Qld 4352 **Region** Queensland Zone
T 0427 203 660 **Open** Not
Winemaker Steve Oliver **Est.** 2005 **Dozens** 600 **Vyds** 1.6ha
Doyle and Vicki Thompson are ex cotton farmers from the Moree district of NSW. In the early 1990s they sold their farm and purchased Rosalie House on the outskirts of Toowoomba, where their three daughters went to boarding school. Initially they continued with contract work on farms, along the way owning three hotels, selling the last in '13. In '05 they planted 0.5ha each of shiraz and chardonnay, 0.4ha grenache and 0.2ha of viognier, making their first wine in '08. They are at the point of finishing building the cellar door and farmhouse restaurant (Vicki is a chef) which are expected to open in the spring of '16.

Rosby ★★★★

122 Strikes Lane, Mudgee, NSW 2850 **Region** Mudgee
T (02) 6373 3856 **www**.rosby.com.au **Open** By appt
Winemaker Tim Stevens **Est.** 1996 **Dozens** 2000 **Vyds** 9ha
Gerald and Kay Norton-Knight have 4ha of shiraz and 2ha of cabernet sauvignon established on what is truly a unique site in Mudgee. Many vignerons like to think that their vineyard has special qualities, but in this instance the belief is well based. It is situated in a small valley, with unusual red basalt over a quartz gravel structure, encouraging deep root growth, making the use of water far less critical than normal. Tim Stevens of Huntington Estate has purchased some of the ample production, and makes the Rosby wines.

ŶŶŶŶŶ Mudgee Shiraz 2012 Plenty of depth to the fruit, no mean feat for the difficult vintage in Mudgee; the American oak is not oppressive, and indeed adds to the nuances of plum cake behind the overall freshness of the wine. Screwcap. 13.5% alc. **Rating** 90 **To** 2022 $17 ○

Mudgee Cabernet Sauvignon 2013 Mid-red; brambly fruit, mulberry and a leafy note; softly textured and well balanced. Screwcap. 13.5% alc. **Rating** 90 To 2020 $20 ✪

ΨΨΨΨ **Mudgee Shiraz 2013 Rating** 89 To 2017 $20
Mudgee Cabernet Sauvignon 2012 Rating 89 To 2022 $17 ✪

Rosemount Estate ★★★★★

114 Chaffeys Road, McLaren Vale, SA 5171 **Region** McLaren Vale
T (08) 8323 6220 **www**.rosemountestate.com **Open** Mon–Sat 10–5, Sun 11–5
Winemaker Matt Koch, Andrew Locke, Randall Cummins **Est.** 1888 **Dozens** NFP
Rosemount Estate has vineyards in McLaren Vale, Fleurieu, Coonawarra and Robe that are the anchor for its top-of-the-range wines. It also has access to other TWE estate-grown grapes, but the major part of its intake for the Diamond Label wines is supplied by contract growers across SA, NSW, Vic and WA. As the tasting notes show, the quality and range of the wines has greatly improved over the past few years as Rosemount Estate endeavours to undo the damage done to the brand around the new millennium. Ironically, the large onsite winery was closed in November 2014, winemaking transferred to other major wineries owned by TWE. Exports to all major markets.

ΨΨΨΨΨ **Balmoral McLaren Vale Syrah 2014** An icon of the region for decades with great parcels of grapes to choose from, matured for 10 months in French and American oak. Bright crimson-purple; iron fist in a velvet glove stuff; sumptuously fleshy black cherry and blackberry fruit fills the mouth in a split second, and the impression remains there long after it has been swallowed. Yet it's not the least bulky or extractive, just seductive. Screwcap. 14% alc. **Rating** 97 To 2039 $75 ✪

ΨΨΨΨΨ **Little Berry McLaren Vale Shiraz 2014** Radically new and appealing packaging/labels. Deep crimson-purple, this has a particularly complex bouquet, the full-bodied palate a mirror image of the bouquet, adding emphatic, savoury tannins to a wine bristling with attitude and energy. Will live for decades; bargain. Screwcap. 14% alc. **Rating** 95 To 2044 $25 ✪
GSM McLaren Vale Grenache Syrah Mourvedre 2014 A 70/17/13% blend, for long one of the go-to examples; it combines spicy/savoury notes on the one hand, cherry/raspberry on the other. Oak plays a silent tune, leaving it to gently earthy tannins to provide structure for what is a complex and complete wine. Screwcap. 14% alc. **Rating** 94 To 2024 $40

ΨΨΨΨΨ **Seven Trick Pony McLaren Vale Shiraz 2014 Rating** 92 To 2029 $20 ✪
Diamond Label Shiraz 2014 Rating 90 To 2020 $15 ✪

Rosenthal Wines ★★★★☆

24 Rockford Street, Denmark, WA 6333 **Region** Great Southern
T 0417 940 851 **www**.rosenthalwines.com.au **Open** Not
Winemaker Luke Eckersley, Coby Ladwig **Est.** 2001 **Dozens** 5000 **Vyds** 4ha
Rosenthal Wines is a small part of the much larger 180ha Springfield Park cattle stud situated between Bridgetown and Manjimup. Dr John Rosenthal acquired the property from Gerald and Marjorie Richings, who in 1997 had planted a small vineyard as a minor diversification. The Rosenthals extended the vineyard, which is equally divided between shiraz and cabernet sauvignon. The wines have had significant show success, chiefly in WA-based shows. Rosenthal Wines is now owned by Luke Eckersley (winemaker at Willoughby Park) and Coby Ladwig (winemaker at Rockcliffe). Exports to China.

ΨΨΨΨΨ **Richings Great Southern Chardonnay 2015** Hand-picked, chilled, whole bunch-pressed direct to French oak, wild-fermented, matured for 9 months. The bouquet has a deliberate touch of reduction quickly swept aside by the rapier intensity of the grapefruit and white peach fruit flavours; oak plays a pure support role, and doesn't overreach. Screwcap. 13.5% alc. **Rating** 95 To 2023 $42

The Marker Pemberton Manjimup Southern Forest Shiraz Cabernet 2013 Strong colour, deep and clear; medium to full-bodied, rich and purposeful, with layers of black cherry, plum, licorice and pepper, the tannins plentiful but soft, oak doing its duty. Screwcap. 14.5% alc. **Rating** 94 **To** 2033 $32

PPPPP The Marker Great Southern Riesling 2015 **Rating** 93 **To** 2027 $32
The Marker Great Southern Pinot Noir 2015 **Rating** 93 **To** 2030 $32
The Marker Great Southern Chardonnay 2014 **Rating** 91 **To** 2020 $32
Garten Series Cabernet Sauvignon 2014 **Rating** 91 **To** 2030 $25
Richings Pemberton Southern Forest Shiraz 2013 **Rating** 90 **To** 2023 $42

Rosenvale Wines ★★★★

467 Research Road, Nuriootpa, SA 5355 **Region** Barossa Valley
T 0407 390 788 **www**.rosenvale.com.au **Open** By appt
Winemaker James Rosenzweig, Philip Leggett **Est.** 1999 **Dozens** 3000 **Vyds** 100ha
The Rosenzweig family vineyards, some old and some new, are planted to riesling, semillon, chardonnay, grenache, shiraz, merlot and cabernet sauvignon. Most of the grapes are sold to other producers, but some are retained and vinified for release under the Rosenvale label. Exports to China.

PPPPP Old Vines Reserve Barossa Valley Semillon 2015 Sweet-but-lively fruit flavour and lots of it, cut with citrussy acidity. It feels unremarkable until the finish, where it soars on, forcing you to take greater notice. Screwcap. 13% alc. **Rating** 92 **To** 2022 $39 CM
Barossa Rose 2015 It's generous in its fruit and floral aspects and yet, more unusually, there's a suggestion of restraint too. It grabs your attention, but then makes you wait for more, which it duly delivers. Screwcap. 13% alc. **Rating** 92 **To** 2017 $24 CM ✪
Old Vines Reserve Barossa Valley Cabernet Sauvignon 2013 Sweet, dark fruit does the grunt work but chains of tannin add much-needed control. It's generous to a fault but it manages to make the style work. Diam. 14% alc. **Rating** 92 **To** 2026 $39 CM

PPPP Estate Barossa Cabernet Sauvignon 2014 **Rating** 89 **To** 2022 $24 CM
Barossa Cabernet Sauvignon Shiraz 2014 **Rating** 89 **To** 2024 $39 CM
Estate Barossa Shiraz 2014 **Rating** 88 **To** 2021 $24 CM
Barossa Grenache Shiraz Mataro 2014 **Rating** 88 **To** 2020 $24 CM

Rosily Vineyard ★★★★☆

871 Yelverton Road, Wilyabrup, WA 6284 **Region** Margaret River
T (08) 9755 6336 **www**.rosily.com.au **Open** 7 days Dec–Jan 11–5
Winemaker Mick Scott **Est.** 1994 **Dozens** 6100 **Vyds** 12.28ha
The partnership of Mick and Barb Scott and Ken and Dot Allan acquired the Rosily Vineyard site in 1994, and the vineyard was planted over three years to sauvignon blanc, semillon, chardonnay, cabernet sauvignon, merlot, shiraz, grenache and cabernet franc. The first crops were sold to other makers in the region, but by '99 Rosily had built a 120-tonne capacity winery. It has gone from strength to strength, all of its estate-grown grapes being vinified under the Rosily Vineyard label, substantially over-delivering for their prices.

PPPPP Margaret River Cabernet Sauvignon 2013 Excellent crimson-purple colour, this nails its colours to the mast the moment you take the first sip, its cassis and mulberry fruit driving through the long medium-bodied palate, meeting died in the wool cabernet tannins and notes of dried herb on the finish. Screwcap. 14% alc. **Rating** 95 **To** 2033 $25 ✪
Margaret River Chardonnay 2015 Smoky, nutty oak jumps out of the glass, but deeper aromas of grapefruit and white peach are not far behind. Glycerous mouthfeel embraces varietal citrus and stone fruit flavours. Beautifully balanced and very Margaret River. Screwcap. 13.5% alc. **Rating** 94 **To** 2022 $25 ✪

Margaret River Chardonnay 2014 The estate chardonnay block has seven clones planted, building complexity from the word go. Evident oak is no more important than the grapefruity acidity that enlivens the palate; above all, it has that special Margaret River depth. Screwcap. 13.5% alc. **Rating** 94 **To** 2022 $23 ❍

Margaret River Cabernet Sauvignon 2014 Fleshy aromas of blackcurrant and red fruit with a cedary overlay of French oak on a leafy background; flavours of cassis, black olive and green herb saturate the palate, the tannins sitting in perfect balance. Screwcap. 14% alc. **Rating** 94 **To** 2030 $25 ❍

🍷🍷🍷🍷🍷 **The Other Side of the Moon 2014** Rating 93 To 2022 $18 ❍
The Other Side of the Moon 2013 Rating 93 To 2023 $18 ❍
Margaret River Merlot 2012 Rating 92 To 2025 $20 ❍
Margaret River Shiraz 2010 Rating 91 To 2020 $23 ❍
Margaret River Sauvignon Blanc 2015 Rating 90 To 2016 $20 ❍
Margaret River Semillon Sauvignon Blanc 2015 Rating 90 To 2020 $20 ❍

Ross Hill Wines   ★★★★★

134 Wallace Lane, Orange, NSW 2800 **Region** Orange
T (02) 6365 3223 **www**.rosshillwines.com.au **Open** 7 days 10.30–5
Winemaker Phil Kerney **Est.** 1994 **Dozens** 25 000 **Vyds** 18.2ha
Peter and Terri Robson planted chardonnay, merlot, sauvignon blanc, cabernet franc, shiraz and pinot noir on north-facing slopes of the Griffen Road Vineyard in 1994. In 2007, their son James and his wife Chrissy joined the business, and the Wallace Lane Vineyard (pinot noir, sauvignon blanc and pinot gris) was planted next to the fruit packing shed which is now the winery. No insecticides are used, and the grapes are hand-picked and the vines are hand-pruned. Exports to Singapore, Bali, Hong Kong and China.

🍷🍷🍷🍷🍷 **The Griffin 2012** 41/51/8% cabernet sauvignon, merlot and cabernet franc. It's the kind of wine to give sturdiness a good name. It's imposingly structured but perfumed and ripe; the burst of peppermint through blackcurrant, mulberry and dried herbs takes the firmness of the foundations and adds a prettiness. Cedary/creamy oak essentially sits hand in glove. Witness this as it unfolds in the glass and it's difficult not to marvel. Screwcap. 14.5% alc. **Rating** 97 **To** 2040 $95 CM ❍

🍷🍷🍷🍷🍷 **Pinnacle Series Orange Shiraz 2014** Has a lot to say for itself. Juicy fruits spanning red, blue and black, pronounced pepper/spice notes, and oak playing a role throughout; the tannins, too, are carefully stage-managed. Screwcap. 14.1% alc. **Rating** 95 **To** 2030 $40

🍷🍷🍷🍷🍷 **Pinnacle Series Orange Sauvignon Blanc 2015** Rating 92 To 2017 $30
Pinnacle Series Orange Cabernet Sauvignon 2014 Rating 92 To 2029 $40
Pinnacle Series Orange Cabernet Franc 2014 Rating 92 To 2030 $40

 # Rouleur   ★★★★★

150 Bank Street, South Melbourne, Vic 3205 (postal) **Region** Yarra Valley/McLaren Vale
T 0419 100 929 **www**.rouleurwine.com **Open** Not
Winemaker Rob Hall, Matthew East **Est.** 2015 **Dozens** 700
Owner Matt East's interest in wine began at an early age, growing up in the Yarra Valley and watching his father plant a vineyard in Coldstream. Between February 1999 and December 2015 his daytime job was in sales and marketing, culminating in his appointment in '11 as National Sales Manager for Wirra Wirra Vineyards (which he had joined in '08). Following his retirement, he formed Mr East Wine Industry Consulting, and also set in motion the wheels of Rouleur. He lives in Melbourne, with the Yarra within easy striking distance, and has an agreement with Rob Hall to make the wines and help source the grapes. He also has wines made in McLaren Vale, using the facilities at Dennis Winery, drawing on the expertise/assistance of personal winemaking friends when needed. Back in Melbourne he is transforming a dilapidated milk bar in North Melbourne into the inner city cellar door for Rouleur.

ＹＹＹＹＹ **Yarra Valley Chardonnay 2015** Hand-picked, 80% whole bunch-pressed, 20% fermented on skins for 5 days, matured in French oak (25% new). A notably elegant style with white peach, nectarine and melon; the oak isn't obvious, even though it has played a major role, likewise the fermentation of part on skins. All coherent and empathetic. Screwcap. 12.5% alc. **Rating** 95 **To** 2024 $32 ⊙

Yarra Valley Pinot Noir 2015 30yo vines, 20% whole bunches, 80% crushed on top, open-fermented, matured in French oak (25% new) for 9 months. Predominantly cherry, some plum, fruit supported on the palate by high quality tannins and oak extract. A very good wine reflecting the vintage. Screwcap. 13% alc. **Rating** 95 **To** 2027 $32 ⊙

McLaren Vale Grenache 2015 A delicious grenache with a lighter touch than many, the whole bunch component providing perfume. A great deal of thought went into making 85 dozen, and the supple cascade of red fruits for soonish drinking are the reward. Screwcap. 14.5% alc. **Rating** 94 **To** 2025 $32

ＹＹＹＹＹ **McLaren Vale Grenache 2014 Rating** 92 **To** 2025 $32

Route du Van

PO Box 1465, Warrnambool, Vic 3280 **Region** Various Vic
T (03) 5561 7422 **www**.routeduvan.com **Open** Not
Winemaker Tod Dexter **Est.** 2010 **Dozens** 8000
The Dexter (Todd and Debbie) and Bird (Ian and Ruth, David and Marie) families have been making or selling wine for over 30 years. They were holidaying in the picturesque vineyards and ancient Bastide villages of southwest France when they decided to do something new that was all about fun: fun for them, and fun for the consumers who bought their wines, which would have a distinctive southern French feel to them. The prices are also friendly, bistros one of the target markets. The business is obviously enjoying great success, production up from 3500 dozen to its present level off the back of expanded export markets. Exports to the UK, the US, Norway, Sweden and Poland.

ＹＹＹＹＹ **Yarra Valley Chardonnay 2013** It presents a refreshing face to the world, and a pleasing one. You'd be happy for it to take a seat at your dining table. Screwcap. 13% alc. **Rating** 90 **To** 2020 $27 CM

King Valley Gioia Bianco 2015 Fruit-driven first and foremost, but with briney, spicy edges to give it an extra kick along. Classy in an understated way. Screwcap. 12.5% alc. **Rating** 90 **To** 2017 $18 CM ⊙

Heathcote Shiraz 2014 Freshness is the key. There's a sizeable serve of fruit here and it's been given free rein; there isn't a great deal of tannin or oak, the result vibrant with various (delicious) berries, earth and dried spices. Refreshing face of Heathcote shiraz. Screwcap. 13.9% alc. **Rating** 90 **To** 2021 $20 CM ⊙

Rowanston on the Track

2710 Burke & Wills Track, Glenhope, Vic 3444 **Region** Macedon Ranges
T (03) 5425 5492 **www**.rowanston.com **Open** 7 days 10–5
Winemaker Laura Sparrow, John Frederiksen **Est.** 2003 **Dozens** 5000 **Vyds** 9.3ha
John and Marilyn Frederiksen are no strangers to grapegrowing and winemaking in the Macedon Ranges. They founded Metcalfe Valley Vineyard in 1995, planting 5.6ha of shiraz and going on to win gold medals at local wine shows. They sold the vineyard in early 2003 and moved to their new property, which now has over 9ha of vines (shiraz, riesling, sauvignon blanc, merlot and pinot noir). The heavy red soils and basalt ridges hold moisture, which allows watering to be kept to a minimum. Rowanston has joined the Wine Export Initiative (WEXI), a co-operative of 36 small wineries across Australia that has recently opened two retail outlets in Singapore. Exports to Hong Kong, Singapore and China.

ＹＹＹＹ **Macedon Ranges Riesling 2015** Hand-picked, whole bunch-pressed, cultured yeast, cool-fermented in stainless steel. This is an embryonic wine, everything tuned down by the used of whole bunch-pressing. All it needs to transform itself is time. Screwcap. 13% alc. **Rating** 89 **To** 2025 $22

Heathcote Viognier 2012 Hand-picked, whole bunch-pressed, cultured yeast, cool-fermented in stainless steel. Has defied convention by having improved with age as a dry white wine, but still has little varietal character. Screwcap. 14% alc. **Rating** 88 **To** 2017 $20

Rowlee Wines

19 Lake Canobolas Road, Orange, NSW 2800 **Region** Orange
T 0438 059 108 **www**.rowleewines.com.au **Open** By appt
Winemaker PJ Charteris (Consultant) **Est.** 2000 **Dozens** 1600 **Vyds** 7.8ha
Rowlee first evolved as a grazing property of 2000 acres in the 1850s. It is now 80 acres, but still with the original homestead built circa 1880. The property has retired from its grazing days and is now home to 20 acres of vineyards, first planted in 2000 by the Samodol family. Varieties include pinot noir, pinot gris, nebbiolo, arneis, chardonnay, riesling and sauvignon blanc. The Rowlee Vineyard is situated on the sloping northerly aspect of an extinct volcano, Mt Canobolas, and at 920m is rich in basalt soils. Wine production commenced in 2013, in partnership with viticulturist Tim Esson and family.

 Orange Sauvignon Blanc 2014 A wine with a particularly powerful drive to and through the length of the palate after a slightly challenging bouquet. A lateral take on the undoubted suitability of the Orange climate for sauvignon blanc. Screwcap. 13% alc. **Rating** 94 **To** 2016 $20 ○

Orange Pinot Gris 2014 Rating 90 **To** 2017 $25
Orange Arneis 2014 Rating 90 **To** 2016 $28 CM

Ruckus Estate ★★★★★

PO Box 167, Penola, SA 5277 **Region** Wrattonbully
T 0437 190 244 **www**.ruckusestate.com **Open** Not
Winemaker Sue Bell **Est.** 2000 **Dozens** 650 **Vyds** 40ha
Ruckus Estate was established in 2000 after a protracted search for high quality viticultural land, with a particular focus on the production of merlot utilising recently released clones that hold the promise of producing wine of a quality not previously seen. However, it's not a case of all eggs in the same basket, for malbec, cabernet sauvignon and shiraz have also been planted. It was not until '13 that the first small amount of wine was made (most of the grapes were, and will continue to be, sold to other winemakers). Given the quality of the Merite Merlot, the plan to increase production to 2000 dozen should be achieved with ease, with Shiraz Malbec released in May '16, and Cabernet Sauvignon in the pipeline.

Single Vineyard Wrattonbully Merite Merlot 2013 Two clones were selected from the four planted on the 18ha of estate merlot, and a partial whole bunch, wild yeast, open fermentation was basket-pressed to French oak (50% new). The wine has a brightness and lightness of touch that can elude Wrattonbully vignerons; the cassis fruit has a distinct black olive/bay leaf character, the complexity augmented by the French oak. Cork. 13.5% alc. **Rating** 96 **To** 2028 $50 ○

Rudderless ★★★★★

Victory Hotel, Main South Road, Sellicks Beach, SA 5174 **Region** McLaren Vale
T (08) 8556 3083 **www**.victoryhotel.com.au **Open** 7 days
Winemaker Pete Fraser (Contract) **Est.** 2004 **Dozens** 450 **Vyds** 2ha
It's a long story how Doug Govan, owner of the Victory Hotel (circa 1858), came to choose the name Rudderless for his vineyard. The vineyard, planted to shiraz, graciano, grenache, malbec, mataro and viognier, surrounds the hotel, which is situated in the foothills of the Southern Willunga Escarpment as it falls into the sea. The wines are mostly sold through the Victory Hotel, where the laidback Doug Govan keeps a low profile.

 Sellicks Hill McLaren Vale Shiraz 2013 Dense blackberried fruit flavour comes wrapped in velvety, creamy vanilla. It's not rocket science but it's both highly effective and high quality. Length of flavour through the finish is upper echelon. Screwcap. 14.5% alc. **Rating** 96 **To** 2032 $35 CM ⭕

Sellicks Hill McLaren Vale Malbec 2013 A leathery voluptuousness sweeps spice, earth and coffee-cream notes/textures extravagantly through the palate. Beautifully fine, filigreed tannin keeping everything where it should be. Gorgeous release. Screwcap. 14% alc. **Rating** 96 **To** 2028 $35 CM ⭕

🍷🍷🍷🍷︎ **Sellicks Hill McLaren Vale Graciano 2013** Rating 93 **To** 2028 $35
Sellicks Hill McLaren Vale Mataro 2013 Rating 92 **To** 2023 $35 CM

Rusty Bike Wines   ★★★☆

27 Range Road South, Houghton, SA 5131 **Region** Adelaide Hills
T 0420 841 404 **www**.rustybike.com.au **Open** Not
Winemaker Michael Goulden **Est.** 2010 **Dozens** 400

Michael Goulden persuaded his wife Lesley that it's possible to fit in winemaking on a (small) commercial scale with full-time work in medical science and family. The name Rusty Bike came after consuming a few glasses of wine and looking at an old rusty bike leaning on their garden fence. If you look at the website, the bike is indeed very rusty. Michael is a self-taught winemaker, relying on trusty mates to hand-pick the grapes and help with the winemaking and bottling when the time comes. He is always looking for small amounts of grapes from well-run vineyards to buy, and the sources do vary somewhat from year to year.

🍷🍷🍷🍷︎ **The Dragster Shiraz 2014** Matured for 12 months in American oak (40% new). Good colour; there's much to like in this wine, even if (or due to) its traditional make-up. The barrels are made by AP John, a master with American oak, and the wine fits seamlessly into the fabric of the perfectly ripened shiraz fruit. Screwcap. 14% alc. **Rating** 93 **To** 2029 $25 ⭕

🍷🍷🍷🍷 **The Tricycle Rose 2015** Rating 89 **To** 2017 $22

Rusty Mutt   ★★★★

26 Columbia Avenue, Clapham, SA 5062 (postal) **Region** McLaren Vale
T 0402 050 820 **www**.rustymutt.com.au **Open** Not
Winemaker Scott Heidrich **Est.** 2009 **Dozens** 800

Scott Heidrich has lived under the shadow of Geoff Merrill for 20 years, but has partially emerged into the sunlight with his virtual micro-winery. Back in 2006 close friends and family (Nicole and Alan Francis, Stuart Evans, David Lipman and Phil Cole) persuaded Scott to take advantage of the wonderful quality of the grapes that year and make a small batch of Shiraz. The wines are made at a friend's micro-winery in McLaren Flat. The name Rusty Mutt comes from Scott's interest in Chinese astrology, and feng shui; Scott was born in the year of the dog, with the dominant element being metal, hence Rusty Mutt. What the ownership group doesn't drink is sold through fine wine retailers and selected restaurants, with a small amount exported to the UK, Singapore and China.

🍷🍷🍷🍷︎ **Rocky Ox GSM 2014** 60/30/10%, open-fermented, 10–12 days on skins, matured for 12 months in used French and American oak. Has more structure and texture than many, this going hand in hand with more savoury tannins than usual, and no hint of confected fruit. Although slightly left field, I think it works well. Screwcap. 14.5% alc. **Rating** 91 **To** 2022 $29

🍷🍷🍷🍷 **Original Shiraz 2013** Rating 88 **To** 2028 $29

Rutherglen Estates   ★★★★☆

Tuileries, 13 Drummond Street, Rutherglen, Vic 3685 **Region** Rutherglen
T (02) 6032 7999 **www**.rutherglenestates.com.au **Open** 7 days 10–5.30
Winemaker Marc Scalzo **Est.** 1997 **Dozens** 12000 **Vyds** 26.5ha

Rutherglen Estates is one of the larger growers in the region. The focus of the business has changed: it has reduced its own fruit intake while maintaining its contract processing.

Production has turned to table wine made from parcels of fruit hand-selected from five Rutherglen vineyard sites. Rhône and Mediterranean varieties such as durif, viognier, shiraz and sangiovese are a move away from traditional varieties, as are alternative varieties including zinfandel, fiano and savagnin. Exports to the UK, the US, Canada, Thailand and China.

🍷🍷🍷🍷🍷 **Single Vineyard Arneis 2015** A seriously good wine; there is depth to the palate, but without any coarseness. Citrus, stone fruit and pear all intermingle, the all-important acidity on the finish perfectly balanced. Whither now? I don't know, but will be an interested observer if I get the chance. Gold medal Victorian Wines Show '15. Screwcap. 13.5% alc. **Rating** 95 **To** 2028 $18 🟠

🍷🍷🍷🍷🍷 **Renaissance Durif 2013** Rating 92 To 2030 $50
Single Vineyard Tempranillo 2014 Rating 91 To 2024 $22 🟠
Renaissance Viognier Roussanne Marsanne 2014 Rating 90 To 2017 $32

Rymill Coonawarra   ★★★★★

Riddoch Highway, Coonawarra, SA 5263 **Region** Coonawarra
T (08) 8736 5001 **www.**rymill.com.au **Open** 7 days 10–5
Winemaker Sandrine Gimon, Federico Saina **Est.** 1974 **Dozens** 40 000 **Vyds** 144ha
The Rymills are descendants of John Riddoch and have long owned some of the finest Coonawarra soil, upon which they have grown grapes since 1970. Champagne-trained Sandrine Gimon is a European version of a Flying Winemaker, having managed a winery in Bordeaux, and made wine in Champagne, Languedoc, Romania and WA. Sandrine became an Australian citizen in 2011. The winery building also houses the cellar door and art exhibitions, which, together with viewing platforms over the winery, make it a must-see destination for tourists. Exports to all major markets.

🍷🍷🍷🍷🍷 **The Surveyor Cabernet Sauvignon 2013** As compelling as it is commanding. It would be brutish if it wasn't so svelte. Blackcurrant, black olive, loganberry and fresh mint notes rush through to the two-thirds point of the palate, where tannin has marshalled in force. A star of a wine. A long life is in store. Diam. 14.5% alc. **Rating** 97 **To** 2035 $90 CM 🟠

🍷🍷🍷🍷🍷 **Shiraz 2013** This speaks volumes about its variety and place, and little about its vinification, very sensibly. Bright crimson-purple through to the rim; the bouquet and palate bring spice, pepper and French oak to the party; it is medium-bodied, its black cherry and blackberry fruits with fine-grained tannins and a reprise of the oak. Diam. 14.5% alc. **Rating** 95 **To** 2033 $32 🟠
Cabernet Sauvignon 2013 Clean and pure. A flood of blackcurrant and mint with subtle tobacco notes drifting over the top. Classic flavour profile and with the structure to match, though it remains fluid, even seductive. Will mature gracefully and well. Diam. 14.5% alc. **Rating** 94 **To** 2030 $32 CM

🍷🍷🍷🍷🍷 **Sandstone Cabernet Sauvignon 2013** Rating 93 To 2025 $60 CM
GT Gewurztraminer 2015 Rating 91 To 2018 $20 🟠
The Dark Horse Cabernet Sauvignon 2014 Rating 90 To 2025 $24

Saddler's Creek   ★★★★★

Marrowbone Road, Pokolbin, NSW 2320 **Region** Hunter Valley
T (02) 4991 1770 **www.**saddlerscreek.com **Open** 7 days 10–5
Winemaker Brett Woodward **Est.** 1989 **Dozens** 6000 **Vyds** 10ha
Saddler's Creek is a boutique winery that is little known outside the Hunter Valley but has built a loyal following of dedicated supporters. It came onto the scene over 25 years ago with some rich, bold wines, and maintains this style today. Fruit is sourced from the Hunter Valley and Langhorne Creek, with occasional forays into other premium regions.

🍷🍷🍷🍷🍷 **Aged Release Classic Hunter Semillon 2009** Gleaming straw-
green; still amazingly fresh and youthful, but has developed another leg to its

lemon/citrus/lemongrass fruit flavours, acidity there as ever. The treasure trove of mature Hunter Valley semillons continues to grow. Screwcap. 11% alc. **Rating** 96 To 2024 $40 ☉

Aged Release Classic Hunter Semillon 2004 Gleaming gold, tinged with green; a screwcapped 12yo semillon which has entered the plateau of a long life based on lightly buttered toast and a nice whisk of honey, then an auto-cleansing finish of (seemingly) soft acidity. Screwcap. 10.5% alc. **Rating** 96 **To** 2024 $46 ☉

Ryan's Reserve Vanessa's Vineyard Shiraz 2014 Excellent hue; this is at the elegant end of the '14 vintage scale, and none the worse for that. It is deliciously juicy on the first sip, and then proceeds to add both texture and flavour to its fruit foundation, with earthy flecks of (or with) fine tannins on the finish and aftertaste. Screwcap. 13.5% alc. **Rating** 95 **To** 2039 $40

Ryan's Reserve Stephanie's Vineyard Chardonnay 2015 Picked that little bit earlier than the Reserve, and with a hint of struck match, it has the edge its sibling lacks, adding to the length of its white peach, nectarine and cashew flavours. Screwcap. 12.8% alc. **Rating** 94 **To** 2023 $36

♟♟♟♟♟ **Wheels Rose 2015** Rating 93 To 2017 $24 ☉
Reserve Chardonnay 2015 Rating 90 To 2021 $36
Single Vineyard Hunter Shiraz 2014 Rating 90 To 2028 $55
Reserve Langhorne Cabernet 2013 Rating 90 To 2028 $65

🍇 Sailor Seeks Horse ★★★★☆

102 Armstrongs Road, Cradoc, Tas 7109 **Region** Southern Tasmania
T 0418 471120 www.sailorseekshorse.com.au **Open** Not
Winemaker Paul and Gilli Lipscombe **Est.** 2010 **Dozens** 400 **Vyds** 6.5ha
While I was given comprehensive information about the seriously interesting careers of Paul and Gilli Lipscombe, and about their vineyard, I am none the wiser about the highly unusual and very catchy name. The story began in 2005 when they resigned from their (unspecified) jobs in London, did a vintage in Languedoc, and then headed to Margaret River to study oenology and viticulture. While combining study and work, their goal was to learn as much as possible about pinot noir. They worked in large, small, biodynamic, conventional, minimum and maximum intervention vineyards and wineries, Woodlands, Xanadu, Beaux Freres, Chehalem and Mt Difficulty all household names. By '10 they were in Tasmania working for Julian Alcorso's Winemaking Tasmania and found a derelict vineyard that had never cropped, having been abandoned not long after being planted in '05. It was in the Huon Valley, precisely where they had aimed to begin. They are working as winemakers for Home Hill and manage Jim Chatto's vineyard in Glaziers Bay – if that doesn't mean anything to you, have a look at their entries. Exports to Singapore.

♟♟♟♟♟ **Pinot Noir 2013** Wild yeast, 10% whole bunches, unfined. Pinot noir like this is never a fluke. It's good and it knows it. Aroma up to here, upright posture, intimidatingly pretty. Slip of a thing but it makes it work. Boysenberry, cranberry and red cherry. Undergrowth. Herbs. Smoky reduction. Brings out the silk and wraps it around the glass. Juicy, tangy length. Tasmanian pinot noir to hunt down and devour. Screwcap. 12.8% alc. **Rating** 96 **To** 2025 $45 CM ☉

♟♟♟♟♟ **Pinot Noir 2014** Rating 92 To 2021 $48

St Anne's Vineyards ★★★

Cnr Perricoota Road/24 Lane, Moama, NSW 2731 **Region** Perricoota
T (03) 5480 0099 www.stanneswinery.com.au **Open** 7 days 9–5
Winemaker Richard McLean **Est.** 1972 **Dozens** 80 000 **Vyds** 182ha
The McLean family has a multi-pronged grapegrowing and winemaking business, with 182ha of vines on the Murray River. All the mainstream varieties are grown, the lion's share to chardonnay, shiraz, cabernet sauvignon and merlot, with lesser quantities of semillon, sauvignon blanc, durif and petit verdot. There is also a very small planting at Myrniong in the Pentland Hills, a 50-minute drive from the heart of Melbourne, where the main cellar door

is situated. There are three other cellar doors: Moama (Cnr 24 Lane and Perricoota Road), Lorne (150 Mount Joy Parade) and Echuca (53 Murray Esplanade). Exports to China.

St Hallett ★★★★★

St Hallett Road, Tanunda, SA 5352 **Region** Barossa
T (08) 8563 7000 **www**.sthallett.com.au **Open** 7 days 10–5
Winemaker Toby Barlow, Shelley Cox, Darin Kinzie **Est.** 1944 **Dozens** 210 000
St Hallett sources all grapes from within the Barossa GI, and is synonymous with the region's icon variety, shiraz. Old Block is the ultra-premium leader of the band (using old-vine grapes from Lyndoch and Eden Valley), supported by Blackwell (Greenock, Ebenezer and Seppeltsfield). The winemaking team headed by Toby Barlow continues to explore the geographical, geological and climatic diversity of the Barossa, manifested through individual processing of all vineyards and single vineyard releases. Exports to all major markets.

🍷🍷🍷🍷🍷 **Old Block Barossa Shiraz 2013** A picture of good health, balance, flavour and length. It bristles with freshness, with power, with authority. The fruit – blueberry and blackberry, splashed with earth and ground coffee – is soft, but the tannin is ropey and firm, like arms around a bountiful harvest. A very long life is in store. Screwcap. 13.9% alc. **Rating** 97 **To** 2040 $100 CM ✪

🍷🍷🍷🍷🍷 **Single Vineyard Release Scholz Estate Barossa Valley Shiraz 2015** A monster of fruit and tannin and with the length to match. St Hallett is in mighty form. Blue and black berries, pepper, wood spice, cocoa and coal. Oak is not a major player. Tannin certainly is. This is the kind of wine that could take your breath away. Screwcap. 14.5% alc. **Rating** 96 **To** 2040 $50 CM ✪
Single Vineyard Release Materne Barossa Valley Shiraz 2015 It gets you in a bear hug. It's an embracing wine. It's bold with blackberried, coal-like fruit, the presence of smoky oak detectable, but only just; it has largely disappeared into the folds of darkness. Floral notes lift from the wine as it slowly opens up. Monumental. Screwcap. 14.5% alc. **Rating** 96 **To** 2040 $50 CM ✪
Single Vineyard Release Wyncroft Eden Valley Shiraz 2015 Toasty oak, clove notes, gunmetal, pepper and ample, dark, blackberried fruit. All in perfect proportion. All begging to be both admired and consumed. This is value with a capital V. From the first sniff to the final linger of flavour, it nails it. Screwcap. 14% alc. **Rating** 96 **To** 2030 $30 CM ✪
Single Vineyard Release Dawkins Eden Valley Shiraz 2015 The prettiness of this wine is quite extraordinary. It's floral and blueberried and it just bounces from the glass, happy to see you, eager to create an attractive first impression. It does, and then continues on seamlessly, the fruit and the weight feeling 'just right' throughout. Screwcap. 13.5% alc. **Rating** 95 **To** 2035 $50 CM
Butcher's Cart Barossa Shiraz 2014 Barossa shiraz to a tee. Rich, bold, awash with blackberried flavour, kissed with creamy/toasty oak. The volume of flavour sees firmish tannin folded through the fruit without the slightest bulge. In the zone, as they say. Screwcap. 14% alc. **Rating** 94 **To** 2028 $30 CM ✪
Blackwell Barossa Shiraz 2014 This sits on the luscious side of the ledger. It's all about sweet, dark-berried fruit, fresh and more-ish, with a melt of tannin and an easy flow of flavour through the finish. Oak is not prominent; it's all about pure Barossa shiraz. Screwcap. 14.5% alc. **Rating** 94 **To** 2030 $40 CM

🍷🍷🍷🍷🍷 **Garden of Eden Barossa Shiraz 2015** Rating 93 To 2025 $25 CM ✪
Mattschoss Eden Valley Shiraz 2015 Rating 93 To 2030 $50 CM
Old Vine Barossa Grenache 2015 Rating 93 To 2021 $30 CM
Faith Barossa Shiraz 2015 Rating 92 To 2024 $19 CM ✪
Butcher's Cart Barossa Shiraz 2013 Rating 92 To 2033 $30
Eden Valley Riesling 2015 Rating 91 To 2028 $19 ✪
Western Front Barossa Shiraz 2015 Rating 91 To 2021 $15 CM ✪
Black Clay Barossa Valley Shiraz 2015 Rating 91 To 2021 $18 CM ✪
Barossa Touriga Nacional 2014 Rating 91 To 2021 $30 CM

St Huberts

Cnr Maroondah Highway/St Huberts Road, Coldstream, Vic 3770 **Region** Yarra Valley
T (03) 5960 7096 **www**.sthuberts.com.au **Open** 7 days 10–5
Winemaker Greg Jarratt **Est.** 1966 **Dozens** NFP **Vyds** 20.49ha
The St Huberts of today has a rich 19th century history, not least in its success at the 1881
Melbourne International Exhibition, which featured every type of agricultural and industrial
product. The wine section alone attracted 711 entries. The Emperor of Germany offered a
Grand Prize, a silver gilt epergne, for the most meritorious exhibit in the show. A St Huberts
wine won the wine section, then competed against objects as diverse as felt hats and steam
engines to wine the Emperor's Prize, featured on its label for decades thereafter. Like other
Yarra Valley wineries, it dropped from sight at the start of the 20th century, was reborn in 1966,
and after several changes of ownership, became part of what today is TWE. The wines are
made at Coldstream Hills, but have their own, very different, focus. St Huberts is dominated by
Cabernet and the single vineyard Roussanne. Its grapes come from warmer sites, particularly
the valley floor, that are part owned and part under contract. Oak use, too, is different, albeit
100% French.

Yarra Valley Roussanne 2015 Has that Yarra Valley focus and length, opening
with apple, pear and mouthwatering citrussy/flinty acidity on the long finish. A
cut above the rest, and certain to age gracefully (as Yeringberg has proven over the
years). Screwcap. 12.5% alc. **Rating** 96 **To** 2023 $33 ✪

Yarra Valley Chardonnay 2014 Yarra Valley stamped in large letters. It has
greater than average intensity and purity, the use of oak more restrained – a
means to an end, not an end in itself; grapefruit opens the batting, and remains
undefeated, although white peach/stone fruit nuances also help the cause of the
varietal fruit expression. Screwcap. 13% alc. **Rating** 95 **To** 2024 $27 ✪

Hubert the Stag Yarra Valley Pinot Noir 2015 Early bottling, and tasting
soon thereafter, hasn't robbed the stag of its antlers. It has all the ingredients to
flourish in bottle, and needs no excuses for its depth of perfectly balanced plum-
infused flavours backed by ripe, fine tannins and a feather duster of French oak.
Screwcap. 13% alc. **Rating** 95 **To** 2030 $24 ✪

Yarra Valley Cabernet Merlot 2014 Bright crimson; the low yield of the
vintage has underwritten the intensity of the wine without diminishing its
elegance and poise; cassis fruit is the white stallion charging through the vinous
landscape, supple tannins and subtle French oak in close attendance. A wine that
stands out the moment you taste it. Screwcap. 13% alc. **Rating** 95 **To** 2034 $27 ✪

Yarra Valley Late Harvest Viognier 2015 Combines fruit, acid and alcohol
in a balanced and harmonious package; dried fruits, Christmas spices, apricot and
citrus all run through a palate that is only moderately sweet. 375m. Screwcap.
10% alc. **Rating** 94 **To** 2020 $27 ✪

Yarra Valley Cabernet Sauvignon 2014 **Rating** 93 **To** 2028 $35 CM

St Ignatius Vineyard ★★★★

5434 Sunraysia Highway, Lamplough, Vic 3352 **Region** Pyrenees
T (03) 5465 3542 **www**.stignatiusvineyard.com.au **Open** 7 days 10–5
Winemaker Enrique Diaz **Est.** 1992 **Dozens** 2000 **Vyds** 9ha
Silvia Diaz and husband Enrique began establishing their vineyard (shiraz, cabernet sauvignon,
malbec and chardonnay), winery and restaurant complex in 1992. The vineyard has received
three primary production awards. Wines are released under the Hangmans Gully label. Exports
to the UK.

Contemplation Shiraz 2012 Estate-grown, matured for 12 months in American
oak. Good depth to the colour heralds a powerful, full-blown shiraz in typical
St Ignatius style, redolent with black fruits, licorice and plum cake surrounded by
plush tannins and vanillan oak. Cork. 14% alc. **Rating** 91 **To** 2032 $60

Contemplation Reserve Shiraz 2013 Deep, bright colour; better balanced and structured than the '14, with a convincing interplay between juicy red and black fruits, licorice and a flick of bramble; the length and balance are likewise good. Cork. 15% alc. **Rating** 90 **To** 2028 $50

ㅝㅝㅝㅝ   Contemplation Shiraz 2011 Rating 89 To 2021 $28
Contemplation Reserve Shiraz 2014 Rating 88 To 2024 $40

St John's Road   ★★★★★
Kapunda-Truro Road, St Kitts, SA, 5356 **Region** Barossa Valley
T (08) 8362 8622 **www.**stjohnsroad.com **Open** Not
Winemaker Phil Lehmann **Est.** 2002 **Dozens** 20000 **Vyds** 20ha
St John's Road is now part of WD Wines Pty Ltd, which also owns Hesketh Wine Company and Parker Coonawarra Estate. After drifting for a while following the death of founder Martin Rawlinson, St John's Road is now back in the game, the vineyards increased to 20ha, production and quality also rising. Exports to the UK, Canada and Europe.

ㅝㅝㅝㅝㅝ   Block 3 Old Vine 1935 Plantings Resurrection Vineyard Barossa Valley Shiraz 2014 From a very early ripening block, matured in French hogsheads. Has class stamped all over it: mouthfilling, yet perfectly balanced and harmonious, fruit, oak and tannins all on the one page. Screwcap. 14.5% alc. **Rating** 95 **To** 2049 $38
Block 8 Maywald Clone Resurrection Vineyard Barossa Valley Shiraz 2014 Matured in used French hogsheads. The vineyard was planted with cuttings from 100+yo vines known as the Maywald Selection, the decision to use old oak to highlight the vibrantly fragrant black fruits resulting in a totally delicious spring-fresh wine. Screwcap. 12.7% alc. **Rating** 95 **To** 2034 $38

ㅝㅝㅝㅝㅚ   Workhorse Shiraz Cabernet 2014 Rating 92 To 2024 $22 CM ✪
Line & Length Cabernet 2014 Rating 92 To 2024 $22 CM ✪
Peace of Eden Riesling 2015 Rating 91 To 2024 $22 CM ✪
PL Wild Yeast Reversed Ferment Eden Valley Chardonnay 2014
Rating 91 To 2020 $38
Motley Bunch GMS 2014 Rating 91 To 2023 $22 CM ✪
Blood & Courage Barossa Shiraz 2014 Rating 90 To 2021 $22 CM

St Leonards Vineyard   ★★★★☆
St Leonards Road, Wahgunyah, Vic 3687 **Region** Rutherglen
T 1800 021 621 **www.**stleonardswine.com.au **Open** Thurs–Sun 10–5
Winemaker Nick Brown, Chloe Earl **Est.** 1860 **Dozens** 5000 **Vyds** 12ha
An old favourite, relaunched in late 1997 with a range of premium wines cleverly marketed through an attractive cellar door and bistro at the historic winery on the banks of the Murray. It is run by Eliza Brown (CEO), sister Angela (online communications manager) and brother Nick (vineyard and winery manager). They are perhaps better known as the trio who fulfil the same roles at All Saints Estate. Exports to the UK and the US.

ㅝㅝㅝㅝㅝ   Wahgunyah Shiraz 2013 The flagship of the St Leonards table wines, 15 barriques selected for this wine. It shows its breeding, with red and black fruits contributing in tandem on the impressively long palate that has the hallmark of barrel ferment adding to its appeal. Screwcap. 14.4% alc. **Rating** 95 **To** 2028 $62

ㅝㅝㅝㅝㅚ   Shiraz 2013 Rating 90 To 2020 $27
Cabernet Franc 2014 Rating 90 To 2021 $30
Classic Rutherglen Muscat NV Rating 90 To 2018 $35 CM

St Mary's   ★★★★
V & A Lane, Penola, SA 5277 **Region** Limestone Coast Zone
T (08) 8736 6070 **www.**stmaryswines.com **Open** 7 days 10–4
Winemaker Barry Mulligan, Ian Mulligan **Est.** 1986 **Dozens** 4000 **Vyds** 12ha

The Mulligan family has lived in the Penola/Coonawarra region since 1909. In '37 a 250ha property 15km west of Penola, including an 80ha ridge of terra rossa over limestone, was purchased for grazing. The ridge was cleared; the remainder of the property was untouched and is now a private wildlife sanctuary. In '86 Barry and Glenys Mulligan planted shiraz and cabernet sauvignon on the ridge, followed by merlot in the early '90s. The outcome of the protracted litigation on the boundaries of Coonawarra included some land that should have been excluded, the reverse of the outcome for St Mary's. Exports to the UK, the US and other major markets.

ΨΨΨΨΨ **Carillon 2013** Cabernet sauvignon, shiraz, cabernet franc and merlot. The vibrant colour and controlled alcohol point to a lively, energetic wine with crisp, juicy red fruits taking total command of the stage. It will be at its best over the next 5 years with anything Italian. Cork. 13.5% alc. **Rating** 92 **To** 2020 $40

House Block Cabernet Sauvignon 2013 An elegant medium-bodied wine with clear varietal expression, the vineyard's proximity to Coonawarra obvious from the word go, with the tempered ripeness of the fruit flavours; the ultra-fresh finish pleases, too. Cork. 14% alc. **Rating** 90 **To** 2025 $30

Saint Regis

35 Waurn Ponds Drive, Waurn Ponds, Vic 3216 **Region** Geelong
T 0432 085 404 **www.**saintregis.com.au **Open** Thurs–Sun 11–5
Winemaker Peter Nicol **Est.** 1997 **Dozens** 500 **Vyds** 1ha
Saint Regis is a family-run boutique winery focusing on estate-grown shiraz, and locally sourced chardonnay and pinot noir. Each year the harvest is hand-picked by members of the family and friends, with Peter Nicol (assisted by wife Viv) the executive onsite winemaker. Peter, with a technical background in horticulture, is a self-taught winemaker, and has taught himself well, also making wines for others. His son Jack became the owner of the business in 2015 and took on the management of the newly constructed restaurant and wine bar. Peter continues to be the winemaker.

ΨΨΨΨΨ **Geelong Shiraz 2015** Well put together. Ripe cherry-plum flavours with mint, pepper and assorted florals. Makes cool climate shiraz look easy. Screwcap. 14% alc. **Rating** 92 **To** 2025 $25 CM ✪

ΨΨΨΨ **Geelong Chardonnay 2015** **Rating** 88 **To** 2019 $25 CM

Salomon Estate

17 High Street, Willunga, SA 5171 **Region** Southern Fleurieu
T 0412 412 228 **www.**salomonwines.com **Open** Not
Winemaker Bert Salomon, Mike Farmilo **Est.** 1997 **Dozens** 6500 **Vyds** 12.1ha
Bert Salomon is an Austrian winemaker with a long-established family winery in the Kremstal region, not far from Vienna. He became acquainted with Australia during his time with import company Schlumberger in Vienna; he was the first to import Australian wines (Penfolds) into Austria, in the mid-1980s, and later became head of the Austrian Wine Bureau. He was so taken by Adelaide that he moved his family there for the first few months each year, sending his young children to school and setting in place an Australian red winemaking venture. He retired from the Bureau and is now a full-time travelling winemaker, running the family winery in the northern hemisphere vintage, and overseeing the making of the Salomon Estate wines at Chapel Hill. Salomon Estate now shares a cellar door with Hither & Yon, just a few steps away from the Saturday farmers' market in Willunga. Exports to all major markets.

ΨΨΨΨΨ **Aestatis GMS 2013** 50% mourvedre, 25% each of grenache and shiraz. The flavour ensemble ranges through plum, black cherry and raspberry couched in a medium-bodied palate with powdery tannins, French oak evident, but not dominant. A really attractive wine. Screwcap. 14.5% alc. **Rating** 95 **To** 2033 $48

Braeside Vineyard Finniss River Cabernet Sauvignon 2013 Hand-picked, destemmed, crushed, open-fermented, wild yeast, matured for 18 months in French oak (20% new). An interesting wine, the key to its individuality its 5-week maceration in skins, then being pressed direct to barrel. It finally comes out of oak and into bottle, bringing with it a fine stream of juicy dark fruits and fine-grained tannins. Cork. 14.5% alc. **Rating** 95 **To** 2043 $35 ⚫

Sea Eagle Vineyard Finniss River Shiraz 2013 Very good colour; a bouquet of perfectly balanced dark fruits, dark chocolate and oak is replayed on the medium to full-bodied palate; the tannins that accompany the fruit are substantial, but ripe and balanced. Cork. 14.5% alc. **Rating** 94 **To** 2039 $40

🍷🍷🍷🍷🍷 **The Verve Free Red 2014 Rating** 93 **To** 2029 $30
Fleurieu Peninsula Syrah V 2014 Rating 92 **To** 2034 $30

Saltire Wines

113 Wilderness Road, Lovedale, NSW 2320 **Region** Hunter Valley
T (02) 4930 7594 www.swishwine.com **Open** 7 days 10–5
Winemaker Darren Atkinson **Est.** 2008 **Dozens** 5000 **Vyds** 6ha
The Warraroong vineyard was planted in 1978, the name an Aboriginal word for 'hillside', reflecting the southwesterly aspect of the property, which looks back towards the Brokenback Range and Watagan Mountains. In 2007 Katrina and Russell Leslie moved to the Hunter Valley, buying existing wineries and/or brands, with the early stages under the Swish Wine umbrella. Tin Soldier came and went, and Wandin Valley Estate also became part of the group. Warraroong Estate is now at the head of the businesses. Exports to China.

🍷🍷🍷🍷🍷 **Semillon 2009** Saltire is on home turf here, and it shows; the intensity, power, length and grip of the lemongrass and citrussy/minerally acidity drive the wine at high speed along the palate and lingering finish. Still a pup, but don't hesitate to drink some, keep some. Screwcap. 10.8% alc. **Rating** 95 **To** 2029 $30 ⚫

🍷🍷🍷🍷🍷 **The Mighty Mouse Reserve Shiraz 2013 Rating** 90 **To** 2033 $45

Saltram

Murray Street, Angaston, SA 5353 **Region** Barossa Valley
T (08) 8561 0200 www.saltramwines.com.au **Open** 7 days 10–5
Winemaker Shavaughn Wells, Richard Mattner **Est.** 1859 **Dozens** 150 000
There is no doubt that Saltram has taken strides towards regaining the reputation it held 30 or so years ago. Grape sourcing has come back to the Barossa Valley for the flagship wines. The red wines, in particular, have enjoyed great show success over the past decade, with No. 1 Shiraz and Mamre Brook leading the charge. Exports to all major markets.

🍷🍷🍷🍷🍷 **Pepperjack Porterhouse Graded Shiraz 2013** A well-constructed and balanced medium-bodied wine, fruit, oak and tannins all singing from the same page. The more you explore the palate, the more you realise its elegance and balance. No need for patience. Screwcap. 14.5% alc. **Rating** 95 **To** 2033 $50

No. 1 Barossa Shiraz 2012 Over the years a flag-bearer for Saltram in vintages where its power and intensity are matched by its complexity, '12 being such a vintage. The colour is that of a 1yo, and the complex array of black fruits is welded to the oak and tannins. Screwcap. 14.5% alc. **Rating** 95 **To** 2037 $99

Edward Salter Cabernet Sauvignon 2012 It has an intensely complex and powerful bouquet of red and dark fruits, earth, spice and a hint of tobacco. The palate delivers that and more, intense and powerful, but beautifully poised between extract and fruit. Decades ahead of it. Screwcap. 14% alc. **Rating** 95 **To** 2030 $100

Mr Pickwick's Particular Tawny NV Crushing intensity and length. Sour and nutty with slick, sweet, fresh toffee, dried fruits, rancio and coffee notes. Dances out through the finish. Irrepressible. Cork. 19.5% alc. **Rating** 95 **To** 2016 $75 CM

Metala Black Label Langhorne Creek Shiraz 2014 Primarily from the original 1891 plantings, matured in new and used French oak. An intense and focused full-bodied shiraz that probes every corner and crevice of the mouth with its spicy/savoury black fruits, firm tannins and long finish. A classic from two centuries ago. Screwcap. 14% alc. **Rating** 94 **To** 2040 $65

ŸŸŸŸ♀ Mamre Brook Eden Valley Riesling 2015 Rating 93 To 2025 $23 ✪
1859 Barossa Shiraz 2014 Rating 93 To 2029 $21 ✪
Mamre Brook Barossa Shiraz 2013 Rating 93 To 2030 $38
Pepperjack Barossa Shiraz 2014 Rating 90 To 2034 $30
Mamre Brook Cabernet Sauvignon 2013 Rating 90 To 2025 $38 CM

Sam Miranda of King Valley   ★★★★

1019 Snow Road, Oxley, Vic 3678 **Region** King Valley
T (03) 5727 3888 **www.**sammiranda.com.au **Open** 7 days 10–5
Winemaker Sam Miranda **Est.** 2004 **Dozens** 20 000 **Vyds** 15ha
Sam Miranda, grandson of Francesco Miranda, joined the family business in 1991, striking out on his own in 2004 after Miranda Wines was purchased by McGuigan Simeon. The High Plains Vineyard is in the Upper King Valley at an altitude of 450m; estate plantings are supplemented by some purchased grapes. The cellar door and restaurant were designed by leading Sydney architect Alex Popov. Exports to the UK, Fiji and China.

ŸŸŸŸ♀ **Single Vineyard Verduzzo 2015** Good value. Good wine. Fruit-forward but with plenty left to give the finish a kick. Dry, but generous. Works an absolute treat, sans fuss. Screwcap. 12.5% alc. **Rating** 92 **To** 2017 $22 CM ✪
Estate Vineyard Tannat 2011 A reef of tannin comes swaddled in dark, leathery, black cherry flavour. It feels purposeful and distinctive, and while just starting to mellow, its development seems appropriate to its age. Screwcap. 13.9% alc. **Rating** 92 **To** 2021 $35 CM
Estate Vineyard Barbera 2014 Cuts an attractive groove. Plenty of perfume and acidity, for which the variety is renowned, but with the fruit and tannin to match. Screwcap. 14% alc. **Rating** 91 **To** 2020 $35 CM
Alpine & King Valleys Pinot Grigio 2015 Crisp with apple, pear and candied grapefruit-like flavour. Admirable intensity without being OTT. Screwcap. 12.3% alc. **Rating** 90 **To** 2016 $22 CM

ŸŸŸŸ **Single Vineyard Riesling 2015** Rating 89 To 2020 $22 CM
Rosato 2015 Rating 89 To 2017 $20 CM
La Prova King Valley Prosecco 2015 Rating 89 To 2016 $25 TS
Prosecco 2015 Rating 88 To 2016 $20 TS

Samuel's Gorge   ★★★★★

193 Chaffeys Road, McLaren, SA 5171 **Region** McLaren Vale
T (08) 8323 8651 **www.**gorge.com.au **Open** 7 days 11–5
Winemaker Justin McNamee **Est.** 2003 **Dozens** 3500 **Vyds** 10ha
After a wandering winemaking career in various parts of the world, Justin McNamee became a winemaker at Tatachilla in 1996, where he remained until 2003, leaving to found Samuel's Gorge. He has established his winery in a barn built in 1853, part of the old Seaview Homestead. The historic property was owned by Sir Samuel Way, variously Chief Justice of the South Australian Supreme Court and Lieutenant Governor of the state. The grapes come from small contract growers spread across the ever-changing (unofficial) subregions of McLaren Vale, and are basket-pressed and fermented in old open slate fermenters lined with beeswax. Exports to the US, Canada, Hong Kong and NZ.

ŸŸŸŸŸ **McLaren Vale Grenache 2014** This is a full-on McLaren Vale grenache in all its glory: layer upon layer of every red fruit in the book, yet no hint of over-extraction, and – even less – dead fruit or confection. There is something about the synergistic/symbiotic link of terroir and variety here that eludes all the other parts of Australia. Cork. 14.5% alc. **Rating** 95 **To** 2029 $40

ŸŸŸŸ **Mosaic of Dreams GMS 2013** Rating 89 To 2023 $75
Comet Tail Sparkling Shiraz 2013 Rating 88 To 2018 $50 TS

Sandalford

3210 West Swan Road, Caversham, WA 6055 **Region** Margaret River
T (08) 9374 9374 **www.**sandalford.com **Open** 7 days 9–5
Winemaker Hope Metcalf **Est.** 1840 **Dozens** 60 000 **Vyds** 105ha

Sandalford is one of Australia's oldest and largest privately owned wineries. In 1970 it moved beyond its original Swan Valley base, purchasing a substantial property in Margaret River that is now the main source of its premium grapes. Wines are released under the Element, Winemakers, Margaret River and Estate Reserve ranges, with Prendiville Reserve at the top. Exports to all major markets.

Prendiville Reserve Margaret River Cabernet Sauvignon 2014 Matured for 12 months in new (50%) and 2yo French barriques, only 10 barriques chosen for this wine. It combines elegance and power, with a silky/juicy quality not obvious in its '13 sibling. The ability of the wine to absorb the new oak is another string to its bow. I am hugely impressed with the elegance that runs from the first sip to the aftertaste. Screwcap. 14.5% alc. **Rating** 97 **To** 2039 $90 ✪

Prendiville Reserve Margaret River Chardonnay 2015 The complex bouquet balances toast and grilled cashew notes with very intense pink grapefruit and stone fruit aromas, the palate providing an instant replay as the flavours ricochet around the mouth, and a very long finish. Amid all this frenetic activity the wine actually remains calm and elegant. Screwcap. 12.5% alc. **Rating** 96 **To** 2028 $60 ✪

Estate Reserve Margaret River Shiraz 2013 The wine finished fermentation in new and 1yo French barriques, followed by 18 months in those barrels. The fragrant bouquet has red fruits in the ascendant, but the balance shifts to black on the long, medium-bodied palate. There is no question the vinification adds a silkiness to the tannins as well as perfectly integrating the oak. A seductive drink now or whenever style. Screwcap. 14% alc. **Rating** 96 **To** 2033 $35 ✪

Estate Reserve Margaret River Sauvignon Blanc Semillon 2015 From the mature estate-grown vineyard; brings a vibrant wine to the table that happily flaunts its peacock's tail display of citrus, passionfruit and gooseberry flavours, lengthened and braced by bright acidity. You can't ask for more. Screwcap. 12.5% alc. **Rating** 95 **To** 2018 $25 ✪

Estate Reserve Margaret River Chardonnay 2015 Fermented in French oak (20% new) and matured on lees for 8 months. Bright straw-green, the bouquet is of white peach, apple and vanilla, a long, intense and finely boned palate adding grapefruity acidity. Screwcap. 12.5% alc. **Rating** 95 **To** 2025 $35 ✪

Estate Reserve Margaret River Chardonnay 2014 Fermented in new French oak and given extensive lees contact in barrel. The oak is front and centre on the bouquet, but is swept aside by the power of the fruit on the palate, with its platter of grapefruit, white peach, nectarine and peach; savoury acidity wraps up the finish. Screwcap. 13.5% alc. **Rating** 95 **To** 2022 $35 ✪

Estate Reserve Margaret River Cabernet Sauvignon 2010 Developing slowly but surely, its general attitude unchanged; quality cabernet's innate austerity (particularly its tannins) has to be accepted. The price for a 5yo wine of this quality is fair. Screwcap. 14.5% alc. **Rating** 95 **To** 2030 $45

Estate Reserve Margaret River Verdelho 2015 Has intense fruit captured by the direct, no-frills winemaking approach and Margaret River's terroir. It lifts this verdelho well above most of its peers. Screwcap. 12.5% alc. **Rating** 94 **To** 2018 $25 ✪

Margaret River Cabernet Merlot 2014 How one could afford to mature a wine in new French oak for this price is beyond me, but it doesn't stop there, for the quality of the fruit deserved this oak. There is an abundance of cassis, black olive and all-up savoury flavours on the medium to full-bodied palate, ripe tannins a further bonus. Screwcap. 14.5% alc. **Rating** 94 **To** 2029 $20 ✪

Estate Reserve Margaret River Cabernet Sauvignon 2014 If you enjoy savoury cabernet with black olive/bay leaf jostling for space along with

blackcurrant fruit and gravelly tannins, this will please you mightily, the reason being enjoyment of Bordeaux. Screwcap. 14.5% alc. **Rating** 94 **To** 2029 $45
Prendiville Reserve Margaret River Cabernet Sauvignon 2013 A full-bodied Margaret River cabernet, with all the focus on fully ripened single varietal fruit still in primary expression, shading complexity from oak and tannins. Onwards and upwards from here. Screwcap. 14.5% alc. **Rating** 94 **To** 2043 $90

🍷🍷🍷🍷🍷   Margaret River Shiraz 2014 Rating 93 To 2029 $20 ✪

Sandhurst Ridge   ★★★★☆

156 Forest Drive, Marong, Vic 3515 **Region** Bendigo
T (03) 5435 2534 **www**.sandhurstridge.com.au **Open** 7 days 11–5
Winemaker Paul Greblo **Est.** 1990 **Dozens** 3000 **Vyds** 7.3ha
The Greblo brothers (Paul is the winemaker, George the viticulturist), with combined experience in business, agriculture, science and construction and development, began the establishment of Sandhurst Ridge in 1990, planting the first 2ha of shiraz and cabernet sauvignon. Plantings have increased to over 7ha, principally cabernet and shiraz, but also a little merlot, nebbiolo and sauvignon blanc. As the business has grown, the Greblos have supplemented their crush with grapes grown in the region. Exports to Norway, Malaysia, Taiwan, Hong Kong, Japan and China.

🍷🍷🍷🍷🍷   **Reserve Bendigo Shiraz 2013** Excellent crimson-purple; a powerful, intense, black-fruited shiraz that has managed to absorb the new oak; it exudes flavour from every pore, but is light on its feet, allowing red fruits, spice and licorice to sidle up to the black fruit core and be heard; the finish reaffirms the quality of this wine. Diam. 13.6% alc. **Rating** 95 **To** 2038 $45

🍷🍷🍷🍷   **Fringe Bendigo Shiraz 2014** Rating 89 To 2024 $24
Fringe Bendigo Shiraz Classic Blend 2014 Rating 89 To 2024 $24
Bendigo Cabernet Merlot 2014 Rating 89 To 2029 $30
Bendigo Shiraz 2014 Rating 88 To 2034 $32

Sanguine Estate   ★★★★★

77 Shurans Lane, Heathcote, Vic 3523 **Region** Heathcote
T (03) 5433 3111 **www**.sanguinewines.com.au **Open** W'ends & public hols 10–5
Winemaker Mark Hunter **Est.** 1997 **Dozens** 10 000 **Vyds** 21.57ha
The Hunter family – parents Linda and Tony at the head, and their children Mark and Jodi, with their respective partners Melissa and Brett – began establishing the vineyard in 1997. It has grown to 21ha of shiraz, with token plantings of chardonnay, viognier, merlot, tempranillo, petit verdot, cabernet sauvignon and cabernet franc. Low-yielding vines and the magic of the Heathcote region have produced Shiraz of exceptional intensity, which has received rave reviews in the US, and led to the 'sold out' sign being posted almost immediately upon release. With the ever-expanding vineyard, Mark has become full-time vigneron and winemaker, and Jodi has taken over from her father as CEO and general manager. Exports to Singapore and China.

🍷🍷🍷🍷🍷   **D'Orsa Heathcote Shiraz 2013** Named in honour of Pietro D'Orsa, great-grandfather of the parents of today's Hunter family, and is a selection of the best barrels of the vintage. This is a mighty, full-bodied wine that dances like a butterfly, stings like a bee. Licorice, black pepper and a cupboard of spices drive the flavour caravan, plus sultry tannins and a generous, but integrated, veneer of oak. Cork. 14.8% alc. **Rating** 97 **To** 2038 $60 ✪

🍷🍷🍷🍷🍷   **Inception Heathcote Shiraz 2014** The flagship wine. 30% new oak makes its mark, but otherwise, little difference from its siblings, unless it be the sole wine in a Burgundy-shaped bottle. On multiple retastings of the line-up, this emerged in front. Screwcap. 14.8% alc. **Rating** 95 **To** 2034 $40
Wine Club Heathcote Shiraz 2014 Some red fruits and spice peep from the depths of the dark plum/black fruit flavours, giving a juicy lift to the back-palate

and finish. Two groups of Sanguine's best customers are given the same four batches of shiraz, and each creates their preferred blend. The *Wine Companion* scores are then compared, and this year the Wine Club emerged with the highest scores. Screwcap. 14.8% alc. **Rating** 94 **To** 2034 $30 ✪

Music Festival Heathcote Shiraz 2014 Black fruits, anise, licorice, blackberry and plum are at the core. Full-bodied, but you can't get away from the feeling that less alcohol would have been better – mind you, all Sanguine Shirazs from '13 and '14 are 14.8%, suggesting some intervention of man or divine providence. Screwcap. 14.8% alc. **Rating** 94 **To** 2030 $30 ✪

♟♟♟♟♟ Robo's Mob Heathcote Shiraz 2014 **Rating** 93 **To** 2023 $30
Heathcote Rose 2015 **Rating** 91 **To** 2017 $20 ✪
Progeny Heathcote Shiraz 2014 **Rating** 91 **To** 2034 $25
Heathcote Tempranillo 2015 **Rating** 90 **To** 2025 $30

Santa & D'Sas

2 Pincott Street, Newtown, Vic 3220 **Region** Various
T 0417 384 272 **www**.santandsas.com.au **Open** Not
Winemaker Andrew Santarossa, Matthew Di Sciascio **Est.** 2014 **Dozens** 5000

Santa & D'Sas brings together two winemakers who met while studying for their Bachelor of Applied Science (Wine Science) degrees. Their first collaboration was to make a student wine as part of their formal studies. Thereafter they went their separate ways, Andrew Santarossa as far afield as Houghton, then returning to the Yarra Valley to work for Giant Steps and Domaine Chandon. Currently he is winemaker for his own Santarossa Vineyards label, and consults to Mandala Wines. Matthew Di Sciascio, with dual degrees in wine science and viticulture, was one of the proprietors, winemaker and viticulturist at Bellbrae Estate in Geelong (2000–'10) as well as winemaker at Otway Estate ('08–'09). Since '11 he has been a vintage winemaker at Galli Estate, consultant winemaker at Clyde Park and has developed Di Sciascio Family Wines. Late in '12 Andrew and Matthew decided they should make another wine together, and one thing has led to another in quick succession. Production of the Santa & D'Sas wines has increased from 1500 cases to its present (2015) level of 5000 dozen, with 12 wines from five different regions across Victoria.

♟♟♟♟♟ Valentino Heathcote Shiraz 2013 Substantial flavours delivered in velvety form. Blackberry, satsuma plum and the cream of toasty, resiny oak. It doesn't hold back, and the oak application is too liberal, but there's substance to its smooth talk. Screwcap. 14% alc. **Rating** 93 **To** 2028 $35 CM

Yarra Valley Chardonnay 2013 Combination of oak and fruit is impressive. Give this a reasonable (but not excessive) chill and you have yourself a glass full of pear and apple flavour, complemented by flashy/sweet oak. Screwcap. 13% alc. **Rating** 92 **To** 2020 $30 CM

Valentino Heathcote Shiraz 2014 Blackberried fruit comes well – but appropriately – infused with smoky vanillan oak. This sits right in the sweet spot, neither overdone nor underdone, with firmish tannin keeping a close eye on it all. Screwcap. 14% alc. **Rating** 92 **To** 2025 $35 CM

Henty Riesling 2015 Riesling with a body of flavour; attractive lime and slate with hints of mandarin. Compact but highly pleasurable. Screwcap. 12% alc. **Rating** 91 **To** 2021 $30 CM

Nuovo Rosso 2015 King Valley sangiovese. Strong savoury overtones, clear touches of charcuterie and a core of cherried fruit. Bang on for early drinking. Screwcap. 13.5% alc. **Rating** 91 **To** 2020 $22 CM ✪

Henty Pinot Gris 2015 Pretty upfront, weighty through the middle and slightly tart on the finish. There's a good deal going on and on offer, and it works reasonably well as a result. Screwcap. 12.6% alc. **Rating** 90 **To** 2017 $30 CM

King Valley Rosato 2015 Pale copper-crimson. Juicy and refreshing with a gentle nod towards savouriness. Dry finish. Above average. Screwcap. 12.5% alc. **Rating** 90 **To** 2016 $22 CM

Yarra Valley Pinot Noir 2014 The inherent complexity of the variety, with sweetness, tanginess and savouriness working in unison, has the drinkability meter pointing to high. Screwcap. 13.5% alc. **Rating** 90 **To** 2019 $30 CM

Heathcote Shiraz 2014 Solid flavours, largely in the blackberry and dark chocolate spectrum, with suggestions of ground coffee and tar. It doesn't quite get the heart racing but you can hardly quibble over the volume of flavour. Screwcap. 14% alc. **Rating** 90 **To** 2023 $30 CM

ΨΨΨΨ **King Valley Prosecco NV Rating** 89 **To** 2016 $22 TS

Santarossa Vineyards ★★★★☆

2 The Crescent, Yea, Vic 3717 (postal) **Region** Yarra Valley/Heathcote
T 0419 117 858 **www.**betterhalfwines.com.au **Open** Not
Winemaker Andrew Santarossa **Est.** 2007 **Dozens** NFP **Vyds** 16ha

Santarossa Vineyards, formerly known as Fratelli, started out as a virtual winery business, owned and run by three brothers of Italian heritage. It is now solely owned by winemaker Andrew and wife Megan Santarossa, and the wines are of impressive quality. The Yarra Valley and Heathcote will henceforth be the focus of the business.

ΨΨΨΨΨ **Better Half Yarra Valley Chardonnay 2015** Beautifully put together. There's a trumpet of flavour, a trill of acidity, a texture that seems to hum with softness. It has a cuddly aspect and yet there's plenty of race to it. Citrus, white peach, oatmeal, toast. One sip and you're hooked. Screwcap. 13% alc. **Rating** 95 **To** 2020 $35 CM ✪

ΨΨΨΨΨ **RedCote Heathcote Shiraz 2013 Rating** 92 **To** 2025 $40 CM
RedCote Heathcote Shiraz 2012 Rating 92 **To** 2022 $40 CM
Better Half Yarra Valley Pinot Noir 2015 Rating 91 **To** 2021 $35 CM

Santolin Wines ★★★★★

c/- 21–23 Delaneys Road, South Warrandyte, Vic 3136 **Region** Yarra Valley
T 0402 278 464 **www.**santolinwines.com.au **Open** Not
Winemaker Adrian Santolin **Est.** 2012 **Dozens** 500

Adrian Santolin grew up in Griffith, NSW, and has worked in the wine industry since he was 15. He moved to the Yarra Valley in '07 with wife Rebecca, who has worked in marketing roles at various wineries. Adrian's love of pinot noir led him to work at wineries such as Wedgetail Estate, Rochford, De Bortoli, Sticks and Rob Dolan Wines. In '12 his dream came true when he was able to buy 2 tonnes of pinot noir from the Syme-on-Yarra Vineyard, increasing production in '13 to 4 tonnes, split between chardonnay and pinot noir. The Boy Meets Girl wines are sold through www.nakedwines.com.au. Exports to the UK and the US.

ΨΨΨΨΨ **Willowlake Vineyard Yarra Valley Chardonnay 2015** Willowlake was the first vineyard to be planted in the Upper Yarra, and has imparted its subregional mark of greater pungency, length and grip. Here grapefruit takes the reins, and it (together with white peach) strongly increases the flavour impact on the back-palate and finish. Screwcap. 13.7% alc. **Rating** 95 **To** 2026 $35 ✪

Menage a Trois Lower Yarra Pinot Noir 2015 Good depth and hue to the colour; a rich and generous pinot with lashings of plum and black cherry; by some distance there is more flavour, texture and overall substance. The Menage a Trois Pinots are sold as a three-pack. Screwcap. 13% alc. **Rating** 95 **To** 2030 $30 ✪

Yarraland Vineyard Yarra Valley Chardonnay 2015 Apart from its single vineyard status in the heart of the Yarra Valley floor (and closest to the Melbourne metro boundary), the slightly higher alcohol here seems to provide a clearer voice, with stone fruit in the lead, grapefruit providing a citrussy bite to the acidity. Screwcap. 13.7% alc. **Rating** 94 **To** 2023 $30 ✪

Menage a Trois Upper Yarra Pinot Noir 2015 Bright, clear hue. Pretty and perfumed, it has excellent length and line, and clear red fruit varietal character, the tannins present but silky. Screwcap. 13% alc. **Rating** 94 **To** 2027 $30 ✪

🍷🍷🍷🍷🍸 **Family Reserve Chardonnay 2015** Rating 93 To 2022 $23
Menage a Trois Macedon Ranges Pinot Noir 2015 Rating 90 To 2022 $30
Family Reserve Pinot Noir 2015 Rating 90 To 2021 $23

Saracen Estates   ★★★☆

Level 10, 225 St Georges Terrace, Perth, WA 6000 **Region** Margaret River
T (08) 9486 9410 **www**.saracenestates.com.au **Open** Mon–Fri 9–5
Winemaker Paul Dixon, Bob Cartwright (Consultant) **Est.** 1998 **Dozens** 2500
The sale of the Saracen Estate property has left a cloud of uncertainty over how the business intends to operate into the future. Maree Saraceni and her brother Dennis Parker are running a virtual winery operation through their Perth office, employing contract winemaker Bob Cartwright, who is buying Margaret River harvest and making wine at Thompson's Estate.

🍷🍷🍷🍷🍸 **Margaret River Sauvignon Blanc Semillon 2015** 95/5% blend. Brave but admirable decision not to simply label it as varietal sauvignon blanc. Plump passionfruit and lemongrass flavours with tips of steel through the finish. No shortage of body. Screwcap. 13% alc. Rating 92 To 2019 $22 CM

🍷🍷🍷🍷 **Margaret River Cabernet Merlot 2014** Rating 89 To 2022 $26 CM
Maree 2010 Rating 88 To 2017 $38 TS

Sarsfield Estate   ★★★

345 Duncan Road, Sarsfield, Vic 3875 **Region** Gippsland
T (03) 5156 8962 **www**.sarsfieldestate.com.au **Open** By appt
Winemaker Dr Suzanne Rutschmann **Est.** 1995 **Dozens** 1000 **Vyds** 2ha
Owned by Suzanne Rutschmann, who has a PhD in chemistry, a Diploma in Horticulture and a BSc (Wine Science) from CSU, and Swiss-born Peter Albrecht, a civil and structural engineer who has also undertaken various courses in agriculture and viticulture. For a part-time occupation, these are exceptionally impressive credentials. Their vineyard includes pinot noir, cabernet semillon, shiraz, cabernet franc and merlot. Sarsfield Pinot Noir has enjoyed success in both domestic and international wine shows. No insecticides are used in the vineyard; the winery runs on solar and wind energy and relies entirely on rainwater.

🍷🍷🍷🍷 **Pinot Noir 2013** A gold medal in Vienna '15 has to be treated with caution even though it is the only show entered, but this is a nice wine, its red fruits with notes of spice, and fine tannins. Its only issue is its relatively short finish. Screwcap. 13.6% alc. Rating 89 To 2020 $26
Cabernets Shiraz Merlot 2012 A lively light to medium-bodied wine with cassis and darker fruits set against notes of leaf and mint. You look for a little more flesh and structure. Screwcap. 13.3% alc. Rating 89 To 2022 $22

🌿 Sassafras Wines   ★★★☆

20 Grylls Crescent, Cook, ACT 2614 (postal) **Region** Canberra District
T 0476 413 974 **www**.sassafraswines.com.au **Open** Not
Winemaker Paul Starr, Hamish Young **Est.** 2015 **Dozens** 300
Paul Starr and Tammy Braybrook brought unusual academic knowledge with them when they established Sassafras Wines. Tammy has a science degree, has worked as an economist, and is now an IT professional and part-time florist. Paul has a PhD in cultural studies and intended to be an academic in the humanities before a detour into environment work in government. Tammy knew Mark Terrell, of Quarry Hill, so the pair ended up working in the Terrell Vineyard with pruning and vintage work, leading to local college courses in winemaking. Paul helped out Eden Road with its cellar door on weekends for four years. History is an interest for both of Paul and Tammy, and when thinking of heading in an altogether new wine direction, they read of what they describe as the ancestral method of making sparkling wine using the original yeast and fermentable sugar to create the mousse, bypassing disgorgement altogether.

ΨΨΨΨΨ Canberra Sagrantino 2013 Excellent colour; starts moderately, but then ignites on the palate with black cherry and bitter chocolate, with dusty, drying tannins on the finish almost coming as a relief after the bombardment of the fruit. Screwcap. 14% alc. **Rating** 90 **To** 2023 $24

Sassy Wines ★★★☆

569 Emu Swamp Road, Orange, NSW 2800 **Region** Orange
T 0409 311 395 www.sassywines.com.au **Open** Sat 10–5, Sun 10–4
Winemaker Peter Logan, Rob Coles **Est.** 2005 **Dozens** 600 **Vyds** 6.5ha
Rob and Felicia (Fliss) Coles first established a vineyard in the Cowra region in 1997, but decided to move to Orange to pursue cooler climate varieties, making that move in 2005, with the establishment of 6.5ha of vines more or less equally split to sauvignon blanc, arneis, riesling, pinot gris, viognier, pinot noir and shiraz. Organic and biodynamic principles are used in the vineyard.

ΨΨΨΨΨ The Ivor Orange Arneis 2015 50/50% hand-picked/machine-harvested, whole bunch-pressed, 60% wild-fermented in tank, 40% with small French oak balls (similar effect to staves or chips), 6 months lees stirring. Complexity is the result, precisely as intended, of course; it is as much to do with texture as flavour. Screwcap. 13.3% alc. **Rating** 90 **To** 2017 $24

ΨΨΨΨ Orange Riesling 2015 **Rating** 89 **To** 2025 $22
Orange Pinot Noir Rose 2015 **Rating** 89 **To** 2017 $22
Orange Late Harvest Arneis 2015 **Rating** 89 **To** 2017 $20

Savaterre

PO Box 337, Beechworth, Vic 3747 **Region** Beechworth
T (03) 5727 0551 www.savaterre.com **Open** Not
Winemaker Keppell Smith **Est.** 1996 **Dozens** NA
Keppell Smith embarked on a career in wine in 1996, studying winemaking at CSU and (at a practical level) with Phillip Jones at Bass Phillip. He purchased the 40ha property on which Savaterre has been established, and has close-planted (7500 vines per hectare) 1ha each of chardonnay and pinot noir at an elevation of 440m. Organic principles govern the viticulture, and the winemaking techniques look to the Old World rather than the New. Smith's stated aim is to produce outstanding, individualistic wines far removed from the mainstream.

ΨΨΨΨΨ Pinot Noir 2013 More delicate than previous releases. More perfumed and floral. Less Italianate, which it has tended to be in the past. This displays notes of cranberry, cherry-plum twigs and herbs, with smoked chicory notes wafting through. Seductive. Screwcap. 13.4% alc. **Rating** 94 **To** 2024 $70 CM
Shiraz 2013 The second release and another strong one. Smoky bacon, cherry-plum, earth and cloves. A savoury style with a heart of fruit. Girders of tannin add a force of their own. Screwcap. 13.4% alc. **Rating** 94 **To** 2026 $70 CM

ΨΨΨΨΨ Chardonnay 2013 **Rating** 92 **To** 2019 $70 CM

Savina Lane Wines

90 Savina Lane, Severnlea, Qld 4380 **Region** Granite Belt
T (07) 4683 5377 www.savinalanewines.com.au **Open** Wed–Sat 10–5
Winemaker Mike Hayes **Est.** 2012 **Dozens** 800 **Vyds** 3.5ha
Brad and Cheryl Hutchings established Savina Lane Wines in 2012 by extending and rehabilitating an existing, much older vineyard. The cellar door includes a 250km^2 underground cellar providing year-round stable temperatures. As well as multiple trophies for the '12 Old Vine Shiraz (ex 40yo dry grown vines), Savina Lane has had conspicuous success with various of its alternative varieties, which include viogner, fiano, petit manseng, tempranillo, graciano and montepulciano. The business has an Inner Circle membership, which already has 400 members and is likely to be the sole avenue for purchasing the wines in the future.

♥♥♥♥♀ **Reserve Granite Belt Graciano 2014** Not an easy variety to handle, but it's been well done here; bright, juicy/silky red fruits run the length of the palate, unencumbered by tannins or oak. Screwcap. 13.3% alc. **Rating** 93 **To** 2024 $55
Reserve Millenium Granite Belt Shiraz 2014 Due for release Nov '16, tasted barely 3 months after being bottled. At the moment it is a wine still searching for itself, but prior history, and the quality of the vintage, tells us it should do well. Given the benefit of the doubt. Screwcap. 13.1% alc. **Rating** 90 **To** 2029 $45

SC Pannell   ★★★★★

60 Olivers Road, McLaren Vale, SA 5171 **Region** McLaren Vale
T (08) 8271 7118 www.scpannell.com.au **Open** 7 days 11–5
Winemaker Stephen Pannell **Est.** 2004 **Dozens** 15 000 **Vyds** 22ha
The only surprising piece of background is that it took (an admittedly still reasonably youthful) Stephen (Steve) Pannell (and wife Fiona) so long to cut the painter from Constellation/Hardys and establish their own winemaking and consulting business. Steve radiates intensity, and extended experience has resulted in wines of the highest quality right from the first vintage. The Pannells have purchased two vineyards in McLaren Vale, the first planted in 1891 with a precious 3.6ha of shiraz. A second property was purchased in 2014, lifting the estate vineyards to a total of 22ha. Steve manages the vineyard with the aim of generating full flavour ripeness as close to 13% as possible. The future for the Pannells is limitless, the icon status of the label already established. Exports to the UK.

♥♥♥♥♥ **Adelaide Hills Syrah 2014** Spicy, peppery notes are liberally sprinkled on the expressive black cherry fruit of the bouquet, the sheer volume of that fruit not imperilling the medium-bodied nature of the palate, simply setting the scene for the remarkable drive and intensity of the finish and cleansing aftertaste. Screwcap. 14% alc. **Rating** 96 **To** 2039 $35 ✪
McLaren Vale Grenache 2014 High quality grapes picked at precisely the right time; has perfectly pitched red fruits, supple yet savoury tannins, hints of herbs and chocolate, and immaculate poise and balance ex the tannin support. Screwcap. 14% alc. **Rating** 96 **To** 2029 $55 ✪
Adelaide Hills Nebbiolo 2013 From five clones grown in the Gumeracha district. 'Should be decanted 2 hours before serving', and I did just that. It has exceptional varietal expression on the bouquet and palate, sultry red fruits, and tannins that are woven through the fruit on the palate so cleverly you almost forget their presence. Screwcap. 14% alc. **Rating** 96 **To** 2023 $45 ✪
Adelaide Hills Sauvignon Blanc 2015 There is a subliminal savoury edge to the bouquet and palate, possibly from more than one yeast at work, and also crisp, crunchy acidity. You pick up the extra level of flavour from ripe (not overripe) fruit on the back-palate and finish. Has the X-factor many sauvignon blancs lack. Screwcap. 13.5% alc. **Rating** 95 **To** 2016 $25 ✪
The Vale 2014 Old vine shiraz grenache. The colour is vivid and deep, its promise fully realised with this medium+-bodied blend; it exudes a sense of place, yet does so without the usual garnish of dark chocolate, giving the fruit a larger field to play in; red and black cherry, soused raspberry, and supple, generous tannins have been exactly measured. Screwcap. 14% alc. **Rating** 95 **To** 2034 $45
Aromatico 2015 An Adelaide Hills blend, predominantly gewurztraminer, with lesser amounts of riesling and pinot gris. I really don't understand how Steve Pannell has managed to extract all the floral, spicy, rose petal and lychee aromas and flavours, but he has. Screwcap. 13% alc. **Rating** 94 **To** 2020 $28 ✪
McLaren Vale Grenache Shiraz Touriga 2014 This blend has bits of just about everything, none getting in the way of the others, but all nonetheless asserting their right to be there; in no particular order of importance: raspberry, sour cherry, licorice, spice, pepper and (yes) dark chocolate. Don't waste time trying to deconstruct it, just enjoy it. Screwcap. 14% alc. **Rating** 94 **To** 2024 $28 ✪

♥♥♥♥♀ **Adelaide Hills Pinot Grigio 2015** Rating 93 **To** 2017 $25 ✪
Arido Adelaide Hills Rose 2015 Rating 93 **To** 2017 $25 ✪

Scarborough Wine Co   ★★★★☆

179 Gillards Road, Pokolbin, NSW 2320 **Region** Hunter Valley
T (02) 4998 7563 **www.**scarboroughwine.com.au **Open** 7 days 9–5
Winemaker Ian and Jerome Scarborough **Est.** 1985 **Dozens** 25 000 **Vyds** 14ha
Ian Scarborough honed his white winemaking skills during his years as a consultant, and has brought all those skills to his own label. He makes three different styles of Chardonnay: the Blue Label is a light, elegant, Chablis style for the export market; a richer barrel-fermented wine (Yellow Label) is primarily directed to the Australian market; the third is the White Label, a cellar door-only wine made in the best vintages. The Scarborough family also acquired a portion of the old Lindemans Sunshine Vineyard (after it lay fallow for 30 years) and planted it with semillon and (quixotically) pinot noir. Exports to the UK and the US.

 The Obsessive Gillards Road Vineyard Hunter Valley Chardonnay 2013
Matured in new French oak for 15 months. Has the bluff character of Ian Scarborough, in whose honour The Obsessive range has been developed. One can't help but wonder what earlier picking and less time in less new oak would have achieved. Screwcap. 14% alc. **Rating** 91 **To** 2017 $40

Schild Estate Wines   ★★★★☆

Cnr Barossa Valley Way/Lyndoch Valley Road, Lyndoch, SA 5351 **Region** Barossa Valley
T (08) 8524 5560 **www.**schildestate.com.au **Open** 7 days 10–5
Winemaker Scott Hazeldine **Est.** 1998 **Dozens** 40 000 **Vyds** 163ha
Ed Schild is a Barossa Valley grapegrower who first planted a small vineyard at Rowland Flat in 1952, steadily increasing his vineyard holdings over the next 50 years to their present level. The flagship wine is made from 150-year-old shiraz vines on the Moorooroo Block. The cellar door is in the old ANZ Bank at Lyndoch, and provides the sort of ambience that can only be found in the Barossa Valley. Exports to all major markets.

 Prämie Barossa Valley Shiraz 2013 From the Liebich (80%) and Angus Brae (20%) vineyards; matured in new and used French hogsheads. A very classy, high quality wine that manages to display its power and complexity with a fresh but compelling touch; navigating the many black and blue fruit flavours is relatively easy and very pleasurable. Cork. 14.7% alc. **Rating** 96 **To** 2038 $70 ✪
Moorooroo Limited Release Barossa Valley Shiraz 2012 Packaged in the biggest, heaviest bottle I have ever encountered. The wine is less weighty than the Ben Schild Reserve, daring to be described as elegant – which is why it hasn't gained gold medals in its journey through the wine shows of the world. Plum, dark cherry and blackberry fruits are the drivers of a remarkable wine. Cork. 14.5% alc. **Rating** 94 **To** 2042 $100

⟡⟡⟡⟡⟡ **Ben Schild Reserve Shiraz 2012** **Rating** 92 **To** 2020 $40

Schubert Estate   ★★★★★

261 Roennfeldt Road, Marananga, SA 5355 **Region** Barossa Valley
T (08) 8562 3375 **www.**schubertestate.com **Open** By appt
Winemaker Steve Schubert **Est.** 2000 **Dozens** 3300 **Vyds** 14ha
Steve and Cecilia Schubert are primarily grapegrowers, with 12ha of shiraz and 2ha of viognier. They purchased the 25ha property in 1986, when it was in such a derelict state that there was no point trying to save the old vines. Both were working in other areas, so it was some years before they began replanting, at a little under 2ha per year. Almost all the production is sold to Torbreck. In 2000 they decided to keep enough grapes to make a barrique of wine for their own (and friends') consumption. They were sufficiently encouraged by the outcome to venture into the dizzy heights of two hogsheads a year (since increased to four or so). The wine is made with wild yeast, open fermentation, basket-pressing and bottling without filtration. Exports to Germany, Malaysia, Hong Kong and China.

⟡⟡⟡⟡⟡ **Goose-yard Block Barossa Valley Shiraz 2013** Open-fermented, matured in barrel for 18 months. Has the same dark chocolate/McLaren Vale flavours as prior vintages, adding a welcome savoury edge to the well of luscious black fruits; the tannins return to dark chocolate, helping the wine to leap over the hurdle of its alcohol with ease. Screwcap. 15% alc. **Rating** 95 **To** 2033 $65

The Lone Goose Barossa Valley Shiraz 2012 Co-fermented with 3% viognier in open pots, hence the vibrant colour; this approach doesn't always succeed in the Barossa Valley, and isn't common. It succeeds here emphatically, giving the wine a light foot and a rare freshness of flavour, and an almost spicy finish to the long palate. Screwcap. 15% alc. **Rating** 95 **To** 2027 $32 ✪

🍷🍷🍷🍷🍷 **The Sentinel Barossa Valley Shiraz 2011** Rating 93 To 2021 $36
The Lone Goose Barossa Valley Shiraz 2011 Rating 91 To 2021 $32
The Gosling Barossa Valley Shiraz 2013 Rating 90 To 2025 $20 ✪

Schulz Vignerons ★★★★☆

PO Box 121, Nuriootpa, SA 5355 **Region** Barossa Valley
T (08) 8565 6257 **Open** By appt
Winemaker Marcus Schulz, Neville Falkenberg **Est.** 2003 **Dozens** 500 **Vyds** 58.5ha
Marcus and Roslyn Schulz are the fifth generation of one of the best-known (extended) wine families in the Barossa Valley. Four generations of grapegrowing and winemaking precede them, but they went down a new path by initiating 'biological farming' in 2002. They have moved away from irrigation and extensive spraying and now the vines are virtually dry grown, producing generous yields of high quality grapes, using natural nitrogen created by the active soil biology, and minimal chemical input. The vineyard is planted to 12 varieties, shiraz, mourvedre, grenache and cabernet sauvignon leading the band. As might be imagined, the lion's share of the grapes is sold to other producers (some finding their way to Torbreck).

🍷🍷🍷🍷🍷 **Benjamin Shiraz 2013** It takes Barossa shiraz and connects it to an amplifier. Berried fruit, thick and furiously well ripened, comes slathered in minty, creamy oak. This has both feet in the big end of town but, thankfully, doesn't come with any sign of alcohol burn. Tannin has enough mettle to stand up to the onslaught of fruit. The full Monty. Screwcap. 14.6% alc. **Rating** 95 **To** 2035 $30 CM ✪

Marcus Old Vine Shiraz 2010 Thoroughly seductive. Bright but dense, soft but full of intent. Sweet plums, peppermint, violets, cedar wood, spiced raspberries. The combination of black and red berries is quite beautiful; so too the floral aspects. A flourish to the finish is all it wants. Screwcap. 14.8% alc. **Rating** 94 **To** 2028 $60 CM

🍷🍷🍷🍷🍷 **Maria Mataro 2013** Rating 92 To 2021 $25 CM ✪
DR's Grenache 2014 Rating 91 To 2020 $25 CM
Johann Primitivo 2011 Rating 91 To 2020 $25 CM

Schwarz Wine Company ★★★★★

PO Box 779, Tanunda, SA 5352 **Region** Barossa Valley
T 0417 881 923 **www.**schwarzwineco.com.au **Open** At Artisans of Barossa
Winemaker Jason Schwarz **Est.** 2001 **Dozens** 3500
The economical name is appropriate for a business that started with 1 tonne of grapes making two hogsheads of wine in 2001. Shiraz was purchased from Jason Schwarz's parents' vineyard in Bethany, the vines planted in 1968; the following year half a tonne of grenache was added, once again purchased from the parents. In '05, grape sale agreements to another (larger) winery were terminated, freeing up 1.8ha of shiraz and 0.8ha of grenache. From this point on things moved more quickly: in '06 Jason formed a partnership (Biscay Road Vintners) with Peter Schell of Spinifex, giving them total control over production. Exports to the US, Canada, France, Singapore, Hong Kong and China.

🍷🍷🍷🍷🍷 **Meta Barossa Shiraz 2014** From Eden Valley, Moppa and Stone Well, hand-picked, wild-fermented, 24% whole bunches, 18 months in French oak. This adds finesse and class to its Barossa Valley sibling. In one sense classic, in another avant garde. Pay your money, take your choice, either way the answer's top class. Screwcap. 14.2% alc. **Rating** 96 **To** 2039 $35 ✪

Meta Barossa Valley Grenache 2015 Average vine age 80yo, matured in French puncheons. Very light colour is totally deceptive: this is vibrantly fresh, with a compelling juxtaposition of bright red fruits, a spiderweb of tannins – and praise the Lord – no confection. This will divide opinions to an unprecedented degree, its magic ex 13.6% alcohol. Screwcap. **Rating** 95 **To** 2023 $35

Barossa Valley Shiraz 2014 Thirteen parcels from six districts, open-fermented, 15% whole bunches, 15 months in French oak. No holds barred, crammed full of black fruits, fresh, poached and dried, yet holds its line very well. Screwcap. 14.2% alc. **Rating** 94 **To** 2034 $30

Barossa Valley GSM 2014 Despite its controlled alcohol, this has hairs on its chest, what legendary English writer George Saintsbury would have described as a manly/manliest wine, intended as high praise. It's got years to run. Screwcap. 14.1% alc. **Rating** 94 **To** 2034 $28

ŦŦŦŦ̣ **Thiele Road Barossa Valley Grenache 2014** **Rating** 91 **To** 2021 $38 CM
Meta Barossa Valley Mataro 2015 **Rating** 90 **To** 2023 $35

Scion Vineyard & Winery ★★★★

74 Slaughterhouse Road, Rutherglen, Vic 3685 **Region** Rutherglen
T (02) 6032 8844 **www.**scionvineyard.com **Open** 7 days 10–5
Winemaker Rowly Milhinch **Est.** 2002 **Dozens** 1650 **Vyds** 3.2ha
Scion Vineyard was established by retired audiologist Jan Milhinch, who is a great-great-granddaughter of GF Morris, founder of the most famous Rutherglen wine family. Jan has now handed the baton on to son Rowland (Rowly), who continues to manage the vineyard, planted on a quartz-laden red clay slope to durif, viognier, brown muscat and orange muscat, and make the wines.

ŦŦŦŦŦ **Rutherglen Rose 2015** Made mostly with durif though with a dab of cabernet. The wine hangs together well. Gentle dusty notes add a savouriness to iodine, anise and black cherry flavour. Salmon coloured. Perfectly balanced. Tangy, tasty finish. Screwcap. 12.5% alc. **Rating** 94 **To** 2016 $27 CM
Rutherglen Durif Viognier 2013 Durif taken to a modern, fresh-faced place. It's not heavy, but it offers a power of dark-berried fruit. It also has floral overtones and a clear sense of juicy, free-flowing momentum; it satisfies but it also makes you want to come back for more. Screwcap. 13.6% alc. **Rating** 94 **To** 2025 $42 CM

ŦŦŦŦ̣ **Rutherglen Durif 2014** **Rating** 90 **To** 2029 $39

Scorpiiion ★★★★

575 Royal Esplanade, Manly, Qld 4179 **Region** Barossa
T 0409 551 110 **www.**scorpiiionwines.com.au **Open** Not
Winemaker Pete Schell **Est.** 2002 **Dozens** 800
Scorpiiion Wines is the concept of Mark Herbertt, who decided to buy a small quantity of McLaren Vale and Barossa grapes in 2002 and have the wine made for himself, friends and family. In '04 Paddy Phillips and Michael Szwarcbord – with Mark Herbertt, they share the Scorpio birth sign – joined the partnership. It is a virtual winery, with the grapes purchased, and the wines contract-made by the brilliant Peter Schell. They say, 'We share a number of likes and dislikes in relation to Australian red wines – apart from that, we don't really agree on anything… We aim for a fruit-driven style with elegant oak, rather than a big, oak-driven style.'

ŦŦŦŦŦ **Barossa Valley Shiraz 2013** It's hard to imagine a lover of Barossa shiraz being anything other than besotted by this. It's a thick, juicy, black-hearted wine with concentrated blackberry, tar and plum fruit and a sheer, masterfully applied coating of creamy, toasty oak. It tests the outer limits of ripeness but it remains sure of itself throughout. Screwcap. 15% alc. **Rating** 94 **To** 2026 $36 CM

ŦŦŦŦ̣ **Barossa Valley Rose 2015** **Rating** 93 **To** 2017 $25 CM

Scorpo Wines

23 Old Bittern-Dromana Road, Merricks North, Vic 3926 **Region** Mornington Peninsula
T (03) 5989 7697 **www**.scorpowines.com.au **Open** By appt
Winemaker Paul Scorpo **Est.** 1997 **Dozens** 3500 **Vyds** 9.64ha

Paul Scorpo has a background as a horticulturist/landscape architect, working on major projects ranging from private gardens to golf courses in Australia, Europe and Asia. His family has a love of food, wine and gardens, all of which led to their buying a derelict apple and cherry orchard on gentle rolling hills between Port Phillip and Westernport bays. They have established pinot gris (4.8ha), pinot noir (2.8ha), chardonnay (1ha) and shiraz (1ha). Exports to Singapore and Hong Kong.

🍷🍷🍷🍷🍷 **Mornington Peninsula Chardonnay 2012** It takes excellence and challenges it to reach higher. It's complex and flinty, with grapefruit and white peach flavours running pure and bright from start to finish. Fennel and cream notes play throughout, as do struck match/sulphide characters. Four years young. Brilliant. Screwcap. 13.5% alc. **Rating** 97 **To** 2020 $45 CM ✪

🍷🍷🍷🍷🍷 **Aubaine Mornington Peninsula Chardonnay 2015** It has a come-hither aspect but the back half is elegant and long. A class act. Beautiful white peach, apple and pear with seamless integration of cedary/spicy oak. Delightful. Screwcap. 13% alc. **Rating** 95 **To** 2021 $32 CM ✪

Mornington Peninsula Pinot Gris 2015 Very pale pink; Paul Scorpo has a well-deserved reputation for his Pinot Gris, and this isn't going to let him down. Clear pear/poached pear fruit provides excellent mouthfeel, and the finish is long and well structured. Screwcap. 14% alc. **Rating** 95 **To** 2022 $35 ✪

Noirien Mornington Peninsula Pinot Noir 2015 The word 'integration' springs to the front of your mind. This is meaty, spicy and complex but it carries its various facets easily, the fruit flowing at a fair clip. It feels skilful. It tastes terrific. Screwcap. 13.5% alc. **Rating** 95 **To** 2022 $32 CM ✪

Mornington Peninsula Pinot Noir 2014 This is taking the slow road to maturity, due to small bunches and berries, ex rain-ravaged flowering. The depth and balance to its black cherry and foresty tannins assure rewards to those who are patient. Screwcap. 13.5% alc. **Rating** 95 **To** 2027 $50

Mornington Peninsula Rose 2015 It's pippy and spicy and strawberried, its pale salmon colour at one with its savoury/elegant personality. Cracks of fennel build on the charm. Screwcap. 13.5% alc. **Rating** 94 **To** 2018 $32 CM

Scotchmans Hill

190 Scotchmans Road, Drysdale, Vic 3222 **Region** Geelong
T (03) 5251 3176 **www**.scotchmans.com.au **Open** 7 days 10.30–4.30
Winemaker Robin Brockett, Marcus Holt **Est.** 1982 **Dozens** 50 000

The change of ownership and management of Scotchmans Hill, now owned by a group of Melbourne investors, in no way reflected any shortcoming in the consistency and quality of the wines produced by long-serving winemaker Robin Brockett, assisted by Marcus Holt. Exports to Asia and other major markets.

🍷🍷🍷🍷🍷 **Pinot Noir 2014** Deep crimson; loaded with cherry kernel, spice, a touch of undergrowth complexity and a lick of dried herbs, the palate rounded, silky and persistent. Given the variability of the '14 vintage across southern Vic, this is a great effort. Screwcap. 13.5% alc. **Rating** 95 **To** 2025 $30 ✪

Shiraz 2014 Geelong shiraz has lot to offer, and this effort is a great showcase for why. Powerful, spice-laden, with black and red fruits flowing seamlessly through the savoury and finely poised palate. Screwcap. 14.5% alc. **Rating** 95 **To** 2030 $30 ✪

Cornelius Single Vineyard Bellarine Peninsula Syrah 2013 A further argument for the future of the Geelong region will be forged on the back of shiraz. This is a compelling wine, full of red and black fruits, spice and with a superbly silky and fine palate. Screwcap. 14.5% alc. **Rating** 95 **To** 2028 $65

Cornelius Sutton Vineyard Bellarine Peninsula Chardonnay 2013 There is a lot to enjoy in this wine. It is generously proportioned on the palate, with layers of flavour and a creamy texture. The acid line holds everything in check; long, fine and persistent. Screwcap. 12.5% alc. **Rating** 94 **To** 2025 $55

♀♀♀♀♀ **Cornelius Sauvignon 2014 Rating** 93 **To** 2020 $46
Cornelius Norfolk Vineyard Pinot Noir 2013 Rating 92 **To** 2025 $55

Scott ★★★★★
102 Main Street, Hahndorf, SA 5245 **Region** Adelaide Hills
T (08) 8388 7330 **www**.scottwines.com.au **Open** 1st w'end of the month 11–5
Winemaker Sam Scott **Est.** 2009 **Dozens** 4000
Sam Scott's great-grandfather worked in the cellar for Max Schubert, and passed his knowledge on to Sam's grandfather. It was he who gave Scott his early education. Sam enrolled in business at university, continuing the casual retailing he had started while at school with Booze Brothers, picking up the trail with Baily & Baily. Next came wine wholesale experience with David Ridge, selling iconic Australian and Italian wines to the trade. This then led to a job with Michael Fragos at Tatachilla in 2000, and since then he has been the 'I've been everywhere man', working all over Australia, and in California. He moved to Bird in Hand winery at the end of '06, where Andrew Nugent indicated that it was about time he took the plunge on his own account, and this he has done. Scott is a star in the making. Best Cellar Door, Adelaide Hills Wine Show '14. Exports to the UK and Singapore.

♀♀♀♀♀ **La Prova Adelaide Hills Pinot Grigio 2015** Trophy Best Pinot Gris/Grigio Adelaide Hills Wine Show '15. The varietal expression (pear and spiced apple) on the bouquet is good, but it's the texture and structure of the palate that must surely have earned the trophy. To describe a white wine as grippy is normally a criticism; here it is the opposite. This is a truly remarkable wine, not the normal anodyne grigio. Screwcap. 12.7% alc. **Rating** 97 **To** 2018 $25 ✪

♀♀♀♀♀ **La Prova Adelaide Hills Fiano 2015** Gold medals Australian Alternative Varieties Wine Show '15 and Sydney International Wine Challenge '15. Its gold medals were well and truly justified. It is interesting until the aftertaste, when lemon pith, juice and chalky acidity cause you to sit bolt upright and go back to the start of the wine to better understand its overall flavour and structure, almond notes joining the fray. Screwcap. 13.5% alc. **Rating** 95 **To** 2019 $26 ✪
Adelaide Hills Shiraz 2014 Crunchy acidity, dried herbs, twiggy characters. There is also a wealth of dark-berried/cherried fruit flavour and smoky/clovey oak notes buried deep therein. It might be savoury, but it's not light; indeed it feels powerful. Bankable quality. Screwcap. 14% alc. **Rating** 95 **To** 2032 $40 CM
La Prova Adelaide Hills Aglianico Rosato 2015 Bright salmon-pink; the wine has well above average complexity to its bouquet and palate alike, strongly reminiscent of Italian panforte, acidity cleansing the finish. Screwcap. 12.5% alc. **Rating** 94 **To** 2017 $25 ✪
La Prova King Valley Prosecco 2015 A fine, persistent mousse is, like everything else in this wine, impressive; pear flavours come through with utmost clarity on the long, perfectly balanced palate. Is there anything this man can't do? Crown seal. 11% alc. **Rating** 94 **To** 2017 $25 ✪

♀♀♀♀♀ **La Prova Bianco 2015 Rating** 93 **To** 2017 $20 ✪
La Prova Barossa Valley Nero d'Avola 2014 Rating 93 **To** 2020 $25 CM ✪
La Prova Adelaide Hills Pinot Nero 2014 Rating 92 **To** 2022 $25 CM ✪
La Prova Rosso 2014 Rating 90 **To** 2020 $20 ✪

Sedona Estate ★★★★☆
182 Shannons Road, Murrindindi, Vic 3717 **Region** Upper Goulburn
T (03) 9730 2883 **www**.sedonaestate.com.au **Open** Wed–Sun & public hols 11–5
Winemaker Paul Evans **Est.** 1998 **Dozens** 2600 **Vyds** 4ha

Sedona Estate, established by Paul Evans and Sonja Herges, is located in the picturesque Yea Valley, gateway to Victoria's high country. The unique combination of abundant sunshine, cool nights and low rainfall in this elevated wine region provides a true cool climate for growing premium-quality fruit.

♟♟♟♟♟ **Reserve Yea Valley Shiraz 2014** Matured for 18 months in 80% new American and French oak. It's very easy to see why this is a Reserve: its power and focus is awesome. Midnight-black inky fruits have iron bands of ripe tannins wrapped around them. New American oak is visible once you know it's there, but the usual coconut/vanillan flavour has sunk in the volume of the fruit. Screwcap. 14% alc. **Rating** 95 **To** 2039 $35 ✪

♟♟♟♟♟ **Yea Valley Shiraz 2013 Rating** 90 **To** 2033 $22

See Saw Wine | Jarretts of Orange   ★★★

Annangrove Park, 4 Nanami Lane, Cargo, NSW 2800 **Region** Orange
T (02) 6364 3118 **www**.seesawwine.com **Open** By appt
Winemaker Contract **Est.** 1995 **Dozens** 4000 **Vyds** 170ha
Justin and Pip Jarrett have established one of the largest vineyards in the Orange region. Varieties include chardonnay (51ha), sauvignon blanc (28ha), shiraz and merlot (22ha ea), pinot gris (15ha), cabernet sauvignon (14ha), pinot noir (11ha), gewurztraminer and prosecco (3ha ea), and marsanne (2ha). They also provide management and development services to growers of another 120ha in the region. A substantial part of the annual production is sold to others. One of the purchasers of Jarretts' grapes was See Saw, a venture owned by Hamish MacGowan (of Angus the Bull) and Andrew Margan. In 2014 Hamish and Andrew decided to concentrate on other wine activities, and Jarretts of Orange was the logical purchaser. Exports to the UK.

♟♟♟♟ **See Saw Orange Hunter Valley Sauvignon Blanc Semillon 2015** A surprise, because the blend might have been expected to reduce the impact of the sauvignon blanc, but instead it (seemingly) has had the opposite effect. Certainly it is mouthfilling, and as rich as this blend could ever be, with tropical fruits doing all the heavy lifting. Screwcap. 12.2% alc. **Rating** 89 **To** 2017 $20
See Saw Orange Chardonnay 2015 Free-run juice fermented in stainless steel and French oak with a small portion undergoing mlf, matured for 9 months. This is the no-frills, low-cost vinification that is the See Saw philosophy; citrus, not stone fruit, is the driver. Screwcap. 12.5% alc. **Rating** 89 **To** 2020 $20

Semprevino   ★★★★

1 Waverly Drive, Willunga, SA 5171 **Region** McLaren Vale
T 0417 142 110 **www**.semprevino.com.au **Open** Not
Winemaker Russell Schroder **Est.** 2006 **Dozens** 1000
Semprevino is the venture of Russell Schroder (mechanical engineering) and Simon Doak (science), who became close friends while studying at Monash University in the early 1990s – although both branched in different directions after graduating. The prime mover is Russell, who, after working for CRA/Rio Tinto for five years, left on a four-month trip to Western Europe and became captivated by the life of a vigneron. Returning to Australia, he enrolled in part-time wine science at CSU, obtaining his wine science degree in 2005. Between '03 and '06 he worked vintages in Italy and Vic, coming under the wing of Stephen Pannell at Tinlins (where the Semprevino wines are made) in '06.

♟♟♟♟♟ **McLaren Vale Shiraz 2014** Sweet-edged but substantial. Caramel, tar and sweet plum notes combine to fill the mouth with rich, dark, malty flavour. No holding back. Screwcap. 14.7% alc. **Rating** 92 **To** 2024 $28 CM
McLaren Vale Pinot Gris 2014 Rich, spicy style. Stone fruit and ginger aplenty. Dry to the point of chalkiness through the finish. Accomplished. Screwcap. 13.1% alc. **Rating** 90 **To** 2015 $18 CM ✪

ΨΨΨΨ   Adelaide Hills Gewurztraminer 2015 Rating 89 To 2016 $22 CM
McLaren Vale GSM 2015 Rating 89 To 2021 $24

Sentio Wines   ★★★★☆

23 Priory Lane, Beechworth, Vic 3437 (postal) **Region** Various Vic
T 0433 773 229 **Open** Not
Winemaker Chris Catlow **Est.** 2013 **Dozens** 800
This is a winery to watch. Owner and winemaker Chris Catlow was born (1982) and raised
in Beechworth, and says, 'A passion for wine was inevitable'. He drew particular inspiration
from Barry Morey of Sorrenberg, working there in his late teens. He moved to Melbourne
and enrolled at LaTrobe University in 2011, completing a double-major in viticulture science
and wine science in 2008, and working with Paringa Estate, Kooyong and Portsea Estate from
2006–13. Here Sandro Mosele led him to his fascination with the interaction between place
and chardonnay, and he in turn worked with Benjamin Leroux in Burgundy during vintage
'13, '14 and (prospectively) '16.

ΨΨΨΨΨ   **Lusatia Park Vineyard Yarra Valley** Chardonnay 2014 The best of the
Beechworth and Macedon releases rolled into one. Both generous and cutting
with stone fruit, pear, oatmeal and smoky oak flavours charging through to an
emphatic finish. Lay down misere. Screwcap. 12.8% alc. **Rating** 96 **To** 2021
$42 CM
Beechworth Chardonnay 2014 Announces its quality from the outset. It
drips with succulent pear-like flavour and finishes with cracks of quartz and spice.
Oatmeal and toasty oak make appropriate cameos. Style, flavour, balance; ticks in
all boxes. Screwcap. 13.5% alc. **Rating** 94 **To** 2021 $42 CM
Cope Williams Vineyard Macedon Chardonnay 2014 Takes time to unfurl
but this wine's future looks bright. Lime, honeysuckle, lemon and grapefruit
flavours with splashes of nashi pear. It seeks to impress more through the finish
than upfront; it's an uncompromised wine, its sights set on the years to come.
Screwcap. 12.4% alc. **Rating** 94 **To** 2021 $42 CM
Saxon Vineyard Beechworth Shiraz 2014 Warm style in terms of its fruit
profile, if not in alcohol, though there are plenty of dried- and pepper-spice
characters here, keeping it lively. It's otherwise nutty, black-cherried, licked with
fennel and gently smeared in smoky oak. It would be better though to simply
describe it as complex but seamless. Both tannin and oak melt through the wine.
Further evidence that we have a new top-flight producer in our midst. Screwcap.
13.5% alc. **Rating** 94 **To** 2026 $45 CM

ΨΨΨΨΨ   Beechworth Pinot Noir 2014 Rating 93 To 2024 $35 CM

Seppelt   ★★★★★

36 Cemetery Road, Great Western, Vic 3377 **Region** Grampians
T (03) 5361 2239 **www.**seppelt.com.au **Open** 7 days 10–5
Winemaker Adam Carnaby **Est.** 1851 **Dozens** NFP **Vyds** 500ha
Seppelt once had dual, very different, claims to fame. The first was as Australia's foremost
producer of both white and red sparkling wine, the former led by Salinger, the latter by Show
Sparkling and Original Sparkling Shiraz. The second claim, even more relevant to the Seppelt
of today, was based on the small-volume superb red wines made by Colin Preece from the
1930s through to the early '60s. These were ostensibly Great Western-sourced, but – as the
laws of the time allowed – were often region, variety and vintage blends. Two of his labels
(also of high quality) were Moyston and Chalambar, the latter recently revived. Preece would
have been a child in a lolly shop if he'd had today's viticultural resources to draw on, and
would be quick to recognise the commitment of the winemakers and viticulturists to the
supreme quality of today's portfolio. At the time of going to press, it was highly likely that
Ararat businessman Danial Ahchow will lease the cellar door and surrounds, including the
underground drives. Seppelt will continue to keep the vineyards in the best possible condition.
Exports to the UK, Europe and NZ.

⚛⚛⚛⚛⚛ **Drumborg Vineyard Riesling 2015** Captures you by stealth; the bouquet is reticent, the fore-palate following suit for a split second before expanding dramatically on the way through to the back-palate, where a whirlpool of flavours explodes, the intensity of the lime juice and acidity almost shocking. Screwcap. 12% alc. **Rating** 98 To 2040 $40 ✪

St Peters Grampians Shiraz 2014 The run of scintillating form continues. This builds complexity in lockstep with depth, its black pepper, clove and gun smoke notes sunk deep into the perfectly ripened, smooth-skinned, cherry-plum fruit. Tannin, firm but exquisitely fine, is but one of its many exemplary qualities. A sensational wine. Screwcap. 14% alc. **Rating** 97 To 2040 $80 CM ✪

⚛⚛⚛⚛⚛ **Drumborg Vineyard Henty Chardonnay 2014** Oatmeal, lemongrass, white peach, grapefruit and mineral; it comes across as seamless and silken and, in the end, pretty much sensational. The price makes it ridiculously attractive. Screwcap. 12.5% alc. **Rating** 96 To 2023 $40 CM ✪

Chalambar Grampians Heathcote Shiraz 2014 The lines of acid and tannin, the colouring in of flavour, the light and shade of berried/clovey fruit and savoury-peppery spice. This is that rare moment on the wine map where balance runs into X-factor. Screwcap. 14% alc. **Rating** 96 To 2034 $27 CM ✪

Mount Ida Heathcote Shiraz 2014 This is a wine of high quality. Redcurrant and plum, mint and clove, a slide of saucy, smoky oak. It has both lift and depth, churning tannin and juicy, rushing momentum. It will seduce. There's no stopping it. Screwcap. 14.5% alc. **Rating** 96 To 2036 $55 CM ✪

Great Western Riesling 2015 Extreme purity. Granny Smith apple, ripe lime and slate, perhaps some spice. It shoots through the mouth with clean precision. It's accessible; it will age. It's a beaut. Screwcap. 10.5% alc. **Rating** 95 To 2030 $27 CM ✪

Jaluka Chardonnay 2015 Tangy citrus and green apple flavours never seem sharp or cutting, but they do keep the line of the wine tight. Lactose, honey and sweet spices are all minor but delicious players. The end result of these various facets is a gorgeous wine. Screwcap. 12.5% alc. **Rating** 95 To 2022 $27 CM ✪

Drumborg Vineyard Pinot Noir 2014 Cool, calm and collected. It has power and length but it presents them with an air of nonchalance. Spiced cherries, macerated plums, herbs, a simmer in the corner of smoky wood. It's one of those 'born in the cool, low light of autumn' pinot noirs; there's nothing 'heat of summer' about this. Screwcap. 12.5% alc. **Rating** 95 To 2022 $45 CM

Jaluka Henty Chardonnay 2014 A wine that makes a mockery of its price; just when you think the grapefruit/citrus flavours are verging on monolithic, a surge of white peach appears on the back-palate and finish. While it may not improve greatly with age, it's not going to broaden any time soon. Screwcap. 12.5% alc. **Rating** 94 To 2024 $27 ✪

⚛⚛⚛⚛⚛ **Salinger Vintage Cuvee 2011 Rating** 93 To 2017 $30
Original Sparkling Shiraz 2013 Rating 93 To 2023 $27 TS ✪
Original Sparkling Shiraz 2012 Rating 93 To 2022 $27 ✪
Salinger Vintage Cuvee 2012 Rating 91 To 2020 $30 TS

Seppeltsfield   ★★★★★

Seppeltsfield Road, Seppeltsfield via Nuriootpa, SA 5355 **Region** Barossa Valley
T (08) 8568 6200 **www**.seppeltsfield.com.au **Open** 7 days 10.30–5
Winemaker Fiona Donald **Est.** 1851 **Dozens** 10000 **Vyds** 100ha
This historic Seppelt property and its treasure trove of fortified wines dating back to 1878 was purchased by Janet Holmes à Court, Greg Paramor and Kilikanoon Wines in 2007, from Foster's Wine Estates (now Treasury Wine Estates). Foster's kept the Seppelt brand for table and sparkling wines, mostly produced at Great Western, Vic (see separate entry). In '09 Warren Randall (ex sparkling winemaker for Seppelt at Great Western in the 1980s) acquired 50% of Seppeltsfield and became Managing Director. In February '13, Randall increased his shareholding in Seppeltsfield to over 90%. The change also marks a further commitment to

the making of table wine as well as more focused marketing of the treasure trove of fortified wines. Exports to Hong Kong and China.

🍷🍷🍷🍷🍷 **100 Year Old Para Liqueur 1916** This release should by rights be 100+ points; it adds another layer of velvety richness, and flavours of chocolate and preserved figs, which join the more usual treacle, burnt toffee and molasses. The bouquet has signalled these flavours and more before you take the first sip. The other X-factor with this vintage is the way this glorious array first fills the mouth without the normal (extreme) level of rancio, but swings into top gear with rancio verve and bite on the back-palate, finish and aftertaste, which is very nearly without end. 100ml. Cork. 21% alc. **Rating** 100 **To** 2017 $700

Para Tawny 1995 Matured for 21 years. Curiously, slightly more red-brick-tawny than the younger Para Rare Tawny. Extremely intense, focused and long; the rancio is extreme. Screwcap. 21% alc. **Rating** 97 **To** 2017 $88 ✪

Vintage Tawny Para Liqueur 1986 Full golden-tawny colour; by far the most luscious and rounded of the Paras, in true liqueur style. Coffee, marsala, raisins, spice, the acidity cutting across the palate like a beacon to provide balance and freshness. Cork. 20% alc. **Rating** 97 **To** 2017 $110 ✪

🍷🍷🍷🍷🍷 **Über Shiraz 2014** Has singular and focused concentration; from the oldest estate plantings, vinified in small open concrete fermenters, with no new oak. Whatever role was played in the winery, it is the outcome that matters – and this is amazing, its longevity unknowable. Screwcap. 14.5% alc. **Rating** 96 **To** 2054 $150

Para Rare Tawny NV Minimum average age 18 years. Some hints of olive-brown; very different bouquet, more biscuity; super intense and powerful; extremely long. Some will find this confronting, not comforting (as the Grand Para is). Screwcap. 21% alc. **Rating** 96 **To** 2017 $75 ✪

Barossa Shiraz 2014 Fermented in the 1888 gravity cellar, matured in used French oak. Spectacularly full-bodied, but with no hint of overripe/dead fruit, just tannins running alongside and barking at the black fruits; these tannins are firm, but not the least dry. Screwcap. 14.5% alc. **Rating** 94 **To** 2034 $38

Grand Para NV The average age is a minimum of 10 years; a very luscious and complex wine with intense spicy dried fruit/fruit peel/biscuit/Christmas cake; long, drying, spicy finish with gentle rancio. No significant change since previously tasted. Screwcap. 21% alc. **Rating** 94 **To** 2017 $36

🍷🍷🍷🍷 **Barossa Grenache 2015** **Rating** 92 **To** 2025 $30

Serafino Wines ★★★★★

Kangarilla Road, McLaren Vale, SA 5171 **Region** McLaren Vale
T (08) 8323 0157 **www**.serafinowines.com.au **Open** Mon–Fri 10–4.30, w'ends & public hols 10–4.30
Winemaker Charles Whish **Est.** 2000 **Dozens** 30 000 **Vyds** 100ha

After the sale of Maglieri Wines to Beringer Blass in 1998, Maglieri founder Serafino (Steve) Maglieri acquired the McLarens on the Lake complex originally established by Andrew Garrett. The operation draws upon 40ha each of shiraz and cabernet sauvignon, 7ha of chardonnay, 2ha each of merlot, semillon, barbera, nebbiolo and sangiovese, and 1ha of grenache. Part of the grape production is sold. Serafino Wines has won a number of major trophies in Australia and the UK. Exports to the UK, the US, Canada, Hong Kong, Malaysia and NZ.

🍷🍷🍷🍷🍷 **Terremoto Single Vineyard McLaren Vale Syrah 2013** Still exceptionally inky purple-crimson; paints every crevice of the mouth with infinite care, every brush stroke evenly weighted. It is a magician's wine, its dark blue and black fruits disappearing as you try to take hold of them for further inspection and description; no matter how many times you come back, it moves more quickly than you, leaving no build-up of unwanted flavour. A great McLaren Vale syrah, its future way in the distance. Screwcap. 14.5% alc. **Rating** 97 **To** 2053 $150 ✪

♥♥♥♥♥ **Scarce Earth Malpas Vineyard McLaren Vale Shiraz 2013** This deep and bright crimson-purple wine is all about its place – not just McLaren Vale, but also the dark brown soil over limestone – the wine responding with a layered palate of dark to black-berry fruits, spices and supple tannins. The choice of 4yo oak and limited maturation time might have seemed counterintuitive, but has precisely captured what winemaker Charles Whish was seeking. Screwcap. 14.5% alc. Rating 95 To 2033 $45

Sorrento McLaren Vale Shiraz 2014 The first whiff of the bouquet establishes its region, the first sip reinforcing the message of the bouquet: dark chocolate and McLaren Vale, with a common umbilical chord. It has very good texture and structure that are rarely encountered in a wine of this price. Screwcap. 14.5% alc. Rating 94 To 2034 $20 ✪

Reserve McLaren Vale Grenache 2014 Colour (or lack thereof) is no guide to the quality of the wine; this isn't deep, but is bright, and the palate is in fact remarkably intense, juicy red fruits engaged in an Indian armwrestle with fine, savoury tannins. It's the real deal. Screwcap. 14.4% alc. **Rating** 94 To 2024 $45

GSM McLaren Vale Grenache Shiraz Mataro 2014 Just as Margaret River dominates SSB/SBS and cabernet merlot blends, so does McLaren Vale achieve consistently more than any other region with this GSM blend. 14.5% alcohol suits the medium to full-bodied wine and its Joseph's coat of plum, black cherry, spice and a hint of dark chocolate. Screwcap. **Rating** 94 To 2030 $28 ✪

♥♥♥♥♡ **McLaren Vale Shiraz 2014** Rating 93 To 2034 $28
Sharktooth McLaren Vale Shiraz 2013 Rating 93 To 2030 $80
Magnitude McLaren Vale Shiraz 2012 Rating 92 To 2032 $45
BDX McLaren Vale Cabernet Sauvignon Merlot Carmenere Cabernet Franc 2014 Rating 92 To 2024 $28
Bellissimo Tempranillo 2015 Rating 90 To 2025 $20 ✪

Serrat   ★★★★★

PO Box 478, Yarra Glen, Vic 3775 **Region** Yarra Valley
T (03) 9730 1439 **www**.serrat.com.au **Open** Not
Winemaker Tom Carson **Est.** 2001 **Dozens** 450 **Vyds** 2.7ha
Serrat is the family business of Tom Carson (after a 12-year reign at Yering Station, now running Yabby Lake and Heathcote Estate for the Kirby family) and wife Nadege Suné. They have close-planted (at 8800 vines per hectare) 0.8ha each of pinot noir and chardonnay, 0.4ha of shiraz, and a sprinkling of viognier. Most recent has been the establishment of an esoteric mix of 0.1ha each of malbec, nebbiolo, barbera and grenache. As well as being a consummate winemaker, Tom has one of the best palates in Australia, and a deep understanding of fine wines of the world, which he and Nadege drink at every opportunity (when they aren't drinking Serrat). Viticulture and winemaking hit new heights with the 2014 Yarra Valley Shiraz Viognier named 2016 *Wine Companion* Wine of the Year (from a field of 8863 wines).

♥♥♥♥♥ **Yarra Valley Chardonnay 2015** Hand-picked, whole bunch-pressed, wild-fermented in French puncheons (20% new), matured for 11 months. Yarra Valley deeply embedded in its DNA; it is super-intense and almost impossibly long, the oak merely a vehicle. Despite all its energy, it has a flowery delicacy. Screwcap. 13% alc. **Rating** 98 To 2027 $42 ✪

Yarra Valley Shiraz Viognier 2015 95% shiraz (Best old clone 1866 planting/ BVRC 15) and 5% viognier co-fermented, matured for 11 months in French oak (25% new). Deep crimson-purple; a worthy successor to the '14 (Wine of the Year *Wine Companion* '16); very complex, deep and powerful, seemingly reflecting its clonal heritage ex Best's (unless it's vine maturity). Spice and pepper are threaded through the red/black cherry and plum fruit; fine tannins and entirely integrated and balanced oak complete a story that has to be personally experienced. Remember, all this achieved at 13% alcohol. Screwcap. 13% alc. **Rating** 98 To 2045 $42 ✪

🍷🍷🍷🍷🍷 **Yarra Valley Pinot Noir 2015** Light, clear and bright colour; a particularly fragrant, spicy bouquet, then a palate with great drive and intensity, small red fruits with fine, lipsmacking tannins providing length and aftertaste. Screwcap. 13% alc. **Rating** 96 **To** 2027 $42 ✪

Fourre-Tout 2015 Since Serrat – and its two owner/winemakers – walk on water, why shouldn't they lead the world by blending 60% malbec with 40% nebbiolo (and a splash of grenache) for a grand total of absolutely delicious plum and cherry fruit? It's almost sacrilegious to subject it to points. Screwcap. 13% alc. **Rating** 95 **To** 2025 $30 ✪

Yarra Valley Grenache Noir 2015 Light, bright colour; lively crunchy red fruit flavours and texture; crisp finish; cool climate grenache is a very different proposition from McLaren Vale grenache. Screwcap. 13% alc. **Rating** 94 **To** 2025 $42

Sevenhill Cellars

111c College Road, Sevenhill, SA 5453 **Region** Clare Valley
T (08) 8843 4222 **www.**sevenhill.com.au **Open** 7 days 10–5
Winemaker Liz Heidenreich, Brother John May **Est.** 1851 **Dozens** 25 000 **Vyds** 95.8ha
One of the historical treasures of Australia; the oft-photographed stone wine cellars are the oldest in the Clare Valley, and winemaking remains an enterprise within the Jesuit Province of Australia. All the wines reflect the estate-grown grapes from old vines. Notwithstanding the difficult economic times, Sevenhill Cellars has increased its vineyard holdings from 74ha to 95ha, and, naturally, production has risen. Exports to the UK, Switzerland, Indonesia, Malaysia, Vietnam, Japan and Hong Kong.

🍷🍷🍷🍷🍷 **St Ignatius 2015** Cabernet sauvignon, merlot, malbec and cabernet franc. This makes it neat, manageable, presentable, perfectly suitable for any table, anywhere. None of this of course does anything to lessen its considerable size, here expressed as fierce intensity of blackberried fruit, but it adds layers, as do chunky bolts of tannin. Screwcap. 14.5% alc. **Rating** 95 **To** 2040 $45 CM

St Francis Xavier 2015 Very cool fermentation in stainless steel preserves the high natural acidity and minerality of riesling on the one hand, a circus ring of citrus fruits on the other. The aftertaste tells you what will emerge in 5+ years. Screwcap. 13% alc. **Rating** 94 **To** 2030 $35

Brother John May Reserve Shiraz 2010 Big, warm, blackberried fruit, screwed tight. Not a lot of charm, but an enormous amount of brooding flavour. Spearmint, peppercorns, melted dark chocolate; they all get a run. A long life in the bottle is assured. Screwcap. 15.5% alc. **Rating** 94 **To** 2038 $95 CM

🍷🍷🍷🍷🍷 **Inigo Clare Valley Riesling 2015** **Rating** 91 **To** 2025 $22 ✪
Estate Grown Clare Valley Barbera 2013 **Rating** 91 **To** 2020 $28 CM

Seville Estate

65 Linwood Road, Seville, Vic 3139 **Region** Yarra Valley
T (03) 5964 2622 **www.**sevilleestate.com.au **Open** 7 days 10–5
Winemaker Dylan McMahon **Est.** 1972 **Dozens** 7500 **Vyds** 8.08ha
Dr Peter McMahon and wife Margaret commenced planting Seville Estate in 1972, part of the resurgence of the Yarra Valley. Peter and Margaret retired in '97, selling to Brokenwood. Graham and Margaret Van Der Meulen acquired the property in 2005, bringing it back into family ownership. Graham and Margaret are hands-on in the vineyard and winery, working closely with winemaker Dylan McMahon, who is the grandson of Peter and Margaret. The philosophy is to capture the fruit expression of the vineyard in styles that reflect the cool climate. Exports to the US and China.

🍷🍷🍷🍷🍷 **Yarra Valley Chardonnay 2015** This is very different from The Barber; the fruit profile is much tighter, the length is greater, the flavours more intense and longer. Was clearly barrel-fermented, not so much from the point of view of flavour as mouthfeel. It really sings. Screwcap. 13% alc. **Rating** 96 **To** 2028 $36 ✪

Reserve Yarra Valley Chardonnay 2015 This is a very good wine, but the difference between it and the estate Chardonnay is much less than that between the estate and The Barber. It's about the future, which may well lie with this wine. In the meantime, the value lies with the Estate. Screwcap. 13% alc. **Rating** 96 To 2030 $70 ✪

Old Vine Reserve Yarra Valley Cabernet Sauvignon 2014 Very good hue; a lovely wine from 42yo vines, no mint or green characters whatsoever, just fragrant cassis blossoming out of the glass on the first whiff, everything flowing on calmly and inexorably thereafter. A very different world since the '70s and '80s for red soil cabernets. Screwcap. 13% alc. **Rating** 96 To 2034 $70 ✪

Yarra Valley Pinot Noir 2015 Bright crimson-purple; the bouquet and palate both throw down the gauntlet with a riveting display of black cherry, spice and a (pleasantly) stalky/vegetal background. Makes a convincing claim for more time in bottle – like lots more. Screwcap. 13.5% alc. **Rating** 95 To 2025 $36

Old Vine Reserve Yarra Valley Shiraz 2014 Densely coloured and flavoured, the bouquet brings in red and black cherry fruit encased in a sheen of spicy/savoury/brambly nuances, the path to the palate simply bringing all the texture and structure into play, but the wine is just too young. Screwcap. 13% alc. **Rating** 95 To 2044 $70

Yarra Valley Shiraz 2014 Fermented with 20% whole bunches, with a substantial amount of estate-grown fruit. A very fragrant bouquet of red and black cherries is liberally laced with spice and pepper; the palate brings home the bacon with very good texture from skilled handling of the tannins giving structure, and a reprise of the fruits of the bouquet. Screwcap. 13% alc. **Rating** 95 To 2034 $36

Old Vine Reserve Yarra Valley Pinot Noir 2015 The lightest colour of Seville Estate's trio of '15 Pinots, but still above average; the bouquet is intensely perfumed, but the palate takes it up another decibel with its drive and intensity. A savoury whole-bunch edge lifts the profile and length of an extremely good pinot noir. Screwcap. 13.5% alc. **Rating** 94 To 2023 $70

The Barber Yarra Valley Pinot Noir 2015 Deep, vibrant crimson-purple, unusual for pinot noir; potent and rich, with plum and strawberries all on parade; remarkable for its third-tier status, particularly as the savoury back-palate and finish come into play. Screwcap. 13.5% alc. **Rating** 94 To 2023 $24 ✪

♀♀♀♀♀ **Yarra Valley Riesling 2015** Rating 93 To 2025 $36
The Barber Yarra Valley Chardonnay 2015 Rating 92 To 2020 $24 ✪
The Barber Yarra Valley Shiraz Cabernet 2013 Rating 91 To 2020 $24 CM

Seville Hill   ★★★★

8 Paynes Road, Seville, Vic 3139 **Region** Yarra Valley
T (03) 5964 3284 **www**.sevillehill.com.au **Open** 7 days 10–6
Winemaker Dominic Bucci, John D'Aloisio **Est.** 1991 **Dozens** 3000 **Vyds** 6ha
John and Josie D'Aloisio have had a long-term involvement in the agricultural industry, which ultimately led to the establishment of Seville Hill in 1991. Plantings of cabernet sauvignon replaced the old apple and cherry orchard on the site. A small winery was established, with long-term friend Dominic Bucci and John D'Aloisio making the wines. In 2011 1ha of the original 6ha was grafted over to nebbiolo, barbera, sangiovese and tempranillo. John and Josie's sons Christopher, Jason and Charles are also involved in all aspects of the business.

♀♀♀♀♀ **No. 8 Shiraz 2012** An attractive wine, easily approached, with all its components balanced and integrated; dark cherry and plum, soft tannins and clever use of oak all sit well. Cork. 14% alc. **Rating** 92 To 2027 $60

Reserve Yarra Valley Chardonnay 2014 Has the length of flavour on the palate typical of the Yarra Valley, the accent firmly on fruit, not oak; that said, there are some cashew and spice flavours that add to the appeal. Cork. 13.5% alc. **Rating** 91 To 2020 $30

Reserve Yarra Valley Shiraz 2013 Hand-picked, open-fermented, 14 days on skins, matured in French oak (25% new) for 12 months. Has vibrant, red soil/cool climate fingerprints all over it; its fragrance is intense, juicy red fruits likewise, oak an incidental extra. Cork. 14.6% alc. **Rating** 91 **To** 2025 $40

Yarra Valley Sangiovese 2013 Bright hue; a New World sangio, with buckets of red cherry fruit and supple, fine tannins; it's also about to build perfume. Cork. 13% alc. **Rating** 91 **To** 2023 $35

Yarra Valley Barbera 2013 Dark cherry with a slightly savoury twist is the dominant player on the medium-bodied palate, the acidity fresh and cleansing. Cork. 13.5% alc. **Rating** 90 **To** 2020 $35

Yarra Valley Tempranillo 2013 One size fits all vinification, but this has the deepest colour of the Seville Hill trio of alternative varieties. Intriguing coffee ground aromas and poached fruits with spices – unusual, but not unpleasant. Cork. 13.8% alc. **Rating** 90 **To** 2025 $35

Sew & Sew Wines

PO Box 1924, McLaren Flat, SA 5171 **Region** Adelaide Hills
T 0419 804 345 **www.**sewandsewwines.com.au **Open** Not
Winemaker Jodie Armstrong **Est.** 2004 **Dozens** 630
Co-owner and winemaker Jodie Armstrong works as a viticulturist by day, consulting to vineyards in the Adelaide Hills and McLaren Vale, at night making small amounts of wine. Grapes are chosen from the vineyards that Jodie manages, and she makes the wines in garagiste facilities in the Adelaide Hills and McLaren Vale, with the support of local oenological talent and her Sydney-based partner Andrew Mason. Exports to Denmark.

ΨΨΨΨΨ **Adelaide Hills Syrah 2013** A frighteningly beautiful wine. It strikes out at you with rich fruit flavour but then seduces via highlights of dried spice and assorted florals. There's no way to escape, but there's no way you'd want to. It's like being leg-roped by an all-consuming idea. Tannin, firm and ripe, makes the embrace certain. Screwcap. 13.7% alc. **Rating** 97 **To** 2036 $35 CM ✪

ΨΨΨΨΨ **Adelaide Hills Shiraz 2014** Immaculate. Power and glory. Strong, rich, plum-shot fruit, toasty/cedary oak, nuances of spice and a liberal sprinkling of X-factor. Drink it now or drink it in 20 years; it will run to your schedule (appropriately stored, of course). Screwcap. 13.8% alc. **Rating** 95 **To** 2034 $25 CM ✪

Adelaide Hills Chardonnay 2015 Breath of fresh air. Completely different style from the '14. This is balanced, sure-footed, full of style and length. A beautiful chardonnay just starting to spread it wings; a long flight lies ahead. Screwcap. 13.5% alc. **Rating** 94 **To** 2021 $35 CM

ΨΨΨΨΨ **Adelaide Hills Pinot Noir 2014 Rating** 92 **To** 2020 $35 CM

Shadowfax

K Road, Werribee, Vic 3030 **Region** Geelong
T (03) 9731 4420 **www.**shadowfax.com.au **Open** 7 days 11–5
Winemaker Matt Harrop **Est.** 2000 **Dozens** 15 000
Shadowfax is part of an awesome development at Werribee Park, a mere 20 minutes from Melbourne. The truly striking winery, designed by Wood Marsh Architects and built in 2000, is adjacent to the extraordinary private home built in the 1880s by the Chirnside family and known as The Mansion. It was then the centrepiece of a 40 000ha pastoral empire, and the appropriately magnificent gardens were part of the reason for the property being acquired by Parks Victoria in the early 1970s. The Mansion is now The Mansion Hotel, with 92 rooms and suites. Exports to the UK, Japan, NZ and Singapore.

ΨΨΨΨΨ **Macedon Ranges Chardonnay 2014** Pale straw; melon, grapefruit and white peach with a lick of spicy oak. Superfine and beautifully balanced, the palate is seamless, with a complex array of fruits coupled with minerality, texture and real presence and length. Screwcap. 13% alc. **Rating** 96 **To** 2030 $32 ✪

Geelong Riesling 2015 Quartz-green; the wine has energy and drive, with lime and grapefruit both having their say on the long palate, flinty acidity the cream on the cake. Surprise packet. Screwcap. 13% alc. **Rating** 95 **To** 2030 $26 ✪

Geelong Chardonnay 2015 Lemon, grapefruit and an intriguing spice note are coupled with a complex background of lees and well-framed oak. The palate has an abundance of concentrated and beautifully textured fruit tightly bound by the mineral line. Screwcap. 13% alc. **Rating** 95 **To** 2020 $30 **○**

Geelong Pinot Noir 2015 Bright, full purple-crimson; genteel power, with the full range of red, blue and purple pinot fruits; the length and balance are impeccable, the price an absolute steal. Screwcap. 13% alc. **Rating** 95 **To** 2028 $30 **○**

♥♥♥♥♀ **Minnow 2015 Rating** 93 **To** 2016 $25 CM **○**
Macedon Ranges Pinot Noir 2014 Rating 92 **To** 2027 $30

Shaw + Smith   ★★★★★

136 Jones Road, Balhannah, SA 5242 **Region** Adelaide Hills
T (08) 8398 0500 **www**.shawandsmith.com **Open** 7 days 11–5
Winemaker Martin Shaw, Adam Wadewitz **Est.** 1989 **Dozens** NFP **Vyds** 80.9ha
Cousins Martin Shaw and Michael Hill Smith MW already had unbeatable experience when they founded Shaw + Smith as a virtual winery in 1989. The brand was firmly established as a leading producer of Sauvignon Blanc by the time they acquired a 42ha property at Woodside known as the M3 Vineyard (as it is owned by Michael and Matthew Hill Smith and Martin Shaw). In '99 Martin and Michael purchased the 36ha Balhannah property, building the superbly designed winery in 2000 and planting more sauvignon blanc, shiraz, pinot noir and riesling. It is here that visitors can taste the wines in appropriately beautiful surroundings. Exports to all major markets.

♥♥♥♥♥ **Adelaide Hills Pinot Noir 2014** Excellent clarity and hue; resonates exceptional winemaking choices, the bouquet ultra-fragrant, the palate silky and sibilant, the full array of red fruits led by strawberry and red cherries, but not stopping there. Next to Ashton Hills, King of the Adelaide Hills pinots. Screwcap. 12.5% alc. **Rating** 96 **To** 2023 $45 **○**

Adelaide Hills Shiraz 2014 Has established a consistent reputation as one of Australia's best cool climate shirazs, low yields (especially in 2014) and site selection all-important. A super-fragrant red cherry bouquet, with notes of mulberry, licorice and plum joining the vibrant red fruits of the palate, backed by firm, precisely framed tannins. Screwcap. 14% alc. **Rating** 96 **To** 2030 $44 **○**

Balhannah Vineyard Shiraz 2013 Inaugural release from a vineyard planted to 5550 vines per hectare. It's an exotic wine, developing slowly. Truffles, cloves, olives and saltbush on a bed of dark cherry-plum fruit. Tannin: ultrafine. Length: to burn. It's complex already but new worlds of aroma/flavour will open up given time. Screwcap. 14% alc. **Rating** 96 **To** 2035 $85 CM

Adelaide Hills Riesling 2015 Quartz-white shouldn't deceive: this has beautifully tempered citrus/lime and green apple flavours of the kind you expect from Germany. It has almost feline grace to its mouthfeel, the perfect balance of titratable acidity and pH, with the alcohol doing the trick. Screwcap. 11.5% alc. **Rating** 95 **To** 2027 $30 **○**

M3 Adelaide Hills Chardonnay 2014 Wild fermented in new and used French barriques; 9 months maturation. Makes its presence felt the first millisecond it enters the mouth, but doesn't threaten. A seamless fusion of white peach, biscuity oak and fresh acidity. Screwcap. 12.5% alc. **Rating** 95 **To** 2023 $44

Adelaide Hills Sauvignon Blanc 2015 Adelaide Hills enjoyed a picture-perfect vintage, with moderate yields ripening to perfection. The wine verges on fleshy on the mid-palate, then finishes with a swagger of limey natural acidity on the long, fresh finish. Flavours? Grapefruit and a touch of passionfruit. Screwcap. 12.5% alc. **Rating** 94 **To** 2016 $26 **○**

Shaw Family Vintners

Myrtle Grove Road, Currency Creek, SA 5214 **Region** Currency Creek/McLaren Vale
T (08) 8555 4215 **www**.shawfamilyvintners.com **Open** 7 days 10–5
Winemaker John Loxton **Est.** 2001 **Dozens** 100000 **Vyds** 461ha
Richard and Marie Shaw ventured into the wine industry by planting shiraz in the early 1970s
at McLaren Flat. They still have the original vineyards, and during the Vine Pull Scheme of
the '80s saved several neighbours' valuable old shiraz and grenache. Their three sons are also
involved in the family business. Extensive vineyards are now held in Currency Creek (350ha)
and McLaren Vale (64ha), with a modern winery in Currency Creek. RMS is the flagship
release, named in honour of founder Richard Morton Shaw. Shaw Family has a second
cellar door and café at Signal Point, Goolwa. Exports to the UK, the US, Canada, Fiji, NZ
and China.

🍷🍷🍷🍷🍷 **Stonemason Currency Creek Cabernet Sauvignon 2014** Bright hue; this
has all of the delicious, fine cassis fruit allied with superfine tannins that neighbour
Langhorne Creek has at its best. The oak, too, has been expertly handed. Screwcap.
14.5% alc. **Rating** 95 **To** 2029 $16 ⬩
Rusty Plough Single Vineyard McLaren Vale Grenache 2013 Crushed and
destemmed, cultured yeast, 5 days on skins, matured for 18 months in French oak.
Another take on McLaren Vale grenache, with extended maturation in French oak
adding to, not detracting from, the flavour spectrum. It also adds to the structure
behind the cherry and raspberry fruits, spices completing the picture. Cork.
15.5% alc. **Rating** 94 **To** 2023 $35

🍷🍷🍷🍷🍷 **Currency Creek Estate Ostrich Hill Shiraz 2014** **Rating** 92 **To** 2034 $35

Shaw Vineyard Estate

34 Isabel Drive, Murrumbateman, NSW 2582 **Region** Canberra District
T (02) 6227 5827 **www**.shawvineyards.com.au **Open** Wed–Sun & public hols 10–5
Winemaker Graeme Shaw, Tony Steffania **Est.** 1999 **Dozens** 12000 **Vyds** 33ha
Graeme and Ann Shaw established their vineyard (cabernet sauvignon, merlot, shiraz, semillon
and riesling) in 1998 on a 280ha fine wool-producing property established in the mid-1800s
and known as Olleyville. It is one of the largest privately owned vineyard holdings in the
Canberra area. Their children are fully employed in the family business, Michael as viticulturist
and Tanya as cellar door manager. Shaw Vineyard Estate operates a 'wine shop' cellar door in
conjunction with Suntay Wines in Hainan Island, China, with plans for further cellar doors in
Shi Jia Zuang and Changzhi. Exports to The Netherlands, Vietnam, Singapore, Thailand, the
Philippines, South Korea, Hong Kong and China.

🍷🍷🍷🍷🍷 **Estate Canberra Riesling 2015** Three trophies at the Cool Climate Wine
Show '15: Best Riesling, Best White Wine and Best Wine of Show. It's not the
least surprising: this has all the marks of great riesling. The bouquet is flowery/
estery (kaffir lime leaf is the Shaw Vineyard description and is spot on), the palate
a concerto of citrus and crystalline acidity, the finish as fresh as a daisy. The value
needs no comment. Screwcap. 13% alc. **Rating** 97 **To** 2030 $25 ⬩

🍷🍷🍷🍷🍷 **Reserve Merriman Canberra District Merlot 2013** A firm, assertive wine,
eager to impress but equally keen to do it the right way, rather than striking simply
at size. Nutty dark cherry and blackberry flavours, edging into mulberry, with
silty/nutty tannin keeping the strings pulled tight. Undergrowth character adds yet
more complexity. It's a wine that slowly but surely gets under your skin. Screwcap.
13% alc. **Rating** 95 **To** 2028 $60 CM
Reserve Canberra District Semillon 2015 This is the first varietal Reserve
release. It's a wild affair on the bouquet before settling in to a palate sizzling with
lemongrass, stone fruit and citrus. There's nothing neutral about this wine; it makes
a statement, all the while remaining fine. Lovely persistence too. Screwcap. 13% alc.
Rating 94 **To** 2020 $35 CM

🍷🍷🍷🍷🍷 Winemakers Selection 2015 Rating 90 To 2017 $16 ❍
Estate Canberra Merlot 2013 Rating 90 To 2020 $25

Shaws Road   ★★★☆

225 Shaws Road, Arthurs Creek, Vic 3099 **Region** Yarra Valley
T (03) 9439 4144 **www**.shawsroad.com.au **Open** 3rd Sun each month 11–5
Winemaker George Apted, John Graves **Est.** 1990 **Dozens** 1000 **Vyds** 4.5ha
This enterprise has grown in stages since the first vines (chardonnay) were planted at the
Eltham Vineyard in 1982, followed by cabernet sauvignon in '83. In '86 a second vineyard
at Shaws Road, Arthurs Creek, was established, with larger plantings of chardonnay, pinot
noir, cabernet sauvignon, cabernet franc and merlot. This vineyard was expanded in '97 with
additional plantings of pinot noir and chardonnay. In 2007 a new winery on the Shaws Road
vineyard was completed. The following year Strathewen Hills winery and vineyard were
purchased from the Christophersen family.

🍷🍷🍷🍷🍷 **Reserve Yarra Valley Cabernet Sauvignon 2006** Is hanging on well, the
colour only marginally more advanced than the '12, cassis running down the
middle of the long palate in fine fashion, the tannins as they should be. Cork.
13.2% alc. **Rating** 90 **To** 2020 $28

Shearer's Hill   ★★★

179 Strathalbyn-Milang Road, Langhorne Creek, SA 5255 **Region** Langhorne Creek
T (08) 8536 4573 **Open** Not
Winemaker Peter Pollard **Est.** 2005 **Dozens** 7000 **Vyds** 360ha
This former grazing property, owned by the Crawford family, underwent a major change
when planting of 360ha of grapes began. The substantial plantings include shiraz (135ha),
chardonnay (82ha), cabernet sauvignon (31ha), with smaller plantings of sauvignon blanc,
pinot gris, pinot noir and merlot. Not all the grapes are used for the Shearer's Hill label, the
excess being sold to other winemakers.

🍷🍷🍷🍷 **Prestige Shiraz 2013** This is a very different wine from its Premium sibling,
with more flavour to start with, then significantly longer time in the upgraded oak.
That said, there is an unusual gritty texture to the palate, sometimes caused by oak
chips or staves. Screwcap. 14.5% alc. **Rating** 88 **To** 2025 $35

Shingleback   ★★★★★

3 Stump Hill Road, McLaren Vale, SA 5171 **Region** McLaren Vale
T (08) 8323 7388 **www**.shingleback.com.au **Open** 7 days 10–5
Winemaker John Davey, Dan Hills **Est.** 1995 **Dozens** 160 000 **Vyds** 120ha
Brothers Kym and John Davey planted and nurture their family-owned and sustainably
managed vineyard on land purchased by their grandfather in the 1950s. Shingleback has been
a success story since its establishment. Its 110ha of estate vineyards are one of the keys to that
success, winning the Jimmy Watson Trophy '06 for the '05 D Block Cabernet Sauvignon. The
well-made wines are rich and full-flavoured, but not overripe (and, hence, not excessively
alcoholic). Exports to the UK, the US, Canada, Cambodia, Vietnam, China and NZ.

🍷🍷🍷🍷🍷 **Unedited McLaren Vale Shiraz 2014** The flag-bearer for Shingleback, tasted
over a year before its release in Mar '17. There is no reason whatsoever why it
shouldn't emulate its illustrious predecessors, for it has that all-important quality of
balance, and while powerful, isn't the least bit extractive. May well deserve higher
points when released. Cork. 14.5% alc. **Rating** 95 **To** 2044 $80
The Gate McLaren Vale Shiraz 2014 Matured in used American (80%) and
French oak for 15 months, a barrel selection. Vibrant colour, and powerfully
built from its bootstraps up; inky black fruits, tar, licorice and classy tannins all
agree with each other – this will be in cruise mode for decades to come. Cork.
14.5% alc. **Rating** 95 **To** 2039 $35 ❍

D Block Reserve McLaren Vale Cabernet Sauvignon 2013 As is entirely appropriate, the wine first expresses its variety, and second its place of origin, the latter taking some of the edge off the mouthfeel, although leaving the tannins to have their say. It's a medium to full-bodied cabernet with crowd-pleaser appeal. Cork. 14.5% alc. **Rating** 94 **To** 2033 $55

 Davey Estate Reserve Shiraz 2014 Rating 93 To 2034 $23 **○**
D Block Reserve McLaren Vale Shiraz 2013 Rating 93 To 2033 $55
Davey Estate Reserve Cabernet 2014 Rating 92 To 2029 $23 **○**
Kiss me Kate Adelaide Hills Chardonnay 2015 Rating 91 To 2021 $23 **○**
Davey Brothers McLaren Vale Shiraz 2014 Rating 91 To 2024 $18 **○**

Shirvington   ★★★★☆

PO Box 220, McLaren Vale, SA 5171 **Region** McLaren Vale
T (08) 8323 7649 **www**.shirvington.com **Open** Not
Winemaker Kim Jackson **Est.** 1996 **Dozens** 950 **Vyds** 23.8ha
The Shirvington family began the development of their McLaren Vale vineyards in 1996 under the direction of viticulturist Peter Bolte, and now have almost 24ha under vine, the majority to shiraz and cabernet sauvignon, with small additional plantings of mataro and grenache. A substantial part of the production is sold as grapes, the best reserved for the Shirvington wines. Exports to the UK and US.

McLaren Vale Shiraz 2012 Beefy shiraz with tar, plum and leather characters bristling beneath a veneer of resiny oak. It's an old-school style but there's no denying the power of fruit. Cork. 14.5% alc. **Rating** 92 **To** 2024 $38 CM
McLaren Vale Cabernet Sauvignon 2012 Mellow cabernet with leather and blackcurrant flavours easing into bay leaf and toasty oak. Heft of both tannin and fruit and in that sense, mouthfilling. Makes its point without trying to finesse the situation at all. Cork. 14% alc. **Rating** 91 **To** 2024 $32 CM

Shoofly | Frisk   ★★★★

PO Box 119, Mooroolbark, Vic 3138 **Region** Various
T 0405 631 557 **www**.shooflywines.com **Open** Not
Winemaker Ben Riggs, Garry Wall **Est.** 2003 **Dozens** 15 000
This is a far-flung, export-oriented, business. It purchases a little over 620 tonnes of grapes each vintage, the lion's share (surprisingly) riesling (250 tonnes), followed by shiraz (200 tonnes) and chardonnay (50 tonnes); the remainder is made up of pinot noir, gewurztraminer, merlot, dolcetto and muscat gordo blanco. Ben Riggs makes Shoofly Shiraz and Chardonnay at Vintners McLaren Vale; Frisk Riesling is made by Garry Wall at King Valley Wines. The bulk of exports go the the US, Canada and Ireland.

Shoofly Adelaide Hills Chardonnay 2013 Bright straw-green; a stylish wine with clear-cut grapefruit/white peach flavours and an airbrush of oak. A steal at the price. Screwcap. 13.5% alc. **Rating** 91 **To** 2017 $15 **○**
Shoofly Pinot Noir 2014 Light, clear colour; there aren't many pinots from the Yarra and King Valleys buzzing around with this degree of varietal fruit, its varietal purity suggesting little or no oak. It's a drink tonight bargain of some magnitude. Screwcap. 13.5% alc. **Rating** 90 **To** 2016 $15 **○**

Shoofly Adelaide Hills Chardonnay 2015 Rating 89 To 2017 $15 **○**
Shoofly Victoria Pinot Noir 2015 Rating 89 To 2020 $15 **○**
Shoofly Shiraz 2014 Rating 89 To 2020 $15 **○**

Shottesbrooke   ★★★★★

Bagshaws Road, McLaren Flat, SA 5171 **Region** McLaren Vale
T (08) 8383 0002 **www**.shottesbrooke.com.au **Open** Mon–Fri 10–4.30, w'ends & public hols 11–5
Winemaker Hamish Maguire **Est.** 1984 **Dozens** 12 000 **Vyds** 30.64ha

Founded by Nick Holmes, who has since passed the winemaking baton on to Flying Winemaker stepson Hamish Maguire, who completed two vintages in France, and one in Spain before settling permanently at Shottesbrooke. The capacity of the winery has been increased to 1200 tonnes annually, and it has a storage capacity for almost 1 million litres. This is far in excess of the amount made under the Shottesbrooke label, the remainder for contract winemaking for a number of other independent brands. Hamish also travels both nationally and internationally promoting the Shottesbrooke brand. Exports to all major markets.

🍷🍷🍷🍷🍷 **Single Vineyard Blewitt Springs Shiraz 2013** A richly coloured and flavoured tapestry in the cooler mode of Blewitt Springs; black fruits, spice and a wisp of bitter chocolate (80% cacao) are underpinned by firm tannins. A full-bodied class act with a long future. Screwcap. 14.5% alc. **Rating** 95 **To** 2038 $50

Eliza Reserve McLaren Vale Shiraz 2012 It's an unreconstructed style, 'unashamedly old school' in the words of winemaker Hamish Maguire, with essency plum lavishly coated and infused with milk chocolate (oak) flavour. Baby smooth. Firm enough, with fine tannin. It has the balance and texture to drink well now, but will of course mature well over many years. Screwcap. 14.5% alc. **Rating** 95 **To** 2027 $50 CM

The Proprietor Reserve 2012 49% cabernet sauvignon, 42% merlot, 9% malbec. It's soft and fluid, but dry herb characters and dusty tannin help afford it some seriousness. This isn't going to let anyone down. Dark-berried fruit, well formed and structured, is the hero. Screwcap. 14.5% alc. **Rating** 95 **To** 2032 $60 CM

🍷🍷🍷🍷♀ **Punch Reserve Cabernet 2012 Rating** 93 **To** 2028 $60 CM
Adelaide Hills Chardonnay 2015 Rating 92 **To** 2021 $35 CM
Adelaide Hills Sauvignon Blanc 2015 Rating 91 **To** 2016 $20 CM ✪
McLaren Flat Cabernet Sauvignon 2012 Rating 90 **To** 2025 $40

Shut the Gate Wines ★★★★

2 Main North Road, Watervale, SA 5452 **Region** Clare Valley
T 0488 243 200 **Open** 7 days 10–4.30
Winemaker Contract **Est.** 2013 **Dozens** 5000
Shut the Gate is the venture of Richard Woods and Rasa Fabian, which took shape after five years' involvement in the rebranding of Crabtree Watervale Wines, followed by 18 months of juggling consultancy roles. During this time Richard and Rasa set the foundations for Shut the Gate, with striking and imaginative labels (and parables) catching the eye. The engine room of the business is the Clare Valley, where the wines are contract-made and the grapes for many of the two ranges of wines are sourced. They have chosen their grape sources and contract winemakers with considerable care. Exports to Canada and Hong Kong.

🍷🍷🍷🍷🍷 **Fur Elise Clare Valley Grenache Rose 2015** Vivid, pale crimson-purple; the highly perfumed bouquet is filled with Turkish delight and rose hip, the lively, bone-dry palate offering a cornucopia of red fruits, the lipsmacking finish demanding another glass. Screwcap. 13% alc. **Rating** 94 **To** 2017 $20 ✪

For Hunger Single Site Clare Valley Grenache 2013 There is a well of red fruits and a fine-spun web of tannins. Like many good grenaches, the mouthfeel has similarities to that of pinot noir, even though the flavours are very different. The more you retaste this wine, the more you become aware of its length and finesse. Screwcap. 14.5% alc. **Rating** 94 **To** 2023 $25 ✪

🍷🍷🍷🍷♀ **Rosie's Patch Watervale Riesling 2015 Rating** 92 **To** 2027 $20 ✪
For Hunger Single Site Clare Valley Shiraz 2012 Rating 92 **To** 2027 $45
For Freedom Polish Hill River Riesling 2015 Rating 91 **To** 2030 $25
For Love Watervale Riesling 2015 Rating 91 **To** 2030 $25
The Forager Clare Valley Shiraz 2012 Rating 90 **To** 2032 $20 ✪

Sidewood Estate ★★★★★

Maximilian's Restaurant, 15 Onkaparinga Valley Road, Verdun, SA 5245
Region Adelaide Hills
T (08) 8389 9234 **www**.sidewood.com.au **Open** Wed–Sun 11–5
Winemaker Darryl Catlin, Natasha Mooney **Est.** 2000 **Dozens** NFP **Vyds** 93ha
Sidewood Estate is part-vineyard and part-horse stables and racehorse training. Owned by Owen and Cassandra Inglis since 2004, both aspects of the business are flourishing. Sidewood Estate lies in the Onkaparinga Valley, with the vines weathering the coolest climate in the Adelaide Hills. Significant expenditure on regeneration of and increase in the size of the vineyards was already well underway when Sidewood obtained a SA State Regional Government Fund grant of $856 000, being part of a $3.5 million expansion of the winery capacity from 500 to 2000 tonnes each vintage. The expenditure will include new bottling and canning facilities capable of handing 400 000 bottles of wine and cider annually by '17. Wines are released under the Sidewood Estate, Stable Hill and Mappinga labels, the last the Reserve range. Exports to the UK, the US and other major markets.

🍷🍷🍷🍷🍷 **Sauvignon Blanc 2015** Whole bunch-pressed, free-run juice cool-fermented, matured on lees for 5 months. The bouquet is correct, the palate with unusual length and persistence to gently tropical fruits. Gold medal Melbourne Wine Awards '15. Screwcap. 12.5% alc. **Rating** 95 **To** 2016 $20 ✪

Mappinga Sauvignon Blanc 2014 Whole bunch-pressed, free-run juice fermented on full solids, matured for 10 months in French oak, made by Darryl Catlin. Given a larger than normal lease of life by its extended maturation in French oak, the flavours of fruit and oak are seamlessly joined, both contributing to a palate that is at once joyous and disciplined. Screwcap. 12.5% alc. **Rating** 95 **To** 2018 $35 ✪

Mappinga Chardonnay 2013 Dijon clones 95 and 76, matured for 8 months in new French oak, 35% mlf, made by Natasha Mooney. This is well made and very complex; the oak might well have been overplayed, but hasn't. Certainly it is there, but the profusion of citrus (mainly, though not entirely, pink grapefruit) and stone fruit (white peach and nectarine) matches the nutty/toasty characters of the oak. Screwcap. 13.5% alc. **Rating** 95 **To** 2023 $35 ✪

Stable Hill Adelaide Hills Palomino Pinot Grigio 2015 An intriguing label with a smartly dressed female with a palomino horse head. It is in true grigio style with grainy/rocky acidity surrounding nashi pear fruit. Is a pinot grigio with that rare commodity, character. Gold medal Melbourne Wine Awards '15. Screwcap. 12.5% alc. **Rating** 95 **To** 2017 $15 ✪

Adelaide Hills Shiraz 2014 Made by Darryl Catlin. Deep, bright crimson; the bouquet, with deep, dark cherry and spice fruit, draws you into a medium to full-bodied wine, with dark cherry and plum fruit underscored by licorice and sweet spices; the tannins are an important part of the mix. Screwcap. 14% alc. **Rating** 94 **To** 2034 $25 ✪

🍷🍷🍷🍷 **Adelaide Hills Pinot Noir 2014** **Rating** 92 **To** 2026 $25 ✪
Sparkling Pinot Noir Chardonnay NV **Rating** 90 **To** 2016 $25 TS

Sieber Road Wines ★★★★

Sieber Road, Tanunda, SA 5352 **Region** Barossa Valley
T (08) 8562 8038 **www**.sieberwines.com **Open** 7 days 11–4
Winemaker Tony Carapetis **Est.** 1999 **Dozens** 4500 **Vyds** 18ha
Richard and Val Sieber are the third generation to run Redlands, the family property, traditionally a cropping/grazing farm. They have diversified into viticulture with shiraz (14ha) the lion's share, the remainder viognier, grenache and mourvedre. Son Ben Sieber is the viticulturist. Exports to Canada and China.

🍷🍷🍷🍷 **Barossa Valley Shiraz Mataro 2013** It's a smooth operator upfront. Weighty leather and blackberry flavours have plenty of impact; creamy/musky oak plays an understated but silken role. Alcohol on the finish thins matters slightly, but if you're looking for a mouthful of smooth-skinned flavour, this delivers it at a relatively modest price. Screwcap. 14.8% alc. **Rating** 92 **To** 2022 $20 CM ○

Ernest Barossa Valley Shiraz 2013 Syrupy and smooth, but then taut to close. Sweet plum and redcurrant, saucy oak, velvety tannin. Crowd-pleasing. Screwcap. 14.9% alc. **Rating** 91 **To** 2022 $25 CM

ᵀᵀᵀᵀ **Grenache Shiraz Mourvedre 2013 Rating** 89 **To** 2021 $20 CM

Silent Way   ★★★★☆

PO Box 630, Lancefield, Vic 3435 **Region** Macedon Ranges
T 0409 159 577 **www**.silentway.com.au **Open** Not
Winemaker Matt Harrop **Est.** 2009 **Dozens** 1000 **Vyds** 1.2ha
This is a busman's holiday for partners Matt Harrop and Tamara Grischy, who purchased their small property in 2007, 10 years after they were married. They have planted 1.2ha of chardonnay, and buy semillon and pinot noir from the Quarry Ridge Vineyard at Kilmore. The name comes from a Miles Davis record made in February '69, regarded as a masterpiece and one of the most inventive recordings of all time. The labels feature artwork originally created by friend Daniel Wallace for their wedding, turned into labels by friend Mel Nightingale. Earthworms, birds, snakes, friendship and love are the symbols for Silent Way.

ᵀᵀᵀᵀᵀ **Macedon Ranges Chardonnay 2014** Has more texture and structure than
        many Macedon Ranges producers (with two obvious exceptions, Bindi and Curly
        Flat). Screwcap. 13% alc. **Rating** 94 **To** 2022 $35
        Pinot Noir 2015 Bright, clear crimson-purple; the fragrant bouquet is red-
        fruited, but with some spicy, savoury trimmings; does have good length, and the
        fruit is ripe, depth the only question. Screwcap. 14% alc. **Rating** 94 **To** 2020
        $25 ○

ᵀᵀᵀᵀᵀ **Macedon Ranges Gewurztraminer 2015 Rating** 93 **To** 2019 $29

Silkman Wines   ★★★★★

c/- The Small Winemakers Centre, McDonalds Road, Pokolbin, NSW 2320 **Region**
Hunter Valley
T 0414 800 256 **www**.silkmanwines.com.au **Open** 7 days 10–5
Winemaker Shaun and Liz Silkman **Est.** 2013 **Dozens** 1000
Winemaking couple Shaun and Liz Silkman (one-time dux of the Len Evans Tutorial) were both born and raised in the Hunter Valley, and worked many vintages (both in Australia and abroad) before joining forces at First Creek Wines, where Liz is senior winemaker. This gives them the opportunity to make small quantities of the three classic varieties of the Hunter Valley: Semillon, Chardonnay and Shiraz. Unsurprisingly, the wines so far released have been of outstanding quality.

ᵀᵀᵀᵀᵀ **Single Vineyard Blackberry Hunter Valley Semillon 2015** A strikingly pure
        and fragrant lemongrass-infused semillon; the palate is precise and laden with
        limey acidity and drive. Another pitch-perfect wine from the rising stars. Screwcap.
        10.5% alc. **Rating** 96 **To** 2030 $35 ○
        Reserve Hunter Valley Semillon 2015 Bursting with lemongrass, lime and
        fennel, the palate flows effortlessly with momentum and energy through to a
        crystal clear finish. A long future guaranteed. Screwcap. 10.5% alc. **Rating** 96
        To 2030 $35 ○
        Reserve Chardonnay 2015 The very worthy follow-up to the James Halliday
        Chardonnay Challenge winner of last year. Exceptionally complex, mealy,
        grapefruit and white peach leading to a superbly pithy, lengthy and mineral-
        infused palate. Screwcap. 12.5% alc. **Rating** 96 **To** 2025 $45 ○
        Reserve Huon Valley Pinot Noir 2014 This Tasmanian pinot is a beautifully
        detailed and fragrant effort. Lithe and perfectly balanced, it flows with red fruits
        and rose petals wrapped in the finest of tannins. Long, precise and with class
        stamped all over it. Screwcap. 13.5% alc. **Rating** 96 **To** 2025 $40 ○

Reserve Hunter Valley Shiraz 2014 Mulberry, raspberry, spice and a lick of dried herbs on the bouquet, but it is on the palate where the incredibly fine and chalky tannins drive on and on, coupled with layers of black fruits. Decades assured. Screwcap. 14% alc. **Rating** 96 **To** 2034 $45 **✪**

Silkwood Wines ★★★★

9649 Channybearup Road, Pemberton, WA 6260 **Region** Pemberton
T (08) 9776 1584 **www**.silkwoodwines.com.au **Open** Fri–Mon & public hols 10–4
Winemaker Blair Meiklejohn **Est.** 1998 **Dozens** 10000 **Vyds** 23.5ha
Silkwood Wines has been owned by the Bowman family since 2004. The vineyard is patrolled by a large flock of guinea fowl, eliminating most insect pests and reducing the use of chemicals. In '05 the adjoining vineyard was purchased, lifting the estate plantings to 23.5ha; plantings include shiraz (5.4ha), cabernet sauvignon (4.3ha) and merlot (3.5ha), with smaller amounts of sauvignon blanc, chardonnay, pinot noir, riesling and zinfandel. The cellar door, restaurant and four luxury chalets overlook the large lake on the property. Exports to Malaysia, Singapore and China.

♀♀♀♀♀ **Pemberton Dry Riesling 2015** A pleasant combination of lime, grapefruit and apple, with enough fruit flavour to warrant cellaring, but this is an optional extra. Screwcap. 11.3% alc. **Rating** 91 **To** 2025 $30
Pemberton Shiraz 2014 Relatively light but bright colour; there is a spicy/peppery backdrop for the red berry flavours, the tannins fine, the oak subtle and integrated. Freshness is a key asset. Screwcap. 13.4% alc. **Rating** 91 **To** 2029 $30
Pemberton Sauvignon Blanc 2015 6% matured in new French oak for 1 month. The wine does have good depth of citrus/tropical fruit, with no obvious uptake from oak. Hefty price. Screwcap. 13.1% alc. **Rating** 90 **To** 2017 $30

Silver Spoon Estate ★★★★

503 Heathcote-Rochester Road, Heathcote, Mount Camel, Vic 3523 **Region** Heathcote
T 0412 868 236 **www**.silverspoonestate.com.au **Open** By appt
Winemaker Peter Young **Est.** 2008 **Dozens** 700 **Vyds** 22ha
When Peter and Tracie Young purchased an existing shiraz vineyard on the top of the Mt Camel range in 2008, they did not waste any time. They immediately planted a second vineyard, constructed a small winery, and in '13 acquired a neighbouring vineyard. The name comes from the Silver Spoon fault line that delineates the Cambrian volcanic rock from the old silver mines on the property. Peter became familiar with vineyards when working as a geologist in the 1970s in the Hunter Valley, and he more recently completed the Master of Wine Technology and Viticulture degree at Melbourne Uni.

♀♀♀♀♀ **Heathcote Grenache 2015** Grenache doesn't always need to reach 15% alcohol or more to express ripe flavours. Here exuberant raspberry and red cherry fruit is given free rein, and responds with alacrity. This is an attractive wine with excellent varietal character, and good mouthfeel. Screwcap. **Rating** 92 **To** 2020 $30
Heathcote GSM 2014 A full-bodied GSM that works well. It has a juicy character which binds the components seamlessly, and takes the attention away from the alcohol. While primarily in a raspberry, red cherry and rhubarb spectrum, the shiraz provides a darker fruit counterpoint that works well. Screwcap. 15% alc. **Rating** 90 **To** 2020 $30

♀♀♀♀ **Hallmark Heathcote Shiraz 2014 Rating** 89 **To** 2024 $55
Heathcote Shiraz 2014 Rating 88 **To** 2024 $28
Heathcote Shiraz Viognier 2014 Rating 88 **To** 2020 $30

Simão & Co ★★★★

PO Box 231, Rutherglen, Vic 3685 **Region** Northeast Victoria
T 0439 459 183 **Open** Not
Winemaker Simon Killeen **Est.** 2014 **Dozens** 800

Simão is Portuguese for Simon, an inspiration far from Rutherglen where Simon Killeen was born and bred. He grew up with vines all around him, and knew from an early age he was going to become a winemaker. After working in wineries across Australia, France and Portugal he returned home to establish Simão & Co in 2014. It leaves time for him, by one means or another, to watch every minute of every game played by the Geelong Cats and hunt down the ruins of ghost wineries around Rutherglen.

🍷🍷🍷🍷🍷 **Alpine Valleys Tempranillo 2014** This tempranillo is from Mark Walpole's vineyard at Whorouly in the Alpine Valleys region (not to be confused with Walpole's Beechworth vineyard). It was whole bunch-fermented and saw 30% new French oak. It's modern, slippery smooth, gently reductive and immediately appealing, but also boasts strong, boney fingers of tannin and more than enough plush fruit. An irresistible package all round. Screwcap. 13.5% alc. **Rating** 94 To 2023 $29 CM

Vintage Fortified 2014 Shiraz, tempranillo, alicante bouschet, tinta barocca, touriga nacional and durif. Alpine Valleys and King Valley. 'Co-fermented, fully foot stomped, 100% stalks and 100% wild.' Bitumen, raspberry, sweet-sour cherries, herbs. Bold, warm and quite beautiful, with rushes of dark chocolate as the final credits. 375ml. Screwcap. 20.5% alc. **Rating** 94 To 2028 $46 CM

🍷🍷🍷🍷🍷 **Old Vine Glenrowan Shiraz 2014** Rating 93 To 2026 $29 CM
Ugni Blanc 2015 Rating 91 To 2016 $29 CM
White 2015 Rating 91 To 2017 $24 CM
Sauvignon Blanc 2015 Rating 90 To 2016 $24 CM

Simon Whitlam & Co   ★★★☆

PO Box 1108, Woollahra, NSW 1350 **Region** Hunter Valley
T (02) 9007 5331 **Open** Not
Winemaker Edgar Vales (Contract) **Est.** 1979 **Dozens** 2000
My association with the owners of Simon Whitlam – Andrew and Hady Simon, Nicholas and Judy Whitlam, and Grant Breen – dates back to the late 1970s, at which time I was a consultant to the Simons' leading wine retail shop in Sydney, Camperdown Cellars. The association continued for a time after I moved to Melbourne in '83, but ceased altogether in '87 when Camperdown Cellars was sold; it was later merged with Arrowfield Wines. The Simon Whitlam label was part of the deal, and it passed through a number of corporate owners until 20 years later, when the original partners regained control of the business.

🍷🍷🍷🍷🍷 **Hunter Valley Semillon 2012** On the march towards maturity, but with years still in front of it; very marked citrus/lemongrass flavours. Screwcap. 11.5% alc. **Rating** 91 To 2022 $22 **◒**

Sinapius Vineyard   ★★★★☆

4232 Bridport Road, Pipers Brook, Tas 7254 **Region** Northern Tasmania
T 0417 341 764 **www.**sinapius.com.au **Open** Thur–Mon 12–5
Winemaker Vaughn Dell **Est.** 2005 **Dozens** 800 **Vyds** 3.5ha
Vaughn Dell and Linda Morice purchased the former Golders Vineyard in 2005 (originally planted in 1994). More recent vineyard plantings include 13 clones of pinot noir and eight clones of chardonnay, as well as a small amount of gruner veltliner. The new vineyard is close-planted, ranging from 5100 vines per hectare for the gruner veltliner to 10 250 vines per hectare for the pinot noir and chardonnay. The wines are made with a minimalist approach: natural ferments, basket-pressing, extended lees ageing and minimal fining and filtration.

🍷🍷🍷🍷🍷 **Home Vineyard Chardonnay 2014** Whole bunch-pressed, wild-fermented, partial mlf, 10 months in French oak (40% new). A complex wine that ticks all the boxes as it should with Tasmanian acidity – including a brisk finish. Screwcap. 13% alc. **Rating** 95 To 2022 $48

🍷🍷🍷🍷🍷 **Home Vineyard Pinot Noir 2014** Rating 93 To 2024 $48
Clem Blanc 2015 Rating 91 To 2020 $38

Singlefile Wines

90 Walter Road, Denmark, WA 6333 **Region** Great Southern
T (08) 9840 9749 **www**.singlefilewines.com **Open** 7 days 11–5
Winemaker Mike Garland, Coby Ladwig **Est.** 2007 **Dozens** 6000 **Vyds** 3.75ha

In 1968 geologist Phil and Viv Snowden moved from South Africa to Perth, where they developed their successful multinational mining and resource services company, Snowden Resources. Following the sale of the company in 2004, they decided to turn their attention to their long-held desire to make and enjoy fine wine. In '07 they bought an established vineyard (planted in '89) in the beautiful Denmark subregion. They pulled out the old shiraz and merlot vines, kept and planted more chardonnay, and retained Larry Cherubino to set up partnerships with established vineyards in Frankland River, Porongurup, Denmark, Pemberton and Margaret River to make the rest of the wines in the distinguished Singlefile portfolio. The cellar door, tasting room and restaurant are strongly recommended. The consistency of the quality of the Singlefile wines is outstanding, as is their value for money. Exports to the US, Japan and China.

ȲȲȲȲȲ **The Philip Adrian Frankland River Cabernet Sauvignon 2013** Singlefile's flagship, made in small quantities (170 dozen) in exceptional vintages. Given a nail-biting 6-week cold soak before fermentation commenced, matured in French barriques (60% new) for 17 months. The brocaded, sumptuous palate has royal purple and black fruits, layers of almost luscious tannins and high quality oak. Screwcap. 14.2% alc. **Rating** 98 **To** 2063 $80 ✪
Family Reserve Denmark Chardonnay 2014 Whole bunch-pressed, fermented and matured in French barriques (40% new). This is gaining a reputation second to none in the Great Southern; it is intense and tightly focused, yet supremely elegant, the finish long and fresh. Screwcap. 13.7% alc. **Rating** 97 **To** 2024 $50 ✪
Clement V 2014 62% shiraz, 33% mataro, 5% grenache from the Riversdale Vineyard in Frankland River. Redefines what is possible with this blend from Frankland River. While shiraz provides black fruits and fine-grained tannins, the other varieties are seamlessly joined with subtle, spicy red fruits. Great value. Screwcap. 14.3% alc. **Rating** 97 **To** 2034 $30 ✪

ȲȲȲȲȲ **Pemberton Fume Blanc 2014** Wild-fermented in stainless steel, then 60% transferred for maturation in French barriques (half new, half 1yo). A strikingly rich, complex and powerful wine, its sauvignon blanc fruit base almost irrelevant. European in its feel. Screwcap. 13.7% alc. **Rating** 95 **To** 2018 $30 ✪
Porongurup Riesling 2015 Free-run juice was cool-fermented, finishing with a pH of 2.94, explaining the minerally acidity that forms the backdrop for a wine of great fruit intensity and persistence, citrus in the vanguard, a wisp of fresh-cut apple in the rear. Screwcap. 12.2% alc. **Rating** 95 **To** 2028 $25 ✪
Mount Barker Riesling 2015 Remarkably textural. It's almost grippy with lime pith characters, though there's yet plenty of juicy citrus, fennel and lime blossom notes. It's quite a beautiful combination. It feels fresh, perfumed and elegant and yet there's a gravitas. Screwcap. 11.2% alc. **Rating** 95 **To** 2026 $30 CM ✪
Run Free Great Southern Chardonnay 2014 The drive, the flesh, the X-factor. This is a chardonnay to seek out. Stone fruit, minerals, quartz-like acidity and a veneer of creamy/cedary oak. Glittering. Screwcap. 13.5% alc. **Rating** 95 **To** 2020 $25 CM ✪
Frankland River Shiraz 2014 The dense crimson-purple colour heralds a wine with a cabernet-like austerity, brooking no argument as the sombre black fruits and firm tannins roll out across a full-bodied palate. Will richly repay extended cellaring. Screwcap. 14.2% alc. **Rating** 95 **To** 2044 $37
Pemberton Fume Blanc 2015 Wild-fermented before 50% went into oak (20% new), the remainder into stainless steel. The result is elegance itself. It shows composure, (enough) intensity and (plenty of) length and it does so in charming fashion. Screwcap. 13.1% alc. **Rating** 94 **To** 2019 $30 CM ✪

Run Free Shiraz 2014 Silken fruit and an amount of it. Chewy with tannin, luscious with satsuma plum, anise and black cherried fruit, and smattered with spicy oak. Pure pleasure as it smoothes along the tongue. Not, though, for the tannin averse. Screwcap. 13.9% alc. **Rating** 94 To 2028 $25 CM ✪

♟♟♟♟♟ Denmark Semillon Sauvignon Blanc 2015 Rating 92 To 2018 $25 CM ✪
Pemberton Pinot Gris 2015 Rating 90 To 2017 $30 CM

Sirromet Wines   ★★★★☆

850–938 Mount Cotton Road, Mount Cotton, Qld 4165 **Region** Granite Belt
T (07) 3206 2999 **www**.sirromet.com **Open** 7 days 9–4.30
Winemaker Adam Chapman, Jessica Ferguson **Est.** 1998 **Dozens** 50 000 **Vyds** 98.7ha
This ambitious venture has succeeded in its aim of creating Qld's premier winery. The founding Morris family retained a leading architect to design the striking state-of-the-art winery; the state's foremost viticultural consultant to plant three major vineyards (in the Granite Belt); and the most skilled winemaker practising in Qld, Adam Chapman, to make the wine. It has a 200-seat restaurant, a wine club, and is firmly aimed at the tourist market, taking advantage of its situation, halfway between Brisbane and the Gold Coast. Exports to Sweden, South Korea, Papua New Guinea, Hong Kong, China and Japan.

♟♟♟♟♟ Wild Granite Belt Chardonnay 2014 Estate-grown, wild-fermented in new French barriques, 20% mlf, 11 months on lees, 8% fermented and matured in a clay amphora for 8 months. The avant garde winemaking was 100% successful; the funky struck match edge to the bouquet and the strong textural play to the palate go well with the grapefruit, apple and white peach fruit; good acidity. Screwcap. 12.9% alc. **Rating** 95 To 2024 $80
Signature Collection Terry Morris Granite Belt Chardonnay 2013 Sirromet's modus operandi for chardonnay is fine-tuned, often with a lateral play on the way through from grapes to wine, as here with grapefruit zest and cedary oak. Screwcap. 13.5% alc. **Rating** 94 To 2022 $35
Signature Collection Terry Morris Granite Belt Cabernet Sauvignon 2014 A very well made cabernet with a feminine touch; cassis is the driver, black olive and bay leaf the passengers, fine-grained tannins and cedary notes the wheels. Screwcap. 13.8% alc. **Rating** 94 To 2030 $35

♟♟♟♟♟ Bald Rock Creek Verdelho Blanc 2015 Rating 93 To 2020 $35
Terry Morris Shiraz Viognier 2014 Rating 93 To 2024 $35
Saint Jude's Road Grand Reserve Merlot 2012 Rating 92 To 2017 $390
Vineyard Selection Cabernet Sauvignon 2014 Rating 90 To 2018 $21 ✪

Sister's Run   ★★★★

PO Box 382, Tanunda, SA 5352 **Region** Barossa
T (08) 8563 1400 **www**.sistersrun.com.au **Open** Not
Winemaker Elena Brooks **Est.** 2001 **Dozens** NFP
Sister's Run is owned by noted Barossa Valley vignerons Carl and Peggy Lindner (owners of Langmeil), directly employing the skills of Elena Brooks as winemaker, and, indirectly, the marketing know-how of husband Zar Brooks. The Stiletto and Boot are those of Elena, and the motto 'The truth is in the vineyard, but the proof is in the glass' is, I would guess, the work of Zar Brooks. Exports to all major markets.

♟♟♟♟♟ Epiphany McLaren Vale Shiraz 2014 Black jelly bean, asphalt, raspberry and coffee flavours provide plenty of entertainment on a well-powered palate. Screwcap. 14.5% alc. **Rating** 90 To 2020 $20 CM ✪
Bethlehem Block Gomersal Cabernet 2014 Curranty fruit with tips of raspberried sweetness. Dusty tannin. Oak plays a minor role at most, though there's a gentle creaminess. No alarms or surprises and decent heft. Screwcap. 14.5% alc. **Rating** 90 To 2021 $20 CM ✪

ᵀᵀᵀᵀ Cow's Corner GSM 2014 Rating 89 To 2020 $20 CM
Old Testament Cabernet 2014 Rating 88 To 2021 $20 CM

Sittella Wines ★★★★★

100 Barrett Street, Herne Hill, WA 6056 **Region** Swan Valley
T (08) 9296 2600 **www**.sittella.com.au **Open** Tues–Sun & public hols 11–5
Winemaker Colby Quirk, Yuri Berns **Est.** 1998 **Dozens** 8000 **Vyds** 10ha
Simon and Maaike Berns acquired a 7ha block (with 5ha of vines) at Herne Hill, making
the first wine in 1998 and opening a most attractive cellar door facility. They also own the
Wildberry Estate vineyard in Margaret River. Consistent and significant wine show success
has brought well-deserved recognition for the wines. Exports to the US, Japan and China.

ᵀᵀᵀᵀᵀ **Reserve Margaret River Chardonnay 2015** 50/50% clones 95 and 96,
hand-picked, whole bunch-pressed, wild-fermented and matured for 9 months in
French oak (20% new). Elegant and pure first up, then the drive and length take
hold of the palate. This is a very distinguished wine made by someone who has
both understanding of, and confidence in, his craft. Screwcap. 13.5% alc. **Rating** 96
To 2025 $35 ✪
Berns Reserve 2014 95% cabernet sauvignon, 3% malbec, 2% petit verdot,
matured for 18 months in French oak (30% new). The ultra-fragrant bouquet is
flooded with cassis, the medium-bodied palate flowing on with cedary oak and
fine-grained tannins completing what is a high quality wine by any standards.
Screwcap. 14% alc. **Rating** 96 To 2034 $48 ✪
Coffee Rock Swan Valley Shiraz 2014 Ultra-complex and painstaking
vinification of fruit ex 65yo vines has repaid all the effort (which included
fermentation in French oak following the removal of the heads). The key features
of the wine are its freshness and balance, which in turn frame the plum and
blackberry fruit. Screwcap. 15% alc. **Rating** 95 To 2029 $48
Margaret River Cabernet Sauvignon 2014 Includes 5% malbec and petit
verdot. Opens with rich, almost voluptuous, cassis, but then turns smartly around
as you arrive at the cabernet tannins on the finish, before the cycle begins again.
Then, unexpectedly, the tannins relax and the fruit emerges triumphant. Screwcap.
14% alc. **Rating** 94 To 2034 $28 ✪
Avant-Garde Series Swan Valley Tempranillo 2015 Hand-picked and sorted,
70% whole berries, 30% whole bunches, wild open ferment, 10 months in French
oak (25% new), 25 dozen made. A very fragrant and complex fruit profile with
both cherry and exotic plum; the whole berry/whole bunch fermentation has
worked very well. Screwcap. 14% alc. **Rating** 94 To 2023 $30 ✪

ᵀᵀᵀᵀ♀ **Pinot Noir Chardonnay 2009** Rating 93 To 2017 $32 TS
The Wild One Sauvignon Blanc 2015 Rating 92 To 2019 $22 ✪
Swan Valley Shiraz 2014 Rating 92 To 2025 $26
Berns and Walsh Swan Valley Rose 2015 Rating 91 To 2017 $19 ✪
Methode Traditionnelle Blanc de Blancs NV Rating 91 To 2018 $32 TS
Berns and Walsh Cane Cut Verdelho 2013 Rating 90 To 2018 $19 ✪
Show Reserve Liqueur Muscat NV Rating 90 To 2015 $39 CM

Six Acres ★★★★★

20 Ferndale Road, Silvan, Vic 3795 **Region** Yarra Valley
T 0408 991 741 **www**.sixacres.com.au **Open** W'ends 10–4
Winemaker Aaron and Ralph Zuccaro **Est.** 1999 **Dozens** 470 **Vyds** 1.64ha
Ralph and Lesley Zuccaro, who have a successful optical dispensing business, decided to
plant a vineyard in 1999 with pinot noir (0.82ha), cabernet sauvignon (0.62ha) and merlot
(0.2ha). Son Aaron, a biochemist, grew restless in the confines of a laboratory, and started his
winemaking career in 2007, graduating in '12 from CSU. During his time at CSU he worked
at Chandon Australia. The small size of the property means that all the work is carried out
by the family.

ΥΥΥΥΥ Yarra Valley Pinot Noir 2014 Very odd square Melbourne Wine Awards '15
gold medal sticker on the bottle. Full of rich, juicy plummy fruit. A great example
of wine show gold medals going to those with the most fruit and extract.
Irresistible. Screwcap. 13.3% alc. **Rating** 95 **To** 2025 $28 **O**

Skillogalee   ★★★★☆
Trevarrick Road, Sevenhill via Clare, SA 5453 **Region** Clare Valley
T (08) 8843 4311 **www**.skillogalee.com.au **Open** 7 days 7.30–5
Winemaker Dave Palmer, Emma Walker **Est.** 1970 **Dozens** 15 000 **Vyds** 50.3ha
David and Diana Palmer have fully capitalised on the exceptional fruit quality of the
Skillogalee vineyards. All the wines are generous and full-flavoured, particularly the reds. In
2002 the Palmers purchased next-door neighbour Waninga Vineyards, with 30ha of 30-year-
old vines, allowing an increase in production without any change in quality or style. Exports
to the UK, Denmark, Switzerland, Malaysia, Thailand and Singapore.

ΥΥΥΥΥ Clare Valley Gewurztraminer 2015 Australian gewurztraminer often seems to
me to be an insipid, washed-out version of Alsace, but 'insipid' is not a word to be
used in describing this wine. It is stacked with musk, lychee, rosewater and exotic
spices, yet has a dry finish; just what the doctor ordered. Screwcap. 14.7% alc.
Rating 95 **To** 2028 $29 **O**
Clare Valley Riesling 2015 Several blocks at the top of the estate slopes were
separately vinified, the best lots blended. There is a juicy, mouthwatering blend of
lime, lemon and a hint of grapefruit; in the long term, the natural acidity of the
year will be a blessing. Screwcap. 13.3% alc. **Rating** 94 **To** 2030 $24 **O**

ΥΥΥΥႜ Basket Pressed Clare Valley The Cabernets 2013 **Rating** 93 **To** 2038 $33

Smallfry Wines   ★★★★★
13 Murray Street, Angaston, SA 5353 **Region** Barossa Valley
T (08) 8564 2182 **www**.smallfrywines.com.au **Open** By appt tel 0412 153 243
Winemaker Wayne Ahrens **Est.** 2005 **Dozens** 1500 **Vyds** 27ha
The engagingly named Smallfry Wines is the venture of Wayne Ahrens and partner Suzi
Hilder. Wayne is from a fifth-generation Barossa family; Suzi is the daughter of well-known
Upper Hunter viticulturist Richard Hilder and wife Del, partners in Pyramid Hill Wines.
Both have degrees from CSU, and both have extensive experience – Suzi as a senior
viticulturist for TWE, and Wayne's track record includes seven vintages as a cellar hand at
Orlando Wyndham and other smaller Barossa wineries. Their vineyards in the Eden Valley
(led by cabernet sauvignon and riesling) and the Vine Vale area of the Barossa Valley (shiraz,
grenache, semillon, mourvedre, cabernet sauvignon and riesling) are certified biodynamic/
organic. Exports to the UK, the US, the Philippines, Singapore, Hong Kong, Japan and China.

ΥΥΥΥΥ Eden Valley Cabernet Sauvignon 2014 18yo vines, matured in French (80%)
and American oak for 22 months. The cooler growing conditions of the Eden
Valley suit cabernet far better than the Yarra Valley; this is a genuinely elegant
cabernet with a hint of eucalypt, the major player cassis; superfine tannins are
another plus. Screwcap. 14.2% alc. **Rating** 94 **To** 2029 $32

ΥΥΥΥႜ Stella Luna Barossa Cinsault Shiraz 2015 **Rating** 93 **To** 2018 $28
Schliebs Garden 2014 **Rating** 93 **To** 2018 $32
Eden Valley Riesling 2015 **Rating** 92 **To** 2025 $25 **O**
Barossa Shiraz 2015 **Rating** 92 **To** 2030 $32
Barossa Shiraz 2014 **Rating** 92 **To** 2039 $32
Joven Barossa Tempranillo and Garnacha 2015 **Rating** 92 **To** 2020 $25 **O**
Barossa Riesling 2015 **Rating** 91 **To** 2025 $25

Smidge Wines

62 Austral Terrace, Malvern, SA 5061 (postal) **Region** South Eastern Australia
T (08) 8272 0369 **www**.smidgewines.com **Open** Not
Winemaker Matt Wenk **Est.** 2004 **Dozens** 1000

The business is owned by Matt Wenk and wife Trish Callaghan, and was for many years an out-of-hours occupation for Matt; his day job was as winemaker for Two Hands Wines (and Sandow's End). In 2013 he retired from Two Hands, and plans to increase production of Smidge to 8000 dozen over the next few years. His retirement meant the Smidge wines could no longer be made at Two Hands, and the winemaking operations have been moved to McLaren Vale, where Smidge is currently leasing a small winery. Smidge owns the vineyard in Willunga which provides the grapes for all the Cabernet Sauvignon releases and some of the McLaren Vale Shiraz. The vision is to build a modern customised facility on the Willunga property in the not-too-distant future. Exports to the UK and the US.

ŸŸŸŸŸ **Magic Dirt Greenock Barossa Valley Shiraz 2013** Three Magic Dirt Shirazs were made in '13, each a best-barrel selection, transferred to older French oak after mlf for 24 months maturation. Deeply coloured, as are all the Magic Dirt wines. Black fruits; intrigue of charred meat; very powerful; full-bodied; the flavours flow on directly from the bouquet. Screwcap. 15% alc. **Rating** 96 **To** 2039 $100

Magic Dirt Willunga Barossa Valley Shiraz 2013 The bouquet of pure, fresh-picked wild blackberry becomes the essence of the full-bodied palate. Oak maturation has rounded the tannins to the point where they are welded to the fruit. Screwcap. 14.8% alc. **Rating** 96 **To** 2039 $100

The GruVe Adelaide Hills Gruner Veltliner 2015 Hurray! An Australian gruner veltliner that does have a dab of white pepper on the bouquet, and lots of juicy citrus fruit on the expressive palate – and length, too. Screwcap. 12.5% alc. **Rating** 95 **To** 2025 $30 ✪

Magic Dirt Moppa Barossa Valley Shiraz 2013 Warmth of cedar and wood smoke curls out of the bouquet, and the palate picks up the oak line without any hesitation or prevarication. This is the most elegant of the Magic Dirt trio. Screwcap. 14.6% alc. **Rating** 95 **To** 2033 $100

S Barossa Valley Shiraz 2013 Exceptionally powerful, luscious and velvety, the oak and tannins standing back to allow the fruit unfettered freedom to express itself. A juicy replay unexpectedly appears long into the aftertaste. Screwcap. 14.6% alc. **Rating** 95 **To** 2038 $65

Magic Dirt Stonewell Barossa Valley Shiraz 2013 This is particularly complex, with rich blackberry and plum fruit, sufficient to carry both the new oak and the alcohol without complaint. The ripe, powerful and balanced tannins are at one with the fruit. Screwcap. 14.6% alc. **Rating** 95 **To** 2033 $100

Magic Dirt Eden Valley Shiraz 2013 The cooler climate of the Eden Valley has facilitated harvest at a somewhat lower alcohol level, which gives the black fruits a lift, but the oak flavour intrudes somewhat – a pity, because the overall feel and structure are very elegant. Screwcap. 14.2% alc. **Rating** 94 **To** 2033 $100

ŸŸŸŸŸ **The Ging McLaren Vale Shiraz 2013** Rating 93 To 2043 $30
Houdini McLaren Vale Shiraz 2014 Rating 92 To 2034 $23 ✪

Smith & Hooper

Caves Edward Road, Naracoorte, SA 5271 **Region** Wrattonbully
T 0412 847 383 **www**.smithandhooper.com **Open** By appt
Winemaker Peter Gambetta **Est.** 1994 **Dozens** 15000 **Vyds** 62ha

On one view of the matter, Smith & Hooper is simply one of many brands within various of the Hill-Smith family financial/corporate structures. However, it is estate-based, with cabernet sauvignon and merlot planted on the Hooper Vineyard in 1994, and cabernet sauvignon and merlot planted on the Smith Vineyard in '98. Spread across both vineyards are 9ha of trial varieties. Exports to all major markets.

ŸŸŸŸ♀ Reserve Merlot 2014 This Wrattonbully vineyard has consistently shown an ability to produce merlot with the X-factor, a rare talent. The colour is bright and full, the fruit rich, but not jammy, and there is enthusiastic support from the oak – strange knowing the eagle eye of the ultimate owner of the vineyard, who is not given to lavish spending. Screwcap. 13% alc. **Rating** 91 **To** 2029 $27

Wrattonbully Merlot 2014 Light, bright hue; no info on vinification, and in particular clones, but it is a very attractive cassis, cherry and briar wine, tannins and oak where they should be – and a bargain. Screwcap. 13.5% alc. **Rating** 90 **To** 2020 $20 **❂**

ŸŸŸŸ Wrattonbully Cabernet Sauvignon Merlot 2013 **Rating** 89 **To** 2023 $20

Snake + Herring   ★★★★★

PO Box 918, Dunsborough, WA 6281 **Region** South West Australia Zone
T 0419 487 427 **www**.snakeandherring.com.au **Open** Not
Winemaker Tony Davis **Est.** 2010 **Dozens** 7000

Tony (Snake) Davis and Redmond (Herring) Sweeny both started university degrees before finding that they were utterly unsuited to their respective courses. Having stumbled across Margaret River, Tony's life changed forever; he enrolled at Adelaide University, thereafter doing vintages in the Eden Valley, Oregon, Beaujolais and Tasmania, before three years at Plantagenet, next Brown Brothers, then a senior winemaking role at Yalumba, a six-year stint designing Millbrook Winery in the Perth Hills, and four years with Howard Park in Margaret River. Redmond's circuitous course included a chartered accountancy degree and employment with an international accounting firm in Busselton, and the subsequent establishment of Forester Estate in 2001, in partnership with Kevin McKay. Back on home turf he is the marketing and financial controller of Snake + Herring. Exports to China.

ŸŸŸŸŸ Corduroy Karridale Margaret River Chardonnay 2015 Gingin, and Dijon clones 76, 95, 96 and 277, combined with the cool Karridale district, provide grapes with remarkable intensity. Saliva runs in an automatic reaction to the flavours of the wine as it enters the mouth, flavours that linger on the aftertaste. Screwcap. 13% alc. **Rating** 96 **To** 2027 $40 **❂**

High + Dry Porongurup Riesling 2015 Only 100 dozen made due to the low yield of 470 litres per tonne. Typical Porongurup: intense but beautifully balanced, with lime juice, zest and pith, acidity as built-in as any cupboard in the house. Screwcap. 12% alc. **Rating** 95 **To** 2025 $28 **❂**

Perfect Day Margaret River Sauvignon Blanc Semillon 2015 A 70/30% blend, 63% barrel-fermented. The wine has wonderful drive, intensity and length, with layers of fruit flavour supported by crunchy acidity and oak. A lot of winemaking of very good fruit was invested here, and it paid off. Screwcap. 13% alc. **Rating** 95 **To** 2018 $25 **❂**

The Distance Higher Ground Porongurup Cabernet Merlot 2014 This is a deadly serious wine made to challenge, rather than comfort you; it has blackcurrant/cassis, redcurrant, dried herbs, graphite, tar and, of course, tannins. It is these that challenge most stridently, but they will be tamed by time, long before the fruit shows any sign of defeat. Screwcap. 14% alc. **Rating** 95 **To** 2039 $65

The Distance Black Betty Margaret River Cabernet Sauvignon 2013 A beautifully detailed, medium-bodied cabernet that pushes all the right buttons at exactly the right time; blackcurrant, black olive and dried herbs are all on show, but it is the unusually fine tannins that seal the deal. Screwcap. 14.5% alc. **Rating** 95 **To** 2043 $65

Tough Love Margaret River Great Southern Chardonnay 2015 67% Gin Gin clones from Margaret River, 33% Dijon clones from Denmark, whole bunch-pressed, wild-fermented, 41% in tank, 59% in French oak (14% new), matured on lees for 10 months. Yes, it's very complicated, something borrowed, something blue; I'd also add that it's very long and very cool, lipsmacking stuff, a bargain at its price. The fruit flavours run through stone fruit, melon and citrus, yet are pure. Screwcap. 13.5% alc. **Rating** 94 **To** 2026 $25 **❂**

The Hard Road Porongurup Pinot Noir 2015 One parcel 100% whole bunch-fermented, the second wild-fermented on 20% whole bunches with plunging, matured in French puncheons (50% new) for 10 months. Good colour and fragrance; a complex wine with spice, plum, cherry and fine tannins all ticking boxes, ditto length and balance. Screwcap. 13% alc. **Rating** 94 **To** 2025 $40
Blue Monday Frankland River Grenache Mourvedre Shiraz 2014
A 57/38/5% blend. This is deadly serious stuff, the mourvedre contributing a lavish superstructure of tannins for the other two varieties to hang their red fruits on; the palate is extremely long, and will carry the wine's message for years to come. Screwcap. 14% alc. **Rating** 94 **To** 2044 $40
Vamos Frankland River Margaret River Tempranillo 2014 A 51/49% regional blend of 95% tempranillo and 5% grenache. Deeply coloured, this is not to be undertaken lightly: the expansive core of dried and fresh black cherry on the long palate tracks the bouquet, the finish with stern tannins that in the final analysis do stand back and yield to the fruit. Great things around the corner? Yes. Screwcap. 14% alc. **Rating** 94 **To** 2029 $25 **✪**

ఄఄఄఄ౽ Tainted Love Grenache Rose 2015 Rating 93 To 2018 $25 **✪**
Wide Open Road Pinot Noir 2015 Rating 92 To 2023 $25 **✪**

Snobs Creek Wines   ★★★★

486 Goulburn Valley Highway, via Alexandra, Vic 3714 **Region** Upper Goulburn
T (03) 9596 3043 **www.**snobscreekvineyard.com.au **Open** W'ends 11–5
Winemaker Marcus Gillon **Est.** 1996 **Dozens** 1500 **Vyds** 5ha
The vineyard is situated where Snobs Creek joins the Goulburn River, 5km below the Lake Eildon wall. The varieties grown are shiraz (2.5ha), sauvignon blanc (1.5ha) and chardonnay (1ha); all manage to produce no more then 7.4 tonnes per hectare. Is described as a 'cool climate vineyard in a landscaped environment'.

ఄఄఄఄ౽ Reserve Pinot Noir 2012 The highly expressive bouquet has spice, dark cherry and oak aromas playing tag with each other, a game that continues on the palate. Has developed well in bottle, with foresty/savoury characters. Screwcap. 13.2% alc. Rating 93 To 2020 $24 **✪**
The Artisan Pyrenees Shiraz 2012 Has abundant blackberry and plum fruit supported by fine, ripe tannins and notes of pepper and spice on the finish. Excellent value. Screwcap. 14.2% alc. Rating 91 To 2025 $19 **✪**

ఄఄఄఄ Cordwainer Chardonnay 2013 Rating 89 To 2018 $21

Sons & Brothers Vineyard   ★★★★☆

Spring Terrace Road, Millthorpe, NSW 2798 **Region** Orange
T (02) 6366 5117 **www.**sonsandbrothers.com.au **Open** Not
Winemaker Dr Chris Bourke **Est.** 1978 **Dozens** 300 **Vyds** 2ha
Chris and Kathryn Bourke do not pull their punches when they say, 'Our vineyard has had a chequered history, because in 1978 we were trying to establish ourselves in a non-existent wine region with no local knowledge and limited personal knowledge of grapegrowing and winemaking. It took us about 15 years of hit and miss before we started producing regular supplies of appropriate grape varieties at appropriate ripeness levels for sales to other NSW wineries.' Chris has published two fascinating papers on the origins of savagnin in Europe; he has also traced its movements in Australia after it was one of the varieties collected by James Busby – and moved just in time to save the last plantings in NSW of Busby's importation.

ఄఄఄఄ౽ Cabernet of Millthorpe 2014 95% cabernet sauvignon, 5% savagnin. The colour is light and clear, pinot-ish rather than cabernet, and very fragrant; indeed, the pinot comparison comes up at every point along the way despite its extended maceration and time in barrel. I really like the wine, but don't agree with the suggested drinking peak between '21 and '28 – it's hard to imagine it will ever be more enjoyable than it is today. Crown seal. 13.5% alc. Rating 93 To 2020 $30

Sons of Eden

Penrice Road, Angaston, SA 5353 **Region** Barossa
T (08) 8564 2363 **www**.sonsofeden.com **Open** 7 days 11–6
Winemaker Corey Ryan, Simon Cowham **Est.** 2000 **Dozens** 9000 **Vyds** 60ha
Corey Ryan and Simon Cowham both learnt and refined their skills in the vineyards and
cellars of Eden Valley. Corey is a trained oenologist with over 20 vintages under his belt,
having cut his teeth as a winemaker at Henschke. Thereafter he worked for Rouge Homme
and Penfolds in Coonawarra, backed up by winemaking stints in the Rhône Valley, and in
2002 took the opportunity to work in NZ for Villa Maria Estates. In '07 he won the Institute
of Masters of Wine scholarship. Simon has had a similarly international career, covering
such diverse organisations as Oddbins, UK and the Winemakers' Federation of Australia.
Switching from the business side to grapegrowing when he qualified as a viticulturist, he
worked for Yalumba as technical manager of the Heggies and Pewsey Vale vineyards. With this
background, it comes as no surprise to find that the estate-grown wines are of outstanding
quality. Exports to the UK, the US, Germany, Switzerland, Hong Kong, the Philippines,
Taiwan and China.

🍷🍷🍷🍷🍷 **Remus Old Vine Eden Valley Shiraz 2013** From low-yielding 50+yo vines,
open-fermented, some whole bunches, in predominantly new French hogsheads
for 22 months. The low yield and vinification haven't led to dead fruit and/or
over-extraction; this wine has exceptional intensity and power, the whole-bunch
inclusion providing some lift, the French oak a flavour counterbalance for a wine
of the highest quality. Screwcap. 14.5% alc. **Rating** 97 **To** 2053 $70 ❂

🍷🍷🍷🍷🍷 **Zephyrus Shiraz 2014** 61% Barossa Valley, 39% Eden Valley. A beautifully
wrought and detailed palate, so supple it literally glides through to the finish and
aftertaste without even a momentary pause for thought. Will live for decades, but
can also be consumed tonight. Screwcap. 14.5% alc. **Rating** 96 **To** 2038 $45 ❂
Romulus Old Vine Barossa Valley Shiraz 2013 From three low-yielding
vineyards, matured in mainly new American hogsheads for 20 months. The come-
hither message of the bouquet leads into an even more seductive palate with folds
of velvet and satin around dark cherry and plum fruit, soft tannins a constant
undertow. Screwcap. 14.5% alc. **Rating** 96 **To** 2038 $70 ❂
Freya Eden Valley Riesling 2015 Still crystal white; a floral blossom bouquet;
intensely focused and equally long on the palate and aftertaste; lime zest and juice
have an electrifying acidity, marking the quality of the wine now and into the
future. Screwcap. 12.5% alc. **Rating** 95 **To** 2035 $27 ❂
Marschall Barossa Shiraz 2014 Matured for 18 months in new and used oak.
Deep crimson-purple; a layered, complex and utterly coherent wine, fruit, oak
and tannins waltzing across the palate. A Barossa Valley wine in Eden Valley drag.
Screwcap. 14.5% alc. **Rating** 95 **To** 2039 $31 ❂
Kennedy Barossa Valley Grenache Shiraz Mourvedre 2014 55/35/10%,
vines 17–100yo, all components fermented and matured separately. The relatively
deep colour tells you this is not your average Barossa GSM, the bouquet and palate
shout agreement from the rooftops. This is a very high quality blend worthy of
comparison to Chateau Rayas of the Rhône Valley (albeit without challenging the
incomparable Rayas). Screwcap. 14.5% alc. **Rating** 95 **To** 2029 $31 ❂
Eurus Eden Valley Cabernet Sauvignon 2013 The skilled winemaking, and
very good fruit, doesn't miss a beat. Blackcurrant, bay leaf and cedary oak are
moulded together with the cement provided by fine tannins that are often part of
cabernet. Screwcap. 14.5% alc. **Rating** 94 **To** 2038 $65

🍷🍷🍷🍷🍷 **Pumpa Cabernet Sauvignon Shiraz 2013** **Rating** 92 **To** 2043 $31

Sorby Adams Wines

51 Murray Street, Angaston, SA 5353 **Region** Eden Valley
T (08) 8564 2993 **www**.sorbyadamswines.com **Open** 7 days 10–5
Winemaker Simon Adams **Est.** 2004 **Dozens** 15 000 **Vyds** 11.65ha

In 1996 Simon Adams and wife Helen purchased a 3.2ha vineyard that had been planted by Pastor Franz Julius Lehmann (none other than Peter Lehmann's father) in 1932. Peter Lehmann always referred to it as 'Dad's Block'. They have added 0.25ha of viognier, which, as one might expect, is used in a shiraz viognier blend. Most recent plantings are of shiraz (2.5ha), riesling (1.7ha), cabernet sauvignon (0.7ha) and traminer (1.5ha). Nonetheless, the top red wines, The Family Shiraz and The Thing Shiraz, need no assistance from viognier. The Adams have opened the Sorby Adams Wine Room & Pantry in Angaston. Exports to Germany, Singapore, Hong Kong, China and NZ.

The Reverend Canon Cabernet Shiraz 2010 The barely stained, high quality, cork has only recently been inserted, but we don't know how long the wine spent in oak or tank. It doesn't matter, for the medium-bodied wine has a juicily fresh array of cassis, blackberry and sour cherry fruit, oak and tannins watching on from the sidelines. 14% alc. **Rating** 94 **To** 2025 $38

Jazz Cabernet Rose 2015 Rating 89 **To** 2016 $20

Sorrenberg

Alma Road, Beechworth, Vic 3747 **Region** Beechworth
T (03) 5728 2278 **www**.sorrenberg.com **Open** By appt
Winemaker Barry and Jan Morey **Est.** 1986 **Dozens** 1600 **Vyds** 4.8ha
Barry and Jan Morey keep a low profile, but the wines from their vineyard at Beechworth have a cult following not far removed from that of Giaconda; chardonnay, sauvignon blanc, semillon, pinot noir, merlot, cabernet franc, cabernet sauvignon and gamay are the principal varieties planted on the north-facing granitic slopes. Gamay and Chardonnay are the winery specialties. Exports to Japan.

Beechworth Sauvignon Blanc Semillon 2014 80/20% blend. 100% barrel-fermented without inoculation. Shows its oak but maintains its elegance. Tropical fruits, lemongrass, green melon and creamy cedar. Delicious mouthfeel. Mellifluous. Cork. 13.4% alc. **Rating** 93 **To** 2021 $37 CM
Gamay 2014 Firm and precise with sweet, undergrowthy fruit admirably intermingled with twiggy spice. Ultrafine tannin and a spine of refreshing acidity. A beautiful wine; alcohol warmth (despite the stated reading) the only possible caveat. Cork. 13.3% alc. **Rating** 93 **To** 2024 $47 CM
Cabernet Sauvignon Cabernet Franc Merlot 2012 Classic Bordeaux blend with redcurrant, blackcurrant and cigar box aromas/flavours moving in mid-weight style though a palate grumpy with herb-strewn tannin. Best days are ahead of it. Cork. 13.6% alc. **Rating** 93 **To** 2026 $52 CM

Soul Growers

218–230 Murray Street, Tanunda, SA 5352 **Region** Barossa Valley
T 0410 505 590 **www**.soulgrowers.com **Open** Thurs–Sat 11–4 or by appt
Winemaker Paul Heinicke, Stuart Bourne **Est.** 1998 **Dozens** 5000 **Vyds** 4.85ha
In January 2014 Paul Heinicke (one of the four founders of the business) purchased the shares previously held by David Cruickshank and James and Paul Lindner. The vineyards are mainly on hillside country in the Seppeltsfield area, with shiraz, cabernet sauvignon, grenache and chardonnay the most important varieties, and lesser plantings of mataro and black muscat; there are then pocket-handkerchief blocks of shiraz at Tanunda, mataro at Nuriootpa and a 1.2ha planting of grenache at Krondorf. Exports to the US, Canada, Singapore, Hong Kong and China.

106 Vines Barossa Valley Mourvedre 2013 110 numbered bottles. It is the opposite of the tannic wine I expected; instead it's fruit-sweet and supple, and carries its alcohol with ease. Made from a tiny survivor patch of vines planted in the 1880s, hand-picked and sorted, destemmed, matured for 18 months in an old 90l American oak barrel. Diam. 15% alc. **Rating** 95 **To** 2023 $100

ŸŸŸŸŸ The Forgotten Soul Cabernet 2013 Rating 93 To 2028 $25 CM ✪
Cellar Dweller Cabernet Sauvignon 2013 Rating 93 To 2028 $50 CM
Black Cellar Sparkling Shiraz 2006 Rating 92 To 2018 $55 TS
Single Vineyard Eden Valley Riesling 2015 Rating 90 To 2028 $25

Soumah   ★★★★★

18 Hexham Road, Gruyere, Vic 3770 **Region** Yarra Valley
T (03) 5962 4716 **www**.soumah.com.au **Open** 7 days 10–5
Winemaker Scott McCarthy **Est.** 1997 **Dozens** 10000 **Vyds** 19.5ha
Unravelling the story behind the exotically named Soumah, and its strikingly labelled Savarro
(reminiscent of 19th-century baroque design), was a voyage of discovery. Soumah is in fact
an acronym meaning South of Maroondah (Highway), and Savarro is an alternative name
for savagnin. This is the venture of Brett Butcher, who has international experience in the
hospitality industry as CEO of the Langham Group, and a long involvement in retailing
wines to restaurants in many countries. Tim Brown is viticultural director. The many varieties
planted have been clonally selected and grafted onto rootstock with the long-term future
in mind, although some of the sauvignon blanc is already being grafted over to bracchetto.
Exports to Canada, South Korea, Singapore, Hong Kong, Japan and China.

ŸŸŸŸŸ Single Vineyard Yarra Valley Chardonnay 2014 An altogether serious
chardonnay, all the winemaker cards played at the right time and in the right way;
the creamy/figgy nuances from the partial mlf are held in place by white peach
fruit, gently toasty oak and grapefruity acidity on the finish. Extra complexity from
the mlf showing as the wine continues to develop. Screwcap. 13.1% alc. **Rating** 96
To 2022 $38 ✪
Hexham Yarra Valley Pinot Noir 2015 MV6, 777 and D4V2 clones, matured
in French oak (27% new) for 11 months. Many Burgundians believe there is
synergy in a clonal mix. It may be this, or the Hexham site, but either way, I have a
slight preference for the more silky, supple mouthfeel and fractionally riper flavours
of this wine. Screwcap. 13.3% alc. **Rating** 95 To 2027 $34 ✪
Single Vineyard Yarra Valley Chardonnay 2015 From the Hexham Vineyard,
wild-fermented in French oak (20% new), matured for 9 months. An attractive
wine, even if it's mainly about stone fruit and honeydew melon, with citrus
playing a minor support role. Its overall balance is good (particularly the oak) and
the length is there. Screwcap. 13% alc. **Rating** 94 To 2021 $38
Blue Stone Single Vineyard Yarra Valley Pinot Noir 2015 MV6 clone,
matured in French oak (27% new) for 9 months. Plummy fruit drives the
expressive bouquet and the supple palate that sneaks up on you, surprising with
its length, fine tannins and persistent aftertaste. The savoury cast to the flavour is a
plus. Screwcap. 13.2% alc. **Rating** 94 To 2028 $34
Single Vineyard Yarra Valley Syrah 2014 5% viognier co-fermented,
10% whole bunches, matured in French oak (35% new) for 18 months. A full-
bodied syrah, deep in colour and with the full kitbag of black fruits, some licorice
and incipient black pepper thrown in for good measure, joining forces with the
oak. An almost limitless future. Screwcap. 13.8% alc. **Rating** 94 To 2040 $37

ŸŸŸŸŸ Wild Yarra Valley Savagnin 2015 Rating 93 To 2022 $33 CM
Yarra Valley Pinot Grigio 2015 Rating 92 To 2016 $26 CM
Yarra Valley Savarro 2015 Rating 92 To 2018 $28 CM
Yarra Valley Sauvignon Blanc 2015 Rating 91 To 2016 $25 CM
Yarra Valley Ai Fiori 2015 Rating 91 To 2017 $26 CM
Yarra Valley Viognier 2015 Rating 90 To 2018 $33
Yarra Valley Brachetto d'Soumah 2015 Rating 90 To 2016 $29 CM

Spence ★★★☆

760 Burnside Road, Murgheboluc, Vic 3221 **Region** Geelong
T (03) 5265 1181 **www**.spencewines.com.au **Open** 1st Sun each month
Winemaker Peter Spence **Est.** 1997 **Dozens** 400 **Vyds** 3.2ha
Peter and Anne Spence were sufficiently inspired by an extended European holiday, which included living on a family vineyard in Provence, to purchase a small property and establish a vineyard and winery. They have planted 3.2ha on a north-facing slope in a valley 7km south of Bannockburn; the lion's share to three clones of shiraz (1.83ha), the remainder to chardonnay, pinot noir and fast-diminishing cabernet sauvignon (it is being grafted over to viognier for use in the Shiraz). The vineyard attained full organic status in 2008, since then using complete biodynamic practices.

ɤɤɤɤɤ **Geelong Shiraz 2014** Excellent flavour upfront: black cherries, black pepper and black licorice. It hits and seduces quick smart, the effect maintained through a sweet-savoury palate high on charm. The finish has a gentle twiggy bitterness; blink and you miss it. Screwcap. 13.6% alc. **Rating** 93 **To** 2026 $30 CM

Spinifex ★★★★★

PO Box 511, Nuriootpa, SA 5355 **Region** Barossa Valley
T (08) 8564 2059 **www**.spinifexwines.com.au **Open** At Artisans of Barossa
Winemaker Peter Schell **Est.** 2001 **Dozens** 6000
Peter Schell and Magali Gely are a husband and wife team from NZ who came to Australia in the early 1990s to study oenology and marketing at Roseworthy College. They have spent four vintages making wine in France, mainly in the south, where Magali's family were vignerons for generations near Montpellier. The focus at Spinifex is the red varieties that dominate in the south of France: mataro (more correctly mourvedre), grenache, shiraz and cinsaut. The wine is made in open fermenters, basket-pressed, with partial wild (indigenous) fermentation and relatively long post-ferment maceration. This is a very old approach, but nowadays à la mode. Exports to the UK, Canada, Belgium, Singapore, Hong Kong, China and NZ.

ɤɤɤɤɤ **La Maline 2013** Improbably, this shiraz takes the Bête Noir onto another level of depth, richness and complexity, although the flavours are in the same style family. It has harmony and supreme balance to its array of black fruits, black pepper and savoury backbone. Quite simple: cellar this for as long as you can, and drink the Bête Noir in the interim. Screwcap. 14.5% alc. **Rating** 97 **To** 2040 $60 ✪

ɤɤɤɤɤ **Bête Noir 2013** Deep, but bright, crimson; right from the first whiff, this shiraz proclaims 'I am Spinifex', the fragrant bouquet of spice, black fruits, licorice and a whisper of oak leading into a palate of exceptional texture, structure, balance; awesome length and freshness. Screwcap. 14.5% alc. **Rating** 96 **To** 2030 $40 ✪
Indigene 2013 The deluxe, weighty bottle for this shiraz mataro blend is not out of place; the colour is exceptional, and is no false dawn for a wine of extreme complexity. First up there is a deep ocean swell of dark berry and plum fruit, then a crosscurrent of savoury flavours and fine, but insistent, tannins; a long finish to close. All class. Screwcap. 14.5% alc. **Rating** 96 **To** 2043 $60 ✪
Esprit 2013 63/21/16% grenache, mataro and cinsaut. This brings the Barossa Valley into close contact with high quality Rhône Valley wines, its intensity and vibrancy wonderful to see; it flows in a mouthfilling stream of red fruits, both fresh and poached, with a garland of spice and dusty tannins providing a savoury finish. Screwcap. 14.5% alc. **Rating** 96 **To** 2025 $35 ✪
Adelaide Hills Aglianico 2014 Normally, if I use the word 'confection' it's a polite way of being impolite about a wine. Here the confection is a sugar-free glaze of dark cherry inside bitter chocolate. There's also the question of texture, which runs down the same track. Screwcap. 13.5% alc. **Rating** 95 **To** 2023 $30 ✪
Barossa Valley Rose 2015 52% grenache, 30% cinsaut, 14% mataro, 4% ugni blanc. A strong and complex array of exotic spices and pressed dried flowers gently finds every corner of the mouth. Fine as an aperitif, even better with tapas. Screwcap. 13.5% alc. **Rating** 94 **To** 2017 $28 ✪

Papillon 2015 A spicy, fresh blend of grenache and cinsaut, which has altogether surprising length and tenacity. Oak? Maybe yes, maybe no. But if yes, it's well worn. Screwcap. 13.5% alc. **Rating** 94 **To** 2020 $28 ✪
Papillon 2014 A light-coloured grenache cinsaut, but the hue is good; there is a will-o'-the-wisp character to the wine, small red fruits, an Indian chef's assortment of spices, and a hard to pin down, but utterly satisfying, exclamation mark on the finish. Screwcap. 13.5% alc. **Rating** 94 **To** 2020 $26 ✪

🍷🍷🍷🍷 **Barossa Valley Rose 2014** **Rating** 93 **To** 2016 $24 ✪
Barossa Valley Pinot Noir 2015 **Rating** 90 **To** 2020 $28 CM

Spook Hill Wines ★★★☆

12 River Terrace, Cadell, SA 5321 **Region** Riverland
T 0428 403 235 **www**.spookhillwines.com **Open** By appt
Winemaker Jock Gordon **Est.** 1999 **Dozens** 1000 **Vyds** 10ha
Owner and winemaker Jock Gordon Jr's family have been grapegrowers for three generations, but in 1999 Jock took the plunge into commercial winemaking after a successful career as an amateur winemaker. He has 8ha of shiraz, 1ha of alicante bouschet and 1ha split between mourvedre and durif, supplemented by grapes from local growers. The Spook Hill vineyard is situated in the Cadell Valley, a former oxbow of the Murray River now bypassed by the river channel; silt soil deposited in the ancient river valley is especially suited to viticulture.

🍷🍷🍷🍷 **Nor'West Blend Mourvedre Durif 2013** It keeps its shape better than its Spook Hill siblings and makes a gentle play at complexity. Raspberry, blackberry, wood spice and earth notes do a pretty good job of both keeping your interest and satisfying. Screwcap. 14.8% alc. **Rating** 90 **To** 2021 $56 CM

Spring Vale Vineyards ★★★★

130 Spring Vale Road, Cranbrook, Tas 7190 **Region** East Coast Tasmania
T (03) 6257 8208 **www**.springvalewines.com **Open** 7 days 11–4
Winemaker Matt Wood **Est.** 1986 **Dozens** 8000 **Vyds** 17.6ha
Rodney Lyne has progressively established pinot noir (6.5ha), chardonnay (2ha), gewurztraminer (1.6ha), pinot gris and sauvignon blanc (1ha each). Spring Vale also owns the Melrose Vineyard, which is planted to pinot noir (3ha), sauvignon blanc and riesling (1ha each) and chardonnay (0.5ha). Exports to Singapore and Hong Kong.

🍷🍷🍷🍷🍷 **Gewurztraminer 2015** It has overdrive as an option but it remains in fourth gear. It's a good way to drive gewurz. It has power, personality and length without revving the charm, or drinkability, out of it. Screwcap. 13.5% alc. **Rating** 94 **To** 2017 $28 CM ✪

🍷🍷🍷🍷 **Chardonnay 2015** **Rating** 91 **To** 2023 $28

Springton Hills Wines ★★★☆

41 Burnbank Grove, Athelstone, SA 5076 (postal) **Region** Eden Valley
T (08) 8337 7905 **www**.springtonhillswines.com.au **Open** Not
Winemaker John Ciccocioppo **Est.** 2001 **Dozens** 2000 **Vyds** 6.5ha
The Ciccocioppo family migrated from central Italy in the 1950s; as is so often the case, wine was in their veins. In 2001, second-generation John and wife Connie purchased a grazing property at Springton, and began the planting of shiraz and riesling. Each year they increased the shiraz and riesling blocks, but also added smaller amounts of cabernet sauvignon, grenache and a smaller amount still of montepulciano. The wines are available for tasting at Taste Eden Valley in Angaston. Good label design and packaging.

🍷🍷🍷🍷🍷 **Koop Creek Reserve Eden Valley Shiraz 2012** This really pumps up the jam. It's full of rich, dark fruit and lavish, coffeed oak, the style and intent abundantly clear from the outset. There's too much oak, but the force of flavour is undeniable. Diam. 14.4% alc. **Rating** 94 **To** 2026 $33 CM

ŢŢŢŢ   Eliza's Eden Valley Riesling 2015 Rating 89 To 2020 $22 CM
       Adelaide Hills Sauvignon Blanc 2015 Rating 89 To 2017 $22 CM

Squitchy Lane Vineyard   ★★★★☆

Medhurst Road, Coldstream, Vic 3770 **Region** Yarra Valley
T (03) 5964 9114 **www**.squitchylane.com.au **Open** W'ends 11–5
Winemaker Robert Paul **Est.** 1982 **Dozens** 2000 **Vyds** 5.75ha
Mike Fitzpatrick acquired a taste for fine wine while a Rhodes scholar at Oxford University
in the 1970s. Returning to Australia he guided Carlton Football Club to two premierships
as captain, then established Melbourne-based finance company Squitchy Lane Holdings.
The wines of Mount Mary inspired him to look for his own vineyard, and in '96 he found
a vineyard of sauvignon blanc, chardonnay, pinot noir, merlot, cabernet franc and cabernet
sauvignon, planted in '82, just around the corner from Coldstream Hills and Yarra Yering.

ŢŢŢŢŢ   **Yarra Valley Cabernet Sauvignon 2014** 75% crushed, 25% destemmed,
       matured for 16 months in French barriques (40% new). Very good colour; rich
       cassis fruit is matched with quality French oak and velvety tannins. Seriously
       attractive wine. Screwcap. 13.5% alc. **Rating** 96 To 2034 $55 ✪
       Yarra Valley Chardonnay 2014 P58 and I10V1 clones, hand-picked, wild-
       fermented in French oak (30% new), matured for 11 months. Shows that the great
       Yarra Valley '14 chardonnay vintage isn't losing its form. This is all about restraint
       and elegance. Screwcap. 13.5% alc. **Rating** 94 To 2022 $26 ✪
       Yarra Valley Chardonnay 2013 Shows the site is able to consistently perform
       well. It really is delicious, still sailing in smooth waters, and represents the best
       value of the Squitchy Lane Chardonnays. Screwcap. 13.5% alc. **Rating** 94 To 2021
       $26 ✪
       Yarra Valley Cabernet Sauvignon Cabernet Franc Merlot 2014
       55/25/20%. This and the Cabernet Sauvignon have seriously attractive cassis-
       related fruit flavours. Here the inclusion of a majority role for the cabernet franc
       and merlot has given the wine a delicacy, yet in no way emasculated it. Great for
       early consumption. Screwcap. 13.5% alc. **Rating** 94 To 2024 $26 ✪

ŢŢŢŢŢ   Yarra Valley Fume Blanc 2014 Rating 91 To 2017 $26

Stage Door Wine Co   ★★★★★

22 Whibley Street, Henley Beach, SA 5022 **Region** Eden Valley
T 0400 991 968 **www**.stagedoorwineco.com.au **Open** Not
Winemaker Graeme Thredgold **Est.** 2013 **Dozens** 2500
It took a long time for Graeme Thredgold to establish this still-embryonic wine business.
Having been a successful professional musician for 15 years during the 1980s and '90s, he
developed vocal nodules in the early '90s, putting an end to his musical career. Having spent
so much time working in hotels and nightclubs, a new occupation stared him in the face: the
liquor industry. In '92 he began working for Lion Nathan as a sales representative; then five
years with SA Brewing, and in '98 venturing into the world of wine as national sales manager
for Andrew Garrett before moving on to the more fertile pasture of Tucker Seabrook as state
sales manager for SA around 2000. Further roles with Barossa Valley Estate and as general
manager of Chain of Ponds Wines added to an impressive career in sales and marketing, before
he made his final move – to general manager of Eden Hall Wines, which just happens to be
owned by his sister and brother-in-law, David and Mardi Hall. Exports to Canada.

ŢŢŢŢŢ   **Eden Valley Shiraz 2014** Heady and floral, with meaty blackberry/anise
       flavours swinging in from behind. Doesn't leave anything in the tank. It curls with
       tannin but the fruit is on a mission, and will not be slowed, let alone stopped.
       Gorgeousness in a bottle. Screwcap. 14.5% alc. **Rating** 95 To 2032 $50 CM
       Eden Valley Cabernet Sauvignon 2014 It fans out with bright, jubey flavour.
       Eden Valley to a tee. It's floral and spicy too, but that deep-but-bright trademark
       of the region's finest reds is here in spades. It's not just the fruit; it's the interplay of

tannin and acid, the succulence, the dry firmness. This puts elegance on the map, and stakes delicious fruit to it. Screwcap. 14.5% alc. **Rating** 95 **To** 2032 $50 CM
Front & Centre Barossa Shiraz 2014 This is how you do it. Plenty of dark-berried fruit, ripe and sweet without being overdone, is combined with savoury, earthen, coffeed flavours aplenty. The flavours are complex but the appeal is simple; perfectly balanced, too. Screwcap. 14.5% alc. **Rating** 94 **To** 2025 $25 CM ❂

Full House Cabernet Sauvignon 2014 Rating 92 To 2023 $25 CM ❂
The Green Room Eden Valley Riesling 2015 Rating 91 To 2022 $25 CM

Staindl Wines ★★★★

63 Shoreham Road, Red Hill South, Vic 3937 (postal) **Region** Mornington Peninsula
T 0419 553 299 **www.**staindlwines.com.au **Open** By appt
Winemaker Rollo Crittenden (Contract) **Est.** 1982 **Dozens** 400 **Vyds** 3.1ha
As often happens, the establishment date for a wine producer can mean many things. In this instance it harks back to the planting of the vineyard by the Ayton family, and the establishment of what was thereafter called St Neots. Juliet and Paul Staindl acquired the property in 2002, and have extended the plantings to 2.6ha of pinot noir, 0.4ha of chardonnay and 0.1ha of riesling, the vineyard run biodynamically. Ironically, all the 30-year-old chardonnay vines have been removed (and replanted) due to eutypa, a die-back disease that decimates the crop, and that is an increasing problem in many parts of Victoria and SA.

Mornington Peninsula Riesling 2015 There is a power of citrus fruit packed into this wine; the ever-present issue with a full maritime climate such as the Mornington Peninsula is lack of finesse. It's all to do with the vineyard, not the winery. Screwcap. 12% alc. **Rating** 90 **To** 2020 $25
Mornington Peninsula Pinot Noir 2014 Good hue, although light; a strongly spicy/savoury pinot with an ephemeral presence of red fruits; it suggests it might have been helped by bottling just before the arrival of the '15 vintage. Screwcap. 13% alc. **Rating** 90 **To** 2020 $55

Staniford Wine Co ★★★★★

20 Jackson Street, Mount Barker, WA 6324 **Region** Great Southern
T 0405 157 687 **www.**stanifordwineco.com.au **Open** By appt
Winemaker Michael Staniford **Est.** 2010 **Dozens** 500
Michael Staniford has been making wine in the Great Southern since 1995, principally as senior winemaker for Alkoomi at Frankland River, with additional experience as a contract maker for other wineries. The business is built around single vineyard wines; a Chardonnay from a 20+-year-old vineyard in Albany and a Cabernet Sauvignon from a 15+-year-old vineyard in Mount Barker. The quality of these two wines is every bit as one would expect. Michael plans to introduce a Riesling and a Shiraz with a similar individual vineyard origin, quality being the first requirement.

Great Southern Reserve Chardonnay 2013 60% Mendoza clone from Albany, 40% Bernard clones from Mount Barker. Gloriously intense, long and fine; riveting, with grapefruit and white peach entangled in a flamenco dance. Wow! Screwcap. 13.5% alc. **Rating** 97 **To** 2025 $38 ❂

Great Southern Reserve Cabernet Sauvignon 2013 Includes merlot, petit verdot and cabernet franc; matured in French oak for 18 months. A nicely composed and balanced blend, the centre of attention being the pure cassis of the cabernet, the other varieties adding to texture more than flavour; the main player here is the cedary French oak, which plays precisely the right role. Screwcap. 13.5% alc. **Rating** 95 **To** 2033 $38

Stanton & Killeen Wines   ★★★★★

440 Jacks Road, Murray Valley Highway, Rutherglen, Vic 3685 **Region** Rutherglen
T (02) 6032 9457 **www**.stantonandkilleenwines.com.au **Open** Mon–Sat 9–5, Sun 10–5
Winemaker Andrew Drumm **Est.** 1875 **Dozens** 15 000 **Vyds** 38ha

In 2015 Stanton & Killeen celebrated its 140th anniversary, with a number of changes throughout the business. Andrew Drumm, formerly the CSU winemaker, was in place for his first vintage at Stanton & Killeen. He joined Ruston Prescott, who had been appointed vineyard manager in December '13. The business is owned by Wendy Killeen and her two children, Simon and Natasha. Wendy had embraced the role of CEO in July '11, using skills learnt working in the business community in North East Victoria. Natasha manages the website, newsletter production and all consumer-focused communications. Simon has chosen to broaden his winemaking knowledge and skills by working outside the company. Exports to the UK, Switzerland and Hong Kong.

ŸŸŸŸŸ **Rare Rutherglen Muscat NV** Fabulous intensity and length. You could be inspired to argue that this is where character starts and ends. It pours it on but leaves time for nuance; it fills the palate with concentrated flavour but keeps something up its sleeve for the finish. One sip and it has you convinced. 375ml. Screwcap. 18.5% alc. **Rating** 97 **To** 2017 $110 CM **✪**
Grand Rutherglen Muscat NV The flavours reach back into the past and pull out into the future. The history has been rich. This is a flame of flavour, monumentally intense and yet precisely well judged. Dust off the word 'tremendous'; its services are required. Screwcap. 18.5% alc. **Rating** 97 **To** 2017 $85 CM **✪**

ŸŸŸŸŸ **Rare Rutherglen Topaque NV** Phenomenal intensity and length. Sweet tea leaves meet rancio meet leatherwood honey and candied orange. The full hedonistic experience at the twist of a cap. Screwcap. 18.5% alc. **Rating** 96 **To** 2017 $110 CM
Grand Rutherglen Topaque NV It's not as open and obvious as many of its regional brethren. There are fresh tea leaves and toffee flavours with clear blooms of butterscotch running the length of the palate. The finish then rings with coffee. It seems absurd to say it, but you'd almost put this in the 'acquired taste' category. 500ml. Screwcap. 18.5% alc. **Rating** 94 **To** 2017 $85 CM
Classic Rutherglen Muscat NV Lusciously sweet, but with real intensity and finish. It takes all the required components and slots them into the correct places. Leather, toffee, rancio, spice. Cleansing acidity sits at one with the overall wine. In a word: seamless. 500ml. Screwcap. 18% alc. **Rating** 94 **To** 2017 $35 CM

ŸŸŸŸŸ **Classic Rutherglen Topaque NV Rating** 90 **To** 2017 $35 CM

Stargazer Wine   ★★★★★

Back Tea Tree Road, Tee Tree, Tas 7017 **Region** Tasmania
T 0408 173 335 **www**.stargazerwine.com.au **Open** By appt
Winemaker Samantha Connew **Est.** 2012 **Dozens** 1000 **Vyds** 1ha

Samantha (Sam) Connew has racked up a series of exceptional achievements, commencing with Bachelor of Law and Bachelor of Arts degrees, majoring in political science and English literature, from the University of Canterbury, Christchurch, NZ, but showing her future direction by obtaining a postgraduate diploma of oenology and viticulture from Lincoln University, Canterbury, NZ. Sam moved to Australia, undertaking the advanced wine assessment course at the Australian Wine Research Institute in 2000, being chosen as a scholar at the '02 Len Evans Tutorial, winning the George Mackey Award for the best wine exported from Australia in '04; and in '07 was made International Red Winemaker of the Year at the International Wine Challenge, London. After a highly successful and lengthy position as chief winemaker at Wirra Wirra, Sam moved to Tasmania (via the Hunter Valley) to make the first wines for her own business, something she said she would never do. The emotive name (and label) is in part a tribute to Abel Tasman, the first European to sight Tasmania before proceeding to the South Island of NZ, navigating by the stars. Exports to the UK and the US.

ɭɭɭɭɭ **Tamar and Derwent Chardonnay 2014** Matured in oak, none of it new. It's an elegant wine with a moreishness to the fruit and an impressive carry of steely, minerally flavour to the finish. Its deliciousness is immediately obvious, but its sheer quality becomes more and more apparent as you spend time with it. Screwcap. 13% alc. **Rating** 95 **To** 2022 $40 CM

Huon Valley Pinot Noir 2014 Single vineyard. 200-odd dozen. Wild ferment. Inherently complex style with twists of herbs and turns of twiggy tannin. One for the structuralists. Tight with raw tannin, fleshed with rhubarb and cherry-plum flavour, and accented by a nutty bitterness. Needs time, but there is a whole lot to explore here. Screwcap. 13.5% alc. **Rating** 95 **To** 2026 $50 CM

Derwent Valley Riesling 2015 Fermented wild. Soft and juicy with an assortment of citrus juice and rind flavours. Spicy. Suggests sweetness and opens up with a serious burst of fruit on the finish. Quite irresistible. Screwcap. 12.5% alc. **Rating** 94 **To** 2026 $30 CM ✪

ɭɭɭɭ♀ **Tupelo 2015** **Rating** 91 **To** 2019 $30 CM

Steels Creek Estate ★★★★

1 Sewell Road, Steels Creek, Vic 3775 **Region** Yarra Valley
T (03) 5965 2448 **www**.steelsckestate.com.au **Open** W'ends & public hols 10–6
Winemaker Simon Peirce **Est.** 1981 **Dozens** 400 **Vyds** 1.7ha
The Steels Creek vineyard (chardonnay, shiraz, cabernet sauvignon, cabernet franc and colombard), family-operated since 1981, is located in the picturesque Steels Creek Valley, with views towards the Kinglake National Park. All the wines are made onsite by winemaker and owner Simon Peirce, following renovations to the winery. Exports to China.

ɭɭɭɭɭ **Yarra Valley Cabernet Sauvignon 2013** In a good place. Medium-bodied and brightened by cranberry/redcurrant flavours, but it's the core of blackcurrant that gets this wine rolling. Eucalypt notes add lift; infusions of herbs are little more than glancing blows. Tannin keeps the picture neat. Diam. 13.5% alc. **Rating** 94 **To** 2028 $35 CM

ɭɭɭɭ♀ **Blanc de Blanc 2012** **Rating** 92 **To** 2022 $40 TS
Yarra Valley Chardonnay 2014 **Rating** 91 **To** 2019 $30 CM
Yarra Valley Colombard 2014 **Rating** 90 **To** 2018 $22 CM
Yarra Valley Cabernet Franc 2014 **Rating** 90 **To** 2024 $35 CM

Stefani Estate ★★★★★

122 Long Gully Road, Healesville, Vic 3777 **Region** Yarra Valley/Heathcote
T (03) 9570 8750 **www**.stefaniestatewines.com.au **Open** By appt
Winemaker Peter Mackey **Est.** 1998 **Dozens** 6700 **Vyds** 28.5ha
Stefano Stefani came to Australia in 1985. Business success has allowed Stefano and wife Rina to follow in the footsteps of Stefano's grandfather, who had a vineyard and was an avid wine collector. The first property they acquired was at Long Gully Road in the Yarra Valley, planted to pinot grigio, cabernet sauvignon, chardonnay and pinot noir. The next was in Heathcote, where they acquired a property adjoining that of Mario Marson (ex Mount Mary), built a winery and established 14.4ha of shiraz, cabernet sauvignon, merlot, cabernet franc, malbec and petit verdot. In 2003 a second Yarra Valley property, named The View, reflecting its high altitude, was acquired and Dijon clones of chardonnay and pinot noir were planted. In addition, 1.6ha of sangiovese, mammolo bianco, malvasia, aleatico, trebbiano and crepolino bianco have been established, using scion material from the original Stefani vineyard in Tuscany. Exports to China.

ɭɭɭɭɭ **Barrel Selection Heathcote Vineyard Shiraz 2014** From the higher slopes of the vineyard, matured in new and used French barrels for 12 months, a best-oak selection. Densely coloured; this is a particularly concentrated, yet fine, full-bodied wine, with blackberry, plum and licorice running through the long, beautifully composed palate. Diam. 14.5% alc. **Rating** 96 **To** 2034 $55 ✪

The View Yarra Valley Vineyard Chardonnay 2013 Has started to develop some very attractive characters, fig, creamy cashew and a fleck of honey all contributing, assisted by Yarra Valley minerally acidity. Screwcap. 13.5% alc. **Rating** 95 **To** 2020 $55

Heathcote Marsanne 2015 Has the classic varietal honeysuckle plus, of course, complexity ex barrel fermentation. This has exceptional development potential. Screwcap. 13.5% alc. **Rating** 94 **To** 2028 $30 ✪

The View Yarra Valley Vineyard Pinot Noir 2014 Gamey/charcuterie nuances on the bouquet, then a powerful and complex palate; plum and wild blackberry floating over a foresty/earthy bedrock of flavours. Will go the distance. Diam. 14% alc. **Rating** 94 **To** 2025 $55

Heathcote Shiraz 2014 A very attractive, well-balanced and structured medium-bodied palate, the tannins soft but persistent; spicy plum fruits do the talking, tannins coming through on the finish. Screwcap. 14% alc. **Rating** 94 **To** 2030 $35

The Gate Yarra Valley Cabernet Sauvignon 2013 It is a convincingly ripe (not overripe) cabernet with hints of black chocolate and plum underlying the blackcurrant fruit. Authentic Yarra Valley cabernet. Diam. 13.5% alc. **Rating** 94 **To** 2028 $55

ᵀᵀᵀᵀᵀ **Boccallupo Yarra Valley Sangiovese 2015** Rating 93 To 2025 $45

Stefano Lubiana ★★★★★

60 Rowbottoms Road, Granton, Tas 7030 **Region** Southern Tasmania
T (03) 6263 7457 **www**.slw.com.au **Open** Thurs–Mon 11–4 (closed Jul)
Winemaker Steve Lubiana **Est.** 1990 **Dozens** NFP **Vyds** 25ha
Monique and Steve Lubiana moved from the hot inland of a brown Australia to the beautiful banks of the Derwent River in 1990 to pursue Steve's dream of making high quality sparkling wine. The sloping site allowed them to build a gravity-fed winery, and his whole winemaking approach since that time has been based on attention to detail within a biodynamic environment. The first sparkling wines were made in 1993 from the first plantings of chardonnay and pinot noir. Over the years they have added riesling, sauvignon blanc, pinot gris and merlot. The Italian-inspired Osteria restaurant is based on their own biodynamically produced vegetables and herbs, the meats (all free-range) are from local farmers, and the seafood is wild-caught. In 2016 the Lubianas purchased the Panorama Vineyard, first planted in 1974, in the Huon Valley. Exports to the UK, Singapore, Indonesia, Japan, Hong Kong and China.

ᵀᵀᵀᵀᵀ **Riesling 2014** As from '14 riesling will always be fermented and matured in a large Austrian oak cask for 4–6 months. This is a riveting wine, with searing acidity wrapped around lime and apple fruit in Rheingau/Pfalz style. Screwcap. 12% alc. **Rating** 95 **To** 2030 $28 ✪

Estate Chardonnay 2013 This is a lovely, easy-to-appreciate chardonnay, fully deserving its top-gold at the International Organic Wine Awards '15 (Germany). While still important to the structure of the wine, acidity is not in your face. The main story is the stone fruit, plus fig and cashew flavours, oak playing long in harmony with the others. Screwcap. 14% alc. **Rating** 95 **To** 2024 $48

Settebello Single Block Pinot Noir 2013 A seamless fusion of red and black cherries, a slash of satsuma plum, and that cool finish many Tasmanian pinots have, thanks to good natural balance. There are also strands of stem adding a degree of complexity. Cork. 13.5% alc. **Rating** 95 **To** 2027 $70

Late Disgorged 1996 After a decade on lees and a further 9 years on cork, this cellar-door-only release must be the oldest current release sparkling in the country, and for all it represents it is grossly underpriced. Its flavours encompass an expansive universe of complexity: grilled pineapple, dried peach, ginger nut biscuits, burnt butter, glacé fig, baked apple and mixed spice. Nuances of smoky tertiary complexity are beginning to emerge. At 20yo it has attained the wonderful

twilight of its life, and has done so with integrity and grace. Cork. 12.5% alc.
Rating 95 **To** 2016 $45 TS

Biodynamic Sauvignon Blanc 2015 A hyper-intense sauvignon blanc, citrus peel zest, pith (you name it), most obviously Tasmanian acidity embellished by the biodynamic practices, no doubt. The oak cask has had an impact on the texture, but not the flavour. Screwcap. 12.5% alc. **Rating** 94 **To** 2017 $30 ✪

Primavera Biodynamic Chardonnay 2014 95% fermented in French oak (60% new), matured for 8–10 months. Very crisp and intense, the acidity in full-blown Tasmanian style, a mix of mineral, citrus and slate. The oak has been reduced to a minor role in shaping the all-up flavour and structure of the wine and its bracing freshness. Screwcap. 13% alc. **Rating** 94 **To** 2028 $30 ✪

Primavera Pinot Noir 2015 Deep colour; a very complex wine, with a spicy/flowery background to the cherry and plum fruits that inhabit both the bouquet and palate; while it needs time, the potential is plain to see – this will always have that little bit extra. It is supple, but has tannin support, and will reach its drink-to date with greater ease than the Estate. Screwcap. 13% alc. **Rating** 94 **To** 2023 $34

Estate Pinot Noir 2014 Identical clonal mix, and the vinification nigh-on identical to that of the '15 Primavera. This has the advantage of an extra year in bottle, but there is still a suite of secondary, earthy characters to fully develop. Screwcap. 13% alc. **Rating** 94 **To** 2026 $48

Grande Vintage 2007 Seven years on lees followed by a year on cork makes for a particularly toasty, nutty cuvee of medium straw-yellow hue. It's beautifully creamy in texture, laced with spice and even a hint of early tertiary complexity in wisps of pipe smoke. A long finish is sustained by well-integrated Tasmanian acidity. 12.5% alc. **Rating** 94 **To** 2018 $55 TS

🍷🍷🍷🍷🍷 **Brut Rose 2010** Rating 93 To 2016 $45 TS
Pinot Gris 2014 Rating 92 To 2017 $30
Reserve Merlot 2013 Rating 92 To 2020 $40
Reserve Brut NV Rating 92 To 2017 $34 TS
Gruner Veltliner 2014 Rating 90 To 2017 $38

Steinborner Family Vineyards ★★★

91 Siegersdorf Road, Tanunda, SA 5352 **Region** Barossa Valley
T 0414 474 708 **www**.sfvineyards.com.au **Open** By appt
Winemaker David Reynolds **Est.** 2003 **Dozens** 2000 **Vyds** 12ha
Steinborner Family Vineyards is owned and operated by David and Rebecca Reynolds and Rebecca's father, Michael Steinborner. Their Ancestry Vineyards are located on the floor of the Barossa Valley in Vine Vale. Shiraz (some over 90 years old) accounts for two-thirds of the total plantings, with equal quantities of marsanne, viognier, durif and semillon making up the rest. Exports to Indonesia, Hong Kong, Singapore, Malaysia and China.

🍷🍷🍷 **Barossa Deutsche Shiraz 2012** Estate-grown on the old Vine Vale family vineyard, matured for 3 years in French and American oak. It is in traditional style, and might have been better with 18 months in oak, but it is fairly priced. Cork. 14% alc. **Rating** 89 **To** 2022 $28

Stella Bella Wines ★★★★★

205 Rosabrook Road, Margaret River, WA 6285 **Region** Margaret River
T (08) 9758 8611 **www**.stellabella.com.au **Open** 7 days 10–5
Winemaker Luke Jolliffe, Michael Kane, Stuart Pym (Consultant) **Est.** 1997
Dozens 50 000 **Vyds** 87.9ha
This enormously successful winemaking business produces wines of true regional expression, with fruit sourced from the central and southern parts of Margaret River. The company owns and operates six vineyards, and also purchases fruit from small contract growers. Substantial quantities of wines covering all styles and price points make this an important producer for Margaret River. Exports to all major markets.

♚♚♚♚♚ **Serie Luminosa Margaret River Cabernet Sauvignon 2013** The three-tier system of Stella Bella is managed with great skill and considerable experience. The wine is not based on weight or size, but on finesse, length, finish and aftertaste all harmoniously balanced. Screwcap. 13.5% alc. **Rating** 97 **To** 2038 $75 ○

♚♚♚♚♚ **Margaret River Chardonnay 2014** It bursts with life and sparkling energy, the grapefruit/citrus rapier thrust on the palate ultimately parried by the underlying stone fruit and benison of subtle French oak; the finish is gloriously fresh and long. Screwcap. 13% alc. **Rating** 96 **To** 2025 $32 ○

Serie Luminosa Margaret River Chardonnay 2014 Pale straw-green; this is pure class, in one sense understated, in another absolutely compelling in its purity, focus and length. It will revel in the security of its screwcap, gaining complexity over the years ahead as its mix of grapefruit and stone fruit expand. Drink some now, some later, and some much later. 12.5% alc. **Rating** 96 **To** 2024 $65 ○

Serie Luminosa Margaret River Chardonnay 2013 A wonderful chardonnay, immediately and insistently proclaiming its class; a perfect fusion of fragrant, juicy pink grapefruit, white peach, nectarine, cashew, oak and all-important crisp acidity on the very long finish. Screwcap. 12.5% alc. **Rating** 96 **To** 2025 $65 ○

Suckfizzle Margaret River Cabernet Sauvignon 2012 This has the Suckfizzle DNA down to its roots. It is perfectly balanced, constructed and structured, elegant yet powerful, and has supple blackcurrant fruit with its own inbuilt, natural tannins. The length is impeccable, as is the clarity of expression. Screwcap. 13.5% alc. **Rating** 96 **To** 2032 $55 ○

Suckfizzle Margaret River Cabernet Sauvignon 2011 A distinguished Margaret River cabernet, the fragrant bouquet and palate of flowery cassis with counterpoints of quality French oak and bay leaf. The silky, supple mouthfeel is an uncommon plus for this style, making it a 'whenever you feel like it' bottle. Screwcap. 14% alc. **Rating** 96 **To** 2031 $55 ○

Margaret River Sauvignon Blanc 2015 Picked at precisely the right moment(s), allowing passionfruit, gooseberry and guava free rein, given context and structure by grainy acidity. A classy wine: don't leave it on the shelf. Screwcap. 13% alc. **Rating** 95 **To** 2016 $24 ○

Suckfizzle Margaret River Sauvignon Blanc Semillon 2013 This has so much depth, power and complexity that it's in an altogether different league. Tropical fruits are shrouded in subtle French oak, and given an exit trajectory courtesy of the lime-riddled acidity. Screwcap. 13.5% alc. **Rating** 95 **To** 2020 $45

Suckfizzle Margaret River Sauvignon Blanc Semillon 2012 Rides high on its complexity and depth, proving beyond doubt that longevity can be achieved with this blend. At once luscious yet restrained (by soft acidity), its flavours span citrus, brioche and white peach. Screwcap. 12.5% alc. **Rating** 95 **To** 2020 $45

Margaret River Semillon Sauvignon Blanc 2015 The grass, green pea and lemon signature of Margaret River semillon comes through on the bouquet, but is blown away by the seductive array of tropical fruits on the palate, with gooseberry, guava and creamy notes (is there a touch of barrel ferment?). Screwcap. 13% alc. **Rating** 95 **To** 2018 $24 ○

Suckfizzle Margaret River Cabernet Sauvignon 2013 Manages to have the best of both worlds, with its beautifully etched and juicy fruit backed by the structure one expects from top class cabernets. There is fruit in abundance matched by high quality oak and tannins, the length, finish and aftertaste all harmoniously balanced. Screwcap. 13.5% alc. **Rating** 95 **To** 2033 $55

Skuttlebutt Margaret River Sauvignon Blanc Semillon 2015 A kaleidoscopic, ever-changing rivulet of green pea, capsicum, citrus, gooseberry and passionfruit and gentle, but cleansing, acidity. The fruit has been allowed to do all the work, courtesy of cool fermentation in tank. Screwcap. 13.5% alc. **Rating** 94 **To** 2018 $18 ○

Margaret River Shiraz 2014 A fresh, lively and totally balanced medium-bodied shiraz with a delightful juiciness achieved without losing texture or structure; poached plum/cherry flavours and fine tannins fill the mouth, yet leave it fresh. Screwcap. 14% alc. **Rating** 94 **To** 2029 $27 ○

Margaret River Cabernet Merlot 2014 The highly fragrant bouquet leads directly into the clearly defined pathway of medium-bodied red berries, cassis and tannins which have a finer mouthfeel. It all adds up to a wine that towers over almost all others at this price. Screwcap. 13.5% alc. Rating 94 To 2034 $24 ✪

Margaret River Cabernet Merlot 2013 60/40%. This wine (and its blend) is the red wine equivalent of Margaret River's SSB/SBS blends, here great colour and seamlessly blended cassis/blackcurrant, bay leaf and black olive have just the right amount of tannin support. Screwcap. 13.5% alc. Rating 94 To 2033 $24 ✪

Margaret River Sangiovese Cabernet Sauvignon 2014 The cabernet doesn't come over the top of the sangiovese, which is exactly as it should be. The fruit flavours play tag with each other, and it's fun to be part of the cherry cassis game, all of which doesn't take the focus away from the truly engaging nature – and quality – of this wine. Screwcap. 14.5% alc. Rating 94 To 2029 $30 ✪

🍷🍷🍷🍷🍷 Sangiovese Cabernet Sauvignon 2013 Rating 93 To 2025 $30 CM
Margaret River Tempranillo 2014 Rating 93 To 2024 $30
Skuttlebutt Margaret River Rose 2015 Rating 92 To 2017 $18 ✪
Margaret River Cabernet Sauvignon 2013 Rating 92 To 2028 $32
Skuttlebutt Cabernet Shiraz 2013 Rating 90 To 2018 $18 ✪

Steve Wiblin's Erin Eyes   ★★★★★

58 Old Road, Leasingham, SA 5452 **Region** Clare Valley
T (08) 8843 0023 www.erineyes.com.au **Open** Not
Winemaker Steve Wiblin **Est.** 2009 **Dozens** 2200
Having sold his share of Neagles Rock Vineyards, Steve Wiblin has struck out on his own with Erin Eyes. He explains the name thus: 'In 1842 my English convict forebear John Wiblin gazed into a pair of Erin eyes. That gaze changed our family make-up and history forever. In the Irish-influenced Clare Valley, what else would I call my wines but Erin Eyes?'

🍷🍷🍷🍷🍷 Pride of Erin Single Vineyard Reserve Clare Valley Riesling 2015 For the nerds, 7.75g/l acid, 4.3g/l residual sugar, and a pH of 2.95, numbers that help explain the poise and intensity of the wine, and its rainbow of citrus flavours, both juice and pith on display; great acidity, too. Exceptional wine. Screwcap. 12% alc. Rating 97 To 2035 $35 ✪

🍷🍷🍷🍷🍷 Clare Valley Riesling 2015 From three vineyards at Sevenhill, Penwortham Polish Hill. The bouquet is fine, the palate outstanding, full of drive, energy and – above all – length to its array of multi-citrus flavours and vividly crisp acidity. Screwcap. 12% alc. Rating 95 To 2030 $25 ✪

🍷🍷🍷🍷🍷 Celtic Heritage Cabernet Shiraz 2014 Rating 93 To 2024 $30
Ballycapple Cabernet Sauvignon 2014 Rating 91 To 2021 $30
Blarney Stone Shiraz 2014 Rating 90 To 2024 $30

Sticks Yarra Valley   ★★★★★

206 Yarraview Road, Yarra Glen, Vic 3775 **Region** Yarra Valley
T (03) 9925 1911 www.sticks.com.au **Open** Not
Winemaker Travis Bush **Est.** 2000 **Dozens** 30 000
Sticks acquired the former Yarra Ridge 3000-tonne capacity winery in 2005, and 24ha of estate vineyards, mainly planted in 1983. The estate production is significantly supplemented by contract-grown grapes sourced elsewhere in the Yarra Valley and surrounding regions. Sticks also provides substantial contract-making facilities for wineries throughout the Yarra Valley. Exports to the UK, the US, Hong Kong and China.

🍷🍷🍷🍷🍷 Pinot Noir 2015 A staple on many Melbourne restaurant wine lists, this classic Yarra pinot from the highly regarded '15 vintage ticks all the boxes: cherry, spice and a silky voluminous palate that carries and persists, lovely balance. Screwcap. 12.8% alc. Rating 94 To 2020 $19 ✪

ΨΨΨΨ♀ Chardonnay 2014 Rating 92 To 2020 $19 ⊙
Cabernet Sauvignon 2013 Rating 92 To 2023 $19 ⊙

Stockman's Ridge Wines   ★★★☆

21 Boree Lane, Lidster, NSW 2800 **Region** Orange
T (02) 6365 6512 **www**.stockmansridge.com.au **Open** Thurs–Mon 1105
Winemaker Jonathan Hambrook **Est.** 2002 **Dozens** 3000 **Vyds** 3ha
Stockman's Ridge Wines, founded and owned by Jonathan Hambrook, started its wine life in
Bathurst, before relocating to its present vineyard on the northwest slopes of Mt Canobolas,
at an elevation of 800m. Here he has planted 1.2ha of pinot noir and 1ha of gruner veltliner.
His next door neighbour is the Booree Lane Vineyard, owned by Bob Clark, who has 21.6ha
of shiraz, merlot, cabernet franc, chardonnay and gewurztraminer – a significant part of the
grapes go next door to Stockman's Ridge. Exports to the US and China.

ΨΨΨΨ **Rider Central Ranges Pinot Gris 2015** Green apples, ripe pears, honeysuckle;
it's both tart and pretty at once. It drinks well. Screwcap. 11.8% alc. **Rating** 89
To 2017 $23 CM

Stomp Wine   ★★★★☆

1273 Milbrodale Road, Broke, NSW 2330 **Region** Hunter Valley
T (02) 6579 1400 **www**.stompwine.com.au **Open** Fri–Sun 10.30–4.30
Winemaker Michael McManus **Est.** 2004 **Dozens** 1000
After a lifetime in the food and beverage industry, Michael and Meredith McManus moved to
full-time winemaking. They have set up Stomp Winemaking, a contract winemaker designed
to keep small and larger parcels of grapes separate through the fermentation and maturation
process, thus meeting the needs of boutique wine producers in the Hunter Valley. The addition
of their own Stomp label is a small but important part of their business.

ΨΨΨΨΨ **Limited Release Hunter Valley Shiraz 2014** Matured in new French and
American barriques for 18 months. Twice as good as its sibling? Well, it doesn't
really matter. The fact is it has the finesse the other lacks, making short work of the
new oak. Juicy, slurpy red berry fruits are a (very attractive) puzzle; if the alcohol
levels of the two wines were swapped, it would be easy to explain the appearance
of finer red fruits here. Screwcap. 14% alc. **Rating** 95 To 2035 $48

ΨΨΨΨ♀ Hunter Valley Shiraz 2014 Rating 92 To 2035 $24 ⊙
Limited Release Hunter Valley Fiano 2015 Rating 90 To 2017 $28

Stone Bridge Wines   ★★★★

Section 113 Gillentown Road, Clare, SA 5453 **Region** Clare Valley
T (08) 8843 4143 **www**.stonebridgewines.com.au **Open** Thurs–Mon 10–4
Winemaker Craig Thomson, Angela Meaney **Est.** 2005 **Dozens** 6000 **Vyds** 29ha
Stone Bridge Wines started out as a hobby but has turned into a commercial enterprise for
its owners, Craig and Lisa Thomson. They say that Craig's 16 years as a baker have assisted
in the art of winemaking: 'It's all about the mix.' Their own patch of shiraz provides part of
the annual crush; riesling, pinot gris, cabernet sauvignon and malbec are purchased from local
growers. The cellar door is a rammed-earth and iron building with picturesque surrounds,
where on Sundays Sept–May (weather permitting), visitors can relax and enjoy a gourmet
wood-oven pizza. Exports to Canada, Denmark, Singapore and China.

ΨΨΨΨ♀ **Clare Valley Shiraz 2013** Deep colour; it is exceptionally powerful and
concentrated, way into full-bodied territory; licorice, boot leather, briar, tar and
spice surround the blackberry essence of the fruit. It's possible, although not
certain, that 25 years hence those still opening bottles will suddenly have a group
of new-found friends. Screwcap. 14.5% alc. **Rating** 93 To 2041 $30
Clare Valley Riesling 2015 A most attractive wine for drinking tonight or later
down the track; it overflows with lime, pineapple and lemon zest fruit, the acidity
present but soft. Screwcap. 12.2% alc. **Rating** 92 To 2022 $22 ⊙

Clare Valley Grenache Mataro 2014 'Yes, we left the shiraz out', say Stone Bridge, and I would add, 'having picked the grenache and mataro at precisely the right moment'. It is light to medium-bodied, fresh as a daisy, with the red fruits of the grenache tempered by more savoury nuances of mataro; good balance and length. Screwcap. 14% alc. **Rating** 91 **To** 2020 $26

Bowerbird Old Tawny NV The average 25 years age claim is borne out by the tawny colour, with no hint of red from young material; it is exceptionally fine, the spirit virtually invisible – as is the rancio. A fascinating exercise in contradictions, but compulsive drinking. 500ml. Screwcap. 18.5% alc. **Rating** 91 **To** 2017 $30

Clare Valley Cabernet Malbec 2013 80/20%. The blackberry jam flavour (not intended as a pejorative description) definitely expresses itself; by the time you have explored the wine, you realise that it is really only medium-bodied; it has a certain beguiling grace. Screwcap. 14.8% alc. **Rating** 90 **To** 2020 $24

ŸŸŸŸ   The Gardener Clare Valley Rose 2015 Rating 89 To 2017 $22

Stonefish   ★★★★★

24 Kangarilla Road, McLaren Vale, SA 5171 **Region** Various
T (02) 9668 9930 www.stonefishwines.com.au **Open** Not
Winemaker Contract, Peter Papanikitas **Est.** 2000 **Dozens** 10 000
Peter Papanikitas has been involved in various facets of the wine industry for the past 30+ years. Initially his contact was with companies that included Penfolds, Lindemans and Leo Buring, then he spent five years working for Cinzano, gaining experience in worldwide sales and marketing. In 2000 he established Stonefish, a virtual winery operation, in partnership with various grapegrowers and winemakers, principally in the Barossa Valley and Margaret River, who provide the wines. The value for money has never been in doubt, but Stonefish has moved to another level with its Icon and Reserve Barossa wines. Exports to China, Thailand, Vietnam, Hong Kong, Indonesia, the Philippines, the Maldives, Singapore and Fiji.

ŸŸŸŸŸ   Icon Barossa Valley Shiraz 2013 An ultra full-bodied shiraz; hand-picked, open-fermented and matured in new and used French oak. The mass of savoury extract is so intense it approaches (although ultimately falls short of) outright bitterness. Cork. 15% alc. **Rating** 95 **To** 2043 $90

Reserve Margaret River Cabernet Sauvignon 2014 Margaret River is the go-to region par excellence if you are prepared to pay for quality at a win-win price. This has it all: bell-clear blackcurrant fruit, black olive and dried herbs, and tannins that are round and ripe. Screwcap. 14% alc. **Rating** 95 **To** 2034 $36

Raffaele Margaret River Cabernet Sauvignon 2012 The first signs of moving out of primary into secondary mode look as if they may soon gather pace; there are some earthy/briary notes (and violets) joining the fruit. Screwcap. 14.3% alc. **Rating** 95 **To** 2027 $36

ŸŸŸŸ♀   Reserve Barossa Shiraz 2013 Rating 90 To 2028

Stoney Rise   ★★★★★

96 Hendersons Lane, Gravelly Beach, Tas 7276 **Region** Northern Tasmania
T (03) 6394 3678 www.stoneyrise.com **Open** Thurs–Mon 11–5
Winemaker Joe Holyman **Est.** 2000 **Dozens** 2000 **Vyds** 7.2ha
The Holyman family had been involved in vineyards in Tasmania for 20 years, but Joe Holyman's career in the wine industry, first as a sales rep, then as a wine buyer, and more recently working in wineries in NZ, Portugal, France, Mount Benson and Coonawarra, gave him an exceptionally broad-based understanding of wine. In 2004 Joe and wife Lou purchased the former Rotherhythe Vineyard, which had been established in 1986, and set about restoring it to its former glory. There are two ranges: the Stoney Rise wines, focusing on fruit and early drinkability, and the Holyman wines, with more structure, more new oak and the best grapes, here the focus on length and potential longevity. Exports to the UK, The Netherlands, Singapore and Japan.

🍷🍷🍷🍷🍷 **Holyman Project X Pinot Noir 2013** The bouquet is extremely fragrant, and the palate has a juicy quality that doesn't need to ram the point home; the tannins are superfine, and the finish speaks as much of the purity of the fruit as of the undoubtedly good structure. Has revelled in the extra 6 months since first tasted, its power and soaring finish gaining a well-deserved extra point. Screwcap. 13% alc. **Rating** 97 **To** 2028 $90 ✪

🍷🍷🍷🍷🍷 **Holyman Chardonnay 2014** At the upper end of Tasmanian chardonnay, with no hint of high acidity to challenge the balance of this style. There is no gainsaying the grapefruit pith component (and why should there be?), but it is accompanied by stone fruit and a touch of cashew, all in balance. Screwcap. 13% alc. **Rating** 95 **To** 2025 $50

Pinot Noir 2015 Vibrant colour, and a vibrantly juicy wine from start to finish. First up there is a rolling wave of red fruits, then a move to more savoury/spicy territory. The end result is a wine that is beautiful now and will remain so into the future. Screwcap. 12.5% alc. **Rating** 95 **To** 2030 $29 ✪

Holyman Pinot Noir 2014 Excellent depth and clarity of colour; this is certainly the vin de garde of Holyman, with the structure and depth to carry it forward for many years. The fruit profile is (like Stoney Rise) in the satsuma plum and cherry register, with ripe tannins adding some savoury notes. Its best years are in front of it. Screwcap. 12% alc. **Rating** 95 **To** 2029 $50

Gruner Veltliner 2015 You need to be on a footpath restaurant in Vienna, then order a gruner veltliner and unscrew the cap (yes, they've got the message) to really have the white pepper assail your nostrils. There's not much of it here, but you do get a surge of citrus fruit on the palate that more than compensates. Screwcap. 12% alc. **Rating** 94 **To** 2025 $29 ✪

Stonier Wines ★★★★★

Thompson's Lane, Merricks, Vic 3916 **Region** Mornington Peninsula
T (03) 5989 8300 **www**.stonier.com.au **Open** 7 days 11–5
Winemaker Michael Symons, Will Byron, Luke Burkley **Est.** 1978 **Dozens** 30 000
Vyds 17.6ha
This may be one of the most senior wineries on the Mornington Peninsula, but that does not stop it moving with the times. It has embarked on a serious sustainability program that touches on all aspects of its operations. It is one of the few wineries in Australia to measure its carbon footprint in detail, using the officially recognised system of WFA; it is steadily reducing its consumption of electricity; it uses rainwater, collected from the winery roof, for rinsing and washing in the winery, as well as supplying the winery in general; it has created a balanced ecosystem in the vineyard by strategic planting of cover crops and reduction of sprays; and has reduced its need to irrigate. All the Stonier wines are estate-grown and made with a mix of wild yeast (from initiation of fermentation) and cultured yeast (added towards the end of fermentation to ensure no residual sugar remains), and almost all are destemmed to open fermenters; all have a two-stage maturation, always French oak and variable use of barriques and puncheons for the first stage. Exports to Europe, Canada, Malaysia, Vietnam, Hong Kong and China.

🍷🍷🍷🍷🍷 **Reserve Mornington Peninsula Chardonnay 2014** A complex bouquet and palate, the mlf impact obvious, arguably a little too much so when first tasted, less so on retasting – it really came into its own on the third time through. Screwcap. 13% alc. **Rating** 95 **To** 2024 $45

Thompson Vineyard Mornington Peninsula Chardonnay 2014 Finely built and structured with an understated purity to its green apple and honeydew melon fruit; the steely acidity is starkly different from its siblings. Screwcap. 13% alc. **Rating** 95 **To** 2023 $55

KBS Vineyard Mornington Peninsula Chardonnay 2014 Has considerable drive, intensity and length, tangy citrus, green apple and some cashew all collaborating. It's easy to see why 33% was taken through mlf, for there is still a substantial reservoir of acidity. All of the Stonier Chardonnays are elegant. Screwcap. 13.5% alc. **Rating** 95 **To** 2022 $50

Reserve Mornington Peninsula Pinot Noir 2014 Has an exceptionally bright hue and an extremely long, intense and complex palate; red and black cherry fruits have a strongly savoury/foresty counterpoint providing both flavour and texture balance. Will be long-lived. Due for release Sept '16. Screwcap. 13% alc. **Rating** 95 To 2024 $55

Lyncroft Vineyard Mornington Peninsula Chardonnay 2014 Has pleasing generosity; stone fruits, fig and cashew are tempered by some citrus; good persistence and aftertaste. Screwcap. 13.8% alc. **Rating** 94 To 2022 $45

♀♀♀♀♀ **Mornington Peninsula Chardonnay 2014** Rating 91 To 2020 $25
Mornington Peninsula Pinot Noir 2014 Rating 91 To 2021 $28

Stormflower Vineyard ★★★★

3503 Caves Road, Wilyabrup, WA 6280 **Region** Margaret River
T (08) 9755 6211 **www**.stormflower.com.au **Open** 7 days 11–5
Winemaker Stuart Pym, Ian Bell **Est.** 2007 **Dozens** 1800 **Vyds** 9ha
Stormflower Vineyard is owned by David Martin, Howard Cearns and Nic Trimboli, three friends better known as co-founders of Little Creatures Brewery in Fremantle. They thought the location of the property (and the vineyard on it that had been planted in the mid-'90s) was ideal for producing high quality wines. Whether they knew that storms hit the property on a regular basis, with hail and wind impacting the crop in most seasons, isn't known. What is known is the investment they have made in the vineyard by pulling out one-third of the vines planted in the wrong way, in the wrong place, leaving the present 9ha of cabernet sauvignon, shiraz, chardonnay, sauvignon blanc, semillon and chenin blanc in place. The driving force in the vineyard is David Martin, with a family background in agriculture. They have moved the management focus towards organic compost and natural soil biology, gaining certified 'organic in conversion' status by NASAA in '15.

♀♀♀♀♀ **Margaret River Sauvignon Blanc 2015** Select harvester, 20% barrel-fermented at 6° baume (40% new French oak), returned to tank once fermented, bottled Sept. Oh, so clever; has given a level of complexity normally ex 100% barrel fermentation, yet retained varietal fruit. Lovely stuff, fantastic value. Screwcap. 13% alc. **Rating** 94 To 2017 $20 ✪

♀♀♀♀♀ **Margaret River Cabernet Shiraz 2013** Rating 93 To 2038 $25 ✪
Margaret River Chardonnay 2013 Rating 91 To 2020 $35

Studley Park Vineyard ★★★★

5 Garden Terrace, Kew, Vic 3101 (postal) **Region** Port Phillip Zone
T (03) 9254 2777 **www**.studleypark.com **Open** Not
Winemaker Llew Knight (Contract) **Est.** 1994 **Dozens** 250 **Vyds** 0.5ha
Geoff Pryor's Studley Park Vineyard is one of Melbourne's best-kept secrets. It is on a bend of the Yarra River barely 4km from the Melbourne CBD, on a 0.5ha block once planted to vines, but for a century used for market gardening, then replanted with cabernet sauvignon. A spectacular aerial photograph shows that immediately across the river, and looking directly to the CBD, is the epicentre of Melbourne's light industrial development, while on the northern and eastern boundaries are suburban residential blocks.

♀♀♀♀♀ **Rose 2015** Bright, pale pink; you are in no doubt about the redcurrant/blackcurrant varietal fruit, perfectly framed by the dry, crisp finish and aftertaste. Screwcap. 12.5% alc. **Rating** 92 To 2017 $18 ✪

Cabernet Sauvignon 2010 Bright colour; the palate is juicy and faintly minty, the tannins fine, the finish long, oak long since absorbed into the fabric of the wine. Screwcap. 13.5% alc. **Rating** 92 To 2025 $25 ✪

Cabernet Sauvignon 2009 Relatively little difference in colour from the '10, this with a little more cassis on the way through, likewise oak, but that's splitting hairs. Melbourne sommeliers should be falling over each other to offer this unique wine by the glass. Screwcap. 13.5% alc. **Rating** 92 To 2025 $25 ✪

Summerfield

5967 Stawell-Avoca Road, Moonambel, Vic 3478 **Region** Pyrenees
T (03) 5467 2264 **www**.summerfieldwines.com **Open** 7 days 10–5
Winemaker Mark Summerfield **Est.** 1979 **Dozens** 6000 **Vyds** 40.5ha
Founder Ian Summerfield handed over the winemaker reins to son Mark several years ago. Mark has significantly refined the style of the wines with the introduction of French oak, and by reducing the alcohol without compromising the intensity and concentration of the wines. If anything, the longevity of the wines produced by Mark will be even greater than that of the American-oaked wines of bygone years. Exports are now directed solely to China.

🍷🍷🍷🍷🍷 **Saieh Shiraz 2014** Matured in American oak (30% new) for 18 months. Exceptional colour, deep, dense purple; has the multilayered texture that marks all the wines from Summerfield; here intense pepper, spice and licorice combine to give flavour and texture in the same breath; the American oak has been manipulated with the skill of a surgeon. Screwcap. 14% alc. **Rating** 97 **To** 2049 $55 ○

🍷🍷🍷🍷🍷 **Sahsah Shiraz 2014** Expressive black and blood plum fruits, licorice and spice populate an undeniably full-bodied palate, that still has elegance and freshness thanks to its modest alcohol. A certain coolness is present throughout as you retaste the wine, starting with the first whiff of the bouquet. Screwcap. 13.4% alc. **Rating** 96 **To** 2044 $55 ○
Reserve Shiraz 2014 Dense, inky crimson-purple; 30% whole bunches immersed in the layers and folds of this strikingly powerful, full-bodied shiraz. One can visualise the small berry fruit size that front-end loads the palate with ripe tannins, and cries out for decades in the bottle. The balance is there to repay patience. Screwcap. 14.2% alc. **Rating** 95 **To** 2040 $55
Shiraz 2014 The saints be praised: a winemaker who uses cork (of high quality) in his cheapest red, screwcaps for the best. Superb, deep crimson-purple, with the complex texture shared to a lesser or greater degree by all the Summerfield Shirazs; also spice, pepper and licorice stitched through the primary plum and black fruit flavours. Screwcap. 14.1% alc. **Rating** 94 **To** 2039 $35
Taiyo Cabernet Sauvignon 2014 The use of whole bunches, let alone 50%, is unusual with cabernet, but it works very well here, trimming the amount of extract. The best of the three Summerfield Cabernets, even bordering on elegance, while not losing its wealth of cassis. Screwcap. 13.8% alc. **Rating** 94 **To** 2039 $63

🍷🍷🍷🍷🍷 **Tradition 2014 Rating** 92 **To** 2030 $35
Cabernet Sauvignon 2014 Rating 91 **To** 2021 $35
Reserve Cabernet Sauvignon 2014 Rating 90 **To** 2035 $55

Sunshine Creek

350 Yarraview Road, Yarra Glen, Vic 3775 **Region** Yarra Valley
T (03) 9818 5142 **www**.sunshinecreek.com.au **Open** Not
Winemaker Mario Marson, Chris Lawrence **Est.** 2009 **Dozens** 7000 **Vyds** 20ha
Packaging magnate James Zhou has a wine business in China, and, over the years, has worked with an A–Z of distinguished Australian winemakers, including Grant Burge, Philip Shaw, Phillip Jones, Pat Carmody, Geoff Hardy and Mario Marson, in bringing their wines to China. It was a logical extension to produce Australian wine of similar quality, and he commissioned Mario Marson to find an appropriate existing vineyard. They discovered Martha's Vineyard, which was planted in the 1980s by Olga Szymiczek. The site was a particularly good one, which compensated for the need to change the existing spur-pruned vineyard (for mechanisation) to vertical shoot position (VSP) for increased quality and hand picking. At the same time, an extensive program of grafting was undertaken and new clones planted. In 2011 Andrew Smith (formerly of Lusatia Park Vineyard) was appointed vineyard manager to change the focus of management to sustainability and minimal interference. In '13 winemaker Chris Lawrence joined the team, and an onsite winery (capable of handing 275 tonnes) was completed prior to the '16 vintage. Exports to Hong Kong and China.

🍷🍷🍷🍷🍷 **Heathcote Shiraz 2012** Matured in French barriques (30% new) for 15 months. Combines elegance with an impressive array of flavours from blackberry to spiced plum, and quality oak underpinned by ample, but soft, tannins. Diam. 14.5% alc. **Rating** 94 **To** 2027 $45

Yarra Valley Cabernets 2012 Cabernet sauvignon, merlot, cabernet franc, malbec and petit verdot. An elegant light to medium-bodied wine that reflects Mario Marson's early years as winemaker at Mount Mary under the tutelage of the late Dr John Middleton. This will develop slowly and serenely, its seamless array of red and black fruits, tannins and oak always in balance. Diam. 13% alc. **Rating** 94 **To** 2027 $45

🍷🍷🍷🍷🍷 **Yarra Valley Chardonnay 2012 Rating** 92 **To** 2019 $45
Yarra Valley Pinot Noir 2012 Rating 92 **To** 2020 $45

Surveyor's Hill Vineyards ★★★☆

215 Brooklands Road, Wallaroo, NSW 2618 **Region** Canberra District
T (02) 6230 2046 **www**.survhill.com.au **Open** W'ends & public hols
Winemaker Brindabella Hills, Greg Gallagher **Est.** 1986 **Dozens** 1000 **Vyds** 10ha
Surveyor's Hill vineyard is on the slopes of the eponymous hill, at 550–680m above sea level. It is an ancient volcano, producing granite-derived, coarse-structured (and hence well-drained) sandy soils of low fertility. This has to be the ultimate patchwork-quilt vineyard, with 1ha each of chardonnay, shiraz and viognier; 0.5ha each of roussanne, marsanne, aglianico, nero d'Avola, mourvedre, grenache, muscadelle, moscato giallo, cabernet franc, riesling, semillon, sauvignon blanc, touriga nacional and cabernet sauvignon.

🍷🍷🍷🍷🍷 **Hills of Hall Cabernet Franc Rose 2015** Pretty, perfumed and leafy at once. Raisin, rose petal and tobacco with a kick of flavour to the finish. Doesn't pander to sweetness but isn't short on fruit either. Screwcap. 13% alc. **Rating** 92 **To** 2017 $18 CM ✪

🍷🍷🍷🍷 **Sauvignon Blanc 2015 Rating** 89 **To** 2017 $20 CM
Hills of Hall Riesling 2015 Rating 88 **To** 2021 $22 CM

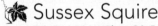 Sussex Squire ★★★☆

PO Box 1361, Clare, SA 5453 **Region** Clare Valley
T 0458 141 169 **www**.sussexsquire.com.au **Open** At The Little Red Grape, Sevenhill
Winemaker Daniel Wilson, Mark Bollen **Est.** 2014 **Dozens** 500 **Vyds** 6ha
There's a long family history attached to this embryonic wine business. The history began with Walter Hackett (1827–1914), a Sussex farmer; next came Joseph Hackett (1880–1958), followed by Joseph Robert Hackett (1911–98), and now fourth-generation Mark and Skye Bollan. Over the generations, the family worked in a successful major grain and seed business, then established the Nyora grazing property near Mintaro and Wyndham Park near Sevenhill, which is still farmed today with herds of black and red Angus cattle. Mark and Skye returned to the Clare Valley after spending 25 years working in other pursuits, Mark in wine sales and marketing, Skye in 5-star hotels for a decade before embarking on a successful career in recruitment. In 1998 Mark and Skye planted 6ha of dry-grown, organically managed, shiraz, and in lieu of Angus cattle, have a flock of Black Suffolk sheep that roam the vineyard during winter to provide natural weed control and fertilise the soil.

🍷🍷🍷🍷🍷 **Thomas Block Single Vineyard Clare Valley Shiraz 2014** Open-fermented, hand-plunged, basket-pressed, matured in French and American oak for 12 months. A very interesting and impressive full-bodied wine awash with black and red cherries and berries, yet retaining shape, elegance and balance, the savoury tannins providing a balanced farewell. Screwcap. 14.5% alc. **Rating** 94 **To** 2025 $25 ✪

Sutherland Estate   ★★★★★

2010 Melba Highway, Dixons Creek, Vic 3775 **Region** Yarra Valley
T 0402 052 287 **www**.sutherlandestate.com.au **Open** W'ends & public hols 10–5
Winemaker Cathy Phelan, Angus Ridley, Rob Hall **Est.** 2000 **Dozens** 1500 **Vyds** 4ha
The Phelan family established Sutherland Estate in 2000 when they purchased a mature
2ha vineyard at Dixons Creek. Further plantings followed: the plantings now consist of 1ha
each of chardonnay and pinot noir, and 0.5ha each of gewurztraminer, cabernet sauvignon,
tempranillo and shiraz. Ron Phelan designed and built the cellar door, which enjoys stunning
views over the Yarra Valley, while daughter Cathy studied Wine Science at CSU. The sparkling
wines are made by Phil Kelly, the reds by Cathy and partner Angus Ridley (who has been at
Coldstream Hills for the last decade), and the Chardonnay by Rob Hall.

♥♥♥♥♥ **Reserve Yarra Valley Shiraz 2015** Spectacularly deep purple-crimson; the first
Reserve wine (any variety) from Sutherland Estate; the palate is superb, tannins
sewn through the spicy black fruits, oak crooning in the backdrop. Sophisticated,
yet lovely. Screwcap. 13.5% alc. **Rating** 97 **To** 2035 $50 ✪

♥♥♥♥♥ **Daniel's Hill Vineyards Yarra Valley Pinot Noir 2015** Bright, clear crimson;
a fragrant and highly expressive bouquet, the palate singing the same tune with
the backing of red and black cherry fruit; the structure is admirable, with superfine
tannins and great length. The best yet. Screwcap. 12.9% alc. **Rating** 96 **To** 2027
$30 ✪
Daniel's Hill Vineyard Yarra Valley Shiraz 2015 Elegant, yet complex texture
and flavour, lush dark-berry fruit, and some oak influence despite none being new;
exceptional bright tannins. Screwcap. 13.2% alc. **Rating** 95 **To** 2030 $30 ✪
Daniel's Hill Vineyard Yarra Valley Cabernet Sauvignon 2015 Deliberately
picked on the edge of maturity, and succeeded – there's nothing green here, just
a slightly leathery/earthy edge to the deliciously fine-boned cassis/blackcurrant
fruit, the length and balance impeccable. Screwcap. 13.1% alc. **Rating** 95 **To** 2035
$30 ✪
Daniel's Hill Vineyard Yarra Valley Tempranillo 2015 Tempranillo should do
very well in the cool Yarra Valley climate, and this certainly has; a lovely assemblage
of cherries for DIY tastings; balance and length. Screwcap. 13.6% alc. **Rating** 94
To 2020 $30 ✪

Sutton Grange Winery   ★★★★☆

Carnochans Road, Sutton Grange, Vic 3448 **Region** Bendigo
T (03) 8672 1478 **www**.suttongrange.com.au **Open** Sun 12–4
Winemaker Melanie Chester **Est.** 1998 **Dozens** 5000 **Vyds** 12ha
The 400ha Sutton Grange property is a horse training facility acquired in 1996 by Peter
Sidwell, a Melbourne businessman with horse racing and breeding interests. A lunch visit to
the property by long-term friends Alec Epis and Stuart Anderson led to the decision to plant
shiraz, merlot, cabernet sauvignon, viognier and sangiovese. The winery is built from WA
limestone. Exports to the UK, the US, Canada, Switzerland and China.

♥♥♥♥♥ **Estate Ram's Horn Block Syrah 2012** Big but exquisite. No caveats or qualms:
this is a beauty. Violets, anise, blackberries and assorted peppers and spices. It's bold,
it's integrated, it's firm, it's ready for anything. Screwcap. 13.8% alc. **Rating** 96
To 2030 $60 CM ✪

♥♥♥♥♀ **Fairbank Syrah 2015 Rating** 93 **To** 2021 $25 CM ✪
Estate Syrah 2012 Rating 93 **To** 2026 $50 CM
Estate Viognier 2014 Rating 91 **To** 2016 $25 CM

Swan Valley Wines

261 Haddrill Road, Baskerville, WA 6065 **Region** Swan Valley
T (08) 9296 1501 **www**.swanvalleywines.com.au **Open** Thurs–Sun & public hols 10–5
Winemaker Paul Hoffman **Est.** 1999 **Dozens** 1500 **Vyds** 6ha

Peter and Paula Hoffman, with sons Paul and Thomas, acquired their property in 1989. It had a long history of grapegrowing, the prior owner having registered the name Swan Valley Wines in '83. Courageously, the Hoffmans decided they would try to emulate the producers of chenin blanc in the Loire Valley, who use a classification system of Sec, Demisec, Moelleux (continuing with Doux and Liquoreux) in ascending order of sweetness. From Moelleuc and above, the wines cruise through 30 years, the rare Liquoreux 100 years. Swan Valley Wines only attempted the first three, but seem to have abandoned it.

ＹＹＹＹＹ Extent Heirloom Blend Mataro Grenache Shiraz 2014 Deep colour for such a blend; very powerful and complex, with the shiraz outperforming its contribution; licorice, anise and ripe tannins are all in the game. Screwcap. 14.3% alc. **Rating** 93 **To** 2029 $20 ❂

Sec Chenin Blanc 2013 Wild-fermented in French puncheons, followed by a further 12 months maturation on lees. While the fruit salad characters of conventionally fermented chenin blanc are much reduced, there is even greater compensation in complexity. The wine has more texture, structure, length and balance than conventionally made chenin, making it very food-friendly. Screwcap. 12.9% alc. **Rating** 92 **To** 2020 $25 ❂

ＹＹＹＹ Sec Tendres Chenin Blanc 2014 Rating 89 **To** 2019 $17 ❂

Swinging Bridge

33 Gaskill Street, Canowindra, NSW 2804 **Region** Central Ranges Zone
T 0409 246 609 **www**.swingingbridge.com.au **Open** Fri–Sun 11–6
Winemaker Tom Ward **Est.** 1995 **Dozens** 4000 **Vyds** 45ha

Swinging Bridge was founded by Mark Ward, who immigrated to Australia in 1965 from the UK with an honours degree in agricultural science from Cambridge University. Its original purpose was to grow grapes for others, with a small winemaking business alongside. Since then, under the direction of Mark's son, Tom, and daughter-in-law, Georgie, it has moved to effectively become an Orange winery. The 45ha of vines are all planted in Orange. In addition, Tom Ward has been involved with Justin Jarrett in the Balmoral Vineyard at Orange since 2012.

ＹＹＹＹＹ Museum Release Reserve Orange Chardonnay 2011 A classy wine that has developed well over 5 years, and has a minimum of another 5 to go. Bright straw-green, it brings together grapefruit, white peach and crisp apple flavours, bright acidity providing the structure for a prosperous future. The oak is good, too. Screwcap. 13.2% alc. **Rating** 95 **To** 2021 $50

ＹＹＹＹ G&A Orange Blanc de Blancs NV Rating 88 **To** 2018 $38 TS

Swings & Roundabouts

2807 Caves Road, Yallingup, WA 6232 **Region** Margaret River
T (08) 9756 6640 **www**.swings.com.au **Open** 7 days 10–5
Winemaker Brian Fletcher **Est.** 2004 **Dozens** 20 000 **Vyds** 5.86ha

The Swings & Roundabouts name comes from the expression used to encapsulate the eternal balancing act between the various aspects of grape and wine production. Swings aims to balance the serious side with a touch of fun. There are four ranges: Kiss Chasey, Life of Riley, Swings & Roundabouts and Backyard Stories. Exports to the US and China, Canada and Japan.

ＹＹＹＹＹ Backyard Stories Margaret River Chardonnay 2015 Hand-picked, whole bunch-pressed, wild-fermented in French oak (35% new, 65% 1yo), matured for 8 months. A prime example of the power of Margaret River chardonnay fruit to handle new oak and everything else that might get in its way in the winery; grapefruit, white peach and nectarine ride the tightrope of acidity with ease. Screwcap. 14% alc. **Rating** 95 **To** 2023 $35 ✪

Backyard Stories Margaret River Cabernet Sauvignon 2014 Matured in French oak (45% new) for 12 months. A classy cabernet, fruit, oak and tannins precisely calibrated; blackcurrant/cassis and dried herb flavours are in the heartland of varietal expression; its balance assures a very long future. Screwcap. 14% alc. **Rating** 95 **To** 2034 $39

Backyard Stories Semillon Sauvignon Blanc 2014 Oak-matured. Gravel and thistle notes move freely among pure, intense grapefruit and pineapple/tropical fruit. Powerhouse style. You'd almost describe this as thrilling. Screwcap. 12.5% alc. **Rating** 94 **To** 2018 $32 CM

🍷🍷🍷🍷♀ **Margaret River Sauvignon Blanc Semillon 2015** **Rating** 93 **To** 2017 $22 ✪
Backyard Stories Rose 2015 **Rating** 93 **To** 2018 $32
Margaret River Cabernet Merlot 2014 **Rating** 92 **To** 2029 $22 ✪
Backyard Stories Chardonnay 2014 **Rating** 91 **To** 2019 $35 CM
Backyard Stories Sparkling NV **Rating** 90 **To** 2017 $35 CM

Swinney Vineyards   ★★★★☆

325 Franland-Kojimup Road, Frankland River, WA 6396 **Region** Frankland River
T (08) 9200 4483 **www.**swinneyvineyards.com.au **Open** Not
Winemaker Cherubino Consulting **Est.** 1998 **Dozens** 1500 **Vyds** 111.2ha
The Swinney family (parents Graham and Kaye, and son and daughter Matt and Janelle) has been resident on their 2500ha property since it was settled by George Swinney in 1922. In the '90s they decided to diversify, and have since planted a very substantial, high quality vineyard on undulating ironstone gravel and loam soils, home to jarrah and red gums. The lion's share of the plantings go to shiraz (45ha) and cabernet sauvignon (37ha), followed by semillon (5ha) and chardonnay (5ha), and they lease 1ha of riesling. They also pushed the envelope by establishing grenache (3.5ha), tempranillo (4ha) and mourvedre (1.6ha) as bush vines, a rarity in this part of the world. In 2015 The Swinney family and former Hardys winemaker Peter Dawson formed a partnership to purchase the Powderbark Ridge Vineyard in Frankland River planted in 1998. With Larry Cherubino making the wines, it is not surprising that they are as good as they are. Exports to the UK.

🍷🍷🍷🍷🍷 **Ingenue Tirra Lirra Red 2014** Cabernet sauvignon, tempranillo, grenache. Flashy with redcurrant, raspberry and cherry-cola flavours, a wave of dusty/spicy tannin then crashing through the back half. Milk chocolate characters play a role too. There's a lot to suggest that this will mature exceptionally well. Screwcap. 14.5% alc. **Rating** 95 **To** 2028 $33 CM ✪

🍷🍷🍷🍷♀ **Tirra Lirra White 2015** **Rating** 92 **To** 2020 $30 CM
Tirra Lirra Grenache Mourvedre 2014 **Rating** 92 **To** 2023 $33 CM

Symphonia Wines   ★★★★

1699 Boggy Creek Road, Myrrhee, Vic 3732 **Region** King Valley
T (03) 4952 5117 **www.**symphoniafinewines.com.au **Open** By appt
Winemaker Lilian Carter **Est.** 1998 **Dozens** 1500 **Vyds** 28ha
Peter Read and his family are veterans of the King Valley, commencing the development of their vineyard in 1981. As a result of extensive trips to both Western and Eastern Europe, Peter embarked on an ambitious project to trial a series of grape varieties little known in this country. Current owners Peter and Suzanne Evans are committed to continuing Peter Read's pioneering legacy, making Arneis, Petit Manseng, Pinot Grigio, Savagnin, Tannat, Tempranillo and Saperavi.

🍷🍷🍷🍷🍷 **King Valley Arneis 2015** Some dare, some drama, and plenty of flavour. This is both rich and refreshing at once, its notes of candied lime, barley and pear rumbling through the palate with purpose and style. Don't hesitate. Screwcap. 12.2% alc. **Rating** 92 **To** 2017 $25 CM ✪

Las Triadas Tempranillo 2014 Polish, poise, oodles of juicy flavour. Right here we have a medium-weight wine of terrific drinkability, its red-fruit-and-spice characters more-ish, to say the least. Screwcap. 13.6% alc. **Rating** 92 **To** 2020 $35 CM

King Valley Pinot Grigio 2015 A bit slim, perhaps, but the flavours of pear and spiced apple are certainly appealing. Indeed, as it rests in the glass it gives up more and more. Screwcap. 12% alc. **Rating** 90 **To** 2017 $25 CM

♀♀♀♀ King Valley Tannat 2013 **Rating** 88 **To** 2023 $35 CM

Symphony Hill Wines   ★★★★☆

2017 Eukey Road, Ballandean, Qld 4382 **Region** Granite Belt
T (07) 4684 1388 **www**.symphonyhill.com.au **Open** 7 days 10–4
Winemaker Mike Hayes **Est.** 1999 **Dozens** 6000 **Vyds** 3.5ha
Ewen Macpherson purchased an old table grape and orchard property in 1996. A partnership with his parents, Bob and Jill Macpherson, led to development of the vineyard, while Ewen completed his Bachelor of Applied Science in viticulture (2003). The vineyard (now much expanded) was established using state-of-the-art technology; vineyard manager/winemaker Mike Hayes is a third-generation viticulturist in the Granite Belt region, and became an equal co-owner of Symphony Hill in '14. He also has impressive academic achievements, with a degree in viticulture, followed by a Masters in Professional Studies – Viticulture, and was awarded a Churchill Fellowship (in '12) to study alternative wine grape varieties in Europe. Symphony Hill has firmly established its reputation as one of the Granite Belt's foremost wineries. Exports to China.

♀♀♀♀♀ Reserve Lagrein 2014 Hand-picked, crushed and destemmed, 11 days cold soak, wild yeast, then cultured, pressed, matured for 10 months in French hogsheads (30% new). Bright hue; fills the mouth to overflowing with its velvety array of plum, cassis and cherry fruits, the tannins all but hidden, the oak a positive contributor to the overall package. Screwcap. 12.7% alc. **Rating** 95 **To** 2024 $65

Gewurztraminer 2015 Top-gold Melbourne Wine Awards '15. Grown in the New England GI, not the Granite Belt. I have no quarrel with its top gold, but it's one of those wines that will shine brightly one day, and be ignored the next (in wine shows). Screwcap. 13.5% alc. **Rating** 94 **To** 2023 $40

♀♀♀♀♀ Reserve Granite Belt Cabernet Sauvignon 2014 **Rating** 93 **To** 2034 $45
Barrel Fermented Gewurztraminer 2015 **Rating** 92 **To** 2022 $45
The Rock Reserve Granite Belt Shiraz 2014 **Rating** 92 **To** 2026 $65
Reserve Merlot 2014 **Rating** 92 **To** 2029 $45
Wild Child Granite Belt Viognier 2013 **Rating** 91 **To** 2017 $45
Fiano 2015 **Rating** 91 **To** 2019 $30
Reserve Granite Belt Petit Verdot 2014 **Rating** 91 **To** 2024 $65
Granite Belt Viognier 2015 **Rating** 90 **To** 2017 $45
Reserve Granite Belt Shiraz 2014 **Rating** 90 **To** 2024 $65

Syrahmi   ★★★★☆

PO Box 438, Heathcote, Vic 3523 **Region** Heathcote
T 0407 057 471 **www**.syrahmi.com.au **Open** Not
Winemaker Adam Foster **Est.** 2004 **Dozens** 1700
Adam Foster worked as a chef in Vic and London before moving to the front of house and becoming increasingly interested in wine. He then worked as a cellar hand with a who's who in Australia and France, including Torbreck, Chapoutier, Mitchelton, Domaine Ogier, Heathcote Winery, Jasper Hill and Domaine Pierre Gaillard. He became convinced that the Cambrian soils of Heathcote could produce the best possible Shiraz, and since 2004 has purchased grapes from the region, using the full bag of winemaking techniques. Exports to the US and Japan.

ㅜㅜㅜㅜㅜ X Heathcote Shiraz 2013 Deep crimson-purple; the very complex bouquet skips around black fruits, spices and tarry charcuterie notes without ever stopping to alight, leaving it to the long palate to join the dots of a superb wine that has risked all but emerged triumphant with great texture, structure and length. A tour de force of winemaking. Screwcap. 13.8% alc. **Rating** 97 **To** 2038 $55 ○

ㅜㅜㅜㅜㅜ Garden of Earthly Delights Pinot Noir 2013 Matured for 10 months in French puncheons (50% new). Has held its light, bright crimson hue very well, and the apparent ease with which the fruit has absorbed the new oak is equally impressive. The perfumed bouquet has red berries, with a generous pinch of allspice, the back-palate and finish notable for their length and balance. Adam Foster must be thinking, 'What's all the fuss about? This is easy.' Screwcap. 13.4% alc. **Rating** 94 **To** 2021 $42

ㅜㅜㅜㅜ♀ Heathcote Mourvedre 2014 **Rating** 91 **To** 2024 $42

T'Gallant

1385 Mornington-Flinders Road, Main Ridge, Vic 3928 **Region** Mornington Peninsula
T (03) 5931 1300 **www.**tgallant.com.au **Open** 7 days 9–5
Winemaker Adam Carnaby **Est.** 1990 **Dozens** NFP **Vyds** 8ha
Husband and wife consultant winemakers Kevin McCarthy and Kathleen Quealy carved out such an important niche market for the T'Gallant label that in 2003, after protracted negotiations, it was acquired by Beringer Blass (now part of TWE). The acquisition of a 15ha property and the planting of 8ha of pinot gris gave the business a firm geographic base, as well as providing increased resources for its signature wine.

ㅜㅜㅜㅜㅜ Tribute Pinot Gris 2014 It's a ribald affair. It tastes of a wide assortment of fruits and spices and throws honeysuckle in for good measure. It's one of those wines where you feel your way along the palate, as much as taste. It's most definitely a gris with attitude. Screwcap. 14.5% alc. **Rating** 94 **To** 2017 $34 CM

ㅜㅜㅜㅜ♀ Grace Pinot Grigio 2015 **Rating** 92 **To** 2017 $25 CM ○
Imogen Pinot Gris 2014 **Rating** 92 **To** 2017 $25 CM ○
Cape Schanck Pinot Grigio 2015 **Rating** 91 **To** 2017 $20 CM ○

Tahbilk ★★★★★

254 O'Neils Road, Tabilk, Vic 3608 **Region** Nagambie Lakes
T (03) 5794 2555 **www.**tahbilk.com.au **Open** Mon–Sat 9–5, Sun 11–5
Winemaker Alister Purbrick, Neil Larson **Est.** 1860 **Dozens** 100 000 **Vyds** 221.5ha
A winery steeped in tradition (with National Trust classification), which should be visited at least once by every wine-conscious Australian, and which makes wines – particularly red wines – utterly in keeping with that tradition. The essence of that heritage comes in the form of the tiny quantities of Shiraz made from vines planted in 1860. Serendipitous, perhaps, but the current release wines are absolutely outstanding. A founding member of Australia's First Families of Wine. 2016 *Wine Companion* Winery of the Year. Exports to all major markets.

ㅜㅜㅜㅜㅜ 1860 Vines Shiraz 2010 The colour is very bright, the bouquet intriguing and complex, but it's the palate that sends the senses into overdrive. Rarely has a wine had such intense power and drive built on such a pure fruit core, relegating the 100% new French oak and tannins to a background role. Even better than the '09. 191 dozen made. Screwcap. 13.5% alc. **Rating** 99 **To** 2040 $298 ○
1927 Vines Marsanne 2008 Pale straw-green; perfectly balanced in every respect; honeysuckle and citrus engage like lovers on the bouquet and palate alike. Is even more youthful than semillon or riesling held back for 8 years prior to release. You have to wonder just how long this wine will live for. As it is, it's utterly exceptional. Screwcap. 11.5% alc. **Rating** 97 **To** 2028 $46 ○
1927 Vines Marsanne 2007 Backed up its gold medal at the Sydney Wine Show '14 with a trophy and gold medal this year, Adelaide also awarding gold. Pale green-straw, it is as fresh as a daisy, the long sibilant palate with a perfect mix of

honeysuckle and perfectly balanced acidity. It's anyone's guess how long the wine will continue to give such pleasure; the drink-to date is a conservative stab in the dark. Screwcap. 10.5% alc. **Rating** 97 **To** 2027 $45 ❂

Eric Stevens Purbrick Shiraz 2010 Produced in limited quantities from old vines, matured in French and American oak. This is a full-bodied shiraz, speaking loudly of its place and variety, yet totally comfortable in its own skin, not needing to raise its voice. A symphony of red and black fruits, gently earthy tannins and a support role of integrated oak are all in complete harmony, the future limitless. Screwcap. 13% alc. **Rating** 97 **To** 2045 $70 ❂

🍷🍷🍷🍷🍷 **Eric Stevens Purbrick Cabernet Sauvignon 2010** The wine speaks with clarion purity of its place and variety, with a complex fusion of blackcurrant, dried herbs and earthy tannins before a final burst of fruit on the farewell, French oak never obvious. Screwcap. 13.5% alc. **Rating** 96 **To** 2035 $70 ❂

Marsanne 2015 The honeysuckle aroma bursts out of the glass when swirled; perhaps a hint of jasmine or field flowers too. The palate lives up to the promise and then some: the variety is often sotto voce when young, but here it is exuberant, aided by chalky acidity. Screwcap. 12.5% alc. **Rating** 95 **To** 2035 $18 ❂

Museum Release Marsanne 2010 Gleaming green-gold; just a lovely wine, with the best bits of youth and incipient maturity to its mix of honeysuckle and perfectly balanced citrussy acidity. Screwcap. 12.5% alc. **Rating** 95 **To** 2025 $24 ❂

Roussanne Marsanne Viognier 2015 A 39/35/26% blend, the roussanne spending 6 months in French oak, the marsanne and viognier fermented in stainless steel. You know with certainty that year by year this wine will grow in weight, complexity and flavour. Screwcap. 13% alc. **Rating** 95 **To** 2029 $26 ❂

Sibling Rivalry King Valley Pinot Gris 2014 Cool-fermented with cultured yeast. Distinct pink hue tinged with bronze; this is remarkably concentrated in its array of strawberry, pear, apple and cinnamon. A truly interesting (and enjoyable) wine. Screwcap. 14% alc. **Rating** 94 **To** 2017 $26 ❂

Roussanne Marsanne Viognier 2014 This is crisp but powerful, with nectarine, spice and citrus notes trending positively through the palate. More than a touch of class about it. Screwcap. 13% alc. **Rating** 94 **To** 2019 $25 CM ❂

Grenache Shiraz Mourvedre 2014 45/40/15%. Heightened fruit/spice aromatics with licorice and raspberry hitting the palate. A wine of verve and polish. Acid and tannin just so. Screwcap. 14.5% alc. **Rating** 94 **To** 2024 $25 CM ❂

Cabernet Sauvignon 2013 Herb and bay leaf announce their presence on the bouquet, blackcurrant quickly following and taking control on the palate. A very successful Tahbilk Cabernet. Screwcap. 14% alc. **Rating** 94 **To** 2033 $25 ❂

🍷🍷🍷🍷🍸 **Riesling 2015 Rating** 92 **To** 2025 $19 ❂
Cane Cut Marsanne 2011 Rating 92 **To** 2018 $25 ❂
Shiraz 2013 Rating 91 **To** 2035 $25
Chardonnay 2015 Rating 90 **To** 2022 $19 ❂
Sibling Rivalry Pinot Noir 2013 Rating 90 **To** 2020 $26

Talbots Block Wines   ★★★★

62 Possingham Pit Road, Sevenhill, SA 5453 **Region** Clare Valley
T 0402 649 979 **www**.talbotsblock.com.au **Open** By appt
Winemaker Contract **Est.** 2011 **Dozens** 800 **Vyds** 5ha

Thanks to careers in government and the oil industry, Alex and Bill Talbot started their journey to wine in 1997 while working and living at Woomera in the SA desert. They purchased land in the Sevenhill area of the Clare Valley, having fallen in love with the place, and dreamed of some day making wine for their friends. They then moved to various places in Asia, including Kuala Lumpur, Jakarta and Singapore, their minds always returning to their Sevenhill vineyard. They now live in the house they built high on the block, giving views across the vineyard, and have the opportunity to tend the vines whenever they please. Initially the grapes were sold, but in 2012 they kept enough of the production to have 800 dozen made across their two distinctly different Shiraz styles. The labels are striking and evocative.

🍷🍷🍷🍷🍷 **The Prince Clare Valley Shiraz 2014** It sits on the rich side of medium–weight and offers all the smoothness and softness lovers of dark-coloured shiraz often seek out. Mint, plum, blackberry and dark chocolate; it's all in good working order. Screwcap. 14.2% alc. **Rating** 92 **To** 2023 $25 CM ●
The Sultan Clare Valley Shiraz 2013 Higher price, higher alcohol, bigger bottle. More (overt) oak too. Coffee cream notes dominate the mainstays of mint, plum and blackberry, with acidity and alcohol then trailing out the finish. Screwcap. 14.7% alc. **Rating** 92 **To** 2026 $36 CM

Talisman Wines

PO Box 354, Cottesloe, WA 6911 **Region** Geographe
T 0401 559 266 **www.**talismanwines.com.au **Open** Not
Winemaker Peter Stanlake **Est.** 2009 **Dozens** 2700 **Vyds** 9ha
Kim Robinson (and wife Jenny) began the development of their vineyard in 2000, and now have cabernet, shiraz, malbec, zinfandel, chardonnay, riesling and sauvignon blanc. Kim says that 'after eight frustrating years of selling grapes to Evans & Tate and Wolf Blass, we decided to optimise the vineyard and attempt to make quality wines'. The measure of their success has been consistent gold medal performance at (and some trophies) the Geographe Wine Show. They say this could not have been achieved without the assistance of vineyard manager Victor Bertola and winemaker Peter Stanlake. Exports to the UK.

🍷🍷🍷🍷🍷 **Gabrielle Ferguson Valley Chardonnay 2014** This is a high quality chardonnay buzzing with energy and drive, pink grapefruit in the driver's seat, but it's a large car, allowing melon, white peach, grilled cashew and oak to all hop on board. Screwcap. 14% alc. **Rating** 96 **To** 2025 $35 ●
Aged Release Ferguson Valley Riesling 2010 Gleaming straw-green; lightly browned toast nuances on the bouquet are followed by an enriched palate, honey starting to develop. Another 2 or 3 years will likely see it reach the plateau of its development. Screwcap. 13% alc. **Rating** 94 **To** 2020 $25 ●
Arida 2015 An unusually complex rose, the spicy bouquet with red flower flecks that persist through the long, striking palate. A real wine, as it were, with undoubted ability to age. Screwcap. 13% alc. **Rating** 94 **To** 2018 $20 ●

🍷🍷🍷🍷🍷 **Ferguson Valley Riesling 2015 Rating** 90 **To** 2025 $22

Tallavera Grove | Carillion

749 Mount View Road, Mount View, NSW 2325 **Region** Hunter Valley
T (02) 4990 7535 **www.**tallaveragrove.com.au **Open** Thurs–Mon 10–5
Winemaker Gwyn Olsen **Est.** 2000 **Dozens** 5000 **Vyds** 188ha
Tallavera Grove is one of the many wine interests of Dr John Davis and family. The family is a 50% owner of Briar Ridge, and also owns a 12ha vineyard in Coonawarra, the 100ha Stonefields Vineyard at Wrattonbully and a 36ha vineyard at Orange (the Carillion wines are sourced from this vineyard). The 40ha Hunter Valley vineyards are planted to chardonnay, shiraz, semillon, verdelho, cabernet sauvignon and viognier.

🍷🍷🍷🍷🍷 **Tallavera Grove Fenestella Hunter Valley Shiraz 2014** This is a top-flight example of the great '14 vintage. It is exceptionally complex, with black and red fruits, detailed tannins and cedary French oak. The depth and length of flavour are exceptional, and the wine is certainly going to have a 40-year life. Screwcap. 13.5% alc. **Rating** 97 **To** 2054 $60 ●

🍷🍷🍷🍷🍷 **Tallavera Grove Hunter Valley Shiraz 2014** Good colour; the fragrant red fruits and spices of the bouquet flow seamlessly into the medium-bodied palate, joined there by purple fruits and perfectly weighted tannin; the wine soars on its gloriously juicy finish. Great value. Screwcap. 13.5% alc. **Rating** 96 **To** 2044 $30 ●

Stonefields Block 22 Wrattonbully Cabernet Sauvignon 2013 Deeply coloured, it is just about as seductive as is possible for cabernet with unalloyed varietal character; blackcurrant/cassis, warm tannins and quality French oak are joined in seamless harmony. Screwcap. 14% alc. **Rating** 96 **To** 2038 $45 ✪
Tallavera Grove Hunter Valley Semillon 2015 Quartz-white; has intense and mouth-cleansing lemon juice, lemon zest and lemongrass all tethered by the crystalline acidity. The long-term quality of the wine is a gold-plated certainty. Screwcap. 12% alc. **Rating** 95 **To** 2035 $25 ✪
Carillion The Volcanics Orange Cabernet Sauvignon 2013 This speaks loud and clear of its cool climate origins, but is unequivocally ripe. Cassis has a garland of bay leaf, dried herb and black olive, and a base of integrated French oak joined with fine, gravelly cabernet tannins. Screwcap. 14% alc. **Rating** 95 **To** 2033 $45
Stonefields Arbitrage Wrattonbully Cabernet Merlot Shiraz 2013 Only produced in exceptional vintages, which '13 clearly was. This stamps its imprint of quality from the first whiff and first sip. The red fruits are crowned with a laurel wreath of perfectly balanced tannins and oak. Screwcap. 14.5% alc. **Rating** 95 **To** 2038 $38

🍷🍷🍷🍷🍷 **Davis Premium Vineyards Rogue Series Moon Child Orange Aglianico 2014** **Rating** 90 **To** 2025 $30

Taltarni ★★★★★

339 Taltarni Road, Moonambel, Vic 3478 **Region** Pyrenees
T (03) 5459 7900 **www**.taltarni.com.au **Open** 7 days 11–5
Winemaker Robert Heywood, Peter Warr **Est.** 1969 **Dozens** 80 000 **Vyds** 78.5ha
The American owner and founder of Clos du Val (Napa Valley), Taltarni and Clover Hill (see separate entry) has brought the management of these three businesses and Domaine de Nizas (Languedoc) under the one roof, the group known as Goelet Wine Estates. Taltarni is the largest of the Australian ventures, its estate vineyards of great value and underpinning the substantial annual production. In Nov 2014, Taltarni's viticulturist, Matthew Bailey, received the prestigious Viticulturist of the Year Award from the Australian Society of Viticulture and Oenology. During his tenure at Taltarni he has established what he calls 'insectariums', continuing, 'These are like insect holiday resorts. The good insects eat the bad insects that eat the vines.' The insectariums are established in permanent vegetation corridors, each containing around 2000 native plants, that provide a pollen and nectar source for the beneficial insects, reducing the need for chemicals and other controls of the vineyards. Exports to all major markets.

🍷🍷🍷🍷🍷 **Old Block Estate Pyrenees Shiraz 2014** This rolls out the velvet. It's rich with plum, tar, mint and crushed dry leaf-like flavours, but it's the suede-like softness that takes it to another level. Tannin, acid, fruit and length come fully integrated. Screwcap. 14.5% alc. **Rating** 96 **To** 2036 $40 CM ✪
Estate Pyrenees Cabernet Sauvignon 2013 The days of excessively tannic Taltarni Cabernets are long gone but the web of beautifully integrated tannin here is certainly a highlight. This is a class act. It's both rich and juicy, comes laden with dark-berried flavour, and curls impressively out through the finish. Screwcap. 14% alc. **Rating** 96 **To** 2033 $30 CM ✪
Fume Blanc 2015 The flavours feel crystal clear, the intensity is good, and it rings impressively out through the finish. Oak obviously plays a role here but it's fundamentally hand in glove. Screwcap. 13.5% alc. **Rating** 94 **To** 2018 $25 CM ✪
Estate Pyrenees Shiraz 2014 Flush with blackberry and dark chocolate, rich earth and mint-like characters. A dab of viognier adds floral lift. Grainy tannin rumbles through the back half. It's a wine with a lot in its favour. Screwcap. 14.5% alc. **Rating** 94 **To** 2030 $30 CM ✪

🍷🍷🍷🍷🍷 **Estate Pyrenees Shiraz 2013** **Rating** 93 **To** 2033 $40
Reserve Pyrenees Shiraz Cabernet 2012 **Rating** 93 **To** 2036 $65 CM

Reserve Pyrenees Shiraz Cabernet 2009 Rating 93 To 2028 $65 CM
Methode Traditionnelle Cuvee Rose 2011 Rating 93 To 2016 $25 TS ✪
Petit Verdot 2014 Rating 92 To 2026 $25 CM ✪
Brut 2012 Rating 92 To 2017 $25 TS ✪
Tache Methode Traditionnelle Chardonnay Pinot Noir Pinot Meunier 2012 Rating 92 To 2017 $25 TS ✪
Sparkling Shiraz 2014 Rating 92 To 2024 $25 TS ✪
Mourvedre 2014 Rating 91 To 2022 $25 CM
Blanc des Pyrenees 2015 Rating 90 To 2017 $25 CM
Cabernet Merlot Petit Verdot 2013 Rating 90 To 2021 $25 CM
Blanc de Blancs 2012 Rating 90 To 2017 $25 TS

Tamar Ridge | Pirie ★★★★★

1a Waldhorn Drive, Rosevears, Tas 7277 **Region** Northern Tasmania
T (03) 6330 0300 **www.**brownbrothers.com.au **Open** 7 days 10–5
Winemaker Tom Wallace **Est.** 1994 **Dozens** 14000 **Vyds** 120ha
In August 2010 Brown Brothers purchased Tamar Ridge from Gunns Limited for $32.5 million. While Dr Andrew Pirie has retired from his former position of CEO and chief winemaker, he points out that the end of his five-year tenure happened to coincide with the acquisition. Tasmania is the one region of Australia with demand for grapes and wine exceeding supply. Tamar Ridge was well managed during the seven years it was owned by Gunns, avoiding the financial meltdown of Gunns. Exports to all major markets.

🍷🍷🍷🍷🍷 **Tamar Ridge Pinot Gris 2014** Gold Tas Wine Show '15. Has exceptional line, length and integrity; superb acidity within the context of a freakishly good class in the show. The original belief (first tasted Jan '15) that the wine would go the distance in the cellar proved correct 8 months later, with a brilliant finish. Screwcap. 13.5% alc. **Rating** 95 To 2019 $26 ✪
Pirie Traditional Method 2009 The fresh vivacity of Tasmania shines from a pale straw hue and delightful purity of lemon, apple and pear fruit that belies 7 years of maturity. Toasty, nutty complexity is subtle considering its age, culminating in a well-honed finish, sustained by bright Tasmanian acidity and the wonderfully mouthfilling texture of long lees age. Trophy Best Vintage Sparkling Tas Wine Show '15. Cork. 12% alc. **Rating** 95 To 2019 $40 TS
Pirie Traditional Method Rose 2009 Rose petal fragrance and enchanting red cherry, wild strawberry, pink grapefruit and pink pepper flavours. 7 years of maturity has built wonderfully integrated texture without any impact on fruit purity, while a long and bright acid line hones an epic finish. Benchmark rose. Cork. 12% alc. **Rating** 95 To 2019 $48 TS
Tamar Ridge Riesling 2015 In the stand-and-deliver style of young Tasmanian riesling which takes no prisoners. Acid and fruit are both thumping their drums, and will continue to do so for some years to come. And then? Likely superb. Screwcap. 12.5% alc. **Rating** 94 To 2025 $24 ✪
Pirie Traditional Method Blanc de Blancs 2009 You'd never guess its age from its pale straw hue, but such thrilling layers of toast, ginger nut biscuits, exotic spice, honey and enticingly creamy texture can come from nowhere else. In the midst of this marvel of maturity, the spine and verve of Tasmanian chardonnay radiates in grapefruit and apple, with well-focused acidity providing tone and calm to a generous and persistent finish. Cork. 12.5% alc. **Rating** 94 To 2019 $58 TS

🍷🍷🍷🍷🍷 **Tamar Ridge Pinot Noir 2014** Rating 93 To 2026 $30
Tamar Ridge Pinot Gris 2015 Rating 90 To 2017 $26

Tambo Estate ★★★★

96 Pages Road, Tambo Upper, Vic 3885 **Region** Gippsland
T (03) 5156 4921 **Open** By appt
Winemaker Alastair Butt **Est.** 1994 **Dozens** 800 **Vyds** 5.11ha

Bill and Pam Williams returned to Australia in the early 1990s after seven years overseas, and began the search for a property which met the specific requirements for high quality table wines established by Dr John Gladstones in his masterwork *Viticulture and Environment*. They chose a property in the foothills of the Victorian Alps on the inland side of the Gippsland Lakes, with predominantly sheltered, north-facing slopes. They planted a little over 5ha of chardonnay (the lion's share of the plantings, with 3.4ha), sauvignon blanc, pinot noir, cabernet sauvignon and a splash of merlot. They are mightily pleased to have secured the services of Alastair Butt (one-time maker at Seville Estate).

ΨΨΨΨΨ **Gippsland Lakes Sauvignon Blanc 2015** You know there's lots of complex flavour there, but it's like a python: slow to move, but then folding itself around you inexorably – here with a happier end. Screwcap. 12.8% alc. **Rating** 94 To 2017 $26 ✪

Gippsland Lakes Pinot Noir 2014 Has good mouthfeel and depth to fruit tightly focused on plums (of various types); the finish and aftertaste have the juicy feel encountered on first tasting the wine. Screwcap. 12.9% alc. **Rating** 94 To 2027 $35

ΨΨΨΨ♀ **Gippsland Lakes Cabernet Sauvignon 2013** Rating 92 To 2028 $26

Tamburlaine

358 McDonalds Road, Pokolbin, NSW 2321 **Region** Hunter Valley
T (02) 4998 4200 **www.**mywinery.com **Open** 7 days 9.30–5
Winemaker Mark Davidson, Ashley Horner **Est.** 1966 **Dozens** 60 000 **Vyds** 125ha
A thriving business that (until exports started to grow significantly) sold over 90% of its wine through the cellar door and by mailing list (with an active tasting club members' cellar program). The maturing of the estate-owned Orange vineyard led to the introduction of reserve varietals across the range. Both the Hunter Valley and Orange vineyards are now certified organic. Exports to Malaysia, South Korea, Nepal, Japan and China.

ΨΨΨΨ♀ **Reserve Orange Syrah 2014** Peppery and black-cherried with good weight and carry. Appropriately firm to close. Very good wine, for now or later. Screwcap. 14.2% alc. **Rating** 93 To 2026 $44 CM

Reserve Orange Chardonnay 2015 Fruit intensity is excellent but it comes with noticeable alcohol warmth. That's the caveat, but the truth is the flavours still win the day. Grapefruit, fig, yellow stone fruit and sweet, spicy oak. To be served alongside rich dishes. Screwcap. 14.7% alc. **Rating** 92 To 2019 $33 CM

Reserve Hunter Valley Semillon 2015 Pale but with a tinge of green; light and lemon-accented with woolly aspects in the background. Sound, elegant length. Aftertaste of red apples. Steady as she blows. Screwcap. 10.4% alc. **Rating** 91 To 2026 $33 CM

Reserve Orange Riesling 2015 Mineral, lime and talc with edges of sweet apple. Finishes well. Screwcap. 12.1% alc. **Rating** 90 To 2021 $33 CM

Reserve Orange Malbec 2014 Sweet boysenberried fruit with touches of raspberry and earth. Cuts a decent figure. Mid-weight, tidy with tannin, relatively simple but easy to like/drink. Screwcap. 14.1% alc. **Rating** 90 To 2021 $44 CM

ΨΨΨΨ **Reserve Orange Sauvignon Blanc 2015** Rating 89 To 2017 $33 CM
Block 15 Single Vineyard Chardonnay 2015 Rating 89 To 2019 $25 CM
Reserve Hunter Valley Verdelho 2015 Rating 89 To 2017 $33 CM
Block 10 Single Vineyard Pinot Noir 2015 Rating 89 To 2020 $25 CM
Reserve Orange Cabernet Sauvignon 2014 Rating 89 To 2024 $44 CM
Reserve Hunter Valley Chardonnay 2015 Rating 88 To 2018 $33 CM
Reserve Hunter Valley Syrah 2014 Rating 88 To 2020 $44 CM

Taminick Cellars ★★★★☆

339 Booth Road, Taminick via Glenrowan, Vic 3675 **Region** Glenrowan
T (03) 5766 2282 **www.**taminickcellars.com.au **Open** Mon–Sat 9–5, Sun 10–5
Winemaker James Booth **Est.** 1904 **Dozens** 2000 **Vyds** 19.7ha
Peter Booth is a third-generation member of the Booth family, who have owned this winery since Esca Booth purchased the property in 1904. James Booth, fourth generation and current winemaker, completed his wine science degree at CSU in 2008. The red wines are massively flavoured and very long-lived, notably those from the 9ha of shiraz planted in '19. Trebbiano and alicante bouschet were also planted in '19; the much newer arrivals include nero d'Avola.

🍷🍷🍷🍷🍷 **Durif 2013** It has two faces, the first its colour, the second extreme elegance (for durif), coupled with perfect balance and length. By any standards a bargain, but by those of durif, utterly exceptional. PS no fining! Screwcap. 14.5% alc. **Rating** 95 To 2028 $20 ◐

🍷🍷🍷🍷🍷 **Family Reserve Muscat NV** Rating 93 To 2017 $35
Cliff Booth Glenrowan Shiraz 2013 Rating 91 To 2033 $24

Tanglewood Vines ★★★

RMB 383, Bridgetown, WA 6255 (postal) **Region** Blackwood Valley
T (08) 9764 4051 **www.**tanglewood-wines.com.au **Open** Not
Winemaker Hamish Hume, Bernie Stanlake **Est.** 1999 **Dozens** 500 **Vyds** 6.2ha
Hamish and Caroline Hume have established cabernet sauvignon (2.2ha), merlot and viognier (2ha each). While they have hitherto been content to keep a low profile and have not sent wines for appraisal, their recent wine show success has led them to take the plunge. Exports to the Philippines.

🍷🍷🍷🍷 **Blackwood Valley Viognier 2014** There are plenty of viognier makers in Australia who would be happy to have this as their own, the only issue a slightly hot finish. Well done. Screwcap. 14% alc. **Rating** 89 To 2016 $24
Blackwood Valley Merlot 2014 Only light-bodied, but has some cassis, plum and herb varietal character that has not been overworked, and the finish is fresh. Screwcap. 14% alc. **Rating** 88 To 2019 $22

Tapanappa ★★★★★

15 Spring Gully Road, Piccadilly, SA 5151 **Region** Adelaide Hills
T (08) 7324 5301 **www.**tapanappawines.com.au **Open** Thurs–Mon 11–4
Winemaker Brian Croser **Est.** 2002 **Dozens** 2500 **Vyds** 16.7ha
Tapanappa has come home in many ways in 2015. It has the original Petaluma winery back, and a cellar door at the picturesque Tiers Vineyard. Equally importantly, it is now wholly owned by Brian and Ann Croser, albeit with the involvement of daughter and son-in-law Lucy and Xavier Bizot. The business as usual components are the Whalebone Vineyard at Wrattonbully (planted to cabernet sauvignon, shiraz and merlot over 30 years ago), the Tiers Vineyard at Piccadilly in the Adelaide Hills (chardonnay), and the Foggy Hill Vineyard on the southern tip of the Fleurieu Peninsula (pinot noir). Exports to the UK, France, the UAE, Vietnam, Hong Kong and China.

🍷🍷🍷🍷🍷 **Whalebone Vineyard Merlot Cabernet Franc 2012** 66/34%, matured for 21 months in French oak (70% new). Spent close on 3 years making its way into bottle, an especially long time for a blend such as this, but it clearly needed it; there is a complex interplay between rich blackcurrant, cedar, cigar box and dried herbs, and a persistent tattoo of fine-grained tannins on the very long palate. Cork. 14.6% alc. **Rating** 96 To 2037 $80
Whalebone Vineyard Cabernet Shiraz 2013 85/15%. The first thing you notice is the liveliness of it; the second is the easygoing complexity; the third is the long chains of tannin. Tobacco and earth run through boysenberry and blackcurrant; smoky oak plays a subtle role. Cork. 14% alc. **Rating** 96 To 2030 $55 CM ◐

Tiers Vineyard Chardonnay 2014 Allow this time to breathe and a world of flavour opens up to you. It stares you straight in the eye, as unflinching as it is intense. It shows malty, smoky oak, especially at first, but as it rests in the glass the seams smooth, and then disappear. Stone fruit rises. Pears. Grapefruit. Apples. It enriches as it refreshes. Screwcap. 13.6% alc. **Rating** 95 **To** 2023 $79 CM
Whalebone Vineyard Merlot Cabernet Franc 2013 56/44% blend matured in 90% new French oak. Balance of fruit, acid and tannin is arguably its key trait, though you can see its charismatic personality getting in a humph over such a call. Choc-spearmint helps bring leather, game, twiggy herbs and sheer cassis flavours together. Cork. 14.8% alc. **Rating** 95 **To** 2030 $80 CM

♀♀♀♀♀ **Foggy Hill Vineyard Pinot Noir 2014** Rating 91 To 2024 $55

Tar & Roses   ★★★★

61 Vickers Lane, Nagambie, Vic 3608 (postal) **Region** Central Victoria Zone
T (03) 5794 1811 **www**.tarandroses.com.au **Open** Not
Winemaker Don Lewis, Narelle King **Est.** 2006 **Dozens** 18 000 **Vyds** 5ha
While Don Lewis and Narelle King have made and marketed the Tar & Roses wines for some years, the business is owned by Tar & Roses Pty Ltd, a company in which neither has a financial interest. It's all rather complicated, but life wasn't meant to be simple.

♀♀♀♀♀ **Heathcote Sangiovese 2014** Enormously drinkable. Leaps from the glass with spiced cherry fragrance and keeps the show going in the mouth. Cherry-plum, leather, undergrowth, roasted nuts. A gentle meatiness. Not a big wine, but a thoroughly engaging one. Screwcap. 13.9% alc. **Rating** 93 **To** 2020 $24 CM ❂
Heathcote Tempranillo 2014 Crushed to a static fermenter, pumped over twice daily, pressed to French oak (13% new) for maturation. A full-bodied tempranillo with strong varietal expression; red, black and sour cherry; firm tannins, and some cedar. Screwcap. 13.8% alc. **Rating** 92 **To** 2024 $24 ❂
Pinot Grigio 2015 Rich and textural. More gris than grigio. Pale pink with notes of strawberry, melon, nashi pear and zesty lemon. Oomph aplenty. Slight warmth to the finish. Screwcap. 14.3% alc. **Rating** 90 **To** 2016 $18 CM ❂
Heathcote Shiraz 2014 An attractive array of juicy red and black fruits, the tannin and oak contributions purely in support mode. Will repay cellaring as the balance is good. Screwcap. 14.5% alc. **Rating** 90 **To** 2029 $20 ❂
Heathcote Nebbiolo 2013 There's a delayed reaction from the tannins, which hold back until you lower your guard – and then strike. Tar & Roses give a brilliant 'wet fern and fennel' description of the bouquet, the palate more a matter of opinion, except for rebellious tannins. Screwcap. 14.2% alc. **Rating** 90 **To** 2023 $45

Tarrahill.   ★★★★★

340 Old Healesville Road, Yarra Glen, Vic 3775 **Region** Yarra Valley
T (03) 9730 1152 **www**.tarrahill.com **Open** By appt
Winemaker Jonathan Hamer, Geof Fethers **Est.** 1992 **Dozens** 700 **Vyds** 6.5ha
Owned by former Mallesons Lawyers partner Jonathan Hamer and wife Andrea, a former doctor and daughter of Ian Hanson, who made wine for many years under the Hanson-Tarrahill label. Ian had a 0.8ha vineyard at Lower Plenty, but needed 2ha to obtain a vigneron's licence. In 1990 the Hamers purchased a property in the Yarra Valley and planted the requisite vines (pinot noir – ultimately destroyed by the 2009 bushfires). In '92 Jonathan planted a further 2ha, and spent all his weekends looking after the vineyard. This became increasingly difficult, so the Hamers planted yet more vines to justify the employment of a vineyard manager. Nonetheless, he and company director friend Geof Fethers continued to work weekends in the vineyard, and in '04 decided that they would undertake a wine science degree (at CSU); they graduated in '11. In '12 Jonathan retired from law and planted more vineyards (cabernet sauvignon, cabernet franc, merlot, malbec and petit verdot, to make a Bordeaux blend), and Ian (aged 86) retired from winemaking. Andrea has also contributed, with a second degree (horticulture); she is a biodynamics advocate.

ΨΨΨΨΨ **Cabernet Sauvignon 2014** Includes 15% shiraz, matured in François Frères French oak (30% new). This is the mirror image of the Shiraz, a wine of immense distinction, driven by the quality and style of the cabernet fruit. I cannot evaluate the impact of the shiraz, not being present at the blending trials (or any other time), but this is the epitome of Yarra Valley cabernet. Screwcap. 14.1% alc. **Rating** 97 **To** 2044 $40 ✪

ΨΨΨΨΨ **Shiraz 2014** Includes 15% cabernet sauvignon, matured in François Frères French oak (30% new). The highly fragrant bouquet lights the way for a light to medium-bodied palate that tastes and feels like 13%, not 14.2%; it has vibrantly fresh red fruits, fine tannins and good oak integration. The cabernet has not pulled the rug from under the feet of the shiraz. Screwcap. **Rating** 95 **To** 2029 $40

Pinot Noir 2014 Some early colour development is evident in a wine with both flavour and textural complexity, this in turn reflecting the use of 40% new Mecurey barrels. I don't want to nitpick, but I'd like to see less oak and/or more fruit evident, regardless of the (high) hedonism factor. Screwcap. 13.8% alc. **Rating** 94 **To** 2024 $40

Pinot Noir 2013 Pinot noir is forever laying traps for both the wary and the unwary. This has riper fruit flavours, yet its alcohol is significantly less than its '14 sibling, with juicy, plummy fruit to the fore, the oak correspondingly less obvious. Screwcap. 13% alc. **Rating** 94 **To** 2023 $30 ✪

Cabernet Sauvignon 2013 Elegant, medium-bodied, cassis-driven; fine, supple tannins, integrated oak, good length. Simply not in the same class as the Olympian '14. Screwcap. 13.4% alc. **Rating** 94 **To** 2030 $30 ✪

TarraWarra Estate ★★★★★

311 Healesville-Yarra Glen Road, Yarra Glen, Vic 3775 **Region** Yarra Valley
T (03) 5962 3311 **www**.tarrawarra.com.au **Open** Tues–Sun 11–5
Winemaker Clare Halloran **Est.** 1983 **Dozens** 15 000 **Vyds** 28.98ha
TarraWarra is, and always has been, one of the top-tier wineries in the Yarra Valley. Founded by Marc Besen AO and wife Eva, it has operated on the basis that quality is paramount, cost a secondary concern. The creation of the TarraWarra Museum of Art (twma.com.au) in a purpose-built building provides another reason to visit; indeed, many visitors come specifically to look at the ever-changing displays in the Museum. Changes in the vineyard include the planting of shiraz and merlot, and in the winery, the creation of a four-tier range: a deluxe MDB label made in tiny quantities and only when the vintage permits; the single vineyard range; a Reserve range; and the 100% estate-grown varietal range. Exports to France, the Maldives, Vietnam, Singapore Hong Kong and China.

ΨΨΨΨΨ **Chardonnay 2014** 50% tank-fermented, 50% in barrel. All natural ferments. 10% new oak. As the winemaking would suggest, the clear emphasis here is on fruit and freshness. It has a slatey, white peach and lemon character, a chalky dryness then fitting in with the general theme. It's both reserved and classy at once; it will build given extra time in the bottle. Quality is a given. Screwcap. 12.5% alc. **Rating** 95 **To** 2021 $28 CM ✪

Roussanne Marsanne Viognier 2014 This powerful mouthfilling wine comes from just seven rows of vines, the flavours starting with apple and apricot, finishing with a powdery acidity that lends it real character. This blend often lacks the X-factor that this wine has. Screwcap. 12.2% alc. **Rating** 95 **To** 2020 $30 ✪

ΨΨΨΨΨ **Pinot Noir 2014 Rating** 93 **To** 2023 $28 CM
Pinot Noir Rose 2015 Rating 90 **To** 2016 $25

Tatachilla ★★★★☆

151 Main Road, McLaren Vale, SA 5171 **Region** McLaren Vale
T (08) 8563 7000 **www**.tatachillawines.com.au **Open** Not
Winemaker Jeremy Ottawa **Est.** 1903 **Dozens** 43 000 **Vyds** 12.4ha

Tatachilla was reborn in 1995 but has had a tumultuous history going back to 1903. Between then and '61 the winery was owned by Penfolds; it was closed in '61 and reopened in '65 as the Southern Vales Co-operative. In the late '80s it was purchased and renamed The Vales but did not flourish; in '93 it was purchased by local grower Vic Zerella and former Kaiser Stuhl chief executive Keith Smith. After extensive renovations, the winery was officially reopened in '95 and won a number of tourist awards and accolades. It became part of Banksia Wines in 2001, in turn acquired by Lion Nathan in '02. Exports to all major markets.

ŸŸŸŸŸ **Foundation McLaren Vale Shiraz 2013** A rich, full-bodied shiraz that provocatively proclaims its McLaren Vale origin from the first whiff through to the aftertaste: black fruits are wrapped in a coat of dark chocolate and licorice, the all-up consequence a seductively rich wine. Its controlled alcohol keeps all its charms in a bra with moderate uplift. A sure future ahead. Screwcap. 14% alc. **Rating** 95 **To** 2038 $50

ŸŸŸŸŸ **McLaren Vale Cabernet Sauvignon 2014 Rating** 92 **To** 2026 $25 CM **O**
McLaren Vale Shiraz 2014 Rating 91 **To** 2023 $25 CM
Pinot Grigio 2015 Rating 90 **To** 2016 $13 **O**

Tatler Wines

477 Lovedale Road, Lovedale, NSW 2321 **Region** Hunter Valley
T (02) 4930 9139 **www**.tatlerwines.com **Open** 7 days 10–5
Winemaker Daniel Binet **Est.** 1998 **Dozens** 6000 **Vyds** 15ha
Tatler Wines is a family-owned company headed by Sydney hoteliers, brothers Theo and Spiro Isak (Isakidis). The name comes from the Tatler Hotel on George Street, Sydney, which was purchased by father James (Dimitri) Isak in 1974 and operated by the family until its closure in '86. In '98 the Tatler name was reborn with the purchase of a 40ha property in Lovedale. The vineyard is planted to 7ha of chardonnay and 4ha each of semillon and shiraz, and the wines are made onsite in the recently renovated winery. Exports to the US.

ŸŸŸŸŸ **Over the Ditch Semillon Sauvignon Blanc 2015** Notwithstanding the implications of the name, this is not a blend with Marlborough sauvignon blanc – it comes from Orange (a well-trodden path). The semillon is from the Hunter Valley. Orange comes up trumps, for there's a healthy infusion of tropical fruits into the semillon without compromising the mouthfeel or flavour. It works well. Screwcap. 12.5% alc. **Rating** 92 **To** 2017 $27
McLaren Vale Shiraz 2014 Why a long-term Hunter Valley winemaker would go to McLaren Vale to buy shiraz in a stellar Hunter vintage is a mystery. It's true this is a good medium to full-bodied shiraz, with that regional gash of dark chocolate opening its centre, but … Screwcap. 14.5% alc. **Rating** 91 **To** 2034 $35

Taylors

Taylors Road, Auburn, SA 5451 **Region** Clare Valley
T (08) 8849 1111 **www**.taylorswines.com.au **Open** Mon–Fri 9–5, w'ends 10–4
Winemaker Adam Eggins, Phillip Reschke **Est.** 1969 **Dozens** 250000 **Vyds** 400ha
The family-founded and owned Taylors continues to flourish and expand – its vineyards are now by far the largest holding in the Clare Valley. There have also been changes in terms of the winemaking team and the wine style and quality, particularly through the outstanding St Andrews range. With each passing vintage, Taylors is managing to do for the Clare Valley what Peter Lehmann did for the Barossa Valley. Recent entries in international wine shows have resulted in a rich haul of trophies and gold medals for wines at all price points. A founding member of Australia's First Families of Wine. No wines received for this edition, but the rating has been maintained. Exports (under the Wakefield brand due to trademark reasons) to all major markets.

TeAro Estate

20 Queen Street, Williamstown, SA 5351 **Region** Barossa Valley
T (08) 8524 6860 **www**.tearoestate.com **Open** Fri–Mon 10–5
Winemaker Todd Rowett, Russell Johnson **Est.** 2001 **Dozens** 2000 **Vyds** 58.2ha
TeAro Estate is a family-owned and operated wine business located in the southern Barossa
Valley. In 1919 great-grandfather Charlie Fromm married Minnie Kappler, who named their
home block TeAro. They planted shiraz and semillon, their only equipment a single crowbar
(and their bare hands). Under the guidance of second and third-generation Ron and Trevor,
the vineyard has grown to just over 58ha. Until 2001 the grapes were sold, but in that year
Trevor decided to have a tonne of shiraz made for the local football club. It has been the fourth
generation, including vigneron Ryan Fromm and brother-in-law Todd Rowett, that has been
responsible for the proliferation of varieties. The vineyards are planted (in descending amount
order) to shiraz, cabernet sauvignon, semillon, chardonnay, pinot noir, riesling, viognier,
sauvignon blanc, pinot gris, tempranillo, merlot, mourvedre and grenache. Exports to China.

ΥΥΥΥΩ **Two Charlies G.S.M. 2013** Well-proportioned and finished. A polished, fruit-
filled wine with plenty of savoury inputs. It's appreciably firm too; in a positive
way. Licorice, raspberry, twigs and five spice. Flecks of orange peel give it a gently
exotic edge. It finishes warm but full of flavour. Screwcap. 14.8% alc. **Rating** 93
To 2022 $28 CM
Pump Jack Cabernet Sauvignon 2014 This is as full-bodied as the message
on the back label, sticks of gelignite part of the story. The alcohol has been
controlled, and every effort has been made (and rewarded) to control the tannin
structure. The future of the fleshy, dense blackcurrant fruit is far distant. Screwcap.
14% alc. **Rating** 92 **To** 2044 $35
Charred Door Shiraz 2014 A ghetto blaster boring through half-shut eyelids
in a frenzied nightclub. New oak (French and American) has added a dimension
to the super-powerful black fruits (not a glimmer of red to be seen) and licorice
essence. A white flag has to be waved vigorously. Any proud parent or grandparent
wishing to celebrate a '14 birth year need look no further. Screwcap. 14.8% alc.
Rating 91 **To** 2035 $35
1946 The Charging Bull Tempranillo 2014 Both savoury and sweet, with
medium-weight choc-berry flavours walking through a field of earth and spice
notes. Effective it is, too. Screwcap. 14.3% alc. **Rating** 90 **To** 2018 $35 CM

ΥΥΥΥ **Iron Fist Grenache 2014 Rating** 88 **To** 2016 $28

Telera ★★★★

PO Box 3114, Prahran East, Vic 3181 **Region** Mornington Peninsula
T 0407 041 719 **www**.telera.com.au **Open** Not
Winemaker Michael Telera **Est.** 2007 **Dozens** 40 **Vyds** 0.4ha
The claim to have the smallest commercial winemaking business in Australia is frequently
made, but I would put my money on this being the smallest, just under half a hectare (an
acre) of sauvignon blanc and pinot noir sufficient to produce 40 dozen bottles a year. It was
established by Michael and Susanne (Lew) Wynne-Hughes, who planted the vines in 2000,
naming the venture MLF Wines. In '11 Michael Telera leased the vineyard, and, following
the death of Michael Wynne-Hughes in that year, the name was changed to Telera. He has
learnt the trade through 6 vintages as a cellar hand/assistant winemaker at Dr George Mihaly's
Paradigm Hill winery, and produces shiraz sourced from other growers on the Peninsula. He
plans to plant 12 rows of pinot noir on the leased property, making the total 20 rows of pinot
noir and 9 rows of sauvignon blanc.

ΥΥΥΥ **Mornington Peninsula Fume Sauvignon Blanc 2015** Crushed and
destemmed into an open vat, the juice settled, cultured yeast added, fermentation
completed in French oak, matured for 6 months. It's certainly created attitude and
flavour, but keeping part in stainless steel might have given the wine the crispness
it lacks. Screwcap. 12.3% alc. **Rating** 89 **To** 2016 $25

Mornington Peninsula Pinot Noir 2014 Deeply coloured and richly fruited, with black cherry and plum to the fore; unquestionably varietal and fault-free, but tends to sit in the mouth, not drive through to the finish. Will improve in bottle for 3–4 years. Screwcap. 13.5% alc. **Rating** 89 **To** 2024 $55

Tellurian ★★★★★

408 Tranter Road, Toolleen, Vic 3551 **Region** Heathcote
T 0431 004 766 **www.tellurianwines.com.au Open** By appt
Winemaker Tobias Ansted **Est.** 2002 **Dozens** 3000 **Vyds** 21.87ha
The vineyard is situated on the western side of Mt Camel at Toolleen, on the red Cambrian soil that has made Heathcote one of the foremost regions in Australia for the production of shiraz (Tellurian means 'of the earth'). Viticultural consultant Tim Brown not only supervises the Tellurian estate plantings, but also works closely with the growers of grapes purchased under contract for Tellurian. Further Rhône red and white varieties were planted on the Tellurian property in 2011. Exports to the UK and China.

🍷🍷🍷🍷🍷 **Block 3 TLR Shiraz 2014** It saw much the same oak handling as several other of the '14 releases but this one has swallowed it whole; it seems to have barely touched the sides. The result is a scorcher. Full of fruit but savoury at heart. Intricately tannic. Lively, fresh and accessible but with more than enough richness and length. Screwcap. 14.5% alc. **Rating** 95 **To** 2030 $39 CM
Pastiche Shiraz 2014 A powerhouse, but not overdone; excellent texture and structure ex high quality, ripe, but fine, tannins; considerable length. Gold medal Victorian Wines Show '15. Screwcap. 14.5% alc. **Rating** 95 **To** 2039 $27 ✪
Fiano 2015 Fruit sourced from Chalmers; the estate's fiano plantings are expected to come on line from '17. This '15 release, though, delivers plenty. Grapefruit, citrus, both the pulp and juice of fresh-cut nectarine; this drips with delicious flavour. Screwcap. 13.5% alc. **Rating** 94 **To** 2017 $27 CM ✪
Block 3 SR Shiraz 2014 Matured in large-format French oak, 50% of which was new. Said oak has made a dramatic impression, with smoky/creamy characters slathered over cherry-plum fruit. You wouldn't say there's too much oak, but you would say it's pushing it. The end result, though, is as luscious as it is seductive. Screwcap. 14.5% alc. **Rating** 94 **To** 2028 $39 CM

🍷🍷🍷🍷🍸 **Tranter Shiraz 2014 Rating** 93 **To** 2028 $39 CM
Grenache Shiraz Mourvedre 2014 Rating 92 **To** 2020 $27 CM
Redline Shiraz 2014 Rating 90 **To** 2019 $22 CM

Tempus Two Wines ★★★★☆

Broke Road, Pokolbin, NSW 2321 **Region** Hunter Valley
T (02) 4993 3999 **www.tempustwo.com.au Open** 7 days 10–5
Winemaker Andrew Duff **Est.** 1997 **Dozens** 55 000
Tempus Two is a mix of Latin (Tempus means time) and English. It has been a major success story, production growing from 6000 dozen in 1997 to 55 000 dozen today. Its cellar door, restaurant complex (including the Oishii Japanese restaurant) and small convention facilities are situated in a striking building. The design polarises opinion; I like it. Exports to all major markets.

🍷🍷🍷🍷🍷 **Uno Hunter Valley Shiraz 2014** It's a character-based drama. It hits with blackberry and dark cherry flavour, as if lulling you into a false sense of security, then twists game, star anise, roasted nuts and burnt rubber flavours at you in rapid succession. In short time you're not feeling so comfortable, and you're gripped to the glass. What happens in the end, only time will tell, but it's a wine you'll want to tell your friends about. Diam. 13.5% alc. **Rating** 95 **To** 2032 $75 CM
Copper Series Wilde Chardonnay 2015 Hunter Valley/Adelaide Hills. Pitch perfect in all respects. Flavoursome, but lengthy. Direct in its appeal, but with flashes of sophistication. One for all seasons and comers. Screwcap. 13% alc. **Rating** 94 **To** 2020 $25 CM ✪

ΨΨΨΨΨ Pewter Hunter Valley Chardonnay 2015 Rating 93 To 2020 $45 CM
Uno Hunter Valley Pinot Shiraz 2014 Rating 93 To 2040 $75 CM
Pewter Hunter Valley Semillon 2015 Rating 92 To 2023 $34 CM
Copper Series GSM 2014 Rating 91 To 2021 $25 CM
Copper Series Tempranillo 2015 Rating 91 To 2020 $25 CM

Ten Minutes by Tractor ★★★★★

1333 Mornington-Flinders Road, Main Ridge, Vic 3928 **Region** Mornington Peninsula
T (03) 5989 6455 **www**.tenminutesbytractor.com.au **Open** 7 days 11–5
Winemaker Richard McIntyre, Martin Spedding, Jeremy Magyar **Est.** 1999
Dozens 9000 **Vyds** 34.4ha
The energy, drive and vision of Martin Spedding have transformed Ten Minutes by Tractor since he acquired the business in early 2004. In mid-'06 Ten Minutes By Tractor purchased the McCutcheon Vineyard; it also has long-term leases on the other two original home vineyards (Judd and Wallis), thus having complete control over grape production. Three new vineyards have been added in recent years: the one at the cellar door and restaurant site is organically certified and is used to trial organic viticultural practices that are progressively being employed across all the vineyards; the others are in the north of the Peninsula. There are now three ranges: Single Vineyard, from the home Judd, McCutcheon and Wallace Vineyards; Estate, the best blend of pinot and of chardonnay from the home vineyards; and finally 10X, from the other estate-owned Mornington Peninsula vineyards. The restaurant has one of the best wine lists to be found at any winery. Exports to the UK, Canada, Sweden and Switzerland.

ΨΨΨΨΨ Wallis Chardonnay 2014 Hand-picked, wild-fermented, matured in French oak for 10 months. Doesn't disavow its paternity – indeed it embraces it, with fruit, oak and acidity in a fluid line; flavours of stone fruit, fig and citrus all make their contribution, again respecting each other's importance. Screwcap. 13.6% alc. **Rating** 95 To 2024 $65
Estate Pinot Noir 2014 Hand-picked, destemmed, 4–6 days cold soak, wild yeast-fermented, 18–22 days on skins, matured for 16 months in French oak (25% new). Bright colour, clear and full; a fragrant red fruit bouquet; the palate ratchets the impact up several notches, introducing spice and hints of forest, adding plum to the flavour spectrum. Not content with that, the lift of the finish has yet another dimension. Lovely pinot. Screwcap. 13.6% alc. **Rating** 95 To 2024 $46

ΨΨΨΨΨ 10X Sauvignon Blanc 2014 Rating 93 To 2016 $28 CM
10X Chardonnay 2014 Rating 93 To 2020 $30 CM
Estate Chardonnay 2014 Rating 93 To 2021 $42
10X Pinot Gris 2014 Rating 93 To 2016 $28 CM
10X Pinot Noir 2014 Rating 93 To 2020 $32 CM
10X Rose 2015 Rating 92 To 2017 $26 CM

Tenafeate Creek Wines ★★★★

1071 Gawler-One Tree Hill Road, One Tree Hill, SA 5114 **Region** Adelaide Zone
T (08) 8280 7715 **www**.tcw.com.au **Open** Fri–Sun & public hols 11–5
Winemaker Larry and Michael Costa **Est.** 2002 **Dozens** 3000 **Vyds** 1ha
Larry Costa, a former hairdresser, embarked on winemaking as a hobby in 2002. The property, with its 1ha of shiraz, cabernet sauvignon and merlot, is situated on the rolling countryside of One Tree Hill in the Mount Lofty Ranges. The business grew rapidly, with grenache, nebbiolo, sangiovese, petit verdot, chardonnay, semillon and sauvignon blanc purchased to supplement the estate-grown grapes. Michael Costa, Larry's son, has now joined his father as co-owner of the business, and has 15 vintages under his belt, mainly in the Barossa Valley, with Flying Winemaker stints in southern Italy and Provence. The red wines have won many medals over the years.

ΨΨΨΨΨ Adelaide Hills Sauvignon Blanc 2015 From a single vineyard, machine-picked – very quickly given the total make of only 250 dozen – pressed and cold-settled for 3 days, racked off lees and very cool fermented for 12 days with a cultured yeast. Has an abundance of tropical fruit flavours neatly balanced by natural acidity. Screwcap. 11.5% alc. **Rating** 91 To 2016 $20 ✪

ℙℙℙℙ **Eden Valley Pinot Grigio 2015 Rating** 89 To 2016 $20
Tempranillo Rose 2015 Rating 89 To 2016 $20
Sticky Sem Late Harvest Semillon 2015 Rating 89 To 2017 $20
Basket Press GSM 2014 Rating 88 To 2017 $25

Terindah Estate   ★★★★☆

90 McAdams Lane, Bellarine, Vic 3223 **Region** Geelong
T (03) 5251 5536 **www**.terindahestate.com **Open** 7 days 10–4
Winemaker Chris Sargeant **Est.** 2003 **Dozens** 2500 **Vyds** 5.6ha
Retired quantity surveyor Peter Slattery bought the 48ha property in 2001, intending to plant the vineyard, make wine and develop a restaurant. He has achieved all of this (with help from others, of course), planting shiraz, pinot noir, pinot gris, picolit, chardonnay and zinfandel. Picolit is most interesting: it is a highly regarded grape in northern Italy, where it makes small quantities of high quality sweet wine. It has proven very temperamental here, as in Italy, with very unreliable fruit set. In the meantime, he makes classic wines of very high quality from classic grape varieties – not wines for sommeliers to drool over because they're hip.

ℙℙℙℙℙ **Road Block Pinot Noir 2014** Brighter, clearer hue than Hill Block; lively and extroverted, with red and darker fruits beating a tattoo on the long palate; complex but true to its variety, its balance protecting its future. Screwcap. 13% alc. **Rating** 95 To 2024 $45
Reserve Single Vineyard Bellarine Peninsula Pinot Noir 2013 Impressive colour, aroma and palate for a 3yo pinot; a gently spiced red berry bouquet, the palate juicy, and yet savoury, new French oak driving a stake into the ground to mark its presence. Screwcap. 13% alc. **Rating** 94 To 2023 $80
Single Vineyard Bellarine Peninsula Shiraz 2014 Full-on cool climate fruit, savoury and peppery, starting with an intense impact on the mouth, that intensity increasing as the wine is retasted. Not for an idle glass, but for a serious carnivorous event. Screwcap. 13.5% alc. **Rating** 94 To 2034 $65

ℙℙℙℙℙ **Hill Block Pinot Noir 2014 Rating** 91 To 2022 $45
Single Vineyard Pinot Gris 2014 Rating 90 To 2017 $30

Terra Felix   ★★★★

52 Paringa Road, Red Hill South, Vic 3937 (postal) **Region** Central Victoria Zone
T 0419 539 108 **www**.terrafelix.com.au **Open** Not
Winemaker Ben Haines **Est.** 2001 **Dozens** 12 000 **Vyds** 7ha
Long-term industry stalwarts Peter Simon and John Nicholson, with an involvement going back well over 30 years, have built on the estate plantings of pinot noir (5ha) and chardonnay (2ha) through purchases from Coonawarra, McLaren Vale, Barossa Valley, Langhorne Creek, Yarra Valley and Strathbogie Ranges. Terra Felix exports 70% of its production to China.

ℙℙℙℙℙ **Heathcote Shiraz 2014** Brightly coloured; an elegant and lively wine, showing its many wares without hesitation; its juicy black and red fruits are neatly held in a fine skein of ripe tannins, oak adding another verse to its song. Screwcap. 13.8% alc. **Rating** 92 To 2025 $18 ✪
Alpine Valleys Chardonnay 2014 A vibrant and fresh wine with grapefruit, stone fruit and melon all in play, the oak judged to perfection, the acidity likewise. Value plus. Screwcap. 13.5% alc. **Rating** 90 To 2017 $18 ✪
McLaren Vale Shiraz 2013 It has very good hue and depth; the medium to full-bodied palate is supple, spherical and smooth, lazily filling the mouth with flavours of blackberry, plum and chocolate. Easygoing style, ready now or whenever. Diam. 14.5% alc. **Rating** 90 To 2028 $29

ℙℙℙℙ **Yarra Valley Pinot Noir 2014 Rating** 89 To 2024 $24
Barossa Valley Shiraz 2012 Rating 88 To 2022 $29
Heathcote Shiraz Viognier 2014 Rating 88 To 2020 $18 CM

Terre à Terre

PO Box 3128, Unley, SA 5061 **Region** Wrattonbully/Adelaide Hills
T 0400 700 447 **www.**terreaterre.com.au **Open** At Tapanappa
Winemaker Xavier Bizot **Est.** 2008 **Dozens** 5000 **Vyds** 16ha

It would be hard to imagine two better-credentialled owners than Xavier Bizot (son of the late Christian Bizot of Bollinger fame) and wife Lucy Croser (daughter of Brian and Ann Croser). 'Terre à terre', incidentally, is a French expression meaning down to earth. The close-planted vineyard is on a limestone ridge, adjacent to Tapanappa's Whalebone Vineyard. The vineyard area has increased (3ha each of cabernet sauvignon and sauvignon blanc and 1ha each of cabernet franc and shiraz), leading to increased production. In 2015, Terre à Terre secured the fruit from one of the oldest vineyards in the Adelaide Hills, the Summertown vineyard, which will see greater quantities of Daosa, and a Piccadilly Valley pinot noir. Wines are released under the Terre à Terre, Down to Earth, Sacrebleu and Daosa labels. Exports to Taiwan and Hong Kong.

🍷🍷🍷🍷🍷 **Crayeres Vineyard Wrattonbully Shiraz 2014** Includes 9% '14 Reserve Cabernet Sauvignon from the Crayeres Vineyard. The immediate energy and drive the wine has lifts it out of the ruck, extending the length of the palate and allowing the undeniably complex black fruits full airplay. This is a classy wine, period, full stop. Screwcap. 14.5% alc. **Rating** 96 **To** 2034 $42 **✪**

Single Vineyard Wrattonbully Cabernet Sauvignon 2013 Includes 5% cabernet franc. A thoroughly elegant and poised cabernet, opening with cassis/blackcurrant, then a matrix of oak, cedar, dried herb and savoury tannins taking the wine through to a powerful conclusion. First tasted a month after it was bottled (Mar '15), it has filled out even more; the perfect, long cork will see the wine through another 20 years without batting an eyelid, allowing the tannins to soften. The colour is yet another plus. 14.4% alc. **Rating** 96 **To** 2035 $40 **✪**

Crayeres Vineyard Wrattonbully Cabernet Franc 2014 A great example of a light to medium-bodied wine that has complexity coming out of its ears, the scene set by its clear, vivid crimson-purple colour, the aromas and mouthwatering flavours with more or less equal portions of sour and red cherries. Screwcap. 14.5% alc. **Rating** 96 **To** 2029 $42 **✪**

Crayeres Vineyard Wrattonbully Sauvignon Blanc 2015 A bold decision to let the grapes ripen to the degree they have, but it's paid dividends, the exotic array of guava, passionfruit and green pineapple balanced by the impact of oak fermentation and maturation. Much in the mould of prior vintages. Screwcap. 13.9% alc. **Rating** 95 **To** 2018 $35 **✪**

Rouge 2014 60% cabernet sauvignon, 28% shiraz, 12% cabernet franc. Is at once supple, yet savoury/spicy, with vibrant red and black fruits neatly tied together by fine tannins and oak. A complete wine. Screwcap. 14.5% alc. **Rating** 95 **To** 2029 $35 **✪**

Down to Earth Wrattonbully Sauvignon Blanc 2015 Before you know it, you're dancing. This is a fruity white wine, done with style. Flint, tropical fruit, slate, subtle grass. It races through the mouth but there's a bit of grip, a bit of mouthfeel. Flavoursome without being in-your-face. Wouldn't hesitate. Screwcap. 13.5% alc. **Rating** 94 **To** 2017 $26 CM **✪**

Crayeres Vineyard Wrattonbully Cabernet Sauvignon 2014 Includes 5% cabernet franc from the Crayeres Vineyard. Good colour, bouquet and palate; the mouthfeel is silky and fluid until fine-grained tannins make their appearance on the back-palate and finish; elegance is its watchword. Cork. 14.5% alc. **Rating** 94 **To** 2029 $55

🍷🍷🍷🍷 **Daosa Blanc de Blancs 2011 Rating** 89 **To** 2026 $55 TS
Blanc 2015 Rating 88 **To** 2020 $35

Tertini Wines

Kells Creek Road, Mittagong, NSW 2575 **Region** Southern Highlands
T (02) 4878 5213 **www**.tertiniwines.com.au **Open** Thurs–Mon 10–5
Winemaker Jonathan Holgate **Est.** 2000 **Dozens** 3000 **Vyds** 7.9ha
When Julian Tertini began the development of Tertini Wines in 2000, he followed in the footsteps of Joseph Vogt 145 years earlier. History does not relate the degree of success that Joseph had, but the site he chose then was, as it is now, a good one. Tertini has pinot noir and riesling (1.8ha each), cabernet sauvignon and chardonnay (1ha each), arneis (0.9ha), pinot gris (0.8ha), merlot (0.4ha) and lagrein (0.2ha). Winemaker Jonathan Holgate, who is responsible for the outstanding results achieved at Tertini, presides over High Range Vintners, a contract winemaking business also owned by Julian Tertini. Exports to Asia.

🍷🍷🍷🍷🍷 **Private Cellar Collection Pinot Noir 2013** The asking price may be a bridge too far, but there's a lot to admire here. It's savoury first and foremost, with autumn leaves and marzipan characters rushing to all corners of the mouth. Dry-but-tangy red and black cherry flavours offer solid support, and the finish doesn't let go without a fight. Indeed it's hard not to come away impressed. Screwcap. 13.5% alc. **Rating** 94 **To** 2020 $70 CM

🍷🍷🍷🍷🍷 **Southern Highlands Riesling 2014 Rating** 93 **To** 2021 $30 CM
Southern Highlands Arneis 2015 Rating 93 **To** 2017 $28 CM
Southern Highlands Chardonnay 2014 Rating 91 **To** 2020 $26 CM
Southern Highlands Pinot Gris 2015 Rating 91 **To** 2016 $26 CM
Southern Highlands Pinot Noir 2013 Rating 90 **To** 2019 $45 CM

Teusner   ★★★★★

29 Jane Place, Tanunda, SA 5352 (postal) **Region** Barossa Valley
T (08) 8562 4147 **www**.teusner.com.au **Open** At Artisans of Barossa
Winemaker Kym Teusner, Matt Reynolds **Est.** 2001 **Dozens** 15 000
Teusner is a partnership between former Torbreck winemaker Kym Teusner and brother-in-law Michael Page, and is typical of the new wave of winemakers determined to protect very old, low-yielding, dry-grown Barossa vines. The winery approach is based on lees ageing, little racking, no fining or filtration, and no new American oak. As each year passes, the consistency, quality (and range) of the wines increases; there must be an end point, but it's not easy to guess when, or even if, it will be reached. Exports to the UK, the US, Canada, The Netherlands, Malaysia, Singapore and Japan.

🍷🍷🍷🍷🍷 **The Bilmore Barossa Valley Shiraz 2014** Good colour; a rich, fruit-slapping mouthful that draws you swiftly back for a second mouthful, and in no time the bottle is empty, especially if you have shared it with another. The finish is remarkable: light and almost airy, yet with a savoury note that serves to highlight the fruit. Screwcap. 14.5% alc. **Rating** 96 **To** 2039 $26 ✪
Big Jim Barossa Valley Shiraz 2014 An impressive shiraz, medium to full-bodied, but with seriously attractive savoury nuances throughout, giving it a character all its own, with a fusion of blackberry/plum flavours ex the Barossa Valley, and earthy/bitter chocolate à la McLaren Vale. Screwcap. 14.5% alc. **Rating** 96 **To** 2039 $65 ✪
Albert 2013 Steps up and delivers the goods. Slashing shiraz. Ripped with blue and black berries and hugged tight by sweet, smoky, cedary oak. Tannin is all class. Nothing about this shiraz disappoints; everything about it impresses. Screwcap. 14.5% alc. **Rating** 96 **To** 2033 $65 CM ✪
Righteous FG Barossa Valley Shiraz 2012 This surely is as powerful and focused as it was when first bottled, its future as far away as Pluto, starting to reveal its secrets in 9½ years from now, but with more to come thereafter. Despite all this, the wine is calm, and you don't feel its alcohol in the endless folds of black fruits, graphite, licorice and clove flavours. Cork. 15% alc. **Rating** 96 **To** 2037 $150

The Dog Strangler 2013 70yo mataro, hand-picked, crushed/destemmed, open-fermented with cultured yeast, 5 days on skins, 15 months in oak. Terrific colour; a sumptuous, rich, succulent mix of red and black fruits; fine tannins add more to the package than the oak. Screwcap. 14.5% alc. **Rating** 95 **To** 2028 $35 ❂

The Wark Family Shiraz 2014 Good hue and depth to the colour. No namby-pamby wine here: it comes at you with a rush, but has balance, texture and structure forming the sure framework for the medley of black and red fruits with plum cake richness, tannins and oak under sure-handed control. Screwcap. 14.5% alc. **Rating** 94 **To** 2039 $26 ❂

The Riebke Barossa Valley Grenache 2014 Matured for 12 months in oak. This is a fine grenache with good colour, red fruits standing proud and sending sparklets of flavour into the mouth, adding to the complexity of this medium-bodied wine, now and in the future. Screwcap. 14.5% alc. **Rating** 94 **To** 2029 $27 ❂

Joshua 2015 60% grenache (100yo), 35% mataro (70yo), 5% shiraz (20yo), matured in stainless steel. (An echo of traditional southern Rhône wines made and matured in concrete tanks.) A totally delicious array of fresh red fruits: plum, cherry, raspberry and strawberry. Drink now, or soonish. Screwcap. 14.5% alc. **Rating** 94 **To** 2020 $35

Teusner & Page Barossa Cabernet Sauvignon 2012 2 years in French oak (50% new). That time in oak has left a deep impression, though the quality of the fruit is high enough to more or less stand up to it. Needless to say, the wine would have been better given more judicious winemaking. Fruit is in the mulberry, boysenberry, pure blackcurrant spectrum, with creamy, smoky cedar wood slathered throughout. Tannin is ultrafine and length is excellent. Screwcap. 14.5% alc. **Rating** 94 **To** 2032 $65 CM

🍷🍷🍷🍷🍷 **Gabrielle Old Vine Barossa Valley Semillon 2011** Rating 93 To 2021 $38
The Empress Eden Valley Riesling 2015 Rating 92 To 2023 $23 CM ❂
The Empress Eden Valley Riesling 2014 Rating 92 To 2029 $23 ❂
Woodside Sauvignon Blanc 2015 Rating 92 To 2017 $23 CM ❂
The Riebke Barossa Valley Shiraz 2014 Rating 92 To 2034 $26
The Independent Shiraz Mataro 2014 Rating 92 To 2029 $27
Vin de Plaisir 2013 Rating 91 To 2020 $25 CM
The Gentleman Cabernet Sauvignon 2014 Rating 91 To 2024 $26
Salsa Barossa Valley Rose 2015 Rating 90 To 2016 $23 CM

The Alchemists ★★★★

PO Box 74, Cowaramup, WA 6284 **Region** Margaret River
T (08) 9755 5007 **www**.alchemistswines.com.au **Open** Not
Winemaker Dave Johnson **Est.** 2009 **Dozens** 3000 **Vyds** 13.6ha
Brad and Sarah Mitchell were metallurgists for 15 and 20 years respectively, working on gold and hydro-metallurgical plants, having studied metallurgy and chemistry at university. Now they see themselves as alchemists, changing grapes into wine. When they purchased the vineyard in 2007 it was already 11 years old, the prior owners having sold the grapes to various well-known Margaret River wineries. Since taking control of the vineyard, they have removed vines on unsuitable soil, and grafted others, moves that have paid dividends, and allowed contract winemaker Dave Johnson (Credaro Family Estate) to make a series of wines that have been consistent medal winners at significant wine shows.

🍷🍷🍷🍷🍷 **Reserve Elixir Margaret River Chardonnay 2014** It starts lean but slowly builds as it travels along the palate. White peach, chalky spice, fennel, toasty-sweet oak. It's balanced and harmonious, is neither over nor under-powered, and feels refreshing through the finish. Screwcap. 13% alc. **Rating** 93 **To** 2022 $35 CM
Margaret River Merlot 2011 In a good place. Blackcurrant and chocolate notes come attractively slung with black olive and wild herb notes. It covers off nicely on both oomph and complexity. Screwcap. 14% alc. **Rating** 91 **To** 2021 $25 CM

Reserve Elixir Margaret River Cabernet Sauvignon 2010 Developing steadily, but the balance and control of the palate are worthy of note. Leather, dusty herbals, signs of fresh blackcurrant. At its peak now. Screwcap. 14% alc. **Rating** 91 To 2021 $35 CM

The Bridge Vineyard ★★★★

Shurans Lane, Heathcote, Vic 3552 **Region** Heathcote
T (03) 5441 5429 **www**.thebridgevineyard.com.au **Open** Select w'ends
Winemaker Lindsay Ross **Est.** 1997 **Dozens** 1000 **Vyds** 4.75ha
This venture of former Balgownie winemaker Lindsay Ross and wife Noeline is part of a broader business known as Winedrops, which acts as a wine production and distribution network for the Bendigo wine industry. The wines are sourced from long-established vineyards, providing shiraz (4ha), malbec (0.5ha) and viognier (0.25ha). The viticultural accent is on low cropping, and thus concentrated flavours, the winemaking emphasis on finesse and varietal expression.

🍷🍷🍷🍷 Shurans Lane Heathcote Shiraz Viognier 2012 93% shiraz. Voluptuous upfront but then firm and spicy to finish. Best of many worlds. Blueberry, violet and blackberry flavours cascade through the mouth. Easy tick. Diam. 14% alc. **Rating** 93 To 2025 $35 CM

🍷🍷🍷🍷 Shurans Lane Shiraz Sangiovese 2012 Rating 88 To 2020 $35 CM

The Grapes of Ross ★★★★

PO Box 14, Lyndoch, SA 5351 **Region** Barossa Valley
T (08) 8524 4214 **www**.grapesofross.com.au **Open** Not
Winemaker Ross Virgara **Est.** 2006 **Dozens** 2000
Ross Virgara spent much of his life in the broader food and wine industry, taking the plunge into commercial winemaking in 2006. The grapes come from a fourth-generation family property in the Lyndoch Valley, and the aim is to make fruit-driven styles of quality wine. His fondness for frontignac led to the first release of Moscato, followed in due course by Rose, Shiraz, Sparkling Shiraz, Grenache Shiraz and The Charmer Sangiovese Merlot Cabernet Sauvignon. Exports to China.

🍷🍷🍷🍷🍷 Limited Release Spirit of Endurance 100 Year Old Vine Barossa Valley Shiraz 2013 This is unapologetically full-bodied, its layers of black fruits framed by oak and ripe tannins, but this is not a Barossa Valley monster; there is light and shade to the texture, and some lively juicy fruit notes on the long palate and aftertaste. I have no quarrel with the alcohol, which sits comfortably in the panoply of flavours. Screwcap. 15% alc. **Rating** 95 To 2053 $70

🍷🍷🍷🍷 Brown Mule Liqueur Muscat NV Rating 89 To 2017 $30

The Hairy Arm ★★★★

18 Plant Street, Northcote, Vic 3070 (postal) **Region** Sunbury/Heathcote
T 0409 110 462 **www**.hairyarm.com **Open** Not
Winemaker Steven Worley **Est.** 2004 **Dozens** 600 **Vyds** 2ha
Steven Worley graduated as an exploration geologist, then added a Master of Geology degree, followed by a postgraduate Diploma in Oenology and Viticulture. Until December 2009 he was general manager of Galli Estate Winery, The Hairy Arm having started as a university project in '04. It has grown from a labour of love to a commercial undertaking; he has an informal lease of 1.5ha of shiraz at Galli's Sunbury vineyard, which he manages, and procures 0.5ha of nebbiolo from the Galli vineyard in Heathcote. The hairy arm, incidentally, is Steven's. Exports to Canada.

🍷🍷🍷🍷🍷 Heathcote Nebbiolo 2013 Its light, developed hue is all nebbiolo, giving little clue about the wine within; it is a Persian carpet with polar opposites of fruit flavours (sour cherry and earth) and texture (robust tannins and lively acidity).

Released May '16, 5 months after tasting, and will be sought by nebbiolo nerds. Screwcap. 14% alc. **Rating** 94 **To** 2034 $45

♟♟♟♟♟ **Sunbury Shiraz 2014 Rating** 93 **To** 2034 $35

The Islander Estate Vineyards ★★★★★

PO Box 868, Kingscote, SA 5223 **Region** Kangaroo Island
T (08) 8553 9008 **www**.iev.com.au **Open** 12–5 Wed–Sun Dec–Feb or by appt
Winemaker Jacques Lurton **Est.** 2000 **Dozens** 10 000 **Vyds** 10ha
Established by one of the most famous Flying Winemakers in the world, Bordeaux-born and trained and part-time Australian resident Jacques Lurton. He has established a close-planted vineyard; the principal varieties are cabernet franc, shiraz and sangiovese, with lesser amounts of grenache, malbec, semillon and viognier. The wines are made and bottled at the onsite winery in true estate style. After several vintages experimenting with a blend of sangiovese and cabernet franc, Jacques has settled on cabernet franc as the varietal base of the signature wine, The Investigator. Exports to the UK, the US and other major markets.

♟♟♟♟♟ **The Investigator Cabernet Franc 2013** A fragrant dark-berry bouquet with spice to the fore; the most striking aspect of the palate is the fine, yet firm, tannins woven throughout; most would guess an Old World origin, the fruit just part of a much bigger whole. Lovely sophisticated wine (and a perfect cork). 14% alc. **Rating** 96 **To** 2038 $150
The Investigator Cabernet Franc 2012 Quite superb. Aristocratic. Luscious with both fruit and tannin, if a wine can boast such a thing, and as a direct result it feels impeccably well balanced. Grassy, licoricey tones to dark, curranty fruit. Pure power. Crackerjack. Cork. 14% alc. **Rating** 96 **To** 2032 $150 CM
Old Rowley 2014 60% shiraz, 40% grenache, hand-picked and sorted on a vibrating sorting tale, destemmed for whole berries, wild-fermented, 5 weeks on skins, then in used French demi-muids for 18 months maturation. An utterly unique style, dark-fruited and with firm, detailed tannins on the long, balanced palate. Screwcap. 14% alc. **Rating** 95 **To** 2034 $35 ✪
The Wally White Semillon 2013 French oak has a dramatic impact but the fruit is interesting and powerful in itself. It tastes of spearmint, malt and smoked spices, all from oak, but these characters are teamed to lemon and melon and gravel. It's a theatrical wine; it has stemware presence. Screwcap. 13.5% alc. **Rating** 94 **To** 2022 $35 CM
Cygnet River 2013 The cool climate is obvious in the spicy, peppery, savoury nature of the background to the black cherry fruit, which is not surprising. What is surprising is the amount of oak, although the cause (maturation in 50% new oak for 30 months) is clear. This shiraz is built for the long haul. Cork. 14% alc. **Rating** 94 **To** 2029 $150

♟♟♟♟♟ **The White 2015 Rating** 93 **To** 2018 $20 CM ✪
The Red 2014 Rating 92 **To** 2021 $19 CM ✪
Bark Hut Road 2014 Rating 92 **To** 2029 $25 ✪
Majestic Plough Kangaroo Island Malbec 2013 Rating 92 **To** 2033 $35

The Lake House Denmark ★★★★★

106 Turner Road, Denmark, WA 6333 **Region** Denmark
T (08) 9848 2444 **www**.lakehousedenmark.com.au **Open** 7 days 10–5
Winemaker Harewood Estate (James Kellie) **Est.** 1995 **Dozens** 8000 **Vyds** 5.2ha
Garry Capelli and Leanne Rogers purchased the property in 2005 and have restructured the vineyard to grow varieties suited to the climate – chardonnay, pinot noir, semillon and sauvignon blanc – incorporating biodynamic principles. They also manage a couple of small family-owned vineyards in Frankland River and Mount Barker, with a similar ethos. Wines are released in three tiers: the flagship Premium Reserve range, the Premium Block range, and the quirky He Said, She Said easy-drinking wines. The combined cellar door, restaurant and gourmet food emporium is a popular destination.

ŸŸŸŸŸ **Premium Reserve Single Vineyard Frankland River Shiraz 2013**
Navigating around the very similar labels and names of these two Reserve wines isn't easy, particularly given that Denmark and Frankland River are separate subregions of the Great Southern. This has the most complex and satisfying bouquet of the siblings; here dark chocolate makes its first (obvious) appearance without obscuring all the other activity on the absolutely delicious full-bodied, supple palate. A steal at this price. Screwcap. 14.5% alc. **Rating** 97 **To** 2048 $45 ✪

ŸŸŸŸŸ **Premium Reserve Premium Selection Frankland River Mount Barker Shiraz 2013** You only have to pick up the heavyweight bottle to know something extra is coming with its contents, toasty French oak (just for starters) augmenting the pre-existing spice notes, introducing licorice and highlighting the intense black fruits. Despite all this, it retains an airy elegance. Screwcap. 14.5% alc. **Rating** 96 **To** 2038 $40 ✪
Premium Reserve Single Vineyard Semillon Sauvignon Blanc 2015 The barrel-ferment input and lower alcohol make this a very different proposition from all the other Lake House SSBs and SBSs. It has greater drive, and you can find just about any white fruit flavour you like. For me, grapefruit, lime and lemongrass (ok, not strictly fruit) are the leaders in this impressive wine. Screwcap. 12% alc. **Rating** 95 **To** 2020 $35 ✪
Premium Reserve Single Vineyard Chardonnay 2014 Super-elegant style; barrel-fermented, but without a lot of new oak, which leaves room for all the finesse and length of the fruit to be seen: white peach, nectarine and grapefruit to the fore, the acidity measured down to the smallest fraction. Screwcap. 13% alc. **Rating** 95 **To** 2025 $40
Premium Block Selection Cabernet Sauvignon 2014 Particularly juicy and welcoming, flooded with cassis, black cherry, spice and dark chocolate, the tannins as tame as a pussy cat; oak conspires to introduce toasty notes to continue the welcome. Great value. Screwcap. 14% alc. **Rating** 95 **To** 2034 $28 ✪
Premium Reserve Premium Selection Riesling 2015 A remarkable wine with an almost Alsace richness and textured mouthfeel, but an Australian flavour and aroma profile generated by its passionfruit overlay to the more conventional fruits in the lime/lemon/apple quadrant. Is there too much of a good thing? Screwcap. 12% alc. **Rating** 94 **To** 2020 $40
Premium Reserve Single Vineyard Pinot Noir 2014 Bright crimson hue; red fruits and spices float upwards out of the glass of their own accord, and the silky red fruits of the palate expand as the forest floor arrives; there is a hint of stem too. Screwcap. 13.5% alc. **Rating** 94 **To** 2023 $45

ŸŸŸŸŸ **Single Vineyard Selection Chardonnay 2014** Rating 93 **To** 2019 $25 ✪
Premium Block Selection Shiraz 2013 Rating 93 **To** 2028 $25 ✪
Premium Block Selection Riesling 2015 Rating 92 **To** 2020 $25 ✪
Premium Block Selection Sauvignon Blanc 2015 Rating 90 **To** 2017 $25
Premium Block Selection SBS 2015 Rating 90 **To** 2019 $25
Single Vineyard Selection Unwooded Chardonnay 2015 Rating 90 **To** 2022 $20 ✪

The Lane Vineyard   ★★★★★

Ravenswood Lane, Hahndorf, SA 5245 **Region** Adelaide Hills
T (08) 8388 1250 **www**.thelane.com.au **Open** 7 days 10–4.30
Winemaker Michael Schreurs, Martyn Edwards **Est.** 1993 **Dozens** 25 000 **Vyds** 75ha
After 15 years at The Lane Vineyard, Helen and John Edwards, and sons Marty and Ben, took an important step towards realising their long-held dream – to grow, make and sell estate-based wines that have a true sense of place. In 2005, at the end of the (now discontinued) Starvedog Lane joint venture with Hardys, they commissioned a state-of-the-art 500-tonne winery, bistro and cellar door overlooking their vineyards on picturesque Ravenswood Lane. Having previously invested in Delatite, and much earlier established Coombe Farm in the Yarra Valley, the Vestey Group (UK), headed by Lord Samuel Vestey and the Right Honourable Mark

Vestey, have acquired a significant shareholding in The Lane Vineyard. The remaining shares are owned by Martyn Edwards and Ben Tolstoshev. Exports to the UK, the US, Canada, The Netherlands, Belgium, the UAE, Hong Kong and China.

♀♀♀♀♀ Reginald Germein Single Vineyard Adelaide Hills Chardonnay 2012

Full straw-green; there's no doubting the class and complexity of this wine, but it was tasted against the might of the greatest Margaret River and Yarra Valley chardonnays at a similar (or lower) price point, and didn't come out the winner. This is a tough call for a wine with lots of varietal flavour and good acidity, but it's a tough world out there. Screwcap. 13% alc. **Rating** 95 **To** 2022 $100

Block 14 Single Vineyard Basket Press Adelaide Hills Shiraz 2014 A whole-berry, wild yeast fermentation is completed in large-format used French oak, matured in oak for 10–12 months, blended and returned to stainless steel for 4–6 months. As fresh as a daisy, and as juicy as a light to medium-bodied shiraz can be, its red fruits and spice leading the way, the tannins soft and fine. Gold medal Adelaide Hills Wine Show '15. Screwcap. 13.5% alc. **Rating** 95 **To** 2034 $39

Reunion Single Vineyard Adelaide Hills Shiraz 2013 Hand-picked, destemmed and berry-sorted, wild-fermented, 25% post-ferment maceration up to 65 days, matured for 18 months in French puncheons (30% new). A compelling wine, showing how much flavour/texture can be obtained with shiraz at a modest alcohol level, the result an elegant, light-footed, spicy/savoury, complex shiraz. Screwcap. 14% alc. **Rating** 95 **To** 2033 $65

19th Meeting Single Vineyard Adelaide Hills Cabernet Sauvignon 2013 An attractive, precisely modulated and balanced medium-bodied cabernet with juicy cassis fruit, hints of oak spice and bay leaf adding texture and complexity; the tannins are superfine but persistent. Screwcap. 13.5% alc. **Rating** 95 **To** 2033 $65

Gathering Single Vineyard Adelaide Hills Sauvignon Blanc Semillon 2014 The sauvignon blanc included 15% whole bunches, the remainder crushed and destemmed, the semillon all destemmed but not crushed, wild-fermented, 70% matured in French oak (15% new), 30% in stainless steel barrels, blended after 6 months, with a further 6 months in tank pre bottling. All this work has paid handsome dividends, the wine with complex texture and flavours and compelling drive; multi-citrus, lesser tropical fruits, and powerful, racy acidity. Screwcap. 13% alc. **Rating** 94 **To** 2020 $35

Block 5 Single Vineyard Adelaide Hills Shiraz 2014 Elegance is the keyword for this wine; its fragrant and expressive red cherry, spice and pepper aromas flow through the opening of the medium-bodied palate, with fine-grained, gently savoury tannins then joining in to provide textural and flavour complexity. Screwcap. 13.5% alc. **Rating** 94 **To** 2024 $25 ✪

Block 8 Single Vineyard Adelaide Hills Merlot 2013 That quality merlot and the Adelaide Hills are highly compatible is beyond dispute; this joins a certain rectitude (bay leaf and dried herb notes) to the embracing juiciness of cassis at the core of the palate; the length and balance are very good indeed. Screwcap. 13.5% alc. **Rating** 94 **To** 2025 $39

♀♀♀♀♀
Beginning Adelaide Hills Chardonnay 2014 Rating 93 To 2023 $39
Cuvée Helen Blanc de Blancs 2009 Rating 92 To 2017 $55 TS
Block 10 Sauvignon Blanc 2015 Rating 91 To 2016 $25 CM
Block 1A Chardonnay 2015 Rating 90 To 2017 $20 CM ✪
Block 2 Pinot Gris 2015 Rating 90 To 2016 $25 CM

The Old Faithful Estate ★★★★

281 Tatachilla Road, McLaren Vale, SA 5171 **Region** McLaren Vale
T 0419 383 907 **www.**nhwines.com.au **Open** By appt
Winemaker Nick Haselgrove, Warren Randall **Est.** 2005 **Dozens** 2000 **Vyds** 5ha
This is a joint venture of American John Larchet, Nick Haselgrove (see separate entry) and Warren Randall. John has long had a leading role as a specialist importer of Australian wines into the US, and guarantees the business whatever sales it needs there. Its shiraz, grenache and

mourvedre come from old, single-site blocks in McLaren Vale. Exports to the US, Canada, Switzerland, Russia, Hong Kong and China.

ŸŸŸŸŸ **Cafe Block McLaren Vale Shiraz 2012** Grown on vines planted in the 1950s. There's a hint of game and a slight drying aspect to the finish, but it's otherwise awash with black-hearted fruit, dense but fresh. Will be interesting to see which way this jumps as it develops. Cork. 14.5% alc. **Rating** 91 **To** 2028 $50 CM

The Other Wine Co ★★★★

136 Jones Road, Balhannah, SA 5242 **Region** South Australia
T (08) 8398 0500 **www**.theotherwineco.com **Open** At Shaw + Smith
Winemaker Martin Shaw, Adam Wadewitz **Est.** 2015 **Dozens** 1000
This is the venture of Michael Hill Smith and Martin Shaw, established in the shadow of Shaw + Smith, but with an entirely different focus and separate marketing. The name reflects the two wines, a McLaren Vale Grenache and an Adelaide Hills Pinot Gris, both intended for casual consumption, the whole focus being freshness combined with seductive mouthfeel. The concept of matching variety and place is one without any particular limits, and there may well be other wines made by The Other Wine Co in years to come. Exports to the UK, Canada and Germany.

ŸŸŸŸŸ **Grenache 2015** Super-fresh (and refreshing) style with spice and aromatic herb notes giving plenty of lift to the punchy, crunchy red-berried flavours. Light but insistent and, most of all, engaging. Excellent example of a 'drink-now' grenache. Screwcap. 13% alc. **Rating** 93 **To** 2020 $27 CM ✪
Pinot Gris 2015 Crisp and zippy but with just enough flavour. Citrus and pear. Gris with more than a nod to grigio. Will be a hit. Screwcap. 12.5% alc. **Rating** 91 **To** 2016 $27 CM

The Pawn Wine Co. ★★★★☆

10 Banksia Road, Macclesfield, SA 5153 **Region** Adelaide Hills
T 0438 373 247 **www**.thepawn.com.au **Open** Not
Winemaker Tom Keelan **Est.** 2002 **Dozens** 5000 **Vyds** 54.92ha
This is a partnership between Tom and Rebecca Keelan and David and Vanessa Blows. Tom was for some time manager of Longview Vineyards at Macclesfield in the Adelaide Hills, and consulted to the neighbouring vineyard, owned by David and Vanessa. In 2004 Tom and David decided to make some small batches of Petit Verdot and Tempranillo at the Bremerton winery, where Tom is now vineyard manager. The wines are sourced from grapes grown on their Macclesfield vineyards; the remainder of the grapes supply brands such as Shaw + Smith, Penfolds, Orlando and Scott Winemaking.

ŸŸŸŸŸ **The Austrian Attack Adelaide Hills Gruner Veltliner 2015** White wine to get excited over. It's an essay on purity and elegance. Slate, citrus, apple and spice notes steam through the palate with the slow, penetrating control of a heavy roller. And yet it's elegant. It's sleight of hand, in the form of a wine. Screwcap. 11.5% alc. **Rating** 95 **To** 2018 $24 CM ✪

ŸŸŸŸŸ **El Desperado Pinot Grigio 2015 Rating** 92 **To** 2017 $19 CM ✪
El Desperado Tempranillo Sangiovese Rose 2015 Rating 92 **To** 2016 $20 CM ✪
El Desperado Tempranillo Shiraz Sangiovese 2015 Rating 92 **To** 2020 $19 CM ✪
El Desperado Sauvignon Blanc 2015 Rating 90 **To** 2016 $20 CM ✪
El Desperado Sangiovese Tempranillo Shiraz 2014 Rating 90 **To** 2018 $20 CM ✪

The Story Wines

1/407 Wattletree Road, Malvern East, Vic 3145 (postal) **Region** Grampians
T 0411 697 912 **www**.thestory.com.au **Open** Not
Winemaker Rory Lane **Est.** 2004 **Dozens** 2500
Over the years I have come across winemakers with degrees in atomic science, doctors with specialties spanning every human condition, town planners, sculptors and painters, and Rory Lane adds yet another to the list: a degree in ancient Greek literature. He says that after completing his degree, and 'desperately wanting to delay an entry into the real world, I stumbled across and enrolled in a postgraduate wine technology and marketing course at Monash University, where I soon became hooked on ... the wondrous connection between land, human and liquid'. Vintages in Australia and Oregon germinated the seed, and he zeroed in on the Grampians, where he purchases small parcels of high-quality grapes. He makes the wines in a small factory where he has assembled a basket press, a few open fermenters, a mono pump and some decent French oak.

Whitlands Close Planted Riesling 2015 Grown at 800m. A smidge of residual gives strong apple/lime flavours an extra push. This is a mighty tasty young riesling. Soft but lengthy and incredibly pure. It will age, but full enjoyment is available now. Screwcap. 12% alc. **Rating** 93 **To** 2024 $28 CM

The Trades

13/30 Peel Road, O'Connor, WA 6163 (postal) **Region** Margaret River
T (08) 9331 2188 **www**.terrawines.com.au **Open** Not
Winemaker Bruce Dukes (Contract) **Est.** 2006 **Dozens** 770
Thierry Ruault and Rachel Taylor have run a wholesale wine business in Perth since 1993, representing a group of top-end Australian and foreign producers. By definition, the wines they offered to their clientele were well above $20 per bottle, and they have decided to fill the gap with a contract-made Shiraz and Sauvignon Blanc from Margaret River.

Butchers Margaret River Cabernet Merlot 2014 77/23% (and 0.19% cabernet franc), matured in French oak (33% new) for 14 months, fined and filtered, needing the former for sure, as the tannins are still to resolve themselves. Rustic, but flavoursome. Screwcap. 13.7% alc. **Rating** 88 **To** 2020 $18

The Vintner's Daughter

5 Crisps Lane, Murrumbateman, NSW 2582 **Region** Canberra District
T 0439 486 419 **www**.thevintnersdaughter.com.au **Open** Not
Winemaker Stephanie Helm **Est.** 2014 **Dozens** 800 **Vyds** 3ha
The Vintner's Daughter is Stephanie Helm, daughter of Ken Helm, who made her first wine when she was 9, and won her first trophy when she was 14. But on finishing school she enrolled in an arts/law degree at the Australian National University, thereafter pursuing a career outside the wine industry until 2011, when she began the wine science degree at CSU. Along the way, while she was at ANU she met a young bloke from Lightning Ridge at a pub, and introduced him to the world of wine. It wasn't too long before he was vineyard manager (with his background as a qualified horticulturist and landscaper) for Ken Helm. In late '14 all the wheels came full circle when a vineyard, originally planted in 1978 with traminer, crouchen and riesling, extended to 3ha in '99, came on the market. It was in an immaculate position between Clonakilla and Eden Road, and they purchased it in a flash and set about some urgently need rejuvenation. Stephanie (and Ben) waltzed into the trophy arena at the Canberra International Riesling Challenge '15, winning the trophy for Best Canberra District Riesling, and for good measure, winning the trophy for Best Riesling at the Winewise Small Vignerons Awards '15. Gewurztraminer is also part of the estate-based portfolio. And yes, they are life partners.

Riesling 2015 Trophies Canberra International Riesling Challenge and Winewise Small Vignerons Awards '15. The structure and texture of this wine are striking, doubtless part of the reason for its spectacular debut; the precision of the citrus and green apple fruit flavours and the crisp acidity on the long finish could hardly be improved on. Screwcap. 11% alc. **Rating** 96 **To** 2030 $28

🍷🍷🍷🍷🍷 Gewurztraminer 2015 Rating 91 To 2020 $26
Gewurztraminer 2014 Rating 91 To 2019 $26

The Willows Vineyard ★★★★

Light Pass Road, Light Pass, Barossa Valley, SA 5355 **Region** Barossa Valley
T (08) 8562 1080 **www.**thewillowsvineyard.com.au **Open** Wed–Mon 10.30–4.30
Winemaker Peter and Michael Scholz **Est.** 1989 **Dozens** 6500 **Vyds** 42.74ha
The Scholz family have been grapegrowers for generations and have over 40ha of vineyards, selling part of the crop. Current-generation winemakers Peter and Michael Scholz make rich, ripe, velvety wines under their own label, some marketed with some bottle age. Exports to the UK, Canada, Switzerland, China and NZ.

🍷🍷🍷🍷🍷 Bonesetter Barossa Shiraz 2013 Uncompromisingly full-bodied, with fruits, tannins and oak all fighting for primacy, none winning. Has all the potential in the world, but needs a minimum of 10 years to really open up. Cork. 14.8% alc. Rating 94 To 2043 $60

🍷🍷🍷🍷🍷 Barossa Valley Shiraz 2013 Rating 90 To 2028 $28

Thick as Thieves Wines ★★★★★

355 Healesville-Kooweerup Road, Badger Creek, Vic 3777 **Region** Yarra Valley
T 0417 184 690 **www.**tatwines.com.au **Open** By appt
Winemaker Syd Bradford **Est.** 2009 **Dozens** 1100 **Vyds** 1ha
Syd Bradford is living proof that small can be beautiful, and, equally, that an old dog can learn new tricks. A growing interest in good food and wine might have come to nothing had it not been for Pfeiffer Wines giving him a vintage job in '03. In that year he enrolled in the wine science course at CSU; he moved to the Yarra Valley in '05. He gained experience at Coldstream Hills (vintage cellar hand), Rochford (assistant winemaker), Domaine Chandon (cellar hand) and Giant Steps/Innocent Bystander (assistant winemaker). In '06 Syd achieved the Dean's Award of Academic Excellence at CSU and in '07 was the sole recipient of the A&G Engineering Scholarship. Aged 35, he was desperate to have a go at crafting his own 'babies', and in '09 came across a small parcel of arneis from the Hoddles Creek area, and Thick as Thieves was born. The techniques used to make his babies could only come from someone who has spent a long time observing and thinking about what he might do if he were calling the shots. Exports to Japan and Singapore.

🍷🍷🍷🍷🍷 Levings Yarra Valley Pinot Noir 2015 Glorious intensity. A body of tangy cherry, anise and wood smoke; laces of spice and herbs; a bow of firm tannin to keep it all in place. You keep hearing its voice long after you've swallowed. Screwcap. 12.5% alc. Rating 96 To 2026 $60 CM ✿
Driftwood Yarra King Valley Pinot Noir Gamay 2015 A mix of whole bunches (clones 114 and 115) and destemmed (MV6) pinot noir, (65%, from the Yarra Valley) and 35% gamay from the King Valley. The bouquet is a fragrant mix of spice and red fruits, the palate long and satisfying, the aftertaste adding conviction to an adventurous blend à la Burgundy passe tout grains. Screwcap. 12.8% alc. Rating 95 To 2019 $30 ✿

🍷🍷🍷🍷🍷 La Vie Rustique Pinot Noir Rose 2015 Rating 93 To 2017 $25 ✿
Plump Yarra Valley Pinot Noir 2015 Rating 93 To 2022 $35 CM
The Don Heathcote Nero d'Avola 2015 Rating 91 To 2020 $35 CM
The Love Letter King Valley Sylvaner 2015 Rating 90 To 2020 $25
King Valley Gamay 2015 Rating 90 To 2020 $35 CM

Third Child

134 Mt Rumney Road, Mt Rumney, Tas 7170 (postal) **Region** Southern Tasmania
T 0419 132 184 **www.**thirdchildvineyard.com.au **Open** Not
Winemaker John Skinner, Rob Drew **Est.** 2000 **Dozens** 750 **Vyds** 3ha
John and Marcia Skinner planted 2.5ha of pinot noir and 0.5ha of riesling in 2000. It is very
much a hands-on operation, the only concession being the enlistment of Rob Drew (from
an adjoining property) to help John with the winemaking. When the first vintage ('04) was
reaching the stage of being bottled and labelled, the Skinners could not come up with a name
and asked their daughter Claire. 'Easy,' she said. 'You've got two kids already; considering the
care taken and time spent at the farm, it's your third child.'

🍷🍷🍷🍷🍷 **Benjamin's Reserve Pinot Noir 2014** Has more of everything than its Thomas
Nicholas sibling, plus supple mouthfeel and a coherent flow of plum, spice
and fine-grained tannins; the new oak component has been totally integrated.
Screwcap. 13.5% alc. **Rating** 94 **To** 2025 $44

🍷🍷🍷🍷🍷 **Riesling 2015 Rating** 92 **To** 2022 $22 ○
Thomas Nicholas Pinot Noir 2014 Rating 90 **To** 2022 $28

Thistledown Wines

c/- Revenir, Peacock Road North, Lenswood, SA 5240 **Region** South Australia
T +44 7778 003 959 **www.**thistledownwines.com **Open** Not
Winemaker Peter Leske, Giles Cook MW, Fergal Tynan MW **Est.** 2010 **Dozens** 3000
Giles Cook MW and Fergal Tynan MW are based in Scotland, and have a collective 40 years'
experience in buying and selling Australian wines. They have been friends since 1998, when
they met over a pint of beer on the evening before the first Master of Wine course they
were about to embark on. In 2006 they established Alliance Wine Australia, which purchases
Australian wines for distribution in the UK; they took the process one step further when
Alliance began the Thistledown Wines venture. This focuses on Barossa Valley Shiraz, McLaren
Vale Grenache, and smaller amounts of Chardonnay from the Adelaide Hills. The wines are
made under Peter Leske's direction at his Revenir small batch winery in the Adelaide Hills.
Giles says he has particular affection for grenache, and is precisely right (in my view) when he
says, 'McLaren Vale grenache is world class, and it best expresses itself when made in the mould
of pinot noir.' Small wonder, then, that they are moving to 500-litre puncheons, looking
for attractive, aromatic styles with elegance and energy rather than dense dry red character.
Exports to the UK, the US and NZ.

🍷🍷🍷🍷🍷 **Thorny Devil Old Vine Gorgeous Barossa Valley Grenache 2015** The
mid-palate bursts with raspberried sweetness, pure and exuberant. Outriders of
earth, crushed dry spices and licorice add both complexity and breadth. In the end,
it cuts a fine figure. Screwcap. 14.5% alc. **Rating** 93 **To** 2022 $30 CM
The Vagabond Old Vine McLaren Vale Grenache 2014 From Blewitt
Springs. It's light in colour but they've nailed the palate. Licorice and raspberry
with spice woven through, but it's just that little something extra – difficult to
define – that this wine most certainly has. It's pretty and light, but it has substance.
Screwcap. 14.5% alc. **Rating** 93 **To** 2023 $35 CM
The Basket Case Old Vine Barossa Valley Shiraz 2013 Smooth-skinned,
clean, polished and well put together. Whether or not there's a personality
lurking within is for time to decide. It tastes of plum, earth, raspberry and leather,
with integrated clovey/cedary oak evident but in the distance. It's impeccable;
it's correct; it's like a shot on goal from directly in front. Screwcap. 14.5% alc.
Rating 92 **To** 2025 $35 CM
The Vagabond Old Vine McLaren Vale Grenache 2015 Red-berried fruits,
bright and lively, swoosh through the palate, engaging as they go. It's not complex,
but it's effective. Dry spice, florals and swirls of anise take the idea and run with it.
It's not heavy, but it's insistent. Screwcap. 15% alc. **Rating** 92 **To** 2021 $35 CM
Great Escape Adelaide Hills Chardonnay 2015 You want more? This
delivers it. Oak and fruit, laid on. Peach, pear, custardy vanilla, even mint. It's not

subtle or even lengthy, but it gives it to you with both barrels. Screwcap. 13% alc.
Rating 90 **To** 2018 $25 CM

The Cunning Plan Langhorne Creek Shiraz 2015 Robust with blackberry,
gum leaf and vanillan oak flavours. You want richness? This delivers it, bam,
nothing fancy, straight at you. Screwcap. 14.5% alc. **Rating** 90 **To** 2023 $25 CM

The Cunning Plan Langhorne Creek Shiraz 2014 Generous offering with
soft-hearted flavours of plum, mint and caramel oozing through the palate. Will
please many. Screwcap. 14% alc. **Rating** 90 **To** 2021 $25 CM

The Basket Case Old Vine Barossa Valley Shiraz 2014 For starters it's
medium to full-bodied with blackberry, asphalt and brighter red-berried notes.
It's ripe and appealing and it won't leave anyone disappointed, but nor will it get
anyone terribly excited. Screwcap. 14.5% alc. **Rating** 90 **To** 2024 $35 CM

**The Thorny Devil Old Vine Single Vineyard Barossa Valley Grenache
2014** Licorice and raspberry with a touch of spice. This is all about ripe,
mellifluous fruit, the texture satiny and the emphasis on drinkability. Screwcap.
14.5% alc. **Rating** 90 **To** 2022 $30 CM

Thomas Vineyard Estate   ★★★★

PO Box 490, McLaren Vale, SA 5171 **Region** McLaren Vale
T (08) 8557 8583 **www**.thomasvineyard.com.au **Open** Not
Winemaker Trevor Tucker **Est.** 1998 **Dozens** 1000 **Vyds** 5.26ha
Merv and Dawne Thomas thought long and hard before purchasing the property on which
they have established their vineyard. It is 3km from the coast of the Gulf of St Vincent on the
Fleurieu Peninsula, with a clay over limestone soil known locally as 'Bay of Biscay'. They had
a dream start to the business when the 2004 Shiraz won the trophy for Best Single Vineyard
Wine (red or white) at the McLaren Vale Wine Show '05, the Reserve Shiraz also winning a
gold medal. Exports to the US, Hong Kong and Singapore.

♥♥♥♥♀ **McLaren Vale Sparkling Shiraz NV** The back label makes various comments,
none giving any details of the vinification/maturation/age/oak, etc of the wine
– which is pretty good in a full-bodied fashion. Great for bbqs, beach parties, etc.
Diam. 14% alc. **Rating** 90 **To** 2020 $25

Thomas Wines   ★★★★★

28 Mistletoe Lane, Pokolbin, NSW 2320 **Region** Hunter Valley
T (02) 4998 7134 **www**.thomaswines.com.au **Open** 7 days 10–5
Winemaker Andrew Thomas, Scott Comyns **Est.** 1997 **Dozens** 8000 **Vyds** 3ha
Andrew Thomas came to the Hunter Valley from McLaren Vale to join the winemaking team
at Tyrrell's. After 13 years, he left to undertake contract work and to continue the development
of his own label. He makes individual-vineyard wines, underlining the subtle differences
between the various subregions of the Hunter. Plans for the construction of an estate winery
have been abandoned for the time being, and for the foreseeable future he will continue to
lease the James Estate winery on Hermitage Road. Until Dec 2016 the cellar door will be as
shown above, but from then Andrew will have part of the Tuscany Wine Estate complex, on
the corner of Hermitage Road and Mistletoe Lane, as a long-term cellar door. The major part
of the production comes from long-term arrangements with growers of semillon (15ha) and
shiraz (25ha); an additional 3ha of shiraz is leased. The quality of the wines and the reputation
of Andrew Thomas have never been higher; the appointment of Scott Comyns as winemaker
is also a significant step. Exports to the US and Japan.

♥♥♥♥♥ **Kiss Limited Release Hunter Valley Shiraz 2014** Velvet wrapped in silk;
cream splashed on chocolate; fruit polished and presented to perfection. Many
of the best wines seem effortless, and this is one such. It's all cherry-plum and
earth, its tannin both terrifically fine and wonderfully well integrated. Screwcap.
14.2% alc. **Rating** 97 **To** 2040 $75 CM

♥♥♥♥♥ **Braemore Individual Vineyard Hunter Valley Semillon 2015** Is everything
expected of winemaker Andrew Thomas and the Braemore Vineyard. The bouquet

has an extra measure of complexity brought into context by the detail of the flavours on the long, satisfying palate, where lemongrass, lime, lemon and a whisk of vanilla repose on a cushion of perfectly balanced acidity. Screwcap. 10.3% alc. **Rating** 96 **To** 2030 $30 ✪

Cellar Reserve Braemore Individual Vineyard Hunter Valley Semillon 2010 Just entering the perfect drinking zone, but with many years of life and development ahead. This is being released at the optimal time. It tastes of citrus, hay and candied orange but mostly it seems controlled, taut and lengthy. Impressive it certainly is. Screwcap. 11.3% alc. **Rating** 96 **To** 2025 $50 CM ✪

Elenay Barrel Selection Hunter Valley Shiraz 2014 Musk-ridden, sweet and soft, but the finesse of the tannin and the easygoing plushness of the fruit have this playing clearly and cleanly in a high quality arena. Screwcap. 13.8% alc. **Rating** 96 **To** 2040 $45 CM ✪

Murphy's Individual Hunter Valley Semillon 2015 Departs from the usual with extended lees contact to build approachability without compromising longevity. This is purity personified, with a stainless-steel strand of acidity at its core, discreetly covered by lemon, apple and lemongrass fruit flavours. Now or much, much later – you won't be disappointed. Screwcap. 10.7% alc. **Rating** 94 **To** 2030 $24 ✪

Synergy Vineyard Selection Hunter Valley Shiraz 2014 Meaty at first and spicy throughout, but with air it opens wings of cherried, cranberried flavour that are as refreshing as they are scrumptious. Earthen tips to the tannin profile; this isn't at all hard to take. Screwcap. 13.7% alc. **Rating** 94 **To** 2026 $25 CM ✪

♟♟♟♟♟ **Synergy Hunter Valley Semillon 2015 Rating** 93 **To** 2030 $20 ✪
Sweetwater Hunter Valley Shiraz 2014 Rating 93 **To** 2025 $35 CM
Six Degrees Hunter Valley Semillon 2015 Rating 93 **To** 2018 $23 ✪
Two of a Kind Semillon Sauvignon Blanc 2015 Rating 92 **To** 2018 $20 ✪
Deja Vu Hunter Valley Shiraz 2014 Rating 91 **To** 2024 $30 CM

Thompson Estate   ★★★★★

299 Tom Cullity Drive, Wilyabrup, WA 6284 **Region** Margaret River
T (08) 9755 6406 **www.**thompsonestate.com **Open** 7 days 11–5
Winemaker Bob Cartwright, Paul Dixon **Est.** 1994 **Dozens** 10000 **Vyds** 28.63ha
Cardiologist Peter Thompson planted the first vines at Thompson Estate in 1997, inspired by his and his family's shareholdings in the Pierro and Fire Gully vineyards, and by visits to many of the world's premium wine regions. The vineyard is planted to cabernet sauvignon, cabernet franc, merlot, chardonnay, sauvignon blanc, semillon, pinot noir and malbec. Thompson Estate wines are made by Bob Cartwright (former Leeuwin Estate winemaker) at its state-of-the-art winery. Exports to Canada, Singapore, Hong Kong and China.

♟♟♟♟♟ **Margaret River Chardonnay 2014** An exemplary Margaret River chardonnay; white peach and grapefruit are the clay, citrussy acidity and integrated oak the mould forming the shape of a wine that has both depth and length. Screwcap. 13.5% alc. **Rating** 95 **To** 2023 $50

Margaret River Cabernet Merlot 2013 62% cabernet sauvignon, 27% merlot, 6% malbec, 5% cabernet franc, matured in used French oak for 18 months. Very good structure and texture underlying the complex interplay of cassis/blackcurrant, redcurrant and earthy/forest fruits. The decision to only employ used French oak is the key to its succes. Screwcap. 14% alc. **Rating** 95 **To** 2033 $35 ✪

Margaret River Cabernet Sauvignon 2013 85% cabernet sauvignon, 5% each of malbec, cabernet franc and merlot. Good hue; this is pure cassis, not blackcurrant per se. This fruit is given another dimension by its oak and silky tannins. Screwcap. 14% alc. **Rating** 95 **To** 2033 $50

Andrea 2013 64% cabernet sauvignon, 16% merlot, 10% each malbec and cabernet franc. There is a broad spectrum of fruit flavours here, plum, spice, redcurrant and bay leaf joining cassis. Controlled alcohol is a plus. Screwcap. 14% alc. **Rating** 94 **To** 2030 $50

ŶŶŶŶŶ SSB Semillon Sauvignon Blanc 2015 Rating 92 To 2021 $35
Four Chambers Shiraz 2014 Rating 91 To 2024 $20 ✪

Thorn-Clarke Wines ★★★★★

Milton Park, 266 Gawler Park Road, Angaston, SA 5353 **Region** Barossa Valley
T (08) 8564 3036 **www.**thornclarkewines.com.au **Open** Mon–Fri 9–5, w'ends 11–4
Winemaker Susan Mickan **Est.** 1987 **Dozens** 80000 **Vyds** 268ha
Established by David and Cheryl Clarke (née Thorn), and son Sam, Thorn-Clarke is one of
the largest family-owned estate-based businesses in the Barossa. Their winery is close to the
border between the Barossa and Eden valleys, and three of their four vineyards are in the Eden
Valley: the Mt Crawford Vineyard is at the southern end of the Eden Valley, while the Milton
Park and Sandpiper vineyards are further north in the Eden Valley. The fourth vineyard is at
St Kitts, at the northern end of the Barossa Ranges. In all four vineyards careful soil mapping
has resulted in matching of variety and site, with all the major varieties represented. The
quality of grapes retained for the Thorn-Clarke label has resulted in a succession of trophy and
gold medal-winning wines at very competitive prices. Exports to all major markets.

ŶŶŶŶŶ Eden Trail Riesling 2015 The impact is obvious. This is a stunning riesling. Pure,
bright, quartz-like, penetrating. Lime, spice and bath salts. Mouthwatering, to say
the least. Screwcap. 11% alc. Rating 96 To 2030 $24 CM ✪
Sandpiper Barossa Cabernet Sauvignon 2014 An elegant cabernet. The
touch of dark chocolate comes as a surprise, but the blackcurrant fruit and
fine-grained, cedary tannins do not. Great value. Screwcap. 14% alc. Rating 95
To 2025 $19 ✪

ŶŶŶŶŶ Terra Barossa Shiraz 2014 Rating 93 To 2025 $19 ✪
Eden Trail Shiraz 2014 Rating 93 To 2024 $28 CM
Barossa Valley Malbec 2012 Rating 93 To 2027 $30
Sandpiper Barossa Shiraz 2014 Rating 92 To 2022 $19 CM ✪
Shotfire Barossa Cabernet Sauvignon Shiraz 2013 Rating 90 To 2030 $25

Three Dark Horses ★★★★☆

49 Fraser Avenue, Happy Valley, SA 5159 **Region** McLaren Vale
T 0405 294 500 **www.**3dh.com.au **Open** Not
Winemaker Matt Broomhead **Est.** 2009 **Dozens** 1500
Three Dark Horses is the new project for former Coriole winemaker Matt Broomhead. After
vintages in southern Italy and the Rhône Valley he returned to McLaren Vale in 2009 and,
with his father Alan, buys quality grapes, thanks to the long experience they both have in
the region. The third dark horse is Matt's 92-year-old grandfather, a vintage regular. Exports
to China.

ŶŶŶŶŶ McLaren Vale Shiraz 2014 A brilliant wine at the price. Bold, luscious, ripped
with (red and black) fruit and tannin, and then strikingly long-flavoured. The
back label says 'Never underestimate a dark horse'; rarely is marketing text so apt.
Screwcap. 14.5% alc. Rating 95 To 2035 $24 CM ✪
McLaren Vale Grenache 2014 Delicious, lively, spicy and fresh red cherry,
strawberry and raspberry fruit make this a compulsory drink-immediately-
and-copiously wine. With utmost responsibility, of course. Screwcap. 14.5% alc.
Rating 94 To 2020 $25 ✪

ŶŶŶŶŶ McLaren Vale Mataro 2014 Rating 93 To 2024 $25 ✪
McLaren Vale Shiraz Grenache Touriga 2014 Rating 92 To 2018 $20 ✪
GT McLaren Vale Grenache Touriga 2015 Rating 91 To 2020 $25 CM
Langhorne Creek Touriga 2015 Rating 91 To 2025 $25
McLaren Vale Grenache Mataro Rose 2015 Rating 90 To 2016 $25 CM

3 Drops ★★★★★

PO Box 1828, Applecross, WA 6953 **Region** Mount Barker
T (08) 9315 4721 **www**.3drops.com **Open** Not
Winemaker Robert Diletti (Contract) **Est.** 1998 **Dozens** 5000 **Vyds** 21.5ha

The three drops are not the three founders (John Bradbury, Joanne Bradbury and, formerly, Nicola Wallich), but wine, olive oil and water, all of which come from the substantial property at Mount Barker. The plantings are riesling, sauvignon blanc, semillon, chardonnay, cabernet sauvignon, merlot, shiraz and cabernet franc, irrigated by a large wetland on the property. 3 Drops also owns the 14.7ha Patterson's Vineyard. Exports to Canada, Singapore, Hong Kong and China.

🍷🍷🍷🍷🍷 **Great Southern Cabernets 2014** 60% cabernet sauvignon, 40% cabernet franc, fermented in 2-tonne open vats with 14 days on skins, matured in French barriques (25% new) for 14 months. Bright crimson-purple; it's pretty clear cabernet sauvignon leads the way. A very good wine that punches far above its price weight, it has a heady dark-fruit fragrance, and a medium-bodied palate that toys with the idea of autocracy, but doesn't go that far, and delivers in spaces on the long finish. Screwcap. 14% alc. **Rating** 97 **To** 2039 $25 ✪

🍷🍷🍷🍷🍷 **Great Southern Riesling 2015** Crushed and destemmed, entirely free-run juice from the press, cold-settled with a clear juice fermentation and early bottling, residual sugar below threshold. Impressive depth to the citrus fruit already on the march, the length even better, with an emphatic finish due to crunchy acidity. Seriously good wine. Screwcap. 12.5% alc. **Rating** 95 **To** 2025 $24 ✪

Great Southern Chardonnay 2014 The elegance of this wine has not been achieved at the expense of complexity; the fresh, grapefruit-accented varietal fruit has subtexts of cashew and a certain savoury spice, the bow tied by citrussy acidity; all up, excellent length. Screwcap. 13% alc. **Rating** 94 **To** 2024 $26 ✪

🍷🍷🍷🍷♀ **Great Southern Sauvignon Blanc 2015** **Rating** 93 **To** 2016 $22 ✪
Great Southern Shiraz 2013 **Rating** 93 **To** 2024 $26 ✪
Mount Barker Merlot 2014 **Rating** 92 **To** 2024 $26
Great Southern Pinot Noir 2014 **Rating** 90 **To** 2026 $28

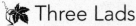 Three Lads ★★★★

46 Rylstone Crescent, Grace, ACT 2911 **Region** Canberra District
T 0408 233 481 **www**.threelads.com.au **Open** Not
Winemaker Bill Crowe, Aaron Harper, Luke McGaghey **Est.** 2013 **Dozens** 500

The three lads are Luke McGaghey, Aaron Harper and Bill Crowe, who fortuitously met at a local food and wine event in 2012, and decided they should have some fun. Their business plan was simplicity itself: buy small amounts of grapes from vineyards in the Canberra District and turn them into wine. Bill Crowe had spent 10 years working at Scott Harvey Wines in Napa Valley and came to Australia to join his wife Jaime Crowe at Four Winds Vineyard, where he (Bill) is winemaker (his real job).

🍷🍷🍷🍷🍷 **Canberra District Shiraz 2013** Fragrant and juicy berry fruits on the bouquet and medium-bodied palate share distinct notes of spice and pepper that lift and lengthen the finish and aftertaste. The DIY label doesn't do justice to the wine. Screwcap. 13.8% alc. **Rating** 94 **To** 2028 $25 ✪

🍷🍷🍷🍷♀ **Canberra District Shiraz 2014** **Rating** 91 **To** 2029 $25
Canberra District Riesling 2015 **Rating** 90 **To** 2025 $22
Gundagai Rose 2015 **Rating** 90 **To** 2017 $20 ✪

3 Oceans Wine Company ★★★★

Cnr Boundary Road/Bussell Highway, Cowaramup, WA 6284 **Region** Margaret River
T (08) 9756 5656 **www**.3oceans.com.au **Open** 7 days 10–5
Winemaker Ben Roodhouse, Jonathan Mettam **Est.** 1999 **Dozens** 160 000

After a period of spectacular growth and marketing activity, Palandri went into voluntary administration in February 2008. In June of that year the Ma family, through their 3 Oceans Wine Company Pty Ltd, acquired the Margaret River winery, the 30-year-old Margaret River vineyard and 347ha of Frankland River vineyards. In October '08 it also acquired the Palandri and Baldivis Estate brands. There is a strong focus on the emerging markets of the Asia Pacific region, but no neglecting of the domestic market. Given the size of production, the quality of the wines is impressive. Exports to the UK and other major markets.

🍷🍷🍷🍷🍷 **The Explorers Margaret River Frankland River Sauvignon Blanc Semillon 2012** 60/40%, hand-picked, wild-fermented in new French oak, matured for 5 months. The smoky, slightly funky, complex bouquet promises much, and the palate over-delivers; it has tremendous drive and intensity, with some white Bordeaux characters. You would never guess it was 4yo – 12 months would be more like it. Striking wine. Screwcap. 12% alc. **Rating** 94 **To** 2019 $35

🍷🍷🍷🍷🍷 **The Rivers Frankland River Rose 2015** Rating 93 To 2017 $15 ✪
The Estates Sauvignon Blanc Semillon 2015 Rating 92 To 2017 $20 ✪
The Estates Frankland River Margaret River Cabernet Sauvignon Merlot 2013 Rating 91 To 2025 $20 ✪
The Rivers White Classic Frankland River Margaret River Sauvignon Blanc Semillon 2015 Rating 90 To 2017 $15 ✪

Tidswell Wines   ★★★★

14 Sydenham Road, Norwood, SA 5067 **Region** Limestone Coast Zone
T (08) 8363 5800 **www**.tidswellwines.com.au **Open** By appt
Winemaker Ben Tidswell, Wine Wise **Est.** 1994 **Dozens** 3000 **Vyds** 136.4ha
The Tidswell family (now in the shape of Andrea and Ben Tidswell) has two large vineyards in the Limestone Coast Zone near Bool Lagoon; the lion's share is planted to cabernet sauvignon and shiraz, with smaller plantings of merlot, sauvignon blanc, petit verdot, vermentino and pinot gris. Tidswell is a fully certified member of WFA's environmental sustainability program. Wines are released under the Jennifer, Heathfield Ridge and The Publicans labels. Exports to Canada, Denmark, Germany, Singapore, Japan and China.

🍷🍷🍷🍷🍷 **Jennifer Limited Release Cabernet Sauvignon 2013** Open-fermented, 7 days on skins, matured for 2 years in French hogsheads (70% new). This introduces an additional level of tannins ex oak, and there may well have been some fruit selection. It needs at least 5 years to settle down, and even then won't be at its peak. Cork. 14.5% alc. **Rating** 94 **To** 2033 $65
Jennifer Limited Release Cabernet Sauvignon 2010 Strange business: the new label of this re-release has dropped its reference to American oak, and now only lists French, and has replaced its three bronze medals with replaced by a Decanter '13 gold, and trophy for Best Regional Wine, even though the Limestone Coast Zone is the only region shown. The constant is the luscious cassis fruit, still going strong. Cork. 14.5% alc. **Rating** 94 **To** 2025 $65

🍷🍷🍷🍷🍷 **Heathfield Cabernet Sauvignon 2013** Rating 91 To 2023 $28

Tilbrook Estate   ★★★★☆

17/1 Adelaide Lobethal Road, Lobethal, SA 5241 **Region** Adelaide Hills
T (08) 8389 5318 **www**.tilbrookestate.com.au **Open** Fri–Sun & public hols 11–5
Winemaker James Tilbrook **Est.** 1999 **Dozens** 1500 **Vyds** 3.97ha
James and Annabelle Tilbrook have almost 5ha of multi-clone chardonnay and pinot noir, plus sauvignon blanc and pinot gris, at Lenswood. The winery and cellar door are in the old Onkaparinga Woollen Mills building in Lobethal; this not only provides an atmospheric home, but also helps meet the very strict environmental requirements of the Adelaide Hills in dealing with winery waste water. English-born James came to Australia in 1986, aged 22, but a car accident led to his return to England. Working for Oddbins and passing the WSET diploma set his future course. He returned to Australia, met Annabelle, purchased the vineyard and began planting it in '99. Exports to the UK and Singapore.

ŸŸŸŸŸ **Adelaide Hills Chardonnay 2014** Hand-picked, whole bunch-pressed, wild-fermented in French oak (25% new), 12 months maturation. Has excellent focus, drive and length; same estate vineyard source as the Reserve, and I prefer the greater restraint of this wine; the acidity is still part of the picture, but only part. Screwcap. 13.5% alc. **Rating** 95 **To** 2022 $30 ●
Reserve Lenswood Estate Adelaide Hills Chardonnay 2014 Slightly unsettling colour development, deeper than its varietal sibling; the acidity is at the upper end of toleration, even for an acid-tolerant palate such as mine. Difficult to point. Screwcap. 13.5% alc. **Rating** 94 **To** 2020 $45

ŸŸŸŸŸ **Reserve Adelaide Hills Botrytis Riesling 2013 Rating** 93 **To** 2023 $25 ●

Tim Adams   ★★★★☆

Warenda Road, Clare, SA 5453 **Region** Clare Valley
T (08) 8842 2429 **www**.timadamswines.com.au **Open** Mon–Fri 10.30–5, w'ends 11–5
Winemaker Tim Adams, Brett Schutz **Est.** 1986 **Dozens** 60000 **Vyds** 145ha
Tim Adams and partner Pam Goldsack preside over a highly successful business. Having expanded the range of estate plantings with tempranillo, pinot gris and viognier, in 2009 the business took a giant step forward with the acquisition of the 80ha Leasingham Rogers Vineyard from CWA for a reported price of $850000, followed in '11 by the purchase of the Leasingham winery and winemaking equipment (for less than replacement cost). The winery is now a major contract winemaking facility for the region. Exports to the UK, The Netherlands, Sweden, Russia, Hong Kong, China and NZ.

ŸŸŸŸŸ **Reserve Clare Valley Riesling 2010** Still in its primary phase, fresh and vibrant, still pale in colour; that said, it has intensity and prodigious length. There can be no question about its future, with some honey just peeping around the corner, toast still far away. Irresistible, especially at this price. Screwcap. 11% alc. **Rating** 96 **To** 2030 $29 ●
Clare Valley Cabernet Malbec 2012 Excellent release. Not particularly deep, but aflame with personality, regionality and life. It's dusty, curranty, shows elements of gun smoke and gum leaf, and swings decisively through the finish. Don't hesitate. Screwcap. 14.5% alc. **Rating** 94 **To** 2030 $24 CM ●

ŸŸŸŸŸ **Clare Valley Riesling 2015 Rating** 93 **To** 2025 $20 ●
Clare Valley Semillon 2012 Rating 93 **To** 2022 $22 CM ●
Clare Valley Pinot Gris 2015 Rating 93 **To** 2016 $22 CM ●
Aberfeldy Shiraz 2012 Rating 93 **To** 2030 $65 CM
The Fergus 2013 Rating 93 **To** 2021 $24 CM ●

Tim Gramp   ★★★★

Mintaro/Leasingham Road, Watervale, SA 5452 **Region** Clare Valley
T (08) 8344 4079 **www**.timgrampwines.com.au **Open** W'ends 12–4
Winemaker Tim Gramp **Est.** 1990 **Dozens** 6000 **Vyds** 16ha
Tim Gramp has quietly built up a very successful business, and by keeping overheads to a minimum provides good wines at modest prices. Over the years the estate vineyards (shiraz, riesling, cabernet sauvignon and grenache) have been expanded significantly. Exports to Malaysia, Taiwan and China.

ŸŸŸŸŸ **Basket Pressed Watervale Grenache 2014** The fruit rushes in faster than a fool. Light colour, but raspberry and spice notes flood through the palate, chipper and chirpy. Firmish tannin makes sure things don't get too far out of control. You'd have to say this wine achieves everything it set out to. Screwcap. 15% alc. **Rating** 91 **To** 2019 $22 CM ●
Watervale Riesling 2015 A slightly closed bouquet breaks free of its bonds on the positive lime/lemon/grapefruit flavours of the palate. Given the vintage, one might have expected the acidity to be a little brighter, but it underlines its early-drinking style. Screwcap. 12.5% alc. **Rating** 90 **To** 2020 $21 ●

ŸŸŸŸ **Basket Pressed Watervale Tempranillo 2014 Rating** 89 **To** 2024 $21

Tim McNeil Wines   ★★★★☆

71 Springvale Road, Watervale, SA 5452 **Region** Clare Valley
T (08) 8843 0040 **www.**timmcneilwines.com.au **Open** Fri–Sun & public hols 11–5
Winemaker Tim McNeil **Est.** 2004 **Dozens** 1500 **Vyds** 2ha
When Tim and Cass McNeil established Tim McNeil Wines, Tim had long since given up his
teaching career, graduating with a degree in oenology from Adelaide University in 1999. He
then spent 11 years honing his craft at important wineries in the Barossa and Clare valleys.
In Aug 2010 Tim McNeil Wines became his full-time job. The McNeils' 16ha property at
Watervale includes mature dry-grown riesling. The cellar door overlooks the riesling vineyard,
with panoramic views of Watervale and beyond. Exports to Canada.

ΨΨΨΨΨ **Reserve Watervale Riesling 2015** This takes up where its sibling left off. The
citrus blossom of the bouquet is not happy if left in the glass, demanding to have
its say – which it does – but it's the palate where this wine clears out. The supple
citrus fruits tinkle on the piano keys as lemon, lime and grapefruit paint your
mouth with an almost glossy feel. Definitiely a two or (if you're lucky) three-glass
wine (with thanks to Michelin). Screwcap. 12.5% alc. **Rating** 95 **To** 2030 $32 ✪
Watervale Riesling 2015 Small wonder many Clare/Eden/Barossa winemakers
have been waxing lyrical about the '15 vintage, for this has the Watervale district
in the crosshairs of its rifle sight. The flavour hits straight up, and builds quickly
as the wine is tasted and retasted, acidity moving to the beat of the same drum.
Screwcap. 12.5% alc. **Rating** 94 **To** 2025 $23 ✪

ΨΨΨΨΨ **On the Wing Clare Valley Shiraz 2013 Rating** 91 **To** 2028 $22 ✪
Clare Valley Shiraz 2013 Rating 90 **To** 2030 $34

Tim Smith Wines   ★★★★★

PO Box 446, Tanunda, SA 5352 **Region** Barossa Valley
T 0416 396 730 **www.**timsmithwines.com.au **Open** Not
Winemaker Tim Smith **Est.** 2002 **Dozens** 5000 **Vyds** 1ha
With a talent for sourcing exceptional old-vine fruit from the Barossa floor, Tim Smith
has created a small but credible portfolio of wines, currently including Mataro, Grenache,
Shiraz, Viognier, and more recently Eden Valley Riesling and Viognier. Tim left his full-time
winemaking role with a large Barossa company in 2011, allowing him to concentrate 100%
of his energy on his own brand. In '12 Tim joined forces with the team from First Drop (see
separate entry), and has moved winemaking operations to a brand-new winery fondly named
'Home of the Brave', in Nuriootpa. Exports to the UK, the US, Canada, Denmark, Taiwan
and Singapore.

ΨΨΨΨΨ **Barossa Shiraz 2014** This is a beauty. Packed to the rafters with dark-berried
fruit yet both bright and savoury as a bonus. Tannin takes careful control as the
wine moves through the palate. Perfumed oak plays a role, and an important one,
but almost without you even knowing it. From the first sip you know you're onto
a good one here. Screwcap. 14% alc. **Rating** 96 **To** 2032 $38 CM ✪
Eden Valley Riesling 2015 Excellent intensity. Clearly a quality release. Citrus,
talc, the rind of lime. Bursts out of the blocks but keeps plenty of thrust for the
finish. Screwcap. 12% alc. **Rating** 95 **To** 2028 $25 CM ✪
Barossa Valley Grenache 2014 Has exemplary varietal character, but with
ululating red fruits of every shape and size, the tannins no more than a silken
web. Slips down the throat so easily most will disappear early in its life. Screwcap.
14.5% alc. **Rating** 95 **To** 2024 $38

ΨΨΨΨΨ **Barossa Mataro Grenache Shiraz 2014 Rating** 93 **To** 2023 $28 CM
Bugalugs Barossa Valley Shiraz 2014 Rating 92 **To** 2022 $20 CM ✪
Bugalugs Barossa Grenache 2014 Rating 91 **To** 2021 $20 CM ✪
Barossa Mataro 2014 Rating 91 **To** 2022 $38 CM
Eden Valley Viognier 2015 Rating 90 **To** 2016 $28 CM

Tinklers Vineyard ★★★★★

Pokolbin Mountains Road, Pokolbin, NSW 2320 **Region** Hunter Valley
T (02) 4998 7435 **www**.tinklers.com.au **Open** 7 days 10–5
Winemaker Usher Tinkler **Est.** 1946 **Dozens** 5000 **Vyds** 41ha
Three generations of the Tinkler family have been involved with the property since 1942.
Originally a beef and dairy farm, vines have been both pulled out and replanted at various
stages, and part of the adjoining 80-year-old Ben Ean Vineyard has been acquired. Plantings
include semillon (14ha), shiraz (11.5ha), chardonnay (6.5ha) and smaller areas of merlot, muscat
and viognier. The majority of the grape production continues to be sold to McWilliam's and
Tyrrell's. Usher has resigned his roles as chief winemaker at Poole's Rock and Cockfighter's
Ghost to take on full-time responsibility at Tinklers, and production has been increased to
meet demand. Exports to Sweden, Singapore and China.

🍷🍷🍷🍷🍷 **Reserve Hunter Valley Semillon 2015** Hand-picked, whole bunch-pressed.
One of those young Hunter semillons that are already complete in their youth,
their future path written in stone. Citrus, lemongrass and apple flavours are
wreathed by acidity, investing the wine with excellent length and balance.
Screwcap. 10.9% alc. **Rating** 95 **To** 2035 $35 ✪
Old Vines Hunter Valley Shiraz 2014 Bright, clear colour; a delicious
medium-bodied wine, red fruits dominant, backed by fine tannins on a graceful
palate. Has length that might escape the casual observer, as may its likely longevity.
Despite this, the wine is already good to go, its modest alcohol a key. Screwcap.
13.5% alc. **Rating** 95 **To** 2025 $35 ✪
U and I Hunter Valley Shiraz 2014 Slightly deeper colour than its Old Vines
sibling; predominantly black fruits led by blackberry and plum, with cedary French
oak making a major contribution, as do ripe tannins. The balance is excellent; this
is made for long-term cellaring. A testament to the vintage. Screwcap. 14.5% alc.
Rating 95 **To** 2044 $45
School Block Hunter Valley Semillon 2015 From Tinkler's oldest vineyard
on sandy gravel soils. Very good drive and length, the flavours of lemongrass and
citrus zest, lively acidity the king of the castle. Onwards and upwards from here.
Screwcap. 10.8% alc. **Rating** 94 **To** 2035 $22 ✪

🍷🍷🍷🍷🍷 **School Block Hunter Valley Semillon 2014** **Rating** 93 **To** 2034 $22 ✪
Poppys Hunter Valley Chardonnay 2015 **Rating** 92 **To** 2023 $25 ✪
Lucerne Paddock Verdelho 2015 **Rating** 90 **To** 2016 $18 ✪

Tintilla Wines ★★★★★

725 Hermitage Road, Pokolbin, NSW 2320 **Region** Hunter Valley
T (02) 6574 7093 **www**.tintilla.com.au **Open** 7 days 10.30–6
Winemaker James and Robert Lusby **Est.** 1993 **Dozens** 4000 **Vyds** 6.52ha
The Lusby family has established shiraz (2.2ha), sangiovese (1.6ha), merlot (1.3ha), semillon
(1.2ha) and cabernet sauvignon (0.2ha) on a northeast-facing slope with red clay and
limestone soil. Tintilla was the first winery to plant sangiovese in the Hunter Valley (in 1995).
The family has also planted an olive grove producing four different types of olives, which are
cured and sold from the estate.

🍷🍷🍷🍷🍷 **Angus Hunter Semillon 2014** It gets the flavour, the feel and the finish right.
This lights up the glass with racy flavour but it smoothes and caresses as it flows.
Grass-light notes add speckle to the flavour. It's all quite delicious, it has to be said.
Screwcap. 11.9% alc. **Rating** 94 **To** 2024 $30 CM ✪
Museum Release Angus Hunter Semillon 2009 Ageing gracefully. Still with
a tinge of green. A combination of primary and secondary characters build steadily
through the palate before flowing faithfully out through the extended finish. At its
peak now. Screwcap. 10.5% alc. **Rating** 94 **To** 2018 $40 CM
Pebbles Brief Hunter Valley Chardonnay 2014 Full-flavoured and yet
lengthy. Cream, toast and cedar spice characters work to enhance the performance

of peachy, citrussy fruit. It's a mouthful of flavour with more than a touch of irresistibility about it. Screwcap. 13% alc. **Rating** 94 To 2020 $30 CM **O**

ΨΨΨΨΩ **Reserve Hunter Valley Shiraz 2013** Rating 92 To 2026 $30 CM
Patriarch Hunter Valley Syrah 2014 Rating 91 To 2026 $60 CM

Tipperary Estate   ★★★☆

167 Tipperary Road, Moffatdale via Murgon, Qld 4605 **Region** South Burnett
T (07) 4168 4802 **www**.tipperaryestate.com.au **Open** Fri 12–3, w'ends & public hols 10–4
Winemaker Clovely Estate (Sarah Boyce) **Est.** 2002 **Dozens** 400 **Vyds** 2ha
The Tipperary Estate vineyard, planted to shiraz (1ha), verdelho and viognier (0.5ha each), has been established high on the northern slopes overlooking the Barambah Valley. Additional grapes are purchased from other growers in the South Burnett region.

ΨΨΨΨΩ **South Burnett Shiraz Viognier 2014** Maturation in new and 1yo French oak is well matched with this light to medium-bodied wine, its fragrant bouquet likewise lifted by the viognier. Sophisticated stuff from the often forgotten South Burnett region. Screwcap. 14% alc. **Rating** 90 To 2024 $25

ΨΨΨΨ **South Burnett Tempranillo 2015** Rating 89 To 2025 $20

Tobin Wines   ★★★★

34 Ricca Road, Ballandean, Qld 4382 **Region** Granite Belt
T (07) 4684 1235 **www**.tobinwines.com.au **Open** 7 days 10–5
Winemaker Adrian Tobin **Est.** 1964 **Dozens** 1500 **Vyds** 5.9ha
In the early 1960s the Rica family planted table grapes, followed by shiraz and semillon in '64–66: these are said to be the oldest vinifera vines in the Granite Belt region. The Tobin family (headed by Adrian and Frances) purchased the vineyard in 2000 and has increased the plantings, which now consist of shiraz, cabernet sauvignon, merlot, tempranillo, semillon, verdelho, chardonnay, muscat and sauvignon blanc, with some remaining rows of table grapes.

ΨΨΨΨΩ **Max Shiraz Block Two 2014** A wine that serves up very complex flavours largely hidden by the extract and tannins. It has excellent colour, and if paired with a man-sized T-bone, the black pepper, licorice and blackberry fruit might knock your socks off. Screwcap. 14.7% alc. **Rating** 92 To 2039 $45

ΨΨΨΨ **Elliot Merlot 2014** Rating 88 To 2018 $45

Tokar Estate   ★★★★★

6 Maddens Lane, Coldstream, Vic 3770 **Region** Yarra Valley
T (03) 5964 9585 **www**.tokarestate.com.au **Open** 7 days 10.30–5
Winemaker Martin Siebert **Est.** 1996 **Dozens** 4000 **Vyds** 12ha
Leon Tokar established 12ha of now mature chardonnay, pinot noir, shiraz, cabernet sauvignon and tempranillo at Tokar Estate, one of many vineyards on Maddens Lane. All the wines have performed well in regional shows, with early success (and continued) for the Tempranillo, and very distinguished Cabernet Sauvignon.

ΨΨΨΨΨ **Yarra Valley Cabernet Sauvignon 2014** Estate-grown, small batches, wild yeast fermentation, extended post-ferment maceration, matured in French oak (40% new). Deep purple-crimson; a classic cabernet with cassis, dried herb and bay leaf, the oak well integrated and the tannins firm, but fine. Gold medal Melbourne Wine Awards '15. Screwcap. 14.5% alc. **Rating** 96 To 2039 $40 **O**
Yarra Valley Tempranillo 2014 Good hue; one of the first movers with the variety in the Yarra Valley, and the wine shows the advantages of some vine maturity; full and fleshy in the mouth, it has excellent length and structure to its black cherry and plum fruit. Screwcap. 14.6% alc. **Rating** 95 To 2029 $35 **O**
Yarra Valley Pinot Noir 2014 Three trophies at the Yarra Valley Wine Show, including Best Red Wine of Show. Is all about flavour and texture

complexity; it has dealt with the challenges of an ultra low-yielding vintage, with a strongly foresty/whole bunch base for the dark cherry fruits. It isn't entirely clear where this will head in the long term, but it will benefit in the short to medium term from more time in bottle. Screwcap. 13.2% alc. **Rating** 94 **To** 2025 $40

🍷🍷🍷🍷🍷 **Yarra Valley Chardonnay 2014** Rating 92 To 2020 $35
Yarra Valley Rose 2015 Rating 90 To 2017 $25

Tolpuddle Vineyard ★★★★★

37 Back Tea Tree Road, Richmond, Tas 7025 **Region** Southern Tasmania
T (08) 8398 0500 **www**.tolpuddlevineyard.com **Open** At Shaw + Smith
Winemaker Martin Shaw, Adam Wadewitz **Est.** 1988 **Dozens** 1800 **Vyds** 20ha
If ever a winery was born with blue blood in its veins, Tolpuddle would have to be it. The vineyard was established in 1988 on a continuous downhill slope facing northeast, and in '06 won the inaugural Tasmanian Vineyard of the Year Award. Michael Hill Smith MW and Martin Shaw are joint managing directors, with Matthew Hill Smith the third shareholder. David LeMire looks after sales and marketing; Adam Wadewitz, one of Australia's brightest winemaking talents, is senior winemaker; and Ray Guerin, one of Australia's most experienced viticulturists, with specialist expertise in cool climate vineyards, is group viticulturist. Vineyard manager Carlos Souris loses nothing in comparison, with over 30 years of grapegrowing in Tasmania under his belt, and an absolutely fearless approach to making a great vineyard even greater. Exports to the US, the UK, Canada, Denmark, China, Japan and Singapore.

🍷🍷🍷🍷🍷 **Chardonnay 2014** Truly beautiful. It flows effortlessly but then feels tight and reserved. It's going to be a humdinger once it's had time to flesh out and grow properly into its skin. White peach, lemon, flint and grilled nuts. It's all there, contained, elegant, harmonious. Grapefruit to the finish. Ever so stylish. Screwcap. 13% alc. **Rating** 97 **To** 2025 $65 CM ◯
Chardonnay 2013 The most remarkable part of this wine is its combination of finesse, length and intensity of varietal fruit flavour, in turn based on the laser etching of Tasmanian acidity. The drink-to date may prove conservative. Screwcap. 12.5% alc. **Rating** 97 **To** 2025 $65 ◯
Pinot Noir 2014 Excellent colour; the bouquet is highly expressive and fragrant, with red fruits wrapped in notes of spice and forest that will continue to increase as the wine develops; the palate is similarly poised between primary fruit flavours and savoury secondary characters. Its greatest assets are its balance and, above all, length. Screwcap. 12.5% alc. **Rating** 97 **To** 2029 $75 ◯

Tomboy Hill ★★★★★

204 Sim Street, Ballarat, Vic 3350 (postal) **Region** Ballarat
T (03) 5331 3785 **Open** Not
Winemaker Scott Ireland (Contract) **Est.** 1984 **Dozens** 600 **Vyds** 3.6ha
Former schoolteacher Ian Watson seems to be following the same path as Lindsay McCall of Paringa Estate (also a former schoolteacher) in extracting greater quality and style than any other winemaker in his region. Since 1984 Ian has patiently built up a patchwork quilt of small plantings of chardonnay and pinot noir. In the better years, single vineyard Chardonnay and/ or Pinot Noir are released; Rebellion Chardonnay and Pinot Noir are multi-vineyard blends, but all 100% Ballarat. After difficult vintages in '11 and '12, Tomboy Hill returned in top form with the '13 wines, and Ian is equally happy with his '14s.

🍷🍷🍷🍷🍷 **Rebellion Ballarat Chardonnay 2014** Hand-picked, matured in new and used French barriques. Ballarat strikes again; it really does invest this wine with a rapier thrust of intensity akin to Premier Cru (and some Grand Cru) Chablis. This is a seriously good chardonnay. Screwcap. 13% alc. **Rating** 95 **To** 2026 $35 ◯
William's Picking Ballarat Chardonnay 2013 The similarity of the fruit intensity to that of the '14 Rebellion Chardonnay is uncanny. It has profound depth, built around a deep well of very special acidity – which gives the fruit

free rein to express itself, as it does here, grapefruit to the fore, framed by oak. Screwcap. 12.6% alc. **Rating** 95 **To** 2025 $50

ɣɣɣɣɣ Rebellion Ballarat Pinot Noir 2014 Rating 93 To 2024 $35
The Tomboy Ballarat Pinot Noir 2014 Rating 93 To 2022 $75

Tomfoolery   ★★★★☆
517 Stockwell Road, Light Pass, SA 5355 **Region** Barossa
T 0447 947 782 **www**.tomfoolerywines.com.au **Open** By appt
Winemaker Ben Chipman **Est.** 2004 **Dozens** 5500 **Vyds** 6.5ha
This business has significantly evolved since 2004 when Ben Chipman crushed half a tonne of shiraz – tomfoolery. In '06 he met wife-to-be Sarah while they were working together at Rockford Wines. In '11 they purchased the homestead and vineyard on the eastern slopes of the Barossa; in '14 they built the winery. Ben had commenced working full-time with Sarah in '13 in a business which is deadly serious. Exports to the UK.

ɣɣɣɣɣ Burla Negra Barossa Tempranillo 2014 The ooze of licoricey flavour pouring through the palate, splashed with dark chocolate, might lead you to think this is a one-trick pony. But the reach of tannin and the overall balance suggest it's anything but. Screwcap. 13.9% alc. **Rating** 94 **To** 2025 $25 CM ❂

ɣɣɣɣɣ Black & Blue Barossa Shiraz 2014 Rating 93 To 2028 $40 CM
Young Blood Grenache 2015 Rating 91 To 2018 $23 CM ❂
Son of a Gun Cabernet Shiraz 2014 Rating 91 To 2024 $25 CM
Skullduggery Barossa Mataro Shiraz 2014 Rating 90 To 2023 $30 CM

Tomich Wines   ★★★★★
87 King William Road, Unley, SA 5061 **Region** Adelaide Hills
T (08) 8299 7500 **www**.tomichhill.com.au **Open** Wed–Sat 12–5
Winemaker Randall Tomich, Ben Riggs **Est.** 2002 **Dozens** 30 000 **Vyds** 180ha
Patriarch John Tomich was born on a vineyard near Mildura, where he learnt firsthand the skills and knowledge required for premium grapegrowing. He went on to become a well-known Adelaide ear, nose and throat specialist. Taking the wheel full circle, he completed postgraduate studies in winemaking at the University of Adelaide in 2002, and embarked on the Master of Wine revision course from the Institute of Masters of Wine. His son Randal is a cutting from the old vine (metaphorically speaking), having invented new equipment and techniques for tending the family's vineyard in the Adelaide Hills, resulting in a 60% saving in time and fuel costs. Exports to the US, Singapore and China.

ɣɣɣɣɣ Woodside Vineyard Q96 Chardonnay 2014 Made from the distinguished Dijon clone 96, hand-picked, 30% wild-fermented, matured in French oak (60% new). Another ravishing chardonnay made from this clone; all the right decisions were made during vinification, not easy given the tiny berries and bunches of the vintage. Cork. 12.5% alc. **Rating** 96 **To** 2019 $60 ❂
Woodside Vineyard Shiraz 2013 First come dark-berry aromas, then a palate initially following directly behind the fruit aromas; it is on the finish and aftertaste that this wine takes off, spicy/savoury tannins the space rockets providing a near endless replay. Screwcap. 14% alc. **Rating** 95 **To** 2043 $25 ❂

ɣɣɣɣɣ Woodside Vineyard Chardonnay 2014 Rating 92 To 2021 $25 ❂
Wing and a Prayer Sauvignon Blanc 2015 Rating 91 To 2017 $18 ❂
Woodside Vineyard Pinot Noir 2014 Rating 91 To 2023 $25
Tomich Hill Sauvignon Blanc 2015 Rating 90 To 2017 $22
Woodside Vineyard 1777 Pinot Noir 2014 Rating 90 To 2024 $60

Toolangi Vineyards

PO Box 9431, South Yarra, Vic 3141 **Region** Yarra Valley
T (03) 9827 9977 **www**.toolangi.com **Open** By appt
Winemaker Various contract **Est.** 1995 **Dozens** 7000 **Vyds** 12.2ha

Garry and Julie Hounsell acquired their property in the Dixons Creek area of the Yarra Valley, adjoining the Toolangi State Forest, in 1995. The primary accent is on pinot noir and chardonnay, accounting for all but 2.7ha, which is predominantly shiraz and a little viognier. Winemaking is by Yering Station (Willy Lunn), Giaconda (Rick Kinzbrunner), Hoddles Creek Estate (Franco D'Anna), Andrew Fleming (Coldstream Hills) and Oakridge (David Bicknell), as impressive a quintet of winemakers as one could wish for. Exports to the UK, Hong Kong, Singapore, Japan and China.

ΨΨΨΨΨ **Block F Reserve Yarra Valley Chardonnay 2012** Gleaming straw-green; virtually stands alone with the power and depth of its complexity, layer upon layer, as much a red as a white wine in terms of its structure and texture. Made by Rick Kinzbrunner. Screwcap. 13.5% alc. **Rating** 97 **To** 2024 $125 ✪

Reserve Yarra Valley Chardonnay 2010 Made by Rick Kinzbrunner, who is happy to walk the later-picking high-wire, bringing together grapefruit zest and juice, white peach and cashew, all bound together by strong minerally acidity. It shares the length with other Yarra Valley chardonnays, but was far less easy to recognise. Typical funky bouquet and a highly structured/layered palate. Screwcap. 14% alc. **Rating** 97 **To** 2020 $80 ✪

Block E Yarra Valley Pinot Noir 2013 Made at Giaconda from the best block on the vineyard. The perfumed bouquet of roses and cherry blossom sets the scene for all that follows; elegance and purity are the cornerstones of the perfectly balanced palate, spicy/powdery tannins and cedary oak providing the structure for the now and the hereafter. Screwcap. 13.5% alc. **Rating** 97 **To** 2025 $100 ✪

ΨΨΨΨΨ **Estate Yarra Valley Chardonnay 2014** Made by David Bicknell. Has a particular feel and flavour that is hard to differentiate from others in the superb chardonnay vintage of '14 – perhaps a little more white peach and nectarine flesh, but not losing finesse or length. Screwcap. 13.5% alc. **Rating** 96 **To** 2025 $45 ✪

Block F Reserve Yarra Valley Chardonnay 2013 Made by Rick Kinzbrunner. Struck match/reductive aromas are highly distinctive, and carry through unabated to the very complex palate. Lovers of white Burgundy will understand what this is all about, others may find it difficult, or actively dislike it – I am not one of those. Screwcap. 14.5% alc. **Rating** 96 **To** 2025 $90

Pauls Lane Yarra Valley Chardonnay 2013 Made by Franco D'Anna at Hoddles Creek Estate. This is an exercise in taking high quality grapes, making the wine without expense, but with incredible attention to detail, and ending up with exquisite harmony and balance, the length a celebration of the essence of Yarra Valley chardonnay. Screwcap. 13.8% alc. **Rating** 96 **To** 2025 $52 ✪

JTH Reserve Yarra Valley Shiraz 2014 A wine made to celebrate the birth of Garry and Julie Hounsell's grandson in '14 (JTH appears in small print on the back label). Made at Dominique Portet. Significantly more powerful than its siblings, with blackberry and black cherry fruit held in the arms of high quality cedary oak linked with fine, but firm tannins. Screwcap. 13.5% alc. **Rating** 96 **To** 2039 $125

Estate Yarra Valley Pinot Noir 2014 Made at Coldstream Hills. Detailed viticulture and careful winemaking have paid handsome dividends. This is a very good pinot with excellent structure and texture, the varietal flavours ripened to perfection, with spice, plum and cherry all having their say. An unhesitating 95 points. Screwcap. 13.5% alc. **Rating** 95 **To** 2029 $45

Yarra Valley Pinot Noir 2013 Part estate-grown, part from a vineyard in Yarra Glen. Made at Yering Station, and matured in French oak for 12 months. Has excellent colour, clear and deep; silky and supple, its varietal expression is flawless, as are its balance and length. Screwcap. 13.5% alc. **Rating** 95 **To** 2023 $28 ✪

Estate Yarra Valley Shiraz 2014 Made at Dominique Portet. An exercise in elegant restraint, the supple medium-bodied palate with a pure stream of juicy black fruits, tannins and oak guards standing by if needed – and they aren't. Just because it can be enjoyed now is no reason to dissuade you from cellaring as much as you drink. Screwcap. 13.5% alc. **Rating** 95 **To** 2034 $40

Yarra Valley Shiraz 2014 Made at Yering Station. This is quite an entry point shiraz, the bouquet immediately grabbing attention with its black fruits, pepper, licorice, spice and cedary oak, every bit of which comes through in 3D on the medium-bodied palate. The line, length and balance are perfect. Screwcap. 14% alc. **Rating** 95 **To** 2035 $26

Reserve Yarra Valley Shiraz 2012 Made by Rick Kinzbrunner. The opening stanza of the wine is all about elegance, the colour bright, the bouquet fragrant and the entry to the mouth with red cherry and spice to the fore. Then the mood changes dramatically as fine, savoury tannins take a grip, and black cherry sashays along with the tannins. Screwcap. 13.5% alc. **Rating** 95 **To** 2030 $75

Yarra Valley Pinot Noir 2014 Made at Coldstream Hills. This is a delicious pinot, only a small margin behind its Estate sibling, and in similar confident style. Will go the distance. Screwcap. 13.5% alc. **Rating** 94 **To** 2025 $30 ✪

🍷🍷🍷🍷🍷 **Emanai 2015 Rating** 93 **To** 2018 $26 ✪

Toorak Winery   ★★★☆

Vineyard 279 Toorak Road, Leeton, NSW 2705 **Region** Riverina
T (02) 6953 2333 **www**.toorakwines.com.au **Open** Mon–Fri 10–5, w'ends by appt
Winemaker Robert Bruno, Martin Wozniak **Est.** 1965 **Dozens** 200 000 **Vyds** 145ha
A traditional, long-established Riverina producer with a strong Italian-based clientele. Production has increased significantly, utilising substantial estate plantings and grapes purchased from other growers in the Riverina and elsewhere. Wines are released under the Willandra Estate, Willandra Leeton Selection and Amesbury Estate labels. Over recent vintages there has been a shift in emphasis away from bulk and buyers-own-brand sales and towards improving quality of Toorak's own brands. Exports to the US, China and other major markets.

🍷🍷🍷🍷🍷 **Willandra Estate Autumn Leaf Botrytis Semillon 2015** Precocious
development; very sweet, very fruity, some complexity, but will develop at a rate of knots. Screwcap. 11.5% alc. **Rating** 90 **To** 2016 $15 ✪

🍷🍷🍷🍷 **Willandra Estate Riverina Durif 2013 Rating** 89 **To** 2030 $18 ✪

Topper's Mountain Wines   ★★★★☆

5km Guyra Road, Tingha, NSW 2369 **Region** New England
T 0411 880 580 **www**.toppers.com.au **Open** By appt
Winemaker Mike Hayes **Est.** 2000 **Dozens** 1500 **Vyds** 9.79ha
Topper's Mountain is named after brothers Edward and William Topper, who were employees of George Jr and Alwyn Wyndham (sons of George Wyndham, founder of Wyndham Estate). They previously owned 'New Valley Station', which included the present day 'Topper's Mountain'. These days, Topper's Mountain is owned by Mark Kirkby. Planting began in the spring of 2000, with the ultimate fruit salad trial of 15 rows each of innumerable varieties and clones. The total area planted was made up of 28 separate plantings, many of these with only 200 vines in a block. As varieties proved unsuited, they were grafted over to those that held the most promise. Thus far, Gewurztraminer and Sauvignon Blanc hold most promise among the white wines, the Mediterranean reds doing better than their French cousins. The original 28 varieties are now down to 16; chardonnay, gewurztraminer, sauvignon blanc, tempranillo, shiraz and merlot are the commercial varieties, the remainder in the fruit salad block still under evaluation. Integrated pest management has been successfully adopted throughout the vineyard. Exports to Germany.

🍷🍷🍷🍷🍷 **Gewurztraminer 2015** Crammed with spice, lychee, musk and lavender, yet
retains freshness and brisk acidity; the aftertaste lifts this right out of the ruck. Screwcap. 13.9% alc. **Rating** 95 **To** 2025 $35 ✪

ŸŸŸŸ♀ **Barrel Ferment Gewurztraminer 2015** Rating 91 To 2020 $35
Barrel Ferment Petit Manseng 2013 Rating 90 To 2019 $34

Torbreck Vintners   ★★★★★

Roennfeldt Road, Marananga, SA 5352 **Region** Barossa Valley
T (08) 8562 4155 **www.torbreck.com Open** 7 days 10–6
Winemaker Craig Isbel, Scott McDonald **Est.** 1994 **Dozens** 70 000 **Vyds** 86ha
Torbreck Vintners was already one of Australia's best-known high quality red wine makers
when, in Sept 2013, wealthy Californian entrepreneur and vintner Peter Kight (of Quivira
Vineyards) acquired 100% ownership of the Torbreck business. The winemaking team headed
by Craig Isbel, supported by Scott McDonald and Russell Burns, all in place for some years,
continue to make the wines. The brand structure remains as before: the top quartet led by The
Laird (single vineyard Shiraz), RunRig (Shiraz/Viognier), The Factor (Shiraz) and Descendant
(Shiraz/Viognier); next The Struie (Shiraz) and The Steading (Grenache/Mataro/Shiraz).
Exports to all major markets.

ŸŸŸŸŸ **The Gask 2012** An immaculately made shiraz with a disciplined and light touch,
making the alcohol irrelevant; it sinuously weaves its way through the black fruits
of the medium to full-bodied palate, which make more impact than tannins or
oak (or alcohol). Perfect length, line and balance will give the wine a very long
future. Screwcap. 15% alc. **Rating** 97 To 2052 $75 ○

ŸŸŸŸŸ **Descendant 2013** The headiness of warm blackberried fruit, anise, clovey oak
and dark chocolate is impossible to resist. High alcohol is noticeable but essentially
taken in the wine's stride; tannin, acid and a great flood of flavour offer great
assistance. You'd pick it every time as a Torbreck wine, as shiraz viognier, and as
high quality. Cork. 15.5% alc. **Rating** 96 To 2028 $125 CM
The Loon 2014 The colour is intensely deep, suggesting this blend of shiraz and
roussanne was co-fermented. In the Torbreck fiefdom, this is a bargain, its infinitely
complex array of blackberry, licorice, spice, tar and charcuterie all having their say.
There are ripe tannins aplenty, a swish of oak, and the alcohol doesn't throw its
weight around. Screwcap. 15% alc. **Rating** 96 To 2034 $30 ○
The Struie 2013 Deep crimson; a blend of Barossa Valley and Eden Valley
shiraz, showing the Torbreck style to maximum advantage; the alcohol is simply a
fact, neither an asset or a liability per se, and Torbreck would doubtless say it is a
product of the multiple layers of black fruits, licorice and high quality tannins that
are in tight-knit balance. Screwcap. 15% alc. **Rating** 95 To 2038 $48 ○
The Factor 2013 Dates, prunes, saltbush and blackberry. It's not the freshest
or most defined of styles, but both intensity and depth are excellent, tannin is al
dente, and the linger of flavour through the finish is not to be sneezed at. Indeed
all up, it's most impressive. Cork. 15.5% alc. **Rating** 95 To 2030 $125 CM
The Laird 2010 Ranks in the top league of mega-powerful Barossa Valley shirazs,
sultry black fruits, graphite, rocky/mineral notes, oak and tannins all sequestered in
the hot embrace of alcohol. Can only be judged within its own terms of reference.
Cork. 15.5% alc. **Rating** 95 To 2050 $750
Les Amis 2013 A beast of sweetness and spice. Alcohol warmth is a clear player
too. Raspberries, black cherries, floats of anise, dry/sweet spices, cedar wood. It all
comes at you like a swarm of bees, with gamey, undergrowthy characters arriving
on the finish. It's a red-fruited wine with high alcohol attitude; within its style, it's
hard to deny. Cork. 15.5% alc. **Rating** 95 To 2024 $187 CM
The Steading 2012 Torbreck occupies a place all of its own; in the context of
the unbridled richness if its wines, this wine's varietal make-up of grenache, shiraz
and mourvedre is subservient almost to the point of irrelevance. Ultra-ripe fruit of
high quality from the best vineyards is the raison d'etre of these wines, so if you
are looking for cool climate elegance, don't waste your money here. Screwcap.
15.5% alc. **Rating** 95 To 2037 $38
Barossa Valley Marsanne 2015 Barrel-fermented. It's marsanne at full throttle
but it's beautifully polished and crafted and has to be admired. Ginger, melon,
lemon curd, spice, cedar wood smeared with cream. Quartz characters to the

finish. It gets under your skin and enters your head. Screwcap. 14% alc. **Rating** 94
To 2020 $48 CM

The Struie 2014 Earth, briary blackberries, anise, sweet raspberry. It's a tried and
true formula for Torbeck but it works. The alcohol is high but the finish remains
fresh; it almost feels refreshing. Chocolate and dried date characters add to the
impression of power. Cork. 15% alc. **Rating** 94 To 2028 $48 CM

Cuvee Juveniles 2014 Step back: this is how you do it. Licorice, raspberry, earth
and dried spice notes are in cahoots with one another, the ambition simple: to
provide pure drinking pleasure. The aroma, the mouthfeel, the flavour: it's all spot
on. 85% grenache, 8% shiraz, 7% mataro. Screwcap. 14.5% alc. **Rating** 94 To 2025
$25 CM ✪

ŶŶŶŶŶ **Barossa Valley Viognier 2015** Rating 93 To 2018 $48 CM
Woodcutter's Barossa Valley Shiraz 2014 Rating 93 To 2022 $25 CM ✪
The Gask 2013 Rating 93 To 2026 $75 CM
RunRig 2012 Rating 92 To 2042 $225
Woodcutter's Barossa Valley Semillon 2014 Rating 90 To 2018 $20 ✪
The Steading Blanc 2015 Rating 90 To 2019 $38 CM

Torzi Matthews Vintners

Cnr Eden Valley Road/Sugarloaf Hill Road, Mt McKenzie, SA 5353 **Region** Eden Valley
T 0412 323 486 **www**.torzimatthews.com.au **Open** By appt
Winemaker Domenic Torzi **Est.** 1996 **Dozens** 3000 **Vyds** 10ha
Domenic Torzi and Tracy Matthews, former Adelaide Plains residents, searched for a number
of years before finding a block at Mt McKenzie in the Eden Valley. The block they chose is in
a hollow; the soil is meagre, but they were in no way deterred by the knowledge that it would
be frost-prone. The result is predictably low yields, concentrated further by drying the grapes
on rack, thus reducing the weight by around 30% (the Appassimento method is used in Italy
to produce Amarone-style wines). Newer plantings of sangiovese and negro amaro, and an
extension of the original plantings of shiraz and riesling, have seen the wine range increase.
Exports to the UK and Denmark.

ŶŶŶŶŶ **Schist Rock Eden Valley Shiraz 2014** Power and personality. Floral and meaty
but bulging with dark-berried fruit. Draws you in and keeps you there. Eden
Valley written all over it. The pretty face, the powerful body. The finish is not a
disappointment, the value exceptional. Screwcap. 14.5% alc. **Rating** 94 To 2023
$20 CM ✪

ŶŶŶŶŶ **Frost Dodger Eden Valley Riesling 2015** Rating 93 To 2024 $25 CM ✪

Totino Estate

982 Port Road, Albert Park, SA 5014 (postal) **Region** Adelaide Hills
T (08) 8349 1200 **www**.totinowines.com.au **Open** Not
Winemaker Don Totino, Damien Harris **Est.** 1992 **Dozens** 15 000 **Vyds** 29ha
Don Totino migrated from Italy in 1968, and at the age of 18 became the youngest barber in
Australia. He soon moved on, into general food and importing and distribution. Festival City,
as the business is known, has been highly successful, recognised by a recent significant award
from the Italian government. In 1998 he purchased a rundown vineyard at Paracombe in the
Adelaide Hills, since extending the plantings to 29ha of chardonnay, pinot grigio, sauvignon
blanc, sangiovese and shiraz. Various family members, including daughter Linda, are involved
in the business. Exports to Italy and China.

ŶŶŶŶŶ **Francesco Reserve Shiraz 2012** Medium to full-bodied; dark fruits intertwine
with fine, persistent tannins, oak now absorbed into the essence of the long, firm,
well-balanced palate and its savoury finish. From Paracombe in the Adelaide Hills.
Cork. 14.5% alc. **Rating** 93 To 2032 $60

Adelaide Hills Sauvignon Blanc 2015 Some colour development is interesting;
was there skin contact? A rich style, the accent firmly on the tropical end of the

spectrum with just a fleck of herb; passionfruit, guava and mango will do for a start. Drink up soon. Screwcap. 13% alc. **Rating** 92 **To** 2016 $19
Adelaide Hills Pinot Grigio 2015 Pale bronze-pink; well above average; distinct pear and apple flavours; citrus acidity also contributes. Screwcap. 13% alc. **Rating** 91 **To** 2017 $19
Adelaide Hills Shiraz 2014 A powerful, medium-bodied wine, still unfolding and barely ready to judge. The black fruits and tannins are fine, but the coconut/vanillan oak jars somewhat. Screwcap. 14.5% alc. **Rating** 90 **To** 2034 $24
Adelaide Hills Cabernet Sauvignon 2013 A medium-bodied cabernet with clear varietal expression courtesy of blackcurrant and mulberry fruit, oak playing a minor savoury role. Screwcap. 13% alc. **Rating** 90 $24

Tower Estate ★★★★★

Cnr Broke Road/Hall Road, Pokolbin, NSW 2320 **Region** Hunter Valley
T (02) 4998 7989 **www.**towerestatewines.com **Open** 7 days 10–5
Winemaker Andrew Leembruggen, Usher Tinkler **Est.** 1999 **Dozens** 10000 **Vyds** 12.6ha
Tower Estate was founded by the late Len Evans, with the award-winning 5-star Tower Lodge accommodation and convention centre a part of the development. In Oct 2013 the winery and lodge were purchased by Karen and Michael Hope, who had many years previously purchased Rothbury Estate, renaming it Hope Estate. Its winemaking custodians are doing a fine job. Exports to the UK.

🍷🍷🍷🍷🍷 **Reserve Hunter Valley Shiraz 2007** Has retained very good hue; the power and intensity of the wine are admirable, and belie the alcohol and 9 years since vintage; black fruits (berry and cherry) lead the way on the full-bodied palate, the tannins obvious, but in balance. This is a real sleeper, with a wonderful 20–30 years ahead. Screwcap. 13% alc. **Rating** 96 **To** 2045 $45
Tasmania Pinot Noir 2014 Matured for 11 months in French oak. This has the power and focus Tasmania so effortlessly brings to the table; the bouquet already has some spice and flowers, with more to come, but it is the depth and polish of the plum and black cherry fruit of the palate that gives the wine its class – and its future. Screwcap. 13.5% alc. **Rating** 95 **To** 2027 $45
Coonawarra Cabernet Sauvignon 2012 Had the misfortune to be tasted after the Parker Coonawarra First Growth, but wasn't humiliated. The varietal fruit is there just as it should be, the structure built on accommodating tannins, only leaving the question of the oak to be answered, and it's ok. Screwcap. 13% alc. **Rating** 94 **To** 2032 $35

🍷🍷🍷🍷🍷 **Hilltops Shiraz 2013 Rating** 90 **To** 2028 $30

Tractorless Vineyard ★★★

McVitty Grove, 424 Wombeyan Caves Road, Mittagong, NSW 2575
Region Southern Highlands
T (02) 4878 5522 **www.**tractorlessvineyard.com.au **Open** Wed–Sun 10–4
Winemaker Jeff Aston, Mark Bourne, Ian McDonald **Est.** 2013 **Dozens** 2000 **Vyds** 12ha
The winery name puts the philosophy of winemakers and owners Jeff Aston, Mark Bourne and Ian McDonald into high relief. All the vineyard work is now done in accordance with biodynamic practices, in particular involving the integration of intensive cell grazing of sheep in the growing season. This means the elimination of weed control and mid-row grass management, at the same time producing 100% grass-fed lamb. It has to be said that the Southern Highlands' temperamental summer weather provides challenges for biodynamic management in wet vintages. This to one side, Tractorless Vineyard now joins an ever-growing number of producers claiming various carbon certifications, each billed as unique, depending on which organisation (if any) is responsible for certification. Tractorless goes in its own way by becoming the first carbon negative producer (as opposed to carbon neutral).

ŶŶŶŶ **Rose 2015** Made with pinot noir and shiraz. Bright coloured and flavoured. The word 'effusive' comes to mind. Strawberries with streaks of both green and dried herbs. Gentle bitterness to the aftertaste but most will enjoy this, particularly with food. Screwcap. 12% alc. **Rating** 88 **To** 2017 $20 CM

The Lost Flock 2013 A blend of red grape varieties though none is mentioned. 18 months in French oak. Sweet raspberried characters meet pure cassis. Musky oak sits over the top. It's not entirely cohesive, but it's ripe and well weighted. Screwcap. 13.8% alc. **Rating** 88 **To** 2021 $30 CM

Trapeze

2130 Kinglake Road, St Andrews, Vic 3761 (postal) **Region** Yarra Valley
T (03) 9710 1155 **Open** Not
Winemaker James Lance, Brian Conway **Est.** 2011 **Dozens** 900
This is the venture of friends James Lance (Punch) and Brian Conway (Izway Wines). While James is firmly attached to the Yarra Valley, Brian divides his time between the Barossa Valley and Melbourne, having made wine from the Rhône varietals for many years. He wanted to tackle the Burgundy varieties but realised this was not going to happen just because he felt the need; thus the partnership came about.

ŶŶŶŶŶ **Yarra Valley Chardonnay 2014** Rich with flavour and high on life. Grapefruit, peach and citrus flavours come adorned with slippery/creamy oak. Pleasure plus. Screwcap. 13% alc. **Rating** 92 **To** 2018 $32 CM

ŶŶŶŶ **Yarra Valley Blanc 2015 Rating** 89 **To** 2016 $32

Travertine Wines ★★★

78 Old North Road, Pokolbin, NSW 2320 **Region** Hunter Valley
T (02) 6574 7329 **www**.travertinewines.com.au **Open** Wed–Sun 10–4
Winemaker Liz Jackson **Est.** 1988 **Dozens** 3000 **Vyds** 10.73ha
This is the reincarnation of Pendarves Estate, originally planted by medico-cum-wine historian-cum-wine health activist Dr Phillip Norrie. It was purchased by Graham Burns in January 2008, and vineyard manager Chris Dibley, who had previously worked in the vineyard, was brought back to 'get the place back up to scratch'. There is a Joseph's coat of plantings including pinot noir (2.35ha), verdelho (2.25ha), chardonnay (1.25ha) and chambourcin (1.7ha), and lesser plantings of tannat, semillon, shiraz and merlot.

ŶŶŶŶŶ **Hunter Valley Chardonnay 2014** Pale mid-straw; peachy, citrus, melon, bright and pure; the palate is rounded, driven by the peach-accented fruit, and finishes generously. Screwcap. 13% alc. **Rating** 90 **To** 2020 $20 **○**

ŶŶŶŶ **Hunter Valley Fiano 2015 Rating** 88 **To** 2017 $20

Traviarti

39 Elgin Road, Beechworth, Vic 3747 **Region** Beechworth
T 0439 994 075 **www**.traviarti.com **Open** By appt
Winemaker Daniel Balzer, Simon Grant **Est.** 2011 **Dozens** 400 **Vyds** 0.43ha
After 15 years in the wine trade, first as a buyer in retail, followed by sales and marketing roles for producers, Simon Grant and partner Helen spent several years looking for the right place to grow nebbiolo, the wine which had the greatest appeal for them. When they moved to Beechworth to run a grapegrowers' co-operative, they found the site and planted both nebbiolo and tempranillo in 2011. At around 600m on the red decomposed shale and mudstone soils just above the town of Beechworth, they have planted multiple clones on a combination of rootstocks and their own roots. Until these vines come into bearing, they source cabernet sauvignon and tempranillo from Mark Walpole's Beechworth vineyard.

ŶŶŶŶŶ **Beechworth Tempranillo 2014** Grown on the Fighting Gully Road Vineyard. Sees no new oak. Light to medium-bodied but blessed with an intriguing array of flavours. Dates, aniseed, fresh cherries, earth. Taut, ultrafine tannin adds tension. Every step along the palate feels considered and deliberate. Screwcap. 13.8% alc. **Rating** 93 **To** 2021 $35 CM

Trentham Estate ★★★★☆

Sturt Highway, Trentham Cliffs, NSW 2738 **Region** Murray Darling
T (03) 5024 8888 **www**.trenthamestate.com.au **Open** 7 days 9.30–5
Winemaker Anthony Murphy, Shane Kerr **Est.** 1988 **Dozens** 70 000 **Vyds** 49.9ha
Remarkably consistent tasting notes across all wine styles from all vintages attest to the expertise of ex-Mildara winemaker Tony Murphy, a well-known and highly regarded producer, with estate vineyards in the Murray Darling. With an eye to the future, but also to broadening the range of the wines in offer, Trentham Estate is selectively buying grapes from other regions with a track record for the chosen varieties. The value for money is unfailingly excellent. Exports to the UK, China and other major markets.

🍷🍷🍷🍷🍷 Family Reserve Heathcote Shiraz 2013 From a single vineyard, crushed, fermented in tank, matured in French oak for 18 months. Great value, but I might have shortened the time in oak to 12 months, notwithstanding the depth of the juicy plum-accented fruit. Others are likely to disagree, particularly on the glass half full paradigm. Screwcap. 14.5% alc. **Rating** 95 **To** 2028 $26 ✪

🍷🍷🍷🍷 Estate Pinot Noir 2014 **Rating** 93 **To** 2017 $16 ✪
The Family Vermentino 2015 **Rating** 92 **To** 2017 $15 ✪
Family Reserve Coonawarra Cabernet Sauvignon 2013 **Rating** 91 **To** 2028 $26
Estate Shiraz 2014 **Rating** 90 **To** 2024 $16 ✪
Estate Noble Taminga 2013 **Rating** 90 **To** 2017 $16 ✪

Trevelen Farm ★★★★★

506 Weir Road, Cranbrook, WA 6321 **Region** Great Southern
T (08) 9826 1052 **www**.trevelenfarm.com.au **Open** By appt
Winemaker Harewood Estate (James Kellie) **Est.** 1993 **Dozens** 3500 **Vyds** 6.5ha
In 2008 John and Katie Sprigg decided to pass ownership of their 1300ha wool, meat and grain-producing farm to son Ben and wife Louise. However, they have kept control of the 6.5ha of sauvignon blanc, riesling, chardonnay, cabernet sauvignon and merlot planted in 1993. When demand requires, they increase production by purchasing grapes from growers in the Frankland River subregion. Riesling remains the centrepiece of the range. Exports to the US, Japan and China.

🍷🍷🍷🍷🍷 506 Frankland Reserve Shiraz 2014 Deep, vivid crimson-purple; plucks all the strings of the cello that celebrates Frankland River shiraz, the melody soaring and descending, the drums providing the heartbeat of the wine. It so mesmerises you that the alcohol escapes unnoticed, just the fused black and red cherry fruits, licorice and pepper remain. Screwcap. 14.7% alc. **Rating** 96 **To** 2039 $40 ✪
Estate Riesling 2015 Quartz-green; a complex wild flower blossom bouquet introduces a crisp and crunchy palate, acidity the cornerstone for intense citrus fruit flavours that will expand dramatically over the next decade, however delicious it is now. Screwcap. 12% alc. **Rating** 95 **To** 2030 $25 ✪
Aged Release Riesling 2005 Green-gold; honey, beeswax and crushed lime leaf aromas translate directly into a very complex, long and finely tuned palate. Its crunchy acidity will prove a rock of ages for the future of the wine. Screwcap. 13% alc. **Rating** 95 **To** 2020 $50

🍷🍷🍷🍷 The Maritime Pinot Noir 2014 **Rating** 92 **To** 2020 $23 ✪
Frankland Reserve Merlot 2012 **Rating** 92 **To** 2027 $23 ✪
The Maritime Chardonnay 2014 **Rating** 91 **To** 2022 $20 ✪

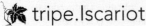 tripe.Iscariot ★★★★

74 Tingle Avenue, Margaret River, WA 6285 **Region** Margaret River
T 0414 817 808 **www**.tripeiscariat.com **Open** Not
Winemaker Remi Guise **Est.** 2013 **Dozens** 250

This has to be the most way out winery name of the century. It prompted me to email South
African-born and trained winemaker/owner Remi Guise asking to explain its derivation and/
or meaning, and he courteously responded with a reference to Judas as 'the greatest black sheep
of all time', and a non-specific explanation of tripe as 'challenging in style'. He added 'I hope
this sheds some light, or dark, on the brand.' The wines provide a better answer, managing to
successfully harness highly unusual technique at various points of their elevage. His day job as
winemaker at Naturaliste Vintners, the large Margaret River contract winemaking venture of
Bruce Dukes, provides the technical grounding, allowing him to throw the 'how to' manual
out of the window when the urge arises. His final words on his Syrah Malbec are 'So, suck
the marrow from the bone, fry the fat, and savour the warm, wobbly bits.'

Aspic Margaret River Grenache Rose 2013 Pale salmon colour; it is hardly
surprising that the palate challenges the norms for a grenache rose, with bramble,
crushed leaves, spice and crumbly acidity all riding high on the very long palate.
Screwcap. 12.8% alc. **Rating** 94 **To** 2017 $29 ✪

Brawn Margaret River Chardonnay 2013 Rating 93 **To** 2025 $39
Marrow Margaret River Syrah Malbec 2013 Rating 93 **To** 2017 $39

Trofeo Estate ★★★★

85 Harrisons Road, Dromana, Vic 3936 **Region** Mornington Peninsula
T (03) 5981 8688 **www**.trofeoestate.com **Open** 7 days 10–5
Winemaker Richard Darby **Est.** 2012 **Dozens** 4000 **Vyds** 18.7ha

This property has had a chequered history. In the 1930s Passiflora Plantations Company
was set up to become Australia's leading exporter of passionfruit and associated products.
By '37, 120ha was covered with 70 000 passionfruit vines, and a processing factory was in
operation. The following year a disease devastated the passionfruit and the company went into
receivership, never to be seen again. In '48 a member of the Seppelt family planted a vineyard
on the exact site of Trofeo Estate, and it was thereafter acquired by leading Melbourne wine
retailer and wine judge the late Doug Seabrook, who maintained the vineyard and made
the wine until the vines were destroyed in a bushfire in '67. In '98 it was replanted, but
passed through several hands and fell into and out of neglect until new owner, Jim Manolios,
developed the property as a café restaurant, vineyard and winery, with pinot noir (6.7ha),
chardonnay (4.9ha), pinot gris (2.6ha), shiraz (2.3ha), cabernet sauvignon (1.2ha) and muscat
(1ha). Trofeo Estate is the exclusive Australian distributor of terracotta amphorae made in Italy,
hence the involvement of amphorae in the making of a number of the wines.

Aged in Terracotta Mornington Peninsula Chardonnay 2014 The palest
colour; the tangy, zesty palate has an edge of grapefruity acidity, and you certainly
don't notice the absence of oak; the wine grows each time you go back to it.
Cork. 13.8% alc. **Rating** 94 **To** 2019 $55
Aged in Terracotta Mornington Peninsula Shiraz 2014 This is an attractive,
cool grown shiraz, the colour bright, the red berry bouquet fragrant, the fruit fresh,
the balance good, as is the texture. Although unoaked, it has none of the cold/
closed characters of red wines made entirely in stainless steel. Cork. 13.9% alc.
Rating 94 **To** 2034 $55

Mornington Peninsula Chardonnay 2014 Rating 93 **To** 2019 $45
Mornington Peninsula Chardonnay 2013 Rating 91 **To** 2017 $50
Traditional Method Vintage Cuvee 2008 Rating 90 **To** 2020 $38

Truffle & Wine Co. ★★★★☆

Seven Day Road, Manjimup, WA 6248 **Region** Pemberton
T (08) 9777 2474 **www**.truffleandwine.com.au **Open** 7 days 10–4
Winemaker Mark Aitken, Ben Haines **Est.** 1997 **Dozens** 4000 **Vyds** 9ha

Owned by a group of investors from various parts of Australia who have successfully achieved their vision of producing fine wines and black truffles. The winemaking side is under the care of Mark Aitken, who, having graduated as dux of his class in applied science at Curtin University in 2000, joined Chestnut Grove as winemaker in '02. The truffle side of the business is run under the direction of Harry Eslick, with 13 000 truffle-inoculated hazelnut and oak trees on the property. Truffle Hill is now the premium label for a range of wines that is sold domestically; the Truffle & Wine Co. label is the ultra-premium label, the best from the Yarra Valley, with 50% of this range exported to international restaurant clients through the exclusive distributors of the truffles. Exports to Hong Kong and Singapore.

🍷🍷🍷🍷🍷 **Margaret River Cabernets 2013** 70% cabernet sauvignon, 15% merlot, 10% cabernet franc, 5% petit verdot. A very successful and interesting wine, which – despite its complexity – takes immediate hold of your concentration with its unusual combination of extreme elegance and extreme intensity (or vice versa). In best Margaret River fashion, there is no point trying to deconstruct the components; just accept, and enjoy it for what it is. Diam. 14% alc. **Rating** 96 **To** 2038 $65 ✪

🍷🍷🍷🍷 **Margaret River Chardonnay 2014** **Rating** 93 **To** 2024 $45
Truffle Hill Shiraz 2013 **Rating** 91 **To** 2028 $28
Yarra Valley Pinot Noir 2014 **Rating** 90 **To** 2021 $55
Truffle Hill Pemberton Merlot 2014 **Rating** 90 **To** 2029 $30
Truffle Hill Cane Cut Pemberton Riesling 2015 **Rating** 90 **To** 2021 $35

Trust Wines ★★★☆

PO Box 8015, Seymour, Vic 3660 **Region** Central Victoria Zone
T (03) 5794 1811 **www**.trustwines.com.au **Open** Not
Winemaker Don Lewis, Narelle King **Est.** 2004 **Dozens** 800 **Vyds** 5ha

Partners Don Lewis and Narelle King had been making wine together for many years at Mitchelton, and Priorat, Spain. Don came from a grapegrowing family in Red Cliffs, near Mildura, and in his youth was press-ganged into working in the vineyard. When he left home he swore never to be involved in vineyards again, but in 1973 found himself accepting the position of assistant winemaker to Colin Preece at Mitchelton, where he remained until his retirement 32 years later. Narelle, having qualified as a chartered accountant, set off to travel, and while in South America met a young Australian winemaker who had just completed a vintage in Argentina, and who lived in France. The lifestyle appealed greatly, so on her return to Australia she obtained her winemaking degree from CSU and was offered work by Mitchelton as a bookkeeper and cellar hand. The estate-based wines are a reflection of Central Victorian style. They also make the Tar & Roses wines.

🍷🍷🍷🍷 **Shiraz 2014** From Don Lewis' Crystal Hill Vineyard, crushed/destemmed, small open fermenters, hand-plunged, 10 days on skins, matured for 12 months in French barriques. Deep colour; a potent and complex bouquet, then a firm, medium to full-bodied palate with black and red fruits on even terms, concluding with chalky, textured tannins. Screwcap. 14.5% alc. **Rating** 91 **To** 2034 $26

Tscharke ★★★★

376 Seppeltsfield Road, Marananga, SA 5360 **Region** Barossa Valley
T 0438 628 178 **www**.tscharke.com.au **Open** Thurs–Mon 10–5
Winemaker Damien Tscharke **Est.** 2001 **Dozens** 5000 **Vyds** 28ha

Damien Tscharke grew up in the Barossa Valley among the vineyards at Seppeltsfield and Marananga. In 2001 he began the production of Glaymond, four estate-grown wines based on what he calls the classic varieties (following the trend of having catchy, snappy names), followed by wines under the Tscharke brand using the alternative varieties of tempranillo, graciano, zinfandel, montepulciano and savagnin. Like the Glaymond wines, these are estate-grown, albeit in limited quantities. Exports to the US, Canada, Denmark, Belgium, Germany, Israel, Indonesia, Singapore and China.

ŸŸŸŸŸ **Project Marananga Montepulciano 2014** This has light and shade, texture to the fruit, and some oak. It's still only medium-bodied, but the balance is good, as is the length. It was wild yeast whole bunch-fermented with treading and plunging by hand; 12 months in used French oak, minimal SO$_2$ the only addition. Cork. 13% alc. **Rating** 92 **To** 2019 $40

The Master Marananga Montepulciano 2013 Confusion reigns supreme: this is The Master Montepulciano, yet subservient to the '14 Project Montepulciano. I give up on that one. It has retained excellent colour, and a red fruit salad of most attractive flavours. Screwcap. 14% alc. **Rating** 91 **To** 2018 $25

ŸŸŸŸ **Project Marananga Savagnin 2014 Rating** 89 **To** 2017 $40
Girl Talk Marananga Savagnin 2014 Rating 89 **To** 2016 $20
Only Son Marananga Tempranillo 2014 Rating 88 **To** 2017 $25

Tuck's Ridge ★★★★★

37 Shoreham Road, Red Hill South, Vic 3937 **Region** Mornington Peninsula
T (03) 5989 8660 **www.**tucksridge.com.au **Open** 7 days 11–5
Winemaker Michael Kyberd, Matthew Bisogni **Est.** 1985 **Dozens** 6000 **Vyds** 3.4ha
Tuck's Ridge has changed focus significantly since selling its large Red Hill vineyard. It retained the Buckle Vineyards of chardonnay and pinot noir that consistently provide outstanding grapes (and wine). The major part of the production is purchased from the Turramurra Vineyard. Exports to the US and Hong Kong.

ŸŸŸŸŸ **Buckle Pinot Noir 2014** If you look at the stitching you notice that it's incredibly fine and intricate. It has all the hallmarks of high quality tailoring. It's shredded with herbs, spices, woods and fruits, but its various aspects and components come across as a unified team. It's a beautiful wine. Screwcap. 13.4% alc. **Rating** 96 **To** 2026 $100 CM

Turramurra Chardonnay 2014 75 dozen. Beautiful chardonnay. Effortless. Mellifluous. Seamless. All those things. Pear and yellow stone fruit with licks of spicy oak and chalk. Screwcap. 13.9% alc. **Rating** 95 **To** 2022 $45 CM

Mornington Peninsula Pinot Gris 2015 Don't hesitate. If you see this around and pinot gris is called for, this is a beautiful example of the variety. Chalk, nashi pear, honeysuckle and red apple all add up to succulent fruit, plus a crunchy dryness and assorted savoury inputs that really sets the fireworks off. Screwcap. 13.2% alc. **Rating** 95 **To** 2017 $32 CM ✪

Mornington Peninsula Pinot Noir 2014 Clearly reductive but just as clearly complex and lengthy. There's a lot going on here and it carries you along with it. Smoky herbs, twigs, forest floor and black cherry. There's some velvet to the texture and more than a little tang to the acidity. It makes you want to like it and then gives you good reason to. Screwcap. 13.6% alc. **Rating** 95 **To** 2023 $43 CM

Mornington Peninsula Shiraz 2014 Peanut shells and black cherries, wood smoke and black peppers. These are just a few of the cool climate delights on offer here. It has body, it does not sting with alcohol, it's complex and yet it's pretty with fragrance. It is yet another ripping release from a resurgent Tuck's Ridge. Screwcap. 14% alc. **Rating** 95 **To** 2028 $38 CM

Mornington Peninsula Sauvignon Blanc 2015 This is right in the zone, as focused as it is flavoursome, with gunmetal and pippy passionfruit flavours riding the palate all the way through to the lemongrass-inflected palate. Screwcap. 13.8% alc. **Rating** 94 **To** 2017 $28 CM ✪

Buckle Chardonnay 2014 Fresh green pineapple drips from an open steel blade. It's steely and dramatic at once. Searing grapefruit-splashed length emphasises its slashing style. Screwcap. 13.7% alc. **Rating** 94 **To** 2022 $55 CM

Mornington Peninsula Savagnin 2015 Fennel, baked apple, perhaps cloves, definitely dried/woody spice. It's like a dessert of autumn fruits, minus the sweetness. It's exotic, it packs plenty of flavour, and yet it remains racy. Quite a wine. Screwcap. 13.5% alc. **Rating** 94 **To** 2017 $45 CM

♀♀♀♀♀ **Mornington Peninsula Chardonnay 2014** **Rating** 90 **To** 2018 $32 CM

Tulloch ★★★★★

Glen Elgin, 638 De Beyers Road, Pokolbin, NSW 2321 **Region** Hunter Valley
T (02) 4998 7580 **www.**tullochwines.com.au **Open** 7 days 10–5
Winemaker Jay Tulloch, First Creek **Est.** 1895 **Dozens** 35 000 **Vyds** 80ha
The Tulloch brand continues to build success on success. Its primary grape source is estate vines owned by part-shareholder Inglewood Vineyard in the Upper Hunter Valley. It also owns the JYT Vineyard established by Jay Tulloch in the mid-1980s at the foot of the Brokenback Range in the heart of Pokolbin. The third source is contract-grown fruit from other growers in the Hunter Valley and further afield. Skilled winemaking by First Creek Winemaking Services has put the icing on the winemaking cake, and Christina Tulloch is a livewire marketer. Exports to Belgium, the Philippines, Singapore, Hong Kong, Malaysia, Thailand, Japan and China.

♀♀♀♀♀ **Hector of Glen Elgin Shiraz 2014** Might be said to have no fixed abode – it is simply made from the best parcel from any given vineyard(s) in the parish of Pokolbin. This is more elegant than the fuller-bodied wines made in '14, and may have a last laugh, if not the last laugh. Screwcap. 14% alc. **Rating** 95 **To** 2049 $95
Private Bin Pokolbin Dry Red Shiraz 2014 The first reaction is to say this wine has less depth and complexity than Hector, but you soon realise it has remarkable length, and is the personification of traditional Hunter shiraz: black fruits, earth and leather all combined. The quality of this and Hector can't be denied. Screwcap. 14.5% alc. **Rating** 95 **To** 2044 $55
Limited Release G3 Hunter Valley Shiraz 2014 An elegant, lively and lush bouquet; the medium-bodied palate has finesse, intensity and length. Screwcap. 14.4% alc. **Rating** 95 **To** 2039 $110
Limited Release G4 Hunter Valley Chardonnay 2014 Light straw-green; a generous wine, one foot in the old camp, one in the new; stone fruit, cashew, fig and apple all ask to be heard, and absorb the oak in the ensuing hubbub. Screwcap. 13.3% alc. **Rating** 94 **To** 2024 $55

♀♀♀♀♀ **JYT Selection 2014** **Rating** 93 **To** 2030 $40 CM
Hunter River White Semillon 2015 **Rating** 91 **To** 2022 $25 CM
Limited Release EM Chardonnay 2015 **Rating** 90 **To** 2022 $30
Pokolbin Dry Red Shiraz 2014 **Rating** 90 **To** 2024 $30

Turkey Flat ★★★★★

Bethany Road, Tanunda, SA 5352 **Region** Barossa Valley
T (08) 8563 2851 **www.**turkeyflat.com.au **Open** 7 days 11–5
Winemaker Mark Bulman **Est.** 1990 **Dozens** 20 000 **Vyds** 47.83ha
The establishment date of Turkey Flat is given as 1990 but it might equally have been 1870 (or thereabouts), when the Schulz family purchased the Turkey Flat vineyard, or 1847, when the vineyard was first planted to the very old shiraz that still grows there today alongside 8ha of equally old grenache. Plantings have since expanded significantly, now comprising shiraz (24ha), grenache (10.5ha), cabernet sauvignon (5.9ha), mourvedre (3.7ha), and smaller plantings of marsanne, viognier and dolcetto. The business is run by sole proprietor Christie Schulz. Exports to the UK, the US and other major markets.

♀♀♀♀♀ **Barossa Valley Shiraz 2014** All the mainstream red winemaking options are used, demanding (and receiving) unrelenting attention to detail. This is a hero Barossa Valley shiraz, with great colour, profound complexity, yet retaining a calm personality within its array of primary, fresh flavours. Screwcap. 14.1% alc. Rating 97 To 2044 $47 ✪

🍷🍷🍷🍷🍷 **Barossa Valley Rose 2015** 92% grenache, 3% cabernet, 2% each of shiraz and dolcetto and 1% mataro reflects the intense care that is taken with this rose. Raspberry, strawberry and red cherry flavours are given an edgy freshness by crisp acidity. Screwcap. 13.5% alc. **Rating** 95 **To** 2017 $20 ✪

Butchers Block Red 2014 48% shiraz, 28% grenache, 24% mataro. Without question one of the best Barossa Valley examples of this blend, synergy its hallmark as it brings its array of red berries, plum, and blackberry/cherry flavours onto the stage, emphatically leaving confection behind. Great value. Screwcap. 14.4% alc. Rating 94 To 2025 $20 ✪

Barossa Valley Mataro 2015 Matured for 8 months in French puncheons. Not specified, but I reckon new oak is minimal, simply because of the intensity of the fruit. That said, it also has very good structure and texture. Turkey Flat is in a happy place. Screwcap. 14.2% alc. **Rating** 94 **To** 2030 $32

🍷🍷🍷🍷🍷 **Barossa Valley Grenache 2014** Rating 93 To 2020 $30
Barossa Valley White 2015 Rating 92 To 2023 $25 ✪

Tweedies Gully Wines ★★★★☆

277 Tweedies Gully Road, Williamstown, SA 5351 **Region** Barossa Valley
T 0413 583 742 **Open** By appt
Winemaker Trevor Jones **Est.** 1996 **Dozens** 500 **Vyds** 7ha
Mary and Peter Eriksen purchased 45ha of land at the eastern end of the Barossa Valley, halfway between Lyndoch and Williamstown, in 1994. They say that after two years of raising Murray Grey cattle they decided vines would be a more compatible use of the land, as they were regularly telephoned by neighbours while they were in Adelaide, advising that their cattle were on roadways or trespassing into neighbours' properties. They realised that vines would not jump fences and escape, and planted 7ha of shiraz in '96. Since 2005 limited quantities of wine have been made each year from the low yield of 1.5 tonnes per acre. So successful has the venture been with the 2010 and '12 vintages that they intend to increase the production of wine under the direction of Trevor Jones.

🍷🍷🍷🍷🍷 **Eriksen's Eden Valley Riesling 2015** Whole bunch-pressed, cultured yeast, cool-fermented in stainless steel. Good quality fruit was the essential starting block, and has been very well made; it is intense and long, steely acidity woven through lime/lemon juice flavours on the long palate; the lingering aftertaste reaffirms the quality of the wine. Screwcap. 12% alc. **Rating** 95 **To** 2030 $30 ✪

 # Twinwoods Estate ★★★★★

Brockman Road, Cowaramup, WA 6284 **Region** Margaret River
T 0419 833 122 **www.**twinwoodsestate.com **Open** Not
Winemaker Deep Woods Estate (Julian Langworthy), Aldo Bratovic **Est.** 2005
Dozens 2500 **Vyds** 8.5ha
This is a winery that was bound to succeed. It is owned by the Jebsen family, for many years a major player in the importation and distribution of fine wine in Hong Kong, more recently expanded into China. Fifteen years ago Jebsen invested in a NZ winery, following that with the acquisition of a vineyard in Margaret River in 2005. It brings together senior Jebsen managing director, Gavin Jones, and peripatetic winemaker Aldo Bratovic, who began his career decades ago under the tutelage of Brian Croser. Its widespread distribution is interesting, not all the eggs being put in the Hong Kong/China markets. The quality of the wines I have tasted fully lives up to what one would expect. (I tasted the wines without any knowledge of the background of Twinwoods.) It commenced selling wine in Australia in '14, with Terroir Selections its Australian partner, another intersection with Brian Croser. Exports to Denmark, Germany, Singapore, Taiwan, Hong Kong, China and NZ.

ŸŸŸŸŸ Optivus Reserve Cabernet Sauvignon 2010 The classy bouquet doesn't prepare you for the mouthfilling opulence of the palate; cassis, redcurrant and cedar all strut their stuff, applauded by the high quality oak and ripe tannins. Cork. 14% alc. **Rating** 96 **To** 2040 $38 ✪

Shiraz 2012 Deep crimson-purple, with little sign of development. Its entire life is stretched out before it, with layer upon layer of black fruits on the full-bodied palate, etched with ripe, but savoury, tannins, oak framing the picture. Ridiculously good value. Screwcap. 14% alc. **Rating** 95 **To** 2032 $25 ✪

ŸŸŸŸŸ Cabernet Sauvignon 2012 **Rating** 93 **To** 2025 $25 ✪
Chardonnay 2013 **Rating** 90 **To** 2017 $22

Twisted Gum Wines   ★★★☆

2253 Eukey Road, Ballandean, Qld 4382 **Region** Granite Belt
T (07) 4684 1282 **www**.twistedgum.com.au **Open** W'ends 10–4
Winemaker Andy Williams (Contract) **Est.** 2007 **Dozens** 700 **Vyds** 2.8ha
Tim and Michelle Coelli bring diverse and interesting backgrounds to this venture. During his university days in the early 1980s Tim began reading weekly wine columns of a certain journalist and bought recommended red wines from Wynns and Peter Lehmann, liked the wines, and with wife Michelle 'bought dozens and dozens …' Tim became a research economist, and during periods of living and working in Europe, he and Michelle became well acquainted with the wines of France, Spain and Italy. Michelle has a degree in agricultural science which, she says, 'has not been well utilised because four children came along'. When they found a beautiful 40ha bush property on a ridge near Ballandean (at an altitude of 900m) with dry grown vines already planted, they did not hesitate.

ŸŸŸŸŸ Single Vineyard Granite Belt Chardonnay 2014 The flexi-tank system works well for white wines, so given the issues Twisted Gum has had to deal with in recent times (in '14 a bushfire burned 1ha of the vineyard), this wine must be a comfort. Screwcap. 13% alc. **Rating** 90 **To** 2018 $25

ŸŸŸŸ Single Vineyard Granite Belt Shiraz 2014 **Rating** 89 **To** 2029 $35

Two Hands Wines   ★★★★★

273 Neldner Road, Marananga, SA 5355 **Region** Barossa Valley
T (08) 8562 4566 **www**.twohandswines.com **Open** 7 days 10–5
Winemaker Ben Perkins **Est.** 2000 **Dozens** 50 000 **Vyds** 15ha
The 'hands' in question are those of SA businessmen Michael Twelftree and Richard Mintz, Michael in particular having extensive experience in marketing Australian wine in the US (for other producers). On the principle that if big is good, bigger is better, the style of the wines has been aimed squarely at the palate of Robert Parker Jr and *Wine Spectator*'s Harvey Steiman. Grapes are sourced from the Barossa Valley (where the business has 15ha of shiraz), McLaren Vale, Clare Valley, Langhorne Creek and Padthaway. The emphasis is on sweet fruit and soft tannin structure, all signifying the precise marketing strategy of what is a very successful business. Exports to the US and other major markets.

ŸŸŸŸŸ Secret Block Single Vineyard Wildlife Road Moppa Hills Barossa Valley Shiraz 2014 Quite superb. Revs of tannin, blooms of dark-berried fruit, smoky nuances, woody spice, malt. It builds and flows, layers and lingers. Structure, flavour, interest, length – this excels at them all. Diam. 13% alc. **Rating** 96 **To** 2034 $100 CM

Bella's Garden Barossa Valley Shiraz 2014 Bang on. A beauty. Thick with fruit, sturdy with tannin, and complex enough to suggest an interesting future. Colour here is a pool of ink; balance is such that you don't think about it; and fruit-drenched length is a non-issue, to say the least. Cork. 13.5% alc. **Rating** 96 **To** 2034 $60 CM ✪

Sophie's Garden Padthaway Shiraz 2014 The full biscuit. This has the X-factor and more. It's brilliant with sweet, syrupy plum, mint and clove-like flavours, though mostly it presents as seamless. The shape of this wine, the firm-but-integrated structure, the length: this does its darndest to steal the 'Garden Series' show. Diam. 14.3% alc. **Rating** 96 **To** 2034 $60 CM ✪

Mystic Block Single Vineyard Benbournie Road Clare Valley Cabernet Sauvignon 2014 Drastically rich and, to boot, beautifully polished. This is a cracking wine. Earth, bitumen, blackcurrant, eucalypt and dusty clove notes smoke their way through a seriously concentrated palate. Tannin uncurls slowly but surely. Everything here is in a good place. Diam. 13% alc. **Rating** 96 **To** 2032 $100 CM

The Boy Eden Valley Riesling 2015 Thrilling acidity, with the flavour and length to match. Cellaring classic. Elegant but intense. Bath salts, citrus, mineral. Slight spritz, as a positive. Screwcap. 12.5% alc. **Rating** 95 **To** 2028 $25 CM ✪

Gnarly Dudes Barossa Valley Shiraz 2014 Bright hue and depth; the bouquet is fragrant and complex, with red fruits, spice and pine needles floating somewhere in the background, the elegant palate lifted and freshened by the low alcohol. The wine will outlive the patience of most who purchase it, but a drink-now decision is no crime. Screwcap. 13.8% alc. **Rating** 95 **To** 2034 $27 ✪

Wazza's Block Single Vineyard Seppeltsfield Road Barossa Valley Shiraz 2014 The stated alcohol gives no clear indication of the wine. This is dark, squishy and super intense, the boom of berries pushing flavour to the limits of freshness, but not beyond. It works, like magic, like escapism, like a world unto itself. Diam. 13.8% alc. **Rating** 95 **To** 2030 $100 CM

Lily's Garden McLaren Vale Shiraz 2013 Whatever pretensions the Langhorne Creek or Barossa Valley siblings of this wine might have had to adopt, some of the clothing (chocolate) of McLaren Vale are blown out of the water by this wine, its river of black and nut chocolate flowing insistently through the palate from start to finish. As a lover of chocolate, I am smitten by this wine. Cork. 14.5% alc. **Rating** 95 **To** 2033 $60

Bella's Garden Barossa Valley Shiraz 2013 Deep colour; a richly robed, medium to full-bodied wine, with strong textural plays the moment the wine enters the mouth; there are black fruits, plum cake and licorice in abundance; both the tannin and oak contributions are well controlled. Cork. 14.5% alc. **Rating** 95 **To** 2035 $60

Twelftree barr Eden Barossa Shiraz 2013 A Barossan beauty. Dark and substantial but firm, bright and disciplined. Blackberry and wads of earth, dark chocolate and graphite. Spiced raspberry. It grabs your interest and refuses to let it waver. Ropes of tannin are a critical part of the spell, but the quality of fruit is the key. Screwcap. 13.5% alc. **Rating** 95 **To** 2028 $55 CM

Angels' Share McLaren Vale Shiraz 2014 While there are no half measures with the weight or shape of this wine, it has a touch of elegance running alongside its blackberry, blood plum and dark chocolate fruit; the tannins wait until the last moment, joining forces with the oak to speak clearly of the long future ahead. Great value. Screwcap. 14.8% alc. **Rating** 94 **To** 2040 $27 ✪

Yacca Block Menglers Hill Eden Valley Shiraz 2014 Restrained power. Squeaky clean blueberry and blackberry fruit flavours combine well with smoky, spicy oak. Balance here is spot on. Tannin is so fine you could play music on it. Length takes care of it. Diam. 13.8% alc. **Rating** 94 **To** 2028 $100 CM

Lily's Garden McLaren Vale Shiraz 2014 Hearty offering with warm blackberry pie and saltbush-like flavours filling the palate to the hilt. This won't ever be skipped over unremarked. What really elevates it, though, is the frame of tannin, which stands firm, dry, ferrous and commanding. Diam. 13.8% alc. **Rating** 94 **To** 2030 $60 CM

Dave's Block Single Vineyard Blythmans Road Blewitt Springs McLaren Vale Shiraz 2014 Inky colour and flavour. It's shiraz cut in thick, meaty slices. It tastes of saturated plums, cloves and malty/toasty oak, and comes twirled with ripe, spicy tannin. Flaws, it has none. Diam. 14.5% alc. **Rating** 94 **To** 2030 $100 CM

Max's Garden Heathcote Shiraz 2014 The fruit is sweet and dense, the tannin a melt throughout, the oak downplayed but at one with the fruit. The fruit profile tends towards jamminess, regardless of the stated alcohol, but for sheer it's-all-there-on-its-sleeve seduction this takes some beating. This is where simple meets saucy. Diam. 13.5% alc. **Rating** 94 **To** 2026 $60 CM

Samantha's Garden Clare Valley Shiraz 2013 The play revolves around blackberry and blackcurrant fruit, with a balanced, savoury display of earthy tannins; oak is certainly present, but not as insistent as it is in most of its siblings; medium-bodied, and very well structured and balanced. Cork. 14.5% alc. **Rating** 94 **To** 2033 $60

Twelftree barr Eden Barossa Shiraz Mataro 2014 Character writ large. Clumps of earth, dry licorice, a subtle meatiness, and then of course berried notes galore. There's a chatter of savouriness but fruit controls the centre. You could build a meal, a conversation, an evening around this. Screwcap. 13.5% alc. **Rating** 94 **To** 2025 $55 CM

♆♆♆♆♀ The Wolf Clare Valley Riesling 2015 Rating 93 To 2024 $25 CM ✪
Heartbreak Hill Shiraz 2014 Rating 93 To 2028 $100 CM
Coach House Block Shiraz 2014 Rating 93 To 2026 $100 CM
Samantha's Garden Clare Valley Shiraz 2014 Rating 93 To 2029 $60 CM
Max's Garden Heathcote Shiraz 2013 Rating 93 To 2030 $60
Sophie's Garden Padthaway Shiraz 2013 Rating 92 To 2030 $60
Harry & Edward's Garden Shiraz 2013 Rating 92 To 2030 $60
Twelftree Ryan Road Mourvedre 2014 Rating 92 To 2022 $45 CM
Sexy Beast Cabernet Sauvignon 2014 Rating 90 To 2020 $27

2 Mates   ★★★★☆

Cnr Kangarilla Road/Foggo Road, McLaren Vale, SA 5171 **Region** McLaren Vale
T 0411 111 198 **www**.2mates.com.au **Open** 7 days 11–5
Winemaker Matt Rechner, Mark Venable, David Minear **Est.** 2003 **Dozens** 500
The two mates are Mark Venable and David Minear, who say, 'Over a big drink in a small bar in Italy a few years back, we talked about making "our perfect Australian Shiraz". When we got back, we decided to have a go.' The wine ('05) was duly made, and won a silver medal at the *Decanter* World Wine Awards in London, in some exalted company. Exports to the UK and China.

♆♆♆♆♆ McLaren Vale Shiraz 2013 Cold-soaked, open-fermented with 21 days on skins, matured for 24 months in new and used French oak. Excellent retention of crimson-purple hue to the deep colour; there's no compromise here: this is a distillation of all things McLaren Vale shiraz, but despite its density (and alcohol), has very good balance and length. Will live longer than most who buy it. Screwcap. 15.1% alc. **Rating** 95 **To** 2043 $35 ✪

Two Rivers   ★★★★★

2 Yarrawa Road, Denman, NSW 2328 **Region** Hunter Valley
T (02) 6547 2556 **www**.tworiverswines.com.au **Open** 7 days 11–4
Winemaker Liz Silkman **Est.** 1988 **Dozens** 12 000 **Vyds** 67.5ha
A significant part of the viticultural scene in the Upper Hunter Valley, with 67.5ha of vineyards, involving an investment of several million dollars. Part of the fruit is sold under long-term contracts, and part is made for the winemaking and marketing operations of Two Rivers. The emphasis is on Chardonnay and Semillon, its 2011, '13 and '15 semillons all rated 95 or 96 points. It is also a partner in the Tulloch business, together with the Tulloch and Angove families, and supplies much of the grapes for the Tulloch label. A contemporary cellar door adds significantly to the appeal of the Upper Hunter Valley as a wine-tourist destination. The appointment of immensely talented winemaker Liz Silkman as winemaker has had an immediate impact.

♆♆♆♆♆ Stones Throw Hunter Valley Semillon 2011 A spray of six gold medals and a trophy tell 99% of the story, one of the golds from the National Wine Show, the trophy from the NSW Wine Awards – all the medals from '11. When tasted in Mar '12 it received 96 points; the only question now is whether it should get an additional point, for it is as fresh as a dawn sky. It beggars belief that it's only $24. Screwcap. 11.8% alc. **Rating** 96 **To** 2026 $24 **◯**

Stones Throw Hunter Valley Semillon 2015 A gold medal at the Hunter Valley Wine Show '15, then trophies at the Hunter Valley Boutique and Small Winemakers shows. The bouquet has a lanolin overlay, the palate soaring off on a very different tangent, with intense lemon/lemongrass flavours achieved effortlessly. You don't need to look at the record of the '13 and '11 to know this will run forever. Screwcap. 10.5% alc. **Rating** 95 **To** 2030 $16 **◯**

Stones Throw Hunter Valley Semillon 2013 Has a juicy feel and flavour stolen from riesling, doubtless responsible for its three trophies and numerous gold medals; the grapes were picked at a higher baume than usual, which is often part of the Two Rivers style; also has a seductive hint of tropical fruit tucked in behind. Screwcap. 11.6% alc. **Rating** 95 **To** 2025 $24 **◯**

🍷🍷🍷🍷 **Reserve Hunter Valley Chardonnay 2015 Rating** 89 **To** 2020 $24
Solera Verdelho NV Rating 88 **To** 2016 $30

Twofold   ★★★★

142 Beulah Road, Norwood, SA 5067 (postal) **Region** Various
T (02) 9572 7285 **Open** Not
Winemaker Tim Stock, Nick Stock, Neil Pike (Contract) **Est.** 2002 **Dozens** 500
This is the venture of brothers Nick and Tim Stock, both of whom have had varied backgrounds in the wine industry (primarily at the marketing end, whether as sommeliers or in wholesale) and both of whom have excellent palates. Their contacts have allowed them to source single vineyard Rieslings from Sevenhill in the Clare and Eden valleys and a single vineyard Shiraz from Heathcote.

🍷🍷🍷🍷🍷 **Clare Valley Riesling 2015** A cracking riesling in anyone's language. Flavour, length, texture; the holy trinity are well taken care of here. It's (highly) accessible now, but of course it will age. Screwcap. 12.5% alc. **Rating** 94 **To** 2024 $27 CM **◯**

Clare Valley Riesling 2013 Exaggerated lime, spice and honeysuckle aromas/flavours lend this a keen sense of drama. It then sizzles with citrussy flavour through the finish, sealing the deal in style. Screwcap. 11% alc. **Rating** 94 **To** 2023 $25 CM **◯**

🍷🍷🍷🍷🍷 **Heathcote Shiraz 2010 Rating** 93 **To** 2022 $40 CM

Tyrrell's   ★★★★★

Broke Road, Pokolbin, NSW 2321 **Region** Hunter Valley
T (02) 4993 7000 **www.tyrrells.com.au Open** Mon–Sat 8.30–5, Sun 10–4
Winemaker Andrew Spinaze, Mark Richardson **Est.** 1858 **Dozens** 200000 **Vyds** 158.22ha
One of the most successful family wineries, a humble operation for the first 110 years of its life that has grown out of all recognition over the past 40. Vat 1 Semillon is one of the most dominant wines in the Australian show system, and Vat 47 Chardonnay is one of the pacesetters for this variety. It has an awesome portfolio of single vineyard Semillons released when 5–6 years old. Its estate plantings are over 116ha in the Hunter Valley, 15ha in the Limestone Coast and 26ha in Heathcote. A founding member of Australia's First Families of Wine. Exports to all major markets.

🍷🍷🍷🍷🍷 **Winemaker's Selection 4 Acres Shiraz 2014** Vines planted in 1879. 290 dozen. It's about as good as it gets. Power and length, complexity woven with a thread count in the 1000s. It's a wine that commands the glass, and the dinner table, and yet is friendly to both. It's medium-bodied and yet it's extraordinarily powerful through the finish. It doesn't tire easily; it saves its best till last, and for the future. Screwcap. 14% alc. **Rating** 98 **To** 2045 $75 CM **◯**

Museum Release Vat 1 Hunter Semillon 2011 Bright, gleaming straw-green; this is a beautiful Vat 1, just starting its journey towards maturity. Its balance and harmony allow it to float effortlessly along the palate and into a finish that caresses that taste buds. It will develop slowly, but give pleasure whenever it is tasted. Screwcap. 11.5% alc. **Rating** 97 **To** 2031 $80 ✪

Vat 9 Hunter Shiraz 2014 This is stellar. The length, the breadth, the form, the immaculate rollout of tannin. It shows cherry plum, earth, violet and spice, but the sum of such humble parts is so much more than that. Milk chocolate from oak simply goes with the flow. We stand in the presence of something resembling greatness. Screwcap. 13.9% alc. **Rating** 97 **To** 2040 $85 CM ✪

♟♟♟♟♟ **Johnno's Semillon 2015** Produced from 106yo vines on the HVD Vineyard, with only 250 dozen made. Hand-picked, basket-pressed unclarified juice gives the wine an extra degree of texture and structure, and underwrites its longevity; traditional cut-grass and lemongrass flavours are punctuated by zesty acidity on the long, crystal-clear palate. A bottle of liquid history, cheap at the price. Screwcap. 10.5% alc. **Rating** 96 **To** 2035 $60 ✪

Single Vineyard Short Flat Semillon 2015 From some of Tyrrell's oldest vines. The flavours of lime citrus, wrapped in a cloud of acidity, reverberate back and forth across the palate at all angles. While its greatest years are decades away, this gives so much already that the temptation to drink it will be intense. Due for release '21. Screwcap. 10% alc. **Rating** 96 **To** 2030 $60 ✪

Single Vineyard Stevens Hunter Semillon 2011 Pour a glass of this for the unwary, and half will think it's a cool climate riesling, the lemon juice acidity suggesting the Eden Valley as one possibility, Porongurup another. It is really hard to spit out, and I console myself by thinking it's only 11% alcohol as I sneak a micro-swallow. Screwcap. **Rating** 96 **To** 2026 $35 ✪

Single Vineyard Stevens Hunter Shiraz 2014 A more powerful expression of this vineyard than we've come to expect. It's tangy with acid, flush with fruit and bursting with firm, ferrous, earthen tannin. Great vineyards stamp their authority in great years; this release from this year sends a clear message about its rightful status. Screwcap. 13.8% alc. **Rating** 96 **To** 2035 $40 CM ✪

Single Vineyard NVC Hunter Shiraz 2014 It's made from a vineyard planted in '21. It reeks of red earth and rust, black cherry and ferrous, clovey spices. It shows chocolate, licorice, boysenberry and violets. It has personality, it has oomph, it has regionality, it has X-factor. It's a steal. The only problem is that less than 300 dozen were made. Screwcap. 13.9% alc. **Rating** 96 **To** 2040 $40 CM ✪

Vat 1 Hunter Semillon 2015 From old, dry grown vineyards dating as far back as '23. Hand picking and sorting eliminated botrytis, leaving a pure display of citrus fruits headed by lemon, with lime and grapefruit also in the mix, all framed by hallmark acidity. A wine in its infancy, its best years a long way into the next decade and beyond. Screwcap. 11% alc. **Rating** 95 **To** 2040 $80

HVD Old Vines Chardonnay 2015 The vines were planted in 1908, making them the oldest in Australia (and possibly the world), producing 500 dozen. Hand-picked, basket-pressed, solids-fermented with extended lees contact – no mention of oak. It is richly textured and appears riper than 12.5%, so it's perfectly possible the wine did not see oak. Screwcap. **Rating** 95 **To** 2030 $60

Vat 47 Hunter Chardonnay 2013 Tyrrell's made its first Vat 47 in '71 and soon embraced barrel fermentation in French oak, to all intents and purposes the leader of the pack, playing the same role that Max Lake had played with cabernet in '65–'66. So it's hardly surprising Tyrell's a skilled practitioner. Screwcap. 13% alc. **Rating** 95 **To** 2027 $70

Johnno's Hunter Valley Shiraz 2014 Iron-bar tannin. Raspberry tipping into aniseed. Dark, loamy earth. A touch of toasty oak. At first it doesn't seem like much; it seems light; as it breathes it expands and imposes. It's almost the definition of the 'destined for the cellar' wine. Screwcap. 14% alc. **Rating** 95 **To** 2040 $75 CM

Old Patch Hunter Valley Shiraz 2014 Musky vanillan oak sits above the spiced red and black cherries with ferrous edges. Anise rises through the wine as it breathes. Tannin and acid are keen players, in a positive sense. Come back

in 10+ years and it will be all the better for the sleep. Screwcap. 13.9% alc.
Rating 95 **To** 2040 $75 CM

Vat 8 Hunter Valley Shiraz Cabernet 2014 If you put this in the cellar the chances of your being disappointed when it reaches maturity are almost zilch. It has character and balance and, from such an excellent year, enough fruit to keep the engine humming for a long, long time. A beautiful medium-weight, filigreed wine. Screwcap. 14% alc. **Rating** 95 **To** 2035 $80 CM

Single Vineyard Belford Hunter Semillon 2011 Gleaming straw-green; while lemongrass and lemon citrus are very much in the frame, there are some honeyed notes starting to develop. They encourage a second glass, and a third … Given its alcohol level, one of the strong points of Hunter Valley semillon, that's not as unwise as it might seem at first blush. A lovely mouthfilling style. Screwcap. 10.5% alc. **Rating** 94 **To** 2026 $35

Single Vineyard Old Hut Hunter Shiraz 2014 In an excellent place. Lots of fruit, especially in a regional context, with black cherry leading into plum, almost anise. Spice notes and sweet raspberry play a role too; this is the most accessible of the '14 Tyrrell's single vineyard shirazs. Screwcap. 14.2% alc. **Rating** 94 **To** 2030 $40 CM

🍷🍷🍷🍷🍷 **Hunter Valley Semillon 2015** Rating 93 **To** 2025 $23 ✪
Special Release Hunter Valley Shiraz 2014 Rating 91 **To** 2034 $40
Rufus Stone Heathcote Shiraz 2013 Rating 91 **To** 2022 $25 CM
Vat 63 Chardonnay Semillon 2015 Rating 90 **To** 2020 $50
Vat 6 Hunter Pinot Noir 2014 Rating 90 **To** 2020 $70

Ulithorne   ★★★★★

The Mill at Middleton, 29 Mill Terrace, Middleton, SA 5213 **Region** McLaren Vale
T 0419 040 670 **www**.ulithorne.com.au **Open** W'ends & public hols 10–4
Winemaker Rose Kentish, Brian Light **Est.** 1971 **Dozens** 2500 **Vyds** 7.2ha

Ulithorne produces small quantities of red wines from selected parcels of grapes from a vineyard in McLaren Vale planted by Rose Kentish's father-in-law, Frank Harrison, over 40 years ago. Rose's dream of making small batch, high quality wines from exceptional grapegrowing regions around the world has taken her to France, where she has made a Vermentinu on the island of Corsica and a Rose in Provence under the Ulithorne label. In 2013 Sam Harrison and Rose Kentish purchased an old vineyard in the heart of McLaren Vale, with 4ha of shiraz and 3.2ha of grenache dating back to 1945. They expect to have a winery and cellar door built on their Kay's Road Vineyard by late '16. Exports to the UK, Canada, The Netherlands, Malaysia and China.

🍷🍷🍷🍷🍷 **Prospera McLaren Vale Shiraz 2014** Primarily from Ulithorne's 65yo dry-grown vineyard in Blewitt Springs, matured in French oak for 17 months. Manages to up the tempo of Familia without falling prey to Parkerism. Black and blue fruits join hands with a touch of regional chocolate, the tannins fine in best Blewitt Springs style, oak no more than a conveyance. Screwcap. 14.5% alc. **Rating** 95 **To** 2034 $55

Dona McLaren Vale Grenache Shiraz Mourvedre 2014 60/30/10%, machine or hand-harvested according to growers' vineyard requirements, the parcels aged separately for 12 months in used French oak and stainless steel. Bright, spicy and juicy red fruits are joined by fine-spun tannins on the light to medium-bodied palate. Screwcap. 14% alc. **Rating** 95 **To** 2024 $25 ✪

McLaren Vale Familia Shiraz 2014 An elegant, medium-bodied shiraz true to both its place of birth and its breeding, the feminine touch of winemaker Rose Kentish another factor in allowing the fruit full freedom to express itself. Screwcap. 14% alc. **Rating** 94 **To** 2029 $40

Paternus McLaren Vale Cabernet Shiraz 2013 80/20% from the Old Ulithorne Vineyard, the parcels kept separate, open-fermented, matured for 16 months in French oak (20% new). Still to emerge as an adult, with bright fruits covering a wide spectrum of flavours, oak and tannins still to settle down.

The balance is there, guaranteeing the long-term future of the wine. I just hope the cork makes the distance. 14.5% alc. **Rating** 94 **To** 2043 $85

♥♥♥♥ **Frux Frugis McLaren Vale Shiraz 2013 Rating** 89 **To** 2028 $85
NV Flamma McLaren Vale Sparkling Shiraz NV Rating 89 **To** 2025 $65 TS

Ulupna Winery ★★★★

159 Crawfords Road, Strathmerton, Vic 3641 **Region** Goulburn Valley
T (03) 9533 8831 **www**.ulupnawinery.com.au **Open** Mon–Fri 11–3, 1st Sat month 10–4
Winemaker Vio Buga **Est.** 1999 **Dozens** 16 500 **Vyds** 22ha
Ulupna started out as a retirement activity for Nick and Kathy Bogdan. The vineyard on the banks of the Murray River is planted to shiraz (50%), cabernet sauvignon (30%) and chardonnay (20%), the plantings allowing for expansion in the years ahead. The wines are made under the direction of Vio Buga, who also designed and planted the vineyard. Exports are primarily directed to China, followed by Hong Kong, South Korea and Singapore.

♥♥♥♥♡ **Special Reserve Shiraz 2014** Input of creamy vanillan oak is high here. It gives the wine a feeling of luxury, even if it has been overdone. It's supported by a mid-weight serve of cherry-plum fruit, ripe and just substantial enough. It will be best consumed young. Cork. 14.3% alc. **Rating** 90 **To** 2020 $32 CM
Limited Edition Cabernet Sauvignon 2014 The alcohol is high but the fruit covers it well. Pure blackcurrant comes surrounded by whispers of resiny vanilla. It's soft-hearted, even gentle, but there's no lack of flavour and the finish is sound and, thankfully, firm. Cork. 15.3% alc. **Rating** 90 **To** 2021 $32 CM

♥♥♥♥ **Phoenix Royal Shiraz 2009 Rating** 89 **To** 2023 $49 CM
Single Vineyard Cabernet Sauvignon 2014 Rating 89 **To** 2020 $27 CM
Limited Edition Shiraz 2014 Rating 88 **To** 2020 $32 CM

Umamu Estate ★★★★★

PO Box 1269, Margaret River, WA 6285 **Region** Margaret River
T (08) 9757 5058 **www**.umamuestate.com **Open** Not
Winemaker Bruce Dukes (Contract) **Est.** 2005 **Dozens** 2000 **Vyds** 16.5ha
Chief executive Charmaine Saw explains, 'My life has been a journey towards Umamu. An upbringing in both eastern and western cultures, graduating in natural science, training as a chef, combined with a passion for the arts and experience as a management consultant have all contributed to my building the business creatively yet professionally.' The palindrome Umamu, says Charmaine, is inspired by balance and contentment. In practical terms this means an organic approach to viticulture and a deep respect for the terroir. In 1997, Charmaine's parents fell in love with the property and its plantings, dating back to '78, of cabernet sauvignon (6ha), chardonnay (3.5ha), shiraz (1.7ha), semillon (2.2ha), sauvignon blanc (1.5ha), merlot (0.9ha) and cabernet franc (0.7ha). Exports to the UK, Hong Kong, Malaysia, Indonesia, the Philippines and Singapore.

♥♥♥♥♥ **Margaret River Cabernet Sauvignon 2013** Filled to overflowing with all the goodies cabernet can offer; lashings of dark fruits centred on blackcurrant, layered tannins and high quality oak; the finish conjures up a savoury edge that adds another dimension. Screwcap. 13.8% alc. **Rating** 96 **To** 2043 $58 ✪
Margaret River Chardonnay 2013 While still youthful and tightly framed, the balance and length of the wine leave no doubt whatsoever about its future. Nectarine, white peach, fig and rockmelon are braced by crisp acidity and sensitive oak handling. Screwcap. 13.8% alc. **Rating** 95 **To** 2025 $50
Margaret River Sauvignon Blanc 2013 You might have expected the wine to show some signs of tiring, but the bright straw-green hue tells otherwise, and nothing after that changes the message much – the finish does drop ever so slightly, taking away from the complexity of the well-balanced palate. Screwcap. 12.5% alc. **Rating** 94 **To** 2016 $35

Ann's Margaret River Cabernet Sauvignon 2012 The fragrant bouquet offers cedary/cigar box aromas coupled with blackcurrant, the savoury medium-bodied palate picking up the theme without a break, the blackcurrant with a crosshatch of bay leaf and dried herbs. A complex and complete wine. Screwcap. 13.8% alc. **Rating** 94 **To** 2027 $58

Underground Winemakers   ★★★★☆

1282 Nepean Highway, Mt Eliza, Vic 3931 **Region** Mornington Peninsula
T (03) 9775 4185 **www**.ugwine.com.au **Open** 7 days 10–5
Winemaker Peter Stebbing **Est.** 2004 **Dozens** 10 000 **Vyds** 12ha
Owned by Adrian Hennessy, Jonathon Stevens and Peter Stebbing. Each has made wine in Alsace, Burgundy, Northern Italy and Swan Hill. Each has extensive experience in the vineyards and wineries of the Mornington Peninsula. Their first step, in 2004, was to lease a small winery at Mt Eliza that had closed years earlier, but still had a vineyard with some of the oldest plantings of pinot noir, pinot gris and chardonnay on the Peninsula. Their portfolio is nothing if not eclectic: Pinot Gris, Pinot Noir and Chardonnay from the Mornington Peninsula, and Durif, Moscato, Cabernet Merlot and Shiraz from northern and Central Victoria.

♟♟♟♟♟ San Pietro Pinot Noir 2013 Flashes of cranberry and raspberry are mere teasers to what is a stern, spicy, savoury palate, marked by dry tannin and a keen intent to keep its best for the flourish of the finish. Excellent shape but could use a little more flesh. Screwcap. 13% alc. **Rating** 91 **To** 2021 $25 CM
San Pietro Pinot Grigio 2015 Musk, spice, pear, melon. It has punch and personality, impact and texture. No matter what they do, this grigio wants to be a gris. Either way, the quality is decent. Screwcap. 12.5% alc. **Rating** 90 **To** 2017 $25 CM
Mornington Peninsula Pinot Noir 2014 Personality plus and depth of flavour rarely seen at this price level; within varietal bounds. Woody herbs, smoked meats, black cherry. Plenty of tang, and character. Not for cellaring but an excellent early drinker. Screwcap. 13.5% alc. **Rating** 90 **To** 2019 $18 CM ✪

♟♟♟♟ Offspring Pinot Gris 2015 **Rating** 88 **To** 2016 $19 CM
Mornington Peninsula Pinot Grigio 2015 **Rating** 88 **To** 2016 $18 CM

Vasse Felix   ★★★★★

Cnr Tom Cullity Drive/Caves Road, Cowaramup, WA 6284 **Region** Margaret River
T (08) 9756 5000 **www**.vassefelix.com.au **Open** 7 days 10–5
Winemaker Virginia Willcock **Est.** 1967 **Dozens** 150 000 **Vyds** 232ha
Vasse Felix was the first winery to be built in the Margaret River. Owned and operated by the Holmes à Court family since 1987, Vasse Felix has undergone extensive changes and expansion. Chief winemaker Virginia Willcock has energised the winemaking and viticultural team with her no-nonsense approach and fierce commitment to quality. The estate vineyards contribute all but a small part of the annual production, and are scrupulously managed, quality the sole driver. Wines include top of the range Heytesbury (a cabernet blend) and Heytesbury Chardonnay; the Premier range of mainly varietal wines; Filius Chardonnay and Cabernet Merlot; and Classic Dry White and Dry Red. Limited quantities of specialty wines include Cane Cut Semillon, Viognier and Tempranillo. Exports to all major markets.

♟♟♟♟♟ Heytesbury Margaret River Chardonnay 2014 The leader of a great trio of Vasse Felix Chardonnays, hand-picked, chilled, basket-pressed to French barriques (64% new), with some natural, although unintended, mlf. Here energy and drive are easily matched by the complexity that is the ever-present fingerprint of Heytesbury. A magical combination of grace and power, with prodigious length to close. Screwcap. 13% alc. **Rating** 97 **To** 2024 $75 ✪
Heytesbury 2012 Cabernet sauvignon, malbec and petit verdot. The perfumed bouquet stands on its own considerable merits, but it is the implacable insistence of the blackcurrant fruit, wrapped around the juicy malbec, that lifts this wine onto

another plane. Is it medium-bodied, medium to full-bodied or full-bodied? It all depends on which facet you concentrate on, but for my money, it's a remarkable medium-bodied wine. Screwcap. 14.5% alc. **Rating** 97 **To** 2050 $90 ✪

🍷🍷🍷🍷🍷 **Margaret River Chardonnay 2014** This is more about complexity than single-minded energy, and suggests some accidental mlf may form a part of the blend assembled at the end of maturation. It is rich, with cashew, fig and white peach fruit flowing seamlessly through the palate. Screwcap. 13% alc. **Rating** 95 **To** 2025 $37

Margaret River Cabernet Sauvignon 2013 Interesting, very interesting. The colour, the freshness of the aromas and flavours, the finely sculpted tannins and the overall harmony suggest 13.5% alcohol, not 14.5%. All this conjecture is, of course, irrelevant: it is the outcome that matters – here a distillation of elegance. Screwcap. **Rating** 95 **To** 2028 $45

Margaret River Sauvignon Blanc Semillon 2015 57/43%. The undergrowth of herb, grass and capsicum to the canopy of gently tropical fruits produces a complex wine, delicately pointing to the 20% fermented in new French oak and matured there for 14 weeks. Screwcap. 12.5% alc. **Rating** 94 **To** 2017 $24 ✪

Filius Margaret River Chardonnay 2014 Throws down the gauntlet with its mouthwatering energy and power. Its acidity guarantees that it will thrive in bottle, but there is a strong argument to say that it is as ready as it will ever be right now. Screwcap. 12.5% alc. **Rating** 94 **To** 2024 $28 ✪

Margaret River Shiraz 2013 Let no one doubt the potential of this wine, but I was slightly surprised that the tannins weren't polished a little more – this has a slightly savoury shroud to its flavours. Perhaps I jump before I looked, for there is also a pepper/licorice/earth component that is very attractive. Screwcap. 14.5% alc. **Rating** 94 **To** 2028 $37

🍷🍷🍷🍷 **Classic Dry White Margaret River Semillon Sauvignon Blanc 2015** **Rating** 93 **To** 2019 $19 ✪

Classic Dry Red Margaret River Shiraz 2014 **Rating** 92 **To** 2024 $19 ✪

Filius Margaret River Cabernet Merlot 2014 **Rating** 92 **To** 2024 $28

Veronique ★★★★☆

PO Box 599, Angaston, SA 5353 **Region** Barossa Valley
T (08) 8565 3214 **www**.veroniquewines.com.au **Open** Not
Winemaker Peter Manning **Est.** 2004 **Dozens** 2000

Peter Manning, general manager of Angas Park Fruits, and wife Vicki moved to Mt McKenzie in the 1990s. His wine consumption soon focused on Barossa shiraz, and he quickly became a close drinking partner, with Domenic Torzi, of all things shiraz. By 2004 the Mannings decided it was high time to produce a Barossa shiraz of their own, and, with the help of Torzi, sourced grapes from three outstanding blocks. The vineyards also include mataro and grenache (thoroughly excusable in the context) and sauvignon blanc. Exports to Hong Kong.

🍷🍷🍷🍷🍷 **Old Vine Barossa Grenache Shiraz Mataro 2013** 42% grenache and 41% mataro from Greenock dating back to 1904, 17% shiraz from Greenock and Eden Valley, crushed and open-fermented, basket-pressed, matured in French and American oak for 21 months. Excellent crimson-purple hue; one from left field, and staring McLaren Vale down with its lush assemblage of juicy red and black fruits undiminished by 21 months in barrel. It has excellent mouthfeel (no hint of alcohol heat), balance and length. In a word, remarkable. Screwcap. 14.5% alc. **Rating** 96 **To** 2028 $22 ✪

🍷🍷🍷🍷 **Foundation Barossa Shiraz 2013** **Rating** 92 **To** 2033 $22 ✪

Barossa Cabernet Sauvignon 2013 **Rating** 92 **To** 2033 $22 ✪

Vickery Wines   ★★★★☆

28 The Parade, Norwood, SA 5067 **Region** Clare Valley/Eden Valley
T (08) 8362 8622 **www**.vickerywines.com.au **Open** Not
Winemaker John Vickery, Phil Lehmann **Est.** 2014 **Dozens** 2000 **Vyds** 12ha

It must be a strange feeling for John Vickery to begin at the beginning again, 60 years after his first vintage, in 1951. His interest in, love of, and exceptional skills with riesling began with Leo Buring in 1955 at Chateau Leonay. Over the intervening years he became the uncrowned but absolute monarch of riesling makers in Australia until, in his semi-retirement, he passed the mantle on to Jeffrey Grosset. Along the way he had (unsurprisingly) won the Wolf Blass Riesling Award at the Canberra International Riesling Challenge 2007, and had been judged by his peers as Australia's Greatest Living Winemaker in a survey conducted by *The Age Epicure* in '03. His new venture has been undertaken in conjunction with Phil Lehmann, with 12ha of Clare and Eden Valley riesling involved, and wine marketer Jonathon Hesketh moving largely invisibly in the background. The Da Vinci code letters and numerals are easy when it comes to EVR (Eden Valley Riesling) and WVR (Watervale Riesling), thereafter the code strikes. The numerics are the dates of harvest, thus '103' is 1 March, '172' is 17 February. The two initials that follow are even more delphic, standing for the name of the vineyard or those of the multiple owners. In 2015 'ZV' translates as Zander Vineyard, while 'CK' is the Castine and Koemer families, who jointly own the vineyard. Da Vinci freaks will be buzzing with excitement when they find that the option of leaving 'B' for Brazel as a further ownership recognition was left out because only a small proportion of the fruit came from that vineyard.

🍷🍷🍷🍷🍷 **Eden Valley Riesling 2015** EVR 103 ZV. Beautifully refined style. Gives
generosity both a nod and a wink via juicy/blossomy lemon and lime flavours,
but then drills down to a dry, slatey, talc-like finish. Right in the zone. Screwcap.
12.5% alc. **Rating** 95 **To** 2030 $23 CM ✪

🍷🍷🍷🍷🍷 **Watervale Riesling 2015 Rating** 93 **To** 2028 $23 CM ✪

Victory Point Wines   ★★★★★

4 Holben Road, Cowaramup, WA 6284 **Region** Margaret River
T 0417 954 6555 **www**.victorypointwines.com **Open** By appt
Winemaker Mark Messenger (Contract) **Est.** 1997 **Dozens** 2500 **Vyds** 13ha

Judith and Gary Berson have set their sights high. They established their vineyard without irrigation, emulating those of the Margaret River pioneers (including Moss Wood). The fully mature plantings comprise 4.2ha chardonnay and 0.5ha of pinot noir, the remainder Bordeaux varieties, with cabernet sauvignon (6.2ha), cabernet franc (0.5ha), malbec (0.8ha) and petit verdot (0.7ha).

🍷🍷🍷🍷🍷 **Margaret River Cabernet Sauvignon 2012** Hand-picked, open-fermented,
27 days on skins, 18 months in French oak (50% new), when 6.5% malbec,
4.5% petit verdot and 3% cabernet franc were blended in. The time on skins has
increased the tannin level significantly, but it remains in balance with the complex
and intense suite of black fruit flavours. A carefully assembled wine with a great
future. Screwcap. 14% alc. **Rating** 96 **To** 2042 $40 ✪
Margaret River Cabernet Sauvignon Malbec Petit Verdot 2011 77%
cabernet sauvignon, 15% malbec and 8% petit verdot. Has retained excellent hue;
an extremely elegant medium-bodied wine made from high quality grapes treated
with skill in the winery; there isn't a hair out of place; blackcurrant/cassis, dried
herb and black olive flavours wend their way in a silky stream across the palate,
guided by fine, savoury tannins. Screwcap. 13.5% alc. **Rating** 96 **To** 2031 $40 ✪
Margaret River Chardonnay 2012 Mendoza, Dijon, 76, 95, 96 and 277 clones,
whole bunch-pressed, 50/50% wild and cultured yeast barrel-fermented, mlf,
10 months on lees in French oak (30% new). In the centre of Margaret River
chardonnay style, celebrating depth and complexity courtesy of grapefruit juice
and zest, fig, stone fruit and melon. Screwcap. 12.5% alc. **Rating** 95 **To** 2022 $40
Margaret River Rose 2015 Made from malbec and cabernet franc, with a small
amount barrel-fermented, which has not led to any salmon tinge to the colour.

It has a distinctive flavour profile, not surprising given its varietal base; spiced plum comes to the fore of both its bouquet and palate, and continues in an unbroken stream through to the finish. Screwcap. 13% alc. **Rating** 95 **To** 2017 $23 **✪**

The Mallee Root Malbec Cabernet Sauvignon Petit Verdot 2014
44/31/25%, the varieties vinified separately, spending 17 months in French oak (50% new) before blending trials completed. Blackcurrant, plum and black cherry all contribute, and collectively push oak and tannins onto the back of the stage. Screwcap. 14% alc. **Rating** 95 **To** 2029 $28 **✪**

♥♥♥♥ Margaret River Malbec 2013 **Rating** 89 **To** 2020 $35

View Road Wines   ★★★★

Peacocks Road, Lenswood, SA 5240 **Region** Adelaide Hills
T 0402 180 383 **www.**viewroadwines.com.au **Open** Not
Winemaker Josh Tuckfield **Est.** 2011 **Dozens** 500
View Road Wines sources prosecco, arneis, chardonnay, sangiovese, merlot, sagrantino and syrah from Adelaide Hills vineyards; shiraz, aglicanico and sagrantino from McLaren Vale vineyards; and nero d'Avola and fiano from the Riverland. All of the wines are wild yeast-fermented, and matured in used oak.

♥♥♥♥♥ The International Syrah Sangiovese 2014 75/25%. Extended time on skins prior to maturation in older French oak. It injects savoury, peppery elements into fresh black cherry and blackberry flavours. A fair amount of character to be tucked into here. The odd (fresh) leathery, nutty note wafts in the background. Firm tannin. Highly accomplished. Screwcap. 13.2% alc. **Rating** 94 **To** 2028 $35 CM

♥♥♥♥♡ McLaren Vale Shiraz 2014 **Rating** 93 **To** 2025 CM
Adelaide Hills Syrah 2014 **Rating** 92 **To** 2020 $37 CM
Piccadilly Valley Chardonnay 2014 **Rating** 90 **To** 2020 CM
Piccadilly Valley Rosato 2015 **Rating** 90 **To** 2017 $32 CM

Vigna Bottin   ★★★★

Lot 2 Plains Road, Sellicks Hill, McLaren Vale, SA 5171 **Region** McLaren Vale
T 0414 562 956 **www.**vignabottin.com.au **Open** Not
Winemaker Paolo Bottin **Est.** 2006 **Dozens** 800 **Vyds** 16ha
The Bottin family migrated to Australia in 1954 from Treviso in northern Italy, where they were grapegrowers. The family began growing grapes in McLaren Vale in 1970, focusing on mainstream varieties for sale to wineries in the region. When son Paolo and wife Maria made a trip back to Italy in '98, they were inspired to do more, and, says Paolo, 'My love for barbera and sangiovese was sealed during a vintage in Pavia. I came straight home to plant both varieties in our family plot. My father was finally happy!' They now trade under the catchy phrase 'Italian Vines, Australian Wines'.

♥♥♥♥♡ McLaren Vale Sangiovese 2014 Cracking example of an early-drinking sangiovese. Ribbed with tannin, but it's mostly about jubey cherry and chicory flavours. It hits, runs and doesn't let up until you're well and truly satisfied, if not impressed. Screwcap. 13.5% alc. **Rating** 93 **To** 2020 $28 CM
McLaren Vale Shiraz 2013 Rich, sweet plum and blackberry flavours come folded with coffee grounds and chocolate. It's a tried and true formula and it's executed well here. Tannin slips a firm noose around it all. Big Red drinkers will like what they find here. Screwcap. 14.5% alc. **Rating** 92 **To** 2022 $40 CM
McLaren Vale Nero d'Avola 2015 It pulls licorice, date and rich blackberried flavour through a well-proportioned palate. You have a rich red on your hands and you're made fully aware of it. It's a good example of the variety. Screwcap. 14% alc. **Rating** 90 **To** 2018 $35 CM

♥♥♥♥ McLaren Vale Vermentino 2015 **Rating** 88 **To** 2016 $24 CM
McLaren Vale Rose 2015 **Rating** 88 **To** 2017 $24 CM

Vignerons Schmolzer & Brown

39 Thorley Road, Stanley, Vic 3747 **Region** Beechworth
T 0411 053 487 **www**.vsandb.com.au **Open** By appt
Winemaker Tessa Brown **Est.** 2014 **Dozens** 500 **Vyds** 2ha

Winemaker/viticulturist Tessa Brown graduated from CSU with a degree in viticulture in the late 1990s, and undertook postgraduate winemaking studies at Adelaide Uni in the mid-2000s. Her self-description of being 'reasonably peripatetic' covers her winemaking in Orange in '99, and Canberra, SA, Rioja, Strathbogie Ranges and Central Otago before joining Kooyong and Port Phillip Estate in '08. She and architect partner Jeremy Schmolzer have kept an eye on North East Victoria for a number of years, and in '09 Mark Walpole showed them a property that he described as 'the jewel in the crown of the GI'. When it came onto the market unexpectedly in '12, they were in a position to jump. The property (named Thorley) was a 20ha cleared property; they began planting chardonnay and shiraz in Oct '14, and have also planted riesling and nebbiolo. By sheer chance, just across the road from Thorley was a tiny vineyard, a bit over 0.4 hectares, with dry-grown pinot and chardonnay around 20 years old. When they realised it was not being managed for production, they struck up a working relationship with the owners, getting the vineyard into shape, and made their first (very good) wines in '14.

♀♀♀♀♀ **Pret-A-Rose Rose 2015** Salmon-onion in colour. Intensity of aroma and flavour is up a gear on last year's release. Savoury cherry, earth and spice notes with a tangy cranberried burst to the finish. Dry style. Eminently food-friendly. Screwcap. 13.5% alc. **Rating** 93 **To** 2017 $27 CM ✪

Brunnen Beechworth Pinot Noir 2014 Bright, clear colour of good depth; a plummy bouquet and fore-palate before a savoury/stalky/earthy back-palate and finish. Give it a few years, and all the pieces will grow and fuse together. Screwcap. 13% alc. **Rating** 92 **To** 2024 $39

Vinaceous Wines

49 Bennett Street, East Perth, WA 6004 (postal) **Region** Various
T (08) 9221 4666 **www**.vinaceous.com.au **Open** Not
Winemaker Gavin Berry, Michael Kerrigan **Est.** 2007 **Dozens** 25 000

This is the somewhat quirky venture of wine marketer Nick Stacy, Michael Kerrigan (winemaker/partner Hay Shed Hill) and Gavin Berry (winemaker/partner West Cape Howe). The fast-moving and fast-growing brand was originally directed at the US market, but has changed direction due to the domestic demand engendered (one might guess) by the decidedly exotic/erotic labels and, more importantly, by the fact that the wines are of seriously good quality and equally good value. They're not just inflatable dolls. Margaret River provides over half of the production, the remainder from McLaren Vale and the Adelaide Hills. With only two exceptions (Shiraz Grenache Tempranillo and Semillon Sauvignon Blanc) they are single varietals. Yet more labels, ranges and wines are in the pipeline; the website is the best method of keeping you up to date. Exports to the UK, the US, Canada, South America, Denmark, Finland, Indonesia, the Philippines, Thailand, Singapore and Hong Kong.

♀♀♀♀♀ **Right Reverend V Benevolentia Syrah 2014** Stern with tannin but flush with black-cherry fruit. Liberal doses of black pepper and meaty spice notes add layers of interest and complexity. This is a wine of beauty and presence that will live and mature terrifically over the next decade and (well) beyond. The price makes it a steal. Screwcap. 14.5% alc. **Rating** 95 **To** 2030 $25 CM ✪

Red Right Hand Margaret River Shiraz Grenache Tempranillo 2014 Exceptionally well crafted. Just the right amount of this, and just the right amount of that. Curvaceous red and black-berried fruit, belts of tannin, clovey/cedary inputs and a gentle creaminess to the texture. Vivid and alive. Spice notes from the grenache work a treat. Screwcap. 14.5% alc. **Rating** 94 **To** 2024 $25 CM ✪

Right Reverend V Patientia Cabernet Sauvignon 2014 An elegant, almost tangy cabernet with a clear serious side. This has been well crafted. It tastes of boysenberry and blackcurrant, carries herb and dust notes in good measure, and has an application of smoky oak that is just right. Excellent buying. Screwcap. 14.5% alc. **Rating** 94 **To** 2028 $25 CM ✪

Voodoo Moon Margaret River Malbec 2014 From the Wilyabrup district. Matured in all-French oak. It pours on leathery, blackberried flavours and does so in fine style. Gravel/earth/gum leaf notes build on the wine's beautiful foundation. And rusty tannin helps lead it out through the finish. Grunty and polished at once; a cut diamond of a wine. Screwcap. 14% alc. **Rating** 94 **To** 2024 $25 CM ✪

🍷🍷🍷🍷🍷 **Raconteur Cabernet Sauvignon 2014 Rating** 92 **To** 2028 $25 CM ✪
Right Reverend V Castitas WBX Semillon Sauvignon Blanc 2015 Rating 91 **To** 2017 $25 CM
Sirenya Adelaide Hills Pinot Grigio 2015 Rating 90 **To** 2016 $22 CM
Snake Charmer McLaren Vale Shiraz 2014 Rating 90 **To** 2021 $25 CM

Vinden Estate ★★★★

17 Gillards Road, Pokolbin, NSW 2320 **Region** Hunter Valley
T (02) 4998 7410 **www.**vindenestate.com.au **Open** Wed–Sun 10–5
Winemaker Guy Vinden, John Baruzzi **Est.** 1998 **Dozens** 1000 **Vyds** 6.5ha
Sandra and Guy Vinden have a beautiful home and cellar door, landscaped gardens and a vineyard that includes shiraz (2.5ha), merlot and alicante bouschet (2ha each), with the Brokenback mountain range in the distance. The wines are made onsite, using estate-grown red grapes; semillon and chardonnay are purchased from other growers. The reds are open-fermented, hand-plunged and basket-pressed.

🍷🍷🍷🍷🍷 **The Vinden Basketcase Hunter Valley Shiraz 2015** A horror season has turned out a delicious wine. Cherried, earthen, cut with mineral and splashed with wood smoke. It's vibrant and yet it has gravitas. Don't let the light colour put you off; this drinks like a charm. Drink it young. Screwcap. 13.8% alc. **Rating** 94 **To** 2020 $30 CM ✪

🍷🍷🍷🍷🍷 **Basket Press Hunter Valley Shiraz 2013 Rating** 93 **To** 2026 $35 CM
Hunter Valley Semillon 2015 Rating 91 **To** 2024 $25 CM
Hunter Valley Chardonnay 2015 Rating 91 **To** 2019 $30 CM

Vinea Marson ★★★★★

411 Heathcote-Rochester Road, Heathcote, Vic 3523 **Region** Heathcote
T 0417 035 673 **www.**vineamarson.com **Open** By appt
Winemaker Mario Marson **Est.** 2000 **Dozens** 2500 **Vyds** 7.12ha
Owner-winemaker Mario Marson spent many years as the winemaker/viticulturist with the late Dr John Middleton at the celebrated Mount Mary. He purchased the Vinea Marson property in 1999, on the eastern slopes of the Mt Camel Range, and has planted shiraz and viognier, plus Italian varieties, sangiovese, nebbiolo, barbera and refosco dal peduncolo rosso. Since leaving Mount Mary he has undertaken vintage work at Isole e Olena in Tuscany, worked as winemaker at Jasper Hill, and as consultant and winemaker for Stefani Estate. Exports to China.

🍷🍷🍷🍷🍷 **Viognier 2013** Whole bunch-pressed, settled for 24 hours, fermented in French barriques (25% new) with cultured yeast, matured for 6 months. This is a very smart viognier. It has juicy citrus, apricot and ginger flavours, subtle oak and a long, well-balanced palate. Bravo. Diam. 13% alc. **Rating** 95 **To** 2017 $29 ✪
Rose 2013 75% sangiovese, 25% nebbiolo, the sangiovese pressed and treated as a white wine, the nebbiolo bled off after crushing, both components fermented in used French barriques and matured for 9 months. Light salmon colour; a wave of complexity crashes through the mouth, with a wash of spices first up, then a bowl of cherries of every imaginable type and style. Outstanding food style. Screwcap. 13.5% alc. **Rating** 95 **To** 2017 $29 ✪

🍷🍷🍷🍷🍷 **Sangiovese 2012 Rating** 91 **To** 2021 $40
Syrah 2012 Rating 90 **To** 2029 $40

Vinifera Wines

194 Henry Lawson Drive, Mudgee, NSW 2850 **Region** Mudgee
T (02) 6372 2461 **www**.viniferawines.com.au **Open** Mon–Sat 10–5, Sun 10–4
Winemaker Jacob Stein **Est.** 1997 **Dozens** 1200 **Vyds** 12ha
Having lived in Mudgee for 15 years, Tony McKendry (a regional medical superintendent)
and wife Debbie succumbed to the lure; they planted their small (1.5ha) vineyard in 1995. In
Debbie's words, 'Tony, in his spare two minutes per day, also decided to start Wine Science at
CSU in 1992.' She continues, 'His trying to live 27 hours per day (plus our four kids!) fell to
pieces when he was involved in a severe car smash in 1997. Two months in hospital stopped
full-time medical work, and the winery dreams became inevitable.' Financial compensation
finally came through and the small winery was built. The now-expanded vineyard includes
chardonnay, cabernet sauvignon (3ha each), semillon, tempranillo, grenache (1.5ha each) and
smaller plantings of graciano and monastrell.

ŸŸŸŸŸ **Organic Mudgee Semillon 2015** Light-fingered and bodied; crisp apple
blossom and fresh fruit join with classic lemon/lanolin varietal characters. It
justified an early raid on the cellar, but it definitely has its best years to come in the
next decade. Screwcap. 12.4% alc. **Rating** 90 **To** 2027 $23
Reserve Mudgee Chardonnay 2015 Barrel fermentation has given the
bouquet a distinct smoky/funky edge that works well with the more gentle stone
fruits and grilled nut flavours of the well-balanced palate. Screwcap. 13% alc.
Rating 90 **To** 2016 $23

Vinrock

1/25 George Street, Thebarton, SA 5031 (postal) **Region** McLaren Vale
T (08) 8408 8900 **www**.vinrock.com **Open** Not
Winemaker Michael Fragos (Consultant) **Est.** 1998 **Dozens** 13 000 **Vyds** 30ha
Owners Don Luca, Marco Iannetti and Anthony De Pizzol all have backgrounds in the wine
industry, none more than Don, a former board member of Tatachilla. He also planted the Luca
Vineyard in 1998 (21ha of shiraz, 5ha grenache and 4ha cabernet sauvignon). The majority of
the grapes are sold, but steadily increasing quantities of wine have been made from the best
blocks in the vineyard, many at tempting prices.

ŸŸŸŸŸ **Block 4 McLaren Vale Shiraz 2014** Red and black-berried fruit flavours are
on the sweet, jubey side but there's more than enough tannin to give it a sense of
sturdiness. This isn't going to fall over in a hurry. A veneer of (integrated) oak adds
just enough razzle. Screwcap. 14.5% alc. **Rating** 93 **To** 2027 $50 CM
McLaren Vale Shiraz 2014 Dense, deep colour; an ultra-concentrated wine
in the style that many '14 SA reds will have willy nilly; it is well balanced and
will respond well to time in the cellar. How well, only time will tell. Screwcap.
14.5% alc. **Rating** 90 **To** 2029 $25

ŸŸŸŸ **Bayliss Road McLaren Vale Shiraz 2014** **Rating** 89 **To** 2039 $20
McLaren Vale Grenache 2014 **Rating** 89 **To** 2019 $25
McLaren Vale Grenache Shiraz Mataro 2014 **Rating** 89 **To** 2017 $25

Vinteloper

195 Norton Summit Road, Norton Summit, SA 5135 **Region** Adelaide Hills
T 0415 297 787 **www**.vinteloper.com.au **Open** By appt
Winemaker David Bowley **Est.** 2008 **Dozens** 1500 **Vyds** 3.5ha
In David Bowley's words, 'Vinteloper is a winery started by a guy who decided, on instinct,
to skip through his own daisy fields.' Vineyards and wineries had permeated David's mind
before he left school, so it was inevitable that he would obtain his oenology degree at Adelaide
University (in 2002). After several years training in both Australia and France, with some of the
biggest and smallest players in the game, he founded Vinteloper in 2008. Wife Sharon draws
the unique labels. Vinteloper continues to handcraft wines styled with a light touch and upbeat
aromatics. Exports to the UK and NZ.

ŸŸŸŸ♀ **Adelaide Hills Shiraz 2014** A high-yielding, cool-grown shiraz that has been well treated in the winery. Predominantly black fruits – blackberry to the fore – are coralled by an ever-changing circle of spice, pepper, licorice, briar, cedar and, most importantly, tannins, oak in the background. Busy? Yes. Screwcap. 13.9% alc. Rating 93 To 2034 $40

McLaren Vale Shiraz 2013 Good hue; a medium to full-bodied shiraz with considerable depth and tannins; the usual McLaren Vale chocolate has gone on leave, allowing the savoury nuances of the blackberry fruit to express themselves, along with clearly defined tannins. Screwcap. 14% alc. Rating 92 To 2038 $40

Langhorne Creek Touriga Nacional 2013 Wild-fermented, 21 days on skins, matured in 50/50% used French and American oak for 24 months. Opulent touriga, rich fleshy cherry/berry fruits having largely absorbed the oak. Screwcap. 13% alc. Rating 91 To 2020 $28

Langhorne Creek Touriga Nacional 2012 Finer than the '13, perhaps due to just the extra year in bottle. Some attractive spicy notes on top of cherry fruit. Screwcap. 13% alc. Rating 91 To 2019 $28

Odeon Lenswood Pinot Noir 2014 Deeper colour than the '13, but with many of the hallmarks of it, not surprising given the unique nature of the site age and planting density. Another low-yielding year has also had an impact, but there is more fruit. This is tiger country, and will always be a challenge for David Bowley to control. Cork. 15% alc. Rating 90 To 2020 $95

Adelaide Hills Pinot Noir 2014 Light colour and overall flavour suggest relatively quick development; spicy/savoury/whole bunch stemmy notes tell a consistent story. No lack of effort, just a work in progress. Screwcap. 13.5% alc. Rating 90 To 2022 $40

Odeon Lenswood Pinot Noir 2013 The light colour belies the intensity of the wine; the bouquet has spicy/savoury/smoky aromas, the palate dragging some purple fruits forward, although these remain subservient to the main game. A striking wine that needs to calm down and let the fruit have more freedom to speak. Cork. 14% alc. Rating 90 To 2019 $95

Adelo 2013 A field blend (planted '03) of 62% touriga national, 26% shiraz, 7% grenache and 5% pinot noir, fermented separately. A robust, full-bodied blend that has a lot going for it, notably its balance and length, down to the All Black fruits. Screwcap. 13.8% alc. Rating 90 To 2030 $28

ŸŸŸŸ **Odeon Riesling 2015** Rating 89 To 2023 $42
Watervale Riesling 2014 Rating 89 To 2019 $28
Southern Fleurieu Pinot Gris 2015 Rating 89 To 2017 $28
Watervale Riesling 2015 Rating 88 To 2020 $28

Vintners Ridge Estate ★★★★

Lot 18 Veraison Place, Yallingup, Margaret River, WA 6285 **Region** Margaret River
T 0417 956 943 **www.**vintnersridge.com.au **Open** By appt
Winemaker Flying Fish Cove (Simon Ding) **Est.** 2001 **Dozens** 500 **Vyds** 2.1ha
When Maree and Robin Adair purchased the Vintners Ridge vineyard in 2006 (cabernet sauvignon), it had already produced three crops, having been planted in Nov '01 (which is a perfectly permissible establishment date). The vineyard overlooks the picturesque Geographe Bay.

ŸŸŸŸ♀ **Margaret River Cabernet Sauvignon 2014** Blackcurrant, mulberry and boysenberry notes meet mint and creamy oak. It flows effortlessly and well but could do with a touch more drive to the finish. It will cellar handily. Screwcap. 14.5% alc. Rating 91 To 2027 $30 CM

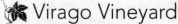

Virago Vineyard ★★★☆

23 Green Street, Wangaratta, Vic 3677 (postal) **Region** Beechworth
T 0411 718 369 **www**.viragobeechworth.com.au **Open** Not
Winemaker Karen Coats, Rick Kinzbrunner **Est.** 2007 **Dozens** 175 **Vyds** 1ha
Virago Vineyard brings together two people with very different backgrounds. Karen Coats was a tax accountant in her previous life, but is now in her final year of a 6-year Bachelor of Wine Science degree at CSU. It was her love of nebbiolo and the Beechworth region that made Virago Vineyard her new office of choice. Prue Keith is an orthopaedic surgeon by day, night and weekend, devoting her free time (whatever is not occupied by mountain biking, skiing and trekking to the peaks of mountains) to Virago Vineyard. She clearly has the same star sign as I do. The vines had been removed from the property long before they purchased it, but the existing terracing, old posts and broken wires laid down a challenge that was easily accepted, although the planting of nebbiolo was not so easy. The one and only Rick Kinzbrunner has a more than passing interest in nebbiolo, so it was inevitable that he would be the contract winemaker.

🍷🍷🍷🍷🍷 **Beechworth Nebbiolo 2011** Similar colour to the '12, and the wine is every bit as fresh; here, though, the tannins are finer, more likely due to the vintage than an extra year in bottle, but I may well be wrong on that. What matters is the most attractive red cherry/berry palate, and the balance and length of the wine. Cork. 14% alc. **Rating** 94 **To** 2026 $45

🍷🍷🍷🍷 **Beechworth Nebbiolo 2012** **Rating** 89 **To** 2022 $45

Virgara Wines ★★★★

143 Heaslip Road, Angle Vale, SA 5117 **Region** Adelaide Plains
T (08) 8284 7688 **www**.virgarawines.com.au **Open** Mon–Fri 9–5, w'ends 11–4
Winemaker Tony Carapetis **Est.** 2001 **Dozens** 50 000 **Vyds** 118ha
In 1962 the Virgara family – father Michael, mother Maria and 10 children – migrated to Australia from southern Italy. Through the hard work so typical of many such families, in due course they became market gardeners on land purchased at Angle Vale ('67), and in the early '90s acquired an existing vineyard in Angle Vale. The plantings have since expanded to almost 120ha of shiraz, cabernet sauvignon, grenache, malbec, merlot, riesling, sangiovese, sauvignon blanc, pinot grigio and alicante bouschet. In 2001 the Virgara brothers purchased the former Barossa Valley Estates winery, but used it only for storage and maturation. The death of Domenic Virgara in a road accident led to the employment of former Palandri (and, before that, Tahbilk) winemaker Tony Carapetis, and the full re-commissioning of the winery. Exports to the US, Canada, China, Thailand, Malaysia and Japan.

🍷🍷🍷🍷½ **Adelaide Shiraz 2013** This is more of everything: colour, fruit, oak, tannins and alcohol – except that the 15.8% on the label is said to be a typo, the correct figure 14.8%. Against the odds, and while it is well into full-bodied territory, there is a coherence and balance to its tumble of black fruits, licorice, dark chocolate fruit, soft tannins and twitch of oak. Screwcap. **Rating** 90 **To** 2028 $18 ✪

Gran Reserve Adelaide Merlot Cabernet Sauvignon Malbec 2013 A wine about power, first, foremost and last. It's a remarkable effort from the Adelaide Plains; if there is any Adelaide Hills fruit in it, it's not disclosed, and is in the Adelaide super zone in any event. Regardless, the three varieties are also estate-grown. The only issue is the tannins, demanding much patience. Diam. 13.8% alc. **Rating** 90 **To** 2043 $50

🍷🍷🍷🍷 **Sangiovese Alicante Bouschet Rose 2015** **Rating** 89 **To** 2017 $13 ✪
Gran Reserve Adelaide Cabernet Sauvignon 2014 **Rating** 89 **To** 2034 $30

Vogel ★★★★

324 Massey Road, Watchem West, Vic 3482 (postal) **Region** Grampians
T (03) 5281 2230 **Open** Not
Winemaker Sam Vogel **Est.** 1998 **Dozens** 150
Sam Vogel is a graduate in wine science from CSU, and worked in Margaret River and the Rhône Valley before joining Scott Ireland at Provenance Wines in Geelong. The eponymous winemaking venture focuses on cool climate shiraz using both Old and New World practices; he generally includes 20% whole bunches, believing this provides greater complexity, in terms of both structure and aromas.

🍷🍷🍷🍷🍷 **Geelong Pinot Noir 2014** Hand picked and tipped straight into a fermenter onto stems from the same block. As a result the wine's working title was '150% stem'. There's certainly a lot of stem influence here but whether or not it's excessive will be down to personal preference. It carries it; tannin is long and stringy and there are earthen/herbal notes aplenty, but they're hitched to succulent cherry/plum/violet fruit. It puts on a show. Screwcap. 13.4% alc. **Rating** 93 To 2025 $35 CM
Otways Sauvignon Blanc 2014 Fermented and matured in old French oak. Tropical fruit rises to greet you before lemongrass, gravel and sweet pea flavours get a look in. Mouthfeel is certainly a highlight. Tending towards richness, in a good way. Screwcap. 13% alc. **Rating** 92 To 2017 $32 CM
Noisy Ritual King Valley Pinot Gris 2015 Barrel-fermented, but released young. Attractive pink tinge. Apples and spice with an edge of rosewater. Good performer. Screwcap. 13% alc. **Rating** 91 To 2016 $25 CM

Voyager Estate ★★★★★

Lot 1 Stevens Road, Margaret River, WA 6285 **Region** Margaret River
T (08) 9757 6354 **www**.voyagerestate.com.au **Open** 7 days 10–5
Winemaker Steve James, Travis Lemm **Est.** 1978 **Dozens** 40 000 **Vyds** 110ha
The late mining magnate Michael Wright pursued several avenues of business and agriculture before setting his sights on owning a vineyard and winery. It was thus an easy decision when he was able to buy what was then called Freycinet Estate from founder and leading viticulturist Peter Gherardi in 1991. Peter had established the vineyard in '78, and it was significantly expanded by Michael over the ensuing years. Apart from the Cape Dutch-style tasting room and vast rose garden, the signpost for the estate is the massive Australian flag pole – after Parliament House in Canberra, the largest flag pole in Australia. Michael's daughter, Alexandra Burt, has been at the helm of Voyager Estate for many years, supported by general manager Chris Furtado and a long-serving and committed staff. Michael is remembered as a larger-than life character, more at home in his favourite work pants and boots than a suit, and never happier than when trundling around the estate on a four-wheeler or fixing a piece of machinery. Exports to the UK, the US, Canada, Germany, Indonesia, Singapore, Japan, Hong Kong and China.

🍷🍷🍷🍷🍷 **Tom Price Margaret River Chardonnay 2014** A barrel selection from Block 6 (57%) and Block 5 (43%). Has wonderful focus, drive and intensity to the fruit, aromas and flavours; clone 95 seems the major contributor, but the percentages aren't far from 50/50% with the Gingin clone. Whatever and however, this is a beautiful Margaret River chardonnay. Screwcap. 12% alc. **Rating** 96 To 2024 $85
Broadvale Block 6 Margaret River Chardonnay 2014 Clone 95, hand-picked, cooled overnight, whole bunch-pressed, wild yeast fermentation in French barriques (60% new, 40% 1yo) plus 11 months maturation; the high natural acidity of Clone 95 led to mlf and lees stirring every 4 weeks during the maturation period. A great demonstration of the quality of clone 95, singing vibrantly and freshly, grapefruit and white peach happily joining the song on the long palate. Screwcap. 11.5% alc. **Rating** 95 To 2022 $60
Margaret River Cabernet Sauvignon Merlot 2012 91% cabernet sauvignon, 6% merlot, 3% petit verdot, the parcels kept separate during 20 months maturation

in French oak (50% new). A powerful, dense wine full of rich, plushy fruit, seeming riper than Girt by Sea, when the opposite is the case – or perhaps it's just the greater intensity and drive. This will certainly improve with further time (5+ years) in bottle. Screwcap. 13.5% alc. **Rating** 95 **To** 2037 $70

Project V9 Old Block Margaret River Cabernet Sauvignon 2012 Matured for 20 months in French barriques (50% new). While there is no shortage of structure, the tannins are less strident than those of Project U12; the cassis fruits are given more playtime, the balance better, the wine more approachable. Screwcap. 13.5% alc. **Rating** 95 **To** 2030 $90

Tom Price Margaret River Cabernet Sauvignon 2012 A 50/50% barrel selection of the Old Block and North Block, the barrels selected and blended after 12 months maturation, then returned to oak for a further 10 months. Rings true to the Tom Price style with no concessions, savoury tannins running around the blackcurrant and bay leaf fruits; the balance is there, and the wine's best days are still ahead of it. Screwcap. 13.5% alc. **Rating** 95 **To** 2035 $150

Margaret River Sauvignon Blanc Semillon 2015 68/32%, from 10 estate vineyard blocks, the semillon matured for 2 months in French oak. It has that extra level of depth that is the birthmark of all Voyager Estate wines, providing fuel for much discussion about the finer details of the blend percentages and so forth. Will stay the distance. Screwcap. 13% alc. **Rating** 94 **To** 2018 $24 ✪

Margaret River Chardonnay 2014 From seven blocks with clones 95, 96, 76 and Gin Gin, hand-picked over 2 weeks between 11° and 12.5° baume, whole bunch-pressed, 85% wild ferment, 11 months in French barriques (40% new). Has the richest array of fruit flavours of the '14 Voyager Chardonnays, even if its structure is less complex. Screwcap. 13% alc. **Rating** 94 **To** 2022 $45

Margaret River Shiraz 2014 A classy, complex shiraz with an intense bouquet and a persistent palate of blackberry, licorice and briar. The low level of tannins means (paradoxically) that the wine is a now or later proposition. Screwcap. 14% alc. **Rating** 94 **To** 2034 $38

Project U12 North Block Margaret River Cabernet Sauvignon 2012 Destemmed, open-fermented, the static fermenters with pump-overs during 16 days, then macerated on skins for a further 21 days, matured for 20 months in French barriques (50% new). The long skin contact/maceration has given the wine a strong tannin structure that lovers of young Bordeaux will think is perfectly justified. Screwcap. 14% alc. **Rating** 94 **To** 2032 $90

ŶŶŶŶŶ **Girt by Sea Margaret River Cabernet Merlot 2014** Rating 92 To 2029 $28
Broadvale Block 5 Margaret River Chardonnay 2014 Rating 91 To 2020 $60

Walter Clappis Wine Co ★★★★

Rifle Range Road, McLaren Vale, SA 5171 **Region** McLaren Vale
T (08) 8323 8818 **www**.hedonistwines.com.au **Open** Not
Winemaker Walter and Kimberley Clappis **Est.** 1982 **Dozens** 15 000 **Vyds** 35ha
Walter Clappis has been making wine in McLaren Vale for well over 30 years, and over that time has won innumerable trophies and gold medals, including the prestigious George Mackey Memorial Trophy with his 2009 The Hedonist Shiraz, chosen as the best wine exported from Australia for the year in question. He now has daughter Kimberley and son-in-law James Cooter, both with impressive CVs, supporting him on the winery floor. The estate plantings of shiraz (14ha), cabernet sauvignon (10ha), merlot (9ha) and tempranillo (2ha) are the cornerstone of his business, which provides the home for the Amicus and The Hedonist wines. Exports include the UK, the US, Canada and China.

ŶŶŶŶŶ **The Hedonist Reserve McLaren Vale Shiraz 2012** Certified biodynamic; destemmed, open-fermented, 12 days on skins, matured in French oak (50% new) for 2 years. Has retained very good colour; full-bodied and crammed to the gills with black fruits, licorice, some dark chocolate and oak. Bottled Dec '15, the missing 8 months (presumably) in tank. Needs yet more time to fulfil its undoubted potential. Screwcap. 14% alc. **Rating** 94 **To** 2037 $65

Amicus Shiraz Cabernet 2012 75/25%, 90% from McLaren Vale, 10% Langhorne Creek, matured in 1yo French and 2yo American oak for 2 years. Attractive wine; the colour is good, the bouquet fragrant, the palate with blackberry, blackcurrant, licorice and spice moving at a fast clip across the long, medium-bodied palate. The vintage shines through. Screwcap. 14.5% alc. **Rating** 94 **To** 2032 $30 ✪

ŸŸŸŸŸ **Down the Rabbit Hole Friends & Lovers McLaren Vale Rose 2015** **Rating** 93 **To** 2017 $25 ✪
The Hedonist McLaren Vale Shiraz 2014 Rating 93 **To** 2029 $25 ✪
The Hedonist McLaren Vale Tempranillo 2014 Rating 91 **To** 2024 $25

Wandin Valley Estate ★★★★

12 Wilderness Road, Lovedale, NSW 2320 **Region** Hunter Valley
T (02) 4930 9888 **www.**wandinvalley.com.au **Open** 7 days 10–5
Winemaker Darren Atkinson **Est.** 1973 **Dozens** 8000 **Vyds** 8ha
After some uncertainty, and changes of heart, Wandin Valley Estate is now owned by Warraroong Estate (which in turn was formerly known as Swish Wine), and is part of an impressive portfolio of vineyards and brands. The cards have been thoroughly shuffled, and it will be interesting to see how they play out. Exports to China.

ŸŸŸŸŸ **Pinot Gris 2014** From Orange; the wine has a distinct pink-grey hue ex skin contact. The back label identifies white nectarine, raspberry, spice, ginger, honey, pear and musk. While I won't attempt to compete with that, it is certainly an attractive pinot gris that will match virtually any cold dish and most Asian cuisines. Screwcap. 13.5% alc. **Rating** 91 **To** 2016 $25
Shiraz 2013 Wandin Valley Estate has come and gone over the years, this return providing a light-bodied shiraz with red fruits to the fore, the oak and tannin support perfectly judged so as not to overwhelm the fruit. Scores for its elegance and balance. Screwcap. 14.5% alc. **Rating** 90 **To** 2025 $35

ŸŸŸŸ **McLaren Vale Barbera 2013 Rating** 89 **To** 2018 $30
Muscat NV Rating 89 **To** 2016 $35

Wangolina ★★★★

Cnr Southern Ports Highway/Limestone Coast Road, Kingston SE, SA 5275
Region Mount Benson
T (08) 8768 6187 **www.**wangolina.com.au **Open** 7 days 10–5
Winemaker Anita Goode **Est.** 2001 **Dozens** 5000 **Vyds** 11ha
Four generations of the Goode family have been graziers at Wangolina Station, but now Anita Goode has broken with tradition by becoming a vigneron. She has planted sauvignon blanc, shiraz, cabernet sauvignon, semillon and pinot gris. Exports to the UK.

ŸŸŸŸŸ **Single Vineyard Mt Benson Syrah 2013** Good depth and hue; black fruits rule the roost along with black pepper, whispers of bitter chocolate and licorice, tannins chiming in precisely when needed. This has a long, prosperous future. Screwcap. 14.5% alc. **Rating** 94 **To** 2038 $30 ✪

ŸŸŸŸŸ **Single Vineyard Cabernet Sauvignon 2013 Rating** 90 **To** 2025 $30

Wantirna Estate ★★★★★

10 Bushy Park Lane, Wantirna South, Vic 3152 **Region** Yarra Valley
T (03) 9801 2367 **www.**wantirnaestate.com.au **Open** Not
Winemaker Maryann and Reg Egan **Est.** 1963 **Dozens** 830 **Vyds** 4.2ha
Reg and Tina Egan were among the early movers in the rebirth of the Yarra Valley. The vineyard surrounds the house they live in, which also incorporates the winery. These days

Reg describes himself as the interfering winemaker, but in the early years he did everything, dashing from his legal practice to the winery to check on the ferments. Today much of the winemaking responsibility has been transferred to daughter Maryann, who has a degree in wine science from CSU. Both have honed their practical skills among the small domaines and chateaux of Burgundy and Bordeaux, inspired by single-vineyard, terroir-driven wines. Maryann was also winemaker for many years in Domaine Chandon's infancy. Tina keeps the mailing list and accounts under control, as well as having that all-important role of looking after the pickers during vintage.

ȲȲȲȲȲ **Isabella Yarra Valley Chardonnay 2014** Plenty of straw-like colour and with the flavour to match, in an elegant context. White peach, pear, cashew and earthen/hay/mineral-like notes. Supple almond milk characters, subtly applied. Quality at its most delightful. Screwcap. 13% alc. **Rating** 95 **To** 2022 $60 CM
Amelia Yarra Valley Cabernet Sauvignon Merlot 2013 Excellent colour; Wantirna Estate always has a gentle hand with its wines, and this is no exception. But that doesn't negate the accumulation of intensity in the cassis and crosscut of chalky tannins, nor the contribution of cedary oak and allied tannins. Diam. 13% alc. **Rating** 95 **To** 2033 $70
Hannah Yarra Valley Cabernet Franc Merlot 2013 Given the price, Wantirna Estate considers this outstanding, and it is a tour de force in elegance and red fruits to burn. My feeling is that it is just a little angular, picked a few days too early. Diam. 12.5% alc. **Rating** 94 **To** 2028 $135

ȲȲȲȲȲ **Lily Yarra Valley Pinot Noir 2014** **Rating** 91 **To** 2024 $70

Warner Glen Estate ★★★★★

PO Box 218, Melville, WA 6956 **Region** Margaret River
T 0457 482 957 **www**.warnerglenestate.com.au **Open** Not
Winemaker Various **Est.** 1993 **Dozens** 6000 **Vyds** 34.6ha
The primary fruit source for Warner Glen Estate is its Jindawarra Vineyard, located south of Karridale. With north-facing slopes and soils of gravelly loams it is the ideal site for high quality grapes. The 100ha property has a large tract of pristine bushland and a winter creek. Planted in 2000, the vines are mature, balanced, and of moderate vigour. The vineyard is only 6km from the Southern Ocean and 4km from the Indian Ocean, and avoids extreme temperatures as a result of the cooling sea breezes. Plantings are of shiraz, chardonnay, sauvignon blanc, pinot noir, viognier and pinot gris. Premium cabernet sauvignon is sourced from the Warner Glen-managed vineyard at Wilyabrup.

ȲȲȲȲȲ **Margaret River Shiraz 2014** Bright crimson; spice, licorice, blackberry and French oak all leap from the glass with the first whiff and the first sip. If there is a criticism it is the over-generous use of new oak, doubly surprising given the price. Its relatively full body also adds to the case for patience: reward is certain. Screwcap. 14.8% alc. **Rating** 92 **To** 2034 $20 ✪
Frog Belly Margaret River Cabernet Sauvignon 2014 This is a heist on a grand scale, true to variety with its luscious blackcurrant fruit balanced by bay leaf and firm, savoury tannins. Moreover, it has a real cellaring future. Screwcap. 14% alc. **Rating** 92 **To** 2029 $13 ✪
Margaret River Chardonnay 2015 Given the price, it seems churlish to be overly critical, but the wine is mildly disappointing – the oak seems out of sync with the fruit, the finish cluttered. Screwcap. 13% alc. **Rating** 90 **To** 2020 $20 ✪
Frog Belly Margaret River Shiraz Cabernet Sauvignon 2014 Bright colour; it's amazing that a quality Margaret River blend such as this can be made at this price (it has the structure of good Great Southern blends, but that's another story). All I can say is glory in its blackberry/blackcurrant fruit, and use it as your house wine. Screwcap. 14% alc. **Rating** 90 **To** 2024 $13 ✪

ȲȲȲȲ **Smokin' Gun Margaret River Great Southern Semillon Sauvignon Blanc 2015** **Rating** 89 **To** 2017 $10 ✪
Frog Belly Semillon Sauvignon Blanc 2015 **Rating** 89 **To** 2017 $13 ✪

Frog Belly Sauvignon Blanc 2015 Rating 88 To 2016 $13 ○
**Smokin' Gun Margaret River Great Southern Shiraz Cabernet Merlot
2014** Rating 88 To 2019 $10 ○

Warner Vineyard ★★★★

PO Box 344, Beechworth, Vic 3747 **Region** Beechworth
T 0438 331 768 **www**.warnervineyard.com.au **Open** Not
Winemaker Gary Mills **Est.** 1996 **Dozens** 350 **Vyds** 4.48ha
The Warner family – Graeme, Gwen, Stuart and Katie – planted their vineyard in 1996,
astutely choosing shiraz (2.3ha) and chardonnay (1.4ha) as their main game, with 0.8ha of
roussanne and marsanne as a side bet. As the vines began to move to maturity, it became clear
that their choice of the decomposed granitic soils was 100% correct, and the grapes were
much in demand, Giaconda taking the shiraz and Jamsheed the chardonnay. In the lead-up
to the '12 vintage, the family decided to keep enough grapes to have Gary Mills (Jamsheed)
make around 200 dozen of each wine.

🍷🍷🍷🍷⚲ **The Rest Chardonnay 2013** Gleaming straw-green; a complex, reductive
bouquet is followed by a palate with some of the same characters, which will
polarise opinions. I am firmly wedged on the fence, not a position I frequently
occupy. Screwcap. 13.5% alc. **Rating** 91 **To** 2022 $33
The Rest Shiraz 2013 A medium-bodied palate with red and black cherry,
licorice, spice and a black olive savoury complexity. An understated wine that will
develop slowly but surely. Screwcap. 14.5% alc. **Rating** 91 **To** 2028 $36

Warrabilla ★★★★

6152 Murray Valley Highway, Rutherglen, Vic 3685 **Region** Rutherglen
T (02) 6035 7242 **www**.warrabillawines.com.au **Open** 7 days 10–5
Winemaker Andrew Sutherland Smith **Est.** 1990 **Dozens** 10 000 **Vyds** 20.4ha
Andrew Sutherland Smith and wife Carol have built a formidable reputation for their wines,
headed by the Reserve trio of Durif, Cabernet Sauvignon and Shiraz, quintessential examples
of Rutherglen red table wine at its most opulent. Their vineyard has been extended by
the planting of riesling and zinfandel. Andrew spent 15 years with All Saints, McWilliam's,
Yellowglen, Fairfield and Chambers before setting up Warrabilla, and his experience shines
through in the wines. You either accept or regret the alcohol; no half measures.

🍷🍷🍷🍷🍷 **Reserve Shiraz 2014** The deep colour is as expected, but there is more freshness
than is usual with wine at this alcohol level – yet it is absolutely within the full-
bodied style Andrew Sutherland Smith proudly makes. If you enjoy fleshy, rich
shiraz, this will give you great pleasure, and because the tannins are so soft there
is no need for extended cellaring. Judged as it is. Diam. 15.5% alc. **Rating** 94
To 2024 $25 ○
Reserve Durif 2014 Intense, deep crimson-purple; there is no messing about
with this wine; it is built like Arnold Schwarzenegger, and you have to marvel
at the grapes grown by Warrabilla. There is no middle ground: love it or leave it.
Diam. 16% alc. **Rating** 94 **To** 2034 $27 ○

🍷🍷🍷🍷⚲ **Reserve Muscat NV** Rating 92 To 2018 $42

Warramunda Estate ★★★★☆

860 Maroondah Highway, Coldstream, Vic 3770 **Region** Yarra Valley
T 0412 694 394 **www**.warramundaestate.com.au **Open** Fri–Sun 10–6
Winemaker Ben Haines **Est.** 1998 **Dozens** 1200 **Vyds** 19.2ha
Ted Vogt purchased the original Warramunda property in 1975, on which a cattle and sheep
stud known as 'Warramunda Station' was run, and extended the property by 320 acres in '80.
A large dam was built in '81, and the property now supports three vineyards and a grazing
property. The Magdziarz family acquired Warramunda from the Vogt family in 2007. The
Magdziarz family have built on the existing solid foundations with a deep respect for the
surrounding landscape, and a vision for terroir-driven wines. In '13, the family enjoyed their

first solo vintage, under the guidance of well-known winemaker Ben Haines. Exports to the UK, the US, Canada and Asia.

♀♀♀♀♀ **Yarra Valley Syrah 2014** The vines are Best's Old Clone (1860s) shiraz, and this is a syrah (I think the name is fully justified) that positively sings with joy from the first sip to the last with silky – and slinky – red fruits on parade: cherry, raspberry and even a hint of strawberry; fine-ground tannins and perfectly judged French oak complete a picture to be proud of. Diam. 13.5% alc. **Rating** 95 **To** 2034 $40
Yarra Valley Pinot Noir 2014 Riddled with exotic spices through both the bouquet and the palate, the rose petals and violets of the bouquet backed by a relatively delicate palate. Has more life and freshness than some of the door-stoppers of the vintage. Diam. 12.5% alc. **Rating** 94 **To** 2021 $40

♀♀♀♀♀ **Yarra Valley Viognier 2014** Rating 92 To 2017 $35

Warrenmang Vineyard & Resort   ★★★★

Mountain Creek Road, Moonambel, Vic 3478 **Region** Pyrenees
T (03) 5467 2233 **www**.warrenmang.com.au **Open** 7 days 10–5
Winemaker Sean Schwager **Est.** 1974 **Dozens** 15000 **Vyds** 32.1ha
Luigi and Athalie Bazzani continue to watch over Warrenmang; a new, partially underground barrel room with earthen walls has been completed, wine quality remains high, and the accommodation for over 80 guests, plus a restaurant, underpin the business. Over the 40 years that Luigi and Athalie have been at Warrenmang, a very loyal clientele has been built up. The business is quietly on the market, Luigi and Athalie having long since earned their retirement. However, they have taken one step to reduce their workload: employing the highly experienced Sean and Cathy Dunn to manage the resort. Exports to Denmark, The Netherlands, Poland, Taiwan, Singapore, Malaysia and China.

♀♀♀♀♀ **Grand Pyrenees 2010** Very good retention of colour; shows you just how good Warrenmang's wines can be. This perfectly balanced and structured blend of cabernet sauvignon, merlot cabernet franc and shiraz is full of rounded dark fruits – blackcurrant/cassis will do for a start – sitting nicely with ripe tannins and totally integrated oak. Screwcap. 13.7% alc. **Rating** 94 **To** 2035 $35

♀♀♀♀♀ **Luigi Beyond 2010** Rating 93 To 2025 $80
Black Puma Pyrenees Shiraz 2012 Rating 92 To 2027 $80
Vinello by Bazzani Barbera Nebbiolo Dolcetto Brunello 2010 Rating 90 To 2020 $25

Warwick Billings   ★★★★

c/- Post Office, Lenswood, SA 5240 (postal) **Region** Adelaide Hills
T 0405 437 864 **www**.wowique.com.au **Open** Not
Winemaker Warwick Billings **Est.** 2009 **Dozens** 250
This is the venture of Warwick Billings and partner Rose Kemp. Warwick was a cider maker in the UK who came to study at Roseworthy, and got diverted into the wine world. He completed postgraduate oenology at Adelaide University in 1995, and worked for Miranda Wine, Orlando and Angove Family Winemakers from 2002 to '08, along the way moonlighting in France and Spain for 12 vintages. Warwick's approach to his eponymous label is self-deprecating, beginning with the name Wowique, and saying, 'Occasionally a vineyard sings to the winemaker. [We] have taken one of these songs and put it into a bottle.' The vineyard in question is an unusual clone of chardonnay nurtured on a sloping hilltop site in Mt Torrens. Warwick's final word on all of this is, 'The winemaking is unashamedly inspired by Burgundy, but care is taken to acknowledge that the soil is different, the clones are often different, the climate is definitely different, and the end consumer is usually different.'

♀♀♀♀♀ **Wowique Single Vineyard Adelaide Hills Chardonnay 2014** Fermentation of partly settled juice starts with wild yeast, then cultured yeast in used French oak (25% new), full mlf, aged for 11 months. If the acidity wasn't increased after the conclusion of mlf, the wine must have been very acidic to start with, which is quite possible given its low alcohol. Whatever the case, it is a slender and willowy wine that has some charm, but needs an extra cm or two around its body. Screwcap. 12% alc. **Rating** 90 **To** 2018 $33

Water Wheel ★★★★

Bridgewater-on-Loddon, Bridgewater, Vic 3516 **Region** Bendigo
T (03) 5437 3060 www.waterwheelwine.com **Open** Mon–Fri 9–5, w'ends 12–3
Winemaker Peter Cumming, Bill Trevaskis **Est.** 1972 **Dozens** 30 000 **Vyds** 136ha
Peter Cumming, with more than two decades of winemaking under his belt, has quietly built on the reputation of Water Wheel year by year. The winery is owned by the Cumming family, which has farmed in the Bendigo region for 50+ years, with horticulture and viticulture special areas of interest. Over half the vineyard area is planted to shiraz (75ha), followed by chardonnay, sauvignon blanc (15ha each), cabernet sauvignon, malbec (10ha each), and smaller plantings of petit verdot, semillon, roussanne and grenache. Water Wheel continues to make wines that over-deliver at their modest prices. Exports to the UK, the US, Canada, Denmark, China and NZ.

♟♟♟♟♟ **Bendigo Shiraz 2014** Excellent, deep crimson-purple hue; the big brother of Memsie, everything at twice the volume, in particular savoury/briary/spicy black fruits and firm tannins. Will be all there in a decade, or longer, after most have moved along, buying each release and having consumed all they have previously bought. Screwcap. 14.1% alc. **Rating** 92 **To** 2029 $18 ❂

♟♟♟♟ **Bendigo Primitivo 2014 Rating** 89 **To** 2020 $18 ❂
Memsie Homestead Bendigo Shiraz 2014 Rating 88 **To** 2024 $12 ❂

Watershed Premium Wines ★★★★★

Cnr Bussell Highway/Darch Road, Margaret River, WA 6285 **Region** Margaret River
T (08) 9758 8633 www.watershedwines.com.au **Open** 7 days 10–5
Winemaker Severine Logan, Conrad Tritt **Est.** 2002 **Dozens** 100 000 **Vyds** 137ha
Watershed Wines has been set up by a syndicate of investors, with no expense spared in establishing the substantial vineyard and striking cellar door, with a 200-seat café and restaurant. Situated towards the southern end of the Margaret River region, its neighbours include Voyager Estate and Leeuwin Estate. The vineyard development occurred in three stages (2001, '04 and '06), the last in Jindong, well to the north of stages one and two. The first stage of the winery was completed prior to the '03 vintage, with a capacity of 400 tonnes, increased the following year to 900 tonnes, then another expansion in '05 to 1200 tonnes. March '08 saw the crush capacity reach 1600 tonnes; wine storage facilities have increased in lockstep with crush capacity, but were lifted by a further 170 000 kilolitres. Exports to Germany, Indonesia, Fiji, Thailand, Papua New Guinea, Singapore, Hong Kong and China.

♟♟♟♟♟ **Awakening Single Block A1 Margaret River Chardonnay 2014** Glittering personality and beauty, in the full flush of youth. A joy to behold. Grapefruit, oatmeal, spicy oak and white peach flavours rush and dance and entertain their way through the palate. Absolutely gorgeous, flavour-filled length. Screwcap. 13.5% alc. **Rating** 96 **To** 2021 $45 CM ❂
Senses Margaret River Shiraz 2013 Begins the conversation on sweet, friendly terms but beware, seriousness lurks. This is not to be taken lightly. Coffeed oak, condensed milk, fresh cherries, plums. Dry leaf matter is spread throughout. Tannin is firm; fine; unyielding. Mid-weight wine with a long future. Screwcap. 14.5% alc. **Rating** 94 **To** 2030 $30 CM ❂

♟♟♟♟♟ **Shades Margaret River Sauvignon Blanc Semillon 2015 Rating** 93 **To** 2018 $19 CM ❂
Senses Margaret River Cabernet Merlot 2013 Rating 93 **To** 2032 $30 CM
Senses Margaret River Sauvignon Blanc 2015 Rating 91 **To** 2017 $30 CM
Shades Margaret River Unoaked Chardonnay 2015 Rating 90 **To** 2017 $19 CM ❂
Margaret River Blanc de Blanc 2011 Rating 90 **To** 2017 $25 TS

WayWood Wines

67 Kays Road, McLaren Vale, SA 5171 **Region** McLaren Vale
T (08) 8323 8468 **www.**waywoodwines.com **Open** Fri–Mon 11–5
Winemaker Andrew Wood **Est.** 2005 **Dozens** 1500
This is the culmination of Andrew Wood and Lisa Robertson's wayward odyssey. Andrew left
his career as a sommelier in London, and retrained as a winemaker, working in Portugal, the
UK, Italy and the Granite Belt (an eclectic selection), settling in McLaren Vale in early 2004.
Working with Kangarilla Road winery for the next six years, while making small quantities of
shiraz, cabernets and tempranillo from purchased grapes, led them to nebbiolo, montepulciano
and shiraz. Andrew and Lisa opened a new cellar door in '15, Lisa's business, Luscious Red,
offering food at the cellar door.

ΨΨΨΨΨ   **McLaren Vale Shiraz 2014** The bright colour accurately signals a super-fresh
wine with vibrant red fruit flavours cosseted by a glance of French oak, fine
tannins and bright acidity. A long way in front of the plodders of full-bodied
shiraz. Screwcap. 14% alc. **Rating** 95 **To** 2030 $24 **◐**
McLaren Vale Cabernet 2013 Rich, archetypal McLaren Vale cabernet full of
generous blackcurrant fruit in best regional style, not OTT, nor filled with dark
chocolate. Its restrained alcohol no doubt plays a role in this, as it does in most of
WayWood's wines. Screwcap. 14% alc. **Rating** 95 **To** 2038 $28 **◐**
McLaren Vale Tempranillo 2014 The positive colour is a good start, and it's
onwards and upwards thereafter, the bouquet promising the raft of red, black and
morello cherries that follow in full song, tannins and oak providing the right
amount of structure. Screwcap. 14% alc. **Rating** 95 **To** 2034 $35 **◐**
McLaren Vale Montepulciano 2014 Good colour; a lyrebird dance of
spicy red fruits, the flavours flashing past your eyes with raspberry, cherry and
forest strawberries consistently rearranging themselves, engaging in animated
conversation in doing so. Enjoy it before it slows up. Screwcap. 13.5% alc.
Rating 95 **To** 2024 $35 **◐**
McLaren Vale Cabernet Sangiovese 2014 The two varieties are
co-fermented, and the marriage works well, the cherry family of sangiovese fitting
snugly with the cassis family of the cabernet, not doubling the impact of tannins –
indeed the reverse. Screwcap. 14.4% alc. **Rating** 94 **To** 2034 $35

ΨΨΨΨ **McLaren Vale Monastrell 2014 Rating** 93 **To** 2024 $35
Quattro Vini 2014 Rating 92 **To** 2029 $24 **◐**
Fluzi Quattro 2015 Rating 91 **To** 2017 $20 **◐**
Quattro Bianca 2015 Rating 90 **To** 2017 $24

Wedgetail Estate

40 Hildebrand Road, Cottles Bridge, Vic 3099 **Region** Yarra Valley
T (03) 9714 8661 **www.**wedgetailestate.com.au **Open** First w'end each month
Winemaker Guy Lamothe **Est.** 1994 **Dozens** 1500 **Vyds** 5.5ha
Canadian-born photographer Guy Lamothe and partner Dena Ashbolt started making wine
in the basement of their Carlton home in the 1980s. The idea of their own vineyard took hold,
and the search for a property began. In their words,'one Sunday, when we were "just out for a
drive", we drove past our current home. The slopes are amazing, true goat terrain, and it is on
these steep slopes that in 1994 we planted our first block of pinot noir.' While the vines were
growing Guy enrolled in the wine-growing course at CSU, having already gained practical
experience working in the Yarra Valley (Tarrawarra), the Mornington Peninsula and Meursault
(Burgundy). Exports to the UK, Canada, Singapore, Hong Kong and China.

ΨΨΨΨΨ **Reserve Pinot Noir 2015** The last vintage made was '10. This is the most
elegant of the Wedgetail '15 Pinot trio, and has made light of its 50% new
French oak; the fruit flavours are mid-range between red and black, and there is a
complex savoury twist on the finish and aftertaste. Screwcap. 13% alc. **Rating** 95
To 2025 $85

Single Vineyard Yarra Valley Chardonnay 2015 10V1 clone, hand-picked, whole bunch-pressed, fermented and matured for 7 months in oak (30% new). Comes together very well; there is good tension to the wine, fruit, oak and acidity all applying separate forces; white peach, apple and grapefruit. Screwcap. 13% alc. **Rating** 94 **To** 2023 $42

Single Vineyard Yarra Valley Pinot Noir 2015 22yo vines, a mix of clones, hand-picked and vinified separately with a mix of whole berries and whole bunches, wild open ferment, 20 days on skins, matured in French oak for 12 months (25% new). A substantially more complex bouquet than the standard Yarra Valley Pinot, with darker fruit aromas and more oak; the palate, too, is in a different league – the 100% price differential is thoroughly justified. Screwcap. 13% alc. **Rating** 94 **To** 2026 $52

🍷🍷🍷🍷 **Yarra Valley Pinot Noir 2015 Rating** 89 **To** 2020 $26

Welshmans Reef Vineyard ★★★☆

Maldon-Newstead Road, Welshmans Reef, Vic 3462 **Region** Bendigo
T (03) 5476 2733 **www**.welshmansreef.com **Open** W'ends & public hols 10–5
Winemaker Ronald Snep **Est.** 1986 **Dozens** 6000 **Vyds** 15ha

The Snep family (Ronald, Jackson and Alexandra) began developing Welshmans Reef Vineyard in 1986, planting cabernet sauvignon, shiraz and semillon. Chardonnay and merlot were added in the early '90s, sauvignon blanc and tempranillo later. The vineyard is certified organic. For some years the grapes were sold to other wineries, but in the early '90s the Sneps decided to share winemaking facilities established in the Old Newstead Co-operative Butter Factory with several other small vineyards. When the Butter Factory facility closed down, the Sneps built a winery and mudbrick tasting room onsite. Exports to China.

🍷🍷🍷🍷🍷 **Cabernet Sauvignon 2013** Very good colour; has that subtle minty aroma that has waxed and waned in Bendigo wines for 150 years, described by one contemporary observer in the 1860s as evocative of sandalwood. More conventional (but not compelling) theory says it comes from gum leaves. This has vilified it, but more balanced thinking (Kiwis, go back home) is that it can be very attractive, as it is here. Screwcap. 13.8% alc. **Rating** 91 **To** 2028 $22 ✪

🍷🍷🍷🍷 **Shiraz 2013 Rating** 89 **To** 2028 $22

Wendouree ★★★★★

Wendouree Road, Clare, SA 5453 **Region** Clare Valley
T (08) 8842 2896 **Open** Not
Winemaker Tony Brady **Est.** 1895 **Dozens** 2000 **Vyds** 12ha

An iron fist in a velvet glove best describes these extraordinary wines. They are fashioned with commitment from the very old vineyard (shiraz, cabernet sauvignon, malbec, mataro and muscat of alexandria), with its unique terroir, by Tony and Lita Brady, who rightly see themselves as custodians of a priceless treasure. The 100-year-old stone winery is virtually unchanged from the day it was built; this is in every sense a treasure beyond price. Wendouree has never made any comment about its wines, but the subtle shift from the lighter end of full-bodied to the fuller end of medium-bodied seems to be a permanent one (always subject to the dictates of the vintage). The best news of all is that I will drink some of the Wendourees I have bought over the past 10 years before I die, and not have to rely on my few remaining bottles from the 1970s (and rather more from the '80s and '90s).

West Cape Howe Wines ★★★★★

Lot 14923 Muir Highway, Mount Barker, WA 6324 **Region** Mount Barker
T (08) 9892 1444 **www**.westcapehowewines.com.au **Open** 7 days (various hours)
Winemaker Gavin Berry, Andrew Vasey **Est.** 1997 **Dozens** 60 000 **Vyds** 310ha

West Cape Howe is owned by a partnership of four West Australian families, including winemaker/managing partner Gavin Berry (28 vintages in the Great Southern) and viticulturist/partner Rob Quenby. Grapes are sourced from estate vineyards in Mount Barker and Frankland River. The Langton Vineyard (Mount Barker) has 100ha planted to cabernet sauvignon, shiraz, riesling, sauvignon blanc, chardonnay and semillon, and the Russell Road Vineyard (Frankland River) has 210ha planted. West Cape Howe also sources select parcels of fruit from valued contract growers. Best Value Winery 2016 *Wine Companion*. Exports to the UK, the US, Denmark, Switzerland, South Korea, Singapore, Japan, Hong Kong and China.

ŶŶŶŶŶ **Book Ends Mount Barker Cabernet Sauvignon 2014** From several vineyards, each portion fermented and matured (18 months) separately in new and used French barriques. Deep, bright crimson-purple; a great example of the vitality and varietal clarity that West Cape Howe brings to its wines, terroir riding high. Its cassis fruit is mouthwatering, not a phrase you would normally use with cabernet, but true here. Screwcap. 14.5% alc. **Rating** 96 **To** 2034 $28 ❂

Shiraz 2014 High quality shiraz from what I would guess to be some or all of the subregions of Great Southern. Great colour; it is a wine of purity and power; used oak rather than new for its maturation. It is bizarre that its price should be so low – this is an extraordinary bargain, even by the over-delivery standards West Cape Howe has set itself. Screwcap. 14.5% alc. **Rating** 95 **To** 2034 $17 ❂

Two Steps Mount Barker Shiraz 2014 Strong crimson-purple; a medium to full-bodied wine with considerable depth and texture to its black fruits, these with high points of cracked pepper and licorice; the tannins (part fruit, part oak) seal the deal, injecting some sweet/savoury (not sweet/sour) nuances on the back-palate. Screwcap. 14.5% alc. **Rating** 95 **To** 2039 $28 ❂

Book Ends Mount Barker Cabernet Sauvignon 2013 A pure, powerful and perfectly balanced cabernet at the start of what will be a very long life. It oozes blackcurrant, bay leaf and savoury notes on its long palate and aftertaste, the oak certainly evident, but equally subservient to the fruit and tannin of the wine. Screwcap. 14% alc. **Rating** 95 **To** 2033 $28 ❂

Mount Barker Riesling 2015 From Block 6 on the Langton Vineyard, the best estate riesling. If tasted in a hurry, it would be easy to miss the quality of the wine, for it leaves it to the finish and aftertaste for its lime juice, zest and pith to join forces with the acidity. Screwcap. 12% alc. **Rating** 94 **To** 2030 $20 ❂

Cabernet Merlot 2014 80% cabernet sauvignon, 20% merlot. The colour is excellent – as is everything else about the wine; black and redcurrant, bay leaf and black olive hop into bed with each other, and snuggle under the covers, the French oak and tannins left to their own devices. The value transcends belief. Screwcap. 14.5% alc. **Rating** 94 **To** 2025 $17 ❂

ŶŶŶŶŶ **Semillon Sauvignon Blanc 2015 Rating** 91 **To** 2018 $17 ❂
Chardonnay 2015 Rating 91 **To** 2018 $17 ❂
Mount Barker Sauvignon Blanc 2015 Rating 90 **To** 2016 $20 ❂
Two Peeps Sauvignon Blanc Semillon 2015 Rating 90 **To** 2017 $20 ❂
Old School Mount Barker Chardonnay 2015 Rating 90 **To** 2017 $20 ❂
Tempranillo Rose 2015 Rating 90 **To** 2017 $17 ❂

Westlake Vineyards   ★★★★★

Diagonal Road, Koonunga, SA 5355 **Region** Barossa Valley
T 0428 656 208 **www**.westlakevineyards.com.au **Open** By appt
Winemaker Darren Westlake **Est.** 1999 **Dozens** 500 **Vyds** 36.2ha

Darren and Suzanne Westlake tend 22ha of shiraz, 6.5ha of cabernet sauvignon, 2ha of viognier, and smaller plantings of petit verdot, durif, mataro, grenache and graciano planted on two properties in the Koonunga area of the Barossa Valley. They do all the vineyard work personally, and have a long list of high-profile winemakers queued up to buy the grapes, leaving only a small amount for production under the Westlake label. Suzanne is a sixth-generation descendant of Johann George Kalleske, who came to SA from Prussia in 1838; the 717 Convicts label draws on the history of Darren's ancestor Edward Westlake, who was transported to Australia in 1788.

🍷🍷🍷🍷🍷 **Eleazar Barossa Valley Shiraz 2014** Here the licorice goes and is replaced by bitter chocolate coming from McLaren Vale – well, not literally. The Westlake Shirazs all have deep, bright colour, which is a compelling start, but doesn't help in trying to work out how these wines come from the same estate vineyard. Whatever, this has an overall savoury elegance that is most appealing, possibly coming from the lower alcohol. Screwcap. 14.5% alc. **Rating** 96 **To** 2030 $60 ✪

Albert's Block Barossa Valley Shiraz 2014 Licorice and pepper are unexpected (semi) leaders of the fragrant pack. This intro, and the supple tannins on the finish, cause you to walk straight past the alcohol. It's not broken, and doesn't need fixing. Only 100 dozen made, more's the pity. Screwcap. 15% alc. **Rating** 95 **To** 2025 $30 ✪

🍷🍷🍷🍷 **717 Convicts The Felon Shiraz 2014 Rating** 91 **To** 2020 $25

Whicher Ridge ★★★★☆

200 Chapman Hill East Road, Busselton, WA 6280 **Region** Geographe
T (08) 9753 1394 **www**.whicherridge.com.au **Open** Thurs–Mon 10–5
Winemaker Cathy Howard **Est.** 2004 **Dozens** 1500 **Vyds** 5ha

It is hard to imagine a founding husband-and-wife team with such an ideal blend of viticultural and winemaking experience accumulated over a combined 40+ years. Cathy Howard (née Spratt) was a winemaker for 16 years at Orlando and St Hallett in the Barossa Valley, and at Watershed Wines in Margaret River. She now has her own winemaking consulting business covering the southwest regions of WA, as well as making the Whicher Ridge wines. Neil Howard's career as a viticulturist spans more than 25 years, beginning in the Pyrenees region with Taltarni Vineyards and Blue Pyrenees Estate, before moving to Mount Avoca as vineyard manager for 12 years. When he moved to the west, he managed the Sandalford vineyard in Margaret River for several years, then developed and managed a number of smaller vineyards throughout the region. Whicher Ridge's Odyssey Creek Vineyard at Chapman Hill has sauvignon blanc, cabernet sauvignon and viognier. The Howards have chosen the Frankland River subregion of the Great Southern to supply shiraz and riesling, and also buy grapes from Margaret River.

🍷🍷🍷🍷🍷 **Geographe Sauvignon Blanc 2014** Smoky oak, velvety texture, grassy overtones and pure, gravelly, intense fruit flavour. There is no mistaking the quality of it. Screwcap. 12.8% alc. **Rating** 94 **To** 2017 $25 CM ✪

🍷🍷🍷🍷 **Museum Frankland River Riesling 2009 Rating** 93 **To** 2019 $45 CM
Elevation Cabernet Sauvignon 2012 Rating 91 **To** 2022 $38 CM

Whiskey Gully Wines ★★★☆

25 Turner Road, Severnlea, Qld 4380 **Region** Granite Belt
T (07) 4683 5100 **www**.whiskeygullywines.com.au **Open** Fri–Tues 10–5
Winemaker Rod MacPherson (Contract) **Est.** 1997 **Dozens** NA **Vyds** 2.5ha

Close inspection of the winery letterhead discloses that The Media Mill Pty Ltd trades as Whiskey Gully Wines. It is no surprise, then, to find proprietor John Arlidge saying, 'Wine and politics are a heady mix; I have already registered the 2000 Republic Red as a voter in 26 marginal electorates and we are considering nominating it for Liberal Party preselection in Bennelong.' John decided to sell Whiskey Gully in 2010 and move to Paris (a sea/cultural change of awesome proportions), but the brand has not been run down, and business is continuing as usual with the same winemaking team.

🍷🍷🍷🍷 **Black Rod Granite Belt Shiraz 2012** Exudes power, but not consistently; there's a catch on the finish that tends to break the line of the wine. However, there's more to like than dislike. Screwcap. 14.6% alc. **Rating** 90 **To** 2032 $30

🍷🍷🍷🍷 **Beverley Granite Belt Chardonnay 2014 Rating** 89 **To** 2018 $25

Whistle Post

PO Box 340, Coonawarra, SA 5263 **Region** Coonawarra
T 0408 708 093 **www**.whistlepost.com.au **Open** Not
Winemaker John Innes **Est.** 2012 **Dozens** 5000 **Vyds** 63ha

Whistle Post is the venture of Brian and Jennifer Smibert, together with their son Angus. The establishment date is correct, but there is in fact a quarter of a century of Smibert grapegrowing: 32ha of cabernet sauvignon, 22ha of chardonnay, 8ha of merlot and 1ha of sauvignon blanc. The grapes were the subject of a 25-year contract to supply Hardys, and when that finished, the Whistle Post brand began serious production. The family put its toe into the water in 2010, with a small amount of wine made on an experimental basis. Part of the annual grape production is sold to others, and one would expect this arrangement to continue into the future.

ΨΨΨΨΨ **Reserve Coonawarra Cabernet Sauvignon 2013** Has spent more time in oak than the varietal version, and more new oak for good measure; the power and complexity of the blackcurrant, mulberry and mint aromas and flavours are obvious. A feature is the fine tannin structure, allowing the wine freedom to move. The oak, too is of high quality. Screwcap. 13.7% alc. **Rating** 95 **To** 2038 $40

ΨΨΨΨΨ **Coonawarra Cabernet Sauvignon 2013 Rating** 90 **To** 2028 $20 ✪

Whistler Wines

Seppeltsfield Road, Marananga, SA 5355 **Region** Barossa Valley
T (08) 8562 4942 **www**.whistlerwines.com **Open** 7 days 10.30–5
Winemaker Josh Pfeiffer **Est.** 1999 **Dozens** 5000 **Vyds** 14.5ha

Four generations of Pfeiffers, spanning 80 years, have been growing grapes in SA. Third-generation brothers Chris and Martin established Whistler Wines in 1999, and in 2013 'retired' (their word and quotation marks) from managing the business, inviting children Matt (finance and distribution), Mel (cellar door, one year later winning the peer-judged Best Cellar Door in the Barossa Region) and Josh (winemaking and viticulture) to 'step up'. Exports to Canada, Denmark, Taiwan, Hong Kong and China.

ΨΨΨΨΨ **Get in my Belly Barossa Valley Grenache 2015** Attitude and character but clean and bright. This is a grenache and a half. It strings herbs through bright red fruits, and carries ironstone-like notes through dry licorice. It's not deep or thick but it insists; it's perfumed and pinot-esque but essentially varietal. And just look at the glide of tannin: both seamless and irrepressible at once. Cork. 14% alc. **Rating** 95 **To** 2026 $35 CM ✪

ΨΨΨΨΨ **Albert Heinrich Barossa Shiraz 2015 Rating** 93 **To** 2024 $25 CM ✪
Shiver Down My Spine Shiraz 2014 Rating 92 **To** 2022 $35 CM
Barossa Shiraz 2013 Rating 92 **To** 2026 $40 CM
Stacks On Grenache Shiraz Mourvedre 2015 Rating 91 **To** 2020 $35 CM
Barossa Cabernet Sauvignon 2013 Rating 91 **To** 2026 $30 CM
Barossa Valley Sparkling Merlot 2012 Rating 91 **To** 2027 $35 TS

Whistling Eagle Vineyard

2769 Heathcote-Rochester Road, Colbinabbin, Vic 3559 **Region** Heathcote
T (03) 5432 9319 **www**.whistlingeagle.com **Open** By appt
Winemaker Ian Rathjen **Est.** 1995 **Dozens** 950

This is a remarkable story. Owners Ian and Lynn Rathjen are fourth-generation farmers living and working on the now famous Cambrian red soil of Heathcote. Henning Rathjen was lured from his birthplace in Schleswig Holstein by the gold rush, but soon decided farming provided a more secure future. In 1858 he made his way to the Colbinabbin Range, and exclaimed, 'We have struck paradise.' Among other things, he planted a vineyard in the 1860s, expanding it in the wake of demand for the wine. He died in 1912, and the vineyards disappeared before being replanted in '95, with 20ha of immaculately tended vines. The core wine is Shiraz, with intermittent releases of Sangiovese, Viognier, Cabernet Sauvignon and Semillon.

🍷🍷🍷🍷 **Heathcote Sangiovese 2013** Good depth to the colour; a powerful wine giving the impression of higher alcohol than it in fact has; fruits include liqueur as well as the usual cherries and some dried fruit notes; a slight herbal fleck on the finish adds further interest. Screwcap. 13.8% alc. **Rating** 91 **To** 2023 $35

Heathcote Botrytis Semillon 2011 Gleaming gold-green; this is very complex, with a touch of pickled ginger giving an appealing savoury/peppery edge to the palate. The sugar/acid balance is very good, so stopping the ferment earlier (to take 1% or so off the alcohol) was probably not an option. It's a very unusual botrytis semillon, far more interesting than the usually cloyingly sweet confection fruit bombs going around, and has developed at a more decorous rate than most. 375ml. Screwcap. 13.8°alc. **Rating** 91 **To** 2020

Eagles Blood Heathcote Shiraz 2013 There's a double helping of everything in this wine, with exotic spice and pepper overtones to the thundering herd of black fruits; the tannin and oak balance is good; the Achilles heel that permeates the wine is its alcohol heat. So near and yet so far. Cork. 14.8% alc. **Rating** 90 **To** 2025 $60

Eagles Blood Heathcote Shiraz 2012 This is a carbon copy of the '13; the heat isn't immediately apparent, but hopes for a great wine are dashed on the second taste. As the points indicate, there's a glass more than half full here. Cork. 14.8% alc. **Rating** 90 **To** 2024 $60

Whistling Kite Wines ★★★

73 Freundt Road, New Residence via Loxton, SA 5333 **Region** Riverland
T (08) 8584 9014 **www**.whistlingkitewines.com.au **Open** By appt
Winemaker 919 Wines (Eric and Jenny Semmler) **Est.** 2010 **Dozens** 360 **Vyds** 16ha
Owners Pam and Tony Barich have established their vineyard and house on the banks of the Murray River, a haven for wildlife. They believe custodians of the land have a duty to maintain its health and vitality – their vineyard has had organic certification for over a decade, and biodynamic certification since 2008.

🍷🍷🍷 **Unwooded Chardonnay 2012** This is a powerful testament to biodynamics, for it has excellent flavour and an illusion of barrel-derived texture (no oak used). It must also be unique as an unwooded Riverland chardonnay selling for $25 a bottle. Screwcap. 13.5% alc. **Rating** 89 **To** 2017 $25

Montepulciano 2013 Hand-picked, crushed, wild yeast, open-fermented, hand-plunged for 7 days, basket-pressed, matured for 9 months in French barriques. A go along to get along variety, here with cherry fruit wrapped in ripe, woolly tannins and oak. Screwcap. 15% alc. **Rating** 89 **To** 2018 $38

White Rock Vineyard ★★★★

1171 Railton Road, Kimberley, Tas 7304 (postal) **Region** Northern Tasmania
T 0407 972 156 **www**.whiterockwine.com.au **Open** At Lake Barrington Estate
Winemaker Winemaking Tasmania, Frogmore Creek **Est.** 1992 **Dozens** 400 **Vyds** 3ha
Phil and Robin Dolan have established White Rock Vineyard in the northwest region of Tasmania, which, while having 13 wineries and vineyards, is one of the least-known parts of the island. Kimberley is 25km south of Devonport, in the sheltered valley of the Mersey River. The Dolans have planted pinot noir, chardonnay, riesling, pinot gris and dornfelder, the lion's share going to the first two varieties. It has been a low-profile operation partly because of its location. The wines are sold online and through local restaurants, and through the cellar door at Lake Barrington Estate.

🍷🍷🍷🍷 **Riesling 2015** Apples. Crisp, pure, dripping with juice. Sipping on this is like biting into a beautiful green apple, the flavours ripe but crunchy. It makes you feel good to be alive. Screwcap. 11.5% alc. **Rating** 93 **To** 2026 $25 CM

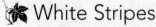 # White Stripes

179 Glenview Road, Yarra Glen, Vic 3775 **Region** Alpine Valleys
T 0432 021 668 **Open** Not
Winemaker Callie Jemmeson **Est.** 2015 **Dozens** 900

Callie Jemmeson has the sort of background that many young winemakers would give their right arm for, as she has crammed so much into a relatively young life. Callie has grown up with wine in her blood, her father David with a lifetime of experience in the industry. A family holiday in Chianti and tastings at Louis Roederer in Champagne set the spark when Callie was still very young. However, she studied psychology and criminology at Melbourne University, then qualified as a chef, and thereafter fell to the lure of grapegrowing and winemaking. She is currently studying wine science at CSU (the extension course) and has already gained experience working at De Bortoli in the Yarra Valley, Littorai Wines in Sonoma, California, Fattoria Zeribina in Emilia Romagne, Italy, and Lavau in the Rhône Valley.

Wicks Estate Wines

21 Franklin Street, Adelaide, SA 5000 (postal) **Region** Adelaide Hills
T (08) 8212 0004 **www**.wicksestate.com.au **Open** Not
Winemaker Leigh Ratzmer **Est.** 2000 **Dozens** 20 000 **Vyds** 38.1ha

Tim and Simon Wicks had a long-term involvement with orchard and nursery operations at Highbury in the Adelaide Hills prior to purchasing their 54ha property at Woodside in 1999. They planted fractionally less than 40ha of chardonnay, riesling, sauvignon blanc, shiraz, merlot and cabernet sauvignon, following this with the construction of a winery in 2004. Wicks Estate has won more than its fair share of wine show medals over the years, the wines priced well below their full worth. Exports to The Netherlands, Singapore, Hong Kong and China.

🍷🍷🍷🍷🍷 **CJ Wicks Adelaide Hills Shiraz 2013** Estate grown at Woodside, a lovely example of Adelaide Hills shiraz. Spice, pepper, red and dark fruits flow effortlessly to the silky, finely extracted tannins on the palate. A really fine effort in power and subtlety. Screwcap. 14.5% alc. **Rating** 95 **To** 2026 $45

CJ Wicks Adelaide Hills Cabernet Sauvignon 2013 Mid-deep red; cassis, earth, mint and briary fruit dominate the bouquet, but there are layers of flavour waiting in the wings; supple and long, with fine tannins, the weight and structure are pitch perfect. Screwcap. 14.5% alc. **Rating** 95 **To** 2030 $45

Adelaide Hills Riesling 2015 Quartz-white; while the bouquet is reticent, the palate is uninhibited in its array of intense, layered citrus fruit flavours, Give it another 12 months and it will be prancing around like a filly on a spring day. Screwcap. 12.5% alc. **Rating** 94 **To** 2028 $18 ✪

Adelaide Hills Shiraz 2014 Revels in its cool climate region, bringing black cherry to the table wreathed in a bevvy of spices, licorice and cedary oak, the overall mouthfeel of freshness. Utterly ridiculous value. Screwcap. 14.5% alc. **Rating** 94 **To** 2029 $20 ✪

🍷🍷🍷🍷🍷 **Adelaide Hills Pinot Noir 2015** **Rating** 93 **To** 2025 $20 ✪
Adelaide Hills Sauvignon Blanc 2015 **Rating** 91 **To** 2016 $18 CM ✪
Adelaide Hills Chardonnay 2015 **Rating** 90 **To** 2020 $18 ✪

Wignalls Wines

448 Chester Pass Road (Highway 1), Albany, WA 6330 **Region** Albany
T (08) 9841 2848 **www**.wignallswines.com.au **Open** 7 days 11–4
Winemaker Rob Wignall, Michael Perkins **Est.** 1982 **Dozens** 7000 **Vyds** 18.5ha

While the estate vineyards have a diverse range of sauvignon blanc, semillon, chardonnay, pinot noir, merlot, shiraz, cabernet franc and cabernet sauvignon, founder Bill Wignall was one of the early movers with pinot noir, producing wines that, by the standards of their time, were well in front of anything else coming out of WA (and up with the then limited amounts being made in Vic and Tas). The establishment of an onsite winery, and the assumption of the winemaking role by son Rob, with significant input by Michael Perkins, saw the quality and range of wines increase. Exports to Denmark, Japan, Singapore and China.

ŸŸŸŸŸ Albany Shiraz 2014 Alive with fragrance. Both beefy and buoyant in the mouth, with fresh pepper and floral notes met solidly by blackberry and black cherry. It has substance and savouriness and yet at all times it seems lively, eager, upbeat. Champion Dry Red Wine at the '15 National Cool Climate Wine Show, and it's easy to see why. Screwcap. 14.6% alc. **Rating** 96 **To** 2034 $29 CM ✪

ŸŸŸŸ Single Vineyard Albany Sauvignon Blanc 2015 Rating 89 **To** 2017 $20 CM
Great Southern Cabernet Merlot 2014 Rating 88 **To** 2022 $18 CM

Wild Dog Winery ★★★★☆

Warragul-Korumburra Road, Warragul, Vic 3820 **Region** Gippsland
T (03) 5623 1117 **www**.wilddogwinery.com **Open** 7 days 11–5
Winemaker Max Marriott **Est.** 1982 **Dozens** 3000 **Vyds** 10.1ha
Wild Dog is a family-owned business operated by Gary and Judy Surman. Since acquiring the business in 2005 much work has been done in the vineyard (planted in 1982) with grafting, replanting and retrellising, and winery expansion (all wines are now made onsite). They have also built a restaurant overlooking the vineyard. Now one of the larger wineries in Gippsland, and one of the more consistent producers of good-quality wines.

ŸŸŸŸŸ Gippsland Cabernet Franc 2014 Typical light colour (outside Margaret River), but the hue is bright, and the floral aromas of rose petals have some pipe tobacco. If judged as a light-bodied red – and it should be – this is utterly delicious, its red fruits sunbeams in the mouth. If you try it, like it and buy it, drink it sooner rather than later, before the magic fades. Screwcap. 13% alc. **Rating** 95 **To** 2020 $25 ✪
Estate Chardonnay 2013 An elegant wine, very different from (and better than) its '14 sibling, a strange outcome. Here fine strands of grapefruit, apple and white peach are woven together by even finer strands of oak, the finish long and fresh. Screwcap. 13% alc. **Rating** 94 **To** 2023 $23 ✪
Wild Ice 2011 Considerable concentration, richness and sweetness from freezing the juice prior to fermentation, peach and apricot flavours suggesting part or all ex viognier, chardonnay as a lesser component. The balance is very good, the acidity spot on. It's harder to get balance than you might imagine. 375ml. Screwcap. 11% alc. **Rating** 94 **To** 2020 $25 ✪

ŸŸŸŸŸ Estate Cabernet Sauvignon 2014 Rating 93 **To** 2029 $25 ✪
Gippsland Riesling 2014 Rating 91 **To** 2024 $23 ✪
Gippsland Viognier 2014 Rating 90 **To** 2018 $23

Will Taylor Wines ★★★★

1B Victoria Avenue, Unley Park, SA 5061 **Region** Various
T (08) 8271 6122 **www**.willtaylor.com.au **Open** By appt
Winemaker Various contract **Est.** 1997 **Dozens** 300
Will Taylor is a partner in the leading Adelaide law firm Finlaysons, and specialises in wine law. He and wife Suzanne have established a classic negociant wine business, having wines contract-made to their specifications. They choose what they consider the best regions for each variety; thus Clare Valley Riesling, Adelaide Hills Sauvignon Blanc, Hunter Valley Semillon, Coonawarra Cabernet Sauvignon and Yarra Valley Pinot Noir. Exports to China.

ŸŸŸŸŸ Coonawarra Cabernet Sauvignon 2012 Coonawarra cabernet sauvignon (90%) and merlot (5%) with a 5% addition of cabernet from McLaren Vale. It doesn't put a foot wrong. It sits in the upper reaches of medium-weight and flows blackcurrant, redcurrant, dry herbs and mint flavours confidently through the palate. Oak is integrated, so too tannin. It will age with ease. Diam. 14% alc. **Rating** 94 **To** 2032 $45 CM

Willem Kurt Wines

Croom Lane, Beechworth, Vic 3747 **Region** Beechworth
T 0428 400 522 **www**.willemkurtwines.com.au **Open** Not
Winemaker Daniel Balzer **Est.** 2014 **Dozens** 300

This is the venture of Daniel and Marije Balzer, he with a German background, she Dutch. The name of the winery is drawn from the middle names of their two children: Willem (Dutch) and Kurt (German), in each instance reflecting long usage in the two families. Daniel moved into the wine industry in 1998, having already obtained a science degree, working first at Yarra Ridge (including a vintage in Germany) before moving to Gapsted Wines in 2003, then completing his Bachelor of Wine Science at CSU the following year. Seven years were given over to contract winemaking for smaller producers, and it was inevitable that sooner or later they would start making wine for their own brand. They currently lease a vineyard in Beechworth, and buy select parcels of fruit. Beechworth is the region they know and love best, the plan being to buy land and establish their own vineyard and winery. The quality of the wines made to date suggests it should succeed.

ΨΨΨΨΨ **Shiraz 2013** Beautifully polished and weighted. Pure silk. Mid-weight cherry plum flavours with clove and cedar oak highlights. Good wine doesn't have to be rocket science. Screwcap. 13.8% alc. **Rating** 93 **To** 2022 $32 CM

Chardonnay 2014 Mellow in Beechworth chardonnay terms. Modest flavours of stone fruit, vanilla pod, green herbs and lemon. Plenty of life and length, if not weight. Drinkability is high. Screwcap. 12.6% alc. **Rating** 90 **To** 2018 $34 CM

Alpine Valleys Vermentino 2015 Pale straw; citrus and spiced pears with a hint of ginger; rounded and softly textured with the phenolics coming late in the palate; nicely balanced. Screwcap. 12% alc. **Rating** 90 **To** 2017 $25

Willespie

555 Harmans Mill Road, Wilyabrup via Cowaramup, WA 6284 **Region** Margaret River
T (08) 9755 6248 **www**.willespie.com.au **Open** 7 days 10.30–5
Winemaker Loren Brown **Est.** 1976 **Dozens** 3000 **Vyds** 17.53ha

One of the pioneer wineries in Margaret River, established by local school headmaster Kevin Squance and wife Marian in 1976. They built their house from local timber and stone, set among the natural forest; it now (inter alia) houses the cellar door. Kevin and Marian have retired, and their four children, who are based in Perth and the southwest, will have an active involvement in the business going forward. They will be developing and activating the domestic and export markets in the short to medium term. Exports to Japan and Singapore.

ΨΨΨΨΨ **Basket Pressed Margaret River Shiraz 2008** First tasted 3 years ago, when the alcohol was stated to be 15%, but on a lab label – and to be fair, lab labels often use DIY alcohol levels. The wine has an elegance and balance more akin to 14% than 15%. It is continuing its steady development (the hue is still bright), and it represents excellent value for a wine to be enjoyed now or much later. Diam. 14% alc. **Rating** 94 **To** 2028 $30 ❂

ΨΨΨΨΨ **Basket Pressed Margaret River Merlot 2009** **Rating** 90 **To** 2020 $27

Willoughby Park

678 South Coast Highway, Denmark, WA 6333 **Region** Great Southern
T (08) 9848 1555 **www**.willoughbypark.com.au **Open** 7 days 10–5
Winemaker Luke Eckersley **Est.** 2010 **Dozens** 13 000 **Vyds** 19ha

Bob Fowler, who comes from a rural background and had always hankered after a farming life, stumbled across the opportunity to achieve this in early 2010. Together with wife Marilyn, he purchased the former West Cape Howe winery and surrounding vineyard that became available when West Cape Howe moved into the far larger Goundrey winery. In '11 Willoughby Park purchased the Kalgan River vineyard and business name, and winemaking operations have been transferred to Willoughby Park. There are now three labels: Kalgan River single vineyard range (Kalgan River Ironrock from single sites within the Kalgan River vineyard); Willoughby

Park, the Great Southern brand for estate and purchased grapes; and Jamie & Charli, a sub-$20 Great Southern range of wines. Exports to China.

ꝚꝚꝚꝚꝚ **Ironrock Kalgan River Albany Riesling 2015** Hand-picked from the best patch of the vineyard, chilled, whole bunch-pressed, wild-fermented, a portion in used French oak. There is more of everything: texture, structure, minerally acidity, lime zest and leaf as well as juice. Screwcap. 12.5% alc. **Rating** 97 **To** 2030 $35 ✪

ꝚꝚꝚꝚꝚ **Kalgan River Albany Cabernet Sauvignon 2013** Classic cool grown cabernet at the sharp end of cool; the bouquet is fragrant, the cassis and bay leaf flavours of the palate make the French oak seem irrelevant. Has a monastic purity that is utterly compelling – as is its value. Screwcap. 13.5% alc. **Rating** 96 **To** 2038 $30 ✪

Ironrock Kalgan River Albany Cabernet Sauvignon 2013 An exceptional cabernet with multiple layers of fruit, tannins and oak sliding against, around and through each other as you taste and retaste the wine. Its greater degree of ripeness and more new oak than its sibling make comparisons invidious: each has its own strength, here a luscious complexity. Screwcap. 14% alc. **Rating** 96 **To** 2043 $55 ✪

Ironrock Kalgan River Albany Chardonnay 2014 Plenty of funk, plenty happening here in general. Stone fruit, melon and citrus wound in with barrel-ferment and lees characters, all in the right proportions. An attractive textural feel to the palate with nutty oak and flavours of pink grapefruit pushing through, the acidity quite brisk but in balance. Complex and still evolving. Screwcap. 13.5% alc. **Rating** 95 **To** 2021 $40

Kalgan River Great Southern Pinot Noir 2015 A seriously powerful pinot that has admirable varietal character, proving the cool Kalgan River Vineyard can achieve the holy grail. The colour is deep, but bright, and this sets the pace; there is no question it will open up in fine fettle over the next 2–3 years, and go well beyond that with its savoury/foresty/spicy characters joining hands with its red fruits. Screwcap. 14.5% alc. **Rating** 95 **To** 2025 $30 ✪

Ironrock Albany Shiraz 2013 Cool climate shiraz in essence, but of many dimensions. Peppery, spicy and savoury first up, richer characters of blueberry and blackcurrant emerging with encouragement. Creamy coffee oak is in the background, adding to the picture, and the tannin weaves its way through the palate without distracting. Screwcap. 13% alc. **Rating** 95 **To** 2035 $55

Kalgan River Albany Riesling 2015 Flush with lime juice fruit on both bouquet and palate; balancing and live-giving acidity is evident, but not strident. Screwcap. 12.5% alc. **Rating** 94 **To** 2025 $27 ✪

ꝚꝚꝚꝚꝚ **Kalgan River Albany Chardonnay 2014** Rating 93 To 2019 $30
Kalgan River Albany Shiraz 2013 Rating 93 To 2023 $30

Willow Bridge Estate ★★★★★

178 Gardin Court Drive, Dardanup, WA 6236 **Region** Geographe
T (08) 9728 0055 **www.**willowbridge.com.au **Open** 7 days 11–5
Winemaker Kim Horton **Est.** 1997 **Dozens** 20 000 **Vyds** 59ha
Jeff and Vicky Dewar have followed a fast track in developing Willow Bridge Estate since acquiring the spectacular 180ha hillside property in the Ferguson Valley: chardonnay, semillon, sauvignon blanc, shiraz and cabernet sauvignon were planted, with merlot, tempranillo, chenin blanc and viognier following. Many of its wines offer exceptional value for money. On 22 March 2015, Willow Bridge's 44-year-old senior winemaker, Simon Burnell, died in a windsurfing accident off the coast of Margaret River. It revived memories of the death of Craggy Range winemaker Doug Wiser in Hawke's Bay in '04 while kite-surfing. Kim Horton, with extensive experience in WA, most recently as Senior Winemaker at Ferngrove, has been appointed to take Simon's place. Exports to the UK, China and other major markets.

ꝚꝚꝚꝚꝚ **Gravel Pit Geographe Shiraz 2014** Includes small amounts of grenache and mataro, matured in French oak (20% new). A potent array of savoury, spicy notes drive the bouquet and palate alike, tannins appearing from the word go on the full-bodied palate and persisting through to the finish, but at no stage threatening the fruit. Sophisticated and confident winemaking is at work here. Screwcap. 13.8% alc. **Rating** 96 **To** 2039 $30 ✪

G1-10 Geographe Chardonnay 2015 Hand-picked, whole bunch-pressed, wild-fermented, matured in French oak (25% new) for 10 months. The complex bouquet and intense palate lay it out in large letters: white peach and nectarine, grapefruit/citrus and a dash of cashew oak, the length and balance faultless. Screwcap. 13.4% alc. **Rating** 95 **To** 2028 $30 ✪

Dragonfly Geographe Chardonnay 2015 50% wild-fermented in used French oak, 50% in tank, an approach that has paid a handsome dividend; the palate has an excellent tactile quality that highlights the complexity of flavours, ranging through struck match, white peach and a burst of grapefruit zest on the long finish. Screwcap. 13% alc. **Rating** 94 **To** 2022 $22 ✪

Dragonfly Geographe Shiraz 2014 Matured in new and used French oak. Bursting with energy and drive, spice, licorice and dark chocolate aromas lead into an intense palate rippling with juicy black cherry, plum and licorice fruit; the modest alcohol confers brightness on the lingering finish. Screwcap. 13.5% alc. **Rating** 94 **To** 2029 $22 ✪

Dragonfly Geographe Cabernet Merlot 2014 71% cabernet, 27% merlot and 2% shiraz. Excellent depth and clarity to the colour; the fragrant dark berry fruits of the bouquet set the agenda that the medium-bodied palate follows without hesitation. Typical Willow Bridge over-delivery of quality. Screwcap. 13.5% alc. **Rating** 94 **To** 2029 $22 ✪

Solana Geographe Tempranillo 2014 A full-bodied and expressive example of the variety, black fruits, anise, earth and a spicy kick leading to a chunky and punchy palate. Demands food. Screwcap. 13.9% alc. **Rating** 94 **To** 2025 $28 ✪

ŸŸŸŸ **Dragonfly Sauvignon Blanc Semillon 2015 Rating** 89 **To** 2017 $22

Willow Creek Vineyard ★★★★★

1/33 Cook Street, Flinders, Vic 3929 **Region** Mornington Peninsula
T (03) 5989 7448 **www**.willow-creek.com.au **Open** Thurs–Sun 11–5
Winemaker Geraldine McFaul **Est.** 1989 **Dozens** 5000 **Vyds** 18ha
Significant changes have transformed Willow Creek over the past 7 years. In 2008, winemaker Geraldine McFaul, with many years of winemaking in the Mornington Peninsula under her belt, was appointed, and worked with viticulturist Robbie O'Leary to focus on minimal intervention in the winery; in other words, to produce grapes in perfect condition. In '13 the Li family arrived from China and expanded its portfolio of hotel and resort properties in Australia by purchasing Willow Creek, with plans to develop a luxury 39-room boutique hotel on the site. This will be the 7th in the Li hotel group.

ŸŸŸŸŸ **O'Leary Block Mornington Peninsula Pinot Noir 2013** MV6 and D2V5 clones, matured for 15 months in French oak (25% new). The first time this block has been bottled (ie not blended), and it's not hard to see why. The fragrant cherry blossom bouquet heralds the red fruits of the elegant, but intense, palate, with nuances of forest floor providing the framework for the long, lingering finish. Screwcap. 13.5% alc. **Rating** 96 **To** 2028 $75 ✪

Mornington Peninsula Sauvignon Blanc 2015 A thoroughly impressive and powerful sauvignon in the style of the late Didier Dageneau (Loire Valley, France). Its flavour spectrum is on the savoury side, oak imparting texture and not subverting the complex and intense mix of herb and blackcurrant (yes!) flavours. Screwcap. 12% alc. **Rating** 95 **To** 2018 $35 ✪

Mornington Peninsula Chardonnay 2014 Tiny berries gave rise to a derisory 1t/ha (less than half a tonne per acre) crop – hence the intensity of this wine; grapefruit leads the way, white peach and nutty notes also in close attendance. The cost of production must have been greater than the price of the wine. Screwcap. 13% alc. **Rating** 95 **To** 2027 $40

Mornington Peninsula Pinot Noir 2014 Destemmed and open-fermented, with 21 days on skins, matured in French oak (25% new). Five clones, picked between 14 and 26 Mar, marry elegance and intensity, red berries with a brocade of multi-spices and a lingering, fresh finish. Screwcap. 13.2% alc. **Rating** 95 To 2025 $40

Malakoff Vineyard Shiraz 2014 Gorgeous shiraz. Textural, smoky, complex and plain delicious. Blackberries and plums, graphite and cloves. Fine, elegant stitches of tannin. Everything in complete harmony. Take a bow. Screwcap. 13.5% alc. **Rating** 95 To 2030 $30 CM ◐

ΨΨΨΨΨ **Mornington Peninsula Pinot Gris 2015 Rating** 91 To 2018 $35
Mornington Peninsula Rose 2015 Rating 90 To 2016 $28

Wills Domain ★★★★★

Cnr Brash Road/Abbey Farm Road, Yallingup, WA 6281 **Region** Margaret River
T (08) 9755 2327 **www.**willsdomain.com.au **Open** 7 days 10–5
Winemaker Naturaliste Vintners (Bruce Dukes) **Est.** 1985 **Dozens** 12 500 **Vyds** 20.8ha
When the Haunold family purchased the original Wills Domain vineyard in 2000, they were adding another chapter to a family history of winemaking stretching back to 1383 in what is now Austria. Remarkable though that may be, more remarkable is that Darren, who lost the use of his legs in an accident in 1989, runs the estate (including part of the pruning) from his wheelchair. The vineyard is planted to shiraz, semillon, cabernet sauvignon, sauvignon blanc, chardonnay, merlot, petit verdot, malbec, cabernet franc and viognier. Exports to Canada, Indonesia, Hong Kong and China.

ΨΨΨΨΨ **Cuvee d'Elevage Margaret River Shiraz 2014** The perfumed bouquet literally leaps from the glass; the palate, while medium-bodied at best, has terrific energy and drive, spice, pepper, cedary French oak (from the new oak) and red/black cherry fruits whirling through from the opening stanza through to the fanfare of trumpets on the finish. Screwcap. 14% alc. **Rating** 96 To 2034 $80

Cuvee d'Elevage Margaret River Chardonnay 2014 Has many things in common with Block 8, not the least balance; here the fruit is a little richer, the oak infinitesimally more obvious. This is the better wine, but the old question remains: is it twice as good? Screwcap. 13.5% alc. **Rating** 95 To 2024 $65

Cuvee d'Elevage Margaret River Matrix 2013 59% cabernet sauvignon, 21% merlot, 8% petit verdot, 6% each of malbec and cabernet franc. Has the Wills Domain stamp on its flavour profile and structure, the fragrant cassis-laden bouquet leading into an elegant, medium-bodied palate; silky tannins are sewn through the supple fruit, the oak by no means oppressive. Screwcap. 14% alc. **Rating** 95 To 2038 $100

Block 8 Margaret River Chardonnay 2014 Matured for 9 months in French oak (40% new). Vibrant and juicy white-fleshed fruits to the fore; exactly pitched acidity gives the palate drive and freshness, the oak merely a means to an end. Screwcap. 13% alc. **Rating** 94 To 2022 $30 ◐

Block 5 Margaret River Shiraz 2014 Good colour; the fragrant bouquet offers both cedary oak and spicy, peppery dark fruits, characters that seize and define the long, intensely focused palate. Makes you sit up and take notice, not snuggle back in for a comfortable journey through to the finish – and all the better for that. Screwcap. 14% alc. **Rating** 94 To 2034 $30 ◐

Block 3 Margaret River Cabernet Sauvignon 2014 What can one say? It's Margaret River and cabernet, and there is only one outcome: a fragrant bouquet, cassis fruit, balanced tannins and length. The real question, I suppose, is how good each of those contributing factors is. The answer here is that that all are in perfect harmony with each other on a finely wrought frame. Screwcap. 14% alc. **Rating** 94 To 2034 $30 ◐

Cuvee d'Elevage Margaret River Cabernet Sauvignon 2013 A complex wine with a mix of texture and flavour that is peculiar to Wills Domain, higher toned (not volatile) and finer in the mouth (not light-bodied). The net effect is impressive and enjoyable (for me; others may scratch their heads). Screwcap. 14.5% alc. **Rating** 94 **To** 2028 $90

🍷🍷🍷🍷♀ **Margaret River Semillon Sauvignon Blanc 2015** Rating 93 To 2018 $20 ✪
Margaret River Shiraz 2014 Rating 92 To 2029 $20 ✪

Willunga 100 Wines   ★★★★★

PO Box 2427, McLaren Vale, SA 5171 **Region** McLaren Vale
T 0414 419 957 **www**.willunga100.com **Open** Not
Winemaker Tim James, Mike Farmilo **Est.** 2005 **Dozens** 9500
Willunga 100 is solely owned by Liberty Wines UK, sourcing its grapes from McLaren Vale and from Adelaide Hills (pinot gris and a portion of its viognier). The winemaking team these days is decidedly high-powered, with the hugely experienced Tim James and Mike Farmilo the conductors of the band. The focus is on the diverse districts within McLaren Vale, and the resource of dry grown bushvine grenache. Exports to the UK, Canada, Singapore, Hong Kong and NZ.

🍷🍷🍷🍷🍷 **The Tithing Grenache 2013** The colour is exceptionally bright and lively for grenache, and sets the scene for gloriously juicy red berry fruits that race headlong along the palate and into the finish and aftertaste, its vibrant acidity the key to its rare quality. Screwcap. 14.5% alc. **Rating** 96 **To** 2025 $40 ✪
McLaren Vale Shiraz Viognier 2014 Bright crimson-purple; the bouquet has spice and licorice to the fore, its plum and blackberry fruit on the palate with fine, dusty tannins running through its length. The clever winemaking has allowed the fruit to retain its freshness, the French oak to sit alongside. Screwcap. 14% alc. **Rating** 95 **To** 2029 $22 ✪
The Hundred McLaren Vale Grenache 2014 It is far harder to make an unoaked red wine than it might seem, particularly to achieve a sense of completeness. This fills the mouth with a spherical texture and structure, the journey from start to finish and back again without a break. And yes, the red fruits do have seamless tannins. Screwcap. 14.5% alc. **Rating** 94 **To** 2029 $30 ✪
McLaren Vale Grenache 2014 A potent and powerful wine, with rare drive and grip, that only McLaren Vale can produce. It does so without in any way subjugating the varietal character, the savoury tannin structure something to behold. Radically different from The Hundred. Screwcap. 14.5% alc. **Rating** 94 **To** 2034 $22 ✪

🍷🍷🍷🍷♀ **McLaren Vale Grenache Rose 2015** Rating 91 To 2017 $22 ✪
McLaren Vale Cabernet Shiraz 2014 Rating 91 To 2034 $22 ✪

Wilson Vineyard   ★★★★★

Polish Hill River, Sevenhill via Clare, SA 5453 **Region** Clare Valley
T (08) 8843 4310 **Open** W'ends 10–4
Winemaker Daniel Wilson **Est.** 1974 **Dozens** 3000 **Vyds** 11.9ha
In 2009 the winery and general operations were passed on to son Daniel Wilson, the second generation. Daniel, a graduate of CSU, spent three years in the Barossa with some of Australia's largest winemakers before returning to Clare in '03. Parents John and Pat Wilson still contribute in a limited way, content to watch developments in the business they created. Daniel continues to follow John's beliefs about keeping quality high, often at the expense of volume, and rather than talk about it, believes the proof is in the bottle. At Daniel's side are wife Tamara and daughters Poppy and Isabelle.

🍷🍷🍷🍷🍷 **DJW Clare Valley Riesling 2015** From a small estate block that has always produced a wine with its own special character, although the back label description of generosity isn't a word I would use. This is a very fine and detailed riesling that progressively picks up power to its lime and lemon fruit on the way to the finish, excellent acidity continuing the drive through to the aftertaste. Screwcap. 12.5% alc. **Rating** 95 **To** 2030 $24 ✪

Polish Hill River Riesling 2015 Has the X-factor that Polish Hill River riesling is blessed with, protected by whole bunch pressing of near-frozen grapes and a very cool 6-week fermentation. It is precisely balanced and articulated, fruit and acidity holding hands and moving in lockstep. Given time, this will shout from the rooftops. Screwcap. 12.5% alc. **Rating** 95 **To** 2035 $29 **◑**

Watervale Riesling 2015 Pause before you leap to judgement on this wine, and let the strength and length of the finish and aftertaste illuminate the faintly herbal citrus fruit of the bouquet and fore-palate. This is a wine bred to stay, and will come into full flower around 7 years hence. Screwcap. 12.5% alc. **Rating** 94 **To** 2024 $19 **◑**

Museum Release Polish Hill River Riesling 2008 Gleaming green-gold; now fully developed, with toasty nuances adding complexity to a wine that always had expression of its particular place on the banks of a meandering stream that runs in winter, but not summer or autumn. Screwcap. 12% alc. **Rating** 94 **To** 2018 $36

Pepperstone Clare Valley Shiraz 2014 An unusual Clare Valley shiraz, constantly looking out towards the chocolate and plum cake flavours of McLaren Vale, but presenting them in a more elegant costume. The alcohol seems much lower than 14.5% (unambiguously good), the tannins finer, the oak absorbed. In short, a really attractive wine requiring no patience. Screwcap. **Rating** 94 **To** 2029 $26 **◑**

Stonecraft Clare Valley Cabernet Sauvignon 2014 Good hue of moderate depth; the fragrant bouquet speaks truly of the elegant palate that follows, with blackcurrant/cassis tripping gracefully along the stepping stones of fine, chalky tannins and pleasing oak. Screwcap. 14.5% alc. **Rating** 94 **To** 2029 $26 **◑**

Wily Trout Vineyard ★★★★

Marakei-Nanima Road, via Hall, NSW 2618 **Region** Canberra District
T (02) 6230 2487 **www**.wilytrout.com.au **Open** 7 days 10–5
Winemaker Nick Spencer, Hamish Young **Est.** 1998 **Dozens** 2500 **Vyds** 12.7ha
The Wily Trout vineyard, owned by Robert and Susan Bruce, shares its home with the Poachers Pantry, a renowned gourmet smokehouse. The quality of the wines is very good, and a testament to the skills of the contract winemakers. The northeast-facing slopes, at an elevation of 720m, provide some air drainage and hence protection against spring frosts.

♟♟♟♟♟ **Canberra District Sauvignon Blanc 2015** Passionfruit coupled with
tropical fruits lead to a rich and powerful varietal expression. Rounded, fine and concentrated, held in check by a fine line of mineral acids. Screwcap. 13.5% alc. **Rating** 94 **To** 2017 $24 **◑**

Canberra District Pinot Noir 2015 Particularly deep colour, and a healthy dose of cherry-scented fruit, this is a delicious pinot, single vineyard no less, for a bargain $25. Impressive depth and character. Screwcap. 13.5% alc. **Rating** 94 **To** 2020 $25 **◑**

♟♟♟♟♟ **Canberra District Chardonnay 2014** **Rating** 91 **To** 2020 $24
Canberra District Shiraz 2014 **Rating** 91 **To** 2020 $25

Wimbaliri Wines ★★★☆

3180 Barton Highway, Murrumbateman, NSW 2582 **Region** Canberra District
T (02) 6227 5921 **www**.wimbaliri.com.au **Open** W'ends 10–5
Winemaker Scott Gledhill **Est.** 1988 **Dozens** 600 **Vyds** 2.2ha
John and Margaret Andersen moved to the Canberra District in 1987, establishing their vineyard at Murrumbateman in '88, bordering Clonakilla. The vineyard is close-planted with chardonnay, pinot noir, shiraz, cabernet sauvignon and merlot (plus a few cabernet franc vines). In 2009 the winery was purchased by Scott and Sarah Gledhill. Scott, born in Wallsend (NSW), is a sixth-generation descendant of German vine dressers who emigrated to the Hunter Valley in the 1850s; Sarah draws upon her science background to assist in the vineyard and winemaking.

♀♀♀♀♀ **35th Parallel Murrumbateman Chardonnay 2014** A distinctive wine; always a good thing. Oatmeal, honeysuckle, melon and cooked apple flavours run into a rush of bacony oak. It's not overly rich, but it's well flavoured; it's not seamless, but the flavours are teamed well enough. Value is certainly in the buyer's favour. Diam. 12.5% alc. **Rating** 91 **To** 2019 $20 CM ✪

♀♀♀♀ **Murrumbateman Shiraz Viognier 2014 Rating** 88 **To** 2021 $40 CM

Windance Wines   ★★★★☆

2764 Caves Road, Yallingup, WA 6282 **Region** Margaret River
T (08) 9755 2293 **www**.windance.com.au **Open** 7 days 10–5
Winemaker Tyke Wheatley **Est.** 1998 **Dozens** 3500 **Vyds** 7.25ha
Drew and Rosemary Brent-White own this family business, situated 5km south of Yallingup. Cabernet sauvignon, shiraz, sauvignon blanc, semillon and merlot have been established, incorporating sustainable land management and organic farming practices where possible. The wines are exclusively estate-grown. Daughter Billie and husband Tyke Wheatley now run operations: Billie, a qualified accountant, was raised at Windance, and manages the business and the cellar door, and Tyke (with winemaking experience at Picardy, Happs and Burgundy) has taken over the winemaking and manages the vineyard.

♀♀♀♀♀ **Shiraz 2014** Full-bodied but riddled with spice. It's a lifted, perfumed style with blackberry, anise and black cherry flavours and sweet florals doing the rounds. Plenty of spicy/meaty tannin. A whisper of menthol. Ripper. Screwcap. 14% alc. **Rating** 95 **To** 2033 $28 CM ✪

♀♀♀♀♀ **Reserve Cabernet Sauvignon 2013 Rating** 93 **To** 2030 $40 CM

Windowrie Estate   ★★★

Windowrie Road, Canowindra, NSW 2804 **Region** Cowra
T (02) 6344 3234 **www**.windowrie.com.au **Open** At The Mill, Cowra
Winemaker Antonio D'Onise **Est.** 1988 **Dozens** 30 000 **Vyds** 240ha
Windowrie Estate was established by the O'Dea family in 1988 on a substantial grazing property at Canowindra, 30km north of Cowra. A portion of the grapes is sold to other makers, but increasing quantities are being made for the Windowrie Estate and The Mill labels. The cellar door is in a flour mill – built in 1861 from local granite – that ceased operations in 1905 and lay unoccupied for 91 years until restored by the O'Dea family. Exports to Canada, China, Japan and Singapore.

♀♀♀♀ **The Mill Orange Sauvignon Blanc 2015** Crowd-pleasing style with sweet pear, passionfruit and lemongrass flavours flowing more or less seamlessly through the palate. Clean and tidy. Screwcap. 12.5% alc. **Rating** 88 **To** 2016 $18 CM

Windows Estate   ★★★★★

4 Quininup Road, Yallingup, WA 6282 **Region** Margaret River
T (08) 9756 6655 **www**.windowsestate.com **Open** 7 days 10–5
Winemaker Chris Davies **Est.** 1996 **Dozens** 3500 **Vyds** 6.3ha
Chris Davies planted the Windows Estate vineyard (cabernet sauvignon, shiraz, chenin blanc, chardonnay, semillon, sauvignon blanc and merlot) in 1996, at the age of 19, and has tended the vines ever since. Initially selling the grapes, Chris moved into winemaking in 2006 and has had considerable show success for the consistently outstanding wines. Exports to Germany, Singapore and Taiwan.

♀♀♀♀♀ **Margaret River Chardonnay 2014** Bright straw-green; a totally beautiful Margaret River chardonnay, with the poise of a ballet dancer; its fruit flavours are gloriously juicy, with citrus and stone fruit so tightly bound it's impossible to deconstruct them: just glory in their impact. And for the sake of completeness, oak is part of the story. Screwcap. 13% alc. **Rating** 97 **To** 2025 $39 ✪

🍷🍷🍷🍷🍷 **Small Batch Margaret River Chardonnay 2013** Bright straw-green, just a hint of the extreme quality, complexity and finesse on display from start to finish; the intensity of the varietal fruit has soaked up the new oak in the way very good White Burgundies do. Still only part of the way to full maturity. Screwcap. 14% alc. **Rating** 96 **To** 2025 $55 ✪

Estate Grown Margaret River Sauvignon Blanc 2015 The wine keeps the door closed until it enters the long palate and lingering aftertaste, with excellent tension between juicy fruits and texture from the oak fermentation. A superior wine in every respect. Screwcap. 12% alc. **Rating** 95 **To** 2017 $22 ✪

Estate Grown Margaret River Semillon Sauvignon Blanc 2015 50% barrel-fermented in new French barriques. The barrel ferment impacts on both the flavour and structure, heightening the role of the semillon in the blend; snow pea, green bean and citrus are drivers, but the greatest impact comes from the invigorating electric acidity. A good few years will add fruit flesh as it matures. Screwcap. 12% alc. **Rating** 95 **To** 2020 $26 ✪

Basket Pressed Margaret River Cabernet Merlot 2013 50% cabernet, 40% merlot and 5% each of malbec and petit verdot. This is elegance with a capital E, red and blackcurrant fruit in a savoury web of tannins; good length is almost a given. Screwcap. 14.5% alc. **Rating** 94 **To** 2028 $32

Basket Pressed Margaret River Cabernet Sauvignon 2013 Margaret River cabernet can come in many shapes and sizes, here full-bodied, yet essentially plush and soft thanks to its ripe tannins and cedary French oak. Give it time to slim down a touch, and you will be well pleased. Screwcap. 14.5% alc. **Rating** 94 **To** 2038 $37

🍷🍷🍷🍷🍷 **Basket Pressed Margaret River Syrah 2013** Rating 93 To 2028 $32

Wines by Geoff Hardy   ★★★★★

327 Hunt Road, McLaren Vale, SA 5171 **Region** South Australia
T (08) 8383 2700 **www**.winesbygeoffhardy.com.au **Open** 7 days 11–5
Winemaker Geoff Hardy, Shane Harris **Est.** 1980 **Dozens** 90 000 **Vyds** 43ha
Geoff Hardy's great-great-grandfather, the original Thomas Hardy, first planted grapes in SA in the 1850s and was one of the founding fathers of the Australian wine industry. In 1980, Geoff left the then family company, Thomas Hardy & Sons, to make his own way in all sectors of the Australian wine business, together with wife Fiona. Wines by Geoff Hardy is made up of three ventures/brands founded by Geoff: Pertaringa in McLaren Vale, K1 by Geoff Hardy in the Adelaide Hills (Tynan Rd, Kuitpo) and Hand Crafted by Geoff Hardy, sourced from a variety of premium regions across SA. Exports to Canada, the UK, Sweden, Finland, India, Thailand, Malaysia, South Korea, Indonesia, Japan, Taiwan, Hong Kong and China.

🍷🍷🍷🍷🍷 **Pertaringa Over The Top Shiraz 2014** Despite the name (and the alcohol), this has unexpected elegance and balance; black cherry and blackberry fruit have a dusting of spice, the tannins fine and supple (an unusual combination). It all adds up to a coherent message. Diam. 14.7% alc. **Rating** 95 **To** 2032 $40

Hand Crafted by Geoff Hardy Tempranillo 2013 It's not often a light to medium-bodied wine can have the power, intensity and length of this wine; the vibrant red and sour cherry fruits have persistent fine-grained tannins and exemplary length. The cool climate is perfect for this early-ripening variety. Screwcap. 14.5% alc. **Rating** 95 **To** 2028 $30 ✪

Hand Crafted by Geoff Hardy Langhorne Creek Graciano 2014 Sourced from Langhorne Creek, made in a nouveau fashion, 10% barrel-matured, 90% in stainless steel before blending and bottling 12 months later. This is seriously clever, indeed sensitive, winemaking, protecting the bright red fruits and crisp, fresh acidity; the low alcohol has no green fruit downside whatsoever. Screwcap. 12.5% alc. **Rating** 95 **To** 2024 $30 ✪

Hand Crafted by Geoff Hardy Lagrein 2013 Deep, dense crimson-purple; the very complex bouquet has a fresh-picked wild blackberry and smoky meat combination, the full-bodied palate establishing itself on the mid-palate, not the finish, tannins not in the game. A fascinating wine, but make sure there is plenty of meat to accompany it. Screwcap. 15% alc. **Rating** 95 **To** 2030 $30 ✪

K1 by Geoff Hardy Adelaide Hills Gruner Veltliner 2015 This has as much varietal character as one can expect from young vines, and shows why gruner veltliner has a guaranteed future – even if it has the same struggle as riesling to gain broad-based acceptance. It has length and excellent mouthfeel, the finish bright and fresh. Screwcap. 12.5% alc. **Rating** 94 **To** 2020 $25 ✪

K1 by Geoff Hardy Adelaide Hills Shiraz 2014 All the '14 wines have what at first sight are two gold medals on their front, but in fact tell the consumer that the SA-based *Winestate* magazine announced Wines by Geoff Hardy as Australian Wine Company of the year in both '12 and '14. The bouquet and palate pull no punches with their display of red and black fruits, spice and high quality tannins. Will develop for many years. Screwcap. 14.5% alc. **Rating** 94 **To** 2034 $40

Pertaringa McLaren Vale Shiraz Mataro 2014 Good colour; a richly robed blend, its succulent array of predominantly black fruits, dark chocolate and supple tannins seamlessly welded together on a full-bodied palate that has exceptional length. This wine really hums, and will do so for years to come. Screwcap. 14.5% alc. **Rating** 94 **To** 2034 $35

Pertaringa Coonawarra Cabernet Sauvignon 2014 Good colour; it immediately establishes its varietal character and place of origin; the fruit has been picked at optimum ripeness, the medium-bodied palate replete with cassis and redcurrant, bay leaf just so, the tannins likewise. Oak? Yes, just as needed. Screwcap. 14% alc. **Rating** 94 **To** 2034 $35

Hand Crafted by Geoff Hardy Montepulciano 2013 Light but bright crimson; the fragrant bouquet and light to medium-bodied palate have the full suite of red fruits, the texture a mix of silk and velvet. Definitely an each-way bet, now or at any time over the next 10 years. Screwcap. 13.5% alc. **Rating** 94 **To** 2023 $30 ✪

Hand Crafted by Geoff Hardy Adelaide Aglianico 2013 There is a flamboyant brocade of red fruits on the bouquet and palate before a finish and aftertaste that are broody and very savoury, considerably lengthening the palate, albeit with minimal tannins. Screwcap. 13% alc. **Rating** 94 **To** 2023 $30 ✪

♟♟♟♟♟ K1 Sauvignon Blanc 2015 Rating 93 To 2016 $22 ✪
Hand Crafted Shiraz 2014 Rating 93 To 2034 $30
Hand Crafted McLaren Vale Nero d'Avola 2014 Rating 93 To 2025 $30
Hand Crafted Gruner Veltliner 2015 Rating 92 To 2020 $25 ✪
Pertaringa Undercover Shiraz 2014 Rating 92 To 2034 $22 ✪
Pertaringa Understudy McLaren Vale Cabernet Sauvignon 2014
Rating 92 To 2029 $22 ✪
Hand Crafted Teroldego 2014 Rating 92 To 2024 $30

Wines by KT   ★★★★★

Main North Road, Watervale, SA 5452 **Region** Clare Valley
T 0419 855 500 **www**.winesbykt.com **Open** By appt
Winemaker Kerri Thompson **Est.** 2006 **Dozens** 1400
KT is winemaker Kerri Thompson. Kerri graduated with a degree in oenology from Roseworthy Agricultural College in 1993, and thereafter made wine in McLaren Vale, Tuscany, Beaujolais and the Clare Valley, becoming well known as the Leasingham winemaker in the Clare Valley. She resigned from Leasingham in 2006 after seven years at the helm, and after a short break became winemaker at Crabtree. Here she is also able to make Wines by KT, sourcing the grapes from two local vineyards, one biodynamic, the other farmed with sulphur and copper sprays only. Exports to the UK.

♟♟♟♟♟ Churinga Vineyard Watervale Riesling 2015 The floral bouquet is thrown into the shade by the sheer power of the palate, with squeaky acidity patrolling the borders, ripe lemon and lime contained within; the intense aftertaste seals the deal.

Patience will be repaid many times over. Screwcap. 12.5% alc. **Rating** 96 **To** 2035 $33 ✪

Peglidis Vineyard Watervale Riesling 2015 This is the most potent and strongly structured of the four Rieslings I have tasted from Kerri Thompson in this vintage, and the most in need of time, however seductive the lingering aftertaste may be. Screwcap. 12% alc. **Rating** 95 **To** 2039 $35 ✪

Melva by KT Wild Fermented Riesling 2015 The kaleidoscopic palate has a light and shade show, delicate lime-infused flavours one minute, more slatey/mineral notes the next, the overall outcome one of freshness and exuberance. The message of the label design? Screwcap. 12% alc. **Rating** 95 **To** 2025 $30 ✪

Rosa by KT Garnacha Tempranillo Rosada 2015 An intriguing palate, with faint touches of fairy floss and Turkish Delight peeping through before a surge of seamless red fruits and acidity pours through the finish and exceptionally persistent aftertaste. Screwcap. 12.5% alc. **Rating** 95 **To** 2017 $23 ✪

5452 by KT Shiraz 2013 5452 is the postcode shared by Leasingham and Watervale. The Clare Valley is not noted for the elegance of its red wines, but this goes perilously close to achieving precisely that. Red and black cherry, redcurrant, fine-grained tannins and a hint of oak all make their contribution to a seductive style, balance and length impeccable. Screwcap. 13.8% alc. **Rating** 95 **To** 2028 $25 ✪

Churinga Vineyard Watervale Shiraz 2013 It is a radically different style from its 5452 sibling, full-bodied and full of inky/sultry/savoury black fruits in a boxing ring of raw-boned tannins and oak. Balance emerges as the winner, but it demands patience. Screwcap. 14% alc. **Rating** 95 **To** 2048 $40

Churinga Vineyard Watervale Cabernet Sauvignon 2013 By Clare Valley standards, the supple cassis fruit is wonderfully juicy and accessible. There won't be many with enough bottles to play the now or later game, but even if there were, there would be no losers. Screwcap. 13.5% alc. **Rating** 95 **To** 2038 $40

5452 Riesling 2015 A bucket of aromas and flavours, with a full range of lime/citrus, and an elusive hint of fennel/herb on the aftertaste to add interest. A snappy wine to act as the financial base of the business. Screwcap. 12% alc. **Rating** 94 **To** 2025 $23 ✪

5452 by KT Grenache Mataro 2013 If I can politely do so, I will bypass 90% of Clare Valley grenache, with or without mataro, but here the feminine wiles of winemaker Kerri Thompson have wound the varieties around her little finger, keeping dead fruit/alcohol at bay, and bringing this posy of bright red fruits centre stage. Ready now or soonish. Screwcap. 14% alc. **Rating** 94 **To** 2020 $25 ✪

Wines for Joanie ★★★★

163 Glendale Road, Sidmouth, Tas 7270 **Region** Northern Tasmania
T (03) 6394 7005 **www.**winesforjoanie.com.au **Open** Fri–Mon 10–5
Winemaker Contract **Est.** 2013 **Dozens** 250 **Vyds** 5ha
Andrew (Rew) and Prue O'Shanesy lived on a small cattle and cropping farm in Queensland, but they realised it wasn't a viable stand-alone business. They sold it, and had no idea what to do next. Northern Territory? A coffee plantation at Byron Bay? Then someone mentioned that a vineyard was for sale in northern Tasmania. Look no further: Rew is a viticulturist and both love drinking wine. In the blink of an eye they were heading across Bass Strait 'with the ute, two cattle dogs, a horse and a prissy cat'. They started working on a budget for a vineyard, trying to make the budget tell them what they wanted to hear. They eventually tore up the budget, took the plunge and bought Glendale, the little farm they now call home. They now have three dogs, two horses, the prissy cat, a couple of chooks, some sheep, a few cows and a baby boy called Angus. Joanie was Rew's mother, an inspiring, vivacious, creative and strong woman.

🍷🍷🍷🍷🍷 **Vintage Sparkling 2014** Pink-copper tinge. Strawberry and sweet doughy flavour but don't settle in, citrussy acidity is on the march. Very long. Very much in need of a year or so in bottle. Very fine bead. Diam. 12.5% alc. **Rating** 92 **To** 2020 $38 CM

Chardonnay 2014 An attractive, well-made Chardonnay that offers a point of difference from most other Tasmanian chardonnays: its flavour core of ripe stone fruit. Oak, acidity and tannins are incidental in their own right, but important in the overall scheme of things. Screwcap. 13.5% alc. **Rating** 91 **To** 2020 $48

Pinot Gris 2015 In an expensive bottle. The colour has only the barest hint of skin contact, and the flavour is firmly fixed on varietal character; this plays to its strengths of length and pleasing grip to the finish. Seafood, tapas, Chinese – bring it all on. Screwcap. 13.5% alc. **Rating** 90 **To** 2018 $28

Winetrust Estates   ★★★

Murray Valley Highway, Swan Hill, Vic 3585 **Region** Swan Hill
T (02) 9949 9250 **www**.winetrustestates.com **Open** Not
Winemaker Callum Peace, Marion Peligri, Rob Moody **Est.** 1999 **Dozens** 59 000
Vyds 88.9ha
Mark Arnold is the man behind Winetrust Estates, drawing on a lifetime of experience in all aspects of the wine industry. Production of the wines from all vineyards in the group is centralised at the Garacama Winery at Swan Hill, the grapes either self-grown, contract-grown or produced under a joint venture across regions in Vic, SA and WA. The top-of-the-range Picarus red wines come from the Limestone Coast; the Ocean Grove, Argon Bay and Firebox Ridge ranges cover all the major varietal wines plus a few newcomers. Exports to the UK, the US, Canada, Vietnam, Singapore, Thailand, Japan, Hong Kong and China.

 Argon Bay Vineyards Regional Selection Reserve Langhorne Creek Cabernet Sauvignon 2013 You get plenty for your dollar with this wine: the typically softly rich fruit of Langhorne Creek, a generous helping of French and American oak (not necessarily ex barrel) and soft tannins. Screwcap. 14% alc. **Rating** 88 **To** 2017 $17 ✪

Winstead   ★★★★

75 Winstead Road, Bagdad, Tas 7030 **Region** Southern Tasmania
T (03) 6268 6417 **www**.winstead.com.au **Open** By appt
Winemaker Neil Snare **Est.** 1989 **Dozens** 700 **Vyds** 3ha
The good news about Winstead is the quality of its generous and rich Pinot Noirs, notable for the abundance of their fruit flavour without any sacrifice of varietal character. In the 2012 Pinot Noir class at the Tasmanian Wine Show '16 only two gold medals were awarded, Winstead Lot 7 top of the class, edging out the other gold, Winstead Lot 13. The bad news is that production is so limited, with only 1.7ha of pinot noir, 0.7ha sauvignon blanc, 0.5ha riesling and 0.1ha of merlot being tended by fly fishing devotee Neil Snare and wife Julieanne.

 Lot 16 Pinot Noir 2013 Good colour for age, slightly brighter than Lot 7; a powerful, rich, and faintly peppery wine with whole bunch/foresty elements giving the palate drive and considerable length. Screwcap. 13.5% alc. **Rating** 92 **To** 2021 $39

Lot 7 Riesling 2015 Light straw-green; layered lime juice, zest and pith pushes the normally strong acidity into a secondary role. Ready now, and I wouldn't be tempted to hold it for more than a few years. Screwcap. 12.5% alc. **Rating** 90 **To** 2019 $22

Lot 7 Pinot Noir 2013 Like Lot 16, has a spicy, peppery element to it, and shares some of its generous textural/structural elements. Screwcap. 13.6% alc. **Rating** 90 **To** 2020 $39

Wirra Wirra   ★★★★★

McMurtrie Road, McLaren Vale, SA 5171 **Region** McLaren Vale
T (08) 8323 8414 **www**.wirrawirra.com **Open** Mon–Sat 10–5, Sun & public hols 11–5
Winemaker Paul Smith, Paul Carpenter, Tom Ravech **Est.** 1894 **Dozens** 180 000
Vyds 51.31ha

Long respected for the consistency of its white wines, Wirra Wirra has now established an equally formidable reputation for its reds. The wines are of exemplary character, quality and style, The Angelus Cabernet Sauvignon and RWS Shiraz battling each other for supremacy, with The Absconder Grenache one to watch. Long may the battle continue under the direction of managing director Andrew Kay and the winemaking team of Paul Smith, Paul Carpenter and Tom Ravech, who forge along the path of excellence first trod by the late (and much loved) Greg Trott, the pioneering founder of modern-day Wirra Wirra. Its acquisition of Ashton Hills in April 2015 adds a major string to its top quality bow. Exports to all major markets.

♥♥♥♥♥ RSW McLaren Vale Shiraz 2014 The continued refinement of the flagship wines from Wirra Wirra is evident in the '14 RSW. Darkly coloured and darkly fruited, the palate is finely poised with grainy, slatey tannins saturated in blackberry-laden fruit, the finish long, savoury and extremely fine. Screwcap. 14.5% alc. **Rating** 96 **To** 2038 $70 ✪

The Absconder McLaren Vale Grenache 2014 Light, but fresh, red hue; this is a very serious grenache, with a rarely encountered drive and length based entirely on its varietal fruit, the oak and tannins whispering in the background. Will flourish with age, but that's no reason for a hands-off policy today. Screwcap. 14.5% alc. **Rating** 96 **To** 2024 $70 ✪

The Angelus McLaren Vale Cabernet Sauvignon 2014 Underrated by many, McLaren Vale produces some very fine cabernet sauvignons, and this is one of them. Beautifully fragrant with red berry/mulberry and a leafy note. The palate is medium to full-bodied, superfine tannins rolling on and on, ably backed by blackcurrant and cassis. Screwcap. 13.5% alc. **Rating** 96 **To** 2034 $70 ✪

Hiding Champion Adelaide Hills Sauvignon Blanc 2015 Pale quartz-green; the fragrant bouquet and vivacious palate range through snow pea, lemon peel, passionfruit and kiwi fruit, all bouncing around on a trampoline of bright natural acidity. Difficult to ask for more. Screwcap. 12.5% alc. **Rating** 95 **To** 2016 $24 ✪

The 12th Man Adelaide Hills Chardonnay 2015 It doesn't take long at all for the intensity and length of this wine to make its mark. While it's also elegant, it is no wannabe sauvignon blanc; there are layers of white peach and grapefruit on offer here. Screwcap. 13.5% alc. **Rating** 95 **To** 2026 $31 ✪

Woodhenge McLaren Vale Shiraz 2014 Darkly coloured and jam-packed with blackberry, tar, anise and a lick of dried herbs. Plush and expansive, with finely grained tannins holding everything in check. Long, and requiring many years. Screwcap. 14.5% alc. **Rating** 95 **To** 2028 $35 ✪

The Lost Watch Adelaide Hills Riesling 2015 'Each grape is picked by hand', declares the back label, a curious bit of marketing spin, but there you go. It's one of many SA cool region wines with a high natural acidity that will underpin its long-term development potential; 5 years will be enough for the light within to burst into life. Screwcap. 12.5% alc. **Rating** 94 **To** 2030 $24 ✪

Original Blend McLaren Vale Grenache Shiraz 2014 70/30%. The name harks back to the first vintage in '74, otherwise not a year to remember. Bright crimson-purple, it manages to give each variety equal footing; it's the full bucket of red, blue and black fruits that provide its flavour and its tannins, oak irrelevant. Screwcap. 14.5% alc. **Rating** 94 **To** 2024 $25 ✪

♥♥♥♥♡ Catapult McLaren Vale Shiraz 2014 Rating 93 To 2027 $25 ✪
Church Block McLaren Vale Cabernet Sauvignon Shiraz Merlot 2014 Rating 91 To 2023 $20 CM ✪
Mrs Wigley Grenache Rose 2015 Rating 90 To 2016 $20 CM ✪

Wise Wine   ★★★★★

237 Eagle Bay Road, Eagle Bay, WA 6281 **Region** Margaret River
T (08) 9750 3100 **www**.wisewine.com.au **Open** 7 days 11–5
Winemaker Andrew Siddell, Matt Buchan, Larry Cherubino (Consultant) **Est.** 1986
Dozens 12 000 **Vyds** 6ha

Wise Wine, headed by Perth entrepreneur Ron Wise, has been a remarkably consistent producer of high quality wine. The vineyard adjacent to the winery in the Margaret River is supplemented by contract-grown grapes from Pemberton, Manjimup and Frankland River. The estate plantings are (in descending order of size) cabernet sauvignon, shiraz and zinfandel. The value for money of many of the wines is extraordinarily good. Exports to the UK and Singapore.

🍷🍷🍷🍷🍷 **Wilyabrup Margaret River Cabernet Sauvignon 2014** The high quality of each of the components – fruit, oak and tannins – create all the synergy you might imagine, the vivid crimson colour waving a flag in case you weren't paying attention. Cabernet can be autocratic and forbidding, but this is the opposite, its waves of flavour surging smoothly through the mouth. Screwcap. 14% alc. **Rating** 96 **To** 2040 $65 ✪

Wilyabrup Margaret River Cabernet Sauvignon 2013 A single site within a single vineyard, matured in new and 1yo French barriques for 18 months. Perfect colour; has flicked off the mantle of oak without any effort whatsoever; firm tannins remain to give the palate the requisite texture and structure, adding to the long length and aftertaste. Screwcap. 13.5% alc. **Rating** 96 **To** 2043 $65 ✪

Lot 80 Margaret River Cabernet Sauvignon 2014 A medium to full-bodied cabernet, excellent colour and firm tannins pointers from opposite ends of the compass. It is highly fragrant, with cassis occupying much of the playing field, but welcoming the tannin contribution with open arms. Screwcap. 14% alc. **Rating** 95 **To** 2034 $45

Margaret River Sauvignon Blanc 2014 Intense and complex, the complexity largely from the fruit, oak contribution of lesser note; there is a riot of citrus, lavender (believe it or not) and passionfruit on the bouquet, the palate thrusting forward with crushed lime leaf, guava and green pineapple. It is certain to develop well in bottle – all for a song. Screwcap. 13% alc. **Rating** 94 **To** 2019 $19 ✪

Margaret River Cabernet Sauvignon 2014 Cassis fruit leaps out of the glass on the bouquet and first sip; the cassis fruit is so fresh it is crunchy and mouthwatering, the tannins fine and – like the French oak – integrated. Very good wine. Screwcap. 14.5% alc. **Rating** 94 **To** 2029 $28 ✪

🍷🍷🍷🍷🍷 **Margaret River Malbec 2014 Rating** 92 **To** 2029 $28
Reserve Margaret River Chardonnay 2014 Rating 90 **To** 2021 $20 ✪

Witches Falls Winery   ★★★★★

79 Main Western Road, Tamborine Mountain, Qld 4272 **Region** Queensland Zone
T (07) 5545 2609 **www**.witchesfalls.com.au **Open** Mon–Fri 10–4, w'ends 10–5
Winemaker Jon Heslop, Arantza Milicua Celador **Est.** 2004 **Dozens** 12 000 **Vyds** 0.4ha
Witches Falls is the venture of Jon and Kim Heslop. Jon has a deep interest in experimenting with progressive vinification methods in order to achieve exceptional and interesting results. He has a degree in applied science (oenology) from CSU, and experience working in the Barossa and Hunter valleys as well as at Domaine Chantel Lescure, Burgundy, and a Napa-based wine grower. Witches Falls grapes are sourced from the Granite Belt, and it is one of the consistently good performers in that context. Exports to the US, South Korea, Taiwan and China.

🍷🍷🍷🍷🍷 **Wild Ferment Granite Belt Garnacha 2014** Light, clear colour, no issue given the variety – which rings loud and clear from the outset of the bouquet and palate alike. Really has its act together, its red fruits with a mere hint of Turkish Delight, offset by fine, savoury tannins. Screwcap. 14.5% alc. **Rating** 95 **To** 2021 $32 ✪

Wild Ferment Granite Belt Monastrell 2014 Attractive wine in every way: the colour is excellent, the palate elegant, abounding with cherries (red and black) and blackberries, the tannins fine, the acidity bright and the length exemplary. Screwcap. 13% alc. **Rating** 95 **To** 2029 $32 ✪

Wild Ferment Granite Belt Viognier 2014 Considerable depth to the colour; the wild fermentation and a cloudy/solids barrel-ferment component results in a notably complex bouquet, mouthfeel and structure; tasted blind there would be many different guesses about its base, particularly given the dry, finely etched, finish. Screwcap. 13.6% alc. **Rating** 94 **To** 2019 $32

Wild Ferment Granite Belt Fiano 2014 Bright, light green hue is a come-hither look, and the wine doesn't disappoint; it adds an extra dimension to the majority of fianos with an almond overlay to the citrus peel/zest often encountered. Jon Heslop also sees apricot and nectarine. Screwcap. 12.6% alc. **Rating** 94 **To** 2022 $32

🍷🍷🍷🍷 **Granite Belt Merlot 2012 Rating** 89 **To** 2018 $28
Granite Belt Cabernet Sauvignon 2013 Rating 88 **To** 2020 $28

Witchmount Estate

557 Leakes Road, Plumpton, Vic 3335 **Region** Sunbury
T (03) 9747 1055 **www**.witchmount.com.au **Open** Wed–Sun 11–5
Winemaker Steve Goodwin **Est.** 1991 **Dozens** 8000 **Vyds** 25.5ha
Witchmount Estate, with its restaurant and function centre, is only 30 minutes from Melbourne in the Sunbury region. The vineyard is planted to shiraz (12ha), cabernet sauvignon (6ha) and chardonnay (2ha), with lesser amounts of sauvignon blanc, pinot gris, merlot, tempranillo and barbera. The quality of the wines has been consistent, the prices very modest. Exports to China.

🍷🍷🍷🍷🍷 **Reserve Shiraz 2010** Has flourished over the past 2 years, albeit still in the full flush of youth, which is utterly exceptional for a 5yo wine. Red berries have morphed into black, perhaps due in part to the savoury backbone of the wine, high quality tannins also part of this full-bodied shiraz. Screwcap. 13.8% alc. **Rating** 95 **To** 2030 $44
Shiraz 2013 Deep crimson-purple, it is extremely intense, with midnight black fruits, pepper and savoury black olive notes, the last borrowed from cool grown cabernet, the finish of exceptional drive and length, French oak absorbed into the fabric of the wine. Great future. Screwcap. 14.5% alc. **Rating** 94 **To** 2038 $32

🍷🍷🍷🍷🍷 **Shiraz Sangiovese Rose 2013 Rating** 93 **To** 2018 $21 ⭕
Shiraz 2013 Rating 93 **To** 2025 $32 CM
Pinot Gris 2015 Rating 92 **To** 2017 $21 ⭕
Lowen Park Chardonnay 2014 Rating 91 **To** 2020 $17 ⭕
Shiraz Grenache 2013 Rating 91 **To** 2020 $21 ⭕
Olivia's Paddock Chardonnay 2013 Rating 90 **To** 2023 $32

Wolf Blass ★★★★★

97 Sturt Highway, Nuriootpa, SA 5355 **Region** Barossa Valley
T (08) 8568 7311 **www**.wolfblasswines.com **Open** 7 days 10–4.30
Winemaker Chris Hatcher, Steve Frost, Marie Clay **Est.** 1966 **Dozens** NFP
Although merged with Mildara and now under the giant umbrella of TWE, the brands (as expected) have been left largely intact. The Wolf Blass wines are made at all price points, ranging through Red, Yellow, Gold, Brown, Grey, Sapphire, Black, White and Platinum labels, at one price point or another covering every one of the main varietals. In 2016 a new range of wines labelled BLASS was introduced. The style and range of the wines continues to subtly evolve under the leadership of chief winemaker Chris Hatcher. Exports to all major markets.

🍷🍷🍷🍷🍷 **White Label Eden Valley Riesling 2015** From a single vineyard; its monastic purity and austerity focuses on chalky acidity as much as on the lime/lemon fruit. Then you can discover rose petals and heady spices far from the usual tightly circumscribed path. Screwcap. 11.5% alc. **Rating** 96 **To** 2035 $34 ⭕
Black Label Cabernet Sauvignon Shiraz 2013 An archetypal Black Label, which over many decades continues to deliver. This is intensely fruited, with lashings of oak to support. With its almost impenetrable colour, it is set for a very

long life. The palate is where it all comes together, with a mouthcoating array of fruits, oak and tannins. Super long. Screwcap. 15% alc. **Rating** 96 **To** 2035 $130

White Label Piccadilly Valley Chardonnay 2015 Pale straw; mealy, citrus, grapefruit, spice framed by sophisticated oak handling. The intense palate is driven by mineral acids and layers of flavour. Polished, and finishes long and distinctly minerally. Screwcap. 13% alc. **Rating** 94 **To** 2025 $34

Brown Label Classic Shiraz 2013 From McLaren Vale, Clare Valley and Barossa Valley. A complex, full-bodied shiraz, with layers of fruit, layers of oak and layers of tannins, all created with some care. The wine ends up with surprising elegance and length, although the style won't appeal to everyone. Screwcap. 14.5% alc. **Rating** 94 **To** 2033 $50

BLASS Noir Coonawarra Cabernet Sauvignon 2014 Mid-dark red; pure-fruited and loaded with mulberry and a lick of spicy oak. The brooding palate is firm, expansive and impressively concentrated. It retains its balance despite the concentration and fullness. Screwcap. 14.5% alc. **Rating** 94 **To** 2025 $35

Grey Label Langhorne Creek Cabernet Shiraz 2014 Darkly fruited with mulberry and cassis, this Grey Label is impressively concentrated. The firm, cherry, and ever so slightly dusty tannins, ensure that this is one for the long term. Screwcap. 14.5% alc. **Rating** 94 **To** 2030 $45

 TTTTT **BLASS Black Spice Barossa Shiraz 2014** Rating 91 **To** 2029 $35
Gold Label Riesling 2015 Rating 90 **To** 2020 $28

Wollombi Village Vineyard ★★★

2971 Payne's Crossing Road, Wollombi, NSW 2325 **Region** Hunter Valley
T 0419 997 434 **www**.wollombivillagevineyard.com.au **Open** W'ends & public hols 9–4
Winemaker First Creek Wines **Est.** 1996 **Dozens** 600 **Vyds** 2ha

Alan and Maria Roe started planting their vineyard in 1996, completing the plantings in 2000. After 32 years of owning and running plumbing supplies shops and a bathroom showroom, they decided it was time to retire, and built the cellar door in '06. The wines have been made by First Creek, as has the exotic range of fruit-based liqueurs using family recipes from Maria's relatives in Italy.

TTTT **Shiraz 2014** Raw oak sits separate from a decent serve of cherry-plum fruit. A little extra time in bottle won't do it any harm. Screwcap. 12.2% alc. **Rating** 88 **To** 2024 $30 CM

Wolseley Wines ★★★★

1790 Hendy Main Road, Paraparap, Vic 3240 **Region** Geelong
T 0412 990 638 **www**.wolseleywines.com **Open** Wed–Sun 11–5
Winemaker Will Wolseley **Est.** 1992 **Dozens** 2000

Will Wolseley grew up in Somerset, England, and from an early age made blackberry wine at home. He came to Australia in 1986 and enrolled in wine science at CSU, gathering vintage experience at various wineries over the next five years. A two-year search for an ideal vineyard site resulted in the acquisition of property on the gently sloping hills of Paraparap, inland from Bells Beach, Torquay. He established 6.5ha of pinot noir, cabernet sauvignon, chardonnay, shiraz, cabernet franc and semillon. Hail storms, frost and drought delayed the first commercial vintage, but the solar-powered winery is now in full production.

TTTTT **Geelong Pinot Noir 2014** Mass of varietal character. Complexity is in no way questioned. It's a savoury, stemmy, undergrowthy wine with nut shells and spice splattered through sweet-sour cherries, red and black. Most pinot noir fanciers would enjoy this. Screwcap. 13.5% alc. **Rating** 92 **To** 2022 $40 CM

Geelong Pinot Noir 2013 Lacks the power of the upcoming '14 but still manages to give a healthy scratch to any pinot noir itch. It's spicy and complex, with tangy, sweet-sour fruit maintaining a lively conversation all the way along the palate. Screwcap. 13.5% alc. **Rating** 90 **To** 2020 $25 CM

Wood Park

263 Kneebones Gap Road, Markwood, Vic 3678 **Region** King Valley
T (03) 5727 3778 **www**.woodparkwines.com.au **Open** At Milawa Cheese Factory
7 days 10–5
Winemaker John Stokes, Richard Tevillian **Est.** 1989 **Dozens** 7000 **Vyds** 16ha
John Stokes planted the first vines at Wood Park in 1989 as part of a diversification program
for his property at Bobinawarrah, in the hills of the Lower King Valley, east of Milawa. The
vineyard is managed with minimal chemical use, winemaking a mix of modern and traditional
techniques (what wine isn't?). The reach of Wood Park has been expanded with Beechworth
Pinot Noir, and a mix of mainstream and alternative varieties, all well made. It also has a cellar
door in Ford St, Beechworth. Wines were received too late for the book, but tasting notes
can be found on www.winecompanion.com.au. Exports to Taiwan, Singapore, Hong Kong
and China.

Woodgate Wines

43 Hind Road, Manjimup, WA 6258 **Region** Manjimup
T (08) 9772 4288 **www**.woodgatewines.com.au **Open** Thurs–Sat 10–4.30, Sun 12.30–4.30
Winemaker Mark Aitken **Est.** 2006 **Dozens** 2000 **Vyds** 7.9ha
Woodgate is the family-owned business of Mark and wife Tracey Aitken, Tracey's mother
Jeannette Smith, and her brother Robert and his wife Linda Hatton. Mark became a mature-
age student at Curtin University, obtaining his oenology degree in 2001 as Dux, earning a
trip to Bordeaux to undertake vintage, returning to work at Manjimup's Chestnut Grove
winery from '02. In '05 he and Tracey began their own contract winemaking business, as well
as making wine for their Woodgate brand. Most of the grapes come from the estate plantings
of cabernet sauvignon, chardonnay, sauvignon blanc, pinot noir and merlot, supplemented by
grapes from a leased vineyard. The name of the sparkling wine, Bojangles, reflects the family's
musical heritage, which stretches back three generations and includes vocalists, guitarists,
pianists, a trumpeter, a saxophonist, two drummers and a double bass player.

ΨΨΨΨΨ **Reserve Pemberton Shiraz 2014** A complex wine, part juicy and supple, part
savoury, with tannins joining the fray. This is crawling with potential, especially
the juicy red cherry, which would send rivers of red juice down your fingers if
you could bite into it, and hold the half-eaten berry in those fingers. Screwcap.
14.5% alc. **Rating** 94 **To** 2034 $35
Pemberton Tempranillo 2014 The bouquet is accurately described as leathery,
earthy and dusty on the back label; the palate is also full of interest, with pleasantly
grippy tannins studded through cherry fruits. Screwcap. 14% alc. **Rating** 94
To 2022 $25 **©**

ΨΨΨΨΨ **Reserve Pemberton Fume Blanc 2015 Rating** 91 **To** 2020 $28
Pemberton Viognier 2015 Rating 90 **To** 2017 $25

Woodhaven Vineyard

87 Main Creek Road, Red Hill, Vic 3937 **Region** Mornington Peninsula
T 0421 612 178 **www**.woodhavenvineyard.com.au **Open** By appt
Winemaker Lee and Neil Ward **Est.** 2003 **Dozens** 150 **Vyds** 1.6ha
Woodhaven is the venture of Lee and Neil Ward, both qualified accountants for 30 years in
Melbourne, albeit working in different fields. They then spent two years looking for a suitable
site on the Mornington Peninsula, and ultimately found one high on Red Hill. Bringing the
venture to the point of production has been a slow and, at times, frustrating business. They
decided from the outset to be personally responsible for all aspects of growing the grapes
and making the wines, relying on the advice readily given to them by George and Ruth
Mihaly of Paradigm, David and (the late) Wendy Lloyd of Eldridge, John and Julie Trueman
of Myrtaceae and Nat and Rose White of Main Ridge. They also decided to grow the vines
organically and biodynamically, and it took 8 years for them to produce their first two barrels
of wine, in 2010. In '13 the 0.8ha each of pinot noir and chardonnay finally produced more
than one barrel of each wine.

ΨΨΨΨΨ **Pinot Noir 2014** Firm and sinewy. This is a prime candidate for the cellar. Macerated cherry, smoked meats, spice and clovey oak flavours, teamed with assertive tannin, lend this a keen sense of gravitas. Tie your hands behind your back if you must; this needs to be left alone. Screwcap. 12.8% alc. **Rating** 94 **To** 2023 $50 CM

ΨΨΨΨΨ **Chardonnay 2012 Rating** 93 **To** 2019 $40 CM

Woodlands   ★★★★★

3948 Caves Road, Wilyabrup, WA 6284 **Region** Margaret River
T (08) 9755 6226 **www.**woodlandswines.com **Open** 7 days 10–5
Winemaker Stuart and Andrew Watson **Est.** 1973 **Dozens** 17 000 **Vyds** 26.58ha
Founder David Watson had spectacular success with the Cabernets he made in 1979 and the early '80s. Commuting from Perth on weekends and holidays, as well as raising a family, became all too much, and for some years the grapes from Woodlands were sold to other Margaret River producers. With the advent of sons Stuart and Andrew (Stuart primarily responsible for winemaking), the estate has bounced back to pre-eminence. The wines come in four price bands, the bulk of the production under the Chardonnay and Cabernet Merlot varietals, then a series of Reserve and Special Reserves, then Reserve de la Cave, and finally Cabernet Sauvignon. The top-end wines primarily come from the original Woodlands Vineyard, where the vines are over 40 years old. Exports to the UK, the US, Sweden, The Netherlands, Indonesia, Malaysia, the Philippines, Singapore, Japan and China.

ΨΨΨΨΨ **Margaret River Cabernet Sauvignon 2013 (Benjamin)** 94% cabernet sauvignon, 4% malbec, 2% cabernet franc, hand-picked, passed over a vibrating sorting table to small closed tanks for fermentation, 35 days post-ferment maceration, matured for 19 months in new French oak. Having gone to this time, trouble and expense, it is logical to build the wine for future generations to enjoy, and that is certainly the case here, with mega-helpings of high quality cabernet fruit (plus bits and pieces), oak and tannins, and the all-important balance. Screwcap. 13.5% alc. **Rating** 96 **To** 2043 $150

Reserve de la Cave Margaret River Cabernet Franc 2014 Continues the fabulous track record of the Reserve de la Cave wines of Woodlands, challenging – as does this one – normal beliefs: how on earth is it possible for a cabernet franc to have such vivid colour, fragrantly sweet berry fruits, fine tannins, balance and length? 25 dozen (1 barrique) made. Screwcap. 13.5% alc. **Rating** 96 **To** 2034 $90

Chloe 2014 From a shaded, south-facing 0.8ha plot in the estate vineyard. Still fresh and lively, at the dawn of its life; the oak management has been exemplary, leaving white peach, nectarine and grapefruit in command of the long palate and aftertaste. Screwcap. 13.5% alc. **Rating** 95 **To** 2022 $90

Margaret 2014 79% cabernet sauvignon, 13% merlot, 8% malbec. Good hue; this is a dead-centre mainstream Margaret River Bordeaux blend; like its SSB, it is a style that Margaret River achieves effortlessly (well, almost), with cassis, dried herb and black olive in a crib of ripe tannins and a dab of new French oak. Screwcap. 13.5% alc. **Rating** 95 **To** 2034 $45

Emily 2014 47% cabernet franc, 42% merlot, 6% malbec, 3% petit verdot, 2% cabernet sauvignon. An extremely elegant wine with pristine cassis fruit from an unusual Bordeaux blend; spicy tannins and oak are cleverly woven through the silky fabric of the predominantly red fruits. Complete in every way. Screwcap. 13.5% alc. **Rating** 95 **To** 2034 $45

Margaret River Chardonnay 2015 Cane damage and poor flowering caused by 50mm rain and high winds in Nov reduced the crop level by 40%. Elegant, but flavour-filled; white peach, nectarine and touch of fig, citrussy acidity following with a splash of oak. Screwcap. 13.5% alc. **Rating** 94 **To** 2023 $25 **۞**

ΨΨΨΨΨ **Margaret River Cabernet Merlot 2014 Rating** 93 **To** 2029 $25 **۞**
Reserve de la Cave Margaret River Malbec 2014 Rating 92 **To** 2029 $90

Woods Crampton

PO Box 417, Hamilton, NSW 2303 **Region** Barossa Valley
T 0417 670 655 **www**.woods-crampton.com.au **Open** Not
Winemaker Nicholas Crampton, Aaron Woods **Est.** 2010 **Dozens** 10 000
This is one of the most impressive ventures of Nicholas Crampton (his association with
McWilliam's is on a consultancy basis) and winemaking friend Aaron Woods. The two make
the wines at the Sons of Eden winery with input advice from Igor Kucic. The quality of the
wines, and the enticing prices, has seen production soar from 1500 to 10 000 dozen, with
every expectation of continued success.

♥♥♥♥♥ **High Eden Riesling 2015** Hand-picked from two High Eden vineyards (over
500m), whole bunch-pressed and only free-run juice (500l per tonne) cool-
fermented (12°C). Lovely wine, very long and intense, its purity outstanding.
Drinking well now, but with a rosy future. 330 dozen made. Screwcap. 12.5% alc.
Rating 95 **To** 2030 $27 ✪
Old Vine Barossa Valley Shiraz 2014 A deliciously fragrant and supple shiraz
that throws down the gauntlet to the Barossa Valley stereotype. Its silky smooth,
medium-bodied palate has boundless berry and plum fruit adroitly framed by
cedary oak and superfine tannins. Screwcap. 13.5% alc. **Rating** 95 **To** 2029 $20 ✪
Barossa Valley Shiraz 2014 Plays as much to complexity as to fruit weight.
A cerebral style. Boysenberry and blueberry flavours lead into dried herbs, florals,
snapped twig. It needs air/decanting. But given time it shines through, via various
twists and turns. Screwcap. 13.5% alc. **Rating** 94 **To** 2026 $20 CM ✪
Burns and Fuller Langhorne Creek Shiraz 2014 85% from Langhorne
Creek, 15% from McLaren Vale. Utterly ridiculous value for an utterly seductive,
mouthfilling, plum and juicy wine; the tannin management makes the quality
embarrassingly good. Screwcap. 14% alc. **Rating** 94 **To** 2029 $15 ✪

♥♥♥♥♡ **Eden Valley Riesling 2015 Rating** 93 **To** 2023 $20 CM ✪
March & Batten Old Vine Eden Valley Shiraz 2013 Rating 93 **To** 2033 $45
The Big Show Shiraz Mataro 2014 Rating 93 **To** 2034 $25 ✪
Old Vine Barossa Valley Mataro 2014 Rating 93 **To** 2022 $27 CM ✪
Third Wheel Barossa Valley Rose 2015 Rating 92 **To** 2016 $24 ✪
The Primrose Path Shiraz 2014 Rating 92 **To** 2020 $16 CM ✪
Pedro GSM 2015 Rating 91 **To** 2020 $23 CM ✪
Sleeping Dogs Barossa Valley Dry Red 2014 Rating 91 **To** 2029 $23 ✪
Three Barrels Barossa Valley Graciano 2014 Rating 91 **To** 2019 $27 CM
Limited Edition Hogshead Black Moon GSM 2014 Rating 90 **To** 2019
$16 ✪

Woodsoak Wines ★★★★

9 Woolundry Road, Robe, SA 5276 **Region** Robe
T 0437 681 919 **www**.woodsoakwines.com.au **Open** Not
Winemaker Peta Baverstock, Don Berrigan **Est.** 2010 **Dozens** 1450 **Vyds** 22ha
The Woodsoak farming property has been in the Legoe family for over 60 years, grazing cattle
and sheep. In 1998 Will and Sonia Legoe diversified into grapegrowing, followed (inevitably)
by a small batch of wine made in 2006 for family and friends; and finally the commercial
establishment of Woodsoak Wines in '10. The vineyard includes cabernet sauvignon, shiraz,
merlot and pinot noir; the Cabernet, Shiraz and Rose are named after their three children,
the Pyaar Pinot Noir after the Hindi word for love. The Legoes say, 'We ran out of children,
and there was no call for more.'

♥♥♥♥♡ **Raj Robe Shiraz 2013** A very good example of the quality of fruit that comes
easily to this cool part of the Limestone Coast. Energetic red and black cherry
fruits are sprinkled with pepper and spice, lifting the medium-bodied palate. Good
length, great value. Screwcap. 13.5% alc. **Rating** 92 **To** 2033 $19 ✪
Pyaar Robe Pinot Noir 2015 The colour is good, and the wine has voluminous
fruit depth. The question is the presence, or absence, of positive pinot flavour and

texture. After much argument with myself, I came down on the side of the wine, but counsel you to leave it alone for a year or two. Screwcap. 13% alc. **Rating** 91 To 2025 $19 ○

Blanc de Noirs 2013 For a 3yo blanc de noirs its hue is pale, testimony to careful fruit handling. Zesty lemon and pink grapefruit flavours are layered with more bottle age complexity and mouthfilling texture than might be expected for two-and-a-half years on lees filled with toasted marshmallow and bubblegum flavour. It finishes long with well-defined acidity and subtle dosage. Diam. 12.5% alc. **Rating** 90 To 2018 $39 TS

ΨΨΨΨ **Rani Robe Rose 2015** Rating 89 To 2017 $19 ○
Vijay Robe Cabernet Sauvignon 2013 Rating 89 To 2023 $19 ○
Sparkling Shiraz 2012 Rating 89 To 2017 $39 TS

Woodstock ★★★★★

215 Douglas Gully Road, McLaren Flat, SA 5171 **Region** McLaren Vale
T (08) 8383 0156 **www**.woodstockwine.com.au **Open** 7 days 10–5
Winemaker Ben Glaetzer **Est.** 1905 **Dozens** 22000 **Vyds** 18.44ha
The Collett family is among the best known in McLaren Vale, the late Doug Collett AM for his World War II exploits flying Spitfires and Hurricanes with the RAF and RAAF, returning to study oenology at Roseworthy Agricultural College, and rapidly promoted to take charge of SA's largest winery, Berri Co-operative. In 1973 he purchased the Woodstock Estate, built a winery, and crushed its first vintage in '74. Son Scott Collett, once noted for his fearless exploits in cars and on motorcycles, became winemaker in '82, and won numerous accolades; equally importantly, he purchased an adjoining shiraz vineyard planted circa 1900 (now the source of The Stocks Shiraz) and a bushvine grenache vineyard planted in '30. In '99, he joined forces with Ben Glaetzer; Scott passed responsibility for winemaking to Ben, but retained the responsibility for the estate vineyards. Exports to most major markets.

ΨΨΨΨΨ **Collett Lane Cabernet Sauvignon 2014** Crushed and destemmed, cultured yeast, matured in new and used American and French oak for 18 months. Ramps up its varietal sibling on all sides – not dramatically, but consistently and convincingly. I can only assume new American oak has been kept off the blending bench, for there are no echoes in this sybaritic cabernet. Screwcap. 14.5% alc. Rating 95 To 2034 $75

ΨΨΨΨΨ **Vintage Fortified McLaren Vale Grenache 2013** Rating 93 To 2033 $25 ○
Pilot's View McLaren Vale Shiraz 2013 Rating 92 To 2038 $38
The Octogenarian Grenache Tempranillo 2013 Rating 92 To 2025 $32
McLaren Vale Cabernet Sauvignon 2014 Rating 92 To 2029 $25 ○
Old Fortified McLaren Vale Tawny NV Rating 92 To 2018 $25 ○
McLaren Vale Chardonnay 2015 Rating 90 To 2019 $20 ○

Woody Nook ★★★★★

506 Metricup Road, Wilyabrup, WA 6280 **Region** Margaret River
T (08) 9755 7547 **www**.woodynook.com.au **Open** 7 days 10–4.30
Winemaker Neil Gallagher, Craig Dunkerton **Est.** 1982 **Dozens** 7500 **Vyds** 14.23ha
Woody Nook, with a backdrop of 18ha of majestic marri and jarrah forest, doesn't have the high profile of the biggest names in Margaret River, but has had major success in wine shows over the years. It was purchased by Peter and Jane Bailey in 2000, and major renovations have transformed Woody Nook, with a new winery, a gallery tasting room for larger groups and an alfresco dining area by the pond. A link with the past is Neil Gallagher's continuing role as winemaker, viticulturist and minority shareholder (Neil is the son of founders Jeff and Wynn Gallagher). Exports to the UK, the US, Canada, Bermuda, Hong Kong and China.

ΨΨΨΨΨ **Gallagher's Choice Margaret River Cabernet Sauvignon 2014** Great colour; in almost identical style to previous vintages, very powerful, sombre blackcurrant fruit set within a necklace of cabernet tannins that stand apart from other tannins; the palate is very long, intense and impeccably balanced. Diam. 14.5% alc. **Rating** 96 **To** 2039 $55

Single Vineyard Margaret River Cabernet Merlot 2014 A totally sybaritic and luscious blend, cassis and plum rolling through the mouth, tannin and oak helping build the medium to full-bodied palate, but still leaving the fruit in the vanguard. It turns the possible fault of high alcohol into a virtue, and there's no need to be patient. Diam. 15% alc. **Rating** 95 **To** 2034 $32

Single Vineyard Margaret River Shiraz 2013 The fragrant, berry-filled bouquet promises the fresh, lively medium-bodied palate that duly follows; you might have thought (as did I) that the oak would be too obvious, but it's not: it fits seamlessly in behind the delicious duo of red and black fruits. Diam. 13.5% alc. **Rating** 94 **To** 2033 $32

Limited Release Margaret River Merlot 2013 From 31yo estate vines. A real charmer, with a vibrant and juicy array of cassis and redcurrant fruit on its finely detailed and long palate; the oak and tannins are precisely weighted. Screwcap. 13.5% alc. **Rating** 94 **To** 2023 $26

ȲȲȲȲȳ **Single Vineyard Margaret River Chardonnay 2014** Rating 93 To 2022 $32
Killdog Creek Margaret River Tempranillo 2014 Rating 93 To 2029 $22
Graciano & Tempranillo 2013 Rating 91 To 2020 $26

Word of Mouth Wines ★★★★

145 Kite Street, Orange, NSW 2800 **Region** Orange
T (02) 6362 0318 **www.**wordofmouthwines.com.au **Open** 7 days 11–5
Winemaker David Lowe (Contract), Liam Heslop **Est.** 1991 **Dozens** 2000 **Vyds** 9ha
The 1991 plantings (made by the former Donnington Vineyard) have changed over the years, and, in particular, since the business was acquired by Word of Mouth Wines in 2003. Pinot gris, riesling, chardonnay, sauvignon blanc, merlot, pinot noir and cabernet sauvignon are all in bearing, and were joined by plantings of petit manseng in the winter of '08. Word of Mouth is the venture of Peter Gibson, Deborah Upjohn, Jamie Gordon and Sharyn Pussell.

ȲȲȲȲȳ **Orange Chardonnay 2015** The fruit has very good supple mouthfeel and equally good flavour; barrel fermentation in used oak has supplied texture without stifling the fruit. Screwcap. 12.5% alc. **Rating** 93 **To** 2022 $40
Orange Pinot Gris 2015 Fermented in used barrels, plus 9 months maturation in that oak. It has a bite to it that is interesting or challenging (you choose), providing good texture – and something different. Screwcap. 14% alc. **Rating** 90 **To** 2018 $25
Orange Viognier 2015 Natural acidity (never high with viognier) is detectable, and gives a cut to the apricot, peach and citrus flavours. Points for effort. Screwcap. 12.7% alc. **Rating** 90 **To** 2017 $25

Wykari Wines ★★★★

PO Box 905, Clare, SA 5453 **Region** Clare Valley
T (08) 8842 1841 **www.**wykariwines.com.au **Open** Not
Winemaker Neil Paulett **Est.** 2006 **Dozens** 1200 **Vyds** 20ha
Local Clare families Rob and Mandy Knight and Peter and Robyn Shearer own two vineyards, one to the north, the other to the south of Clare. The vineyards were first planted in 1974, and are dry-grown and hand-pruned. In all there is shiraz, riesling, cabernet sauvignon and chardonnay.

ȲȲȲȲȲ **Clare Valley Riesling 2015** Estate dry-grown 41yo vines have their signature fairly and squarely stamped on this wine. It has layers and folds of blossomy bouquet and rich palate, giving no excuse for not drinking (at least some) right now, filling your senses with lemon/lime fruit. Screwcap. 11.8% alc. **Rating** 94 **To** 2025 $22

ȲȲȲȲȳ **Clare Valley Cabernet Sauvignon 2013** Rating 91 To 2028 $24

Wynns Coonawarra Estate   ★★★★★

Memorial Drive, Coonawarra, SA 5263 **Region** Coonawarra
T (08) 8736 2225 **www.**wynns.com.au **Open** 7 days 10–5
Winemaker Sue Hodder, Sarah Pidgeon **Est.** 1897 **Dozens** NFP
Large-scale production has not prevented Wynns (an important part of TWE) from producing excellent wines covering the full price spectrum, from the bargain-basement Riesling and Shiraz through to the deluxe John Riddoch Cabernet Sauvignon and Michael Shiraz. Even with steady price increases, Wynns offers extraordinary value for money. Large investments since 2000 in rejuvenating and replanting key blocks, under the direction of Allen Jenkins, and skilled winemaking by Sue Hodder, have resulted in wines of far greater finesse and elegance than most of their predecessors. Exports to the UK, the US, Canada and Asia.

🍷🍷🍷🍷🍷 **John Riddoch Limited Release Cabernet Sauvignon 2013** A potent, rich, complex, full-bodied cabernet that has a signature as indelible as that of Grange. Cassis/blackcurrant fruit, with touches of earth, tar and licorice, pours in a rush along the palate, not held up by oak or tannins, both subsumed into the fabric of the wine. Screwcap. 13.5% alc. **Rating** 97 **To** 2053 $150 ○

Harold Single Vineyard Cabernet Sauvignon 2013 The Harold Vineyard was planted 45 years go, and has always produced high quality cabernet – this vintage stood out, hence its single vineyard status. It has a deliciously supple juicy mouthfeel and flavour, and I believe it will prove to be one of the best releases since this program of ever-changing single vineyards began a decade ago. Beautiful cabernet, perfectly made. Screwcap. 13% alc. **Rating** 97 **To** 2043 $80 ○

🍷🍷🍷🍷🍷 **Michael Limited Release Shiraz 2013** This is a rare full-bodied wine with finesse. The coupling comes about courtesy of the way the oak is integrated and the tannins honed, though not with any apology from the blackberry and black cherry fruit. Screwcap. 13.8% alc. **Rating** 96 **To** 2043 $150

Black Label Cabernet Sauvignon 2014 Wynns say this is Australia's most important cabernet, based on volume and value of each vintage. It's a model for the flavour and structure of cool grown cabernet with the ace in the hole cards of blackcurrant fruit, firm tannins and balanced oak. Screwcap. 13.5% alc. **Rating** 96 **To** 2039 $45 ○

V&A Lane Selected Vineyards Shiraz 2014 V&A Lane bisects the Coonawarra red soil halfway between its ends, and was also the border between the Victoria and Albert local government areas. Wynns has vineyards on either side of the lane. Bright crimson; this perfectly formed and weighted medium-bodied shiraz has striking purity, appropriately with half red and half dark fruit flavours. Tannins and oak have been deliberately controlled at a low level. Screwcap. 12.5% alc. **Rating** 95 **To** 2039 $60

🍷🍷🍷🍷🍷 **V&A Lane Cabernet Shiraz 2014** **Rating** 93 **To** 2030 $60

Wynwood Estate   ★★★★

310 Oakey Creek Road, Pokolbin, NSW 2320 **Region** Hunter Valley
T (02) 4998 7885 **www.**wynwoodestate.com.au **Open** 7 days 10–5
Winemaker Peter Lane **Est.** 2011 **Dozens** 7000 **Vyds** 28ha
Wynwood Estate is owned by Winston Wine Pty Ltd, the Australian arm of what is described as one of the largest and fastest-growing wine distributors in China, with 100 wine stores established across the country. Wynwood has almost 30ha of low-yielding vineyards, including shiraz (8ha), merlot (5ha), chardonnay (4ha), verdelho (3ha) and muscat (1ha). It has some dry-grown 95-year-old shiraz vines that only produce an average of 0.75 tonnes of fruit each vintage. Plantings were extended in 2014 with durif (3ha), malbec and roussanne (1ha each). Wynwood also sources cabernet, franc, grenache and merlot from company-owned vineyards in the Barossa Valley. Winemaker Peter Lane has had a long career in the Hunter Valley, beginning at Mount Pleasant for six years, moving to Tulloch in the early 1990s, then Tyrrell's until 2012.

ŢŢŢŢŢ **Reserve Hunter Valley Shiraz 2014** From 70yo estate vines in Pokolbin, matured for 14 months in French hogsheads. A potent, full-bodied shiraz with the stamp of the great vintage, still in swaddling clothes. The tannins are a trifle edgy, but the overall balance is good, and it will mature in measured steps for years to come. Screwcap. 14.2% alc. **Rating** 94 **To** 2039 $70

ŢŢŢŢŢ **Grey Gum Limited Release Barossa Valley Cabernet Franc Merlot Cabernet Sauvignon 2014 Rating** 90 **To** 2024 $40

Xabregas   ★★★★☆

Spencer Road, Mount Barker, WA 6324 **Region** Mount Barker
T (08) 6389 1382 **www.xabregas.com.au Open** Not
Winemaker Mike Garland, Andrew Hoadley **Est.** 1996 **Dozens** 10 000 **Vyds** 80ha
The Hogan family have five generations of WA history and family interests in sheep grazing and forestry in the Great Southern, dating back to the 1860s. Terry Hogan, founding Xabregas chairman, felt the Mount Barker region was 'far too good dirt to waste on blue gums', and vines were planted in 1996. The Hogan family concentrates on the region's strengths – shiraz and riesling. Exports to the US, Singapore, Japan, China and NZ.

ŢŢŢŢŢ **X by Xabregas Figtree Riesling 2014** Surely the most minimalist of all minimalist labels. Quartz-white; a lively and fresh wine, with passionfruit nuances, possibly from the 11g/l of residual sugar; it has good balance and length, with just enough acidity to brighten the finish. Very different in style from Artisan, but of the same quality. Screwcap. 12.2% alc. **Rating** 94 **To** 2025 $40
Artisan Riesling 2014 One of four rieslings from Xabregas, wild yeast barrel-fermented, finishing totally dry, but not painfully so; the length and finish come into ever greater focus the more the wine is tasted, lees contact having laid the groundwork. Screwcap. 12.8% alc. **Rating** 94 **To** 2024 $31
X by Xabregas Spencer Riesling 2014 A crystal-clear wine built for the next decade; there is residual sugar sweetness, but it is largely hidden by the crisp, minerally acidity; Granny Smith apple, lime and lemon fruit flavours will grow exponentially over the next 5 years, and go on for years thereafter. Screwcap. 10.3% alc. **Rating** 94 **To** 2029 $40

Xanadu Wines   ★★★★★

Boodjidup Road, Margaret River, WA 6285 **Region** Margaret River
T (08) 9758 9500 **www.xanaduwines.com Open** 7 days 10–5
Winemaker Glenn Goodall **Est.** 1977 **Dozens** 70 000 **Vyds** 109.5ha
Xanadu Wines was established in 1977 by Dr John Lagan. In 2005 it was purchased by the Rathbone family, and together with Glenn Goodall's winemaking team they have significantly improved the quality of the wines. The vineyard has been revamped via soil profiling, precision viticulture, improved drainage and reduced yields, with production bolstered through the acquisition of the Stevens Road Vineyard in '08. In '15 the new entry point Exmoor range replaced the Next of Kin range, made from both estate and contract-grown grapes. Exports to most major markets.

ŢŢŢŢŢ **Stevens Road Margaret River Chardonnay 2013** From the Lagan Vineyard at Wilyabrup, Gingin clone, hand-picked, whole bunch-pressed, wild yeast-fermented in French oak (35% new), lees-stirred during 9-month maturation, no mlf, a selection of the best barrels. This is the most complex of the '13 Xanadu Chardonnays, yet retains the hallmark precision and elegance of its siblings. 7 months after its first tasting, its power, intensity and extreme length have come into full focus, gaining another point. Screwcap. 13% alc. **Rating** 98 **To** 2025 $70 ✪
Reserve Margaret River Cabernet Sauvignon 2013 Includes 5% each of malbec and petit verdot, all components matured for 14 months in French barriques (50% new) before a best-barrel selection. Cabernet doesn't come more intense than this without losing its shape; here it parlays into purity and precision.

The fruit and tannins have well and truly absorbed the oak. You might think this can't be consumed now, but it can – the final achievement. Screwcap. 14% alc. **Rating** 98 **To** 2043 $85 **☉**

Stevens Road Margaret River Chardonnay 2014 From 20 rows of Gingin clone on the Stevens Road Vineyard. This is a twin to the Reserve, having far more things in common than points of difference. This is slightly finer and more open, but you wouldn't say that if it was any other wine in the comparison. The flavour spectrum and balance are nigh-on identical, and to force the issue, this wine is readier than the Reserve. Screwcap. 13.5% alc. **Rating** 97 **To** 2024 $70 **☉**

Reserve Margaret River Chardonnay 2014 Gingin clone from the oldest estate vineyard, hand-picked. It's possible to suggest that Xanadu has its own style of Margaret River chardonnay, as it has with cabernet. There is an extra degree of precision and length, the Yarra Valley taking the place of Great Southern for the comparison. Pink grapefruit, white peach and striking minerally acidity drive this wine at a furious pace. Screwcap. 13% alc. **Rating** 97 **To** 2026 $85 **☉**

Stevens Road Margaret River Cabernet Sauvignon 2013 Bright crimson; this has the Stevens Road DNA at its most expressive and triumphant; Xanadu has carved out a cabernet style all its own, as if the Great Southern has crept in under the bedclothes one night. It is awesome in its focus and precision, which allow it to tread lightly, seemingly impossible for a young cabernet of supreme class. Screwcap. 14% alc. **Rating** 97 **To** 2048 $70 **☉**

ΨΨΨΨΨ **Margaret River Chardonnay 2014** Predominantly estate-grown on the Stevens Road and Lagan Vineyards. There is an inevitability about the very high quality of the Xanadu wines these days; thus this very intense and powerful, yet perfectly delineated and balanced wine is no surprise; nor is its extreme length. Screwcap. 13% alc. **Rating** 96 **To** 2025 $35 **☉**

Margaret River Cabernet Sauvignon 2013 Xanadu paints an unerring landscape of intense, elegant Margaret River cabernet, with a stream of cassis fruit bordered by gravelly but fine tannins, oak insistently completing the picture. Great value. Screwcap. 14% alc. **Rating** 96 **To** 2038 $35 **☉**

Margaret River Chardonnay 2015 Poised and elegant, the aromas and flavours are in the citrus and stone fruit spectrum, the oak beautifully integrated and providing texture as much as anything. Grapefruit-like acidity runs evenly through the palate, gathering and lingering on the finish. Screwcap. 13% alc. **Rating** 95 **To** 2022 $38

DJL Margaret River Sauvignon Blanc Semillon 2015 It has a bit of presence about it. It's fruit-driven and accessible but its reach through the finish is uncommonly long, its notes of cool alpine herbs serving to refresh. The word 'layered' (used on the back label) is apt. Screwcap. 12.5% alc. **Rating** 94 **To** 2017 $24 CM **☉**

DJL Margaret River Chardonnay 2015 The lowish alcohol (12.5%) is a pointer towards the style, as is the absence of mlf. This is precise, uncluttered chardonnay despite the winemaking input. The primary flavours are of grapefruit and white peach with subtle cashew and lees texture, the citrus acidity stiletto-like. Screwcap. **Rating** 94 **To** 2020 $24 **☉**

DJL Margaret River Shiraz 2013 The wine doesn't disappoint, and the inclusion of a Frankland River component has given the mouthfeel and flavour an edge of authority that drives the long, agile palate with its sparkling array of red and black fruits. Screwcap. 14% alc. **Rating** 94 **To** 2028 $24 **☉**

Next of Kin Margaret River Cabernet Sauvignon 2013 87% Margaret River, 13% Frankland River. This is simply one of the bargains of the year, a cabernet of verve and length, with delicious cassis fruit flavours built on a scaffold of balanced tannins. Screwcap. 14% alc. **Rating** 94 **To** 2033 $18 **☉**

DJL Margaret River Cabernet Sauvignon 2013 90% cabernet sauvignon, the balance equal proportions of cabernet franc and petit verdot. Blackcurrant is the prominent varietal marker on bouquet and palate, the more lifted and floral notes contributed (most likely) by the minor partners. A touch of green herb and toasty

oak along with the modulating tannin completes an attractive package. Diam.
14% alc. **Rating** 94 To 2025 $24 ✪

🍷🍷🍷🍷🍷 Next of Kin Margaret River Chardonnay 2014 Rating 93 To 2020 $18 ✪
DJL Margaret River Rose 2015 Rating 93 To 2016 $24 CM ✪
DJL Margaret River Shiraz 2014 Rating 93 To 2026 $24 CM ✪
Margaret River Petit Verdot 2012 Rating 93 To 2032 $60
Exmoor Sauvignon Blanc Semillon 2015 Rating 92 To 2018 $18 ✪
Exmoor Cabernet Sauvignon 2013 Rating 92 To 2023 $18 ✪
Next of Kin Cabernet Sauvignon 2015 Rating 91 To 2022 $18 CM ✪

Yabby Lake Vineyard ★★★★★

86–112 Tuerong Road, Tuerong, Vic 3937 **Region** Mornington Peninsula
T (03) 5974 3729 **www**.yabbylake.com **Open** 7 days 10–5
Winemaker Tom Carson, Chris Forge **Est.** 1998 **Dozens** 3350 **Vyds** 50.8ha
This high-profile wine business was established by Robert and Mem Kirby (of Village
Roadshow), who had been landowners in the Mornington Peninsula for decades. In 1998
they established Yabby Lake Vineyard, under the direction of vineyard manager Keith Harris;
the vineyard is on a north-facing slope, capturing maximum sunshine while also receiving sea
breezes. The main focus is the 25ha of pinot noir, 14ha of chardonnay and 8ha of pinot gris;
3h of shiraz, merlot and sauvignon blanc take a back seat. The arrival of the hugely talented
Tom Carson as Group Winemaker has added lustre to the winery and its wines, making the
first Jimmy Watson Trophy-winning Pinot Noir in 2014, and continuing to blitz the Australian
wine show circuit with Single Block Pinots. Exports to the UK, Canada, Sweden, Singapore,
Hong Kong and China.

🍷🍷🍷🍷🍷 Single Block Release Block 6 Mornington Peninsula Chardonnay 2015
100% Mendoza clone. The difference in the clonal make-up is immediately
obvious on the palate, here with greater precision to the grapefruit/grapefruit
pith, almond and minerally acidity; the overall line, length and balance is perfect.
Screwcap. 12.5% alc. **Rating** 97 To 2030 $95 ✪
Single Block Release Block 6 Mornington Peninsula Pinot Noir 2015
75% Pommard clone, 25% MV6. High-toned spicy notes are the cornerstone of
a highly expressive and elegant wine, providing a launch pad for the silky and
elegant, but long and insistent palate. Screwcap. 13% alc. **Rating** 97 To 2030
$95 ✪

🍷🍷🍷🍷🍷 Single Vineyard Mornington Peninsula Chardonnay 2015 40% Mendoza
clone, 40% P58, 20% B76. A fragrant and pure bouquet leads into a supremely
elegant, understated palate that departs from Mornington Peninsula orthodoxy
by preventing mlf and relying on natural acidity, steps that will underwrite the
longevity of the wine. Screwcap. 12.5% alc. **Rating** 96 To 2025 $45 ✪
Single Vineyard Mornington Peninsula Chardonnay 2014 There's not a
solitary hair out of place in this perfectly delineated and balanced wine, the fusion
of fruit, oak and acidity absolute. All of that said, it is the white peach and cashew
fruit that sits at the heart of the wine, and it will always remain so. Screwcap.
12.5% alc. **Rating** 96 To 2026 $45 ✪
Single Block Release Block 2 Mornington Peninsula Pinot Noir 2015
MV6. The depth of the black cherry and plum fruit soaks up the oak without
leaving a trace; it is hard not to keep on returning to the succulent and seamless
mouthfeel of the palate. Screwcap. 13% alc. **Rating** 96 To 2030 $95
Single Block Release Block 1 Mornington Peninsula Pinot Noir 2015
100% MV6, 100% whole bunches. Bright crimson; the hallmark power of Yabby
Lake Pinot immediately imprints itself, here with the forest floor/sous bois impact
of the whole bunches; great length and balance. Impressive depth to the plummy
fruit at the core of the wine. Screwcap. 13% alc. **Rating** 96 To 2030 $95
Single Vineyard Mornington Peninsula Pinot Noir 2014 A perfectly
manicured pinot, as are all the wines made by Tom Carson. The bouquet is highly

fragrant, with red fruits, rose petal and spice all in play; the palate has immaculate balance, the fruit purity retained even though there are savoury crosscuts that build texture and complexity. Screwcap. 12.5% alc. **Rating** 96 **To** 2024 $60 ✪

Single Vineyard Mornington Peninsula Syrah 2014 Hand-picked from Blocks 2 and 3. Excellent colour; this is a syrah of quite exceptional intensity that takes no prisoners, yet does so from a medium-bodied base of black fruits, spice, pepper and licorice; oak and tannins also in play, but of secondary importance. Screwcap. 14% alc. **Rating** 96 **To** 2030 $30 ✪

Single Vineyard Mornington Peninsula Pinot Noir 2015 95% MV6, 5% D4V2 clone. Supple and smooth; red fruits in the ascendant on the expressive bouquet and palate. Gentle spices will grow over time, adding another dimension to an already compelling wine. Screwcap. 13.5% alc. **Rating** 95 **To** 2028 $60

Red Claw Mornington Peninsula Chardonnay 2015 I suppose you have to see this as an entry point wine, for that's what it is. But many producers would be happy to have a wine of this quality and style as their icon wine because of its energy and drive, achieved without any tricks used such as (say) 40% new oak. Screwcap. 13% alc. **Rating** 94 **To** 2025 $27 ✪

Red Claw Mornington Peninsula Pinot Noir 2015 Excellent colour sets the scene for a wine loaded with pinot varietal fruit, but needing another year or so to open up fully, especially on the finish. Screwcap. 14% alc. **Rating** 94 **To** 2025 $27 ✪

🍷🍷🍷🍷🍸 **Pink Claw Heathcote Grenache Rose 2015** **Rating** 93 **To** 2017 $27 ✪
Red Claw Heathcote Shiraz 2014 **Rating** 92 **To** 2034 $27
Single Vineyard Cuvee Nina 2011 **Rating** 91 **To** 2026 $45 TS

Yal Yal Estate   ★★★★

15 Wynnstay Road, Prahran, Vic 3181 (postal) **Region** Mornington Peninsula
T 0416 112 703 **www.**yalyal.com.au **Open** Not
Winemaker Glen Hayley **Est.** 1997 **Dozens** 1000 **Vyds** 2.63ha
In 2008 Liz and Simon Gillies acquired a vineyard planted in 1997 to 1.6ha of chardonnay and a little over 1ha of pinot noir. Since 2000 the wines have been made at Port Philip Estate (under the watchful eyes of the Gillies).

🍷🍷🍷🍷🍷 **Yal Yal Rd Chardonnay 2014** A vibrantly arresting and complex wine, the flavours building throughout the length of the palate, reaching a crescendo on the finish as the acidity clicks in alongside the fruit. There are aspects of Coche Dury in play here. Screwcap. 13.5% alc. **Rating** 95 **To** 2025 $30 ✪

🍷🍷🍷🍷 **Yal Yal Rd Mornington Peninsula Pinot Noir 2014** **Rating** 88 **To** 2019 $30

Yalumba   ★★★★★

40 Eden Valley Road, Angaston, SA 5353 **Region** Eden Valley
T (08) 8561 3200 **www.**yalumba.com **Open** 7 days 10–5
Winemaker Louisa Rose (chief), Peter Gambetta, Kevin Glastonbury **Est.** 1849
Dozens 930 000 **Vyds** 180ha
Family-owned and run by Robert Hill-Smith, Yalumba has a long commitment to quality and great vision in its selection of vineyard sites, new varieties and brands. It has always been a serious player at the top end of full-bodied (and full-blooded) Australian reds, and was a pioneer in the use of screwcaps. While its estate vineyards are largely planted to mainstream varieties, it has taken marketing ownership of viognier. However, these days its own brands revolve around the Y Series and a number of stand-alone brands across the length and breadth of SA. A founding member of Australia's First Families of Wine. Exports to all major markets.

🍷🍷🍷🍷🍷 **Steeple Vineyard Light Pass Barossa Valley Shiraz 2013** This estate vineyard was planted in 1919, immediately after the end of the First World War. The wine is special, with a fragrant bouquet of spice and licorice that come through on the medium-bodied palate, and with really attractive fresh black fruits and supple, silky tannins. It represents good value, as wines of this category are increasingly routinely priced over $100. Cork. 13.5% alc. **Rating** 97 To 2048 $68 **⊙**

Steeple Vineyard Light Pass Barossa Valley Shiraz 2012 You want to use some English wine writers' phrases such as 'charming', liable to give the wrong impression in Australia, but it's true of this wine (and the '13 vintage). Part of the special quality of this vineyard is its evident ability to fully ripen shiraz at 13.5%, retaining shape and structure as it does so. 13.5% alc. **Rating** 97 To 2037 $68 **⊙**

Ringbolt 21 Barriques Margaret River Cabernet Sauvignon 2012 Richer and riper than the '11. As a result it's stunning in a different way. Eucalypt plays a leading role here but so too do beautifully ripened blackcurrant, plum and bay leaf flavours. Cedary-spicy oak has melted straight down into the fruit, and tannin is fine but ever-so-firm. We have something special here. Cork. 14.5% alc. **Rating** 97 To 2040 $38 CM **⊙**

♟♟♟♟♟ **The Virgilius Eden Valley Viognier 2014** Hand-picked, whole bunch-pressed, fermented and matured for 12 months in used French barriques and puncheons. Bright straw-green; shows why Virgilius is accepted as the standard for all others to seek to achieve, with varietal expression crystal clear in a complex structural web. Screwcap. 13.5% alc. **Rating** 96 To 2019 $48 **⊙**

The Octavius Old Vine Barossa Shiraz 2012 This wine used to be full-bodied, with a 'more of everything' philosophy. Inevitably, given the small barrels used, it has obvious oak, but the integrity and strength of the fruit carries the oak, and the tannins are no issue whatsoever. Cork. 13.5% alc. **Rating** 96 To 2032 $112

Eden Valley Viognier 2014 Yalumba set the bar very high when it decided to make viognier its champion variety. Its Virgilius is Australia's best (and priced accordingly), and this has the characters expected of Virgilius, with its complex pear and biscuity aromas; there is no oak, even though the bouquet has barrel ferment-like complexity; the palate is luxuriantly rich before the coup de grace of its fresh, crisp finish. Screwcap. 14.1% alc. **Rating** 95 To 2017 $24 **⊙**

Ringbolt 21 Barriques Margaret River Cabernet Sauvignon 2011 Medium-bodied, but oh how gorgeous this is. Curranty fruit and musky oak, traces of leaf and a slink of sweetness. It's one of those smells/tastes/feels/is good wines. Fully integrated tannin franks the quality. Cork. 14% alc. **Rating** 95 To 2035 $38 CM

Eden Valley Roussanne 2014 Gleaming straw-green; the expressive bouquet ranges through orange blossom to baker's spices, the palate retaining shape and freshness through to the long, citrussy/minerally acidity on the finish. If Yalumba had set out to make roussanne its flagship, its ride to victory might have been faster. Screwcap. 12.5% alc. **Rating** 94 To 2022 $24 **⊙**

♟♟♟♟♟ **Paradox Northern Barossa Shiraz 2013** Rating 93 To 2033 $45
The Signature Cabernet Shiraz 2013 Rating 93 To 2033 $60
Running With Bulls Tempranillo 2015 Rating 93 To 2021 $22 CM **⊙**
FSW8B Wrattonbully Botrytis Viognier 2015 Rating 93 To 2024 $30
The Menzies Cabernet Sauvignon 2013 Rating 92 To 2033 $55
Running With Bulls Barossa Tempranillo 2014 Rating 92 To 2019 $23 **⊙**
Menzies The Cigar Cabernet Sauvignon 2013 Rating 91 To 2028 $26
Running with Bulls Barossa Garnacha 2015 Rating 90 To 2017 $23

Yangarra Estate Vineyard   ★★★★★

809 McLaren Flat Road, Kangarilla SA 5171 **Region** McLaren Vale
T (08) 8383 7459 **www.**yangarra.com.au **Open** 7 days 10–5
Winemaker Peter Fraser, Shelley Torresan **Est.** 2000 **Dozens** 15 000 **Vyds** 89.3ha
This is the Australian operation of Jackson Family Wines, one of the leading premium wine producers in California, which in 2000 acquired the 172ha Eringa Park vineyard from Normans Wines (the oldest vines dated back to 1923). The renamed Yangarra Estate Vineyard

is the estate base for the operation, which built a state-of-the-art premium red wine facility in '10, and is moving to certified organic status with its vineyards. Peter Fraser has taken Yangarra Estate to another level altogether with his innovative winemaking and desire to explore all the possibilities of the Rhône Valley red and white styles. Thus you will find grenache, shiraz, mourvedre, cinsaut, carignan, tempranillo and graciano planted, and picpoul noir, terret noir, muscardin and vaccarese around the corner. The white varieties are roussanne and viognier, with grenache blanc, bourboulenc and picpoul blanc planned. Then you see ceramic eggs being used in parallel with conventional fermenters. In '15 Peter was named Winemaker of the Year at the launch of the 2016 *Wine Companion*. Exports to the UK, the US and other major markets.

ŸŸŸŸŸ **Small Pot Whole Bunch McLaren Vale Shiraz 2014** Great aromas don't prepare you for the full-bodied palate, every crevice of the mouth filled with velvety black fruits, bitter chocolate, licorice and spice. The balance is such that drinking it now is no crime, however far into the distant future the wine will run. Screwcap. 14.5% alc. **Rating** 97 **To** 2049 $50 ✪

Ironheart McLaren Vale Shiraz 2013 Sombre, earthy black fruits are so intense they momentarily stop the heart from beating. The texture and mouthfeel are such that they throw down the gauntlet to anyone seeking to drink more than a glass at this early (indeed far too early) stage of its life. The balance is spot on the money, so the long-term future is assured. Screwcap. 14.5% alc. **Rating** 97 **To** 2053 $100 ✪

High Sands McLaren Vale Grenache 2013 This is in another league altogether. There is total fusion between the fruit and tannins first up, oak likewise subsumed by the fruit. There is a bright display of a blaze of red fruits, so vivid that the structural components are relegated to the back of the stage, where they will remain for the life of the wine. Screwcap. 14.8% alc. **Rating** 97 **To** 2033 $130 ✪

ŸŸŸŸŸ **Small Pot Ceramic Egg McLaren Vale Grenache 2014** The fruit comes into play early, and continues its dominance through the length of the palate, its juicy red berry/compote fruits not letting the ever-present tannins gain control. Whether it's the eggs or the fruit, it has more overall power than its siblings. Screwcap. 14.5% alc. **Rating** 96 **To** 2030 $50 ✪

GSM McLaren Vale Grenache Shiraz Mourvedre 2014 65/27/8%. Excellent depth to the colour; this is a mighty mouthful, somewhere between Guigal and Chateau Rayas in style, a veritable volcano of red and purple fruits that do, however, want to be enjoyed sooner rather than later. First-class wine. Screwcap. 14.5% alc. **Rating** 96 **To** 2020 $30 ✪

McLaren Vale Shiraz 2014 Everything falls into place, the design of the jigsaw puzzle taking shape post haste. McLaren Vale fruit essence, with black fruits and potent dark chocolate looking as much to the sky as the earth, the whole bunch elements adding a twist to the main design, eloquent tannins also making a significant contribution. Screwcap. 14% alc. **Rating** 95 **To** 2034 $30 ✪

Old Vine McLaren Vale Grenache 2014 The lightish colour is misleading: the wine has a cascade of red fruits, with a slightly unexpected brush fence of ripe tannins, important now as much as in the future, when they will fuse back into the wine. Screwcap. 14.5% alc. **Rating** 95 **To** 2029 $32 ✪

ŸŸŸŸŸ **PF McLaren Vale Shiraz 2015 Rating** 93 **To** 2018 $25 ✪
McLaren Vale Mourvedre 2014 Rating 93 **To** 2029 $35
McLaren Vale Viognier 2015 Rating 92 **To** 2017 $28
McLaren Vale Roussanne 2015 Rating 92 **To** 2021 $32

Yarra Burn   ★★★★

4/19 Geddes Street, Mulgrave, Vic 3170 **Region** Yarra Valley
T 1800 088 711 **www.yarraburn.com.au Open** Not
Winemaker Ed Carr **Est.** 1975 **Dozens** NFP

At least in terms of name, this is the focal point of Accolade's Yarra Valley operations. However, the winery was sold, and the wines are now made elsewhere. The Upper Yarra vineyard largely remains. The lack of interest in the brand and its quality is as sad as it is obvious.

ΨΨΨΨΨ **Pinot Noir Chardonnay Pinot Meunier 2010** A full five-and-a-half years on lees brings all the joy of biscuity, honeyed complexity, while upholding a core of cool climate Yarra Valley citrus and stone fruit integrity. Phenolic presence brings a little grip to the finish, but it holds it with even persistence. Cork. 12.5% alc. **Rating** 91 **To** 2017 $28 TS

Premium Cuvee Brut NV Based on the '13 vintage, a full two-and-a-half years on lees in bottle makes this one of the most sophisticated sparkling wines on the bottom shelf. A creamy bead and textured palate brings dimension to citrus and stone fruit flavours, finishing long and well integrated. Cork. 12.5% alc. **Rating** 91 **To** 2017 $17 TS ✪

Yarra Yering ★★★★★

Briarty Road, Coldstream, Vic 3770 **Region** Yarra Valley
T (03) 5964 9267 **www.**yarrayering.com **Open** 7 days 10–5
Winemaker Sarah Crowe **Est.** 1969 **Dozens** 3000 **Vyds** 26.37ha

In September 2008, founder Bailey Carrodus died, and in April '09 Yarra Yering was on the market. It was Bailey Carrodus's clear wish and expectation that any purchaser would continue to manage the vineyard and winery, and hence the wine style, in much the same way as he had done for the previous 40 years. Its acquisition in June '09 by a small group of investment bankers has fulfilled that wish. The low-yielding, unirrigated vineyards have always produced wines of extraordinary depth and intensity. Dry Red No. 1 is a cabernet blend; Dry Red No. 2 is a shiraz blend; Dry Red No. 3 is a blend of touriga nacional, tinta cao, tinta roriz, tinta amarela, alvarelhao and souzao; Pinot Noir and Chardonnay are not hidden behind delphic numbers; Underhill Shiraz (planted in 1973) is from an adjacent vineyard purchased by Yarra Yering over a decade ago. Sarah Crowe, who had carved a remarkable reputation as a winemaker in the Hunter Valley in a relatively short time, was appointed winemaker in the wake of Paul Bridgeman's departure to Levantine Hill after the '13 vintage. She has made red wines of the highest imaginable quality from her first vintage, and to the delight of many, myself included, has offered all the wines with screwcaps. For good measure, she introduced the '14 Light Dry Red Pinot Shiraz as a foretaste of that vintage, and an affirmation of the exceptional talent recognised by her Winemaker of the Year in this edition of the *Wine Companion*. Exports to the UK, the US, The Netherlands, Malaysia, Singapore, Hong Kong and China.

ΨΨΨΨΨ **Carrodus Shiraz 2014** From the tiny '69 planting. The bouquet is highly charged and perfumed, with both red and black fruits spanning plums and berries, and French oak chiming in on the background. It's only on the palate that the very special quality of the wine is laid bare, spelling finesse and length in diamond-encrusted block letters. It soars on the finish line like a great Burgundy, the aftertaste virtually endless. Screwcap. 13% alc. **Rating** 99 **To** 2044 $250 ✪

Carrodus Cabernet Sauvignon 2014 From the topmost '69 plantings on a westerly slope. The purity and the intensity of the gaze of this wine as you look at it, and it looks back at you, is daunting and humbling. Cassis, bay leaf and cedar are the aroma and flavour headstones; ripe, but finely honed cabernet tannins of a quality no 2yo First Growth Bordeaux could possibly aspire to, provide the texture and structure. Screwcap. 13.5% alc. **Rating** 99 **To** 2044 $250 ✪

Light Dry Red Pinot Shiraz 2015 A 50/50% blend. Superb colour and clarity, startlingly bright crimson. A piercing bouquet of incredible vitality, drive and intensity, the aromas and flavours anchored on red cherries, with subtexts of strawberry and fresh-picked raspberries, which come through in pristine fashion on the vibrantly fresh palate. Spring dawn dew drops on the vines' new season shoots, an ode to the great Mount Pleasant winemaker, Maurice O'Shea. I am besotted with this wine. Screwcap. 13% alc. **Rating** 98 **To** 2030 $86 ✪

Underhill 2014 From 8ha of shiraz planted in '73 on a westerly slope. Vivid crimson purple; counterintuitively slightly deeper than '14 Carrodus. Spectacular intensity and power, yet the detail is so precise that you can smell and taste each tile in the mosaic of the wine: black cherry, licorice, spice, pepper, tannins, blackberry. Paradoxically, because it is due to this detail that the wine cries out for more time. Screwcap. 13% alc. **Rating** 98 **To** 2044 $92 ✪

Dry Red No. 2 2014 Largely shiraz, with a small amount of mataro added and co-fermented with viognier and marsanne. Brought back an instant recollection of the Bayeux Tapestry. It commences with a Catherine wheel of aromas, flavours and textures which are astounding and – you think – leave nothing more to be said. But there's more, much more. For one thing, it is a sacrilege to spit out any of the wine when tasting it, for the autopilot is still working furiously trying to capture the interplay between the infinitely complex fruit flavours, the charcuterie, the spices, the earth, the tannins, the oak and the licorice. Screwcap. 13% alc. **Rating** 98 **To** 2039 $92 ✪

Dry Red No. 1 2014 A blend of cabernet sauvignon (dominant), merlot, malbec and petit verdot. Fabulous colour, deep crimson; the bouquet is so intense it sets the antennae waving furiously. The palate is an essay. Sheer, unadulterated power; the four components have bonded so symbiotically and synergistically with each other, and the 100% new French oak, that it will be a decade at the very least before the wine opens up to display the intricacy of its inner workings. When it does, this wine may emerge as the greatest of the vintage. Screwcap. 13.5% alc. **Rating** 98 **To** 2049 $92 ✪

Pinot Noir 2014 Four clones, planted in '69, '81 and '84. Relatively light colour; the bouquet is supercharged with floral perfume that fills the senses and paves the way for the gloriously fine and beautifully detailed palate. Here red fruits of every description dance a pas de deux with gossamer, yet persistent, tannins. The length is prodigious, the line of almost painful precision, the balance perfection. French oak. Well, I know it's there, but trying to verbalise it is a waste of time. Screwcap. 13% alc. **Rating** 97 **To** 2029 $92 ✪

♀♀♀♀♀ **Dry Red No. 3 2014** A blend of the Portuguese varieties touriga nacional, tinta cao, tinta roriz, tinta amarela, alvarelhao and souzao. Its deep colour seems inevitable in the context of the other wines, but its suite of aromas, flavours and texture are – inevitably – very different. Intensely spicy, it brings supple and seductive plum fruits into play, with a counterpoint of sour cherry. It glides along the tongue in a dangerous fashion, encouraging rapid consumption. Screwcap. 12.5% alc. **Rating** 96 **To** 2020 $86

Dry White No. 1 2014 No mlf. A semillon-based white Bordeaux style. While already very complex, toasty and full-bodied, its acidity (left intact by the exclusion of mlf) slices through the palate like King Arthur's sword, giving the illusion of green lemon and herb/green capsicum flavours. Will be fascinating to watch its development. Screwcap. 13.5% alc. **Rating** 95 **To** 2025 $50

Chardonnay 2014 Crushed, skin-contacted, basket-pressed, fermented (100% mlf) and matured in French oak. Bright straw-green; a throwback to an almost forgotten style, incredibly rich and textured, with multiple layers of peachy fruit, honey and cashew balanced by fresh, natural acidity. Almost impossible to point as it will polarise opinions. The screwcap will be the wine's salvation as it ages. Screwcap. 13% alc. **Rating** 94 **To** 2022 $86

♀♀♀♀♀ **Dry White No. 2 2014** **Rating** 93 **To** 2021 $50

Yarrabank

38 Melba Highway, Yarra Glen, Vic 3775 **Region** Yarra Valley
T (03) 9730 0100 **www**.yering.com **Open** 7 days 10–5
Winemaker Michel Parisot, Willy Lunn, Darren Rathbone **Est.** 1993 **Dozens** 5000
Vyds 4ha

Yarrabank is a highly successful joint venture between the French Champagne house Devaux and Yering Station, established in 1993. Until '97 the Yarrabank Cuvee Brut was made under Claude Thibaut's direction at Domaine Chandon, but thereafter the entire operation has been conducted at Yarrabank. There are 4ha of dedicated 'estate' vineyards at Yering Station (planted to pinot noir and chardonnay); the balance of the intake comes from growers in the Yarra Valley and southern Vic. Wine quality has consistently been outstanding, frequently with an unmatched finesse and delicacy. A representative range of wines was not received for this edition, but the rating has been maintained. Exports to all major markets.

 Cuvee 2011 A full yellow hue with copper tints introduces a cuvee of surprising development for fruit sourced largely in the Upper Yarra Valley in the cool '11 vintage. It's well into the secondary phase of its life, already toasty, biscuity, spicy and honeyed, and while it's reached this point faster than expected, it's otherwise a compelling, mature Yarra style. Diam. 12.5% alc. **Rating** 90 **To** 2016 $38 TS

YarraLoch ★★★★☆

11 Range Road, Gruyere, Vic 3770 **Region** Yarra Valley
T 0407 376 587 **www**.yarraloch.com.au **Open** By appt
Winemaker David Bicknell **Est.** 1998 **Dozens** 2000 **Vyds** 6ha
This is the ambitious project of successful investment banker Stephen Wood. He has taken the best possible advice, and has not hesitated to provide appropriate financial resources to a venture that has no exact parallel in the Yarra Valley or anywhere else in Australia. Twelve hectares of vineyards may not seem so unusual, but in fact he has assembled three entirely different sites, 70km apart, each matched to the needs of the variety/varieties planted on that site. Pinot noir (4.4ha) is planted on the Steep Hill Vineyard, with a northeast orientation, and a shaley rock and ironstone soil. Cabernet sauvignon (4ha) has been planted at Kangaroo Ground, with a dry, steep northwest-facing site and abundant sun exposure in the warmest part of the day, ensuring full ripeness. Just over 3.5ha of merlot, shiraz, chardonnay and viognier are planted at the Upper Plenty Vineyard, 50km from Kangaroo Ground. This has an average temperature 2°C cooler and a ripening period 2–3 weeks later than the warmest parts of the Yarra Valley. Add skilled winemaking and some sophisticated (and beautiful) packaging, and you have a recipe for 5-star success.

Stephanie's Dream Whole Bunch Pinot Noir 2013 80% whole bunch. 150 dozen. An outstanding wine in all respects. Ripped with herbs, awash with wood smoke, plush with fruit and undergrowth and strung with tannin. Everything is firm, purposeful, dripping with character. There's a velvety aspect to the texture, for good measure. This is what it's all about. Screwcap. 13% alc. **Rating** 97 **To** 2025 $50 CM ●

Single Vineyard Chardonnay 2014 Ripe stone fruit flavour leads the charge, and while it picks up support from nutty, creamy oak along the way, fruit is still the driver through the long finish. An entirely satisfying chardonnay. Screwcap. 13% alc. **Rating** 94 **To** 2022 $35 CM

Single Vineyard Pinot Noir 2014 **Rating** 93 **To** 2021 $30 CM
LaCosette Pinot Noir 2014 **Rating** 91 **To** 2020 $25 CM

Yarrambat Estate ★★★☆

45 Laurie Street, Yarrambat, Vic 3091 (postal) **Region** Yarra Valley
T (03) 9717 3710 **www**.yarrambatestate.com.au **Open** By appt
Winemaker Rob Ellis (Contract) **Est.** 1995 **Dozens** 1350 **Vyds** 2.6ha
Ivan McQuilkin has pinot noir, cabernet sauvignon, chardonnay and merlot in his vineyard in the northwestern corner of the Yarra Valley, not far from the Plenty River. It is very much an alternative occupation for Ivan, whose principal activity is as an international taxation consultant to expatriate employees. While the decision to make wine was at least in part triggered by falling grape prices, hindsight proves it to have been a good one. Exports to Singapore and China.

ꬰꬰꬰꬰꬰ Single Vineyard Harcourt Pinot Gris 2015 Just a touch of grey-pink; a
surprise packet with its crisp green apple and pear fruit braced by talcy acidity;
good length. Screwcap. 13% alc. **Rating** 90 **To** 2017 $17 **☉**

ꬰꬰꬰꬰ Single Vineyard Cabernet Merlot 2013 **Rating** 89 **To** 2028 $22
Single Vineyard Bendigo Shiraz 2013 **Rating** 88 **To** 2020 $23
Brut Rose 2013 **Rating** 88 **To** 2016 $25 TS

Yarran Wines ★★★★

178 Myall Park Road, Yenda, NSW 2681 **Region** Riverina
T (02) 6968 1125 **www**.yarranwines.com.au **Open** Mon–Sat 10–5
Winemaker Sam Brewer **Est.** 2000 **Dozens** 8000 **Vyds** 30ha
Lorraine Brewer (and late husband John) were grapegrowers for over 30 years, and when son
Sam completed a degree in wine science at CSU, they celebrated his graduation by crushing
1 tonne of shiraz, fermenting the grapes in a milk vat. The majority of the grapes from the
estate plantings are sold, but each year a little more has been made under the Yarran banner;
along the way a winery with a crush capacity of 150 tonnes has been built. Sam worked for
Southcorp and De Bortoli in Australia, and overseas (in the US and China), but after 10 years
(in 2009) decided to take the plunge and concentrate on the family winery, with his parents.
The majority of the grapes come from the family vineyard, but some parcels are sourced
from growers, including Lake Cooper Estate in the Heathcote region. It is intended that the
portfolio of regions will be gradually increased, and Sam has demonstrated his ability to make
silk purses out of sow's ears, and sell them for the price of the latter. Exports to Singapore
and China.

ꬰꬰꬰꬰꬰ Leopardwood Limited Release Heathcote Shiraz 2014 As ever, Yarran –
and winemaker Sam Brewer – comprehensively over-deliver; you can taste the
concentration of the blackberry fruit ex the low-yielding vines (the '14 vintage),
spice and licorice joining hands with French oak as the wine marches purposefully
towards the rich finish. Screwcap. 14.5% alc. **Rating** 94 **To** 2034 $20 **☉**
B Series Yenda Durif 2015 Vivid crimson; densely textured, powerful, full-
bodied oceans of black fruits, licorice, spice and vanilla; no sign of heat ex alcohol.
Big handlebars to hold onto. Screwcap. 14.5% alc. **Rating** 94 **To** 2030 $22 **☉**

ꬰꬰꬰꬰꬰ Chardonnay 2015 **Rating** 90 **To** 2017 $12 **☉**
Heathcote Cabernet Sauvignon 2015 **Rating** 90 **To** 2030 $12 **☉**

Yarrawood Estate ★★★☆

1275 Melba Highway, Yarra Glen, Vic 3775 **Region** Yarra Valley
T (03) 9730 2003 **www**.yarrawood.com.au **Open** Mon–Fri 10–5, w'ends 8–5
Winemaker Contract **Est.** 1996 **Dozens** 25 000 **Vyds** 40.6ha
Yarrawood Estate has pinot noir (10.6ha), cabernet sauvignon (7.9ha), chardonnay (7.2ha),
merlot (5.3ha), shiraz (4.5ha) and lesser amounts of sauvignon blanc, riesling and verdelho. The
Tall Tales wines are contract-made from the estate-grown grapes. The cellar door and café are
located on the Melba Highway, 3km north of Yarra Glen, overlooking the vineyard. Exports
to Singapore, Malaysia, Japan and China.

ꬰꬰꬰꬰ Tall Tales Rose 2015 Made using merlot grapes. Fun and fruity but (thankfully)
without being too sweet. Redcurrant and cherry flavours with woody spice notes
to close. Simple but effective. Screwcap. 13.5% alc. **Rating** 88 **To** 2017 $19 CM

Yarrh Wines ★★★★

440 Greenwood Road, Murrumbateman, NSW 2582 **Region** Canberra District
T (02) 6227 1474 **www**.yarrhwines.com.au **Open** Fri–Sun 11–5
Winemaker Fiona Wholohan **Est.** 1997 **Dozens** 2000 **Vyds** 6ha

Fiona Wholohan and Neil McGregor are IT refugees, and both now work full-time running the Yarrh Wines vineyard and making the wines. Fiona undertook the oenology and viticulture course at CSU, and has also spent time as an associate judge at wine shows. They say they have spent the last 5 years moving to a hybrid organic vineyard, with composting, mulching, biological controls and careful vineyard floor management. The vineyard was planted in three stages between 1997 and 2000, and now includes cabernet sauvignon, shiraz, sauvignon blanc, riesling, pinot noir and sangiovese. They have recently tripled their sangiovese plantings with two new clones, and are planning to plant nero d'Avola, montepulciano and aglianico. And just to put the record straight, Yarrh was the original Aboriginal name for the Yass district.

ＹＹＹＹＹ **Shiraz 2013** A positive, medium to full-bodied shiraz with very good depth without going OTT; spice and licorice notes on the bouquet turn more savoury on the palate, dark chocolate joining with the tannins of the black fruits. It all comes together very well. Screwcap. 13.5% alc. **Rating** 93 **To** 2033 $28
Sauvignon Blanc 2015 While the varietal expression isn't complex (simply tropical), the wine has been well made, particularly with the line, length and balance of the fruit that is there. It's the sort of wine that will please almost everyone, including sauvignon blanc apostates. Screwcap. 11.5% alc. **Rating** 90 **To** 2016 $20 ●

ＹＹＹＹ **Mr Natural Shiraz 2015 Rating** 89 **To** 2023 $25
Canberra District Sangiovese 2013 Rating 89 **To** 2020 $27

Yeates Wines   ★★★★

138 Craigmoor Road, Mudgee, NSW 2850 **Region** Mudgee
T 0427 791 264 **www**.yeateswines.com.au **Open** By appt
Winemaker Jacob Stein **Est.** 2010 **Dozens** 500 **Vyds** 16ha
In 2010 Alexander (Sandy) and Victoria Yeates purchased the vineyard known as Mountain Blue under the aegis of Rosemount Estate. Part of the condition of sale imposed by vendor Foster's was that the vineyard name remain the property of Foster's, the last Mountain Blue vintage being '06. By '10 the vineyard was very rundown, with no continuity of vineyard management, the vines riddled with trunk disease. A program of bringing the vines back to full health is underway, but it is clear that this is going to take some time. Most of the grapes are sold, 3–5 tonnes a year retained for the Yeates wine brand.

ＹＹＹＹＹ **The Gatekeeper Reserve 2014** Matured for 15 months in French and American oak, 5% cabernet sauvignon blended in. Jacob Stein's skills make this light to medium-bodied blend of red and blue fruits ready to go any time. Screwcap. 14.5% alc. **Rating** 90 **To** 2034 $25

Yelland & Papps   ★★★★★

Lot 501 Nuraip Road, Nuriootpa, SA 5355 **Region** Barossa Valley
T (08) 8562 3510 **www**.yellandandpapps.com **Open** Mon–Sat 10–4
Winemaker Michael Papps **Est.** 2005 **Dozens** 4000 **Vyds** 1ha
Michael and Susan Papps (née Yelland) set up this venture after their marriage in 2005. It is easy for them to regard the Barossa Valley as their home, for Michael has lived and worked in the wine industry in the Barossa Valley for more than 20 years. He has a rare touch, the wines consistently excellent, but also pushing the envelope; as well as using a sustainable approach to winemaking with minimal inputs, he has not hesitated to challenge orthodox approaches to a number of aspects of conventional fermentation methods.

ＹＹＹＹＹ **Devote Greenock Barossa Valley Shiraz 2014** An intensely focused, powerful full-bodied shiraz that resolutely stays within the boundaries of balance and – to stretch the point just a little – elegance. Would other Greenock growers please look at the alcohol and taste the wine? Screwcap. 13.3% alc. **Rating** 96 **To** 2049 $35 ●

Second Take Barossa Valley Shiraz 2015 A fragrant spicy/peppery bouquet; a savoury black fruit palate with finely chiselled tannins and oak adding to the length on the palate. This is an exceptional Barossa Valley shiraz, humming with the unexpected. Screwcap. 14.3% alc. **Rating** 95 **To** 2035 $40

Second Take Barossa Valley Mataro 2015 Red and blue fruit is wholesome, but it's the fluid mouthfeel that sets this wine apart, with tannins that flit about like glow worms in the night, vanishing and reappearing so quickly it's impossible to track individual flight paths. Screwcap. 14.2% alc. **Rating** 95 **To** 2028 $40

Eden Valley Riesling 2015 From two vineyards. 3 months lees contact, 353 dozen made. Savoury/pithy lemon, lime and mineral flavours come together seamlessly on the long palate and aftertaste; firm, but balanced, acidity points the way for the future. Screwcap. 11.7% alc. **Rating** 94 **To** 2025 $25 ☉

ΨΨΨΨ♀ **Barossa Valley Vermentino 2015** Rating 93 To 2018 $25 ☉
Devote Old Vine Barossa Valley Grenache 2014 Rating 92 To 2020 $35
Vin de Soif 2014 Rating 92 To 2024 $25 ☉
Devote Barossa Valley Roussanne 2015 Rating 91 To 2020 $35
Barossa Valley Cabernet Sauvignon 2014 Rating 91 To 2024 $25

Yellowglen   ★★★☆

The Atrium, 58 Queensbridge Street, Southbank, Vic 3006 **Region** South Eastern Australia
T 1300 651 650 **www**.yellowglen.com **Open** Not
Winemaker Trina Smith **Est.** 1971 **Dozens** NFP
Yellowglen is not only the leading producer of sparkling wine in the TWE group, but the largest producer of sparkling wine in Australia. In 2012 it announced a major restructuring of its product range, adding single vineyard traditional-method wines under the Exceptional Vintage XV label. Trina Smith is a highly accomplished winemaker. Exports to the UK, the US, Canada, Japan and NZ.

ΨΨΨΨΨ **Vintage Perle Rose 2008** 60% pinot meunier, 27% pinot noir and 13% chardonnay from Henty, Tumbarumba and the Adelaide Hills, spending 6 years on lees in bottle. Stacked with crushed red fruits and spice aromas and flavours, with a biscuity lees contact edge. No addition of red wine was needed. Surely selling below the cost of production. Cork. 12% alc. **Rating** 94 **To** 2017 $25 ☉

ΨΨΨΨ **Vintage Perle 2012** Rating 89 To 2022 $20 TS

Yeowarra Hill   ★★★☆

152 Drapers Road, Colac, Vic 3250 **Region** Geelong
T (03) 5232 1507 **www**.yeowarrahill.com.au **Open** By appt
Winemaker Dinny Goonan **Est.** 1998 **Dozens** 140 **Vyds** 1ha
Bronwyn and Keith Thomas planted pinot noir (two-thirds) and chardonnay over 1998 and '99. They say the early vintages were consumed by family and friends, and as the vines have gained maturity and moved to full cropping, part of the production has been sold to other wineries in the region. The business is part of a function venue which has expansive views of Colac, with the vineyard in the foreground.

ΨΨΨΨ♀ **Limited Release Pinot Noir 2013** A wine of savoury complexity. This is a fine release. Cherries and plums on the one hand, pepper-spice and stems on the other. The hands are well linked. From start to finish, it's good. Screwcap. 13% alc. **Rating** 92 **To** 2021 $25 CM ☉

Yering Station   ★★★★★

38 Melba Highway, Yarra Glen, Vic 3775 **Region** Yarra Valley
T (03) 9730 0100 **www**.yering.com **Open** 7 days 10–5
Winemaker Willy Lunn, Darren Rathbone **Est.** 1988 **Dozens** 60 000 **Vyds** 112ha

The historic Yering Station (or at least the portion of the property on which the cellar door sales and vineyard are established) was purchased by the Rathbone family in 1996 and is also the site of the Yarrabank joint venture with French Champagne house Devaux (see separate entry). A spectacular and very large winery was built, handling the Yarrabank sparkling and the Yering Station table wines, immediately becoming one of the focal points of the Yarra Valley, particularly as the historic Chateau Yering, where luxury accommodation and fine dining are available, is next door. Willy Lunn, a graduate of Adelaide University, has more than 25 years' cool-climate winemaking experience around the world, including at Petaluma, Shaw + Smith and Argyle Winery (Oregon). Exports to all major markets.

ΨΨΨΨΨ **Reserve Yarra Valley Shiraz Viognier 2013** The colour is exceptionally deep and bright, setting the scene for an exotic and compelling bouquet, the multilayered, medium to full-bodied palate lifting the bar even further. Here plum, black cherry, spice and cracked pepper join forces with ripe tannins, all in seamless balance. Screwcap. 14% alc. **Rating** 98 **To** 2043 $120 **✪**
Reserve Yarra Valley Shiraz Viognier 2014 98/2% co-fermented, 10% Old Beenak Road Shiraz blended in. Given that viognier is only 2%, it technically can't be shown on the front label (5% minimum), but its impact is little different from 5%. The vivid crimson-purple colour is great, the tannins are super supple and smooth, the oak present and correct, which leaves the fruit as lord of all of it surveys, its heart beating strong and true. Great wine. Screwcap. 13.9% alc. **Rating** 97 **To** 2039 $120 **✪**

ΨΨΨΨΨ **Reserve Yarra Valley Chardonnay 2014** Still pale straw-green; the bouquet is reductive, but the palate has an explosive powerhouse of grapefruit, flinty acidity and quality French oak. This was a great vintage for Yarra Valley chardonnay, and the wine has a great future. Screwcap. 13% alc. **Rating** 96 **To** 2029 $120
Reserve Yarra Valley Cabernet Sauvignon 2014 Bright crimson; elegance, balance and purity are the watchwords for this cabernet; it shows just how suited the Yarra Valley can be for cabernet if – as here – the right sites are chosen for it. Lateral winemaking has also paid off handsomely. Screwcap. 13.8% alc. **Rating** 96 **To** 2040 $120
Yarra Valley Chardonnay 2014 As might be expected, attests to the quality of the vintage first and foremost. This is a first-class illustration of the inherent strength of high quality Yarra chardonnay, fruit, acidity and oak all singing from the same page. Screwcap. 12.5% alc. **Rating** 95 **To** 2024 $40
Yarra Valley Pinot Noir 2014 Light, bright colour; it has a perfumed bouquet, then a pure stream of cherry and plum fruit running confidently through to the finish, its banks of earthy tannins merely suggesting which way the stream should flow. Screwcap. 12.8% alc. **Rating** 95 **To** 2023 $40
Single Vineyard Old Beenak Road Shiraz 2014 A medium-bodied cool climate shiraz packing a considerable punch without apparent effort. The layers of dark fruits (berries and plums) build progressively, but the tannins stay in their hutch, leaving oak to provide the context, fruit the length. Screwcap. 13.9% alc. **Rating** 95 **To** 2039 $60
Yarra Valley Shiraz Viognier 2013 Bright hue; red cherries and spices play tip and run on the expressive and inviting bouquet; the palate texture is a mix of silk and taffeta, the juicy gently spiced red fruit flavours a sheer delight. A first-class now-or-later style Screwcap. 13.8% alc. **Rating** 95 **To** 2033 $40
Reserve Yarra Valley Cabernet Sauvignon 2013 From a single vineyard near Spring Lane in Coldstream, open-fermented with 21–30 days on skins, matured in French oak (30% new) for 18 months. A distinguished cabernet with an autocratic edge that will please cabernet/Bordeaux lovers. It needs time to fully open up, but will be around for decades thereafter. Screwcap. 14% alc. **Rating** 94 **To** 2043 $120
Yarra Valley Cabernet Sauvignon 2013 Open-fermented, 80% with 21 days on skins, 20% for 42 days (fermentation 21 days), matured in French oak (25% new) for 18 months. This bold approach, seeking to extract every bit of fruit, has worked, moving the wine into its own course: left of centre of the usual Yarra

Valley elegance, but making up for that through its intensity. Screwcap. 14.3% alc.
Rating 94 **To** 2028 $40

ŸŸŸŸŸ **Village Yarra Valley Pinot Noir 2014** Rating 92 To 2020 $24 **✪**
Village Yarra Valley Pinot Noir 2013 Rating 91 To 2020 $24
Village Yarra Valley Chardonnay 2015 Rating 90 To 2020 $24
Village Yarra Valley Shiraz Viognier 2012 Rating 90 To 2022 $24

Yeringberg   ★★★★★

Maroondah Highway, Coldstream, Vic 3770 **Region** Yarra Valley
T (03) 9739 0240 **www**.yeringberg.com **Open** By appt
Winemaker Guill and Sandra de Pury **Est.** 1863 **Dozens** 1500 **Vyds** 3.66ha
Guill de Pury and daughter Sandra, with Guill's wife Katherine in the background, make
wines for the new millennium from the low-yielding vines re-established in the heart of
what was one of the most famous (and infinitely larger) vineyards of the 19th century. In the
riper years, the red wines have a velvety generosity of flavour rarely encountered, while never
losing varietal character; the long-lived Marsanne Roussanne takes students of history back to
Yeringberg's fame in the 19th century. Exports to the US, Switzerland, Hong Kong and China.

ŸŸŸŸŸ **Yarra Valley Chardonnay 2014** A lovely Yarra Valley chardonnay from a great
vineyard site and mature vines. White peach, grapefruit and nectarine are braced
by brilliant acidity that lengthens the palate and the aftertaste to dizzy heights;
the new oak has disappeared into the innermost fabric of the wine. Screwcap.
12.5% alc. **Rating** 96 **To** 2024 $50 **✪**
Yarra Valley Marsanne Roussanne 2014 59/41%, crushed and destemmed,
fermented in French oak, as are all the Yeringberg white wines, but with a
relatively small percentage of new barrels. Barrel ferment and the synergy between
the two varieties, neither of which is aromatic, give the wine its mouthfeel and
flavours, all of which will continue to grow for 20 years or more. Screwcap.
13% alc. **Rating** 95 **To** 2034 $50
Yarra Valley Shiraz 2013 Bright, clear crimson-purple, doubtless assisted by
the co-fermentation of 3% viognier. Over 30 years ago, Yeringberg pulled out its
original shiraz because no one wanted to buy it; Vine Pull without any subsidy, but
regretted as much here as in SA. Purity, intensity and length are the keywords for
this lovely medium-bodied cool climate shiraz. Screwcap. 13.5% alc. **Rating** 95
To 2033 $65
Yarra Valley Viognier 2014 One of the best viogniers around (after Yalumba,
of course). It is very complex and rich, with both barrel ferment and varietal fruit
(apricot and fresh ginger) to the fore, the force of the finish and aftertaste unique
to Yeringberg, seeming to be alcohol warmth, but it can't be. Screwcap. 13.5% alc.
Rating 94 **To** 2019 $35
Yeringberg 2013 65% cabernet sauvignon, 12% cabernet franc, 10% merlot,
7% malbec, 6% petit verdot. Bright, although relatively light, crimson; there's
nothing lacking in the complexity of the bouquet or palate; there is a wealth of
primarily red fruits, but with some blue and black adding their say, and a savoury
dressing to accompany the palate and aftertaste; the tannins are fine, but persistent,
and oak is there, but no more. Screwcap. 13.5% alc. **Rating** 94 **To** 2033 $75

ŸŸŸŸŸ **Yarra Valley Pinot Noir 2013** Rating 91 To 2021 $75

Yes said the Seal   ★★★★☆

1251–1269 Bellarine Highway, Wallington, Vic 3221 **Region** Geelong
T (03) 5250 6577 **www**.yessaidtheseal.com.au **Open** 7 days 10–5
Winemaker Darren Burke **Est.** 2014 **Dozens** 1000 **Vyds** 2ha
This is a new venture for David and Lyndsay Sharp, long-term vintners on Geelong's Bellarine
Peninsula. It is situated onsite at the Flying Brick Cider Co's Cider House in Wallington. The
2ha of estate vineyard were planted to shiraz in 2010; the remaining varieties are purchased
from growers on the Bellarine Peninsula.

🍷🍷🍷🍷♀ **The Bellarine Rose 2015** Machine-harvested shiraz and a little chardonnay, 24 hours skin contact, then fermented in stainless steel, 20% taken to used French oak for completion of fermentation and 4 months maturation. Bright colour with just a hint of salmon; delivers the complexity in the mouth that the winemaking suggests, the chardonnay giving a citrus note behind the dominant red cherry fruits; crisp and dry. Screwcap. 13.5% alc. **Rating** 93 **To** 2017 $25 ❂

The Bellarine Sauvignon Blanc 2015 Trophy Best Sauvignon Blanc Concours des Vines de Victoria '15, bronze medal Geelong Wine Show. I find myself a pig in the middle: the wine is complex and mouthfilling, but is a barrel-fermented white wine with minimal varietal character needing more acidity. Screwcap. 12.8% alc. **Rating** 90 **To** 2017 $25

🍷🍷🍷🍷 **Reserve Blanc de Blanc 2009 Rating** 89 **To** 2024 $40 TS

Yilgarnia   ★★★★

1847 Redmond West Road, Redmond, WA 6327 **Region** Denmark
T (08) 9845 3031 www.yilgarnia.com.au **Open** W'ends & school hols 11–5 Oct–Apr
Winemaker Peter and Anthony Buxton, Michael Staniford (Consultant) **Est.** 1997
Dozens 4000 **Vyds** 13.5ha
Melbourne-educated Peter Buxton travelled across the Nullarbor over 40 years ago and settled on a bush block of 163ha on the Hay River, 6km north of Wilson Inlet. For the first 10 years Peter worked for the Department of Agriculture in Albany, surveying several of the early vineyards in WA; he recognised the potential of his family's property. The vineyard (chardonnay, sauvignon blanc, shiraz, cabernet sauvignon, semillon and merlot) is planted on north-facing blocks, the geological history of which stretches back 2 billion years. Exports to the UK, India and Singapore.

🍷🍷🍷🍷♀ **Denmark Semillon 2014** For delivery of texture and flavour it's hard to fault this. Tinned tropical fruits come infused with lemongrass. It continues the parade all the way along the palate. Screwcap. 13% alc. **Rating** 91 **To** 2018 $19 CM ❂

Denmark Merlot 2014 Leather, chocolate, orange, briar and earth. It's sturdy, savoury and pretty all at once. It puts X-factor before substance but there's a good deal of that too. Screwcap. 15% alc. **Rating** 91 **To** 2024 $24 CM

Denmark Cabernet Merlot 2014 Rich with melted chocolate, coffee and blackberry flavour, licorice and jellied plum flavours fleshing it out. An audience won't be hard to find. Screwcap. 15% alc. **Rating** 91 **To** 2023 $21 CM ❂

Denmark Semillon Sauvignon Blanc 2015 It feels a little awkward but there's ample flavour and length. A punch bowl of tropical fruits with wisps of wood smoke to close. Screwcap. 14% alc. **Rating** 90 **To** 2017 $17 CM ❂

Denmark Shiraz 2014 Dark, liquid choc-orange oozes through blackberry and black jelly bean flavours. It's hard not to enjoy it. The flavours carry through to a warm but satisfying finish. Screwcap. 15.5% alc. **Rating** 90 **To** 2026 $24 CM

🍷🍷🍷🍷 **Denmark Sauvignon Blanc 2015 Rating** 89 **To** 2017 $19 CM ❂
Denmark Cabernet Sauvignon 2014 Rating 89 **To** 2025 $24 CM
Due South Semillon Sauvignon Blanc 2015 Rating 88 **To** 2017 $15 CM ❂
Denmark Chardonnay 2015 Rating 88 **To** 2017 $19 CM

Z Wine   ★★★★☆

PO Box 135, Lyndoch, SA 5351 **Region** Barossa Valley
T 0422 802 220 www.zwine.com.au **Open** By appt
Winemaker Janelle Zerk **Est.** 1999 **Dozens** 5500 **Vyds** 1ha
Sisters Janelle and Kristen Zerk are the dynamic duo behind Z Wine. The Zerk family has been growing grapes in the Barossa Valley since 1846, but fifth-generation Janelle is the first family member to pursue a winemaking career, and has made wine in Tuscany, Burgundy (Puligny Montrachet) and Sonoma, California. Kirsten has a wine marketing degree from Adelaide University. Grapes are sourced from the family's Lyndoch vineyard. The Rustica wines are sold exclusively through Dan Murphy. Exports to China.

ŶŶŶŶŶ **Aveline Barossa Valley Rose 2015** Juicy drinkability but with a bit extra. It's essentially raspberried and floral, but spice and earth notes, and a bit of grip, elevate it. Screwcap. 13% alc. **Rating** 92 **To** 2017 $20 CM ◑

Eden Valley Riesling 2015 Serves the flavours on a platter, or so you think; it's a fair bet that more is in store given time. Lemon, lime and talc are ready to be tucked into now. But it has the length and poise to cellar. Screwcap. 11.5% alc. **Rating** 91 **To** 2022 $25 CM

Rustica Reserve Barossa Valley Shiraz 2013 Coffeed oak stands on the shoulders of blackberried fruit and calls attention to itself. It's a mouthfilling wine, soft and rich. No holds barred, so to speak. Screwcap. 14.5% alc. **Rating** 91 **To** 2019 $30 CM

ŶŶŶŶ **Rustica Barossa Valley Cabernet Sauvignon 2014** Rating 89 To 2019 $20 CM

Rustica Barossa Valley Shiraz 2014 Rating 88 To 2016 $15 CM ◑

Zema Estate

14944 Riddoch Highway, Coonawarra, SA 5263 **Region** Coonawarra
T (08) 8736 3219 **www**.zema.com.au **Open** Mon–Fri 9–5, w'ends & public hols 10–4
Winemaker Greg Clayfield **Est.** 1982 **Dozens** 20 000 **Vyds** 61ha
Zema is one of the last outposts of hand-pruning in Coonawarra, with members of the Zema family tending the vineyard set in the heart of Coonawarra's terra rossa soil. Winemaking practices are straightforward; if ever there was an example of great wines being made in the vineyard, this is it. Exports to the UK, Vietnam, Hong Kong, Japan, Singapore and China.

ŶŶŶŶŶ **Family Selection Coonawarra Cabernet Sauvignon 2012** Classic cigar box, mint and blackcurrant flavours come infused with smoky vanillan oak. It's mid-weight but it finishes strong and varietally proud. This should develop beautifully. Screwcap. 14% alc. **Rating** 96 **To** 2036 $46 CM ◑

Coonawarra Shiraz 2013 There's a bit more throttle to this release than we've come to expect of shiraz under this label. It works a treat, too. Grainy cherry-plum flavours with beefier notes/aspects, bolstered further by sweet, toasty, cedary oak. We're in business. Screwcap. 14.5% alc. **Rating** 95 **To** 2030 $25 CM ◑

Coonawarra Cabernet Sauvignon 2013 There's a tiny amount of strut to this wine. It's a good thing. It tastes of blackcurrant, ground coffee, mint and fresh herbs, and while it's generally elegant, it powers confidently through the finish. Screwcap. 14.5% alc. **Rating** 95 **To** 2033 $29 CM ◑

Family Selection Coonawarra Shiraz 2012 Fresh and svelte. Musky vanillan oak slips over redcurrant, plum and mint flavours. It turns tangy and firmish on the finish, with notes of crushed/dry tobacco evident, but you have to describe this wine as smooth. Screwcap. 14% alc. **Rating** 94 **To** 2030 $46 CM

ŶŶŶŶ **Cluny Coonawarra Cabernet Merlot 2013** Rating 89 To 2023 $25 CM

🍃 Zerella Wines

182 Olivers Rd, McLaren Vale, SA 5171 **Region** McLaren Vale
T (08) 8323 8288/0488 929 202 **www**.zerellawines.com.au **Open** By appt
Winemaker Jim Zerella **Est.** 2006 **Dozens** 2000 **Vyds** 58ha
In 1950 the Ercole Zerella left his native Campania in southern Italy to seek a better life in SA. With a lifetime of farming and grapegrowing, the transition was seamless. Ercole's son Vic followed in his father's footsteps, becoming an icon of the SA farming and wine industries. He founded Tatachilla, where his son Jim began as a cellar hand, eventually controlling all grape purchases. While working there, Jim purchased land in McLaren Vale and, with help from family and friends, established what is now the flagship vineyard of Zerella Wines. He also established a vineyard management business catering to the needs of absentee owners. When Tatachilla was purchased by Lion Nathan in 2000 he declined the opportunity of continuing his role there, and by '06 had purchased two more vineyards, and become a shareholder in

a third. These all now come under the umbrella of Zerella Wines and its 58ha of vines. The winemaking techniques used are thoroughly à la mode, and definitely not traditional Italian.

ΨΨΨΨΨ La Gita Etrurian McLaren Vale Sangiovese 2013 If you leave the wine in the mouth long enough as you are ruminating on all the complex cherry fruit flavours and styles, the tannins will come and find you: not necessary and not advisable. To look for more, the luxurious bouquet helps. Screwcap. 14.5% alc. **Rating** 95 **To** 2033 $60
La Gita McLaren Vale Nero d'Avola 2014 Hand-picked, destemmed, 5 days cold soak, wild ferment, 20 days on skins, matured for 15 months in French oak (18% new). Splendidly juicy, with a complex web of red fruits, dark chocolate and multi-spice overtones. The winemaking has brought out the best in it. Screwcap. 14% alc. **Rating** 95 **To** 2021 $35 ✪

ΨΨΨΨΨ McLaren Vale Grenache Mataro Shiraz 2013 **Rating** 92 **To** 2030 $35
Olivers Road McLaren Vale Grenache 2013 **Rating** 91 **To** 2019 $60
McLaren Vale Mataro Shiraz 2013 **Rating** 91 **To** 2028 $25
La Gita McLaren Vale Barbera 2014 **Rating** 91 **To** 2024 $35

Zig Zag Road ★★★★

201 Zig Zag Road, Drummond, Vic 3446 **Region** Macedon Ranges
T (03) 5423 9390 **www**.zigzagwines.com.au **Open** Thurs–Mon 10–5
Winemaker Eric Bellchambers, Llew Knight **Est.** 1972 **Dozens** 600 **Vyds** 4.5ha
Zig Zag Road's dry-grown vines produce relatively low yields, and until 1996 the grapes were sold to Hanging Rock Winery. In 2002 Eric and Anne Bellchambers became the third owners of this vineyard, planted by Roger Aldridge in '72. The Bellchambers have extended the plantings with riesling and merlot, supplementing the older plantings of shiraz, cabernet sauvignon and pinot noir.

ΨΨΨΨΨ Blanc de Noir 2012 A fruity sparkling pinot noir of faint blush tint, delivering the body and fleshiness of this variety with all the texture of 4 years on lees. Fruit sweetness more than its low dosage of just 5.5g/l evenly balances its acidity and phenolic grip. A generous and appealing style. Diam. 13% alc. **Rating** 91 **To** 2017 $38 TS
Macedon Ranges Shiraz 2012 Bright hue; a delicious combination of red and morello cherry on the bouquet leaves you in no doubt it will replay on the palate, and so it does; there is no problem at all with the extract, the fine-spun tannins utterly subservient to the fruit. It's remarkably fresh, and will never be better than it is now. Screwcap. 13.5% alc. **Rating** 90 **To** 2020 $23s

Zilzie Wines ★★★★

544 Kulkyne Way, Karadoc, Vic 3496 **Region** Murray Darling
T (03) 5025 8100 **www**.zilziewines.com **Open** Not
Winemaker Hayden Donohue **Est.** 1999 **Dozens** NFP **Vyds** 572ha
The Forbes family has been farming since the early 1990s; Zilzie is currently run by Ian and Ros Forbes, with sons Steven and Andrew, and the diverse range of farming activities now includes grapegrowing from substantial vineyards. Having established a dominant position as a supplier of grapes to Southcorp, Zilzie formed a wine company in '99 and built a winery in 2000, expanding it in '06 to its current capacity of 45 000 tonnes. The wines consistently far exceed expectations, given their enticing prices, that consistency driving the production volume to 200 000 dozen (the last known publicised amount) – this in an extremely competitive market. The business includes contract processing, winemaking and storage. Exports to the UK, Canada, Hong Kong and China.

ΨΨΨΨΨ Ferghana Shiraz 2014 A medium to full-bodied shiraz with blackberry, satsuma plum and spice aromas and flavours; has good mouthfeel and balance, oak and tannins supporting the fruit. Good wine with a long future. Cork. 13.5% alc. **Rating** 92 **To** 2034 $50

Regional Collection Barossa Shiraz 2014 Sends a compelling message: it is possible to make balanced, medium-bodied shiraz in the Barossa Valley with 13.5% alcohol. Sure, the colour isn't deep, and there's scant evidence of oak or tannins, but it has supple cherry and plum fruit in abundance, with no hint of green/minty unripe flavours. Screwcap. **Rating** 90 **To** 2018 $18 ❂

ŶŶŶŶ Yarra Valley Chardonnay 2015 Rating 89 To 2020 $18 ❂
Estate Pinot Grigio 2015 Rating 89 To 2017 $12 ❂
Adelaide Hills Pinot Gris 2015 Rating 89 To 2017 $18 ❂
Estate Shiraz 2015 Rating 89 To 2019 $12 ❂
Selection 23 Rose 2015 Rating 88 To 2016 $11 ❂
Adelaide Hills Pinot Noir 2015 Rating 88 To 2019 $18
Selection 23 Shiraz 2015 Rating 88 To 2018 $11 ❂
Estate Shiraz 2014 Rating 88 To 2017 $12 ❂
Selection 23 Cabernet Merlot 2015 Rating 88 To 2018 $11 ❂

Zitta Wines   ★★★★☆

3 Union Street, Dulwich, SA 5065 (postal) **Region** Barossa Valley
T 0419 819 414 www.zitta.com.au **Open** Not
Winemaker Angelo De Fazio **Est.** 2004 **Dozens** 3000 **Vyds** 26.3ha
Owner Angelo De Fazio says that all he knows about viticulture and winemaking came from his father (and generations before him). It is partly this influence that has shaped the label and brand name: Zitta is Italian for 'quiet', and the seeming reflection of the letters of the name Zitta on the bottle is in fact nothing of the kind; turn the bottle upside down, and you will see it is the word 'Quiet'. The Zitta vineyard dates back to 1864, with a few vines remaining from that time, and a block planted with cuttings taken from those vines. Shiraz dominates the plantings (22ha), the balance made up of chardonnay, grenache and a few mourvedre vines; only a small amount of the production is retained for the Zitta label. The property has two branches of Greenock Creek running through it, and the soils reflect the ancient geological history of the site, in part with a subsoil of river pebbles, reflecting the course of a long-gone river. Exports to Denmark and China.

ŶŶŶŶŶ Single Vineyard Greenock Barossa Valley Shiraz 2013 Has a deep well of crimson-purple colour; powerful, full-bodied, with savoury black fruits sweeping all before them. Screams loudly for at least 5 years grace before opening a bottle, but does manage the alcohol well, with no heat obvious. Screwcap. 14.7% alc. **Rating** 95 **To** 2048 $55

ŶŶŶŶŶ Union Street Barossa Valley Shiraz 2013 Rating 93 To 2034 $25 ❂
Bernardo Barossa Valley Shiraz 2013 Rating 91 To 2033 $40

Zonte's Footstep   ★★★★

PO Box 2424, McLaren Vale, SA 5171 **Region** McLaren Vale
T (08) 8383 2083 www.zontesfootstep.com.au **Open** Not
Winemaker Ben Riggs **Est.** 1997 **Dozens** 20 000 **Vyds** 214.72ha
Zonte's Footstep has been very successful since a group of long-standing friends, collectively with deep knowledge of every aspect of the wine business, decided it was time to do something together. Along the way there has been some shuffling of the deck chairs, all achieved without any ill feeling from those who moved sideways or backwards. The major change has been a broadening of the regions (Langhorne Creek, McLaren Vale, the Barossa and Clare valleys and elsewhere) from which the grapes are sourced. Even here, however, most of the vineyards supplying grapes are owned by members of the Zonte's Footstep partnership. Exports to the UK, Belgium, Sweden, The Netherlands, South Korea, Thailand, Singapore and China.

ŶŶŶŶŶ Z-Force 2013 85% shiraz, 15% petite syrah from McLaren Vale. Deep, gleaming inky purple; all about hedonism: this bypasses the head, travelling through the heart and establishing a lasting friendship with the stomach. It's the outcome of some very clever winemaking. Screwcap. 15% alc. **Rating** 94 **To** 2033 $50

Avalon Tree Fleurieu Peninsula Cabernet 2014 From Langhorne Creek and Blewitt Springs, gold medal Perth Wine Show '15. A typically rich, open and generous Langhorne Creek style with red and black currant fruits, plus a little spice ex the oak. Screwcap. 14.5% alc. **Rating** 94 **To** 2030 $25 ✪

Chocolate Factory Vale Shiraz 2014 Rating 92 **To** 2034 $25 ✪
Doctoressa Di Lago Pinot Grigio 2015 Rating 90 **To** 2017 $18 ✪
Lake Doctor Langhorne Creek Shiraz 2014 Rating 90 **To** 2034 $25
Violet Beauregard Malbec 2014 Rating 90 **To** 2029 $25

Index

Adelaide Hills (SA)